D0789148

A Companion to Aesthetics

Blackwell Companions to Philosophy

This outstanding student reference series offers a comprehensive and authoritative survey of philosophy as a whole. Written by today's leading philosophers, each volume provides lucid and engaging coverage of the key figures, terms, topics, and problems of the field. Taken together, the volumes provide the ideal basis for course use, representing an unparalleled work of reference for students and specialists alike.

Already published in the series

1. The Blackwell Companion to Philosophy, Second Edition
   Edited by Nicholas Bunnin and Eric Tsui-James

2. A Companion to Ethics
   Edited by Peter Singer

3. A Companion to Aesthetics, Second Edition
   Edited by Stephen Davies, Kathleen Marie Higgins, Robert Hopkins, Robert Stecker, and David E. Cooper

4. A Companion to Epistemology
   Edited by Jonathan Dancy and Ernest Sosa

5. A Companion to Contemporary Political Philosophy (two-volume set), Second Edition
   Edited by Robert E. Goodin and Philip Pettit

6. A Companion to Philosophy of Mind
   Edited by Samuel Guttenplan

7. A Companion to Metaphysics, Second Edition
   Edited by Jaegwon Kim and Ernest Sosa

8. A Companion to Philosophy of Law and Legal Theory
   Edited by Dennis Patterson

9. A Companion to Philosophy of Religion
   Edited by Philip L. Quinn and Charles Taliaferro

10. A Companion to the Philosophy of Language
    Edited by Bob Hale and Crispin Wright

11. A Companion to World Philosophies
    Edited by Eliot Deutsch and Ron Bontekoe

12. A Companion to Continental Philosophy
    Edited by Simon Critchley and William Schroeder

13. A Companion to Feminist Philosophy
    Edited by Alison M. Jaggar and Iris Marion Young

14. A Companion to Cognitive Science
    Edited by William Bechtel and George Graham

15. A Companion to Bioethics
    Edited by Helga Kuhse and Peter Singer

16. A Companion to the Philosophers
    Edited by Robert L. Arrington

17. A Companion to Business Ethics
    Edited by Robert E. Frederick

18. A Companion to the Philosophy of Science
    Edited by W. H. Newton-Smith

19. A Companion to Environmental Philosophy
    Edited by Dale Jamieson

20. A Companion to Analytic Philosophy
    Edited by A. P. Martinich and David Sosa

21. A Companion to Genethics
    Edited by Justine Burley and John Harris

22. A Companion to Philosophical Logic
    Edited by Dale Jacquette

23. A Companion to Early Modern Philosophy
    Edited by Steven Nadler

24. A Companion to Philosophy in the Middle Ages
    Edited by Jorge J. E. Gracia and Timothy B. Noone

25. A Companion to African-American Philosophy
    Edited by Tommy L. Lott and John P. Pittman

26. A Companion to Applied Ethics
    Edited by R. G. Frey and Christopher Heath Wellman

27. A Companion to the Philosophy of Education
    Edited by Randall Curren

28. A Companion to African Philosophy
    Edited by Kwasi Wiredu

29. A Companion to Heidegger
    Edited by Hubert L. Dreyfus and Mark A. Wrathall

30. A Companion to Rationalism
    Edited by Alan Nelson

31. A Companion to Ancient Philosophy
    Edited by Mary Louise Gill and Pierre Pellegrin

32. A Companion to Pragmatism
    Edited by John R. Shook and Joseph Margolis

33. A Companion to Nietzsche
    Edited by Keith Ansell Pearson

34. A Companion to Socrates
    Edited by Sara Ahbel-Rappe and Rachana Kamtekar

35. A Companion to Phenomenology and Existentialism
    Edited by Hubert L. Dreyfus and Mark A. Wrathall

36. A Companion to Kant
    Edited by Graham Bird

37. A Companion to Plato
    Edited by Hugh H. Benson

38. A Companion to Descartes
    Edited by Janet Broughton and John Carriero

39. A Companion to the Philosophy of Biology
    Edited by Sahotra Sarkar and Anya Plutynski

40. A Companion to Hume
    Edited by Elizabeth S. Radcliffe

41. A Companion to the Philosophy of History and Historiography
    Edited by Aviezer Tucker

42. A Companion to Aristotle
    Edited by Georgios Anagnostopoulos

43. A Companion to the Philosophy of Technology
    Edited by Jan-Kyrre Berg Olsen, Stig Andur Pedersen, and Vincent F. Hendricks

Also under contract

A Companion to Philosophy of Literature
   Edited by Garry L. Hagberg and Walter Jost

A Companion to Schopenhauer
   Edited by Bart Vandenabeele

A Companion to Relativism
   Edited by Steven D. Hales

A Companion
to Aesthetics

Second edition

Edited by
Stephen Davies, Kathleen Marie Higgins,
Robert Hopkins, Robert Stecker,
and David E. Cooper

WILEY-BLACKWELL

A John Wiley & Sons, Ltd., Publication

This second edition first published 2009
© 2009 Blackwell Publishing Ltd
Edition history: Blackwell Publishing Ltd (1e, 1992)

Blackwell Publishing was acquired by John Wiley & Sons in February 2007. Blackwell's publishing program has been merged with Wiley's global Scientific, Technical, and Medical business to form Wiley-Blackwell.

Registered Office
John Wiley & Sons Ltd, The Atrium, Southern Gate, Chichester, West Sussex, PO19 8SQ, United Kingdom

Editorial Offices
350 Main Street, Malden, MA 02148–5020, USA
9600 Garsington Road, Oxford, OX4 2DQ, UK
The Atrium, Southern Gate, Chichester, West Sussex, PO19 8SQ, UK

For details of our global editorial offices, for customer services, and for information about how to apply for permission to reuse the copyright material in this book please see our website at www.wiley.com/wiley-blackwell.

The right of Stephen Davies, Kathleen Marie Higgins, Robert Hopkins, Robert Stecker, and David E. Cooper to be identified as the author of the editorial material in this work has been asserted in accordance with the Copyright, Designs and Patents Act 1988.

Library of Congress Cataloging-in-Publication Data
A companion to aesthetics : edited by Stephen Davies . . . [et al.]. — 2nd ed.
    p. cm. — (Blackwell companions to philosophy)
  Includes bibliographical references and index.
  ISBN 978–1–4051–6922–6 (hardcover : alk. paper)   1. Aesthetics—Encyclopedias.
  BH56.C65 2009
  111′.8503—dc22

                                                    2008051223

A catalogue record for this title is available from the British Library.

Set in 9.5/11pt Photina
by Graphicraft Limited, Hong Kong
Printed in Singapore by Fabulous Printers Ltd Pte

01   2009

Contents

Contributors   xi
Preface   xv

Historical Overviews   1
    art of the Paleolithic Gregory Currie   1
    aesthetics in antiquity Stephen Halliwell   10
    medieval and renaissance aesthetics John Marenbon   22
    eighteenth-century aesthetics Paul Guyer   32
    nineteenth- and twentieth-century Continental aesthetics Robert Wicks   51
    twentieth-century Anglo-American aesthetics Stephen Davies & Robert Stecker   61

The Arts   74
    architecture Edward Winters   74
    dance Julie Van Camp   76
    drama James Hamilton   78
    drawing, painting, and printmaking Patrick Maynard   82
    literature David Davies   85
    motion pictures Noël Carroll   88
    music and song John Andrew Fisher and Stephen Davies   91
    opera Paul Thom   95
    photography Patrick Maynard   98
    poetry Anna Christina Ribeiro   101
    sculpture Erik Koed   104

A   107
    abstraction Robert Hopkins   107
    Adorno, Theodor W(iesengrund) Paul Mattick   109
    aesthetic attitude David E. Cooper   111
    aesthetic education Pradeep A. Dhillon   114
    aesthetic judgment Andrew Ward   117
    aesthetic pleasure Jerrold Levinson   121
    aesthetic properties Alan H. Goldman   124
    aestheticism David Whewell   128
    aesthetics of food and drink Carolyn Korsmeyer   131
    aesthetics of the environment Allen Carlson   134
    aesthetics of the everyday Sherri Irvin   136

African aesthetics John Ayotunde (Tunde) Isola Bewaji   139
Amerindian aesthetics Anthony K. Webster   142
Aquinas, Thomas John Haldane   145
Aristotle Stephen Halliwell   147
art history David Carrier   149
artifact, art as George Dickie & Robert Stecker   152
"artworld" Anita Silvers   155
authenticity and art Theodore Gracyk   156

B   160
Barthes, Roland Mary Bittner Wiseman   160
Baumgarten, Alexander G(ottlieb) Nicholas Davey   162
Beardsley, Monroe C(urtis) Donald Callen   163
beauty Mary Mothersill   166
Bell, (Arthur) Clive (Heward) Ronald W. Hepburn   172
Benjamin, Walter Martin Donougho   174
Burke, Edmund Patrick Gardiner   177

C   179
canon Stein Haugom Olsen   179
catharsis Stephen Halliwell   182
Cavell, Stanley Timothy Gould   183
censorship Bernard Williams   185
Chinese aesthetics Marthe Chandler   188
cognitive science and art William P. Seeley   191
cognitive value of art Matthew Kieran   194
Collingwood, R(obin) G(eorge) Michael Krausz   197
comedy Noël Carroll   199
conceptual art Peter Goldie   202
conservation and restoration David Carrier   205
creativity Berys Gaut   207
critical monism and pluralism Robert Kraut   211
criticism Michael Weston   215
Croce, Benedetto Douglas R. Anderson   219
cultural appropriation James O. Young   222

D   226
Danto, Arthur C(oleman) David Novitz & Stephen Davies   226
deconstruction Stuart Sim   229
definition of "art" Kathleen Stock   231
Deleuze, Gilles Nicholas Davey   234
depiction Katerina Bantinaki   238
Derrida, Jacques Mary Bittner Wiseman   241
Dewey, John Thomas M. Alexander   244
Dickie, George Noël Carroll   247
Dufrenne, Mikel Wojciech Chojna & Irena Kocol   249

E   252

  emotion Malcolm Budd   252
  erotic art and obscenity Matthew Kieran   256
  evolution, art, and aesthetics Stephen Davies   259
  expression Derek Matravers   261
  expression theory Derek Matravers   264

F   267

  feminist aesthetics Peg Zeglin Brand   267
  feminist criticism Renée Lorraine & Peg Zeglin Brand 269
  feminist standpoint aesthetics A. W. Eaton   272
  fiction, nature of Robert Stecker   275
  fiction, the paradox of responding to Alex Neill   278
  fiction, truth in Paisley Livingston   281
  fictional entities Diane Proudfoot   284
  forgery Robert Hopkins   287
  formalism Nick Zangwill   290
  Foucault, Michel Robert Wicks   293
  function of art David Novitz   297

G   302

  Gadamer, Hans-Georg Robert Bernasconi   302
  gardens David E. Cooper   304
  genre Andrew Harrison   306
  Gombrich, Sir Ernst (Hans Josef) David E. Cooper   308
  Goodman, Nelson Catherine Z. Elgin   311

H   314

  Hanslick, Eduard Malcolm Budd   314
  Hegel, Georg Wilhelm Friedrich Gary Shapiro   315
  Heidegger, Martin Robert Bernasconi   321
  hermeneutics Joseph Margolis   324
  horror Amy Coplan   328
  Hume, David Theodore Gracyk   331
  humor John Lippitt   334
  Hutcheson, Francis Peter Kivy   338

I   341

  iconoclasm and idolatry David Freedberg   341
  illusion Robert Hopkins   343
  imagination Roger Scruton   346
  imaginative resistance Tamar Szabó Gendler   351
  implied author Peter Lamarque   354
  Indian aesthetics Kalyan Sen Gupta   356
  ineffability David E. Cooper   360
  Ingarden, Roman Wojciech Chojna   364

intention and interpretation Colin Lyas & Robert Stecker 366
"intentional fallacy" Colin Lyas & Robert Stecker 369
interpretation Joseph Margolis 371
interpretation, aims of David Davies 375
irony David E. Cooper 378
Islamic aesthetics Oliver Leaman 381

J 384

Japanese aesthetics Yuriko Saito 384

K 388

Kant, Immanuel David Whewell 388
Kierkegaard, Søren Ann Loades 392
kitsch Kathleen Marie Higgins 393
Kristeva, Julia Laura Marcus 396

L 400

Langer, Susanne Thomas M. Alexander 400
Lessing, Gotthold Ephraim Anthony Savile 402
Lewis, C(larence) I(rving) Paisley Livingston 405
Lukács, Georg Tom Rockmore 408

M 411

Margolis, Joseph Richard Shusterman 411
Marxism and art Tom Rockmore 412
mass art Noël Carroll 415
meaning constructivism Robert Stecker 418
Merleau-Ponty, Maurice John J. Compton 421
metaphor Samuel R. Levin 423
modernism and postmodernism Stuart Sim 425
morality and art Berys Gaut 428
museums Paul Mattick 431

N 435

narrative Stein Haugom Olsen 435
Nietzsche, Friedrich (Wilhelm) Julian Young 438
notations Stephen Davies 441

O 444

objectivity and realism in aesthetics Robert Hopkins 444
ontological contextualism Theodore Gracyk 449
ontology of artworks Nicholas Wolterstorff 453
originality George Bailey 457

P 460

performance Stephen Davies 460
performance art David Davies 462

perspective John Hyman   465
picture perception Katerina Bantinaki   469
Plato Stephen Halliwell   472
Plotinus John Haldane   474
popular art Richard Shusterman   476
pornography Bernard Williams   478
pragmatist aesthetics Richard Shusterman   480
psychoanalysis and art Kathleen Marie Higgins   484

R   489

race and aesthetics Monique Roelofs   489
rasa Kathleen Marie Higgins   492
realism John Hyman   495
relativism Nicholas Davey   498
religion and art Robert Grant   500
representation Robert Hopkins   504
Ruskin, John Michael Wheeler   508

S   511

Santayana, George Morris Grossman   511
Sartre, Jean-Paul John J. Compton   512
Schelling, Friedrich Wilhelm Joseph von Andrew Bowie   514
Schiller, (Johann Christoph) Friedrich von Margaret Paton   517
Schlegel, August Wilhelm von Tom Rockmore   519
Schlegel, Friedrich von Tom Rockmore   520
Schopenhauer, Arthur Michael Tanner   522
science and art Anthony O'Hear   525
Scruton, Roger Anthony O'Hear   528
senses and art, the Robert Hopkins   530
sentimentality Deborah Knight   534
Shaftesbury, Lord Dabney Townsend   537
Sibley, Frank Noel Colin Lyas   538
structuralism and poststructuralism Stuart Sim   540
style Andrew Harrison   544
sublime Mary Mothersill   547
symbol Charles Molesworth   551

T   554

taste Robert Hopkins   554
technology and art John Andrew Fisher   556
testimony in aesthetics Robert Hopkins   560
text Richard Shusterman   562
theories of art Ronald W. Hepburn   565
Tolstoy, Leo David Whewell   570
tradition Anthony O'Hear   573
tragedy Susan L. Feagin   575
truth in art Eddy M. Zemach   578

U   581
  universals in art Kathleen Marie Higgins   581

W   586
  Wagner, Richard Michael Tanner   586
  Walton, Kendall L(ewis) Alessandro Giovannelli   588
  Wilde, Oscar David E. Cooper   591
  Wittgenstein, Ludwig Malcolm Budd   593
  Wollheim, Richard Malcolm Budd   596

Index   600

List of Contributors

Thomas M. Alexander
Southern Illinois University–Carbondale

Douglas R. Anderson
Southern Illinois University–Carbondale

George Bailey
East Carolina University

Katerina Bantinaki
University of Crete

Robert Bernasconi
University of Memphis

John Ayotunde (Tunde) Isola Bewaji
University of the West Indies

Andrew Bowie
Royal Holloway, University of London

Peg Zeglin Brand
*Indiana University–Purdue University
Indianapolis*

Malcolm Budd
University College London (Emeritus)

Donald Callen
Bowling Green State University

Allen Carlson
University of Alberta

David Carrier
*Case Western Reserve University/Cleveland
Institute of Art*

Noël Carroll
City University of New York Graduate Center

Marthe Chandler
DePauw University

Wojciech Chojna
La Salle University

John J. Compton
Vanderbilt University (Emeritus)

David E. Cooper
University of Durham

Amy Coplan
California State University–Fullerton

Gregory Currie
University of Nottingham

Nicholas Davey
University of Dundee

David Davies
McGill University

Stephen Davies
University of Auckland

Pradeep A. Dhillon
University of Illinois–Urbana–Champaign

George Dickie
University of Illinois–Chicago (Emeritus)

Martin Donougho
University of South Carolina

A. W. Eaton
University of Illinois–Chicago

Catherine Z. Elgin
Harvard Graduate School of Education

Susan L. Feagin
Temple University

John Andrew Fisher
University of Colorado–Boulder

David Freedberg
Columbia University

Patrick Gardiner
Magdalen College, Oxford
(Deceased)

Berys Gaut
University of St. Andrews

Tamar Szabó Gendler
Yale University

Alessandro Giovannelli
Lafayette College

Peter Goldie
University of Manchester

Alan H. Goldman
College of William & Mary

Timothy Gould
Metropolitan State College of Denver

Theodore Gracyk
Minnesota State University–Moorhead

Robert Grant
University of Glasgow

Morris Grossman
University of Fairfield (Emeritus)

Kalyan Sen Gupta
Jadavpur University

Paul Guyer
University of Pennsylvania

John Haldane
University of St. Andrews

Stephen Halliwell
University of St. Andrews

James Hamilton
Kansas State University

Andrew Harrison
University of Bristol
(Deceased)

Ronald W. Hepburn
University of Edinburgh
(Deceased)

Kathleen Marie Higgins
University of Texas at Austin

Robert Hopkins
University of Sheffield

John Hyman
The Queen's College, Oxford

Sherri Irvin
University of Oklahoma

Matthew Kieran
University of Leeds

Peter Kivy
Rutgers University

Deborah Knight
Queen's University, Ontario

Irena Kocol

Erik Koed
Independent scholar

Carolyn Korsmeyer
University at Buffalo

Michael Krausz
Bryn Mawr College

Robert Kraut
Ohio State University–Columbus

Peter Lamarque
University of York

Oliver Leaman
University of Kentucky

Samuel R. Levin
City University of New York

Jerrold Levinson
University of Maryland, College Park

John Lippitt
University of Hertfordshire

Paisley Livingston
Lingan University

Ann Loades
University of Durham

Renée Lorraine
University of Tennessee–Chattanooga

Colin Lyas
Independent scholar

Laura Marcus
University of Edinburgh

John Marenbon
Trinity College, Cambridge

Joseph Margolis
Temple University

Derek Matravers
Open University

Paul Mattick
Adelphi University

Patrick Maynard
University of Western Ontario (Emeritus)

Charles Molesworth
Queen's College, City University of New York

Mary Mothersill
Barnard College
(Deceased)

Alex Neill
University of Southampton

David Novitz
University of Canterbury, New Zealand
(Deceased)

Anthony O'Hear
University of Buckingham

Stein Haugom Olsen
University of Bergen

Margaret Paton
Independent scholar

Diane Proudfoot
University of Canterbury, New Zealand

Anna Christina Ribeiro
Texas Tech University

Tom Rockmore
Duquesne University

Monique Roelofs
Hampshire College

CONTRIBUTORS

Yuriko Saito
Rhode Island School of Design

Anthony Savile
King's College, University of London

Roger Scruton
Independent scholar

William P. Seeley
Bates College

Gary Shapiro
University of Richmond

Richard Shusterman
Florida Atlantic University

Anita Silvers
San Francisco State University

Stuart Sim
University of Sunderland

Robert Stecker
Central Michigan University

Kathleen Stock
University of Sussex

Michael Tanner
Corpus Christi College, Cambridge

Paul Thom
University of Sydney

Dabney Townsend
Armstrong Atlantic State University

Julie Van Camp
California State University–Long Beach

Andrew Ward
University of York

Anthony K. Webster
Southern Illinois University

Michael Weston
University of Essex

Michael Wheeler
University of Southampton

David Whewell
Independent scholar

Robert Wicks
University of Auckland

Bernard Williams
Corpus Christi College, Oxford
(Deceased)

Edward Winters
West Dean College

Mary Bittner Wiseman
Brooklyn College, City University of New York

Nicholas Wolterstorff
Yale University (Emeritus)

James O. Young
University of Victoria

Julian Young
University of Auckland

Nick Zangwill
University of Durham

Eddy M. Zemach
Hebrew University

Preface

Welcome to the second edition of *A Companion to Aesthetics*. Like the first edition of 1992, it consists primarily of short entries arranged alphabetically with the aim of covering as many topics and perspectives on aesthetics and the philosophy of art as possible. These include issues and authors prominent in both Anglo-American and Continental traditions and in both Western and non-Western thought about art. The goal is to provide an entrée to whatever issue in this increasingly vibrant field of inquiry a scholar, student, or layperson might desire to explore.

There is also much that is new to this edition and that provides a more systematic understanding of the discipline. Most prominently, there are six overview essays tracing the origins of art in the Paleolithic period and the history of aesthetics in the West from ancient times to the present day. There is also a greatly expanded group of essays on non-Western thought about art including new essays on African, Amerindian, Chinese, Islamic, and Japanese aesthetics as well as an essay on the concept of rasa, crucial in Indo-Asian aesthetics. The first edition contained no essays on individual art forms, which is remedied here by 11 new ones. Also new is a table of contents listing all 185 essays so that readers can see at glance what is on offer in this volume and better navigate it.

We have also expanded the list of short entries to reflect recent developments in aesthetics. One of these developments has perhaps shaped this volume more than any other. This is a debate between those who believe that the concept of art is peculiarly Western and relatively recent in origin, arising in the eighteenth century, and those who think that it is found in almost every culture, is ancient in origin, and derives from practices directly tied to human evolution. As well as motivating a new entry on evolutionary aesthetics, the suspicion that the second of these views is more likely true provides one rationale for the scope of the overview essays and the decision to give considerable coverage to non-Western aesthetics. Some proponents of the first view find support for it in the anthropology and sociology of art, while some proponents of the second view appeal to evolutionary psychology. This debate is symptomatic of a wider development in aesthetics, viz., the importation into aesthetics of ideas from the sciences, especially from evolutionary theory, anthropology, psychology, and cognitive studies. This reflects a trend in philosophy generally to take a greater interest in developments in the empirical sciences and to see philosophy as continuous with those disciplines.

A related development since the 1990s is the interaction between aesthetics and other areas of philosophy, including ethics, metaphysics, and the philosophy of mind and language. In part because of this interaction, there have been several "growth areas" in the discipline over the last 20 years, including the ontology of art, the multifaceted role of emotion in art, the role of pretense and make-believe in art, the interaction of ethics and aesthetics, feminist perspectives on art and the role of race and gender in art, environmental and everyday aesthetics, the nature of pictorial representation, and the nature of literary interpretation. There has also been a burst of new work on certain art forms, especially music and cinema. Many new entries analyze these developments.

Finally, we should mention that nearly every entry in the second edition is new in some way. Many of those carried over from the first edition have been revised and the rest have been updated to reflect new work done since their original appearance.

We would like to thank Daniel Wilson and Jennifer Saul, and from Wiley-Blackwell, Jeff Dean, Tiffany Mok, Barbara Duke, Janey Fisher, and Jacqueline Harvey.

Historical Overviews

art of the Paleolithic In 1789 John Frere, a Suffolk landowner, wrote to the Society of Antiquities describing stone implements discovered in a quarry at Hoxne. He did not draw attention to their appearance, focusing presciently on the vast age suggested by their position under a layer of sand and sea shells, and below the fossil remains of a large, unknown animal. They came, he surmised, from "a very remote period indeed, even beyond that of the present world" (Frere 1800). These objects are now known as Acheulean hand axes: tools made, in this case around 400,000 years ago (400k BP). Among them is a piece of worked stone, shaped as an elongated tear drop, roughly symmetrical in two dimensions, with a twist to the symmetry which has retained an embedded fossil. In size and shape it would not have been a useful butchery implement, and is worked on to a degree out of proportion to any likely use. While it may be too much to call it an "early work of art," it is at least suggestive of an aesthetic sensibility.

The origin of art is generally dated later than this: 360,000 years later. While prehistory is defined simply as that period of human habitation of a place for which there is no written record, studies of prehistoric art have tended to focus on the Upper Paleolithic, that period in European prehistory associated with the entry, around 40k BP, of *Homo sapiens*. The period ends with the Magdalenian culture of 18–10k BP that gave us the cave paintings of northern Spain and southern France. These extraordinary and mysteriously situated products of ice age Europe have generated vast art-historical speculation and are popularly represented as marking the dawn of art.

Later we will look back into the more distant past – as well as giving a brief sideways glance at Neanderthal neighbors – to examine the evidence for aesthetic production in the African Middle Stone Age, and then at stone artifacts as old as 1 million years before the present. Before doing so I will highlight two issues important for an understanding of the origin of artistic activity, and provide a brief account of human evolution.

BIOLOGY AND CULTURE

There are different kinds of explanations to hand for the innovations we find associated with the growth of art. One view has it that the dramatic changes to artistic and other practices we find in the Upper Paleolithic mark a development in human cognitive capacities consequent on biological change (Klein 2000). Another seeks the explanation in the nonbiological sphere, emphasizing, say, the relationship between increasing group size and such variables as efficiency of innovation or the growth in quantity and quality of children's pretend play, considered as a training ground for innovative activity. But the simple dichotomy between cognitive and cultural change breaks down if we accept that human cognition is itself partly a function of the environment in which the individual operates; on this view, the functional architecture of mind can change without change in the underlying biology. Michael Tomasello (1999) has argued that the biological difference between a baby human and a baby chimp is small, and that what makes for most of the eventual difference in cognitive power is that the human child is heir to a massive fortune in retained cultural innovation made possible by human tendencies to imitate one another. (Other researchers have recently suggested that chimps have more imitative ability than previously thought, however.) Further, cultural change may itself alter the distribution of genes in a population, as has been the case with increased lactose tolerance among cattle herders. One form that this change

1

may take is of especial interest. If, for example, changes to group size and pretend play intensify the degree of imaginative innovation in a population, and those who display this capacity in salient ways benefit in terms of survival and reproduction, then individuals born with greater capacities for imagination will benefit in ways they would not have done before the cultural change. This will change the pattern of genes' relative contributions to fitness, and intensify the selection for imagination-relevant genes. This effect – the Baldwin Effect – can look like Lamarckian evolution, since an acquired improvement in some ability can seem to give rise directly to the inheritance of that ability (see Papineau 2005).

Whatever humans do, they must have a biological make-up that allows them to do it, but it is generally not profitable to seek specific associations between biological and cultural change. The point, if there is one, at which we identify the first significant artistic activity may be of no biological significance. Still, as we look further and further back into the evolutionary past, changes to brains and other bodily structures may be of special relevance in explaining the beginning of activities that suggest themselves as precursors of art-making.

ART AND THE AESTHETIC

On visiting Altamira Cave, Picasso is reported to have said "We have learned nothing," powerfully encapsulating the thought that these great works represent what European art has struggled to achieve in its painful path to – and beyond – pictorial realism. Thus the cave paintings were easily incorporated into a conception of "high art" that spoke to classical and modernist sensibilities. More recent tendencies in art practice and theory have questioned this; to the extent that we take these developments seriously, they undermine the assumptions that make it appropriate to see the products of Upper Paleolithic cultures as art.

In a move which gained its impetus from Duchamp's ready-mades of the early twentieth century, conceptual artists and others have been in revolt against the idea that art involves the production of beautiful or aesthetically pleasing objects, opting instead for activities which are in various ways provocative, especially by way of challenging our assumptions about

art itself. In a philosophical move made partly to accommodate these practices, it has been asserted that what is art depends, not on the look of the object, but on its place in an institutional structure, the "artworld." A different accommodation is offered by those who argue that art is a historical concept in the sense that what we may legitimately count as art now depends on how the objects in question are related to the art of the past. Is it possible, for instance, to tell a coherent narrative that links this object with the aspirations productive of earlier work? While we may choose carefully among these doctrines, together they offer something like the following challenge: while we can find in the very distant past objects which please us aesthetically and which may have had a similar effect on their makers and audience, we cannot on these grounds assume that these things are art, especially when we do not find either any meaningful historical link between these objects and that which we antecedently recognize as art, or any developed institutions of art in the societies that produced them. Further, there are regular denunciations of the idea that "art" is a concept we may apply to societies very different from our own. These arguments are often directed at our treatment of preliterate societies of the present and recent past, but have been taken up by paleoanthropologists who insist that "'Art' as a modern Western construct is anachronistic with the Paleolithic" (Nowell 2006: 244).

This suite of objections cannot be replied to here in detail; instead I will make the following general remarks. First, the separation (if there is one) between the aesthetic and the artistic seems to be extremely recent and it can hardly be a criticism of any theory that it looks for connections between art and the aesthetic in the distant past, when virtually all but the last 50 years of art history reinforces that connection. It is true that our current and recent artistic practices and institutions are different from those of preliterate societies of which we know anything, and doubtless very different from those of prehistory. This cannot be grounds for saying that the concept "art" has no application to other societies. It is allowed that peoples in all conditions and at all times have both technology and religion, though theirs may differ greatly from our own. A culture's technology may be seen as underpinned by magical forces, or as subject to the will of gods. Religions may be polytheistic and suffused with magical elements in ways that make them far distant from the systematic and official doctrines some of us subscribe to today. Our art is not obviously more distant from that of the Upper Paleolithic than Anglicanism is from the religion of, say, the San people of southern Africa well into the twentieth century – a system of belief that, it has been suggested, is the best model we now have for religion in the Upper Paleolithic (Lewis-Williams 2002). Anyway, opponents of aesthetic approaches to culture find the extreme clash of artistic conceptions they are looking for only by failing to compare like with like: they compare the beliefs and practices common among members of preliterate societies with the notions of a contemporary cultural elite whose formulations correspond hardly at all to conceptions of art, beauty, and the aesthetic in the rest of their populations.

This highly selective suspicion about art and the aesthetic may derive from the thought that appeal to aesthetic values is an explanatory dead end. But ethical ideas and practices are regularly subject to interrogation using economic and other models without their ceasing thereby to count as values. Treating Stone Age objects as aesthetic, and even as art, is not inconsistent with trying to understand them in a broader economic, demographic, cultural, and evolutionary perspective – as we shall see. Sometimes emphasis on the aesthetic dimension of Stone Age cultures is associated with the discredited idea that early people produced these objects to fill their leisure hours (Lewis-Williams 2002: 42). Again, this is by no means a burden that an advocate of the aesthetic approach must carry. Certainly, we ought to question the anthropologist's assumption that the "symbolic" is an explanatory category always to be preferred to the aesthetic, and one which is to be invoked any time we find something with no apparent utilitarian function (d'Errico et al. 2003: 18). It is unclear, for example, why early musical practices or bodily adornments should be assumed to symbolize anything. Depictive paintings such as we find in the Upper Paleolithic represent things, but it is a further step to conclude that they are symbolic. This is a particularly relevant point given that, as we shall see,

there is evidence of aesthetic activity that massively predates any evidence of symbolic behavior.

HUMAN ANCESTRY AND PREHISTORY
The most recent common ancestor of humans and chimpanzees lived some 7 million years ago in Africa. We have evidence for about 20 species on the human side of this divide (the *hominina*); all evolved in Africa, and only one has survived, ours (*Homo sapiens*). Around 2.5 million years ago (2.5m BP) several coexisted; the pathway of our own descent through these species is not well understood. At this time, human species – *Homo ergaster*, called *erectus* in Asia, and *Homo antecessor* – moved into Asia and Europe. Some time around 200k BP anatomically modern humans evolved in Africa. By 80k BP they had moved into the Middle East, and by 40k BP into Europe and Australia. In Europe they lived alongside *Homo Neanderthalis*, a much earlier immigrant species, which disappeared around 30k BP.

Our period is the Old Stone Age, or Paleolithic, which begins around 2.5m BP with the production of crude stone tools created by striking. At this time there were several species of *hominina* living: our own relatively large-brained ancestor *Homo habilis*, together with species of an older genus, *Australopithecus*, which had smaller brains and larger teeth. While it is fair to assume that *Homo habilis* was an early toolmaker, these other species may have been also. Styles of tool-making did not change until around 1.5m BP when *Homo ergaster* introduced the Acheulean technology that involved taking off small flakes from the surface to produce a symmetrical implement. This technology went with the African emigrant communities to Europe and Asia: Frere's hand ax, found in England, is a late example. No clear evidence of culturally determined differences in style is available for the Acheulean industry. Around 300k BP the Acheulean gave way to the Levallois industry marked by the pre-shaping of a stone core from which flakes are successively struck. This time marks the beginning of the Middle Stone Age (called the Middle Paleolithic in Europe), where we find the shaping and marking of shells and soft stone, the making of hafted weapons, and clear indications of cultural variation in production. With the Late Stone Age (Upper Paleolithic in Europe) from 40k BP, we have increased economy and complexity in stone tool manufacture, evidence of tailored clothing, sophistication in hunting, and greater population density. The Upper Paleolithic begins with the Aurignacian culture in western Europe from about 40–28k BP; this culture has been said both to represent a significant qualitative shift in sophistication (sometimes called the cultural Big Bang) as compared with that of the Middle Stone Age, and to be associated exclusively with the *Homo sapiens* newcomers into Europe. Both of these claims are disputed. The Paleolithic is conventionally reckoned to end about 10k BP after the last glaciation and with the beginnings of farming.

DOES ART BEGIN IN THE UPPER PALEOLITHIC?
Schematic outline depictions of animal parts have been found from times early in the Upper Paleolithic, around 35k BP, in the Aurignacian period. Given that the cave paintings at Altamira and Lascaux are dated around 15k BP, it was once possible to believe that the Upper Paleolithic enclosed the development, over many thousands of years, of pictorial style from crude Aurignacian to mature Magdalenian. But in 1994 paintings were discovered at Chauvet Cave in southern France, many with the same startling realism, fluidity, and individuality of style as those found at Lascaux. Some of the Chauvet cave pictures were quickly dated at 31k BP. These dates have been questioned, largely on the grounds that the depictions in the cave have stylistic features in common with known work from the Magdelanian, while being, it is claimed, at odds with the other evidence available of the Aurignacian (Pettit & Bahn 2003). We await the outcome of this debate; I will assume the dating is correct.

At Chauvet Cave there is a predominance of large, fierce animals that contrasts with the later (Magdalenian) representation of hunted species, creating difficulty for theories that explained cave paintings as ritual invocation of magic to aid hunters: a view associated particularly with Abbé Breuil who, in the first half of the twentieth century, was a dominant figure in the study of prehistoric art. There are groups of animals occluding one another; a group of horses thus displayed has been argued, intriguingly, to represent a single animal at

various times, rather than a series of animals laid out in space. There is a bison with the head twisted to one side, looking out of the picture plane. It has been said that the use of natural surface features of the rock that are suggestive in shape of the animals then painted on them is a feature of later Magdalenian depiction, but this technique is found at Chauvet also. Chauvet was impeccably treated from the moment of its discovery and may deliver important clues to the purpose of the depictions.

At Chauvet, as at other, later, sites, there are puzzling aspects to the execution of the work; figures are sometimes painted one on top of another, with no apparent regard to overall coherence; some depictions are so placed they can hardly be seen at all; elsewhere great trouble has been taken to enhance viewing conditions for a particular work; anamorphic representation occasionally defines a specific viewing point. The animals often have a "floating" quality; the creatures seem to stand in no physical place and legs are generally schematically represented. Nor is there generally any narrative content to the picture, an Aurignacian depiction of two rhinos face to face at Chauvet being a possible exception. Human figures are rare in cave art and, when they occasionally appear, are schematically represented, in marked contrast to the sometimes sharp individuality of the animals. In addition to the depictive representations there are various geometrical markings for which it has been difficult to find an interpretation. Some of these features are addressed by theories to be described later.

It is worth bearing in mind that photographic reproduction gives no idea of what viewing *in situ* is like, sometimes in places very difficult of access, in acoustically resonant chambers, lit only, as they then would have been, by flickering torches. Nor can the effort of these depictive projects be easily exaggerated; the surface of the wall was often elaborately prepared; heat to 1000 °C was needed for certain ochre preparations; at Lascaux, wooden scaffolding has been used to get the artist to the required height.

In addition to their dramatic cave paintings, the Aurignacians provided grave goods for the dead, used bodily adornment, and crafted their artifacts according to an aesthetic of skillful and sometimes witty representation: a popular item, mass produced by the standards of the day, was a spear-thrower shaped as an animal in the act of defecating. From 34k BP there is an exquisite horse in ivory from Vogelherd, Germany. From 28–30k BP there is a human figure with the head of a lion carved in ivory; from 28–25k BP a tiny limestone figure of a grotesque human female; from 25–23k BP a bas relief in limestone of a woman. Chimeric figures speak of a developed imaginative sense; one depiction at Chauvet seems to be a bison-headed man.

Recent research has chipped away, somewhat, at the artistic uniqueness of the Upper Paleolithic. There is evidence from earlier periods and distant places, as well as intriguing evidence of activity among the Neanderthal people whose habitation of Europe greatly preceded that of *Homo sapiens*. At Blombos Cave (southern Cape) we have perforated shells, which are most likely personal ornaments, as well as many thousands of ochre crayons, two with systematic, apparently abstract markings, all reliably dated at around 74k BP. Perforated shells claimed to have been used as beads have now been reported from north African sites dated to 82k BP and 100–135k BP. Pigments of various kinds are found in layers datable much earlier even than this, possibly around 400k BP, and some scholars are willing to infer their use in aesthetic activity, perhaps bodily adornment.

In one respect the Upper Paleolithic does, on current evidence, cling precariously to a significant first: depiction. Here we need to distinguish between work in two and three dimensions; the situation as regards sculpture is a little ambiguous. The earliest two-dimensional depictions we have in an African context are those from Apollo 11 cave (Namibia): a number of freestanding slabs of rock on which animal figures have been painted: rhinoceros, zebra, large cat. There is a suggestion that the last of these is a hybrid with human legs, but this is far from certain. Dating has been disputed, but 26k BP remains the most likely, compared with 35k BP for the Upper Paleolithic. Agreed dates for the Australian context are hard to find, but there is little direct evidence for depictive marking

before about 20k BP. It is to be emphasized that new discoveries in any of these places could radically alter the picture. Turning to sculpture, a puzzling item is the so-called Berekhat Ram figurine, a small piece of basalt reminiscent of a female head and body, dated prior to 200k BP. The most likely hypothesis is that the natural shape of the rock suggested the human form, and this has been made slightly clearer by deliberate but minimal abrasion and incision (d'Errico & Nowell 2000).

If the Berekhat Ram figurine does represent an early attempt at mimetic representation, the idea does not seem to have caught on; we have no other such objects from the period, or any time before 35k BP. And while sophisticated tool-making in stone and bone is visible in the Middle Stone Age, the various innovations found there were not preserved and accumulated in the way they were in the Upper Paleolithic; they make their appearance and are absent from the later record (Zilhão 2007). What may be distinctive about the Upper Paleolithic are its robust patterns of cultural and technological reproduction, which helped communities to turn individual innovation into sustained practices.

If the Aurignacians had aesthetic precursors they may also have had contemporary competitors. The recent consensus has been that Neanderthal symbolic activity, such as it was, was merely imitation of *Homo sapiens* neighbors. But the argument is put that there are small but significant amounts of ornamental material, such as perforated animal teeth, from the time before *Homo sapiens* entered Europe, and that much in evidence thereafter cannot be explained simply as low-level imitation (Zilhão 2007).

Something needs to be said about arts other than the visual. Pieces of hollow bone with holes in them have been interpreted as wind instruments; in many cases it is likely that the holes were made by carnivores. The earliest instruments we can be confident of are from Isturitz (France) and Geissenklosterle (Germany), some of which have likely dates of 35–30k BP. D'Errico et al. (2003) argue that these instruments are sophisticated and must emerge from a long tradition of musical development of which we currently have no artifactual evidence. Storytelling is undatable earlier than the written record, but if the cave paintings of the

Upper Paleolithic have religious or magical associations as many suppose (see below), narrative must have been in place by then. Indeed, it is probably much older; as old, perhaps, as language. If, as some suppose (Dunbar 1996), language began as social cement, the narrative form may have been in place very early in its development, since gossip – telling A about the doings and motives of B – is naturally conveyed in narrative. Since the function of gossip is as much to manipulate as to inform, the earliest narratives may have included deliberate falsehoods. The ability to construct a plausible but false narrative seems to require imaginative capacities of some kind, but we can only speculate as to how and when the construction of highly elaborated and even avowedly fictional narratives emerged, and what the precise cognitive preconditions for them were.

Returning to the visual domain: Can we find evidence of aesthetic production even earlier than the perforated shells and marked crayons of 70–135k BP? Recalling John Frere and his hand ax, we find evidence of a very deep history of aesthetic production: a history so long that it makes the Upper Paleolithic look positively contemporary. This history extends back long before our species emerged, long before language developed, long – apparently – before any genuinely symbolic activity of any kind.

The first stone tools were made by *Homo habilis*; we find stone artifacts at African sites going back to 2.5m BP, the so-called Oldowan technology. Before about 1.4m BP we do not find anything aesthetic about them; they are simply stones on which a cutting edge has been made, with no attention to anything but practical need. It seems likely that people at this time used both the cores and the flakes cut from them, the cores for dismembering and smashing bones, and the flakes for cutting off meat.

It is with the Acheulean industry first attributed to *Homo ergaster* and beginning around 1.4m BP that we see objects with a deliberately and systematically imposed symmetry, created by removing flakes all over the stone's surface. Some are finely shaped, thin and highly symmetrical in three dimensions, with flakes taken off by using, successively, stone, antler, and wooden implements. One elegantly elongated piece in phonolite (green volcanic

lava) from Olduvai is dated at 1.2m BP (British Museum, P&E PRB 1934.12-14.49); another from the same place, dated at 800k BP, is an extraordinarily crafted piece of quartz with amethyst bands, a difficult material to work (British Museum, P&E PRB 1934.12-14.83). Size and shaping are often not consistent with practical use, and indeed many such objects are found with no evidence of wear. There are examples, as with the Hoxne axe, of an apparently intentional twist to the symmetry and a retained fossil. In addition to the standard tear-shaped hand ax there are dagger-like ficrons and cleavers with a transverse cutting blade; a recent find in the UK has located one of each, described as "exquisite, almost flamboyant," and so placed as to suggest their having been made by the same individual (Wenban-Smith 2004). The obvious question is "why hominids went to all that bother when a simple flake would have sufficed?" (White 2000).

One answer is that hand ax technology was partly an investment in the creation of something pleasurable to look at, and for that a simple flake does not suffice. Now there is another question. When we find creatures investing scarce resources in an activity, we want to know what is adaptive about it. So what is adaptive about making beauty? One answer is that *costly signals* may benefit both parties in a communicative situation when the evident cost of the signal is a reliable indicator of some relevant quality in the signaler. Gazelles pursued by predators may stop their flight to leap in the air; this stotting behavior, which puts the prey at greater risk, indicates the strong likelihood that the prey is healthy enough to escape with a margin for safety; the chase – costly to both in energy and likely get the predator nowhere – may then be broken off.

If overworked hand axes are reliable signals, what do they signal? There is a range of possibilities here: the best known takes us from natural to sexual selection, those forces shaping reproductive advantage by conferring a certain degree of attractiveness as a mate. Ax construction requires significant spatial skills to produce a symmetrical object; skill at resource location; and time, which in turn implies general efficiency and security in social matters. Marak Kohn and Steven Mithen (1999) suggest that symmetrical, aesthetically wrought ax production was a means of reliably advertising these qualities to prospective mates. Supposing these creatures already possessed a tendency to like their conspecifics better if they did or made likable things, one mechanism to ensure that the maker seems attractive is to ensure that the products themselves are pleasing. None of this assumes that our ancestors *saw* hand axes as signs of fitness; all that is required is that they admire the hand axes in ways that enhance the maker's chance of reproducing. Costly displays may secure other advantages: social power within the group, or better resources from caregivers. While finding direct evidence for any of these hypotheses may be difficult, the important point is that the emergence of capacities for skillful, nonutilitarian production is by no means inconsistent with Darwinism.

Attentiveness to the visual form of artifacts will not explain much about the particular direction that aesthetic styles and genres have subsequently taken; our story is merely one about the source of a river the subsequent detailed course of which cannot be predicted from its starting point. But once a tendency to make pleasing things, and to contemplate the things and their making, is established, other evolved capacities will feed into determining the shape of these activities. Evolutionary psychologists have emphasized the importance of habitat choice in the survival of our species, and it is to be expected that pleasure would accrue to us on contemplating those scenes most likely to have nurtured us during the Pleistocene. A popular form of landscape art is said to be the beneficiary of this preference. What then of our liking for mountainous and inhospitable scenes of the sublime? The situation here parallels the relation between ethical preference and tragedy: we enjoy the good outcomes of comedy but also – in different ways – the bad ones of tragedy. The most we ought to say is that our sense of what is and is not a hospitable environment contributes to the *kind* of pleasure we take in a scene; it does not mark the divide between what is aesthetically pleasing and what is not.

DEPICTION AND THE SYMBOLIC

On current evidence, there was no systematic practice of depiction, in two or three dimensions, before 40k BP. By 30k BP there was carving of figures, painting, and drawing, with mastery of realist techniques that capture the spirit of fierce lions and gentle horses. There is for this period no record, as yet, of anything like the painful steps toward naturalistic representation that brought Western art to the Renaissance. How did the discovery, or the invention, of depiction come about?

The possibility of depiction depends on the phenomenon of *seeing-in*, our capacity to see a figure or a face in the pattern of lines and colors on a surface (Wollheim 1980: supp. essay V). We can also see a person's face in the shape of a pebble, or a head in a sculptured piece of clay. Seeing-in depends partly on the fact that the human visual system, like any perceptual mechanism, is subject to false positives. The visual system uses the input from the eyes to identify the object seen, and may come up with the answer "person" when there is in fact no person there but instead merely a pattern of lines on a surface or a shaped solid which triggers the visual system's person-recognition capacity. Being able to recognize something goes with being prone to misrecognize it.

This does not mean that pictures create illusions of the presence of depicted objects; it is the visual system, a subpersonal mechanism, that is fooled, not the person in the gallery who possesses the mechanism. The agent knows full well that there is no person really there, and information from the visual system serves merely to help the person recognize the content of what is depicted. Animals are also subject to false-positives; birds and fish will flee when shown the outline shapes of their predators. But this is not seeing-in, since the bird or fish does not realize that this is not really a predator. Great apes are capable, however, of seeing the contents of pictures without always being fooled into thinking that the content is actually present, and some human-reared apes have shown a capacity to sort pictures by subject matter. If the capacity to see things in pictures is one we share with our ape relatives, it is likely to be much older in our lineage than 40,000 years.

The capacity for seeing-in is not enough to make one capable of depiction – something other great apes do not seem to be capable of. You need to be able – and motivated – to produce arrangements of lines or colors within

7

which things can be seen. Creatures who are able to see things in other things do not need depictions in order to have the experience of seeing-in; we see people's faces in clouds, frost, and many other natural phenomena. Indeed, so prone are humans to recognize a face that a pattern on a pebble very vaguely resembling the arrangement of eyes, nose, and mouth will produce the experience of seeing a face in the pebble's surface. And there are other such stimuli around: footprints and animal hoof marks, which constitute photograph-like impressions of the things of which they are traces; protuberances on cave walls which are in the shape of an animal (as noted, the cave artists exploited these shapes); shadows thrown by sun and firelight (many caves contain "shadow" depictions, where paint has been sprayed on the wall over which a hand has been placed). We may assume that people have a very long history of attending to objects within which things could be seen. It is surprising then that we have not found stones whereon someone has chipped a vaguely face-like arrangement of marks. Yet we know that for 1 million years our ancestors worked skillfully in stone to shape it both for use and – apparently – for aesthetic pleasure (see above). Whitney Davis (1986) has argued that it was the sheer accumulation of nondepictive marks on surfaces that provoked seeing-in and led to the invention of depiction during the Upper Paleolithic. But it is not the experience of seeing-in that needs explaining; that can be assumed to be available, and common, well before the Upper Paleolithic. Rather it is the invention of ways deliberately to create something in which something else can be seen. This seems to have been surprisingly elusive.

Other explanations of depiction focus on cultural developments in the Upper Paleolithic. It has long been suggested that cave art was connected with magical and religious practices. Partly on the basis of ethnographic studies of living hunter-gatherer communities and their shamanistic practices, David Lewis-Williams (2002) has argued that these caves were thought of as boundaries between the natural and supernatural worlds, where the images, often in relief and dramatically illuminated by the movement of a torch, and seen under conditions of altered psychological states, con-

tributed to experiences of magical connection to the other world. Lewis-Williams then suggests that these altered states explain the origin of depiction. These states include ones in which mental images appear to be projected onto external surfaces; people, he suggests, reached out to "touch" and preserve these images, producing image-like marks on soft surfaces – the first depictions. This accounts, says Lewis-Williams, for the strange geometrical markings, which correspond to imagistic experiences typical of such altered states. One question that arises here is whether the development and understanding of a capacity for depiction is likely when the people concerned were taking mind-altering drugs and thought themselves in the presence of magical beings. Lewis-Williams offers a plausible account of some opportunities for seeing-in. But this is not what needs explaining, since, as I have indicated, people would have had such opportunities on many occasions prior to the development of shamanistic culture.

This approach associates the development of pictorial art with the growth of relatively sophisticated cultural practices such as story-telling and religion. An entirely different explanation is offered by Nicholas Humphrey (1998), who notes striking similarities between the paintings at Chauvet (and other Upper Paleolithic sites) and the precocious drawings of a young autistic girl, Nadia, whose depictions have been extensively documented. Like the cave painters, Nadia tended to draw one thing on top of another, and sometimes produced apparently chimerical figures; this may have been due simply to the fact that her focus on detail at the expense of gestalt left her vulnerable to changing tack midway through a picture. Nadia's drawing declined as she acquired language, consistent with the idea that having a language-based schema of knowledge about things derails the attempt to reproduce the way they look, a capacity typically developing children acquire only by painful and culturally scaffolded learning. While it is generally assumed that language was fully developed by the Upper Paleolithic, Dunbar (1996) and Mithen (1996) have suggested that it did not evolve as a whole, but in stages corresponding to the mind's then distinctive modular structure, with "social language" first off the blocks.

Drawing these thoughts together, Humphrey argues that the cave artists, while not autistic, had minds as radically different from ours as Nadia's was from the typically developing child's. Language, he suggests, was at that time only partly developed, being social, and not yet available to the "natural history" module. That way we can see the cave painters as having a Nadia-like capacity for linguistically unencumbered naturalism in depicting the animal world, while the absence of convincing human figures from the corpus is explained by the derailing effect of their intact social (inter-personal) language. Humphrey's suggestion is highly revisionary, since it places a lower bound on fully developed language later than the naturalistic school of cave painting. Also, the supposed transition from a modular to a gen-eral-purpose mind cannot now be invoked, as it is by Mithen, to explain the cultural break-throughs of 40–30k BP (but see Currie 2004: ch. 12). Nonetheless, Humphrey's observation that the pictorial sophistication of cave paint-ings cannot be proof of the modernity of their makers' minds is well taken. And for reasons I will come to immediately, his challenge to received wisdom is very welcome.

Part of Humphrey's challenge is to the pre-sumption that the Upper Paleolithic represents the transition to a "symbolic" culture wherein decoration of grave sites, cave walls, and implements speaks of a richly meaningful con-nection to a spiritual world, the values it imparts to us, and the narratives we tell of it – things scarcely possible without a language that integrates thought about the natural and the social. Over the last 100 years there have been regular if not very successful challenges to the idea that cave art and its associated artifacts have spiritual or symbolic meaning. Labeled by its enemies "art for art's sake," and hence woundingly associated with "fin-de-siècle decadence" (Halverson 1987), this challenge has often taken the form of a *general* denial of meaning to these artifacts. While this position does not strike me as obviously wrong, it is important to see that it is the extreme end of a spectrum of views that make explanatory appeal to the idea of the aesthetic. We might hold instead that a certain object provides aesthetic pleasure as well as having some symbolic func-tion (or indeed a function of some other kind),

and that its characteristics are not explicable in terms of just one of these factors. Nor is it mandatory to hold that the symbolic must have primacy over the aesthetic, in the sense of carrying the greater explanatory burden, or corresponding to a deeper, more urgent, or phylogenetically older motivation. If the evid-ence of the Acheulean technology is anything to go by, the order of priority is likely to be the other way around. Indeed, aesthetic sensibility may play its part in explaining the develop-ment of symbolic culture. If aesthetic sense is a sensitivity to "good making," as the costly sig-naling hypothesis suggests, the design-like fea-tures of the natural world can be expected to trigger aesthetic responses and to create illusions of purpose, leading to ideas of magic and reli-gion. Nor, finally, is the idea of an irreducibly aesthetic motive to be written off as a roman-tic belief in our enduring recognition of the value of beauty. Aesthetic preference may be basic – people seeking aesthetic experience simply for the pleasure it brings – and at the same time fully and naturalistically explicable in terms of, say, the entirely contingent way that sexual selection has shaped our tendencies to be delighted.

ART AND THE AESTHETIC

Implicit in the above account is a budget of problems to which philosophers of art may contribute some clarification, but which are empirical and on which we shall expect the sciences to lead the way. Among them are questions about what explains, and what is explained by, the aesthetic sensibilities of Stone Age peoples. Other questions concern the ways in which aesthetic activity was organized, understood, and integrated with other activities. What sense, within this framework, should we give to the familiar question "When did art begin?" If we allow that not all aesthetic making is art-making, we might try to decide whether there is some significant shift in the pattern of human aesthetic activity which identifies a point at which "art" becomes a sen-sible label to apply. Given the contested nature of the concept "art," agreement on this will not be easily found. I suggest we take our cue from the two sets of questions distinguished above, and look at the archaeological record for evid-ence that aesthetic activity has, at certain times and places, become a community practice, reflected upon in communal discourse and to some extent institutionalized through division of labor. It is likely always to remain a matter of very indirect inference as to whether such conditions were met in the Upper Paleolithic or Late Stone Age.

For information on the Acheulean industry and a digital archive of images see http://antiquity.ac.uk/ProjGall/marshall/marshall.html. For Blombos see http://www.svf.uib.no/sfu/blombos/. For Apollo 11 see http://images.google.co.uk/imgres?imgurl=http://www.klaus-dierks.com/images/Namibia_Karas_ApolloXI_4.jpg&imgrefurl=http://www.klausdierks.com/Chronology/1.htm&h=629&w=799&sz=199&hl=en&start=40&um=1&tbnid=Od2Z-c2KOVJV_M:&tbnh=113&tbnw=143&prev=/images%3Fq%3Dapollo%2B11%2Bcave%2B%26start%3D20%26ndsp%3D20%26um%3D1%26hl%3Den%26safe%3Dactive%26sa%3DN. For Chauvet see http://www.culture.gouv.fr/culture/arcnat/chauvet/en/. For Lascaux see http://www.culture.gouv.fr/culture/arcnat/lascaux/en/. For Altamira see http://museodealtamira.mcu.es/ingles/index.html.

See also "ARTWORLD"; COGNITIVE SCIENCE AND ART; DEFINITION OF "ART"; EVOLUTION, ART, AND AESTHETICS; FUNCTION OF ART; PICTURE PERCEPTION; UNIVERSALS IN ART.

BIBLIOGRAPHY
Currie, Gregory. 2004. *Arts and Minds*. Oxford: Oxford University Press.
Davis, Whitney. 1986. "The Origins of Image Making," *Current Anthropology*, 27, 193–215.
d'Errico, F. et al. 2003. "Archaeological Evidence for the Emergence of Language, Symbolism, and Music: An Alternative Multidisciplinary Perspective," *Journal of World Prehistory*, 1, 1–70.
d'Errico, F. & Nowell, A. 2000. "A New Look at the Berekhat Ram Figurine: Implications for the Origins of Symbolism," *Cambridge Archaeological Journal* 10, 123–67.
Dunbar, Robin. 1996. *Grooming, Gossip and the Evolution of Language*. Cambridge, MA: Harvard University Press.
Frere, John. 1800. "Account of Flint Weapons Discovered at Hoxne in Suffolk," *Archaeologia*, 13, 204–5.
Halverson, J. 1987. "Art for Art's Sake in the Paleolithic," *Current Anthropology*, 28, 63–89.
Humphrey, Nicholas. 1998. "Cave Art, Autism, and the Evolution of the Human Mind," *Cambridge Archaeological Journal*, 8, 165–91 (with commentaries and replies from Humphrey).
Klein, R. G. 2000. "Archaeology and the Evolution of Human Behavior," *Evolution of Anthropology*, 9, 17–36.
Kohn, Marak & Mithen, Steven. 1999. "Handaxes: Products of Sexual Selection," *Antiquity*, 73, 518–26.
Lewis-Williams, David. 2002. *The Mind in the Cave: Consciousness and the Origins of Art*. London: Thames & Hudson.
Mithen, Steven. 1996. *The Prehistory of the Mind*. London: Thames & Hudson.
Nowell, A. 2006. "From a Paleolithic Art to Pleistocene Visual Cultures," *Journal of Archaeological Method and Theory*, 13, 239–49.
Papineau, D. 2005. "Social Learning and the Baldwin Effect." In *Cognition, Evolution, and Rationality*. A. Zilhão (ed.). London: Routledge, 40–60.
Pettit, P. & Bahn, Paul. 2003. "Current Problems of Dating Palaeolithic Cave Art: Candamo and Chauvet," *Antiquity*, 77, 134–41.
Tomasello, Michael. 1999. *The Cultural Origins of Human Cognition*. Cambridge, MA: Harvard University Press.
Wenban-Smith, F. 2004. "Handaxe Typology and Lower Palaeolithic Cultural Development: Ficrons, Cleavers and Two Giant Handaxes from Cuxton," *Lithics*, 25, 11–21.
White, M. 2000. "The Clactonian Question: On the Interpretation of Core-and-Flake Assemblages in the British Lower Palaeolithic," *Journal of World Prehistory*, 14, 1–63.
Wollheim, Richard. 1980. *Art and Its Objects*. 2nd edn. Cambridge: Cambridge University Press.
Zilhão, João. 2007. "The Emergence of Ornaments and Art: An Archaeological Perspective on the Origins of 'Behavioral Modernity'," *Journal of Archaeological Research*, 15, 1–54.

GREGORY CURRIE

aesthetics in antiquity Although "aesthetics" is a word of Greek derivation (*aisthêtikos*, adj.: "relating to perception"), there is no specific ancient usage, nor any explicit branch of ancient thought, which corresponds to the modern sense of the term. When Baumgarten coined the word for the sensory cognition of beauty, he was aware of a Greek philosophical contrast between the perceptual and the "noetic" or intellectual. But that contrast is employed by thinkers such as Plato and Aristotle without any necessary reference either to beauty or to the group of arts (poetry, music, painting, etc.) that have become central to modern aesthetics. To conclude from this, however, that there was no aesthetics *tout court* in antiquity would be premature.

Greco-Roman culture produced, in fact, a complex tradition of reflections both on beauty and on the principles of poetic, musical, and figurative art forms. These reflections emerged within and between various frameworks of thought: poetics, rhetorical theory, cultural critique, systems of metaphysics, as well as technical treatises (outside the scope of this article) on painting, music, and architecture. On any nondoctrinaire understanding of the concept, antiquity plays a formative, influential role in the history of aesthetics. The challenge is to trace the ancient phases of this history in a spirit that can identify affinities and continuities without forcing the past into the mold of the present, and to recognize that the status of ancient aesthetics is important in part precisely because of its refusal to constitute a single domain of thought.

ARCHAIC ORIGINS

Many of the questions, problems, and ideas which stimulated ancient impulses in aesthetics were generated by the "song culture" of archaic Greece (eighth to sixth centuries BCE) – a culture in which poetry, music, and dance were a major means of expressing religious, political, ethical, and erotic values, often in special social contexts such as festivals and feasts. Homeric epic, with its narrative of a distant world of heroic myth, contains resonant images of the psychological potency of song. These include the remarkable scene where Odysseus, though paradoxically overcome by "grief" when hearing a song about his own prominence as a warrior, feels a profound need to repeat the experience (*Odyssey* 8.62–92, 485–531): song reveals his life to him in a new light. In archaic Greece generally, song at its finest is regarded as a gift from the gods: a gift, often, of "inspiration" by the Muses (which can still leave room, however, for human skill), but also a quality of radiant loveliness (sometimes called *charis*, inadequately translated "grace") which emanates from anything touched by the divine. Whatever its sources,

song has the capacity to induce states of rapt enthrallment, even quasi-magical "enchantment." Such emotional intensity, sometimes conceived as a quasi-erotic longing in response to the beauty of words and music, defies easy definition and can involve a mixture of pleasure and pain: Sappho's songs of "bittersweet" erotic memory and desire are a salient illustration of this sensibility. In early Greece, musico-poetic performances themselves frequently incorporate reflections on their own seductive power.

Ideas of rapt absorption and deep emotional engagement remain a premise of most ancient forms of aesthetics; notions of aesthetic distance, detachment, or "disinterested" judgment are largely foreign to antiquity. From an early date, Greek culture also looks to the power of song to disclose some kind of "truth." But this is a problematic expectation: in Hesiod, perhaps contemporary with Homer, the Muses proclaim that "we know how to tell many falsehoods that resemble the truth, and we know, when we choose, how to utter the truth" (*Theogony* 27–8). These much debated lines elude stable interpretation; they imply the difficulty, for human singers and audiences, of knowing where "inspired" truth begins and ends. Moreover, they suggest that even "falsehoods" may have the divine power to draw audiences into engrossing world-like *semblances* of truth. Archaic Greece laid the basis for a lasting tension between an aesthetics of truth and an aesthetics of compelling fiction.

By around 500 BCE, comparisons between poetic and figurative art emerge as one means of articulating proto-aesthetic considerations about representation and expression. The poet Simonides described poetry as "speaking painting," painting as "silent poetry" (Plutarch, *Moralia* 346f). Such comparisons, positing a shared category of image-making but marking differences of capacity between verbal and visual media, became common (e.g., Plato, *Republic* 10 and Aristotle, *Poetics* 25 employed them) and later gave rise to the tradition of *ut pictura poesis*, "just as with painting, so with poetry" (the Latin phrase from Horace, *Ars Poetica* 361), the tradition which Lessing's *Laocoön* set itself to overhaul. Convergence on a cohesive concept of representational art was strengthened by the idea of mimesis, whose origins are obscure but which came to be applied to pictorial, poetic, choreographic, musical, and some other kinds of representation. The translation "imitation," though standard, does scant justice to the ways in which Greeks used interpretations of mimesis to wrestle with problems, in modern terms, both of representation and of expression. The status of mimesis intersects, moreover, with issues of truth and falsehood/fiction, especially in poetry, and different versions of mimesis cover a spectrum stretching from "world-reflecting" realism to "world-creating" idealism (Halliwell 2002).

While much of archaic Greek culture was prepared to ascribe special truth-telling powers to poets, whether resulting from divine support or human insight (or both), some philosophers raised objections. Heraclitus poured scorn on the belief that Homer and Hesiod possessed any authentic wisdom; Xenophanes (a rare Greek critic of polytheism), writing in verse himself, complained that these same poets had attributed gross immorality to the gods. The importance of such polemics is twofold: they imply that representational art is open to scrutiny on epistemological and ethical grounds, and they show the development of what Plato would later call "the ancient quarrel between philosophy and poetry" (*Republic* 10.607b).

CLASSICAL FRAMEWORKS AND DEBATES
In the classical period (fifth to fourth centuries BCE), Greek attitudes to poetry, music, painting, and sculpture did not lose contact with their archaic roots but became open to new forms of (partly) rationalistic theorizing and judgment. There is an increasing tendency to recognize a family of figurative and musico-poetic practices, each of which typically counts as a *technê* or specialized expertise (see below) and whose common feature is mimetic depiction, simulation, or enactment of world-like properties (things "resembling the truth," in the Greek phrase). This is apparent in the classification of mimesis in the opening chapters of Aristotle's *Poetics*; and when in that work Aristotle aligns poetry with "the other mimetic arts" (8.1451a30), he clearly assumes familiarity with a well-established category. It was also possible to characterize part of this category with the term *mousikê*, literally "art of the Muses," a word which could denote music per se but also a larger consortium of musico-poetic arts. This use of the term is particularly prominent in Plato's *Republic*, but it is not original there. In Aristophanes' *Frogs*, for instance, the creative activity of tragic playwrights is called *mousikê*.

The nature and implications of mimesis are most extensively and intricately explored in this period by Plato and Aristotle. But there are traces of a wider culture of discussion on the subject. In Xenophon, *Memorabilia* 3.10.1–8, a partly fictionalized collection of memories of Socrates, the latter asks the painter Parrhasius whether his "imaging of the visible" can include depiction of strictly nonsensory qualities such as a person's "character": Parrhasius at first resists but is brought round by a suggestion that such qualities might be shown "through" physical expressions, especially on the face. In a further conversation, Socrates asks the sculptor Cleiton how he "renders the sense of life" in his figures. In both cases, the philosopher probes the (blurred) boundary between representation and expression. He asks how "colors and shapes" can be seen as conveying nonsensory properties and meanings; and there are intimations of a view which will be spelt out in a later period (see below on Philostratus), that mimetic effects require imaginative cooperation from viewers prepared to project significance onto the appearances of a work. Mimesis uses material media to produce readable semblances of a world (whether real or fictive), a process that could be either celebrated for what Greeks sometimes called its "soul-drawing" allure (*psychagôgia*) or distrusted for its speciousness.

Too much should not be made of the linguistic fact that the sense in which poetry, music, and painting could count as "arts," *technai* (plural of *technê*), does not coincide with the generalized modern usage of "art." It is true that the concept of *technê*, a skill or expertise based on rationally expoundable principles, can be used of activities as diverse as shoemaking and medicine. But its implication of mastery of materials and practices in a particular domain does still contribute one strand of modern usage; beyond that, modern usage itself is problematic, since it masks widespread disagreement about what constitutes "art." Furthermore, the unitary notion of art that emerged in the eighteenth century is a synthesis of the category of "fine arts" or *beaux-arts*, and that grouping closely matches the "mimetic arts" of Aristotle's *Poetics*: a fact made explicit in Batteux's pivotal work, *Les beaux-arts réduits à un même principe* (1746).

Nonetheless, even in the classical period itself the question of whether the makers of mimetic works *did* possess a special expertise was a focus for competing views. The claim was unproblematic in certain respects: no one doubted that sculptors or professional instrumentalists could reliably exercise identifiable competences. But older Greek notions of the skill of poets, in particular, had tended to blur the distinction between technical facility (e.g., in versification) and cognitive insight. Such ambiguities became entangled in an overlapping set of debates about the creative sources, the qualities, and the value of poetry. In the fifth century, the atomist philosopher Democritus described Homer as having been "endowed with a god-like nature" but as having used it to "build a beautiful construction of words": the proposition combines the ideas of a special (though perhaps metaphorical) gift and a meticulously cultivated expertise. Somewhat differently, in a famous passage of Plato's *Apology* (22a–c) Socrates explains how he interrogated poets to see if they could explain what their works *meant*; he concluded that they could not, and inferred that they had produced their works (which he accepts are "beautiful") not by rational expertise but by nonrational intuition or inspiration.

In his *Ion*, Plato foregrounds these issues in a way that is deliberately, provocatively polarized between discursive knowledge and divine inspiration. The dialogue avoids a decisive answer: it includes a lyrical evocation of inspiration as involuntary "possession" or madness; but it also presses for an account of "the art of poetry as a whole" (532c), leaving the impression that an interlocutor more acute than Ion might get closer to meeting Socrates' challenge. Aristotle, in the *Poetics*, thinks he is doing just that. The *Poetics* is built on the premise that poetry (like painting) is a teachable *technê*; and while Aristotle still allows for exceptional creative excellence, such as Homer's, he understands this in terms of powers of imaginative vision and emotional concentration (*Poetics* 17), eliminating any supposition of an external force channeled through the artist's mind. Throughout antiquity, in fact, thinkers of many persuasions continued to operate with models of creativity that balance elements of learned skill against more instinctive, "natural" abilities (Horace's *Ars Poetica* 408–18 is a standard specimen). Modern dichotomies of "technique" and "originality" have inherited similar underlying concerns.

Another evolving issue in the classical period concerned the status of poems, paintings, etc. in relation to truth and falsehood. The debate is made harder to follow by sometimes blurred distinctions, in particular between historical-descriptive and ethical-normative truth: both kinds could be ascribed (or denied) to the traditional stories ("myths") which formed a large part of the subject matter of Greek art. A longstanding awareness of the uncertainty of poetic truth, seen above in Hesiod, developed into a set of fluid arguments. Pindar, himself a poet, could detect quasi-historical "falsehoods" in Homeric myth while nonetheless recognizing their beguiling appeal (*Nemean* 7.20–3): this is not outright censure but an indication of ambiguity about what matters in poetry's creation of impressive paradigms of human experience. The historian Thucydides is hesitant about using Homer as factual evidence for the past (e.g., 1.10.3), yet he does rely on him up to a point; at the same time, he contrasts temporary poetic gratification with the permanence of historical truth (2.41.4). Thucydides seems almost to resent the indeterminacy of poetry's contents. But during this same period there were also attempts to move toward something like a positive conception of fiction as a special language game that falls between simple truth and falsehood.

One such attempt can be glimpsed in the sophist Gorgias, who described tragic drama as a paradoxical "deception" in which "the deceiver [i.e., the successful playwright] is better than the non-deceiver, and the deceived [i.e., the enthralled spectator] is wiser than the undeceived" (Plutarch, *Moralia* 348c). An anonymous treatise of around the same date (late fifth century), adducing "the arts (*technai*) and the works of the poets," states that "in tragic poetry and in painting the best person is the one who deceives the most by making things that resemble reality" (*Dissoi Logoi* 3.10).

In both these texts, the notion of "deception" seems to combine a work-centered concept of fiction (the presentation of an artfully invented world) with an audience-centered notion of compelling psychological involvement.

In another of his writings, the *Encomium of Helen* (an imaginary defense speech for the heroine), Gorgias uses poetry as a prime example of the power of language to overcome the soul with emotion: he clearly has tragedy again in mind when he speaks of the fear, pity, and grief induced by poetry "at the affairs of others." Gorgias ascribes a comparable power to images; they enter the eyes and imprint themselves on the mind with the same kind of irresistible effect (including erotic desire) as words. What is more, he gestures toward, without working out systematically, a conception of both language and vision as turning all experience into a kind of narrative-cum-emotional construction of the world. He speaks of vision "painting images in the mind" and he leaves the impression that all language aspires to the intense condition of poetry. Whatever the status of this controversial work, the *Encomium of Helen* gives the flavor of a sophistic milieu of thought in which quasi-aesthetic enthrallment becomes a kind of lens through which to see life as a whole.

It has sometimes been thought that a work by Gorgias might have been a source for the contest of tragedians in the second half of Aristophanes' *Frogs* (405 BCE). This is doubtful, but *Frogs* is certainly a vibrant testimony to the aesthetic debates surrounding one particular art form, tragedy, in the agonistic theatrical culture of classical Athens. The play picks up the problems, indicated above, of calling poetry a *technê*: by making the contest range from the choice of individual words to the putative political messages of whole plays, Aristophanes throws up a set of puzzles about what kind of "expertise" the creation of tragic drama might be. Set in Hades (thereby applying a sort of "test of time" to the genre), the competition turns playwrights of different generations, Aeschylus and Euripides, into representatives of different artistic standards (as seen from both sides, by their advocates and opponents): grand, heroic, uplifting Aeschylean theater (alternatively: bombastic, portentous obscurity) versus realistic, rhetorical, "modern" Euripidean

drama (alternatively: banal, immoral decadence). The arguments move back and forth between "technical" details and larger cultural mentalities: it is no accident that *Frogs* influenced Nietzsche's conception of tragedy's history in *Birth of Tragedy*, including its alleged "death" at the hands of the rationalist Euripides. Although the contest in *Frogs* is a comic *tour de force*, it shrewdly exposes the challenge, even the *impossibility*, of "objective" aesthetic judgment (Dionysus' eventual decision is an arbitrary whim). It uses its own comic aesthetic (of exaggeration, irony, absurdity) to emphasize both that an art form can change radically over time and that its values cannot be divorced from the expectations of its audiences. *Frogs* was designed to stimulate a theatrical public used to arguing over the meanings and merits of plays.

Among much else, *Frogs* is a reminder of the need to avoid homogenization of classical Greek aesthetics. Disagreement about fundamental values was part of the culture. Much of the debate revolved round a tension between competing ideas of what mimetically created "worlds" might offer their audiences: on the one hand, an intense immediacy of experience, an imaginative immersion in the structured universe of the individual work; on the other, the disclosure of truths which might inform and edify experience outside the work as well. This pair of ideas, which could be set against one another or combined in various ways, forms part of the backdrop to the two most important philosophies of art of the period (and of antiquity as a whole), those of Plato and Aristotle.

The complexity of thoughts about poetry, music, and visual art in Plato's dialogues has too often been translated into monolithic hostility to these cultural practices. But careful reading uncovers a subtle dialectic between suspicion of claims for art's self-sufficiency and recognition of the psychological power of its resources. At *Republic* 10.596d–e, for instance, painting is notoriously compared to the passive mirroring of appearances. Historians of aesthetics usually present this as a fixed Platonic tenet. But not only do we encounter different views in other dialogues – see, for example, the stress on compositional selection, design, and beauty at *Gorgias* 503d–e – earlier in the *Republic* itself, Socrates used painting as a metaphor for idealistic philosophical vision, acknowledging the existence of figurative art which does much more than replicate the surfaces of things (see esp. 5.472d, 6.500e–501c): an art, indeed, whose beauty of form can be "full" of ethically charged expressiveness (3.400e–401a). So an alert reader of the whole dialogue is primed to treat book 10's mirror analogy not as an unequivocal rejection of painting but a rhetorical provocation to readers to grasp the need for a better justification of visual (and, by analogy, poetic) mimesis than the mere "semblance" of the real. A comparable point emerges from Socrates' explicit request for a new defense of poetry later in the same book: after supposedly confirming the banishment of poetry as subversive of rationality, he voices a cautious but fervent hope for a way of harmonizing the "bewitchment" of poetic language and feeling with an ethical conception of how best to live (607–8). Plato's dealings with mimetic art never reach a definitive conclusion.

Aristotle's was the most influential response to Plato's challenge to elaborate an aesthetics that could unite intense pleasure and emotion with philosophically acceptable truth. In the *Poetics* he undertakes this task principally with reference to tragedy and epic, but with clear indications that his principles could be extended to other mimetic art forms as well. Aristotle's position on poetic "truth" is complicated. Clearly he does not require, though he allows for, empirical truth in poetry: the objects of mimesis, according to *Poetics* 25, include the actual, the hypothetical, and the ideal. Like Pindar (above), Aristotle can explicitly admire the Homeric use of "falsehood" (*Poetics* 24), by which he means the artful design of scenes that are emotionally convincing despite underlying inconsistencies. Aristotle takes poetry to be a representation of "life" (*Poetics* 6), yet he does not equate this with sustained realism (*Poetics* 8) but connects it to what he counts as poetry's quasi-philosophical capacity to incorporate "universals" into its narrative structures. He believes, moreover, that mimesis is a medium of understanding (*Poetics* 4). All this seems to yield the inference that poetry is not a duplication of actual particulars but can nonetheless be "true to" the essential patterns of causality and significance in

human experience. At the same time, Aristotle is emphatic that the cognitive experience of mimetic works brings with it powerful emotions and perhaps even the potential to make a lasting difference to the emotional dispositions of individuals.

Insofar as anything like a standard model of aesthetic experience emerges from the debates of classical Greek culture, it can be characterized as the engaged imaginative contemplation of the artistically shaped universe of a mimetic work. From such a perspective, beauty tends to count not as a separate category of value but rather as completeness of excellence of the relevant kind: a beautiful song or statue, therefore, is one which satisfies whatever the observer takes to be the most important criteria of value (including formal unity, finesse of detail, emotional expressiveness, ethical idealism) applicable to such an object or performance. Even when distinct criteria of beauty are stipulated, they normally function in this way. When, for instance, in *Poetics* 7 Aristotle says that beauty resides in the ordering of parts in relation to one another, together with the appropriate magnitude for the object in question, he makes it clear that he is specifying conditions that allow something to be appreciated as the thing that it should be. He thus thinks of a beautiful body as relative to the changing tasks of different periods of life (*Rhetoric* 1.5). In the case of a tragic plot, his direct concern in *Poetics* 7, beauty is inextricably related to mimesis of a unified structure of human action of a certain kind and is therefore not independent of representational and expressive value. This is in keeping with Aristotle's general construal of unity of poetic form as a principle of intelligibility.

It is only when the human sphere is transcended that more abstract ideas of beauty come into play in Greek culture. In a passage of Plato's *Republic* 5 (475–6), "lovers of beautiful sights and sounds" addicted to drama, music, etc. are contrasted with the true philosopher who loves only pure beauty "in itself." Comparably, in Plato's *Symposium* the ultimate vision of beauty stands at the top of a spiritual ascent that leaves beautiful artworks, together with the human scene as a whole, far behind. Yet even here it is significant that Diotima's account figures the mystical vision as contemplation of a symbolic natural panorama, "the vast ocean of beauty" (210d), rather as in Plato's *Phaedrus* the soul's vision of ultimate reality, including beauty, is pictured in terms of a celestial festival (247–8). Even these important Platonic gestures toward a kind of transcendent "aesthetic" require metaphors from embodied experience to convey their significance.

HELLENISTIC DEVELOPMENTS AND BEYOND

The Hellenistic period, conventionally dated from the death of Alexander the Great (322 BCE) to the first century BCE, sees a considerable diffusion of Greek thought and values across an expanded cultural landscape. In the second half of this period and beyond, when Rome becomes politically dominant in the Mediterranean world, that diffusion translates itself increasingly into a Greco-Roman phenomenon. During this extended stretch of antiquity, earlier Greek paradigms of mimetic art, beauty, and criticism were both maintained and reworked by new types of thinking. On the philosophical side, the most important development was the growth of Epicureanism and Stoicism. The contrast between the two schools marks a divergence between strong tendencies toward aesthetic hedonism and aesthetic cognitivism. But there are complications to this contrast.

Epicureanism provided a complete philosophy of life on the basis of just two main tenets: one, an atomic physics (all reality is reducible to atoms and void); the other, the principle that the only criterion of human value is pleasure (including freedom from pain and care). This framework encouraged a downgrading of the capacities of poetry, music, and other traditional art forms. Epicurus himself (341–270 BCE) rejected a system of education built around them, partly because such education was superfluous to the simple pleasures of the best life, partly because poetry in particular propagated false myths about the gods (who, according to Epicurus, do not actively interfere in human lives) and the afterlife (which has no existence, since death is the end of individual identity and consciousness). To escape traditional Greek pessimism ("best never to be born") or to free oneself from fear of death, much myth-based poetry (and visual art) had to be rejected (Epicurus, *Letter to Menoeceus* 126–7; *Principal*

Doctrines 12). Tragedy, for instance, could have no value for an Epicurean.

But this critique of a mythological world-view, a critique that follows in the older tradition of Xenophanes and Plato, itself implies that poetry can have a cognitive-cum-emotional impact on its audiences' beliefs. It does not look, then, as though poetry could give pleasure to an Epicurean without a judgment on its philosophical content. One possibility is that poetry could be made a medium for Epicureanism itself. Epicurus seems both to have anticipated and to have resisted this: he thought that only the Epicurean philosopher could discuss music and poetry correctly, but that he would not take writing poetry seriously himself (Diogenes Laertius, *Lives* 10.120). But in the first century BCE Lucretius' great poem, *De rerum natura*, reverting in this respect to the practice of some of the Greek Pre-Socratic philosophers, showed that an Epicurean aesthetic could marry philosophical content with poetic form for overtly persuasive purposes. Despite their defining emphasis on the criterion of pleasure, Epicureans could not advocate pure aestheticism, it seems, where representational art was concerned.

In practice, Epicurean attitudes to art were not inflexible. Epicurus himself, while dismissive of the cultural prestige of poetry, music, etc., nonetheless said that the true philosopher would be a "lover of spectacle" capable of enjoying the great Dionysiac festivals at which, among other things, drama was standardly performed (Plutarch, *Moralia* 1065c): this seems like a pointed retort to the idealism of Plato's devaluation of "lovers of beautiful sights and sounds" (see previous section). While uncertainties remain about the nuances of Epicurus' pronouncements in this area (Asmis 1991), our best chance of understanding the intricate moves of which an Epicurean aesthetics was capable comes from the writings of Philodemus (first century BCE): many of those writings, found on charred papyri from Herculaneum (engulfed by the great eruption of Vesuvius in the year 79), are currently being expertly reconstructed.

The extensive but difficult fragments of Philodemus' polemical treatise *On Poems* suggest that his own position stood poised between conceptions of poetic excellence as self-contained form and attempts to equate poetic value with intellectual or moral benefit. Philodemus takes poetry to provide the mind with a pleasure that depends on the combination of carefully chosen thought with well-matched language; he sees style and content as integrated and equally important. He accepts poetry as an art in its own right, but he keeps it compatible with Epicureanism by making it a kind of mimetic echo of "useful" (i.e., philosophical) discourse. Some have discerned in Philodemus, who himself wrote elegant epigrams, an aesthetic in which poetic form and matter are "organically" fused, a sort of Hellenistic "New Criticism."

Philodemus also wrote a polemical treatise *On Music* in which he contested the common view (shared by Pythagoreans, Platonists, Aristotelians, and at least some Stoics) that music was a species of (mimetic) expression, using audible "likenesses" or correlates of emotions to shape and convey ethically contoured feelings. For Philodemus the materialist, music is nothing but "irrational," that is, meaningless, patterns of sound; it merely "tickles the hearing"; and when it accompanies poetry, any emotional effect on the soul stems entirely from the thoughts contained in the words. Once mimesis (whether as representation or expression) has been denied to music, we are left with an art that for the Epicurean Philodemus, anticipating Hanslick, amounts to pure (tonal) form whose experience is restricted to an auditory pleasure without any significance beyond itself.

Among Philodemus' many targets in *On Music* were Stoic thinkers who regarded music, as well as poetry and painting, as providing fundamentally cognitive experiences that could enhance perception and judgment of reality. Much of the primary evidence for Stoic aesthetics has not survived; treatises on poetry, for instance, by the first three heads of the school – Zeno of Citium, Cleanthes, and Chrysippus – have been lost. But the holistic cast of Stoic thinking makes reconstruction easier than it might otherwise have been. Stoics were powerfully committed to seeing the cosmos as a rational, providential unity, permeated by an active, divine "spirit." They therefore had reason to regard both the natural world and the products of mimetic art as valuable insofar as they were reflections or expressions of the goodness of the cosmos. The idea of beauty as a harmonious conjunction of parts (Cicero,

De officiis 1.98, deriving from the Greek Stoic Panaetius) is not original with the Stoics; Aristotle, as we have seen, had propounded a similar view. But in the hands of Stoics the idea carries a larger impetus to integrate all aspects of reality into a single vision of value; "beauty," in Stoic vocabulary, is always synonymous with "goodness" per se.

Such a perception of beauty required a good deal of actively interpretative "seeing"; the vision was available only to those in possession of full wisdom. Thus Marcus Aurelius (*Meditations* 3.2) claims that all sorts of natural phenomena, even those which look unattractive in isolation, can manifest a special beauty and appeal, even a sort of enthralling quality, to the eyes of those who have a "deeper conception" of the unity of nature. When he adds that such a person will take as much pleasure in nature itself as in graphic or sculptural representations of it, he voices an aesthetic not of sensual appearances but of nature as a system of harmonious significance. And he accordingly indicates that this way of reading the natural world is closed to those who do not possess the Stoic key to the system.

Stoics took over from earlier philosophy, especially Plato's *Timaeus* (where the visible world is a temporal image of eternity made by the "demiurge," the divine craftsman), the notion of the cosmos as the "work of art" created by the ideas in god's mind (e.g., Seneca, *Epistles* 65). This brought with it the implication of human artistry as the rationally purposive production of objects possessing both "utility" (i.e., for Stoics, moral value) and beauty. Although such a model of productive art could be purely analytical, as in Aristotle's conception of the artisan working from an idea in his mind (*Metaphysics* 988a4, 1032a32), Stoics, like some Platonists and, subsequently, Neoplatonists (see below), developed the model into an aesthetic of metaphysical idealism, regarding the meaning of an artwork, like the significance of the cosmos itself, as residing not in sensory appearances as such but in the truth encoded in its beautiful form and readable by a philosophically attuned mind. At the same time, the holistic mentality of Stoicism treated beauty, whether in nature or in representational art, as integrating appearance and meaning, not splitting them apart.

We can glimpse some of the consequences of this stance in Stoic treatments of poetry, the art which, because of its cultural-cum-educational prestige and its capacity to be (re)interpreted philosophically, interested them more than any other. Stoics were highly assertive, even interventionist, readers. They employed a repertoire of critical techniques – including allegorical interpretation, to reconcile anthropomorphic deities with their own more abstract conception of the divine, and even, on occasion, the active "rewriting" of certain passages – to maximize the utility of poetry for philosophical purposes. In this respect the Stoics were responding to a Platonic challenge to show that moral "benefit" and poetically aroused pleasure could work together. But their response sometimes involved an almost total privileging of the cognitive-cum-moral over the emotional.

A remarkable illustration of this can be found in the Stoic geographer Strabo (c.64 BCE–21 CE). At the start of his *Geography* (1.1–2), he repudiates the view that poetry offers a psychological captivation of its own and argues that Homer is a fundamentally reliable purveyor of historical, geographic, political, and other scientific knowledge. For Strabo, reading Homer is (or can be) a quasi-philosophical exercise in tracking an essentially veridical, which is not to say always literal, picture of reality. He concedes in passing the permissibility of an element of creative invention or fiction; he recognizes, as other Stoics did, the importance of poetic "composition" and style; and he allows that poetry can provide some pleasures that are not reducible to truth. But he firmly subordinates such considerations to the imperatives of his Stoic agenda, even though his position requires him to admit that the emotional charge of poetic myths makes them most suitable as instruction for minds incapable of dealing with philosophical knowledge in a purer form.

There are suggestions elsewhere of a more nuanced Stoic conception of poetry. Among these is the view ascribed to Cleanthes (c.330–230 BCE) that, while philosophical prose can adequately state the truth of religious doctrines, poetry has additional resources of language, including its rhythmical-cum-musical organization: these bring the mind closer to a vivid contemplative engagement with the truth. Cleanthes, who wrote poems himself on themes from Stoic theology and ethics, appears more capable than Strabo of recognizing the need for a philosophical aesthetics to treat the possibilities of an art form as more than a functional vehicle for things which could exist just as well without it. One brief report of Cleanthes' position, speaking of how the "compressed necessity" of poetry can intensify meaning and its impact on the mind, occurs in Seneca the Younger (*Epistles* 108.10). It remains a major but unresolved question whether Seneca's own tragedies, with their extraordinarily stark evocations of human suffering and depravity, should count as expressions of a Stoic aesthetics (and therefore ethics). Are they poetic enactments of the Stoic doctrine of the need for virtuous independence from all the passions, with their deleterious attachment to "externals"? There is no doubt that other Stoics saw the genre that way: Epictetus is a case in point (*Discourses* 1.4.24–7). To sustain such a view apparently means making the tragic theater a form of aversion therapy, as Marcus Aurelius *Meditations* 11.6 does. There is, however, an enigma here. If those aspiring to Stoic virtue can witness in tragedy the false values that lead to extreme suffering, do they do so by passing through but beyond pity and fear, or by resisting such feelings altogether? It remains unclear whether Stoics wanted to reinterpret the emotional experience of tragedy or replace it with a didactic alternative (Halliwell 2005: 405–9). This may reflect a general tension between cognition and emotion in their thinking about poetry.

One final development in Hellenistic aesthetics deserves mention here. Both Stoics and Platonists probably contributed to it, though the details are uncertain. This is the emergence of a concept of creative imagination that becomes associated in some texts with the term *phantasia*. Much attention has been paid in this respect to Philostratus' *Life of Apollonius of Tyana*, a third-century work containing a passage (6.19) in which *phantasia* is said to be capable of giving artistic form to "even what it has never seen," while mimesis is said to be restricted to "what it has seen." But it is probably exaggerated to see this contrast as representing a radical break with older traditions of thought. Those traditions had always allowed, even within the parameters of mimesis, for representation and expression of the imaginary or the idealized; see, for instance, the idealistic beauty of painting at Plato, *Republic* 5.472d, or the schema of different objects of mimesis in Aristotle, *Poetics* 25 (both cited earlier). Philostratus' text pits two kinds of representation against one another, and it uses mimesis in a narrower sense (*qua* empirical realism) to sharpen the contrast. But it does so specifically in connection with images of the *divine* and cannot therefore be taken as the formula for an entire aesthetic of visual art.

As it happens, another passage from Philostratus' book (2.22) actually uses the vocabulary of mimesis to denote a fundamentally imaginative capacity required not just by makers but also by viewers of visual art: viewers must use their own mental image-forming powers to project and fill out the significance of what they see. This idea, echoed by Lessing in *Laocoön*, makes imagination a process in which the artist's source of ideas must be complemented by the actively interpretative response of the beholder. This is a principle borne out in the descriptions of (probably fictional) paintings, the *Imagines*, also written by someone called Philostratus (whether the same person remains uncertain). This work, influential in the Renaissance, frequently carries the notion of active interpretation beyond the optically possible, for example, by projecting movement onto figures in the paintings. What is at stake in both the Philostratean texts mentioned is the workings and limits of creative imagination. But that is a subject on which some Greek thinkers, as the next section will show, adopted more far-reaching positions.

TOWARD TRANSCENDENCE

The treatise *On the Sublime* (which survives incomplete) was possibly the work of Cassius Longinus, a rhetorician and Platonizing philosopher of the third century. Most scholars doubt this, however, and posit an anonymous author (often called "Pseudo-Longinus") of the first century. I use the name "Longinus" here agnostically. Whatever the truth, the treatise is a remarkable document. While grounded in the traditions of rhetorical analysis (discussing the persuasive effect of such things as figures of speech and word order), the work breaks the bounds of those traditions with its concept of a sublimity "beyond persuasion" which produces a transfigured, quasi-ecstatic state of consciousness in those who experience it. Longinus opens up a kind of transcendental aesthetic whose possibilities were further developed, but also modified, in the eighteenth century, not least by Burke and Kant.

Longinian sublimity is a quality of language, thought, and feeling which cuts across genres; it is common to all the greatest writings, whether prose or verse. The impact it makes on the minds of readers or hearers is described in terms that go beyond anything found earlier in antiquity. Particularly striking is the claim in chapter 7 that the sublime induces the mind to feel "that it has itself given birth to what it has in fact heard," and the formulation in chapter 9 that sublimity is "the echo of greatness of mind." The quality Longinus wants to define is therefore a kind of creative resonance of the mind itself: it "echoes" from its creator in the expressive intensity of language, and then re-echoes in the mind of the receiver. But Longinus stresses, not least in chapter 3 (on *failure* to achieve sublimity) and chapter 8 (on the five sources of the sublime), that this is a matter not of generalized, amorphous feeling, but of moments of concentrated elevation of mind whose content can be directly grasped in thought and emotion. And Longinus is no subjectivist: he treats the authentically sublime as triumphantly *inter*-subjective, a great connector of minds.

A further dimension of the treatise's aesthetic philosophy can be brought out by specific contrast with Burke. In chapter 9, Longinus cites a passage from *Iliad*, book 17 where Ajax pleads with Zeus to disperse the thick mist which shrouds the battlefield: "kill us at least in the daylight," he screams to the sky-god. Here as elsewhere, Longinus associates the sublime with heroism; Ajax's self-affirmation, demanding the right to fight and die with unflinching courage, is treated as manifesting a capacity within the mind itself to transcend material limits. When Burke cites the same passage in his *Essay on the Sublime and Beautiful* (iv.14), he uses it, by contrast, to reinforce the "terrible" associations of darkness, which is itself here the source of the sublime. One thing this illustrates is how the Longinian sublime is forcefully positive and (self-)creatively elevating: it is not incompatible with an atmosphere of "fearful" grandeur, but it is always located in the greatness of mind which asserts itself in the face of such things. Even where extreme states of suffering are depicted, the sublime redeems these by finding ways of expressing exhilarating nobility and defiance, and thereby arousing a joyous exhilaration in the minds of those who contemplate it.

Longinus' aesthetic thrusts into the realms of the metaphysical. In chapter 35, a key passage with both Platonic and Stoic overtones, he pronounces that humans have been made to be "spectators" of the entire cosmos; great writers are "demigods" whose visionary powers exercise this potential, and enable others to exercise it, to the highest degree. (Longinus, more than any other ancient, foreshadows later ideas of "genius.") In fact, the mind can do more than contemplate the cosmos: it can exceed it in thought. Longinus' treatise is replete with religious language for experience of the sublime. But in as bold a move as is to be found anywhere in the history of aesthetics, it ultimately articulates something like a divinization (half-literal, half-metaphorical) of the creative mind. For Longinus, the greatest moments of literature, whatever their subject matter, somehow internalize the greatness and beauty of the cosmos within the infinite spaces of the mind itself. This idea seems to represent a translation of religious impulses into an aesthetic paradigm where both truth and "ecstasy" are encountered in direct experience of the unlimited creativity of language.

If the aesthetic effectively subsumes the theological in Longinus, the reverse is the case in some of the texts of Neoplatonism, the broad phase of revitalized interest in Plato's work which flourished from the third to the sixth century. One of many strands in this movement was a rethinking of questions about mimesis, art, and beauty raised in Plato's dialogues. The two most important positions to emerge on the subject were those of Plotinus (205–70) and Proclus (412–85). Both thinkers created complex philosophical systems of their own. The aesthetic component in their work cannot be separated from their overarching metaphysics; only some pointers can be given here.

Everything in Plotinus' *Enneads* belongs to a unified, hierarchical cosmos, in which reality emanates creatively from the ultimate source of being (the One) through the levels of "intellect" and "soul"; part of soul is nature, which produces a spatiotemporal world within the negative receptacle of matter. It is significant that Plotinus frequently uses the vocabulary of "mimesis" for the way in which, within his system, every lower element reflects and tries to assimilate itself to a higher element: every level, other than the One itself, bears the image or imprint of its source. A key dynamic of Plotinus' worldview is therefore a process by which reality is constantly aspiring to model itself on, and return to, its divine origin. Whatever the larger philosophical implications of this picture, it sets the scene for a view of mimetic art as a potential medium of expressiveness that can reach beyond representation of the material world.

This can best be seen at *Enneads* 5.8.1, where Plotinus tries to explain contemplation of the beauty of intellect by an analogy with sculpture. A beautiful statue is made beautiful, he says, by the "form" imposed on it by the maker's skilled art; but the form exists in the sculptor's mind before it is in the work (see "Hellenistic developments," above), and there is a beauty "in the art" itself prior to, and finer than, that of the particular statue. This exemplifies a more general Plotinean principle, that everything creative is superior to what it creates. So the beauty of the visible derives from, and draws the viewer toward, a higher beauty. Furthermore, Plotinus defends arts that produce likenesses of nature ("imitate" it, on the conventional translation) by proposing, first, that they belong to the larger mimetic processes of reality (nature itself is a mimesis of higher principles), and, second, that they are not limited to producing simulacra of appearances: "they return to the principles at the root of nature itself" and employ imagination to add beauty to what they depict. So Plotinus both accepts and reinterprets artistic mimesis into an aesthetic of expressive, beautiful form produced by acts of skillful but also intuitive creativity.

Unfortunately Plotinus does not develop his aesthetic of the mimetic arts in much further detail. Passing hints sometimes suggest that he did not regard all such art as possessing the kind of value envisaged in 5.8, but also that other factors complicate his position (such as acceptance of allegorical meaning in some poetry, 1.6.8). But together with Plotinus' general commitment to a Platonic conception of beauty as capable of drawing the soul up the hierarchical ladder of reality, *Enneads* 5.8 is enough to delineate a philosophy of artistic form not as an idealism of enhanced appearances but an idealism of spiritual expressiveness. This feature of his thought was to exercise some influence not only on the Middle Ages (partly via Augustine) and on Renaissance Neoplatonism, but also on later thinkers too, including Coleridge and Goethe.

Where Plotinus has little to say directly about poetry, Proclus expends much energy on the subject; in particular, he elaborately reworks the *Republic*'s two critiques of poetry. His main aim is (or becomes) to resolve the "ancient quarrel" between philosophy and poetry, to effect a reconciliation between Plato and (in particular) Homer. He does this partly by arguing that there is more to poetry than its literal meaning, and partly by reconfiguring some of the critical terms in Plato's various treatments of poetry. The result is a tripartite scheme of types of poetry: "inspired" (capable of conveying divine truth through symbols and allegory), "knowledge-based" (capable of educating the soul in contemplation of noetic essences), and "mimetic" (tied to depiction of the phenomenal world and its human passions).

But there are complications. For one thing, these types do not seem to be entirely intrinsic to poetry; they depend on the varying intellectual capacities of its readers. In part at least, Proclus' scheme is an account of different ways of *interpreting* poetry and the different cognitive states they entail. (There is a partial parallelism here with Augustine's famous typology of methods of interpretation.) One implication of this, which Proclus sometimes seems happy to admit, is that *all* poetry, even that which is "inspired," retains what he counts as a mimetic surface, that is, a prima facie representation of the world. Proclus draws attention to the fact that in this sense Plato himself is a highly mimetic writer and shares this quality with Homer. In places he is also prepared, like Plotinus and under the influence of Plato's

Timaeus (see earlier), to regard poetic mimesis as akin to the "cosmic" mimesis by which nature itself embodies images of a transcendent, eternal reality.

Overall, then, Proclus' use of the concept of mimesis fluctuates in weight and significance. But there is no doubt that his dominant aim is to find ways of reading poetic images of the material world as symbolic microcosms, intimations of a higher realm. It is hardly surprising, therefore, that despite his relative inaccessibility Proclus has appealed to some modern devotees of a transcendentalist aesthetic, including Emerson. Such an aesthetic marks the furthest reach of the trajectory of Greek ideas that this essay has tried to trace: a trajectory which, for all its variations of emphasis and evaluation, was centrally preoccupied with the relationship between the psychological immediacy of representational art and the meanings that might be found in (or beyond) it by its contemplatively engaged audiences.

See also ARISTOTLE; BURKE; CATHARSIS; PLATO; PLOTINUS; THEORIES OF ART; TRAGEDY.

BIBLIOGRAPHY
Asmis, E. 1991. "Epicurean Poetics," *Proceedings of the Boston Area Colloquium in Ancient Philosophy*, 7, 63–93.
Beardsley, Monroe C. 1966. *Aesthetics from Classical Greece to the Present*. New York: Macmillan.
Büttner, Stefan. 2006. *Antike Ästhetik*. Munich: C. H. Beck.
Bychkov, O. & Sheppard, A. 2009. *Greek and Roman Aesthetics*. Cambridge: Cambridge University Press.
Carchia, G. 1999. *L'estetica antica*. Rome: Editori Laterza.
Coulter, J. A. 1976. *The Literary Microcosm: Theories of Interpretation of the Later Neoplatonists*. Leiden: Brill.
Halliwell, Stephen. 2002. *The Aesthetics of Mimesis. Ancient Texts and Modern Problems*. Princeton: Princeton University Press.
Halliwell, Stephen. 2005. "Learning from Suffering: Ancient Responses to Tragedy." In *A Companion to Greek Tragedy*. J. Gregory (ed.). Oxford: Blackwell, 394–412.
Lombardo, G. 2002. *L'estetica antica*. Bologna: il Mulino.
Nussbaum, Martha C. 1993. "Poetry and the Passions." In *Passions and Perceptions*. J. Brunschwig & M. C. Nussbaum (eds.). Cambridge: Cambridge University Press, 97–149.

Panofsky, Erwin. 1968. *Idea: A Concept in Art Theory*. J. Peake (trans.). New York: Harper & Row.

Russell, D. A. & Winterbottom, M. 1972. *Ancient Literary Criticism*. Oxford: Oxford University Press.

Schaper, Eva. 1968. *Prelude to Aesthetics*. London: George Allen & Unwin.

STEPHEN HALLIWELL

medieval and renaissance aesthetics   The first and longer part of this entry looks at aesthetics in the Middle Ages (c.500–c.1500). The topic is not a straightforward one, since there is no body of arguments and theories that can be uncontroversially identified as medieval aesthetics. I shall describe the Standard Approach to solving this problem adopted by most writers, and then a Revisionary Approach advocated by some, according to which there was no aesthetics in the Middle Ages, and finally present a New Approach, which saves the idea of medieval aesthetics and also links it closely to contemporary developments in the field. The second part of the entry is devoted to the period 1500–1700. The period of "renaissance" is often regarded as one in which, by contrast with the previous millennium, poets, painters, sculptors, and architects revived the traditions of antiquity and gained a new consciousness of themselves as artists. Moreover, the accepted historiography of philosophy sharply distinguishes at least the second of these two centuries as "early modern" as opposed to medieval philosophy. I shall consider whether these two apparent differences mean that renaissance aesthetics needs to be approached differently from that of the Middle Ages.

MEDIEVAL AESTHETICS: THE STANDARD
APPROACH

Many branches of contemporary philosophy, such as metaphysics, ethics, and logic, existed as distinct and recognized subjects in the Middle Ages. Aesthetics did not, even under some other name. Exponents of the Standard Approach believe that, nonetheless, there was a medieval aesthetics. They take as their starting point an assumption about the nature of aesthetics, which is based on how modern aesthetics – that is to say, the subject from c.1700 to c.1950 – has usually been conceived and

practiced. Aesthetics, they believe, concerns beauty, especially as manifested in works of art (literature, painting, sculpture, architecture, music). They recognize that, in this sense, medieval authors did not produce explicit aesthetic theories, but they themselves aim to construct a medieval aesthetics from medieval theories about beauty and technical treatises about the different arts, often along with observations about the medieval artifacts themselves. Exponents of this Standard Approach include Edgar de Bruyne, Erwin Panofsky, Wladyslaw Tatarkiewicz, Rosario Assunto, and Umberto Eco. I shall look at its two main elements in turn, before presenting the case against it made by the Revisionists.

MEDIEVAL THEORIES OF BEAUTY

Some theologians in the thirteenth-century universities developed fairly elaborate theories of beauty, usually in their discussions of God, his attributes, and their relation to created things. Behind their treatments lay two important sources. One was a definition found in Augustine and Cicero: beauty consists in the congruence of parts along with delightfulness (*suavitas*) of color. The other was a passage in chapter 4 of *On the Divine Names*, a text that had been issued under the name of Dionysius, the Areopagite converted by Paul, and so enjoyed great authority, although in fact it was the work of a fifth-century writer, influenced by late Neoplatonism. God, says Pseudo-Dionysius, is beautiful because he transmits beauty to all things according to their own characteristics. The Beautiful and the Good, he adds, are the same – all things desire them and there is nothing that does not participate in them. On the strength of this passage, beauty was discussed along with the group of "transcendental attributes," properties such as unity, truth, and goodness that all things were supposed to have simply in virtue of existing, and according to the Standard Approach, many thirteenth-century thinkers regarded beauty as itself a transcendental (Pouillon 1946; but see below).

In the first half of the thirteenth century, William of Auvergne, the followers of Alexander of Hales, and Robert Grosseteste each developed thoughts about beauty using these sources. For example, Grosseteste used his metaphysics of light as a way of explaining how all things possess the Augustinian marks of beauty, color, and symmetry. Like most medieval thinkers, Grosseteste thought of color as an effect of light, and he envisaged the whole universe in terms of light radiating out from its primal source. Since Grosseteste also believed that the universe is designed according to the laws of geometry, it followed that everything in it is symmetrically proportioned. The three most important discussions, however, are those from later in the century by Albert the Great (1200–80) and two of his pupils, Ulrich of Strasbourg (d.1272) and Thomas Aquinas (d.1274). They are all based on Aristotle's hylomorphism, according to which every particular of a natural kind is analyzed as matter informed by a substantial form or essence, which makes the whole the sort of thing it is (so Fido is matter informed by the form of dogness); the matter–form concrete whole is then informed by various accidental forms (e.g., the brownness of Fido's fur, his having such and such a weight, his lying down).

Albert's fullest treatment of beauty is in his commentary on Pseudo-Dionysius *On the Divine Names* (c.1250; the section is printed, wrongly attributed to Aquinas, in Aquinas 1927: 417–43). Albert is therefore talking about the beauty that derives from God and in which everything participates. Like Pseudo-Dionysius, he insists that beauty is the same as goodness, but he allows (question 1, article 2) that conceptually ("by reason") it differs in certain ways. In especial, something is beautiful because of "the resplendence of the substantial or accidental form over proportioned and bounded parts of matter." As an analogy for this metaphysical conception of beauty he suggests the way in which "a body is said to be beautiful from the resplendence of color over proportioned limbs" – a conception of beauty close to Augustine's definition. The unstated difference between "beauty" in this common sense and in Albert's metaphysical sense is that a body may fail to be beautiful, if the limbs are ill-proportioned or it lacks color. But a substantial form or an accidental one by informing matter is – Albert seems to suggest – "resplendent" over it, and the Aristotelian hylomorphism he is adopting would mean that, by being informed, the matter is proportioned to the form and bounded. Albert has thus found a way of explaining Pseudo-Dionysius' claim that everything is beautiful, but at the cost of making this use of the word only loosely analogical with its ordinary usage.

When Ulrich of Strasbourg discusses beauty in his *De summo bono* ("On the Highest Good," c.1262–72; 1987–9: II.4), he follows his teacher Albert's idea that beauty is found in the way forms inform their matter. But he does not, like him, treat this as a type of metaphysical beauty, different from beauty in the ordinary sense. Although Ulrich accepts that all things are beautiful, just as they are good, to some extent, they vary in the degree to which they are beautiful, and some things are ugly (although presumably also, in some respect, beautiful). This variable beauty can be spiritual or bodily, accidental or essential. Ulrich says little about spiritual beauty, which is that of noncorporeal things, such as souls or angels, and their attributes, such as knowledge. Accidental corporeal beauty, he says, is what fits Augustine's definition, "congruence of parts and delightfulness of colour." His idea seems to be that any sort of physical object will gain in accidental beauty if it displays the characteristics of symmetry and colorfulness, which it has through accidental forms of quantity (e.g., it has such and such dimensions) and quality (e.g., it is red and gold). Essential corporeal beauty, by contrast, depends on the relation between the substantial form and the matter it informs. Ulrich explains this idea in terms of a fourfold consonance that is required for perfect beauty: in disposition, quantity, the number of parts, and the relation of each part's size to the whole. He gives the balance of humors in a human as an example of consonant disposition – the principle seems to be that the internal physical constituents of a given sort of thing need to be in their proper proportions. Consonance in quantity means having a body of the right size for the species of thing – if Fido is a toy poodle, then for Ulrich he is far from beautiful. By missing one of the usual parts of the body, a thing is "deformed": having all the usual parts is prerequisite for perfect beauty. And if any part of a body is out of its usual proportions, then that thing will lack perfect beauty. Ulrich, then, sees essential corporeal beauty as greater the more a particular corresponds to the general pattern of its species.

Aquinas sets out his ideas about beauty in passing and even less systematically than Albert or Ulrich. Like both of them, he finds beauty in the relationship between form and matter and, like Ulrich, he distinguishes things that are more and less beautiful, using Augustine's definition of beauty to suggest his criteria. He adds the suggestion that, although everything is both good and beautiful, a thing's beauty is related to its being contemplated, whereas its goodness is related to its desirability. This idea has been seized on by the exponents of the Standard Approach, as a warrant to discover in Aquinas an aesthetic theory that anticipates aspects of Kant's (e.g., *see* AQUINAS). Umberto Eco (1970) has made a particularly ingenious, thorough – and unusually self-conscious – attempt to construct a theory about the beauty of art from Aquinas's scattered remarks.

At much the same time as Aquinas was writing, a Polish scientist Witelo was composing his treatise on perspective, based on the work of an eleventh-century Arabic writer Ibn al-Haytham, which had been translated into Latin. Al-Haytham (II.3) thinks that an object is visually beautiful if it has properties that have an effect on viewers so that the form seems beautiful to them. His, then, is a type of naturalistic theory. Certain sensory properties are such, he thinks, that viewers will be affected in the particular, undefined way that makes them label what they see as beautiful. Of the simple characteristics of beauty, some, such as color, are traditional, but most are pairs of opposites: so, for example, separateness produces beauty – separate stars are more beautiful than nebulae – but continuity produces beauty too – a meadow with continuous vegetation is more beautiful than one where it is sparse. Al-Haytham also recognizes that these properties produce beauty in combination, and that there are certain, special harmonious combinations that produce beauty, even when what are combined are not completely beautiful. Al-Haytham's categories are, in fact, just a way to organize certain strong preferences – but he takes no account of the possibility of cultural differences in the perception of beauty, and confidently pronounces (III.7), to the dismay of latter-day Brünnhildes, that blond hair and blue eyes are ugly. Witelo (IV.148, edited in Baeumker 1908) follows most of these views, but he has an awareness of the cultural relativism of judgments of beauty lacking in his source and uncommon in the Middle Ages:

In many of these things, however, it is custom that makes beauty. This is why each race of humans considers its form of beauty as that which in itself is beautiful and attains the end of beauty. A Moor approves of different colors and proportions in human bodies or pictures than a Dane . . .

TREATISES ON THE ARTS

There were technical treatises written in the Middle Ages on various of what are now called the "arts." Music was considered to be a branch of mathematics (along with arithmetic, geometry, and astronomy), and there were theoretical texts on it by two of the great late ancient authorities, Augustine and Boethius. Boethius's *De musica* was widely studied and glossed in the earlier part of the Middle Ages, and study of musical theory in this tradition continued in the arts faculties of the universities. There were also many treatises on music of a more practical kind (almost all can be read at www.chmtl.indiana.edu/tml/start.html) written throughout the period. Treatises on painting and the decorative arts were even more obviously technical manuals – a wide-ranging example is *De diversis artibus* ("On Different Arts") written by a certain Theophilus, probably in the twelfth century, which discusses painting, pigments, glues, and varnishes, in books, on walls, and on panels, and then glass, ordinary and stained, and then metalwork. Aside from a theological passage on the gifts of the Holy Spirit, it has no pretensions except to instruct artisans how to perform their tasks. There seems, however, to be an exception to the rule that medieval authors wrote only technical manuals about the arts of building and decoration. In the 1140s, Abbot Suger wrote an account of how he rebuilt St. Denis: *De rebus in sua administratione gestis* ("Of the Things Done under His Direction"). In a well-known essay introducing his translation and commentary of this text (Suger 1946), Erwin Panofsky connects Suger's description of the building and its ornaments with Neoplatonism and the metaphysics of light. According to Panofsky's presentation, Suger reaches original solutions to architectural problems, inspired by aesthetic ideas that manifest themselves in his writings.

The treatises on poetry (often themselves versified) which were written in the later twelfth and thirteenth centuries – the most famous of them is Geoffrey of Vinsauf's *Poetria nova* (after 1199) – contain some general reflections on how a poet should go about planning and forming his poem, but they are mostly devoted to presenting the rhetorical figures which adorn poetry. They too, therefore, are very definitely craft manuals. There are, however, reasons to think that at least one later treatise on poetry, Dante's *De vulgari eloquentia* ("On Eloquence in the Vernacular") contains some interesting and original philosophical speculation about language (see Dante 2007: xv–xix).

THE REVISIONARY APPROACH: THERE IS NO MEDIEVAL AESTHETICS

The claim made by exponents of the Standard Approach is that, from these elements – theories of beauty and discussions of individual arts – they can derive a medieval aesthetics. Usually they also make use of medieval artifacts themselves as evidence for their theoretical accounts, since they are held to reflect the aesthetic ideals in concrete form. Panofsky's *Gothic Architecture and Scholasticism* (1957) is the most striking example of this side of the approach. He traces a pattern of intellectual development, leading to the comprehensive, clear, and highly articulated synthesis of philosophy and religion he claims to see in Aquinas, which he finds exactly paralleled in architecture by the achievement in the Gothic cathedral of a unified space combined with a clear differentiation of elements.

The Revisionists (such as Paul Oskar Kristeller, Andreas Speer, Jan Aertsen, and Olivier Boulnois), like the exponents of the standard approach, describe aesthetics in characteristically modern terms, as the theory of beauty especially in art. But they believe that, understood in this sense, aesthetics did not exist in the Middle Ages. Their objection is not merely to the way in which the Standard Approach takes material of disparate kinds and various origins and assembles it into medieval aesthetics. They are not making – or,

at least, need not make – the radically historicist claim that historians of philosophy must organize their research according to the disciplinary categories of the time they are studying. The Revisionists could, for instance, distinguish between the case of philosophy of language – not a medieval category, but a contemporary category to which, arguably, a body of medieval material belongs – and that of aesthetics. Their criticism is not that no one in the Middle Ages engaged in aesthetics as a distinct branch of philosophical inquiry. They did not engage in it at all. It is simply not there to be discovered and put together by contemporary historians of philosophy.

The Revisionists argue as follows: when medieval thinkers discussed beauty, they were clearly not mainly considering the beauty of artifacts. Their theories of beauty were usually framed in a theological context, and considered beauty as a property of natural things created by God. (Ulrich of Strasbourg's theory is a good example: most of it makes little sense except with regard to members of natural kinds). Moreover, even the view that medieval thinkers elaborated an independent theory of beauty needs to be scrutinized. Aquinas, whose theory of the beautiful has been treated as central in medieval aesthetics, makes only some brief, scattered remarks on the subject (Speer 1990). And the claim that beauty was considered one of the transcendentals can be questioned (Aertsen 1991), since it is not considered an independent attribute of all things, like unity, truth, and goodness, but rather as just an aspect of goodness.

As for the arts, the system of "fine arts," which connects together (at least) poetry, painting, music, sculpture, and architecture, did not exist in the Middle Ages (see Kristeller 1980). At this time, the "arts" were understood to be the seven liberal arts that formed the basis of the medieval curriculum up to the end of the twelfth century: the three linguistic arts of the trivium – grammar, logic, and rhetoric – and the four mathematical arts of the quadrivium – arithmetic, geometry, astronomy, and music. The arts of poetry were related to grammar, and the study of music, but only in the theoretical tradition of Boethius, was part of the quadrivium. But, not only the visual arts, but the practice of writing and performing music and, indeed, poetry, were considered as crafts – practical skills. Such skills were much less esteemed than the pursuit of knowledge through the arts. In his *Didascalicon*, from the mid twelfth century, Hugh of St. Victor takes an unusual step by adding seven "mechanical" arts to the seven "liberal" (1961: II.21–8): here, along with agriculture, sailing, weaving, hunting, and medicine, Hugh has "theatrical knowledge" (though this includes gymnastics and athletics); and, as one of the subdivisions of *armatura*, literally "arms-making" but extended to making any sort of artifact, he includes, along with other types of construction, sculpture and painting. It is not simply, however, that the "fine" arts were not distinguished and grouped in the way they are now. Any sort of human artifice was considered to be subordinate to what was natural – that is to say, created. Artifice recovered a certain dignity by following Augustine's view that the human makers depended on ideas in the mind of God (Boulnois 2008: 342–4), but it remained on a lower level than nature.

The fault of the Standard Approach, then, lies at a deeper level than that of intruding aesthetics, a theoretical consideration of beauty in art, into a period where it was not practiced. It rests on taking medieval artifacts as if they were works of art, a type of entity that had no place within the categories of medieval culture. Interpreted carefully, the very sources that have been used to present medieval artifacts as artworks tell the opposite story – as for instance with a recent presentation of Suger's text on St. Denis (Suger 1995), which shows that his account fits into the context of his political, liturgical, historical, and ecclesiological ideas, and has nothing to do with envisaging his building as a work of art.

The Revisionists conclude that we should, therefore, abandon the idea of medieval aesthetics altogether. It is as empty a subject as medieval nuclear physics or biotechnology.

A NEW APPROACH TO MEDIEVAL AESTHETICS

Should we accept the Revisionists' conclusion? Their arguments against the Standard Approach are, collectively, very powerful, but their position has one important weakness: like the Standard Approach, it understands aesthetics as modern aesthetics – the subject as it grew up in the eighteenth century and was practiced up until the mid twentieth century, which was centered on beauty as found in works of art. But modern aesthetics is not contemporary aesthetics. Both the Standard Approach and the Revisionist one are based on an understanding of aesthetics nearer to Croce or Collingwood than to the subject as it is now studied, at least by Anglophone philosophers. Today's looser approach to the coherence of the subject may allow a place for medieval discussions, without forcing them into an alien mold.

Beauty, especially natural beauty, is indeed studied by some aesthetic philosophers today, but only a few wish to insist on an important connection between art and beauty. It is therefore wrong to exclude medieval discussions of beauty from aesthetics, in its contemporary meaning, because medieval philosophers too did not make a connection between beauty and human artifacts. As for the medieval lack of a conception of works of art, many philosophers today deny that there are any intrinsic properties that distinguish works of art from other things. When contemporary philosophers consider individual first-order topics in aesthetics, such as representation, expression, style, intention, narrative, humor, metaphor and symbolism, truth and fiction, the question of what, if anything, constitutes a work of art does not usually play an important part in their discussions. They base their analyses around poems, or pieces of music, or paintings, or sculptures – for the most part simply taking what is uncontroversially accepted as art without attaching any theoretical weight to this concept. It would, therefore, seem reasonable to regard medieval treatments of, for example, representation in pictures and sculptures, or metaphor and symbolism, or truth and fiction and narrative in poetry, as being topics in aesthetics.

It remains true, as the Revisionists insist, that aesthetics does not constitute a distinct area in medieval philosophy. Each of the inquiries that can be described as "aesthetic" fits into some other, particular context – for example, analysis of beauty into theological treatment of God's relation to his creatures or else into optics, pictorial representation and symbolism into other, again mainly theological, contexts, and metaphor into semantic theory as developed within logic. Yet, just because of these very dissimilarities, rather than in spite of them, there is something to be gained both for historians of medieval philosophy and contemporary aesthetic philosophers by making a link between contemporary aesthetics and these medieval discussions that belong to so different an intellectual context. For the medievalists, there is the chance to understand the texts as philosophy in a way that is hard to do without connecting them to the questions that seem philosophically important to us now (even if this process ends by showing us the radical difference of some medieval problems, questions, and answers). For contemporary aestheticians, the connections medieval thinkers made between topics now in aesthetics and metaphysics, logic, politics, and theology should help in questioning how much the way in which they approach topics is narrowed by a conception of aesthetics as a unitary discipline they no longer themselves accept. Maybe the medieval thinkers' understanding of the philosophical problems raised by the sorts of artifacts we regard as works of art was in some respects improved by their lack of aesthetics as a category, and this is a lesson that philosophers of art are now ready to learn.

What this New Approach proposes is, therefore, in principle not a view about how to go about writing the history of medieval aesthetics – there is clearly no such history to be written – but a series of research projects on bodies of medieval material, linked by subject or theme, where the questions raised can be related interestingly, and perhaps provocatively, to those discussed by contemporary aesthetic philosophers. None of these projects has yet been carried out, and in most the ground has hardly been prepared. Here are just a few of them:

(1) Questions about interpretation and meaning in artifacts, especially literary, are considered in contemporary aesthetics. There was much thinking in the Middle Ages about the interpretation of texts, both the Bible and classical pagan texts, and also visual images and natural objects. At times, the discussion moves to a level of abstraction on which questions about authorial intention, the meaning of

texts, and the aims a reader should have are considered. Important writers include Augustine in late antiquity, John Scottus Eriugena in the ninth century, William of Conches in the twelfth, Aquinas and Bonaventure in the thirteenth, Dante in the fourteenth.

(2) Music is very often discussed separately from the other arts in contemporary aesthetics. In the Middle Ages, the distinction was even sharper, because music was seen as a type of mathematics. Did medieval thinkers' freedom from the preconception of music as like painting or literature give them a valuable insight that may have become hidden? It would be interesting, especially, to investigate whether, in the theoretical tradition of writing about music in the Middle Ages, there is reflective material which could counter the tendency among some aestheticians now to concentrate on music's supposed role in expressing or arousing emotion.

(3) Metaphor is another topic considered in aesthetics today. Strangely, perhaps, to modern eyes, the treatment of metaphor in medieval writing on literature tends to be disappointing (Lorusso 2005), but there is, by contrast, a variety of sophisticated analyses in logical texts (see Ashworth 2007).

(4) Indeed, in the Arabic tradition, poetics and rhetoric were considered to be part of the logical curriculum (see Black 1990). It was thought that there was a whole range of different types of syllogism, ranging from the demonstrative syllogisms of scientific discourse treated in the *Prior* and the *Posterior Analytics* to the imaginative syllogisms of poetry. It has recently been argued (Kemal 2003) that the great Arabic philosophers, al-Fârâbî, Avicenna, and Averroes, built this idea into a full account of the aims and value of poetry and its place in a well-ordered community. The theory touches on many questions debated in aesthetics now, ranging from the problem of fiction and truth to the moral dangers of and justification for literature.

(5) Aestheticians today are interested in the problem of representation: at its simplest, what does it mean to say that a picture represents a certain landscape or a statue a certain person? Throughout the Middle Ages, there was sophisticated debate about images and their relationship to reality (a fascinating treatment is given in Boulnois 2008). It centered around a

theological problem: to what extent do images help – or hinder – us in knowing God? But it also involved issues in philosophy of mind, such as Aristotle's view that we cannot think intellectually without an accompaniment of mental images. The discussion often concerned pictures or figurative language: the very fact that this concern was not in the context of what is now regarded as aesthetics should make this area of thought especially valuable to investigate with the discussions of contemporary aesthetics in mind.

AESTHETICS FROM 1500 TO 1700:
A RENAISSANCE IN AESTHETICS?

Readers may be surprised to see aesthetics in the sixteenth and seventeenth centuries treated as an appendage to medieval aesthetics. The decision cuts across the accepted periodization, both in philosophy and in the arts. Historians of philosophy tend to make a sharp distinction between the period of early modern philosophy, beginning in the seventeenth century, and what went before. In the history of literature, the visual arts, and architecture (though less so for music), the break is usually seen as one occurring a century or so earlier, as medieval styles and aspirations gave way to those of the renaissance. Both of these changes promise, at first sight, to have implications for aesthetics. Descartes, Locke, Spinoza, and Leibniz are often considered, unlike the medieval thinkers, to have engaged in a rationally based philosophy, separate from theology and linked to the new science, and so to have established a tradition that leads directly to contemporary philosophy. Renaissance writers, painters, sculptors, and architects did not differ from their medieval predecessors merely by using new styles, which were heavily influenced by ancient models. They also had a new, and far more elevated, conception of their role and the independent value of what they produced. For these reasons, it might seem that the special methodology proposed above for making it possible to talk at all of aesthetics in the Middle Ages is unnecessary from the period from 1500.

There was, indeed, a significant change in how writers and artists in the renaissance conceived their work. A new value was given to fabrication, which broke down the very sharp medieval distinction between creation, as the work of God alone, and artifacts, the work of humans. In his *Platonic Theology*, written 1469–74, Marsilio Ficino (2004: XIII.3) shows the soul's domination over the body from the way in which humans fashion "all the world's materials . . . elements, stones, metals, plants and animals" into many forms and figures, which include not just fabrics and buildings, but also pictures and sculptures. Moreover, it became common to associate poetry, painting, sculpture, and music, and to consider them as noble activities, very different from the work of craftsmen (Kristeller 1980: 180–6). Leonardo da Vinci (1452–1519), for example, was keen to argue that painting is superior to poetry, sculpture, and music. By casting the argument in this way, he suggests that, though others might not accept the pre-eminence of painting, the special links between it and sculpture, music, and poetry were generally accepted (Leonardo da Vinci 1989: 20–46).

Overall, to speak of "works of art" is not the anachronism with regard to the sixteenth and seventeenth centuries that it is for the Middle Ages. Thinkers of the renaissance did, therefore, unlike medieval philosophers, have one of the conceptual prerequisites for formulating aesthetic theories in the modern style. But this preparedness did not in fact result in an aesthetics on modern lines from the renaissance or seventeenth century. The characteristic concentration of seventeenth-century philosophers on epistemology and the new scientific understanding of the physical world made mainstream philosophy less accommodating to topics with links to aesthetics than medieval philosophy, with its strong leaning to questions about language and meaning. Renaissance philosophy – the work of those thinkers in the fifteenth and sixteenth centuries strongly influenced by the new availability of Plato and a whole range of other classical philosophy – seems more promising, but also turns out to disappoint. For example, Agostino Nifo (d.1538) wrote a book *De pulchro* ("On the Beautiful"). It turns out to be concerned with the beauty of the human body and linked to the debate about Platonic love provoked by works such as the *Symposium*. Although it is an interesting philosophical question to consider how and why humans might be considered beautiful, Nifo is content to assert (ch. 37) that it is only in them that is found the measure and balance of parts that constitute beauty. And other important aesthetic issues raised in passing – such as (ch. 17) whether beauty is an attribute of the object deemed beautiful or of the representation (*species*) of it in the beholder's mind – are given similarly cursory treatment.

Renaissance aesthetics needs, therefore, to be investigated in the same way as suggested for the Middle Ages. But the field of material on which research projects can be focused is wider. As well as the writings of philosophers, there is a rich and varied sixteenth- and seventeenth-century literature of treatises or other discussions on the individual arts. Although not without precedent in the Middle Ages, this literature is different in three important respects. First, among its authors are painters, sculptors, and poets themselves (Dante, here, is a forerunner). Second, the treatment of the visual arts is far more reflective and sophisticated than in any of the medieval treatises. Leonardo da Vinci, in his discussion of painting and the other arts, or Alberti, in his long treatise on architecture, or Vasari in his *Lives of the Artists* provide a subtle account of the first-level features of judgments in these areas, which they weave into a historical and political framework. Gian Paolo Lomazzo, a painter who turned to theoretical writing when he went blind, combines technical discussion with philosophical passages indebted to Ficino in his *Idea del Tempio della Pittura* ("Idea of the Temple of Painting," 1590). Third, there is the development of a tradition of Aristotelian literary theory. For the history of aesthetics, it is the third point that is most important because, despite the speculative interests in the background of some works in the visual arts, they do not contain much of the type of abstract reflection that would link with the concerns of philosophers of art, rather than art historians or artists today.

The literary treatises are full of theoretical discussion. During the Middle Ages, Aristotle's *Poetics*, though translated in the late thirteenth century, was almost never studied in the universities of western Europe. It was known through a translation of Averroes's paraphrase commentary, which was occasionally glossed but not widely studied. In 1498, Giorgio Valla's translation of the *Poetics* was

published, and it was succeeded by other, more accurate versions. Fifty years later appeared the first of the great renaissance commentaries on the *Poetics* by Francesco Robortelli. Along with commentaries, in Latin and the vernacular (the first was Lodovico Castelvetro's, published in 1570), were written treatises on poetic theory (Weinberg 1970 – collecting those from Italy), drawing on and considering problems raised by Aristotle, but also influenced by the new knowledge of Plato and the need to respond to his apparently low estimation of poetry. Many of the debates in these works involve issues still current in aesthetics, even if the terms in which they are framed seem antiquarian. For example, the argument over whether Empedocles and Lucretius should be considered poets (see Hathaway 1962: 65–86 and Aristotle, *Poetics* 1451b) brings up questions about the distinctions between art and nonart and between truth and fiction; and the disagreements over the meaning of "catharsis" (*Poetics* 1449b) led writers to think about the emotive effect of drama and its moral justification (see below).

In order to illustrate how renaissance discussions of literature can be usefully related to the concerns of aesthetics, as practiced now, I end by looking at two sample passages, both from writings by literary practitioners.

SIDNEY'S REVERSAL OF PLATO: ART, MORALITY, AND REPRESENTATION

Sir Philip Sidney probably wrote his *Apology for Poetry* three or four years before his death in 1586. Cast in the form of an oration, it sets out to defend poetry, in its various genres, against its detractors (the most eminent of whom, of course, was Plato) while freely admitting the shortcomings of the poetry of his own time in England – a strategy that, in itself, puts the main part of his defense on a theoretical plane.

Sidney's first main argument for the value of poetry runs as follows: all the arts but poetry have nature as their object. For example, astronomers find out the order in which nature has established the stars, physicians are concerned with the nature of human bodies, and metaphysicians "build upon the depth of Nature." "Only the poet," continues Sidney

> disdaining to be tied to any such subjection, lifted up with the vigour of his own invention, doth grow

in effect into another nature, in making things either better than Nature bringeth forth, or quite anew, forms such as never were in Nature . . . Nature never set forth the earth in so rich a tapestry as divers poets have done; neither with pleasant rivers, fruitful trees, sweet-smelling flowers, nor whatsoever else may make the too much loved earth more lovely. Her world is brazen, the poets only deliver a golden. (1963: 100–1)

Sidney then turns to consider poetic presentation of humans, and he claims that nature never produced examples of people so valiant, constant in friendship, or in every way excellent as can be found in poetry. He makes the theory underlying his comments more explicit when he considers an objection to his position. His claims, it might be said, cannot be taken seriously, because nature produces real things and the poet only imitations of them. He answers that what shows a poet's or any artificer's skill is not the object produced but the mental concept ("Idea or fore-conceit") of it. And, he suggests, when the poet introduces, for instance, an ideally just prince like Cyrus, he is doing more than nature might have done, because he bestows "a Cyrus upon the world to make many Cyruses, if they will learn aright why and how that maker made him."

Sidney is drawing on a background of ideas that are found in the literary theorist Julius Scaliger (d.1558) and Ficino, but he is giving, more pointedly than any of them, a response to Plato's most direct criticism of poets. Despite some resemblances, his theory is not one of the sort suggested by the Neoplatonists (see esp. Plotinus, *Ennead* V.8.1), in which the world of Ideas, as described in the middle books of the *Republic*, is made graspable through artifacts. Rather, Sidney is addressing himself to the argument of *Republic* X, where Plato uses a rather different conception of Ideas. When Plato condemns poets in *Republic* X for imitating an imitation, his point is that we learn skills, ranging from shoemaking to government, by intellectually grasping the function of the task and so how it should be performed: it is these Ideas in virtue of which the particular shoemaking or governing can take place. Whereas shoemakers or rulers imitate such Ideas, poets merely imitate the external performance of these imitators – an imitation of an

imitation: when Homer gives a statesman's speech, he is not drawing on the intellectual principles of good government but just on the way statesmen in fact speak. Sidney argues that poets are in fact able to draw on Ideas, which he sees, in terms closer to *Republic* X than to other texts, as the knowledge of how to behave virtuously in different aspects of life and positions in it (including that of ruler). Through their writing, poets can present these Ideas more directly than they are found in nature – in particular, virtuous people – and so in a way that serves better the purpose of moral instruction and formation. In proposing this theory, Sidney is therefore taking a position both about what would now be called the question of art and morality, and also about representation.

CORNEILLE, ARISTOTLE, AND THE ORIGINS OF MODERN AESTHETICS

Sidney was a leading English poet in a generation quickly overshadowed by the next. Pierre Corneille is recognized as one of the two great seventeenth-century French tragedians. When he published an edition of his plays in 1660, he wrote long theoretical prefaces to each volume. The second, the *Discourse on Tragedy*, considers in detail how catharsis should be interpreted in Aristotle's *Poetics*. When Aristotle presents his definition of tragedy (*Poetics* 1449b), he ends by saying that a tragedy "through pity and fear brings out the *catharsis* of [pity and fear]." This remark seems to be giving what he takes to be the proper effect of tragedy, and so it is central to an understanding of his thought on the area, and yet it is not at all clear what he meant, especially since, on the one other occasion when he uses the term "catharsis" in a similar context (*Politics* 1341b), he refers back to the *Poetics* – perhaps to a different version from that we have – as if there were a fuller explanation there. Scholars today are still divided about how to interpret the term, and in the sixteenth and seventeenth centuries, there were many conflicting views. Corneille begins his second *Discourse* by giving a confident account of how to interpret Aristotle's enigmatic remark.

Quoting Aristotle's assertion in his *Rhetoric* that we pity those who suffer an undeserved misfortune and fear that the same thing may happen to ourselves, Corneille says that pity is felt with regard to the person we see suffering, and fear with respect to ourselves. This distinction, he believes, shows how catharsis should be understood:

> Pity for the misfortune into which we see those like us fall brings us to fear similar misfortune for ourselves, this fear to the desire to avoid it, and this desire leads us to purge, moderate, rectify and even uproot the passion in ourselves which we see plunging those whom we lament into misery before our eyes, because of this common, but natural and indubitable argument, that to avoid the effect it is necessary to remove the cause. (1999: 96)

If this were in fact Corneille's view about how tragedy works, then it would be no more worth quoting than many other of the interpretations current at the time – perhaps, indeed, less so, because some of the renaissance and seventeenth-century writers produced considerably more plausible readings than this overtly moralizing one. But Corneille does not himself at all accept Aristotle's theory.

Aristotle, in his view, is wrong from the start, because tragedies do *not* purge the passions. If they did, then the way he has described, he believes, is how it would have to happen. But in practice, even the very few tragedies that meet Aristotle's condition of having a hero who is neither evil nor wholly innocent fail to have the effect he claims. Corneille takes the example of his own *Le Cid*. There the tragic misfortune is brought about by a couple's love for each other: we pity them, and this pity should – by the theory of catharsis as he has reconstructed it – lead us to fear a similar misfortune and so purge in us the excess of love which is the cause of their downfall. "But I do not know that it produces fear in us, or purges us of this excess," Corneille continues, "and I greatly fear that Aristotle's reasoning on this matter is no more than a beautiful idea, which is never brought to effect in reality" (1999: 99–100). Corneille goes on to propose a way of saving Aristotle, by understanding him to mean that the purgation is achieved by *either* pity *or* fear. In his discussion, however, Corneille uses this formula to explain the workings of, on the one hand, tragedies that teach morally by showing an evil person punished (and so make us fear to be evil) and, on the other, of tragedies that simply cause pity, without morally instructing. Despite initial appearances, therefore, Corneille

is willing to go beyond the usual insistence in his day that serious poetry and drama must always instruct, as well as pleasing.

Tragedy and its purposes is still a subject discussed on the borderline of aesthetics and literary theory, and philosophers are certainly concerned with the wider question of why we choose to witness representations (in drama or pictures or films) of events that are harrowing. But there is another reason for giving a place in the history of aesthetics to Corneille's second *Discourse*. As is illustrated by the essay *Of Tragedy* written less than a century later by David Hume, perhaps the first great figure in modern aesthetics, one of the bases of this new development was the discussion of traditional themes of literary theory in a freely speculative way, liberated from the need to interpret Aristotle. Corneille has not yet reached that stage, but by turning his back on the *Poetics* and thinking about tragedy in terms of how real audiences are affected by different types of plot and characters, he is taking a significant step to making modern aesthetics possible.

See also TWENTIETH-CENTURY ANGLO-AMERICAN AESTHETICS; AQUINAS; ARISTOTLE; CATHARSIS; PLATO; PLOTINUS; RELIGION AND ART.

BIBLIOGRAPHY

Primary sources

Albert the Great. 1972. *Super Dionysium de divinis nominibus* (c.1250). P. Simon (ed.). Münster: Aschendorff.

Aquinas, Thomas. 1927. *Opuscula omnia*. 5 vols. P. Mandonnet (ed.). Paris: Lethielleux.

Assunto, Rosario. 1961. *La Critica d'Arte nel pensiero medievale*. Milan: Il Saggiatore.

Corneille, Pierre. 1999. *Trois discours sur le poème dramatique*. B. Luvat & M. Ecola (eds.). Paris: Flammarion.

Dante Alighieri. 2007. *De vulgari eloquentia*. Book I: *Über die Beredsamkeit in der Volkssprache*. R. Imbach, I. Rosir-Catach, & T. Suarez-Nani (eds.). Hamburg: Meiner.

Ficino, Marsilio. 2004. *Platonic Theology*, vol. iv. M. J. B. Allen & J. Hankins (eds. & trans.). Cambridge, MA: Harvard University Press.

Hugh of St. Victor. 1961. *The Didascalicon of Hugh of St. Victor: A Medieval Guide to the Arts*. J. Taylor (trans.). New York: Columbia University Press.

Ibn al-Haytham. 1989. *The Optics of Ibn al-Haytham. Books I–III: On Direct Vision*. A. I. Sabra (trans. & comm.). London: Warburg Institute.

Ibn al-Haytham. 2001. *Alhacen's Theory of Visual Perception: A Critical Edition, with English Translation and Commentary, of the First Three Books of Alhacen's "De aspectibus," the Medieval Latin Version of Ibn al-Haytham's Kitâb al-Manâzir*. A. Mark Smith (ed.). *Transactions of the American Philosophical Society*, 91(4); 91(5).

Leonardo da Vinci. 1989. *Leonardo on Painting: An Anthology of Writings by Leonardo da Vinci with a Selection of Documents relating to His Career as an Artist*. M. Kemp (ed.). M. Kemp & M. Walker (sel. & trans.). New Haven: Yale University Press.

Nifo, Agostino. 1549. *Augustini Niphi medicis libri duo De pulchro, primus. De amore, secundus*. Lyons: apud Godefridum & Marcellum Beringos.

Sidney, Philip. 1973. *An Apology for Poetry*. G. Shepherd (ed.). Manchester: Manchester University Press.

Suger. 1946. *Abbot Suger on the Abbey Church of St.-Denis and its Arts Treasures*. E. Panofksy (ed.). Princeton: Princeton University Press.

Suger. 1995. *De consecratione*. G. Binding & A. Speer (eds.). Cologne: Vertrieb Abt. Architekturgeschichte.

Ulrich of Strasbourg. 1987–9. *De summo bono*, II.1–4. A. de Libera (ed.). Hamburg: Meiner.

Secondary sources

Aertsen, Jan A. 1991. "Beauty in the Middle Ages: A Forgotten Transcendental?" *Medieval Philosophy and Theology*, 1, 68–97.

Ashworth, E. Jennifer. 2007. "Metaphor and the Logicians from Aristotle to Cajetan," *Vivarium*, 45, 311–27.

Assunto, Rosario. 1961. *La Critica d'Arte nel pensiero medievale*. Milan: Il Saggiatore.

Baeumker, Clemens. 1908. *Witelo: Ein Philosoph und Naturforscher des XIII. Jahrhunderts*. Münster: Aschendorff.

Black, Deborah L. 1990. *Logic and Aristotle's "Rhetoric" and "Poetics" in Medieval Arabic Philosophy*. London: Brill.

Blunt, Anthony. 1940. *Artistic Theory in Italy 1450–1600*. Oxford: Oxford University Press.

Boulnois, Olivier. 2008. *Au-delà de l'image: une archéologie du visuel au Moyen Âge, Ve–XVIe siècle*. Paris: Seuil.

De Bruyne, Edgar. 1998. *Études d'esthétique médiévale*. Paris: Albin Michel. (Reprints, with new introduction and afterword, both the *Études* of 1946, and *L'Esthétique du moyen âge* of 1947, trans. as *The Esthetics of the Middle Ages* by E. B. Hennessy. New York: Ungar, 1969.)

Eco, Umberto. 1970 [1956]. *Il Problema estetico in Tommaso d'Aquino*. 2nd edn. Milan: Bompiani. (*The Aesthetics of Thomas Aquinas*. H. Bredin (trans.). London: Radius, 1988.)

Eco, Umberto. 1986. *Art and Beauty in the Middle Ages*. H. Bredin (trans.). New Haven: Yale University Press. (Translation of a section, "Sviluppo dell'estetica medievale" in *Momenti e problemi dell'estetica* (1959); Eco has published an updating: *Arte e bellezza nell'estetica medievale*. Milan: Bompiani, 1987.)

Hathaway, Baxter. 1962. *The Age of Criticism: The Late Renaissance in Italy*. Ithaca: Cornell University Press.

Kemal, Salim. 2003. *The Philosophical Poetics of Alfarabi, Avicenna and Averroës: The Aristotelian Reception*. London: Routledge Curzon.

Kristeller, Paul Oskar. 1980. "The Modern System of the Arts." In *Renaissance Thought and the Arts*. Princeton: Princeton University Press, 163–227.

Lorusso, A. M. (ed.). 2005. *Metafora e conoscenza*. Milan: Bompiani.

Panfosky, Erwin. 1957. *Gothic Architecture and Scholasticism*. London: Thames & Hudson.

Pouillon, Henri. 1946. "La Beauté, propriété transcendentale chez les scolastiques (1220–1270)," *Archives d'histoire doctrinale et littéraire du moyen âge*, 15, 263–329.

Speer, Andreas. 1990. "Thomas Aquin und die Kunst: Eine hermeneutische Anfrage zur mittelalterlichen Ästhetik," *Archiv für Kulturgeschichte*, 72, 323–45.

Speer, Andreas. 1993. "Vom Verstehen mittelalterlicher Kunst." In *Mittelalterliches Kunsterleben nach Quelen des 11. Bis 13. Jahrhunderts*. G. Binding & A. Speer (eds.). Stuttgart and Bad Cannstatt: Fromman & Holzboog, 13–52.

Speer, Andreas. 1994. "*Kunst* und *Schönheit*: Kritische Überlegungen zur mittelalterlichen Ästhetik." In *"Scientia" und "ars" in Hoch- und Spätmittelalter*. I. Craemer-Ruegenberg & A. Speer (eds.). Berlin: de Gruyter, 946–66.

Tatarkiewicz, Wladyslaw. 1970. *History of Aesthetic*, vol. ii. The Hague: Mouton. (Translation by A. & A. Czerniawki of *Historia Estetyki*, vol. ii. *Estetyka Sredniowieczna*.)

Weinberg, Bernard (ed.). 1961. *A History of Literary Criticism in the Italian Renaissance*. Chicago: University of Chicago Press.

Weinberg, Bernard (ed.). 1970. *Trattati di poetica e retorica del cinquecento*. Bari: Laterza.

JOHN MARENBON

eighteenth-century aesthetics Alexander Gottlieb Baumgarten (1714–62) coined the term "aesthetics" in 1735 in his master's thesis, *Philosophical Meditations on Some Matters Pertaining to Poetry*. But the field had hardly waited for this baptism to commence, and the entire century saw extensive publication in aesthetics, not only in Germany but also in France and Britain (even though the new name for the field was not incorporated into English until the nineteenth century). Historical periodization is always somewhat arbitrary, and the boundaries of eighteenth-century aesthetics are debatable, especially at the later end, where typical eighteenth-century modes of thought continued in Britain past 1800 while ideas more characteristic of nineteenth-century thought began to appear in Germany during the 1790s. Here eighteenth-century aesthetics will be treated as extending from 1709 to 1810, from the first publication of *The Moralists* (subsequently incorporated into his *Charackeristicks of Men, Manners, Opinions, Times*) by Anthony Ashley Cooper, Third Earl of Shaftesbury (1671–1714), to the publication of the *Philosophical Essays* of Dugald Stewart (1753–1828), then emeritus professor of moral philosophy at the University of Edinburgh. During these 101 years, a vast number of books were published by philosophers, divines, critics of art and literature, and men of letters in general (in spite of the fact that writing about aesthetics by no means took place only in the exclusively male universities of Britain and Europe, the texts of eighteenth-century aesthetics were nevertheless produced only by men) that can be considered part of the literature of aesthetics because they deal in a reflective and analytical way with the origins, objects, value, and intersubjective validity of human experiences of nature and art that cannot be simply subsumed under the categories of knowledge on the one hand or prudential and moral action on the other hand. While many of the texts of this century have fallen into obscurity, several have become cornerstones of subsequent aesthetics, and many of the issues discussed in both better- and lesser-known works of the period have remained central to the field.

Any number of explanations might be offered for the immense outburst of activity in aesthetics during this period. It might be thought of as the theoretical response to the revival of the arts after their puritanical suppression in the seventeenth century, especially in Protestant areas such as Britain and the German regions where much of the activity took place. It might be associated with the rise of a prosperous bourgeoisie, whose wealth and leisure created the opportunity for indulgence in both the fine arts and in nature as a site for recreation and appreciation as opposed to mere toil, a demand for the theorization of these new pleasures, and the wealth to support a cadre of writers to undertake this theorization. It might be conceived of as the attempt to argue for the possibility of common cultural ground in an increasingly stratified society, or conversely as the attempt of the newly empowered bourgeoisie to establish its cultural hegemony over other strata of society (for alternative liberal and Marxist accounts, see Ferry 1993 and Eagleton 1990). This entry, however, will eschew any historical explanation of the flourishing of aesthetics in the eighteenth century and confine itself to describing some of the main issues and accomplishments of the period.

A common view of the period assumes a widely shared consensus that aesthetic experience consists in a disinterested contemplation of the forms of objects, whether of nature or of fine art, producing a pleasure that can be expected to be shared by all who have troubled to refine their taste in readily specifiable and accessible ways, and that the disinterested character of aesthetic experience and judgment grounds the autonomy of art, or the freedom of artistic practices and projects from criticism and constraint from external theoretical or practical standpoints, especially from moral, political, or religious standpoints. Suggestions of such a view can be found in Francis Hutcheson (1694–1746) early in the century and in Immanuel Kant (1724–1804) toward its end, but Hutcheson's aesthetic theory was not widely accepted, Kant's is far more complicated than this caricature suggests, and there were many alternatives to every element of this supposed consensus. This entry will aim to convey a sense of the wealth and variety of views that were offered on the central issues in aesthetic theory during the century rather than to regiment them under some simplistic scheme. Borrowing titles from the period, views about the objects and organs of aesthetic experience and judgment will be discussed under the heading "The Pleasures of the Imagination," views about the possibility of intersubjective validity in judgments of taste under the heading "The Standard of Taste," and views about the relations between aesthetic experience and morality under the rubric "The Aesthetic Education of Humankind."

THE PLEASURES OF THE IMAGINATION

One author who might fit the caricature of eighteenth-century aesthetics as reducible to a formalist theory of beauty is Denis Diderot (1713–84), or at least the Diderot who in 1752 wrote the article "On the Origin and Nature of the Beautiful" for the great *Encyclopedia* that he edited with Jean le Rond d'Alembert (1717–83). In this article Diderot termed "beautiful" "everything that contains the power of awakening the notion of relation in my mind," regardless of what that relation might be, thus relations among the various parts of a building, the sounds of a piece of music, "the relations apparent in men's actions" or among the parts of "the works of nature": differences in the nature of the relata might give rise to names of different species of beauty, such as moral beauty, literary beauty, musical beauty, or natural beauty, but none of these differences affects the real character of beauty, which is simply "the ease with which we grasp" any relations "and the pleasure that accompanies their perception" (1966: 54–5). But most theorists of the period offered more complicated catalogues of the sources of aesthetic pleasure than that (as did Diderot himself in his famous *Salons*, Diderot 1995).

The variety of eighteenth-century conceptions of both the objects and the organs of aesthetic experience – about what we respond to in such experience and by means of what capacities we do so – is already evident in a comparison of the views of Shaftesbury and Francis Hutcheson: although Hutcheson originally presented his 1725 *Inquiry into the Original of Our Ideas of Beauty and Virtue* (divided into two treatises, the first *Concerning Beauty, Order, Harmony, Design* and the second *Concerning Moral Good and Evil*) as an explanation and defense of the principles of Shaftesbury, there are many differences between their positions, a fact that Hutcheson tacitly acknowledged by dropping the reference to Shaftesbury from the title page of the second and later editions of his book. Although his education was supervised by the empiricist John Locke (1632–1704), who

was employed as both a physician and a political adviser by his grandfather, the first earl, Shaftesbury was a Neoplatonist who held that the true, the good, and the beautiful are all manifestations of the harmonious order of the universe and of the divine intelligence that is its source, the former of which may initially be apprehended by our senses but the latter of which is ultimately apprehended by our own intellect, while Hutcheson in fact hewed more closely to Locke, holding that our apprehension of beauty is an immediate, sensory response to a variety of relations that may be subsumed under the general conception of "unity amidst variety," and which are analogous but by no means identical to the forms of unity amid variety that are the objects of knowledge on the one hand and of moral sentiment on the other. Hutcheson thus recognized a wider variety of objects of aesthetic response and drew a firmer distinction between the organs of aesthetic response and our other capacities than did Shaftesbury. Shaftesbury introduced the concept of disinterestedness in his moral philosophy, arguing that our approbation of virtuous actions is not interested or mercenary, that is, based on an expectation of an increase to our own happiness from such actions in this life or the next (e.g., *Moralists* II.2; 1999: 268–9), and suggested that our pleasure in a beautiful scene in nature is also not interested in the sense of being founded in an expectation of pleasure from the personal use or consumption of those natural objects (III.2; 1999: 318–19). But Shaftesbury did not intend disinterestedness to be the explanation of our pleasure in beauty, only a consequence and therefore a sign of it; the explanation of our pleasure in beauty is that in apprehending something beautiful we apprehend an instance of "nature's order in created beings" and beyond that "the source and principle of all beauty and perfection" (III.1; 1999: 298). More fully, Shaftesbury held that in taking pleasure in beauty we respond to a hierarchy of principles of form or unity: in works of nature or human art, the immediately perceivable unified form of the object, but that is only "*dead form*"; in the case of works of art, the "*forms which form*, that is, which have intelligence, action and operation," that is, human artistry, but then in both cases the ultimate source of form, "*that third order of beauty, which forms not only such as we call mere forms but even the forms which form*" (III.2; 1999: 323). Although the immediate object of our pleasure in a beautiful object may be the form perceived by our senses, the ultimate object of our pleasure is the divine source of that form, inferred by our intellect. Hutcheson, by contrast, even though unlike Shaftesbury he was actually a minister, and was certainly a pious man, offered a more empiricist and less theological aesthetic theory. Hutcheson held that our pleasure in beauty is a feeling that accompanies our "complex Ideas of Objects" that are "Regular" or "Harmonious," as opposed to the pleasures that accompany "the simple Ideas of Sensation" (I.viii; 2004: 22); indeed, sometimes he went so far as to identify the property of beauty with the pleasurable "Idea rais'd in us" (I.ix; 2004: 23), although in practice, like anyone else, he often spoke of beauty as the order in an object that produces pleasure in us rather than as the feeling of pleasure itself. Hutcheson argued that our apprehension of beauty "is justly called a sense," because although our pleasure is a response to the order that we find in objects, it "does not arise from any Knowledge of Principles, Proportions, Causes, or of the Usefulness of the Object, but strikes us at first with the Idea of Beauty" (I.xiii; 2004: 25). Because the beauty of an object pleases us independently of any such knowledge, no "Prospect of Advantage or Disadvantage" can "vary the Beauty or Deformity of an Object" (I.xiv; 2004: 25): our pleasure in a beautiful object is disinterested because it is immediate and therefore precedes any possible calculation of advantage or disadvantage. Hutcheson goes on to argue that it can be empirically ascertained that "what we call Beautiful in Objects . . . seems to be in a compound Ratio of Uniformity and Variety" (II.iii; 2004: 29), but we do not respond to it as a part of the larger order of the universe or as a sign of the divine intelligence that has created the universe. Hutcheson then introduces a complexity into the objects of aesthetic appreciation that Shaftesbury had not recognized: he divides beauty into "Original or Absolute," where what we respond to is uniformity amid variety perceived within an object taken by itself, and "Relative or Comparative," where we take pleasure in the uniformity amid variety that we perceive in a relation between

one object and another. Under this rubric Hutcheson treats the beauty of representational works of art, where we appreciate "a kind of unity between the Original and the Copy" (IV.i; 2004: 42), as well as works of nature where our "fruitful Fancy" finds resemblances of all sorts of things (IV.iv; 2004: 44), and also our appreciation of artistry, where we take pleasure in "Correspondence to Intention" and the successful execution of a "Design" by "curious Mechanism" or skill (IV.vii; 2004: 45). Thus Hutcheson both separates the order that pleases us in beautiful objects, whether of nature or fine art, from the order of the universe as a whole, while at the same time recognizing a greater variety of beauties than did Shaftesbury, including the beauty of form in objects, the beauty of content in objects, whether intended as in works of art or imputed as in works of nature, and the beauty of artistry. (On Hutcheson's aesthetics, see Kivy 2003.)

Other authors recognized an even larger variety of objects of aesthetic experience. A seminal text was the series of essays on "The Pleasures of the Imagination" written by the English critic Joseph Addison (1672–1719) and published in June and July of 1712 in the *Spectator*, the journal that he coedited with Richard Steele (1672–1729) from 1711 to 1714 that would become the model for "moral weeklies" throughout Europe. By "pleasures of the imagination," Addison meant pleasures that "arise from visible objects, either when we have them actually in our view, or when we call up their ideas into our minds by paintings, statues, descriptions, or any the like occasion," and he held that such pleasures

> do not require such a bent of thought as is necessary to our more serious employments, nor, at the same time, suffer the mind to sink into that negligence and remissness, which are apt to accompany our more sensual delights, but, like a gentle exercise of the faculties, awaken them from sloth and idleness, without putting them upon any labour or difficulty. (Addison & Steele 1965: no. 411)

Addison did not use the term "disinterestedness," but by describing the pleasures of the imagination as a "gentle exercise" of our mental faculties falling between our "serious employments" and merely "sensual delights," he

35

suggested a way of characterizing the independence of aesthetic experience from straightforward cognition on the one hand and straightforward sensation on the other: eight decades later, Kant would support his explicit claim that our pleasure in beauty is disinterested by distinguishing it from merely sensory "agreeableness" on the one hand and our pleasure in the conceptually mediated cognition of goodness, whether merely prudential or moral, on the other (Kant 2000: §§2–5). Addison then took an equally influential step when he divided "those pleasures of the imagination which arise from the actual view and survey of outward objects" into those proceeding "from the sight of what is great, uncommon, or beautiful" (Addison & Steele 1965: no. 412): the pleasures of the sublime, the novel, and the beautiful. By the great or the sublime he meant whatever gives us "an image of liberty, where the eye has room to range abroad, to expatiate at large on the immensity of its views, and to lose itself amid the variety of objects that offer themselves to its observation"; by the novel, what "fills the soul with an agreeable surprise, gratifies its curiosity, and gives it an idea of which it was not before possessed"; and by the beautiful, whatever "immediately diffuses a secret satisfaction and complacency through the imagination, and gives a finishing to any thing that is great or uncommon." He divided beauties into two further kinds, those that make members of a species beautiful to others of its own kind, especially creatures of one sex to the other, and those that we find throughout "the several products of nature and art . . . in the gayety or variety of colours, in the symmetry and proportion of parts, in the arrangement and disposition of bodies, or in a just mixture and concurrence of all together," among which the beauty of colors are particularly pleasing.

Addison's scheme would be influential throughout the century. Sometimes the pleasure of novelty would disappear from the list, as when Edmund Burke (1729–97), in his *Philosophical Enquiry into the Origin of Our Ideas of the Sublime and Beautiful* of 1757, and following him Kant, would divide the sources of aesthetic appreciation into two main groups, those of the beautiful and the sublime, rather than three, but no one other than Hutcheson

failed to emphasize the importance of the sublime alongside the beautiful. (The concept of the sublime was popularized by translations of the ancient treatise "On the Sublime" by Pseudo-Longinus, into French by Nicolas Boileau in 1674 and English by William Smith in 1743; see Longinus 1964, Monk 1935, Zelle 1995, and Ashfield & de Bolla 1996.)

In spite of this common division, there were also great differences between the theories of Kant and Burke. Burke based his division on the empirical psychology of the day, arguing that there is an immediate and positive pleasure in anything that gratifies our fundamental passion for society and a negative pleasure at our escape from potential pain in the gratification of our passion for self-preservation. The sublime is then "Whatever is fitted to excite the ideas of pain, and danger, that is to say, whatever is in any sort terrible," but does not actually harm us and therefore affords us negative delight (I.viii; 1958: 39), and the beautiful is whatever suggests the pleasures of society. Following Addison's hint, Burke divides beauty into two kinds, namely the sorts of features that we find sexually attractive in members of our own species and that thus ground specific sexual relations (I.ix; 1958: 41–2) (his list of such beauties is actually a list of properties that men are supposed to find beautiful in women, such as delicacy and smoothness; see III.xii–xviii), and the sorts of features that we find attractive in other human beings generally or even in other sorts of creatures (such as grace and elegance; see III.xix–xxvi), and that can ground nonsexual social relations. Burke goes beyond this psychological account of the beautiful and the sublime to a more purely physiological account, in which he argues that the pleasure of the approach to but ultimate avoidance of pain that is characteristic of the sublime stems from the invigoration of our fibers (IV.vii; 1958: 136), while "beauty acts by relaxing the solids of the system" (IV.xix; 1958: 149). This sort of speculative physiology might seem to be a by-way in eighteenth-century aesthetics, but it would recur four decades later in the *Letters on the Aesthetic Education of Mankind* by Friedrich Schiller (1759–1805) – who began his career as a student of medicine and physiology – in his distinction between "melting" and "energizing" beauty, the former of which "restores harmony to him who is over-tensed" and the latter of which restores "energy to him who is relaxed" (Letter XVII; 1967: 117). Burke would add another crucial element to eighteenth-century aesthetics in the final part of his book, where he argued that poetry works because its words affect us with the same emotions that the actual view of the objects they describe or refer to would affect us with (V.i; 1958: 165): in other words, literature works through the association of ideas, or more precisely through the association of emotions with signs: Burke held that the emotion is immediately caused by the literary sign, not through an intermediate image of the object invoked by the sign. The association of ideas would become a central part of aesthetics in such subsequent works as the *Elements of Criticism* of 1762 by Henry Home, Lord Kames (1696–1782) (about which more shortly) and the *Essays on the Nature and Principles of Taste* of 1790 by Archibald Alison (1757–1839) (see Dickie 1996).

While following Burke's division of the objects of aesthetic response into the beautiful and the sublime, Kant rejected what he explicitly called Burke's "empirical" and "physiological exposition" in favor of what purported to be an a priori and "transcendental" explanation of our aesthetic responses and judgments: this consisted in the attempt to show that these responses and judgments arise from the same faculties of mind that we use in ordinary theoretical and practical judgment, but not from the ordinary, determinate use of these faculties to satisfy specific theoretical or practical goals. Kant began with the analysis of judgments of taste about beauty. He contrasted the disinterested pleasure of beauty with the interested pleasures of the agreeable and the good (2000: §§2–5), as already noted, and argued that the pleasure of beauty is the effect of the "free play" between the cognitive faculties of imagination – the ability to have and recall particular images of objects – and understanding – the ability to connect and unify such objects, ordinarily but not in this case by subsuming them under particular concepts – with which we may respond to the perception of an object (§§vii: 9, 20; General Remark following §§22, 35). Because such an experience satisfies our general cognitive aim of finding unity in the manifold of our experience of any object without subsuming it under a concept, Kant called this response "purposiveness without purpose," "subjective purposiveness," or "formal purposiveness" (§12), but also identified this with "purposiveness of form," and thus held, without adequate argument, that beauty properly lies in the "drawing" rather than color of works of visual art (here Kant rejected Addison's suggestion of the preeminence of color among sources of visual beauty) or of "composition" rather than particular tones or instrumentation in music (§14). Kant also supposed that under ideal conditions, the same objects should produce the same free play of imagination and understanding in all who experience them, thus that judgments of beauty could claim "universal subjective validity" (§8) and "exemplary necessity" (§18), a point to be discussed below. Kant then argued that our experience of the sublime rests on a complex relationship between the faculties of imagination and reason rather than imagination and understanding, a relationship that begins as a painful disharmony but culminates in a pleasurable harmony. Whereas Addison and Burke had divided beauty into two kinds, Kant (following many other writers, including Moses Mendelssohn; see Mendelssohn 1997: 194) divided the sublime into two kinds. In the experience of the "mathematical sublime," the imagination is initially stymied in its attempt to apprehend all of some vast natural vista in a single image, but we are then gratified by the sense (it cannot be a determinate conceptualization if this experience is to remain aesthetic) that it is our own capacious faculty of (theoretical) reason that has set the imagination this impossible task (§§25–6); in the experience of the "dynamical sublime," the imagination is initially threatened by the vista of some mighty and destructive natural object, but we are then gratified by the sense that even the threat of physical injury or destruction cannot determine or constrain our capacity to make moral choices on the basis of (practical) reason alone (§28). Finally, paralleling Burke's addition of poetry to his scheme through the mechanism of the association of ideas, Kant adds an account of the beauty of fine art to his accounts of natural beauty and sublimity with the argument that a work of art always "ventures to make sensible rational ideas," such as moral ideas, but does so, at least if it is a product of genius, by means of a

> representation of the imagination . . . which by itself stimulates so much thinking that it can never be grasped in a determinate concept, hence which aesthetically enlarges the concept itself in an unbounded way, [and] then the imagination is creative, and sets the faculty of intellectual ideas (reason) into motion. (§49)

A work of art that does this is one that contains an "aesthetic idea," that is, makes an idea aesthetic by stimulating the free play of the imagination with an idea of reason rather than constraining the imagination by a rule-like concept. The artist who can create such free play in his or her own mind and express it through a publicly accessible work is a genius, but part of the genius of such a work is precisely that it leaves room for and stimulates a free play of the imagination in the minds of its audience, including subsequent artists, rather than completely dictating their response. (On Kant, see Guyer 1979, 1993, 2005.)

Burke and Kant (for example) thus diversify Hutcheson's focus on beauty alone with the addition of the sublime. Others enumerated an even greater variety of objects of aesthetic pleasure and, at least in the British tradition, corresponding "senses" for them. In a prizewinning *Essay on Taste* first published in 1759 (the same year as the second edition of Burke's *Enquiry*), Alexander Gerard (1728–95), professor of philosophy (later of divinity) at Marischal College, Aberdeen, enumerated seven such objects and corresponding senses, namely "the sense or taste" of Novelty, Grandeur and Sublimity, Beauty, Imitation, Harmony, Ridicule, and Virtue (1978: part I). Three years later, the Scottish justice Henry Home, Lord Kames, a distant relative of David Hume (1711–76) and a founder of the society that had awarded Gerard's prize, published his *Elements of Criticism*, a book that went through six editions in Kames's lifetime and remained a college textbook in the United States until well into the nineteenth century. He carefully omitted a definite article from the title of his book to indicate that his list of aesthetic qualities was intended to be open-ended, but even so he went beyond Gerard in enumerating Beauty, Grandeur and Sublimity, Motion and Force,

Novelty "and the unexpected appearance of Objects," Risible Objects, Resemblance and Dissimilitude, Uniformity and Variety, Congruity and Propriety, Dignity and Grace, Ridicule, Wit, and Custom and Habit as objects of aesthetic pleasure (2005b: table of contents), the unifying bond among all of these diverse qualities being that all of them can stimulate pleasing "Perceptions and Ideas in a Train" (ch. 1). Natural objects can stimulate pleasing trains of ideas directly through such features, but works of (representational) art can double our pleasure through our awareness of the correspondence between the train of ideas stimulated by the artistic representation and that which would be stimulated by the represented object: "Every work of art that is conformable to the natural course of our ideas, is so far agreeable; and every work of art that reverses that course, is so far disagreeable." In other words, our response to the correspondence between an artistic representation and what it represents is itself another pleasing train of ideas.

However, the greatest addition of Kames's *Elements of Criticism* to the diversity of objects of aesthetic response recognized in the eighteenth century lies in his recognition that the arousal of our emotions through works of art is our most fundamental source of pleasure in them. Here Kames brings into the British tradition in aesthetics the central idea of the French Abbé Jean-Baptiste Du Bos (1670–1742). Du Bos's widely influential *Critical Reflections on Poetry, Painting and Music*, first published in French in 1719 and translated into English in 1748, held that "The arts of poetry and painting are never more applauded, than when they are most successful in moving us to pity" (1748: part 1, 1). Du Bos argued that the "heaviness," *ennui*, or boredom "which quickly attends the inactivity of the mind" is displeasing (part I, ch. 1, 5), and that we seek out all sorts of amusements, including gambling, bullfights, and the like, in order to relieve ourselves of it through the stimulation of passions, but that many such means of stimulation can have unacceptably high costs, such as financial ruin. However, the representational arts can "separate the dismal consequences of our passions from the bewitching pleasure we receive in indulging them" because through their "imitation of objects capable of exciting real passions" such arts can "contrive to produce objects that would excite artificial passions, sufficient to occupy us while we are actually affected by them, and incapable of giving us afterwards any real pain or affliction" (part I, ch. 3, 21–2). Du Bos's theory was that the depiction of various sorts of human conduct and their pleasurable or painful consequences in literature or painting raise in us the very same sorts of passions that seeing such events in real life would raise, but within limits – we walk away from the theater once the tragedy is over – so that the pleasure of the stimulation of our emotions is not outweighed by the painful consequences that the sort of events depicted would have in real life. So artificial passions are not make-believe emotions, but real, stimulating emotions kept within bearable limits by the artificiality of their objects.

Du Bos's conception of artificial passions was widely taken up. Moses Mendelssohn (1729–86), for example, who made his mark with his writings on aesthetics in the 1750s long before his famous work on Jewish emancipation (*Jerusalem*, 1783) and his leadership of the German Jewish Enlightenment, argued against Du Bos that it is not the sheer stimulation of our emotions but rather our sympathy with the perfections revealed by characters even under adversity that pleases us in drama, but agreed with Du Bos that the artistic challenge of drama lies precisely in the fact that it must both stimulate our passions through successful illusion yet at the same time keep those passions in check by reminders that it is "artistic deception" (Mendelssohn 1997: "On Sentiments," 75). Kames's position was even closer to that of Du Bos. He shared Du Bos's view that mental activity in general – "trains of ideas" – is a source of pleasure to us, and, as already noted, enumerated a large variety of qualities of objects that could stimulate such activity. But he certainly agreed with Du Bos that the stimulation of our emotions through the depiction of the actions and feelings of human beings is the foremost source of our pleasure in representational art. In an essay on "Our Attachment to Objects of Distress" that began his 1751 *Essays on the Principles of Morality and Natural Religion* and that itself began with a reference to Du Bos (2005: 11), Kames argued that "history, novels, and plays" are

"the most universal and favourite entertainments" because in our response to them "We enter deep into [the] concerns" of those they depict, "take a side . . . partake of joys and distresses," and argued that a good tragedy, although it is obviously artificial, produces even deeper emotions than we usually experience in ordinary life:

> Tragedy is an imitation or representation of human characters and actions. It is a feigned history, which commonly makes a stronger impression than what is real; because, if it be a work of genius, incidents will be chosen to make the deepest impressions; and will be so conducted as to keep the mind in continual suspense and agitation, beyond what commonly happens in real life. By a good tragedy, all the social passions are excited. (2005a: 17)

But he resolved the threat of paradox in tragedy – that we should find it painful rather than pleasurable to observe the depiction of painful events – by distinguishing between painfulness and aversion, arguing that "the moral affections, even such of them as produce pain, are none of them attended with any degree of aversion . . . Sympathy in particular attaches us to an object in distress so powerfully as even to overbalance self-love . . . Sympathy accordingly, though a painful passion, is attractive." From this he concluded that tragedy can "seize the mind with all the different charms which arise from the exercise of the social passions, without the least obstacle from self-love" (2005a: 18). In his chapter on "Emotions and Passions" in the *Elements of Criticism*, by far the longest chapter in the work, Kames puts the point by distinguishing between emotion, "an internal motion or agitation of the mind [that] passeth away without desire," and passion, a motion or agitation that is followed by desire (ch. 2; 2005b: 37), and then arguing that works of art raise emotions but not passions. They do this by what Kames calls "ideal presence," their ability to make us "recall any thing to [our] mind in a manner so distinct as to form an idea or image of it as present," to raise in us "ideas no less distinct than if [we] had originally been an eye-witness" and to "insensibly transform" us into spectators, which in turn produces in us the emotions (but not passions) that the real object would and thereby engage our sympathy: "ideal presence supplies the want of real presence; and in idea we perceive persons acting and suffering, precisely as in an original survey; if our sympathy be engaged by the latter, it must also in some degree be engaged by the former (2005b: 67–9). Not all forms of fine art stimulate pleasing trains of ideas by representation of human actions at all, and among those that do, not all do it to the same degree, but "Of all the means for making an impression of ideal presence, theatrical representation is the most powerful" (2005b: 71) because it combines the power of words and the power of visual images to affect our feelings, and is thus more powerful than either literature or painting alone – but Kames leaves no doubt that the enjoyment of emotions stimulated by ideal presence is the greatest of the enjoyments that art has to offer.

There can be no question, then, that many French and British writers in the eighteenth century regarded the depiction of human action and the consequent arousal of emotion as at least as important in our experience of the fine arts as our enjoyment of forms or colors in the naturally or artistically beautiful or our enjoyment of magnitude and force in the sublime, and that it would thus be a profound error to reduce eighteenth-century aesthetics to the theory of the beautiful. This is true in the perfectionist tradition of eighteenth-century German aesthetics as well. This tradition began with Christian Wolff (1679–1754), and was carried on by Alexander Gottlieb Baumgarten and his student Georg Friedrich Meier (1718–77), Moses Mendelssohn, and Johann Georg Sulzer (1720–79), the author of a massive encyclopedia of the arts and aesthetics (Sulzer 1994) which remains an unsurpassed source for eighteenth-century aesthetics. Wolff did not write a treatise on aesthetics, but he initiated the German tradition in the subject by accepting the definition of sense-perception as clear but confused cognition of that which could at least in principle be known clearly and distinctly from Gottfried Wilhelm Leibniz (1646–1716), defining pleasure as the sensory perception or clearly but confused cognition of perfection (Wolff 2003: §404), which he defined in formal terms as the consensus of the parts of the relevant object with each other (§152). If all pleasure is the sensory response to perfection and perfection is just the agreement

of parts with one another, this would seem to leave room only for a purely relational or formal theory of beauty as the object of aesthetic pleasure, like Diderot's theory, but in practice Wolff interpreted perfection as the consensus of the parts of an object with its ground or, in the case of an artifact, with its purpose, and suggested a path for aesthetics with his illustrations. Thus one of his examples of perfection was the perfection of painting, which consists in its similarity to its intended object (2003: note §129 to §404), and in a treatise on architecture that he included in his *Encyclopedia of Mathematical Sciences*, Wolff argued that works of architecture have the dual aim of being both convenient for their intended use and formally beautiful as well, and that our pleasure in works of architecture arises from our sensory perception of the joint satisfaction of both of these aims.

Wolff's recognition of the importance of utility to our pleasure in architecture introduces yet another entry into the eighteenth-century catalogue of aesthetic values. That will be discussed shortly; here let us see how the German tradition made room for the recognition of the importance of the arousal of emotions in aesthetic experience in spite of the formalist conception of beauty suggested by Wolff's conception of perfection. This happens in the work of Baumgarten and Meier. In his 1735 thesis on poetry, where he first defined aesthetics as the "science that guides the lower faculty of knowledge" or "the science of how something is to be cognized sensitively" (Baumgarten 1983: §115), Baumgarten defined a poem as a "perfect sensitive discourse" (§IX), or a verbal artifact that maximizes the potential of sense perception to fuse a great deal of particularized "marks" or images together clearly yet without marking the differences between them by general concepts (§XVII); thus "singular representations" – or representations of particulars "are especially poetic" (§XIX). In Leibnizian terms, poems are or convey "clear but confused cognition." In his large but uncompleted treatise *Aesthetica*, the two extant volumes of which were published in 1750 and 1758, Baumgarten generalized his earlier treatment of poetry into a theory of all art (although his examples continued to be drawn exclusively from poetry). Here he equated aesthetics as the science of sensitive cognition with the "theory of the liberal arts, the theory of lower cognition, the art of thinking beautifully, and the art of the analogue of reason" (2007: §1), and defined the "goal of aesthetics as the perfection of sensitive cognition as such," which he in turn analyzed as consisting in "the consensus of thoughts among themselves insofar as we abstract from their order and significance," the "consensus of the order in which we reflect upon beautifully thought things," and the "internal consensus of the signs with the order and the things" (§§18–20). Here Baumgarten transformed Wolff's conception of aesthetic pleasure as the "sensitive cognition of perfection" into a conception of it as arising from the "perfection of sensitive cognition," that is, he recognized that the representation of things through images rather than through concepts offers its own particular opportunities and standards for excellence and enjoyment, different from those offered by the project of the scientific analysis, classification, and explanation of things. In this way, Baumgarten made conceptual space for the new discipline of aesthetics. But his account of the nature of aesthetic excellence, as just outlined, seems highly formalistic, and this impression seems only strengthened by his more detailed list of aesthetic qualities as the "analogues" of the perfections of "logical" or scientific cognition. The latter include wealth or range (*ubertas*), magnitude, truth, illumination (*lux*), certitude, and liveliness (*vita cognitionis*), and so the aesthetic qualities include aesthetic wealth, aesthetic magnitude, aesthetic truth, aesthetic illumination, aesthetic certitude, and aesthetic liveliness (2007: synopsis). Given the logical origin of these concepts, they can be expected to concern various formal features of artworks, and Baumgarten does give much space to formal considerations. However, the concept of "aesthetic magnitude" in particular turns out to be more complex than that. The criteria for this aspect of aesthetic quality include "the weight of the [represented] objects and their significance, the weight and significance of the thoughts appropriate to these, and the fruitfulness of taking both together," and these qualities are in turn measured by "what can hardly and not even hardly be banned from our mind, but which is rather constantly, firmly, and indelibly preserved in our memory"

(§177; Baumgarten is quoting from Longinus' "On the Sublime"). And the latter phenomenon is in turn a consequence of moral or emotional impact: what possesses "aesthetic magnitude" is above all themes of great moral importance, or "aesthetic dignity" (§182). So, in spite of the "logical" origin of Baumgarten's categories, emotionally significant content is as important in his conception of aesthetic qualities as is perceptual form.

This is also clear in the works of Baumgarten's disciple Meier, who published a compendious German treatise based on his master's lectures, *The Foundations of All Beautiful Sciences*, in 1748–50, even before his master's Latin treatise, but who both earlier and later also published numerous essays that demonstrate that the formalism of the Baumgartian approach is superficial, and that the real aim of art even on this approach is emotional impact. Thus, in one essay from 1751 Meier wrote that "The inner essence of the art of literature consists in sensible representations and in affect, which can arouse affect, in representations that impress lively images on our fancy and work on our heart and arouse passions. The poet must treat matters that work on the passions" (2002: iii.163). Another essay, from 1757, shows how the Baumgartian list of aesthetic qualities includes emotional impact as well as formal features: in addition to wealth of representation, truth of cognition, liveliness and brilliance of cognition, certainty of cognition, beautiful order, and beautiful designation, Meier includes in the second spot on his list "the magnitude of cognition, or the noble, the sublime, etc.," the representation of "great, upright, important, noble objects," and, further down the list, the "touching" or "moving" (*das Rührende*), by which he means that a "beautiful cognition must not please as much as possible merely through itself," that is, its formal features, "but must also cause a suitable satisfaction or dissatisfaction over its object" (2002: iii.192–3).

The more popular essays of Moses Mendelssohn, first appearing in the same years, also manifest the same emphasis on emotional arousal within the Baumgartian framework to which he too subscribed. The work that first brought Mendelssohn widespread attention in 1755 was entitled "On

Sentiments," and here Mendelssohn introduced his conception of "mixed sentiments" as central to aesthetic experience: we can take pleasure in the virtues of a depicted character along with our pain at his misfortunes, and we can take pleasure in the skill of the artist along with our pain at depicted events, and in both ways combine pleasure in the perception of perfections with displeasure in imperfections in a way that is on balance pleasing, in which, indeed, "If a few bitter drops are mixed into the honey-sweet bowl of pleasure, they enhance the taste of the pleasure and double its sweetness" (1997: 74). In the "Rhapsody or additions to the Letters on Sentiment" which he added to the first collection of his essays in 1761, Mendelssohn provided a metaphysical framework for what might otherwise have been merely an empirical observation by exploiting Wolffian perfectionism. He argued that every representation "stands in a twofold relation" to "the matter before it as object . . . and then to the soul or the thinking subject (of which it constitutes a determination)," and that there is potential for pleasure in perfection in either of these: we might or might not take pleasure in the perfection of the represented object, but we can also take pleasure in a good representation of it as "an affirmative determination" of the soul, so even a "representation of evil" can be "a picture within us that engages the soul's capacities of knowing and desiring" and thus be a pleasing "element of the soul's perfection" that can contribute to the overall pleasure of the experience of the artistic representation of painful objects or events (1997: 132–4). This is perfectionism but not formalism. In a 1757 essay "On the Main Principles of the Fine Arts and Sciences" which he also included in his 1761 collection, Mendelssohn expanded this twofold analysis of the sources of aesthetic pleasure into a fourfold analysis: in a work of art, we can potentially enjoy the perfections of the depicted object (or be dissatisfied by its imperfections), but we can also enjoy the "faithfulness or similarity of the imitation" (the artistic imitation but also the mental representation of that), the perfection of the artist who can produce such an imitation, and finally the pleasing effect of the harmonious mental representation on our own bodily condition (1997: 172–6). In the case of natural beauty, of course, our admiration of

the skill of a human artist is replaced by our even greater admiration of the divine artist. The crucial point in all of this, however, is just that Mendelssohn's analysis is one more indication that the eighteenth-century conception of the aesthetic response includes far more than disinterested pleasure in the perceivable form of a work of art or nature alone.

As already mentioned, Wolff has included utility among the sources of beauty in architecture. That is hardly surprising, since the practical role of architecture is inescapable. But some theories counted utility, or at least the appearance of utility, as a source of beauty in arts beyond architecture. Hutcheson had excluded utility as a source of beauty by means of his argument that the response to beauty is an immediate sensory response that leaves no time or place for calculations of advantage. This position was rejected by George Berkeley (1685–1753) in his 1733 *Alciphron*, an attack on Shaftesbury that included an attack on this point in Hutcheson, who then defended his position in the fourth edition of his *Inquiry* in 1738. Burke also rejected the idea that beauty has anything to do with utility with the colorful argument that the snout of a swine may be very useful to it in rooting for food, but is hardly beautiful (1958: III.vi: 195); this followed his rejection of the theory that beauty arises from proportion, however, which could be taken as an attack on Hutcheson's formalist theory that beauty arises from a proportion between unity and variety, and Burke's own theory that beauty lies in properties that we find socially and especially sexually attractive might well be thought to come closer to a utility- than a form-based theory of beauty.

David Hume took a Solomonic position in this debate by arguing, shortly after Hutcheson's reply to Berkeley but long before Burke's *Enquiry*, that there are two kinds of beauty: "the beauty of all visible objects causes a pleasure pretty much the same, tho' it be sometimes deriv'd from the mere *species* and appearance of the objects; sometimes from sympathy, and an idea of their utility" (2000: 3.3.5: 393). By the former, Hume means "such an order and construction of parts, as either by the *primary constitution* of our nature, by *custom*, or by *caprice*, is fitted to give a pleasure and satisfaction to the soul," or something like the beauty of form in the broad sense in which Hutcheson understood it; by the latter he means the "great part of the beauty, which we admire either in animals or in other objects, [that] is deriv'd from the idea of convenience and utility," such as "a shape which produces strength" in one animal, one that "is a sign of agility in another," or the "order and convenience of a palace" as contrasted to "its mere figure and appearance" (2.1.8: 195). About the first kind of beauty, Hume thinks there is not very much that can be said, because "it is only the effect, which [a] figure produces upon the mind, whose particular fabric or structure renders it susceptible of such sentiments" ("The Sceptic"; 1987: 165; app. I; 1998: 87); he thus tacitly resists Hutcheson's attempt to explain all cases of beauty immediately perceived by the senses with some specific as a particular proportion between unity and variety (even if that is not itself terribly specific). But Hume offers a more elaborate discussion of the beauty of utility, which can be taken as an attempt to explain what makes the recognition of utility in an object an aesthetic property rather than a subject of merely practical approbation. The questions about the beauty of utility that Hume explicitly raises are why persons other than the owner of a useful object should take pleasure in it, why anyone should take pleasure in a useful object that will not in fact be used, and why anyone should take pleasure in an object that looks useful but is not actually so, such as a painting of a useful object. His answers to these questions are illustrations of his general theories of sympathy and imagination: we take pleasure in the utility of an object that belongs to someone else because through sympathy we share the pleasure the other takes in that object, because "the minds of men are mirrors to one another" (2.2.5; 2000: 235–6). And we take pleasure in useful objects that cannot actually be used (such as an athlete in chains) or in the nonuseful representation of a useful object because of the imagination's tendency to generalize, or its tendency to pass from a cause (the object) to its effect (pleasure in its utility) "without considering that there are still some circumstances wanting to render the cause a complete one" (3.3.1; 2000: 374). But we might interpret Hume's theory more broadly to suggest that under

certain circumstances we take pleasure in the *appearance* of utility, or as he himself says "the idea of utility," remembering that by "idea" Hume means in the first instance a copy of a sensible impression rather than something more abstract and intellectual; and then it would be the fact that our pleasure is in an appearance rather than in a reality, and in the activity of the imagination with that appearance rather than in the actual use of the object, that makes the pleasure in the appearance of utility an aesthetic response.

Kant's opening statements of his analysis of beauty suggests that he must have completely rejected Hume's account of the beauty of utility: his explication of the claim that "the satisfaction that determines the judgment of taste is without any interest" is that "if the question is whether something is beautiful, one does not want to know where there is anything that is or that could be at stake, for us or for someone else, in the existence of the thing, but rather how we judge it in mere contemplation (intuition or reflection)" (2000: §2). However, Kant subsequently accommodates Hume's recognition of two kinds of beauty, although he does not explain the second variety in the same way Hume does. Kant distinguishes between "free beauty" and "adherent beauty," stating that the former "presupposes no concept of what the object ought to be" but the "second does presuppose such a concept and the perfection of the object in accordance with it" (§16). His examples of the latter include the beauty of humans, of animals such as horses, and of buildings such as churches, palaces, arsenals, or summerhouses, as contrasted to such beautiful things as some birds, crustaceans, designs *à la grecque*, foliage for borders and wallpapers, and so on. Since he does not simply reject adherent beauty as a kind of beauty at all, as his initial discussion of disinterestedness might seem to have required, his theory must be that the recognition of the intended purpose of the object that is inescapable in the case of adherent beauty is not incompatible with the occurrence of the free play of imagination and understanding that is the hallmark of the experience of the beautiful in general. There are several ways in which this might be true: the intended purpose of the object might set constraints on its form within which there is still room for invention and free play, or the requirements of satisfying the intended purpose of the object might themselves enter into a non-rule-governed yet harmonious interaction with the form of the object to which we respond with a free play (see Guyer 2005: chs. 4, 5). Whatever the details, however, the point remains that even Kant did not reduce beauty to a simple quality of pure form, but recognized a variety of kinds of beauty.

In sum, Francis Hutcheson's reduction of all cases of beauty to cases of uniformity amid variety was not the norm but rather an extreme position in eighteenth-century aesthetics, which more generally recognized a variety of sources of aesthetic pleasure, including at least formal beauty, beauty in or connected with the appearance of utility, the sublime, the pleasures of emotional arousal through works of art, and pleasure in the recognition of artistic skill.

THE STANDARD OF TASTE

A central issue throughout the century was that of the possibility of a "standard of taste," or the rationality of asserting universal validity for judgments of taste in spite of the perceived variety in actual tastes (a variety obvious for many reasons, including the increasing familiarity with cultures radically different from European ones) and the fact that many accounts of beauty and other aesthetic properties, such as Kant's, implied that these qualities could not be subsumed under rules that could ground noncontrovertible judgments.

For Hutcheson, the possibility of consensus in judgments of taste seemed nonproblematic. He held that empirical evidence shows that all people like the same sort of quality in objects of taste, namely uniformity in variety (VI.iv; 2004: 63), that differences in their particular preferences for instances of this quality show only differences in their education and exposure (VI.v; 2004: 64), which can be corrected, or different associations of ideas, which may make something naturally pleasurable unpleasant or vice versa (VI.xi; 2004: 67), and which may or may not be correctible, but which should not, apparently, trouble our confidence that under ideal conditions, that is, apart from such associations, all would find the same degrees of unity amid variety pleasing

to the same degree. Hutcheson also argued that custom and education cannot be the original source of our aesthetic responses, although they can modify them in various ways; "But all this presupposes our Sense of Beauty to be natural" (VII.iii; 2004: 73).

Others saw the problem as more difficult. Hume addressed it in his famous essay "Of the Standard of Taste," inserted at the last minute in a volume of *Four Dissertations* in 1757, along with his essay on tragedy, when it seemed too dangerous to include his essays on suicide and immortality. Hume presents the problem of taste as a conflict – what Kant would subsequently call the "antinomy of taste" (2000: §56) – between a "species of philosophy" and a "species of common sense," the former the inference that, since "Beauty is no quality of things themselves" but only a "sentiment" that "exists merely in the mind" and "All sentiment is right," there is no hope of "a decision . . . confirming one sentiment, and condemning another," the latter the view that some preferences are genuinely preferable to others, for example that "Whoever would assert an equality of genius and elegance between OGILBY and MILTON . . . would be thought to defend no less an extravagance, than if he had maintained a mole-hill to be as high as TENERIFFE" (Hume 1987: 229–31). Hume argued that the latter position is in fact true, but that since the former position is correct in assuming that aesthetic properties cannot be reduced to objective properties of objects in accordance with any "reasonings *a priori*" or fixed rules, the distinction between reasonable and extravagant preferences in taste can be made only by appeal to the consensus that he assumes to obtain among the verdicts of qualified critics throughout history (1987: 238). Who those are, in turn, Hume believes can be settled by objective criteria – "questions of fact, not of sentiment" (1987: 242). The "finer emotions of the mind" that constitute aesthetic responses are, Hume holds, "of a very tender and delicate nature, and require the concurrence of many favourable circumstances to make them play with facility and exactness, according to their general and established principles," and qualified critics are those who have the delicate faculties necessary to experience these delicate emotions and who are also capable of the "perfect serenity of mind, . . . recollection of thought, [and] due attention to the object" necessary for the optimal enjoyment of that object (1987: 232). More fully, Hume holds that qualified critics are distinguished by their "*delicacy* of imagination" (1987: 234), their "*practice* in a particular art" and careful and extended perusal of any "individual perform-ance" or object (1987: 237), the extensive "*comparisons* between the several species and degrees of excellence" they have been able to make (1987: 238), and the "*good sense*" that enables them to preserves their minds "free from all *prejudice*" or, more precisely, to approach any given work with the *right* "pre-judices" or presuppositions that are necessary to understand its intentions and its success in realizing those (1987: 239–40). And the ver-dicts of such qualified critics are normative for the rest of us because although "Many men, when left to themselves, have but a faint and dubious perception of beauty," they are "yet capable of relishing any fine stroke, which is pointed out to them" (1987: 243). For Hume, the consensus of qualified critics over time cre-ate a standard of taste not in the form of a set of rules for the judgment of objects, but rather in the form of a canon of objects of good taste, a set of objects that will bring the rest of us increased pleasure.

Recent discussion of Hume's proposal has focused on whether his criteria for good cri-tics are in fact objective, or rather whether his solution is circular, allowing us to agree on who the good critics are only if we have already agreed on what good art is (see Kivy 1967; Korsmeyer 1976; Carroll 1984; Townsend 2001; Guyer 2005: ch. 2; and Costelloe 2007). Hume's Scottish successors, however, raised questions about the indirectness of his approach and the adequacy of his list of the qualities that a good judge of art must have. They sought a list of attainments by means of which all could improve their taste, not criteria for a privileged class of critics, and many authors also expanded the lists of attain-ments necessary for good taste in order to reflect their increasing recognition of the vari-ety of aesthetic qualities. Gerard's 1759 *Essay on Taste* provides a good example of the former tendency: Gerard writes that "We are scarce pos-sessed of any faculty of mind or body that is not improveable" (II.iii; 1978: 91), and "Thus taste, like every other human excellence, is of a progressive nature; raising by various stages, from its seeds and elements to maturity," although to be sure, "like delicate plants, liable to be checked in its growth and killed, or else to become crooked and distorted, by negli-gence, or improper management" (1978: 95). He then reduced Hume's list of the qualities required for the "maturity and perfection" of taste, now transformed into targets for all of us, into "*sensibility, refinement, correctness*, and the *proportion* or *comparative adjustment of its separ-ate principles*" (1978: 95). In 1783, James Beattie agreed with Gerard in treating taste as something that can be improved in all of us, but emphasized the diversity of the objects of taste and therefore amplified the list of the components of improved taste. He observed that "sublimity, beauty, and elegance, are not the only things in art and nature, which gratify taste. There is also a taste in imitation, in harmony, and in ridicule," for example (2004: 161). Reflecting especially the widespread recognition of the centrality of the arousal of emotion in the experience of art that had begun with Du Bos, Beattie then wrote that

> To be a person of taste, it seems necessary, that one have, first a lively and correct imagination; secondly, the power of distinct apprehension; thirdly, the capacity of being easily, strongly, and agreeably affected, with sublimity, beauty, harmony, exact imitation, &c., fourthly, sympathy, or sensibility of heart; and fifthly, judgement, or good sense, which is the principal thing, and may not very improperly be said to comprehend all the rest. (2004: 162)

"Sympathy or sensibility of heart" is Beattie's main addition to Hume's list of the conditions for good taste; given Hume's emphasis on sym-pathy in his own explanation of our enjoy-ment of beauty, one might have thought that Hume could have added it to his own list, although Beattie probably means something different by sympathy than Hume did, not the transmission of feeling from one enjoyer of an object to another, but rather the "sensibility of heart" to be moved by the plight or the prosperity of characters depicted or described in works of art, in other words, sensitivity to what Du Bos had called "artificial emotions."

As late as 1810, Dugald Stewart still followed the model of enumerating criteria for the self-improvement of taste rather than for the identification of qualified critics, and added the idea that excessive refinement of critical capacities actually gets in the way of the enjoyment of many objects, so where taste "exists in its highest perfection" we need to find "an understanding, discriminating, comprehensive, and unprejudiced . . . a love of truth and of nature," but also "a temper superior to the irritation of little passions" and hypercritical expectations of perfection in art (1811: 473). A further response to the problem of taste among British authors was to recognize that there is also good reason to expect and allow for some diversity of taste. In the concluding chapter on the "Standard of Taste" in the *Elements of Criticism*, Kames argued that there is a common nature underlying a common taste among mankind, thus that "with respect to the fine arts, there is less difference of taste than is commonly imagined" (ch. 25; 2005b: 728). He argued that such "uniformity of taste" is necessary in order to provide an audience for the laborious works of single artists and even to make possible those works that require extensive collaboration, such as "sumptuous and elegant buildings" and "fine gardens"; he also argued that shared objects of taste, such as "public spectacles, and . . . amusements that are best enjoyed in company," offer at least some resistance to "The separation of men into different classes, by birth, office, or occupation," which, "however necessary, tends to relax the connection that ought to be among members of the same state" (2005b: 724). However, like Hume, he also recognized that the "Many circumstances [that] are necessary to form . . . a judge" of fine art, including both gifts of nature such as "delicacy of taste" and gifts of fortune such as "education, reflection, and experience," all of which "must be preserved in vigour by living regularly, by using the gifts of fortune with moderation, and by following the dictates of improved nature," are by no means available to all, and thus that "The exclusion of classes so many and numerous, reduces within a narrow compass those who are qualified to be judges in the fine arts" (2005b: 727). But he then argued that it is a good thing that nature "hath wisely and benevolently

filled every division with many pleasures," for in spite of the core of taste that is naturally widely shared, the many differences of rank and employment among human beings requires a variety of objects of taste "in order that individuals may be contented with their own lot, without envying that of others" (2005b: 720). In Kames's view, then, commonalities of taste make it possible to overcome social divisions to a certain extent, but variations in taste also make it possible to accept social divisions that cannot readily be overcome.

Another thinker whom many consider to have stood apart from the widespread search for some standard of taste is Johann Gottfried Herder (1744–1803), often regarded as the founder of cultural relativism. In a famous essay on Shakespeare published in a 1773 collection *On German Style and Art* (*Von deutscher Art und Kunst*), which also included an equally famous essay on Gothic architecture by Johann Wolfgang von Goethe (1749–1832), Herder argued that modern art could not be an imitation of ancient art, for example Shakespeare could not imitate Greek tragedy, because the circumstances of life in Elizabethan and Jacobean England were so different from those of ancient Attica: "neither action, nor customs, nor language, nor purpose" in the two epochs have anything in common (1999: 165), so the art of those two epochs inevitably differs. This might suggest that the taste of the two epochs must differ, so that the audiences of the later epoch could not appreciate the works of the earlier epoch in the same way and with the same intensity as its original audience. However, this does not seem to be Herder's conclusion. Rather, he suggests that beneath the superficial differences in their works, Shakespeare and, for example, Sophocles, had the same fundamental aim, to mirror their times in their art: "Shakespeare is Sophocles's brother, precisely where he seems to be so dissimilar, and inwardly he is wholly like him. His whole dramatic illusion is attained by means of this authenticity, truth, and historical creativity" (1985: 172). This in turn suggests that insofar as audiences at different times approach works of art with the same underlying principle, they can equally appreciate the success of superficially different works at mirroring their own times and enjoy them equally. The differences among historically or geographically diverse cultures do not affect the underlying principles of art, and therefore do not preclude a canon of taste valid for different times and places.

Kant's insistence on the possibility of universality in taste is much closer to the surface than that of Herder, his one-time student and later critic. Although Kant had many targets in his aesthetic theory, Hume was a more important target for him than Herder (see Guyer 2008: ch. 5 and, for the contrary view, Zammito 1992): Hume's *Four Dissertations* was translated into German as early as 1759, and Hume's approach to the standard of taste was certainly one of Kant's chief targets; indeed, Kant's presentation of the "peculiarities" of the judgment of taste (2000: §§32–4) and the "antinomy" of the judgment of taste (§§55–7) are clearly modeled on Hume's conflict between the species of philosophy and common sense. Kant also follows Hume in holding that, because judgments of taste concern our sentiment or feeling in response to objects, the standard of taste cannot consist in conceptually formulated rules for the judgment (or production) of objects of taste (the latter is the core of Kant's theory of genius in §§46–9). But he did not think that Hume's confidence that many a person can appreciate the fine strokes that the critics point to him, or for that matter Hutcheson's confidence that experience reveals at most a difference in degree in the kinds of things that all find pleasing, is sufficient to ground the reasonableness of claiming the assent of all to our own judgments of beauty, our claim to speak with a "universal voice" when we make a judgment of taste (§8). Kant insisted on an a priori foundation for the commonality of taste that is asserted by an aesthetic judgment. He claimed to find such a foundation by means of the argument – his "deduction of judgments of taste" – that because the response to beauty is a free play of imagination and understanding, it involves the same faculties that are involved in cognition in general, and because every normal human being is certainly capable of cognition of any given object, we must all also find the pleasure of beauty in the same objects, at least under optimal conditions when our imaginations and understandings can play freely and are not distracted by irrelevant

interests, charms, and so on (§§21, 35). Even among those who have found Kant's concept of the free play of imagination and understanding (or imagination and reason, in the case of the sublime) a convincing analysis of aesthetic experience, Kant's assumption that, because we all have the same general capacities for cognition, the very *same* objects that induce the state of their free play in one person can reasonably be expected to do so in all others as well, even under optimal conditions, has certainly been contested (compare Guyer 1979: chs. 8–9 and Allison 2001: ch. 8).

Another issue that has been debated is whether Kant's claims for the moral significance of aesthetic experience depend on the existence of an a priori ground for intersubjectively valid judgments of taste (see Crawford 1974; Rogerson 1986; Guyer 1993: intro.). But instead of pursuing that, we may turn here to a broader discussion of eighteenth-century views about the relations between the aesthetic and the moral.

THE AESTHETIC EDUCATION OF HUMANKIND

Hutcheson argued for the sense of beauty in order to support his argument that there is a natural sense of virtue and vice, or a moral sense, but did not argue for any direct moral value of aesthetic experience. In this he was not paradigmatic, but rather an exception to the rule in eighteenth-century aesthetics. Another exception to the general assumption of the moral value of aesthetic experience was Jean-Jacques Rousseau (1712–78) whose attack on D'Alembert's recommendation that Geneva drop its prohibition of the theater outdid its model, Plato's exclusion of drama from the education of the guardians of his ideal Republic: Rousseau warned that allowing theater into Geneva "would only serve to destroy the love of work . . . render a people inactive and slack . . . prevent it from seeing the public and private goals with which it ought to busy itself . . . turn prudence to ridicule . . . substitute a theatrical jargon for the practice of the virtues," and "make metaphysic of all morality" (2004: 298). But most authors recognized some significant role for aesthetic experience in moral development, even if Schiller's claim that, if the moral and political problems of mankind are ever to be solved, "it must take the aesthetic path, because it is through beauty that one makes his way to freedom" (Letter II; 1967: 8–9), or that the "aesthetic education of mankind" is the only path to its moral education, was extreme. Given the emphasis in most authors on the arousal of emotions through art, it was only natural for them to think that the experience of art could be used to develop morally beneficial emotions; the emphasis on the sublime also led to an assumption of the moral value of aesthetic experience, since the experience of the sublime was commonly divided into an admiration for the magnitude of nature, which would lead to morally valuable reflection on the greatness of the creator of nature, and an admiration for the moral magnitude of depicted heroes, which would naturally lead to a desire to emulate them (e.g., see Beattie and Ussher in Ashfield & de Bolla 1996). Archibald Alison, for example, held that wherever the "objects of the material world . . . afford us delight, they are always the signs or expressions of higher qualities, by which our moral sensibilities are called forth" (1811: ii.437), and argued that it is of the utmost "consequence in the education of the Young, to encourage their instinctive taste for the Beauty and Sublimity of Nature." "It is to provide them," he continued,

> amid all the agitations and trials of society, with one gentle and unreproaching friend, whose voice is ever in alliance with goodness and virtue, and which . . . is able both to sooth misfortune, and to reclaim from folly. It is to identify them with the happiness of that Nature to which they belong; to give them an interest in every species of being which surrounds them; and, amid the hours of curiosity and delight, to awaken those latent feelings of benevolence and sympathy, from which all the moral or intellectual greatness of man finally arises. (1811: ii.447)

Alison's confidence in the value of the aesthetic stimulation of moral sentiments depended on his acceptance of the British view that moral sentiments are the foundation of virtue.

After an early dalliance, Kant firmly rejected the attempt to ground the principles of morality on sentiment, but neither did he attack the moral value of aesthetic experience like Rousseau did; he offered a more nuanced assessment of the moral value of aesthetic experience (see Guyer 1993: ch. 1). While he insisted that the moral law can be (and is) known by pure reason alone and that morally estimable action must be motivated by respect for that law alone, he allowed that "the beautiful prepares us to love something . . . without interest; the sublime, to esteem it, even contrary to our (sensible) interest" (2000: general remark following §29), both of which we must be able to do in order to act as morality commands; in the mature phenomenology of moral action that he offered in his late *Metaphysics of Morals*, on which the dictates of pure practical reason are always effected *through* the cultivation and regulation of appropriate natural inclinations, Kant stated that a natural feeling for the beauties of nature is "a disposition of sensibility that greatly promotes morality or at least prepares the way for it: the disposition, namely, to love something . . . even apart from any intention to use it" ("Doctrine of Virtue," 1996: §17). In these remarks he suggested that aesthetic experience is psychologically conducive to acting in accordance with morality. In other remarks, he suggested that aesthetic experience could be cognitively relevant to morality: we take an interest in the beauty of nature, Kant argued, as a sign that nature is amenable to the realization of our objectives in general, but foremost our moral objectives, an assumption we need to be able to make in order to pursue our moral objectives rationally (§42), and we take the beautiful as a symbol of the morally good because of analogies between our experience of beauty and key elements of morality, especially between the freedom of the imagination in aesthetic experience and the freedom of the will in moral action (§59). Kant never argued that aesthetic sensitivity is a necessary condition of morality, but he did argue that it is only insofar as aesthetic experience is conducive to morality that we have a right to demand taste from others "as if it were a duty" (§40). Even if it is conceded that aesthetic sensitivity is conducive to morality, however, it is not evident that all must enjoy the *same* objects of taste in order to derive these moral benefits, thus that Kant's analysis of the moral benefits of aesthetic experience depends on or contributes to the success of his deduction of judgments of taste (for a contrary view, see Savile 1987: ch. 6).

Schiller, as already noted, did assert that aesthetic education is a necessary condition of successful moral development and the resolution of the outstanding political tensions of modernity (for his analysis of the latter, see esp. 1967: Letter VI). When he came to details, however, what he actually argued is that cultivation of the key ability necessary for the appreciation of beauty, especially in art, namely, the ability to be sensitive to both general principles and the particularities of the object before one at the same time, is also conducive to the development of that ability for application in both scientific and especially moral contexts. The appreciation of the beautiful requires both "receptivity" and "activity," both sensitivity to particulars and the ability to abstract general principles out of particulars, and so does successful action elsewhere, but especially in morality: the "culture" or education of the human being "will therefore consist, *firstly*, in creating for his receptive faculty the most manifold contacts with the world . . . *secondly*, in acquiring for the determining faculty the utmost independence from the receptive and intensifying activity on the side of reason to the utmost. Where both these qualities are united, then will the human being combine the utmost independence and freedom with the utmost fullness of existence" (Letter XIII; 1967: 86–7). But Schiller did not actually attempt to prove that this goal can be accomplished only through aesthetic education, and not directly through scientific or moral education, so all that he actually proved, like Kant, is that aesthetic education may be conducive to morality. But both certainly argued against Rousseau that the cultivation of aesthetic sensitivity need not be in tension with the demands of morality, and under proper conditions may be helpful to morality.

*

There are many other themes and issues in eighteenth-century aesthetics worthy of discussion, including the paradox of tragedy, first named by Du Bos and then discussed by Kames, Hume, Mendelssohn, and many others; the differences among artistic media, the subject of Gotthold Ephraim Lessing's (1729–81) critique of Winckelmann in his *Laocoön*

(1766), in turn criticized by Herder in his first *Critical Forest* (1769) and his essay on *Sculpture* (1778); the classification or "system" of the fine arts, a topic for nearly every aesthetic treatise in the century (see Kristeller 1965); the nature of artistic creation or genius (Gerard 1966 [1774] was the target for Kant's theory); and more. Many of those topics are engaged in individual entries; the topics discussed here are only the most general issues for eighteenth-century aesthetics.

See also AESTHETIC ATTITUDE; AESTHETIC EDUCATION; AESTHETIC JUDGMENT; AESTHETIC PROPERTIES; BAUMGARTEN; BEAUTY; BURKE; FORMALISM; FUNCTION OF ART; HUME; HUTCHESON; KANT; LESSING; SCHILLER; SHAFTESBURY; SUBLIME; THEORIES OF ART.

BIBLIOGRAPHY

Primary sources
Addison, Joseph & Steele, Richard. 1965 [1712–15]. *The Spectator*. D. F. Bond (ed.). Oxford: Clarendon.
Alison, Archibald. 1811. *Essays on the Nature and Principles of Taste*. 2 vols. 2nd edn. Edinburgh: Bell & Bradfute.
Ashfield, Andrew & de Bolla, Peter (eds.). 1996. *The Sublime: A Reader in British Eighteenth-Century Aesthetic Theory*. Cambridge: Cambridge University Press.
Baumgarten, Alexander Gottlieb. 1983 [1735]. *Meditationes philosophicae de nonnullis ad poema pertinentibus*. H. Paetzold (ed.). Hamburg: Meiner.
Baumgarten, Alexander Gottlieb. 2007 [1750–8]. *Aesthetica*. D. Mirbach (ed.). 2 vols. Hamburg: Meiner.
Beattie, James. 2004. *Selected Philosophical Writings*. J. A. Harris (ed.). Exeter: Imprint Academic.
Burke, Edmund. 1958 [1759]. *A Philosophical Enquiry into the Origin of Our Ideas of the Sublime and Beautiful*. J. T. Boulton (ed.). 2nd edn. London: Routledge & Kegan Paul.
Diderot, Denis. 1966 [1752]. "On the Origin and Nature of the Beautiful." In *Diderot's Selected Writings*. L. G. Crocker (ed.). New York: Macmillan.
Diderot, Denis. 1995. *Diderot on Art*. J. Goodman (trans.). 2 vols. New Haven: Yale University Press.
Du Bos, Jean-Baptiste. 1748. *Critical Reflections on Poetry, Painting and Music*. T. Nugent (trans.). 3 vols. London: John Nourse.
Gerard, Alexander. 1966 [1774]. *An Essay on Genius*. B. Fabian (ed.). Munich: Wilhelm Fink.

Gerard, Alexander. 1978 [1780]. *An Essay on Taste*. W. J. Hipple (ed.). 3rd edn. Delmar: Scholars' Facsimiles & Reprints.

Herder, Johann Gottfried. 1985 [1773]. "Shakespeare." Joyce P. Crick (trans.). In *German Aesthetic and Literary Criticism: Winckelmann, Lessing, Hamann, Herder, Schiller, Goethe*. H. B. Nisbet (ed.). Cambridge: Cambridge University Press, 161–76.

Herder, Johann Gottfried. 2002 [1778]. *Sculpture: Some Observations on Shape and Form from Pygmalion's Creative Dream*. J. Gaiger (ed. & trans.). Chicago: University of Chicago Press.

Herder, Johann Gottfried. 2006 [1769]. "First Critical Forest." In *Selected Writings on Aesthetics*. G. Moore (ed. & trans.). Princeton: Princeton University Press.

Hume, David. 1987 [1777]. *Essays Moral, Political, and Literary*. Final edn. E. F. Miller (ed.). Indianpolis: Liberty Fund.

Hume, David. 1998 [1751]. *An Enquiry concerning the Principles of Morals*. T. L. Beauchamp (ed.). Oxford: Clarendon.

Hume, David. 2000 [1739–40]. *A Treatise of Human Nature*. D. Fate & M. J. Norton (eds.). Oxford: Oxford University Press.

Hutcheson, Francis. 2004 [1725]. *An Inquiry into the Original of Our Ideas of Beauty and Virtue*. W. Leidhold (ed.). Indianapolis: Liberty Fund.

Kames, Henry Home, Lord. 2005a [1751]. *Essays on the Principles of Morality and Natural Religion*. M. C. Moran (ed.). Indianapolis: Liberty Fund.

Kames, Henry Home, Lord. 2005b [1785]. *Elements of Criticism*. 6th edn. P. Jones (ed.). Indianapolis: Liberty Fund.

Kant, Immanuel. 1996 [1797]. *Metaphysics of Morals*. In *Practical Philosophy*. M. J. Gregor (ed. & trans.). Cambridge: Cambridge University Press.

Kant, Immanuel. 2000 [1790]. *The Critique of the Power of Judgment*. P. Guyer (ed.). P. Guyer & E. Matthews (trans.). Cambridge: Cambridge University Press.

Longinus. 1964 [1743]. *Dionysius Longinus on the Sublime*. D. A. Russell (ed.). W. Smith (trans.). Oxford: Clarendon.

Meier, Georg Friedrich. 1999–2002. *Frühe Schriften zur ästhetischen Erziehung der Deutschen*. H.-J. Kertscher & G. Schenk (eds.). 3 vols. Halle: Hallescher.

Mendelssohn, Moses. 1997 [1761]. *Philosophical Writings*. D. O. Dahlstrom (ed.). Cambridge: Cambridge University Press.

Rousseau, Jean-Jacques. 2004 [1758]. *Letter to d'Alembert on the Theater*. In *Collected Writings of Rousseau*, vol. x: *Letter to D'Alembert and Writings for the Theater*. A. Bloom, C. Butterworth, & C. Kelly (eds. & trans.). Hanover: University Press of New England.

Schiller, Friedrich. 1967 [1795]. *Letters on the Aesthetic Education of Man*. E. M. Wilkinson & E. M. Willoughby (trans.). Oxford: Clarendon.

Shaftesbury, Anthony Ashley Cooper, Third Earl of. 1999 [1713]. *Characteristicks of Men, Manners, Opinions, Times*. L. E. Klein (ed.). Cambridge: Cambridge University Press.

Stewart, Dugald. 1811 [1810]. *Philosophical Essays*. Philadelphia: Anthony Finley.

Sulzer, Johann Georg. 1994 [1771–4; enlarged 2nd edn. 1792–4]. *Allgemeine Theorie der schönen Künste*. 4 vols. G. Tonelli (ed.). Hildesheim: Georg Olms.

Wolff, Christian. 2003 [1751]. *Vernünftige Gedancken von Gott, der Welt, und der Seele des Menschen*. New edn. in *Metapysica Tedesca*. R. Ciafardone (ed.). Milan: Bompiani.

Secondary sources

Allison, Henry E. 2001. *Kant's Theory of Taste: A Reading of the Critique of Aesthetic Judgment*. Cambridge: Cambridge University Press.

Carroll, Noël. 1984. "Hume's Standard of Taste," *Journal of Aesthetics and Art Criticism*, 43, 181–94.

Costelloe, Timothy M. 2007. *Aesthetics and Morals in the Philosophy of David Hume*. London: Routledge.

Crawford, Donald W. 1974. *Kant's Aesthetic Theory*. Madison: University of Wisconsin Press.

Dickie, George. 1996. *The Century of Taste: The Philosophical Odyssey of Taste in the Eighteenth Century*. New York: Oxford University Press.

Eagleton, Terry. 1990. *The Ideology of the Aesthetic*. Oxford: Basil Blackwell.

Ferry, Luc. 1993. *Homo Aestheticus: The Invention of Taste in the Democratic Age*. R. de Loaiza (trans.). Chicago: University of Chicago Press.

Guyer, Paul. 1979. *Kant and the Claims of Taste*. Rev. edn. Cambridge: Cambridge University Press, 1997.

Guyer, Paul. 1993. *Kant and the Experience of Freedom*. Cambridge: Cambridge University Press.

Guyer, Paul. 2005. *Values of Beauty: Historical Essays in Aesthetics*. Cambridge: Cambridge University Press.

Guyer, Paul. 2008. *Knowledge, Reason, and Taste: Kant's Response to Hume*. Princeton: Princeton University Press.

Kivy, Peter. 1967. "Hume's Standard of Taste: Breaking the Circle," *British Journal of Aesthetics*, 7, 57–66.

Kivy, Peter. 2003. *The Seventh Sense: Francis Hutcheson and Eighteenth-Century British Aesthetics*. 2nd edn. Oxford: Clarendon.

Korsmeyer, Carolyn. 1976. "Hume and the Foundations of Taste," *Journal of Aesthetics and Art Criticism*, 35, 201–15.

Kristeller, Paul Oskar. 1965 [1951–2]. "The Modern System of the Arts." In *Renaissance Thought and the*

Arts: Collected Essays. Princeton: Princeton University Press, 163–227.

Monk, Samuel. 1935. *The Sublime*. 2nd edn. Ann Arbor: University of Michigan Press.

Rogerson, Kenneth F. 1986. *Kant's Aesthetics: The Role and Form of Expression*. Lanham: University Press of America.

Savile, Anthony. 1987. *Aesthetic Reconstructions: The Seminal Writings of Lessing, Kant and Schiller*. Oxford: Blackwell.

Townsend, Dabney. 2001. *Hume's Aesthetic Theory: Taste and Sentiment*. London: Routledge.

Zammito, John. 1992. *The Genesis of Kant's Critique of Judgment*. Chicago: University of Chicago Press.

Zelle, Carsten. 1995. *Die doppelte Ästhetik der Moderne: Revisionen des Schönen von Boileau bis Nietzsche*. Stuttgart: J. B. Metzler.

PAUL GUYER

nineteenth- and twentieth-century Continental aesthetics sets forth from Immanuel Kant's *Critique of the Power of Judgment* – a master text that appeared one year after the leading inspirational event of the age, the French Revolution. Subsequent to France's 1789 upheaval, Europe saw the rise of Napoleon, the advance of the industrial revolution, the development of photography, the emergence of the life sciences, Charles Darwin's evolutionary theory, Karl Marx's communism, Sigmund Freud's psychoanalysis, the twentieth century's two devastating world wars, and the turbulent events of 1968, all of which influenced Continental aesthetics during this 200-year period, as the Age of Progress passed into the Age of Language.

KANTIANISM AND NEOCLASSICISM

Kant's third *Critique* – the *Critique of the Power of Judgment* (1790) – begins our presentation, although it lies thematically near the end of Kant's philosophy. This work follows the *Critique of Pure Reason* (1781–7) and *Critique of Practical Reason* (1788), which reveal the universal foundations of empirical knowledge and morality respectively. The third *Critique*'s topic is beauty and teleology, and its aesthetics circumscribes the principle, *de gustibus non est disputandum* (there is no disputing about taste) to establish universal foundations for objective, discussion-amenable differences of opinion about pure beauty.

To delineate this famous principle's proper bounds, Kant distinguishes between two kinds of pleasures, namely, those whose source and content is essentially sensory, and those that issue exclusively from our nonsensory, intellectual functions. He associates *de gustibus non est disputandum* with sensory pleasures, since people's taste, hearing, visual, olfactory, and tactile sensitivities differ physiologically, and since these variations undermine meaningful discussion about the shared, objective quality of some food, drink, sound quality, color contrast, perfume, etc.

Among nonsensory pleasures, Kant recognizes a special kind of intellectually grounded pleasure that occurs when our mind is well tuned toward knowing some object in a factual or scientific sense, that is, when we are disposed to categorize it as a thing of a certain kind and to locate it within our system of knowledge. This pleasure becomes salient, he believes, when we reflect disinterestedly and exclusively on the rational, systematic quality of an object's design, while disregarding what type of object it is. To appreciate a rose's pure beauty, we need know neither what kind of flower it is, nor that it is a flower at all, since here, only the impact of the object's design determines its pure beauty.

Kant's restriction of pure beauty to an object's spatial and/or temporal design may seem austere and contrary to how we judge an object's beauty. In the case of the rose, we would ordinarily consider its formal design, but also equally its pastel color, its soft texture, its delicate aroma and perhaps its feminine or love-related symbolic quality. Notwithstanding these associations, Kant has some sharp reasons for setting them aside in judgments of pure beauty.

Specifically, his motivation and rationale is epistemological: Kant needs to identify a set of perceivable features that everyone can uniformly recognize, and he realizes that this cannot include the charming qualities of tastes, odors, sounds, or colors, since these vary with individual structures of the tongue, nose, ears, and eyes. More promising are intersubjectively invariant, geometrical and arithmetical features, for whether you, or I, or someone else perceives a square as such, its four sides will be equal and the notion of aesthetic balance will apply to each of our experiences. By restricting judgments of pure beauty to the contemplation of spatial and/or temporal forms, Kant establishes an objective, universally shared basis for agreement and disagreement about pure beauty, and he shows how a thoroughgoing relativism in reference to such judgments is not necessary.

The formal systematicity of purely beautiful designs is at the basis of some parallels between judgments of pure beauty and judgments of moral value. First, Kant regards both types of judgment as universal, disinterested, freedom-related, and based on an immediate satisfaction, and claims accordingly that beauty is the symbol of morality. Second, the formal systematicity of beautiful objects structurally parallels the system of moral laws, and beauty symbolizes morality in this further sense.

Human beauty is among the most influential intersections between beauty and morality in Kant's aesthetics. He observes that when we contemplate the beauty of a human form, but judge it abstractly as a pure design without respecting that the form is specifically human, pure beauty and morality can clash. Human beings deserve unconditional respect according to Kant, and if we do not aesthetically appreciate a human being explicitly as a human, we introduce the possibility of neglecting our moral dictate to treat the humanity in everyone as an end in itself, and not merely as a means to some other end. This would occur if the human form were decorated with purely beautiful designs that obscure or conflict with natural, morally expressive, bodily forms, as Kant believes happens in the case of heavily tattooed faces. Human beauty requires that we always take the concept of the human being into account, and that our judgment respect, depend on, or adhere to that concept, and not contradict it.

Kant's aesthetics has been described at some length, since his association between empirical knowledge, beauty, and morality is the origin of a long line of Continental aesthetic philosophizing. His influence predominates in the neoclassical tradition, and it also affects the history of romanticism and expressionism. The neoclassical influence is immediately discernible in Friedrich Schiller's writings, whose *Letters on the Aesthetic Education of Man* (1795)

apply Kant's aesthetics to social philosophy. Schiller writes with distress in view of how the French Revolution degenerated into tyranny, and he concludes that the 1793–4 Reign of Terror could have been prevented, had people's mentalities been more balanced between their instinctual and moral sides. To him, the French revolutionaries were neither mature nor civilized enough to manage their newly found power responsibly.

Hoping to foster a spiritual balance in future generations, Schiller prescribes an "aesthetic education" that highlights the awareness of beauty, assuming with Kant, that beauty mediates between our sensuous and our moral faculties. He believes that beauty can introduce a more idealizing and civilizing content into sensation and instinct, while also providing a concrete place for abstract, rational, moral ideas to adhere, so they can come into closer contact with our sensuous, instinctual side.

Schiller's faith is that the cultivation of character through beauty will give rise to a beautiful soul – a harmonious spiritual condition where instinctual and rational sides are coordinated and mutually supportive, and whose realization helps facilitate a social world that is agreeable, nonoppressive and free. A person with a beautiful soul acts with energy, grace, composure, dignity, and proportion, and displays the threefold integration of natural instinct, beauty, and morality. Schiller envisioned that a population of beautifully composed people could promote an ideally structured society, much as Plato imagined, and, indeed, Schiller's celebratory impression of ancient Greek civilization underlies his model of the beautiful soul.

This neoclassical vision flows into G. W. F. Hegel's *Lectures on Fine Art*, which were given at the University of Berlin in the 1820s. Like Schiller, Hegel espouses the integration of the human personality and society, but within a wider quest to organize all knowledge into a single, rational and living totality. Part of his insight is to realize that this grand integration requires a historical perspective and philosophy of history where each time period's main ideas are set next to those of their predecessors and successors to comprise a whole, much like a tree or animal that grows in successive stages. Hegel uses the bud–blossom–fruit image to convey his teleological ideas, and asserts that we contemporaries are, at least to date, the most mature, self-aware beings the cosmos has yet produced.

Within this developmental, quasi-biological framework, Hegel regards beauty, along with religion and philosophy, as expressive of a culture's highest interests. Following Kant and Schiller, he arranges art, religion, and philosophy in a developmental sequence that begins with the sensuous sphere, and ascends gradually in an increasingly reflective, conceptually abstract and nonsensory path. The three-dimensional, sensuous expression of metaphysical knowledge is the task of art; the more inward, feeling-oriented, mental-imagistic expressions of metaphysical knowledge are the work of religion; fully abstracted, nonsensuous knowledge is the goal of philosophy. Ancient Greek culture was ideal for art's realization; Christian medieval Europe was the prime soil for religion. Philosophy's era remains that of the French Revolution and thereafter. Such a schema explains why twentieth-century art is highly philosophical, where we witness art about art, writing about writing, painting about paint, conceptual art, artworks that make philosophical statements, and related artistic phenomena.

Perceivable, rational forms predominate in Hegel's conception of beauty, and he describes ideally beautiful objects as standing before their audiences like the statues of the ancient gods, filled with meaning, surrounded by a holy aura, and exuding tranquillity, contentment, emotional control, and inner bliss. Since his philosophy of history regards the human spirit as becoming more reflective after the decline of ancient Greek civilization, and artistic culture as giving way to a more inward, feeling-oriented Christian world as the predominant way to express the newly emerging social interests, he states that in this day and age, artworks lack the cultural impact they once had. This is the "end of art," not in the sense that artistic production has ceased or will cease, but in the sense that art's cultural significance has been overshadowed by religious and philosophical modes of expression. For Hegel, natural science counts as a rudimentary philosophical mode of expression, so contemporary science's role as a source of leading cultural values accords with Hegel's end of art thesis and philosophy of history.

The ruling notions of the nineteenth century include those of historical progress and goal-orientedness, and they express the form in which the concept of "life" enters into the cultural spirit at the end of the 1700s, as it conveys ideas of growth, developmental stages, ascending and descending patterns, organic unity, and, in some instances, dialectical development. Well within this optimistic atmosphere, Karl Marx develops a social theory based on material activity and economic relationships, claiming that after society passes through feudal and capitalistic stages, a future communal, mature, and more realistic social stage will emerge where exploitation and selfish profiteering will become a thing of the past.

Art's place within Marx's historical progress compares to Hegel's conception: the art of each historical time period expresses the social and economic realities of the time, either reinforcing them or pointing beyond them in support of revolution and social change. Hegel and Marx advocate different metaphysical theories, but they share the legacy of Kant's ideal social order where harmony and respect prevails, and where a heavenly condition is held to be a virtual inevitability in an upcoming kingdom of ends.

At the close of the nineteenth century, we find Leo Tolstoy's aesthetic theory continuing to resonate with the soon-to-fade notion of historical progress. In *What is Art?* (1897), Tolstoy writes that art's main purpose is to communicate emotion, whereas language's is to communicate ideas. The more effective an artwork is at infecting others with the emotion the artist experienced, the better the artwork is as art. Invoking the communication of brotherly, Christian love through art, Tolstoy adds that the more effectively an artwork conveys socially integrating love, the better it is in terms of its content. He envisages a world united by Christian values and maintains that art's highest purpose is to convey those values. In the course of this account, he celebrates folk art and popular art, and condemns elitist, socially divisive art, which for him includes Beethoven's symphonies, opera, and ballet, whose usual audiences are wealthy and privileged.

During the twentieth century, neoclassical ideals extend into the 1930s as one of the cornerstones of the National Socialists' theory of art. Echoing Schiller's beautiful soul with its classical proportions, and adding content from Marx's communist ideal with its strong connection to the earth and to work, the Nazis advocate healthy bodies; willful minds; powerful, athletic men; and enduring, fertile women who bear children and remain at home to raise them in a traditional family setting. They advocate these values, however, with an extraordinarily prejudicial restriction to distinctively German versions of them, and a hard exclusion, not to mention murderous persecution, of competing aesthetic mentalities and individuals. Nazi aesthetics takes the combination of neoclassical and earth-centered ideals to a vicious extreme, where the nineteenth-century Greek revival images related to bodily proportions, health, and balance between instinct and reason receive a nationalistic presentation, and where without reservation, all competing alternatives are marked for subjugation or annihilation.

SUBLIMITY AND THE RISE OF INSTINCT

Although progress is among the leading nineteenth-century historical themes, it is not the most long-ranging in Continental aesthetic theory's trajectory from the nineteenth into the twentieth century. To appreciate the origins of this more sustained theme, we can recall Kant's theory of the sublime, and how life's aspects accord not only with rationality, proportion, systematicity, organic unity, and development, but involve powerful and standing instinctual forces as well – forces that can spin out of control at any given time within a developmental process.

Kant observes that the experience of the sublime arises in relation to objects perceived to be very large or very powerful. Both lead us to apprehend our physical being's limits, either by bringing it to imaginative exhaustion, as when we try to trace the extent of infinite space or time, or by presenting it with possible physical destruction and the loss of consciousness, as when we encounter a threatening explosion, thunderstorm, whirlpool, precipice, or fall. Upon realizing the weakness of our imagination or the fragility of our physical bodies in a sublime experience, Kant maintains that we apprehend yet another aspect of ourselves that withstands all sensory limits and threats – viz., our reason and moral essence – and that signals how our moral constitution is unconditional, how it transcends the sensory world, and how it renders the sensory world, life, and death meaningless without its presence. Kant associates morality not only with beauty but with sublimity, and his aesthetic theory aims to reinforce our moral awareness through both types of aesthetic experience.

Kant stands only at the outset of this development, however, for a sublime experience also creates psychological tension, typically between our desire to protect ourselves from danger and our desire for intense aesthetic experiences. In pursuit of the sublime, a person will edge closer and closer to a thunderstorm or tornado to feel the thrill of the powerful natural energies, to the point where the strong likelihood of being hurt or, worse, death halts the advance. Reason is no longer the center or end of the sublime experience, for it becomes overshadowed by a life-invigorating enthusiasm that welcomes pain and danger to our physical wellbeing. The experience compares to that of the moth, whose excitement increases as it draws closer to a bright fire that, if it comes too close, will also incinerate it.

Sublime experiences accordingly promote a conception of life that is more bursting with instinct, feelings of expansion, irrationality, the surging of power, and unconscious energies. No later than a decade after Kant's third *Critique*, the notion of the unconscious enters into aesthetic theorizing in F. W. J. Schelling's description of the artistic genius in his *System of Transcendental Idealism* (1800). Here, the genius is a cosmic figure who embodies a primordial synthesis and "infinite contradiction" of unconscious and conscious energies, and who works those energies into the fabric of a great work of art.

Less than 20 years later, the unconscious presents itself once more at the center of Arthur Schopenhauer's philosophy (c.1818) – a philosophy within which art is a vehicle to achieve salvation from the frustrating pressures of the unconscious, constantly driving Will. The Schopenhauerian artistic genius transcends the ordinary constraints of scientific reason to apprehend timeless truths, or Ideas, which he or she then reproduces in artworks to communicate to others, helping them toward their own salvation. The goal is to spread metaphysical knowledge and tranquility through the presentation of idealized images that lift a person out of the stream of mundane, persistent striving.

Schopenhauer complements his aesthetics of the visual and literary arts with an independent characterization of music as the direct reflection of the Will, claiming that when we listen to music we experience an interplay of universal forces, fused with the detached forms of human emotion. His theory of music is an instance in nineteenth-century Continental aesthetics where literalistic modes of thought are subordinated to artistic modes within the context of an aesthetic experience that conveys metaphysical knowledge.

Friedrich Nietzsche revalues Schopenhauer's metaphysical Will by venerating, rather than deprecating, the feral, creative and destructive energies that surge through us, adding that these energies can be artistically tempered, sublimated, and civilized through our rational powers of organization and idealization. In *The Birth of Tragedy* (1872), he states that ancient Greek art achieved this balance to perfection, echoing Schiller's laudatory attitude toward the Greeks. In contrast to Kant, however, Nietzsche no longer describes the sublime as an aesthetic indicator of reason and morality, but as a way to present overwhelming natural forces, both inner and outer, as manageably tempered by reason. Nietzsche wants to listen to, and to feel the energies of life surging through all things in what amounts to a maximally sublime, virtually superhuman experience, without having these energies break him into a thousand pieces. Like Schopenhauer, he is concerned to explore what it feels like to be within another person's or entity's perspective, and this leads him to downplay literalistic modes of expression in favor of literary, metaphor-filled ones in the majority of his works.

Sigmund Freud's ideas on art closely follow Nietzsche's, except that Freud translates them into a more clinical, psychologically oriented framework. Freud similarly identifies an instinctual source of life energy – later (c.1920) referred to as the "it" (*das Es*) or Id – and maintains that artistic activity, like metaphor-filled dreams, is the refined, moderated, legitimized, morally digestible expression of aggressive, reproductive, frightening, unconscious, repulsive, and socially confusing energies. His 1908 essay "The Relation of the Poet to Daydreaming" encapsulates his position.

Artistic activity and artistic perception reveal basic psychological structures, and they express and dissipate psychological tensions. Freud maintains that we all experience aggression toward our same-sexed parent, for example, and that in the paradigm case of Shakespeare's Hamlet, the latter's well-known hesitation to bring his uncle to justice after the latter had poisoned his beloved father and usurped his throne is easily explained, along with our satisfaction in reading the play (*The Interpretation of Dreams*, 1900). Throughout the work, Hamlet might want to kill his uncle to balance the scales, but he also feels a positive attraction to him, for it is none other than his uncle who does exactly what Hamlet unconsciously always wished to do, namely, kill his father and marry his mother. Hence we find Hamlet suspended in indecision throughout the play, torn between two opposing desires.

Freud's and Nietzsche's theories inform the twentieth-century Surrealists of the 1920s and 1930s. As we read in André Breton's Surrealist manifesto of 1924, the Surrealists are interested in freedom, and are intent on painting dreamscapes that arise from the unconscious and on supplementing these with the psychoanalytically inspired methods of automatic writing. In such writing, one records the first, often seemingly random, thoughts that enter one's mind to reveal the psychological reality of one's unconscious life. Virtual kin to the Dada artists who preceded them, the Surrealists likewise regarded rationality as an impediment to the expression of psychological truth, and as a sinister force in its instrumental guise as the genius behind military weaponry.

Although the assumption is now often questioned, emotion and reason have been conceived as distinct and opposed forces for centuries. This division allows us to interpret turn-of-the-century expressionism as a further extension of Schelling's, Schopenhauer's, Nietzsche's, and Freud's combined interest in nonrational energies. Schopenhauer's theory of music is particularly revealing, since it anticipates Vassily Kandinsky's view in *Concerning the Spiritual in Art* (1911) that the function of painting is to express subtle emotions, and that these emotions have a metaphysical or spiritual content. Kandinsky explores the analogy between music and color, where colors are the like a piano's keyboard, our eyes, its hammers, and the soul, the piano itself that sounds with its many strings. Each color has its symbolic and associative content for Kandinsky, and he prescribes the use of color in painting as a means to convey emotion, consistent with how Tolstoy imagines the formal purpose of art.

Martin Heidegger's aesthetics enters at this juncture as a twentieth-century version of the position that art reveals metaphysical truth, and that this truth is not reducible to formulas, concepts, or definitions. As he writes in "The Origin of the Work of Art" (1935, and later revised), a Greek temple is a meaning-rich artifact that exudes and discloses the ancient Greek world of which it was an integral part. Like a person's unconscious, this perpetually resonant world is too complex and profound to be captured in formulas or to be rendered fully explicit. The embodied Greek world discloses itself, but always only partially, as it stands shrouded in layers of mystery, owing to our finite location in history and our limited knowledge.

Elaborating and enhancing Heidegger's notion of "world" through a French phenomenological lens, are Mikel Dufrenne's discussions in *The Phenomenology of Aesthetic Experience* (1953), which also address the nature of aesthetic experience and the work of art. Dufrenne's approach compares to, and is preceded by the work of one of Edmund Husserl's finest students, the Polish aesthetician, Roman Ingarden, who is known for his 1931 study, *The Literary Work of Art*. Ingarden analytically stratifies the literary work of art into four levels of signification, and characterizes aesthetic value, and the work itself, as a polyphonic harmony between these strata.

Contrasting with Ingarden's proposal that literary value arises from a harmony between strata of meaning, Mikhail Bakhtin provides an alternative in his 1934 article, "Discourse in the Novel." Employing the notion of "heteroglossia," he emphasizes how literary works – especially the novel – employ internal conflict between a variety of discourses to achieve their aesthetic impact.

HISTORICAL CONCRETENESS, HERMENEUTICS, AND MODERNITY

The enthusiastic attention to life and its attendant concepts that begins during the 1790s and becomes salient thereafter, helps define a new spirit of an age within which we arguably still remain. The prevailing attitude involves surveying a subject – whether it happens to be a rock, plant, animal, discourse, social structure, or academic discipline – and understanding it in terms of its historical antecedents and projected historical path. Historical order replaces abstract logical order, and instead of conceiving of some animal, for example, by means of a definition of the animal's species, we consider the animal in terms of its developmental stages, physiology, ancestors, and future potentialities.

When intensified, the focus on historical considerations transforms into an attitude where a privileged value attaches to the immediate moment, its rich perceptual detail, and its inherent fluctuation, with the effect of subordinating more static, idealized, conceptualized and abstracted approaches to experience. In nineteenth-century Continental aesthetics, this attitude is discernible in a variety of theories and movements that include Søren Kierkegaard's 1840s characterization of the aesthetic mentality, Gustave Courbet's Realist writings of the 1860s, the French Impressionist painters' 1870s emphasis on the immediately perceived moment, the Pointillist painters' emphasis on the same in the 1880s, and the decadent movement's lush, sensory self-indulgence of the 1880s and 1890s.

Despite their differences, these aesthetic perspectives share a preference for immediately perceivable subject matter, an attention to perceptual detail for its own sake, a tendency toward superficiality, a reluctance to present grand philosophical ideas, and an increasing disengagement from moral issues. They also invert the academic hierarchy of genres prevalent since the 1600s, where history painting is the most respected, followed by scenes from everyday life, portraits, landscapes, and, most insignificantly, still lifes.

Contributing to the perceptual atmosphere is the continued influence of morally and politically neutral scientific thinking, paradigmatic during the seventeenth and eighteenth centuries, in its close attention to physical phenomena and its mathematical, quantitative approach. Pointillism in French painting is an example: resonating with the late seventeenth- and early eighteenth-century British empiricist theories of knowledge that took simple sensory impressions as foundational, later painters such as Georges Seurat (1859–91) and Paul Signac (1863–1935) divide color analytically into its elemental points, and juxtapose these points on the canvas so that they can mix visually in the eye for a more intense aesthetic experience. The French Impressionists used similar techniques.

Although academic painting sustained its polished and idealizing presence during the nineteenth century in figures such as Jean-Auguste-Dominique Ingres, and later William-Adolphe Bouguereau, it nonetheless gave way to the Impressionist, Post-Impressionist, and Expressionist movements. Writing in 1945 from a phenomenological standpoint in his essay, "Cezanne's Doubt," Maurice Merleau-Ponty describes Cezanne's Post-Impressionist works as prime examples of this down-to-earth attitude, citing his ability to attend closely to the immediately presented qualities of the visual experience in his landscapes, portraits, and in particular, his still lifes.

The discovery of photography (c.1826, but becoming more popular by the 1840s) also influenced these developments insofar as photographs capture the moment and present the exact details of an object or scene. Photography's power to capture exact detail motivated aspiring artists to break away from preconceived, cartoon-like procedures of how to paint objects, and to paint them less schematically in a more experientially faithful manner. Initially painting captured light effects better, but by the end of the century the availability and improvement of photographic methods led painters to explore the expressive powers of painting beyond what photographs could convey, and this contributed to the development of Expressionism.

The nineteenth century's greater attentiveness to historical presence was a factor in the widespread spiritual crisis that had been threatening traditional moral values since the beginning of that century. In the early decades, efforts to resurrect Greek ideals in an attempt to reinvigorate the culture prevailed in Germany. The initial spark was set by the eighteenth-century art historian, Johann Winckelmann, whose *History of Ancient Art* (1764) introduced an image of classical Greek and Roman sculpture into German culture that was both informed and highly idealized. Goethe, Schiller, Schelling, and later Nietzsche helped realize this renaissance, but hermeneutical reflections soon made it obvious that each person is a child of his or her historical age, and that a complete Greek revival was impossible.

There seemed to be no choice but to be modern, for as historical awareness increases, traditional strategies for attaining salvation lose their attractiveness: one cannot revive the ancient Greeks, or the garden of Eden, or the days of the noble savage, for their times have passed; neither can one live in the future, since the future is never present. Otherworldly heavens also turn to gray, as their inaccessibility undermines their believability. Only the present moment remains from which to derive life's value, and although this present is vibrant, it is continually reappearing, is permeated with accidental properties, is not moving clearly in any direction, and seems to be thin on reliable universal structure, noticeably within the social sphere. With a stronger emphasis on an individual's contingent existence, God becomes less of a reality, along with moral values and expectations of salvation or punishment in an afterlife. Nihilistic feelings eventually emerge, leading either to despair, to a decadent immersion in sensory detail, to a compromising contentment with a middle class existence, or to an effort to find salvation in creating something absolutely new.

Kierkegaard's writings integrate these ideas illuminatingly. His description of the aesthetic character in *Either/Or* (1843) represents one extreme: the self-centered aesthete revels in sensory detail, cares little for others, and is bored, cynical, and directionless. Complementing this is the religious character – described in *Fear and Trembling* (1843) and *Concluding*

Unscientific Postscript (1846) – who, longing for contact with something absolute within a world of contingency, discovers the sublime power of personal choice, and learns to savor the thrilling, anxiety-filled, nonrational experience of making ungrounded choices, or leaps of faith, that maximize creativity and personal responsibility.

Implicitly postulated here is an absolute freedom that enables one to interpret the world as one wills, to change one's personality, one's values, or one's lifestyle. Jean-Paul Sartre later strikes this existentialist keynote in his early philosophy, where he also combines an interest in appreciating sensory detail to its fullest and sometimes most frightening aspects (*Nausea*, 1938) with the presence of absolute freedom (*Being and Nothingness*, 1943).

Kierkegaard prefigures Sartre's existentialism and reveals at a relatively early date (the 1840s) an attitude that plots the course for Continental aesthetic theories of the first few decades of the twentieth century. This is the modernist quest for what is new, where one rids oneself of antecedent trappings, tradition, and ornamentation. Individuality is paramount, and objective universal rules that predetermine one's possibilities, for the most part, are absent.

When the notions of freedom and contingency dominate the cultural atmosphere, theories emerge that ground themselves on changeability, accidentality, and ultimately, artifactuality, in the sense that artifacts are not natural products, but human constructions, typically the result of plans freely projected in view of the whole. Although the modernist aesthetic prescribes a sharp break from the past, an undercurrent of hermeneutic awareness – much like the one that undermines the early nineteenth-century efforts to institute a Greek revival – yields a more tempered attitude toward the possibility of becoming thoroughly modern. The situation is paradoxical: it is impossible to resurrect the ancient Greeks or any other cultural milieu, for we must be our own contemporaries; it is impossible to be exclusively modern, for we always import the effects of past tradition, given how tradition is the soil from which our contemporary attitudes grow, whenever or wherever we happen to be living.

This dual-aspected hermeneutical awareness intensifies during the nineteenth century and comes to a head in Martin Heidegger's *Being and Time* (1927), where he explains how understanding always presupposes a set of background assumptions that prefigure whatever we are trying to understand. Everyone is born into a specific time period, culture, and language, and these factors constitute the background to any given interpretation. Even if we were to replicate the exact sonic stimuli that some musical audience member experienced three centuries ago, for example, this would not suffice to generate the same experience as that of that past listener, for our contemporary presuppositions about how music should sound inevitably affect our experience. Heidegger articulates these considerations in 1927, and in 1960 his faithful student, Hans-Georg Gadamer, develops them at length in the hermeneutic and aesthetic theory he sets forth in *Truth and Method* – a book that incidentally criticizes Kant's aesthetics for not having secured a rich enough place for taste to be a vehicle of knowledge.

This Heideggerian hermeneutical awareness tempers the modernist quest to produce a new, tradition-free art. Soon realizing that cultural tradition and language inheres in everyone from the start, later theorists appreciate that the quest for the "new" always launches from within a given historical context. The modernist project can be achieved only partially, in other words, and only by acknowledging the very materials of the given historical and linguistic context from which one aims to break free. Rather than attempting impossibly to invent an entirely new language from scratch, one would speak poetically with the language one already has.

Theodor Adorno's aesthetic theory grows out of these concerns, as he observes initially that the majority of accepted contemporary artworks have a strong commodity function that implicitly reinforces objectionable capitalist forces. Adorno argues that genuine artworks are autonomous, are relatively uncommon, are critical of market forces, are not produced by the culture industry, and are antagonistic toward an instrumental conception of rationality that is in league with economic exploitation. Whether such autonomous artworks can withstand the social pressure to become com- modified and absorbed into the oppressive eco- nomic system remains a looming question for him, but he upholds the liberating ideal of works of art that stand as unique, and that defy reductions to formulas and preexisting linguistic categories. He emphasizes unique- ness, individuality, and freedom, as these chal- lenge universal generalizations, regulations, and predictable constancies.

In the 1936 essay, "The Work of Art in the Age of Its Technical Reproducibility," Walter Benjamin adopts a contrary line by associating an artwork's perceived uniqueness, historic- ally generated social authority, and aura, with the exploitative capitalist forces of tradition. Benjamin's view is that when an artwork is mechanically reproduced, its widespread dupli- cation breaks down its aura of elitism, thereby making the general public or proletarian popu- lation familiar with the work and undermin- ing its elitist pretensions. Popular tabloids that publish raw and unflattering photographs of movie stars, taken while they are at home, in restaurants, on vacation, without make-up, in ordinary clothing, etc., erode personal auras in a comparably leveling way.

The juxtaposition of Adorno's and Benjamin's views on mechanical reproduction raises the question of how best to understand the dynamics of revolutionary art, since, con- tra Benjamin, the mechanical reproduction of artworks can also assimilate them into the pre- vailing culture and undermine how they stand critically against the status quo. Benjamin also claims that film is advantageous because its temporal quality opposes the ossifying employ- ment of static concepts. Since the film's images pass by quickly, however, there is often little time to reflect on them, and the audience can absorb their presentation without reflection. This becomes problematic when the films have a propagandist agenda.

ARTIFACTUALITY, LANGUAGE, AND LIBERATION

When the French artist Marcel Duchamp submitted an ordinary, mass-produced urinal to the Society of Independent Artists' exhibi- tion in 1917, held in Manhattan, he signaled that within the right context any object can be interpreted as a work of art. If we couple this notion with the nineteenth-century intensification of historical awareness and the associated emphasis on contingency and indi- viduality, it is a short step to the idea that, if every object can be seen as an artwork, what seems to be natural and fixed can be reframed as a human artifact.

A year earlier, Ferdinand de Saussure's *Course in General Linguistics* (1916) was posthumously published, to great effect. Its ideas immediately changed the course of linguistic theory, and within several decades it captured the interest of French structuralist and poststructuralist theorists. Saussure's claim is that linguistic signs are arbitrary, and that meanings arise primarily from the interrelationships between the signs, rather than from the signs' objective referents. Linguistic meaning is consequently artificial and artifactual and, if we assume fur- ther that human consciousness and the social order rely on language, the upshot – consistent with an existentialist emphasis on freedom – is that nothing is written in stone, that we can radically change social structures, and that untold possibilities await us.

With respect to Continental aesthetic the- ory, such assumptions contribute to a sweep- ing change in the set of aesthetic values that are generally invoked when judging the quality of works of art. In accordance with both the idea that we inherit a linguistic tradition and must acknowledge its parameters, and the thought that breaking through such parameters is the path to greater freedom and truth, thinkers such as Roland Barthes distinguish between texts that adhere to conventional styles and values, and texts that challenge conventions with a promise of greater freedom (*S/Z*, 1970). Writing toward a liberating end about the "death of the author" in his 1968 essay of the same name, he contests the authority of a text's author to determine its meaning, and portrays the author as an oppressive force. Finally, in his 1977 inaugural lecture at the Collége de France, he describes literalistic, categorizing language itself as an oppressive force and prescribes that we employ constant shifting and playfulness to loosen language's freezing grip on us.

Michel Foucault similarly upholds authors who use poetic language to break through the rigidities of linguistic convention, as in *Death and the Labyrinth: The World of Raymond Roussel*

(1962) and *Maurice Blanchot: The Thought from Outside* (1966). Also a champion of freedom, Foucault urges in a later interview (1982) that we can turn our lives into a work of art through creative self-discipline. Underlying his view of art as liberation as well is the assumption that society is an artifact, that social values are conventional, and that creative artistry is at the forefront of releasing us from a conventional, oppressive attitude.

Following Barthes and Foucault, Jacques Derrida produces some novel interpretative construals within the field of literary criticism, assigning to language a pervasive presence, such that the world as a whole assumes a text-like quality and subsequently becomes subject to literary criticism. His approach encapsulates the tendencies in Barthes and Foucault that are antagonistic to rigid meanings, for Derrida understands every linguistic presentation – and we can recall Heidegger's meaning-exuding Greek temple here – as harboring meanings that are in excess of the manifest meaning. What remains unsaid, or what is said but only peripherally, provide him with keys to a text's inexhaustible layers of implicit meaning.

Husserl's phenomenology notes that we cannot apprehend any object without considering a wider context against which it is set. According to Freud's method of interpreting dreams, the most apparently insignificant detail in a dream can be the definitive one. Such ideas enter into Derrida's theory of interpretation, where he shows how any given artwork's or text's context and peripheral elements involve meanings that are in fact central to the work. Since contexts are as important as the manifestly highlighted elements within this perspective, Derrida's thought prohibits exclusionary oppositions, where for instance, one might naturally wish to distinguish between a painting and its frame, where the latter is considered to be nonessential and outside of the work.

In an assortment of highly original writings, Gilles Deleuze accentuates the aesthetic value of innovation and bold imagination, not only in his prescriptions for art, but in his own texts, which he fills with linguistic inventions. He believes that the best literary works, for instance, ought to appear as a foreign language that nonetheless inhabits a familiar linguistic context, as they

break through established conventions with their novel modes of presentation. Such ideas, despite their visionary and challenging quality, essentially cohere with the aesthetic quest for individuality, autonomy, uniqueness, and nonassimilability that we see in earlier theorists, as we witness his attempts to overcome the effects of tradition through a variety of devices that violate standard expectations.

Barthes, Foucault, Derrida, and Deleuze together call for the replacement of traditional aesthetic values associated with closure and definitiveness, with values related to expansion and innovation. Judged in traditional terms, the most valuable works of art ought to be unified, coherent, well planned, determinate, perspicuous in meaning, and, as a rule, associated with beauty. Alternatively, when judged with an interest in undermining convention for the sake of expanding personal, social, and all types of interpretative horizons, the most valuable works of art ought to display a multiplicity of meaning; resist closure; disperse efforts to define single and definitive meanings; exhibit wittiness, playfulness, indeterminacy, evocativeness, and sublimity; while also resisting absorption into an indiscriminate linguistic sea. From the standpoint of these alternative values, a new, seemingly profound, and imaginatively resonant but ultimately mistaken and misleading work would remain aesthetically preferable to a polished, beautiful, understandable, semantically circumscribed, plausible, albeit less resonant one.

The aesthetics of the sublime is at the crux of this transition, for it encourages the propagation of limit-experiences that bring us to the edge of our given, standard, expected, entrenched, or ordinary perspective, and that promise a horizon beyond our present one. This promise combats the despair of facing the deathly possibility – as Jean-François Lyotard mentions in several essays on the sublime from the 1980s – that nothing further will happen. The sublime indicates a contemporary preference for transcendence, expansion, revaluation of old values, newness, originality, novelty, evocativeness, shock quality, and often enough, terror and outrage. Continental aesthetics gravitates to this point, as we reflect on how the nineteenth-century aesthetics of beauty transforms into the early twentieth-century aesthetics of expressiveness, and how, later in the century, expressiveness transforms into the limit-breaking sublime. The latter is not new, original, or novel, since sublime experience has been with us ever since people began to gaze at the starry skies with a sense of humility and awe. Its contemporary attractiveness arises from its specifically linguistic versions, which dwell in the expansive disclosures of sheer creativity and the associated urge to speak differently.

See also EIGHTEENTH-CENTURY AESTHETICS; ADORNO; BARTHES; BENJAMIN; DECONSTRUCTION; DELEUZE; DERRIDA; DUFRENNE; FOUCAULT; GADAMER; HEGEL; HEIDEGGER; HERMENEUTICS; INGARDEN; KANT; KIERKEGAARD; MARXISM AND ART; MERLEAU-PONTY; MODERNISM AND POST-MODERNISM; NIETZSCHE; PSYCHOANALYSIS AND ART; SARTRE; SCHELLING; SCHILLER; SCHOPEN-HAUER; STRUCTURALISM AND POSTSTRUCTURAL-ISM; TOLSTOY.

BIBLIOGRAPHY

Cazeaux, Clive (ed.). 2000. *The Continental Aesthetics Reader*. London: Routledge.

Chytry, Josef. 1992. *The Aesthetic State: A Quest for Modern German Thought*. Berkeley: University of California Press.

Croce, Benedetto. 1964 [1922]. *Aesthetic: As Science of Expression and General Linguistic*. D. Ainslie (trans.). New York: Noonday.

Eagleton, Terry. 1990. *The Ideology of the Aesthetic*. London: Basil Blackwell.

Hammermeister, Kai. 2002. *The German Aesthetic Tradition*. Cambridge: Cambridge University Press.

Krukowski, Lucian. 1992. *Aesthetic Legacies*. Philadelphia: Temple University Press.

Nochlin, Linda. 1971. *Realism*. Harmondsworth: Penguin.

ROBERT WICKS

twentieth-century Anglo-American aesthetics The twentieth century began with all forms of art dominated by a modernist avant-garde that has its roots in the last third of the previous century. Also inherited from the nineteenth century were several important ideas in aesthetics itself. One was a redefinition of aesthetics as the philosophy of art, or at least an almost exclusive focus on art as the subject of aesthetic inquiry. Second, via such figures as Schopenhauer, the idea that art is autonomous from other aspects of human life and is to be appreciated in an experience that was similarly autonomous – aesthetic experience – was taking root. A third development was abandonment of the idea that the question "What is art?" could be answered in terms of representation or mimesis, as it had been for at least a century and arguably since ancient times. This was prompted in part by the advent of photography, in part by painting that aimed to distinguish itself from the photograph, and in part by the recognition of instrumental music as a supreme but nonrepresentational art form. Hence there was a search for a new way of defining art that accommodated modernism and these other developments.

EXPRESSION THEORY

One of these approaches defines art in terms of expression rather than representation. This approach also had roots in late nineteenth-century thought but received much attention in the first half of the twentieth century. Its twentieth-century exponents include most prominently Benedetto Croce and R. G. Collingwood. In 1898, Tolstoy proposed that art is concerned with the communication (or "infection" as he called it) of an emotion experienced by the artist to an audience by means of external signs. A work that fails to do this is not truly art, even if it is in a recognized "art" form. Tolstoy also provided criteria for evaluating artworks. These criteria are both formal and substantive. An artwork is formally good if it is sincere, and it lucidly expresses an individualized emotion. The substantive criteria are moral, but not in a conventional sense. A work is substantively good if it supplies the spiritual message needed in its day and age, and this changes over time. In general, the function of art is to unite human beings in a common, spiritually beneficial feeling. On Tolstoy's criteria, many works considered among the greatest products of Western art, such as Shakespeare's plays, Beethoven's symphonies, and Wagner's operas, are either not art at all or bad art. Many later expression theorists, though they depart from many specifics tenets of Tolstoy, are remarkably influenced by him.

Thus Collingwood, the proponent of the expression theory who is now most read, agrees with Tolstoy that it is essential to distinguish between genuine art and various counterfeits that are often assumed to be art but actually are not. For example, anything made for the purpose of amusement or giving pleasure ("amusement art"), no matter how highbrow, is not art properly so called. Like Tolstoy, many items assumed to be among the greatest artworks are not art at all according to Collingwood.

The mark of true art is, of course, expression, by which Collingwood means something quite specific. Expression is neither the production of an indicator of what one feels, as when one sighs in sadness, nor the intentional arousal of emotion in another. The expression of emotion is the coming to know in full specificity exactly what emotion one is feeling. It is the articulation of the emotion. The creative process by which art comes into existence, for Collingwood, consists in first becoming aware that one is feeling something and then gradually and fully spelling out what this is in one's imagination. Notice that on this account, the artwork is fully realized within the artist's mind. In contrast to Tolstoy, Collingwood thought that is where art exists.

However, Collingwood recognizes that various media – paint, bronze, stone or clay, the written word, etc. – have an important dual role in art-making. First, although strictly speaking an artwork exists in some mind, most notably the artist's, the mental discovery typically occurs only in the process of an artist's using a favored medium. Second, the product of this process – for example, the paint on canvas – is the means by which the emotion might be communicated to an audience. This occurs not by arousing the emotion in them but by allowing them to recreate the emotion in their own imagination and thereby also express it in Collingwood's technical sense.

Like Tolstoy and other proponents of the expression theory such as Croce, Collingwood has an unconventional way of marking the art/nonart distinction. Unlike Tolstoy but like Croce, Collingwood has a hard time finding a way to distinguish good art from bad. Anything that succeeds as expression as Collingwood understands it not only is art but also does exactly what a work of art is supposed to do and hence would seem also to be good art. Collingwood sometimes speaks of failed attempts at expression as bad art, but strictly speaking they should count as failed attempts at art-making.

All three expression theorists assign to art a hugely important but incredibly narrow mission. For Tolstoy, it is the uniting of human being in common, spiritually beneficial feelings. For Croce, it is to create a symbolic expression of an intense feeling – a presentation of the feeling itself rather than a statement about it. For Collingwood, the mission of art is the self-knowledge that comes from the clarification of emotions, which is the "medicine for the worst disease of the mind, the corruption of consciousness" (1938: 336). It is not surprising that so much of what is conventionally considered art falls outside the boundaries drawn by such theories, but this is indicative of a defect more in the theories than in the rejected works.

FORMALISM

Formalism is another approach that attempts to accommodate the rise of modernism and the rejection of mimetic theories of art. Clive Bell and Roger Fry, the most famous proponents of formalism in the early twentieth century, were art critics and they were heavily influenced by the developments in the visual arts, especially the paintings of Cézanne, Picasso, and Braque. (In the second half of the twentieth century, the standard-bearers of formalism were Clement Greenberg, another art critic, and Monroe C. Beardsley, a philosopher heavily influence by the school of literary criticism known as New Criticism.) Through the lens of such works, which these early formalists interpreted as totally devaluing representation in the service of exploring form, they reinterpreted the history of art and developed a formalist aesthetic theory.

This theory has two main points: a new answer to the question "What is art?" and a theory of aesthetic value.

According to Bell, a good theory of what art is identifies a property that all artworks share. Though Bell did not make this point, that is not enough, because if many other things also share this property, we have still failed to pick out all and *only* artworks. It is somewhat plausible to suppose that art's nature has something to do with form, once we reject representation as its defining feature. But all sorts of things that are not artworks also have a form in some sense or other. So we need to find a property possessed by all artworks and not by these other things. Bell's solution to this problem is to say that what makes something a work of art is the possession of *significant* form. This is a form that imbues what possesses it with a special kind of value that consists in the affect produced in those who perceive it. Bell calls this affect the aesthetic emotion.

A common criticism of Bell's attempt to define art is that it is circular. He tells us that art is significant form and this is to be understood as form that creates a certain experience in its audience, the aesthetic emotion, but reference to this emotion is not self-explanatory. The aesthetic emotion, unlike fear and anger, is not a psychological state that everyone recognizes. However, Bell tends, especially when he first introduces his conception of art, to explicate the relevant emotion as that which is caused by significant form. This clearly does not help.

Some sympathetic interpreters of Bell attempt to show that he is not stuck in this circle. They point to what Bell calls the metaphysical hypothesis, which claims that the experience of significant form is much like mystical experience. In both experiences, we encounter a more ultimate reality, which Bell liked to describe in Kantian terminology: we encounter the thing-in-itself. On this proposal, focusing on the explicit representation in artworks distracts us from the more important reality we gain access to through form. More importantly, this view suggests a noncircular account of the aesthetic emotion. It is the emotion felt when one encounters ultimate reality.

There is a problem with this explication of Bell. While it accurately represents his metaphysical hypothesis, it mislocates its place in Bell's theory. Bell recognizes the hypothesis is speculation, and he does not want to tie his definition of art to its being correct. He stands by his definition even if his metaphysics is wrong. This implies that whatever "significant form" does mean, it is not form that creates an encounter with ultimate reality.

There are other problems with Bell's theory. If there are paintings, sculptures, etc. that lack significant form, as Bell clearly believes, they would not be artworks at all. Hence, like the expression theorists, Bell's formalism rules that

many items widely considered art really are not. That is counterintuitive. Also, for this very reason, he too has no place for bad art, since the defining feature of art is also its most important good-making feature.

Fry escapes these last two criticisms because, unlike Bell, he does not attempt to define art in terms of form. He is interested in identifying the right way to appreciate visual art and in what its value consists. He uses the form/representation distinction to answer these questions. He argued that representation inevitably evokes subjective responses depending on the associations such features elicit in the individual viewer. The only way to escape this sort of subjectivity is to focus on formal features. That is the correct way to appreciate art, and it is what gives artworks their objective value. Fry's argument has even more obvious problems than Bell's. He assumes that the only way we can evaluate the representational properties of painting is by creating subjective associations about them. But there is no good justification for this premise.

In fact, while definitions of art in terms of form have not won wide acceptance, formalism is particularly weak as an all-encompassing account of the value of art. This is because it has to treat the most salient feature of countless artworks – their representational content – as irrelevant to their artistic value. They occur incidentally for the sake of the forms that emerge from them. Among the many problems with such an account is that it implausibly distances works from the concerns of the artists who made them and the audiences who receive them.

Before moving on from the topic of formalism, we note a view fashioned from both formalist and expressivist considerations. In 1942, Susanne Langer drew on the early Wittgenstein's picture theory of meaning, Ernst Cassirer's work on symbolic forms, and Bell's view that art is significant form in her *Philosophy in a New Key*, a study of expressiveness in music. She distinguished two opposed and exclusive modes of symbolism, the discursive and the presentational. Discursive symbolism is exemplified by language and mathematics. Here meaning is generated according to the rule-governed combination of units of significance. By contrast, presentational symbols take on their meaning by sharing the form of what they signify, though they realize this in their own, sometimes very different, media. Music operates as a presentational symbol of the form of feeling, according to Langer. That is, music expresses emotions by producing a dynamic, temporal structure that is an iconic transformation of the sensational structure of emotional experience. In *Feeling and Form* (1953), Langer extended her account to all the arts. Even those that are explicitly discursive take their primary significance from operating as presentational symbols of organic emotional processes and rhythms.

Langer's theory long remained popular with music educationists, but is now largely ignored within analytic philosophy of art. Perhaps this is because the philosophies of mind, the emotions, and language that she adopts all look dated, and because the indescribable forms and inarticulable meanings that lie at the heart of her theory remain basically obscure. More generally, despite attracting some attention in the 1950s, semiotic approaches to aesthetics have sometimes been thought to blur distinctions that should be clarified, such as those between depiction and expression, meaning and reference, extension and intension.

AESTHETIC THEORY

A third large-scale theory of art that was prominent in the first half of the twentieth century is the aesthetic theory, the idea that artworks are aesthetic objects, and that their nature and value derives from special experiences they are capable of delivering. Aesthetic theory can be formulated with a formalist or an expressivist bias but part of its strength lies in the fact that it need not have either slant. The general idea behind aesthetic theory leaves open just which properties of an object are responsible for the distinctive aesthetic experience. This has given the theory staying power. It is the only one to remain prominent in the philosophy of art after 1950.

Another element often found in aesthetic theory concerns the attitude that we bring to the situation in which an object is experienced. This idea goes back to eighteenth-century accounts of judgments of taste according to which only those judgments that are disinterested – that is free from bias, and from practical or even theoretical concerns – are capable of being valid judgments of taste. Edward Bullough was an influential early twentieth-century proponent of this idea. The key concept in his view is that of psychical distance. This is initially put forward as a variant of the disinterested attitude. We achieve psychical distance when we put a phenomenon "out of gear with" practical concerns and personal ends which enables us to perceive the phenomenally objective features it possesses (1912: 89). Bullough's famous example is a fog at sea that, from a practical perspective, is both inconvenient in creating delays and dangerous in increasing the likelihood of a collision. In contrast, when one distances oneself from these practical concerns one can appreciate the unique visual quality of the fog – its milky opaqueness, the way it blurs and distorts the shapes of objects – which produce in the observer an "uncanny mingling of repose and terror" (1912: 89). As Bullough develops his idea of psychical distance, it becomes more differentiated from the traditional idea of disinterest. First, it turns out that one can be both under-distanced and over-distanced from the perceived object. In fact, when it comes to the reception of artworks, the ideal is to be as little distanced as possible without being completely without distance (1912: 94). Second, distance is not only a property of an appreciator's attitude but also a property of artworks. Some "in-your-face" ones actually attempt to destroy distance while other, unusually cool works create more distance than normal. Bullough regarded under- and over-distanced works as aesthetically flawed.

A rather different aesthetic theory is proposed by John Dewey in his book *Art as Experience*, published in 1934. Perhaps the starkest difference between Dewey and other aesthetic theorists is his insistence that aesthetic experience is continuous with the "normal processes of living" (1987: 16). Hence, there is not the disengagement from practical and theoretical pursuits that philosophers like Kant, Schopenhauer, and Bullough emphasize. Dewey insists that aesthetic experience has an instrumental value often overlooked or denied by other theorists. For anything to have human value it must serve the needs of human beings in coping with the world they live in.

Dewey's idea here seems be that intrinsically enjoyable aesthetic experience can help us achieve a variety of other human ends: it can sensitize us to features of the environment we might otherwise overlook; it can help us imagine more vividly the cognitive and emotional life of others; perhaps most important for Dewey, it can "invigorate and vitalize us" in the pursuit of whatever other ends we might have (Shusterman 2001: 98). There is a similar continuity between aesthetic and theoretical perspectives. Art, like science, functions to order and make sense of experience. To use the language of a later philosopher influenced by pragmatism, both are "ways of worldmaking" (Goodman 1978).

All this might leave one wondering just what aesthetic experience is for Dewey. The fact is that he is better at noting continuities than sharply defining things. Doing the latter seems to go against the grain for him. Still there are special features of aesthetic experience as Dewey conceives it. Aesthetic experience is *an experience* rather than just an undistinguished segment in the flow of consciousness. It is whole in itself. Such an experience possesses unity and gives a feeling of closure. It is always intense; we are most alive when having such experience. It always seems to have a positive valence, and perhaps is always enjoyable. These features make it valuable in its own right apart from and in addition to the instrumental functions it serves.

AESTHETIC THEORY AFTER 1950

As mentioned above, aesthetic theory remained prominent in both Britain and the United States after 1950. However, it was developed in rather different ways in these two countries.

In Britain, unlike the United States, the leading philosophers of the day did write about art and the aesthetic, if only occasionally. They endorsed a highly eviscerated aesthetic theory, which no doubt unintentionally but inevitably could only leave one to wonder how an artwork could ever be seriously evaluated or be more than a trivial diversion. Peter Strawson followed Kant in arguing against any rules by which artworks can be evaluated and added that aesthetic judgment is devoid of any "interest in what [art] can or should do or what we can do

with it" (1974: 178). Stuart Hampshire asserted that "works of art are gratuitous, something made or done gratuitously, and not in response to any problem posed" (1954: 161).

The most important English philosopher of art to emerge in this period is Frank Sibley. He also took the aesthetic theory of art for granted, but what makes his essays important and influential is their rigorous, detailed investigation of the logic and epistemology of the aesthetic judgment.

Sibley's best-known paper is "Aesthetic Concepts" (1959). Here he distinguishes between nonaesthetic perceptual properties that anyone with normal vision can notice (e.g., being a red patch) and aesthetic properties that are also often perceptual but require taste, sensitivity, or special training to see (e.g., being balanced). Sibley's main point in this paper, however, is that while the aesthetic properties of artworks supervene on the nonaesthetic properties so that a change in the latter would lead to a change in the former, we can never validly infer the existence of an aesthetic property from the fact that it contains a set of nonaesthetic properties. For this reason, he claims that aesthetic disputes cannot be settled by inductive or deductive reasoning from premises about nonaesthetic properties to conclusions about aesthetic ones. Aesthetic properties have to be perceived to ascertain their existence in an artwork or other object.

Do Sibley's conclusions imply that aesthetic judgments lack objectivity and that there can be no general rules or reasons available to support such judgments? In this and later papers, Sibley took up these questions and argued for negative answers to both of them. Perceptual, noninferential judgments can be objective, and for that reason aesthetic judgments can have an objectivity similar to those about color. As for reasons or rules, while nonaesthetic judgments never entail aesthetic ones, there are nontrivial entailments among aesthetic judgments themselves. The existence of certain more specific aesthetic properties can provide reasons for more general aesthetic judgments. That a work is graceful, balanced, or witty are reasons to think it has aesthetic merit. Further, there are always such reasons. But such reasons are capable of being defeated. Wit does not entail overall goodness in a work. Rather it is always a prima facie reason to think a work has a degree of aesthetic merit that might on occasion be defeated in virtue of the way the wit interacts with other properties the work possesses.

In the United States, the most important proponent of the aesthetic theory was Monroe C. Beardsley, who wrote *Aesthetics: Problems in the Philosophy of Criticism* in 1958. Unlike Sibley, whose work is characterized by subtle but piecemeal exploration into the nature of the aesthetic judgment, Beardsley aimed for a comprehensive theory of art. Despite its sub-title, his book considers all the arts and many of the issues of depiction, expression, interpretation, and evaluation that continue to attract atten-tion in the field, and he reviewed and acknow-ledged the philosophical literature on these topics. In subsequent books, he wrote on the his-tory of aesthetics and on literary criticism.

In "The Intentional Fallacy," an article coauthored with William K. Wimsatt in 1946, Beardsley attacked forms of criticism that drew attention away from the artwork to its artist. Only what is manifest in the artwork should be invoked in discussing, analyzing, and inter-preting it, they maintained, in line with the New Critics of literary theory. This anti-intentionalist stance carried over to *Aesthetics*, in which Beardsley consistently defended the autonomy of the artwork. In general, he regarded reference to the circumstances of the work's genesis as irrelevant to its appreciation. In *Aesthetics*, he wrote of "aesthetic objects" and avoided "works of art," and regarded the value of art as tied to the pleasure its aesthetic contemplation provided. In these and other respects, Beardsley continued the aesthetic tra-dition, and he was its most eloquent advocate when it came under attack in the 1960s and 1970s. He differed from some aesthetic theorists, however, in regarding art also as an important source of pragmatic value, and in this was explicitly influenced by John Dewey.

WITTGENSTEINIAN AESTHETICS

In the mid 1950s there was a rash of articles (by Morris Weitz, Paul Ziff, John Passmore, W. E. Kennick, and W. B. Gallie) questioning the possibility and usefulness of defining art. Artworks are related not by individually necessary and jointly sufficient properties they all share but by family resemblance or by their similarity to paradigm artworks, it was held. These views were prompted by Wittgenstein's posthumously published *Philosophical Investigations* of 1953, with its skepticism regarding a metaphysics concerned with Platonic essences. Although the explana-tory power of appeals to family resemblance and the like have been questioned – after all, *family* membership is not established in terms of resemblance – antiessentialism in aesthetics has become a perennial theme. For many people, there is something about art – its creativity, volatility, self-consciousness, rebel-liousness – that is supposed to make it resistant to the strictures of definition.

Another part of *Philosophical Investigations* to attract the attention of aestheticians was the discussion of aspect perception, or "seeing as." This stressed the extent to which how one sees an ambiguous figure is under the control of the will. It seemed to some that this account provided a model for aesthetic experience in general (e.g., see Aldrich 1963 and, for a more sophisticated use of the notion, Scruton 1974). And it seemed to others that pictorial repre-sentation, at least, could be analyzed as a vari-ety of aspect perception; we see the painted surface *as* what it represents. But whereas an ambiguous figure can be seen under only one aspect at a given time, we are simultaneously aware of the painted surface and of what it depicts, which is one reason why later theories of pictorial representation moved beyond the dis-cussion of "seeing as."

Wittgenstein's influence in aesthetics was strengthened by the publication in 1966 of notes taken in his lectures on aesthetics, psy-chology, and religious belief. These rejected the relevance of psychologists' experimental search for the causes of our aesthetic experience. On the positive side, they emphasized the con-text sensitivity and particularity of aesthetic judgments and the indescribability of aesthetic qualities. Meanwhile, some philosophers fol-lowed Wittgensteinian methods of "ordinary language philosophy" to investigate art and the aesthetic, which involved considering how art and the aesthetic are ordinarily discussed and explaining away philosophical puzzles as arising from misunderstandings or misapplica-tions of the "grammar" of this discourse.

Wittgenstein's influence on aesthetics reflects his influence on philosophy more generally. For a time he was a dominant figure and his ideas remain important to the present. But his influence has waned over the decades, as philosophers of art adopted different approaches or considered different issues. He has remained a more prominent and respected philosopher in Britain than in the United States.

COGNITIVISM AND CONTEXTUALISM

In 1968, two significant monographs were published. Richard Wollheim's *Art and Its Objects* explores and rejects the idea that some artworks are physical objects, touching on depiction, expression, and many other topics in the process. The influence of the later Wittgenstein is apparent here, as Wollheim emphasized that art is a form of life, and concluded that it is essentially historical. He made the aesthetic function of art central, but challenged the notion of the aesthetic introduced by Kant and, in the twentieth century, Bullough. Nelson Goodman's *Languages of Art* addressed a range of central topics – depiction, expression, and appreciation – and, via a discussion of symbol systems, provided a new approach to each. In addition, Goodman drew an ontological distinction between singular artworks, such as oil paintings, which are "autographic," and potentially multiple artworks, such as novels or symphonies, which are "allographic," and he developed an account of notation capable of explaining how allographic artworks can be definitively specified by scripts and scores.

Though Wollheim's and Goodman's books are different in purpose, content, and style, with hindsight each can be seen to indicate a radical change of orientation in Anglo-American analytic aesthetics. That shift might be dated to the decade between 1964 and 1974. In brief, it involved a move from regarding artworks as best appreciated as autonomous and isolated from their creators and from the circumstances of their creation (where this approach includes the adoption of a psychologically distinctive mindset, the aesthetic attitude), to regarding their identities and appreciable properties as depending on relations tying them to art traditions, conventions, practices, and artists' intentions. In other words, an ahistorical, psychologistic analysis of art and its appreciation was replaced with a historically contextualized, sociological account of these matters. For Wollheim, this is apparent in his stress on art's historical character and, for Goodman, it emerges from his account of art's identity as relative to the conventions of symbol systems and of art's value as primarily cognitive. This strand is yet more obvious in his *Ways of Worldmaking* (1978), with its emphasis on art as a mode of world-making and its recommendation that the question "When is art?" has more interest and merit than "What is art?"

Not everyone followed the trend, however. *Art and Imagination* (1974), by the British philosopher Roger Scruton, focused on the phenomenology of aesthetic experience rather than the importance of art's social context. Nevertheless, Scruton also contested the traditional characterization of aesthetic properties as simple. With due homage to Wittgenstein, he argued that aesthetic properties are, like aspects, complex and "emergent" from simpler, base properties. And above all, he stressed how engagement with art and aesthetic properties involves the imagination. Another philosopher who began to explore the role of make-believe in our experience of art at this time was Kendall L. Walton (1973). He emphasized more than Scruton the way make-believe must be responsive to the historically variable conventions of the relevant art tradition.

The reorientation within analytic aesthetics from the individual contemplator to the social setting of art's creation and presentation, which dominated for the remainder of the century, had two aspects in its initial phase. One was negative. It involved a sustained attack on the notions of aesthetic properties and aesthetic experience, at least as these had come to be regarded earlier in the twentieth century. The aesthetic theory that was challenged maintained that aesthetic properties are "internal" to the items that possess them and thus are made available through contemplation of that object for its own sake alone. Indeed, the theory held that actively disregarding the intentions of the item's maker, the context of production, and any nonaesthetic functions the item might serve promotes – indeed, is perhaps essential – for its fullest aesthetic appreciation. The adoption of the aesthetic attitude, a distinctive psychological perspective that involves a distanced and disinterested approach to its target, seemed to be mandated by the aesthetic theory.

The positive agenda of the new direction in analytic aesthetics involved demonstrating what relations between the item and its broader context are relevant to its aesthetic character. As part of this project, a sharper distinction was drawn between the aesthetic qualities of humanly produced items, especially works of art, and those of natural objects. The appreciable features of artworks – for instance, ones displaying influence, reference, modes of treating the medium, the solution of technical problems, and the extension or repudiation of an art tradition – were represented as being much richer than those traditionally covered by the term "aesthetic." In particular, it was argued that, for artworks, the art-historical context of their creation, the artists' intentions, genre membership, and individual styles are all significant not only in generating the work's appreciable properties but in shaping its identity as the work it is.

Of the articles that heralded this change in direction, the most cited is Arthur C. Danto's "The Artworld" of 1964. This introduced a term for the nexus of artists, audiences, critics, and the formal and informal institutions through which they create, present, describe, record, and appreciate art. Here and elsewhere Danto made use of what might be called "the argument from indiscernibles," an argument style with an ancient philosophical pedigree. That is, Danto described cases in which an artwork is perceptually indiscriminable from a nonartwork – for instance, Andy Warhol's *Brillo Boxes* and the cartons in which Brillo boxes are delivered to supermarkets – or in which two artworks are perceptually indiscriminable – his hypothetical example is of paintings of Newton's First and Third Laws by artists *A* and *B* – yet, despite the similarity in their appearances, the one has aesthetically significant properties the other lacks. Whereas *A*'s painting depicts the path of a particle through space, *B*'s shows where two masses meet, and whereas Warhol's *Brillo Boxes* make some kind of comment on the material values of the time, including the commodification of art, the supermarket cartons do not. Such examples,

if convincing, clearly count against the idea that an artwork's aesthetically appreciable properties reside solely in its appearance. By describing perceptually identical pieces – that is, pieces that might be mistaken for each other by a person who knows nothing of their functions or origins – that, nevertheless, possess strikingly different artistic features, Danto's argument showed that those features depend for their character on relations they hold to matters lying beyond the work's boundaries. As Danto specified it, the other element in the relation is "an atmosphere of theory."

The choice of the word "theory" was perhaps unwise. It is too easily interpreted as referring to a pseudophilosophical theory held by the artist or critic about the nature of art. As emerged later, what Danto meant could better be characterized as an atmosphere provided by the art-historical context in which the work is produced. And this fits with a point he also stressed, following the art historian Heinrich Wölfflin, that whether something can be art at a given moment within the history of art depends on who offers it and what has become art up to that time. Another aspect of the argument in Danto's article proved too obscure to be helpful. He invoked an "is" of artistic identity that is supposed to be distinct from the "is" of identity, existence, or predication. In addition, the article ended with a controversial claim: not only do current artistic developments alter the art-historical conditions for the works that follow, thereby affecting the properties they may have, they retrospectively alter the properties of works created formerly. This final thought was not one that Danto developed or repeated.

Related views were presented at much the same time by Marshall Cohen, Stanley Cavell, Joseph Margolis, Kendall L. Walton, and George Dickie. And it was Dickie who produced the most telling criticisms of traditional aesthetic theory in a series of articles (1962, 1964, 1965, 1968) that challenge the idea that aesthetic appreciation involves the adoption of a special frame of mind that dissociates its object from its social, practical context. Rather, close attention of the ordinary kind is required, and, in the case of art, familiarity with the appropriate artworld conventions is vital for locating and framing the object of appreciation.

As already noted, these arguments led philosophers to focus less on the state of mind of the individual appreciator and more on the social context in which art is produced and consumed. The outcome was Dickie's institutional definition of art, first heralded in 1969 but achieving its fullest statement in *Art and the Aesthetic: An Institutional Analysis* (1974). According to the institutional definition, arthood is a status conferred on artifacts by agents of the artworld. More specifically, an artwork is "(1) an artifact (2) a set of the aspects of which has had conferred upon it the status of candidate for appreciation by some person or persons acting on behalf of . . . the artworld" (1974: 179–80). The status of art might be merited more or less according to the usual aesthetic or other criteria, but what makes something art is that it is dubbed as such by someone with the authority so to declare it, and not whether it deserves the title.

A similar view was developed by the British philosopher Terry Diffey, also in 1969. The main respect in which his account differs from Dickie's is in maintaining that it is the artworld public who collectively bestow the status of art. Dickie, by contrast, holds that it is individual agents – almost always the artists who created the works – who do this. But it should be noted that Dickie's is not a more elitist account on this score, because he thought almost any member of the artworld could create art and thereby count themselves an artist, and he characterized the art institution as extensive and informal, not confined to academies and professionals.

The institutional theory caused considerable debate among aestheticians, and this persists. Among the major concerns is that the theory tends to be circular and that it loses sight of the point of art-making by attaching too much significance to provocative, anti-aesthetic works, such as Duchamp's *Fountain*. Meanwhile, it is far from clear that the artworld is institutional in structure, so it is difficult to make sense of the idea of agents acting on behalf of the institution. Also, art is made in other cultures and earlier times, often in connection with religious or political institutions, where it is even less plausible to identify an autonomous, structured artworld.

Dickie revised his theory in *The Art Circle: A Theory of Art* (1984) in a way that downplayed talk of baptismal acts of status conferral. He stressed that the artist works not so much as an agent of an institution but against the background of a practice and, through work on an artifact, achieves, rather than confers, the art standing of his or her works. As the title suggests, Dickie flaunts the circularity of his account. By removing the emphasis on institutional authority and structure, he avoids some objections to the earlier version of the theory but also loses much of its explanatory power, because it is less clear how the conventions and social practices that are the background to the artist's work play a role in the achievement of arthood.

Dickie's work stimulated interest in the definition of art more generally. (For an account and critical discussion, see Davies 1991.) In a series of articles from 1979–83, Beardsley developed a definition in terms of art's aesthetic function: an artwork is either an arrangement of conditions intended to be capable of affording an aesthetic experience with marked aesthetic character, or an arrangement of a type that is typically intended to have this capacity. Definitions that make art's aesthetic function central to its nature have been regularly presented since Beardsley's, a more recent example being by Nick Zangwill (1995). Others took up Danto's suggestions regarding the historicity of art to produce recursive definitions with the form: something is art if it stands in the art-defining relation to earlier art, and the first artworks were art because . . . According to Jerrold Levinson (1979), the art-defining relation is that of being intended for a type of regard accorded to earlier art, whereas James Carney (1991) saw it as a matter of shared styles. Noël Carroll (1988), who claimed to be characterizing art's extension rather than defining it, regarded as art those pieces that can be fitted into a true narrative of the ongoing unfolding of art practices. Inevitably, attempts have been made to integrate or combine these different strategies for definition, as in Robert Stecker's *Artworks: Definition, Meaning, Value* (1997). Meanwhile, the antiessentialism of the 1950s is also frequently revived, a recent version being Berys Gaut's cluster theory (2000), which maintains that different subsets of a cluster of features can be sufficient for something's being art, with no single feature being necessary.

As well as stimulating attempts to define art, arguments for the social character of art led also to interest in the ontology of art, which previously was a neglected topic. The Polish philosopher Roman Ingarden, whose works were not translated into English until the 1970s and 1980s, as well as both Wollheim and Goodman, contributed to this awakening, but it was Nicholas Wolterstorff's *Works and Worlds of Art* (1980) that focused on works of art as cultural artifacts and stressed how, rather than being passively contemplated, they are used by their public for world projection. Also in 1980, Jerrold Levinson described the identity of musical works as essentially involving not only sequences of sound but also their composer's identity and their instrumental means of realization.

In the remaining decades of the twentieth century, the ontology of art remained consistently high on the agenda of debate, with Platonists arguing that artworks are abstract types that are discovered rather than created, ontological contextualists arguing that they take their identity in part from relations they hold to their context of creation, and relativists arguing that they have an evolving identity that alters with their ongoing interpretation.

Interest in the historical character of art reflected the influence of Danto's *The Transfiguration of the Commonplace* (1981). In this work, Danto developed some of the main themes of his earlier papers. He emphasized how art, even as it came to resemble "mere real things," like urinals and Brillo boxes, separates itself from them, because it is "about" its nature in a way that mere real things are not about theirs. Inevitably, then, to be appreciated artworks must be distinguished from their material substrate. Meanwhile, the identification of a work's subject and style depends in part on awareness of its art-historical location, including the identity of its artist, because a given element or feature can vary in its significance according to that location. Perceptually indiscernible paintings by a child, a forger, and an established artist would possess very different characteristics, as would look-alikes created within different art traditions or at a historical remove from each other. Somewhat obscurely, Danto compared artworks with metaphors; they are rhetorical devices that are not to be read literally and that are used to convey an attitude toward a subject matter.

Beginning with "The End of Art" (1984), Danto developed a neo-Hegelian account of art's historical essence. According to Hegel, art was one phase of spirit's attempt to understand itself, and when this phase was completed, prior to the Christian era, art had fulfilled its historical destiny and in that sense its history came to an end. In a similar vein, Danto argued that art's historical purpose was to provoke the philosophical analysis of its own nature, and this was achieved with Pop Art in the late 1960s. Such art could not be analyzed in terms of mimesis, representation, or expression, and presented an appearance that did not distinguish it from nonart, so traditional theories of art were defeated and a new account, such as the one Danto proposed, was called for. Danto's observations that, in its posthistorical phase, art could have nothing new to say and that anything could be art do not sit comfortably with the other strand of his historicism, because the significance of any given artistic gesture depended as much on its art-historical location after 1968 as before it. In any case, the historical purpose Danto describes for art looks like only one among many possibilities and a secondary one at that, given art's politico-social significance and use over millennia.

If *The Transfiguration of the Commonplace* was the book of the 1980s, that of the 1990s was Kendall L. Walton's *Mimesis as Make-Believe: On the Foundations of the Representational Arts* (1990). Walton here built on his earlier work on the centrality of make-believe to the appreciation of art. His guiding idea was that artworks are props in games of make-believe, just as dolls or stuffed animals are in children's games. Some of these games are authorized by the work's author or by conventions of the work's kind. For instance, the Sherlock Holmes stories authorize the pretense that there is a brilliant detective who lives on Baker Street in London. Others are more optional or ad hoc. One of the basic virtues of this account is that it transcends the specific media through which artworks are presented, applying equally well to fictional literature, painting, and film among other art forms. The other basic virtue of the account is more important. Walton was able to deploy his guiding idea to provide ingenious solutions to a wide array of issues raised by fictional representation. These range from seeming paradoxes regarding our emotional reactions to fictions – Why should we fear fictional monsters or pity the protagonists of tragedy? – to questions about the ontological status of fictional characters, and to the nature of both pictorial representation and artistic expression. Walton's reliance on the idea of make-believe or pretense also raises general issues about the nature of the imagination and its role in human development and human life.

DEBATE AT THE CLOSE OF THE CENTURY

As in other areas of philosophy, there was a virtual explosion of publications in the final decades of the last century. For this reason, it is not possible to convey the variety of topics covered and the richness of the debate by highlighting a few books or seminal articles. We have already indicated how the definition and ontology of art became extensively discussed, but other trends and movements since the 1980s should also be listed.

The nature of artistic interpretation is another topic reinvigorated by the emphasis of social and historical context. If work identity is context sensitive, it is very plausible that the meaning of a work would also be. That some such features are crucial in fixing meaning is now widely accepted, but which ones, even which contexts, is hotly debated. One debate pits the context of creation against successive contexts of reception as the ones that are crucial for understanding and appreciating works. Those who agree that the context of creation is the crucial one, disagree about which features of this are the meaning-fixing ones. Some give that role to the actual intentions of artists, while others give more weight to other contextual properties.

Philosophical aesthetics traditionally took painting, poetry, drama, and literature as its exemplars, but since the 1980s there has been a major expansion in the discussion of music, including rock and jazz, of film, and of the mass and popular arts. Architecture, sculpture, and dance remain comparatively underrepresented in the discussion.

The emphasis on art's sociocultural location, rather than leading to neglect of natural and environmental aesthetics, stimulated new discussion there. Of leading concern has been consideration of the "frame" or categories under which nature is appropriately to be brought for aesthetic appreciation. Another area of growth is in regard to the connection between art and ethics. The interest here is not so much in the longstanding topics of pornography and censorship, but in art as a source of moral knowledge on the one hand and in the interaction of aesthetic and ethical value within the appreciation of art on the other. Meanwhile, beauty and the aesthetic, rather than being driven from the debate by the 1960s attack on traditional conceptions of these, have been redescribed and reintroduced to the discussion.

Intersecting with some of these trends is the rise of feminist studies within aesthetics. Feminists discussed the social context of art in political terms, noticing how women were systematically excluded from creative roles while they were featured in art as passive subjects for the delectation of an audience assumed to be male. They addressed the role of art in confirming and shaping identity, gender, and sexuality. Again, this led to a questioning of claims made on behalf of traditional aesthetics for the disinterested, distanced objectivity of the aesthetic attitude, for the value of an established canon of *master*works, and for the connection claimed between creativity and egocentric genius. Some feminists reversed or challenged the ranking of fine art over craft, intellect over emotion, the sensory over the sensual. Meanwhile, artworks created by women with art-political feminist agendas, along with attempts to develop styles of criticism based on feminist sensibilities, provided material for theoretical debate and analysis.

Another movement matched elsewhere in philosophy was the naturalization of aesthetics, in which philosophers drew on scientific studies of human nature, of the operation of the brain, of cognitive, perceptual, and affective systems, and of human evolution and child development, in explaining our relation to art and nature. The growth of cognitive science, in particular, has proved relevant to philosophical discussions of creativity, emotion, imagination, language use, sympathy and empathy, synaesthesia and metaphor, and of the principles that govern our organization of sight and sound. In some cases, the scientific data concern art and are imported to aesthetics directly. More often, empirical data that are more generally relevant to issues in the philosophy of mind, epistemology, identity, emotion, ethics, and politics are taken up and applied to the creation, reception, and criticism of art.

STATUS WITHIN THE PROFESSION

Though art received the attention of famous Greek philosophers and, following Kant, featured in the work of many Continental philosophers, such as Hegel, Schopenhauer, and Nietzsche, within Anglo-American academic philosophy of the twentieth century it was largely ignored and sometimes treated with disdain. George Dickie once explained how he first came to teach aesthetics: the course went to the department's most recent and junior appointee. Unless they had a special passion for it, the most rigorously trained analytic philosophers hardly came across analytic aesthetics at all. No one who hoped for academic employment would highlight it as an area of specialty.

In his introduction to *Aesthetics*, Beardsley observed: "Aesthetics has long been contemptuously regarded as a step-sister within the philosophical family. Her rejection is easy to explain, and partially excuse, by the lack of tidiness in her personal habits and by her unwillingness to make herself generally useful around the house. It is plain to even a casual visitor that aesthetics is a retarded child" (1958: 11). Though he seemed here to lay the blame for this situation at the door of aesthetics, rather than at the narrow-mindedness of the profession, he believed aesthetics could raise its game. Indeed, there can be no question that his book contributed enormously to its doing so. And it is pleasing to think, as one surveys the many passionate debates in contemporary aesthetics and the philosophy of art, that work in the area meets an appropriate standard for quality.

Yet if aesthetics has redeemed itself, as one hopes, it remains marginal if not marginalized within Anglo-American analytic philosophy, though more so in the United States and Australasia than in Britain. What has gone, perhaps, is the sense of guilt that once led talented philosophers to apologize for squandering their gifts there.

See also AESTHETIC ATTITUDE; BEARDSLEY; BELL; COLLINGWOOD; CROCE; DANTO; DEWEY; DICKIE; EXPRESSION THEORY; FORMALISM; FUNCTION OF ART; GOODMAN; LANGER; ONTOLOGICAL CONTEXTUALISM; PRAGMATIST AESTHETICS; SCRUTON; SIBLEY; THEORIES OF ART; TOLSTOY; WALTON; WITTGENSTEIN; WOLLHEIM.

BIBLIOGRAPHY

Aldrich, Virgil C. 1963. *Philosophy of Art*. Englewood Cliffs: Prentice-Hall.

Beardsley, Monroe C. 1958. *Aesthetics: Problems in the Philosophy of Criticism*. New York: Harcourt, Brace & World.

Beardsley, Monroe C. 1983. "An Aesthetic Definition of Art." In *What Is Art?* H. Curtler (ed.). New York: Haven, 15–29.

Beardsley, Monroe C. & Wimsatt, William K., Jr. 1946. "The Intentional Fallacy," *Sewanee Review*, 54, 468–88.

Bell, Clive. *Art*. 1914. London: Chatto & Windus.

Bullough, Edward. 1912. " 'Psychical Distance' as a Factor in Art and as an Aesthetic Principle," *British Journal of Psychology*, 5, 87–98.

Carney, James D. 1991. "The Style Theory of Art," *Pacific Philosophical Quarterly*, 72, 273–89.

Carroll, Noël. 1988. "Art, Practice, and Narrative," *Monist*, 71, 140–56.

Collingwood, R. G. 1938. *The Principles of Art*. Oxford: Clarendon.

Croce, Benedetto. 1965. *Guide to Aesthetics*. P. Romanell (trans.). New York: Bobbs-Merrill.

Danto, Arthur C. 1964. "The Artworld," *Journal of Philosophy*, 61, 571–84.

Danto, Arthur C. 1981. *The Transfiguration of the Commonplace*. Cambridge, MA: Harvard University Press.

Danto, Arthur C. 1984. "The End of Art." In *The Death of Art*. B. Lang (ed.). New York: Haven, 5–35.

Davies, Stephen. 1991. *Definitions of Art*. Ithaca: Cornell University Press.

Dewey, John. 1987 [1934]. *Art as Experience*. Chicago: Open Court.

Dickie, George. 1962. "Is Psychology Relevant to Aesthetics?" *Philosophical Review*, 71, 285–302.

Dickie, George. 1964. "The Myth of the Aesthetic Attitude," *American Philosophical Quarterly*, 1, 56–65.

Dickie, George. 1965. "Beardsley's Phantom Aesthetic Experience," *Journal of Philosophy*, 62, 129–36.

Dickie, George. 1968. "Art Narrowly and Broadly Speaking," *American Philosophical Quarterly*, 5, 71–7.

Dickie, George. 1974. *Art and the Aesthetic: An Institutional Analysis*. Ithaca: Cornell University Press.

Dickie, George. 1984. *The Art Circle: A Theory of Art*. New York: Haven.

Diffey, T. J. 1969. "The Republic of Art," *British Journal of Aesthetics*, 9, 145–56.

Fry, Roger. 1956 [1928]. *Vision and Design*. New York: Meridian.

Gaut, Berys. 2000. " 'Art' as a Cluster Concept." In *Theories of Art Today*. N. Carroll (ed.). Madison: University of Wisconsin Press, 25–44.

Greenberg, Clement. 1961. *Art and Culture*. Boston: Beacon.

Goodman, Nelson. 1968. *Languages of Art*. New York: Bobbs-Merrill.

Goodman, Nelson. 1978. *Ways of Worldmaking*. Indianapolis: Hackett.

Hampshire, Stuart. 1954. "Logic and Appreciation." In *Aesthetics and Language*. E. Elton (ed.). Oxford: Blackwell, 161–9.

Langer, Susanne. 1942. *Philosophy in a New Key*. Cambridge, MA: Harvard University Press.

Langer, Susanne. 1953. *Feeling and Form*. New York: Scribner.

Levinson, Jerrold. 1979. "Defining Art Historically," *British Journal of Aesthetics*, 19, 232–50.

Levinson, Jerrold. 1980. "What a Musical Work Is," *Journal of Philosophy*, 77, 5–28.

Scruton, Roger. 1974. *Art and Imagination*. London: Methuen.

Shusterman, Richard. 2001. "Pragmatism: Dewey." In *Routledge Companion to Aesthetics*. B. Gaut & D. McIver Lopes (eds.). London: Routledge, 97–106.

Sibley, Frank. 1959. "Aesthetic Concepts," *Philosophical Review*, 68, 421–50.

Stecker, Robert. 1997. *Artworks: Definition, Meaning, Value*. University Park: Pennsylvania State University Press

Strawson, Peter. 1974. "Aesthetic Appraisal and Works of Art." In *Freedom and Resentment*. London: Methuen, 178–88.

Tolstoy, Leo. 1930. *What is Art?* A. Maude (trans.). Oxford: Oxford University Press.

Walton, Kendall L. 1970. "Categories of Art," *Philosophical Review*, 79, 334–67.

Walton, Kendall L. 1973. "Pictures and Make-Believe," *Philosophical Review*, 82, 283–319.

Walton, Kendall L. 1990. *Mimesis as Make-Believe: On the Foundations of the Representational Arts*. Cambridge, MA: Harvard University Press.

Wittgenstein, Ludwig. 1953. *Philosophical Investigations*. G. E. M. Anscombe (trans.). New York: Macmillan.

Wittgenstein, Ludwig. 1966. *Lectures and Conversation on Aesthetics, Psychology, and Religious Belief*. C. Barrett (ed.). Oxford: Blackwell.

Wollheim, Richard. 1968. *Art and Its Objects*. New York: Harper & Row.

Wolterstorff, Nicholas. 1980. *Works and Worlds of Art*. Oxford: Clarendon.

Zangwill, Nick. 1995. "The Creative Theory of Art," *American Philosophical Quarterly*, 32, 307–23.

STEPHEN DAVIES & ROBERT STECKER

The Arts

architecture   If we think of a range of candidates listed and proposed for admission to the status of architecture, we would find that all or most are buildings. Other designed objects, desks, chairs, shoes, shirts, cars, and carpets might be included for candidature, but buildings would occupy a central place within the list. Let us then consider buildings. There are two ways in which we might think a building beautiful: the first as a natural phenomenon, the second as a work of art. Human beings design buildings within which to prosecute the commerce of their daily lives. However, so too do birds, badgers, bumblebees, and beavers. The nest, the set, the hive, and the dam are all in some sense "built" by their occupants. Moreover, we think of these natural habitats as beautiful. Why should we not think of our buildings along such lines? Or, conversely, why should we not think of nests, sets, hives, and dams as architecture?

There is a single answer to both of these questions. We think of architecture as an art. That is, we do not think of the buildings we design, *as architecture*, being part of nature's beauty, and we do not think of the habitats constructed in the natural world as works of art. A creature's nature is written into it. Its behavior is best understood as compulsive – determined by its genetic program. The birds and the bees have no conception of what they are doing as they build, and no judgment enters into the construction of nest or hive that might critically and crucially alter the appearance of the creature's refuge. We may look on such natural shelters as part of nature's wonder, but nature herself is blind to her beauty. Birds and bees do not look at their work or consider its merits. They are merely driven to inhabit.

By contrast, our regard for architecture is shaped by consideration of what the architect was doing when designing the building. We see the architect's *aesthetic* solution to a problem that the design brief has presented. We do not merely inhabit our built environment. We regard it as a repository of our values, and we see it as imbued with the standing that other works of art have in their respective fields.

Great buildings, works of architecture, are accorded the status of great works of art. If that is so, and we are to think of architecture as an art, we might consider the ways in which we are called on to appreciate its works. Two interrelated questions present themselves immediately: (1) What does architecture have in common with some or all of the other arts? (What makes it an art?) (2) And what is peculiar to architecture as an art? (What makes it the art that it is?)

We have already begun to answer (1). In separating architecture's buildings from the natural habitats of wild creatures we observed that our building – where that is to be considered architecture – includes consideration of the architect's critical response to a perceived aesthetic problem. The judgment of the architect shows up in the building at which we look. Architecture, then, is a visual art. We need to look at its works in order best to understand what it is that the architect has done in building this work. No natural habitat is properly observed under this condition. We might be amused, awed, and amazed at the complexity and regularity to be seen in a hive. We might be dispirited, dejected, and disappointed at the mess in which some sort of animal passes its life. But we cannot heap praise or blame on the animal for its judgment in its choice of environment. For it makes no such judgment. Our amazement or disappointment is directed at nature as a whole and not at the individual animal.

Architecture, like the other arts, engages our understanding. This has persuaded some of the linguistic nature of art. Art, some think, is intrinsically linguistic, and it is because it bears such meaning that it acquires the status of art. The added feature of "reference" is what elevates what would otherwise be a mere building to the status of a work of architecture. Nelson Goodman provides an account of three routes of reference. These are: (1) denotation, as when we come to regard the Sydney Opera House as denoting sailboats; (2) exemplification, as when we understand certain forms of modernist architecture as literally exemplifying their means of construction; and (3) expression, as when a building, say a Gothic cathedral, metaphorically exemplifies properties it could not literally possess, say "soaring" and "singing." It is because we follow these routes of reference that we come to understand the building at which we look (Goodman 1988). The problem of such a view, however, is that it fails to account for the value we place on the building in virtue of the experience we undergo. It elevates the hamburger-shaped hamburger stand to the status of architecture, and leaves us wondering if some great works of architecture are architectural works at all (Winters 2007). (There are some buildings that we seem to appreciate without readily being able to provide the required routes of reference.) The view provides an account of elevation but remains silent concerning evaluation.

Understanding architecture is concerned with our *experience* of its works in ways that the linguistic account leaves out of consideration. In coming to understand architecture – in order to appreciate it – we look at the work and consider the complex and interrelated sets of judgments that the architect has had to deal with in making a coherent and significant work. Like all works of art, architecture requires aesthetic understanding as a component part of appreciation. Such appreciation is an enjoyed understanding. That enjoyment is internal to the special kind of understanding involved in aesthetic appreciation, so that the critical dimension of understanding provides content and character to the enjoyment we gain from contemplating a work. That may seem odd. My enjoyment of marzipan does not require understanding. However, it should be clear that my enjoyment of a novel, film, or piece of music does consist in my understanding the

significance of the particular work within the framework of the art within which it is placed. Since architecture is a visual art, our appreciation is directed toward the look of the building. Hence, the significance of a work of architecture resides in its visual appearance. So architecture, like all the arts, requires appreciation, which consists in a pleasurable contemplation shaped by our understanding of the architect's work. As with the other visual arts, which include painting and sculpture – and distinct from the nonvisual arts such as music and literature – appreciation brings understanding and judgment into contact with the *visual appearance* of the work.

We come now to our second question. Among the arts, what is it that is special to architecture? For the sake of convenience, we can further refine this question. What distinguishes architecture from the other visual arts? What is it that makes something architecture? To that question we can say that architecture is constrained by the need to provide us with accommodation. Architecture, that is, serves a practical purpose, whereas the other arts do not. Since our appreciation of architecture requires us to consider the sets of judgments that the architect makes in designing a building, it is clear that fitness for purpose is one constraint that the architect must observe in the practice of design. This has prompted some to think of architecture as an impure art, hampered in its artistic ambitions by the need to serve some purpose.

The purposefulness of architecture is not a burden but a defining characteristic. Purposefulness provides the resistance peculiar to the architectural project. "The light dove, cleaving the air in her free flight, and feeling its resistance, might imagine that its flight would be still easier in empty space" (Kant 1964: 47). Of course, flight is impossible in empty space, air being the resistance required for flight. Representation (broadly construed) might be considered a defining characteristic of painting, its removal leaving dumb color and pattern, mere pleasantries. The struggle to create an image provides the resistance against which the artist can work, making sense of painting as an artistic activity. So, in architecture the purposefulness of the building proves resistant to the architect's efforts to organize our occupancy of the environment. It is because we understand that works of architecture are built for our purposes that we are able to value them as works of art. (That is why we wondered if cars and carpets might be admitted as candidates for the status of architecture.) Such a view of architecture is not committed to functionalism. It says only that we are constrained in our understanding of architecture by the fact that buildings are made for our occupancy. It makes no commitment to a style or method. The view put simply commends the baroque, the rococo, and the postmodern, as well as the austere building designed as a result of functionalist polemic.

Another essential feature of architecture is its public aspect. Architectural works of art impinge upon a public and ought to be designed in light of this fact. The character of a building, then, must regard a public who might have no choice in confronting it. Thus the need for politeness in the work is written into the discipline. Hence, works of architecture are inappropriate vehicles for the expression of the architect's emotion or the representation of particular scenes. Architecture is neither a fully representational art nor yet a fully expressive art. Architecture, rather, deploys allusion in the frames it provides for our daily commerce. "My ideal is a certain coolness. A temple providing a setting for the passions without meddling with them" (Wittgenstein 1980: 3e). We think of architecture as providing suitable surroundings for the activities we pursue in our public lives. If privacy is dealt with in architecture, it is at the level of the domestic interior. Indeed, the exterior/interior distinction serves well, up to a point, as a metaphor for the public/private. Its functionality and its essential publicity are the two features of architecture that mark it out as a special art. Each of these aspects contributes to its status as an art in which civic values are enshrined. Architecture, like ritual and ceremony, brings people together in the presence of shared value and it is within the embrace of architecture that we are able to feel at home. Hence, in pessimistic mood, Wittgenstein remarked, "Architecture immortalizes and glorifies something. Hence there can be no architecture where there is nothing to glorify" (1980: 64e.)

See also AESTHETIC PLEASURE; AESTHETICS OF THE ENVIRONMENT; AESTHETICS OF THE EVERYDAY; FUNCTION OF ART; GARDENS; MODERNISM AND POSTMODERNISM; TECHNOLOGY AND ART.

BIBLIOGRAPHY
de Botton, Alain. 2006. *The Architecture of Happiness*. London: Hamish Hamilton.
Forty, Adrian. 2000. *Words and Buildings*. London: Thames & Hudson.
Goodman, Nelson. 1988. "How Buildings Mean." In *Reconceptions in Philosophy and Other Arts and Sciences*. Nelson Goodman & Catherine Z. Elgin. London: Routledge, 31–48.
Graham, Gordon. 2000. *Philosophy of the Arts*. 3rd edn. London: Routledge, ch. 7.
Kant, Immanuel. 1964. *The Critique of Pure Reason*. N. Kemp Smith (trans.). London: Macmillan.
Leach, Neil (ed.). 1997. *Rethinking Architecture: A Reader in Cultural Theory*. London: Routledge.
Scruton, Roger. 1979. *The Aesthetics of Architecture*. London: Methuen.
Scruton, Roger. 1994. *The Classical Vernacular*. Manchester: Carcanet.
van Eck, Caroline. 1994. *Organicism in Nineteenth Century Architecture*. Amsterdam: Architectura and Natura.
Winters, Edward. 2007. *Aesthetics and Architecture*. London: Continuum.
Wittgenstein, L. 1980. *Culture and Value*. G. H. von Wright (ed.). Peter Winch (trans.). Chicago: University of Chicago Press.

EDWARD WINTERS

dance The paucity of attention to dance by aestheticians has long been lamented, but recent decades have seen increasing attention from several important vantage points.

While familiar analyses from major art forms, especially music, literature, and visual art, can be extrapolated to dance, the uniqueness of the central role of the human body suggests that special approaches are needed. Studies in music inform our understanding of rhythm and harmony. Our attention to literature elaborates the role of character and plot development. The visual arts address unique and nonverbal symbol systems of communication. Dance draws on all these art forms in varying degrees, yet remains a special challenge in its complexity and its distinctive central use of the human body as instrument.

The range of philosophical questions concerning dance is vast, as familiar debates in Western aesthetics have been applied to dance. What is the definition of "dance"? How does it comport with proposed definitions of "art" in general? Can we identify necessary and sufficient conditions of dance? With the interest in everyday movement, ritual, happenings, and performance art, do institutional definitions of dance better account for our understanding of this art form than focusing on the essential properties of the art object?

The ontological status of dance as a performing art has been especially challenging for philosophers. Live bodies moving in space, typically with musical or rhythmic accompaniment of some kind, resist familiar explanations from other art forms. The identity of individual works of art in dance is also a special challenge, not only because of the recent emergence of notation and techniques for recording movement, but also the still-evolving standards for what counts as a work in the dance world community.

Historic comments on the aesthetics of dance have been identified in the work of Plato, Aristotle, Hegel, and others, although their attention typically was limited and embedded in discussions of other art forms. In the twentieth century, philosophers such as Monroe C. Beardsley, Noël Carroll, Francis Sparshott, Nelson Goodman, Susanne Langer, and Graham McFee focused with more precision on special issues in dance, especially expressive and communicative capacities of the art form.

Of all the arts, dance would seem to have the most natural expressiveness, as it uses the entire human body itself. Expression is not limited to metaphorical or hypothetical or symbolic expression, for the body itself really does express a range of human emotions and attitudes in ordinary life. But this unique situation also raises questions unlike any other art form. What is the difference between the expression of an emotion by a person in an artwork in dance and the expression of an emotion by a person in an everyday life, nonart situation? Do the expressions in the artwork have a special presence or symbolism or universality that we do not experience when identical bodily movements are completed by a person in ordinary life?

While theories of art as expression, representation, or communication have been fruitful in understanding dance, formalism also has been particularly helpful with regard to twentieth-century plotless dance, from the neoclassical ballets of George Balanchine to postmodern dance, as illustrated in the writing of David Michael Levin.

The proper object of criticism, a special focus of Beardsley's approach to aesthetics, also has drawn interest from philosophers looking at dance, including George Dickie and Joseph Margolis. Dance presents a special set of complications because of rehearsal and performing conditions not perceivable during performance.

Aestheticians inclined to Continental and phenomenological approaches have fruitfully pursued distinctive perspectives. Maxine Sheets-Johnstone applies Maurice Merleau-Ponty's work on phenomenology to dance to suggest that the expression of movement is really a form of thinking through the body. Sandra Fraleigh uses existentialist thought to explain dance, and shares the emphasis on dance as a communicative vehicle for nonverbal thought. Susan Leigh Foster's work spawned substantial interest from dance theorists, importing poststructuralist criticism to highlight the active role of audiences interacting with new dance vocabularies and codes of contemporary dance.

Recent attention to the body, especially in feminist and Continental approaches to philosophy generally, has also addressed dance as a performing art from this broad perspective. Pragmatist philosopher Richard Shusterman has taken up a focus on the body in the performing arts in what he calls somaesthetics, emphasizing the role of our own physical experiences as opposed to theorizing or verbal interpretation.

Work in cultural studies has broadened to performance studies, which emphasize the broader historical and cultural context of all performances in the arts, including dance. While more traditional approaches have recognized those contexts, as in John Dewey's emphasis on ordinary experience in understanding art, recent trends in performance studies renew this broad emphasis for interpretative understanding.

Overdue attention to non-Western cultures has further enriched the exploration of the cultural phenomenon of dance, as both a social activity and a performing art. While most work in dance aesthetics still focuses almost exclusively on the Western dance tradition, the landmark *International Encyclopedia of Dance* drew welcome attention to dance aesthetics in African, Asian, and Islamic cultures and the writing of Lois Lamya' al-Faruqi, Frederick Lamp, and A. C. Scott. Of special significance is the integration of religious, cultural, and social dimensions of dance, as well as its interdisciplinary fusion with a broad range of other artistic expression.

Given the marginalized status of the art form for so much of its history, even today, thoughtful work in related disciplines that ventures into philosophical dimensions has been particularly valued. In the eighteenth century, John Weaver and Jean-Georges Noverre were theorists and choreographers whose writing constitutes some of the earliest focused attention to the nature of dance. In the twentieth century, the philosophically informed work of dance historians Selma Jeanne Cohen and Sally Banes has been particularly valuable in this dialogue. The philosophically sensitive criticism of such critics as Arlene Croce has focused on the rationale for evaluative standards used broadly in the art form. Rudolf von Laban, a modern dance choreographer who developed today's most important form of notation, also wrote extensively on the nature of dance, with special emphasis on natural expressiveness.

For philosophers who consider aesthetics to be the study of criticism ("talk about talk about art," as Beardsley said), the breadth and quality of dance criticism has improved dramatically in the twentieth century with such writers as Jack Anderson, Deborah Jowitt, Anna Kisselgoff, Alan Kriegsman, John Martin, Marcia B. Siegel, and Carl Van Vechten.

While dance has not yet achieved the stature and importance of the major art forms of music, literature, and visual art, its complex nature and its historic ties to cultural and religious phenomena ensure that it will remain an intriguing if ever perplexing art form of interest to aestheticians.

See also MUSIC AND SONG; DEFINITION OF "ART"; EXPRESSION; FEMINIST AESTHETICS; NOTATIONS; ONTOLOGY OF ARTWORKS; PERFORMANCE.

BIBLIOGRAPHY

Best, David. 1978. *Philosophy and Human Movement*. London: Allen & Unwin.

Cohen, Selma Jeanne. 1982. *Next Week, Swan Lake: Reflections on Dance and Dances*. Middletown: Wesleyan University Press.

Fancher, Gordon & Myers, Gerald (eds.). 1981. *Philosophical Essays on Dance*. Brooklyn: Dance Horizons.

Foster, Susan Leigh. 1986. *Reading Dancing: Bodies and Subjects in Contemporary American Dance*. Berkeley: University of California Press.

Fraleigh, Sandra. 2004. *Dancing Identity: Metaphysics in Motion*. Pittsburgh: University of Pittsburgh Press.

Lepecki, Andre (ed.). 2004. *Of the Presence of the Body: Essays on Dance and Performance Theory*. Middleton: Wesleyan University Press.

McFee, Graham. 1992. *Understanding Dance*. London: Routledge.

Sheets-Johnstone, Maxine (ed.). 1984. *Illuminating Dance: Philosophical Explorations*. Lewisburg: Bucknell University Press.

Shusterman, Richard. 2008. *Body Consciousness: A Philosophy of Mindfulness and Somaesthetics*. New York: Cambridge University Press.

Sparshott, Francis. 1988. *Off the Ground: First Steps to a Philosophical Consideration of the Dance*. Princeton: Princeton University Press.

JULIE VAN CAMP

drama In recent years, two seemingly insoluble issues have confronted the scholar interested in particular works of drama. The first is the degree to which she should engage with those features a work of drama might possess because it was written for performance. Call this the "constraint problem." The second is whether, because of its peculiar history or nature, drama is a stable *literary* category at all. Call this the "instability problem." The constraint problem is an immediate question concerning the relevant features for an analysis or interpretation. The instability problem is a concern if artistic categories are not just taxonomic but are appealed to in explaining particular works of literature. These issues have a common source, namely, the connections and disconnections between dramatic literature and theatrical performance. So they are not always distinguished.

"Drama" is also beset with definition problems. First, "drama" cannot be defined as a basic *form* of literature, as it is sometimes taken to be, distinct from the two other basic literary forms, poetry and prose. To mark the relevant distinctions among basic forms of literature, one must call attention to some aspect of their characteristic uses of language. For example, poetry is often thought to be separable from other writing because of its attention to the formal features of words in combination: rhythm, alliteration, and meter in particular. Likewise, prose is often thought to be separable from poetic writing by being concerned mainly with features of the senses of words, not with their sensible features. Drama too is frequently said to be a separable basic form of literature. However, what marks that distinction is the manner in which its speakers are identified or individuated. Immediately we see this is a comparatively odd term of contrast. The first two modes of contrast are clear enough, even if they only mark relative emphases. But nothing in poetry or prose, as demarcated above, is clearly contrasted with what is ordinarily taken to be the central mark of dramatic literature: the use of dialogue. Dialogue, even dialogue set out with explicit speech prefixes, does not contrast with a concern for either the forms of words or their senses.

Second, "drama" cannot easily be distinguished as a more specific sort of artistic category like "genre" or "literary kind," where the comparison class would include lyric poetry, epic, the novel, romance, short story, among others. Once again, what must be said about drama to mark the relevant distinctions will be some aspect of its characteristic uses of language. Once again, the manner of its written representation of speech – the use of dialogue – is not the sort of feature in terms of which we can contrast drama with these other genres or literary kinds. For example, there is no principled reason a lyric poem, even a sonnet, could not be written in dialogue. This could be one effective way to give voice to indecision in poem or song.

But suppose we think of a "dramatic work" as any narrative writing that is both script-like – *typically* but not exclusively written in dialogue – and actually read for any literary features or values the work possesses. And suppose we think of a "script," in contrast to a dramatic work, as any writing that is actually used as a source of one or more ingredients in a theatrical production by means of providing words or, more generally, information that is to be presented in some particular order. That is, I am proposing that any given piece of writing may function *either* as a work of literature *or* as a script and I am not insisting that the script-like character of the writing be determined in only one way. I allow that a dramatic work may not be judged to be literature in anything more than the fairly broad sense that it is written language. So some readers may judge a given dramatic work as not having literary features and values in sufficient quantity to warrant being called "literature" in either the sense of belles-lettres or in the yet more restrictive sense of imaginative and creative art. But I define a work of dramatic literature in terms of what it could be: it is prima facie literature in a more robust sense because it is language that can be read for the features and values *of its writing*. To stipulate that a work of dramatic literature be script-like, however that is determined, allows that the object might have been written for use in theatrical performance. Since there is theater without drama, without narrative, and even without scripts of any kind, this stipulation simply notes one possible alternative function of a given piece of writing.

Although this way of marking dramatic literature has kinships with the foregoing definitions, it is a more relaxed approach that has several advantages over those views. By appealing only to typical marks of being script-like, it allows even greater scope for the fact that there is no clean way to distinguish dramatic literature from other forms, genres, or kinds of narrative literature. And it allows for the determination of any quality, and hence any positioning within/outside a literary canon, to be decided or contested by readers on substantive grounds and not by philosophical *fiat*. Further, because it distinguishes between works of dramatic literature and scripts in terms of their functions, it allows for judgments deriving from literary and theatrical analyses of the same piece of writing to overlap but still to be aimed at different functions. Finally, it does not preclude the use of writing that is not typically script-like – ostensibly nondramatic literary texts – as scripts for theater.

In contrast to the definition problems, the constraint and instability problems with which we began initially appear quite insoluble. These problems have to do with the connection between drama as a literary form, kind, or genre, and the extraliterary institution of theatrical performance.

The constraint problem has two aspects. Seen from the side of literature, it can be stated this way: should the fact that a text is written for performance constrain the critical interpretations we can reasonably give it? The fact that it is performed in a specific place and over a specific stretch of time can always be said to constrain the text on that occasion. But this allows that there is always more than one possible meaning to the text and that any given performance can realize only one of them. Moreover, without real information about prior productions and given the historical and imaginative limits of actual literary critics, only a limited number of performance possibilities can actually be in play in a literary analysis or interpretation of a work of dramatic literature. Anyone who offers what is called "stage-centered literary criticism" of dramatic texts – for example, B. Beckerman, A. C. Dessen, and J. L. Styan – attempts to constrain dramatic criticism so that it is responsible only to the possibilities of performance. But this now can seem seriously mistaken.

When seen from the side of theater the constraint problem can be put this way: should the fact that a script is written for performance constrain how it is used? The fact that it is written for performance can always be thought to determine what gets said, in what order, and maybe even by whom so long as the performers agree to use the script in that way. In particular cases they may have good reasons for doing so – reasons having to do with what can be achieved in the performance when it is undertaken in this manner. But this entails no logical demands, only aesthetic and, moreover, disputable demands that performers use a script in that way. Put in those terms, the attempt of H. Berger and others to conduct dramatic criticism by calling attention to the limits of what can be performed amounts to freeing literary criticism from the constraint of what is possible in performance, but at the apparent cost of treating the script as though it were not written for performance after all.

The instability problem can be put this way: Does the historical fact, that where there is no extraliterary institution of theater there is also no literature anyone calls "drama," entail that what counts as dramatic literature is unstable or destabilizing? One might wonder why it should. The first poems were spoken aloud. It is reasonable to think some sort of nonliterary institution of declamation preceded written poetry, since writing emerged in most cultures well after poetic storytelling. And even were that not the case, concerns with the formal features of rhythm and meter just are concerns with how language sounds when spoken. Yet poetry, as a literary type, does not seem to suffer any instability for these reasons. Poetry can exist quite well where there is no institution of declamation. Indeed that is now the case in many cultures. Still, one might think it less likely that dramatic literature could exist without the institution of theater. Works of dramatic literature not intended for performance do exist of course. In western European literature, Percy Bysshe Shelley's *The Cenci* and Karl Kraus's *The Last Days of Mankind* readily come to mind. But that sort of writing is exceptional in every culture that has dramatic literature. Most dramatic literature is written for public performance in a theater. And theater is not literature – it has to do with more, less, and frequently other than language. We can now set forth a simple argument for the claim that theater poses a deep problem for literature. Dramatic literature requires nonliterary action, theatrical performance, in order to fully achieve its effects and meanings. But theatrical performance – because of its materiality and its corresponding modes of apprehension – resists being understood in purely rhetorical and discursive (i.e., in literary) terms. If we recognize that dramatic literature cannot be clearly distinguished from other literary categories, it is hard to see how those other categories could be shown to be immune to the very same worry that theater poses for the category of dramatic literature: in short, can any work of literature be analyzed fully and purely in literary terms? The contingent facts of the history of dramatic literature seem to render the category of dramatic literature itself unstable and thereby to have a destabilizing effect on all of literature.

The solution I have offered to the definition problems also shows us a way to defuse these explosive and seemingly intractable debates recently occupying literary theory. It relaxes an implicit demand underwriting these problems, namely, the demand that we seek a way to take certain writings simultaneously as literary and as theatrical. Instead, I have held that a given piece of writing may be either a work of dramatic literature or a script, either a writing to be *read* for certain literary features and values or a writing to be *used* in a quite different way.

This relaxation in the definition of "drama" immediately undermines the main argument for the instability problem. If a bit of writing functions as a work of dramatic literature, then the relevant effects, features, and values to be analyzed and examined are exactly those analyzed and examined with respect to any other narrative literary work. Crucially, a work of dramatic literature does not require theatrical performance for the realization of those effects, features, or values. The first premise in the argument is false. And the argument for the claim that the category of dramatic literature is unstable and destabilizing for all literature is unsound.

Although this maneuver closes off the main argument for the instability problem for dramatic literature, it does not foreclose on what may be called a "literary theater." The content of a theatrical performance is not fully governed, deliverable, or retrievable by a written text. Still, if we think of scripts as "scores for action" (Saltz 1991), we should also think of them as providing particular orderings of the information an audience will encounter (Stoppard 1999). Some scripts do this to excellent effect; and, in theater parlance, they "have legs." Like some gymnastic or jazz routines, they are frequently repeated and approximated because – together with all the rest without which there is no performance – they yield performances that take our breath away. It is arguable that writing can contribute to this achievement for theater because it allows greater control over the flow and order of information than complex scenarios crafted for improvisational sequences can or, perhaps, even than is possible by means of scenarios and language passed down from performer to performer over time. Whatever the case may be with respect to the value of scripted performances over others, however, a script-driven theater is likely to be a literary theater simply because it will produce some written scripts that can – indeed, will – also be taken to function as works of literature.

Finally, this maneuver allows us to reframe the constraint problem by noting first that literary analyses of any work of dramatic literature that also happens to get used as a script may or may not be useful for performers, and by noting second that the dispute between stage-centered and text-centered *literary* criticism should be resolved, if at all, by appeal to some more general standard concerning the point of the aesthetic appreciation of works of literature and what that standard requires. For example, were the standard to require that we first give literary works their richest possible interpretations, we will favor text-centered literary criticism of works of drama. This might be the case if the goal of aesthetic appreciation is to maximize the aesthetic pleasure we can gain from a literary work. However, were the standard to require constraint by information about the intentions of actual (or hypothetical) authors, this would include the fact that their works were written to be performed and thereby tend to push us toward some version of stage-centered criticism. We might think this if we held an achievement standard for the aesthetic appreciation of literature. But determining which of these, if either, is the right sort of standard and imposes the right sort of restrictions or requirements on the aesthetic appreciation of literary works is not within the scope of this essay.

See also LITERATURE; POETRY; INTERPRETATION; NOTATIONS; PERFORMANCE.

BIBLIOGRAPHY

Beckerman, Bernard. 1979. *Dynamics of Drama: Theory and Method of Analysis.* New York: Drama Book Specialists.

Bennett, Benjamin. 1990. *Theater as Problem.* Ithaca: Cornell University Press.

Bennett, Benjamin. 1992. "Performance and the Exposure of Hermeneutics," *Theatre Journal,* 44, 431–47.

Bennett, Benjamin. 2005. *All Theater is Revolutionary Theater.* Ithaca: Cornell University Press.

Berger, Harry, Jr. 1989. *Imaginary Audition: Shakespeare on Stage and Page*. Los Angeles: University of California Press.

Dessen, Alan C. 1995. *Recovering Shakespeare's Theatrical Vocabulary*. Cambridge: Cambridge University Press.

Hamilton, James R. 2007. *The Art of Theater*. Malden: Blackwell.

Laetz, Brian & Lopes, Dominic McIver. 2008. "Genre." In *The Routledge Companion to Film and Philosophy*. P. Livingston & C. Plantinga (eds.). New York: Routledge, 152–61.

Lamarque, Peter & Olsen, Stein Haugom. 2005. "The Philosophy of Literature: Pleasure Restored." In *The Blackwell Guide to Aesthetics*. P. Kivy (ed.). Malden: Blackwell, 195–214.

Meskin, Aaron. 2001. "Style." In *The Routledge Companion to Aesthetics*. B. Gaut & D. McIver Lopes (eds.). 2nd edn. New York: Routledge, 489–500.

Saltz, David Z. 1991. "Texts in Action/Action in Texts: A Case Study of Critical Method," *Journal of Dramatic Theory and Criticism*, 6, 29–44.

Stoppard, Tom. 1999. "Pragmatic Theater," *New York Review of Books*, 46, 14.

Styan, J. L. 1975. *Drama, Stage and Audience*. Cambridge: Cambridge University Press.

JAMES HAMILTON

drawing, painting, and printmaking This introduction to the aesthetics of three great surface-marking fine arts focuses on drawing, with remarks on painting and printmaking organized around it.

Words for drawing reveal three main aspects: "drawing," the physical action of dragging one thing across another; the *dessin/disegno* group, planning or design; and a link between drawing and writing (*graphêi*). This mixture of connotations of constructive foresight, close-contact physical action, and mental expression seems strikingly appropriate.

Drawing and painting have been closely related since prehistory and the difference between them is often unclear, with countless variations of individual artistic practices. A serviceable distinction may be found by briefly characterizing painting. Color is a crucial factor closely associated with painting, of great meaning, but regarding which difficulty in theorizing is legendary. Fortunately, painting is best understood in terms of paint. Painting is covering surfaces by spreading layers of the stuff, typically successive layers built up from the ground. Thus its association with relatively wet media. By contrast, drawing, like writing, is a matter of dragging markers over surfaces, along roughly linear paths. Significantly, unlike painting, scratching or incising are common drawing techniques, which lead to printmaking. Drawing thereby tends to work by dividing rather than concealing its ground, often by defining distinct enclosures upon it. While painting typically covers its tracks, drawing leaves separately identifiable marks against the reserved ground.

THE NECESSITY OF DRAWING

That drawing, assisted by painting, is a basic human activity may be argued by a few historical observations. First, *Homo sapiens* is identified as an emerging species by its mental and social capacities, and drawing practices provide much of the evidence for that. Locating the emergence of our species-defining linguistic and similar "symbolic" abilities rests most directly on the evidence of prehistoric drawings and paintings, already at levels requiring no improvement.

Second, drawing and painting, linking the most complex human sensory and motor systems of eyes and hands with other structures, proved essential to much later thought, communication, and production. Drawing is an indispensable means of design in most traditional societies, where much of it, called "constructional" drawing, is directly on the worked materials, in order to shape them. Such work disappears in the finished product – the guideline in the saw kerf.

Third, industrialized society is even more dependent on drawings, usually of highly specialized forms. The modern may be marked out from the traditional as that in which any artifact must be drawn in order to be produced: in the process of conceiving, where it will be sketched and resketched; in communicating about production (often as part of a contract); and in guiding it, as a way of relaying measurements between different sites for parts that must fit. Thereafter, diagrams guide use: no circuit diagrams, no modern world. Therefore, philosophically, issues about drawing, having practical, ethical, social, and political dimensions, are not restricted to aesthetics. However, aesthetic matters are inextricable from them all.

DRAWING IN THE FINE ARTS AND AS A FINE ART

Given its importance to human cultures, it is no wonder that drawing should not only be among, but be considered to include, several fine arts. In some traditions, it is the art comprising all design (*disegno*), especially architecture, sculpture, and painting. In others, "the arts of the brush" include calligraphy, thereby linking not only with painting but with poetry and language generally. Overlapping traditions strongly associate design with geometry, and that with constructional drawing: Euclid often directs us how to draw a given shape.

Since drawing and painting as fine arts exist at high levels in most cultures in which fine arts are recognized, we must avoid channeling our conceptions to the figurative, which is not equally valued everywhere. Just as much purely utilitarian drawing is not *of* anything, neither is much artistic work, or only somewhat. This holds for such developed traditions as the Greek Geometric, much Islamic, and great calligraphic cultures in which writing, drawing, and painting are scarcely separable. Therefore the familiar path of investigating these great surface-marking arts through representation goes awry – making it difficult to understand even modern nonfigurative work within the largely figurative tradition of the West. It is misleading even to call the results of much fine drawing, painting, and printmaking "pictures."

Even regarding depictive uses, a second caution concerns spatial studies. If modern cognitive research – following its interests – expands our understanding of drawing largely in terms of spatial representation, philosophy of art needs to insist on a "bigger picture" of depiction. This is particularly important because since the Renaissance an influential habit of thought conceives of pictures as basically perspectival projections onto flat surfaces of three-dimensional situations derived from what is often termed "the real world," however fantastic. This perspective conception interlocks with an even older one, according to which images, as "symbols," refer or "point" like arrows to things other than themselves – an idea which seems flawed, as it pertains to neither Mickey Mouse drawings, nor to well-known pictures (e.g., by Escher and Saul Steinberg) that depict themselves.

As a fine art, painting has so long been the favored of the three in Western practice, history,

and criticism that the very words for art in some modern languages immediately suggest it. Drawing serves so widely for planning as to be associated with the "sketch," something both tentative and instrumental in aid of another finished object, including paintings. Even before painting attained its artistic primacy, Michelangelo's architectural, sculptural, and painting drawings were to him not worth the paper they were on, which he reused, destroyed. Although from his time drawings came increasingly to be appreciated in the West for their show of the movements of thought and hand, it was some time before that tradition reflected something like an Asian interest in process itself.

That came about largely through the medium of oil, whose blending and slow drying features reduced painting's dependence on staged preplanning, with the result that painting assumed some of drawing's process-expressive properties. Drawing took renewed life from a series of new graphic processes – engraving and etching, later wood-engraving, then lithography – and the combination of the older method of woodcut with movable type, all of which provided it with new "ontological" status and wider currency, before the advent of photography, and later photomechanical printing, as surface-marking arts.

AESTHETIC FORMALISM

Contemporary philosophy of these arts has tended to focus on common issues of form, representation, expression, and art status, with less attention to their differences, such as color, material, procedure. In this it has followed concerns in the artworld, and in particular modernism's emphasis on aesthetic or immediate features of "the work itself" combined with questioning age-old ideas of representation. The ancient referential or "pointing" conception of representation noted above suggested to some that representational interest could not be interest in "the works themselves," but only in what they "referred to," and was therefore nonaesthetic. Some aesthetic theories treat self-expression similarly, arguing that interest in the works' production, whether located in the artist or society, while important, is extrinsic. Formalist philosophy has proved valuable for several reasons. It draws attention to the paramount issue of artistic form, and assists access to nonfigurative art as well as to a diversity of world imagery, for modern audiences, for whom much subject content, process, and use may be esoteric, even unacceptable.

Nonetheless several problems arise. Conceptually, the existence of such centrally representational arts as poetry and drama, the statistical evidence of the three visual arts as overwhelmingly mimetic, and growing cultural skepticism about universalities and museum "decontextualization" from social contexts pose serious challenges to formalism. In addition, enormous growths in travel, the museum world (entries outstripping those for sports), and art-book publication make formalism too practically restrictive for our irrepressible interest in contexts and creators. Finally, the three modern visual art practices have returned to figuration and to social contexts.

PICTORIAL REPRESENTATION AS ART

Perhaps inspired by historian-theorist Ernst Gombrich's *Art and Illusion* (1960), which owed much to cognitive psychology, philosophical thought about representation in the three arts has sought new starting points. A beginning has been made in attempting to provide, in various ways, a better definition of visual representation itself. Advances in cognitive research into the perception of space have inspired philosophical work, though their relevance for art is always moot. However, a battery of aesthetic-formalist challenges needed response – challenges that do not presuppose formalism's positive theses. One is that, if what Gombrich called "convincing representation," or even representation itself, is neither necessary nor sufficient for art, how could it be artistically relevant? Another is how we are to distinguish interest in objects as depicted in pictures from interest in those objects themselves. A related challenge to artists' self-expression is to distinguish interest in biography from interest in the product before us.

Philosophers have taken several courses in response. Some reject formalism, even any focus on the aesthetic. Others accept aesthetic constraints but try to show how interest in subject matter can meet them. One approach is to insist that, where a picture is representational, attention to it as representation is

attention to it "for itself," since that is what it is. This argument may appeal to research that stresses perceptual contexts, including those of category. As shown by simple experiments, sight organizes the shapes and colors depicting objects, including their orientations and groupings – literally deciding which way is up – partly according to subject-recognition categories. It may add that, as Kant observed, when we identify something in a bog as a board not a branch, we take its cause to be something "with an end in view, to which it owes its form" (2000: §43). Merely taking something to be an artifact greatly affects its appearance. This effect of artifact perception, the argument may continue, is even greater with works of fine art, whose "end in view" includes appearing to us in certain ways. According to such arguments, aesthetic form could not be entirely separable from either depictive content or artists' purposes.

Even if effective, such replies do not yet address how perception of subject matter in pictures could be itself aesthetic or distinctively artistic. Here common sense invokes artists' "ways of seeing" subject matter, possibly also introducing an expressive aspect. Consider the contrasts between flowers in a garden and flowers as seen by Chao Meng-chien, Dürer, Rachel Ruysch, Van Gogh, or Redon. Can philosophers not only articulate this reply but develop it in illuminating ways? Here treatment of our three great marking arts, particularly through drawing, may benefit philosophy of visual art in a number of ways. This might be shown by exploiting, in ways there is only space here to sketch, the three connotations of drawing's name with which we began: design, physical action, and mental, "symbolic" content.

Regarding design, much of visual art lies in form. And although there is much form that is not shape, shape is a very significant instance of form. Drawing, with direct emphasis on finding interesting shapes, is an excellent place to investigate this difficult but most important matter. One clear meaning of a distinct "way of seeing" in pictures is the shapes through which depicted objects are presented to us. Existing theoretical traditions for understanding form as meaningful shape include the classical geometrical or proportional mentioned above, the visual-dynamic (including gestalt), and the depth-psychological.

As to physical action, drawing provides ideal data for investigating how artists' physically formative actions – as intentional – can be evident in the products of those actions, and therefore how complex mental and psychological attitudes can appear in, and guide understanding of, their work. Unlike in real environments, objects in pictures can be experienced as "described" through artists' physical actions.

Finally, anthropology, as earlier noted, appreciates prehistoric drawing as evidence of capacities for "symbolic thought": the ability to conceive of situations in diverse ways, and to share this rather than only to respond to them. The wealth of world drawing furnishes varieties of individuation and categorization of events and entities, their modes and parts, as well as qualification by temporal relations, causal connections, mental and psychological states, through narrative. Explanation of how there can be such distinct "ways of seeing" in different works should begin to show how a few scratches on a surface can produce reference, allusion, warmth, intelligence, even moral greatness, without recourse to language – as prelude to addressing the wider resources of painting for generating meaning.

See also ART OF THE PALEOLITHIC; ABSTRACTION; CHINESE AESTHETICS; COGNITIVE SCIENCE AND ART; DEPICTION; FORMALISM; PERSPECTIVE; PICTURE PERCEPTION; TECHNOLOGY AND ART.

BIBLIOGRAPHY
Arnheim, Rudolf. 1974. *Art and Visual Perception: A Psychology of the Creative Eye.* 2nd edn. Berkeley: University of California Press.
Gombrich, Ernst. 1960. *Art and Illusion: A Study in the Psychology of Pictorial Representation.* Princeton: Princeton University Press.
Ivins, William. 1978. *Prints and Visual Communication.* 2nd edn. Cambridge, MA: MIT Press.
Kant, Immanuel. 2000 [1790]. *Critique of the Power of Judgement.* P. Guyer & E. Matthews (trans.). Cambridge: Cambridge University Press.
Maynard, Patrick. 2005. *Drawing Distinctions: Varieties of Graphic Expression.* Ithaca: Cornell University Press.
Podro, Michael. 1998. *Depiction.* New Haven: Yale University Press.
Rawson, Philip. 1969. *Drawing.* Oxford: Oxford University Press.
Taylor, Joshua. 1981. *Learning to Look: A Handbook for the Visual Arts.* 2nd edn. Chicago: University of Chicago Press.
Willats, John. 1997. *Art and Representation.* Princeton: Princeton University Press.
Wollheim, Richard. 1987. *Painting as an Art.* London: Thames & Hudson.

PATRICK MAYNARD

literature   The term "literature" has at least three different senses. In the broadest sense, it refers to any body of writing that has a shared topic. It is in this sense that we talk of the literature on global warming. In the right context, almost any piece of writing can count as literature in the broadest sense. The term is also used, however, to pick out narrower classes of writings that possess, or are claimed to possess, some qualities that we value. Often, when questions are raised about the nature of literature, our interest is in those writings that might be studied in "literature" courses taught at colleges and universities. To be literature, in this "artistic" sense of the term, is to be a literary artwork. But the term "literature" is also often used with normative import in an extended sense, to include not only literary artworks but also writings in nonartistic genres – travel writing, essays, some works of philosophy and history – that are taken to share with literary artworks some of the qualities for which the latter are valued. It is in this sense that Terry Eagleton (1983: 1) cites, as examples of seventeenth-century English literature, not just the works of Shakespeare, Webster, Marvel, and Milton, but also "the essays of Francis Bacon, the sermons of John Donne, Bunyan's spiritual autobiography," and even philosophical and historical works such as Hobbes's *Leviathan* and Clarendon's *History of the Rebellion.* Eagleton concludes that literature in the extended sense is just "a highly valued kind of writing" (1983: 10), and thus culturally relative given the plurality of things that are valued in different cultures.

Even if we agree with Eagleton that there is no objective criterion of literariness in the extended sense, we can still wonder whether there are any distinguishing characteristics of the literary artwork. While some would argue that the notion of literary art is as culturally inflected as the notion of literature in the extended sense, and that the distinction between literary artworks and other works of literature in the extended sense is a matter of convenience and convention rather than of principle, it is worth considering how a more principled distinction between literary artworks and other kinds of (valued) writing might be drawn (e.g., see Stecker 1996).

Literary artworks might be thought to differ in their *content*, being *fictional*. But this is clearly neither sufficient nor necessary for being a work of literary art. On the one hand, jokes, thought experiments, and comic strips are usually viewed as fictions, but not as literary artworks. On the other hand, some literary works, such as works of lyric poetry, seem to be nonfictional in their subject matter.

This suggests an alternative criterion of literary art, namely, the *style* of a piece of writing. Roman Jakobson, one of the Russian Formalists, defined literature as organized violence committed on ordinary speech. On such a view, literature in the artistic sense deliberately departs from ordinary speech, and relies for its effects on this disruption. A related view was defended by the American "New Critics," who took as their focus the "literary use" of language – the use of distinctive rhythms, syntax, sound patterns, imagery, metaphor, tropes, ambiguity, and irony. Literary artworks, it was claimed, differ from other writings in their possession of these features, in virtue of which they lend themselves to a particular kind of close reading that focuses on relationships internal to the text.

A first difficulty with such a view is that, even if we restrict ourselves to the field of poetry, we can find parts of poems, and even entire poems, that do not seem to commit any violence on ordinary speech, but merely to reflect it, and that are not distinctive in their use of "literary language." For example, there are contemporary "prose poems" that are composed entirely of what might pass as ordinary prose and eschew standard prosodic conventions. This testifies to a more fundamental problem with any attempt to characterize literary art – even poetry – in terms of stylistic features of the writing. In literature, as in the other arts,

accepted features of artistic style are always open to challenge by artists who produce artworks that deliberately depart from the received style. We see this, for example, in the intentionally "flat" writing of French "new novelists" such as Alain Robbe-Grillet, and in the short stories of Jorge Luis Borges, which deliberately adopt for fictional purposes the academic style of professional journals, complete with scholarly footnotes and erudite references. Furthermore, writers in fields that we would not naturally classify as artistic – "new journalists" like Truman Capote, Norman Mailer, and Tom Wolfe – can employ stylistic devices of the sort celebrated by the Formalists.

Some have concluded that there is no distinctive class of "literary artworks," but only distinctive "literary" ways of *reading* texts – for example, attending to the very features of "writing" to which the Formalists and the New Critics drew our attention. A text, then, is a literary artwork just in case we choose to read it in a certain way. Ways of reading might be regarded as institutionalized and historically contingent sets of operations and procedures to which texts are subjected by those who belong to particular critical traditions. Michel Foucault associated the kinds of critical practices celebrated by the New Critics with the contemporary conception of an author. Certain classes of texts, Foucault (1986) maintained, become associated with what he termed the "author function," something we must reject in order to allow greater freedom to readers and a proliferation of interpretations of works. But this seems to elide an important distinction between something *being* a literary artwork, and its being *treated as* a literary artwork. Also, the decision to adopt a particular strategy in reading a particular text seems to reflect a prior expectation that the text in question is profitably approached through such a strategy, an expectation which seems to reflect, in turn, a prior classification of certain texts as literary artworks.

This suggests that we might try to distinguish literary artworks from other texts not in terms of how they are or might be read, but in terms of how their authors *intended* them to be read. Suppose that, as has just been suggested, there exist, in given cultural contexts, established ways of treating certain classes of texts, corresponding to the sorts of reading strategies described by the New Critics. Perhaps such reading strategies enhance the apprehension of certain sorts of "aesthetic" values through the reader's attention to formal properties of texts. It could then be argued that works of literary art are texts that are intended by their authors to furnish such values to readers who adopt the relevant kinds of reading strategies (e.g., see Lamarque & Olsen 1994). This allows both for something being treated as a literary artwork when it is not (because the required general intentions were not instrumental in its history of making), and also for flawed or downright bad works of literary art (where an author fails to produce something that readers find valuable in the relevant ways when they adopt the intended reading strategies).

The challenge then is to say what is distinctive about the ways in which literary artworks are intended to be read, especially given the broad disagreement in the scholarly community as to how such works *should* be read. Is there any common core to the reading strategies that have been proposed by literary theorists, and will this allow us to distinguish an intention that a work be read as literature in the artistic sense from the intention that a text be read as a work of literature in the extended sense?

Parallel questions arise concerning other art forms. In the case of the visual arts and dance, for example, theorists appeal to intended function to account for artworks that are perceptually indistinguishable from nonartworks. In watching a dancer, we are expected to attend to her movements, however mundane, with a particular kind of care and intensity, and to have an "artistic" interest in grasping the *point* of the movements. An instance of an artwork is intended to function as an artistic vehicle by means of which certain things are represented, expressed, or exemplified. The artist assumes that the receiver will know that she is supposed to treat the artistic vehicle in particular kinds of ways. What makes something an artwork is not, per se, the elements of which it is composed or the way in which those elements are put together, but how the assemblage of elements that make up the artistic vehicle is intended to function in the articulation of content. Cases where the artistic vehicle shares its perceptible properties with something that does not serve

as an artistic vehicle serve to clarify this point. But most artistic vehicles do have distinctive perceptible features that distinguish them from other entities, and artists presumably confer these features on their vehicles because they are particularly apposite for the articulation of content in an "aesthetic" way, given the shared understandings within the relevant artistic community as to how one should "take" an artistic vehicle.

Applying this to the distinguishing features of literary art, we can say that literary texts demand, for their appreciation, techniques of reading that allow the texts to articulate their content in particular ways. In the case of poetry, for example, we are intended to take account of a much fuller range of properties of the words used – their cultural resonance, their associations, their sounds, for example – and we take account of what a given string of words can be taken to exemplify, qua string, and not merely of what the words "mean." We also take the content articulated at more immediate levels to contribute toward the higher-order thematic content of the piece, the "point" of the piece that we expect to uncover in our reading. Furthermore, the higher-level content is not articulated explicitly, as might be the case if we were simply giving examples in support of a general conclusion, but has to be determined by the reader through close attention to the lower-level articulatory functions performed by the artistic vehicle. As with dance and visual art, then, it is our understanding, in encountering a poem, that we are supposed to attend to it in these sorts of ways that explains the different kinds of functions that a given text performs if it is taken to be the vehicle of a poetic artwork. Of course, poems are only one kind of literary artwork, and most of us are more familiar with prose works such as novels and performed works such as plays. It would therefore also be necessary to show how, for example, our attempts to understand the narratives in fictional works of literary art require that we take account of the more thematic content of the work.

In summary, then, it can be argued that literary artworks are to be distinguished not in terms of their distinctive contents, nor in terms of their distinctive style or syntax, but in terms of how they are intended to function as vehicles for the articulation of content. The more manifest features of literary artworks – the prosodic structures of poems, the syntactic dislocation of certain works of which the Formalists spoke, the use of certain figures of speech, of metaphor, and of ambiguity – are means whereby content is articulated, but can serve as such means only given shared understandings as to how the linguistic text is to be read.

See also DRAMA; POETRY; CANON; FOUCAULT; INTENTION AND INTERPRETATION; INTERPRETATION; INTERPRETATION, AIMS OF; TEXT.

BIBLIOGRAPHY
Eagleton, Terry. 1983. *Literary Theory: An Introduction.* Oxford: Blackwell.
Foucault, Michel. 1986. "What is an Author?" In *The Foucault Reader.* P. Rabinow (ed.). New York: Pantheon, 101–20.
Lamarque, Peter & Olsen, Stein Haugom 1994. *Truth, Fiction, and Literature: A Philosophical Perspective.* Oxford: Oxford University Press.
Stecker, Robert. 1996. "What is Literature?" *Revue Internationale de Philosophie*, 198, 681–94.

DAVID DAVIES

motion pictures Although presaged by entertainments like the magic lantern, with its moving dissolves, and various visual toys, such as zoetropes, motion pictures in the form of photographic films broke onto the scene between 1889 and 1895. Initially, these motion pictures came in the form of kinetoscopes – viewing boxes into which customers peered, one at a time, in order to see short clips of things like Annie Oakley shooting at targets. Kinetoscopes were developed by Thomas Edison and his assistant W. K. L. Dickson between 1889 and 1891 and the first kinetoscope parlor was opened in New York on April 14, 1894.

The next important event in the birth of the motion picture, as we know it, was the development of motion picture projection by the Lumière Brothers. They staged their first public screening of a series of short films on December 28, 1895 in Paris. By screening films instead of presenting them via individual viewing boxes, the Lumières were able to engage larger audiences and, thereby, enhance the financial feasibility of motion pictures. One screening could now accommodate 10, 20, 100, and then more viewers at a time. And with the expansion of the potential profitability of motion pictures, the practice of motion-picture-making extended in every direction – including fiction and nonfiction, poetic experimentation, and so forth – until it became, according to many, a (if not *the*) major art form of the twentieth century.

Because the practice of motion-picture-making represents such a large contribution to culture, it is a topic for many different branches of philosophy. However, the two central questions that philosophers have asked about the motion picture are: what is a motion picture and can motion pictures be art?

WHAT IS A MOTION PICTURE?
Since we often speak in terms of "the philosophy of *X*" – as in the case of the philosophy of motion pictures – the first order of business, in doing the philosophy of whatever, is to define what the whatever is. One way of doing this is to say what conditions or criteria a candidate has to meet in order to count as a member of the whatever. So, in our case, we want to know what features something must possess in order to fall under the concept of motion picture.

First of all, a motion picture should be a picture. But what is a picture? Let us say that a picture is a visual representation whose referents we recognize by simply looking – without recourse to arbitrary codes or conventions – in cases where we are already capable of recognizing that kind of object or event in the world outside of pictures. A picture of a horse is such that I can recognize it as of a horse by looking, where I am able to recognize that kind of thing – say, four-legged animals – in terms of my ordinary powers of object recognition.

The earliest motion pictures were photographic. As we shall see, this led some people to charge that they could not be art, because a photograph, it was held, was merely the mechanical reproduction of reality. Photography left no room for expression, imagination, or formal invention. It remained too tied to the reality that had given rise to the photograph. Photography was too close to reality. Looking at a photograph, moving or otherwise, is allegedly tantamount to looking at the reality that gave rise to it. Thus, we need to pinpoint the difference between looking at a horse and looking at a photograph of a horse.

Looking at a horse is different than looking at a photograph of the same horse insofar as the former experience comes automatically with a built-in, egocentric orientation to the horse, whereas my experience of the photograph does not. By "egocentric orientation" I mean that on seeing the horse I can point my body in its direction and walk toward it. I cannot do that with a photograph of a horse. Suppose the photo were taken on a space station orbiting the earth. I cannot point my body to the location of the horse when the photo was snapped; the space between me and the horse as represented by the photo is discontinuous. For the space represented by the photo, like that of all pictures, is a "detached display" – the place of its referent is epistemically unavailable to me, since it has been, so to speak, detached from the spatiotemporal continuum that I inhabit.

Inasmuch as motion pictures are pictures, then, they are representations, specifically detached displays, whose referents we recognize simply by looking. But this is true of ordinary pictures – including not only photographs but paintings, engravings, and so forth. So the next question becomes: what is the difference between motion pictures and pictures *simpliciter*? Ordinary language alerts us to the key differentiae here. It is motion. We call them motion pictures, or moving pictures, or just movies in light of the fact that they possess the technological capacity to engender the impression of movement in viewers.

Note that the requirement here is only that candidates for the status of motion picture have the capacity to deliver the impression of movement. They need not literally do so. There are motion pictures that do not move, such as *Band of Ninja* (1967) – a film by Nagisa Oshima of a comic strip. Perhaps one could show the same comic strip, panel by panel or page by page, by means of a series of slides. Nevertheless, the parade of slides would not be a motion picture, since slides lack the technological capacity to provoke the impression of movement. Oshima's film and a cascade of slides might be indiscernible to the human eye and yet they would belong to different

ontological categories – the slides to the category of *still* pictures and Oshima's film to the category of *motion* pictures. Likewise paintings, engravings, lithographs, photographs, and so forth are still pictures in contrast to motion pictures.

However, this raises the question of the distinction between theater and motion pictures, since theatrical arrays are visual representations that are also detached displays (I cannot orient my body toward Elsinore on the basis of the production at the Guthrie Theater) which have the capacity for movement and whose referents are recognized simply by looking (I recognize Hamlet is a man by looking, not by deciphering a code, reading, or inferring). So what differentiates theater from motion pictures?

Both theater and motion pictures are multiple-instance arts. There can be multiple instances of *Hamlet* being performed at the same time, just as there can be multiple, simultaneous performances (screenings) of *To Kill a Mockingbird* (1962). One way of characterizing this phenomenon is to say that dramas and motion pictures are types that can sustain a multiplicity of token performances, just as there is the design of the $1 bill of which the singles in our wallets are tokens.

Of course, saying that dramas and movies are both multiple-instance arts does not help us to cut the difference between them. But if instead we concentrate on the way in which we get from the types – *Hamlet* (the play type) and *To Kill a Mockingbird* (the movie type) – to their respective token performances, two philosophically striking contrasts begin to emerge. For example, in order to get from the play type *Hamlet*, a literary artifact that acts as a recipe for cooking up performances of *Hamlet*, to the token performance, we require the intentional activities of the playmakers in interpreting the play type and applying it in the thick of performance.

But that which mediates the transit from the motion pictures type *To Kill a Mockingbird* to token performances of it (screenings) is a template, for example, a filmstrip or a DVD, that operates mechanically and/or electronically. So, although theater and motion pictures are both multiple-instance or type arts, they nevertheless differ fundamentally in the way in which they generate token performances of the relevant types. Theater does it through the mediation of intentional states whereas motion pictures generate token performances by means of engaging templates, which are tokens, mechanically (and electronically).

A corollary of this, interestingly, is that the token performance of a theatrical token is a work of performing art whereas a token performance of a motion picture (a screening) is not. For running a template by the numbers through the appropriate mechanism, such as my DVD player, although it may involve routine technical competence, does not involve artistry.

So far then, something is a motion picture only if (1) it is a visual representation of the order of a detached display, (2) whose subject we recognize by merely looking, (3) which possesses the capacity to engender the impression of movement, (4) whose token performances are generated by templates, and (5) whose token performances are not artworks in their own right.

However, this is not sufficient. Imagine a mechanized tableau, as one might find at a theme park, with a robotized Abraham Lincoln delivering the Gettysburg Address. It would meet the five conditions outlined above, but we would not be disposed to call it a motion picture, since it is, rather, a moving sculpture. In order to exclude such phenomena from the order of the motion picture, we should add that the candidate in question be two-dimensional.

Some have argued that the addition of the requirement of two-dimensionality to the formula makes the definition of motion pictures too narrow, since it would exclude holographs. Surely, it may be urged, if one could holographically project the final gun battle of *3:10 to Yuma* (2007) in three dimensions, that would be a motion picture. But would it? Wouldn't it be a moving sculpture, the very category that the addition of the requirement of two-dimensionality was designed to exclude. Against this, it may be objected that sculptures are not made of light. However, the objection is false, if one considers the light sculptures of Dan Flavin.

ARE MOTION PICTURES ART?

Although motion pictures can discharge many services – from surveillance to colonoscopies – it is undoubtedly as art that motion pictures have captured the global imagination. This is not to say that all motion pictures are art, but that some, indeed a great many, motion pictures are artworks. And yet, from the birth of the movies and into our own times, there have been skeptics who contend that motion pictures cannot be art.

Their reservations usually rest on the assumptions that motion pictures are nothing more than moving photographs and that photographs, moving or otherwise, cannot be artworks. Among the reasons that are offered for the demotion of photography, perhaps the central worry is that photographs are nothing more than mindless, mechanical reproductions of whatever stands before the camera. You press a button, you get a photo. The process is one of a series of sheer causal processes with no opportunity for artistic expression. It is like holding a mirror up to nature. Thus, insofar as artistic expression is said to be the hallmark of art, photographs, moving or otherwise, cannot be art.

This argument is plagued by a number of flaws. First, motion pictures are not just moving photographs. They include other dimensions, such as editing, relations between sound and image, musical tracks, and so forth. Therefore, even if the individual images (the shots) in movies were photographs, artistic expression might be available to the motion picture maker in virtue of these other dimensions of creativity.

Of course, another problem with the argument is that, even if the individual shots are photographs, albeit moving ones, this would not preclude artistic expression. For photography itself possesses a wealth of strategies and devices that may be deployed to expressive effect, including camera angles, image scale, lighting, color design, variable framing, camera movement, and so forth. Moreover, the cinematic image can be processed during the postproduction period in many different ways that can make an expressive difference (e.g., by changing the hue of the image, or by adding special effects, among other things).

Moreover, this argument against the possibility of motion picture art is being rendered technologically obsolete by the perfection of computer-generated imagery, such as the CGI mattes in movies like *300* (2006). By means of digital manipulation, images can be created from scratch – and will be with increasing regularity – thereby undermining the presupposition that all motion picture images, in virtue of being photographic, are mindless reproductions of reality. Instead, by means of computers, motion picture images can be as divorced from what is as are paintings.

See also PHOTOGRAPHY; ONTOLOGY OF ARTWORKS; TECHNOLOGY AND ART.

BIBLIOGRAPHY
Allen, Richard & Smith, Murray (eds.). 1997. *Film Theory and Philosophy*. Oxford: Oxford University Press.
Carroll, Noël. 2008. *The Philosophy of Motion Pictures*. Oxford: Blackwell.
Carroll, Noël & Choi, Jinhee (eds.). 2006. *The Philosophy of Film and Motion Pictures*. Oxford: Blackwell.
Cavell, Stanley. 1979 [1971]. *The World Viewed*. Enlarged edn. Cambridge, MA: Harvard University Press.
Currie, Gregory. 1995. *Image and Mind*. Cambridge: Cambridge University Press.
Danto, Arthur C. 1979. "Moving Pictures," *Quarterly Review of Film Studies*, 4, 1–21.
Freeland, Cynthia & Wartenberg, Thomas (eds.). 1995. *Philosophy and Film*. London: Routledge.
Gaut, Berys. 2002. "Cinematic Art," *Journal of Art and Aesthetic Criticism*, 60, 299–312.
Scruton, Roger. 2006. "Photography and Representation." In *The Philosophy of Film and Motion Pictures*. Noël Carroll & Jinhee Choi (eds.). Oxford: Blackwell, 19–34.
Wartenberg, Thomas & Curran, Angela (eds.). 2005. *The Philosophy of Film: Introductory Texts and Readings*. Oxford: Blackwell.

NOËL CARROLL

music and song In ancient Greece, the Pythagoreans were interested in the principles of acoustics and suggested that the harmony of proportions in music echoed a similar cosmic harmony. The Greek philosophers focused on music's effects on the character, attitudes, and emotions of those who heard it (e.g., see Aristotle's *Politics* 8 §6). The consideration of music in the context of cultural critique has always been popular with philosophical pundits, who deplore the impoverished nature and corrupting influence of the day's popular music (e.g., Adorno 1989 on jazz and Scruton 1997 on

rock), or propagandize in favor of one kind or type of music above others (e.g., Adorno 1973). but it was Arthur Schopenhauer (1969) in the nineteenth century who first argued for the preeminence of music among the arts. In its abstract character, he suggested, music is both a direct presentation of the will and a release from the will's constant frustration. Undoubtedly the rise of instrumental, abstract music contributed to the growing status of music as an art at this time.

Overall, the most persistent theme in the philosophy of music, and still the most discussed, is that of whether and how music expresses emotion, how it affects the listener, how it compares in this respect with language, and whether it is thereby a source of value and knowledge. The earliest, sophisticated argument on the topic was offered in the mid nineteenth century by the music critic Eduard Hanslick (1986), who argued that music cannot express emotion because it cannot possess or communicate the cognitive elements essential to emotion. His views continue to be championed by formalists, but a majority of philosophers accept that music is expressive and attempt to explain how this is possible. For instance, in the mid twentieth century, Susanne Langer argued that music employs a distinctive mode of symbolism with which it presents the form of feelings. A range of issues, not only concerning music's expressiveness but also the character of emotion, continue to be presented: for example, whether expressiveness is a literal or metaphoric property of music, whether music arouses in listeners the emotions it expresses, whether the emotions expressed are to be attributed to a hypothetical persona or solely to the musical sounds, whether emotions always involve cognitive commitments and as such are to be distinguished from physiological sensations, and so on.

The ontology of musical works and their relation to the performances that instance them has become a growing area of discussion since it first attracted attention late in the twentieth century (Levinson 1980; Wolterstorff 1980; Ingarden 1986), as have related topics, such as whether musical works are discovered or created (Fisher 1991), what the criteria for authentic performance are, and whether authentic performance is possible or desirable (Kivy 1995; Davies 2001). The role of music in fostering cultural identity has also been discussed in terms of authenticity (Rudinow 1994; Davies 2001; Gracyk 2001; Young 2007).

Further subjects covered under the heading of the philosophy of music include the nature of the material elements of music (Scruton 1997; Davies 2001; Hamilton 2007), representation or depiction in music (Kivy 1984; Davies 1994; Scruton 1997), musical profundity (Kivy 1990), the requirements for and nature of the listener's appreciation of music (Kivy 1990; Davies 1994; Levinson 1997), notation (Davies 2001), differences between live performance and recordings (Brown 2000a; Davies 2001; Kania 2007), and improvisation (Alperson 1984; Hamilton 2007). As well, there are philosophically informed literatures on music's connection with education, health and therapy, the brain, language, evolution, and technology.

Until recently, philosophers have focused their accounts on Western, classical, instrumental works of the eighteenth and nineteenth centuries, considered from the perspective of the listener rather than of the performer (but see Godlovitch 1998), analyst (but see DeBellis 1995), or composer. Careful and sympathetic consideration of the distinctive natures of and aesthetics appropriate to medieval and renaissance music, jazz (e.g., in Brown 2000b; Hamilton 2007), popular music (e.g., in Gracyk 1996, 2001), and non-Western music has been more the exception than the rule, but this situation is changing. As yet, functional music – film music, work songs, devotional music, dance music, lullabies, anthems – has attracted little interest, except in the cultural critique of muzak. And the definition of music has been largely ignored.

SONGS

Songs are the dominant subset of music that is sung. Wherever there is singing, there is song, but not every case of singing – for instance, opera, cantatas, and chants – is a case of singing a song. Most music that people around the world experience consists of songs, but in spite of this universality, songs and song have been overlooked in the philosophy of music until recently. Not only have most accounts

focused on classical music, but the works that have most fascinated theorists have been "pure" or "absolute" music, that is, music without text or story (as criticized in Ridley 2004). Yet, there is no doubt that songs are musical works too, and, as Levinson (1987: 42) says, there "are defensible senses in which song might be said to be the most fundamental music, the most natural music."

The focus on "pure" music results from the traditional preference of aesthetic theorists for high art and the elevation of "absolute" music in the nineteenth century to a supreme position among the arts. In instrumental music, such as string quartets, music could attain complete aesthetic autonomy free from any external constraints, including those that come with any text setting. So, vocal music was demoted in this conception, and popular songs with texts connected to everyday life and emotion are doubly impure, both as low art and because the words can only limit the music. The use of descriptors such as "pure" or "music in itself" (see Kivy 1990; Kania 2007) implies that such music is more primary or fundamental than song, that it is music in its essential form. Yet, all writers (e.g., Kivy 2007: 203) appear to concede that music did not originate that way.

We might regard song as a combination of more primary art forms, poetry and music. This view may be based, however, on the questionable inference that songs are juxtapositions of two forms because we can abstractly consider the text or the music by itself. Is representational painting an impure art form merely because one can intellectually abstract pure visual form from the representational image? Song is often regarded as text-setting, and art songs are almost always settings of preexisting poetic texts, but this characterization is significantly misleading for modern vernacular songs, which are typically offered as a unified structure of lyrics and music, both created together with neither intended to stand alone.

One place the issue of how to conceptualize songs comes up is in considering how to evaluate them. Levinson (1987) suggests that the relations of the text, the vocal line or melody, and the accompaniment determine how successful the song is *as a song*. However, this framework may not be apt for rock music (broadly conceived to include rap, electronica, reggae, etc.), where debate has sprung up about whether the criteria of evaluation echo those for classical music (Frith 1996; Gracyk 1996; Davies 1999). If the primary works in rock are recordings (see below), the whole "wall of sound" on the recording created by the application of recording technology needs to be included, and this is not simply a notated accompaniment. Alternatively, if the abstract song is merely instanced in the recording playback, then we need a thinner notion of a song for the case of rock and popular music, a notion that omits a specific accompaniment (Davies 2001; Kania 2006). Gracyk (1996, 2001) has written an extensive aesthetics of rock music, insisting that the primary work is the recording and defending the quality and value of the best rock music.

THE MANY MEANINGS OF "SONG"

Philosophical examinations of vocal music (Levinson 1987; Kivy 1998, 2007) have overlooked the difference between songs and other kinds of vocal music, such as operas and chants, and thus treat songs as if they do not constitute a significant aesthetic category on their own. Here it is helpful to keep in mind the difference between "song," used to refer to the general category of vocal music of all sorts, and its use as a count noun, as in "*a* song" or "the ten song*s* in the musical." We can say that an opera or chant is song but not that it is *a* song.

Clearly the range of things to which we apply the count noun "song" expanded enormously in the twentieth century. In jazz and rock, purely instrumental works are universally called songs. "Song" has become the term to apply to any short work of popular or mass culture music with or *without* lyrics. This usage reflects the common use of "song" to refer to the instrumental melody of a song with lyrics.

Another crucial extension of "song" occurs in rock music. With groundbreaking recordings by the Beatles, the Rolling Stones, Pink Floyd, Jefferson Airplane, and many others, the recording became a work of art in its own right, not necessarily reflecting live performances. Whereas ethnographic recordings are *of* songs, the recordings of rock music (broadly construed) are themselves called songs. We talk both of the Beatles' recording of "Some-

thing" as a song and of the abstracted song "Something." But are recordings, what Kania (2006) calls "tracks," literally songs, or is this merely a metonymic usage, like referring to the score of a piece of music as "the music"?

THE CORE CONCEPT OF A SONG

If "Revolution Nine" by the Beatles, the extended songs of Bob Dylan, Tin Pan Alley songs, songs in musicals with long introductory verses (usually omitted when performed independently of the musical narrative), Child ballads, work songs, etc., all qualify, it is unlikely that there is a plausible formal definition of the core concept of a song. Nevertheless, it will be useful to outline elements that are typical, frequent, or salient in songs. Songs characteristically involve a *text* that is *sung*. The *text is set to one musical line*, a main melody line, which can involve call and response or verse and chorus. (A song can be *arranged* in complex ways for multiple singers with multiple lines, but the basic song is usually simple – although not in art songs – and can be performed without the complexity.) Also, a song is not typically part of a larger musical work, and can be performed by itself. (Songs in musicals can be detached from their dramatic context.)

Vernacular songs – for example, karaoke, hymns, lullabies – are usually *performable by the larger community* in that anyone can sing them. This feature gives them a wide-ranging capacity to be made the individual expression of any singer in performance. Even when they are regarded as personal expression, as in popular music written by rock musicians and singer-songwriters, other performers are free to vary the meaning and expressive properties of a given song, making it their own, as in Jimi Hendrix's version of Dylan's "All Along the Watch Tower." Their recording becomes as much their creation as it is the original composer's.

With art songs, by contrast, the impetus is to find the essential work specified in the score. They are regarded as expressions of the composer (or her surrogate: the singer) and they are often difficult, requiring professional musicianship to perform. That said, art songs – for example, the songs of Schubert or Charles Ives – are clearly songs; they set texts to accompanied melodies and stand as autonomous musical works. They have roots as deep in the universal song tradition as do popular songs.

In rock, is the main artwork the core song that is instanced or manifested on the recording, or the specific recording of that song, or both? There is reason to think the recording is the main artwork, for it is only the recording that represents the abstract core song (words plus music) *within* an overall sound work that produces the meaning and expressive qualities that the composer-performers intended. Somebody else can take the abstract song and turn it into his or her own expression as a live singer, or a group can create a new recording that "manifests" the same abstract song. Ultimately, Davies (2001: 14) – who holds that rock songs are best thought of as works for studio performance – sorts out the relation of song to recorded work this way: "I believe that most people conceive of rock recordings as (studio) performances of songs, not as purely electronic non-performance works (that might manifest songs).". By contrast, Kania (2006) defends Gracyk's notion that a paradigm song is "manifested" in rock recordings.

INTERPRETATION OF SONGS

One feature of vernacular songs is their public nature; they can be recognized and hummed by many people as well as passed down to future generations. These features open up vernacular songs to a much wider range of interpretations than is true of classical music and art songs. They may be performed in radically different ways, and as the meaning of the lyrics may be partially lost or misunderstood, the result can be a performance with different and even incompatible expressive and other aesthetic properties from the original. Bicknell's notion (2005), that singing in popular music involves self-expression of a public persona or role, implies that within limits performers can bring the song within the ambit of their own musical oeuvres. If the Beatles' "Something" is performed by Frank Sinatra (as it was), we should expect very different results from the Beatles' original release, and when Paul McCartney performed it on the ukulele at a memorial concert for George Harrison, it became different again, an expression of love for a lost friend. Imagine what happens after an even greater period of time when more of the original cultural context is lost. This suggests that vernacular songs are "open texts" in a way that classical musical works are not.

When we shift from the abstract song instanced or manifested in the recording to the *recording* song, the ontological picture changes. The recording – say, the Beatles' "Something" – can be imitated on other recordings or in live performance, but these are copies of the recording, not interpretations. If the recording is sampled and remixed, such would be a sort of interpretation of the recorded work, but also a derived and hence new work. So, this possibility does not imply that the recording song is an especially open work.

As a work with a stable artistic character and regarded by both producers and consumers as a vehicle of self expression, the rock recording has a claim to be an artwork going beyond that of other popular songs. If Gracyk is right that the primary text in rock is the recording, the rock song's claim to belong in the category of artworks seems as strong as that of the art song. Against this thought, however, is Gracyk's (2001) point that popular recordings are *mass art*. As such, he argues, they are open to a special interpretative pluralism; because recordings are listened to in very different times and cultural contexts, they can be interpreted in significantly different ways, as when a new generation takes a nonironic recording to be ironic. This calls into doubt the earlier suggestion that they have a stable enough character to be artworks. Recording songs are prone to being recycled and used in ways unintended by the original artists (e.g., in car commercials). If the arthood of rock songs is to be defended against this observation, it will be necessary to show that some interpretations or uses of recordings are mistaken or inappropriate, that not "anything goes" when it comes to the interpretation of recordings.

See also OPERA; POETRY; ADORNO; CULTURAL APPROPRIATION; EXPRESSION; HANSLICK; LANGER; MASS ART; NOTATIONS; ONTOLOGY OF ARTWORKS; PERFORMANCE; POPULAR ART; SCHOPENHAUER; SCRUTON; WAGNER.

BIBLIOGRAPHY

Adorno, Theodor W. 1973 [1948]. *Philosophy of Modern Music*. A. G. Mitchell & W. V. Blomster (trans.). New York: Seabury.

Adorno, Theodor W. 1989 [1936]. "On Jazz," J. O. Daniel (trans.), *Discourse*, 12, 45–69.

Alperson, Philip. 1984. "On Musical Improvisation," *Journal of Aesthetics and Art Criticism*, 43, 17–30.

Bicknell, Jeanette. 2005. "Just a Song? Exploring the Aesthetics of Popular Song Performance," *Journal of Aesthetics and Art Criticism*, 63, 261–70.

Brown, Lee B. 2000a. "Phonography, Repetition and Spontaneity," *Philosophy and Literature*, 24, 111–25.

Brown, Lee B. 2000b. " 'Feeling My Way': Jazz Improvisation and Its Vicissitudes – A Plea for Imperfection," *Journal of Aesthetics and Art Criticism*, 58, 112–23.

Davies, Stephen. 1994. *Musical Meaning and Expression*. Ithaca: Cornell University Press.

Davies, Stephen. 1999. "Rock versus Classical Music," *Journal of Aesthetics and Art Criticism*, 57, 193–204.

Davies, Stephen. 2001. *Musical Works and Performances: A Philosophical Exploration*. Oxford: Clarendon.

DeBellis, Mark. 1995. *Music and Conceptualization*. Cambridge: Cambridge University Press.

Fisher, John Andrew. 1991. "Discovery, Creation, and Musical Works," *Journal of Aesthetics and Art Criticism*, 49, 129–36.

Frith, Simon. 1996. *Performing Rites: On the Value of Popular Music*. Cambridge, MA: Harvard University Press.

Godlovitch, Stan. 1998. *Musical Performance: A Philosophical Study*. London: Routledge.

Gracyk, Theodore. 1996. *Rhythm and Noise: An Aesthetics of Rock*. Durham: Duke University Press.

Gracyk, Theodore. 2001. *I Wanna be Me: Rock Music and the Politics of Identity*. Philadelphia: Temple University Press.

Hamilton, Andy. 2007. *Aesthetics and Music*. London: Continuum.

Hanslick, Eduard. 1986 [1854]. *On the Musically Beautiful*. G. Payzant (trans.). Indianapolis: Hackett.

Ingarden, Roman. 1986 [1966]. *The Work of Music and the Problem of Its Identity*. J. G. Harrell (ed.). A. Czerniawski (trans.). Berkeley: University of California Press.

Kania, Andrew. 2006. "Making Tracks: The Ontology of Rock Music," *Journal of Aesthetics and Art Criticism*, 64, 401–14.

Kania, Andrew. 2007. "The Philosophy of Music." In *The Stanford Encyclopedia of Philosophy*. E. N. Zalta (ed.). Available at http://plato.stanford.edu/archives/win2007/entries/music/

Kivy, Peter. 1984. *Sound and Semblance: Reflections on Musical Representation*. Princeton: Princeton University Press.

Kivy, Peter. 1990. *Music Alone: Philosophical Reflections on the Purely Musical Experience*. Ithaca: Cornell University Press.

Kivy, Peter. 1995. *Authenticities: Philosophical Reflections on Musical Performance*. Ithaca: Cornell University Press.

Kivy, Peter. 1998. "Speech, Song, and the Transparency of Medium: A Note on Operatic Metaphysics." In *Musical Worlds: New Directions in the Philosophy of Music*. P. Alperson (ed.). University Park: Pennsylvania State University Press, 63–8.

Kivy, Peter. 2007. "In Defense of Musical Representation: Music, Representation, and the Hybrid Arts." In *Music, Language, and Cognition: And Other Essays in the Aesthetics of Music*. Oxford: Clarendon, 199–213.

Levinson, Jerrold. 1980. "What a Musical Work Is," *Journal of Philosophy*, 77, 5–28.

Levinson, Jerrold. 1987. "Song and Musical Drama." In *What is Music?* P. Alperson (ed.). New York: Haven, 283–301.

Levinson, Jerrold. 1997. *Music in the Moment*. Ithaca: Cornell University Press.

Ridley, Aaron. 2004. *The Philosophy of Music: Theme and Variations*. Edinburgh: Edinburgh University Press.

Rudinow, Joel. 1994. "Race, Ethnicity, Expressive Authenticity: Can White People Sing the Blues?" *Journal of Aesthetics and Art Criticism*, 52, 127–37.

Schopenhauer, Arthur. 1969 [1819/44]. *The World as Will and Representation*. 2 vols. E. J. F. Payne (trans.). New York: Dover.

Scruton, Roger. 1997. *The Aesthetics of Music*. Oxford: Clarendon.

Wolterstorff, Nicholas. 1980. *Works and Worlds of Art*. Oxford: Clarendon.

Young, James O. 2007. *Cultural Appropriation and the Arts*. Oxford: Blackwell.

JOHN ANDREW FISHER & STEPHEN DAVIES

opera includes in the widest sense an aesthetically diverse array of music theater in the Western tradition from the late sixteenth century to the present day, including comic and serious forms, with or without spoken dialogue, for performance in large or small venues, indoors or outdoors, to popular or elite audiences – along with several varieties of Asian music theater.

Fundamental to any philosophical inquiry into an art form is the ontological question: what must there *be* in order for there to be art of this kind? In the case of performing arts such as opera, there is also the practical question: what must be *done* in order for there to be art of this kind? A philosophical consideration of these questions should begin by noting that audiences are able to attribute properties to an opera (as distinct from its performance); and they are able to experience the opera in experiencing its performance. If we think of what is performed as the *content* of the performance, these observations should lead us to ask what kind of existence the content of an operatic performance has.

Standardly, in Western aesthetics the content is thought of as an artwork – a particular kind of musical work. But that thought may need some qualification in the light of two further questions. First, if as Goehr (1994) argues, the notion of a musical work was not widely used before 1800, what is the ontological status of pre-1800 operas, and what was it before 1800? Second, if some Chinese opera is performed without the use of a score, are there operatic works in that tradition? Both questions have received careful consideration by Davies (2001).

The fact that the content of one performance can be repeated in another has led many philosophers to think of the content of a performance as a type whose tokens are its performances. However, philosophers disagree about what the relevant types are. Some (e.g., Thom 1993) say they are action types; some (e.g., Dodd 2007) say sound-event types.

An opera may never have been performed, in which case there is no such thing as what *is* performed. Nonetheless, if the opera exists, there is a way of discovering what is *to be done* if the opera is to be performed (namely, by consulting whatever it is that "fixes" the opera – its score, a recording, or the overlapping memories of an oral tradition). Thus we might think of an opera as a set of type actions under the description "to be done if the opera is to be performed." On this view, the existence of an opera implies not only the existence of types but the existence of agents (its authors) who by taking certain actions specify what is to be done in its performances.

The actions involved in performing an opera include the representation of characters and events through singing, stage movement, instrumental playing, and the creation of scenic effects (though in contemporary music theater other types of action may be substituted for some of these). Paramount among these is the act of singing. It is not just the sound of the singers but their production of that sound that is the focus of interest in opera. The extreme physicality that is unique to operatic singing can make watching an operatic performance a little like watching an athletic event.

Because of its representational potential, operatic singing can be considered as having two aspects, corresponding to the vehicle and the object of representation. The object is usually thought of as spoken dialogue or monologue, but it is sometimes itself a song, so that the vehicle at times becomes what Abbate (1991) calls a "voice-object" independent of any representationality. Singing is a topic that should be approached historically and from a cultural perspective, because singing in the age of intimate theaters and small orchestras was different from what it became during the reign of grand opera, and different again from what it has become in the age of the microphone; furthermore, singing to a reverential Western opera audience is a different kind of act from singing to a rowdy audience in China.

Opera is a hybrid form; and there has been some philosophical reflection on hybrid art (e.g., Levinson 1984). The actions that an opera prescribes require diverse skills for their execution. When these diverse actions have to be executed by a single performer, the choice is sometimes made to regard some elements of the operatic mix (e.g., stage movement) as being of secondary or negligible importance. When operatic performances compromise on such matters by using singers deficient in the relevant skills, many audiences experience the result as bad art. This phenomenon is not uncommon in Western opera, though it seems that such compromises are less frequent in Chinese opera.

Opera is not only a hybrid but also a collaborative art, at the level both of authorship and of performance. Some philosophical work has been done on collaborative action in the arts, principally in film; it is yet to be extended into the domain of opera. Among the key issues is the question whether in collaborative arts we should speak of multiple authors, and the question of how to define a successful collaboration.

The common ontology shared by operas from different cultures and historical periods is accompanied by major aesthetic differences. If an opera is an action type comprising the representation of characters and events through singing, stage movement, orchestral playing, and the creation of scenic effects, then different kinds of opera can be distinguished according to the specific form that each of these elements takes, the prominence given to each of them, and their relative subordination.

At times when paradigms of operatic composition are under challenge (e.g., the various periods of Monteverdi, Gluck, Wagner, Berg, and the present time), significant creative choices regarding these matters must be made by librettists and composers. These choices are sometimes labeled "the problem of opera." The problem is how to write an aesthetically good opera, given opera's hybrid nature and its recurrent liability to fall short of its aesthetic ideals. One's solution to the problem will depend on what one takes the elements in the operatic mix to be, which of them if any should be subordinated to others, and what one would count as a "satisfactory" way of combining them. Some writers have thought of opera's elements as music plus narrative (e.g., Abbate 1991); some as music plus drama (e.g., Kivy 1988). To some it has seemed as if all other elements must be subordinated to the music; others have disagreed, making everything else subordinate to the libretto. The *combination* of these elements has also been thought of in various ways – as synthesis (Wagner) or in terms of alienation (Brecht).

Even in times of "normal" opera, when paradigms of composition are apparently stable, the presence of conflicting aesthetic ideals within an existing paradigm may allow for the making of significant creative choices. For instance, some music historians argue that the conflict between romanticism and realism was an undercurrent in the nineteenth century, and that one can detect elements of both ideals in certain nineteenth-century operas.

Because operas comprise specifications of what is to be done – specifications that can never be exhaustive – they require interpretation in performance. Thus, as with any other performing art, the performance of opera poses practical questions of interpretation. These take on a particular urgency in the case of many operas that have remained in the repertoire for a long time. On the one hand, the interpretation of these works may have become stale with repeated performance. On the other hand, much is known about their early performance history. How then should modern interpreters approach the performative interpretation of these works? Some writers believe there is a case for recreating old operas in "authentic" style; others oppose the idea of authenticity, and argue that an element of irony is necessary when staging those pieces in the standard repertoire whose plots now lack plausibility or whose staging requirements now seem gratuitously excessive.

Philosophers have suggested a number of features as being unique to opera. Clément (1988) claims that there is a uniquely operatic way of representing women, especially the death of women. Abbate (1991) finds in opera unique ways of propelling a narrative. The thesis of Tomlinson (1998) is that there is a uniquely operatic way of expressing different historical modes of human subjectivity. Cavell (1994) suggests that it is not so much opera's subject matter as the role music plays in its performance that sets it apart from the other arts. He sees opera as showing "the intervention or supervening of music into the world as revelatory of a realm of significance that either transcends our ordinary realm of experience or reveals ours under transfiguration" (1994: 141). These claims and many others deserve a considered interpretation in a yet to be written comprehensive philosophy of opera as a performing art.

See also MUSIC AND SONG; NOTATIONS; ONTOLOGY OF ARTWORKS; PERFORMANCE; WAGNER.

BIBLIOGRAPHY

Abbate, Carolyn. 1991. *Unsung Voices: Opera and Musical Narrative in the Nineteenth Century*. Princeton: Princeton University Press.

Cavell, Stanley. 1994. *A Pitch of Philosophy: Autobiographical Exercises*. Cambridge, MA: Harvard University Press.

Clément, Catherine. 1988. *Opera; or, The Undoing of Women*. B. Wing (trans.). Minneapolis: University of Minnesota Press.

Davies, Stephen. 2001. *Musical Works and Performances: A Philosophical Exploration*. Oxford: Clarendon.

Dodd, Julian. 2007. *Works of Music: An Essay in Ontology*. Oxford: Oxford University Press.

Goehr, Lydia. 1994. *The Imaginary Museum of Musical Works: An Essay in the Philosophy of Music*. Oxford: Clarendon.

Kivy, Peter. 1988. *Osmin's Rage: Philosophical Reflections on Opera, Drama, and Text*. Princeton: Princeton University Press.

Levinson, Jerrold. 1984. "Hybrid Art Forms," *Journal of Aesthetic Education*, 18(4), 5–13.

Thom, Paul. 1993. *For an Audience: A Philosophy of the Performing Arts*. Philadelphia: Temple University Press.

Tomlinson, Gary. 1998. *Metaphysical Song: An essay on Opera*. Princeton: Princeton University Press.

PAUL THOM

photography presents philosophy with serious issues beyond aesthetics, rooted in ancient problems of the power of visual images over our conceptions, feelings, and desires. In their contemporary forms, these problems are intensified by photography's vastly expanding the range of pictorial subjects, its combination with other technologies, its wide and rapid distribution technologies, and its distinctive kinds of vividness and authority. Although most such topics must fall outside this essay, our work bears on them.

TWO ISSUES

From the moment of the various breakthroughs that led to its invention, photography has had an uneasy status among the arts. In part this reflects its unsettled identity as a kind of image-making. In 1857 Elizabeth Eastlake wrote of "a new form of communication," which "fills up the space between" messages and pictures, while not being quite either – although she went on to ask whether "photographic pictures" could be art. Replies have not divided simply between the pro and con that we will consider. Some have held that the idea of art should be extended to include photography, others that the term "art" has, over recent decades, come to include exhibition photography. Still others have argued that photography constitutes a distinct but equal realm of pictorial arts, that it is greater than previous art, even that it has helped usurp the idea of art.

Another set of questions concerning the veracity or realism of photography reemerges with each development of this constantly evolving technological family. Although photo-fidelity issues extend beyond the range of aesthetics, they not only overlap with them: they have become subject matter for recent art photography. Within philosophy, more attention has been given to these topics than those specific to art, individual photo-aesthetics, or the philosophical contents of particular works or styles. Can we connect these two perennial concerns, art status and photo-fidelity, in a better understanding, thereby clearing the way for other developments of this field?

WHAT IS PHOTOGRAPHY?

Photography is a set of technologies for using light and similar radiations to make physical images, permanent or transient, on receptor surfaces (chemical or electronic), by means of emitters and modulators of the radiation. Modulation includes refraction, diffraction, reflection, transmission, blocking, filtering, and like optical operations. The receptors are physical surfaces, marked either permanently or transiently as receptor screens.

Crucial to its understanding is that photography, as "the art of fixing a shadow" – as one of the first inventors, William Henry Fox Talbot, called it – has many important uses, which combine in numerous ways. Shadows themselves, as modulations of natural light, show how this might be. While there is limited use of shadow-play as a kind of pictorial art, most of our use of shadows is for detecting features of our environments. As photographers in particular know, the mere existence of a cast shadow – its shape, direction, and the sharpness of its edges – are features that carry information about the light source, the nature and position of the shadow-casters, and the surfaces upon which a shadow falls. From its beginnings photography was pressed into similar uses, independent of its uses for picture-making (thus was daguerreotypy presented to the French academies). X-ray and spectroscopy are two well-known means employed in detection, yet the spectroscopic bands registering the chemical composition of a star, even the expansion of the universe, are not depictions of these bodies. While there are many other important uses for such light-markings (e.g., photo-reproduction: one of the earliest and of most continuing importance), "aesthetically" we will consider photography mainly in terms of images made to be looked at for the sake of the looking. Here depiction plays a major role.

PHOTOGRAPHIC DEPICTION

Shadows may also help us understand photo-depiction. Suppose in a hand-shadow play an animal (depicted by the left hand's shadow) is grasped by a large hand (depicted by the shadow of the right hand): we are to imagine of the first shadow that it is an animal, of the second that it is a hand – maybe the hand that casts it. Both shadows depict in this nursery theater, but only the right depicts what casts it, a hand. These shadows each bear double cognitive messages: one by their causal, productive means, the other through prompting our imaginations. Each shadow evokes its fictional situation, while, like any shadow, also providing information about the actual situations that produce it: the light source, "scrim," and screen. So much, literally, is child's play, yet ideas about photo-depiction have been confused by the failure to make correspondingly simple distinctions within photographic depiction. As cinematography makes clear, photographs of things are commonly used to depict entities that were not photographed, or to depict things that were photographed as other than they are.

Despite their role in perceptual detection, shadows can be distorted and confusing. Puzzles about veracity in photographs would be like those about the "veracity" of shadows, imprints, and like traces, except that, unlike shadows, photographs are normally considered artifacts: entities made on purpose, for the purpose of being looked at. With most photos, the main purpose is depictive display, which, as we observed, is a matter of getting people to imagine seeing things. It is easy to see why most photography mixes this use with the evidential. Such photography has always been principally a matter of deriving easy depictions of things and situations, most of which would never have been pictured otherwise. But, given the nature of photo-optics, the causal process of making such depictions necessarily results in a good deal of evidence about their subjects (as well as other factors), willy-nilly, although – unlike closely controlled technical uses of photography – much of that is ambiguous. Nevertheless, the mere fact of there being such potential evidence about subjects seems to make our perception of photographs different from that of other depictions.

Besides the detective, in some cases, another factor related to the formative peculiarity of photo-depictions has long been noted. This is the very causal connection between subject matter and image: the subject's having causally affected the image by the action of light, which likewise affects us when we look at it. As David Hume observed, the connection between cause and effect is an even more powerful force in "enlivening" our conceptions of things than is resemblance. He would likely have held that photos of things provide both sorts of linkages, interwoven in that the causal connection accounts for the resemblance.

ARTISTIC OBJECTIONS: AESTHETIC AND EXPRESSIVE

The causal relationships that photo-depictive images typically bear to their depicted subject matter, which is the source of its evidential and contact connection values, has posed the main obstacle to the acceptance of photography as art. Corresponding to two main components of our ideas of fine art, two "classical" negative arguments recur historically in the literature of the subject – one aesthetic, the other expressive.

On the assumption that art is essentially aesthetic, while "aesthetic" denotes value for its own sake, the detective and contact functions of photography are judged too distracting to allow sufficient attention to the photograph. This argument can permit photographs a degree of aesthetic interest, but accords most of that to its subject matter and therefore not to "the work itself." A second, more influential, argument concerns the expressive component of art, which seems necessary for separating art from the vast aesthetic realm of nature.

The very word "artwork" labels works of art as artifacts – which indicates that they are deliberately contrived entities, typically to serve purposes. To perceive something as an artifact, not as mainly natural or accidental, is therefore to apply to it certain intentional concepts, concepts that strongly shape our experience of it. As the aesthetic argument urges, not everything we produce on purpose is for a purpose; some things must be free of intrinsic value. Even so, artifacts such as artworks are understood purposefully, regarding their parts and aspects. A song is sung for its sake alone; still, its parts and aspects are experienced in terms of what they do for the whole. We understand them in terms of why they are the way they are and in terms of what they are meant to be doing – thus intentionally.

Of course, many aspects of artifacts will be understood to have happened rather than to have been done. "Exekias made me," inscribed on a black-figure amphora, does not mean that the ceramist made the clay. Besides, like all artifacts, many aspects of artworks are not only natural but accidental – works differing as to how much they allow, invite, exploit. The calligraphic strokes of a Chinese artist show more of chance than do the words of the poem they inscribe, not just because of the style but because they, unlike the words, are physical particulars – and not the lesser for that. This raises a question of the extent to which we wish to keep nature and artifice distinct in a given art. Philosophical differences exist among traditions and individuals regarding the relationships of purposeful human productions and natural processes. Photographers provide a philosophically interesting array of such attitudes.

Intentional appearance is only a first step toward expressiveness, and very few artifacts are considered works of fine art, or are meant to be. The standard case from expression against photographic art is that its products, being automatically made, possess too few features that are explicable in terms of purposes for which they were put there, since most were not put there at all: thus that they fail even at an artifactual level. This may be considered consistent with photographs being highly worthwhile aesthetically, even with their requiring aesthetic talent to select: "wildflowers" picked from a visual field. The strategy for responding to this challenge seems clear: to present some photographs as works of human agency which uses photographic materials to perform productive picture-making acts, acts that place the results sufficiently under an intentional understanding that they can bear the kinds of mental, expressive meaning expected of works of art.

This reply, as offered by photographers such as Stieglitz, Weston, and Cartier-Bresson, emphasizes composition. For it to succeed, composition would have to be a relevantly important aspect of the image, and also be experienced as something done by the photographer. Furthermore, to rank photography with other pictorial fine arts, this should go beyond aesthetic results into a range of mental states and attitudes, including conceptions and feelings. Such an argument appears best made through actual photographic practice, by showing that individual styles have emerged, as with other visual arts, and that we experience these styles under the same sorts of mental attributions that we apply to other works of art. The question is empirical, and seems to require answering in the affirmative. We do appear to distinguish some photographers' works stylistically, and to characterize them in the required terms. If this has not always been clear, it is perhaps due to our considering individual photographs in isolation. Lone photographs can be striking, but appreciating them as artworks usually requires putting them in the context of the rest of the photographer's work. Only then do their relevant characteristics emerge as both aesthetically valuable and as due to the photographer. However, photography is not alone in this respect. It is typical of many kinds of modern artworks that it takes time to identify what they have to offer as art. The perception of expression, like that of skill, often requires practice and guidance even to understand what has been done.

OTHER AESTHETICS

Compositional defense of photo-art need not approach the issue expressively. One example is Robert Adams's (1996) distinctly aesthetic defense, based on three principles: that the goal of art is beauty; that beauty exists in form, provided by artists in their compositions; and that form provides consolation regarding meaningfulness in life – given our anxiety about its incoherence – so that suffering is more tolerable. Accordingly, the best art produces "shapes nearest shapelessness," providing reassurance that the feared incoherence has been rendered coherent, and not merely avoided through detachment. Subject matter is essential, since mere perceptual form, although pleasing, is not in this way consoling (although abstract forms can have subject matter). In addition, beauty in art requires "fresh intimations of form," to reassure us that new coherencies may continue to be found; and art should display "apparent ease," suggesting that this is not too difficult. Therefore art is best when it deals with specifics of the "commonplaces" in our lives – with concrete-seeming incoherencies nearest to our experience. Photography, Adams holds, does all this best, in our time.

See also MOTION PICTURES; ARTIFACT, ART AS; BEAUTY; DEPICTION; EXPRESSION; FUNCTION OF ART; SCRUTON; TECHNOLOGY AND ART; TRUTH IN ART.

BIBLIOGRAPHY

Adams, Robert. 1996. *Beauty in Photography: Essays in Defense of Traditional Values*. New York: Aperture Foundation.

Marien, Mary Warner. 2003. *Photography: A Cultural History*. Englewood Cliffs: Prentice-Hall.

Maynard, Patrick. 1997. *The Engine of Visualization: Thinking through Photography*. Ithaca: Cornell University Press.

Newhall, Beaumont. 1982. *History of Photography: From 1839 to the Present*. 5th edn. Boston: Little, Brown.

Trachtenberg, Alan (ed.). 1980. *Classic Essays on Photography*. New Haven: Leete's Island Books.

Walden, Scott (ed.). 2008. *Photography and Philosophy: Essays on the Pencil of Nature*. Oxford: Blackwell.

PATRICK MAYNARD

poetry One of the most ancient art forms, poetry, like other art forms, finds its roots embedded in activities that are not necessarily associated with art today, most notably religious rituals. Still, even while poetry is now commonly enjoyed for its own sake, many poems continue to be made for specific life events: weddings, funerals, presidential swearing-in ceremonies, anniversaries, and so on. Their connection to such events may call into question the *art* status of some poems; indeed, definitions of poetry (as is the case with definitions of art in general) must provide an account that establishes the art status of poems while still acknowledging that some poems may be parasitic upon human activities and events that have no intrinsically *artistic*

goals. Questions of this sort already presuppose a notion of art that divorces artworks from those activities and events and establishes art-making as an endeavor in its own right, one that by definition is independent from any other goals and that, were it to be mixed with other activities or goals, would have its art status threatened. However, just as a notion of art that denied art status to (say) the Vietnam Memorial in Washington DC in virtue of its serving a function beyond the purely artistic would be seriously defective, so a definition of poetry that denied poetry status to W. H. Auden's *Funeral Blues* would be anemic at best. The intention to write a poem, therefore, is the intention to fit one's work into a tradition, one in which, as happens to be the case, poems are written for various occasions. Likewise, the poetic tradition is one in which various formal means have been employed (alliteration, meter, rhyme schemes, etc.); a "transparent" poetic intention (i.e., one in which the poet is aware of the character of her intention) would therefore involve responding to the formal dimension of the tradition in various ways (see Ribeiro 2007).

It has been argued that most, if not all, philosophical issues that arise with respect to poetry are rather pertinent to literature in general, so that a "philosophy of poetry" is not needed beyond a philosophy of literature and criticism (Neill 2003). There are at least two problems with a philosophy of literature that subscribes to this view. The first is that what it amounts to in practice is, frequently, an undue focus on a particular literary genre, at the expense of other forms that may have little to do with it beyond sharing a medium in language. Typically, the philosopher of literature today is a reader of novels, with little to no knowledge about the history of poetry or of the formal devices that are its bread and butter. Despite best intentions, then, the philosophy suffers in virtue of the assumption that what works for one works for all. Nevertheless, one could still claim that there is no need for a philosophy of poetry in addition to a philosophy of literature – that is, so long as philosophers of literature are sufficiently well informed about the various literary arts. However, here the second problem rears its head. For while it may be true for some issues that one philosophy of literature fits

101

all, some facts about poetry suggest that we might do better by compartmentalizing. These include: (1) formal schemes; (2) figurative language (tropes); (3) the first-person perspective of most poetry; and (4) the oral origins of poetry.

Perhaps the most obvious difference between poems and novels, short stories, essays, and plays is that in poetry the use of formal schemes is pervasive. The use of poetic schemes such as meter, rhyme schemes, alliteration, and parallelism is not a typical feature of the novel or the essay. Accordingly, attention to those devices, and to how, and how well, they might be employed by the author, is not a feature of the literary criticism of novels or essays. The presence of formal schemes also has consequences for how readers or listeners comprehend and experience poems. Theories in pragmatics that seek to explain linguistic choices in the process of communication sometimes see the formalization found in poems as cognitive hurdles readers must surpass in order to arrive at a poetic message (see Sperber & Wilson 1995). However, it is just as plausible to see rhyme schemes, for instance, as cognitive facilitators, insofar as they may encourage readers or listeners to draw semantic connections between phonetically similar words. Be that as it may, questions regarding the effects of formal schemes on the cognition and experience of literary works arise with special urgency in poetry; even prose poems and so-called "free" verse make extensive use of poetic schemes. The same cannot be said regarding prose works such as novels and essays.

A second aspect of poetry central to the art form is its use of tropes such as metaphor, simile, metonymy, and many others. The flourishing of philosophy of language in the twentieth century, with its general focus on issues of meaning and truth, led to a plethora of articles on metaphor in the 1970s and 1980s; today, developments in cognitive science are again bringing the issue to the fore. It is certainly true that metaphor (and figurative language in general) is not the exclusive domain of poets; people use tropes in everyday conversation frequently. It is also true, nevertheless, that the most challenging tropes – the most novel and frequently also the most difficult to parse – are typically found in poems. While the question of metaphor in general is an issue for philosophy of language, it is a question why tropes should pervade poetry to the extent that they do. One answer focuses on tropes as a poetic medium (and one may see schemes as a poetic medium as well; both tropes and schemes being ways in which language can be used). That is, tropes such as metaphors encourage the reader to see things differently, thus promoting a search for meaning within the work, and of a poetic message. While this may seem obvious, such an idea contrasts with the view that it is something external to the poem, namely the conventions of reading, that foster in readers a search for poetic meaning and poetic message (see Lamarque & Olsen 1994). While reading conventions may help explain why, once familiar with poems, readers may be more inclined to read them in certain ways, they cannot explain why on a first encounter with poetry one may have a meaning- or message-seeking attitude. In such cases, something internal to the poem must be doing the work: poetic metaphors, similes, etc. challenge readers' typical semantic associations, and thereby force an entertainment of novel ones and of what significance they may have.

Most poetry has been and continues to be lyric poetry (rather than narrative or dramatic), and the lyric poem is almost invariably written in the first person. All of Shakespeare's sonnets, for instance, are written in the first person, and most of them explicitly indicate as much in the first or second line. That lyric poetry is principally written in the first person (either implicitly or explicitly) has immediate consequences for how we experience poems, and in turn for how we evaluate them. This personal mode of expression invites a personal mode of engagement with the content of the work such that the ideal engagement often involves some level of identification, on the part of the listener or reader, with the impressions, thoughts, or feelings expressed in the work. The "I" of the lyric encourages our taking the poetic voice as our own, much as point-of-view shots in films put us in the perspective of the protagonist. Evidence that identification is a central characteristic of our engagement with poems may be found in the common practice of "appropriation," where we borrow poems written by others to express our own ideas or feelings. While appropriation may occur with other art forms, the practice is not widespread in any other art form except the song lyric, which shares historical roots and structural similarities with the lyric poem. Finally, subjective (though not necessarily critical or scholarly) evaluation of the quality of a poem is in part dependent upon the level of identification resultant from one's engagement with the work, where the greater the potentiality for "appropriation," the greater the likelihood of subjective appreciation of the work. *Mutatis mutandis*, the less one is able to identify with a poem (and consequently potentially to "appropriate" it for personal use), the less one may be able to appreciate its qualities, no matter how critically acclaimed the work may be.

Finally, the ontology of literature has suffered because of insufficient attention to the particularities of the poetic tradition. Poetry has its origins in oral cultures, and scholars have long noted that in oral traditions the texts of literary works are considerably more fluid than they have been since the invention of the printing press. An ontology that is to account for this aspect of early literature as well as for literature created since the early modern period must consequently be responsive to the varieties of strictures on what makes a literary work. Literary works created within the context of oral traditions do not rely on written texts and so do not adhere to a strict word-by-word text type in the way that is common in modern literature. Rather, criteria such as story theme and metrical structure individuate works in those contexts. Moreover, in such contexts works are instantiated in their enunciations rather than, as has been claimed, in the text copies that are our usual means of access to those works today.

Other questions that have commanded the attention of philosophers relate to the truth value of poetic statements: can the propositions found in poems be said to be true, especially when they are made by means of metaphors ("Juliet is the sun")? Much has been made of this question (see Budd 1995). On the one hand, it may plausibly be thought that the value of a poem may at least in part depend on the truth of the beliefs expressed in it, and, on the other, it may be objected that the manner of expression is what gives a poem its value as a poem, especially insofar as beliefs should be true or false independently of how they are expressed, and could accordingly at least in principle be expressed otherwise (this too has been contested, most famously in Brooks 1947). This issue, while not peculiar to poetry alone, emerges most pointedly in poems, and especially lyric poems since the modern period, inasmuch as the stability of texts enabled by printing has led to a certain "idolization" of the text, where *these* words and punctuation in *this* specific order make up a given poem, and any alteration would violate its integrity as an instance of the work. It is unlikely that there would have been a heresy of paraphrase for the rhapsodes of antiquity; what was important was not whether Zeus indeed had wide brows or the thought could be expressed differently, but whether the epithet fit the meter on a given line.

These considerations may not warrant a philosophy of poetry segmented from a more general philosophy of literature. They show nevertheless that a substantive philosophy of literature demands attention to the various particularities and histories of literary practices, and that the attention demanded by poetry is *sui generis* among the literary arts.

See also DRAMA; LITERATURE; COGNITIVE VALUE OF ART; CRITICISM; EXPRESSION; METAPHOR.

BIBLIOGRAPHY

Aristotle. 1954. *Rhetoric and Poetics*. R. Roberts & I. Bywater (trans.). New York: Modern Library.
Brooks, Cleanth. 1947. *The Well Wrought Urn*. New York: Harcourt Brace.
Budd, Malcolm. 1995. *Values of Art*. London: Penguin.
Hegel, G. W. F. 1975 [1835–8]. *Aesthetics: Lectures on Fine Art*. 2 vols. T. M. Knox (trans). Oxford: Clarendon, vol. ii (esp. part 3, sec. 3, ch. 3, "Poetry").
Kant, Immanuel. 1987 [1790]. *Critique of Judgment*. W. S. Pluhar (trans.). Indianapolis: Hackett.
Lamarque, Peter & Olsen, Stein Haugom. 1994. *Truth, Fiction and Literature*. Oxford: Clarendon.
Neill, Alex. 2003. "Poetry." In *Oxford Handbook of Aesthetics*. J. Levinson (ed.). Oxford: Oxford University Press, 605–13.
Plato. 1997. *Ion* and *The Republic*. In *Plato: Complete Works*. J. M. Cooper (ed.). Indianapolis: Hackett.
Ribeiro, Anna Christina. 2007. "Intending to Repeat: A Definition of Poetry," *Journal of Aesthetics and Art Criticism*, 65, 189–201.

Sperber, Dan & Wilson, Deirdre. 1995. *Relevance Theory.* 2nd edn. Oxford: Blackwell.

Stecker, Robert. 2001. "Expressiveness in Music and Poetry," *Journal of Aesthetics and Art Criticism,* 59, 85–96.

ANNA CHRISTINA RIBEIRO

sculpture Contemporary accounts of the nature of sculpture have sought to identify distinctive features of works of sculpture, or our experience of them, that are nontrivially necessary and plausibly sufficient for their being sculptures. They have focused variously on the physical properties of work materials, the involvement of specific perceptual modes, or perceptual phenomena, or the relationship to sculpture of a distinctive sensibility. An alternative is to understand the art of sculpture in terms of the ways the use of materials features in practices of producing and appreciating.

MATERIALS
There is a commonsense thought that sculptures are three-dimensional art objects as distinct from, for example, the two-dimensional pictorial arts. The sculptor Naum Gabo asserted that sculpture is three-dimensional *eo ipso*. The problem with this idea is that all embodied artworks, including pictorial works, are three-dimensional in their material construction. Sculptures may typically be less flat than paintings, but the nature of sculpture cannot lie in physical three-dimensionality per se. Alternatively it could be argued that whereas sculptures and paintings are all made of three-dimensional materials, three-dimensional properties are *artistically relevant* to our appreciation of sculptures but not for paintings (where only the two-dimensional surface properties count). Robert Vance, for example, argues that "sculptures are objects designed in three dimensions" and that "what counts for sculpture is real occupancy of space" (1995: 224, 217). Yet other kinds of artworks are also designed and fashioned out of three-dimensional materials, and their "real occupancy of space" matters to us in appreciating them. Paintings, and even photographs and other pictorial arts, take their appearance and embody their two-dimensional properties in virtue of their three-dimensional construction,

and this relationship can sometimes play a role in our appreciation not only as a material condition but as a matter of specific artistic interest. If the three-dimensional has a specific and distinctive relevance in sculpture, it does not follow from the properties of art materials.

PERCEPTION
Perhaps the nature of sculpture and the relevance of the three-dimensional can be understood in terms of the sense modalities, or the content or structure of perceptual experience. Herbert Read, for example, argued that sculpture is an art of palpation. Yet there are many instances of sculpture – most monumental sculpture being an obvious example – that cannot be touched and are not intended to be, and for which it is vision rather than touch that is the primary mode of access. F. David Martin claims that the nature of sculpture lies in a phenomenon he calls "enlivened space," with the space around sculpture a perceptible part of the work in virtue of its location in a space continuous with our own. Susanne K. Langer holds that a unique feature of the art of sculpture is the way the content of our experience of space is structured or organized in our experience of the work, such that "a piece of sculpture is a center of three-dimensional space. It is a virtual kinetic volume, which dominates the surrounding space, and this environment derives all proportions and relations from it, as the actual environment does from oneself" (1959: 91). Robert Hopkins (2004) concurs with Langer, and puts this down to the fact that, unlike pictures, sculptures do not incorporate a perspective on what they represent. This leaves the represented world of the sculpture incomplete and able to interact with the world of the gallery in the way characterized by Langer. However, while much sculpture may indeed "impact" into the space of the appreciator, this is not a universal feature of sculpture. Some frontal sculptures, and works such as statuary high on buildings, may be intended to be viewed from a distance and direction, and often do not seem to fill or energize space, or form an experiential kinetic spatial center in any way specific to the art. Furthermore, some sculptures do have a perspectival structure and offer us a "complete" world into which we look from our own space (e.g., some of the

works of Giacometti). On the other hand, some paintings, including pictorial works, can create an apparent space that imposes itself upon us, or form a kinetic center around which our experience of the space of the work and its location is structured (e.g., some color-field and *trompe-l'oeil* painting). The apparent space of either kind of work can seem (or can be represented) as continuous or discontinuous with, as dominating or dominated by, our own.

SENSIBILITY

Another approach is to suppose that a distinctive sensibility is required in the production or appreciation of sculpture. Read (1956), for example, suggests that sculpture requires the involvement of a specifically plastic sensibility, central to which are perception from depth to surface and the synthetic realization of the mass and ponderability of the object as if held within the hand. Robert Vance (1995) argues that sculptures are dependent on the appreciator's bodily self-awareness in a way that differs significantly from the pictorial, evoking nonpropositional imaginative identification with the sculpture, feeling the work's apparent qualities as if they belonged to the appreciator's own body. L. R. Rogers (1962, 1963) proposes that "sculptural thinking" differs qualitatively from the kind of thinking involved in other kinds of art in its analysis of spatial concepts and manipulation of complex spatial forms involving mass and space. Sculptors (and presumably appreciators) need on this view to be schooled in the "logic of form," which makes the articulation of sculpture intelligible. Yet, while the factors identified by Read may be characteristic of how we ought to approach our experience of some works, such as those of Rodin or Moore, they do not seem necessary to our appreciation of all sculpture, and may be antithetical to some (e.g., those concerned with the arrangement of abstract line and form, the articulation of surfaces, or the absence of substance). Similarly with respect to Vance, it is true not only of some sculptures but also of some paintings that the imagined mass of a work's material construction, or the apparent qualities of its represented content, is integral to our experience of the work. Nonpropositional imaginings of the kind Vance describes some-

times play a role in our appreciation of other kinds of art – we might also imagine the thickness and resistance of the paint in its application to the canvas, or the mass and density of its final hardened state, or in viewing a picture imagine its represented features as being experienced by ourselves, perhaps as features of our own bodies. Nor, with respect to Rogers' notion of "sculptural thinking," is it unusual in the pictorial arts to think with or through three-dimensional spatial concepts or forms, not only in relation to represented forms but also, when the properties of the paint on the canvas are of special practical interest, the material construction of the work.

PRACTICE

A problem that faced accounts of the kinds addressed earlier was that the features of artworks that they identify are either trivially necessary or not plausibly sufficient to account for their being sculptures. An alternative is to understand sculpture in terms of the place of a distinctive "sculptural" way of using materials as an artistic medium within practices of production and appreciation (Koed 2005). What separates painting and sculpture is not the dimensionality of the art materials, or whether three-dimensional space is represented or possesses one or other quality in perception, but the way in which representation (for example) is achieved and the way it is interpreted. Whereas the three-dimensional physical properties of materials and related perceptual properties may be material conditions for the two-dimensional surface properties that function as the artistic medium in painting, within sculptural practices of production and appreciation properties such as thickness or weight themselves function directly as an art medium. Sculpture can be understood as a tradition of art practice to which such a use of materials is standard, in the terms of Kendall Walton's (1970) categories of art. Whether individual works are sculptures will therefore depend on the facts of their relationship to the traditions of art practice out of which they emerge. Works that do not belong to the category of sculpture may well nevertheless involve a sculptural use of materials where this use is (in terms of Walton's categories) variable (e.g., architecture) or contra-standard (e.g., painting) to the traditions of practice out of which they emerge and are to be understood.

In appealing to specific features as essential, the theories canvassed earlier are unable to explain the special relationship to sculpture they suppose such features to have. An account of the kind just outlined, however, enables us to understand general physical and perceptual differences between sculptures and paintings as contingent rather than essential. Sculptures are likely to be more massive or more appropriately touched or moved around than those in which two-dimensional features function as a medium given the sculptural use of materials. Likewise, observations about the general role of ways of thinking or imagining in terms of three-dimensional form, spatial concepts, and real and imagined sensations can be made sense of in terms of their relationship to sculptural use of materials as a medium in the production and appreciation of works.

See also ARCHITECTURE; DRAWING, PAINTING, AND PRINTMAKING; DEPICTION; TRADITION; WALTON.

BIBLIOGRAPHY

Hopkins, Robert. 2004. "Painting, Sculpture, Sight and Touch," *British Journal of Aesthetics*, 44, 149–66.

Koed, Erik. 2005. "Sculpture and the Sculptural," *Journal of Aesthetics and Art Criticism*, 63, 147–54.

Langer, Susanne K. 1959. *Feeling and Form*. London: Routledge & Kegan Paul.

Martin, F. David. 1981. *Sculpture and Enlivened Space*. Lexington: University Press of Kentucky.

Read, Herbert. 1956. *The Art of Sculpture*. London: Faber.

Rogers, L. R. 1962. "Sculptural Thinking," *British Journal of Aesthetics*, 2, 291–9.

Rogers, L. R. 1963. "Sculptural Thinking. 2: A Reply," *British Journal of Aesthetics*, 3, 357–62.

Vance, Robert D. 1995. "Sculpture," *British Journal of Aesthetics*, 35, 217–26.

Walton, Kendall L. 1970. "Categories of Art," *Philosophical Review*, 79, 334–67.

ERIK KOED

A

---

abstraction   Artworks are abstract, we might think, when they do not represent: abstraction is simply the absence of representation. After all, there is a natural contrast between abstract and representational painting; and music, at least in its "absolute" (i.e., abstract) form, does not clearly represent at all. Absolute music, like abstract painting, *expresses* feelings and perhaps thoughts, but, we suppose, expression and representation are different.

However, there are two difficulties with taking this to capture the nature of abstraction. First, on closer inspection it excludes art that intuitively counts as abstract; and second, the definition is only as clear as the rather murky notion of representation itself.

To illustrate the first difficulty, consider Richard Wollheim's argument (1987: ch. 2) that a good deal of abstract painting in fact represents in the same way as painting of other kinds. In looking at a typical Kandinsky, for instance, while I may not see in it everyday objects such as men and buildings, I do see colored shapes arrayed in three-dimensional space. The red trapezium that breaks a long black line is seen as a red rectangle, tilted at an angle to the viewer, and lying in front of a black strip. I am thus simultaneously aware of how marks are distributed on the canvas and of rather different objects arranged in depth. Since for Wollheim pictorial representation just *is* the deliberate generation of experiences with this twofold nature, he concludes that the Kandinsky represents shapes in three-dimensional space. And although the details of Wollheim's argument invoke his views about pictorial representation, his conclusion has independent appeal. Now, Wollheim does not think every abstract painting can be treated in this way. Certain works of Mondrian and Barnett Newman, he says, resist being seen as other than simply marks on a canvas. Thus he accepts that the traditional definition of abstraction does apply to some paintings. The problem is that it does not apply to most of those we think of as abstract.

We can flesh out the second difficulty by considering either abstract painting or music. It is hardly plausible that these never make any reference to things beyond themselves. The idea that they express emotions and ideas is intended to concede as much, without reintroducing representation. But is it clear that expression is not simply another form of representation? Of course, it differs from some kinds of representing – from the depiction that concerns Wollheim, for instance, or from describing things in language. But the notion of representation is both highly general and resists easy analysis. Until we settle whether expression is itself representing, our definition of abstraction leaves us uncertain whether expressive absolute music, for instance, counts as abstract or not. Of course, there is nothing in itself wrong with a definition leaving boundaries vague. Many phenomena exhibit hinterlands where it is simply unclear whether they hold. The problem is rather that defining abstraction as absence of representation leaves the limits of the latter unclear as those of the former, on our intuitive understanding, are not.

The alternative is to see abstraction, not as the absence of representation, but as a matter of *what* is represented. Wollheim suggests that what marks out the Kandinsky from more traditional painting is that the latter is *figurative*. Traditional works represent things of readily identifiable kinds (dogs, houses, battles, one-eyed giants), and individual members of those kinds (Louis XIV or Polyphemus). Much abstract painting instead represents things which themselves belong only to relatively abstract kinds – red rectangles or black strips, for instance. In similar vein, Kendall L. Walton

(1988) explores the idea that what marks out abstract works is that what is represented or conveyed is purely general. While a novel may describe a specific locale and specific events that occur within it, abstract works (Walton's focus is music) convey, for instance, only the general notion of struggle, or the dynamics of an emotion. In the context of painting, a natural relative of Walton's thought lies in the idea that abstraction should be understood as the product of *abstracting from* the specifics of visual phenomena. While a nineteenth-century Realist painter might have sought to capture all the detail of some scene, his more abstract successors seek instead to extract from it the bare essentials of form and structure. This idea is familiar from the work of Cézanne, for instance, in which buildings and natural features are stripped down to their basic geometry. But it also runs through a good deal of later work, such as the drawings of Picasso (in almost any of his periods). Abstraction in this sense need not mean abandoning the representation of particulars – Picasso's own portrait of Françoise Gilot as a flower shows that what can be preserved is the form of an *individual's* look, abstracted from the details of her appearance. What it does necessarily involve is abandoning detail in favor of the basic form, structure, or gestalt.

Although it is perhaps not entirely clear quite what any of these suggestions involves, and thus whether there are one or several proposals here, it is clear that they all tend in the same direction. The result is a definition of abstraction that, in contrast to its predecessor, treats it as a matter of *degree*. It also opens up the prospect of making sense of abstraction in arts, such as literature, in which it is unclear what would be left if representation were absent.

A full account of abstraction will need to deploy both definitions now before us. As Wollheim notes, some, if not many, paintings are abstract in virtue of not representing at all; and perhaps there can be musical art that neither represents in any more straightforward way nor expresses anything. (Some indeed, have considered this to be the true mission of absolute music.) So the first notion cannot be dispensed with entirely. But, equally, we have seen good reason not to rely on it alone.

Never far behind questions about the nature of abstraction are questions concerning its value. Abstraction is sometimes itself a source of value (and not a mere accompaniment to other qualities that are valuable). Where abstract art is profound – in the greatest works of absolute music, or the masterpieces of abstract painting – the abstractness of the works is surely central to their achieving what they do. Something like this thought no doubt underpins the persistent tendency to valorize absolute music as the purest form of that art, and the attempts made during the heyday of Abstract Expressionism to do the same for it in relation to painting (Greenberg 1971). Yet it can seem puzzling how abstraction can be of value. How can eschewing representing altogether, or limiting oneself to representing only what is general, help produce art worth caring about?

Where art is abstract in our second sense, there is no real difficulty in understanding how that promotes value. Less abstract art captures the details of particular things, or of specific types: the precise features of a sitter's face, perhaps, or the character of a typical Victorian pickpocket. But why, apart from historical or psychological curiosity, should we care about representations that capture such features? The sitter is available to be studied for herself, and the pickpocket probably never existed. What are either to me, and what does the painting or novel make of either that I could not make for myself? Surely one of the things to want from art is something more universal, something to take away that can be found in other instances of the types, and in life more generally. For that, however, what matters is the more general content of the artworks. That might be present in nonabstract works – they may represent the general by representing the specific. It is also, however, certainly present in works that are abstract in our second sense.

That leaves untouched, of course, works that are abstract in the other sense, those that do not represent at all. Since abstraction here is conceived purely negatively, the prospects for understanding how it contributes to value are limited. We may instead ask a related question: how can the work have value at all, given that it does not represent anything? But puzzlement over that is only in place to the extent that we understand how in general representation contributes to art's value. Since I doubt our understanding of that issue goes deep, we should not rush to find it mysterious how art can be successful in representation's absence.

See also DRAWING, PAINTING, AND PRINTMAKING; MUSIC AND SONG; COGNITIVE VALUE OF ART; EXPRESSION; PICTURE PERCEPTION; REPRESENTATION.

BIBLIOGRAPHY

Greenberg, Clement. 1971. *Art and Culture*. Boston: Beacon.

Walton, Kendall L. 1988. "What is Abstract about the Art of Music?" *Journal of Aesthetics and Art Criticism*, 46, 351–64.

Wollheim, Richard. 1987. *Painting as an Art*. London: Thames & Hudson.

ROBERT HOPKINS

acquaintance principle   *see* TESTIMONY IN AESTHETICS.

Adorno, Theodor W(iesengrund) (1903–1969)   German philosopher; leading figure in the Frankfurt school of critical theory. Born into a wealthy family in Frankfurt am Main, Adorno received his PhD in philosophy in that city in 1924, but spent the following year in Vienna studying composition with Alban Berg. While remaining involved in the music world, he taught philosophy at Frankfurt University until Hitler's advent to power drove him to the US in 1938, where he joined the Frankfurt Institute for Social Research in exile, working in New York and southern California. He returned to a professorship in Frankfurt in 1953, and succeeded his close collaborator Max Horkheimer as director of the institute, also reinstalled in that city, in 1964. His work, which greatly influenced the German student movement of the 1960s, has since the 1980s become an international touchstone for criticism, especially in the visual arts. The majority of Adorno's works are concerned with aesthetic questions. There are studies of Berg, Mahler, and Wagner; essays on literary and musical matters; an *Introduction to the Sociology of Music* (1962); and two central theoretical works: *Philosophy of Modern Music* (1948) and *Aesthetic Theory*

(1970). His aphoristic style reaches a high point in the wide-ranging *Minima Moralia* (1951), one of the great books of the postwar period.

Adorno's primary aesthetic interest is in the "autonomous" art that emerged from earlier functional contexts at the end of the eighteenth century. This autonomy "was a function of the bourgeois consciousness of freedom that was itself bound up with the social structure" (1997: 225); thus art expressed the autonomy of the individual subject vis-à-vis society. Art's autonomy means a development of its own structures of meaning, independent of direct reference to the social world; hence Adorno suggests that the concept of art is strictly applicable only to music, since literature and painting always include "an element of subject-matter transcending aesthetic confines, undissolved in the autonomy of form" (1974: 223). Paradoxically, it is the very tendency toward the elaboration of its own formal nature that constitutes art's social meaning. As the expression of a subjectivity engaged dialectically with a social reality at once repressive of its desires and defining its conditions of existence, art represents the demand for freedom from repression. Its autonomy, its functionlessness, allow it to stand as a critique of a society dedicated to the domination of nature in the interests of commercial profit. As an element of the modern society to which it stands in this critical relation, aesthetic form is "sedimented" social content, because "artistic labour is social labour" (1997: 5, 236). Its history follows the pattern of social development generally: that of the progressive mastery of nature by humankind, described by Adorno (following Max Weber) as a process of rationalization. Nature is represented in music by what Adorno calls the musical "material" confronting composers at any given time: sound as organized by historically evolved musical form. The drive to control this material led first to the elaboration of the tonal system by the masters of Viennese classicism and then to the total control over the material achieved by Schoenberg. With the second Viennese school, no conventions force the composer "to acquiesce to traditionally universal principles. With the liberation of musical material, there arose the possibility of mastering it technically . . . The composer has emancipated himself along with his sounds" (1973: 52).

The emancipation achieved by modern art through its denial of earlier conventions must be paid for. "In the process of pursuing its own inner logic, music is transformed more and more from something significant into something obscure – even to itself" (1973: 19). From the artist's point of view, "the progress in technique that brought them ever greater freedom and independence of anything heterogeneous, has resulted in a kind of reification, technification of the inward as such" (1974: 214). For the listener, music has lost its transparent meaningfulness and the satisfaction it once gave. To grasp its meaning – what Adorno calls its truth content – now requires, beyond "sensory listening," aesthetic theory, which alone makes possible "the conceptually mediated perception of the elements and their configuration which assures the social substance of great music" (1973: 130) – its resistance to the ideological demand that experience be depicted as the achievement of harmonious totality.

Art that does not confront society in this way is condemned by Adorno as regressive, both in the realm of high art, as with Stravinsky's primitivism and neoclassicism, and in that of the popular music mass produced by the "culture industry." Both are adaptations to social reality: in the former by formally modeling the submission of the individual to social irrationality, in the latter by accepting completely the consequences of the commodity form for musical production. "Classical" music as a whole is drawn into the system of commercialization, as its presentation is adapted to a mass listenership no longer capable of "structural listening" but able only to wait for the appearance of beautiful melodies and exciting rhythms. In this, too, music bears a social meaning – that of the increasing domination of individual experience by the needs of industrial capitalism.

It follows from Adorno's conception of artworks as "concentrated social substance" that a critical aesthetics must seek social significance in the formal properties of individual works. This is a difficult prescription to follow, and Adorno's studies of artworks are typically less persuasive than his theoretical generalizations. Attempts at combining formal analysis with sociological decoding, such as the comparison of serial technique to bureaucratization,

or of the relation between theme and harmony in sonata form to the dialectic of individual and society, are too often "merely verbal analogies which have no basis in fact but owe their origin and a semblance of plausibility to a generously ambivalent use of words like . . . 'general and particular' " (Dahlhaus 1987: 243). In addition, Adorno does not hesitate on occasion to subordinate matters of fact to his philosophical purposes (see Dahlhaus 1970). His clearly inadequate dismissal of Stravinsky and his inexpert and unsubtle treatment of popular music have also come under much (not unappreciative) criticism. Nevertheless, his work remains important as an aesthetics of modernism, both for its general program, the discovery of social meanings in artistic form, and for its many powerful observations and suggestions.

See also NINETEENTH- AND TWENTIETH-CENTURY CONTINENTAL AESTHETICS; ART HISTORY; MARXISM AND ART.

BIBLIOGRAPHY

Primary sources
[1948] 1976. *Philosophy of Modern Music*. A. G. Mitchell & W. V. Blomster (trans.). New York: Continuum.
[1951] 1974. *Minima Moralia*. E. F. N. Jephcott (trans.). London: Verso.
[1962] 1973. *Introduction to the Sociology of Music*. E. B. Ashton (trans.). New York: Continuum.
[1970] 1997. *Aesthetic Theory*. R. Hullot-Kentor (trans.). Minneapolis: University of Minnesota Press.
2002. *Essays on Music*. R. Leppert (ed.). Berkeley: University of California Press.

Secondary sources
Dahlhaus, Carl. 1970. "Soziologische Dechiffrierung von Musik. Zu Theodor W. Adorno's Wagnerkritik" [Sociological deciphering of music: on Theodor Adorno's critique of Wagner], *International Review of Music Aesthetics and Sociology*, 1, 137–47.
Dahlhaus, Carl. 1987. *Schoenberg and the New Music*. D. Puffett & A. Clayton (trans.). Cambridge: Cambridge University Press.
Gendron, Bernard. 1986. "Theodor Adorno meets the Cadillacs." In *Studies in Entertainment*. T. Modleski (ed.). Bloomington: Indiana University Press, 18–36.
Mattick, Paul. 2007. "The Dialectic of Disappointment: Adorno and Art Criticism since the 1980s." In *Value: Art: Politics. Criticism, Meaning and*

Interpretation after Postmodernism. J. Harris (ed.). Liverpool: Liverpool University Press, 347–66.
Paddison, Max. 1993. *Adorno's Aesthetics of Music*. Cambridge: Cambridge University Press.

PAUL MATTICK

aesthetic attitude The question of what it is to adopt a distinctively aesthetic attitude to objects is important in its own right, but also because of the role attributed to this attitude within wider issues. For example, the difficulties, intensified by developments in "modern art," in defining the term "art" have prompted the attempt to characterize works of art as those toward which it is appropriate to adopt the aesthetic attitude. Some philosophers have also tried to define the notions of aesthetic properties, qualities, values, and experience in terms of aesthetic attitude.

Immanuel Kant was not the first person to associate a distinctively aesthetic attitude with "disinterest." (A similar association seems to have shaped Japanese aesthetic theory over many centuries: see Odin 2001.) But in modern Western aesthetics, it is Kant's discussion that has had a decisive influence. Entirely representative, therefore, is the definition of "the aesthetic attitude" as "disinterested and sympathetic attention to and contemplation of any object of awareness whatever" (Stolnitz 1960: 34–5). (Strictly speaking, Kant himself did not employ "disinterest" to distinguish the aesthetic from the nonaesthetic, but to distinguish, within the realm of what he called "the aesthetic," judgments of beauty and sublimity from those of mere pleasantness or agreeableness.)

Kant explains the "disinterested" attitude as one where the subject is "merely contemplative . . . indifferent as regards the existence of an object," and focusing rather upon its "appearance" (Kant 1966: 43). This is intended to capture the insight that when viewing something "disinterestedly," and so aesthetically, will and desire are in abeyance. When so viewing an object, a person is unconcerned with its practical utility, including its role as a source of intellectual or sensuous gratification. From this Kant draws some questionable conclusions. Not only, he says, is emotion a "hindrance" to "pure" appreciation of beauty but the subject must have no concern with the kind of object he is viewing – that is, with the "concept" under which it falls.

There have been several significant variations on Kant's theme. For Schopenhauer, too, the aesthetic attitude is marked by a withdrawal from our usual practical, willful engagement with things. It is, once again, a type of contemplation, but directed toward the Platonic ideas or forms that lie behind "appearances." In contemplating a building, I am indifferent to its function, attending instead to the ideas of space, gravity, and so on. Edward Bullough characterized the aesthetic attitude in terms of "psychical distance." On a fogbound ship, the aesthete distances himself from the fears and practical concerns of the crew, and concentrates on the strange shapes and forms the fog lends to things. Finally, a number of phenomenologists, elaborating on Kant's talk of "indifference" to actual existence, have argued that the true object of the aesthetic attitude is not an actual object in the world but an "intentional object," existing only for the perceiver. Strictly, therefore, there cannot be a single object toward which both aesthetic and nonaesthetic attitudes may be taken, for in the two cases different kinds of object are being considered.

More dramatic are the implications many twentieth-century artists and critics have drawn from Kant's notion of "disinterest" for the proper ambitions and functions of art. One of these is a marked "formalist" hostility to representational art. In "pure" aesthetic experience, wrote Clive Bell in 1914, a painting must be treated as if it "were not representative of anything" (1947: 32). More generally, there should be no concern for content and meaning since this would contradict the required indifference to matters of existence and conceptualization. A second implication drawn – also in the "formalist" spirit – is that art should not aim to be expressive of emotion. The proper response to art is not an emotional one but something like Kant's "restful contemplation." Finally, "disinterest" has been invoked to support the aestheticist or "art for art's sake" estimation of art. Since people are not viewing something *as* art if they are interested in further benefits to be derived from it, no justification is required for art beyond the satisfaction aesthetic contemplation yields.

It is hard to judge how far Kant would endorse such claims, since the bulk of his discussion is about an aesthetic attitude toward nature, not art. Extrapolation to a Kantian theory of art is uncertain. (What, for example, is the analogue in the case of painting to suspension of interest in a thing's actual existence? Indifference to the existence of the canvas and pigments? Or to that of whatever is depicted?) Some of his remarks indicate that he would not accept these alleged extensions of his idea. Thus, while he indeed insists that judgments of beauty should be "independent of emotion," the feeling of the sublime – itself an aesthetic one – is an "outflow of vital powers" and may be "regarded as emotion" (Kant 1966: 83). And, unlike the aestheticists, Kant offers nonaesthetic justifications for aesthetic experience. Most notably, it is "purposive in reference to the moral feeling," since it "prepares us to love disinterestedly" (Kant 1966: 108; see also Guyer 2005: esp. chs. 8–9.)

The formalist and aestheticist programs are surely not entailed by the bare idea of "disinterest." That my concern with a painting must not be practical (pecuniary, say) nor a "conceptual" one of classification (Pre-Raphaelite, say) cannot entail that paintings should eschew representation. Nor can it entail that I should suspend all inquiry into a painting's "point" or content, representational or otherwise. Nor, except on the crude view that a painting only expresses something extraneous to it (like the artist's mood), is there any reason to proscribe attention to its expressive features, including those which are expressive of emotions. For these features may be discerned as belonging, integrally, to the painting itself.

Finally, the doctrine of "art for art's sake" seems guilty of confusing two questions – that of the proper attitude toward a work of art, and that of why it may be desirable for this attitude to be taken. It is perfectly possible to answer the second question by referring to the moral, psychological, or even religious benefits that may accrue, while insisting that the aesthetic gaze itself must not be *motivated* by such considerations. It is only because it is "disinterested" that, as Kant clearly saw, it can succeed in yielding these further benefits.

Even with these unwarranted extensions blocked, the characterization of the aesthetic attitude as "disinterested" indifference to its objects' actual existence and conceptual type remains implausible. The aesthetic satisfaction yielded when one looks at a cathedral may be due, in part, to a projected sense of its solidity, the coolness of its stone, and the peace that obtains within. This enjoyment could not survive the discovery that the "cathedral" is a cardboard facade used in the latest film about Thomas à Becket, and so cannot be an enjoyment that is "indifferent" to the building's real existence. And while Kant may be consistent in concluding that my appreciation of a cathedral is "impure" to the extent that I am conceiving of it *as* a cathedral, his conclusion betrays a peculiarly restricted notion of aesthetic appreciation. It is my aesthetic sensibility, as much as anything, that is offended by the staging of a circus or bingo competition within the cathedral's walls, and this sensibility is not to be abstracted from my consciousness of the building's spiritual purpose, of the prayers and acts of worship it has housed.

Given such considerations, some philosophers prefer to characterize the aesthetic attitude and disinterest in terms of attention to an object "for its own sake." This would not carry the same connotation of indifference to the object's existence, to the kind of thing it is, and to its representational and expressive features. But the notion of an interest in something "for its own sake" has substance only by way of contrast with other sorts of interest. So the first problem will be to specify these other attitudes and interests. Now, while it is easy enough to exclude such obviously pragmatic interests as those in a painting's monetary value and powers of sexual arousal, there remain many noninstrumental attitudes toward things or people that are not aesthetic. I admire a person of high moral caliber simply for what he or she is; the true scholar seeks knowledge for its own sake.

In some of these cases, it will be said, satisfaction of the interest in question (moral, scholarly, or whatever) does not take the form of *enjoyment*, as it must in the case of aesthetic interest. But if "enjoyment" is understood narrowly, it is hardly obvious that aesthetic satisfaction should always be described as enjoyment. I admire, but do not enjoy, Goya's "black paintings." If, however, "enjoyment" is stretched to cover such instances, it is no longer clear that perception of moral quality or the acquisition of new knowledge is not an experience of enjoyment. It might be more promising, then, to employ a variety of criteria for distinguishing these other modes of interest in something "for its own sake" from the aesthetic one. For example, Dufrenne suggests that the difference between love and aesthetic appreciation is that "love requires a kind of union which is not needed by the aesthetic object, because the latter . . . holds [the spectator] at a distance" (1973: 432).

More difficult, arguably, is to distinguish an aesthetic attitude toward, say, a lakeland scene from the simple and utterly familiar experience of passing the time, idly and enjoyably, looking about one, observing the clouds and boats sailing by. This, too, is done for no further reason, but for the mere sake of it, yet "aesthetic" sounds too portentous a term for such a banal occupation.

A further and more radical challenge will question whether "disinterest" or interest in something "for its own sake" is anyway the right place from which to start in trying to characterize the aesthetic attitude. This challenge might focus on the tendency of characterizations like Kant's and Stolnitz's to assimilate the aesthetic attitude to *contemplation*. To begin with, there are paradigm cases of contemplation – "navel-gazing," say – which are not ones of aesthetic appreciation. Second, while some works of art, like Olivier Messiaen's religious works, might reasonably be described as invitations to contemplation, this would be a strange description of, say, the finale of the "Eroica" Symphony. So, at the very least, the contemplation deemed essential to the aesthetic attitude must be contemplation in a very special sense. Third, it has been vigorously argued by Arnold Berleant (1991) that disinterested contemplation is rarely the form taken by aesthetic appreciation of nature. Here, rather, the appreciator is typically participating in and interacting with the landscape, and it is through this engagement, not despite it, that proper appreciation is possible. Berleant goes on to argue that the disinterested contemplation model is a poor one even in the case of art. Typically, neither artworks nor natural scenes are "objects" of detached contemplation, but "occasions" for "active" engagement.

As that final point indicates, much of the problem here has to do with the *passivity* often associated with the contemplative attitude. As one author, echoing many others, puts it, the contemplative spectator "is not concerned to analyze . . . or to ask questions about [an object]" (Stolnitz 1960: 38). But the justification for insisting that this is how spectators should approach works of art is unclear. Typically, they come before works in an active spirit, replete with ambitions to analyze and ask questions, to compare and put into context. "In aesthetic appreciation," Scruton writes, "the object serves as a focal point on which many different thoughts and feelings are brought to bear" (1974: 155). A person looking at *Night Café in Arles* is not looking for the answers to questions about human loneliness available from a sociological tome, but would one dismiss as "nonaesthetic" a response to the painting like "Van Gogh shows what it is like to be lonely, even in the company of others"?

An appropriate comportment toward a work of art requires a certain openness or receptivity toward it, but this point – the element of truth in the idea of "disinterested" contemplation – cannot prohibit approaching a work with active interests, like that of learning how it is to view the world a certain way or how a work embodies the predilections of its creator's times. What matters in such instances – and what makes them instances of aesthetic appreciation, arguably – is the spectator's readiness to employ imagination in attempting to satisfy the interrogative interests with which he or she approaches the work. The painting does not *tell* one about loneliness, nor does a statue *depict* the prejudices of its age. These, rather, are matters an audience must imaginatively reconstruct from the canvas or stone before it.

To understand the aesthetic attitude in terms of a readiness for imagination is, to be sure, to move from one obscure notion to another. But at least imagination incorporates that peculiar blend of will and receptivity, that oscillation between an imposition of structure or meaning and a readiness to be "taken over," which is characteristic of our best moments in the presence of art, or indeed of natural scenes. It may well be that only so much of aesthetic experience can be understood in these terms. And then the conclusion should be that it was mistaken to look for a single phenomenon, *the* aesthetic attitude. This conclusion was reached by George Dickie (1974) in his well-known attacks on "the myth of the aesthetic attitude." Not only, he argued, is there no single state of mind one must induce in oneself – through a feat of "psychical distancing," say – in order to appreciate things aesthetically, but it is impossible to understand where "disinterested" aesthetic attention differs from attention *tout court*. People who focus on, say, the cost of the painting or the moral character of its painter are guilty of plain inattention to it, the work itself.

The implication to draw from Dickie's criticism is not, perhaps, that we should eschew all talk of aesthetic attitude. Something, after all, distinguishes the kind of attention we try to pay to paintings from the kind paid, for example, to incoming shells by soldiers in a trench. A more moderate implication would be that we should content ourselves with describing a motley of attitudes, united more by the range of objects or "occasions" – including, of course, works of art – that tend to invite them than by a single, underlying state of mind. If we do so then the ambition, noted at the outset, of *defining* "art" in terms of a particular attitude toward objects must be abandoned, for that would be a circular enterprise.

See also EIGHTEENTH-CENTURY AESTHETICS; TWENTIETH-CENTURY ANGLO-AMERICAN AESTHETICS; AESTHETIC PROPERTIES; AESTHETICISM; DEFINITION OF "ART"; DICKIE; IMAGINATION; KANT.

BIBLIOGRAPHY

Bell, Clive. 1947. *Art*. London: Chatto & Windus.
Berleant, Arnold. 1991. *Art and Engagement*. Philadelphia: Temple University Press.
Bullough, Edward. 1912. " 'Psychical Distance' as a Factor in Art and an Aesthetic Principle," *British Journal of Psychology*, 5, 87–98.
Dickie, George. 1974. *Art and the Aesthetic*. Ithaca: Cornell University Press.
Dufrenne, Mikel. 1973. *The Phenomenology of Aesthetic Experience*. A. Anderson (trans.). Evanston: Northwestern University Press.
Guyer, Paul. 2005. *Values of Beauty: Historical Essays in Aesthetics*. Cambridge: Cambridge University Press.
Kant, Immanuel. 1966 [1790]. *Critique of Judgment*. J. Bernard (trans.). New York: Hafner.
Odin, Steve. 2001. *Artistic Detachment in Japan and the West: Psychic Distance in Comparative Aesthetics*. Honolulu: University of Hawai'i Press.
Schopenhauer, Arthur. 1966 [1819/44]. *The World as Will and Representation*. E. J. F. Payne (trans.). New York: Dover.
Scruton, Roger. 1974. *Art and Imagination: A Study in the Philosophy of Mind*. London: Methuen.
Stolnitz, Jerome. 1960. *Aesthetics and Philosophy of Art Criticism*. Boston: Riverside.

DAVID E. COOPER

aesthetic education   My main aim in this essay is to clarify the concept of aesthetic education, rather than provide an overview of the recent literature on this topic. (See Smith 1998 for an overview.) The concept refers to the theory, content, and practice of teaching and learning related to issues of aesthetic value and aesthetic experience. In educational disciplines it is often used to cover a range of teaching and learning practices that pertain to what we might properly call art education. On the other hand, within philosophical aesthetics, education is largely seen to be an area of application, particularly that of moral education, for philosophical aesthetics. In addition, within the literature more generally, philosophical aesthetics and philosophy of art are often conflated. The point of clarifying the concept of aesthetic education then is to be able to say more clearly what it is, and how it serves toward an education that is not focused narrowly on the creation and appreciation of artworks in themselves. Its goal is to educate individuals toward the recognition and enhancement of the role that aesthetics can play in human wellbeing, a role that aesthetics plays in all human activity from cognition, through the development of institutions, to our engagement with natural and built environments. This is not to exclude artworks but to recognize them instead as just one form of human activity that engages us aesthetically.

There is a long history of the role of aesthetics in human development and citizenship education, as in Plato's *Symposium* and *The Republic*, and Aristotle's *Poetics*, within the Western philosophical tradition. Regardless of whether these arguments defend an education in the arts or argue against them, they rest on the assumption that aesthetic education bears a strong relationship to our emotional lives and moral and political development. Within non-Western aesthetics, too, a connection between the arts and the moral and political realms is explicit. For example, drama, within the Indian tradition, as in the Greek, was a key vehicle for the imparting of moral and political values. Not surprisingly, then, in these traditions we see the early development of philosophical aesthetics in the writings of Bratahari and Aristotle. More recently, we see similar attempts at linking aesthetics with ethics and moral education, as, for example, Marcia M. Eaton's *Aesthetics and the Good Life* (1989). Jenefer Robinson (1995), taking a more psychological approach, has argued for an education of the emotions through an engagement with the arts that would facilitate moral education.

While the cognitive value of the arts was addressed by the early philosophers, it is with Kant, building on Alexander Baumgarten and responding in part to David Hume, that we see the emergence of modern aesthetics. With the development of modern aesthetics we see an increase in the interest of aesthetics as an aspect of human cognition. This interest has grown considerably in significance with developments in neuroscience (Zeki 2000). David Hume's essay "Of the Standard of Taste" is a classic within aesthetic education but it remains strongly rooted in art. For Hume, the question is how we can set a standard for judgments of taste. For Kant, on the other hand, in making aesthetic judgments we make a determination about human cognition rather than about the object itself. Aesthetic pleasure is our *felt awareness* that the appearance of the object conforms to the most basic conditions of human cognition.

Roughly the argument is that there are structures or categories of the mind that affect what we perceive and construct what we know. For example, in the case of vision "seeing" does not entail a passive reception of perceptual information. Rather, "seeing" is an active process that brings our cognitive apparatus and the visual signal together to construct what we see. For Kant, aesthetics, the cognitive organization of perceptual information, is fundamental to human animals. Hence, aesthetic experiences are not limited to those with refined sensibilities as Hume might have it. Rather, they are available to all. What in particular is appreciated is a matter of taste,

and hence of culture and education. Much of our contemporary philosophical interest in environmental aesthetics could turn to Kant, with some profit, in thinking about aesthetic education and about human development and wellbeing. Moreover, taking a Kantian view of aesthetics is invaluable in understanding formalism, and as Nick Zangwill (2001) so persuasively argues, providing us with a systematic understanding of the relation between aesthetic properties and experience. Above all, taking a Kantian approach makes us aware of the role that aesthetics, as human cognition, plays in all human activity. This, too, is a relatively underdeveloped area within aesthetic education.

Perhaps there is no single philosopher more important to aesthetic education than John Dewey. His *Art as Experience*, a book based on the William James Lectures that he delivered at Harvard University in 1931, lays out the role that aesthetics plays in the development of humans, as complex biological organisms adapted to their environment.

Dewey had always stressed the importance of recognizing the significance and integrity of all aspects of human experience. His repeated complaint against the partiality and bias of the philosophical tradition expresses this theme. Consistent with this theme, Dewey took account of qualitative immediacy in *Experience and Nature*, and incorporated it into his view of the developmental nature of experience. It is in the enjoyment of the immediacy of an integration and harmonization of meanings, in the "consummatory phase" of experience that, in Dewey's view, the fruition of the readaptation of the individual to her environment is realized.

These central themes are enriched and deepened in *Art as Experience*, making it one of Dewey's most significant works. Furthermore, the roots of aesthetic experience lie, he argues, in commonplace experience, in the consummatory experiences that are ubiquitous in the course of human life.

Like Kant, Dewey argues against the conceit cherished by some art enthusiasts that aesthetic enjoyment is the privileged endowment of the few. While Kant remains agnostic regarding the prescription of certain aesthetic experiences over others, Dewey thinks that it is precisely because humans are aesthetically predisposed that certain experiences should be valued over others, so that individuals do not fill this need through less than worthy artworks. While he does not offer any criteria as such for preferring some works or experiences over others, drawing on his overall philosophy it is safe to say that only those aesthetic experiences would be considered educative that foster more meaningful experiences.

More importantly, for Dewey, an "experience" coalesces into an immediately enjoyed qualitative unity of meanings and values drawn from previous experience and present circumstances. Life itself takes on an aesthetic quality and this is what Dewey calls having an experience.

For Dewey, the creative work of the artist, broadly speaking, is not unique. It is a process that requires an intelligent use of materials, the imaginative development of possible solutions to problems issuing in a reconstruction of experience that affords immediate satisfaction. This process, found in the creative work of artists, is also to be found in all intelligent and creative human activity. What distinguishes artistic creation is the relative stress laid upon the immediate enjoyment of unified qualitative complexity as the rationalizing aim of the activity itself, and the ability of the artist to achieve this aim by marshaling and refining the massive resources of human life, meanings, and values. Although Dewey insisted that emotion is not the significant content of the work of art, he clearly understands it to be the crucial tool of the artist's creative activity.

Dewey's aesthetic theory requires education, both formal and informal, to build up these resources that help create artworks, but requires aesthetic education in this sense to appreciate them too. For Dewey, accounts of aesthetic appreciation that portray the artist as an active creator and the audience as passive receiver are flawed. In his view, both the artist and audience are active in producing and appreciating artworks that afford us aesthetic experience.

It is commonplace to think that the senses play a key role in artistic creation and aesthetic appreciation. Dewey, like Kant, however, argues against the view, stemming historically from the sensationalistic empiricism of David Hume, who interprets the content of sense experience simply in terms of the traditionally codified list of sense qualities. Such qualities are not divorced from an individual's history. Rather, they rely on our mental structures and content gained through experiences. Unlike Kant, however, Dewey highlights the role of education in building a content rich in meanings from past experience. Culture is invaluable to the making of such a fund of meanings.

Ever concerned with the interrelationships between the various domains of human activity and interest, Dewey ends *Art as Experience* with a chapter devoted to the social implications of the arts. Because art has its roots in the consummatory values experienced in the course of human life, its values have an affinity to commonplace values, an affinity that gives the arts a critical role in relation to prevailing social conditions. Dewey's specific target is the conditions of workers in industrialized society, conditions that force upon the worker the performance of repetitive tasks that are devoid of personal interest and afford no satisfaction in personal accomplishment. That is, assembly-line routines of work are impoverished aesthetically. Such impoverishment is not necessarily tied to labor as such, as Dewey demonstrates with examples like that of riveters setting up a rhythm in catching and using hot rivets as they build a skyscraper. It is management that needs to be made aware – educated – toward the role that aesthetics plays in all human activity in order to make it meaningful and worthwhile.

Richard Shusterman (2008) has extended and deepened Dewey's aesthetics through his theory of aesthetics related to the body – "somaesthetics." Furthermore, he has extended the educational repertoire of artworks worthy of producing meaningful experiences by including those we might typically not consider worthwhile even though they carry meaning for vast segments of our society. In this he remains true to Dewey's democratic commitments. Arnold Berleant (1997) and Yuriko Saito (2007), on the other hand, have turned their attention to the aesthetic dimensions of our natural and built environments and to everyday life. Dewey's ubiquitous theory of aesthetics, like Kant's cognitive theory, recognizes the role of aesthetics in all human activity and not only in the making and appreciating of high art but also nonart like the environment and the everyday. Aesthetic education in this case might mean not only the enhancing of our awareness of this dimension of our activities and experiences but also serving more humbly, but not less importantly, as a reminder of its pervasive presence.

See also AESTHETIC PROPERTIES; AESTHETICS OF THE EVERYDAY; COGNITIVE VALUE OF ART; DEWEY; HUME; INDIAN AESTHETICS; KANT; MORALITY AND ART.

BIBLIOGRAPHY

Berleant, Arnold. 1997. *Living in the Landscape: Toward an Aesthetics of the Environment*. Lawrence: University of Kansas Press.

Dewey, John. 2005 [1934]. *Art as Experience*. New York: Perigee.

Eaton, Marcia. 1989. *Aesthetics and the Good Life*. Madison: Farleigh Dickinson University Press.

Robinson, Jenefer. 1995. "L'education Sentimentale," *Australasian Journal of Philosophy*, 73, 212–26.

Saito, Yuriko. 2007. *Everyday Aesthetics*. Oxford: Oxford University Press.

Shusterman, Richard. 2008. *Body Consciousness: A Philosophy of Mindfulness and Somaesthetics*. Cambridge: Cambridge University Press.

Smith, Ralph. 1998. "Education, Aesthetic." In *Encyclopedia of Aesthetics*. M. Kelly (ed.). Oxford: Oxford University Press, vol. ii, 93–6.

Zangwill, Nick. 2001. *The Metaphysics of Beauty*. Ithaca: Cornell University Press.

Zeki, Semir. 2000. *Inner Vision: An Exploration of Art and the Brain*. Oxford: Oxford University Press.

PRADEEP A. DHILLON

aesthetic judgment There have been a huge number of attempts to understand the nature of aesthetic judgment. These are placed in two broad categories, and called here objectivism and subjectivism.

SIMPLE OBJECTIVISM

According to a simple objectivism, the truth of an aesthetic judgment is wholly determined by whether certain qualities or relations exist in the object. An important corollary of this account is that when a spectator affirms that an object is, for instance, beautiful, his judgment must imply that everyone who judges the object aesthetically ought to find it beautiful. This implication holds because what he is claiming is only that the object has certain qualities arranged in a given way. If the original judgment is correct, it follows that anyone else ought to judge in the same way.

Simple objectivism has been subjected to several criticisms. Many have found it counterintuitive that one can, in theory, decisively settle the beauty of an object by reference to rules of composition alone. Whatever aesthetic rule of composition is proposed, it is never self-contradictory to accept that the object unequivocally falls under the rule, yet deny that it is beautiful.

Second, the analysis leaves no intrinsic role for a spectator's feelings in the determination of beauty. Admittedly, a defender of the analysis can, and very probably will, allow that the judgment is normally *accompanied* by a feeling of pleasure or displeasure, but an object's beauty exists quite independently of any spectator's feelings. Finally, the evaluative force of the judgment is not adequately accounted for: one is not merely judging that the object possesses certain properties disposed in a given way, but also that it *merits* attention.

SIMPLE AND SOPHISTICATED SUBJECTIVISM

According to simple subjectivism, the correctness of an aesthetic judgment is determined by the pleasure or displeasure that perception of the object arouses in any given spectator. This implies that if, under the same circumstances, one individual judges that an object is beautiful and another judges that it is not, they could never be contradicting each other. Yet it seems evident that at least sometimes they could be. Moreover, an aesthetic judgment is made on the basis of our perception of features in the object. We are normally expected to show that the judgment rests on features that render our response a *justifiable* one. This is not consistent with the judgment depending only on feelings of pleasure or displeasure the perception of the object occasions in any spectator.

In the light of these and other criticisms, subjectivists have usually accepted that the aesthetic judgment cannot be a bare statement of personal liking or disliking. A more sophisticated subjectivist account was defended by Hume, and most subsequent subjectivist theories have remained greatly indebted to it. The basic idea is often introduced by seeking to draw an analogy between color judgments and aesthetic judgments. Even those who construe an object's color as nothing more than an occurrence in the observer's mind allow that there are standards for assessing the appropriateness of particular color judgments. These standards depend on: (1) similar general principles governing most people's color perception, and our accepting that those within the consensus who can make maximum discriminations between colors have the best color vision; (2) widespread agreement among the maximum discriminators about the precise colors of given objects. Similarly, the sophisticated subjectivist urges, we should think of standards in art criticism as resting on: (1) the same, or nearly the same, general principles governing most people's aesthetic taste, and our acknowledging that those within this majority who are capable of experiencing the fullest and most discriminating range of contemplative feelings have the most perfect taste; (2) a large measure of agreement among the maximum discriminators about the precise feelings that are produced by the particular qualities and relations of objects.

If the subjectivists are to make good this analogy, they will need to defend the belief that the majority of people *are* governed by similar principles of taste. They attempt to do this by pointing to the long-running survival of certain admired works among diverse nations; and by arguing that most disagreements are due to factors like prejudice or lack of suitable education.

Even allowing that the analogy with colors can survive the existence of aesthetic disagreement, it still fails to explain why we should talk of the beauties or blemishes of *objects* (the feelings of pleasure/displeasure manifestly belong to the subjects judging). To meet this objection, the sophisticated subjectivist refers to those features of objects, the awareness of which causes the majority's contemplative feelings of pleasure or displeasure. He insists that the capacity to notice intricate relationships between the parts of a complex work of art or natural object is, as a matter of fact, a causally necessary condition for the fullest experience of the appropriate feelings. Accordingly, we learn that in order to *justify* our responses as aesthetic ones, they need to be grounded in the aware-

ness of such features. These features become denominated the "beauties" or "blemishes" of objects, despite their existence being dependent on the sensibilities of discriminating spectators. On this account, any defensible aesthetic rules of composition will simply be empirical generalizations, based on the discovery that features of a certain kind have been found to please discriminating spectators in a variety of different objects.

Sophisticated subjectivism incorporates many of the properties that have been widely seen as central to aesthetic appreciation. It permits a prominent role to reasoning and the comparison of cases in the justification of aesthetic judgments, at least in the finer arts; yet it gives to contemplative feelings of pleasure or displeasure the ultimate determining ground of the judgment. And since any acknowledged general rules are only contingent, it can explain why it is never self-contradictory to admit that certain features fall under an accepted rule, while also denying that they are beautiful. Furthermore, it can account for why we place such a value on aesthetic appreciation: the discriminating feelings, on which judgments in the finer arts depend, are of an intrinsically satisfying nature. Also they have a strong tendency (together with the analytical skill required for their experience) to civilize a person's attitude toward moral and intellectual matters. Since both these consequences are highly desirable, it is not surprising that aesthetic discrimination should be considered an admirable quality and its objects worthy of appreciation.

On the other hand, a subjectivist cannot allow that an aesthetic judgment about any given object claims the *necessary* agreement of everyone. At best, the aesthetic judgment can lay claim only to a contingent universality, or near-universality, based on an *empirical* generalization concerning the sensibilities of human beings. To those of us whose sensibilities may happen to be governed by totally different principles from the majority's, the judgments of discriminating spectators within that majority can have no logical force.

SOPHISTICATED OBJECTIVISM

This position, which was originally developed by Kant, shares with simple objectivism the view that the judgment of taste lays claim to the necessary agreement of everyone without exception, but it shares with sophisticated subjectivism the view that its determining ground must always be the feeling of contemplative pleasure or displeasure. Even if this is, so far as it goes, a correct analysis of the aesthetic judgment, its appearance of having one's cake and eating it raises very acutely the question of whether application of the judgment can ever be justified.

In Kant's case, the justification is intimately linked with his metaphysics. Two people can only be perceiving the same object insofar as they possess the same faculties of understanding and imagination, operating identically in both of them. The feeling of contemplative pleasure or displeasure, by which we determine the aesthetic judgment, also has to arise from the interlocking of these two faculties in an act of perception. We correctly pronounce an object to be beautiful if, and only if, in an act of purely reflective perception upon the relations holding among its formal features, we find – by means of the ensuing feeling – that the imagination is permitted maximum freedom from the rule-governed constraints of the understanding. On this account, it is *impossible* for two people to be perceiving the same object, while making different, equally well-grounded, aesthetic judgments. It is impossible because we make a well-grounded aesthetic judgment on the basis of a feeling that depends on an identical use of necessarily shared perceptual faculties. (Differences in aesthetic judgment arise because people seldom reach a decision solely by allowing the imagination its free play.)

So although we decide upon an object's beauty on the basis of feeling, Kant thinks that what we are thereby estimating is the extent to which the object's mere form or design gives scope to the imagination's free play. But there can be no discoverable general rules for establishing this, precisely because the imagination is here maximally *un*constrained by the faculty of rules (the understanding). Only if we had access to the ground of all experience – the supersensible world – would it be possible to discover the principles governing the free play of the imagination; and, hence, to determine prior to and independently of feeling the extent of an object's beauty. Failing, as we do, to achieve this insight into the supersensible,

each of us can only estimate beauty by means of his own individual feeling.

Kant's theory belongs in the objectivist camp because of his insistence that a well-founded aesthetic judgment ultimately rests on (unknown) principles that obtain independently of any spectator's feelings. Arguably, his position rests on an unjustified metaphysical structure; relatedly, it relies on a narrow formalist conception of beauty. Still, Kant's analysis raises a serious problem for the subjectivist, which is to account for the persisting contention that the aesthetic judgment claims the necessary agreement of everyone without exception.

For the subjectivist, any inclination to claim strict universality for the aesthetic judgment arises from explicable delusion: because the exercise of judgment, especially in the finer arts, requires extensive knowledge and reflection, it is easy to be misled into thinking that the judgment depends wholly on factors belonging to the mere perception of the object (especially since the feelings resulting from careful and practiced aesthetic reflection are frequently so comparatively unobtrusive); and, under such a misapprehension, one will naturally take it that the verdict claims strict universality. In reality, the most that can be claimed is a universality covering all who, *as a matter of fact*, possess a similar sensibility.

FURTHER DEVELOPMENTS
How convincing is the sophisticated subjectivist's position? On two counts, it has been strenuously disputed.

First, it has been held that the spectator must be the final authority on what aspects of an object ground his response. It is always the spectator himself, on the basis of his own experience of the aesthetic object, who must willingly authorize any suggestions from others before they can be considered correct. Yet – the argument runs – on the supposition that the connection between object and response is a causal one, no authorization by the person concerned would be required. Second, it has been held that although the spectator is the final authority on the ground of his response, that response can only be justified as an *aesthetic* one if the reasons for it appropriately fall under aesthetic rules. Perhaps the rules themselves were first laid down because the features that answered to them satisfied the sensibilities of influential people. Whatever their origins, only judgments in accord with these rules are well founded. They have become a constitutive element in manifesting aesthetic appreciation. Consequently, the connection between response and object, insofar as the response is to be thought of as genuinely aesthetic, cannot be merely contingent. If it were, one could identify that response *independently* of knowing whether its grounds were in accord with aesthetic rules. What is crucial is that there exists a fundamental framework of given rules, within which alone it is possible to talk of the making, defending, and criticizing of particular aesthetic judgments.

This dual attack on subjectivism, which derives from the work of Wittgenstein, evidently has affinities with Kant's position. It defends the strict universality of the aesthetic judgment, and it affirms an internal, and not a merely contingent, relation between the spectator's perception of the object and his making an aesthetic judgment.

Despite its ingenuity, it is doubtful whether the attack's central claim – that the connection between object and spectator's response is essentially noncontingent – should be conceded. Admittedly, it does seem right to say that the spectator must willingly authorize any suggestion as to the precise reason for his satisfaction or dissatisfaction, before that suggestion can be considered correct (as the first criticism of subjectivism contended). At the same time, it also seems right to say that any precise identification by him of the ground of his feeling is subject to a familiar form of causal falsification.

For example, we question whether certain features can be the real reason for a spectator's dissatisfaction with an object (even though he identified them as such) if, on another, similar, occasion, their presence, though noted, did not interfere with his pleasure. So whereas the spectator may be able to *rule out* suggestions as to the reason for his response, he cannot justifiably continue to *affirm* that such and such features are the real reason for that response, if it can be shown that his awareness of them formed an insignificant part of its cause.

Once it is admitted that the features which figure as the real reason for a spectator's plea-

sure or displeasure do, after all, carry a causal implication, it would be implausible to hold that any currently accepted aesthetic rules form an immovable framework that serves to define the possible justifiable content of aesthetic judgments (as the second criticism of subjectivism contended). For suppose it is discovered that certain features of an object, although fully in accord with an accepted aesthetic rule, are not the cause of the response of discriminating spectators, despite being picked out by them as its ground; and suppose, further, that other features which they also perceived were acting as the cause. Since it is implied that a spectator's awareness of the properties named in an aesthetic explanation cause his response, this discovery would force a change in the rules, so that they did henceforth pick out the object's causally efficacious features. It follows that aesthetic rules are ultimately dependent on the sensibilities of human beings, in the very manner that the sophisticated subjectivist maintains.

The subjectivist has argued forcefully that, without a causal implication to aesthetic reason giving, there can be no conceivable case where the assignment of aesthetic value would be justified. It turns out, therefore, that if the objectivist tries to analyze the aesthetic judgment without the causal implication, he will be in grave danger of having to deny that its application ever entails an evaluation. This is an absurd consequence. It raises, again, a difficulty that we encountered in connection with simple objectivism: namely, whether an objectivist can provide a comprehensible account of aesthetic value. Unless such an account is forthcoming, no persuasive alternative to sophisticated subjectivism appears to be available; and we shall just have to confess that there is an element of delusion, a tendency to affirm a stricter universality than can be warranted, in our application of the aesthetic judgment.

See also AESTHETIC PLEASURE; BEAUTY; HUME; KANT; OBJECTIVITY AND REALISM IN AESTHETICS; RELATIVISM; TASTE; THEORIES OF ART; WITTGENSTEIN.

BIBLIOGRAPHY
Hume, David. 1985. "The Sceptic" (1742), "Of the Delicacy of Taste and Passion" (1742), and "Of the

Standard of Taste" (1757). Repr. in *Essays Moral, Political and Literary*. Indianapolis: Liberty Classics.

Kant, Immanuel. 1987 [1790]. "Introduction" and "Critique of Aesthetic Judgment." In *Critique of Judgment*, W. Pluhar (trans.). Indianapolis: Hackett.

McDowell, John. 1983. "Aesthetic Value, Objectivity, and the Fabric of the World." In *Pleasure, Preference and Value*. E. Schaper (ed.). Cambridge: Cambridge University Press, 1–16.

Mackie, John L. 1977. *Ethics: Inventing Right and Wrong*. Harmondsworth: Penguin.

Pears, David F. 1975. "Causes and Objects of Some Feelings and Psychological Reactions." In *Questions in the Philosophy of Mind*. D. Pears (ed.). London: Duckworth, 56–79.

Reid, Thomas. 1969 [1785]. "Of Taste." In *Essays on the Intellectual Powers of Man*. Cambridge, MA: MIT Press.

Ward, Andrew. 2006. "A Kantian or an Empiricist Theory of Taste?" In *Kant: The Three Critiques*. Cambridge: Polity, 220–6.

Wittgenstein, Ludwig. 1996. *Lectures and Conversations on Aesthetics, Psychology and Religious Belief*. C. Barrett (ed.). Oxford: Blackwell.

ANDREW WARD

aesthetic pleasure When is pleasure in an object properly denominated "aesthetic"? The characterization of aesthetic pleasure is something that almost every theorist of the aesthetic has attempted. For such a characterization to be accounted a success, it should illuminate the relation between aesthetic pleasure and the taking of an aesthetic attitude to works of art, and make intelligible how aesthetic pleasure can be taken in what are usually labeled nonaesthetic aspects of an item – for instance, its cognitive content, moral import, or political message – without thereby turning into pleasure of a nonaesthetic sort.

Before venturing my proposal, I review briefly some of the prominent suggestions that the tradition of aesthetic thought has thrown up so far. In Kant's influential treatment, aesthetic pleasure is characterized as the by-product of a nonconceptual and disinterested judging, whose focus is exclusively the formal purposiveness of the object judged. In being nonconceptual it is distinguished from pleasure taken in an object as good, since such a judgment always presupposes a concept of the object as of some kind or other. In being

disinterested – that is, not grounded in the subject's personal desires, needs, or susceptibilities – it is distinguished (or so Kant believed) from sensory pleasures such as those of a warm bath or the taste of raspberry. In deriving from an impression of purposiveness – an impression which, in stimulating imagination and understanding to an unaccustomed free play, directly gives rise to the pleasure in question – aesthetic pleasure is shown to reside in forms or appearances per se, and not in an object's real-world status or connections.

Different strands of this complex conception have been stressed by subsequent writers. Schopenhauer agreed with Kant that the pleasure in beholding an object aesthetically is a disinterested one, but claimed that its focus is not an object's pure form as such in relation to the cognitive faculties, but rather some metaphysical *idea* inherent in an object which, in drawing the subject's attention, lifts him temporarily out of the painful striving to which he, as a spatiotemporally bound individual bundle of will, is ordinarily condemned. In a similar vein, Bullough proposed that such pleasure issues upon the subject's metaphorically *distancing* any object of perception, in the sense of bracketing all of its life implications, thus putting the subject's practical self "out of gear" and clearing a space for rapt absorption. Others in the twentieth century, such as Eliseo Vivas and Jerome Stolnitz, have emphasized the *intransitivity* of the mode of attention that yields aesthetic pleasure, by which is meant its not going beyond the object but instead terminating on it.

The formalist strand in Kant's conception has been taken up in different ways in the twentieth century by Clive Bell, J. O. Urmson, and Monroe C. Beardsley. Bell claimed that pleasurable aesthetic emotion is the result solely of contemplation of an object's *significant form*. It is unclear, however, whether Bell had any intelligible, noncircular account to give of when a form is significant, and so the cash value of Bell's pronouncement seems to be just that form, narrowly construed – that is, the pure arrangement of elements in a medium – is the sole legitimate object of aesthetic experience. More liberally, Urmson has suggested that specifically aesthetic pleasure is pleasure deriving from a concern with appearances as such. On such a suggestion the aesthetic includes, but is not restricted to, the narrowly formal. Relatedly, Beardsley has proposed that aesthetic pleasure be defined as pleasure taken in either an object's formal qualities (for instance, balance, unity, tension) or its regional qualities – that is, gestalt qualities of character or expression which attach to structured wholes (for instance, vivacity, serenity, gloominess, grace).

That aesthetic pleasure derives from a wholly nonconceptual engagement with an object, as Kant would have it, has not been as readily accepted as some other parts of his theory. What the balance of thought and feeling in aesthetic experience is or should be was a prominent topic for critical discussion in the twentieth century. Roger Scruton, for instance, has urged that aesthetic experience and the satisfaction inherent in it is necessarily permeated by thought or imagination – that such experience always involves conceptions of objects, of their features, under certain descriptions. An object not consciously construed in one fashion or another cannot, for Scruton, be an object in which one is finding aesthetic, as opposed to merely sensational or instinctive, satisfaction.

I propose the following characterization of aesthetic pleasure. *Pleasure in an object is aesthetic when it derives from apprehension of and reflection on the object's individual character and content, both for itself and, at least in central cases, in relation to the structural base on which such character and content rest.* That is to say, to appreciate something aesthetically is characteristically to attend not only to its forms, qualities, and meanings for their own sakes, but also to the way in which all those things emerge from the particular set of low-level perceptual features that constitute the object on a nonaesthetic plane. We apprehend the character and content of items as anchored in and arising from the specific structure that constitutes it on a primary observational level. Content and character are supervenient on such structure, and appreciation of them, if properly aesthetic, involves awareness of that dependency. To appreciate an object's inherent properties aesthetically is to experience them, minimally, as properties of the individual in question, but also typically as bound up with and inseparable from its basic perceptual configuration.

Especially if a characterization of aesthetic pleasure is to be adequate to our interest in art, it will have to be roughly of the sort I have sketched. Aesthetic pleasure is supposed to be both individualizing and capable of being taken in an object's cognitive and moral aspect, without becoming a fortiori purely cognitive or moral satisfaction. Now, it seems that what is most distinctive about an artwork, and possibly the only thing for which uniqueness might be claimed, is not its artistic character or content per se, but the specific complex of the work's character and content with the particular perceptual substructure that supports it. So, insofar as that is what is attended to, interest in an object carries to what is maximally distinctive about it. And where a work has a prominent intellectual or moral or political content, pleasure in this remains recognizably aesthetic when it results not so much from acquisition of some portion of scientific knowledge or ethical insight or political wisdom per se, but from appreciation of the *manner* in which these are embodied in and communicated by the work's specific elements and organization.

Aesthetic satisfaction in Thomas Mann's *Death in Venice*, for instance, is to be derived from more than its beauty of language, the strikingness of its images, or even the downward curve of its sad narrative; it is had as well in its moral mediation of life and art, and in its symbolism of death and disintegration. But the satisfaction is properly aesthetic in these latter cases precisely when such symbolic or moral content is apprehended in and through the body of the literary work itself – its sentences, paragraphs, and fictive events – and not as something abstractable from it. Aesthetic pleasure in Matisse's *The Red Studio* is not exhausted in delectation of its shapes, planes, and colors; it includes, for one thing, delight in the originality of Matisse's handling of space. But such delight is inseparable from a conception of what that handling amounts to, and how it is based in, or realized by, the particular choices of shape, plane, and color before one.

Aesthetic appreciation of art thus always acknowledges the vehicle of the work as essential, and never focuses merely on detachable meanings or effects. It is a signal advantage of the characterization outlined here that it ensures both that aesthetic pleasure is individualizing or work-centered, and that aesthetic pleasure can be taken in what are, on a traditional reckoning, nonaesthetic aspects of a work, without thereby becoming nonaesthetic.

How, though, are aesthetic pleasures differentiated from sensory and from intellectual ones? When is pleasure in a flavor, for example, aesthetic rather than merely sensory? It seems natural to suggest that what is required is some grasp of the flavor for the quality it is, perhaps in opposition to other flavors not then present, and/or of the flavor as itself founded on other discriminable qualities. To appreciate the taste of raspberry aesthetically is to register not only the brute taste, but also, so to speak, its form – that is, its relation to other, simpler qualities in the taste, or to ones it contrasts with in imagination. A purely sensory pleasure in raspberry taste, insofar as this is possible, would neither focus on the flavor for what it distinctively is nor involve awareness of relationships and dependencies within the experience as a whole. On the other hand, as already remarked, since paradigm aesthetic pleasures always involve an appreciation of contents-in-relation-to-vehicles-or-supports, then although necessarily involving thought of a kind, they do not collapse automatically into pure intellectual pleasures, in which satisfaction is grounded in the acquisition of knowledge or insight as such, for themselves, independent of how they are embodied or conveyed.

Turning now to nature, how is aesthetic pleasure in that related intelligibly to aesthetic pleasure in art? I suggest that, with nature as well as art, the pleasure is usually taken in its experienceable aspects, coupled with a vivid awareness both of the interrelations of such aspects and of their groundedness in the object's structure, history, or function. Aesthetic pleasure in natural objects, like aesthetic pleasure in works of art, is typically a multilevel affair, involving reflection not only on appearances per se, but on the constitution of such appearances and the interaction between higher-order perceptions. The shapes, colors, and expressivenesses of natural objects are appreciated in their complex relation to one another and to the concepts under which we identify such objects. For instance, a landscape scene might provide aesthetic pleasure not solely in its appearance but in the recognition

of this as resulting from geological forces along with patterns of human use.

Some theorists, such as Arthur C. Danto and Nelson Goodman, have stressed the great difference in kind between aesthetic response to nature and to art, while other theorists, such as Richard Wollheim and Anthony Savile, have even proposed that the aesthetic interest in art is logically prior to that in nature, the latter being properly analyzed in terms of the former. While recognizing that there may be two species of aesthetic response here, I suspect there is no priority either way. In any event, my concern has been only to characterize aesthetic satisfaction in such a way as to cover both.

It is clear that aesthetic pleasure as characterized so far in this article comprises more than pleasure in aesthetic qualities per se – that is, those that Frank Sibley has famously identified – and, equally, more than pleasure in mere appearances. Of course, when one is after aesthetic gratification one is interested in appearances, but usually one is equally interested in how, on a phenomenological plane, such appearances are generated; or, alternatively, how aesthetic qualities emerge from an object's structure. Somewhat legislatively, I have sought a notion which would make aesthetic pleasure, where works of art are concerned, something closer to pleasure proper to something as art – that is to say, art-appropriate pleasure. In this broader, art-conscious sense, the relationship of substructure and superstructure in the total impression that an object affords is necessarily of concern when an object is approached aesthetically.

Of course we may still acknowledge, in a traditional vein, a more basic notion of aesthetic pleasure as pleasure taken in sensory or perceptual properties as such, for example, colors, sounds, or shapes, immediately experienced (see Stecker 2005: 46–7). And indeed I framed my proposed characterization of aesthetic pleasure earlier in this essay so as to allow for such cases at the margin, insisting only that in *central* instances of aesthetic pleasure, attention must carry to relationships of dependence between higher-order and lower-order qualities as experienced. And in line with that more basic notion of aesthetic pleasure, appreciation in which awareness of relationships among experienced qualities at different levels was wholly absent might yet be accountable as aesthetic, provided there is an element of focusing on such qualities for what they are, so as to prevent such pleasure from collapsing into purely sensory pleasure. But we must not lose sight of the fact that such appreciation, even if minimally qualifiable as aesthetic, is simply too thin to do justice to art and nature appreciation as such, and that it is two-level, and not one-level, appreciation that should be seen as the paradigm of aesthetic appreciation. Accordingly, it seems useful to have articulated a notion of aesthetic pleasure sufficiently rich to respect the complex contents of its primary objects, art and nature.

Two last points. First, in order to have a notion of aesthetic appreciation applicable to artworks and natural phenomena alike, I invoked in my characterization none of the ingredients specific to the appreciation of art, such as concern with style, personality, intention, and design. The result is a notion that seems to fit what goes on when we regard a natural phenomenon as more than just a source of sensation, but without necessarily treating it as artwork *manqué*. The aesthetic appreciation of nature requires not only attention to manifest appearances but a concern with their perceptual and conceptual underpinnings.

Second, my characterization has the virtue, ironically, of preserving a connection between the aesthetic and the formal in art, reminiscent of Kant, but without reducing the aesthetic to the formal narrowly construed – for instance, as pattern in space or time. For in deriving gratification from the unique *manner* in which a work's content and character, whatever they might comprise, are rooted in and emerge from the work's form *sensu stricto* – the particular arrangement of elements (colors, sounds, words, movements, gestures) through which it conveys whatever else it does – one is focused on something which could fairly well be described as formal, in a wide sense.

Pleasure in an artwork is aesthetic when, whatever aspects of it are attended to, be they psychological or political or polemical, there is also attention to the *relation* between content and form – between what a work expresses or signifies, and the means it uses to do so. This relation, which is the *sine qua non* of aesthetic pleasure in art, is quite obviously a kind of higher

form – which means that Kant, in an oblique fashion, was right about aesthetic pleasure after all.

See also EIGHTEENTH-CENTURY AESTHETICS; AESTHETIC ATTITUDE; AESTHETIC JUDGMENT; AESTHETIC PROPERTIES; AESTHETICS OF THE ENVIRONMENT; BELL; FORMALISM; KANT; SCHOPENHAUER.

BIBLIOGRAPHY
Beardsley, Monroe C. 1982. *The Aesthetic Point of View*. M. Wreen & D. Callen (eds.). Ithaca: Cornell University Press, chs. 1–3.
Bell, Clive. 1914. *Art*. London: Chatto & Windus.
Budd, Malcolm. 1995. *The Values of Art: Pictures, Poetry, and Music*. London: Penguin.
Bullough, Edward. 1912. " 'Physical Distance' as a Factor in Art and as an Aesthetic Principle," *British Journal of Psychology*, 5, 87–98.
Goldman, Alan H. 1995. *Aesthetic Value*. Boulder: Westview.
Kant, Immanuel. 1987 [1790]. *Critique of Judgment*. W. Pluhar (trans.). Indianapolis: Hackett.
Levinson, Jerrold. 1990. *Music, Art, and Metaphysics*. Ithaca: Cornell University Press, chs. 6, 7.
Levinson, Jerrold. 1996. *The Pleasures of Aesthetics*. Ithaca: Cornell University Press, chs. 1, 2.
Savile, Anthony. 1982. *The Test of Time*. Oxford: Oxford University Press.
Schopenhauer, Arnold. 1966 [1819]. *The World as Will and Idea*, book 3. E. F. J. Payne (trans.). New York: Dover.
Scruton, Roger. 1979. *The Aesthetics of Architecture*. Princeton: Princeton University Press.
Stecker, Robert. 2005. *Aesthetics and the Philosophy of Art: An Introduction*. Lanham: Rowman & Littlefield.
Stolnitz, Jerome. 1960. *Aesthetics and Philosophy of Art Criticism*. New York: Houghton-Mifflin.
Urmson, J. O. 1957. "When is a Situation Aesthetic?" *Proceedings of the Aristotelian Society*, supp. vol. 31, 75–92.
Vivas, Eliseo. 1959. "Contextualism Reconsidered," *Journal of Aesthetics and Art Criticism*, 18, 222–40.
Wollheim, Richard. 1980. *Art and Its Objects*. 2nd edn. Cambridge: Cambridge University Press.

JERROLD LEVINSON

aesthetic properties A definition or analysis of aesthetic properties may best be approached by first listing those properties and types of properties that are typically thought to be aesthetic when ascribed to works of art:

1   pure value properties: being beautiful, sublime, ugly;
2   formal qualities: being balanced, tightly knit, graceful;
3   emotion properties: being sad, joyful, angry;
4   behavioral properties: being bouncy, daring, sluggish;
5   evocative qualities: being powerful, boring, amusing;
6   representational qualities: being true-to-life, distorted, realistic;
7   second-order perceptual properties: being vivid or pure (said of colors or tones);
8   historically related properties: being original, bold, derivative.

This list, especially with its inclusion of (8), takes a broader view of aesthetic properties than the one traditionally adopted. The reasons for including such properties as originality or staleness in the list are, first, that they contribute to the value of artworks qua artworks and, second, that, despite not being directly perceived, they influence the ways knowledgeable viewers perceive or experience the works.

Is there any common characteristic of these various properties by which they are all recognized as aesthetic qualities? Several proposals may seem promising, but may be dismissed by counterexample. It might be thought that these are all perceptible properties of the works themselves. But not all the qualities listed above can be perceived in the works themselves. One could not perceive whether a representational work was true to life without knowing the model or type of model represented; one could not know that a work was original without knowing the tradition. Aesthetic properties have also been called regional qualities (Beardsley 1973), qualities of complexes that emerge from qualities of their parts, but vividness of color and purity of tone are just qualities of single colors or tones. Many of the properties in the above list – for example, the emotion and behavior properties – are ascribed literally to humans and perhaps only metaphorically to artworks. But this is not true of the formal or representational properties.

Another influential suggestion has been that aesthetic properties are those that require taste to be perceived (Sibley 1959). Ordinary perceivers do not see sadness, balance, power,

and realism in artworks as readily as they perceive redness or squareness. It seems that they must be more sensitive or knowledgeable to see the former qualities; hence the suggestion that they require taste. But the traditional concept of taste has suggested a special faculty akin to moral intuition. Without some independent description of how the faculty is supposed to work, its existence is no more plausible in the one case than in the other. Furthermore, there are qualities in our list that do not require taste to be perceived (e.g., vividness in color).

Those qualities that do seem to require taste for their appreciation need not lead us to posit a special faculty. The apparent need for taste can be explained, first, by the fact that many of the qualities in question are complex relations. We may require considerable exposure, or training, before we become capable of recognizing such relations in works of art. Second, most of the qualities mentioned in our list are at least partly evaluative. To call an artwork daring, powerful, or vivid is to suggest a positive evaluation of it. To call it sluggish, boring, or drab is to suggest a negative evaluation.

Thus, ascription of these properties expresses some set of aesthetic values. This fact points to a plausible general criterion for identifying aesthetic properties: they are those that contribute to the aesthetic values of artworks (or, in some cases, to the aesthetic values of natural objects) (Beardsley 1973). It has also been plausibly suggested that aesthetic properties are those that make artifacts works of art, or that help to determine what kinds of artworks they are (Sparshott 1982: 478). These two criteria may well be related if "work of art" is itself a partly evaluative concept in at least one of its definitions, so that to call something a work of art is to imply, for example, that it is worthy of sustained perceptual attention. We might conclude that works of art are objects created and perceived for their aesthetic values, and that aesthetic properties are those that contribute to such values. In considering this analysis, we must not forget that there are negative evaluative properties on the list as well. If being ugly, boring, distorted, or dull contribute to an object's value, they normally contribute only to negative value (though not always, e.g., a work's ugliness may contribute to its power or realism).

There are also qualities, such as emotion qualities like sadness, that seem to be evaluatively neutral. It will be argued below that such properties do contribute to aesthetic value, albeit more indirectly or less obviously than some of the others.

If we restrict attention to the positively evaluative properties, it might seem that artists would intend to build as many as possible into their works, and that their works would be better the more such properties they have. But this idea is too simple, since many of these properties do not blend well in particular contexts. In the case of both positive and negative evaluative properties, it is part of the task of critics to point them out and to justify their claims in this regard.

Most of the qualities listed are both relational and (partly) evaluative. In principle, it should be possible to analyze particular references to such properties (although not the property types themselves) into evaluative and descriptive components. A crucial question concerns the relation between these components. The properties on our list differ among themselves in the degree to which they always include (in their instantiations) specific evaluative or descriptive aspects.

These distinctions can be brought out by analyses of the following form: "object O has aesthetic property P" means "O is such as to elicit response of kind R in ideal viewers of kind V in virtue of its more basic properties B." If P is evaluative, then R will be positive or negative, often involving pleasure or displeasure. V will almost always include characteristics such as being knowledgeable of the kind of artworks to which O belongs, being unbiased or disinterested, and being sensitive enough to react to properties of type B. B may be more broadly or narrowly specified. Although the evocative qualities on the initial list most clearly involve reactions of observers, this analysis views many of the other properties there as having similar structure. Ascribing such properties to an object expresses a positive or negative response, suggests that others ought to share the response (ought to approximate to the ideal viewer), and points to certain more or less specific objective properties of the object.

Beauty, for example, is nonspecific on the objective side, but always elicits a pleasurable response in sensitive observers. Philosophers have not always agreed that the objective side of beauty cannot be specified. Perhaps the best-known attempt to do so was that of Hutcheson (1725), who held that it is always uniformity amid variety. But all such attempts fall to counterexamples, in this case ordered complex objects that do not appear beautiful. Although B (from the above formula) is therefore unspecified in the case of beauty, there will always be some properties – usually formal relations – in virtue of which an object is beautiful. Sometimes these more basic properties will themselves be evaluative properties. For example, an artwork may be beautiful in virtue of its grace or power. It may in turn be powerful in virtue of its piercing pathos or graceful in virtue of its smooth lines. A property such as grace, while still generally positively evaluative, is more specific on its objective side. "Graceful" always refers to formal qualities that suggest smooth and effortless movements. Graceful objects will nevertheless differ in their particular formal properties.

Ascriptions of more broadly evaluative and less specifically objective properties, when challenged, are always defended by appeal to less broadly evaluative and more specifically objective properties. Ultimately, a critic or viewer should defend evaluations by pointing to nonevaluative properties of the works in question. These will be formal, expressive, representational, or historical properties of the work (relations of the work to its tradition) that lack evaluative dimensions in themselves. For example, while to say that a painting's composition is balanced may be to evaluate it positively, to say that it is symmetrical is not evaluative; similarly for "poignant" and "sad" when predicated of musical works. Ultimately, appeal may be always to nonevaluative formal properties, but this claim is more controversial.

Sibley (1959) raised the question of how aesthetic qualities relate to nonaesthetic properties, and he claimed that the latter are never sufficient conditions for the former. He did seem to allow for necessary conditions in claiming that aesthetic properties could be "negatively condition governed." His example was that objects with all pastel colors cannot be gaudy (a necessary condition for gaudiness is bright colors). Sibley's question whether aesthetic properties are "condition governed" is equivalent to the question whether there are principles governing their ascription, a central question in aesthetics. We may ask it at the level Sibley does, the relation between aesthetic and nonaesthetic properties, or we may ask how the more specific or less broadly evaluative aesthetic properties relate to the more broadly evaluative ones or to overall evaluations of works.

Not only do there not appear to be necessary or sufficient conditions at either level, but properties at one level do not always contribute in the same direction to properties at the next level. In regard to necessary conditions, Sibley's example fails. The art deco facades in South Beach, Miami are pastel and gaudy. Undoubtedly there are trivial necessary conditions for many aesthetic properties: a tragic poem must contain more than the single word "pussycat." But it is much more difficult to think of nontrivial necessary conditions that could not be counterinstanced by a clever and original artist.

Regarding the relation of narrower evaluative properties to overall evaluations, properties that are normally positive, such as gracefulness, are not always so. A graceful performance of Stravinsky's *The Rite of Spring* might not be better for it, and arguably the graceful prose of Cooper's *The Last of the Mohicans* detracts from the excitement of the story.

Something similar can be said of the relation between nonaesthetic properties and aesthetic properties: again there are no principles governing this relation. The same objective formal properties – for instance, gentle curves and pastel colors – that make one artwork graceful might make another insipid. The same harmonies that make one piece of music powerful might make another strident. From the point of view of a single critic, it would seem that evaluative aesthetic properties must supervene on nonevaluative qualities of artworks; that is, there can be no difference in evaluative properties without some differences in objective qualities. This amounts to a constraint on rational aesthetic judgment: given all the same objective properties, evaluative judgment must remain constant, at least for those with fully developed tastes. But the principle of supervenience fails when we compare judgments across equally competent or even ideal critics.

The examples just noted suggest two reasons why we cannot specify interesting principles of aesthetic evaluation. First, aesthetic properties of parts of artworks are altered or transformed, often in unpredictable ways, when juxtaposed with properties in other works. A curve that is graceful in one sculpture may be insipid in the context of another sculpture. Second, there remain irreconcilable differences in taste, even when we consider the aesthetic judgments of only ideal critics. Aesthetic properties are response dependent – relations between objective properties and responses of observers – and these responses are relative to different tastes. That is why there is no supervenience across different critics, at least if we restrict the supervenience base to objective properties of works.

Aesthetic properties have been identified here primarily as those that contribute to the aesthetic value of artworks (or, in some cases, natural objects), and as those that provide reasons for aesthetic judgments or evaluations. Many of these properties are themselves evaluative, consisting in relations between objective basic properties and evaluative responses of observers. Others have been characterized here as nonevaluative properties that ultimately ground evaluations. It remains to explain briefly how and why these basic properties are ultimate sources of aesthetic value.

Complex formal properties constitute principles of order among the elements they structure. They enable perception and cognition to grasp such elements in larger wholes and to assign them significance in terms of their places and functions within such structures. This recognition of order, especially after being challenged by complexity, is pleasing to those faculties that seek it (although, as noted above, it is not always constitutive of beauty). Likewise, representational and expressive properties engage the imagination and affective capacities in satisfying ways free of the costs and dangers often associated with the latter in real life. Of significance too is the way that these distinct aesthetic properties interact in the context of artworks. Formal properties help to determine expressive, behavioral, and representational qualities, which may in turn enter formal structures at higher levels, and so on. Since elements within works are grasped in terms of their contributions to aesthetic properties and to such complex interactions among them, this makes for an intensely meaningful and rich experience of these elements as they are perceived.

At best, complexes of aesthetic properties in artworks can so engage all our cognitive and affective capacities as to seem to be distinct worlds, intentionally designed to challenge and satisfy these uniquely human capacities or faculties. Basic aesthetic properties create value ultimately by contributing to the constitution of such alternative worlds in which we can become fully and fulfillingly engaged.

See also EIGHTEENTH-CENTURY AESTHETICS; TWENTIETH-CENTURY ANGLO-AMERICAN AESTHETICS; AESTHETIC ATTITUDE; AESTHETIC JUDGMENT; AESTHETIC PLEASURE; BEARDSLEY; BEAUTY; DEFINITION OF "ART"; EXPRESSION; FORMALISM; REPRESENTATION; SENSES AND ART, THE; SIBLEY; TASTE.

BIBLIOGRAPHY
Aagaard-Mogensen, Lars. 1983. "Aesthetic Qualities." In *Essays on Aesthetics*. J. Fisher (ed.). Philadelphia: Temple University Press, 21–34.
Beardsley, Monroe C. 1973. "What is an Aesthetic Quality?" *Theoria*, 39, 50–70.
Beardsley, Monroe C. 1974. "The Descriptivist Account of Aesthetic Attributions," *Revue Internationale de Philosophie*, 28, 336–52.
Budd. Malcolm. 1999. "Aesthetic Judgments, Aesthetic Principles and Aesthetic Properties," *European Journal of Philosophy*, 7, 295–311.
De Clercq. Rafael. 2002. "The Concept of an Aesthetic Property," *Journal of Aesthetics and Art Criticism*, 60, 167–76.
Goldman, Alan H. 1995. *Aesthetic Value*. Boulder: Westview.
Hutcheson, Francis. 1971 [1725]. *An Inquiry into the Origin of Our Ideas of Beauty and Virtue*. New York: Garland.
Isenberg, Arnold. 1949. "Critical Communication," *Philosophical Review*, 58, 330–44.
Levinson, Jerrold. 2006. *Contemplating Art*. Oxford: Oxford University Press.
Mitias, Michael (ed.). 1988. *Aesthetic Quality and Aesthetic Experience*. Amsterdam: Rodopi.
Sibley, Frank. 1959. "A Contemporary Theory of Aesthetic Qualities: Aesthetic Concepts," *Philosophical Review*, 68, 421–50.
Sparshott, Francis. 1982. *The Theory of the Arts*. Princeton: Princeton University Press.
Stecker, Robert. 2005. *Aesthetics and the Philosophy of Art*. Lanham: Rowman & Littlefield, ch. 4.

ALAN H. GOLDMAN

aestheticism The doctrine that art should be valued for itself alone and not for any purpose or function it may happen to serve, and thus opposed to all instrumentalist theories of art. Historically, the idea of art for art's sake is associated with the cult of beauty, which had its roots in Kantian aesthetics and the Romantic movement, although its potential application is wider than that.

The phrase *l'art pour l'art* (art for art's sake) first became current in France in the first half of the nineteenth century as the rallying cry of the aesthetic movement, and was associated with such names as Théophile Gautier and Baudelaire, and later with Flaubert. The doctrine became fashionable in England in the second half of the nineteenth century under the influence first of Walter Pater and later of such luminaries as Oscar Wilde, Whistler, Aubrey Beardsley, and A. J. Symons (author of *The Quest for Corvo*), among others. The movement is famously satirized in the Gilbert and Sullivan operetta *Patience*, where Wilde appears under the guise of the poet Bunthorne. In its earliest and most uncompromising form, the doctrine asserts not merely that a work of art should be judged only on its internal aesthetic properties, but that any extraneous purpose or function it may happen to serve must be counted a serious defect. Thus, in the preface to his novel *Mademoiselle de Maupin*, Gautier argues that "nothing is truly beautiful except that which can serve for nothing; whatever is useful is ugly." This was in part a reaction to the utilitarian and materialistic values of the new industrial age. It can clearly be seen to be an overreaction – to quote Harold Osborne:

> As we survey the art work of the past from the earliest cave art onwards we find that, various as their uses were, by and large all works of art were made for a use . . . They were essentially utensils in the same sort of sense as a suit of armour, a horse's harness or objects of domestic service are utensils, though the purpose they served was not necessarily a material one. (1968: 13)

The very idea of "the fine arts," arts such as painting, poetry, music, sculpture, and ballet, in which the aesthetic properties are thought to be more important than the utilitarian ones, was largely an eighteenth-century innovation. By Gautier's criterion, beauty in its purest form simply did not exist in art prior to the eighteenth century. A far more sensible line is that taken by André Malraux, who has argued that by viewing the art of all times, all places, all cultures as pure aesthetic objects, divorced from their original purposes and functions, we have in effect entered into "an entirely new relationship with the work of art," where "the work of art has no other function than to be a work of art." We have, he says, created for ourselves "a museum without walls" (Malraux 1974).

Clearly, to accept this contextless approach to art as a perfectly legitimate and even desirable one, is to adhere to one of the main tenets of the art for art's sake doctrine. The central core of truth in this doctrine can be summarized in the following way: aesthetic values depend on properties which are internal to the work of art on account of which it is valued for its own sake. In other words, aesthetic merit, thus narrowly defined, is a type of final value but clearly distinguishable from all other final values such as knowledge for its own sake, the love of God, and doing one's duty. As the philosopher Victor Cousin said, "we must have religion for religion's sake, morality for morality's sake, as with art for art's sake . . . the beautiful cannot be the way to what is useful, or to what is good, or to what is holy; it leads only to itself" (Cousin 1854).

It is, then, a necessary condition of a work's being valued for its own sake that it be valued on account of its intrinsic properties and not on its relationship to anything external, such as nature, moral and political systems, audience response, and so on. We deem the internal properties of a work to be aesthetic not because they belong to a distinct class, like the class of color concepts, but because of the way they contribute to or detract from its value. Properties commonly identified as aesthetic include beauty, elegance, grace, daintiness, sweetness of sound, balance, design, unity, harmony, expressiveness, depth, movement, texture, and atmosphere. Not all such properties could accurately be described as formal properties – expressiveness, for example. This is important, because most of those who espouse the doctrine of art for art's sake do so on the basis of some sort of formalistic theory. Take, for example, E. M. Forster: "Works of art, in my opinion, are the only objects in the material universe to possess internal order, and that is why,

though I don't believe that only art matters, I do believe in art for art's sake" (1951: 104). Since the aesthetic movement owed much of its inspiration to Kant's powerfully formalistic theory in the *Critique of Judgment*, it is perhaps not surprising that the two doctrines should be so closely associated.

A major drawback to a strict formalist approach is that while the form/content distinction is clear enough within the narrow confines of Kant's aesthetics, it has a tendency to break down when applied across the board, especially when applied to the literary arts. For instance, if expression in art is treated as an internal property and not defined in terms of self-expression or audience reaction, then no distinction can usefully be drawn between the particular feeling being expressed and the manner of its expression. Nevertheless, as Scruton has observed, "aesthetic expression is always a value: a work that has expression cannot be a total failure" (1974: 213). Other nonformal aesthetic properties might include brilliance of color, sweetness of sound, texture, and felicity of language.

This leads to the question of whether the self-sufficiency of works of art, on which the doctrine of aestheticism depends, is in any way undermined by the presence of affective properties – properties that express or reflect human response, such as those that render works of art moving, exciting, interesting, amusing, enjoyable. Clearly, these properties are not internal in the required sense. The attitude of the aesthete, typified by Oscar Wilde, is to regard their presence as aesthetically harmful, because "all art is quite useless" and has no business with such external effects. As long as a thing affects us in any way, either for pain or for pleasure, or appeals strongly to our sympathies, then it is outside the proper sphere of art.

However, it is a mistake to treat the affective response to art as a specific state of mind that is produced by the object but that might be produced in other ways – as, for example, a relaxed frame of mind might be produced by tranquilizers, meditation, or by reading escapist literature. For the very identity of the affective response depends on the identity of the intentional object, and cannot be independently described. Thus it would be misleading to say that the purpose of a work of art is to interest, amuse, or please, because to find it interesting, amusing, or pleasing on account of its internal properties is, in effect, to value it for its own sake. It is, after all, the work itself that is interesting, amusing, or pleasing, and not the state of mind produced by it.

A related problem that more particularly concerns the aestheticist is how to justify the treatment of aesthetic values, not only as final values, but as ultimate values alongside truth and goodness. Some in the aesthetic movement, of whom Walter Pater is a prime example, see aesthetic values as actually overriding all other values, even moral ones. For Pater, the aesthetic quest is the highest way of life a man can follow. The possibility of such a "philosophy of life" was anticipated and attacked by Søren Kierkegaard in his *Either/Or* (1843). Under the influence of Pater, Wilde's humor is sometimes aimed at subverting morality and elevating what may be broadly termed aesthetic values, as when he says that "people will only give up war when they consider it to be vulgar instead of wicked," or, again, that it is better to be beautiful than to be good. Such remarks may sound flippant, but anyone who acknowledges the supremacy of aesthetic values is bound to take them seriously. Not surprisingly, few have been prepared to defend such an extravagant position, which is usually stigmatized as decadent.

Even if one adopts the less extreme position of treating aesthetic values as taking their place alongside other ultimate values rather than overriding them, one encounters difficulties. What grounds the claims of aesthetic values to occupy such a position? It is not enough to say, as Harold Osborne (1968: 202) does, that aesthetic activity is a self-rewarding and therefore self-justifying activity, because many self-rewarding activities, like smoking and billiards, are relatively trivial. The high seriousness of aesthetic value could perhaps be established in two stages: first, by showing that aesthetic preferences are not merely private and personal but may be correct and incorrect; and second, by linking them, if only indirectly, to overriding moral values or some more general notion of the "good life." The second move would run counter to the spirit of aestheticism. However, if the aestheticists are right to claim that aesthetic values are ultimately important

in and for themselves, that would in itself place us under a moral obligation to preserve them.

Whatever its other defects, the art for art's sake approach is surely too restrictive. The aesthetic standpoint is not the only possible standpoint from which one can approach a work of art, as is shown by the wide diversity of theories about the nature and purpose of art, all illuminating different aspects. To understand a work of art adequately, one may need to consider it from more than one aspect. For example, if one were to view a piece of medieval stained glass from a narrowly aesthetic standpoint, one would be unable to appreciate it as a *religious* work of art. To refuse to take account of that aspect, on the grounds that it is aesthetically irrelevant, would be to diminish rather than to enrich one's appreciation, and would be a kind of aesthetic puritanism.

See also TWENTIETH-CENTURY ANGLO-AMERICAN AESTHETICS; AESTHETIC ATTITUDE; AESTHETIC PROPERTIES; BEAUTY; COGNITIVE VALUE OF ART; FORMALISM; FUNCTION OF ART; KANT; MORALITY AND ART; ONTOLOGICAL CONTEXTUALISM; RELIGION AND ART; WILDE.

BIBLIOGRAPHY

Beardsley, Monroe C. 1958. *Aesthetics: Problems in the Philosophy of Criticism*. New York: Harcourt Brace.

Bradley, A. C. 1909. "Poetry for Poetry's Sake." In *Oxford Lectures on Poetry*. London: Macmillan, 3–36.

Cousin, Victor. 1854. *Lectures on the True, the Beautiful and the Good*. O. W. Wright (trans.). New York: D. Appleton.

Ellman, Richard. 1987. *Oscar Wilde*. Harmondsworth: Penguin.

Forster, E. M. 1951. "Art for Art's Sake." In *Two Cheers for Democracy*. New York: Harcourt Brace & World, 88–95.

Gautier, T. 1981 [1835]. *Mademoiselle de Maupin*. J. Richardson (trans.). Harmondsworth: Penguin.

Johnson, R. V. 1969. *Aestheticism*. London: Methuen.

Malraux, André 1974 [1952]. *The Voices of Silence*. S. Gilbert (trans.). London: Paladin.

Osborne, Harold. 1968. *Aesthetics and Art Theory*. London: Longman.

Pater, Walter. 1873. *The Renaissance: Studies in Art and Poetry*. London: Macmillan.

Scruton, Roger. 1974. *Art and Imagination*. London: Methuen.

Wilde, Oscar. 1983. *Complete Works of Oscar Wilde*. V. Holland (ed.). London: Collins.

DAVID WHEWELL

aesthetics   *see* AFRICAN A.; AMERINDIAN A.; CHINESE A.; EVOLUTION, ART, AND A.; FEMINIST A.; FEMINIST STANDPOINT A.; INDIAN A.; ISLAMIC A.; JAPANESE A.; OBJECTIVITY AND REALISM IN A.; PRAGMATIST A.; RACE AND A.; TESTIMONY IN A.

aesthetics of food and drink   Philosophical attention to food and drink is a relatively recent but burgeoning scholarly enterprise that manifests striking revaluations of what were previously derogated as merely bodily experiences. The sources for these changes are multiple, including reexamination of the senses in cognition, feminist critiques of the concept of rationality, artistic challenges to fine art traditions, and revisions of the parameters of the aesthetic – all of which converge in attention to embodiment.

HISTORICAL BACKGROUND

The traditional exclusion of eating and drinking from the purview of philosophy has ancient and enduring roots. Though a multimodal sensuous experience, eating chiefly and centrally engages the "bodily" senses of taste and smell, which are considered cognitively limited compared to the distance senses of vision and hearing because they provide relatively little information about the world around (Korsmeyer 1999: ch. 1). (The role of touch – the third bodily sense – is somewhat ambiguous because it coordinates with vision.) The bodily senses are the sources of considerable pleasure, but their brand of enjoyment is often dismissed as merely physical gratification that poses risky distractions and temptations. In fact, food, drink, and sex provide the typical exemplars of pleasures that should be governed or avoided. Philosophers from Plato to Hegel have observed that physical enjoyment should be set aside in preference for the mental and spiritual pleasures of true beauty.

In addition, food and drink have not been considered good candidates for aesthetic attention because of the way taste qualities are usually understood. The saying "There's no disputing about taste" sums up the philosophical neglect of qualities that appear to be mere matters of personal preference, different for each individual, and not important enough to demand standards. Indeed, in the eighteenth century when so much aesthetic theory was being developed, the literal sense of taste was the chief point of both comparison and contrast for analyzing aesthetic taste. As Kant put it, literal taste is merely subjective, whereas aesthetic taste is both subjective and universal.

With the aesthetic status of food so in question, the issue of its standing as an art form was more or less moot. Moreover, eating is a necessity for life, and its practical importance may seem to eclipse any claims for food as art, especially as a "fine art" whose chief purpose is aesthetic contemplation. Nonetheless, in the nineteenth century an enthusiastic group of European writers promoted fine dining for its aesthetic importance and gastronomy as an art form, taking as their models the new aesthetic theories (Gigante 2005). Their efforts were little noted by philosophy at the time, although they are now gaining retrospective interest.

TASTE AND TASTE QUALITIES

If eating preferences are indeed solely dependent on individual inclination and taste qualities admit of no standard, then it would be difficult to defend a robust account of the aesthetics of food. However, there is no reason to conclude that the relative "subjectivity" of taste – understood as the complete taste experience that includes smell and touch (and often vision and even hearing) – entails either idiosyncratic privacy or the absence of standards for excellence. By means of taste one discerns properties that are otherwise inaccessible. Hume made this point long ago in his essay "Of the Standard of Taste" (1757) when he introduced his controversial example of a wine-tasting contest to illustrate what he called delicacy of taste – the ability to perceive fine qualities of objects. Contemporary philosophers have further investigated the complexities of subjectivity to vindicate both an "objective" standing for tastes and the aesthetic significance of eating and drinking.

Tastes are undeniably subjective in that they need to be directly experienced by a perceiving subject. This fact appears particularly troublesome for taste because its causal triggers cannot be easily identified externally in the way that visual qualities can (although recent studies in taste chemistry have greatly illuminated the determinants of flavors). In contrast to the "higher" senses of vision and hearing, the objects of taste are never distant; they are literally inside one. Nonetheless, taste registers qualities of food and drink that as a rule normal perceivers are all disposed to detect. In other words, the degree to which taste experience is subjective is consistent with the claim that tastes are also *of* their substances (Sweeney 1999, 2007; Machamer 2007; Smith 2007a; Bender 2008; Shaffer 2007). If there were no objective pole to tasting, there would be no possibility of developing discriminating taste, which entails that there is something out there to discriminate. The possibility of developing expert taste is one dimension of the aesthetic potency of food and drink, one that perhaps has been most recognized with wine (Smith 2007b; Allhoff 2008).

The character of taste qualities extends to include a cognitive dimension to flavors that is often overlooked. Tastes themselves are only fully comprehended when the identity of the substance and its place in culture are in evidence, and this opens the door for claims that tastes themselves impart meaning – meaning that manifests the pervasive and complex roles that eating practices play in ceremonies, rituals, and everyday habits (Heldke 2003). When one attends to the meanings that foods carry, the parameters of aesthetic attention widen to include place of origin and modes of production and preparation. Though at first such matters may appear aesthetically extrinsic, they enter into what might be considered the style of food and drink and their cultural properties. That is, flavor is not just analogous to artistic "form"; it suggests "content" as well. What is more, certain concepts central to art, such as authenticity, are equally relevant to judging food and drink, for taste qualities concern the identity of the sapid substance and how it was made (Jacquette 2007; Gale 2008).

Directing aesthetic attention to food has several implications for the concept of the aesthetic itself, for it erases the traditional distinction between aesthetic and sensuous pleasures. The satisfaction of appetite was for years the paradigmatic "interested" pleasure, and aesthetic pleasure was considered "disinterested" – free from the self-directed concerns that limit judgments to personal relevance. Some of these values linger in aesthetic accounts of food inasmuch as there is a widespread assumption that when eating is worthy of aesthetic attention, it qualifies as fine, gourmet dining rather than the mere satisfaction of appetite. (Indeed, eating when appetite is not acute was for the nineteenth-century gastronomers mentioned above the gustatory equivalent of disinterested contemplation (Gigante 2005).) Nonetheless, the inclusion of eating and drinking in the purview of aesthetic activities still represents an important modification of the old standard of disinterestedness for aesthetic pleasure and an inclusion of bodily experiences in aesthetic practice (Sibley 2001; Brady 2005; Burnham & Skilleås 2008).

FOOD, DRINK, AND ART

While the aesthetic dimension of eating and drinking is a point of agreement among those who theorize on the subject, the standing of food as an art form remains unsettled. Difference on this question pivots around the concept of art and whether or not the values of food and drink are sufficiently similar to the values of (other) art forms. Most disagreement centers on whether culinary art has claims to be considered a fine art, for its qualifications as an applied art are evident.

There are at least two questions that need to be addressed here: Can we approach food and drink in the same appreciative manner as we approach fine arts such as music or painting? And, is it appropriate to consider foods in the category of artworks? To the first question there is a fair degree of assent, for demonstrably one can appreciate the sequence of tastes of a meal or the notes of wine with an attention and discernment that is parallel to the attention and discernment required to listen sensitively to a concert performance (Sweeney 1999; Bach 2007). Frequently the comparisons chosen are from the performance arts, for neither a performance nor a meal endures for more than a short time (Monroe 2007). How far the comparison can be sustained is more disputed, although absent the tradition that emphasizes fine art, foods are more readily accommodated within the concept of art (Saito 2007).

Up until this point the tacit assumption has been that the measure of success in gustatory aesthetics is discriminating pleasure. However, pleasure alone, no matter how sophisticated, is a limited achievement, especially in comparison to the wider scope of values sought in art. Attention to aesthetic savoring suits approaches familiar from Dewey that accentuate experience (Kuehn 2007). Concepts of art that emphasize their meanings may seem to preclude food and drink, which are widely held to exhibit a paucity of message or expression (Telfer 1996; Sibley 2001). However, as mentioned above, a full investigation of taste qualities extends to the meanings of flavors in history and society, which in turn connect to the significant roles that food and drink play in ceremony, hospitality, and daily practice. Whether or not one categorizes food as art, its aesthetic qualities include its cultural significance and the meanings it conveys.

Not only does the aesthetic exercise of the proximal senses draw attention to embodiment, but our bodies themselves are palpably changed by eating and drinking – and by deprivation and excess. The aspect of food that involves growth, change, and death is foregrounded by some contemporary artists who include foodstuffs or other transient substances in their work. Artists who make use of foods often exploit the meanings implicit in decay and putrefaction, in counterpoint to the emphasis on savoring that is more commonly explored in the philosophical aesthetics of food. The fact that eating is a physical activity with perilous borders – including fasting and starvation, not to mention the destruction of sentient creatures that are eaten – can give it a profundity and risk that some argue bears comparison with the sublime (Korsmeyer 1999; Weiss 2002; Lintott, 2007). Eating sustains life and vitalizes community, but at the same time awareness of mortality adds depth to the aesthetic dimensions of food and drink, and philosophic reflection on these elements amplifies comparisons with artworks with profound and difficult import.

See also AESTHETIC ATTITUDE; AESTHETIC PROPERTIES; AESTHETICS OF THE EVERYDAY; JAPANESE AESTHETICS; TASTE.

BIBLIOGRAPHY

Allhoff, Fritz (ed.). 2008. *Wine and Philosophy*. Malden: Blackwell.

Allhoff, Fritz & Monroe, Dave (eds.). 2007. *Food and Philosophy*. Malden: Blackwell.

Bach, Kent. 2007. "Knowledge, Wine, and Taste." In *Questions of Taste*. Barry C. Smith (ed.). Oxford: Signal Books, 21–40.

Bender, John W. 2008. "What the Wine Critic Tells Us." In *Wine and Philosophy*. Fritz Allhoff (ed.). Malden: Blackwell, 125–36.

Brady, Emily. 2005. "Sniffing and Savoring." In *The Aesthetics of Everyday Life*. A. Light & J. Smith (eds.). New York: Columbia University Press, 177–93.

Burnham, Douglas & Skilleås, Ole Martin. 2008. "You'll Never Drink Alone." In *Wine and Philosophy*. Fritz Allhoff (ed.). Malden: Blackwell, 157–71.

Gale, George. 2008. "Who Cares If You Like It." In *Wine and Philosophy*. Fritz Allhoff (ed.). Malden: Blackwell, 172–85.

Gigante, Denise. 2005. *Taste: A Literary History*. New Haven: Yale University Press.

Hales, Steven D. (ed.). 2007. *Beer and Philosophy*. Malden: Blackwell.

Heldke, Lisa. 2003. *Exotic Hungers*. New York: Routledge.

Jacquette, Dale. 2007. "Thirst for Authenticity." In *Beer and Philosophy*. Steven D. Hales (ed.). Malden: Blackwell, 15–30.

Korsmeyer, Carolyn. 1999. *Making Sense of Taste*. Ithaca: Cornell University Press.

Kuehn, Glenn. 2005. "How Can Food be Art?" In *The Aesthetics of Everyday Life*. A. Light & J. Smith (eds.). New York: Columbia University Press,194–212.

Lintott, Sheila. 2007. "Sublime Hunger." In *Food and Philosophy*. Fritz Allhoff & Dave Monroe (eds.). Malden: Blackwell, 58–70.

Machamer, Peter. 2007. "How to Properly Dispute Taste." In *Beer and Philosophy*. Steven D. Hales (ed.). Malden: Blackwell, 52–64.

Monroe, Dave. 2007. "Can Food be Art?" In *Food and Philosophy*. Fritz Allhoff & Dave Monroe (eds.). Malden: Blackwell, 133–44.

Saito, Yuriko. 2007. *Everyday Aesthetics*. Oxford: Oxford University Press.

Shaffer, Michael. 2007. "Taste, Gastronomic Expertise, and Objectivity." In *Food and Philosophy*. Fritz Allhoff & Dave Monroe (eds.). Malden: Blackwell, 73–87.

Sibley, Frank. 2001. "Tastes, Smells, and Aesthetics." In *Approaches to Aesthetics*. Oxford: Oxford University Press, 207–55.

Smith, Barry C. 2007a. "The Objectivity of Taste and Tasting." In *Questions of Taste*. Barry C. Smith (ed.). Oxford: Signal Books, 41–73.

Smith, Barry C. (ed.). 2007b. *Questions of Taste*. Oxford: Signal Books.

Sweeney, Kevin W. 1999. "Alice's Discriminating Palate," *Philosophy and Literature*, 23, 17–31.

Sweeney, Kevin. 2007. "Can a Soup be Beautiful?" In *Food and Philosophy*. Fritz Allhoff & Dave Monroe (eds.). Malden: Blackwell, 117–32.

Telfer, Elizabeth. 1996. *Food for Thought*. London: Routledge.

Weiss, Allen S. 2002. *Feast and Folly*. Albany: State University of New York Press.

CAROLYN KORSMEYER

aesthetics of the environment   Much of our aesthetic appreciation is not limited to art, but rather is directed toward the world at large. Moreover, we appreciate not only pristine nature – sunsets and mountains – but also our more mundane surroundings: the solitude of a neighborhood park on a rainy evening, the chaos of a bustling morning marketplace, the view from the road. Thus, there is a place for the notion of environmental aesthetics, for in such cases – in our appreciation of the world at large – our aesthetic appreciation often encompasses our total surroundings: our environment. Environments may be large or small, more or less natural, mundane or exotic, but in every case it is central that it is an environment that we appreciate. This fact signals several important dimensions of such appreciation, which in turn contribute to the central issues of environmental aesthetics.

These dimensions follow from the delineation of the field of inquiry. The "object" of appreciation, the "aesthetic object," is our environment, our own surroundings, and thus we are in a sense immersed in the object of appreciation. This fact has the following ramifications. We are in that which we appreciate, and that which we appreciate is also that from which we appreciate. If we move, we move within the object of our appreciation and thereby change our relationship to it and at the same time change the object itself. Moreover, as our surroundings, the object impinges upon all our senses. As we reside in it or move through it, we can see it, hear it, feel it, smell it, and perhaps even taste it. In brief, the experience of the environmental object of appreciation from which aesthetic appreciation must be fashioned is intimate, total, and somewhat engulfing.

This aspect of our experience of the environmental object of appreciation is intensified by the unruly nature of the object itself. The object of appreciation is not the more or less discrete, stable, and self-contained object of traditional art. It is rather an environment; consequently, not only does it change as we move within it, it also changes of its own accord. Environments are constantly in motion, in both the short and the long term. Even if we remain motionless, the wind brushes our face and the clouds pass before our eyes; and, with time, changes continue seemingly without limit: night falls, days pass, seasons come and go. Moreover, environments not only move through time, they extend through space, and again seemingly without limit. There are no predetermined boundaries for our environment; as we move, it moves with us and changes, but it does not end; indeed, it continues unending in every direction. In other words, the environmental object of appreciation does not come to us "preselected" and "framed" as do traditional artistic objects, neither in time as a drama or a musical composition, nor in space as a painting or a sculpture.

These differences between environments and traditional artistic objects relate to an even deeper dissimilarity between the two. The latter, works of art, are the products of artists. The artist is quintessentially a designer who creates a work by embodying a design in an object. Works of art are thus tied to their designers not only causally but conceptually; what a work is and what it means has much to do with its designer and its design. However, environments are paradigmatically not the products of designers. In the typical case, both designer and human design are lacking. Rather, environments come about "naturally"; they change, they grow, they develop either by natural processes or by means of human agency, but even in the latter case only rarely are they the result of a designer explicitly embodying a design. Thus, the typical environmental object of appreciation is unruly in yet another way: neither its nature nor its meaning is determined by a designer and a design.

The upshot is that in our aesthetic appreciation of the world at large we are initially confronted by – indeed, intimately and totally engulfed in – something that forces itself upon all our senses, is limited neither in time nor in space, and is constrained concerning neither its nature nor its meaning. We are immersed in a potential object of appreciation, and our task is to achieve some aesthetic appreciation of that object. Moreover, the appreciation must be fashioned anew, without the aid of frames, the guidance of designs, or the direction of designers. Thus, in our aesthetic appreciation of the world at large we must begin with the most basic of questions, those of exactly what and how to aesthetically appreciate. These questions raise the main issues of environmental aesthetics, essentially issues concerning what resources, if any, are available for answering them.

Concerning the questions of what and how to aesthetically appreciate in an environment, there are two main lines of thought. One, which is sometimes characterized as subjectivist or perhaps even as skeptical, holds that, since in the appreciation of environments we seemingly lack the resources normally involved in the aesthetic appreciation of art, these questions cannot be properly answered. That is to say that since we lack resources such as frames, designs, and designers, and the guidance they provide, the aesthetic appreciation of environments, unlike the appreciation of art, cannot be judged to be either appropriate or inappropriate. Moreover, even if it could be so judged, it would remain, in comparison with that of art, at best free and fanciful – or at worst superficial and shallow as opposed to serious and deep. An even more skeptical line suggests that perhaps the appreciation of environments is not genuine aesthetic appreciation at all. Concerning the world at large, as opposed to works of art, the closest we can come to appropriate aesthetic appreciation is simply to give ourselves over to being immersed, to respond as we will, and to enjoy what we can. In contrast to the aesthetic appreciation of art, the aesthetic appreciation of environments is marked by openness and freedom. And whether or not the resultant experience is appropriate in some sense or even really aesthetic in any sense is not of much consequence.

A second line of thought concerning the questions of what to aesthetically appreciate in an environment and how to do so is frequently characterized as objectivist or cognitivist. It argues that there are in fact important resources to draw on in our appreciation of environments, especially the object of appreciation itself, but also the appreciator and the knowledge that the latter has of the former. Thus, in the aesthetic appreciation of an environment, these elements can play roles similar to those played in the aesthetic appreciation of traditional art by the designer and the design. In appreciating the world at large, we typically fulfill some of the roles of a designer and yet let the world provide us with its own "design." Thus, when confronted by an environment, we select the ways that are relevant to its appreciation and set the frames that limit it in time and space. Moreover, as designers creatively interact with that which they design, we likewise creatively interact with an environment in light of our knowledge of it. In this way an environment itself, by its nature, provides its own "design" and can bring us to appreciate it "as what it is" and "on its own terms." In short, the environment offers the necessary guidance in terms of which we, the appreciators, by our selecting and framing, can answer the questions of what and how to appreciate – and thereby fashion our initial and somewhat chaotic experience of an environment into genuine aesthetic appreciation – appreciation that is both appropriate and serious.

As is typical with disputes in aesthetics between subjectivist or skeptical positions and more objectivist ones, the burden of proof falls on the latter. Thus, it is important for the objectivist account to be elaborated and supported by examples. The basic idea of the objectivist position is that our appreciation is guided by the nature of the object of appreciation. Thus, knowledge of the object's nature, of its genesis, type, and properties, is essential for serious, appropriate aesthetic appreciation. For example, in appropriately appreciating a natural environment such as an alpine meadow it is useful to know, for instance, that it has developed under constraints imposed by the climate of high altitude, and that diminutive size in flora is an adaptation to such constraints. This knowledge can guide our appreciation of the environment so that, for example, we avoid imposing inappropriately large frames, which may cause us to simply overlook miniature wild flowers. In such a case, we will neither appreciatively note their wonderful adjustment to their situation nor attune our senses to their subtle fragrance, texture, and hue. Similarly, in appropriately appreciating human-altered environments such as those of modern agriculture, it is helpful to know about the functional utility of cultivating huge fields devoted to single crops. Such knowledge encourages us to enlarge and adjust our frames, our senses, and even our attitudes, so as to more appreciatively accommodate the expansive uniform landscapes that are the inevitable result of such farming practices.

The basic assumption of environmental aesthetics is that every environment – natural, rural, or urban, large or small, ordinary or extraordinary – offers much to see, to hear, to feel, much to aesthetically appreciate. The different environments of the world at large are as aesthetically rich and rewarding as are works of art. However, it also must be recognized that special problems are posed for aesthetic appreciation by the very nature of environments, by the fact that they are our own surroundings, that they are unruly and chaotic objects of appreciation, and that we are plunged into them without appreciative guidelines. Both the subjectivist and the objectivist approaches recognize the problems and the potential involved in the aesthetic appreciation of environments. The main difference is that while the latter attempts to ground an appropriate aesthetic appreciation for different environments in our knowledge of their particular natures, the former simply invites us to enjoy them all as freely and as fully as we can and will. In the last analysis, perhaps both alternatives should be pursued.

See also AESTHETIC ATTITUDE; AESTHETIC JUDGMENT; AESTHETICS OF THE EVERYDAY; ARTIFACT, ART AS; EVOLUTION, ART, AND AESTHETICS.

BIBLIOGRAPHY
Berleant, Arnold. 1992. *The Aesthetics of Environment*. Philadelphia: Temple University Press.
Berleant, Arnold & Carlson, Allen (eds.). 2007. *The Aesthetics of Human Environments*. Peterborough: Broadview.
Brady, Emily. 2003. *Aesthetics of the Natural Environment*. Edinburgh: Edinburgh University Press.
Budd, Malcolm. 2002. *The Aesthetic Appreciation of Nature*. Oxford: Oxford University Press.
Carlson, Allen. 2000. *Aesthetics and the Environment: The Appreciation of Nature, Art and Architecture*. London: Routledge.
Carlson, Allen. 2007. "Environmental Aesthetics." In *The Stanford Encyclopedia of Philosophy*. E. N. Zalta (ed.). Available at http://plato.stanford.edu/entries/environmental-aesthetics/
Carlson, Allen & Berleant, Arnold (eds.). 2004. *The Aesthetics of Natural Environments*. Peterborough: Broadview.
Carlson, Allen & Lintott, Sheila (eds.). 2008. *Nature, Aesthetics, and Environmentalism: From Beauty to Duty*. New York: Columbia University Press.
Kemal, Salim & Gaskell, Ivan (eds.). 1993. *Landscape, Natural Beauty, and the Arts*. Cambridge: Cambridge University Press.
Sepänmaa, Yrjö. 1993. *The Beauty of Environment: A General Model for Environmental Aesthetics*. 2nd edn. Denton: Environmental Ethics Books.

ALLEN CARLSON

aesthetics of the everyday The discipline of aesthetics has tended, especially for the twentieth century, to focus on encounters with the fine arts and, to a lesser extent, with nature. Much attention has been devoted to the projects of defining art and establishing its ontology, and accounts of aesthetic experience and aesthetic properties have been derived primarily from considerations related to Western artworks. In the last few decades, though, there has been a movement away from the narrowly art-oriented approach and toward recognition of the continuity between experiences of fine art and experiences from other domains of life. This movement has given rise to an emerging subdiscipline often known as "everyday aesthetics" or "the aesthetics of the everyday." Theorists in the aesthetics of the everyday typically claim that objects and activities not essentially connected to art or nature can have aesthetic properties and/or that they can give rise to significant aesthetic experiences. Aesthetic analysis, then, is appropriately extended to virtually all areas of life.

John Dewey's (1934) *Art as Experience* has had a great influence on contemporary work in everyday aesthetics. Dewey suggested that the experiences of aesthetic exaltation associated with art can be traced back to processes that predate art and, indeed, that both humans and other animals partake in. Aesthetic experience, according to Dewey, is on a continuum with the deep feelings of fulfillment that arise from interacting with the environment to satisfy one's needs. What distinguishes aesthetic experiences from nonaesthetic aspects of experience, he claims, is not that they involve response to a particular set of objects, as many aesthetic traditionalists would claim, but that they exhibit qualitative unity as well as a sense of closure or consummation. These qualities can belong even to simple experiences like that of lifting a stone, as long as it is done with sufficient attention (1934: 44). Dewey's view is thus highly amenable to the application of aesthetic concepts throughout everyday life.

Despite its significant expansion of the territory of the aesthetic, Dewey's view has been criticized as too restrictive by some aestheticians of the everyday. Mindful of contemporary developments, they observe that many objects in the fine arts lack unity and closure or give rise to experiences that are "disjointed, severed, and jarring" (Novitz 1992: 9), but are nonetheless counted as aesthetic by traditional art-oriented theories. Indeed, their fragmented nature may be precisely what gives them their distinctive aesthetic qualities (Irvin 2008). It cannot, then, be a necessary condition for an experience's being aesthetic that it exhibit unity or closure. This conclusion is in line with recent developments in accounts of aesthetic experience, which no longer tend to claim that an experience must be positive in valence or must have a particular qualitative character to count as aesthetic.

Though particular aspects of Dewey's account may be criticized, the Deweyan strategy of deflating traditional distinctions between the fine arts and other domains of life has remained central to the aesthetics of the everyday. Some theorists have observed that the aesthetic phenomena invoked in traditional discussions of art are also present in other domains of life such as sport, sex, and everyday decision-making (Kupfer 1983). Moreover, aestheticians have increasingly rejected the Kantian notion that the aesthetic attitude involves holding oneself distant from the object of contemplation and remaining indifferent to any nonartistic functions it may serve. Arnold Berleant (1991) argues that the proper attitude toward artworks is one of deep engagement of the whole

person, an attitude which, he suggests, is quite naturally taken toward the objects of ordinary life as well. The traditional division of the senses into "higher" and "lower," and the associated suggestion that aesthetic experience must be exclusively the province of the former, has been challenged as arbitrary, with the result that ordinary activities involving taste and smell (Korsmeyer 1999; Brady 2005: ch. 10) or touch (Shusterman 2000: chs. 7, 10) have been rendered eligible for aesthetic consideration.

The sharp distinction between the fine arts and other domains of life has also been challenged by the observation that art emerges out of, and is in many contexts integrated with, everyday practices. Crispin Sartwell (1995) and Yuriko Saito (2007) observe that, particularly in non-Western cultures, works of art and aesthetically oriented design objects are often made to enhance everyday life. David Novitz (1992) notes the implausibility of seeing popular art forms as segregated from everyday life: works of television and pop music often take the mundane as their subject matter, and their consumption is integrated with the ordinary activities of life. Moreover, recent developments within the Western fine arts have arguably brought art and life closer together, as ordinary objects have been exhibited in gallery settings and ordinary sounds have been integrated into avant-garde musical compositions. These techniques seem to invite us to apply to everyday objects and events the same aesthetic regard traditionally reserved for artworks.

While much of the defense of everyday aesthetics has grown out of observations related to art, another important force has been the burgeoning of environmental aesthetics. While taking its initial impetus from the Kantian interest in the sublime, environmental aesthetics has evolved to include consideration of a wide variety of environments and phenomena. An interest in natural science has moved some environmental aestheticians to acknowledge the difficulty of drawing a principled distinction between the natural and the nonnatural: since humans are animals, and their artifacts, behaviors, and environments arise in large part out of evolved capacities, the natural and nonnatural seem to be best thought of as lying along a continuum rather than on opposite sides of a sharp divide. If an aesthetic regard can properly be cast on natural objects and environments, then there is no obvious reason not to extend it further. More generally, the attention to environments, rather than isolated objects, has led to the recognition of a mode of aesthetic experience that is complex, immersive, and multisensory, and thus readily applicable to everyday life.

Once the barriers separating everyday life from art and nature have been broken down, a positive case remains to be made for the interest of applying aesthetic concepts to ordinary objects and phenomena. The interest is claimed to be both practical and theoretical. From a practical perspective, the claim is often made that a serious interest in the aesthetics of the everyday promises a richer life, as we attend to satisfactions that are readily available but that we may not have tended to notice or take advantage of. Indeed, Shusterman (2000: ch. 10) suggests that everyday aesthetics should include practical training in bodywork and related disciplines, precisely to secure the benefit of a more satisfying life. The aesthetics of the everyday also has moral implications. Kupfer argues that "the aesthetic dimensions in everyday life are . . . instrumental in developing people into more deliberate, autonomous community members" (1983: 3). Irvin (2008) argues that aesthetic satisfactions in everyday life can be harnessed to support moral behavior. And as Sartwell (1995) points out, in many cultural and, especially, spiritual traditions the moral and the aesthetic are seamlessly integrated within everyday life.

From a theoretical perspective, it has been suggested that the aesthetics of the everyday is of special interest because everyday phenomena may require aesthetic insights and concepts distinct from those needed to account for art and nature (Saito 2007: 5). Many of the aesthetic properties exhibited by everyday phenomena, for instance, may be different from those derived from a prominently art-oriented aesthetics (Leddy 1995). At the same time, the aesthetics of the everyday may be used as a source of insights about the nature of art: Sartwell suggests, based on observations about the continuity between art and everyday life in many cultures, that art should be redefined as "skilled and devoted making" that may eventuate in

artifacts that serve a variety of everyday functions (1995: 9).

Attempts to demonstrate the theoretical interest of everyday aesthetics bring out a methodological tension that inheres in the discipline. On the one hand, in order to demonstrate that it really is a subdiscipline of aesthetics, the aesthetics of the everyday must demonstrate that, at some level, it is fundamentally concerned with the same concepts and phenomena that have preoccupied mainstream aesthetics. This is why so much of the discipline has been concerned to break down barriers between art and other domains of life. On the other hand, though, if it is to be of interest, everyday aesthetics must show that it has a distinctive contribution to make to aesthetics by virtue of introducing a distinctive subject matter, methodology, or set of aesthetic concepts. This tension continues to animate the discipline: aestheticians of the everyday continually refer back to and demonstrate connections to traditional aesthetic objects, properties, and experiences, even while suggesting that mainstream aesthetics has been too restrictive in its treatment of them.

The breadth of content and approach advocated within the aesthetics of the everyday leaves the discipline vulnerable to two objections. First, one might suspect that it renders the notion of the aesthetic so broad as to be meaningless. If aesthetic experience can happen at any time, can take anything as its object, and need have no particular qualitative feel, is there really any distinction between the aesthetic aspects of experience and its other aspects? Such a concern is presumably what motivated Dewey to require qualitative unity and closure: these criteria ensure that not every possible experience will fall into the category of the aesthetic, and thus secure the nontriviality of the concept. If such requirements are rejected, it appears that any experience may qualify as aesthetic just by virtue of having a qualitative feel. This is a conclusion that aesthetic traditionalists are likely to find unpalatable, even as aestheticians of the everyday may welcome it. Second, since everyday aesthetics tends to emphasize aesthetic experiences and objects that are not exalted in character, one may wonder if it really warrants our attention. Would it not ultimately be more rewarding to focus on great artworks and the natural sublime, which promise more significant edification? The aesthetician of the everyday may reply that the aesthetic pleasures of everyday life are worth acknowledging because they are available to everyone, even those who lack access to art and untouched nature. Moreover, even if the texture of everyday life is such as to yield aesthetic satisfactions that are relatively subtle, continual awareness of these satisfactions may offer a payoff in quality of life that is very much worth having.

See also AESTHETIC ATTITUDE; AESTHETIC PROPERTIES; AESTHETICS OF FOOD AND DRINK; AESTHETICS OF THE ENVIRONMENT; DEWEY; EVOLUTION, ART, AND AESTHETICS; JAPANESE AESTHETICS; POPULAR ART.

BIBLIOGRAPHY

Berleant, Arnold. 1991. *Art and Engagement*. Philadelphia: Temple University Press.
Brady, Emily. 2005. "Sniffing and Savoring: The Aesthetics of Smells and Tastes." In *The Aesthetics of Everyday Life*. A. Light & J. M. Smith (eds.). New York: Columbia University Press, 177–193.
Dewey, John. 1934. *Art as Experience*. New York: Perigee.
Irvin, Sherri. 2008. "The Pervasiveness of the Aesthetic in Ordinary Experience," *British Journal of Aesthetics*, 48, 29–44.
Korsmeyer, Carolyn. 1999. *Making Sense of Taste: Food and Philosophy*. Ithaca: Cornell University Press.
Kupfer, Joseph H. 1983. *Experience as Art: Aesthetics in Everyday Life*. Albany: State University of New York Press.
Leddy, Thomas. 1995. "Everyday Surface Aesthetic Qualities: 'Neat,' 'Messy,' 'Clean,' 'Dirty'," *Journal of Aesthetics and Art Criticism*, 53, 259–68.
Light, Andrew & Smith, Jonathan M. (eds.). 2005. *The Aesthetics of Everyday Life*. New York: Columbia University Press.
Novitz, David. 1992. *The Boundaries of Art*. Philadelphia: Temple University Press.
Saito, Yuriko. 2007. *Everyday Aesthetics*. New York: Oxford University Press.
Sartwell, Crispin. 1995. *The Art of Living: Aesthetics of the Ordinary in World Spiritual Traditions*. Albany: State University of New York Press.
Shusterman, Richard. 2000. *Pragmatist Aesthetics: Living Beauty, Rethinking Art*. 2nd edn. Lanham: Rowman & Littlefield.

SHERRI IRVIN

African aesthetics   Art is a universal human phenomenon. It is the expression of the compulsive innate human tendency toward creativity. It is one of the main engagements and accomplishments of human beings that distinguishes humans from other beings, as the means by which humans are capable of focusing consciousness to achieve and express their perception, comprehension, apprehension, annotation, demarcation, appreciation, and documentation of their peculiar lived realities. It is in this regard that it is meaningful to speak of African art, while being mindful of the heterogeneity of the natural habitats, languages, ethnicities, and cultures of the many African peoples, as there are some common African cultural affinities and identities that have been manifested over many millennia.

African art encompasses visual and nonvisual, tangible and nontangible elements, such that virtually every aspect of living constitutes a veritable domain for art. It can be conjectured that the two tropes that facilitate the understanding of African aesthetics are beauty and pleasantness. Beauty and pleasantness make the object of art and the process or act of creating worthy art special, distinguishing art from nonart objects, because the latter are not deliberately made by humans to be artistic.

At the time of their production, most art objects often reflect a multiplicity of intention, purpose, utility, and appreciation. These may be masked by the search that pervades contemporary consumerist consciousness for the net financial worth of art objects, with the result that their value is misplaced. In most cases, the makers of African art, in its indigenous setting, set no monetary value on their effort, not because they do not understand that they are incurring costs in the production or because they cannot put a value on the effort they have put into the production, but more importantly because they understand that the beauty and pleasantness of what is produced, the truth and meaning it purveys, and the sentiment and social consciousness invested in it, are beyond financial quantification. In this regard, the art object is a gift to the person who has commissioned it, as well as to the society in which it is produced, reflecting and enriching that society's moral, social, spiritual, and other values. The society collectively owns the art object, as much as does its individual "owner"; hence the unusual reticence with which most Africans sell art objects.

Some of the areas in which art is manifested, showing the twin consciousness of beauty and pleasantness, are in (1) the architecture of used or inhabited space; (2) the dress, appearance, deportment, and adornment of persons for various occasions and vocations; (3) the content of speech and the manner of speaking as befits the audience and occasion; (4) decorations that emphasize and enhance the beauty and pleasantness of homes, spaces, and the wider world; (5) the capacity to appreciate art in nature – such as when animal, tree, river, rock, celestial appearance, and behavior become narratives underlining an architectonic of beauty and pleasure, leading to formation of cosmologies, cosmogonies, ontologies, metonyms, metaphors, and mythologies; (6) the humble display of the performer's skill and talent; (7) efforts to observe the highest professional and moral standards in whatever is done to capture and enrich truth; (8) the display of good habits and respectful mannerisms in private and public spaces; (9) the care taken to ensure the maintenance of equilibrium and moderation in the various modes of being of the living, the dead, and the unborn; (10) the maintenance of proper and edifying relationships within and outside families; and (11) efforts toward the development of future generations and filial bonding with family members and society.

There are three elements that contribute to African aesthetics. First, there is the skill, dexterity, and consciousness and other mental faculties involved in the production of true artistic forms of life. Second, there is the final outcome of the effort, the extent to which it meets the remit that impelled it in terms of finesse, truth of representation, orientation, and integration. Third, there is the moral or ethical element of art – how far it is morally edifying, truthful, and acceptable, or denigrating and unacceptable; how far it conduces to the interests of society as a whole in affirming and promoting harmony and cultural progress. Any art that is skeptically oriented and infused with cynicism, as in carefully choreographed and intelligently orchestrated critiques of power and wealth, has to be not only beautiful but pleasant, even

to those who form the intended target of that critique, in order that the point be properly driven home without alienation or disruption of communal existence.

In Africa, art is the epitome of the culture and civilization of society, representing the human capacity to enjoy the sublime aspects of life, regardless of the wider situation, without leading to a rich/poor divide in cultural consciousness. In fact, most African art functions seamlessly, because it transcends artificial divisions to present itself to every member of society. To this end, it is clear that some artistic expressions record the skepticism of the critical members of society, those who take issue with their society's epistemological, metaphysical, moral, religious, political, and scientific beliefs, its received knowledge. These individuals often find ingenious ways of expressing their alternative views without failing to entertain, regardless of how arcane the views may seem at the time. They may even record their defiance of and nonconformity to the orthodox and popular positions embraced by the majority in various ways, making art not only a means of celebrating the patterns of cooperation of members of society but also a medium of protest. For example, among the Yoruba certain ways in which men wear their caps and women tie their headgear clearly signal a protest against the norm, reflecting their view that in society certain wrongs need redressing. Yoruba artists also question conformity through stories, practical jokes, songs, sculpture, bodily adornment, hairstyle, dress, and music (using both the language and music itself and their choice of instruments to make the point), and even silence, generated at appropriate moments in conversation and theatrical performance.

Essentially, art is an integral part of the conscience of any society. The way its practitioners carry out their trade will help to determine the epistemological engineering and re-engineering that the social fabric must undergo continuously. Even when there is borrowing from others, this has to be done with as much faithfulness and honesty as possible, recognizing the debt (perhaps with tongue in cheek), and acknowledging the reason for the borrowing. Thus there is a tendency to speak of the original artwork by comparing it with copies; even where there are no observable distinctions between them, the original is preferred and attracts a higher accolade.

There is also often a clear distinction between artworks and mere tools. One may have to use a very "ugly" tool to perform a task, and may feel repelled every time one uses it, but if it is the best tool, or the only one available or most suited for the job at hand, one is foolhardy to worry about taste, instead of being clear-sighted about the effectiveness and efficiency of the tool in the performance of the task at hand, as no further consideration is relevant. This is not far from the Yoruba understanding of the difference between beauty in character and physical beauty: the wise Yoruba man or woman recommends that one should marry not for physical beauty but for its ethical form and beauty in behavior, for it can be said that "The lady may be beautiful in looks, but spoil her beauty with bad character." But in the absence of the combination of physical beauty and beauty of character, it is better to marry someone who is not (so) beautiful but who is known to have been properly brought up by his or her parents and acknowledged to have good character (i.e., an *omoluabi*, a well-cultured, highly respectful, and morally upright person).

Whenever comparisons are made in Yoruba culture, acuity of observation is emphasized. Language itself embodies this search for subtle points of comparison, and there is a general insistence that the meaning of any comparative claim be clear, as a corollary of the more general requirement that the young be given clear instruction in the virtues. In all instances of comparison in Yoruba culture, for example, acuity of observation is emphasized. It is important to note that there is a combination of an epistemic discernment that has led to a noting and incorporation of comparative ideas into the corpus of language, and to insistence both on understanding the meaning of the message and on the clarity with which the young are instructed in the virtues.

Order and responsibility are important and unavoidable requisites of all aspects of civilized life in any society and any attempt to compromise them always involves a great human, cultural, and material cost to society. Consequently, the arts to which children and other members of society are exposed should reflect the values that are worthy to be developed, maintained, emulated, and perpetuated. This constitutes a regulatory code of conduct, for leaders and their followers that covers all aspects of life, from dress, eating, and forms of greeting, to games and work ethics, political leadership, relaxation, and festivals. It extends to what can be exhibited in private and public space, how and where they can be exhibited, and so on.

In many African societies, the art of child-rearing is suffused with person-affirming and individuality-developing literature, songs, dance, paintings, and other cultural paraphernalia. Also, while the other-regarding aspect of social existence is emphasized, the need for the individual to acknowledge himself or herself as an individual, and as a *person*, with a name, a destiny, a calling, etc., is instilled in the child from the beginning, such that, while he or she shares a common human destiny of being and of responsibility for the survival of the species, his or her ability to make a difference is never disregarded or compromised.

There is a clear relationship between art and morality, as the different arts are educational media for the training of the young in society. In this regard, there is room for academic discourse to the extent that it will lead to an informed decision as to the proper course of action. This is important because bad art can have deleterious effects: (1) people can be deceived by it into false complacency, similar to what happens when religion becomes the opium of the people; (2) it can be responsible for creating unfounded euphoria, especially in untutored and uncultured minds; (3) it can misrepresent reality; and (4) it can lead people to have false impressions of their capabilities, similar to what happens when people relate to their environment under the influence of drugs. In these ways, such art destroys psychic harmony rather than reinforcing it, and stirs up wrong emotions and false beliefs, thus confusing rather than clarifying reality.

We should remember that the workings of art within a culture involve the appreciation of more than artworks alone; it is equally important to recognize that every artist loves applause. African artists, in all walks of life, are appreciated within their various societies. For, as these societies often recognize, praise begets further excellence, while failure to appreciate can stymie creativity, if not totally destroy it.

See also ART HISTORY.

BIBLIOGRAPHY
Bewaji, J. A. I. 2003. *Beauty and Culture: Perspectives in Black Aesthetics*. Ibadan, Nigeria: Spectrum Books.
Layton, Robert. 1991. *The Anthropology of Art*. 2nd edn. Cambridge: Cambridge University Press.

JOHN AYOTUNDE (TUNDE) ISOLA BEWAJI

Amerindian aesthetics   Franz Boas's (1927: 183–298) monumental *Primitive Art* devotes 115 pages to a discussion of north Pacific coast artistic styles. Boas, as was his method, was largely descriptive in his analysis of Native American aesthetic practices. For example, he writes: "Two styles may be distinguished: the man's style expressed in the art of wood carving and painting and their derivations; and the woman's style which finds expression in weaving, basketry, and embroidery. The two styles are fundamentally distinct. The former is symbolic, the latter formal. The symbolic art has a certain degree of realism and is full of meaning. The formal art has, at most, pattern names and no especially marked significance" (1927: 183). For Boas, the understanding of patterns was the beginning of an understanding of Native American aesthetics. Amerindian aesthetics were not, however, limited to visual arts, but also included verbal arts (song, story, chant, etc.) as well as dance.

Since Boas's early work, anthropologists have been engaged in documenting and understanding Amerindian aesthetic practices. These investigations have been variously termed ethnoaesthetics (B. Tedlock 1986), ethnopoetics (Hymes 1981; D. Tedlock 1983), and ethnomusicology (McAllester 1954). Such approaches have striven to understand what makes various social practices "beautiful." The focus here is on aesthetic practices and the ways that such practices are given value as aesthetically pleasing. In each case, the question of what is and is not considered beautiful becomes an ethnographic question, as does the very question of what it means to say something is "beautiful." What ethnographers have found is that Amerindian peoples often have well-thought-out theories of beauty.

In a short piece it is impossible to cover all of Amerindian aesthetics and aesthetic practices.

For the purposes here, I shall focus on three ethnographic examples. They are the Kuna, the Zuni, and the Navajo. I discuss each in turn. I explore the general by way of the particular. In conclusion, I discuss issues of the appropriation of Amerindian aesthetic practices.

KUNA AESTHETICS
The Kuna, who live along the Atlantic coastal region of primarily Panama and Colombia as well as in Panama City, are traditionally agriculturalists, who practice slash and burn agriculture in the coastal jungles. Their aesthetic practices have been most ably described by Joel Sherzer (1983, 1990).

Perhaps the most famous example of Kuna aesthetic practices are the molas. Molas are multicolored appliqué blouses that were traditionally made and worn by Kuna women. A woman made her own mola. The molas were quintessential emblems of Kuna-ness. More recently, molas have been sold to tourists and collectors. The organizing principle of mola design is that of repetition with variation. Molas are often based on three themes: (1) geometrical designs; (2) representations of Kuna life; and (3) representations of the Western world (copied from magazines). Molas are filled. Empty space is to be avoided. The molas are not representations of Kuna "ancestors, mythical beings or scenes, or good or bad spirits of a supernatural nature" (Sherzer & Sherzer 1976: 32). They are decorative emblems of Kuna-ness, but they are not supernatural in nature. Nor for that matter are they meant to be interpreted.

This aesthetic differs in some substantial ways from the verbal art of the Kuna. Among the Kuna, the use of the paradigmatic litany of objects in chants creates lists of the known. For example, in the "Way of the Hot Pepper" (a Kuna chant) the kinds of peppers known to the Kuna are listed through parallelism, that is, repetition with variation. The "Way of the Hot Pepper" then is a statement of Kuna ecology via parallelism. In going through the various paradigmatic relationships, the Way is lengthened. This is also a part of Kuna aesthetic practices. Long chants, as well as verbal proclivity, are considered aesthetically pleasing. Silence, on the other hand, is something to be avoided. Chants can be performed either in public at the central congress house or in private, when addressed to the spirits. In the public congress there is also much meta-talk about chants. A Kuna chief gives a speech in the central gathering house, and that speech is then interpreted and translated by a ratified interpreter. Kuna chants and speeches are given in esoteric and metaphoric language. The esoteric and metaphoric languages are considered aesthetically pleasing aspects of the chants. They are meant to be interpreted. Curing chants, done in private, are not interpreted.

The Kuna, then, have two poles on a continuum of aesthetic practice. On the one hand, they have the molas, which are seen as beautiful, but are not meant to be interpreted. On the other hand, they have chants and speeches given in the central congress house, which are also beautiful, but which must be interpreted. The organization of both the molas and chants is based on the principle of parallelism. Both attempt to fill emptiness, either with images or with sounds. Finally, both the chants and the molas are understood as the products of creative individuals.

ZUNI AESTHETICS

The Zuni predominately live at Zuni Pueblo and the surrounding area in western New Mexico. The Zuni language, which is still actively spoken, is a language isolate. This has led some amateur scholars to wild speculations concerning the origins of the Zuni, but all that it really means is that the Zuni language cannot be directly connected with other languages based on the methodology of historical linguistics.

Zuni aesthetic practices have been described most usefully by Barbara Tedlock (1984, 1986, 1995) and Dennis Tedlock (1972, 1983). Zuni have two broad ethnoaesthetic categories, *tso'ya* and *attanni*. For purposes here, we can gloss – though these are in no way adequate translations – *tso'ya* as "beautiful" and *attanni* as "dangerous." These categories cross multiple domains, genres, and media. As Barbara Tedlock explains: "In the visual world of the cultural world, *tso'ya* describes flower bouquets, jewelry, pottery, beadwork, the costumes of Zuni Olla Maidens, kachina dance costumes, the arrangement of kachinas in dance line, and the interior decoration of Sha'lako houses, all of which display a great variety of textures,

forms, and colors" (1986: 190). Songs, as well, can be considered *tso'ya*, when they are newly composed, "rich in allegorical meaning . . . sung clearly, and when the basically diatonic melody has a stepped construction beginning low and ending high" (1986: 191).

On the other hand, "*attanni* is a quality of the shaggy, dark, matted hair and costumes of ogres, and of crudely naturalistic designs painted on kiva walls as well as on certain types of ceremonial pottery. In auditory culture, the *attanni* aesthetic occurs in traditional songs of the medicine societies . . . which have relatively simple texts and melodies totally lacking in chromaticism" (1986: 193). Things that are *tso'ya* can be shared. Much of the artistic expressions, the kachina designs sold by Zuni artisans, are understood as *tso'ya* and are, therefore, shareable. The kachina are sacred and *tso'ya* and hence shareable. On the other hand, War God images are *attanni* and because they are dangerous they are not shareable. Understanding Zuni aesthetics allows one to understand that not all sacred items are treated identically, nor are they categorized by Zunis identically (B. Tedlock 1995).

NAVAJO AESTHETICS

Much has been written concerning Navajo aesthetics (see McAllester 1954; Witherspoon 1977; Witherspoon & Peterson 1995). The Navajo were traditionally a Southern Athabaskan-speaking people who resided in what is now the American southwest. Today, Navajos (or Diné) live on the Navajo Nation, a reservation that covers portions of Arizona, New Mexico, and Utah, as well as in urban areas throughout the United States. Navajo is still spoken by nearly 120,000 Navajos. Younger Navajos, though, are no longer learning the language at a rate that will guarantee its continued use.

David McAllester summed up Navajo aesthetics as "beauty is that which *does* something" (1954: 72). The Navajo are famous for their elaborate and complex chantway ceremonies (Matthews 1995). Such chantways as the Enemyway, Blessingway, and Nightway can last many nights and work either as a curative or a prophylactic. *Hózhǫ́* ("beauty, harmony, good") and *nizhóni* ("it is good, it is beautiful") are often used by Navajos to describe things that are beautiful. The Navajo are also known for their weavings and for their silver work.

Chantways are marked by long complex chants and by the use of drypaintings or sandpaintings. Sandpaintings are used immediately after they have been completed in a ritual setting. The patient is placed on the sandpainting almost immediately after the sandpainting has been completed and the sandpainting is destroyed. This lack of reification of the sandpainting as an enduring artistic piece had been one of the hallmarks of Navajo aesthetics. This is a focus on the process and not on the product. With changes in economics that have been conditioned by incorporation into a capitalist economy that objectifies and trades in commodities, sandpaintings are now being done by Navajos to be sold to tourists and collectors. Weavings too, in theory never completed, are also now sold as objects of trade and commerce. Many weavers leave a flaw in the rug's border, a gap. This aesthetic, that no design is ever truly complete, keeps the rug as a process, and not as a product.

In chants, weavings, and sandpaintings, repetition and repetition with variation often mark their forms. The use of repetition and of repetition with variation of formulaic expressions is often considered aesthetically pleasing. Repetition in fours or twos is common and appreciated as aesthetically pleasing. The sandpaintings are often a series of figures or designs that repeat and vary. In principle, they often reflect complementary concepts. Male and female are frequently put into complementary dialogue. The sacred mountains and sacred directions are often presented in a formulaic manner. However, while repetition and parallelism are important components of Navajo chantways, they are not enough. A chant must be aesthetically pleasing as well (Field & Blackhorse Jr. 2002). Deities respond to chants because of aesthetic considerations.

Onomatopoeia is common in chantways as well as in songs, place names, and contemporary poetry. Such sound symbolism is aesthetically pleasing because it allows a listener to imagine a particular moment. Through sound symbolism one can imagine the moment in which the event occurred because one can imagine the sounds of the moment. Navajo expressive culture is most aesthetically pleasing when it allows listeners to engage in imaginative coordination. Silence is also valued. Speech is understood as considered action and speaking should be done in a careful and thoughtful manner. There is a link between aesthetic practices and traditional Navajo religious views. One of the things that beauty does is to heal and to protect.

One feature of Navajo verbal art is that it is localized. That is, stories begin at named locales and events take place at named and knowable locations. Place names are often considered aesthetically pleasing uses of language. Such place names are often descriptive and are also associated with the ancestors who originally named those places. I am reminded of a November afternoon in 2000, when a Navajo friend, his elderly maternal aunt, and I stood out at the crest of a ridge on the Navajo Nation near where both my friend and his aunt had grown up. We were talking about place names. The aunt had asked if I knew the name for the place we were. I had offered the conventional term for what I thought was the place. She corrected me: "That's what people call it now." She paused. "But it's *T'iis 'ii'áí'*." "Tree line," offered my friend. She went on to explain how there used to be a series of trees along the ridge, but that the trees were gone now. The beauty of the place name came partly from its brevity and descriptiveness, but it also came from an association with the words of her elders, and finally there was also the ability, through an association with her elders and due to its descriptiveness, to recall an earlier time. Aesthetically pleasing uses of language "give an imagination to the listener" as one Navajo consultant told me. As the language shifts from Navajo to English, such aesthetic practices are also lost.

Much contemporary written Navajo poetry has links with the oral traditions (Webster 2006) and shares their rhetorical and poetic devices. Parallelism is found in Navajo chantways and can be evoked in written poetry as well. Interpretation is not highly valued, but reflection is. A good poem, as it was explained to me, is one that makes someone think or reflect. Nor are chantways or, for that matter, contemporary poetry, considered to be the sole invention of a creative individual. Rather chantways are considered – given the vagaries of life – to be exact repetitions of prior chants. While the individual is important, this importance is mitigated by acknowledgment of the words of those who have come before.

CONCLUSION

Amerindian aesthetics are not identical across groups or across genres and media. Kuna and the Navajo both value speaking and find displays of repetition with variation to be aesthetically pleasing. Yet Kuna fill the world with sounds, while Navajos appreciate silence. Not every aesthetic practice that Amerindians engage in is sacred or religious. The Kuna mola is an aesthetic practice that is considered beautiful but is not meant for sacred reflection. Zuni War Gods, on the other hand, are sacred and *attanni*, "dangerous," and they cannot be removed from Zuni control. Images of kachinas, on the other hand, are *tso'ya*, "beautiful," and can be shared and, for that matter, sold by Zuni artisans. Understanding Amerindian aesthetic systems can go a long way in aiding understanding of what is and is not meant to be shared cross-culturally. As the Navajos have learned with sandpaintings and the Kuna with molas, aesthetic practices can be adapted by degrees for Western consumerism. The problem of misrecognizing every Amerindian aesthetic practice as "spiritual" continues, however, as does the appropriation of aesthetic practices as well. These problems will continue as long as Amerindians occupy a "spiritual other" place in the Western imagination.

The aim here has been to suggest something of the variety of Amerindian aesthetics, not to summarize an entire hemisphere's aesthetic practices. In the list of further reading below, I suggest contemporary ethnographic accounts of the aesthetic practices from North and South America. The list is eclectic, but I hope that it allows for a motivated rambling through the contemporary literature.

See also AUTHENTICITY AND ART; CULTURAL APPROPRIATION.

BIBLIOGRAPHY
Basso, Ellen. 1985. *A Musical View of the Universe*. Philadelphia: University of Pennsylvania Press.
Boas, Franz. 1927. *Primitive Art*. Cambridge, MA: Harvard University Press.
Field, Margaret & Blackhorse, Taft, Jr. 2002. "The Dual Role of Metonymy in Navajo Prayer," *Anthropological Linguistics*, 44(3), 217–30.
Hill, Jonathan. 1993. *Keepers of the Sacred Chants*. Tucson: University of Arizona Press.
Hymes, Dell. 1981. *In Vain I Tried to Tell You*. Philadelphia: University of Pennsylvania Press.
McAllester, David. 1954. *Enemy Way Music: A Study of Social and Esthetic Values as seen in Navajo Music*. Cambridge, MA: Papers of the Peabody Museum of American Archaeology and Ethnology, 41(3).
Matthews, Washington. 1995. *The Night Chant*. Salt Lake City: University of Utah Press.
Samuels, David. 2004. *Putting a Song on Top of It*. Tucson: University of Arizona Press.
Sherzer, Dina & Sherzer, Joel. 1976. "Mormaknamaloe: The Cuna Mola." In *Ritual and Symbol in Native Central America*. P. Young & J. Howe (eds.). Portland: University of Oregon, 21–42.
Sherzer, Joel. 1983. *Kuna Ways of Speaking*. Austin: University of Texas Press.
Sherzer, Joel. 1990. *Verbal Art in San Blas*. Cambridge: Cambridge University Press.
Tedlock, Barbara. 1984. "The Beautiful and the Dangerous: Zuni Ritual and Cosmology as an Aesthetic System," *Conjunctions*, 6, 246–65.
Tedlock, Barbara. 1986. "Crossing the Sensory Domains in Native American Aesthetics." In *Explorations in Ethnomusicology*. C. Frisbie (ed.). Detroit: Information Coordinators, 187–98.
Tedlock, Barbara. 1995. "Aesthetics and Politics: Zuni War God Repatriation and Kachina Representation." In *Looking High and Low*. B. J. Bright (ed.). Tucson: University of Arizona Press, 151–72.
Tedlock, Dennis. 1972. *Finding the Center*. New York: Dial Press.
Tedlock, Dennis. 1983. *The Spoken Word and the Work of Interpretation*. Philadelphia: University of Pennsylvania Press.
Webster, Anthony. 2006. " 'Aɬk'idą́ą́' Mą́'ii Jooldlosh, Jiní: Poetic Devices in Navajo Oral and Written Poetry," *Anthropological Linguistics*, 48(3), 233–65.
Witherspoon, Gary. 1977. *Language and Art in the Navajo Universe*. Ann Arbor: University of Michigan Press.
Witherspoon, Gary & Peterson, Glen. 1995. *Dynamic Symmetry and Holistic Asymmetry: In Navajo and Western Art and Cosmology*. New York: Peter Lang.

ANTHONY K. WEBSTER

Aquinas, Thomas (1225–1274) Italian Dominican friar whose philosophy and theology ("Thomism") have decisively shaped Catholic thought. Born into an aristocratic Italian family,

Aquinas disappointed his relatives by failing to enter the affluent Benedictine order, instead becoming a friar of the newly founded Dominican Order of Preachers. Under the tutelage of St. Albert the Great in Cologne, he began to study Aristotle and later became a major figure at the University of Paris and at the papal court. He died on his way to the Council of Lyons; and in 1323 he was canonized.

Aquinas is generally regarded as the greatest of the medieval philosophers. This estimate is hard to fault when one takes account of the scale and variety of his intellectual achievements, for he was the first medieval thinker to work out at length the new synthesis between Catholicism and philosophy. He believed in the idea of cumulative philosophical and religious wisdom, and sought to integrate Neoplatonist, Augustinian, and Anselmian ideas, as well as Aristotelian ones, with scripture, patristic teaching, and evolving Catholic doctrine.

He was a prodigious writer on a multitude of topics. With a few exceptions (such as Jacques Maritain and Armand Maurer), however, philosophers inspired by Aquinas have had little to say about aesthetics. This reflects the character of his own writings, for while he offers remarks on the nature of beauty and of art-making, he has no treatises or extensive theory on these subjects. All the same, it is possible to extract from his work ideas of enduring interest for philosophical aesthetics.

The two most important sources of these ideas are brief remarks in his *Commentary on the Divine Names* (*De divinis nominibus*) and in the *Summa theologiae*. In the first of these he observes that something is not beautiful because we like it, but that our liking for it is due to its beauty (c.IV, *lectio* 10), having earlier remarked that anyone who depicts a thing does so for the sake of making something beautiful; and that each thing is beautiful to the extent that it manifests its proper form (c.IV, *lectio* 5). In the *Summa*, this notion of manifest form occurs implicitly within the famous Thomist analysis of beauty: "Three things are required for beauty. First, integrity or perfection [*integritas sive perfectio*], for what is defective is thereby ugly; second, proper proportion or consonance [*proportio sive consonantia*]; and third, clarity [*claritas*]" (*Summa theologiae* 1, question 39, article 8; see also *Summa theologiae*

1–2, q. 54, a. 1: "Beauty is the compatibility of parts in accordance with the nature of a thing").

Before commenting on these ideas, it will be as well to introduce another of Aquinas's interesting claims. This is the suggestion that beauty is a *transcendental* quality identical in an entity to that thing's *being*, its *unity*, its *goodness*, and its *truth*. Moreover, according to Aquinas, it is part of what it is to be a transcendental quality that everything possesses it. Thus, "There is nothing which does not share in goodness and beauty, for according to its form each thing is both good and beautiful" (*De divinis nominibus* c.IV, *lectio* 5).

The key to understanding what otherwise appear obscure remarks is Aquinas's notion of *form* – more precisely, substantial form (*forma rei*), that which makes a thing what it is, constitutes its principle of organization and (in the case of something animate) of life. Carbon, cars, and cats all have organizing forms – chemical, mechanical, and biological, respectively. The form of a thing gives it existence, and inasmuch as its being is an object of value for it or for others it has *goodness*. Equally, when that existence is affirmed in the mind of a thinker the thing has *truth*, and when it is viewed as an object of contemplation it takes on the character of *beauty*. In speaking of goodness and beauty (as of being and truth), therefore, one is not speaking of intrinsically different properties but of one and the same quality considered in relation to different concerns. In contemporary philosophical language the difference is one of sense or "intension" and not of reference or "extension."

In short, beauty is only ascribable in the context of actual or potential contemplation of the form of a thing. This introduces an element of subjectivity but relates it directly to an objective ground, the nature of the object being contemplated. The earlier analysis of beauty now emerges as an account of the necessary conditions under which the meeting of an object and a subject gives rise to aesthetic experience. The thing in question must be possessed of the elements or aspects apt to something having the relevant form or nature (*integritas*), these elements must be properly related to one another (*proportio*), and these states must be manifest when the entity is perceived or contemplated (*claritas*).

This interpretation suggests parallels with Kantian aesthetics. For Aquinas is claiming that the experience of beauty arises directly as a type of intellectual satisfaction taken in the contemplation of elements apt for cognition, when one's present interest in them is neither practical nor scientific. Where Aquinas differs from Kant, however, is in regarding the contemplated forms as being structural elements of a mind-independent reality. On which, if either, of these philosophers this difference reflects greater credit is a matter beyond discussion here. It should be clear, however, that Aquinas has interesting ideas to offer to those who hope to integrate an account of beauty and aesthetic experience within a broadly realist epistemology and metaphysics.

See also MEDIEVAL AND RENAISSANCE AESTHETICS; BEAUTY; KANT.

BIBLIOGRAPHY

Primary sources
1963–75. *Summa theologiae*. 60 vols. Oxford and London: Blackfriars with Eyre & Spottiswoode.
1969. *De divinis nominibus* [Commentary on the Divine Names]: selected translations from this and other relevant works are to be found in *The Pocket Aquinas*. V. Bourke (ed. & trans.). New York: Washington Square. (Also in Wladyslaw Tatarkiewicz, *History of Aesthetics*, vol. ii. The Hague: Mouton, 1970, 257–63.)

Secondary sources
Barrett, Cyril. 1963. "The Aesthetics of St Thomas Re-examined," *Philosophical Studies* (Ireland), 12, 107–24.
Bredin, Hugh & Santoro-Brienza, Liberato. 2000. *Philosophies of Art and Beauty*. Edinburgh: Edinburgh University Press.
Eco, Umberto. 1988. *The Aesthetics of Thomas Aquinas*. H. Bredin (trans.). Cambridge, MA: Harvard University Press.
Kovach, Francis J. 1961. *Die Ästhetik des Thomas von Aquin*. Berlin: de Gruyter.
Maritain, J. 1974. *Art and Scholasticism*. J. W. Evans (trans.). Notre Dame: University of Notre Dame Press.
Maurer, A. 1983. *About Beauty*. Houston: Center for Thomistic Studies.
Phelan, G. 1967. "The Concept of Beauty in St Thomas Aquinas." In *G. Phelan: Selected Papers*. A. Kirn (ed.). Toronto: Pontifical Institute of Mediaeval Studies, 155–80.
Tatarkiewicz, Wladyslaw. 1970. *History of Aesthetics*, vol. ii: *Medieval Aesthetics*. C. Barrett (ed.). The Hague: Mouton.

JOHN HALDANE

Aristotle (384–322 BCE)   Greek philosopher and scientist of immense, enduring influence. After studying in Plato's Academy he founded his own school, the Lyceum. Often regarded as the first philosopher to admit the autonomous character of aesthetic activity and experience, in direct reaction against supposed Platonic moralism. But the full picture is more complex than this. Aristotle's statement in *Poetics* 25 that "correct standards in poetry are not the same as in politics or any other art" asserts a kind of aesthetic independence for individual art forms. But his description of tragedy as "mimesis [i.e., representation] of actions and life" (*Poetics* 6) signals a fundamental link between experience of art and experience of life in general.

The framework of Aristotle's thinking in this area (see *Poetics*, ch. 1) is a classification of certain activities as mimetic, that is representational-cum-expressive forms of image-making. Each of these counts for him as a *technê*, a specialized expertise subject to conscious, rational control. The group in question includes poetry, painting, sculpture, dance, and even music. The latter is mimetic for Aristotle, as it was for many Greeks, in virtue of embodying what he calls tonal and rhythmic "likenesses" (or correlates) of "movements of the soul" (*Politics* 8.5). It is important, however, to distinguish two Aristotelian principles of mimesis that are often confused. Mimetic representation, as in poetry, involves imaginative simulation of aspects of reality. But the principle that "all art is mimesis of nature" (misleadingly translated as "all art imitates nature": "all art follows the pattern of nature" would be better) is of a different order: it applies to the production of all kinds of artifacts and posits a parallelism of teleology, but *without* conscious imitation, between human craftsmanship and what Aristotle sees as the purposive shaping of form into matter by nature. This second principle (found at, e.g., *Physics* 2.2, 2.8) must encompass the musico-poetic and figurative arts as well, but Aristotle never appeals to it in his discussions of them.

Aristotle's conception of mimetic representation is seen most fully in his treatment of tragedy (with subordinate treatment of epic) in the *Poetics*. By analyzing the genre's qualitative constituents (plot, character, etc.), Aristotle works out a normative view of the dynamic relationship between a tragic action, in which human lives are exposed to major suffering through the fallibility (*hamartia*: "error" or "fault") of the agents, and the audience's defining emotional response ("pity and fear"). Although recognizing that tragedy is a highly stylized, elevated art form, Aristotle believes that it deals with *possible* events (esp. ch. 9), events that audiences can understand and judge in ways continuous with those they use to interpret life outside the theater. The *Poetics* repeatedly underlines this point by appealing to criteria of "necessity and/or probability," criteria which call *both* for "internal" consistency in the terms of the represented world, *and* for the intelligibility of that world by the standards of the audience's beliefs about reality as a whole.

But Aristotle goes further. In *Poetics* 9 he states: "Poetry is more philosophical and more serious than history, for it speaks more of universals, while history speaks of particulars." Aristotle does not mean by this that poetry offers abstractions or schematic types of people and events. What he appears to mean is that successful poetic plots differ from the contingency of ordinary life (*individual* lives are not artistically unified, he stresses: *Poetics* 8). They have a purer, more coherent intelligibility; universals are, as it were, woven into their dramatic fabric. The achievement of such intelligibility is undoubtedly connected, in Aristotle's thinking, with the principle of artistic unity. "Just as in the other mimetic arts . . . , so the plot-structure of tragedy . . . should be a representation of a unitary and complete action" (*Poetics* 8).

Aristotle's notion of unity is not strictly formalist in character. All order and beauty depend on the nature and function of the objects in which they are realized (*Politics* 7.4). Unity in mimetic art is the meaningful organization of the representational content of a poem or other work; the criteria of wholeness and completeness which *Poetics* 7 sets out, with the formula of "beginning, middle and end," cannot be detached from the significance of the "actions and life" (*Poetics* 6) the poem depicts. Chapter 9's remarks about "universals" follow directly from the discussion of unity: unity, probability, and the universals built into a poetic structure of action are mutually reinforcing elements in a theory of poetry that endows artistic images with a coherent sense of human meaning. Whether this theory entails a rationalization of "the tragic" remains a challenging question about Aristotle's agenda in the *Poetics*.

Form and content are intertwined in Aristotle's account of aesthetic objects; and his conception of aesthetic experience possesses matching features. *Poetics* 4 (compare with *Rhetoric* 1.11) gives a cognitive grounding to the pleasure that arises from contemplation of mimetic works: the viewer seeks to understand and reason out each element in an image or poem. *Politics* 8.5, discussing music but widening the point, confirms this: "habituation to feeling pain and pleasure in the case of likenesses [i.e., mimesis] is close to being so disposed towards the truth." Aesthetic responses are not *sui generis* but correlated with larger structures of experience. That correlation allows, however, for important variations. *Poetics* 4 registers the pleasure taken in the depiction of objects that would be found painful in life; this, implicitly, is pertinent to tragedy. "Art" can transform, as well as capturing the underlying principles of, "life."

Aristotle's model of aesthetic pleasure remains, even so, resistant to any strong version of aestheticism: it combines the cognitive and the affective. He describes the pleasure of tragedy as "that which comes from pity and fear through mimesis" (*Poetics* 14). Grasping the embodied universals of a poetic representation is not a matter of abstract comprehension; it involves sensitive absorption in the world of the play and carries with it an intensely emotional reaction to the imagined characters and events. Plato had feared that such experience could subvert reason by its "bewitching" power over the emotions; Aristotle believes that good mimetic art elicits responses in which reason and emotion are integrated.

While Aristotle diverges from the more uncompromising of Plato's attempts to subject aesthetic standards to a unified framework of ethical and metaphysical value, he does not aim to establish an outright autonomy for mimetic art. He allows it considerable freedom of scope (on a scale that runs from realism to idealism: see the start of *Poetics* 25) and denies that artistic standards can simply be equated with those of morality or politics in general. But he nonetheless regards both the making and the reception of poetry, painting, and music as special forms of engaged contemplation (*theôria*) through which the human need to understand the world finds one kind of fulfillment.

See also AESTHETICS IN ANTIQUITY; CATHARSIS; PLATO.

BIBLIOGRAPHY

Primary sources
1984. *The Complete Works of Aristotle*. 2 vols. J. Barnes (ed.). Princeton: Princeton University Press.
1995. *Aristotle Poetics*. S. Halliwell (trans.). Cambridge, MA: Harvard University Press.

Secondary sources
Andersen, Ø. & Haarberg, J. (ed.). 2001. *Making Sense of Aristotle: Essays in Poetics*. London: Duckworth.
Halliwell, Stephen. 1998. *Aristotle's Poetics*. 2nd edn. London: Duckworth.
Nussbaum, Martha C. 1986. *The Fragility of Goodness: Luck and Ethics in Greek Tragedy and Philosophy*. Cambridge: Cambridge University Press.
Rorty, A. O. (ed.). 1992. *Essays on Aristotle's Poetics*. Princeton: Princeton University Press.

STEPHEN HALLIWELL

art   *see* ARTIFACT, A. AS; AUTHENTICITY AND A.; COGNITIVE SCIENCE AND A.; COGNITIVE VALUE OF A.; CONCEPTUAL A.; DEFINITION OF "A."; EROTIC A. AND OBSCENITY; EVOLUTION, A., AND AESTHETICS; FUNCTION OF A.; MARXISM AND A.; MASS A.; MORALITY AND A.; PERFORMANCE A.; POPULAR A.; PSYCHOANALYSIS AND A.; RELIGION AND A.; SCIENCE AND A.; SENSES AND A.; TECHNOLOGY AND A.; THEORIES OF A.; TRUTH IN A.; UNIVERSALS IN A.

art and experience   *see* SENSES AND ART, THE.

"art for art's sake"   *see* AESTHETICISM.

art history   What a history requires is a narrative framework relating what comes earlier to what happens later. A culture could have art, and even a concept of art, without having any conception of art history. That culture might make art, and theorize about that activity, without thinking that its art had a history. Writing a history of art requires thinking of its development as having a historical structure.

The first extended history of European art appears in an odd place, book 35 of Pliny's *Natural History*, between the discussion of medicinal drugs in book 34 and the description of stones in book 36. As modern commentators (Kris & Kurz 1979) have observed, the anecdotes that Pliny presents about various Greek painters recur frequently in accounts of Renaissance artists. Pliny's history of naturalistic art is told in terms of progress. Early, later, latest is good, better, best: such is the story of the development of naturalism. Vasari's history of art of the Italian Renaissance from the time of Cimabue and Giotto to his own era, two and a half centuries later, employs a similar framework. In such a history, once image-making begins, it continues, this model suggests, until the tradition dies.

In one way, beginnings and endings have a certain symmetry. Whatever art comes before the beginning, like what comes after the end of the tradition, is not part of the history of art. In another way, however, endings raise special problems. Vasari explains in 1550 that he judges each artist relative to the standards of that man's time: "Although Giotto was admirable in his own day, I do not know what we should say of him or the other ancients if they had lived in the time of Michelangelo" (1963: iv. 291). Insofar as the claim of his account is that Michelangelo is an absolutely great artist, a figure whose work sums up the whole tradition, it is very hard to see what could come next. At earlier times, of course, great artists had successors, but given Vasari's narrative framework one has difficulty in imagining Michelangelo's successors.

Once the cycle is started, it is hard to see how it can conclude, except in decay which, after some interval, may be followed by a rebirth of the tradition. Vasari's working assumption is that the cycle of development in antiquity, as described by Pliny, repeats in his own time.

That repetition is possible only because medieval art marks a break in the tradition, a gap between the development of illusionism in antiquity and the rebirth of that artistic tradition in the Renaissance. A modern historian of technology might think that indefinite progress is possible; when employing Pliny's and Vasari's organic model, such a view of history is hard to imagine.

Here we encounter an important conceptual complication, the development of which began with Winckelmann's *Reflections on the Imitation of Greek Works in Painting and Sculpture* of 1755. Winckelmann both discusses the tradition that concerns him most deeply, the story of Greek sculpture, and explains its relationship to art of the Renaissance. In some ways, he admits, the modern artists are better: "In the science of perspective modern painters are clearly superior . . . Various subjects . . . have likewise been raised to a higher degree of perfection in modern times, for example, landscapes and animal species" (1987: 59).

Gombrich has argued that "rather than Winckelmann's *History of Ancient Art* . . . it is Hegel's *Lectures on Aesthetics* . . . which should be regarded as the founding document of the modern study of art . . . they contain the first attempt ever made to survey and systematize the entire history of art" (1984: 51). While Winckelmann's account remains focused on Greek art, it is Hegel who provides a way of linking art of antiquity to painting of the Renaissance. For Hegel, it should be added, what constitutes "the entire history of art" is defined by the concerns of early nineteenth-century European scholarship. He did not know much about Chinese and Indian art; he does not discuss Japanese painting or African sculpture.

Unlike Pliny, Vasari, and Winckelmann, Hegel does not focus on the history of the development of illusionistic painting and sculpture within one culture. He explains how the art of quite different cultures is part of one continuous story, a universal history of art. Insofar as each culture possesses its own values, it too may express them in its art. The goal of art history is to identify the relationship between a culture and its art. Thus, to understand Dutch art of the Golden Age, "we must ask about Dutch history" (Hegel 1975: 169). The

Dutch struggle against Spanish rule, the feats of their maritime empire, and their pleasure in communal festivities are all expressed in their art. A history of the art of any culture might be written in this way. The Japanese and the Africans can also express themselves in their art.

One consequence of Hegel's approach is to suggest that each culture must have its own independent artistic ideals. Wölfflin develops this idea. The classical and the baroque "are like two languages, in which everything can be said, although each has its strength in a different direction" (1908: 12). Wölfflin's history employs a formalist approach, explaining the development of art as a self-contained process without much reference to the larger culture. Another development of Hegelian art history occurs in the diverse approaches of art historians who focus on the social history of art. As Hegel sees Dutch art as expressing the characteristic political, religious, and social concerns of that culture, so these historians treat each culture as capable of expressing its own values in its art.

Both the formalist approaches and these social histories can describe the art of very diverse cultures. So, for example, American Abstract Expressionist painting of the 1940s can be understood formally as developing the flattened space found earlier in Cubism, and in the early modernist art of Cézanne and Monet (Greenberg 1961). But it may also be explained as an expression of post-World War II American culture. The formalist finds similarities between artists whose work looks different. Thus in Wölfflin's account, not only Rembrandt and Rubens, but also Vermeer and Bernini, must be linked under the rubric "baroque." If the danger of formalism is the need to appeal to such a fiction of a "period style," the problem of a social history of art is that it may link art with the general society in all too facile a fashion. These problems with both formalist and social histories become more pressing as we approach the present. It is difficult enough to identify the common features of the work of Bernini, Pietro da Cortona, Borromini, and all the other artists working in Rome in the era of the baroque. But when we look at the culture of New York during the 1940s, to speak of that as the era of American Abstract Expressionism really is problematic.

We must connect work of quite diverse painters by reference to a period style; we must exclude from the account painters working in other styles; and we need to explain how American philosophy and the larger culture are related to that art.

Recognizing that both formalist and social histories of art must thus employ fictions is only to acknowledge that they, like any history, have to use such devices in order to tell a story (Carrier 1991). It is important to recognize connections between the literary structures of art histories and those employed by creative writers. When Vasari treats the collective creation of artists from Cimabue to Michelangelo as akin to an organism which is born, develops to maturity, and dies, he is only using an analogy. Vasari's analogy has an important influence on how he thinks about art history. An organism must die, but there is, in principle, no reason why an artistic tradition may not continue indefinitely.

Any story must be selective. The art historian, like the creative writer, chooses to describe those events that he can fit into a plausible narrative. But in one essential way, literature and history are different. The stories of the novelist seek merely to be convincing; the narrative of the art historian aims for truth. Wölfflin wants to understand how Raphael's High Renaissance classicism anticipates the baroque, although Raphael could not think of his art in that way; Greenberg seeks to grasp the relationship between Cubism and Abstract Expressionism, although the Cubists could not imagine that later movement.

Can we both exercise our modern sensibility and simultaneously be aware that the artist whose work we study saw it differently? When, for example, we see a Rubens crucifixion, may we apply to it "some concepts derived from psycho-analysis – some such notions as the release of aggression with the displacement of guilt" (Podro 1982: 214), which, though alien to Rubens's culture, express in our vocabulary how his contemporaries saw that work? These questions are unanswerable. Any translation of Christian ideas into a psychoanalytic vocabulary will be controversial. The best we can do is both understand Rubens's culture in its own terms, and interpret it as best we can in our modern vocabulary.

The development of art history by A. Riegl, Wölfflin, and E. Panofsky out of the legacy of Hegel (Podro 1982) requires pruning that theory of Hegel's metaphysics. For the modern art historian to say that a culture expresses itself in its art is only a manner of speaking, not a theory to be taken literally. Modern art historians work within the general framework established by these founding fathers of their discipline, collecting information about artists and periods not yet intensively studied by the precursors, yet without abandoning this historical framework itself. But when now we collect in our museums not only Greek and Italian Renaissance art, the Dutch painting that Hegel discusses, and the baroque works Wölfflin deals with, but also Chinese and Japanese painting, Hindu sculpture, African artifacts, weaving and other decorative work from many cultures, and modernist and postmodernist art, then the claim that it is possible to write a general history of art seems increasingly questionable. Insofar as a history is a story in which all of these artworks are to be set within one narrative framework, the claim that there can be some general interpretative framework adequate to all art now seems highly problematic (Elkins 2002).

Until relatively recently, the best-known English-language survey histories have focused on the story of Western art. Chinese scrolls, Hindu sculpture, and Islamic decorations make only cameo appearances. And while there are elaborate specialist histories of art in China, India, and the Islamic world, and also in Africa and the other cultures without writing, as yet this material is not integrated into these general histories. But it starts to become apparent that we need a world art history (Onians 2004; Elkins 2007). We need it because we have to do justice to art from all cultures, and also because of the legitimate political demands raised within our multicultural societies. How is it possible, then, to develop narratives that take account of art from all cultures without imposing a bias based on the traditional studies of European art (Carrier 2008)? Answering this question is the central concern facing the profession right now.

See also MEDIEVAL AND RENAISSANCE AESTHETICS; AFRICAN AESTHETICS; CHINESE AESTHETICS;

GOMBRICH; HEGEL; INDIAN AESTHETICS; ISLAMIC AESTHETICS; MODERNISM AND POSTMODERNISM; TRADITION.

BIBLIOGRAPHY

Carrier, David. 1991. *Principles of Art History Writing*. University Park: Pennsylvania State University Press.

Carrier, David. 2008. *A World Art History*. University Park: Pennsylvania State University Press.

Elkins, James. 2002. *Stories of Art*. New York: Routledge.

Elkins, James (ed.). 2007. *Is Art History Global?* New York: Routledge.

Gombrich, E. H. 1984. " 'The Father of Art History': A Reading of the Lectures on Aesthetics of G. W. F. Hegel (1770–1831)." In *Tributes: Interpreters of Our Cultural Tradition*. Ithaca: Cornell University Press, 51–69.

Greenberg, Clement. 1961. *Art and Culture*. Boston: Beacon.

Hegel, G. W. F. 1975 [1835–8]. *Aesthetics: Lectures on Fine Art*. 2 vols. T. M. Knox (trans.). Oxford: Clarendon.

Kris, Ernst & Kurz, Otto. 1979 [1934]. *Legend, Myth, and Magic in the Image of the Artist*. A. Laing & L. M. Newman (trans.). New Haven: Yale University Press.

Onians, J. (ed.) 2004. *Atlas of World Art*. London: Laurence King.

Pliny. 1968 [77 CE]. *Natural History*. 10 vols. H. Rackham (trans.). London: Heinemann, vol. ix.

Podro, Michael. 1982. *The Critical Historians of Art*. New Haven: Yale University Press.

Vasari, Giorgio. 1963 [1550]. *The Lives of the Painters, Sculptors and Architects*. A. B. Hinds (trans.). London: Dent.

Winckelmann, J. J. 1987 [1755]. *Reflections on the Imitation of Greek Works in Painting and Sculpture*. E. Heyer & R. C. Norton (trans.). La Salle: Open Court.

Wölfflin, Heinrich. n.d. [1908]. *Principles of Art History*. M. Hottinger (trans.). New York: Dover.

DAVID CARRIER

artifact, art as Until recently, everyone had assumed without question that art is artifactual – that is, that a work of art is a humanly created object. Traditional philosophers of art attempted to defend their claims that art is expressive, symbolic, or of some other nature, but it never occurred to them to defend their common view that art is artifactual. An object need not be physical in order to be humanly created; for example, a poem or a theory are humanly created and hence are nonphysical artifacts.

Why, then, have philosophers of art become concerned in recent times with the question of whether artifactuality is or is not a necessary condition for being art? One reason has its origins in certain developments within the philosophy of language: namely, Ludwig Wittgenstein's view about how certain words apply to their objects. These words apply, Wittgenstein maintains, in virtue of "family resemblances" among the objects to which they apply, rather than in virtue of the objects possessing properties that satisfy necessary and sufficient conditions.

Paul Ziff (1953), Morris Weitz (1956), and William Kennick (1958) were the first to attempt to apply this linguistic thesis to the philosophy of art. These three and subsequently other philosophers claimed that "art" (or "work of art") does not have any necessary and sufficient conditions that must be satisfied in order for something to be a member of the class of works of art. Rather, they maintain that the members of the class of works of art belong to that class in virtue of the "family resemblances" that obtain among the members. Thus, work of art A is a member of the class of artworks because it shares a property with work of art B, and work of art B is a member of the class because it shares a property with work of art C, and so on. Work of art A and work of art Z, however, may not share any property and do not need to. Although work A and work Z do not share any property, they are related to one another through the property-sharing of other members of the class of works of art. Every member of the class of works of art will share a property with at least one other work (and probably many more), but a given pair of works need not share any property. If the members of the class of works of art do not need to share *any* property, then they do not need to share the property of artifactuality. And, in fact, these philosophers claim that there are works of art that are not artifacts, these nonartifacts having become works of art by sharing a property with a prior established work of art. Weitz, for example, claims that a piece of driftwood can become a work of art when someone notices its resemblance to some sculpture and says, "That driftwood is a lovely piece of sculpture." Driftwood, sunsets, and other nonartifacts can become works of art in this way. Thus, according to Ziff, Kennick, Weitz, and company, the traditional assumption that every work of art is an artifact is shown to be false.

There are several difficulties with this way of conceiving of art. First, if resembling a prior established work of art is the basic way that something becomes a work of art, it is going to be virtually impossible to keep everything from becoming a work of art, for everything resembles everything else in *some* way. Second, "the new view" gives the impression that sharing a property with, or resembling, a prior established work of art is the only way that something can become a work of art. If, however, every work of art had to become art by resembling a prior established work of art, then an infinite regress of works receding into the past would be generated and no work of art could ever have come into being. Some other way of becoming a work of art would be required to block the regress, and the only plausible way would be that the regress-blocking work or works came into being as a result of an artifact's being created. Thus, this new view requires two distinct and different kinds of art – art as conceived of by Ziff, Weitz, and Kennick, which may be called "resemblance art," and what may be called "artifactual art."

Artifactual art has a temporal priority. Of course, it is not just that artifactual art is required to block the regress. Even given the new way of conceiving of art, much of the art that has been created has come into being as artifactual art. Thus, artifactual art, with its one necessary condition (artifactuality), forms an unacknowledged basis or core of the new conception of art. The two kinds of art required by the new conception have two very different bases: the one derives from acts of human creativity and the other from acts of noticing similarities. This striking difference suggests that it is the members of the class of artifactual art that we have in mind when we speak *literally* of works of art, and that the other class of objects is a metaphorical derivative.

Suppose, however, that both classes are literally art. This just means that it is and always was the class of artifactual art that philosophers have been interested in theorizing about. Traditional philosophers of art have sought to discover the essential nature of a particular class of human artifacts, and even if the members of this class of objects do not have any other interesting property or properties in common, they are all artifacts. Artifactuality is built into the philosophy of art because philosophers have always been interested in theorizing about a set of objects that are produced by human creativity. The fact that another class of objects can be generated by means of resemblance to the members of the class of artifactual art provides no reason to divert philosophers of art from their traditional task.

There is another reason to challenge the artifactuality of art that is quite different from those based on a Wittgensteinian conception of language. How are philosophers of art to deal with things such as the urinal that Duchamp entered in that now famous art show under the title *Fountain*? The urinal is an artifact of the plumbing trade, but is *Fountain* Duchamp's artistic artifact? Driftwood and urinals are the materials of a class of artworks that can be called "found art." In some instances the material basis of a work is already an artifact when found (the urinal), in others it is not (the driftwood), but in both cases, something further is done by the artist in addition to finding the item. The most minimal thing that could be done is presenting the item as art to an artworld audience by showing it in some manner or other. Assume that this (possibly along with some other conditions that may well be present) is sufficient to make these items artworks. Is it sufficient to make these items artifacts? In the case of the urinal, since it is already an artifact, we can assume that the artwork it becomes is also one. But what about the driftwood? This seems at best a borderline or minimal case of artifactuality, if it is a case of artifactuality at all.

There are at least two other kinds of artworks that might be regarded as good candidates for being nonartifactual artworks: some works that are ontologically abstract and some conceptual works. Ontologically abstract artworks are not those that are nonrepresentational but are those that have more than one instance or occurrence. Musical works are instanced in their performances, novels in their copies. There are some who claim that even ontologically abstract works are artifacts, since they are humanly created entities (such as Levinson 1980; Thomasson 1999). However, there are others who deny this (such as Kivy 1993; Dodd 2000). They claim that musical works, for example, are abstract sound structures that exist eternally and hence are discovered, not created. Some even deny that abstract objects can be created (Dodd 2000). If this view is right, musical works are not artifacts. Of course, this is a conditional claim. It depends on the correctness of a controversial and highly contested view about the ontology of art. So we do not yet have an unchallenged example of clearly nonartifactual art.

Some conceptual artworks provide another set of possible examples. Consider the famous piece by Robert Barry entitled or specified by: *All the things I know but of which I am not at the moment thinking – 1:36 pm, June 15, 1969*. It is not clear just what this piece consists in. Is it the very beliefs referred to by the specification? The set of beliefs is not an artifact. Is it the act of referring to those beliefs or the inscription or utterance of the words? Would any of these be more plausible candidates for being an artifact?

From the first sentence of this entry, it has been assumed that an artifact is anything that is humanly created. Nor have we been very careful to define the extension of the humanly created. Does it include things we do, as well as the products deliberately made in the course our doings? In any case, we have looked for counterexamples to the claim that artworks are necessarily artifacts in things that are not humanly created, such as driftwood, abstract structures, beliefs, or concepts.

Some argue, however, that "artifact" has a much more narrowly circumscribed meaning. According to Randall Dipert, an artifact is something intentionally modified to serve as a means to an end whose modified properties were intended by their maker to be recognized as having been altered for that, or some other, use (1993: 29–30). Stephen Davies claims that an artifact in the primary sense is something modified by work, which, he thinks, implies that it is an object that is manufactured via the direct manipulation of a material item that preexists the creation of the artifact (1991:

123–4). Dipert's and Davies's definition of artifact seem, at first sight rather similar. They both involve reference to modifying something or other. Dipert, however, requires that a genuine artifact has to communicate something, viz., that it is a thing made for some specific use. Davies has no such requirement. Davies claims that artifacts must result from the manipulation of a material object and are themselves material objects. Dipert does not claim this. He thinks some actions are artifacts. It is not clear whether he thinks there are also abstract artifacts.

For someone who agrees with Davies's understanding of "artifact," or who decides to adopt this conception for more pragmatic reasons such as greater precision, the issue of whether all artworks are artifacts becomes crystal clear. Even if all artworks are humanly created, they are not all artifacts.

See also TWENTIETH-CENTURY ANGLO-AMERICAN AESTHETICS; CONCEPTUAL ART; DEFINITION OF "ART."

BIBLIOGRAPHY

Davies, Stephen. 1991. *Definitions of Art*. Ithaca: Cornell University Press.

Dickie, George. 1984. *The Art Circle*. New York: Haven.

Dipert, Randall R. 1993. *Artifacts, Art Works, and Agency*. Philadelphia: Temple University Press.

Dodd, Julian. 2000. "Musical Works as Eternal Types," *British Journal of Aesthetics*, 40, 424–40.

Kennick, William E. 1958. "Does Traditional Aesthetics Rest on a Mistake?" *Mind*, 67, 317–34.

Kivy, Peter. 1993. *The Fine Art of Repetition: Essays in the Philosophy of Music*. Cambridge: Cambridge University Press.

Levinson, Jerrold. 1980. "What a Musical Work Is," *Journal of Philosophy*, 77, 5–28.

Levinson, Jerrold. 2006. "Artworks as Artifacts." In *Contemplating Art*. Oxford: Oxford University Press, 26–37.

Thomasson, Amie. 1999. *Fiction and Metaphysics*. Cambridge: Cambridge University Press.

Thomasson, Amie. 2007. "Artifacts and Human Concepts." In *Creations of the Mind*. E. Margolis & S. Laurence (eds.). Oxford: Oxford University Press, 52–73.

Weitz, Morris. 1956. "The Role of Theory in Aesthetics," *Journal of Aesthetics and Art Criticism*, 15, 27–35.

Ziff, Paul. 1953. "The Task of Defining a Work of Art," *Philosophical Review*, 62, 58–78.

GEORGE DICKIE & ROBERT STECKER

"artworld"   A term that has both a philo-sophical and an ordinary meaning. Philo-sophically, the idea of an "artworld" serves as a device for analyzing "art" and the "aesthetic." Artworld theory makes these concepts the products of certain social practices so specialized that persons engaged in them appear to be operating in an autonomous world. In the ver-nacular, the "artworld" is the actual society of persons whose interactions affect the valu-ation of works of art. What these meanings have in common is an understanding of art as being the consequence of institutionalized activities.

That art should be thought of as situated in a special world of its own is a notion of some-what recent fabrication, and one quite alien to antiquity's robust idea of art as central to prac-tical human life. Plato and Aristotle located artistic activity and appreciative experience among practices meant to promote the goals of cognition and conduct. But, subsequently, at least two lines of thought converged to drive art from this central location.

The first was triggered by Plato's reasons for doubting how effectively art can realize vital practical functions. In response, art's apologists have tended to isolate it from every-day activities or experiences as a stratagem for defending its value. They typically define art (or the appropriate experience of it) as autonomous, arguing that art characteristically induces unique ways of feeling or thinking, or is the pro-duct of a unique kind of activity, or is at least a unique product of ordinary activities. The result is to construe art as independent of prac-tical contexts, and aesthetic value as irreduc-ible. This strategy blunts Plato's complaints by removing art from the constraints usually associated with cognition and conduct, but it also threatens art's place in the everyday world.

A second line of thought which makes the notion of situating art in an environment of its own attractive is fuelled by a widespread skepticism about finding an essential property internal to all artworks. If there is no such property, then whatever warrants the identi-fication of some objects as art must be found in the contexts in which these objects are situated. But if to recognize something as art is also to accept it as independent of contexts occasioned by the everyday world, its being art must be conditional on circumstances that obtain in a special artworld. Several late twentieth-century theorists, notably Arthur C. Danto and George Dickie, develop this thought by arguing that objects qualify as art in virtue of being the subject of practices characteristic of a special world exclusive to art.

In brief, the contemporary philosophical conception of the artworld locates what is definitive of art in the application of some set of practices, whether these be activities which treat art organizationally, historically, or theoretically. To hypothesize an artworld is to explain that objects qualify as art by being "institutionalized' – that is, by operating or being operated on within a definitive institutional framework.

But the relevant institutions need not con-stitute an all-encompassing world that embraces all the kinds of human activities. So such ques-tions as whether the artworld is democratic or elitist are not automatically relevant; they are germane only where there is reason to con-strue artworld systems as political. On the one hand, it seems parochial for philosophers to posit unique aesthetic practices when so wide a range of explanations of institutionalized phenomena is available in the work of other dis-ciplines. The more thoroughly the artworld is conceived in terms of principles which operate also in the world of practical life, the more misguided seems the drive to separate these worlds. On the other hand, to operationalize the artworld in social scientific terms is to accept reductionism.

In the vernacular, to speak of the artworld is to refer to networks of persons engaged either vocationally or avocationally in activities that affect the buying and selling of art. But to re-cognize the power of such persons by no means solves the problem of whether their actions determine, or are determined by, aesthetic or other values. This brings us finally to the ques-tion of whether the conception of the artworld is simply another relativizing notion.

To what kinds of systematized circum-stances is the identification of objects as art to be tied, and may these encompass, or must they exclude, systems that also are constitutive of the practical world? Are the art systems of different times and places frameworks to be thought of as begetting separate worlds?

Fragmenting aesthetic contexts in this way makes it hard to explain the undoubted ease with which cultures adopt and appreciate each other's art. Or are the divergent systems to be incorporated into one complex artworld scheme so as to account for art's demonstrable ability to diffuse transculturally and transhistorically? If this latter alternative is the case, then how are we to decide which systems' values are to be marginalized? Thus, the most vexing disagreements about the interpretation and evaluation of art reappear, unresolved, within artworld theory.

Attempts to define art as the product of the artworld, which is characterized as an informally structured institution, are controversial in ways already indicated. But the idea that identifying and appreciating artworks involves seeing them in relation to art practices and traditions that they continue, develop, or rebel against – which was always an important strand in the accounts of the artworld proposed by both Danto and Dickie – is now widely accepted by philosophers of art and plays an important role in theories of art interpretation and of the ontology of artworks.

See also ARISTOTLE; DANTO; DEFINITION OF "ART"; DICKIE; FUNCTION OF ART; INTERPRETATION; ONTOLOGY OF ARTWORKS; PLATO.

BIBLIOGRAPHY

Danto, Arthur C. 1964. "The Artworld," *Journal of Philosophy*, 61, 571–84.
Danto, Arthur C. 1981. *The Transfiguration of the Commonplace*. Cambridge, MA: Harvard University Press.
Dickie, George. 1974. *Art and the Aesthetic: An Institutional Analysis*. Ithaca: Cornell University Press.
Dickie, George. 1984. *The Art Circle: A Theory of Art*. New York: Haven.
Silvers, Anita. 1976. "The Artworld Discarded," *Journal of Aesthetics and Art Criticism*, 34, 441–54.
Silvers, Anita. 1989. "Once upon a Time in the Artworld." In *Aesthetics: A Critical Anthology*. G. Dickie, R. Sclafani, & R. Roblin (eds.). New York: St. Martin's, 183–95.

ANITA SILVERS

attitude, aesthetic   *see* AESTHETIC ATTITUDE.

authenticity and art   Works of art stand in multiple complex relationships to their originating contexts. Some of these relationships are grouped together as matters of authenticity and inauthenticity. Broadly understood, a work of art possesses authenticity when it is "true" to its authorial and/or cultural origins by reflecting beliefs and values held by its creator and/or creator's community. However, different eras, artforms, and critical traditions emphasize distinct relationships between art and its sociohistorical origins, so prominent species of authenticity display considerable variety.

Individual and cultural authenticities are associated with competing artistic values. Cultural authenticity generally requires conformity with established cultural norms. In contrast, authorial or individual authenticity requires some degree of originality and therefore tends to involve departure from established norms. Evaluating literary texts for authenticity relative to authorial intentions, we can ask which edition of James Joyce's *Ulysses* is most faithful to his intentions. Viewing *Ulysses* relative to contemporaneous cultural practices, its radical innovations are more authentically modernist than Irish. As this example suggests, the same work can be authentic relative to one classification and inauthentic relative to another.

Three important uses of "authentic" fall outside the scope of this entry. The first involves inauthenticity due to forgery. The second involves the degree to which works remain intact following restoration. The third derives from functional accounts of art, where authentic art advances art's proper ends and inauthentic art does not. This broad category is emphasized in Continental philosophy and plays a prominent role in, for instance, writings of Martin Heidegger and Theodor Adorno.

Questions about artistic authenticity seem to have arisen when philosophers and artists began to question eighteenth-century expectations about artistic beauty (Trilling 1971: 92–100). As art came to be valued as a vehicle for self-exploration, standards of beauty came to be regarded as cultural impositions that restricted self-fulfillment and expression. A poem or painting achieved expressive authenticity by challenging prevailing taste. By the end of the nineteenth century, it was commonly thought that authenticity was diluted by any concessions made for the sake of commercial viability. Thus, to experience "authentic" Beethoven we turn to his late string quartets, which baffled his contemporaries, rather than to *Twenty-Five Scottish Songs* (Op. 108), his piano arrangements of existing folk songs undertaken for commercial profit. However, this tradition prioritizes authenticity relative to self-expression – a standard that applies to Beethoven's music but not, for example, to bronze statutes of Buddha produced in seventeenth-century Tibet, which are authentic or not relative to established iconography. Applied to "traditional" and non-Western art, the opposition of commerce and authenticity introduces questionable assumptions about cultural purity and cultural change (Shiner 1994). The opposition of commerce and authenticity is also challenged by the fact that multiple issues about expressive authenticity arise within the commercial marketplace of popular culture, as evidenced by blues music (Rudinow 1994).

The performing arts highlight additional issues of authenticity as issues of work authenticity are supplemented by questions about performance authenticity. Debates about the possibility and desirability of authentic performance of "early" and "period" music have become an especially rich arena for exploring the tensions between different modes of authenticity. Different performances of the same work can be evaluated as more or less authentic by reference to distinct goals and performing styles of different performers, which can, in turn, be evaluated by reference to (and conflict with) goals indicated or presupposed by the work's composer. Hence, the ideal of authentic self-expression puts a performer's expressive authenticity at cross-purposes with the goal of authentically rendering all the work's contemporaneous properties (Kivy 1995:138–42).

These issues have also enriched discussion of the ontology of art. For example, an intuitively simple ontology of the performing arts regards works as structural types. On this model, performances occur in order to make these types accessible to audiences. However, different expressive and aesthetic properties are present in different performances of a common type. Is a musical performance authentic if the musicians play the correct notes but fail to realize the composer's expressive goals? If musical works are pure sound structures, then such questions are trivialized, because expressive authenticity in performance is unrelated to the work's identity and provenance. Alternatively, if we construe authenticity as a matter of the work's essential relationship to its origins, then the variety of questions that are posed about authentic musical performance suggests a corresponding variety in the historically contingent properties that belong to various musical works. Let us explore three of these issues.

First, a sound structure can be performed with different timbres, as when the same piece is played on a harpsichord and then on a piano. Many composers constrain timbre choice by specifying instrumentation. So we do not think that a string quartet receives an authentic performance if the four string parts are performed with a tuba, a kazoo, and two tin whistles. However, a simplistic adherence to composer-specified instrumentation can generate its own sonic inauthenticity. Because Mozart wrote for valve-less horns, the use of modern horns for performances of his horn concertos yields horn lines that are audibly different from those that Mozart expected to be derived from his scores. The violin parts of these concertos also sound different (and louder, altering the balance of instruments) when played with modern synthetic strings in place of historically correct animal-gut strings.

So are performances of Mozart's horn concertos more authentic when performed on valve-less horns and gut-strung violins? Since he wrote with those sounds in mind, it would seem so. Yet he did not specify these expectations. We surmise what Mozart expected the audience to hear by determining what was available to him. Hence, we must consult historical practices in order to combine explicit instructions (e.g., a musical score) with contemporaneous performance conventions in order to achieve authentic realization of a composer's music (Davies 2001: 103–7).

It does not follow that authenticity is fully achieved through sonic authenticity, i.e., by producing the sounds that the composer would anticipate hearing under the best circumstances. Many opera arias in the soprano and alto range in Italian *opera seria* were composed for male castrati. In the nineteenth century, moral qualms led audiences to reject this performance practice. The music can be transposed for tenors, or sung at pitch by male countertenors or by female singers, though none of these reproduces the combination of power and high pitch for which castrati were renowned. More recently, electronic manipulation has been used to duplicate a castrato's unique combination of range, timbre, and volume. Although sonically authentic, this electronically created sonic facsimile is rejected as too inauthentic for actual opera performance. It obliterates the *performance* art that made the best castrati singers into international stars. Human performance, even if not sonically faithful to what the castrato could achieve, is still regarded as more desirable than sonic mimicry.

Second, a musical sound structure is always interpreted by its realization in a performance style. For example, eighteenth-century violinists appear to have used vibrato quite sparingly. In the twentieth century, continuous vibrato became fashionable. Haydn's violin concertos can be played with continuous vibrato or with very little, but either approach will present audiences with the notes and structures that are actually stipulated in Haydn's scores. Hence, performance technique introduces another facet to authenticity.

Although it might seem obvious that a performance always has greater authenticity by virtue of utilizing contemporaneous performance practices with instruments of the intended type and from the composer's era, there are competing considerations. It is tempting to say that historically appropriate instrumentation is authentic because it reflects the composer's intentions. However, it is easy to find examples of composers who recognized the deficiencies of the available instruments. It is unlikely that Beethoven desired that the "Appassionata" piano sonata (Op. 57) should only be played on fortepianos of the sort available to him in 1807, whose strings broke when he played its most tumultuous passages. Hence, some performances might be more authentic by virtue of being performed as the composer would have wanted them had later instruments been available. Extending this line of thought, authenticity of aesthetic or expressive effect might demand radical departures from the instrumentation specified. Bach's idea of massed musical forces was puny by our standards, so realizing Bach's intentions requires rearranging his music (Kivy 1995: 53). However, in the same way that a work composed for strings yields a different, derivative work when played on a mellotron or on wind instruments, it can be argued that sacrificing explicit instructions (e.g., the score) in light of an interpretation of overall intentions results in a substitution of a derivative musical work (Davies 2001: 223–4).

Additional complications arise when we emphasize that music is a performing art. Consider the performer's role when performing the "Appassionata" piano sonata. Pianists engage in a skilled activity and Beethoven wrote piano sonatas that exploit and sometimes challenge that skill. In a word, his sonatas are meant to provide occasions of musicianship. Hence, authentic performances require performers who employ and display the proper technical skill, which in turn requires the right *sort* of instrument, if not the make and model that Beethoven had available. Pianists are ultimately the best judges of the proper balance of innovation and conservatism when performing those works (Godlovitch 1998: 61–78).

Third, recognizing that musical works are more than mere sound structures invites extended debate about which *other* composer-intended features of performances are equally relevant. For example, J. S. Bach intended that particular religious cantatas be performed in a Lutheran church on specific Sundays of the liturgical year. Given his clear intentions, a Friday performance of "Wachet Auf" in a concert hall cannot be authentic. One response is that most music is multifunctional. Secular presentations are authentic whenever a composition is meant to be "an object of interest in its own right" (Davies 2001: 216). Because Bach intended this function for all of his music, our secular performances are authentic in *one* of the ways sanctioned by his intentions. A parallel argument can be made about modern museum displays of religious "art," such as altarpieces and Byzantine icons.

However, the concept of aesthetic autonomy is foreign to many artistic traditions. Although secular performances of Bach's religious cantatas can be defended on the grounds that he intended them to be judged for their aesthetic merit, the same intention does not equally guide all indigenous and traditional "art" (Shiner 1994). Many cultural artifacts are site and event specific. Despite their significant aesthetic value, reproducing or preserving them violates cultural tradition. Their public or "aesthetic" display may be prohibited. Hence, cultural exportation of ceremonial objects often renders them inauthentic. In other cases, the process that makes such "art" available for aesthetic appreciation introduces new values and practices into the originating culture, reducing cultural authenticity.

For example, Navajo sandpaintings are created as part of a healing ritual. These colorful, crushed rock designs are destroyed at the end of the ceremony. Navajo tradition prohibits their preservation or fixed replication. Although these ceremonial artifacts are aesthetically complex and rewarding, they are not produced as works of art. Hence, a sandpainting produced for display or sale is inherently inauthentic with respect to Navajo tradition. Respecting this tradition, Navajos who create sandpaintings for nonritual display will intentionally alter them from their "authentic," ritual-specific counterparts. These "inauthentic," fixed-form sandpaintings can be evaluated for authenticity by regarding them as displays of traditional Navajo symbolism and design principles. However, many collectors and art dealers believe that stylistic authenticity is insufficient. Authenticity requires "traditional" intentions. Seeking authentic indigenous art, they reject the very artifacts that the Navajo produce as works of art, namely, artifacts created to be objects of aesthetic appreciation.

Paradoxically, cultural changes introduced to accommodate foreign expectations and exploitation are challenged as inauthentic whenever the artists evolve new practices as a result of these cultural interactions (Shiner 1994). Yet works rejected as inauthentic may scrupulously adhere to the originating culture's own standards of creativity and authorship (Coleman 2005).

See also MUSIC AND SONG; ADORNO; AMERINDIAN AESTHETICS; CONSERVATION AND RESTORATION; CULTURAL APPROPRIATION; FORGERY; NOTATIONS; ONTOLOGICAL CONTEXTUALISM; ORIGINALITY; PERFORMANCE.

BIBLIOGRAPHY

Bicknell, Jeanette. 2005. "Just a Song? Exploring the Aesthetics of Popular Song Performance," *Journal of Aesthetics and Art Criticism*, 63, 261–70.

Coleman, Elizabeth Burns. 2005. *Aboriginal Art, Identity and Appropriation*. Aldershot: Ashgate.

Davies, Stephen. 2001. *Musical Works and Performances*. Oxford: Clarendon.

Dutton, Denis. 1979. "Artistic Crimes," *British Journal of Aesthetics*, 19, 302–41.

Godlovitch, Stan. 1998. *Musical Performance: A Philosophical Study*. London: Routledge.

Kivy, Peter. 1995. *Authenticities: Philosophical Reflections on Musical Performance*. Ithaca: Cornell University Press.

Rudinow, Joel. 1994. "Race, Ethnicity, Expressive Authenticity: Can White People Sing the Blues?" *Journal of Aesthetics and Art Criticism*, 52, 127–37.

Shiner, Larry. 1994. " 'Primitive Fakes,' 'Tourist Art,' and the Ideology of Authenticity," *Journal of Aesthetics and Art Criticism*, 52, 225–34.

Shiner, Larry. 2003. "Western and Non-Western Concepts of Art: Universality and Authenticity." In *Art and Essence*. S. Davies & A. Sukla (eds.). Westport: Praeger, 143–56.

Trilling, Lionel. 1971. *Sincerity and Authenticity*. Cambridge, MA: Harvard University Press, 81–105.

Young, James O. 1988. "The Concept of Authentic Performance," *British Journal of Aesthetics*, 28, 228–38.

THEODORE GRACYK

B

Barthes, Roland (1915–1980) French semioticist and literary and cultural critic; a leading representative of structuralism. At the Pavillon des Arts in Paris in 1986 there was an exhibition called *Roland Barthes: Le texte et l'image*. It consisted of paintings, photographs, and posters, accompanied by Barthes's writings about them blown up large enough to be comfortably seen from the viewing distance called for by the images. The words overpowered the images, which in turn became illustrations of them, in a fitting exhibition for one for whom words, written or spoken, sounded or seen, were material, physical, affecting each other and whatever encountered them as do all material things. Words had for Barthes a power akin to that of tribal carvings or icons and to that he found in certain photographs. It was the power of the past and of the form without which nothing could work or take effect or make its mark, including the brute, dumb, blind energy of the unconscious and its instincts.

Barthes was a writer for whom writing was the quintessential human activity, because through it the individual participates in the production of sense and experiences the limits of the intelligibility hard won by productive labor; through it she imbricates herself in the structure of birth and death common to meaning and nature alike. By the death of meaning or sense is meant escape from the systems of difference that alone create sense, a leap beyond the limits of the intelligible, cultured world into the raw, the intractable real, the primitive. The experience of the primitive is possible only as an irruption of the cultured; it is, therefore, not the primitive raw that is experienced but the opposition between cultured and raw, between what Barthes calls in his last book, *Camera Lucida: Reflections on Photography* (1980), "the tame and the mad." To appreciate the opposition is to be struck, shaken by the collision of the opposing terms, by the catastrophe that befalls the hitherto privileged term. A successful opposition is as violent or forcible as what it opposes is entrenched, and when the privileged is the set of culturally endorsed beliefs, its unsettling is cataclysmic. The cataclysm occurs in the individual whose beliefs are undone by the incursion of the primitive.

This is the poststructural deconstruction of precisely those received meanings explained by structuralism in terms of Ferdinand de Saussure's linguistic model. Barthes was a preeminent scriptor of this deconstruction, which appears full-blown in *S/Z* (1970), his reading of a Balzac short story fragmented along the lines of language, money, and sex that organize Michel Foucault's *The Order of Things* (1966). Barthes's career is intimately connected with the rise and fall of structuralism in Paris in the 1960s and the skepticism born of the end of what he called "the dream of scientificity" to which structuralism had given rise. A structuralist, Barthes tell us in his primer, *The Elements of Semiology* (1964), is simply one who uses words like "sign," "signifier," "signified" and finds the models of language of Saussure and Hjelmslev helpful in classifying the elements of signification, which are taken to be signs. Signs are arbitrarily connected with that of which they are signs. In this signs are different from meanings, which are held to be necessarily connected with that of which they are meanings. His interest was in the structuring activity, which he described as fragmenting the given and encoding the fragments in a variety of codes – as many as imagination could devise. It was the freedom of the activity of structuring that he sought, not the structures that it produced.

Freedom appears as a value in Barthes's first book, *Writing Degree Zero* (1953), as the freedom of the writer to choose his forms. This is a high modernist tract that identifies writing in its difference from both style, a writer's utterly personal signature born in the depths of his body, and language, an algebra-like system of rules, impersonal and abstract. The modern writer, refusing to inherit tradition's forms of literature, bears the responsibility of choosing the forms in which he shall write. The necessity of positioning himself with respect to the tradition follows from the historicism to which modernism is committed. By the time of *S/Z*, however, Barthes's focus turns from the modern writer's choice of forms to "writerly" reading, and the opposition between classic and modern yields to that between "readerly" and "writerly."

Each is a way of reading that can be used indifferently on classic or modern texts, and the reader is free to choose between the ways. The readerly is the comfortable, familiar way of reading, whereas the writerly is what unsettles all that the readerly assumes: it undoes the reader's "historical, cultural, psychological assumptions, the consistency of his tastes, values, memories, [and] brings to a crisis his relation with language" (1974: 93). The readerly brings pleasure, the writerly bliss, where bliss is an ecstasy in which are dissolved all familiar conceptions, including those along whose lines the reader's identity is drawn. The reader, then, loses herself in the act of reading in the writerly way.

This distinction appears in the last book as the distinction between a photograph's *studium*, what in it is culturally coded, and its *punctum*, what, unbeckoned, rises out of it to pierce, touch, wound its viewer. The *punctum* connects the viewer with the object whose light-drawn image the photograph records, proving the past reality of the object and putting the viewer in touch with the past as nothing else can. Barthes calls light a "carnal skin" enveloping the photographed object and its viewer, thereby carrying the viewer back to the time of the photograph's taking. The ecstatic dissolve of the viewer into the past made present in the photograph can bring madness, madness being the other side of the tame, the civilized – that exists, however, only as an encroachment upon the tame, the sane. Culture and its systems of meanings are always already there, therefore, and the work of Barthes's last five years consists of efforts to trick, outwit, outplay, evade these delimiting systems. Identity questions are raised, only to be shown to be impossible of answer, especially questions about the identity, completeness, and consistency of the self. *A Lover's Discourse* characterizes a discourse warranted neither by the speaker's intentions nor by the rules of language and, driven "into the backwater of the 'unreal' . . . has no recourse but to become the site, however exiguous, of an *affirmation*" (1978: 126). This discourse is pure act, the site of the affirmation of itself, not of its speaker.

For Barthes, the subject, the speaker, vanishes into acts of writing, reading, speaking, as in *Camera Lucida* material objects vanish into their photo-recordable traces of light. Language is put into motion as each word becomes a step along a path to all the other words to which it can be connected by resemblance, by difference, by contiguity, with the result that the materiality of words themselves vanishes into the gathering speed of writerly reading. At the end of *Camera Lucida* Barthes says of whether to view the matter in this mad way or in a manner more familiar: "The choice is mine."

See also NINETEENTH- AND TWENTIETH-CENTURY CONTINENTAL AESTHETICS; DECONSTRUCTION; INTERPRETATION; MEANING CONSTRUCTIVISM; STRUCTURALISM AND POSTSTRUCTURALISM; TEXT.

BIBLIOGRAPHY

Primary sources
[1957] 1972. *Mythologies*. A. Lavers (trans.). New York: Hill & Wang.
[1964] 1972. *Critical Essays*. R. Howard (trans.). New York: Hill & Wang.
[1970] 1974. *S/Z*. R. Miller (trans.). New York: Hill & Wang.
[1973] 1975. *The Pleasure of the Text*. R. Miller (trans.). New York: Hill & Wang.
[1977] 1978. *A Lover's Discourse: Fragments*. R. Howard (trans.). New York: Hill & Wang.
1977. *Image–Music–Text*. S. Heath (trans.). New York: Hill & Wang.
[1980] 1981. *Camera Lucida: Reflections on Photography*. R. Howard (trans.). New York: Hill & Wang.
[1982] 1985. *The Responsibility of Forms: Critical Essays on Music, Art, and Representation*. R. Howard (trans.). New York: Hill & Wang.

Secondary sources
Allen, Graham. 2003. *Roland Barthes*. London: Routledge.

Brown, Andrew. 1992. *Roland Barthes: The Figures of Writing*. New York: Oxford University Press.

Culler, Jonathan. 2002. *Barthes: A Very Short Introduction*. Rev. edn. New York: Oxford University Press.

Wiseman, Mary Bittner. 1989. *The Ecstasies of Roland Barthes*. London: Routledge.

MARY BITTNER WISEMAN

Baumgarten, Alexander G(ottlieb) (1714–1762)

German philosopher and logician; a significant influence on Kant's aesthetics. The "father" of aesthetics and the first to employ the term in a distinctly philosophical context; his pseudonym was Aletheophilus, "friend of truth." Baumgarten's principal doctrines were:

1 that aesthetics comprises a science of sensitive knowing (*scientia cognitionis sensitivae*);
2 that such knowing is not, as Spinoza and Leibniz believed, solely subordinate to logical knowledge but possesses an autonomy of its own;
3 that aesthetic knowledge exhibits its own perfection, here understood in the eighteenth-century manner as a specific activity achieving its fruition (*per-facere*). Baumgarten accordingly conceived of the task of aesthetic knowing as the translation of an obscure sensuous manifold into a clear perceptual image.

A professor of philosophy at Frankfurt and Halle, Baumgarten was known as a formidable logician, theological hermeneuticist, astute critic, and a follower of the rationalist Christian Wolff. Rather unjustly, Baumgarten is remembered solely for his definition of aesthetics as "the science of sensitive knowing" (*Aesthetica* §1), a science that touches neither on the nature of art per se nor on its social import but on the direct sensuous apprehension of its actuality. The context and purpose of his argument is, regrettably, hardly remembered. But given the vehement contemporary debate over the perception of meaning in postmodern aesthetic and hermeneutic theory, his works have much to offer.

Baumgarten's philosophy is shaped by the rationalist conviction, *cognitio vera est realitas*: the world is considered an intelligible totality constituted by the relations of greater and lesser wholes, the logical key to which is the form of the subject–predicate proposition. Just as reality is the greatest unity and variety of its actual states (predications), so, Baumgarten believed, sensuous perfection attains the greatest unity and variety of perceptions within a singular image. Aesthetics springs from a "dark faculty" of the soul, an *ars combinationis*, which intuitively fuses a perceived sensuous manifold into a coherent whole, the perfection of which lies in the degree of its "intensive and extensive clarity" – an argument that cleverly reworks the Cartesian terms "clear" and "distinct."

Descartes insisted that, though we may perceive the sea before us "clearly," we may not know those defining properties which make it "distinct" from other types of water. We might, equally, "know" seawater's distinct properties and yet never have "clearly" seen the sea. Baumgarten departs from this juxtaposition (especially Leibniz's version of it) with his insistence that, though remaining logically indistinct, sensitive knowledge has a perfection of its own that cannot be reduced or dissolved by conceptual knowing. With an ingenious wordplay, Baumgarten names the sensuously perceived realm a "field of confusion" (*campus confusionis*), a point which, though it appears to abide with the rationalist conviction that the sensuous is logically confused (indistinct and muddled), in fact breaks with it by displaying the perceptual world as confluence, convergence, and synthesis (con-fusion), a world in which indiscernible particulars (Leibniz's "dull perceptions") are combined to produce a distinctly "clear" image. The argument is worked out in the *Metaphysica* (1739) and in the incomplete two-volume *Aesthetica* (1750, 1758), but its basis stems from his earliest work, *Meditationes philosophicae de nonnullis ad poema pertinentibus* (1735). In a manner close to Gadamer, he suggests that poetic words have both an intensive and extensive clarity – intensive insofar as they invoke a highly particular object, and extensive inasmuch as the richness of poetic allusions involves making all the implicit associations of an image explicitly clear. Baumgarten's understanding of semiotics was such that he believed there to be no difference between the functioning of visual signs and of poetic words.

It is unclear whether he appreciated the extent to which his insistence on an irreducible perfection proper to aesthetic knowledge disrupted the rationalist program of knowledge as a logically unified science. And yet his merit is that, though by no means a deprecator of reason, he reveals how any transition from the phenomenological experience of the sea's immediacy to an analysis of saltwater involves a great diminishment of the experiential world. The transition might facilitate an advancement of "distinct" knowledge, but only at the cost of weakening our aesthetic sensibility. Baumgarten was one of the first moderns to defend the autonomy not only of aesthetics but also of immediate experience against the encroachments of theory, while his suggestion that sensuous appearance is art's proper terrain opens a line of thinking which leads to Nietzsche, Heidegger, and Gadamer.

Once Kant steered aesthetics toward a transcendental study of the objective preconditions of judgments concerning the beautiful, Baumgarten, despite the proselytizing efforts of G. F. Meier and the admiration of Moses Mendelssohn and J. G. Herder, was fated to fall into obscurity. His location of the aesthetic in the realms of the "sensitive" condemned him in Kant's eyes as an apologist for sensationalism and subjectivism. In the *Critique of Pure Reason*, Baumgarten is referred to as that "admirable thinker" who "attempted to bring the critical treatment of the beautiful under rational principles, and to raise its rules to the rank of a science." Yet Kant dismissed the attempt because "the said rules . . . are empirical and . . . can never serve as determinate *a priori* laws by which our judgment of taste must be directed" (1970: 66). However it is now Kant's star that is waning, for since Gadamer has forcefully undermined the estranged intellectualism of Kant's aesthetic and reasserted the truth claim of the aesthetically immediate, the virtues of Baumgarten's initial position are apparent. Contemporary debates about the distinctness of aesthetic as opposed to scientific knowledge, recent appeals to an intuitive sense of aesthetic wholeness to mitigate between opposing interpretations, and attempts to defend perceptions of unitary meanings in artworks against deconstructive criticism, all indicate that Baumgarten's aesthetics remains not merely relevant but ripe for serious philosophical reappraisal.

See also EIGHTEENTH-CENTURY AESTHETICS; GADAMER; IRONY; KANT.

BIBLIOGRAPHY

Primary sources
[1734] 1974. *Reflections on Poetry.* K. Aschenbrenner & W. Holther (trans.). Berkeley: University of California Press.
[1739–58] 1983. *Texte zur Grundlegung der Aesthetik.* H. R. Schweizer (ed.). Hamburg: Meiner. (Contains a dual Latin and German text of extracts from Baumgarten's *Metaphysica*, Halle, 1739, §§501–623; *Philosophia generalis*, Halle, 1770, §147; and the *Aesthetica*, Frankfurt, 1750/8, §1.)
[1750, 1758] 1983. *Theoreitische Ästhetik: Die grundlegenden Abschnitte der "Aesthetica."* H. R. Schweizer (ed.). Hamburg: Meiner. (Edited collection of extracts from Baumgarten's *Aesthetica*. Frankfurt. 1750/8.)

Secondary sources
Cassirer, Ernst. 1969. *The Enlightenment.* New Haven: Yale University Press, 338–53.
Davey, Nicholas. 1989. "Baumgarten's Aesthetics: A Post Gadamerian Reflection," *British Journal of Aesthetics*, 2, 101–15.
Gross, Steffen W. 2001. *Felix aestheticus: Die Ästhetik als Lehre vom Menschen: zum 250. Jahrestag des Erscheinens von Alexander Gottlieb Baumgartens "Aesthetica".* Würzburg: Königshausen & Neumann.
Kant, Immanuel. 1970 [1781]. *Critique of Pure Reason.* N. K. Smith (trans.). London: Macmillan.
Wessell, Leonard P. 1972. "Alexander Baumgarten's Contribution to the Development of Aesthetics," *Journal of Aesthetics and Art Criticism*, 30, 333–42.
Witte, Eqbert. 2000. *Logik ohne Dornen: Die Rezeption von A. G. Baumgartens Ästhetik im Spannungsfeld von logischen Begriff und asthetischer Anschauung.* Hildesheim: Olms.

NICHOLAS DAVEY

Beardsley, Monroe C(urtis) (1915–1985) American philosopher of art and literary criticism. While having contributed importantly to the philosophy of action, Beardsley developed extensively and defended articulately the twentieth century's most influential aesthetic theory since John Dewey. Growing out of the desire to provide a philosophical foundation for the New Criticism as well as a sense that the arts have a distinctive social and cultural place, the body of Beardsley's aesthetic theory is supported at the heart by a conception of aesthetic experience or an experience having aesthetic character (whatever other character it may have too) and aesthetic value.

The latter notion is to be understood in terms of the former, aesthetic value being, in Beardsley's most considered view, a value owing to a potentiality of artworks and other relevantly similar objects to afford experiences that, through cognition, characteristically involve "attention firmly fixed on a perceptual or intentional object; a feeling of freedom from concerns about matters outside that object; notable affect that is detached from practical ends; the sense of exercising powers of discovery; and integration of the self and of its experiences" (1981: lxii). Objects which have such value provide experiences with aesthetic character in virtue of their "formal unity and/or the [typically human as well as formal] regional qualities of a complex whole" (1982: 22). The interpolation is worthy of special note, since Beardsley was intent on separating himself from formalist views such as those of Clive Bell and Roger Fry (1981: xvii). An artwork itself is to be understood as an arrangement of conditions in such an object intended to afford such an experience.

Now, while "intention" plays an important part in Beardsley's notion of an artwork, his best-known doctrine is that it is a fallacy to hold that appeal to information about the artist's intention is indispensable for determining the meaning or aesthetic character of an artwork (Beardsley & Wimsatt 1946). Whatever the peculiar causal conditions entering into the creation of art, the artist's intentions being among them, the aesthetic features of the work are themselves independently perceivable. This gives the work a critical autonomy.

A central aspect of the theory here, taking the especially difficult case of a literary work, is that the work *as such* be understood to be not itself a speech act but, rather, the imitation or representation of a speech act (Beardsley 1970). (An analogous point could be made concerning any theory of art that considers the work qua work to be an expressive act.) However, that we need not know the intentions of Wordsworth in order to fully appreciate "A slumber did my spirit seal" does not mean that we do not need to know the meanings of words as they were used when Wordsworth was writing. Thus, it would be unreasonable to think that an author could successfully write a piece that is ironical if an educated reader of the author's time could not be reasonably be expected to catch the irony in virtue of knowing how the language works (Beardsley 1982: 188–207). That a later reader should be helped in appreciating the irony by reading the author's private correspondence is compatible with it not being necessary that such help be generally provided for a full appreciation of the work. Any residual indeterminacy of meaning is simply a matter of strict ambiguity.

The artwork, though admittedly often a very complex object, is an object nonetheless, and our reasoning about its value and character is not logically different from other sorts of reasoning about values. Beardsley resists both relativism and Kantian subjectivism in his account of aesthetic judgment. And while artworks can be judged from other points of view – as we can judge literature for its truth value, for example – properly critical judgment is judgment that addresses the work from the aesthetic point of view. It manifests an interest in the aesthetic value of the work and defends its judgments by referring to the aesthetic qualities of the work. These qualities are condition-governed (Beardsley 1982: 99–110). That is, they are causally generated by the nonaesthetic perceptual or intentional qualities of the work in the way that a gestalt is causally conditioned by perceptual and semantic features that constitute the local qualities of a figure. Beardsley thus wants to set strict limits on the contextual determination of the character of the artwork.

The artwork, then, does have contextual and causal conditions, some of which might be called institutional, but Beardsley resists the institutional definition of art most saliently represented in the work of George Dickie. He worries that in gathering a sense of all the cultural dependencies that enter into the practice of art, we will lose a sense of what makes art special (1982: 356). Art is not, he says, *essentially* institutional (1982: 125–43). An essentially institutional act is one that could not take place independent of the existence of an institution – for example, depositing a paycheck in a bank account. Beardsley does not deny that the creation of many artworks takes place within institutions, that is, as part of the day-to-day activity of those institutions. Rather, his point is that art does not require such institutions.

Think of Sunday painters or children's art. It may be that some properties of some artworks – for instance, belonging to a genre – are institutionally conditioned, but that does not make the writing of a poem essentially institutional. Nor is the existence of art essentially dependent on the presence of some theory of art that allows or disallows one to ascribe entitlement to art status, though some artists create with theories in mind about what they are doing. Are there certain normal kinds of aesthetic qualities that are essentially institutional? Beardsley leaves open the possibility that there may be. If so, then art would perhaps turn out to be essentially institutional in certain ways in the normal case (which is perhaps a peculiar kind of essence). But even so, it would not follow that we should not look for how art functions quite generally to satisfy certain basic human needs and interests – that is, aesthetic interests. An answer to the question "What things are called 'art' by artistic establishments?" is no substitute for an answer to the question "What is art?"

The alternative view, to wit that a sufficient condition for creating a work of art is that an action or object be given the status of art by suitably qualified status-conferring actions or persons, makes the creation of an artwork a nearly senseless act. Writing about artistic creation, Beardsley features the importance of a negative critical judgment in the process of creating a work of art. While not having a precise idea of a goal to be achieved in the work, the artist is sensitive to the conditions that make for aesthetic value. The effect of an art-making action will be allowed to stand as part of the work only if it does not produce the judgment that the result weakens expressive regional intensity or formal unity in the object that is taking shape (Beardsley 1982: 239–62). Thus, echoing traditional expressionist theories of art, the artist discovers what her work is about in the process of making it, but the process as a whole has been guided by an aesthetic interest. Of course other interests may be present as

well. Picasso may have wanted to protest the barbaric effects of war in painting *Guernica*, but he understood that the only effective way for him to do this *as an artist* was to make a painting that would be aesthetically satisfying as well. Otherwise, assuming the point could still be made, the "work" would be merely political commentary with no specially qualified expertise to recommend it, the merits of his human lamentation notwithstanding. Speaking of Duchamp's *Fountain* during a seminar, Beardsley quipped that one might be able to rescue the gesture as a minor work of art were we to think of it as a joke pointed at the jury of judges for the exposition. That the joke was made by an artist acting as a critic created not an artwork difficult to understand as such but a critical confusion for generations to come of artists, critics, and philosophers of art. Artists may also be critics, of course, but that does not make criticism art.

See also TWENTIETH-CENTURY ANGLO-AMERICAN AESTHETICS; AESTHETIC ATTITUDE; AESTHETIC PROPERTIES; "ARTWORLD"; BELL; DEFINITION OF "ART"; "INTENTIONAL FALLACY"; INTERPRETATION.

BIBLIOGRAPHY

Primary sources
1946. (& Wimsatt, W. K., Jr.) "The Intentional Fallacy," *Sewanee Review*, 54, 3–23; extensively reprinted.
1966. *Aesthetics from Classical Greece to the Present.* New York: Macmillan.
1970. *The Possibility of Criticism.* Detroit: Wayne State University Press.
1981. *Aesthetics: Problems in the Philosophy of Criticism.* 2nd edn. Indianapolis: Hackett.
1982. *The Aesthetic Point of View.* M. Wreen & D. Callen (eds.). Ithaca: Cornell University Press.

Secondary sources
2005. "Symposium: Monroe Beardsley's Legacy in Aesthetics," *Journal of Aesthetics and Art Criticism*, 63, 175–95.
Davies, Stephen. 1991. *Definitions of Art.* Ithaca: Cornell University Press, ch. 3.
Wreen, Michael. 2005. "Beardsley's Aesthetics." In *The Stanford Encyclopedia of Philosophy*. E. N. Zalta (ed.). Available at http://plato.stanford.edu/entries/beardsley-aesthetics/

DONALD CALLEN

beauty is a topic of great philosophical interest and one that is relatively unexplored. Few would deny its importance, and yet the mere suggestion that it be defined drives intelligent people to witless babble. They suppose that the first and obvious requirement is to prove that beauty is "objective"; that it is not "in the eye of the beholder." They assume that the burden of proof lies on those who maintain that utterances of the form "*O* is beautiful" are either true or false, and they also assume that no proof will be forthcoming, that only very unsophisticated persons think that such judgments are "objective." The suggestion is that, until what is assumed to be impossible has been achieved, there is no point in talking about beauty.

But this is all pretentious nonsense: the unhappy metaphor in which a complex epistemological problem is presented as a question about what is or is not "out there" is multiply ambiguous. As a remedial first step, consider the following: beauty is linked with appreciation, so if all human beings died, then there would be no one to do the appreciating and no claim that something was beautiful would be true. But under such circumstances, no claim of *any* kind would be true since there would *be* no claims – no sentences uttered. If that is the idea, then truth, as well as beauty, is "in the eye of the beholder." On the other hand, if beauty's being in the eye of the beholder is supposed to mean that everything is equally beautiful or that nothing is beautiful, then the hypothesis needs the backing of a developed theory, since in an ordinary way of thinking it is false. Beauty is not more equally distributed than is height or intelligence. Perhaps there are people to whom nothing is beautiful: they are either deprived or very depressed.

Even if it were cleaned up, the inside/outside question would be premature. How the taking of something to be beautiful fits into our overall scheme, whether the cognitive idiom is appropriate to such takings – is a question that presupposes some understanding and interpretation of the phenomena. To prove that *thinking* something beautiful is, so to speak, all there is, or that what we take to be aesthetic pleasure is some other kind of gratification in disguise, we have to be able to characterize the alleged illusion, to explain what it is that people mistakenly take to be the case.

Those who think that beauty is undiscussable have another familiar objection: tastes differ, and of two incompatible judgments it is impossible to prove that one is right. This is an idea that has haunted the literature since the eighteenth century. I believe it comes from assuming that to define a term is to offer a criterion for its application. A definition of *X* is thought of as answering the question, "By what marks can I recognize a case of *X*?" Three observations: First, if what is wanted is a test, then beauty is indefinable, but so are most terms of everyday language. Definitions that tell me how to recognize an *X* are found in legal textbooks, in formal logic, in the physical sciences, but rarely elsewhere. Second, a definition presents two terms as equivalent, but equivalent with respect to what? Do they apply to the same items? Do they have the same meaning? Is the equivalence something discovered, or something stipulated? It all depends on what you want to use the definition for, what function it plays in your inquiry. Developing a philosophical theory is not like putting together a manual for beginners. When Russell and Frege argue about how to define number, they are not thinking about helpful clues that will help the ordinary person *recognize* a number. Third, a term of everyday language – "beauty," say – is indefinable in the sense of lacking criteria for application. You can make up a definition if you want to and perhaps force everyone to adopt it. But then you will have to invent another term to do the job that had been done by "beauty." This is a general point, but it is important for the theory of the beautiful, since we are often tempted to look for rules or principles that would bolster our particular preferences. Kant was the first philosopher to see how empty such attempts must be.

A final and inconsequential obstacle: it is said that "beauty" is not the right *term* to focus on because it carries the suggestion of something mildly pleasing and nonstrenuous, thereby excluding much great art. (How many times have we been told that neither the ceiling of the Sistine Chapel nor *King Lear* nor late Beethoven quartets are "beautiful"?) This is just pedantry: in eighteenth-century critical parlance where, in accord with the now-forgotten theory of genres, the beautiful was divided from the "sublime," the "picturesque," the "pathetic," and so forth, it had a point, although even then it was one known only to insiders. Nonexperts then and now apply the term "beautiful" across the board, and the same is true for its cognate in other languages. Anyone who thinks "aesthetic value" is an improvement is free to adopt it – but then it has to be explained: beauty is a good, so "value" is appropriate, but what do you say about "aesthetic"?

Once we set aside the questions that have been supposed to block inquiry, we are free to consider the role that aesthetic considerations play in our lives. We care a *lot* about good appearance: to be beautiful, to have good-looking children, nice clothes, a fine house – these are accounted blessings. People work long and hard, inspired by the hope that what they achieve may be beautiful – and not just artists but gardeners and industrial designers. Our perceptions of beauty are deeply intertwined in the complexities of our affective lives. Why does a mere house inspire in me feelings of pride? "Because it is mine and because I think it beautiful" is an answer that anyone can understand. Think further of the role that "because it is beautiful" plays in explanations of such emotions as envy, love, ambition, solicitude. It is not only in the theory of affect that such considerations figure. No account of deliberation or practical reason that did not allow them their proper weight could be adequate. What is at issue in particular cases may be momentous (which one shall I marry?) or minor (where shall we spend our vacation?) or trivial (shall I buy this potholder?). But there is no decision in which what Kant calls "the judgment of taste" may not play a role, and in some contexts it is decisive. So there is every reason to recognize that beauty is a basic and indispensable concept in whatever sense one could say the same of knowledge, belief, wrongdoing, logical validity, or virtue.

To say of beauty that it is relatively unexplored is just to observe that many great philosophers treat it in a perfunctory manner or not at all. None of the system-builders of the seventeenth century – not Descartes, Locke, Spinoza, Berkeley, Leibniz – has anything much to say about the beautiful. Who, then, have made significant contributions? Plato, for one, Aquinas and some of the medievals, Hume,

Kant, and, in the present century, Dewey, Santayana, and a handful of later writers. The popular conception – that there is a vast literature, many theories, as many as there are theorists – is false. It is also a mistake to assume that the views that we *do* have are in conflict with one another. On questions of ontology, theory of knowledge, and ethics, Plato, Hume, and Kant represent very different positions, and such differences emerge in their analyses of the beautiful. But with respect to what it is that *needs* analysis, the characterization of the data, their views converge. There are differences of emphasis but, by and large, these are complementary rather than competitive. Furthermore, the philosophers' consensus is in accord with common sense – that is, with the opinion of reflective laypeople.

Certain propositions are taken to need no argument: they are not axioms or a priori truths but commonplaces derived from experience and observation. Some examples:

1　Beauty is a kind of good, a "positive value."
2　Beauty is linked with pleasure: what we take to be beautiful we enjoy. The converse does not hold, since we enjoy things that we do not think beautiful or even seemly.
3　Beauty inspires love and thus acquires its power as an element of motivation.
4　Appreciation of beauty depends on perception or, if abstract entities are in question, on some other form of acquaintance. Hence our findings are, as one might say, all first-personal, and discussions of a piece of music that is described but never heard are necessarily vacuous.
5　The claim, when it is serious, that a particular item is beautiful brings into play a kind of judgment that is distinctive – not to be subsumed under the heading of practical or theoretical judgment. Kant was the first to make it explicit and recognize its importance.

The five propositions listed provide a basis to build on. Taken together, they suggest a number of further propositions. Thus, if, as according to proposition 4, ascription of beauty to an individual, *O*, requires that the ascriber be acquainted with *O*, then it appears that, whatever the warrant for the ascription may be, it cannot depend on inference from general principles. A major premise for a syllogism that had "*O* is beautiful" as its conclusion would have to be of unrestricted generality, like "All roses are beautiful," which, in contrast with "All the roses in this vase are beautiful," requires commitment with respect to an indefinitely large number of hitherto unexamined roses – and this is incompatible with proposition 4.

When it comes to determining what is beautiful, no interesting, law-like generalizations are available. Kant puts it plainly: there are no principles of taste. Kant takes his claim to be self-evident, but it is not – as appears from the manifest convictions of many to the effect that *unless* there are principles of taste, the judgment of taste must be "merely subjective." Kant's greatest contribution is his recognition that what is posed as a dilemma is not a dilemma; that while there is something to be explained, there is no forced option; and that the singular judgment of taste, "*O* is beautiful," despite lack of principled support, is (sometimes at least) a valid judgment. Although Kant puts his negative thesis with respect to principles as an a priori truth that needs no argument, it is perhaps helpful to see that his point can be derived from, or at least supported by, proposition 4. What proposition 4 amounts to is the claim that the judgment of taste is, in a radical sense, an empirical judgment.

The virtual consensus among historical authors with respect to the phenomenal characteristics of the beautiful should not stand in the way of our noting that none of the traditional accounts is wholly adequate. Plato, for instance, appears to believe that spiritual progress, anchored in a love of the beautiful, moves (if all goes well) from appreciation of the particular – as might be, a handsome youth – to the more general – what handsome youths have in common – thence to the beauty of social institutions (the "just state"), and finally to a grasp of the form of absolute beauty. If we grant the five propositions listed above, then beauty belongs only to individuals, and Plato's second step is a false step. Moreover, Plato's account is full of apparent incoherencies: earthly items become beautiful by "participating" in the form, beauty, and that form is said to be itself the most beautiful of all. But the good is also said to be the most beautiful of all forms, and if the good

has to "participate" in beauty, then – well, you can see the difficulties. Maybe the story of the progressive ascent from handsome youth to absolute beauty is not really Plato's considered view; the account comes from the *Symposium*, where it is attributed by Socrates to Diotima, a prophetess.

Or consider Kant, so clear and persuasive on the main points, yet he has the weird idea that when I judge something beautiful, I am focusing not on the *thing* but on what Kant sees as a command (something like the categorical imperative) that every human being must assent to my claim. Admittedly, it is true that if I think I am right, I will *expect* competent peers to concur in my judgment, but to *demand* that everyone agree with me seems a most illiberal and anti-Enlightenment requirement. Here again, there may be a way of squaring Kant's doctrine with commitment to freedom of thought and expression, but what way has yet to be made out.

Hume's mistake was fairly basic: he is probably the originator of the idea of a dilemma – that only if there are principles of taste can we grant that some judgments of taste are true and others false. Hume believed that there was some conflict between holding on the one hand that a speaker, in making a judgment of taste, manifests not his beliefs but his "sentiments" and recognizing, on the other, that some judgments – such as the judgment that Ogilby (a now forgotten poet) is the equal of Milton – are not merely false but absurd. Hume tries to solve the problem by proposing that there *are* principles of taste, but very elusive ones, difficult to discern and impossible to formulate. (This is like claiming that there are moral principles but that it is not possible to cite any examples.) Hume's epistemological commitments lead him to a kind of waffling that Kant was careful to avoid, although when Hume forgets his theories, he is as clear-sighted as anyone has ever been.

In fact, the conflict that worried him need not have arisen: it depends entirely on his assumption that the *motive* of an utterance is decisive in determining its claim to have a truth value. He is therefore led to believe that, given their provenance, judgments of taste, like moral judgments, are beyond the reach of reason and hence neither true nor false. Hume offers no arguments for this claim, one that surely needs defense. It would have astonished Plato and Aristotle. (In a fit of passion, I shout out, "Socrates is a Greek!"; in a moment of cool reflection, I murmur, "Alcibiades is beautiful." There may be questions about truth claims, but they are not questions that are settled by discovery of my emotional state at the time of utterance.)

The preceding observations about Plato, Kant, and Hume are meant to suggest that the philosophers who have contributed most to the analysis of the beautiful have raised issues of consequence and have left us with many problems to solve. They present a challenge to anyone who takes the topic seriously. Why has the discussion languished?

You might think that philosophical aesthetics is the study of the beautiful, but that is not how things have turned out. From its mid-eighteenth-century beginnings when it first became an academic subject in German universities, aesthetics has been mainly concerned with the fine arts. Kant's *Critique of Judgment* (1790) is the first work that can be said to offer a systematic theory of beauty, but Kant was the last philosopher to consider nature on an equal footing with the arts. Indeed, because of his preoccupation with the "sublime" as a bridge between aesthetics and ethics, and his hope of preserving what he felt was valuable in the "Argument from Design," he pays more attention to natural phenomena than to works of art.

The shift of focus from the concept of beauty to the idea of a unitary enterprise called "art" happened gradually, and can escape notice because works of art were always among the items taken as exemplars of the beautiful. The expression "work of art" itself is a honorific title that belongs not just to any old poem or painting but to those that are deemed notably beautiful. But works of art can be studied from many different points of view, and are interesting for reasons other than their aesthetic value. Plato was the first to see that because drama, music, and poetry have powerful emotional effects, statesmen and educators can put the arts to work in support of political goals, worthy or unworthy. Plato also thought that what later ages were to call the "fine arts" were essentially mimetic; that, for instance,

melancholy music causes hearers to feel melancholy by "imitating" melancholy feelings. For reasons connected with his metaphysical doctrines, he supposed such music to be doubly hazardous: first, because it arouses negative emotions, and, second, because what it imitates or represents is not part of true reality but an aspect of the bungled world of appearance and becoming. The practice of the arts, he argues, must be strictly controlled because art is both deceptive and demoralizing.

Aristotle is another who is less concerned with the beauty of the arts than with their psychological effects, which, in contrast to Plato, he takes to be mainly benign. To be moved by an imitation of wrongful action or bad feeling is good: vicarious satisfaction of our own antisocial wishes makes us less rather than more likely to model ourselves on the doomed characters depicted on the Attic stage. Medieval authors, drawing on what was available to them from the classical tradition, take beauty seriously but show a kind of ambivalence about the arts. The delight we take in pageantry, music, ornamentation, and sculpture is seductive and may lead us away from our spiritual vocation. On the other hand, the arts, by way of fable or allegory, prefigure for simple folk truths of faith that are abstract and difficult to grasp. Manifest physical beauty is a clue to and a reminder of the beauty that is higher but less obvious – namely, the beauty of the virtuous soul secure in its faith.

Another persistent theme is that the world as a whole is an object for admiration and pleasure. The creator in Plato's *Timaeus* had wanted to make a *kosmos*, fine in every detail and beautiful as a whole. One article of the Manichaean heresy was the claim that the world is in a constant state of strife between good and evil. Scholastic philosophers bent on refutation of that view found it helpful to emphasize the intimate connection between the beautiful and the good. In the face of the facts, it is harder to argue that God is benevolent and just than to argue that God is an artist who needs contrasts – shadows to make brightness more striking, discords that can be harmoniously resolved.

What properties of the universe as a whole make it beautiful? The answer is going to have to be fairly abstract and not susceptible to disconfirmation, since we have only our own

BEAUTY

world to appreciate and nothing to compare it with. Thus the notion of "unity in variety" comes to the fore, often embellished with fanciful doctrines of ratio and proportion. Presumably Pythagorean in origin, these doctrines exercise a strange fascination over theorists and artists alike; by the time of the Renaissance they are a familiar obsession. As for the beauty of the *kosmos*, you can appreciate it without being a believer or thinking of the *kosmos* as a work of art. Because of the size and duration of the universe, you cannot *grasp* it as a whole, but this is not fatal: it can be seen as a limiting case of the difficulty of getting a fix on extremely long novels or operas. Nonetheless, it is a thought that impressed the medievals more than subsequent generations. It is perhaps echoed on a smaller scale in the reflections of philosophically unpretentious astronauts who have found our planet, seen from afar, fragile, solitary, and beautiful.

The story of the progressive institutionalization of the arts and of their elevation to a social status comparable with that of the professions has been told by historical scholars. Out of the miscellany of crafts and techniques – some messy and manual, like painting and sculpture, some intellectual and refined, like music and poetry – there emerged the notion of art as a unitary enterprise, and with it the belief that it was important to determine what the essential characteristics of art may be. The arts are obviously very different, and yet there does seem to be some bond. A straightforward and seemingly uncontentious suggestion is that works of art are artifacts that are beautiful; and that suggestion, although rarely accepted as adequate, lurks in the background of traditional theories of beauty. This explains the fact that, until the early nineteenth century, there is no sharp distinction between explications of beauty and explications of what we might call artistic excellence or merit. The big break came with Hegel, who worked on such questions as that suggested by passing queries of Horace's – namely, how much of an affinity does narrative poetry have with painting? What does the medium dictate? Is it illuminating to think of architecture as "frozen music"? Hegel's contribution was to propose that, while common people characterize as "beautiful" landscapes, plants, or animals that happen to please them,

this is a loose way of speaking. The only true beauty is that which is "born again of the mind," and hence to be found only in human beings and in the works of art that they create.

Hegel was the first to recognize that, although artistic beauty may be timeless, to understand a work from an alien or bygone culture requires research: you have to learn about the social, economic, and ideological context in which the work was produced. Conversely, once you get the point, you can use the work as a key to what Hegel refers to as "the spirit of the age." To the extent that "the philosophy of X" is conceived as an attempt to discover the meaning of X, Hegel's insight is the discovery that the philosophy of art, rather than being an independent subject, is identical with the history of art – or at any rate its history seen through the eyes of a philosopher. Hegel's own version is interesting. He believed that all history is at bottom a sort of psychobiography of "absolute spirit," in the course of which the subject undergoes dialectical vicissitudes; conflicts and contradictions are resolved and the resolution generates new contradictions. Hegel also put forward the peculiar hypothesis that art is about to come to an end and is to be replaced by a yet higher and more evolved spiritual form: namely, philosophy.

Academic aesthetics has accepted and absorbed one part of Hegel's legacy and ignored another part. What was accepted was the view that mere nature is aesthetically defective and just sits there in its dumb way as subject matter for the creative artist. This assumption, although understandable, has had some bad consequences for aesthetic theory. On the other hand, few aestheticians have appreciated the merit of Hegel's claims about the importance of history – which is why much of the best work in the philosophy of art has been done not by professional philosophers but by philosophically minded art historians and scholars.

What is wrong with taking philosophical aesthetics to be the study of art as distinct from such items as landscapes or persons or the universe as a whole? In a way, there is nothing wrong: when we believe of something marvelous that it was made by another human being, our admiration and interest acquire

170

added dimensions; we raise questions about technique, intentions, motives, feelings that would be inappropriate were the item in question taken to be the accidental product of natural forces. Besides, it may be that some works of art are more beautiful than any such product. Plato did not believe this and neither did Kant, but it still might be true.

The difficulty lies deeper, and has to do with our grasp of what it is to find something beautiful. There are works of art that you cannot appreciate or understand without some background and knowledge of the relevant conventions (Hegel's point): polyphony is chaotic to someone unfamiliar with counterpoint; Picasso looks primitive (or crazy) to someone who has never encountered anything other than anecdotal nineteenth-century painting. And yet, as one might put it, everything that is there *is there*. Acquaintance with Bach's fugues or the preoccupations of Cubist artists may lead you to notice features that you had not noticed before, but beliefs about a picture are not visual properties of the picture, and knowing how a fugue is supposed to work is not like adding a fourth voice. If you look and listen and are patient enough, then, even without instruction, you will eventually see what Picasso or Bach is up to. And then there are cases where you really do not *know*. John Dewey asks us to imagine an interesting little piece of stone that is first classified as a geological accident, then as an artifact, a tool, and then as an artifact that has a symbolic or aesthetic function – asks us to consider how it is moved from one museum to another and how we look at it in different ways depending on how it is described. Changes of belief may, but need not, affect appreciation: if I like the way the little thing looks or how it feels when I hold it in my hand, then my state is one of appreciation and I am on the threshold of a judgment of taste.

To say that only works of art are beautiful is as paradoxical as saying that only wrongful actions are bad. A terrible catastrophe occurs: someone says, "I can't say whether it was bad or not until I know whether it was deliberately brought about by an agent." We find ourselves in an alpine meadow bright with wild flowers: someone says, "I can't tell you whether this is beautiful or not until I know whether it is a garden."

Many people would find it enough to say that aesthetics covers any question that is directly or indirectly connected with criticism or the arts. All right – but then was not Baumgarten mistaken in thinking that he had discovered a new subject? One suggestion: works of art do have something in common, but it is not peculiar to works of art. Works of art are humanly made items that are preeminently beautiful. They exhibit a kind of goodness, although possibly in higher degree, that is also manifest in particular persons, rivers, mountains, animals, and plants. If this is so, philosophical aesthetics needs to return to the question of the nature of beauty and to try to develop the insights of past philosophers in a systematic way.

See also AESTHETICS IN ANTIQUITY; MEDIEVAL AND RENAISSANCE AESTHETICS; EIGHTEENTH-CENTURY AESTHETICS; AESTHETIC ATTITUDE; AESTHETIC JUDGMENT; AESTHETIC PROPERTIES; ARISTOTLE; "ARTWORLD"; DEWEY; HEGEL; HUME; KANT; PLATO; SANTAYANA; SUBLIME; TASTE; TESTIMONY IN AESTHETICS; THEORIES OF ART.

BIBLIOGRAPHY
Aristotle. 1941. *Poetics*. In *The Basic Works of Aristotle*. R. McKeon (ed.). New York: Random House.
Brand, Peg Zeglin (ed.). 2000. *Beauty Matters*. Bloomington: Indiana University Press.
Dewey, John. 1934. *Art as Experience*. New York: Minton, Balch.
Hegel, G. W. F. 1920 [1835–8]. *Philosophy of Fine Art*. 4 vols. F. P. B. Osmaston (trans.). London: G. Bell & Sons.
Hume, David. 1960 [1739]. *A Treatise of Human Nature*. L. A. Selby-Bigge (ed.). Oxford: Clarendon.
Hume, David. 1965 [1757]. *Of the Standard of Taste*. J. W. Lenz (ed.). New York: Bobbs-Merrill.
Kant, Immanuel. 1964 [1790]. *Critique of Judgement*. J. C. Meredith (trans.). Oxford: Clarendon.
Mothersill, Mary. 1984. *Beauty Restored*. Oxford: Clarendon.
Osborne, Harold. 1952. *Theory of Beauty*. London: Routledge.
Plato. 1920. *Ion, Symposium, Phaedrus, Republic*. B. Jowett (trans.). New York: Random House.
Santayana, George. 1902. *The Sense of Beauty*. New York: Scribner.
Zangwill, Nick. 2001. *The Metaphysics of Beauty*. Ithaca: Cornell University Press.

MARY MOTHERSILL

Bell, (Arthur) Clive (Heward) (1881–1964) British art critic; an early champion of Post-Impressionist and abstract art. Convinced that little had been so far achieved in aesthetics, Bell proposed a fresh start: a return to basic personal experience of authentic works of art. In his book *Art* (1914), he took as basic a distinctive "kind of emotion," "aesthetic emotion," and a quality "common and peculiar to all the objects that provoke it." In visual art, Bell's main concern, this quality must arise from certain "forms and relations of forms," "relations and combinations of lines and colours." Why these arouse aesthetic emotion we do not know: we have to postulate "unknown and mysterious laws" whereby particular forms constitute for us "significant form," as Bell labels it.

Creating and responding to significant form is a very different matter from furnishing and receiving *information* through purely descriptive, illustrative painting (e.g., William Powell Frith's *Paddington Station*); different, too, from evoking and reliving the varied emotions of human life. In authentic art, the painted forms are themselves the objects of our (aesthetic) emotion, not the "means of suggesting emotion and conveying ideas." The proper goal of art is not the perfecting of mimetic accuracy through technical virtuosity. For imitation, we now, in any case, have the camera. Where painting is concerned, if "a representative form has value, it is as form, not as representation."

What we should look for and hope to experience in art, then, is what we seldom experience in life outside art – the aesthetic thrill, rapture, or ecstasy. For all the inexhaustible variety of styles, idioms, and media throughout the history of art, the same thrill that testifies to significant form is the vital constant feature of genuine art. It is common to Sumerian sculpture, archaic Greek art, sixth-century Byzantine art; to Giotto, Poussin, and Cézanne, with his "insistence on the supremacy of significant form." But from the High Renaissance to the Impressionists, Bell sees numerous highly regarded painters as failing in the crucial respect. His aesthetic theory supported radical revisions in the estimation of artistic achievement, and in particular gave a theoretical warrant to the efforts of Roger Fry and Clive Bell himself to win acceptance for the artists of the first and second Post-Impressionist exhibitions in 1910 and 1912. (It is worth adding that much later in life, in his preface to the 1949 edition of *Art*, Bell allows that he spoke "absurdly and impertinently of the giants of the High Renaissance.")

With some diffidence, he now ventures a "metaphysical hypothesis." To experience the purely formal, we have to strip off the everyday human significance of objects in the world and abandon seeing them merely as means to our practical ends. To contemplate them as pure forms, as "ends in themselves" or "things in themselves," is to reach a vision of "ultimate reality," to become aware of "the God in everything . . . the all-pervading rhythm." Here "the chatter and tumult of material existence is unheard." Not surprisingly, Bell sets together "art and religion as twin manifestations of the spirit," two roads "to ecstasy." Similarly, there is no special problem, for Bell, in relating the values of art and the values of morality. In fulfilling its proper task of facilitating aesthetic experience, an intrinsically excellent state of mind, art ministers directly to one of the fundamental forms of goodness. Bell explicitly models his thinking here on G. E. Moore's *Principia Ethica* (1903).

Clive Bell's bold, unitary, simple theory of art has been a tempting target for criticism by analytical philosophers, skeptical of speculative systems as such. They have seen it as failing to present a genuinely informative verdict about human experience of art. His main concepts ("work of art," "aesthetic emotion," "significant form") constituted, rather, a self-supporting set, defined in terms of one another: they achieved no triumph of comprehensive explanation, since they were not really open to empirical confirmation or falsification. The analytical philosopher tended thus to dismiss Bell's theory as metaphysical in a bad sense, as simplistic or, indeed, vacuous. Nevertheless, there is some reason to see these critics as themselves simplifying and distorting Bell's position.

Bell certainly believed his theory to be anchored in individual experience – experience of one characteristic type evoked by art from primitives to Post-Impressionists. He cannot give a formula for what evokes it; but he knows that formal structures, not narrative or sentimental matter, are its source. Many readers of Bell, again, deny that there exists any distinctive aesthetic emotion. Should we not speak, instead, of the "aesthetic attitude," contemplatively disengaged from practical concerns (Dickie 1965)? But surely that would be too remote from what Bell meant by "aesthetic emotion," for we can take up an aesthetic attitude to an object which (because of its lack of satisfying formal unity) does not in the event sustain or reward that attitude. Closer to Bell might be a response of admiration, delight, and wonder to an individual achievement of formal unity. That would capture the essential receptivity, without insisting on a specific aesthetic emotion – though that too cannot be dogmatically denied (see Meager 1965).

Art was an eloquent and much needed reappraisal of sentimental, literary, and moralizing painting. Did it, however, react excessively against the according of aesthetic value to representation as such? Bell himself came to realize that there were complexities that he had shied away from in *Art*. More basically, though, the very distinction of "form" and represented "content" cannot be sharply maintained – a fact of high importance to aesthetic theory. In countless paintings, the way we apprehend the represented subject matter – its overall expressive quality – is a function of the design, pattern, and textures in and through which the subject matter is represented. So, too, the emotions, attitudes, and appraisals evoked by the *form* are inseparable from our awareness of what these same forms are representing. Those are, in fact, crucial strategies by which art intensifies and extends human experience. Again, where we perceive formal unity as being won from heterogeneous or conflictful materials, we can appreciate that triumph of the formal only if we also, and first, respond to the diversity and the tensions. We must experience the recalcitrance, the near refusal, of some (perhaps chaotic, or tragic) represented material to be contained and assimilated within any form, before we can appreciate fully the fact that a work of art *has* ordered and subdued it. In a word, the interplay and "fusion" of formal and representational elements needs a more complex and balanced exploration.

There is no doubt that aesthetic experience and religious experience can be very near

neighbors: for instance, a contemplative withdrawal of ordinary concepts and categories may feature in some mystical states of mind. Yet Bell is not a clear-headed guide in this area: he slides, rather than convincingly argues, from talk of nonutility perception to perception of objects as ends in themselves, as things-in-themselves, as reality, and as God in everything.

Bell should not be judged on one book alone. In his later writing, "significant form" became a more elusive quality, and art criticism correspondingly a more difficult and more fallible a task. Significant form may manifest itself in a shock or sudden thrill to the passive spectator, yielding a judgment that subsequent study in detail and depth cannot properly modify or overlay. Conversely, an analytical grasp of a work's form cannot reverse an unfavorable holistic emotional response. Form is "significant" in later Bell if, but only if, it cannot be further worked on, refined, simplified, and intensified by an artist in an artwork. Nature's forms are therefore not in the strong sense significant. They become so only when an artist realizes their potentiality (see also Elliott 1965).

See also TWENTIETH-CENTURY ANGLO-AMERICAN AESTHETICS; AESTHETIC ATTITUDE; AESTHETICISM; FORMALISM; LANGER; RELIGION AND ART.

BIBLIOGRAPHY

Primary sources
[1914] 1987. *Art*. 3rd edn. J. B. Bullen (intro.) Oxford: Oxford University Press.
1922. *Since Cézanne*. London: Chatto & Windus.
1934. *Enjoying Pictures*. London: Chatto & Windus.

Secondary sources
Dean, Jeffrey. 1996. "Clive Bell and G. E. Moore: The Good of Art," *British Journal of Aesthetics*, 36, 136–45.
Dickie, George. 1965. "Clive Bell and the Method of *Principia Ethica*," *British Journal of Aesthetics*, 2, 139–43.
Elliott, R. K. 1965. "Clive Bell's Aesthetic Theory and His Critical Practice," *British Journal of Aesthetics*, 2, 111–22.
Gould, Carroll. 1994. "Clive Bell on Aesthetic Experience and Aesthetic Truth," *British Journal of Aesthetics*, 34, 124–33.
Lake, Beryl. 1954. "A Study of the Irrefutability of Two Aesthetic Theories." In *Aesthetics and Language*. W. Elton (ed.). Oxford: Blackwell, 100–13.

Meager, Ruby. 1965. "Clive Bell and Aesthetic Emotion," *British Journal of Aesthetics*, 2, 123–31.

RONALD W. HEPBURN

Benjamin, Walter (1892–1940) German philosopher and cultural/literary critic; influenced as much by Jewish mysticism as by Surrealism and Marxism. Born in Berlin, he committed suicide at age 48 on the Franco-Spanish border. He is recognized as one of the most important literary critics and aesthetic theorists that Germany produced in the twentieth century.

Such recognition was belated however. Only after T. W. Adorno's 1955 publication of selections from his work did Benjamin become known to a wider public. Following decades of commentary in several languages, backed by a scholarly *Gesammelte Schriften* – from which were excerpted four volumes of *Selected Writings* (1996–2003) – Benjamin's place in the intellectual firmament of our time is assured. Yet his thought is famous for its obscurity, which stems from denseness of expression, the fragmentary nature of even the published works, and the apparent inconsistency of the positions he was drawn to in what he once called "the economy of my existence."

One interpretative problem lies in gauging how far Benjamin should be considered an aesthetic theorist at all. He took art to be subservient to theological, philosophical, and political concerns; he also came to assume it was at an end, its "aura" of authenticity now in decay. The ambiguity of his utterances may be seen in their diverse reception. He was brought to the attention of the Anglophone world by the 1969 publication of *Illuminations*, Hannah Arendt's selection of essays (a volume supplemented in 1978 by a second, *Reflections*). Implicitly – and openly in her introduction – Arendt denominated Benjamin a literary critic and "poetic thinker," so taking issue with other perspectives that would view him as primarily a philosopher (Adorno), a metaphysician of messianic bent (Gershom Scholem), or a political theorist whose engagement with historical materialism was more than "a contingent peccadillo or tolerable eccentricity" (Terry Eagleton).

It is not just Benjamin's legacy that is ambiguous: in his own lifetime he was different things to different friends and correspondents. The bewildering array of sources he drew on – from Kant to Surrealism – makes it especially difficult to characterize his thinking. Benjamin was a collector of both objects and quotations. He refused to follow any fashion or *Fach* (specialty), and it is no surprise that his intended doctoral dissertation on baroque *Trauerspiel* (tragic drama) was rejected as incomprehensible by the faculties of both philosophy and German literature at the University of Frankfurt. Benjamin's preferred method of "immanent criticism" – theoretical principles had to emerge from the material or work being studied – was really no method at all. There are, nevertheless, certain motifs running through his writings, which can be roughly sorted into two phases. The first – more metaphysical or theological – extends as far as his *Trauerspiel* book. A second – more political and materialist in orientation – goes from 1925 almost to the end of his life, and would include the enormous and unfinished *Passagenwerk* ("Arcades" Project).

BENJAMIN'S EARLY AESTHETICS

Benjamin's theory of art was always a theory of *experience* (*Erfahrung*). In his first essays he opposed the Neo-Kantians' reduction of experience to empirical terms and their refusal to allow the suprasensible as a possible object of knowledge. Influenced by Hamann, among others, he viewed language as originally unified but now – after the fall into profane temporality – fragmented, severed from divine law. He thought initially that metaphysical "mimesis" could capture the divine power of creative naming (for Benjamin, naming was the essence of language), so redeeming human experience. By the time of his 1919 thesis on German Romantic *Kritik* ("Concept of Criticism," *Selected Writings*, i. 116–200) he no longer supposed that philosophy could accomplish that. He suggested that art, however, was capable – at least, art completed by a criticism that would reveal its animating form or "idea." Benjamin's practice of "immanent criticism" remained true to this Romantic principle.

The principle found immediate application in a brilliant 1922 essay on Goethe's *Elective*

Affinities (*Selected Writings*, i. 297–360). Only in and through the novel's historical specificity would its inner truth emerge – a truth reminiscent of Benjamin's own Kantian ethic. Art occupies a fragile place between regression to mythic nature and election to moral grace. It offers no more than an image or "semblance" (*Schein*) of human unity with the divine, hence a measure of hope; it cannot itself "create."

Ambivalence toward art is found also in the work that sums up his early career, *The Origin of German Tragic Drama* (1924–5). At times it reads like a parody of the dissertation it was meant to be, scholarly footnotes jostling darkly brilliant insights and generalizations. Yet Benjamin wishes to avoid a universal aesthetics of tragedy; instead he aims to rehabilitate a specific historical genre, that of seventeenth-century Protestant *Trauerspiel*. Only after its specificity is grasped will he expand on its significance, its "truth content": historical commentary precedes interpretive criticism. The converse also holds, however: the historicity of artworks, he wrote, in a letter of December 1923 (1994: 224), emerges not in art history but only in interpretation.

The so-called "epistemo-critical prologue" to the work – one of the densest bits of prose anywhere – offers a unique reflection on his method. Benjamin aims at presentation (*Darstellung*) of the material in such a way that the timeless, monadic "ideas" shine through: "Ideas are to objects as constellations are to stars" (1977: 34). The metaphor of "constellation" supplies one of his main concepts: the configuration of phenomena "saves" them while also presenting their inner truth. The first, more historical section, though, is taken up with the description of *Trauerspiel*. Benjamin notes that this was taken as historical fact, not just theatrical device: the fallen state of history takes dramatic form. History is transposed to spatial form, in the self-enclosed world of stage or court; it is (as he puts it) "petrified" into nature. *Trauerspiel* tells sad stories of the death of kings, whether tyrants or martyrs. Compared with ancient tragedy, death appears radically contingent; the bodies pile up with the ruins of the world. In the second part of his treatise, Benjamin shifts beyond the externals of the artwork toward its inner truth or idea – namely, allegory. This is understood not as

conventional expression but as "expression of convention": that is, it reflects on the finitude of a world that has lost the wholeness of Greek tragedy. In turn, allegory becomes the emblem of a modernity now understood as secularized and mortified history. Here we glimpse what he calls the "smugglers' path" preserving an esoteric past (*Trauerspiel*) within present concerns (disenchantment, reification). Moreover, Protestant and melancholic contemplation is revealed as a historico-political practice – again, a secret path takes us to the political tendency in Benjamin's work.

THE TURN FROM THEORY

The *Trauerspiel* book contains the seeds of much that followed. Benjamin celebrates, yet also delimits, the momentary "semblance" of salvation art affords. The question he grappled with for the remainder of his life was this: how could this essentially theological model of interpretation be transposed into a historical and materialist register? While finishing his dissertation he had begun reading Georg Lukács, which, along with his meeting the young revolutionary Asja Lakis (who later introduced Benjamin to Brecht), helped make him a committed Marxist. Around this time too, he chanced on the work of the Surrealists, whose play on contingent juxtapositions of ordinary objects and investigation of dream logic left a lasting impression on his subsequent projects. The essay "Marseilles" carries an epigraph from André Breton which applies to much that came later: "The street . . . the only valid field of experience" (*Selected Writings*, ii. 232). In addition, fascination with Baudelaire and with dreams led Benjamin to write (2006b) about the experience of taking drugs: he was in search of an "aura" that would merge self and world, detect hidden similarities in all things.

Marxism and Surrealism are central to Benjamin's ultimate project, the intended book called "Paris, capital of the nineteenth century" (also known as the "Arcades" Project, after the glassed-in shopping streets he took as emblematic of emergent modernity). Here a montage of quotations – "citing without quotation marks" – was to take over the function "criticism" had previously performed. Benjamin termed its principle the "dialectical image" or "dialectics at a standstill." "When thinking reaches a standstill in a constellation saturated with tensions, the dialectical image appears. The image is the caesura in the movement of thought" (Benjamin 1999a: 475). In its initial conception the project juxtaposed representative personages (Fourier, Grandville, Louis-Philippe, Baudelaire, Haussmann) with physiognomic descriptions of the modern cityscape (World Exhibition, interior, *flâneur* sauntering through the arcade) taken as the commodified lifeworld, a "phantasmagoria" of nature. Later on, influenced by the support of the Institute for Social Research in New York, he made Baudelaire more central. The two essays he wrote (1973a) are a small but brilliant precipitate from a mass of notes. His formal procedure remains controversial, however. Adorno criticized it as too reductively materialist, suspended between "magic and positivism."

During the 1930s, Benjamin wrote several essays of remarkable originality on, for example, Proust, Nikolai Leskov, and Kafka (to whom he felt especially close). From his association with Brecht came a number of important studies on "epic theatre." Benjamin's materialism is on display in essays on photography, "The Author as Producer" (1934) and "The Work of Art in the Age of its Technological Reproducibility" (1935–6). This last – his most celebrated piece of writing – emphasizes conditions of reception. Technology may be taken as an extension of the lifeworld, but also as its opposite, the congealing or mortification of history. Photography and cinema have, he contends, supplanted the "aura" of traditional art (unique, individual, distanced) by communal experience and the immediate "shocks" of montage, yet may be of use in "politicizing art" and so counteract Fascism's "aestheticizing of politics." This again brought down Adorno's censure: he rejoined that Benjamin had overestimated the emancipatory potential of mass media while ignoring the critical function of autonomous art.

Benjamin's last word and testament (though he might not have considered it ready for publication) is "On the Concept of History" – 18 runic fragments shored against a disastrous time (Hitler–Stalin pact, Nazi occupation of Poland). Meaning and context are more than usually controversial, as Benjamin seems to revisit his initial messianism to invoke a "now-time" that would blast through the continuum of linear history. What remains constant throughout his life, however, is his antihistoricism, a commitment to rescuing the past in the name of the future, and a conviction that (to cite his Goethe essay) "only for the sake of the hopeless ones have we been given hope" (*Selected Writings*, i.356).

See also NINETEENTH- AND TWENTIETH-CENTURY CONTINENTAL AESTHETICS; ADORNO; LUKÁCS; MASS ART; TECHNOLOGY AND ART.

BIBLIOGRAPHY

Primary sources
1969. *Illuminations.* H. Zohn (trans.). New York: Schocken.
1973a. *Charles Baudelaire: A Lyric Poet in the Era of High Capitalism.* H. Zohn (trans.). London: New Left Books.
1973b. *Understanding Brecht.* A. Bostock (trans.). London: NLB.
1977. *The Origin of German Tragic Drama.* J. Osborne (trans.). London: NLB.
1978. *Reflections: Essays, Aphorisms, Autobiographical Writings.* E. Jephcott (trans.). New York: Harcourt Brace Jovanovich.
1979. *One-Way Street.* E. Jephcott & K. Shorter (trans.). London: NLB.
1986. *Moscow Diary.* R. Sieburth (trans.). Cambridge, MA: Harvard University Press.
1989. *The Correspondence of Walter Benjamin and Gershom Scholem, 1932–1940.* A. LeFevere (trans.). New York: Schocken.
1994. *The Correspondence of Walter Benjamin, 1910–1940.* M. Jacobson & E. Jacobson (trans.). Chicago: Chicago University Press.
1996–2003. *Selected Writings.* 4 vols. M. Bullock & M. Jennings (eds.). Cambridge, MA: Harvard University Press.
1999a. *The Arcades Project.* H. Eiland & K. McLaughlin (trans.). Cambridge, MA: Harvard University Press.
1999b. (with Adorno, T. W.) *The Complete Correspondence, 1928–1940.* N. Walker (trans.). Cambridge, MA: Harvard University Press.
2006a. *Berlin Childhood around 1900.* H. Eiland (trans.). Cambridge, MA: Harvard University Press.
2006b. *On Hashish.* Cambridge, MA: Harvard University Press.

Secondary sources
Brodersen, Momme. 1996. *Walter Benjamin: A Biography.* M. Green & I. Ligers (trans.). London: Verso.

Buck-Morss, Susan. 1989. *The Dialectics of Seeing: Walter Benjamin and the Arcades Project.* Cambridge. MA: MIT Press.

Ferris, David (ed.). 2004. *The Cambridge Companion to Walter Benjamin.* Cambridge: Cambridge University Press.

Löwy, Michael. 2005. *Fire Alarm: Reading Walter Benjamin's "On the Concept of History".* London: Verso.

Osborne, Peter (ed.). 2005. *Walter Benjamin: Critical Evaluations in Cultural Theory.* 3 vols. London: Routledge.

Rochlitz, Rainer. 1996. *The Disenchantment of Art: The Philosophy of Walter Benjamin.* New York: Guilford.

MARTIN DONOUGHO

Burke, Edmund (1729–1797)   Irish lawyer, politician, and, through his criticism of the French Revolution, a founder of modern conservative thought. Born and educated in Ireland, Burke graduated from Trinity College, Dublin. His reputation chiefly rests on his political career and writings: elected a Member of Parliament for the first time in the 1760s, he was the author of various trenchant political books and pamphlets, including the famous *Reflections on the Revolution in France* (1790). These have tended to overshadow his early *Philosophical Enquiry into the Origin of Our Ideas of the Sublime and Beautiful*, a contribution to aesthetics that was originally published in 1757 and reissued two years later in an enlarged edition. Some of the views it contains were anticipated by Joseph Addison's 1712 *Spectator* articles on "the pleasures of the imagination," and the introduction that Burke added to his second edition seems also to have been partly prompted by Hume's essay "Of the Standard of Taste," which had recently appeared. Nonetheless, the *Enquiry* was of importance in its own right. It attracted considerable attention in England, and an extended review by Moses Mendelssohn was instrumental in arousing a comparable interest in the book in Germany, where it impressed both Lessing and Kant.

In common with much nineteenth-century British work on aesthetics, Burke's investigation is essentially explanatory and genetic in character. A notable feature of his approach, however, lies in the manner in which he seeks to interpret aesthetic reactions in terms of certain universal instincts and sentiments that are basic to human nature. Drawing upon a division that had already acquired a limited currency but the appeal of which his own essay did a great deal to strengthen, he distinguishes between pleasures of the kind intrinsic to the experience of beauty and the specific form of "delight" that he attributes to the experience of the sublime. The source of the former is to be found in the "social passions," predominantly that of sex but also ones involving friendship and sympathy with others. The latter, by contrast, originates in our instinctual preoccupations with self-preservation, and turns "mostly on pain and danger." The *Enquiry* is largely taken up with showing how such primal proclivities operate to induce these two types of aesthetic response.

So far as the experience of the sublime is concerned, it is requisite that its objects be apprehended as being in some way "terrible" and hence capable of instilling fear or awe. Burke recognizes, however, that it seems paradoxical to suggest that we can derive satisfaction from phenomena that threaten our lives or wellbeing. The solution he offers is that the experience is typically confined to situations in which we are not ourselves placed in dangerous circumstances and only have an "idea" of these. Our sense of the fearful, in other words, is felt at a safe remove from the real thing; in consequence, it is able to tense and set in play "the finer parts of the system" in a fashion that is stimulating and invigorating without being noxious. As opposed to cases where we suffer actual terror, we are here conscious of a "sort of delightful horror," this being principally produced by images evocative of immense power or unfathomable dimensions.

Similar considerations are adduced when Burke comes to connect the awareness of beauty with such fundamental passions as love and sexuality. Just as the sublime is experienced when there is no question of our having to ward off or avoid a present danger, so experiences of the beautiful are distinguishable from those of "desire or lust" that "hurry us on" to the possession of certain coveted objects. Instead, the relevant sentiments are transposed to, and modified within, a setting where they exert no active influence; we are caused to respond to particular things in a purely contemplative frame of mind, the pleasure involved – unlike that of the sublime – deriving from their tendency to relax the "fibers" and "solids" of the whole system. As might be expected, the qualities Burke identifies as being especially well suited to effecting this happy outcome carry erotic overtones: he refers, for example, to smoothness (something explicitly attributed to the skins of "fine women"), gradual variation of the kind exemplified by "waving" and "serpentine" lines, and delicacy or fragility.

In his treatment of beauty Burke is insistent that it requires "no assistance from our reasoning" to appreciate it, and he goes to considerable if sometimes implausible lengths in denouncing classical theorists who invoked mathematical criteria of measurable proportion. Proportion is "a creature of the understanding," and as such it has no share in what properly belongs to "the senses and imagination." And a comparable emphasis on the crucial importance of perceptual immediacy and imaginative potential is also apparent in his account of the sublime. At the same time, however, he is at pains to stress the distinctive role these play in the latter. For there it is not formal grace and elegance, together with their sensuous associations, that elicit a psychophysiological reaction. On the contrary, it is characteristic of sublime objects or works of art that they should often be dark in tone and rugged or indistinct in outline. So presented, they are experienced as mysterious and obscure, conveying intimations whose full import eludes our conscious grasp and whose very indeterminacy is apt to arouse sensations of uncertainty or apprehension.

In making such claims, Burke helped to alter and enlarge the boundaries implicit in the taste and critical canons of his period: he may be regarded, furthermore, as on occasions anticipating themes that were to figure prominently in the subsequent development of Romantic modes of thought. When he insists at one point in the *Enquiry* on the failure of clear ideas or imagery to communicate impressions of grandeur, and when he asserts at another that "it is our ignorance of things that causes all our admiration and chiefly excites our passions," his remarks seem far removed in spirit from that of an age that – in art as elsewhere – put a premium on the ideals of perspicuous representation and rational intelligibility.

See also EIGHTEENTH-CENTURY AESTHETICS; BEAUTY; SUBLIME.

BIBLIOGRAPHY

Primary sources
[1757, 1759] 1958. *A Philosophical Enquiry into the Origin of Our Ideas of the Sublime and Beautiful.* J. T. Boulton (ed.). London: Routledge & Kegan Paul.

Secondary sources
Ayling, S. 1988. *Edmund Burke: His Life and Opinions.* London: John Murray.
Engell, J. 1981. *The Creative Imagination: Enlightenment to Romanticism.* Cambridge, MA: Harvard University Press.
Monk, S. H. 1960. *The Sublime.* Ann Arbor: University of Michigan Press.
Wood, N. 1964. "The Aesthetic Dimension of Burke's Political Thought," *Journal of British Studies,* 4, 41–64.

PATRICK GARDINER

C

canon The idiom of "canon" is relatively new in the theoretical debate about literature and art. Until the early 1960s there were, instead, debates about the nature, content, and value of traditions. The concept of tradition has not, of course, disappeared from the art critical vocabulary, but the concept has ceased to be the focus of an ongoing debate about the nature and value of past artworks and their relation to the art of the present. The concept of canon that came into use in the theory and criticism of art in the 1960s was in its origin theological. This theological concept of canon is applied with two important criteria: authenticity and authority. The canon of scripture has been fixed by the authoritative organs of the Church. No matter how violent the disagreement before such decisions are taken, the official decision settles the matter. The logical basis on which the Christian Church declares a work to be canonical is genetic: it has to be a text dealing with Old Testament or New Testament history which the Church decides is *inspired*. The connection between authority and the condition of authenticity is closely related: the authoritative organ decides whether or not a text fulfills the condition of being inspired. Thus, what appears to be the basic criterion for declaring a text canonical – that is, the criterion of authenticity (a text must be "genuine and inspired") – though it is logically independent from authority, has no independently *valid application*.

It is above all in the field of literary criticism that the concept of canon has been widely used. Within this field it is possible to distinguish three different applications of the concept with different relationships to the theological concept. First, it is used to designate those writings of a secular author accepted as authentic (*Oxford English Dictionary*). This concept, just like the theological one, has as its complementary the concept of apocrypha. There is a Shakespeare canon and a Shakespeare apocrypha. This concept of a secular canon embodies the element of authenticity but it does not have the implicit reference to authority. There is a good reason for this. The criterion of "inspired," which is the only criterion for inclusion in the scriptural canon, does not in itself dictate a protocol for testing whether a text is inspired or not. An authoritative decision is therefore indispensable in identifying an "inspired" text. However, there is a whole battery of tests available for deciding whether a text has been written by a particular individual, from eyewitness accounts and publication records to textual and stylistic evidence. Thus, it is quite clear in the case of literary authorship what would constitute evidence for authenticity, while in the scriptural case the criterion of inspiration provides little guidance as to what would constitute such relevant evidence.

A second concept of canon in use in literary criticism and theory is that of "a sanctioned or accepted group or body of related works" (*Merriam-Webster*). This is the concept of canon that first appears with a catalogue of authors in the fourth century specifically in relation to Christian literature. However, the practice of putting together a catalogue of selected authors arose long before the concept of "canon" was introduced. It can be traced back to the Alexandrian philologists who were the first to put together a selection of earlier literature for the use of grammarians in their schools (Curtius 1953). A catalogue of this kind involved the selection of model authors or, as they later were called, "classics." This notion of canon is closely tied to institutional teaching and learning. It can meaningfully and fruitfully be used about the list of works that various modern teaching institutions set for students of literature. It is different from the notion of a scriptural canon in that it contains no reference to authenticity. It does, however, embody the notion of authority. The choice of books in teaching institutions involves a selection, which has to be made by people in authority. The catalogue of authors and works is *prescribed* by a group of people who are, or who think they are or ought to be, in a position of authority to impose this list on those who are students of literature. However, in spite of the similar logical role which authority plays in fixing the application of the concept of "literary canon" and "canon of scripture," there is a difference between the *type* of authority to which the two concepts appeal as well as to the *scope* of that authority. The authoritative organ that determines the scriptural canon has a status and a role within the Church that the authorities who determine the literary canon do not have. The representatives to the National Conference on Uniform Entrance Requirements that was responsible for drafting the list of texts to be set for college entrance requirements in English in the US in 1894, and which was therefore responsible for establishing a list of canonical works that secondary schools would adopt, can hardly be compared in its authority with the Church Council of Trent. Literature has not developed the characteristics of a universal church with its notion of authority and the reliance upon dogma: there is no authoritative organ within the institution of literature which could constitute a universally valid canon of literature through a decision similar to official decisions taken by the authoritative organs of a worldwide church. There is within the institutions of literature and art a distinction between connoisseurs or adepts and the less able, between highly trained and sensitive practitioners who know how to read and interpret and who also have the necessary fund of knowledge about the institution and its social setting, and those who are less skilled and less knowledgeable. However, there are no rules that confer upon one group an absolute authority to take decisions about a canon.

A third concept of canon involves reference to "a general rule, fundamental principle, aphorism, or axiom governing the systematic or scientific treatment of a subject; *e.g.* canons of descent or inheritance; a logical, grammatical, or metrical canon; canons of criticism, taste, art,

etc." (*Oxford English Dictionary*). This rule or standard replaces the criterion of authenticity as the criterion for inclusion. The canon should comprise what is "best." The logical basis for pronouncing a work to be a canonical text of the scripture was genetic: it had to be authentic (genuine and inspired). Works are included in the literary canon on the basis that they conform to a standard. Thus, in the identification of a literary canon there is not the same close connection between authority and the condition for inclusion as there is in the identification of a canon of scripture. The standard of judgment and the values that a canon of literature is intended to exemplify can be *recognized without reference* to authority.

The canon in this sense is essentially contingent and plural. The choice of the standard to which the authors on the canonical list must conform will be determined by the immediate practical purposes that the catalogue of authors/works is aimed at serving. In antiquity the concept of the model author was oriented upon a grammatical criterion, the criterion of correct speech. The Middle Ages sought in their authors technical information, worldly wisdom, and general philosophy compressed into *sententia* and into descriptions of human excellence and weakness, *exempla*. The two standards invoked in the two different periods necessarily produced very different canons.

When the concept of a canon appeared in literary criticism in the 1960s it was with a new twist. The concept had the element of catalogue of model authors imposed by people in position of authority, but it was lifted out of the traditional context of institutional teaching and learning and applied to what had up to then been labeled the literary tradition. Expressions like "the Western canon" or "the canon of English literature" came into use, and these canons were then attacked for being arbitrary impositions of standards of value that somehow served the aims and purposes of those in authority who imposed these standards. The introduction of the idiom of "canon" into the literary critical debate had an ideological function. A canon, whether scriptural, juridical, or literary, is by its very nature contingent and imposed by authoritative fiat. Applying this notion to the literary tradition as defined through those works that had survived through time, one implied that this tradition was also a social construct embodying an "ideology," a set of values expressing the limited and constraining view of those who "dictated" the canon. There then arose a debate about the canon of literature and art in which some defended the canon, others attacked it for being in its nature pernicious, excluding or marginalizing certain socially defined groups. The question that was not raised was whether the notion of canon was an appropriate term to apply to the literary and artistic traditions and consequently whether the questions raised in the debate about the canon were real or just pseudo-questions.

The inadequacy of the concept of canon as an instrument in art criticism can be illustrated by a comparison with the concept it was replacing, that of "tradition." The notion of "artistic tradition" has four important elements that are absent from the concept of "canon." It is tied to the notion of a practice, to the notion of a way of doing things, a way of writing, a way of painting, a way of reasoning that has built into it a set of standards and a notion of skill. The great works of a tradition are great not because they are pronounced to be great but because they display to a high degree the required skill and meet the requirements of the tradition in an exemplary manner. Second, a tradition has continuity: it is handed down. The notion of tradition captures the continuity as well as the development that is constituted not only through the similarities and differences between literary works since Homer, but also through the acts of authors of all periods of placing themselves self-consciously in relations of opposition and/or discipleship to earlier writers as well as to writers contemporary with themselves. Third, a tradition is anonymous, an "immemorial usage": no named authority is responsible for or can *create* a tradition. A tradition develops. However, it cannot be changed by authoritative fiat as can a "canon." Finally, the notion of tradition is linked to the notion of culture: a tradition is a "cultural continuity in social attitudes, customs, and institutions" (*Merriam-Webster*). Traditions are culturally embedded and are by their nature local and culturally specific. Different cultures and different language communities have different literary traditions closely linked to what is perceived as the identity of a culture and of a language community. That is why literature has sometimes played such an important role in the definition of national identity at times of struggle for political and cultural independence. It is also one of the reasons for the continuity and stability of the literary tradition: it is one of the identity markers of a culture. However, different traditions can be culturally specific and can nevertheless involve the same types of skill and the same standards. To what extent they actually do is an empirical question, and if traditions become too different in the demands they make on their practitioners, they will no longer be the same kind of tradition.

The debate about the canon misses all these points. There will always be debate within a culture about the canon that teaching institutions should use. This discussion can only take place against the background of a recognized tradition. And it cannot be extended into a discussion of the tradition without seriously distorting some of the fundamental issues that a discussion about any artistic tradition will raise.

See also LITERATURE; CRITICISM; FEMINIST AESTHETICS; FEMINIST STANDPOINT AESTHETICS; RACE AND AESTHETICS; TRADITION.

BIBLIOGRAPHY

Alter, Robert. 2000. *Canon and Creativity: Modern Writing and the Authority of Scripture.* New Haven: Yale University Press.

Bloom, Harold. 1994. *The Western Canon: The Books and School of the Ages.* New York: Harcourt Brace.

Crowther, Paul. 2007. *Defining Art, Creating the Canon: Artistic Value in an Era of Doubt.* Oxford: Oxford University Press.

Curtius, Ernst Robert. 1953. *European Literature and the Latin Middle Ages.* W. R. Trask (trans). London: Routledge & Kegan Paul.

Gorak, Jan. 1990. *The Making of The Modern Canon: Genesis and Crisis of a Literary Idea.* London: Athlone.

Hallberg, Robert von (ed.). 1984. *Canons.* Chicago: University of Chicago Press.

Leavis, F. R. 1960 [1948]. *The Great Tradition.* London: Chatto & Windus.

Olsen, Stein Haugom. 2001. "The Canon and Artistic Value," *British Journal of Aesthetics*, 41, 261–79.

Oppel, Herbert. 1937. *Kanon: Zur Bedeutungsgeschichte des Wortes und seiner lateinischen Entsprechungen (regula-norma).* Leipzig: Dieterich'sche Verlagsbuchhandlung.

Ross, Trevor. 1998. *The Making of the English Literary Canon: From the Middle Ages to the Late Eighteenth Century.* Montreal: McGill-Queen's University Press.

Smith, Barbara Herrnstein. 1988. *Contingencies of Value: Alternative Perspectives for Critical Theory.* Cambridge, MA: Harvard University Press.

STEIN HAUGOM OLSEN

catharsis The term (literally, "cleansing") used by Aristotle for part of the psychological experience and effect of tragedy. Its interpretation is fraught with difficulties; the view adopted here is tentative. The definition of tragedy in *Poetics* 6 speaks of the genre "accomplishing through pity and fear the catharsis of such emotions." Aristotle subsequently refers often to pity and fear (a widely accepted Greek formula for responses to tragedy) but no explanation of the term "catharsis" is forthcoming in the work.

In *Politics* 8.7, however, Aristotle says of music that it should be used "both for education and for catharsis," adding: "what I mean by catharsis I shall state simply now; I will discuss it again more clearly in my treatment of poetry." (The cross-reference might be to his early dialogue *On Poets*, now lost, or to the missing second book of the *Poetics*.) He comments there on variable susceptibility to strong emotions such as pity, fear, and "enthusiasm" (here a kind of frenzy), and he notes how, in the case of the last, there are religious rituals in which special music is used to arouse the emotion and allow those gripped by it to find "as it were a cure and a catharsis." But other people experience something of the same kind ("a certain catharsis and pleasurable alleviation") according to their emotional dispositions. So it is important that Aristotle here posits both "pathological" and "normal" emotional catharsis in response to certain kinds of music. Whether there was any link with what Aristotle's pupil Aristoxenus tells us about the Pythagoreans, that they "achieved catharsis of the soul through music," we cannot now be sure.

The relevance of the *Politics* passage to tragic catharsis has sometimes been disputed. But this is unreasonable, since Aristotle explicitly indicates a connection with his views on poetry. It is possible to infer several things about nonpathological catharsis from *Politics* 8.7: first, that it is neither religious nor medical (though it has analogies in both domains); second, that *through* an experience of certain emotions a change occurs *in* (a disposition for) those emotions; third, that where music (and presumably poetry too) is concerned, catharsis is dependent on the art's general capacity to arouse and shape emotion (and thereby, as *Politics* 8.5 puts it, "to change the soul"); fourth, that catharsis is aligned with, and perhaps even consists in, the conversion of *painful* emotions into pleasure.

Those implications, when combined with the fact that for Aristotle emotions are intricately bound up with ethical perceptions and impulses, encourage us to relate tragic catharsis to the *Poetics*' conception of pity and fear as a heightened but cognitively grounded response to the patterns of human suffering embodied in a plot structure. On this reading, tragic catharsis is no mere discharge or "purgation" of emotion, something that makes no sense in terms of Aristotle's moral psychology. Catharsis must be closely associated with, but need not be identical to, tragic pleasure: it is perhaps best interpreted as the cumulative psychological satisfaction and benefit accruing from the transformation of painful into pleasurable emotions through imaginative contemplation of an appropriately unified artwork. This will fit with Aristotle's larger views by making experience of tragedy one way of attuning a spectator's dispositions to an ethical "mean" (i.e., the right degree of feeling): the emotions aroused will be intense but fully justified by the structure of "action and life" enacted.

The lack of a direct Aristotelian explanation of tragic catharsis has stimulated a complex history of interpretation (Halliwell 1998: app. 5). For most sixteenth- and seventeenth-century neoclassicists, the idea became heavily moralized and colored by Stoic presuppositions: catharsis, mediated by the "lessons" of tragedy, involved extirpation of dangerous passions and/or acquisition of emotional fortitude. Something closer to a model of psychological harmonization was advocated by Lessing. Jacob Bernays reacted against such views in an influential monograph of 1857, limiting catharsis to a quasi-medical discharge of feeling. Catharsis as purgation consequently became an academic orthodoxy (now waning); it was adhered to by, among others, Nietzsche, in a series of dismissive references to Aristotle's *Poetics*. Bernays's influence also encompassed Sigmund Freud (who married Bernays's niece). And it is the entanglement of catharsis with psychoanalytic ideas that has given the term a ubiquitous currency in the modern world: one word in the *Poetics* has been transformed into a protean concept of popular aesthetic psychology.

See also AESTHETICS IN ANTIQUITY; MEDIEVAL AND RENAISSANCE AESTHETICS; DRAMA; ARISTOTLE; FICTION, THE PARADOX OF RESPONDING TO; PLATO.

BIBLIOGRAPHY
Halliwell, Stephen. 1998. *Aristotle's Poetics*. 2nd edn. London: Duckworth.
Halliwell, Stephen. 2003. "La psychologie morale de la catharsis: un essai de reconstruction." *Les Études Philosophiques*, 4, 499–517.
Kraut, Richard (trans. & comm.). 1997. *Aristotle: Politics Books VII and VIII*. Oxford: Clarendon.
Lear, J. 1988. "*Katharsis*," *Phronesis*, 33, 297–326.
Nussbaum, Martha C. 1992. "Tragedy and Self-Sufficiency: Plato and Aristotle on Fear and Pity." In *Essays on Aristotle's Poetics*. A. O. Rorty (ed.). Princeton: Princeton University Press, 261–90.

STEPHEN HALLIWELL

Cavell, Stanley (b.1926) American philosopher of skepticism, language, literature, and film at Harvard University. Cavell's contributions to aesthetics move in two directions: (1) toward his own guiding project of diagnosing and undermining skepticism, which he characterizes as an issue not only for philosophy but also for poetry, drama, and film; and (2) toward issues and problems within specific fields of criticism and within works of art or literature. These directions in turn contain prospects for a unity that helps to structure – though it cannot eliminate – the inveterate plurality of Cavell's investigations. Ultimately, this unity derives from the possibility that the various versions of skepticism are, in fact, various guises of a single, self-inflicted threat to human existence. He characterizes the threat of skepticism as the most recent and perhaps the most destructive version of the ancient wish to escape the human being's situation within language and history. What philosophy knows as Cartesian or Humean skepticism is only the most intellectually refined expression of this skeptical wish.

Cavell's most detailed effort to undermine epistemological skepticism takes the form of a reading of Wittgenstein (Cavell 1979). As in Wittgenstein, the terms of Cavell's investigations bear obvious affinities to some of the crucial enterprises and concepts of aesthetics. He modifies the enormous importance that Wittgenstein attaches to the possibilities and necessities of human judgment, including features of what other philosophers take to be its mere contingencies: for instance, its agreements, its evaluations, its publicness, and its persistent privacies. Cavell goes on to characterize the philosophical power of Wittgenstein's *Philosophical Investigations* as resting on written recollections and achievements of the human voice in its most ordinary settings. He thus isolates a dimension of Wittgenstein – and perhaps of philosophizing as such – that is potentially of special interest to students of aesthetics.

Cavell characterizes skepticism as embodying a wish to repudiate the "givenness" of language and the apparent arbitrariness in the fact that human beings must express themselves in order to be understood. Accordingly, he characterizes as skeptical the precarious efforts to reconstruct human language and communication on a more "rational" or more "justified" foundation, one which would avoid the need for the less tidy and more disruptive aspects of ordinary speech. The overcoming of skepticism will occur not as a single theoretical event but as the repeated, practical efforts to recover human expressiveness from its suppression in philosophical and antiphilosophical theorizing. Some philosophers have found Cavell's responses to skepticism to constitute a merely literary solution to an intellectual problem. Students of aesthetics might follow Cavell and Wittgenstein in exploring a less reductive sense of human expression and hence a more interesting access to the literary conditions of philosophical questioning.

Cavell persistently tracks something like an aesthetic dimension of judgment and expression throughout the fields of epistemology, morality, and the philosophy of language. It is therefore not surprising that his work leaves little room for the idea of a set of intrinsically aesthetic problems, which might be treated in isolation from the rest of philosophy. Furthermore, it is of the essence of his approach to aesthetic questions that his work attempts to take on the issues of the critics that matter the most to him. Cavell's primary concern is to address the insights and mystifications of those critics, readers, and viewers (himself included) who have already felt the pull of the particular work or experience in question. His investigations often move directly from the individual work (for instance, of Shakespeare or of film) to the issues of philosophy. Those who have felt the power and the exactness of his readings are unlikely to see the pertinence of the more generalized issues of academic aesthetics. Nevertheless, it is possible to specify some lines of investigation in Cavell's work that either belong explicitly to aesthetics or else can be seen to bear on the wider issues of literature and interpretation that increasingly occupy the attention of philosophers concerned with the arts. These aesthetic investigations can be divided into six major segments.

(1) The essays collected as his first book (1976a) include his most explicit treatments of specific aesthetic questions about intentions, pleasure, metaphor, musical form and "significance," literary or dramatic genres and artistic media, and the relationship of aesthetics to criticism. This first book also includes extended instances of his critical activities (climactically, his essays on Samuel Beckett and *King Lear*), as well as a sort of Wittgensteinian proposal for the centrality of aesthetics within a newly self-critical practice of philosophy.

(2) Cavell's investigations of Shakespeare (2002) have secured him a place as one of the leading literary critics of his generation. He continues to delineate his sense of the isomorphism between the convulsions of philosophy inaugurated in Descartes's methods of representative self-doubt and Shakespeare's preoccupation with the catastrophes in human knowing and with the traumatic constructions of the modern world. Perhaps because of their

resistance to regarding a work of literature as harboring anything like the propensity for rigorous thought, Anglo-American philosophers have found this side of Cavell's project to be essentially inaudible.

(3) His work on film begins with an exploration of the relations between the photographic basis of the movies and their specific incarnation of narrative possibilities (1976b, 1981). He comes to focus on the possibilities contained primarily within two genres: "the comedy of remarriage" and "the melodrama of the unknown woman" (1996).

(4) His work on the relation of literary Romanticism to the critique and transformation of Kant begins with a book on Thoreau (1992) and becomes a central theme of his Beckman lectures (reprinted in 1988a). The issue of Kant's inheritance is at the center of his continuing encounters with Emerson. His stress on an Emersonian, antimetaphysical strand of moral perfectionism – stretching from certain regions of Kant to Wittgenstein and Heidegger – leads him to his most prolonged, recent confrontation (1990) with American philosophy, as represented by John Rawls and Saul Kripke.

(5) Again beginning with Thoreau, Cavell has steadily intensified his excavation of a problematic of reading, with a consequent emphasis on the fact of writing as a source and emblem of human activity and originality (1979, 1988a, 1990).

(6) Finally, there is an increasingly explicit involvement with psychoanalysis that needs to be distinguished from other contemporary approaches. Cavell treats Freud's work neither as a perfected methodology of interpretation nor as the enlargement of our narrative capacity for self-dramatization. In Cavell's account, the goal of a psychoanalytic reading is, above all, a better understanding of our prior seduction or bewitchment by the work, an understanding which frees us for a still more unsheltered engagement with the work's significance and fascination.

Cavell's use of psychoanalysis to create the freedom for a further encounter with the work can thus stand as an expression of one of his earliest motives for thinking about the arts. Already in his concern with the inescapability of intentions in our experience of art and in his related struggles against false pictures of the "inside" and "outside" of the work, Cavell has sought to block the idea that the significance of art can be appreciated from some safely externalized distance. Here, as elsewhere, he sees philosophy as crystallizing the human inclination to imagine ourselves exempt from the seductions of experience on the grounds that we are capable of analyzing it. But philosophy is also a name for the place in which we might learn that there is no separate place from which to learn the significance of human works and expressions, apart from submitting to the specific demands they make on our capacities for understanding and response.

In Cavell's account, the task of aesthetics is to maintain the still more basic and ineradicable demand that we submit ourselves to the experiences that we are drawn to learn from. (This version of Kant demands that we submit the object to our own eyes, for our own judgment.) But this thought goes together with his insistence that we bear in mind those ordinary surfaces of words and concepts and events, without which the struggle with the depths of our experience of a work is bound to lose its sense.

See also CRITICISM; MORALITY AND ART; PSYCHO-ANALYSIS AND ART; WITTGENSTEIN.

BIBLIOGRAPHY

Primary sources
[1969] 1976a. *Must We Mean What We Say?* 2nd edn. Cambridge: Cambridge University Press.
[1971] 1976b. *The World Viewed: Reflections on the Ontology of Film.* Enlarged edn. Cambridge, MA: Harvard University Press.
[1972] 1992. *The Senses of Walden: An Expanded Edition.* Chicago: University of Chicago Press.
1979. *The Claim of Reason: Wittgenstein, Scepticism, Morality and Tragedy.* Oxford: Oxford University Press.
1981. *Pursuits of Happiness: The Hollywood Comedy of Remarriage.* Cambridge, MA: Harvard University Press.
[1987] 2002. *Disowning Knowledge in Seven Plays of Shakespeare.* Expanded edn. Cambridge: Cambridge University Press.
1988a. *In Quest of the Ordinary: Lines of Skepticism and Romanticism.* Chicago: University of Chicago Press.
1988b. *Themes Out of School: Effects and Causes.* Chicago: University of Chicago Press.

1989. *This New Yet Unapproachable America: Lectures After Emerson After Wittgenstein.* Albuquerque: Living Batch.
1990. *Conditions Handsome and Unhandsome: The Constitution of Emersonian Perfectionism.* Carus Lectures, 1988. Chicago: University of Chicago Press.
1996. *Contesting Tears: The Hollywood Melodrama of the Unknown Woman.* Chicago: University of Chicago Press.
2004. *Cities of Words: Pedagogical Letters on a Register of the Moral Life.* Cambridge, MA: Harvard University Press.
2005a. *Cavell on Film.* W. Rothman (ed.). Albany: State University of New York Press.
2005b. *Philosophy the Day After Tomorrow.* Cambridge, MA: Harvard University Press.

Secondary sources
Cohen, Ted & Guyer, Paul (eds.). 1992. *Pursuits of Reason: Essays in Honor of Stanley Cavell.* Lubbock: Texas Tech Press.
Eldridge, Richard (ed.). 2003. *Stanley Cavell.* Cambridge: Cambridge University Press.
Fischer, Michael. 1989. *Stanley Cavell and Literary Skepticism.* Chicago: University of Chicago Press.
Fleming, Richard & Payne, Michael (eds.). 1989. *The Senses of Stanley Cavell.* Lewisburg: Bucknell University Press.
Goodman. Russell B. (ed.). 2005. *Contending with Stanley Cavell.* Oxford: Oxford University Press.
Gould, Timothy. 1998. *Hearing Things: Voice and Method in the Writings of Stanley Cavell.* Chicago: University of Chicago Press.
Hammer, Espin. 2002. *Stanley Cavell: Skepticisim, Subjectivity, and the Ordinary.* Cambridge: Polity.
Mulhall, Stephen (ed.) 1996. *The Cavell Reader.* Cambridge, MA: Blackwell.
Smith, Joseph & Kerrigan, William (eds.). 1987. *Images in Our Souls: Cavell, Psychoanalysis and Cinema.* Baltimore: Johns Hopkins University Press.

TIMOTHY GOULD

censorship In its broadest sense, censorship is any kind of suppression or regulation, by government or other authority, of a writing or other means of expression, based on its content. The main concern with censorship applies to kinds of work intended for sale, display, or other manner of publication, though the term has been applied to the official activity of removing sensitive information from private letters written home by troops serving in war. It seems that the activity has at least to be publicly recognized in order to count as censorship, and interference with the mail by the secret police, or covert intimidation of editors, would be examples of something else. Accordingly, any censorship implies a public claim of legitimacy for the type of control in question.

The most drastic methods of control involve *prior restraint*: a work is inspected before it is published, and publication may be forbidden, or permitted only after changes have been made. Traditional absolutist regimes sought to control book publication by these means, and legal procedures to the same general effect, for the control of material affecting national security, still exist in many states. Until 1968, theatrical performances in England were controlled in this way by a court official, the Lord Chamberlain, whose staff monitored scripts before production, would demand changes on a variety of grounds (including disrespect to the monarchy), and attended performances to see that their instructions were being observed. In many jurisdictions, cinema films are inspected by some official agency before release, and its powers may include that of suppressing some or all of a film. However, the emphasis of these inspections has increasingly moved from suppression to labeling, the agency not so much censoring films as classifying them by their suitability for young people.

Prior restraint is essential when censorship is motivated by official secrecy: once the information is out, the point of censoring it is lost. (The English government attracted ridicule in the 1980s by trying to ban a book on security grounds that had already been published elsewhere.) There are other aims of censorship, however, including those most relevant to aesthetics, which do not necessarily demand prior restraint. If a work is thought objectionable on grounds of indecency, evil moral character, or its possible social effects, the suppression of it after publication may still have a point, in limiting people's exposure to it. Actions of this kind, and laws under which they can be carried out, are also regarded as examples of censorship. This form of censorship avoids some of the objections to prior restraint – notably, its secrecy – and it is in relation to this kind of censorship that questions of principle are now normally discussed. It is important that censorship in this form still aims at suppression.

Schemes of restriction or zoning, which require, for instance, that pornographic materials be sold only in certain shops and only to adults, are analogous to film classification, and are to be distinguished from censorship, strictly understood.

In 1774 Lord Mansfield said "Whatever is *contra bonos mores et decorum* the principles of our laws prohibit, and the King's Court as the general censor and guardian of the public morals is bound to restrain and punish." Although this dictum was approvingly mentioned by another English law lord as recently as 1962, few now would offer quite such a broad justification for censorship. In part, this is because of doubts about what "the public morals" are, and by whom they are to be interpreted: pluralism, skepticism, sexual toleration, and doubts about the social and psychological insight of judges have played their part in weakening confidence in the notion. A more basic point is that, even where there is a high degree of moral consensus on a given matter, it remains a question what that may mean for the law, and what, if anything, can count as a good reason for using the law in an attempt to suppress deviant opinions or offensive utterances. Liberal theories claim that freedom of expression is a right, which can be curtailed only to prevent serious and identifiable harms. This is, in effect, the conclusion reached by John Stuart Mill in his very influential defense of freedom of expression, though he himself did not theoretically favor the notion of a right. Other liberals who are better disposed to that notion insist, further, that the harms that justify suppression must take the more particular form of a threatened violation of someone's rights.

A very strong version of such principles is embodied in United States law, which has interpreted the First Amendment to the Constitution ("Congress shall make no law . . . abridging the freedom of speech or of the press") in such a way as to make censorship on any grounds very difficult. Mr. Justice Holmes in 1919 produced an influential formula. "The question in every case is whether the words used are used in such circumstances and are of such a nature as to create a clear and present danger that they will bring about the substantive evils that Congress has a right to prevent"; and restrictions in such terms have been taken to protect even overtly racist demonstrations, let alone publications. The "clear and present danger" test is not used with regard to pornography, but the effect of Supreme Court decisions in that area has been that, at most, hard-core pornography can be suppressed. In many parts of the US, all that the law enforces are zoning restrictions.

English law allows greater powers of suppression than that of the US: publications designed to arouse racial hatred, for instance, may be illegal, and the same is true in other jurisdictions. In the case of pornography, the main concept used in English law is *obscenity*: in a formula inherited from a judgment of Chief Justice Cockburn in 1868, the principal statute defines a publication as obscene if it has a "tendency to deprave or corrupt" those exposed to it. This professedly causal concept of obscenity implies that the rationale of the law is to be found in the harmful consequences of permitting a particular publication. However, as the House of Lords has itself observed, the courts could not apply this formula in a literal sense, and do not really try to do so. No expert evidence is allowed on the matter of causation, and in practice the question is whether a jury or a magistrate finds the material sufficiently offensive. As critics have pointed out, this not only makes the application of the law arbitrary but reopens the question of its justification. As opposed to the principle that rights to free speech may be curtailed by appealing to harms in the particular case – the principle that Holmes's "clear and present danger" test expresses in a very strict form – the mere fact that a work is found deeply offensive is likely to justify its suppression only to those who think that it is the business of the law to express any correct, or at least shared, moral attitude.

There has been a great deal of controversy about the effects of pornographic and violent publications, and a variety of anecdotal, statistical, and experimental evidence has been deployed in attempts to find out whether there is a causal link between such publications and some identifiable class of social harms, such as sexual crime. It is perhaps not surprising that such studies are inconclusive, and more recent advocates of censorship, such as some radical feminists, have moved away from thinking of censorship in this area on the model of a public

health measure, and concentrate on the idea that certain publications unacceptably express a culture of sexual oppression. This approach tends to treat legal provisions against pornography as like those against publications that endorse racial discrimination. In some systems, of course, this would still not make such censorship constitutional, even if the problem can be solved of making the provisions determinate enough for them not to be void on account of uncertainty.

Censorship laws typically encounter problems about artistic merit. The English law is not alone in allowing a "public good defence," which permits acquittal of a work that possesses serious aesthetic, scientific, or other such merits. (In English law a jury who acquit in a case where this defense has been made are not required to say whether they found the work not to be obscene, or found it meritorious although it was obscene.) Provisions of this kind have certainly helped to permit the publication of serious works such as *Ulysses* and *Lady Chatterley's Lover*, which were previously banned; but there are difficulties of principle, which have been clearly illustrated in the English practice of allowing expert testimony on the merits of the works under prosecution. Besides the inherent obscurity of weighing artistic merit against obscenity, and the fact that evidence bearing on this has to be offered under the conditions of legal examination, the process makes the deeply scholastic assumption that the merit of a given work must be recognizable to experts at the time of its publication. Moreover, the works that can be defended under such a provision must presumably be meritorious, which implies that they are to some considerable degree successful; but if a law is to protect creative activity from censorship, it needs to protect the right to make experiments, some of which will be very unsuccessful.

The idea of making *exceptions* to a censorship law for works with artistic merit seems, in fact, essentially confused. If one believes that censorship on certain grounds is legitimate, then if a work of artistic merit does fall under the terms of the law, it is open to censorship: its merits, indeed, may make it more dangerous, on the grounds in question, than other works. If one believes in freedom for artistic merit, then one believes in freedom, and accepts censorship only on the narrowest of grounds.

See also EROTIC ART AND OBSCENITY; ICONOCLASM AND IDOLATRY; MORALITY AND ART; PORNOGRAPHY.

BIBLIOGRAPHY
Devlin, Lord. 1959. *The Enforcement of Morals*. Oxford: Oxford University Press.
Dworkin, Ronald. 1985. *A Matter of Principle*. Cambridge, MA: Harvard University Press.
Hart, H. L. A. 1963. *Law, Liberty and Morality*. Oxford: Oxford University Press.
Mill, John Stuart. 1983 [1859]. *On Liberty*. In *On Liberty and Other Writings*. S. Collini (ed.). Cambridge: Cambridge University Press, 1–116.

BERNARD WILLIAMS

Chinese aesthetics   In China the arts played much the same role in the history of philosophy that science performed in the West. Classical philosophers in Greece and China investigated the origin of sensory, aesthetic knowledge, assessed its reliability, and debated its importance. In the West, sight was assumed to be the most important sense and wisdom was described in terms of "vision" and "insight." In classical China, hearing was considered at least as important as sight and the Chinese sage was often a person of acute hearing.

METAPHYSICS AND MUSIC
The difference in epistemological metaphors was significant. Western philosophers typically conceived of reality as composed of two kinds of things: visible physical objects and invisible mental ones, understood as a special kind of object, a mental image or picture. Since the epistemological problem was to know when and how the mental objects represented, corresponded to, or otherwise correctly reflected physical reality, philosophers seldom considered the representation of "fictions" as important as the discovery of "facts," that is, scientific and metaphysical truths.

Given the importance of hearing in early Chinese theorizing about the senses, the fundamental metaphysical metaphor was sound and the air or wind that carries it. Wind and sound are powerful forces that influence faraway things with no visible connection between them. Music seems particularly powerful in this respect, since notes from one instrument can resonate with distant instruments causing them to produce the same tone. Like the air we breathe, sound penetrates the human body, creating a harmony between sounds in different places in the world. Because it is difficult to understand sound as "representing" anything, in Chinese metaphysics the cosmos was made up of "psychophysical energy" or *qi*, rather than as a system of discrete objects, one of which copied or represented the other. Unlike Western conceptions of order that classify objects by their relationship to logical concepts, Chinese conceptions of order are described as "aesthetic." An aesthetic order seeks allusions, analogies, and associations reflecting the mutual influence, resonances, and harmonies of *qi* in different locations in the universe. Thus, sound in general, and music in particular, became the key to understanding natural phenomena and the interactions between humankind and nature.

China is the only society where standard measurements were based on the pitches of perfectly tuned bells. The tones of the chromatic scale were correlated to the divisions of the year, establishing a cosmic connection between music and time. Since determining the calendar is particularly important in an agricultural society like China, control of high-quality precisely tuned bells was a symbol of governmental authority.

AESTHETICS AND MORALITY
Moreover, just as the tones of a bell reflected the cosmic order of the seasons, the moral order of a society was reflected in (and influenced by) its music. In early Chinese psychology, humans have a single organ, the "heart-mind" or *xin* that thinks and feels, and according to the ancient *Book of Documents*: "Poetry expresses the heart's intent." The human heart-mind is in a state of tranquility until it responds to something outside itself in poetry, song, and dance. Musicians, poets, and dancers move audiences to respond in similar ways, creating a human community. Because the social harmony between people contributes to the harmony between humanity and the cosmos, the relationship between the arts, morality, and cosmic order are an enduring theme in Chinese aesthetics.

Daoist aesthetics looked for harmony with nature, while the Confucians focused on social harmony; neither of them looked for an abstract set of laws or principles under which behavior could be classified and evaluated. Given the intimate association of music, ritual, and order, the music of a state was said to reflect its moral order. Government officials collected folk songs to understand the ambitions, joys, and complaints of the people. The earliest collection of Chinese poetry, *Classic of Odes*, was said to be such a collection of folk songs and dynastic hymns edited by Confucius himself. Confucius argued that reciting the *Odes* and understanding their many levels of meaning was an essential part of a good education.

Although the *Odes* describe natural scenes, feelings of love and longing, hunting parties, and farming rituals, they were interpreted as allegories and allusions, reminding readers of associated images, historical events, and moral principles and provoking an appropriate range of emotional responses. Chinese poetry is not primarily intended to describe reality or narrate a heroic epic, but to express the poet's emotions and personality and inspire listeners to respond in an appropriate way.

POETRY, CALLIGRAPHY, AND PAINTING

Poetry, calligraphy, and painting were intimately connected because they use a brush to express the moods and feelings of the artist. Just as poetic images are interpreted as allusions rather than descriptions, in calligraphy the subject matter of a piece of writing is all but irrelevant to its aesthetic value. Particular brush strokes are discussed in terms relating to the human body (bone, muscles, blood), the human spirit (strong, vigorous, carefree, honest) and human emotions (writing done by someone in bitter rage, bone deep pain, with a tranquil and soaring spirit).

In early aesthetic theory, painting was not considered a serious art form because it was only decorative or representative. Paintings were portraits or illustrations that did not express the artist's emotional and intellectual responses to the world. When painter-poets began to use the repertoire of brush strokes developed in calligraphy to express their own moods and feelings rather than to represent the things they painted, the status of painting was elevated to that of poetry and calligraphy.

Although the early great landscape paintings of the tenth to thirteenth century were largely representational, Chinese artists never attempted the illusion of reality that led Western artists to develop single-point perspective. Viewers of Chinese paintings cannot identify the place from which the artist observed the scene being painted. Chinese artists use a series of shifting perspectives that invite us to take a journey through the landscape depicted. A small path may start at the bottom of the painting leading the eye past a waterfall to the top of a towering mountain. Tiny human figures often travel up the mountain, passing isolated pavilions or temples along their way. Long handscrolls demand even more active participation from viewers who hold the scroll at arm's length on a table, opening it, unrolling it, and rerolling it as they wander through scene after scene. Writing and seals on paintings add another interpretative dimension, providing a dedication for the painting, descriptions of the occasion on which it was painted, a series of poems by the painter's contemporaries, and inscriptions expressing appreciation of the artist and the work. The meaning of Chinese painting, like that of the older art form of poetry, is found in the many layers of responses and associations it evokes.

The relationship between the vast natural scenes of mountains, rocks, waterfalls, and rivers and the small villages, buildings, and people in a landscape express the Daoist belief in the value of a hermetic life alone in a mountain forest, as well as the belief that people are a part, but only a small part, of the entire cosmos. Chinese paintings also reflect Confucian ideals of our duty to live in the natural world and to revere the past. While Western artists are concerned with originality, Chinese paintings seem to repeat a series of conventional images developed over centuries: mountain, waterfall, a lone scholar walking in the woods, a fisherman drifting in a boat on the river. Moreover painters often claim to be painting "in the style of" an older master. Nevertheless, the greatest paintings are always highly original expressions of the particular painter's personality, moods, and metaphysical insight. Ni Zan, the great Yuan dynasty landscape painter, often neglected to put a human figure or pavilion in his sparse paintings, indicating his deep feelings of alienation and isolation.

PAINTING AND POLITICS

Painters did not always convey lofty metaphysical or cosmic thoughts and moods. Amateur literati artists used paintings to communicate political distress they could not express directly. The literati were scholars who had been educated for government service but were forced into exile by invading foreign dynasties. Paintings of orchids adopted a Buddhist symbol of purity growing out of filth and muck, isolated and unappreciated, to protest the conquest of China by the Mongols of the Yuan dynasty. Bamboo symbolized uprightness, simplicity, and the "hollow-heartedness" obtained by freedom from desire. Pine trees, which remained green in winter, stood for steadfastness in adversity.

Literati paintings of horses relied on the Chinese belief that the ability to judge horses was associated with the ability to judge the character of a government official. Han Gan's Tang dynasty portraits of imperial horses came to symbolize Chinese power at its artistic and military height. Literati painters under the Yuan dynasty eschewed Han Gan's use of color and produced simple ink pictures of horses, representing the plight of Chinese officials under the Yuan conquerors. In the twentieth century, Xu Beihong's exuberant ink paintings of galloping horses represented the courageous Chinese struggle against the Japanese. In 1980, Wang Huaiqing's less spirited but more colorful *Bole, a Wise Old Man who Knows How to Choose Horses* represented China's ambiguous relationship to its past.

AESTHETICS IN THE TWENTIETH CENTURY

The Communist revolution imported Soviet Socialist realism along with Marxism. Although Mao Zedong lectured that art should serve the masses in their struggle for liberation and reject the elite bourgeois art of the past, Mao himself identified with the tradition of Confucian scholars who had led China for 1,000 years. He read traditional literature, wrote poetry, and practiced calligraphy. Despite Mao's condemnation of the "poster and slogan" style of art, the horrors of the Cultural Revolution forced much Chinese art to become pure propaganda.

When the Cultural Revolution ended China experienced an "aesthetics craze." Chinese philosophers asserted the independence of art from ideology and offered the traditional aesthetic values of harmony and personal expression as a welcome relief from the chaos of the preceding decades. Combining Kantian aesthetics with Confucian morality and Marxist materialism, Li Zehou argued that aesthetic experience, not politics or religion, constituted the highest form of human life. Nevertheless Kantian arguments for the autonomy of art may have been taken to mean that art was politically and morally irrelevant, severing the ancient connection between art and morality. At the same time, China has become part of the global art community. The internationally celebrated artist Xu Bing uses pigs and human mannequins painted with English words and Chinese characters to express his ambivalence about the literature of ancient China and the relationship between China and the United States. The imperial horses painted by Han Gan appear on tote bags and Xu Beihong's galloping horses decorate refrigerator magnets. Although traditional Chinese art may have become just another consumer good, Chinese aesthetics has always insisted that the old and new are in harmony. The thoughts and feelings of ancient, and not so ancient, artists resonate with the feelings of twenty-first-century audiences as traditional themes and forms express new ideas, new thoughts, and new feelings about China's place in the world.

See also ART HISTORY; CONSERVATION AND RESTORATION.

BIBLIOGRAPHY

Cahill, James. 1960. "Confucian Elements in the Theory of Painting." In *The Confucian Persuasion.* D. Nivison & A. F. Wright (eds.). Stanford: Stanford University Press, 115–40.

Cai Zong-qi. 2002. *Configurations of Comparative Politics.* Honolulu: University of Hawai'i Press.

DeWoskin, Kenneth J. 1984. *A Song for One or Two: Music and the Concept of Art in Early China.* Ann Arbor: Center for Chinese Studies.

Gao Jianping. 2002. "Chinese Aesthetics in the Past Two Decades," *Acta Orientalia Vilnensia,* 3, 129–38.

Hall, David L. & Ames, Roger T. 1987. *Thinking through Confucius*. Albany: State University of New York Press.

Li Zehou. 1994. *The Path of Beauty: A Study of Chinese Aesthetics*. Hong Kong: Oxford University Press.

Mao Zedong. 1967. "Talks at the Yenan Forum on Literature and Art." In *Selected Works of Mao Tse-Tung*, vol. iii. Beijing: Foreign Language Press, 69–98.

Sullivan, Michael. 1980. *Three Perfections: Chinese Painting, Poetry and Calligraphy*. New York: George Braziller.

Temple, Robert. 1986. *The Genius of China: 3,000 Years of Science, Discovery, and Invention*. New York: Simon & Schuster.

MARTHE CHANDLER

cognitive science and art   Can an understanding of the psychological processes that subserve our engagement with artworks contribute to discussions of the nature of art or the character of aesthetic experience? Engaging with artworks is a canonically psychological task. In this context, cognitive science can help explain the way artworks induce perceptual and expressive effects associated with aesthetic experience and control for semantic associations associated with their meanings. Understanding these processes would seem central to our understanding of art, as both a category of objects and a set of loosely related cultural practices. Therefore, the answer would seem to be yes. However, philosophers have been generally skeptical about the prospects of a productive rapprochement between the philosophy of art and cognitive science. Their skepticism boils down to a question about whether psychological explanations of our engagement with artworks suffice to explain the artistic salience of associated perceptual and cognitive effects. This is a compelling worry. Nonetheless, it may be too strong as an evaluative criterion. Cognitive science need not provide independent explanations of artistic phenomena to contribute to our understanding of them. The question therefore is, what role, if any, can research in cognitive science play in discussions of issues germane to the philosophy of art and aesthetics.

Research at the confluence of cognitive science and philosophy of art rests on two assumptions. First, cognitive science can explain how artworks function as cognitive stimuli. Second, an understanding of how artworks function as cognitive stimuli can contribute to an understanding of how they function as artistic stimuli. The first claim is trivially true. The function of the formal structure of an artwork is to provide viewers, listeners, spectators, and readers with sets of cues to enable them to recognize its formal, representational, and expressive content. We do not need specialized artistic training to recognize these types of features in an artwork. The sets of visual cues embedded in the formal structure of a painting trigger the same sets of visual processes by which viewers perceive depth and recognize objects in ordinary visual contexts. Likewise, sets of cues embedded in the narrative structure of a text trigger the same sets of cognitive processes by which individuals recognize actions and events, interpret the beliefs, desires, and emotions of others, and predict their behavior. Cognitive science can explain how these basic processes work. Therefore cognitive science can explain how artworks work as perceptual and cognitive stimuli.

An artist's formal methods (e.g., maquettes, drawings, and color studies in the visual arts) can be thought of as tools for recovering sets of formal cues sufficient for artistic production in a medium (e.g., realistic representation in landscape painting) from ordinary experience. However, even in the case of realistic pictorial representations, there is no preferred set of image cues for accomplishing this task. Any number of possible formal vocabularies will suffice (e.g., formal differences between Hudson River School and Superrealist paintings). In this context artists choose the formal features and narrative devices they use to construct a work relative to the aesthetic effects or semantic association they intend them to produce. Therefore, explanations of how artworks function as cognitive stimuli should also explain how they function as artistic stimuli.

The strength of this model lies in its appeal to ordinary psychological processes that are transparent to empirical investigation. However, this strength is also its central flaw. Consider Margaret Livingstone's explanation of Mona Lisa's dynamic expression (2008: 68–73). Our ability to discern fine visual detail is far greater in the central, or foveal, region of the visual field than the periphery. However, this important capacity comes at a cost. Foveal vision is insensitive to coarse-grained visual features (e.g., broad contours defined by shading). Livingstone has demonstrated that Mona Lisa's expression is depicted using only coarse-grained image features (Leonardo used a technique called *sfumato* to blur the smile contours around the eyes and mouth of the figure). These coarse-grained features are invisible when one looks directly at Mona Lisa's face, but reappear when one looks away. This entails that the expression perceived on Mona Lisa's face actually changes as a viewer scans the painting. Therefore, Livingstone's research explains how *Mona Lisa* functions to induce the experience of perceiving a dynamic expression.

This case study illustrates the way artists learn to harness the basic psychological processes associated with a spectator's engagement with works in their medium. However, the psychological processes appealed to by cognitive scientists in this case and in explanations of other aesthetic effects are not unique to a viewer's engagement with artworks. Leonardo's formal strategy for *Mona Lisa* works precisely because it harnesses psychological processes involved in everyday face perception. This entails that the explanation Livingstone provides for Mona Lisa's dynamic expression applies equally to aesthetic and nonaesthetic stimuli (e.g., *Mona Lisa* and the laconic expression on a friend's face in a snapshot from 1978). Therefore, these types of explanations fail to differentiate our engagement with artworks from our engagement with ordinary, nonart stimuli, and so also artworks from nonart stimuli.

The solution to this difficulty emerges from an examination of the goals of empirically minded philosophers of art. The purpose of their appeal to research in cognitive science is not to generate a novel biological paradigm for understanding art, but rather to provide data to contribute to theoretical debates in philosophical aesthetics (Raffman 1993: 3). Results from research in cognitive science can be used to explain how particular artworks induce aesthetic effects or guide semantic associations. These data can be used to confirm critical interpretations of existing artworks and adjudicate between competing philosophical theories

about the nature of art and aesthetic experience. In this restricted sense, cognitive science can make a clear contribution to the philosophy of art. Consider *Mona Lisa* again. It is often argued that the aesthetic merit of Leonardo's painting lies in the use of *sfumato* to generate the dynamics of her expression. Livingstone's discussion of the painting supports this interpretation. Therefore, although her research does not itself explain why we assign aesthetic value to our engagement with the painting, it contributes confirming evidence to a theory that does. This in turn entails that it contributes to our understanding of how *Mona Lisa* functions as an artistic stimuli.

Research in cognitive science on art can be loosely taxonomized relative to its methodology. Neuroaesthetics and other research in the cognitive neuroscience of art employ a case study approach. Particular works of art are used to demonstrate correlations between artists' formal productive strategies and the operations of basic neuropsychological processes (e.g., Livingstone's discussion of *Mona Lisa*). These correlations are, in turn, employed to explain a range of psychological issues related to the production, understanding, and appreciation of art, for example, how techniques like half-shadows and irradiation function to enhance the perception of depth in oil paintings. This research is scientifically interesting. However, it is as yet underdeveloped territory in the philosophy of art. The cognitive neuroscience of visual art (Zeki 1999; Livingstone 2002) has received a great deal of attention, much of it skeptical. There is a broad range of focused research in the cognitive neuroscience of music (Peretz & Zatorre 2005). There is also a growing interest in the cognitive neuroscience of dance derived from research on mirror neurons, motor simulation, and our understanding of the intentionality of actions (Montero 2006).

The more prevalent strategy is to apply theories and results from a broad range of research in cognitive psychology and neuroscience to what have traditionally been thought of as uniquely philosophical puzzles. This strategy has been applied to discussions of such diverse issues as narrative understanding in film and literature (Currie 2007), emotional engagement with fictional characters (Goldman 2006), musical comprehension (Raffman 1993), the expression of emotion in music (Robinson 2005), the nature of pictorial representation (Rollins 2001), the nature of creativity (Boden 2003), and aesthetic responses to dance (Montero 2006). Consider our emotional engagements with fictional characters. Our naive intuitions suggest that some form of character identification, or empathy, plays a critical role in our experience and understanding of narrative fictions. However, there are a number of philosophical difficulties with this intuition. For instance, although we often experience the events depicted in narrative fictions vicariously, our responses would be inappropriate for their characters (e.g., we are frightened of quiet, dark places in horror films because we, unlike the protagonists, know what is coming). Further, we recognize that these are fictional characters in fictional contexts. So it would seem that there is nothing for us to be sad about or afraid of, and no one for us to empathize with.

Philosophical discussions of these issues have focused on the role of imagination in narrative understanding. Participants in the debate can be loosely divided into two camps. Proponents of *simulation theory* argue that some form of first-person imaginative experience is critical to our understanding of narrative fictions. Although there are a number of variations on this theme, the central claim is that spectators and readers imaginatively project themselves into narratives, adopt the perspective of either one of the characters or a hypothetical observer, and thereby simulate the experience of a participant in the events depicted. Alternative theories deny the centrality of first-person imaginative experience to narrative understanding. They argue instead that fictional narratives contain cues that that enable spectators and readers to categorize a character's response as belonging to a particular type without adopting his or her perspective. Therefore, understanding our emotional engagement with fictional characters requires no appeal to first-person imaginative experiences. Philosophers in this debate appeal to research from the study of autism, developmental and cognitive psychology, and cognitive neuroscience in support of their theories. For instance, two types of evidence have been offered in support of the simulation approach.

First, readers are quicker to respond to questions about narratives that track characters' perspectives than those that do not. Second, it has been demonstrated that the same brain areas involved in performing an action oneself are involved in perceiving that action performed by others (see Goldman 2006: 51).

The productive rapprochement between philosophical aesthetics and cognitive science should come as no surprise. These fields are, in one sense, natural bedfellows. Cognitive science is concerned with the way organisms acquire, recognize, use, and manipulate information. Cognition can, in this context, be understood in terms of representational structures that encode information about the environment and computational processes that interpret and transform those structures. Artworks are, by virtue of the practical necessities of working in a medium, abstract, or degraded, stimuli. Questions about the production, understanding, and appreciation of art are, in part questions about the way viewers, spectators, listeners, and readers acquire, represent, and transform information from these stimuli in order to recognize, categorize, and evaluate their content. Cognitive science is, by definition, methodologically well suited to answer these types of questions. The goal of the resulting research program is not *reductive*, but rather to expand the range of explanatory tools available for examinations of the nature of art and aesthetic experience.

See also DANCE; CREATIVITY; DEPICTION; EVOLUTION, ART, AND AESTHETICS; EXPRESSION; FICTION, THE PARADOX OF RESPONDING TO; IMAGINATION; NARRATIVE.

BIBLIOGRAPHY
Boden, Margaret A. 2003. *The Creative Mind*. New York: Routledge.
Currie, Gregory. 2007. *Image and Mind*. Cambridge: Cambridge University Press.
Goldman, Alvin. 2006. "Imagination and Simulation in Audience Responses to Fiction." In *The Architecture of the Imagination: New Essays on Pretence, Possibility, and Fiction*. S. Nichols (ed.). New York: Oxford University Press, 41–56.
Livingstone, Margaret. 2002. *Vision and Art: The Biology of Seeing*. New York: Abrams.
Montero, Barbara. 2006. "Proprioception as an Aesthetic Sense," *Journal of Aesthetics and Art Criticism*, 64, 231–42.

Peretz, Elisabeth & Zatorre, Robert (eds.). 2005. *The Cognitive Neuroscience of Music*. New York: Oxford University Press.

Raffman, Diana. 1993. *Language, Music, and Mind*. Cambridge, MA: MIT Press.

Robinson, Jenefer. 2005. *Deeper than Reason*. Oxford: Clarendon.

Rollins, Mark. 2001. "Pictorial Representation." In *The Routledge Companion to Aesthetics*. B. Gaut & D. McIver Lopes (eds.). New York: Routledge, 297–312.

Zeki, Semir. 1999. *Inner Vision*. New York: Oxford University Press.

WILLIAM P. SEELEY

cognitive value of art It is a mark of civilization that the arts are cultivated and promoted. Arts education is important and provision of access to the arts for all is thought to be a *sine qua non* of a good society. The presumption is that art educates and ennobles the mind. It seems that we would know far less if we lived in a world devoid of literature, films, paintings, and music. Yet ever since philosophical reflection about art began, there has been skepticism about the idea that art can teach us anything.

Plato argued that art affords only the illusion of knowledge. The fundamental thought can be articulated independently of Plato's contentious metaphysics. The creation of and engagement with art draws on the imagination. If we read a novel, look at a painting, or watch a movie we engage with a make-believe world. The artistry is designed to promote imaginings and shape our responses. Artists need have no knowledge about what they represent and appreciators may be unconcerned with truth in participating in games of make-believe. Knowledge requires contact with reality but games of make-believe do not. Thus art cannot cultivate knowledge.

Stolnitz (1992) argues that art cannot afford significant knowledge since it yields only banalities or trivial knowledge. As imaginative creations whose function is to sustain games of make-believe, artworks need not reflect the world. Far from being windows onto the world they are props that enable us to imagine beyond the confines of actuality. Moreover, consider the kind of putative insights we glean from fictions. Goya's *Disasters of War* (1810–20) etchings may convey war's horrors or Austen's *Pride and Prejudice* the dangers of self-regard, but do we learn such things from the artworks concerned? The idea that war is horrific or that pride comes before a fall is commonplace and trivial. If we already believe the message of such works then we cannot be said to learn anything from them. If we do not, then how could we learn from make-believe worlds that are not tied to truth about the real world?

First, it is worth noting that many artworks are not fictions. Orwell's *Homage to Catalonia* or Ingres's *Napoleon the Emperor* (1806) are works of nonfiction that do tell us about actuality. Orwell's book reveals much about the infighting among the communists in the Spanish civil war and Ingres's portrait conveys all too well what Napoleon looked like and how he conceived of himself. Second, even if fictions do not give us worthwhile propositional knowledge, it can be argued that art affords significant nonpropositional knowledge (Nussbaum 1990). Artworks can give us practical know-how, phenomenal knowledge, or access to ways of apprehending the world that may not be expressible in straightforward propositional terms. Perhaps there is something about what it is to see another human being as a mere extension of the material world, as a mere organism to be butchered, that Goya's sketches convey to us. Third, it can be argued that art does afford propositional knowledge. Artworks may be thought of as aesthetically detailed thought experiments that cultivate our imaginative understanding (Carroll 2002; Kieran 2004; Gaut 2007). In real life we are in a poor position to know what someone's character or intention in action is. By contrast, the artifice of fiction allows the elaboration of pure cases where hypothetically we know the ways in which someone's thought, action, and character may be intimately related. Consider *Pride and Prejudice*. Elizabeth Bennett and Mr. Darcy are proud in different respects and prejudiced against one another as a result. Darcy's pride is a result of the unqualified admiration of his parents allied to extreme standards of propriety. However, as the story develops, we come to see that his defensiveness, scorn, and solicitations of praise manifest an underlying insecurity. Hence it is clear both why he would assume that Elizabeth admires him (as all others do) and why he is shocked when she rebuffs him. Only when he comes to see his actions from Elizabeth's point of view can Darcy recognize that he has failed to live up to the self-professed ideals of propriety and consideration. We do not merely learn that "pride comes before a fall." Rather, we learn that narcissism and insecurity can combine in mutually reinforcing and self-destructive ways.

However, a problem remains. How can we tell whether or not the beliefs we derive from art are warranted? Looking at a Van Dyck portrait of Charles I or reading Tolstoy's *War and Peace*, we may acquire true beliefs about Charles I or Russian society during the Napoleonic era. Yet we may also acquire false beliefs. The problem is that there is no way of telling from a fiction which beliefs are true and which are false. If we want to know whether Charles I was an authoritative king of England or whether the Russian General Kutzov slept through battles we must look outside the work (e.g., at historical sources). Furthermore, many assumptions integral to artworks might be fundamentally flawed. Situation psychology, for example, suggests that our ordinary conception of character is radically mistaken. Milgram's experiments on authority and Zimbardo's Stanford prison experiments are sometimes taken to show, on the basis of measured behavior, that character traits such as compassion do not exist (Doris 2002). If so, then psychologically "realist" works serve only to embed our illusions about character. *Pride and Prejudice* may perpetuate an illusion rather than afford genuine knowledge. There are different areas of inquiry ranging from history to science and philosophy. Each one is characterized by their distinct objects of study and methods of inquiry. Yet art has neither a distinctive object of study nor distinct methods of inquiry. Hence for any truth claim conveyed through art we should look to the relevant mode of inquiry to check if it is warranted. We cannot learn, for example, from Austen about character – that is a matter for psychology.

Art often concerns how people experience, think about, and respond to the world. Hence we clearly can learn from it. What can we learn? How artists experience, conceive of, and respond to the world. Imaginative experience with art may also give rise to reliably formed beliefs about possibilities (Stokes 2006) and modal knowledge is crucial to scientific, historical, philosophical, and ordinary reasoning. Furthermore, in ordinary life we often imagine hypothetical scenarios to help us find out what we would think and feel. Even if such imaginings do not give us knowledge, they are cognitively useful in terms of testing out how we might think and feel. Artworks can be particularly vivid and enriching means of doing so. This is true even if the conception itself is mistaken. Hence, even if situation psychology is right, we can nonetheless learn from "realist" novels how we tend (falsely) to conceive of the interrelations between thought, action, and character. Furthermore, artworks can themselves show us reason to doubt claims made elsewhere. A large part of the point of Austen's novels is that possessing a trait is insufficient to determine behavior. Characters possessing the same trait may act differently. Practical wisdom is required, to make the appropriate evaluative judgments, and must be underwritten by the higher order virtue of constancy to act continually in accord with virtue. Darcy's compassion leads him to see his actions as inconsiderate but it is his constancy to high ideals that renders him capable of reshaping himself and winning Elizabeth's approval. Failure to do so would not have shown that Darcy lacked compassion but, rather, that he lacked constancy. Austen's novels show how possession of a trait might be insufficient to determine behavior. Hence they give us reason at least to question some of the claims made by situation psychology.

A complementary approach sets aside the question of whether beliefs endorsed in a work are warranted or not. Independently of whether art affords knowledge, works may be cognitively valuable insofar as they cultivate perceptual and cognitive virtues (Kieran 2004; Lopes 2005). Chardin's *Boy Playing Cards* (1740) for example, involves a complex play with our visual attention. It stretches our capacity to see the visual field presented to us as a diamond shape, emphasized by the illumination of the cards, the boy's collar and cuff. The picture cultivates the virtues of patience, close attention, visual discrimination, and adaptation.

Even if it is granted that art affords knowledge, it does not automatically follow that this is relevant to a work's value as art. We delight in the way in which the form of a work is an aesthetically artful and apposite means of portraying its subject matter. Artistic value is constituted by the imposition of form on a subject in such a way as to realize aesthetically valuable features. Aestheticism holds that the content of a work matters only insofar as it relates to the unity, complexity, intensity, elegance, gracefulness, vivaciousness, or other aesthetic qualities of it. Hence we should distinguish between a work's fictive, aesthetic, and cognitive aspects. On this view, the content of a work is relevant only to the extent it promotes or hinders the attainment of properly aesthetic virtues. Good art is, it may be thought, to be distinguished from bad art in terms of its capacity to realize and sustain aesthetic experience. Thus the value of a work as art is not reducible to its message. This explains why we can and do value works that embody incompatible claims. Philip Pullman's *His Dark Materials* trilogy and Michelangelo's *Pietà* (1498–9) embody conflicting claims about divinity. But we can appreciate them both as art since, according to aestheticism, truth is as such irrelevant to artistic value (Lamarque 2006).

Aestheticism is, however, at odds with critical practice. Critics often advert to considerations of truth in evaluating works as art. Critical terms of praise or blame such as profound, insightful, sentimental, shallow, callow, often do pick out the beliefs and attitudes conveyed through a work. It is hard to see how we could make sense of such notions without some kind of relation to truth. Moreover, it is no part of the cognitivist's claim that truth is the only pertinent cognitive value. After all, works can be truthful but banal and partial or mistaken and yet profound. There is a range of cognitive virtues. Hence we can value highly works that are incompatible (in the same way we may value different philosophical theories). What is needed is an account of the criteria that distinguish when the content of a work is relevant to its value as art and when it is not (Gaut 2007). The complexity of art suggests that there will be many. Visual artworks make use of distinctively visual techniques in order to convey modes of apprehension or reflective attitudes through our experience of the work. Where works do so, the mode of apprehension or attitude is relevant to assessing the work's value as art. The anamorphosis of a skull in Hans Holbein's *Ambassadors* (1533) must be viewed from the right, close up to the plane of the canvas, rather than the usual straight-on position required to see the rest of the painting. In the most marked way the distinctiveness of the position required to see the skull casts light on the content of the painting – the pride of the painting's subjects is mere hubris when viewed from the perspective of mortality (Kieran 2004). A different criterion focuses on art's solicitation of emotional responses from us. The content of a work seems relevant to its value as art insofar as it relates to the emotional response solicited. How we evaluate Francis Bacon's work will partly depend on whether the visceral horror solicited at his vision of the human condition is appropriate or not. Thus, not only can works cultivate knowledge, and the capacity to become better knowers, but how they do so seems internally related to their value as art.

See also LITERATURE; AESTHETIC EDUCATION; AESTHETICISM; FICTION, NATURE OF; FICTION, TRUTH IN; FUNCTION OF ART; MORALITY AND ART; TRUTH IN ART.

BIBLIOGRAPHY
Carroll, Noël. 2002. "The Wheel of Virtue: Art, Literature and Moral Knowledge," *Journal of Aesthetics and Art Criticism*, 60, 3–26.
Doris, John. 2002. *Lack of Character*. Cambridge: Cambridge University Press.
Gaut, Berys. 2007. *Art, Emotion and Ethics*. Oxford: Oxford University Press.
Kieran, Matthew. 2004. *Revealing Art*. London: Routledge.
Lamarque, Peter. 2006. "Cognitive Values in the Arts: Marking the Boundaries." In *Contemporary Debates in Aesthetics and the Philosophy of Art*. M. Kieran (ed.). Oxford: Blackwell, 127–39.
Lopes, Dominic M. 2005. *Sight and Sensibility*. Oxford: Clarendon.
Nussbaum, Martha. 1990. *Love's Knowledge*. New York: Oxford University Press.
Plato. 1974 [375 BCE]. *The Republic*. D. Lee (trans.). 2nd edn. Harmondsworth: Penguin.
Stokes, Dustin. 2006. "Art and Modal Knowledge." In *Knowing Art*. M. Kieran & D. M. Lopes (eds.). Dordrecht: Springer, 67–82.

Stolnitz, Jerome. 1992. "The Cognitive Triviality of Art." *British Journal of Aesthetics*, 32, 191–200.

MATTHEW KIERAN

Collingwood, R(obin) G(eorge) (1889–1943) British philosopher, historian, and archaeologist; from 1935 Waynflete Professor of Metaphysics at Magdalen College, Oxford. As a philosopher, Collingwood disassociated himself from the realism and positivism of his colleagues, and in aesthetics pursued a course that drew on the work of Giambattista Vico, Benedetto Croce, and others. Besides his contributions to aesthetics, Collingwood is known especially for his work on philosophy of history, and he wrote extensively as well in metaphysics, philosophical method, philosophy of mind, philosophy of religion, and politics. There is some controversy as to whether there is an essential continuity or discontinuity in the course of his philosophical career, which spans 15 published books. This question colors one's reading of his contributions to specific philosophical topics (see bibliography).

Regarding mind as an activity rather than an entity, Collingwood's works may be viewed as an extended account of different types of mental activities or forms of experience. In his *Speculum Mentis*, he argues against the view that knowledge should be pursued in terms of delineable domains of inquiry, and emphasizes the essential unity of mind by charting the relations between its forms of experience: art, religion, science, history, and philosophy. These forms are not exhaustive, for Collingwood allows the possibility that others might yet develop and that some subforms within this outline might be filled in. The question of the nature of the specific relations between these forms of experience concerned him for most of his philosophical career. In this "map of knowledge" art plays an important role, for the aesthetic infuses all other forms of experience. Collingwood is primarily concerned with the connection between art and mental activity, and not with the defining features of works of art, nor with the criteria of "good" works of art.

Generally, he identifies art with the movement from unreflective to reflective thought. Consequently, while there is a history of artistic achievements, there can be no history of artistic problems. Problems are understood in terms of questions and answers, and unreflective thought does not allow for the formulation of questions to start with.

"The aesthetic experience, or artistic activity, is the experience of expressing one's emotions; and that which expresses them is the total imaginative activity called indifferently language or art" (Collingwood 1938: 275). For Collingwood artistic creation does not answer to his so-called logic of question and answer, which he articulates, for instance, in his *Essay on Metaphysics*. In *The Principles of Art* he is concerned to show that art is not assertion; art predates assertion, and assertion presupposes art. That is, in the creative moment the product cannot be understood as an answer to a question (as such later thinkers as Karl Popper and Ernst Gombrich suggested it can), because creative activity is one in which the unconscious becomes conscious. Consequently, although a critic or art historian may offer a "rational reconstruction" of the creative moment in terms of questions and answers, such reconstructions cannot claim to be *historically* true. This thought undercuts any intentionalist program insofar as the latter seeks to reconstruct the conscious problem situations of creators. Collingwood holds that intentions can exist only in their expression; they do not predate expression.

Further, he holds that there can be no unexpressed emotion. Expression and emotion are dialectically codependent. It is in the expression of emotion that one becomes conscious of it; consciousness of emotion follows its expression. Thus emotions are not objects that are possessed before one's consciousness of them. In this sense, emotion and its expression are one: "What the artist is trying to do is to express a given emotion. To express it and to express it well, are the same thing. To express it badly is not one way of expressing it . . . it is failing to express it" (1938: 282).

Now, one may disown or repress feelings. That is, one may refuse to bring them to expression. Collingwood calls this the "corruption of consciousness" (1938: 216–21). This happens when "the conscious self disclaims responsibility for [feelings], and thus tries to escape being dominated by them without the trouble of dominating them. This is the 'corrupt consciousness,' which is the source of what psychologists call repression" (1938: 224).

In the case of artistic creation, a corrupt consciousness gives rise to bad art. In order to apply this notion of corrupt consciousness in specific cases of works of art, one would expect that rules or guidelines of application would be provided. But Collingwood does not offer any. His intention may not be to provide criteria for distinguishing between particular good or bad artworks, but rather to provide an account of what it is for artworks to be good or bad.

Collingwood identifies "art proper" as an imaginative experience. He holds that "A work of art in the proper sense of that phrase is not an artifact, not a bodily or perceptible thing fabricated by the artist, but something solely in the artist's head, a creature of his imagination; and not only a visual or auditory imagination, but a total imaginative experience. It follows that the painted picture is not the work of art in the proper sense of that phrase" (1938: 305).

A physical painted picture is a necessary accessory for a work of art proper. At the same time, "the picture . . . produces in [the audience] sensuous-emotional or psychical experiences which, when raised from impressions to ideas by the activity of the spectator's consciousness, are transmuted into a total imaginative experience identical with that of the painter" (1938: 308).

Collingwood distinguishes between artistic making or creating, and fabricating. His distinction between creating and fabricating appears to be coextensive with his distinction between imaginary and real. He suggests that while a work of art is made by the artist, it is not made by "transforming a given raw material, nor by carrying out a preconceived plan, nor by way of realizing the means to a preconceived end" (1938: 125). His examples include an artist making a poem, a play, a painting, or a piece of music. He was not especially concerned to discriminate between art forms in this regard. Collingwood tells us that the purpose of making sketches is to inform or remind others or oneself of the plan in one's head.

By Collingwood's account, for a tune to exist it is not necessary for a composer to hum, sing, or play it, nor is it necessary for him to write it down. While these are accessories of the real work and make the tune "public property," they are not necessary for it to exist in the composer's mind. There it exists as an imaginary tune. The actual making of the tune is something that goes on in the composer's head, and nowhere else.

Creating involves making a plan, while fabricating involves imposing that plan on certain matter. A plan can exist only in a person's mind. An engineer's notes and sketches on paper, for example, may serve as an accessory in order for others to share (and retrieve, when necessary) the plan that is in his head. Finally, when the bridge (for instance) is built, the plan is "embodied" in the bridge. The plan or the form was in the engineer's mind. Further, a plan or a work of art need not be made as means to an end, for a person can make these with no intention of executing them. Generally, works of art proper are not made as means to an end (1938: 135).

One might object to Collingwood's distinction between creating a tune and publishing it by suggesting that music may be created through improvisation – that is, through the interaction of a sometimes inchoate musical idea and the materials of music-making. It seems that he assumes that there is a sharp distinction between what is initially in the artist's mind and what is not. Not only do works of art characteristically not present themselves as plans independently of their embodying materials and forms, but such materials and forms characteristically help formulate the plan to start with. Put otherwise, it is in the interaction between the plan and the materials that the work of art comes to emerge.

But such an objection would be misplaced, for Collingwood's distinction allows that the activities of creating (or imagining) and making can go on simultaneously. The latter may be an accessory for the former. Put negatively, he is not committed to the view that creating precludes fabricating. There need be no instance of creating without fabricating: "There is no question of 'externalizing' an inward experience which is complete in itself. There are two experiences, an inward or imaginative one called seeing and an outward or bodily one called painting, which in the painter's life are inseparable, and form one single indivisible experience, an experience which may be described as painting imaginatively" (Collingwood 1938: 304–5). Yet one might press the point by suggesting that while imagining and making may be understood as interacting simultaneously, they are also *emergent* in a sense that is not captured by the idea that they interact. That is, the work of art may well embody properties that are attachable to none of its contributing parts, be they imagining or making. This emergentist view would undermine Collingwood's idea that works of art are essentially expressive of what goes on in the mind of the artist. Correspondingly, it would pose difficulties for the view that the audience recreates what is putatively in the mind of the artist.

See also TWENTIETH-CENTURY ANGLO-AMERICAN AESTHETICS; CREATIVITY; CROCE; EMOTION; EXPRESSION THEORY; ONTOLOGY OF ARTWORKS; RELIGION AND ART; THEORIES OF ART.

BIBLIOGRAPHY

Primary sources
1924. *Speculum Mentis; or, The Map of Knowledge.* Oxford: Clarendon.
[1925] 1964. *Outlines of a Philosophy of Art.* In *Essays in the Philosophy of Art.* A. Donagan (ed.). Bloomington: Indiana University Press. Also repr. Bristol: Thoemmes Press, 1994.
1938. *The Principles of Art.* Oxford: Clarendon.
2005. *The Philosophy of Enchantment: Studies in Folktale, Cultural Criticism and Anthropology.* D. Boucher, W. James, & P. Smallwood (eds.). Oxford: Clarendon.

Secondary sources
Donagan, Alan. 1952. *The Later Philosophy of R. G. Collingwood.* Oxford: Oxford University Press.
Jones, Peter. 1972. "A Critical Outline of R. G. Collingwood's Philosophy of Art." In *Critical Essays on the Philosophy of R. G. Collingwood.* M. Krausz (ed.). Oxford: Clarendon, 42–65.
Knox, T. M. 1946. "Editor's Introduction." In R. G. Collingwood, *The Idea of History.* Oxford: Oxford University Press.
Mink, Lois O. 1969. *Mind, History and Dialectic: The Philosophy of R. G. Collingwood.* Bloomington: Indiana University Press.
Rubinoff, Lionel. 1970. *Collingwood and the Reform of Metaphysics: A Study in the Philosophy of Mind.* Toronto: University of Toronto Press.
Van Der Dussen, W. J. 1981. *History as a Science: The Philosophy of R. G. Collingwood.* The Hague: Martinus Nijhoff.

Wollheim, Richard. 1972. "On an Alleged Inconsistency in Collingwood's Aesthetic." In *Critical Essays on the Philosophy of R. G. Collingwood.* M. Krausz (ed.). Oxford: Clarendon, 68–78.

MICHAEL KRAUSZ

comedy Sometimes in the course of daily events, we come upon things that simply strike us as funny, such as nuns in full regalia shooting at clay pipes in a gaming stall in Coney Island. Here, the disparate elements that strike us as funny have come together in an uncontrived manner – by coincidence, so to speak. The nuns did not stop at the shooting gallery in order to be funny. Their presence just is funny.

Comedy, on the other hand, is composed. It involves the intention to make something that will be funny. If the nuns are an example of found funniness, comedies are instances of invented funniness. The range of things that are comedies include: plays, movies, television programs, like situation comedies or sit-coms, cartoons, comics, songs, poems, such as limericks, stand-up comedy routines, jokes, riddles, parodies, satires, novels, caricatures, sight gags, and much impersonation and puppetry.

This, of course, is by no means an exhaustive list, nor are all the items mentioned so far mutually exclusive. Roughly, comedy in the broad sense belongs to the category of the funny. What differentiates comedy from the other major member of the species – found funniness – is that comic funniness is invented. Of course, the notion of invented funniness is of little use unless we have a handle on funniness. So our first order of business is to explicate the concept of funniness or humorousness, after which we will discuss a question about a category of comedy that has interested philosophers since the ancients, viz., the nature of the comic narrative, or comedy as a genre of the order of tragedy.

INVENTED FUNNINESS
Comedy is invented funniness. Professional comedians or comics are people who make or perform compositions that are funny – such as plays, caricatures, and songs – often for profit, although unpaid amateurs, plain folk like ourselves, also often produce comedy as when we tell a joke or imitate a coworker in an

exaggerated or caricaturistic manner. The notion of invention in this formula amounts to the idea that the composition in question is an intentional construction or creation. However, the concept of funniness, although applied to particulars with surpassing accuracy and competence by most of us, is harder to pinpoint.

One approach to elucidating funniness or the funny is to define it as that which makes us laugh (Morreall 1987). When we go to a comedy club, we expect to laugh and are generally disappointed if we do not. So, one characterization of comedy might be that it is a composition designed with the intention of provoking laughing. Or, to unpack this idea more precisely: X is a comedy if and only if it is a composition created and/or performed with the intention of eliciting laughter. By emphasizing that comedy is an intentional production, we allow for the possibility of bad comedy – comedy that is intended to engender laughter, but fails to do so.

The problem with this formulation is the weight that it places on the phenomenon of laughter. Laughter is taken as the hallmark of funniness. However, there is a great deal of laughter that has nothing to do with funniness. Laughter can be induced by tickling, which, if uninvited and protracted, can be an experience that is anything but funny. Moreover, laughter can be engineered pharmacologically by the appropriate dosages of nitrous oxide, belladonna, atropine, amphetamine, cannabis, or alcohol. Nevertheless, we do not count as comics chemists who intentionally ply us with these drugs.

Laughter may also issue from certain medical conditions, including the gelastic seizures that accompany certain epileptic fits, extreme nervousness, and hebephrenia. But these afflictions are tragic, not comic.

There is, in addition, the laughter of superiority that one warrior or competitor bellows forth on the defeat of his nemesis. This too seems, in principle, divorced from that which we identify as funny, since this species of laughter might resound at the sight of a ghastly victory, as when masses of mangled enemy bodies dispose the conqueror to laugh derisively at the conquered dead.

And finally recent scientific research has discovered that most laughter does not obtain in response to funny constructions, like jokes, or even in reaction to funny remarks, but rather occurs as a kind of conversational glue in everyday conversation (Provine 2000). Short bursts of laughter, that is, serve as feedback between interlocutors, signaling that each is following the other or they are used for emphasis. But since the conversations in question need not be comic constructions, the existence of this sort of phatic laughter provides further evidence that neither laughter nor the intention to elicit it is part of a sufficient condition for comedy. Indeed, the evidence here is overwhelming, since there is putatively more phatic laughter than comic laughter.

Furthermore, it is not clear that laughter or even a disposition to laugh is a necessary condition for funniness, since a funny observation may stimulate no more than a sense of joy or lightness (i.e., levity) in listeners, viewers, and/or readers. That which we find funny is pleasurable, but our enjoyment need not be marked by laughter, even if it often is.

Perhaps one way to get at what comprises funniness is to ask what gives rise to laughter on those occasions where the laughter is comic, rather than, for example, pharmacological. The leading philosophical suggestion here is that comic laughter is directed at constructions perceived to be incongruous. Where pharmacological laughter has a purely physical basis, the laughter that correlates with comedy involves cognition. Specifically, it erupts when one cognizes that the stimulus to which one has been exposed strikes one as being incongruous.

For example, Groucho Marx once said: "These are my principles – but if you don't like them I have others." The incongruity here is based on an absurdity or contradiction or category mistake. Principles are that which you hold onto – come hell or high water. Thus, it is incongruous to treat them as fungible.

But the incongruities that feed comic laughter need not be based solely on strict contradictions. They may merely reverse received wisdom as in the story of the church with the sign outside advising "Come early if you want to sit in the back." Nor need the expectations that are being subverted incongruously merely be propositional. When a comedian uses a tablecloth as a napkin, the effect is comically risible because the gesture is incongruous relative to our standing norms of etiquette.

Thus, we may hypothesize that a composition and/or its performance is an example of invented funniness where it is constructed in such a way that it is perceived to be incongruous. Of course, a recurring objection to this is that not every instance of inventions that are thought to be incongruous is comic. Incongruity can cause anxiety as readily as it may spur delight. What is strange can be threatening, if it is not carefully contextualized. Consequently, the perceived incongruities that are intended to figure in comedy are ones that do not engender distress, but, in contrast, instill pleasure.

Nevertheless, there are, additionally, perceived incongruities that do not inspire anxiety but which are not funny either. We can call these incongruities puzzles, such as mathematical puzzles. Instead of simply relishing these incongruities – as we do with a joke – we attempt to solve them. Puzzle incongruities, that is, mobilize a puzzle-solving attitude in response, one committed to finding the correct answer in contrast to a comic riddle of which we are simply satisfied (indeed, happy) to relish its absurd resolution.

Something, then, is funny or humorous if and only (1) if it is perceived to be incongruous, (2) where the incongruity is not threatening or anxiety-producing, and (3) where the incongruity does not recruit an attitude of committed puzzle-solving, but (4) is simply enjoyed (Carroll 2003). A specimen is comic if and only if the composition and/or a performance thereof is intended to be funny or humorous in the preceding sense. That is, *X* is comic just in case it is a case of invented funniness or humor.

COMIC NARRATIVES

So far we have been discussing comedy broadly in terms of the conditions that a member of any comic genre must meet in order to be considered a comedy. However, traditionally the theoretical discussion of comedy has often focused more narrowly on a particular genre or set of genres within this group – comic plays and narratives, or comedies rather than tragedy with respect to theater.

In this regard, one thought that recurs with almost numbing frequency is that comedy is "a genre in which the ending of a play or a film

script proclaims happiness through a love match, a wedding, a triumph over adversity, or a reconciliation" (Bermal 2003: 293). That is, comedies have happy endings whereas in tragedies the play typically concludes with one or more calamities. *A Midsummer Night's Dream* ends with lots of marriages and reconciliations whereas *Hamlet* finishes off with a rush of deaths, murders, and defeats.

Nevertheless, although the notion that comedy correlates with happy endings has a long history, it cannot be right. A happy ending cannot be a necessary condition for comedy, since there are comedies that end badly, such as *Dr. Strangelove; or, How I Learned to Stop Worrying and Love the Bomb* (1964), which forecasts the total destruction of human life. Nor is a happy ending a sufficient condition for comedy. The plots of many genres other than comedy end well for the protagonists. Every stage version of *Dracula* rounds off with the execution of the count, but, unless we are talking about a parody, no one takes *Dracula* to be a comedy.

If the happy-ending plot structure does not identify comic narratives, are there any plot structures that may turn the trick? In all likelihood we are prone to call a narrative comic if a substantial number of the incidents it represents are intended to be humorous, that is, are presented as instances of invented funniness. Even the ending of *Dr. Strangelove* meets this criterion, since a man riding an atomic bomb to earth as if it were a bucking bronco is surely incongruous.

And, in addition to this quantitative measure of comedy, there are also certain plot structures that have the capability to meet the criteria of invented funniness discussed in the previous section. These include what can be called *the equivocal plot* and *the wildly improbable plot* (Carroll 2005). The wildly improbable plot obtains when, through the machinations of the narrative, some wildly improbable conclusion occurs, often through a wildly improbable string of events – as in *Back to the Future* (1985) when Marty's weak-kneed and timid father defeats the bully and wins the heart of Marty's mother. It is just too incredible, indeed wildly improbable, where improbability, of course, is one source of incongruity. Thus, if this perceived incongruity meets the other conditions for invented funniness, then it will count as a comedy.

This is also the case with the equivocal plot. This kind of plot involves arranging the events that comprise the narrative in such a way that they can be seen from two or more, generally conflicting, points of view. For example, the townspeople in Gogol's *Inspector General* think that Khlestakov is a government official, whereas the audience knows he is not. As happens with a pun, the doubleness in the situations that ensue sparks laughter, in this case, due to the incongruity of the townspeople's mistaken perspective. Given the kind of person Khlestakov is, it is ridiculous that villagers could misread the situation with such regularity.

Of course, not all comic plots are incongruous as a result of being wildly improbable or equivocal throughout. Instead, in a great many cases, we categorize plots as comic when they are comprised predominately of episodes of invented funniness.

Where the ancients were concerned to differentiate only two grand genres – comedy and tragedy – perhaps the notion of a happy ending was (almost) up to the task. But since we now have so many more genres to deal with – many of which can support happy endings, but which are not comedies – our approach to comic plotting needs to become more nuanced.

See also HUMOR; TRAGEDY.

BIBLIOGRAPHY

Bergson, Henri. 1956 [1900]. *Laughter*. C. Brereton & F. Rothwell (trans.). In *Comedy*. W. Sypher (ed.). Baltimore: Johns Hopkins University Press, 61–190.

Bermal, Albert. 2003. "Comedy." In *The Oxford Encyclopedia of Theatre and Performance*. D. Kennedy (ed.). Oxford: Oxford University Press, 293.

Carroll, Noël. 2003. "Humour." In *The Oxford Handbook of Aesthetics*. J. Levinson (ed.). Oxford: Oxford University Press, 344–65.

Carroll, Noël. 2005. "Two Comic Plot Structures," *Monist*, 88, 154–83.

Cohen, Ted. 1999. *Jokes*. Chicago: University of Chicago Press.

Lauter, Paul (ed.). 1964. *Theories of Comedy*. Garden City: Anchor/Doubleday.

Levinson, Jerrold. 1998. "Humour." In *Routledge Encyclopedia of Philosophy*. E. Craig (ed.). London: Routledge, 562–7.

Monro, D. H. 1951. *The Argument of Laughter*. Melbourne: Melbourne University Press.

Morreall, John. 1983. *Taking Laughter Seriously*. Albany: State University of New York Press.

Morreall, John (ed.). 1987. *The Philosophy of Laughter and Humor*. Albany: State University of New York Press.

Provine, Robert R. 2000. *Laughter: A Scientific Investigation*. Harmondsworth: Penguin.

NOËL CARROLL

conceptual art is of particular interest from a philosophical point of view, for two main reasons. First, the approach of many conceptual artists is notably philosophical. Second, and consequently on the first point, thinking about conceptual art raises important challenges to some of the main questions in philosophical aesthetics.

Conceptual art resists precise definition. The term "conceptual art" first came into prominence in the late 1960s, during what might now be thought of as its "high" period, in New York in 1966–72, although the movement has its roots in the "ready-mades" of Marcel Duchamp in the early 1900s, such as his famous *Fountain*, and the movement continues today, in, for example, much of the work of the Young British Artists. Here are some examples of conceptual art from its high period (various images and texts about these works are available from an online search): Vito Acconci, *Following Piece* (1969); Joseph Kosuth, *One and Three Chairs* (1965); Michael Craig-Martin, *An Oak Tree* (1973). Further examples can be found on Tate Online: www.tate.org.uk/collections/glossary/definition.jsp?entryId=73

At the heart of conceptual art is the thought that "the idea or concept is the most important aspect of the work," as the conceptual artist Sol LeWitt once put it. What seems to be involved is a kind of "downgrading" of the importance of the artwork, the physical object (e.g., a picture, a sculpture), as the proper object of aesthetic appreciation: "Conceptual art, for me, means work in which the idea is paramount and the material is secondary, lightweight, ephemeral, cheap, unpretentious, and/or dematerialised" (Lucy Lippard, cited in Godfrey 1998: 14).

I will now consider four challenges that conceptual art raises which are philosophically important: questions of definition, of ontology, of epistemology, and of value.

CONCEPTUAL ART AND DEFINITION

Is conceptual art really art? Characteristically, conceptual artists *intentionally* challenge our everyday ideas of what art is; moreover, they deny that whether or not conceptual art really is art is something to be determined by the art critic or the connoisseur: "If I say it's art, then it's art" is often their refrain.

There are many attempts to define art, but for these purposes they can usefully be divided into three kinds. First, there is the family-resemblance account, according to which art cannot be defined in terms of necessary and sufficient conditions. In spite of this, according to this view, we are able to recognize those things that are works of art and those things that are not, and we are able to do so because of their *perceptual resemblance* to other things that we previously know to be art (Weitz 1956). But this is open to the challenge mounted by Danto (1981), that perceptual resemblance is not necessary for something to be art: Duchamp's *Fountain* illustrates this as it is not like any kind of art that has gone before. Nor is it sufficient: Andy Warhol's *Brillo Boxes* most of all resembles Brillo boxes that are *not* works of art.

The second kind of approach to definition is *functional* (S. Davies 1991), according to which something is a work of art if it has a certain function. This function is often taken to be the capacity to produce in the viewer some kind of aesthetic experience, paradigmatically aesthetic pleasure. The problem is that much conceptual art does not achieve this (consider here Kosuth's *One and Three Chairs*), and yet we do take it to be art. A searching question here is whether this ought to lead to a rejection of this kind of definition of art, or to a rejection of conceptual art as not *really* art.

The third kind of definition of art, often designed specifically in order to be able to encompass conceptual art (Levinson 1989), is *procedural* (S. Davies 1991). One such is the *institutional definition of art*, according to which, roughly, something is an artwork if it is "an artifact of a kind created to be presented to an artworld public" (Dickie 1995). Many philosophers find this kind of procedural definition to be unsatisfactorily *conventional*;

much here hangs on the definition of "artworld." (Some philosophers have tried to accommodate this last concern by introducing a "hybrid" definition of art, in part procedural and in part functional; see Stecker 1997.)

Thinking about conceptual art, then, makes us sharpen up our ideas of what art is, and whether conceptual art has a rightful claim to be art.

CONCEPTUAL ART AND ONTOLOGY

Ontology is concerned with what there is (and questions of ontology are thus not the same as questions of definition). Our everyday notion of art involves thinking of works of art as spatio-temporal objects, of the kind one finds on walls or plinths in museums and art galleries. The object is the means, or the *medium*, by which the artist communicates his or her ideas.

The ontological challenge from conceptual art seems to be in the rejection of the role of the medium in art as being of central importance, a rejection reflected in the conceptual artist Joseph Kosuth's comment that "The 'art idea' and art are the same." This rejection comes in three forms, raising increasing difficulties. First, there is the rejection of the modernist idea that there is a specific medium that is "proper" to each art form; for example, works of conceptual art sometimes incorporate a wide range of media (sometimes known as *mixed-media works*). Second, there is the rejection of the idea that the physical thing is the appropriate object for appreciation; for example, works of conceptual art sometimes consist just of typed words, or very poor photographs, which do not seem to be suitable for this purpose. And third, there is what Lippard (1973) has called the dematerialization of the art object; for example, Robert Barry has a work which consists just of these words: *All the things I know but of which I am not at the moment thinking – 1:36 pm, June 15, 1969.*

Not all artworks are spatiotemporal objects: consider, for example, dance, music, and poetry. Some of these are, arguably, events; others are, perhaps, abstract objects. But intuitively, we also take *some* kinds of artworks to be spatiotemporal objects: paradigmatically pictures and sculptures. We have thus been content to operate with a *mixed ontology*. Where does conceptual art such as Robert

Barry's piece belong in this ontology? We might, for example, think that conceptual art has its own special kind of ontology, whereby it is Barry's *idea* that is the art object: not just the single thought, encapsulated in those words, but the whole series or narrative of thoughts and intentions leading up to, and including, that final thought which is encapsulated in the title to the piece. Alternatively, some philosophers, David Davies (2004) in particular, in considering what we can learn from such examples as the Barry piece, have been drawn to a *single* ontology for all art. This is undoubtedly an extreme move, but considering conceptual art raises ontological questions in an especially pressing way.

CONCEPTUAL ART AND EPISTEMOLOGY

Traditionally, it is considered necessary that one be in direct perceptual contact with a work of art if one is properly to appreciate it; mere testimony that a work is beautiful is not sufficient for one properly to appreciate its beauty (Sibley 1965).

It can readily be seen that the points just made about the ontology of conceptual art and the dematerialization of the art object give rise to a range of epistemological questions about how we are able to appreciate conceptual art. Consider, for example, Vito Acconci's *Following Piece*, where the only "thing" one can be in direct perceptual contact with is a series of poor photographs of people in the street, and a description of what the work is. This still leaves us some epistemic distance from the events of which the photos are "documentation": "Activity, 23 days, varying durations. Choosing a person at random, in the street, any location, each day. Following him wherever he goes, however long or far he travels. (The activity ends when he enters a private place – his home, office, etc.)." We simply cannot gain direct perceptual contact with those events; the best we can do, perhaps, is imagine them.

The epistemological question, then, is how we are properly to engage with works of conceptual art of this kind in order to appreciate them. This immediately leads to questions of the value of art: to questions about how art *ought* to be appreciated. The epistemological answer should in some sense depend on answers to questions of value.

CONCEPTUAL ART AND ARTISTIC VALUE

Traditionally, the value of art has often been assumed to reside in the kind of experience it can give rise to – specifically *aesthetic* experience. This kind of experience is often supposed to arise in perceptual confrontation (thus the term *aesthetic*, first coined in the eighteenth century, from the Greek term for "perceive" or "feel") with an object that is *beautiful* or has other kinds of aesthetic properties that make this kind of experience appropriate – being serene for example. (The connections here with the earlier discussion of definition, of ontology, and of epistemology should be obvious.)

But if conceptual art characteristically eschews this kind of experience, not seeking to produce objects of aesthetic interest, what kind of value can it possibly have? What is important in the first place here is to appreciate at least the possibility that artistic value need not consist only in aesthetic value, even if that is what artistic value has traditionally been taken to be. As Timothy Binkley has put it, with one of Duchamp's works in mind, "Some art (a great deal of what is considered traditional art) creates primarily with appearances . . . On the other hand, some art creates primarily with ideas. To know the art is to know the idea; and to know an idea is not necessarily to experience a particular sensation, or even to have some particular experience" (1977: 266).

So when we come to the value of art, conceptual art helps us at least to appreciate that artistic value can sometimes reside in something other than its physical appearance, with which one must be in direct perceptual contact to appreciate its specifically aesthetic value. The challenge is to spell out quite what that further kind of artistic value might be if it is not aesthetic.

See also ARTIFACT, ART AS; DANTO; DEFINITION OF "ART"; MODERNISM AND POSTMODERNISM; ONTOLOGY OF ARTWORKS; PERFORMANCE ART; TESTIMONY IN AESTHETICS; THEORIES OF ART.

BIBLIOGRAPHY
Binkley Timothy. 1977. "Piece: Contra Aesthetics," *Journal of Aesthetics and Art Criticism*, 35, 265–77.
Danto, Arthur C. 1981. *The Transfiguration of the Commonplace*. Cambridge, MA: Harvard University Press.

Davies, David. 2004. *Art as Performance*. Oxford: Blackwell.

Davies, Stephen. 1991. *Definitions of Art*. Ithaca: Cornell University Press.

Dickie, George. 1995 [1983]. "The New Institutional Theory of Art." In *The Philosophy of Art: Readings Ancient and Modern*. A. Neill & A. Ridley (eds.). New York: McGraw-Hill, 213–23.

Godfrey, Tony. 1998. *Conceptual Art*. London: Phaidon.

Goldie, Peter & Schellekens, Elisabeth (eds.). 2007. *Philosophy and Conceptual Art*. Oxford: Clarendon.

Goldie, Peter & Schellekens, Elisabeth. 2009. *Who's Afraid of Conceptual Art?* London: Routledge.

Levinson, Jerrold. 1989. "Refining Art Historically," *Journal of Aesthetics and Art Criticism*, 47, 21–33.

Lippard, Lucy. 1973. *Six Years: The Dematerialization of the Art Object from 1966 to 1972*. Berkeley: University of California Press.

Sibley, Frank. 1965. "Aesthetic and Nonaesthetic," *Philosophical Review*, 74, 135–59.

Stecker, Robert. 1997. *Artworks: Definition, Meaning, Value*. University Park: Pennsylvania State University Press.

Weitz, Morris. 1956. "The Role of Theory in Aesthetics," *Journal of Aesthetics and Art Criticism*, 15, 27–35.

PETER GOLDIE

conservation and restoration The act of preserving the artwork as the artist intended it to be seen, conserving what he made by restoring losses caused by aging or the effects of time.

Since art history is based on the assumption that what the historian views in the museum is what the artist made, a theory of restoration is a necessary starting point for art history. Unless the artwork we see has been successfully conserved, how can we accurately interpret it? Although restoration and conservation are concerns in every art, they are of special importance in visual art. Jane Austen wrote texts that we interpret; Haydn created scores that the modern orchestra performs. So long as her text or his score has been accurately copied, the artwork is preserved. But in the visual arts the artist traditionally creates a physical thing. Unless the restorer can preserve that object, the artwork does not survive.

The goal of restoration is easy to state. The restorer aims to preserve what the artist made. The difficulties arise when we ask how that goal is to be achieved (Carrier 1985). An artist makes an *artifact* with a certain *appearance*. With time, the picture may darken unless the restorer intervenes. But is the aim to preserve the *original artifact*, which will darken with time? Or should the restorer seek to preserve the *original appearance* of the artifact? In 1644–5 Pieter Saenredam made two paintings of the nave of the Buurkerk, Utrecht. One is now in the Kimbell Art Museum, Fort Worth, Texas, the other in the National Gallery in London. When they were made, the panels were almost certainly similar in appearance. But now the first depicts stark white walls while the second shows a mellow brown interior. Treating these pictures differently, the restorers "have performed . . . a series of changes . . . which have amounted to complete transformations of the aesthetic effect of the two panels" (Schwartz & Bok 1990: 198–9). Both paintings have survived, but until we can determine which of them provides an accurate record of Saenredam's activity, we cannot understand his art.

Often attempts are made to solve this problem by appeal to the artist's intention. Perhaps he wanted his picture to darken, showing its age. Or maybe he would have preferred the original appearance of his artifact to be preserved. On reflection, however, it becomes clear that appeal to intentions cannot solve this problem. In practice, usually the artist must first be concerned with how the work will appear to contemporaries. He is unlikely to be concerned with future viewers and may be unable to predict how his work will appear at a later time. But even if he says explicitly how he desires the work to appear in the future, we need not necessarily accept his viewpoint. Just as the artist is not necessarily the best interpreter of his work, so he may not be the final authority on how it should be conserved.

An analysis of restoration is unavoidably bound up with more general philosophical problems. Some thing, a substance, remains the same entity, though its properties change. We need some way to identify what has changed as the same thing; for, otherwise, speaking of change would be impossible. If we think of change as continuous, then we can describe how a thing gradually changes. That requires some way of identifying the self-same thing, that enduring entity which has changed. Four kinds of different substances have been considered by metaphysicians (Wiggins 1980): artifacts, organisms, persons, artificial entities.

Artifacts can have their parts replaced and remain the same thing so long as that process proceeds slowly. A car is the same car, the same functioning artifact, when its original components are replaced as they wear out. Organisms are substances which change as they mature. The same tree is first tiny, then large, and then decays. These changes involve a natural process of growth in accordance with a built-in plan of development. Human beings also are organisms. But identity of persons may be different from identity of organisms. On some theories, a person can survive the destruction of his body. Artificial entities like states survive if there is enough continuity. Modern France is the same country as ruled by Louis XIII, though it is now a democracy and its borders have changed somewhat. But the Venetian Republic ceased to exist when it was incorporated into Italy and the last doge was deposed. The United States is the same country as the republic created in the late eighteenth century, although slavery has now been abolished, women have the vote, and there are 50 states. There is enough continuity to identify it through these radical changes.

None of these substances are exactly like artworks. If artworks were artifacts, then they could survive the gradual replacement of all of their original parts. But if a fresco is gradually repainted, when none of the original paint survives the artwork has not survived, although the original design has been preserved. Organisms are born, grow to maturity, and die. But since normally artworks do not contain a built-in plan of development, they cannot be organisms. Usually the restorer seeks to arrest natural processes, intervening as the artwork decays. A person can continue to exist through radical changes in his physical qualities, because one test of continuity is memory or continuity of consciousness. An artwork is not that sort of thing.

Perhaps, then, the most promising approach to conservation involves treating artworks like artificial entities. Emphasizing, as it does, the role of convention in restoration, that way of thinking focuses attention on the function of artworks. Most art in our museums was not made for the museum. If what the African tribal artisan made was a magical artifact, the object cannot be preserved when it is treated as an artwork and carefully presented in a temperature-controlled museum environment. Similar problems arise when sacred Christian works are taken from a church to a museum. We conserve in the museum the artwork made by the artist, secularizing what originally was a sacred work. We preserve the artwork by changing its function (Riegl 1984). Like a country, the object treated as an artwork in the museum can survive such radical changes.

Some art historians deny that it is possible for the artwork to survive such changes (Wind 1969). How we see Romanesque carvings is influenced by our experience of early modernist sculpture; the colors in old master art now look subdued because our eyes are accustomed to garish twentieth-century paintings. This implies that to preserve the original artwork we must preserve its effect, which is not the same thing as preserving the object itself. How we see that object depends on our experience of other art that the artist did not know. Even if the artifact is preserved perfectly, it will now look different.

Were this argument correct, it would be impossible to conserve artworks. But it is hard to state this skeptical argument in a consistent way. When an altarpiece is placed in a museum, and set near modern secular art, it looks different from how it looked in a church. But if every such change in context changes how we see the work, then how can we know that? Unless we were able to successfully imagine the original appearance of the work, we could not know that now its appearance has changed.

The settings of the African artifact and the Italian altarpiece are dramatically changed when they are put in the museum. If the identity of these objects depends on their function, then they have not been preserved when they are placed in the museum. The object has survived, but, set in a new context, it has lost its original function. Some aestheticians solve this problem by claiming that artworks possess universally recognizable qualities. On this Kantian view, artworks are not artifacts because they "do not normally, *qua* works of art, have any *function*" (Wiggins 1980: 138). As art-works, the African artifact and Italian altar-piece do not have a function.

This is an ahistorical way of thinking. Until relatively recently, most art had a function. According to a long tradition of what has been called "museum skepticism" (Carrier 2006), art museums fail to preserve the objects they contain. When an altarpiece moves from a church to a museum, its context is changed. No longer do people pray before it. This altarpiece has become a work of art. Even more dramatic changes occur when Chinese scroll paintings, Hindu temple sculptures, or Islamic decorations from mosques are moved into museums. Still, in many (though not all) cases there is some overlap between how artworks were thought of in their original culture and how they are perceived in the museum. There is some connection between the function of these objects in their original culture and their aesthetic qualities which we appreciate in our museum. These artifacts had one function in their original context, and have another in the museum where they are treated as artworks. These changes of function involve enough continuity for us to say that they have survived.

We preserve the artifacts in our museums at the cost of changing rather drastically their function. Something is preserved even while these things are drastically changed. It is important to recognize that the problems of preservation of artworks involve understanding the function of the museum. Although our art museum is a creation of the late eighteenth century, there is enough continuity between the beliefs of that period and ours to permit us to speak of the same institution. A succession of gradual changes in the museum may add up to the effect of a revolution. But those successive changes are changes in the same institution, whereas by definition a revolution involves a break with tradition. Museums have changed radically, but there is enough continuity to permit us to identify them as the same institutions. The function of a museum is to give us knowledge of the past and aesthetic experience of artworks.

These philosophical arguments can seem of tangential importance to the conservator. He must act while philosophers go on talking. But how he proceeds in his important practical activity is ultimately determined by the broader culture's highly elusive ideas about how we should think of the identity of artworks.

See also ART HISTORY; MUSEUMS; ONTOLOGICAL CONTEXTUALISM; ONTOLOGY OF ARTWORKS.

BIBLIOGRAPHY
Carrier, David. 1985. "Art and Its Preservation," *Journal of Aesthetics and Art Criticism*, 43, 291–300.
Carrier, David. 2006. *Museum Skepticism: A History of the Display of Art in Public Galleries*. Durham: Duke University Press.
Riegl, Aloïs. 1984 [1903]. *Le culte moderne des monuments: son essence et sa genèse*. D. Wieczorek (trans.). F. Choay (intro.). Paris: Seuil.
Schwartz, Gary & Bok, Marten Jan. 1990. *Pieter Saenredam: The Painter and His Time*. New York: Abbeville.
Wiggins, David. 1980. *Sameness and Substance*. Oxford: Blackwell.
Wind, Edgar. 1969. *Art and Anarchy*. 2nd edn. New York: Random House.

DAVID CARRIER

creativity has been discussed by several major philosophers of art: Plato, Aristotle, Kant, Schopenhauer, Nietzsche, and Collingwood made important contributions to the topic. But the latter half of the twentieth century, perhaps due to the lingering influence of formalism, saw a relative decline of interest in creativity in comparison to the voluminous writings about the definition and interpretation of art. This relative neglect is odd, since creativity and art are often strongly associated in art-critical discussions and in artists' own self-understandings. However, creativity has begun to reemerge as the object of philosophical attention, as witnessed by two recent anthologies (Gaut & Livingston 2003; Bardsley et al. forthcoming). Several issues can be raised about creativity, but I will concentrate on three: the definition of "creativity," the nature of the creative process, and the value of creativity in art.

DEFINITION
The traditional definition has two parts. A creative act, process, or object must be original. But originality does not suffice, for, as Kant

207

remarks, there can be original nonsense: so the act, process, or object must also be valuable – it must be "exemplary" (Kant 1987: 175). But if originality is simply newness, and since almost all particulars differ from other particulars in some respect or other, more needs to be said about the notion of originality if it is to escape vacuity.

Refining the traditional definition, Boden holds that creative ideas must be not only valuable but also new *and surprising* – the surprise condition answers the problem of trivial differences. Further, an idea may be new to the person who comes up with it (P-creativity, or psychological creativity) or also new in the sense that no one else has thought of it before (H-creativity, or historical creativity). And something may be surprising either because it is an unfamiliar combination of familiar ideas (combinational creativity), because it explores a conceptual space (exploratory creativity), or because it transforms a conceptual space (transformational creativity). In the latter case, the idea could not have been thought of before, since the previous conceptual scheme rendered it unthinkable (Boden 2004: 1–6). A conceptual space is a set of generative rules or constraints, such as the rules of chess or of grammar; and the notion is widely applicable: there are, for instance, rules for generating Frank Lloyd Wright's prairie house architecture. Transformational creativity is more radical than exploratory creativity, since it transforms the generative rules, rather than merely exploring the possibilities within them; and the deeper the constraint that is transformed or dropped, the more radical is the creativity (Boden 1994). Since computers can model generative rules and specify their transformations, this account grounds a computational theory of creativity, in the sense that computers can model creativity, though there is no implication that computers really are creative.

It has been objected to Boden's definition that transforming a conceptual space is not necessary to creativity, since Jenner's invention of the smallpox vaccine was creative, but did not transform a conceptual space, for no conceptual space about vaccines existed prior to his invention. Nor is transforming a conceptual space sufficient for creativity, even when something valuable is produced, since

Goodyear's invention of the vulcanization of rubber transformed the conceptual space governing rubber, but his invention was not creative, since it was produced by mechanically adding to liquid rubber all the substances on which he could lay his hands (Novitz 1999).

Novitz's Jenner objection is more effective against Boden's 1994 position, which comes close to suggesting that transformational creativity is the only kind of creativity; but by 2004 she is explicit that other kinds of creativity exist. However, the Goodyear objection is a problem not just for Boden's account of creativity but also for the two-part definition in general: for it is possible to produce original and valuable objects by luck or mechanical search procedures (such as the mass testing of chemical compounds employed by pharmaceutical companies), but for the results not to be creative. This shows that not just *what* is produced matters in determining whether something is creative, but also *how* it is produced. So the definition of "creativity" should be three-part: a creative idea must be not just original (saliently new) and valuable but also produced by flair, in a sense that rules out pure luck and the use of mechanical search procedures in its generation (Gaut 2003).

THE CREATIVE PROCESS

Probably the two most influential traditional philosophical accounts of the creative process are the inspiration model (Plato) and the imagination model (Kant).

According to Plato, the creative process is a matter of being literally inspired (breathed into) by the gods, so that the creative person does not know what he is doing and cannot explain it; and Plato thinks of inspiration as producing a kind of derangement in the creative person (Plato 1963). The inspiration account was enthusiastically embraced by the Romantic poets, particularly Shelley; and it does capture the feeling of some creative people that their ideas arrive mysteriously and unbidden. Freudian theories of creativity also owe something to the Platonic model, with the unconscious taking the role of the gods.

According to Kant, a genius has an innate talent for allowing his faculties of imagination and understanding to play freely together (i.e., in non-rule-governed fashion) so as to create works of beauty – genius occurs only in the fine arts and not in science according to Kant. In particular, the genius possess *Geist*, spirit, which is an ability to exhibit aesthetic ideas, and "by an aesthetic idea I mean a presentation of the imagination which prompts much thought, but to which no determinate thought whatsoever, i.e., no [determinate] *concept*, can be adequate" (Kant 1987: 182). This account of open-ended imaginative exploration captures an aspect of the creative person's experience, in the sense that the creative person may explore various possibilities in imagination, so that imagination is the vehicle of active creativity (Gaut 2003). Kant also holds that the operations of genius are inexplicable, since the natural talent that is genius is grounded on the subject's supersensible nature, that is, on his nature in the noumenal realm, which does not admit of scientific knowledge (Kant 1987: 217). Thus, though his reasons differ, Kant agrees with Plato that creativity is inexplicable.

An important refinement of traditional models is due to Collingwood. He holds that art is created and "To create something means to make it non-technically, but yet consciously and voluntarily" (1938: 128). Technical making is craft-making, and it involves taking the means to some predetermined end and also skill. Though Collingwood does not explicitly connect creativity to creation, a natural thought prompted by his account is that the creative process cannot involve taking means to some already established end, since, if the end is already established, the creative act is complete. Vincent Tomas has defended this view, holding: "To create is to originate. And it follows from this that prior to creation the creator does not foresee what will result from it . . . [Otherwise he] would have to have the idea of it in mind. But if he already had the idea in mind, all that would remain to be done is to objectify the idea in paint or in stone, and this would be a matter of skill, or work" (1958: 4). In this sense, creativity is "blind," and the creative process is not teleological but generates its own momentum and direction from factors internal to it (Beardsley 1965).

Though influential, this nonteleological model has been challenged. John Hospers objects that the creative person has to know something about what she is trying to do in order to reject some of her attempts at achieving it as unsatisfactory (1985: 245). And it has also been argued that the creative process can be teleological, both because it can involve a more detailed specification of one's end and also because creativity can be shown in choosing the means to one's ends; and this view also allows that creativity is or involves a skill (Gaut 2008). Some writers also note that creativity occurs in a framework of planning and intention-formation without which the creative process could not be effective (Livingston 2005: ch. 2).

The idea that creativity cannot be explained has also been challenged on various grounds. David Novitz (2003) has argued that action-guiding and causal explanations of creativity are not available, but has defended the possibility of biological and social explanations. Jon Elster (2000) develops an account of the creative process in terms of the constrained maximization of artistic value, which makes it a rational process and so also potentially subject to explanation. The possibility of comprehensive explanations is also suggested by computational models of creativity and by explanatory accounts of creativity offered by psychologists.

CREATIVITY AND THE VALUE OF ART

Formalists reject the relevance of creativity as an artistic value, since the originality – a component of creativity – of a work is an extrinsic property of it. So Beardsley (1965), having developed a theory of creativity, goes on to claim that the theory plays no role in understanding or in evaluating art. Nonformalists have also questioned the value of originality. Originality in the sense of mere newness per se has no aesthetic value, since, as Kant notes, there can be original nonsense. And if a work is original by being new in respect of some aesthetically valuable property, then the reason the work is aesthetically valuable is because of the aesthetic value of the property, not because of its newness. For consider the first work in Frans Hals's mature style: this work has aesthetic value by virtue of its valuable style, but this value is possessed by all his later works in the style too; the mere fact that it is the first in that style, in contrast, gives it some historical value, but no aesthetic value (Vermazen 1991; cf. Sibley

1985). It has also been argued that whereas creativity, the maximization of artistic value subject to constraints, has aesthetic value, originality, the mere changing of these constraints, has no intrinsic aesthetic value (Elster 2000). And even if one accords originality some aesthetic value, one can deny that it has the preeminent value that it is sometimes accorded, since some of the greatest artists were less original than lesser ones: Defoe, Fielding, and Richardson were more innovative as novelists than Austen, Dickens, and Eliot, but it is the latter group who are the greater artists (Olsen 2003).

A defense of the aesthetic value of originality can appeal to the fact that artworks are not just objects with properties, but also achievements. So artistically evaluating them involves in part evaluating them as achievements; and the degree of their achievement is partly dependent on how original they are. Thus the originality of a work is part of its artistic value (Levinson 2003). One can also hold that originality is an artistic value, without believing that it is a preeminent one: one can accord originality status as one of several artistic merits that artworks possess.

CONCLUSION

These three issues are only some of those that can fruitfully be raised about creativity: there are also interesting questions to explore about the relation of creativity to rules, to tradition, to moral values, and so on. Also, the relative lack of attention to creativity in aesthetics and philosophy in general contrasts sharply with the large amount of work that has been done by psychologists on the topic (Sternberg 1999). Some of the most important recent work by philosophers has explored computational models of the mind (Boden 2004). But there are many other psychological theories worthy of philosophical investigation, such as Darwinian theories, which consider creativity as the production of random ideational variants, the successful ones of which are selectively retained (Simonton 1999). Given the importance of creativity in art and the psychological theories awaiting philosophical exploration, there is every reason to believe that the recent philosophical revival of interest in creativity will continue to flower and grow.

See also COLLINGWOOD; IMAGINATION; KANT; ORIGINALITY; PLATO; SCIENCE AND ART.

BIBLIOGRAPHY
Bardsley, Karen, Dutton, Denis, & Krausz, Michael (eds.). Forthcoming. The Idea of Creativity. Leiden: Brill.
Beardsley, Monroe C. 1965. "On the Creation of Art," Journal of Aesthetics and Art Criticism, 23, 291–304.
Boden, Margaret. 1994. "What is Creativity?" In Dimensions of Creativity. M. Boden (ed.). Cambridge, MA: MIT Press, 75–117.
Boden, Margaret. 2004. The Creative Mind: Myths and Mechanisms. 2nd edn. London: Routledge.
Collingwood, R. G. 1938. The Principles of Art. Oxford: Clarendon.
Elster, Jon. 2000. Ulysses Unbound: Studies in Rationality, Precommitment, and Constraints. Cambridge: Cambridge University Press.
Gaut, Berys. 2003. "Creativity and Imagination." In Gaut & Livingston, 148–73.
Gaut, Berys. Forthcoming. "Creativity and Skill." In The Idea of Creativity. K. Bardsley, D. Dutton, & M. Krausz (eds.). Leiden: Brill.
Gaut, Berys & Livingston, Paisley (eds.). 2003. The Creation of Art: New Essays in Philosophical Aesthetics. Cambridge: Cambridge University Press.
Hospers, John. 1985. "Artistic Creativity," Journal of Aesthetics and Art Criticism, 43, 243–55.
Kant, Immanuel. 1987 [1790]. Critique of Judgment. W. Pluhar (trans.). Indianapolis: Hackett.
Levinson, Jerrold. 2003. "Elster on Artistic Creativity." In Gaut & Livingston, 235–56.
Livingston, Paisley. 2005. Art and Intention. Oxford: Oxford University Press.
Novitz, David. 1999. "Creativity and Constraint," Australasian Journal of Philosophy, 77, 67–82.
Novitz, David. 2003. "Explanations of Creativity." In Gaut & Livingston, 174–91.
Olsen, Stein Haugom. 2003. "Culture, Convention, and Creativity." In Gaut & Livingston, 192–207.
Plato. 1963. Ion. In Plato: The Collected Dialogues. E. Hamilton & H. Cairns (eds.). Princeton: Princeton University Press.
Sibley, Frank. 1985. "Originality and Value," British Journal of Aesthetics, 25, 169–84.
Simonton, Dean Keith. 1999. Origins of Genius: Darwinian Perspectives on Creativity. New York: Oxford University Press.
Sternberg, Robert (ed.). 1999. Handbook of Creativity. Cambridge: Cambridge University Press.
Tomas, Vincent. 1958. "Creativity in Art," Philosophical Review, 67, 1–15.
Vermazen, Bruce. 1991. "The Aesthetic Value of Originality," Midwest Studies in Philosophy, 16, 266–79.

BERYS GAUT

critical monism and pluralism *Critical pluralism* is the thesis that artworks admit of alternative, equally acceptable interpretations, some of which are incompatible with others; it asserts that if there is a way to get an artwork right then there are many ways. The contrasting thesis is *critical monism*: every artwork is susceptible to a single correct, complete interpretation. Critical pluralism is an exciting thesis: it entails that two critics could lay equal claim to understanding the same artistic phenomenon despite serious interpretative disagreements with one another. It promises *rival interpretations*, complete interpretations, each of which accounts for all the artwork's features, yet all equally correct and genuinely incompatible. Critical monism, in contrast, insists that every instance of interpretative disagreement rests on at least one interpretative error.

A helpful contrast is provided by scientific explanation. Fashionable relativisms and postmodern rhetoric notwithstanding, there is a way the world is: a way to get it right, and many ways to be mistaken. There are determinate facts, for example, about the electrostatic properties of copper, the toxicity levels of arsenic, and the representational significance of dark areas on a photographic plate. No "plurality of equally correct but incompatible" characterizations of such facts should be countenanced. In contrast, critical pluralism denies the existence of a single, correct interpretation of any given artwork: it portrays the artworld as sustaining interpretative pluralism in a way that the physical world does not.

Perhaps the contrast is misleading: artworks are a special domain of objects, and artworld interpretation is not scientific explanation. Ptolemy and Copernicus could not both have been correct about planetary trajectories, but rival critics disagreeing about the aesthetically relevant features of Barnett Newman's paintings, or the expressive properties of Stravinsky's *Firebird Suite*, or the proper interpretation of T. S. Eliot's "The Hollow Men" may be equally correct. Critical pluralism claims that for a variety of artworks, no unique correct interpretation is forthcoming.

Pluralism is intimately related to *tolerance*. A tenet of liberal democratic orthodoxy is that Tolerance is a Good Thing. But once the pluralistic rhetoric is set aside it is difficult to see what the alleged contrast between critical pluralism and critical monism amounts to. Genuinely incompatible theories – artworld interpretative or otherwise – cannot both be correct, unless the pluralist gives "correct" a nonstandard interpretation. Critical pluralism strains at our ordinary concepts of correctness, completeness, disagreement, and incompatibility. In what sense are the touted "rival" interpretations genuinely incompatible? Does one interpretation really affirm (as true) what another denies? In what sense are they "equally correct"? In what sense do they account for all of the artwork's features?

If the coherence and intelligibility of critical pluralism and critical monism are established, the challenge is to locate compelling reasons for accepting one or the other. Although critical monism is not without adherents (Nehamas 1981), pluralism is the dominant sentiment within the artworld. Terry Barrett, for example, claims as a basic principle of interpretation that "artworks attract multiple interpretations and it is not the goal of interpretation to arrive at single, grand, unified, composite interpretations" (2003: 198). Despite his acknowledgment that some interpretations are more coherent, reasonable, convincing, and informative than others – thereby rejecting the idea that all interpretations of an artwork are equally acceptable – Barrett nonetheless insists that "there is a range of interpretations any artwork will allow" (2003: 198). It is not clear, however, what sorts of arguments support his pluralistic preferences.

One way to understand critical pluralism and critical monism is as expressions of conflicting views about the nature of artistic meaning and the purpose of art interpretation. On one view, interpretation aims to *discover* facts about meaning. The meaning is "out there" in the artistic object or performance: an interpreter can be right or wrong about it. Such a "realist" view about meaning carries no commitment as to its nature. Meaning might be a psychological property constituted by artist's intentions, for example, or by experiences prompted by an artwork among the artist's contemporaries. Or meaning might be a sociological property, explicable in terms of communally upheld norms, or a physical property, explicable in terms of reliable signaling and informational content. Whatever the nature and ontological status of meaning, it is a feature as real and objective as the mass of an object or the relative position of a city. The successful interpreter gets it right. Such a picture of meaning is naturally conjoined with critical monism.

A contrasting view is that artistic meaning is "projected," rather than discovered, by the interpreter. The meaning of a painting is no more a real feature of the painting than the taste of an orange is a real feature of the orange. The interpreter's job is to weave narrative stories that facilitate engagement with artworks: meanings properly ascribed to an artwork are constituted by viewer/reader/listener responses, which are mediated by his or her interests, expectations, presuppositions, and contextual situation. Meanings are made, not found. Such a view about meaning is naturally conjoined with critical pluralism (with reservations to be noted below).

Thus, there are two different ways to think about artistic meaning: (1) it is a real feature of an artwork, analogous to the representational significance of tree rings, deflections on an ohmmeter, or height of a mercury column; one can be correct or mistaken about such matters; or (2) it is constituted by subjective psychological responses to a work; meaning is a feature that emerges from the effects of an artwork on an observer, and the narratives and interpretative stories it prompts the observer to tell.

But a projective theory of artistic meaning does not, in fact, provide a ground for critical pluralism. Granted, some interpretative stories are more fruitful and robust than others, and lead to richer aesthetic experiences, heightened awareness of artwork subtleties and complexities, etc.; and beyond this there is nothing for the interpreter to be right or wrong about. But critical pluralism is no consequence, for on this projective view of meaning, interpretative claims are not truth-evaluable (therefore the various interpretations cannot be said to be equally correct). Moreover, the various interpretative stories are not, strictly speaking, incompatible; at most they foreground different features of the interpreted object.

Insofar as the dispute between critical pluralism and critical monism is grounded in disagreement about realist versus projective conceptions of artistic meaning, adjudication requires technical semantic and psychological inquiries; moreover, empirical study is required to identify the notion of interpretative meaning actually sustained within the artworld. Examples: if art historians seek to discover cultural-historical facts about the iconic significance of certain images, this would suggest that critical monism provides a more accurate picture of actual critical practice. If film critics regard late 1950s science fiction movies as "about" cold war anxiety and fear of nuclear radiation – and dismiss contemporary viewers as unable to grasp that content and thus unable to understand the genre – this too would suggest that critical monism provides a more accurate picture of actual critical practice. And so on.

Putting aside the theory of meaning, the term "pluralism" tends to be applied to a variety of phenomena: considerations that appear to validate critical pluralism turn out, on careful scrutiny, to be unexciting and/or unsupportive of pluralistic conclusions.

Consider an analogy between interpreting artworks and understanding persons. Any effort to tell "the whole story" about Robin involves a plurality of complex descriptions connected with various aspects of her life. Perhaps any "monistic" effort to pin down a single, unified story about her is misguided (except in the trivial sense that the conjunction of this plurality of stories is constructible, thereby resulting in a single story). Understanding Robin's complex life requires attention to a plurality of interpretative and explanatory stories; perhaps an analogue of this situation obtains in the realm of artworld interpretation, thereby vindicating critical pluralism.

But the alleged pluralities in Robin's life flow from a single, underlying explanatory ground. Persons are unified entities; the properties manifest throughout her various roles flow from some unifying personal essence – her character. Her patience and compassion, for example, explain *both* her professional *and* her parental temperament; her cleverness explains both her problem-solving skills in hospital settings and in dealing with friends' crises. Understanding Robin requires knowing *why* she exhibits the features she does across various aspects of her life. This in turn involves grasping the underlying personality from which her multifarious properties flow. There is a single, correct psychological theory about Robin, difficult though it may be to discover. Monism vindicated.

Although artworks are not persons, the analogy is provocative. Just as aspects of Robin displayed across a plurality of contexts are manifestations of an underlying, explanatorily unifying character, any alleged plurality of correct interpretations of a given artwork might be subject to unification via a single interpretative story: the correct interpretation of the artwork properly identifies that underlying explanatory essence. Critical monism vindicated. Of course, different observers armed with different interests might focus on different facets of Robin's life, but such interest relativity provides no ground for pluralistic conclusions.

On the other hand, explanatory unification of the envisaged sort is not always possible: some artworld correlate of Donald Davidson's (2001) "anomalous monism" might obtain, whereby different classes of predicates "not made for each other" are applicable to the same artwork and figure into a variety of correct but incommensurable interpretations. (Plausible artworld examples of this phenomenon are worth seeking.) Moreover, the critical pluralist might prefer a different sort of analogy. Perhaps interpreting an artwork is less like understanding a person (or explaining scientific data) and more like planning an extended journey: there is no single, "correct" route to be discovered. The optimal line of travel depends on one's interests and goals (minimize drive time, maximize scenic views, etc.). Critical pluralism vindicated.

But some analogies are more apt than others. And arguments are required. Here we offer additional considerations in support of critical pluralism, and find none to be convincing: the critical monist will have a response to each. This hardly establishes the falsity of critical pluralism; but in light of plausible assumptions about meaning and interpretation – artistic and otherwise – it provides sufficient basis for skepticism. Given the prevalence of pluralistic sentiments within the artworld, this conclusion is nontrivial.

One way to approach the issue is to explore parallel puzzles concerning the metaphysics of linguistic meaning. In the wake of Quine's (1960) arguments for the indeterminacy of translation there is ongoing dispute about the existence of "mutually incompatible but equally correct" translations of sentences in natural language. Quine's results are pluralistic: if there is one correct translation scheme from an alien language to our own, there are many such schemes. If Quine is right – if there is "no fact of the matter" about sentence meaning and the reference of singular terms – perhaps similar considerations apply to the artworld, thereby providing support for interpretative pluralism.

But arguments for critical pluralism modeled on Quinean arguments for the indeterminacy of translation are not likely to be compelling, for several reasons. (1) It is not clear that artistic genres are sufficiently similar to natural languages, and artworld interpretation sufficiently similar to natural language translation, to render Quine's arguments supportive of critical pluralism. (2) Quine's arguments for translational indeterminacy rest on a rigorous (and controversial) specification of "correct translation," but no equally rigorous characterization of "correct artistic interpretation" would likely be agreed on by parties to the dispute between critical pluralism and critical monism (thereby arousing suspicion that critical pluralism and critical monism are not, in fact, conflicting claims about the same phenomenon).

Another possible route to critical pluralism turns on the idea that artworks are cultural artifacts, and that interpretation of cultural phenomena deploys a methodology that does not aspire toward uniqueness of functional characterization. If, for example, correct interpretation of Kasimir Malevich's paintings involves situating them in the context of Russian avant-garde artists, or the social ideals behind the Russian Revolution, or European Post-Impressionism, or aerial photography, then the art-interpretative enterprise emerges as an instance of *historical explanation*. Perhaps there is a compelling argument that such explanation, unlike that in physics or chemistry, involves a hermeneutic methodology that cannot be expected to deliver a single, correct story. Perhaps, as Hayden White suggests, "narrative accounts of real historical events . . . admit of as many equally plausible versions in their representation as there are plot structures available in a given culture for endowing stories, whether fictional or real, with meanings" (1986: 489). But it is vital to distinguish epistemic roadblocks – the difficulties in discerning connections of historical influence and causation – from the metaphysical claim that historical reality is ontologically indeterminate and admits of inconsistent but equally correct characterizations. The latter claim appears implausible (if not unintelligible). Pending an elaborate inquiry into the metaphysics of past events, there seems little reason to endorse it. Thus no argument for critical pluralism is likely to emerge from considerations of historico-hermeneutic methodology. (For further discussion, see Habermas 1971.)

Yet another pluralistic argument highlights the social-institutional constituents of meaning, and draws its power from an analogy. Linguistic communities play an essential role in the constitution of semantic content: it is the word's use within *this* group of speakers that constitutes its meaning. Analogously, art communities play a role in the constitution of artistic content: it is the image's use within *this* group of artists that constitutes its meaning. The interpretative meaning of artistic productions is constituted by facts about artistic norms and stylistic conventions – those sustained within the relevant community.

Therefore an artwork – qua susceptible to interpretation – must be construed as occupying a place within an institutional, normatively constrained context: an artworld. This was Arthur C. Danto's (1964) fundamental insight. But Danto failed to note that there are *many* such artworlds, just as there are many distinct natural languages. This plurality of artworlds provides a ground for critical pluralism: if there is no fact of the matter as to which artworld is relevant to the proper interpretation of a given artwork, any of several interpretations will qualify as equally correct.

But additional argument is required to show that no artistic community is the correct frame of reference for the interpretative task. Moreover, if an artwork is situated at a communal crossroads – perhaps the artist belongs simultaneously to a plurality of relevant artistic communities – then proper interpretation of the work requires specification of *all* of the relevant roads, as well as the interpretative ambiguities and ironies that result. To alter the imagery, if a person enjoys citizenship in a plurality of nations, proper understanding of that person requires the complete story about such multiple citizenship and, perhaps, of the internal tensions that result. There will be a single, correct such story. Critical monism vindicated.

Further reflection on the nature of meaning, purposes of artworld interpretation, methodology of cultural history, and/or the ontology of art might provide compelling grounds for critical pluralism not considered here (see Kraut 2007). But insofar as meaning – artistic and otherwise – is a real phenomenon in the world, and artworld interpretation aspires to discover it, the onus is on the critical pluralist to establish that there is, in any interesting sense, a plurality of equally correct interpretations of an artwork.

See also LITERATURE; "ARTWORLD"; CRITICISM; IMPLIED AUTHOR; INTENTION AND INTERPRETATION; "INTENTIONAL FALLACY"; INTERPRETATION; INTERPRETATION, AIMS OF; MEANING CONSTRUCTIVISM.

BIBLIOGRAPHY
Barrett, Terry. 2003. *Interpreting Art: Reflecting, Wondering, and Responding.* New York: McGraw-Hill.
Danto, Arthur C. 1964. "The Artworld," *Journal of Philosophy,* 61, 571–84.
Davidson, Donald. 2001. "Mental Events." In *Essays on Actions and Events.* New York: Oxford University Press, 207–29.
Habermas, Jürgen. 1971. *Knowledge and Human Interests.* Boston: Beacon.
Kraut, Robert. 2007. *Artworld Metaphysics.* Oxford: Oxford University Press.
Nehamas, Alexander. 1981. "The Postulated Author: Critical Monism as a Regulative Ideal," *Critical Inquiry,* 8, 133–49.
Quine, W. V. O. 1960. *Word and Object.* Cambridge, MA: MIT Press.
Stecker, Robert. 2003. *Interpretation and Construction: Art, Speech and the Law.* Oxford: Blackwell.
White, Hayden. 1986. "Historical Pluralism," *Critical Inquiry,* 12, 480–93.

ROBERT KRAUT

criticism Introducing a collection of papers entitled *Contemporary Criticism* in 1970, Malcolm Bradbury, while noting an increase in what he termed "speculative theory," recorded nevertheless that "today, literary criticism has become *the* method of literary study – its primary methodology, or 'discipline,' the self-conscious tactic of the subject" (1970: 19). Almost 20 years later, however, we find Frank Kermode declaring that "criticism seems to be in rapid decline, and is by many thought moribund, and all the better for that" (1989: 5). Not, of course, that this marks a decline in the productivity of teachers in literature departments, but rather the replacement of "criticism" by "theory." The latter, Kermode thinks, "is often the work of writers who seem largely to have lost interest in literature as such" and to be hostile to criticism, desiring "to destroy the end [it] had in view, which . . . was to deepen understanding of literature, and to transmit to others (including non-professors) interpretations and valuations which could and would be transformed or accommodated to new conditions as time went by" (1989: 5). For both Bradbury and Kermode, "criticism" is to be contrasted with "theory," and while the former is concerned with "literature as such" and is directed toward the interpretation and evaluation of individual works, the latter, at least in its contemporary and dominant mode, intends the destruction of criticism and its goals.

This understanding of the object and goals of criticism is at one with that of the so-called "New Criticism" developed in the writings of John Crowe Ransome, Allen Tate, and especially Cleanth Brooks in the United States during the 1930s and 1940s, and which, through the textbooks *Understanding Poetry* (1938) and *Understanding Fiction* (1941) (both by Brooks and Robert Penn Warren), became the dominant force in the teaching of literature in American universities after World War II. Although the term "New Criticism" was taken from the title of a book by Ransome that did not discuss any of the critics now associated with it, it nevertheless aptly marks the sense of a break with the previous practice of literary study. At the heart of this lay the question of the sense and role of history for literary study. Tate characterized the new criticism as opposed to the "historical method," the research into the historical influence on and of a work of literature, which treated the literary as a historical object about which facts could be gleaned. This approach, however, presupposed a quite different relation to the work, through which its reputation could be established in the first place so that it could become a worthy object for the study of "influences." Such an engagement is essentially interpretative and evaluative.

In *The Well-Wrought Urn*, Brooks went on to argue against the tendency to reduce this evaluative and interpretative activity itself to a species of factual inquiry. "The temper of our times is strongly relativistic," he wrote, for "we tend to say that every poem is an expression of its age . . . that we must judge it only by the canons of its age" (1947: preface). But such a position both conceals its own evaluative character, in determining which authors are to be taken as showing us the relevant canons, and makes impossible an engagement with contemporary work, which must first be evaluated before there can be any conception of a "canon" at all. We can only evaluate current work in terms of standards appropriate for literature *as such*, and it is in terms of these too that we engage with the works of the past insofar as we are evaluatively engaged with them. Great poems, Brooks claims, bear a close relation to each other, in the qualities which make them poems and that determine whether they are good or bad. Poetry, as a distinct form of discourse, embodies general criteria against which poems may be measured. Such judgments, then, will not be relative to their age, nor to our own, but are made in terms of the nature of poetry *as such* (Brooks 1947: 197). I shall return to what this involves shortly.

Now this is, Brooks claims, a new understanding of poetry and the critic's role. There have indeed been critical revolutions in the past, but if now we are to consider literature *as* literature, then these must have shared an essentially nonliterary understanding of the literary work. These revolutions, the neoclassical at the end of the seventeenth century and the Romantic at the turn of the nineteenth, although opposed in many ways in their understanding of poetry, had their differences constituted within a unity. A poem was understood by both as essentially a statement, the test of which is its truth; the poetical aspect of the work lies in the decoration of this information with imagery and appropriate meter and sound. There was thus a distinctive poetry language, although what was taken as poetic changed.

One might justify this in relation to writing inspired by the importation of French neoclassical critics such as Boileau, René Rapin, and Dominique Bouhours at the end of the seventeenth century, by referring to John Dennis's *Grounds of Criticism in Poetry* (1704, in Elledge 1961). Here Dennis claims that poetry is an art, and "if it is an art it follows that it must propose an end to itself and afterwards lay down proper means for the attaining that end . . . those proper means in poetry we call rules." The end of poetry is twofold: "the subordinate one is pleasure, and the final one is instruction . . . in reforming the manners." Poetry is essentially the conveying of moral instruction in a pleasing form which will incline the reader toward virtue and against vice.

The particular kinds of poetry are concerned with different spheres of human life and the virtues and vices relevant to them. The epic thus concerns the highest forms of conduct concerned with the wellbeing of the state or of mankind itself; tragedy, the punishment of great vice or the endurance of great misfortune on the part of the virtuous; comedy, the common foibles and small vices of ordinary people, and so forth. Each kind of poetry has its own rules, determined by the end of pleasing by instruction through the imitation of the appropriate manners, which concern the various parts of the poem: plot, character, speeches, sentiments, imagery, diction, and versification. Criticism brings to bear the appropriate end and rule for the kind of poem at issue, and exercises taste which Addison called "that faculty of the soul which discerns the beauties of an author with pleasure and the imperfections with dislike." Such criticism not only notes conformity with the rules, which Pope said resulted in "exact disposition, just thoughts, correct elocution, polished numbers," but also that "poetical fire" which marks the great from the commonplace in the production of daring and striking imagery, and so forth. The end of moral instruction requires reference to a universal morality and the depiction of individuals with reference to their general humanity, so that Dr Johnson tells us in *Rasselas* that "the business

of the poet is to examine, not the individual but the species; to remark general properties and large appearances"; and, in the preface to his edition of Shakespeare's plays, that "it is always a writer's duty to make the world better, and justice is a virtue independent of time and place."

If the Romantics objected to the production of imagery through fancy – which elaborates, as Wordsworth put it, "the lurking affinities" in dissimilars – in favor of the imagination, and rejected the neoclassical "kinds" of poetry, for Brooks they do so still in the name of a non-literary purpose. Imagination, Coleridge said, acts "by impressing the stamp of humanity, of human feeling over inanimate objects" so that objects are not merely imitated, but "a human and intellectual life is transferred to them from the poet's own spirit" (1960: ch. 11). This is not merely a matter of seeing nature through an emotional coloring, as when in *Lear* "the deep anguish of a father spreads the feeling of ingratitude and cruelty over the very elements of heaven," but a bringing of "the whole soul of man into activity" (1960: ch. 12). Imagination, which "struggles to idealize and to unify," has the essential task of revealing the unity of the human with the universe at large and so, as Wordsworth put it, "to incite and support the eternal." Hence the appropriateness of the Romantic lyric form and the autobiographical poem – Wordsworth's *Prelude* being the greatest exemplar – in which the individual characteristically is shown moving from an instinctive unity with nature to an alienation revealed by man's capacity for freedom, which is in turn remedied through the revelation of a new and higher unity within which the individual achieves, as the *Prelude* (book 14, ll. 113–14) says, "the highest bliss . . . the consciousness / Of whom they are."

Thus, for Brooks, the aim of such poetry is to convey truths about "the eternal," which may equally be transmitted argumentatively in philosophy, in a language and form calculated to incite the appropriate feelings. The critic's task is to enable the reader to participate in such feelings, a project which leads to an "appreciative" criticism which itself conveys the feelings of the critic and which, therefore, itself participates to an extent in the character of literature itself.

The previous critical revolutions, then, understood the poem instrumentally, as directed toward a nonliterary end and to be judged accordingly. Whether it is "to instruct by pleasing" or "to incite and support the eternal," the poem's quality depends on the truth of its teaching and on the effectiveness of its poetic language in achieving the desired end. The poem has not been judged *as* literature but as a means to a nonliterary end. To approach the poem *as* poetry and so noninstrumentally means rejecting the form/content distinction between the truth conveyed and the way it is presented. A poem, Brooks says, is not about whatever ideas it may contain. The imagery, rhythm, and sound are not merely instruments by which a content is conveyed, but rather constitute the *meaning* of the poem itself. Poetry is a particular kind of discourse – figurative discourse – and the poem as poem is a dramatic unity of patterns of figuration. The unity of the poem lies in the ways in which tensions are set up by propositions, tropes, rhythm, and sound and are ultimately resolved, again figuratively. The poem is thus to be understood in close proximity to a musical composition, as when in sonata form tonal tensions are set up, argumentatively developed, and resolved.

The significance of this figurative use of language lies for Brooks in literature's concern not with ideas but with the way a human being may relate to them, which requires figurative expression, as can be seen in our everyday lives when we have resort to simile and metaphor in order to express how we feel. Because the structure of the poem is to be understood in this dramatic way, the central terms of critical discourse are those of "ambiguity," "paradox," "complex of attitudes," "irony," and "wit." The poem is an *enactment* of attitudes and of their conflict and resolution, and the critic's task is to interpret, in the sense of bringing out the nature of the "meaning," figuratively understood, as opposed to the mere paraphrasable content, and to evaluate the poem's success or failure as such enactment.

Brooks considers two critical revolutions prior to the advent of the New Criticism, and one might wonder why not more, given that literature and its discussion have a far longer history. George Watson (1973: 3) notes that it was Dryden who first used the term "criticism"

in relation to literature, at least in print, in the preface to *The State of Innocence* (1677), where he explains it as "a standard of judging well" and claims it was instituted first by Aristotle. But evaluative interpretation of individual works is singularly lacking in ancient and medieval texts. Plato, concerned to dispute the educative value of poetry, and Aristotle, to defend it as a form of knowledge about human life, both take for granted the evaluation of the works they mention but provide little insight into its formation. The same is largely true of the tradition of so-called rhetorical criticism in the Hellenistic period, concerned as it was to preserve a culture of the past by making its accepted masterworks into unquestionable models for imitation, although there are hints of a critical practice at work in the descriptions of the appropriateness of particular rhythms, diction, and sounds to the different "styles" of poetry (e.g., see Demetrius in Russell & Winterbottom 1972). The allegorical interpretation of the Middle Ages, deriving from Neoplatonic models utilized for Christian exegesis, consists in the application of a method to texts already selected on other grounds. One could get no indication from Dante's allegorical account of *The Divine Comedy* of how one could distinguish his work from the mediocre or incompetent, as his contemporaries and successors clearly did.

Let us, however, return to the question of the contemporary confrontation between criticism and theory. What is proposed by this in its various forms is that the practice of criticism involves presuppositions "about language and about meaning, about the relationships between meaning and the world, meaning and people, and . . . about people themselves and their place in the world" (Belsey 1980) which are never explicitly stated and defended. When these presuppositions are revealed by reflective thought, they are shown to be inadequate, and the practice that may then ensue, properly grounded in the appropriate theory, is no longer recognizably criticism. Theory takes a variety of contemporary forms depending on the sort of presuppositions identified and criticized, but perhaps the dominant modes have been deconstruction in the United States, and in Britain a form of poststructuralism centrally concerned with political history.

According to poststructuralist critics of both camps, literary criticism has sought to interpret works of literature and so provide us with access to their meaning. Such a meaning is assumed to be unitary, whether this is taken as a paraphrasable message or as the figurative unity sought by the New Critics, and only on the basis of this assumption are the interpretative practice and its characteristic forms of dispute and agreement intelligible. But this assumption is untenable, it is claimed. The meaning of any sign is produced only through its differing from others, and this process can have no given terminus as such an end would have to be a sign whose meaning was not the result of difference. Any particular determinant meaning is possible only because we have terminated this play of differentiation for practical purposes, and yet that meaning is possible only because the signs concerned can always be incorporated in another nexus of differences, another context, and so come to mean differently, in a way that cannot, in principle, be limited.

Deconstruction thus characteristically tries to show how a text, in trying to limit its meaning, at the same time undoes this work and shows its impossibility. Certain kinds of literary work are sometimes privileged within deconstructive approaches, as showing a reflective awareness of the differential nature of meaning, inviting interpretations that they at the same time resist. Thus, Barbara Johnson in a discussion of Melville's *Billy Budd* tries to show how the different readings of the text produced in literary criticism are replicated in the text itself, in the way Budd, Claggart, Dansker, and Vere read the events of the story and each other. At crucial moments of the text, central to *deciding* a meaning, however, there is only the "empty, mechanical functioning" of language, as when, for example, Vere dies simply repeating Budd's name. It is, Johnson suggests, "these very gaps in understanding," which both provoke interpretation and prevent its success, that "Melville is asking us to understand" (Johnson 1980: 94).

British theorists have tended to regard American deconstruction as a continuation of the New Critical project by other means, within which one can restrict oneself to the formal aspects of a text. "In the constant and repeated assertion of the evaporation of meaning there is no place to analyze the contest of meaning, and therefore no politics, and there is no possibility of tracing changes of meaning, the sliding of the signified, in history" (Belsey 1988: 403). For such theorists, the differential nature of meaning shows it as unfixed, "sliding," and so a matter for political debate. The differential structures of meaning available at any time determine the limits of what it is possible to say and understand, and since the destination of meaning is the subject, "subjectivity is discursively produced and is constrained by the range of subject positions defined by the discourses in which the individual participates" (Belsey 1985: 6). This determines, therefore, what it is possible to *be* at any time. But since the play of meaning cannot be halted, all such determinations of subjectivity are unstable and embattled.

The discourse of literary criticism, in its various forms, assumes a particular form of subjectivity – the unified, autonomous individual for whom there is a unified, determinate, and graspable meaning – the subjectivity of "liberal humanism," which emerges out of conflict with medieval conceptions in the sixteenth century and achieves dominance in the seventeenth. Literature is one of the scenes within which such fundamental determinations of meaning are contested and reinforced. The aim of the work on literature is to undermine the hold of "liberal humanism," through a demonstration of the way its fundamental conceptions have emerged through conflict and have maintained themselves through the suppression of alternative subjectivities. In this way, a contemporary space is to be formed within which radical change becomes possible. This reading practice is directed toward a "political history from the raw material of literary texts" for which "literary value becomes irrelevant: political assassination is problematized in Pickering's play *Horestes* (1567) as well as in *Hamlet*"; fiction is thus "put to work for substantial political ends" (Belsey 1988: 409).

The theoretical approaches to literature that have become a staple part of literary education over the past 30 years in general share this emancipatory ambition. Dominant forms of subjectivity (e.g., patriarchal, heterosexual, white colonial) historically define themselves over against subordinate and so inferior ones (female, homosexual, indigenous) and literature is read in terms of the constitution of, and opposition to, the former, a reading directed toward the liberation of the subordinated others to find their own voice. This has clearly been a liberating exercise itself for the study of literature. It emphasizes the historicality, and so alterability, of conceptions of human life, and foregrounds the historical situatedness of literary works in relation to the formation and contestation of these conceptions, but without objectifying history. Theory stresses, rather, that we are ourselves part of the history of human subjectivities so that to respond appropriately to literature is to do so in an engaged manner, in terms of our own contestations.

But although "criticism" in the sense advocated by the New Critics is a thing of the past, its concerns with the specificity of the literary and with the evaluation of individual works remain to trouble theory and to require an accommodation. Because theory sees literature as merely one way in which representations of subjectivity are constituted and contested, attention is diverted from the character of a work as a poem or short story, say, rather than a piece of journalism, within which, too, representations of subjectivity are formed. Again, it is difficult to see how issues of evaluation and its criteria can be avoided. The question of why we attend to Conrad and Kipling rather than Flora Annie Steel in relation to colonial subjectivities cannot be answered by an appeal to historical inquiry into their readerships, contemporary citations, and so forth. Why such authors still matter to us, and which contemporary works should, remain questions for us as they were for Cleanth Brooks in 1947.

See also LITERATURE; POETRY; AESTHETIC JUDGMENT; CANON; DECONSTRUCTION; FEMINIST CRITICISM; INTERPRETATION; MODERNISM AND POSTMODERNISM; SIBLEY; STRUCTURALISM AND POSTSTRUCTURALISM; TASTE.

BIBLIOGRAPHY
Belsey, C. 1980. *Critical Practice*. London: Methuen.
Belsey, C. 1985. *The Subject of Tragedy*. London: Methuen.
Belsey, C. 1988. "Literature, History, Politics." In *Modern Criticism and Theory*. David Lodge (ed.). London: Longman, 399–410.
Bradbury, Malcolm (ed.). 1970. *Contemporary Criticism*. London: Arnold.
Brooks, Cleanth. 1947. *The Well-Wrought Urn*. New York: Reynal & Hitchcock.
Coleridge, Samuel Taylor. 1960 [1817]. *Biographia Literaria*. G. Watson (ed.). London: Dent.
Cunningham, Valentine. 2002. *Reading After Theory*. Oxford: Blackwell.
Elledge, Scott (ed.). 1961. *Eighteenth-Century Critical Essays*. Ithaca: Cornell University Press.
Johnson, Barbara. 1980. *The Critical Difference*. Baltimore: Johns Hopkins University Press.
Kermode, Frank. 1989. *An Appetite for Poetry*. London: Collins.
Lodge, David (ed.). 1988. *Modern Criticism and Theory*. London: Longman.
Russell, D. A. & Winterbottom, M. 1972. *Ancient Literary Criticism*. Oxford: Oxford University Press.
Watson, George. 1973. *The Literary Critics*. Harmondsworth: Penguin.
Waugh, Patricia. 2006. *Literary Theory and Criticism: An Oxford Guide*. Oxford: Oxford University Press.

MICHAEL WESTON

Croce, Benedetto (1866–1952) Italian idealist philosopher, historian, and critic; a dominant figure in his country's intellectual life in the first part of the twentieth century. Born in the Abruzzo region of Italy, Croce developed in his youth a taste for old books and the life of a self-styled scholar in literature and history. Gradually, a passion for the free thinking that philosophy allowed drew him into writing in a philosophical vein. In 1883 he suffered a tragedy that reoriented his domestic life. He was on holiday with his family when an earthquake struck; his parents and sister were killed and he himself was buried for several hours before being rescued. He went to live in Rome with his uncle and when he finally emerged from the depression brought on by the tragedy and the subsequent displacement, he embarked on his philosophical career.

Croce's thinking drew from a variety of sources. Early on, under the influence of Antonio Labriola, he was led to explore the work of J. F. Herbart and Marx. A more direct influence on his aesthetics, however, was Francesco de Sanctis, whose work he had begun reading as a schoolboy. His continuing attention to de Sanctis led, after the turn of the century, to study of Hegel and Vico and to the refining of his own brand of idealist aesthetics. In tracing the history of Croce's central notion of intuition, it is of interest to note his assertion that he learned from de Sanctis "in a very crude shape this central idea: that art is not a work of reflection and logic, nor yet a product of skill, but pure and spontaneous imaginative form" (1928: 78–9).

Croce's first work in aesthetics, an outline of his initial thoughts, appeared in 1900 as *Thesis of Aesthetics*. This was followed in 1902 by the publication of his central work on the subject, *Aesthetic: As Science of Expression and General Linguistic*. It is in the *Aesthetic* that he first fully describes his account of art as intuition. Intuition, as he understood it, is not a mystical acquisition of transcendent truths, but the immediate knowing, and thereby transforming, of impressions. Since intuitive knowing is active, Croce maintains, it can also be understood as expression. Thus, intuition is expression insofar as expression is the act of transforming impressions by active imagination (*fantasia*) into individual unified images or organic wholes: "Intuition is the undifferentiated unity of the perception of the real and of the simple image of the possible" (1964: 4). The result was that, for Croce, intuition-expression in itself is neither divisible into parts nor subsumable under intellectual genera or categories.

In identifying art as intuition-expression, Croce seemed to champion art for art's sake. The presence or absence of intuition marked off that which was art from nonart. Although he insisted that aesthetic activity is not restricted to artists in the professional sense, he believed it possible to identify them by their "greater aptitude" and "more frequent inclination fully to express certain complex states of the soul" (1964: 13). However, he was also adamant in dismissing two extreme readings of art's autonomy. First, the aesthetic is not the only fundamental realm of the human spirit; rather, it has its place alongside logic, the practical (economics and ethics), and history. Second, despite its autonomy, art as intuition-expression cannot occur without the richness of human spirit in all its manifestations. Thus, aesthetics, although it is foundational, is not the monarch of all sciences, and artistic expression does not occur unfunded by other human activities.

On this foundation in the *Aesthetic* Croce built his fuller account of art as intuition. Scholars, however, disagree how to read the development of his ideas. Some argue that his views changed so drastically that it is best to understand his work as a series of distinct and inconsistent moments. However, he himself held that the development of his ideas was evolutionary, that his later thinking was an extension, not a refutation, of his earlier thinking. This was consistent with his adoption of a kind of historicism that acknowledged the growth of ideas. The evolutionary interpretation seems not only the most fruitful but, at least in the first instance, the one that, given Croce's own endorsement of it, provides the likeliest avenue to understanding him.

Not only the nature of this development, but its method, is significant. In 1903, shortly after publication of the *Aesthetic*, Croce and Giovanni Gentile began publication of their journal *La Critica*. Croce's task was that of criticizing recent Italian literature. Thus, his philosophical development came to be deeply influenced by his work as a practical critic. Indeed, his life's work as a whole exhibits a dialectic of the practical and the theoretical. In his aesthetics, this dialectic resulted in the breaking down of his initial description of art as intuition into three stages: (1) the attribution of a lyrical character to intuition; (2) the defense of cosmic totality in art; and (3) the distinction between poetry and literature.

The first development, begun in 1908 and summed up in *Guide to Aesthetics* in 1913, is perhaps the least problematic. The question that Croce faced was the efficacy of intuition: if intuition is not formed by intellectual concepts, how does it occur? His answer, which he attributed to ideas developed in his role as critic, was that intuition is "lyrical." That is, it is the expression of emotion or feeling. By this, however, he intended neither a "letting-off of steam" nor a simply imitative theory of expression. Rather, the intuition-expression is idealized or transformed emotion. As Orsini puts it: "The lyrical function of art is to express the personality of the artist – not, be it carefully noted, his 'practical personality' as evidenced in his biography, but what Croce calls here the 'soul' of the man" (1961: 48). The lyrical conception of intuition, in pointing to idealized emotion and personality, sets the stage for the second development of Croce's notion of art.

In a 1918 essay entitled "The Character of Totality in Artistic Expression," Croce argued that intuition involves a kind of universality or cosmic totality (*totalità*). To many critics this move appeared problematic, in view of his earlier assertions that logical concepts are universal and expressive intuitions are individual. However, Croce wanted to argue for a special kind of universality in art. In assessing the work of Ariosto, Shakespeare, Corneille, and others, he found himself searching for that which distinguishes their work from confessional, subjective articulations of emotion. What he suggested was that the best works of these artists express, in their individuality, something common to all humanity; they express or reflect a cosmic totality. This does not, as Croce saw it, imply an act of intellectualizing or philosophizing in art. An intuition-expression in itself is still not a general type governing a set of tokens. Rather, the universality or totality of art occurs together with art's individuality in an undifferentiated form, as is not the case in conceptual renderings of universality.

An interesting upshot of Croce's defense of cosmic totality occurred when he began to search for its phenomenological attributes. From the mid 1920s, he began to argue that moral conscience is a condition of intuition-expression. If taken to mean that art depends on morality, this clearly and flatly contradicts one of his fundamental theses: the separation of the realms of the spirit. Moreover, critics saw in this suggestion the possibility of the very kind of moralism that Croce had always sought to reject. It is possible, however, that he had something more expansive in mind: "It is impossible," he said, "to be a poet or an artist without being in the first place a man nourished by thought and by experience of moral ideals and conflicts" (1949: 133). He may have been searching not for a narrow moralism but for the kind of experience, even if imaginative experience, that can engender cosmic totality.

In the final turn in his aesthetics, Croce published in 1936 his *Poetry and Literature: An Introduction to Its Criticism and History*. Here he distinguishes poetry from literature. On the surface such a distinction may appear to contradict his earlier insistence against understanding art through types or genres. However, his project was to return to his distinction between art and nonart. The problem was to locate those items that appear to be poetry, inasmuch as they appropriate artistic expressions, but are not themselves intuition-expressions. He had in mind particular items such as entertainment and prose that are practical or intellectual in nature. To these items he gave the name "literature" to distinguish them from poetry or art. Thus, instead of establishing fixed genres within art, Croce was simply refining a distinction he had made in the *Aesthetic*.

His notion of art as intuition-expression in its various stages of development produced several interesting corollaries. First, it excised external production or the making of artifacts from art proper. For Croce, "externalization" of intuition-expression was a practical affair, not an aesthetic one. This was, and is, anathema for aestheticians for whom the physical making is integral to art. Yet Croce's position is not as strange as it might seem at first glance.

On the one hand, even in his earliest work he recognized that externalization can be used to assist expression. On the other, he never discarded from intuition qualities such as tempo, rhythm, line, and color. The mistake, as he saw it, was an ontological one of assuming that these qualities are merely external, physical items or events. For him they *are* the intuition-expression in their unique unity; and they occur in the intuition prior to any physical recording of them.

This in turn led to Croce's assertion that the role that physical artifacts have to play is that of vehicle for communicating art. Thus, as Dewey independently suggested, critics and observers must use artifacts to re-create the intuition of the artist. As did Dewey, Croce faced opposition here from those who argued that such strict re-creation is impossible. However, it is doubtful that he had in mind anything like a technical isomorphism; rather, the *genius* of the producer and the *taste* of the critic achieve the same intuition of cosmic totality. It is in this way "that our little souls can echo great souls, and grow great with them in the universality of the spirit" (1964: 121).

The adoption of this method of criticism also meant that he rejected the efficacy of criticisms that rest entirely on intellectual categorizations of technique or content. For Croce, such categories, by virtue of their practical or intellectual natures, were incidental to art. Nevertheless, he did come to maintain that critics can use intellectual categories in their practice of criticizing, but only after a re-creation of intuition-expression has occurred.

Much of Croce's work remains under-explored in contemporary Anglo-American aesthetics, perhaps because much of it remains untranslated. Nevertheless, through the work of R. G. Collingwood his aesthetics has been indirectly influential beyond Continental Europe. Moreover, Croce's discussions of the similarities between his ideas and those of John Dewey deserve further investigation. While Dewey attempted to disavow any debt to Croce, the similarities that exist are too compelling to be dismissed. If the flux of Croce's aesthetics makes it difficult to unify, the experiential soundness of its insights insures it future importance.

See also COLLINGWOOD; DEWEY; EXPRESSION THEORY; ONTOLOGY OF ARTWORKS.

BIBLIOGRAPHY

Primary sources
[1902; rev. edn. 1922] 1964. *Aesthetic: As Science of Expression and General Linguistic*. D. Ainslie (trans.). New York: Noonday Press.
[1913] 1965. *Guide to Aesthetics*. P. Romanell (trans.). Indianapolis: Bobbs-Merrill.
[1918] 1928. *Benedetto Croce: An Autobiography*. R. G. Collingwood (trans.). Oxford: Clarendon.
[1936] 1981. *Benedetto Croce's Poetry and Literature: An Introduction to Its Criticism and History*. G. Gullace (trans.). Carbondale: Southern Illinois University Press.
1949. *My Philosophy and Other Essays on the Moral and Political Problems of Our Time*. E. F. Carritt (trans.). London: Allen & Unwin.

Secondary sources
Brown, Merle E. 1966. *Neo-Idealistic Aesthetics: Croce–Gentile–Collingwood*. Detroit: Wayne State University Press.
D'Amico, Jack et al. 1999. *The Legacy of Benedetto Croce*. Toronto: University of Toronto Press.
Moss, M. E. 1987. *Benedetto Croce Reconsidered: Truth and Error in Theories of Art, Literature, and History*. Hanover: University Press of New England.
Orsini, Gian N. G. 1961. *Benedetto Croce: Philosopher of Art and Literary Critic*. Carbondale: Southern Illinois University Press.

DOUGLAS R. ANDERSON

cultural appropriation Cultural appropriation occurs when members of one culture take something from members of another culture. It is particularly controversial when someone from a wealthy or powerful culture takes something from an indigenous culture or from a disadvantaged minority culture. This article differentiates the types of cultural appropriation in the arts and indicates how each of them could be questioned from an aesthetic or moral perspective.

At least three distinct activities have been described as cultural appropriation. One sort involves taking tangible works of art. The transfer of the Parthenon Marbles from Athens to the British Museum is an instance of such appropriation. The appropriation by museums and collectors of artworks (such as totem poles and masks) from indigenous cultures has also proved very controversial. This sort of appropriation can be called *object appropriation*.

A second sort of cultural appropriation occurs when an artist reuses artistic content that originated in another culture. A culturally mainstream Australian who retells stories of aboriginal Australian cultures has engaged in this sort of cultural appropriation, as has the artist from one culture who performs a musical composition from another culture. Call this *content appropriation*. Sometimes artists appropriate less than an entire work of art. For example, a style can be appropriated, as when a non-African American musician composes in a jazz or blues style. Sometimes not even this much is appropriated. For example, Picasso appropriated basic ideas or motifs from west African carvers without producing a work in the style of these carvers. Similarly, Stravinsky and Milhaud appropriated motifs from jazz without producing jazz compositions.

Finally we may identify a sort of appropriation that is somewhat different from the others. This sort of appropriation does not involve the taking of something produced in the context of another culture. Rather, it is the representation of one culture by members of another. The mysteries that Tony Hillerman sets among the Navajo are instances of such appropriation, as is Kipling's *Kim*. Sometimes this is called "voice appropriation." Since a subject matter is appropriated, I will call it *subject appropriation*.

Cultural appropriation gives rise to both aesthetic and moral questions. One aesthetic objection suggests that outsiders (nonmembers of a culture) who appropriate content will produce works or performances that are aesthetically inferior (perhaps because inauthentic in some way) to those produced by insiders (members of a culture). So, for example, some people suggest that non-African Americans will be unable to perform jazz or blues music as well as members of African American culture. A similar claim has been made about subject appropriation. Here the suggestion is that outsiders will necessarily misrepresent or distort insiders and their cultures and that this is an aesthetic flaw.

Some evidence can be adduced in favor of aesthetic objections to cultural appropriation. Many non-African American musicians have failed to produce aesthetically successful performances of the blues. Other artists have appropriated the styles of various aboriginal cultures and then produced poor works of art. On the other hand, artists from a variety of cultures have apparently been very successful when appropriating works, styles, and motifs from other cultures. The Japanese filmmaker Akira Kurosawa successfully reworked plays by Shakespeare in the films *Throne of Blood* (1957) and *Ran* (1985). Non-African American musicians such as Marcia Ball, Eric Clapton, and Stevie Ray Vaughan are widely regarded as accomplished blues musicians.

Cultural appropriation also raises moral questions. Consider the morality of object appropriation. Many instances of object appropriation are unobjectionable. A European tourist who purchases a work of indigenous art from a legitimate dealer in Darwin or Sante Fe transfers an artwork from one culture to another but does not act wrongly. Other cases of object appropriation are obviously wrong because they are instances of theft. The looting of the Benin Bronzes (many of which are in the British Museum) during the punitive expedition of 1897 is a case in point.

In a wide range of instances, the morality of object appropriation is far from clear. In some cases, forebears of a contemporary culture may not have objected to the appropriation of a work. The *Flatejarbók*, which records the voyage of Leif Ericsson to North America, provides an example. When it was taken to Denmark and willed to the University of Copenhagen in the eighteenth century, few Icelanders knew or cared about it. In other cases, works of art were appropriated after they had been lost or abandoned by their original owners. Many archaeological finds fall into this category. The challenge here is to show that the appropriation of a work of art is wrong even though no one initially objected to the appropriation.

Cultures can claim to have inherited property that was not originally its property. Any claim to have inherited property must be based on the testamentary wishes of previous owners. The trouble is that often a work was in the past owned by a state, a religious communion, a clan, or an individual and not a culture. Often cultures will claim ownership of artworks when the claim that the original owners wished or would have wished a culture to inherit them is hard to establish or implausible. Consider, for example, the Parthenon Marbles. They were not originally the property of Greek culture, but rather Athenian civic property. It is unlikely that ancient Athenians would have wanted bitter enemies (such as Spartans) to be among the future owners of the Marbles.

The value that certain works have for a culture can, in some circumstances, give a culture a claim on a work. Consider again the manuscript of the *Flatejarbók*. Icelandic culture did not inherit this work – the University of Copenhagen did. Nevertheless, the *Flatejarbók* is so crucial to Icelandic culture that it has a plausible claim to own it. Denmark recognized this claim and the book was returned to Iceland. A similar case could be made for returning the Parthenon Marbles to Greece or other works of art to various indigenous cultures.

Content appropriation can also give rise to questions about property. Clearly it is wrong to violate legitimate copyright in artworks. Controversy can arise, however, because different cultures have different legal rules about what can be owned. In Western cultures, only specific expressions of an idea can be protected by copyright. Even this sort of copyright expires after a term. In certain indigenous cultures, laws regulate who may tell certain stories (such as creation myths). These laws protect not only particular expressions of the story but also the general idea for a type of story. Often these laws apply in perpetuity, unlike Western copyright. In other indigenous cultures, styles (including the X-ray style of certain Australian aboriginal cultures), patterns of cross-hatching or motifs (such as the koru of Maori art) are regarded as property. When cultures have different rules governing what may be appropriated, we need to ask about the moral basis for claims to own certain items of property.

It is hard to make the case for ownership by a culture of motifs, patterns, or general plot types. Cultures have always interacted and a particular type of story may be told in a variety of cultures. Even when cultures have not interacted, certain patterns and motifs may have developed independently. Under such circumstances, it is difficult to identify one culture as the owner of a plot, pattern, or motif. Defenders of cultural appropriation will also be inclined to argue that Western copyright law captures an important moral truth: a balance ought to be struck between the interests of those who are responsible for the origin of some original creation and the interest everyone shares in innovation, unconstrained creativity, and the free exchange of ideas. Restrictions on the use of styles and plots would not strike the right balance. Everyone would be denied the many interesting innovations that have arisen as a result of cultural appropriation.

Even if cultural appropriation does not involve the harmful violation of property rights, it could be wrong. One often reads that certain forms of subject or content appropriation can lead to distorted pictures of a particular culture. This can, in turn, lead to harm to members of the culture. Consider, for example, old Hollywood Westerns and their caricatures of Native American cultures. These almost certainly fostered discrimination against indigenous people. Similarly, some outsider's clumsy appropriation of content could similarly encourage the formation of harmful stereotypes about the insiders' culture. This could, in turn, lead to harmful treatment of insiders.

The harmful misrepresentation of a culture is often wrong. It is not clear, however, that all appropriation of content or subject matters harms insiders or their cultures. The Navajo have praised Hillerman for his accurate depiction of their culture. Edward Said has argued that outsiders are apt to create stereotypes about insiders and their cultures, but he also maintained that it is possible for members of one culture to understand another. He explicitly denied that "only women can understand feminine experience, only Jews can understand Jewish suffering, only formerly colonial subjects can understand colonial experience" (Said 1993: 31). According to Amiri Baraka (LeRoi Jones), who opposes appropriation of jazz and blues as a kind of theft, Bix Beiderbecke's appropriation of jazz "served to place the Negro's culture and Negro society in a position of intelligent regard it had never enjoyed before" (Jones 1963: 151).

Sometimes cultural appropriation is thought to be wrong because it is offensive. Subject appropriation certainly can be offensive, as when Westerners represent the prophet Muhammad (in the *Jyllands-Posten* cartoons of 2005) or Islam (in Theo van Gogh's film *Submission*, 2004). Content appropriation can also be offensive. For example, the use of story plots, styles, and patterns characteristic of Australian aboriginal cultures has been described as "inappropriate, derogatory, culturally offensive or out of context" (Janke 1998: 19). Many aboriginal communities are offended by the appropriation and display in museums of art objects that they regard as having sacred or ritual significance.

There is a prima facie case against acting in an offensive manner, but the creation of an offensive work of art is not always wrong. Consider two works that have proved deeply offensive: *Piss Christ* by Andres Serrano and Chris Ofili's *Holy Virgin Mary*. The former is a photograph of a crucifix immersed in a tank of the artist's urine. Ofili's work is a multimedia image of Mary. Her breasts are crafted from elephant dung and small pictures of female buttocks and genitalia, cut from pornographic magazines, surround the central image. While these works have proved offensive to many Christians, creating them was arguably not wrong. In creating the works in question, Ofili and Serrano were engaged in acts of self-expression. That some people are offended by their work is unfortunate, but when artists produce offensive works when engaged in self-expression and self-realization, it is not obvious that they act wrongly. This point extends to artists whose work is offensive qua act of cultural appropriation. So long as artists who engage in cultural appropriation are engaged in a project of self-expression or self-realization, it is not obvious that they act wrongly, even if members of the culture from which they appropriate are deeply offended.

See also AMERINDIAN AESTHETICS; AUTHENTICITY AND ART; FORGERY; MUSEUMS.

BIBLIOGRAPHY
Brown, Michael F. 2003. *Who Owns Native Culture?* Cambridge, MA: Harvard University Press.
Coleman, Elizabeth Burns. 2005. *Aboriginal Art, Identity and Appropriation.* Aldershot: Ashgate.
Gracyk, Theodore. 2001. *I Wanna Be Me: Rock Music and Politics of Identity.* Philadelphia: Temple University Press.
Hurka, Thomas. 1994. "Should Whites Write about Minorities?" In *Principles: Short Essays on Ethics.* Toronto: Harcourt Brace, 183–6.
Janke, Terri. 1998. *Our Culture: Our Future: Report on Australian Indigenous Cultural and Intellectual Property Rights.* Australian Aboriginal and Torres Strait Islander Studies and Aboriginal and Torres Strait Islander Commission.
Jones, LeRoi [Amiri Baraka]. 1963. *Blues People.* New York: William Morrow.
Merryman, John. 1985. "Thinking about the Elgin Marbles," *Michigan Law Review*, 83, 1881–923.
Said, Edward W. 1993. *Culture and Imperialism.* New York: Knopf.
Thompson, Jana. 2003. "Cultural Property, Restitution and Value," *Journal of Applied Philosophy*, 20, 251–62.
Young, James O. 2007. *Cultural Appropriation and the Arts.* Oxford: Blackwell.

JAMES O. YOUNG

225

D

Danto, Arthur C(oleman) (b.1924) American philosopher and art critic; for many years at Columbia University. Past president of the American Society of Aesthetics (1989–90) and of the American Philosophical Association (1983), Danto became art critic of *The Nation* in 1984, in whose service he produced a prize-winning array of articles that marry philosophical acumen with a rich knowledge of, and feeling for, the fine arts.

His entry into the philosophy of art was marked by his article "The Artworld" (1964), which brought the term "artworld" from the vernacular into mainstream aesthetics. The term was used by George Dickie and others in the development of institutional theories of art, but for Danto, the artworld is constituted by the art traditions, conventions, and practices that create space for the given artwork. It is in terms of theory and history, not the decrees of a social institution, that Danto hopes to explain what it is that makes an object art.

This theme is taken up and developed in his most important work in aesthetics (Danto 1981). Deeply influenced by Wittgenstein's concern with questions about the difference between indiscernibles – between my arm rising and my raising my arm – Danto posed a related question about art. What, he wanted to know, is the difference between two indiscernible objects – two identical urinals, for instance – one of which is a work of art, the other not? According to Danto, the difference resides in the fact that works of art are *about* the world in a way that ordinary objects are not. Both art and philosophy are about reality in much the way that language is when it is employed descriptively. Hence art is always representational – not merely (if at all) in the sense that it refers to something, but also in the sense that it conveys the artist's way of seeing, viewing, understanding. Art is often about what

has gone before it, and attains what sense it has because of this.

Danto asks us to suppose that Picasso, in a moment of inspiration, painted one of his old neckties a bright blue. This work, were it to exist, would be *about* the history and theory of painting itself. This is why the child who does similar damage to his father's tie will not have produced a work of art: the damaged tie is not about anything. The fact that Picasso's tie is a work of art means that it has properties which "its untransfigured counterpart lacks" (1981: 99). The distinction, then, between the child's imagined tie and Picasso's is an ontological, not an institutional, distinction. It is the historical and theoretical identity of the work – furnished in an interpretation – that gives it the aesthetic properties that it has. Interpretation, Danto argues, is essential to the *existence* of a work of art.

Artworks, in Danto's view, are representations that are self-referential and that require interpretation both by the artist, in the sense that it is partly constituted by such interpretation, and by the viewer, in the sense that the artwork cannot be apprehended as an artwork without interpretation. There remains the obvious objection, though, that some self-referential reports and descriptions are not works of art. An artwork, he writes, is "a transfigurative representation rather than a representation *tout court*" (1981: 172). By commenting on itself, it acquires properties that nonart representations do not possess.

These themes are deeply suggestive, but are not always well worked out. Could not a philosophical text comment on, and so transfigure, itself in just this way? And does this mean that philosophy is art? Some of these issues are picked up and developed in a later work (Danto 1986), although the main concern here is to show that philosophy (as practiced by Plato,

Kant, and Hegel) has traditionally attempted to undermine and so disenfranchise art. Part of Danto's attempt to reenfranchise art involves returning to the relation between art and interpretation in order to show that works of art are not to be attended to merely for the disinterested pleasure they afford. Since it is possible to have two snow shovels both exactly alike, only one of which is a work of art, it cannot be the aesthetic appearance of the snow shovel that makes it a work of art. Rather, indiscernible objects become "quite different and distinct works of art by dint of distinct and different interpretations" (1986: 39).

Danto's treatment of interpretation is puzzling. Recognition that the snow shovel is a work of art depends not on interpretations in any ordinary sense of this word, but on one's knowledge of certain theories and cultural conventions. If one has the requisite knowledge, one recognizes that the snow shovel is a work of art, and one recognizes this quite independently of whether one understands the work. If puzzled by the work, one may venture to explain and in this sense interpret it. This, of course, is an altogether different process, but Danto seems to run the two together.

A second major theme in Danto's philosophy of art concerns the "end of art." Inspired by views presented by Hegel, he (1986) offers the idea that the history of art is the record of its progress toward self-realization through self-understanding. In the twentieth century, art fulfilled its destiny, so that now the history of art is at an end. Art has entered its "posthistorical" stage.

As we have seen, Danto holds that artworks can be identified and appreciated only through their proper location within art-making traditions which generate the atmospheres of theory which make them what they are. A consequence of this is that artistic change is directional and irreversible. The possibilities for artistic change are shaped by both technical innovations that impinge on the "artworld" from the wider culture and the direction in which earlier artists have led the artworld. What is possible at any time depends on what has been achieved in the art of the past. The artworld has to be "ready" for the new movements, because they build on or challenge the possibilities of the art of the past.

Danto rejects two models for progress in art history in favor of a third in which aspects of the first two models are synthesized. The first sees art as aiming at perceptual fidelity, as motivated wherever possible by an imperative to replace inference to perceptual reality with something equivalent to what perceptual reality itself would present. On this view, the history of painting is to be characterized in terms of the development of pictorial conventions the purpose of which is to render space and perspective faithfully. Danto rejects this model because it fails to accommodate not only narrational art forms but also those arts to which it most naturally applies. The invention and development of "moving pictures" in the cinema made clear that optical fidelity might be achieved there more successfully than could be hoped for in painting. Early in the twentieth century, this led painters to question and, ultimately, to abandon the goal of representational accuracy in favor of other concerns.

The second model of progress in art history holds that art is expression. Danto objects that this reduces the history of art to a list of individual acts that are not unified by shared progress toward a common ideal. He notes that, from Fauvism onward, the important common element seemed to be not expression but reliance on a quite complex theory in order that often very minimal objects could be transfigured into art. Art became self-conscious and, from that point on, any distinction between art's nature and a philosophical consideration of its nature was undermined; it was only through conscious attention to its own philosophical character that art could continue to develop. Every work and movement became a kind of theory in action. Nowhere was this more obvious than in Duchamp's presentation of his readymades. Duchamp's works, says Danto, raise the question of the philosophical nature of art from within art, implying that art is already philosophy in a vivid form.

The theory of art history Danto then develops was influenced by Hegel's suggestion that art, through its own development, reaches a stage at which it contributes to the goal of human thought, which is an understanding of its own historical essence. The stage is transitional – a step on the path to self-knowledge which encompasses art as one important aspect of human culture. When the driving forces of history no longer mesh with the driving forces of art, the history of art ends. But whereas Hegel regarded this as occurring at the close of the classic period of Greek art, Danto dates it to the arrival of Pop Art in the 1960s. By aping "mere real things," the works of Pop Art provoked the philosophical question that asks what distinguishes them from their mundane, perceptually indistinguishable counterparts. In his early discussions (1986, 1987), Danto suggests that art somehow answered the question it posed, thereby becoming transmuted into philosophy. Later (1992, 1997), he accepts that art is incapable of responding to the query it spent half a millennium in raising and refining. Pop Art's achievement consists in posing the question in a form that makes it possible for philosophers to address it, whereas they were in no position to do so formerly.

So, art fulfilled its historical destiny in the 1960s, Danto maintains, and the history of art had then come to a close though art continued to be made in its posthistorical phase. Danto (1986) identified the hallmarks of the posthistorical phase as follows: anything can become an artwork. Where all directions are available there no longer can be progress. What art is and what it means have already been revealed, so it is not possible that art should continue to astonish us. As the atmosphere of art theory thickens, so the objects of art become thinner, more minimal, even dispensable. Traditional boundaries between the art forms tend to become radically unstable. The institutions of the artworld, the existence of which is predicated on ideas of artistic history and progress, begin to wither and die. This largely negative characterization was balanced (1987) by the suggestion that having achieved self-comprehension, art could return to the serving of largely human needs.

In questioning Danto's thesis, one might object to the manner in which he marginalizes all popular and non-Western art. Is it only in the rarefied realm of avant-garde Western "high" art that art's nature is revealed?

And one can doubt that his various theses are consistent. While he allows (1986, 1992, 1994) that, since nothing is historically mandated in the posthistorical phase of art, every-

thing is permitted, he also observes (1997) that what artists can achieve by what they do is no less limited now by history than before. Artists are free to adopt any style they like, but if the cultural and intellectual setting that gave that style its significance has passed, they are not free to give their work the content and import that former artists might have done. Invoking a familiar distinction in the philosophy of language, Danto holds that artists can *mention* styles they appropriate, but cannot *use* them.

Now, though, we are bound to wonder what can be meant by the claim that the history of art has come to an end. All it entails, apparently, is that artworks no longer need to impersonate real things, since art's philosophically provocative duty already has been discharged. It does not mean, as one might have supposed, that artists now can make any *artwork* they like, but only that *any thing* might be made into an artwork. What an artwork can be and can mean is no less a function of the times in which it is made than was so prior to 1964.

The universality of art from the earliest times suggests that art answers to some deep human needs, and that art might serve those needs for as long as the fundamental character of human nature remains unchanged. Given that we remain all too human, there is reason to doubt that art can no longer have anything "new to say." If much modern art seems to be empty, this is not because we now understand what art is and what it means. That philosophical knot is no easier to unravel than ever it was.

See also TWENTIETH-CENTURY ANGLO-AMERICAN AESTHETICS; ART HISTORY; "ARTWORLD"; DEFINITION OF "ART"; DICKIE; HEGEL; INTERPRETATION; THEORIES OF ART.

BIBLIOGRAPHY

Primary sources
1964. "The Artworld," *Journal of Philosophy*, 61, 571–84.
1981. *The Transfiguration of the Commonplace: A Philosophy of Art*. Cambridge, MA: Harvard University Press.
1986. *The Philosophical Disenfranchisement of Art*. New York: Columbia University Press.
1987. *The State of the Art*. New York: Prentice-Hall.

1988. *The Politics of Imagination*. Lawrence: University of Kansas Press.

1990. *Encounters and Reflections: Art in the Historical Present*. New York: Farrar, Straus, & Giroux.

1992. *Beyond the Brillo Box: The Visual Arts in Post-Historical Perspective*. New York: Farrar, Straus, & Giroux.

1993. "Responses and Replies." In *Arthur Danto and His Critics*. M. Rollins (ed.). Oxford: Blackwell, 193–216.

1994. *Embodied Meanings*. New York: Farrar, Straus, & Giroux.

1997. *After the End of Art: Contemporary Art and the Pale of History*. Princeton: Princeton University Press.

2003. *The Abuse of Beauty: Aesthetics and the Concept of Art*. Chicago: Open Court.

Secondary sources

Carroll, Noël. 1990. "Review Essay," *History and Theory*, 29, 111–24.

Haapala, Arto, Levinson, Jerrold, & Rantala, Veikko (eds.). 1997. *The End of Art and Beyond: Essays After Danto*. New Jersey: Humanities Press.

Lang, Berel (ed.). 1984. *The Death of Art*. New York: Haven.

Rollins, Mark (ed.). 1993. *Arthur Danto and His Critics*. Oxford: Blackwell.

DAVID NOVITZ & STEPHEN DAVIES

death of art   *see* DANTO; HEGEL.

deconstruction   A form of textual analysis largely derived from the work of the French poststructuralist philosopher Jacques Derrida, basing itself on the following assumptions: texts, like language, are marked by instability and indeterminacy of meaning; given such instability and indeterminacy, neither philosophy nor criticism can have any claim to authority as regards textual interpretation; textual interpretation is a free-ranging activity more akin to game-playing than to traditional analysis.

The point of deconstructive reading is to destroy the illusion of stable meaning in texts. It does this by way of what Derrida calls "active interpretation," an anarchic form of writing that makes extensive use of wit and wordplay. Derrida speaks of the reader engaging in "the joyous affirmation of the play of the world and of the innocence of becoming, the affirmation of a world of signs without fault, without truth, and without origin which is offered to an active interpretation" (1978: 292). Signs that are without fault, truth, or origin are signs whose meaning has not been fixed in advance, as would be the assumption under a structuralist scheme of analysis. Their meaning at any given point will depend on the ingenuity of the reader's "active interpretation." Reading becomes a creative process rather than an exercise in the recovery of meaning.

Deconstruction begins as a form of philosophy concerned to challenge the Western metaphysical tradition in general and its theories of meaning in particular, but it is probably best known in the English-speaking world as a style of literary criticism. Its popularity is largely due to the efforts of the Derrida-influenced "Yale School": Geoffrey Hartman, Harold Bloom, Paul de Man, and J. Hillis Miller. In the hands of these critics, deconstruction becomes a license for a display of linguistic virtuosity that deliberately avoids anything resembling *explication de texte* – "interpretation no longer aims at the reconciliation or unification of warring truths" (Hartman 1981: 51). Active interpretation takes as its goal the proliferation, rather than the reduction to schemes and codes, of meaning. It is questionable whether "interpretation" is even an appropriate word to use in this context, since it is normally taken to mean interpretation in terms of a scheme of some kind, having pretensions to truth of some kind. But such pretensions are precisely what Derrida is arguing are unsustainable.

Derrida sees meaning as being endlessly deferred by the action of *différance*, a concept he constructs from the verb *différer*, which can mean either "to differ" or "to defer." *Différance* cannot be distinguished from the word *différence* when spoken, and for Derrida this illustrates the inherent ambiguity of the linguistic sign. The latter thus has an odd sort of half-life; as Gayatri Spivak has described it: "Such is the strange 'being' of the sign: half of it always 'not there' and the other half always 'not that' " (Derrida 1976: xvii). Deconstructionist critics plunder texts for evidence of *différance* and the indeterminacy of the sign, and playing with language is one of their primary strategies for drawing such phenomena to our attention. Puns and wordplay are used to open up texts because they widen the field of meaning of words, thus suggesting that the sign is indeed always half "not there" and half "not that." A word's sound quality brings to mind like-sounding, although not necessarily like-meaning, words, thereby breaking the notion of a one-to-one relationship between signifier and signified (word and concept). The pun, in effect, defers the union of signifier and signified.

Once we set off on a sequence of punning our frame of reference keeps shifting, thus preventing stable meaning from ever forming. It is an example of paradigmatic relation – or "association of ideas" – in operation, and deconstructionists consider that by undermining a text's linearity of argument they are undermining its pretensions to rationality (which is felt to depend on linear thought process). A typical sequence in Geoffrey Hartman moves by means of punning and association of ideas from the German word *Ecke* (corner) to the French word *coin* (corner), to the English *coin*, to the German word *Kante* (board) and then to the name of the philosopher Kant (1981: 85). This takes place in the context of a supposed commentary on Derrida's *Glas*, and can serve only to disorient an audience habituated to expect logical argument and carefully ordered critique. Only the failure of the critic's ingenuity, or the reader's patience, can end such a sequence.

Hartman is here putting into practice Spivak's plan of operations for the aspiring deconstructionist:

> if in the process of deciphering a text in the traditional way we come across a word that seems to harbor an unresolvable contradiction, and by virtue of being one word is made sometimes to work in one way and sometimes in another and thus is made to point away from the absence of a unified meaning, we shall catch at that word ... We shall follow its adventures through the text and see the text coming undone. (Derrida 1976: lxxv).

The text comes undone because the critic's linguistic ingenuity – punning, wordplay, allusion, association of ideas – demonstrates just how diffuse and unpredictable meaning is at any given moment. "We are tempted to become associative and metaphorical," because "the slippage [of meaning] is all around us, and the principle of stabilization not very conspicuous" (Hartman 1981: 149, 64). The point of deconstructive reading is persistently to reveal that

slippage, the sheer undecidability of textual meaning.

Deconstructionists believe that slippage is inevitably present in all texts, including philosophical ones. In one of the more provocative developments of deconstruction, literary critics have turned the techniques of their own discipline back on philosophy in what Christopher Norris has called "the revenge of literary theory on that old tradition of philosophical disdain or condescension stretching back at least to Plato's *Republic*" (1983: 3). The objective of such an exercise is to challenge philosophy's claims to be an arbiter of truth and knowledge, by exploring "the various ways in which philosophy reveals, negotiates or represses its own inescapable predicament as written language" (1983: 12). This "inescapable predicament" means that philosophical texts are no more able to stabilize meaning than any others are.

Derrida's own aesthetic criticism uses various tricks to defer meaning and textual explication, such as a footnote running the whole length of the text in "Living On: Border Lines," and a dwelling on marginal details such as frames, borders, and signatures when discussing painting (1987). In a very real sense the act of criticism is never allowed to get under way in Derrida, and he argues that, when confronted with a text, the deconstructionist critic should resist the temptation to interpret it: "We should neither comment, nor underscore a single word, nor extract anything, nor draw a lesson from it" (1979: 152). The entire strategy is to frustrate the normal expectations of the reader. Style becomes a battleground for the deconstructionist, who deliberately cultivates an anarchic way of writing for polemical purposes.

Deconstruction had a powerful impact on the American academic scene in the 1970s and 1980s, one critic even arguing that it "effectively displaced other intellectual programs in the minds and much of the work of the literary avant-garde" there (Bove 1983: 6). American deconstruction has, however, come under attack from some quarters for being a debased version of the philosophical original. Several commentators regard it as merely an updated form of New Criticism, and just as open to charges of ahistoricism (neither New Critics nor deconstructionists feel any need to go outside the text in their readings).

Derrida himself has expressed misgivings about what has been done in his name: "this word [deconstruction] which I had only written one or twice . . . all of a sudden jumped out of the text and was seized by others who have since determined its fate in the manner you well know . . . But for me 'deconstruction' was not at all the first or the last word, and certainly not a password or slogan for everything that was to follow" (1988: 86). This raises the interesting specter of a misreading of Derrida by his American followers, which in a theory celebrating the inescapable instability of the sign and the perpetual presence of *différance* within language is more than somewhat ironic; but it does suggest the need to discriminate carefully between deconstruction as philosophy and deconstruction as literary criticism. The former is a serious, if iconoclastic, contributor to the debate on the nature of meaning, the latter arguably more of a license for a display of linguistic virtuosity for its own sake.

A more damaging indictment of the deconstructive enterprise is that it trades on notions of undecidability while arguing its case for undecidability within meaning and language. Most philosophers and critics would be quite willing to admit that slippage of meaning occurs (poetry works on just such a principle), but would draw the line at saying that *nothing but* slippage occurs: it is hard to see how, if that were the case, we could even communicate such a state of affairs.

See also NINETEENTH- AND TWENTIETH-CENTURY CONTINENTAL AESTHETICS; CRITICISM; DERRIDA; INTERPRETATION; INTERPRETATION, AIMS OF; STRUCTURALISM AND POSTSTRUCTURALISM; TEXT.

BIBLIOGRAPHY

Bove, Paul. 1983. "Variations on Authority: Some Deconstructive Transformations of the New Criticism." In *The Yale Critics: Deconstruction in America*. J. Arac, W. Godzich, & W. Martin (eds.). Minneapolis: University of Minnesota Press, 3–19.

Derrida, Jacques. 1976 [1967]. *Of Grammatology*. G. C. Spivak (trans.). Baltimore: Johns Hopkins University Press.

Derrida, Jacques. 1978 [1967]. *Writing and Difference*. A. Bass (trans.). London: Routledge & Kegan Paul.

Derrida, Jacques. 1979. "Living On: Border Lines." In *Deconstruction and Criticism*. H. Bloom et al. (eds.).

J. Hulbert (trans.). London: Routledge & Kegan Paul, 75–176.

Derrida, Jacques. 1987 [1978]. *The Truth in Painting*. G. Bennington & I. McLeod (trans.). Chicago: University of Chicago Press.

Derrida, Jacques. 1988. *The Ear of the Other: Otobiography, Transference, Translation*. C. McDonald (ed.). P. Kamuf (trans.). Lincoln: University of Nebraska Press.

Hartman, Geoffrey. 1981. *Saving the Text*. Baltimore: Johns Hopkins University Press.

Norris, Christopher. 1983. *The Deconstructive Turn*. London: Methuen.

STUART SIM

definition of "art" A definition of art is standardly intended to apply to works unambiguously belonging to Western fine art traditions and to their developments, including those of the avant-garde; and perhaps also to certain objects of alternative cultural provenance (e.g., cave paintings, Shaker textiles). The classic form is that of a small number of individually necessary and jointly sufficient conditions, satisfaction of which is to determine the reference of the concept. For some, a definition enables us to identify art, especially avant-garde works, many of which are not easily differentiable from other things. For others, its use is primarily metaphysical: given that artworks form no obvious natural kind, a definition should engage with the reasons for which art is identified as such by us, in order to show that artworks are a unified (nonnatural) kind of thing.

There is further disagreement about what is to be defined. Some differentiate between a classificatory and an evaluative concept, arguing that sometimes the appellation as art implies that value is present, but that there is also a notion of bad art which a classificatory but not an evaluative concept can accommodate. Against this, others object that an evaluative concept is consistent with there being bad art (e.g., Rowe 1991; Gaut 2000).

With certain exceptions (e.g., Davies 1991), that an artwork must at least be an artifact is widely accepted. There is less of a consensus about further necessary conditions. It is agreed that, given recent art-historical developments and the resultant physical diversity of artworks, definitions in terms of perceivable properties must fail, as must definitions in terms of relatively concrete relational properties, such as beauty, imitation, or expression. Consciousness of these points has produced definitions in terms of more abstract relational properties. I will consider three prominent sorts.

On a functionalist account, art is that which fulfills a particular role in people's lives, or is intended to. Often the role is characterized as aesthetic. For instance, according to Beardsley "[a]n artwork is something produced with the intention of giving it the capacity to satisfy the aesthetic interest" (1983: 21). An attraction of this sort of view is that it apparently engages with the value we find in much art. A problem is that, given traditional views of aesthetic experience, which connect it to beauty or pleasure or disinterestedness, many artworks do not provide any such experience, and are not intended to (see Beardsley's acknowledgment (1983: 26) that he rules out conceptual and other anti-aesthetic visual works from art's extension). Since a definition should be adequate to linguistic practice, this is a serious fault. Recent functionalist definitions define art in terms of more abstract notions of aesthetic experience, aiming at accommodating a maximal range of artworks (for instance, Anderson 2000). A residual problem is that such accounts tend to countenance as art objects that fulfill the designated function but lack relevant connections to the sort of cultural structures many think essential to a thing's arthood (e.g., gardens, jewelry, haute couture).

Those to whom this objection is persuasive are likely to be attracted to a definition that attempts to relate art, explicitly, to the right sort of cultural practice. Historical and institutional definitions both fall under this description.

On a well-known historical definition, Levinson argues that X is an artwork at time t if and only if the person who has a proprietary right over X intends it to be regarded "in any way (or ways) in which objects in the extension of 'artwork' prior to t are or were correctly or standardly regarded" (1979: 236). This account seems attractive insofar as it correctly emphasizes the point that not anything can be an artwork at any time. Moreover, it encompasses avant-garde works, as long as they are made with the relevant intention. However, apart from problems accommodating revolutionary

art, addressed by Levinson in later work, a significant worry is whether, given the untraceability in many cases of the intention cited, the definition incorrectly engages with general reasons for which art is classified as such (Stock 2003).

Instead, one may prefer to define art in terms of an external and so more publicly available historical relation. For instance, Carney defines art as that which "can be linked by those suitably informed, along one or more of various specific dimensions to a past or present general style or styles exhibited by prior artworks" (1991: 273). However, the problem now becomes one of overinclusiveness, since many nonart objects can be so linked (Stock 2003).

Meanwhile, the most well-known version of an institutional definition, offered by Dickie (1974) and since modified, builds on the claim of Danto (1964) that whether something is art or not is partly a function of its relation to an "artworld." Dickie conceives of the artworld as a social institution, on behalf of which certain individuals with relevant authority act to confer the status of "candidate for appreciation" upon aspects of certain artifacts, which count as artworks in virtue of this procedure.

An attraction of this view is its appearance of having roughly the right extension (with the possible exception of art made in cognitive isolation from established practices of art-making, including "first art"). Like historical accounts, it encompasses avant-garde works of any nature, so long as they are related to the sort of act specified. There are worries, however. One is circularity, explicit in a later incarnation of the definition in which Dickie presents *work of art* as one of a set of concepts, each of which uses some other member in its *definiens*. Another concerns his construal of the artworld as an institution: certainly if this is interpreted as one having formally delineated roles, it is implausible; hence it is urged that we understand the institution as an informal one. In turn, this move has prompted worries about whether the notion of a person acting authoritatively "on behalf of" the artworld can be made sense of. These and other issues are discussed at length by Davies (1991).

Earlier it was noted that an aim of many definitions of art is to demonstrate the unity of the concept. Whether institutional definitions can do so is moot. To vary a famous objection of Wollheim (1980) to Dickie, either there is some single or small set of reasons for conferring art status on objects, or there is not (because different reasons tend to inform each decision). If the former, then, assuming the interest of a definition is in such reasons, art should be defined in terms of them rather than in terms of the act of conferral. If the latter, then the class of artworks is no longer a genuinely unified class of objects, even if all and only artworks stand in relation to an act of conferral of the relevant sort.

Of course, though Dickie does not, one might embrace the point that art is not a unified kind of thing, and so cannot be defined. This is the conclusion of Weitz (1956) who argues that art is best understood as a "family resemblance" concept, insofar as every artwork counts as such in virtue of sharing some property with some other member, but there are no properties individually necessary to all.

Weitz's grounds for his antiessentialist conclusion are unpersuasive. He claims that the practice of art is sufficiently innovative to insure that no adequate definition of its disparate products could ever be given. To this it can be replied that the experimental nature of artistic practice is consistent with its products having some relatively abstract set of properties as necessary and sufficient (indeed, this is what modern definitions seek to provide).

However, the antiessentialist conclusion itself is unfairly maligned. An objection often made is that if resemblance to established artworks is sufficient for arthood then, since everything resembles everything else, anything might counts as art, even in virtue of some trivial resemblance. Yet an antiessentialist need not hold that just any property shared with an established artwork is sufficient for arthood, but only that some are. Moreover, such properties, rather than being trivial, may intersect with deep and abiding human interests. Nor need they be manifest properties, as is sometimes complained (Carroll 1993).

A candidate list of such properties is proposed by Gaut (2000), who designates art a "cluster concept" governed by disjointly necessary conditions, all or fewer of which are sufficient for arthood. Though he denies that this amounts to a definition, it is often taken to be

a disjunctive one. Given the relatively large number of conditions listed and their independence from one another, this seems inappropriate if, as was indicated earlier, a definition is aimed at revealing the unity of a concept. (Indeed, the challenge of demonstrating how a set of disjunctive conditions could capture a concept's unity faces any disjunctive definition. For the claim that most current definitions take this form, including his own hybrid historical-functionalist definition, see Stecker 2003).

A more radical antiessentialist position claims that the "reasons" for which the linguistic community classifies particular artworks as such, in terms of shared properties with established artworks, do not automatically extend to other objects that possess those properties, and hence are not always universalizable. Artworks count as such because relations are found between them and other artworks, and not simply because such relations exist. This "radical stipulativist" position (the term is from Davies 2006) is outlined by Stock (2003) though remains to be positively defended in detail. It is not to be confused with the view according to which art is identified as such by the telling of narratives intelligibly connecting a present object to some past artwork(s), via relations of repetition, amplification, or repudiation (Carroll 1993). For Carroll, it seems it is the fact of such relations that is sufficient for arthood, rather than any narrative about them. This admission tends to make his account open to counterexample (Stock 2003). Nor is the view a covert definition, claiming that art is all and only that about which a narrative citing the relevant relations is told. As with the institutional definition, this would appear unsatisfactory, since it would not capture the salient facts about artworks which lead to their classification as such (in this case, the features of works picked out by the narratives in question), which is what a definition should be interested in, insofar as it is interested in showing art to be a unified kind of an interesting sort.

Recently several objections have been made to radical stipulativism by Davies (2006); it remains to be seen whether these can be answered.

See also TWENTIETH-CENTURY ANGLO-AMERICAN AESTHETICS; ARTIFACT, ART AS; "ARTWORLD";

BEARDSLEY; CONCEPTUAL ART; DANTO; DICKIE; FUNCTION OF ART; THEORIES OF ART.

BIBLIOGRAPHY

Anderson, James. 2000. "Aesthetic Concepts of Art." In *Theories of Art Today*. N. Carroll (ed.). Madison: University of Wisconsin Press, 65–92.

Beardsley, Monroe C. 1983. "An Aesthetic Definition of Art." In *What is Art?* H. Curtler (ed.). New York: Haven, 15–29.

Carney, James. 1991. "The Style Theory of Art." *Pacific Philosophical Quarterly*, 72, 273–89.

Carroll, Noël. 1993. "Historical Narratives and the Philosophy of Art." *Journal of Aesthetics and Art Criticism*, 51, 313–26.

Carroll, Noël (ed.). 2000. *Theories of Art Today*. Madison: University of Wisconsin Press.

Danto, Arthur C. 1964. "The Artworld." *Journal of Philosophy*, 61, 571–84.

Davies, Stephen. 1991. *Definitions of Art*. Ithaca: Cornell University Press.

Davies, Stephen. 2006. *The Philosophy of Art*. Malden: Blackwell.

Dickie, George. 1974. *Art and the Aesthetic: An Institutional Analysis*. Ithaca: Cornell University Press.

Gaut, Berys. 2000. " 'Art' as a Cluster Concept." In *Theories of Art Today*. N. Carroll (ed.). Madison: University of Wisconsin Press, 25–44.

Levinson, Jerrold. 1979. "Defining Art Historically." *British Journal of Aesthetics*, 19, 232–50.

Rowe, M. R. 1991. "Why 'Art' Doesn't have Two Senses." *British Journal of Aesthetics*, 31, 214–21.

Stecker, Robert. 2003. "Is It Reasonable to Attempt to Define Art?" In *Theories of Art Today*. N. Carroll (ed.). Madison: University of Wisconsin Press, 45–65.

Stock, Kathleen. 2003. "Historical Definitions of Art." In *Art and Essence*. S. Davies & A. C. Sukla (eds.). Westport: Praeger, 159–76.

Weitz, Morris. 1956. "The Role of Theory in Aesthetics." *Journal of Aesthetics and Art Criticism*, 15, 27–35.

Wollheim, Richard. 1980. *Art and Its Objects*. 2nd edn. Cambridge: Cambridge University Press.

KATHLEEN STOCK

Deleuze, Gilles (1925–1995) is the philosopher of the unruly and feral, the thinker who seeks to un-domesticate the established discourses of art and philosophy by opening them to those impersonal, disruptive energies and forces which conventional intellectual practices invariably struggle to tame.

Deleuze is respected as a prolific poststructuralist philosopher/theorist whose written corpus displays three clear aspects: substantial reinterpretations of major figures in Western philosophy (Spinoza, Leibniz, Hume, Kant, and Nietzsche), significant individual contributions to poststructural thought (e.g., *Difference et Repetition*, 1968; *Logique du Sens*, 1969), and cooperative works of philosophy and literary criticism with Felix Guattari (such as *L'Anti-Oedipe, Capitalisme et Schizophrenie 1* (1972), and *Qu'est-ce que la Philosophie?* (1991). However, throughout his career Deleuze also wrote important works on aesthetics, most notably *Proust et les Signes* (1964), *Francis Bacon: Logique de la Sensation* (1981), *Cinema 1* (1983), and *Cinema 2* (1985), works which have endeared him to many artists attracted to the material and temporal dimensions of art production.

Deleuze does not offer an aesthetic theory in any conventional sense. As a poststructuralist thinker greatly influenced by Nietzsche's philosophy of Becoming, he tends not to be concerned with the intrinsic aesthetic properties of an art object, nor is he enamored with the specific qualities of a spectator's experience. Deleuze attempts to articulate a realm of affectivity in which potent works overreach the circumstances of both their historical production and reception to generate further thought and response. The thesis is affiliated with Heidegger's modernistic claim that "great" works of art are not so much the products of history but announce and define new historical epochs. Within Deleuze's perspective, the compositions of Wagner and Schoenberg become significant for their historical effects: the capacity of their germinal structures to generate musical transformations in the subsequent compositions of Bruckner, Mahler, and Webern.

Deleuze presents the vibrancy and vitality of an artwork as transformative and generative. The transformative aspect reflects the monistic form of his thinking. His theory of *ontogenesis* dissolves the usual dualisms which sever an artwork from the viewer. Deleuze strives, to the contrary, to portray the artwork as a process of transformative emergence. This conception sweeps away conventional distinctions between work, material, content, and artistic intentionality. It also opposes attempts to explain art's emergence by appeal to purposes external to art itself. Deleuze expresses hostility toward teleological accounts of Becoming defended by thinkers such as Aristotle, Hegel, and Marx. Art does not arise to fulfill or realize an externally set historical purpose; its emergence is to be regarded as a spontaneous expression, a transformation and intensification of the forces which sustain its coming to be, a bringing of formative energies into new configurations able to generate unexpected historical effects.

Pace Nietzsche, Deleuze presents individuated works as essentially unstable resultant forms, complex multiplicities that will always imply more than the apparent fixity of their form suggests. The implication here is to the virtual, a grounding concept in Deleuze's thought which denotes that almost unconceptualizable realm of prephenomenal force (flux) which wells up within a work, individuating it by transforming embryonic energies into new and, perhaps, more infectious shape and form. By no means does this dynamic privilege actualization (as if a work were a single bloom, following one developmental trajectory only to become locked in a fixity of form and thought). The signature of Deleuze's thought emphasizes transformation and reanimation: it is what a work sets in motion that is important, its ability not just to express the forces which impel it into being but to reanimate and reactivate them so as to bring new effects into being. In this respect Deleuze can be grouped with those philosophers who, like Nietzsche, Merleau-Ponty, and Heidegger, value art's self-generative ontology as a disruptive challenge to philosophy's fixation with the stable and identical. Deleuze accordingly esteems art's ability to afford a glimpse of the prephenomenal forces of becoming operating as the condition of emergence of all the individuated forms. Mozart's Symphony No. 40 and Mahler's No. 9 are examples of works that push their form to such extremes that it becomes possible to discern the energy that not only drives them into a given shape but also threatens to overwhelm them. Artworks, then, are transformations of prephenomenal energies into more intense and infectious forms. Their emergence can generate new sensibilities. Their distinct visual or sound worlds can be compared to Deleuze's

account of concepts in that, like concepts, they are intellectual formations that, though they may derive from experience, then transform experience in new and unexpected ways.

Deleuze's thought strives to dismantle the customary distinctions between art and theory by stressing that philosophy, like art, is a productive process. It is not that philosophy can "think" art by offering a conceptual representation of the subject but rather that, in the struggle to find new ways of thinking about art, philosophy becomes comparable to art inasmuch as it forms, invents, and articulates concepts. From the multiple cross-currents of all levels of impressions and perceptions, a thinker can (often inexplicably) bring to fruition a concept able to shape and give form to an inchoate mass of thought. Indeed, from within a Deleuzian perspective it would be more appropriate not to say that a film, a novel, or painting gives voice to a historical situation but rather that the situation gains expression in the work it brings forth. Concepts for Deleuze do not serve as mental re-presentations of any extra-mental world, rather they serve to reorganize complex perceptions forming what are in effect new regions of intelligible experience. Furthermore, concepts, like poignant artworks, have an effective transformative power well beyond both what their (alleged) creators may have imagined and the specific circumstances of their production. Plato's *logos*, Descartes's *cogito*, Nietzsche's *Wille*, Hegel's *Geist*, or Wittgenstein's *Lebensform* are not just free-floating ideas but modes of thought that are both indicative and expressive of the social and cultural situations which call them forth. More important, concepts, like artworks, have (often unpredictable) effects: they open "new perspectives on the world" which cannot be wholly reconciled with one another.

Deleuze's aesthetics is distinctly modernist. It emphasizes process, becoming, and the multiplication of worlds. The ontogenetic movement from the virtual to the actual occurs within processes of differentiation. Tension, contradiction, and collision are of the essence. For Deleuze, the purpose of creative thought is not to smooth out contradiction and opposition but rather to intensify them. Once again, the task of philosophical thought is not to seek resolving syntheses but to penetrate appearance, identity, and surface and to reengage with the possibilities of the new within the virtual. Partly because of his poststructuralist orientation, Deleuze regards the intellectual tendency to compromise or overcome differences as an expression of establishment powers. However, as a post-Nietzschean thinker, he is committed to radicalizing and sharpening difference, not to disrupt and discredit ideologies of identity but more to set back into play the impersonal forces and energies within the virtual and the possibilities for new epiphanies they hold. Philosophy must transform the concept as a tool of reduction and generalization into a device for inducing the unpredictable associations and links. Deleuze's most innovative image is of the concept and artwork as a rhizome, a living entity that grows horizontally and vertically in a discontinuous clustering of synthetic associations. The task of both philosophy and art is indeed subversive: to seek out those fault lines, tensions, and contradictions in dominant modes of thinking and practice, to seek out the unsettling which established discourses strive to hide, in order to release the possibilities for becoming that lie within the virtual. The Nietzschean aspect of Deleuze's aesthetic is plain. The creativity of art and philosophy requires instability, disturbance, and excess. And yet, in order to be disruptive and have longevity of effects, a work must achieve a relative stability. The only law of creation, Deleuze argues, is that a work must stand on its own. This he claims is the artist's greatest challenge.

Philosophy makes concepts. Art shapes percepts and affects. Both activities strive to give form to experience in such a way that experience when transformed into concept or work can stand on its own and be autonomous independent of the artist's intentions, feelings, or thinking. In *What is Philosophy?* Deleuze proclaims the artwork as a being of sensation and as existing in itself. A work preserves what is described as a block of sensations, a compound of percepts and affects. In Heidegger's and Adorno's language, Deleuze's artwork "comes to stand" and its authenticity resides in that capacity. Yet though this allows a work to act as an identity, that is, operate as discernible force field of effects, as a synthetic compound it is inherently nonidentical with itself and essentially so. A work, like a concept, is not an abstract entity but is formed from interrelationships between different ideas and fields of association. It is the fact that concept and work allow different components to intersect with each other that allows both in Gadamer's phrase to be historically effective. The contrasts and connections made within a given philosophical or artistic structure can link in historically unpredicted but transformative ways with patterns of intellectual and sensual association not presently connected with it. It is the very nonidentity of concept and work that enables them to be historically effective. The power to affect gives both a concept and a work the semblance of an identity in that "it" becomes a given history of effects and, as such, "appears" to operate as an independent agency. This form of argumentation in fact serves to rewrite notions of tradition and canon. A tradition can be rearticulated as a continuity of generic transformations within an idiom of artistic or intellectual practice. A canonical work can be described as one that continues to have effects in the sense of generating new associated forms and idioms.

It is in his discussion of painting that Deleuze is most insightful and most cherished by certain painters. The essay *Francis Bacon: Logique de la sensation* emphasizes the importance of focusing on how artists deploy their chosen material. Deleuze's antirepresentationalist aesthetic rules make it clear that it is not a matter of coming to judgment about whether the material mode of the work successfully accords with a preexisting conception of a mood, gesture, or subject. It is, therefore, not a question of how Turner uses paint to represent or look like water. For Deleuze, it is much more a matter of how an artist like Turner can use the virtual properties of liquidity within paint in such a way that his canvases appear to swell, and dip, wave-like. The genius of Turner from a Deleuzian perspective involves a certain abandonment of figuration and representation, a succumbing to the materiality of paint, an attention to how the material medium can organize itself as if it were water, such that the painting becomes a visual and material analogue to the massive power of swirling seawater itself. Very material painters, such as Turner, Bacon, and Auerbach, evolve a painterly logic of sensation that serves not so much as an analogue for the represented seascape, figure, or face but for the chaos of prephenomenal forces that form such objects. The challenge that such art poses for philosophers is how the formation of concepts might similarly serve as an analogue for thinking the virtual.

At least two questions can be raised about Deleuze's account of ontogenesis and the formation of artworks. The first reflects a problem characteristic of philosophies of Becoming which affirm the idea of prephenomenal energies and forces underlying individuated beings. Deleuze's thinking runs along lines similar to Nietzsche's reasoning in this respect. A conscious representation of the external world is not a representation of an actual external world at all but an internal interpretative effect of subconscious interactions with forces and affects that extend beyond a subject's individuated being. What is presented in consciousness is, then, an interpretative response of one lifeform being acted on by another. In Nietzsche's words, the external object "is only a kind of effect produced by a subject upon a subject – a modus of the subject" (*Will to Power*, §569). If, however, all we can know are our conscious states, the question arises as to how Deleuze can proclaim the existence of prephenomenal forces that, by definition, cannot be known. For an aesthetics that strives to escape the actual and make visible what normally lies invisible within the virtual, this question poses a serious difficulty.

The second question relates to whether issues of aesthetic meaning and value can be collapsed into assertions of intensity. There are considerable advantages to this stratagem. It avoids all the customary problems associated with debates about aesthetic intentionality, essential content, subjectivity, and meaning. There is, indeed, something persuasively Nietzschean in Deleuze's argumentation: a measure of great art is its ability to animate, to excite, to agitate, and to enliven the activity of the senses and, hence, to intensify our sense of being intensely alive. The question is whether descriptions of such experiential intensity, descriptions that deliberately avoid reference to customary discourses of visual meaning, could ever be recognized as descriptions of art. This is not to deny that art does quicken and enliven. The question is whether art and its understanding can be reduced to an account of processural affects and still be recognized as art. Deleuze's account of aesthetic experience faces similar difficulties to those that confront Clive Bell's famous argument concerning significant form. Bell, like Deleuze, wishes to avoid privileging established discourses about art. He chooses to emphasize a work's significant form, its planes, its surfaces, and its compositional form. The difficulty shared by these positions is that while they laudably endeavor to escape narrow bourgeois prejudices concerning art and its privileged meanings, they produce formal accounts of art and aesthetic experience that threaten to dissolve what is readily understood as art in the first place.

See also NINETEENTH- AND TWENTIETH-CENTURY CONTINENTAL AESTHETICS; STRUCTURALISM AND POSTSTRUCTURALISM.

BIBLIOGRAPHY

Primary sources
[1962] 1983. *Nietzsche and Philosophy*. H. Tomlinson (trans.). New York: Columbia University Press.
[1964] 2003. *Proust and Signs*. R. Howard (trans.). Minneapolis: University of Minnesota Press.
[1968] 1994. *Difference and Repetition*. P. Patton (trans.). New York: Columbia University Press.
[1968] 1992. *Expressionism in Philosophy: Spinoza*. M. Joughin (trans.). New York: Zone Books.
[1969] 1990. *The Logic of Sense*. C. V. Boundas (ed.). New York: Columbia University Press.
[1981] 1994. *Francis Bacon: The Logic of Sensation*. P. Patton (trans.). London: Athlone.
[1983] 1989. *Cinema 1: The Movement-Image*. H. Tomlinson & B. Habberjam (trans.). London: Continuum.
[1985] 1989. *Cinema 2: The Movement-Image*. H. Tomlinson & R. Galeta (trans.). London: Continuum.
[1991] 1994. (with Guattari, Felix) *What is Philosophy*. H. Tomlinson & G. Burchell (trans.). London: Verso.
1993. *The Deleuze Reader*. C. Boundas (ed.). New York: Columbia University Press.

Secondary sources
Ansell-Pearson, Keith. 1999. *Germinal Life: The Difference and Repetition of Deleuze*. London: Routledge.
Bogue, Ronald. 2003. *Deleuze on Music, Painting and the Arts*. London: Routledge.

Colebrook, Clare. 2002. *Gilles Deleuze*. London: Routledge.

NICHOLAS DAVEY

depiction   Philosophical studies of depiction focus on the representational function of figurative pictures: they aim to explain how such pictures represent and how pictorial representation relates to other types of representation. Although contemplation of the nature of pictures has a long history that starts in antiquity, depiction becomes an object of systematic philosophical study only after the middle of the twentieth century. At this time developments in the philosophy of language, but also relevant studies in experimental psychology and visual anthropology, provided philosophers with the incentive and the theoretical tools needed to scrutinize the distinctive way in which pictures serve their representational function. In what follows we will consider the main directions of analysis that pictorial theorists have followed.

THE RESEMBLANCE THEORY

In the *Republic*, Plato contends that pictures are like mirror images; through their lines and colors they imitate the appearance of the objects of the world of sense. This pronouncement is the earliest characterization of depiction, but also the precursor of the resemblance theory, historically the dominant theory of depiction. Proponents of the resemblance theory focus on the relation between pictures and their objects in order to explain the representational function of pictures, identifying this relation as one of resemblance. Specifically, it is assumed that (1) a picture X represents an object Y just in case X notably resembles the appearance of Y; and (2) representing in that way is distinctive of pictorial modes of representation.

The resemblance theory has considerable intuitive appeal; pictures *do* seem to resemble visually the objects or scenes that they depict. However, the conviction that such resemblance explains the representational function of pictures is implausible. On the one hand, pictures visually resemble many other objects apart from the objects that they depict, for instance other pictures; while resemblance can also seem to operate in nonpictorial modes of representation, for instance sculpture. Both considerations entail that resemblance is not sufficient for depiction. On the other hand, some pictures (for instance, some Cubist paintings) do not seem to bear any notable resemblance to what they depict, in which case resemblance is not necessary for depiction either. Finally, the resemblance theory seems to have limited explanatory scope: where there *are* notable resemblances between picture and subject, what seems to resemble the appearance of the subject is the object seen in the picture, rather than the pattern of lines and colors on the canvas. For instance, when I take a portrait to be a good likeness of Queen Elizabeth II, it is the woman in the picture that I see as resembling the Queen, not the color patches on the pictorial surface. But if so, we need to understand how a certain pattern of colors (a certain design) comes to be identified as a depiction of a woman in the first place. In that respect, the resemblance theory takes depiction for granted.

CONVENTIONALISM

The resemblance theory draws a sharp contrast between pictorial and linguistic representation: whereas the latter is governed by convention, the former is thought to be grounded on a relation, that is, resemblance, that holds independently of practice or precept. The presumed radical disparity between pictures and language has been forcefully undermined by Nelson Goodman. Pictorial representation, Goodman argues, is no less conventional than linguistic representation, although the two symbol systems are governed by different conventions, that is, different sets of arbitrary laws that determine the mode of representation as well as what is represented in each case. Specifically, Goodman explains, the pictorial symbol system has the following properties: it is syntactically and semantically dense, and it is relatively replete. What these properties entail respectively is that the pictorial system provides for infinitely many possible characters (i.e., types of pictorial mark), as well as an infinite number of possible referents correlated (by convention) with that set of characters; and, further, that for a relatively wide range of properties of marks on a pictorial surface, the smallest difference in one of those properties affects to which character a mark belongs and thus what reference it is assigned.

Goodman's analysis of depiction has received much criticism. A first point of concern is that it does not provide either sufficient or necessary conditions for depiction. On the one hand, as Goodman himself acknowledged, there are syntactically/semantically dense and relatively replete symbol systems that are not pictorial. (Consider, for instance, a system of representation where pictures in linear perspective are cut up into many pieces and reshuffled according to some rule; such a system is both dense and relatively replete but it is not pictorial.) On the other hand, there are pictures that belong to articulate rather than to dense systems, for instance digital pictures.

A further, perhaps more important, worry about Goodman's account is that his principal assumption that depiction, like language, is entirely governed by convention, fails to comply with practice. There is no doubt that the ability to understand pictures that belong to unfamiliar systems or traditions of depiction may often require some instruction regarding the conventions and regularities that these systems involve. However, pictorial competence is generative. Once a viewer has acquired some familiarity with a system of depiction, she is able to understand any picture in that system without further instruction or learning provided that she has a recognitional capacity for the object the picture depicts. The generative character of pictorial competence undermines Goodman's radical conventionalism: unlike linguistic comprehension, pictorial comprehension does not seem to rely on knowledge of an arbitrary set of conventions.

THE RECOGNITION THEORY

Although the ability to understand pictures in different systems of depiction involves some familiarity with the conventions and regularities pertinent to each system, the above consideration seems to suggest that it also involves a natural capacity, or else, that it has a natural starting point. This insight is central to the recognition theory of depiction. According to recognition theorists, it is distinctive of depiction that it is an essentially visual form of representation as it invokes our perceptual ability to visually recognize the object represented. Pictures, it is suggested, embody information from their objects on the basis of which these can be recognized: they have been designed to trigger roughly the same visual processing that allows a perceiver to recognize the object represented when seen face to face. As Dominic Lopes explains, this entails that "the ability to work out what pictures depict covaries with the ability to recognize their depicta in the flesh" (Lopes 2005: 170). That is, we can recognize in pictures those objects that we can recognize in the flesh and under the same dimensions of variation. Moreover, it is assumed that, given some familiarity with the norms of a given system of depiction, the viewer's recognitional ability for Os is necessary and sufficient for understanding a picture of O in that system.

However, the relation between ordinary and pictorial perception might be a source of worry for the recognition theory. The perceptual achievement in both cases seems to be that we recognize O, but of course (trompe-l'oeil pictures aside) we never take ourselves to see the actual O in a picture; rather we see a depiction of O. Lopes explains that, although pictorial and face-to-face recognition largely overlap and co-vary, they differ in that the former is typically triggered by a flat, marked surface; pictorial competence thus supposedly relies on an ability to recognize objects when they appear in two dimensions. So what is the content of the pictorial act of recognition? Given that in pictorial perception the viewer is (usually) aware of seeing a representation, presumably she identifies this representation as of O, and sees that the representation is two-dimensional. As Robert Hopkins has noted however, this qualification significantly limits the explanatory scope of the recognition theory: "it turns the overlap claim from an interesting assertion about the cognitive processing involved in understanding pictures into the wholly uncontroversial claim that we are able to understand them" (2005: 157).

EXPERIENTIAL THEORIES

A comprehensive theory of depiction, it seems, has to acknowledge the visual nature of depiction, but also the ways in which pictorial perception differs from ordinary perception. This is the central insight of experiential theories, which seek to define depiction in terms of the distinctive visual experience that pictures evoke.

According to Ernst Gombrich, pictorial seeing is a case of illusion: in seeing a picture of a table, for instance, we have an experience *as of seeing* a real table, that is, an experience phenomenologically like that of seeing a real table. The illusion hypothesis has been undermined by Richard Wollheim, who rightly notes that (*trompe-l'oeil* pictures aside) seeing an object in a picture is not like seeing the object face to face in that there is a difference in the phenomenology of the two experiences. The difference, he thinks, consists in the fact that the pictorial marks are perceived along with what is represented in the picture; awareness of the marks and awareness of the object of representation are two distinguishable but inseparable aspects of a single visual experience. The capacity for visual experiences that have this sort of complexity is for Wollheim the capacity for seeing-in. Seeing-in, Wollheim explains, can also be triggered by adequately differentiated surfaces that are not representational. It is distinctive of depiction, however, that there is a standard of correctness for seeing-in (for what is to be recognized in the marked surface) set by the intentions of the artist. It follows that a picture *P* depicts an object *O* if and only if *P* has been intentionally marked so that *O* can be seen in *P*.

Although we may have to concede with Wollheim that depiction ordinarily fosters twofold seeing, the seeing-in theory has not been adequately developed so as to qualify as a complete theory of depiction. On the one hand, Wollheim does not explain how pictures represent, that is, why *X* rather than *Y* can be recognized in a marked surface. Further, he refuses to provide a comprehensive characterization of seeing-in, one that would allow us to understand the precise character and content of this complex experience, thinking that such an endeavor would not be fruitful.

Perhaps, however, the resemblance hypothesis can give us some insight into the nature of seeing-in. Robert Hopkins has argued that the type of resemblance that is salient to depiction is resemblance in outline shape, where outline shape is the solid angle that an object subtends at a point in its surroundings. Since outline shape ignores the third dimension, it is a property that pictures and their objects can share. What matters for depiction though, according to Hopkins, is *not* the actual resemblance in outline shape between the marked surface and the object depicted therein, as the resemblance itself does not entail that the viewer will have the experience appropriate to pictures, seeing-in. Rather, what matters is the *experience* of such resemblance. When a viewer experiences resemblance in outline shape between the marks on a pictorial surface and a familiar object (which she thereby takes the picture to depict), both the marks and the object figure in her awareness, so the experience can be properly characterized as a case of seeing-in.

According to Hopkins, then, a picture *P* depicts an object *O* because (1) *P* is experienced as resembling *O* in outline shape; and (2) *P* has been intentionally marked (or is causally related to *O*, in the case of photographs) so as to promote this experience. However, Hopkins notes, there is not always an exact match between the depictive content of a picture and what can be seen in it. Drawing on her knowledge of the regularities and practices that govern depiction, the viewer may need to take certain details of the object seen in a picture as stylistic traits or simply limitations of the medium, irrelevant to what the picture is intended to convey.

The success of the experienced resemblance theory seems to rest on whether we perceive – that is, are consciously aware of – outline shape; moreover, in the case of depiction, whether we do so before we identify what a picture depicts. As Lopes notes, there is evidence that the features we see a picture surface as having (for instance, subjective contour, perceived relative size, shape, etc.) may depend in part on what we see in a picture; "if the experienced resemblance between P and O is detached from an actual resemblance between P and O, then there is the danger that it is a function of P's depicting O. Experienced resemblance cannot explain depiction if it is beholden to depiction" (2005: 168).

CONCLUSION

Although the existent theories of depiction do not converge in a unitary account of the phenomenon, due to their breadth and depth they have offered us a rich understanding of different aspects of depiction. In order to reach a more comprehensive understanding of the way pictures serve their representational function, we need to gain a better insight into the overall nature of the pictorial experience, one that highlights the points of similarity and the points of contrast with ordinary perception – with regards, for instance, to their phenomenology, or the visual cues that each exploits and the epistemic resources on which each draws. Although individually these phenomena *have* been studied by different theories of depiction, both in the domain of pictorial theory and in experimental psychology, what we do not have is a study that would consider the phenomena in their interrelations. Such an integrating approach would allow us a more broad and uniform understanding of the way depiction functions.

See also DRAWING, PAINTING, AND PRINTMAKING; PHOTOGRAPHY; ABSTRACTION; GOMBRICH; GOODMAN; PERSPECTIVE; PICTURE PERCEPTION; REALISM; REPRESENTATION; WALTON; WOLLHEIM.

BIBLIOGRAPHY
Budd, Malcolm. 1992. "On Looking at a Picture." In *Psychoanalysis, Mind and Art: Perspectives on Richard Wollheim.* J. Hopkins & A. Savile (eds.). Oxford: Blackwell, 259–80.
Gombrich, Ernst. 1977. *Art and Illusion: A Study in the Psychology of Pictorial Representation.* 5th edn. London: Phaidon.
Goodman, Nelson. 1968. *Languages of Art.* Indianapolis: Bobbs-Merrill.
Hopkins, Robert. 1998. *Picture, Image and Experience.* Cambridge: Cambridge University Press.
Hopkins, Robert. 2005. "The Speaking Image: Visual Communication and the Nature of Depiction." In *Contemporary Debates in Aesthetics and the Philosophy of Art.* M. Kieran (ed.). Oxford: Blackwell, 145–59.
Hyman, John. 2000. "Pictorial Art and Visual Experience," *British Journal of Aesthetics,* 40, 21–45.
Hyman, John. 2003. "Subjectivism in the Theory of Pictorial Art," *Monist,* 86, 676–701.
Kulvicki, John. 2006. *On Images: Their Structure and Content.* Oxford: Oxford University Press.
Lopes, Dominic McIver. 1996. *Understanding Pictures.* Oxford: Oxford University Press.
Lopes, Dominic McIver. 2005. "The Domain of Depiction." In *Contemporary Debates in Aesthetics and the Philosophy of Art.* M. Kieran (ed.). Oxford: Blackwell, 160–74.
Peacocke, Christopher. 1987. "Depiction," *Philosophical Review,* 96, 383–410.
Schier, Flint. 1986. *Deeper into Pictures: An Essay on Pictorial Representation.* Cambridge: Cambridge University Press.
Walton, Kendall L. 1990. *Mimesis as Make-Believe.* Cambridge, MA: Harvard University Press.
Wollheim, Richard. 1980. *Art and Its Objects.* 2nd edn. Cambridge: Cambridge University Press.
Wollheim, Richard. 1987. *Painting as an Art.* London: Thames & Hudson.

KATERINA BANTINAKI

Derrida, Jacques (1930–2004) is part of the grand tradition of French *skepticism* that includes Montaigne, Descartes, Mersenne, Pascal, Bayle, Voltaire, Camus. Born in Algeria in 1930, Derrida began to study philosophy in 1950 in a Paris dominated by Camus and Sartre, and received a doctorate in literature in 1980 with the essay "The Inscription of Philosophy: Research on the Interpretation of Writing," having already received one in philosophy in 1967 with *Of Grammatology,* "on the enduring of the Platonic, Aristotelian, and Scholastic conceptions of the written sign." The information about the degrees comes from a three-page typewritten curriculum vitae, current up to 1984, that dramatizes the problem of sources and origins, authorizations and legitimating laws to which Derrida has paid attention, namely: I have seen no other reference to the essay submitted for the degree in literature and the vitae does not name the granting institutions. In "The Time of a Thesis: Punctuations" (1983), a presentation made at the Sorbonne on June 2, 1980 to the examining committee, Derrida draws a map of his career up to the time of the thesis.

Husserl and Hegel were his first interlocutors. The 1967 defense of grammatology was preceded in 1954 by a master's thesis on the problem of genesis in the phenomenology of Husserl and in 1957 by the registration of a first thesis topic, "The Ideality of the Literary Object," to be written under the direction of the Hegel scholar Jean Hyppolite. The task was to fashion a new theory of the literary object with the techniques of transcendental phenomenology.

For Derrida said that his most constant interest has been in how it is that the sheer fact of writing can disturb most fundamental questions about what exists and what whatever exists means. He asks himself rhetorically why he is so fascinated by the trick, the play, the dodge of the inscription and the paradox of the trace, the mark that erases itself in the course of making, performing itself.

The trace is for Derrida that whose existence is proved by a Kantian transcendental deduction to conditions necessary for the possibility of something's being the case. Its invisibility as well as its existence is assured by the occurrence of that of which it is a necessary condition. The trace "carries its other within itself," and here are opened up the fields on which play blindness and insight, presence and absence, death and life. The paradox of the trace is, Derrida would say, not only ungraspable but also unsolvable, with the result that there always is what cannot be grasped; there always is paradox. The effort to uncover the paradoxes that haunt writing, "the literary ruse of inscription," has occupied Derrida from the start, where the ruse is that only in literature is writing opaque and intransitive.

His claim is that not only has all writing density and a life and destiny of its own but also writing is a precondition of speech. There is an arche-writing, an articulation, a spacing, a carving out of what Saussure calls the continuous ribbons of thought and sound that precede speech and make it possible. This is no simple reversal, however, for the crucial step in this deconstruction of the opposition is the shift in the conceptual scheme that follows upon the reinscription of speech and writing within arche-writing. The change this discovery rings on familiar conceptual schemes amounts to their deformation, which is difficult in the extreme to make out unless one performs an experiment in imagination that consists in supposing the standard contract between reader and text to be null and language to have power to resist the intentions of its users. These suppositions made, the experimenter can try out various of Derrida's strategies of reading as Derrida later does on texts other than those of Plato, Condillac, Kant, Rousseau, Hegel, Husserl, Heidegger, Nietzsche, Freud.

Having written a lengthy introduction to Husserl's *The Origin of Geometry* (1962), Derrida no longer looked in phenomenology for a theory of the literary object because he found Husserl to have located writing within mathematical objects without realizing that the logic of the inscription, with its presumption of the same presence to mind of ideal objects (meanings) to which speech lays claim, menaces the whole phenomenological project from the outside. This thesis is worked out in the close readings done in the three works published in 1967 (*Speech and Phenomena*, *Of Grammatology*, *Writing and Difference*), where Derrida shows writing to have a logic of its own that relentlessly governs texts despite their avowals that writing is necessary only because of the limits nature imposes on the range of the voice and is dangerous because it tries to usurp the power of speech, whose handmaiden it is. This notion is akin to that of *pragmatic contradiction*, which occurs when what someone does contravenes what he says, when the performance of a speech act undercuts either what is said or a necessary condition thereof, as when someone says that he is silent or does not exist, with the difference that Derrida locates contradiction between what a text, not a person, does and what it says.

This identification of both a *textual unconscious*, to which dangerous writing is relegated in order to preserve the hegemony of the voice and speech fully present to conscious mind, and the various maneuvers performed by the textual unconscious was the subject of his earlier work. The later work gave way to works of plastic art, institutions, individual lives, and their stories. From 1963 to 1968 Derrida worked in solitude, apart from the structuralism that prevailed in Paris. He said that in 1967 he had had so little inclination to question the necessity of the university and its general principle that he thought to divide his labor between a thesis on Hegel's semiology to be done with Jean Hyppolite on the one hand and the continuation of work that not only did not conform to such requirements as a thesis but also was meant to displace and deform them. He registered this second thesis topic in 1967, but after the May uprising and the death of Hyppolite in 1968, he simply ignored it, publishing three books in 1972 (*Dissemination*,

Positions, Margins of Philosophy) and writing texts that became more and more playful. The play, however, was in the deadly serious service of breaking the habits of reading that refuse to search out the places in a text where what it does undermines what it says.

In 1974 he decided not to write the thesis because doing so would be inconsistent with a political struggle over the place of philosophy in the French curriculum in which he was engaged as a founder of GREPH (Groupe de Recherches sur l'Enseignement Philosophique) and an activist until 1979. During this time, he notes, his work focused on questions of rights, on the proper, the signature, the name, its destination and restitution, and the institutional hold on discourses' internal and external lines of demarcation. In his work, philosophers' texts gave way to their institutional contexts, and the borders between them were shown to be highly pervious. In the time after the final thesis of 1980, these texts are reinscribed in the philosophers' lives, as the issue of Nazism beset the lives of Paul de Man and Heidegger and forced the question of the boundaries between professional, political, and private, between the productions of and by institutions and individuals. In 1989 two books appeared in English: *Memoires: For Paul de Man* and *Of Spirit: Heidegger and the Question*, about which last David Farrell Krell, a scholar translator of Heidegger, asks "Will a more important book on Heidegger appear in our time?" and answers "No, unless Derrida continues to think and write in his spirit."

Derrida's singularity is such that one is not inclined to identify the spirit in which he works as that of anyone but himself. Yet strands other than French skepticism pass through him. One is the modernist preoccupation of early twentieth-century art and philosophy, for example, with what they are that pervaded the art and philosophy of the time. Derrida's difference is that he asks these questions of *every* concept he encounters. Just as the modernist "art is significant form" was read back into the history of art, so Derrida reads any concept on which he is working back into the myriad other concepts on which he has worked. Whether it is something people do (mourn, give hospitality, forgive, decide, take responsibility) or a characteristic of a practice, state of affairs, text (the spectral, death, the future), Derrida takes the concept out of its familiar contexts and destabilizes it. The fact that it can be decontextualized without losing itself shows it to have been already unstable, which exemplifies the principle that nothing can be done or found that was not already done or already there to be found.

Of the concept stripped bare of its context, Derrida asks the Kantian "How is it possible?" and answers that all are possible because they contain their other within themselves. Everything has at its heart what is different-from-itself, and in the latter body of work Derrida turns to explicating the notion of the other, which is different from the opposite. Were death, say, *wholly other* than life, it could not, as such, have anything to do with it. But death is at the very heart of life: only what can die can be said to be alive. That, however, is not the end of the matter. The strangeness of the concept of death is revealed once it too is taken out of its familiar contrast with life. It is also the other of immortality, and of the pair Derrida says "we will never believe in either death or immortality." We cannot decide between them because – and here the Derridian project puts everything at risk because no concept stays still and none has its borders intact – each inhabits the other in the guise of what is different-from-it and is, therefore, neither the same as nor separate from the other.

Derrida's move from the deconstruction of binary oppositions in written texts to the unsettling of the concepts through which we think the world – rife as it is with institutions, politics, globalization, war – is not a move from language to world or from names to things, however. No name is proper to the thing it names: it does not belong to what it names. What we know is that name and named are not and *cannot be the same*. Derrida describes this as the name's being inhabited by the death of the thing, which transforms the name from being appropriate to the thing to being its death. In Derrida's description, death has lost its mooring as the other of life to become instead *the impossibility of being the same*.

"The impossible to think" is the condition for the possibility of the new – which would contravene the principle that everything has always already been done or found – and for the possibility of decision. Decision is called for when reasons for and against a matter do not decide it and when, then, a leap of faith into an unknown future is required. The necessary condition for decision, in turn, is the idea of a future as that which is utterly open and wholly other from what we can think, as that with which we can have nothing to do from where we now stand, but toward which we can, if we dare as Derrida did, make a leap of faith.

See also NINETEENTH- AND TWENTIETH-CENTURY CONTINENTAL AESTHETICS; DECONSTRUCTION; STRUCTURALISM AND POSTSTRUCTURALISM.

BIBLIOGRAPHY

Primary sources
[1962] 1978. *Edmund Husserl's "Origin of Geometry": An Introduction.* J. P. Leavey (trans.). Pittsburgh: Duquesne University Press.
[1967] 1973. *"Speech and Phenomena" and Other Essays on Husserl's Theory of Signs.* D. B. Allison (trans.). Evanston: Northwestern University Press.
[1967] 1967. *Of Grammatology.* G. C. Spivak (trans.). Baltimore: Johns Hopkins University Press.
[1967] 1978. *Writing and Difference.* A. Bass (trans.). London: Routledge & Kegan Paul.
[1972] 1981. *Dissemination.* B. Johnson (trans.). London: Athlone.
[1972] 1981. *Positions.* A. Bass (trans.). London: Athlone.
[1972] 1982. *Margins of Philosophy.* A. Bass (trans.). Chicago: University of Chicago Press.
[1978] 1987. *The Truth in Painting.* G. Bennington & I. McLeod (trans.). Chicago: University of Chicago Press.
[1982] 1985. *The Ear of the Other.* P. Kamuf (trans.). New York: Schocken.
1983. "The Time of a Thesis: Punctuations." *Philosophy in France Today.* Alan Montefiore (ed.). Cambridge: Cambridge University Press, 34–53.
[1986] 1989. *Memoires: For Paul de Man.* C. Lindsay, J. Culler, E. Cadaver, & P. Kamuf (trans.). Rev. edn. New York: Columbia University Press.
[1987] 1989. *Of Spirit: Heidegger and the Question.* G. Bennington & R. Bowlby (trans.). Chicago: University of Chicago Press.
1994. *Specters of Marx: The State of Debt, the Work of Mourning and the New International.* P. Kamuf (trans.). New York: Routledge.
2001. *On Cosmopolitanism and Forgiveness.* M. Dooley & M. Hughes (trans.). New York: Routledge.
2002. *Who's Afraid of Philosophy? Right to Philosophy 1.* J. Plug (trans.). Stanford: Stanford University Press.
2004. *Eyes of the University: Right to Philosophy 2.* J. Plug (trans.). Stanford: Stanford University Press.

Secondary sources
Cohen, Tom. 2002. *Jacques Derrida and the Humanities: A Critical Reader.* Cambridge: Cambridge University Press.
Royle, Nicolas. 2003. *Jacques Derrida.* New York: Routledge.
Stocker, Barry. 2006. *Routledge Philosophy Guidebook to Derrida on Deconstruction.* New York: Routledge.

MARY BITTNER WISEMAN

Dewey, John (1859–1952) American philosopher, educator, and reformer; contributed significantly to every major field of philosophy. Aesthetics and its affiliated subject matters play a central role in the work of C. S. Peirce and William James as well as, and preeminently, of Dewey, all of whom are considered the most prominent members of the school in American philosophy called the "pragmatist movement."

Though Dewey wrote only one book explicitly devoted to aesthetics, *Art as Experience* (1934), it remains one of the most significant and original treatments of the topic. It also offers an insight into the nature of Dewey's general philosophy, illuminating his abiding concern with the aesthetic dimension of experience. Some, however, like Croce, have regarded this book as radically inconsistent with Dewey's pragmatism, while others have thought that it carries within it two inconsistent strands: one idealist, the other naturalist. But it is important to note that the views expressed in this work follow the underlying themes of Dewey's major philosophical opus, *Experience and Nature* (1925), in which is found not only the theoretical context of his aesthetics but also the ramifications for a radically novel metaphysical theory that takes aesthetic experience as central.

By the early years of the twentieth century, Dewey had aligned himself with the naturalistic side of the pragmatist movement. In his essay "The Reflex Arc Concept in Psychology," he provided a successful model of learning activity that takes as primary the idea of an organism constantly acting and responding to its environment in a continuous and developing pattern of experience. By 1925, with *Experience and Nature*, the model had been expanded to account for how members of a community, rather than a single isolated organism, pursue through the use of symbol, expression, and communication the ongoing project of directing experience toward intrinsically fulfilling ends which give human existence its depth of value and meaning. Thus, by Dewey's mature period, the term "experience" had come to mean for him *not* what it connotes to the tradition of British empiricism (the subjective, discrete, static mental image somehow "representing" an "external world"). Rather, it signifies the *shared social activity* of *symbolically mediated behavior* that seeks to discover the *possibilities* of our *objective situations* in the *natural world* for meaningful, intelligent, and fulfilling *ends*. And the skill at doing this Dewey calls "art."

Experience is a process in nature; it embraces potentialities as well as immediate actualities; it can be "civilized" or "cultivated" through education, whereby one becomes a participant in a social world; it can become "intelligent" insofar as it can be directed by recognition of its possibilities, both desirable and undesirable. The idea that experience is such a process, capable of control, so that it can develop continuously rather than be suffered from moment to moment, is the *idea* of art, which Dewey describes as the "greatest intellectual achievement in the history of humanity" (1987: 25, 31).

It is important, Dewey thinks, to understand the origin of art and the quest for aesthetic experience in the natural world of human action, especially since the cultural climate of the "artworld" and its institutions, like the museum or the market value of "great art," have been so uncritically taken as the starting point for aesthetic theory. He sees any theory, such as Clive Bell's, that treats art as an isolated, "high," or "pure" phenomenon standing unrelated to any other mode of human concern or experience, as a victim of a particular historically mediated cultural situation – one of which Dewey himself was highly critical. By separating the *idea* of art from life, we not only mystify art, but we thereby fail to recognize the pervasive *aesthetic* possibilities of human experience in general.

Dewey has been much misunderstood on this point. He is not rejecting the social function of public museums. Nor is he arguing that "ordinary" human experience, left unrefined in all its massive crudities, *is* art in exactly the same way in which "fine art" is art. What he does say is that the origin of art lies in the capacity to develop our ordinary experiences toward fulfilling ends. The traditional fine arts have done this exceptionally well, and thus can serve as a model for any activity that is fraught with the possibilities for truly fulfilling the human desire to exist with a vivid, complex awareness of the meaning and value of life. By putting the *idea* of art on a pedestal, as it were, we lose sight of its continuity as a development from the ordinary world (1987: 8).

Thus Dewey seeks to remind us of the constant involvement of "the live creature" with its world. Our senses are extensions of our need for continuous, organized activity that maintains and develops our equilibrium. There is an underlying vital rhythm to any living being's existence, and these rhythms form an organic matrix out of which our sense of dynamic order arises. Our embodiment as organisms shapes the conditions of the aesthetic. This rhythm of "doing and undergoing," of anticipating, acting, and responding, builds up our overall framework of what a "meaningful world" is. We come to experience in the light of remembered events and foreseen consequences, and cease thereby to be prisoners of the momentary sensation. The objects of our world arise from the temporality of human action constructing interpretations out of immediate events (1987: 13).

This leads to the most significant idea of Dewey's aesthetics: consummatory experience or "*an* experience," as he often referred to it. When the rhythmic interaction of individual and world comes to be consciously experienced as a developmental process culminating in the kind of organic integrity and wholeness which makes the event sensed as deeply meaningful, pervaded by a qualitative continuity which uniquely distinguishes the experience as such, then one has had "*an* experience." Works of art are preeminent examples: the experience of a Bach fugue, the Medici Chapel, Dante's

245

Commedia. But, of course, many experiences also have this consummatory character – even experiences that are not particularly happy or uplifting. There is *"an* experience" of a special day spent with a child, a gourmet meal enjoyed with friends, and of heart-rending grief. What is common to these experiences is that, through their internal qualitative integrity, they have revealed the capacity of experience to be meaningful on a profound level. The enemies of the aesthetic, says Dewey, are mindless habitual repetition at one extreme and random chaos at the other (1987: 40).

Aesthetic experience is not instantaneous or timeless. Its "consummatory" nature lies not in the fact that the experience comes to an end – for all experiences do – but that it is marked off *from the start* by the element of "closure." This is what gives dynamic, growing *continuity* to the experience beyond the mere succession of anticipations and responses. The experience has a sensed movement about it that holds forth the promise of consummation or, in some cases, fails its promise, and so is sensed as a "disappointment" (1987: 41).

Some of the most novel aspects of Dewey's theory lie in his discussions of expression and form. His is often misunderstood, along with other "expression theories," as simply regarding expression as an aspect of the creative act. But Dewey treats expression as the ongoing relationship between the work of art and the public. He distinguishes the "work of art" from the physical "art product," such as the canvas and paint, ink and paper, or sound vibrations; the *work* of art is the result of the interaction of the art product and an appreciator; the "work" becomes the meaningful integration of an art product and a life.

Like Collingwood, Dewey did not believe that "emotions" or "aesthetic intuitions" pre-existed their physical embodiment; as the work became objectified, so did they take on definition. Mere emotional outpouring is not "expressing." Expression is governed by the idea of *communication*, whether the art product is meant to be encountered by anyone else or not. Even while creating, the artist takes on the role of the appreciator in every act of critical assessment and response to what she has done. One is engaged in a dialogue with the self; as the product engages others, it becomes a dynamic dialogue within the experience of the human community – that is, culture. The *work* of art is to be found in the *life* it has within the culture. Thus there is not *one* "real" *Hamlet.* Neither is *Hamlet* a meaningless name for a haphazard variety of subjective reactions. The work of art that is *Hamlet* lies in the continued life of its reception in the culture, which gives rise to many divergent interpretations and readings (1987: 81).

Likewise, Dewey takes form in a very dynamic sense. The work of art is temporal, historical, cultural, and developmental. Its "form" cannot refer to some static underlying skeleton. Rather, its form is the way the work gives organization to experience: it is the pattern of the "working of the work," to use Heidegger's phrase. Form is the process of accumulative richness or, to use another of Dewey's terms, "funding" in *an* experience. Because the work of art is temporally experienced, not only is each moment of the process a "summing up and a carrying forward," but it is *felt* and *perceived* as such (1987: 137).

Dewey also distinguishes the "subject matter" of a work of art from its "substance." The subject is what may be discursively and topically isolated or shared by many different works. *Paradise Lost* and the Sistine Chapel, for example, share the common subject matter of the story of the creation and fall according to Genesis. But each work has disclosed its rendition in an entirely distinct way that can be encountered only through the work itself: this is what each work is really *about*; this is its *substance*. The substance is what is disclosed through the work, and it is this that gives sense to the saying that a work of art is ultimately about itself (1987: 111).

Any philosophy of experience, Dewey states, is ultimately tested by its treatment of aesthetic experience (1987: 274). Because aesthetic experience signifies for him the most integrated and complete mode of experience in which the human quest for meaning directly imbues the events of life with value, any short-sightedness here or lack of attention to vital factors, such as emotion, feeling, and imagination, will be most evident in an aesthetic theory (or lack of one). It is remarkable how many philosophies stand condemned by this requirement. Dewey does not make this comment idly, and surely intends his own philosophy to be judged by it.

It is perhaps one of the starker ironies of the history of philosophy that Dewey's philosophy has largely been judged on other, lesser merits. There are, obviously, weaknesses and problems in Dewey's theory, not least of which are the vagueness and rambling discursiveness of his prose. His heavy reliance on organic metaphors is often excessive or, at least, in need of clarification. He is not the connoisseur of fine art that Bell, Langer, Goodman, or Cavell are. One wishes he dealt more forthrightly with the genuine problem of cross-cultural responsiveness to art, instead of naively believing that art communicates directly where language often fails.

But these are all minor points in the light of the fact that Dewey has given in his discussion of art and aesthetic experience one of the most powerful, original, and challenging theories in the literature. Carried to its conclusion, his theory would have revolutionary effects not only upon the conclusions but also upon the conduct of most Anglo-American philosophy.

See also TWENTIETH-CENTURY ANGLO-AMERICAN AESTHETICS; AESTHETICS OF THE EVERYDAY; BELL; EXPRESSION THEORY; MUSEUMS; PRAGMATIST AESTHETICS.

BIBLIOGRAPHY

Primary sources
1925. *Experience and Nature*. Chicago: Open Court.
[1934] 1987. *Art as Experience*. Carbondale: University of Southern Illinois Press.

Secondary sources
Alexander, Thomas M. 1987. *John Dewey's Theory of Art, Experience, and Nature: The Horizons of Feeling* Albany: State University of New York Press.
Shusterman, Richard. 1992. *Living Beauty, Rethinking Art*. Oxford: Blackwell

THOMAS M. ALEXANDER

Dickie, George (b.1926) American philosopher of art. He was president of the American Society of Aesthetics in 1993–4. Dickie has made contributions to a number of important topics in analytic aesthetics, such as evaluation and intentionalism. However, the two areas of discussion where his work has sparked the most controversy and had the most impact are aesthetic theory and art theory.

Traditionally, aesthetic theory has been concerned with our responses to such things as natural beauties and artworks. The task of aesthetic theory – at least since the eighteenth century – has been to characterize the spectator's share in our commerce with nature and art in such a way that it can be seen as comprising a distinctive or unique mode of experience or perception, or as requiring or activating a distinctive attitude or faculty. Broadly put, aesthetic theory attempts to define a realm or dimension of the spectator's commerce with art and nature that is essentially distinguishable from any other mode of experience or activity such as the religious, the practical, and the moral. Dickie's contribution to this debate has been to argue that the notion of a distinct realm of the aesthetic, such as aesthetic experience, is a myth. No principled distinction can be drawn between so-called aesthetic perception and ordinary perception. And the postulation of special faculties, like taste, or the aesthetic attitude is ill-advised.

Dickie has attacked many diverse attempts to formulate aesthetic theories. One of his central objections has been to the role that the notion of disinterestedness plays in so many aesthetic theories. For example, Jerome Stolnitz (1960: 34) defines an aesthetic attitude as "disinterested and sympathetic attention to any object of awareness whatever for its own sake alone." Here, the idea of the aesthetic is a matter of attending to something in a specifiable way – that is, disinterestedly. "Disinterest," in turn, involves a lack of any ulterior purpose. But, Dickie notes, disinterest tells us something about a spectator's motives; it does not really point to any feature of the spectator's act of attention. If two people listen to a recording of a symphony – one in preparation for a music exam and the other for enjoyment – presumably the former has an interest and the latter is disinterested. Both may attend to the same features of the music and appreciate their structures for the same musicological reasons. There is only one way to attend (albeit with different grades of sophistication) to the music, though there may be different motives for our attention. Thus, notions like interest and disinterest do not specify different modes of attention. Furthermore, there is no reason to invoke these ideas in order to explain why the theatrical producer who watches his production with an eye to the box office is not responding appropriately. The problem is not that he is not attending disinterestedly. Rather, he is not paying attention to the play at all.

Along with his celebrated attacks on theories of disinterested attention, Dickie's attempts to construct a real or essential definition of art are his most noteworthy contribution to analytic aesthetics. It can be said that he reinvigorated the project of art theory in the name of what he initially called an "institutional theory of art." Prior to Dickie's intervention in the debate, aestheticians of the 1950s and 1960s were generally persuaded by the arguments of neo-Wittgensteinian philosophers, like Morris Weitz, who maintained (1) that art cannot be defined because it is an open concept; and (2) that the lack of a real definition of art should raise no philosophical anxieties, for there is an alternative way of identifying art – namely, the family-resemblance method.

Dickie rejected the notion of family resemblance as a serviceable means for telling art from nonart, on a number of grounds. One decisive objection was that the notion of family resemblance is ultimately only the idea of a resemblance, and, since everything resembles everything else in some respect, noting so-called family resemblances will finally force us to count everything as art. Moreover, since the family-resemblance approach is an obviously inoperable method for identifying art, one is compelled to take a second look at the rival method, that of identifying art by means of a definition comprising necessary conditions that are jointly sufficient. Dickie showed that such a definition of art need not place limits on artistic creativity with respect to artifacts. This definition, the "institutional theory of art," states in one of its elaborations: "A work of art in the classificatory sense is (1) an artifact (2) a set of the aspects of which has had conferred upon it the status of candidate for appreciation by some person or persons acting on behalf of a certain social institution (the artworld)" (1974: 34). This definition allows that an artwork could, for instance, look like anything – even a snow shovel – so long as the artifact is introduced by means of the right procedure:

that is to say, by having status conferred upon it by the right persons.

The institutional theory of art was subjected to intense criticism. One such was that the definition is circular insofar as art (the artworld) is an ineliminable element of the *definiens*. Dickie conceded this point, but argued that the circularity is not vicious. Another line of objection is that the underlying analogy with formal institutions, such as the law and religion, is strained beyond breaking point. Formal institutions of this kind have specifiable criteria governing what can be a candidate for a certain position (for instance, a potato cannot be a candidate for President of the United States) as well as specifiable criteria for who may officiate over certain procedures (for instance, only a bishop can confer Holy Orders). The artworld lacks criteria of this sort. Therefore, the artworld is not an institution in any rigorous sense. In other words, the second condition in Dickie's theory relies on the putative existence of altogether bogus roles and procedures.

Feeling the pressure of this line of argument, Dickie jettisoned talk of institutions in favor of talking about the art circle, a practice involving structured relations between artists and their audiences. In this context, he identified a necessary condition for what it is to be an artwork: "A work of art is of a kind created to be presented to an artworld public." This, in turn, is elucidated by the following four propositions: "A public is a set of persons the members of which are prepared in some degree to understand an object which is presented to them"; "An artworld system is a framework for the presentation of a work of art by an artist to an artworld public"; "An artist is a person who participates with understanding in the making of an artwork"; and "The artworld is the totality of artworld systems" (1984: 80–2). Dickie waves aside anticipated charges of circularity here, on the grounds that it is not vicious, while also conjecturing that it is a feature of cultural concepts that they will be circular – or, as he prefers to say, "inflected" – in this way.

Nevertheless, even if the theory of the art circle successfully deflects some of the objections leveled at the institutional theory of art, it would appear to provoke some problems of its own. There is the genuine question, for instance, of whether this theory is indeed a theory of art.

For though Dickie's set of inflected definitions mentions "art" at crucial junctures, the overall framework could be filled in just as readily with the names of other complex, coordinated, communicative practices, such as philosophy. But then the question arises as to whether Dickie has really said anything specific about art, as opposed to producing something like the necessary framework of coordinated, communicative practices of a certain level of complexity, where such practices cannot be identified in terms of their content. In other words, Dickie indicated that art belongs to the genus of complex, coordinated, communicative practices, along with showing, by example, some of the interrelated structures of these practices. This analysis is not without interest, but it does not seem to qualify as a definition of *art* – the very thing that he believes is the point of art theory.

Though Dickie's contributions to aesthetic theory and art theory may appear to be independent, they are not. For in dismissing the viability of the notion of the aesthetic, he undermines the possibility of aesthetic theories of art – theories such as Clive Bell's, that maintain that artworks are artifacts designed to cause aesthetic experiences. Insofar as aesthetic theories of art are rivals to institutional theories, Dickie's rejection of the aesthetic can be seen as a dialectical thrust against a major competing view. The other major competitor to the institutional approach was the neo-Wittgensteinian notion that art might be identified in virtue of family resemblances. In contradistinction to the tendencies of these rival theories of art is the importance Dickie places on social context for art theory. Whether the details of Dickie's theories are finally correct, it is nevertheless the case that he, along with Arthur C. Danto, has put the significance of social context on the agenda of contemporary philosophy of art.

See also TWENTIETH-CENTURY ANGLO-AMERICAN AESTHETICS; AESTHETIC ATTITUDE; ARTIFACT, ART AS; "ARTWORLD"; BELL; DANTO; DEFINITION OF "ART"; THEORIES OF ART; WITTGENSTEIN.

BIBLIOGRAPHY

Primary sources
1971. *Aesthetics: An Introduction.* Indianapolis: Pegasus.

1974. *Art and the Aesthetic: An Institutional Analysis.* Ithaca: Cornell University Press.
1984. *The Art Circle: A Theory of Art.* New York: Haven.
1988. *Evaluating Art.* Philadelphia: Temple University Press.
1989. (ed. with R. Sclafani & R. Roblin) *Aesthetics: A Critical Anthology.* 2nd edn. New York: St. Martin's.
1997. *Introduction to Aesthetics: An Analytic Approach.* Oxford: Oxford University Press.
2001. *Art and Value.* Oxford: Blackwell.

Secondary sources
Aagaard-Mogensen, Lars (ed.). 1976. *Culture and Art.* Atlantic Highlands: Humanities Press.
Davies, Stephen. 1991. *Definitions of Art.* Ithaca: Cornell University Press.
Graves, David C. 1997. "The Institutional Theory of Art: A Survey," *Philosophia*, 25, 51–67.
Stecker, Robert. 1996. "The End of an Institutional Theory of Art," *British Journal of Aesthetics*, 26, 134–42.
Stolnitz, Jerome. 1960. *Aesthetics and Philosophy of Art Criticism.* Boston: Riverside.
Yanal, Robert J. (ed.). 1994. *Institutions of Art: Reconsiderations of George Dickie's Philosophy.* University Park: Pennsylvania State University Press.

NOËL CARROLL

Dufrenne, Mikel (1910–1995) French philosopher, best known for applying phenomenology to the study of visual art. Dufrenne studied under Alain and Souriau, and taught at the universities of Poitiers and Paris–Nanterre, and of Buffalo, Michigan, and Delaware. He was the chief editor of *10/18*, the well-known French aesthetic and art journal transformed in 1974 from the *Revue d'esthétique*, which he had coedited.

His principal Sorbonne thesis, published in 1953 as *Phénoménologie de l'experience esthétique*, is his largest and most comprehensive work of aesthetics, and focuses mostly on the study of aesthetic experience, aesthetic objects, and aesthetic values. Like Ingarden, he rejects the traditional "objectivist" and "subjectivist" aesthetics, and accepts the phenomenological point of departure: the analysis and description of the acts of consciousness and their intentional correlates at the moment of the subject's encounter with a work of art.

Dufrenne follows Husserl in his critique of psychologism, physicalism, and relativism, and in the phenomenological method of description, though he rejects the notion of *pure transcendental ego*, claiming that consciousness is always individualized and concrete, as is its correlate, the aesthetic object. Like Merleau-Ponty, he emphasizes the concrete, lived, corporeal, and sensuous (*sensible*) experience of art. Like Ingarden, he distinguishes between the work of art and the aesthetic object – which is the only true form in which the work of art can be appreciated. Nevertheless, he criticizes Ingarden's thesis of works of art as purely intentional, and Sartre's thesis of *irreality*, though it seems that his critique of Ingarden is based more on terminological than on conceptual differences between them.

The most interesting aspect of Dufrenne's aesthetics seems to be his theory of the categories *affective a priori*, arising out of his interest in "the possibility of a pure aesthetics." Kant's notion of a priori is extended to affective categories a priori as the "conditions under which a world can be felt" (1973: 437). Specifically, Dufrenne distinguishes between the cosmological and existential a priori, the former residing in the object (making it perceivable), and the latter in the subject (making him capable of perceiving aesthetically). We are capable of having an aesthetic experience because we have the existential categories affective a priori which allow us to emotionally penetrate a work of art, to decipher its sense and value, and to feel its unique climate: the pathos of Beethoven's music, the tragic in the works of Sophocles, or the comic in Moliére.

The work of art expresses emotions: the cypresses in Van Gogh's painting are not just trees, but the expression of passion. The affective a priori in a work of art constitutes its value, its "soul," which is always associated with truth, for art grasps the elements of reality that cannot be expressed otherwise. To discover values is to discover the truth of nature. "The artist exists in the service of Nature which seeks to be incarnated in the work through his agency" (1973: 454), for he has a special sensitivity (categories *existential a priori*) for discovering its true sense, which the perceiver will be able to feel, thanks to his categories. "Aesthetic experience can thus become the

basis for the reflection between man and the real" (1973: 456). Thus, the cosmological and the existential are united in the aesthetic experience in which we learn truths about art, nature, and ourselves.

Dufrenne comes back to this theme in his subsequent *Poétique*, where he insists that the aesthetic experience does not stop with the aesthetic object but transcends it to contemplate the truth of nature, accessible in no other way than through the archetypes expressed in art. In this sense nature needs art as much as art needs a spectator for "the glory of appearing." Art can express truths, and man can perceive them sensually because the categories affective a priori are antecedent to both – like human beings, and art, they belong to being itself.

It seems that the project of pure aesthetics has been frustrated in favor of Heideggerian ontology, which actually leads Dufrenne to anthropology (see his *Pour l'homme* ("For Man")), and to ultimately denying the possibility of transcendental philosophy. His statement that the a priori is revealed only in the a posteriori is an ambiguous attempt at combining the empirical and the transcendental, as well as absolutism and relativism, especially when he addresses Max Scheler's antinomy between the absoluteness of values transcending the relativity of history and the "historicity of the feeling of values" (1973: 494).

Dufrenne's works from 1980 provide analyses of those contemporary works of art that, programmatically, go against all traditional schemata, genres, styles, and methods. The work ceases to be the ultimate goal of artistic creativity, and Dufrenne's attention shifts now to illuminate the process of creation as an end in itself. The contemporary work of art, with its elements of improvisation and participation of the perceiver, defies finality and the traditional subject–object structure. It disrupts the limits artificially imposed on art by institutions, and opens up new possibilities for freedom and creativity, whose end is the liberation of humankind from oppressive practices – such as violence, ideology, commercialization, fashion and power structures – that negate human values.

Artistic practices may actually be only marginal to the whole commercialized and institutionalized industry called "the artworld," but for aesthetics they should be of central interest, since spontaneous creation and aesthetic perception are two most important experiences in life. In creation "man reveals himself as capable of escaping the realm of necessity," and in aesthetic experience "man reveals himself capable of wonder" (1987: vii). Thus, what really remains as the end in itself for Dufrenne is humankind and its values, which are revealed in artistic and aesthetic experience, the only "innocent and free praxis" left in "the world sinking into barbarism" (1987: xii). The joy and spontaneity of such experiences, based on love and not domination, are subversive – they go against the established orders, show the possibility of change, and promise liberation.

Dufrenne remains the defender of humanism in his numerous polemics with its critics – namely, Heidegger, Althusser, Lévi-Strauss, and Lacan. His dialogue with French postmodernism is of particular value, and not only to students of aesthetics. Some of his discussion of Barthes, Bachelard, Derrida, and Lyotard can be found in *In the Presence of the Sensuous*. This anthology, the first English collection of Dufrenne's writings, spanning almost the whole of his career, exhibits the unusual versatility of his philosophical interests – imagination, artistic creativity, aesthetic values, the death of art, nature and aesthetic experience, language and reality, literary criticism, humanism, and postmodernism. All of these phenomena are analyzed with his usual depth and honesty and he takes care to reveal what should never be lost: the irreducibility and value of being.

See also NINETEENTH- AND TWENTIETH-CENTURY CONTINENTAL AESTHETICS; "ARTWORLD"; INGARDEN; MERLEAU-PONTY; TRUTH IN ART.

BIBLIOGRAPHY

Primary sources
[1953] 1966. *The Notion of the A Priori*. E. S. Casey (trans.). Evanston: Northwestern University Press.
[1953] 1973. *The Phenomenology of Aesthetic Experience*. E. S. Casey (trans.). Evanston: Northwestern University Press.
1963. *La Poétique*. Paris: Presses Universitaires de France.
1967, 1976, 1981. *Esthétique et philosophie*. 3 vols. Paris: Klincksieck.
1968. *Pour l'homme*. Paris: Seuil.
1987. *In the Presence of the Sensuous*. M. S. Roberts & D. Gallagher (eds. & trans.). Atlantic Highlands: Humanities Press.

WOJCIECH CHOJNA & IRENA KOCOL

E

education, aesthetic   *see* AESTHETIC EDUCATION.

emotion   figures in art and in the aesthetic experience of the natural word in many different ways. Some of these are unproblematic, but others are less easy to understand and their full aesthetic significance more difficult to grasp.

Perhaps the most difficult issues about art and emotion are these. First, there is the problem of the artistic expression of emotion. Works of art can not only describe emotion or depict or otherwise represent its manifestation in the body, but also express it. What is the relation between a work and a certain emotion, when the work expresses that emotion? This question arises in its purest form when the expressive work lacks any representational content, as is usually the case with music. Remarkable claims have often been made about the great superiority of music to language as a vehicle for the expression of emotion, especially in its capacity to express nuances of emotion that elude the net of language.

Whatever the truth of these claims, it is clear that some musical works are valued partly in virtue of their being heard as expressive of emotion; and yet it is by no means clear what this experience is and how, if at all, the emotionally expressive aspect of a work endows it with musical value. Does the experience consist in the recognition of some property of the music (e.g., the music's resemblance to one of the ways in which the emotion can be expressed in the human body or voice), or the recognition of some symbolic relation in which it stands to the emotion it expresses; or does it involve responding to the music with emotion of some kind; or is it some combination of these? Whatever the correct answer to this question may be, there is a further issue about artistic expression: is there a unitary sense in which works of art are experienced as being expressive of emotion, or does the sense change from one art form to another?

Second, there are various problems about the emotions aroused by works of art. One of these concerns the nature of the mental state of someone who reacts with emotion to a fictional state of affairs represented in a work of art. It seems often to be the case – in the cinema, at the theater, in an art gallery, or when reading fiction – that we are moved by what we know not to be real, but only fictional. But how is it possible for a fictional person or state of affairs to be the object of our emotion, when we are fully aware of their unreality? And if we do feel emotions about people or states of affairs that we are conscious of as merely fictional is it rational for us to do so?

Another problem about the artistic arousal of emotion concerns the so-called negative emotions, emotions like fear and horror that involve a negative attitude toward what they are about and are distressing to experience. Aristotle located fear and pity at the heart of the experience of tragic art, identified the tragic *pleasure* with that of fear and pity, and maintained that the arousal of fear and pity by a tragedy effects "catharsis."

There is a long-standing problem about the correct interpretation of Aristotle's conception of catharsis. But there is a further problem, for Aristotle defined both fear and pity as forms of pain, which would appear to preclude their constituting the distinctive pleasure of tragedy. Hume inherited this problem, and tried to resolve it by means of a doctrine about the conditions under which one emotion will be transformed by another, so that a normally painful emotion will lose its painful aspect and increase the strength of the pleasurable emotion that dominates it. But there is a more general issue about the occurrence of negative emotion in the experience of a work of art that is found valuable, which does not presuppose that this experience must be pleasurable: namely why is it ever reasonable to value a work of art for its ability to arouse negative emotions?

Finally, there is a problem about the education of emotion through art. A common justification of art is that it has a beneficial effect on the emotions of both the artist and the public: its successful practice requires the control and development of the artist's emotional life, and its products are unrivaled in their ability to introduce those who appreciate them to unfamiliar and superior forms of feeling, and to encourage in them more adequate or more rewarding feelings about many aspects of the world in which they live. Yet the variety of ways in which art can accomplish these desirable ends, and the sense or senses in which emotion can be refined and educated through artistic practice and appreciation, are not well understood. This is especially true of nonrepresentational works of art.

It is possible to make some progress with aesthetic problems concerning emotion, while remaining unclear about the nature of emotion in general and the various natures of the different emotions. But proposed solutions of these problems are often rendered null by a defective understanding of the emotions, and definitive solutions must be founded on a sound understanding. However, the field of the emotions is highly contentious, within both philosophy and psychology, and it is by no means easy to achieve a firm grasp of the topic.

What are the emotions? As a first approximation: the emotions are attitudes or reactions to how the world is represented as being, and they are distinguished from one another by the different representations or responses they involve. Each emotion requires the world to be represented to its subject in a certain way, as fear requires the representation of a threat, jealousy a rival, and sorrow the death of a loved one, for instance. Such a representation can be realized in many different forms, such as perception, experiential memory, imagination, or thought.

But an emotion requires more than the right kind of representation, for unless the representation induces the response distinctive of the emotion, the subject is not in that emotional condition. Both pity and *Schadenfreude* include the representation of someone's misfortune; but it is possible to be emotionally unaffected by someone's misfortune; and pity and *Schadenfreude* are different emotions because they involve opposite responses to the represented misfortune that is common to them. This encourages the thought that the emotions can be defined in terms of the representations and responses that jointly constitute them. But what kind of response to a representation is an emotional response? What needs to be added to a representation to make it an instance of an emotion?

Now, an emotion can exist in either a dispositional or an experiential form. If you have a general fear (e.g., of dogs), or you are afraid of a particular person or that a certain state of affairs will come about, you need not be undergoing any experience of fear – you might even be dreamlessly asleep, experiencing nothing at all. Your fear is a dispositional state, which is manifested not only in a tendency to avoid the feared object or to reduce the likelihood of the threatening state of affairs or to reduce your vulnerability to the threat it poses, but also in experiences of fear targeted on particular objects or concerned with possible states of affairs. When you experience an emotion, typically you *feel* the emotion – you feel afraid, ashamed, embarrassed, proud, or whatever. This suggests that the specifically emotional ingredient in a mental state is a feeling: an emotion requires the right representation plus the right feeling. Whether or not this is so, the idea of experiencing an emotion is of crucial significance for aesthetics, for the central problems about emotion turn on it. So what is it to feel a certain emotion? What kind of feeling is the feeling of jealousy, admiration, remorse, or amusement, and what makes a feeling a feeling of one of these emotions rather than another?

The best-known account of the nature of emotional feelings identifies the feeling of an emotion with the experience of bodily sensations. A bodily sensation is a feeling of an occurrence in or a state of the body. When you feel a pain in your back or when you feel hot, it feels to you as if something is going on in some part of your body or that your body is in a certain condition; and what is felt to occur or how your body feels to you determines the nature of the sensation you experience. Now, it is true that when you experience an emotion it will often be the case that you experience bodily sensations. But it is mistaken to represent the feeling of sadness, envy, pride, or regret as being composed of bodily sensations.

This suggestion exists in two forms. The stronger claim maintains that for each emotion there is a set of distinctive bodily sensations such that whenever the emotion is felt this set of bodily sensations is experienced: it identifies a type of emotional feeling with a collection of types of bodily sensation. Perhaps the best way for this suggestion to be developed is to maintain that a set of bodily sensations constitutes an emotional feeling, not simply in virtue of the intrinsic character of the set of sensations, but because it has been caused by the right kind of representation of the world. The weaker form of the suggestion maintains only that for each episode of emotion what is felt is a set of bodily sensations: it identifies each instance of an emotional feeling with whatever bodily sensations are caused on that occasion by the representation integral to the emotion. Whereas the stronger version requires that each instance of an emotional feeling of the same kind (admiration, say) consists of bodily sensations of the same kind, the weaker allows bodily sensations to vary across different instances of the same emotional feeling. But neither form is correct.

It is sometimes thought to be sufficient, to refute the identification, to point to the intentionality or directedness of emotions and the lack of intentionality of bodily sensations: whereas emotions are about something or other, bodily sensations are not. But this objection presupposes that bodily sensations are not representations of the body's condition: if they are, they possess intentionality. Perhaps it will be thought that, nevertheless, they would not possess the right intentionality. For, unless the object of an emotion is the subject's own body, as it might be in a case of pride or shame, emotions are directed toward the world outside one's body, whereas bodily sensations indicate the current state of one's body. But this consideration is inconclusive, since it would be possible for an adherent of the identification to reply that an emotional feeling is inherently only body-directed, its world-directed intentionality being derivative from the mental representation intrinsic to the emotion.

It is unnecessary to pursue this issue, however, for there is a more decisive objection. When you feel admiration, amusement, disgust, gratitude, sadness, shame, or shyness, it is unnecessary for you to be aware of any bodily sensations, so that the feeling you are aware of cannot be composed of bodily sensations in either the stronger or the weaker sense. Furthermore, it is never sufficient in order to experience a certain emotion that you should feel various bodily sensations as a result of the representation of the world integral to the emotion: if the perception of danger causes you to feel the pounding of your heart and the bristling of your hair, you might feel afraid of the threat, but you might instead feel excited at the challenge it poses. An emotion is not a causal compound of a mental representation and bodily sensations.

If an emotional feeling is not a set of bodily sensations, what else might it be? A more plausible suggestion emerges if we are guided by the account of the emotions in Aristotle's *Rhetorica*. Aristotle defines the emotions as "all those feelings that so change men as to affect their judgments, and that are also attended by pain or pleasure"; a good illustration is his definition of anger as "an impulse, accompanied by pain, to a conspicuous revenge for a conspicuous slight directed without justification towards what concerns oneself or towards what concerns one's friends" (*Rhetorica* 2.182). The great advantage of Aristotle's account is that it exploits and articulates a crucial feature of the emotions – namely, their power to initiate action and to affect thought. For many emotions involve not only mental representations but forms of desire or aversion, pleasure or pain, or other kinds of pro or con attitudes; as amusement and pride involve pleasure, hope a wish that something is or will be so and regret a wish that things had turned out differently, shame the desire to conceal and anger the desire to oppose or overcome, grief and fear distress, envy an aversion to a perceived inequality and pity the impulse to help. So the suggestion is that what we must feel if we are to experience an emotion is the pleasure or pain or the (apparent) frustration or satisfaction of the desire or wish integral to the emotion.

Note that this allows that when we experience an emotion we may often feel various processes take place in our body; but it denies that this is what the feeling of amusement, anger, envy, fear, grief, hope, pity, pride, regret, or shame amounts to. Rather, it is an experience of satisfaction or frustration, pleasure or pain. It is important to distinguish between what we *must* feel if we are to feel shame, say, and what in fact we feel on some occasion (or even all occasions) when we feel shame. The feeling of shame is the first of these, not the second. Note also that this theory does not rest on the common doctrine that a desire lies at the heart of each emotion: the truth is that some emotions lack constitutive desires. Nor does it presuppose that we always derive satisfaction from the known satisfaction of a desire, and experience displeasure if a desire is thought to be unfulfilled. What it maintains is that we experience an emotion that contains a desire that appears to us to be frustrated or threatened, only if we experience displeasure at that prospect or certainty: to feel the emotion is to experience the displeasure.

Note, finally, that this suggestion does not identify any emotion with a feeling. What it offers is an account of what is felt when an emotion is experienced; but there is more to any emotion than the feeling that partly constitutes it. There is a difference between what is felt when an emotion is experienced and what it is to feel that emotion. Although what it is to feel one emotion is not the same as what it is to feel a different emotion, there is a sense in which what is felt (e.g., pleasure) may be the same in the two cases. The nature of the feeling does not determine the nature of the emotion felt. For an emotion is a causal structure: unless the feeling intrinsic to an emotion is caused by the representation intrinsic to the emotion and is directed at what the representation is about, the emotion is not experienced.

This suggestion maintains that the experience of an emotion is a product of a mental representation, typically a belief, and a positive or negative attitude toward the content of the representation, which attitude either is an affect or combines with the representation to produce one. If this is a true account of what it is to feel the emotions mentioned, does it hold for all emotions? Certainly, it applies to a number of other emotions (e.g., embarrassment). Not only, though, do the emotions form a heterogeneous class, which militates against a unitary account of the kinds of feeling intrinsic to them; but the boundaries of the class are uncertain, so that it is unclear whether certain kinds of reaction fall within the boundaries and therefore are emotions.

For instance, if surprise and amazement are correctly thought of as emotions, what we experience when we undergo them does not conform to the account, since the experience of surprise or amazement is not one of being frustrated by or distressed about something, or in which pleasure or satisfaction is derived from some state of affairs. Even so, these experiences are not bodily sensations. (They are the confounding of expectations – as the experience of wonder is the surpassing of expectations.) So there may well be counterexamples to the suggestion. It may also be necessary to qualify the suggestion by introducing additional kinds of feeling into the analysis of certain of the emotions for which the suggestion holds – felt impulses to action, the feeling of being invigorated or the feeling of lassitude, for example.

I believe that the best strategy is not to attempt to design a theory that captures every member of the accepted class of emotions, since this class may be both ill-conceived and indeterminate. It is better to try to accommodate the great majority of the members within a single theory, and to place the exceptions outside the newly drawn boundaries of the class. This is how the suggestion outlined above should be understood. But even if this suggestion captures most emotional feelings, it does not follow that it is better than any other, for another account might capture equally many, if not more. Furthermore, without an exhaustive list of the emotions, it is unclear whether the suggestion is in fact true of most, or only a minority, of emotional feelings. If it holds only for a minority, a different strategy recommends itself: recognize the diversity of emotional feelings and abandon any attempt to redraw the boundaries of the class in order to impose uniformity on its members. This strategy appears to be especially appropriate within aesthetics, where problems about emotion benefit from a case-by-case approach.

See also AESTHETIC EDUCATION; AESTHETIC PLEASURE; ARISTOTLE; CATHARSIS; EXPRESSION; FICTION, THE PARADOX OF RESPONDING TO.

BIBLIOGRAPHY

Aristotle. 1924. *Rhetorica*. W. R. Roberts (trans.). Oxford: Clarendon.

Budd, Malcolm. 1985. *Music and the Emotions*. London: Routledge & Kegan Paul, ch. 1.

Hepburn, Ronald W. 1984. "The Arts and the Education of Feeling and Emotion." In *"Wonder" and Other Essays*. Edinburgh: Edinburgh University Press, 88–107.

Levinson, Jerrold. 2006. "Emotion in Response to Art." In *Contemplating Art: Essays in Aesthetics*. Oxford: Clarendon, 38–55.

Robinson, Jenefer. 2005. *Deeper than Reason: Emotion and Its Role in Literature, Music and Art*. Oxford: Clarendon.

MALCOLM BUDD

end of art   *see* DANTO; HEGEL.

environmental aesthetics   *see* AESTHETICS OF THE ENVIRONMENT.

erotic art and obscenity   Artworks are sometimes condemned as obscene. In making the judgment that something is obscene, the presumption seems to be that a work is morally repulsive and thereby to be condemned as art. The arts, after all, should educate and refine the mind rather than coarsen and degrade it. Hence, for example, we may praise a work as erotic art while condemning another as pornographic. Yet there is a strong tradition within art of making works that deliberately seek to unsettle and provoke us – in part through getting us to take up interests, imaginings, or responses that we normally would not. It can be a good-making feature of a work that it challenges some of our most fundamental cognitive/affective attitudes. Works often adjudged obscene may challenge us in valuable ways. So what is it for a work to be obscene and just how does this relate to artistic value?

The notion of obscenity cannot be strictly causal (contra MacKinnon 1993). It is true that a lot of obscenity debates around pornography center on whether sexual objectification

is likely to cause immoral attitudes and behavior toward (usually) women. Yet even if we grant that there are causal links from objectifying representations to immoral behavior, the causal assumption would apply to many works we do not judge obscene. Many Klimts or Pre-Raphaelite paintings, film comedies, and books that sexually objectify women are not judged to be obscene. Furthermore, works soliciting a certain interest in the freakish and deformed (Joel-Peter Witkin), children or death (Jake and Dinos Chapman) may still be condemned as obscene without the assumption that they affect anyone's attitudes or behavior to the disabled, young, or the deceased.

Alternatively obscenity is sometimes identified with objectification (Scruton 1994). Yet a medical photograph, Cezanne's portrait of his dead child, or Lucian Freud's nudes may solicit an objectifying interest in our corporeal nature without being judged to be obscene. Obscenity as such should not be conflated with objectification (though the latter may be a typical means of realizing the former). Works judged to be obscene do not always involve objectification (think of sacrilegious art), and works that depend on objectification to achieve their aims are not always obscene.

Paradigms of obscenity manifest a variety of features that we take to be marks of the obscene: subject matter of bodily functions, sex, violence, and death; a lack of self-restraint sought from or elicited in the viewer; the objectification of people and indecency. While these may be potential markers, such features do not capture the fundamental character of obscenity. What further matters is the way the subject matter is treated by the representations to seek or elicit certain kinds of responses from us. It is not enough (contra Feinberg 1985) to say that the features involved or the responses sought are vulgar or deemed to be morally indecent or problematic. There are many representations that may be judged in these terms without thereby attracting a judgment of obscenity. What also seems to be required is the recognition of a central feature of the phenomenology involved in paradigmatic instances: the feelings of repulsion that arise in virtue of both the solicitation or elicitation of responses taken to be morally prohibited and the attraction toward indulging or savoring those very responses (Kieran 2002, 2004). This explains why it is that people tend to get so heated when discussing obscene artworks.

The type of account just sketched faces at least two challenges: (1) what motivation could we have for indulging in responses we take to be morally repulsive, and (2) how is it that we may judge works to be obscene even where we do not ourselves feel the attraction of the morally prohibited responses spoken to? The second challenge is the more straightforward to meet. Although paradigmatic cases are characterized in terms of representations being found to be both morally repulsive and attractive, this is not strictly necessary. We can and do recognize that representations may merit or elicit such responses in others, in ways we take to be morally problematic, even though we ourselves do not so respond. Judging something to be obscene is in this respect similar to judgments of moral offence – we can judge something to be offensive or obscene without ourselves necessarily feeling repulsed and attracted or feeling offended. With respect to meeting the first challenge, there are at least three explanations as to why we may be attracted by a representation we deem to be morally repulsive (Kieran 2002, 2004). First, a representation indulges basic motivating desires deemed to be morally wrong, misdirected, or excessive. Imagine a work that uses explicit genital fixation to solicit a viewer's sexual interest in young girls. Alternatively, consider a representation of rape where the artistry is designed to arouse the viewer through the victim's subjugation. Sexual desire is not as such wrong, and desire for the young or for sexual dominance is not that uncommon. Such representations are repulsive, in virtue of the way in which they are morally abhorrent, and yet attractive, in virtue of arousing and commending certain basic sexual desires. The same kind of characterization generalizes to include, for example, certain kinds of representations of violence, suffering, or death. A photograph, for example, that solicits delight in the annihilation of another and the destruction of the human body is repulsive and yet speaks to base desires in exactly this way. Second, some obscene works engage the desire to be morally transgressive or to delight in the feelings of repulsion

and disgust themselves. A common strand of twentieth-century art is driven by the impulse to shock or repulse. One of the ways a work can do so is through being morally transgressive. Works that seek morally problematic responses may do so to solicit interest and delight in moral transgression as such. Part of the appeal may spring from a common enough desire to break free from basic moral norms. We are not usually attracted to doing so in real life, since the moral costs are high (and often the prudential ones are too). However, such costs are greatly diminished where doing so involves attending to representations that indulge such desires without obviously harming anyone. Third, a work may speak to cognitive interests such as curiosity or fascination. As Leontion in Plato's *Republic* (1974: 439e–440a) sated his curiosity to dwell on the appearance of executed corpses despite his better judgment, so we too may feel the pull of representations of death and disaster out of sheer curiosity even though we may consider how we are invited to do so to be morally repulsive.

Can obscene works, in particular pornographic ones, be any good as art? The received view holds that what is pornographic cannot be artistic. Erotic works may aspire to the rarefied heights of great art but the pornographic, it is often held, can only be bad art (if it is art at all). The erotic engages the imagination and may evoke sensuous feelings, whereas pornography trades in explicitness and mere fantasy in the pursuit of arousal. Thus, by definition, the pornographic cannot make for (good) art (Burgess 1970; Levinson 1998). Two underlying assumptions are questionable. First, it is taken for granted that because the pornographic aims at sexual arousal it cannot have any other aims. Why should we think this is true? Representations made to fulfill one function are often designed with others in mind (to take but one example, consider much religious art). In the case of sexually explicit works, at least some of them clearly seem to be designed with both artistic and pornographic interests in mind (Kieran 2001, 2004). Jeff Koons's controversial 1990s "Made in Heaven" series graphically depicts the artist and his then wife, the former porn start Ilona Staller, having sex. Aubrey Beardsley, Degas, Toulouse-Lautrec, and Klimt, to name but a few, all went in for frank, sexually charged sketches and paintings. Indeed, Egon Schiele sometimes made a living by making pornographic works to order and ran into all sorts of legal troubles. Second, why should we think that sexual explicitness aiming at arousal precludes the exercise of artistic imagination (Kieran 2001, 2004)? To take just one example, the heightened dynamism in Rodin's explicit line drawings is achieved through the innovative use of wash and overscoring.

The strongest consideration in defense of the received view is the claim that pornographic works may be appreciable as art and as pornography but they cannot be appreciated as pornographic art (Longford 1972; Levinson 2005). A pornographic interest pays attention to explicit body parts and behavior in the service of sexual arousal. An aesthetic interest concerns the medium, structural composition, and meaning of a work. Zeroing in on the features that serve to arouse may obliterate the detachment and attention required for aesthetic appreciation. Yet if we consider pornographic works that are truly artistic, there is some reason to doubt this. Torii Kiyonobu I's *Erotic Contest of Flowers: Scenes of Lovemaking* (1704–11), works from the Japanese Ukiyo-e school, Rodin's drawings, or Robert Mapplethorpe's aestheticization of homoerotic desire all seek to convey something about the nature of sexual desire, in part through the solicitation of it via artistic features. The extent to which they are successful is the extent to which there is reason to hold something can be appreciated as pornographic art (Kieran 2001, 2004).

What distinguishes the merely pornographic from pornographic art? Pornographic art is something *more* than pornography (as opposed to not being pornographic at all). Good art draws us in to appreciate particular ways of viewing and responding to the world – often ones that may not be our own. A piece of mere pornography may manifest banal sexual clichés or vicious attitudes in the same way that someone clenching their jaw may manifest anger. Pornographic art, however, cultivates through the artistic solicitation of arousal a way of apprehending and responding to the subjects or states of affairs as represented. Of course, we may not like how we are invited to

respond to the work, and this sometimes gives rise to judgments of obscenity. Mapplethorpe's fetishism of muscle definition, sinew, and, not to put too fine a point on it, size, seems a morally impoverished aestheticization of sexual desire. Rodin's ferocious lust for sexual possession suffers from the fervors of an over-romanticization of sexual desire. But some such works cannot be appreciated as art without seeing that this is what their artistry, albeit sexually explicit and partly in the service of sexual interest, is devoted to evoking. Hence, to appreciate them fully, one cannot but engage with and appreciate such works as pornographic art. Pornographic works, and obscene works more generally, may sometimes be good as art partly in virtue of their pornographic or more generally obscene nature.

See also CENSORSHIP; MORALITY AND ART; PORNOGRAPHY.

BIBLIOGRAPHY

Burgess, Anthony. 1970. "What is Pornography?' In *Perspectives on Pornography*. D. A. Hughes (ed.). New York: St. Martin's.
Feinberg, Joel. 1985. *Offense to Others*. Oxford: Oxford University Press.
Kieran, Matthew. 2001. "Pornographic Art," *Philosophy and Literature*, 25, 31–45.
Kieran, Matthew. 2002. "On Obscenity: The Thrill and Repulsion of the Morally Prohibited," *Philosophy and Phenomenological Research*, 64, 31–56.
Kieran, Matthew. 2004. *Revealing Art*. London: Routledge, ch. 4.
Levinson, Jerrold. 1998. "Erotic Art." In *The Routledge Encyclopedia of Philosophy*. E. Craig (ed.). London: Routledge, 406–9.
Levinson, Jerrold. 2005. "Erotic Art and Pornographic Pictures," *Philosophy and Literature*, 29, 228–40.
Longford, Lord. 1972. *Pornography: The Longford Report*. London: Coronet.
MacKinnon, Catherine. 1993. *Only Words*. Cambridge, MA: Harvard University Press.
Plato. 1974 [375 BCE]. *The Republic*. D. Lee (trans.). 2nd edn. Harmondsworth: Penguin.
Scruton, Roger. 1994. *Sexual Desire*. London: Phoenix.

MATTHEW KIERAN

ethics and art *see* AUTHENTICITY AND ART; CENSORSHIP; CULTURAL APPROPRIATION; EROTIC

ART AND OBSCENITY; FORGERY; MORALITY AND ART; PORNOGRAPHY; RACE AND AESTHETICS.

evaluation of art   *see* COGNITIVE VALUE OF ART; CRITICISM; INTERPRETATION, AIMS OF; OBJECTIVITY AND REALISM IN AESTHETICS; TASTE.

evolution, art, and aesthetics   If our aesthetic preferences and artistic behaviors are directly connected to evolution, then either they are adaptations or they are "spandrels," adventitious by-products of adaptations. An adaptation is some feature produced by chance genetic variation that confers a net advantage to the long-term reproductive success of those individuals that have it, in some cases by appealing to the preferences of potential sexual partners. Adaptations must be reliably transmissible from generation to generation, usually in part via genetic inheritance, so that the feature is perpetuated in the lineages of its possessors. Adaptive behaviors and qualities are often self-motivating or perceived as intrinsically appealing or pleasurable; we enjoy eating nutritious food, having sex, and nurturing babies for their own sakes.

It is not inevitable that successful adaptations will become universal across the species. A behavior or trait might be adaptive only by relating in a stable equilibrium to different, more common adaptations. (Neither is universality sufficient to identify a successful adaptation: spandrels can be universal, as can be features generated by random genetic drift.) Whether a successful human adaptation is displayed pan-culturally depends on whether the necessary environmental and sociohistorical resources for its realization are available in every culture.

Though evolutionary change is an ongoing process – as a result, we are immune to germs and viruses that would have killed our forebears – the perceptual, cognitive, and affective systems that characterize modern-day humans were in place earlier than 50,000 BP. Accordingly, successful adaptations are typically of prehistoric origin, and our basic aesthetic preferences and art behaviors would have to be similarly ancient if they are adaptations or spandrels.

Many of the claims made about the evolutionary status of currently observed human behaviors are dismissed as post hoc speculations. Apart from continuing archaeological and other studies of prehistoric times, four kinds of tests are used to offset such charges: observation of contemporary hunter-gatherers, study of children (because their development is thought to recapitulate the species' evolutionary history), comparison with primates and other animal relatives, and "reverse engineering," which views current behavior as addressing some ancestral challenge and infers backward to what that was. Inevitably, the status of the hypotheses proposed by sociobiologists and evolutionary psychologists often remains controversial.

NATURAL AESTHETIC PREFERENCES
Evolutionary psychologists have discussed the adaptive value of our aesthetic tastes with respect to other humans and natural environments. Our concern with human beauty or attractiveness is assumed to be linked to our interest in others as potential sexual partners or as social allies/rivals (Pinker 1997; Miller 2000). Judgments of human beauty or attractiveness track markers of health and fertility, such as symmetry, hypernormalcy, and youthfulness, that in turn are predictors for the breeding success of offspring. In other words, we find aesthetically appealing those people most likely to be the most successful parents. For instance, studies have shown strong correlations between our finding faces beautiful and their being symmetrical, and it is noted that symmetry is a strong indicator of health, "good genes," and immunity to disease. Matters are not always so straightforward, however. We can also be entranced by features that are unusual in falling at the extremes of (but not beyond) the normal range. Of course, it is not only aspects of physical appearance that are relevant to breeding success. Desirable intellectual and moral qualities, social adeptness, knowledge, physical prowess, creativity, humor, and, indeed, aesthetic sensitivity can all contribute to a person's appeal.

Some evolutionary psychologists may be guilty of equating or confusing aesthetic beauty with sexual attractiveness, but their position need not be reductive. It could be argued that they identify the *roots* of our aesthetic preferences for our fellows as originating in connection with mate selection, and this is consistent with acknowledging that the aesthetic stance is distinct from the sexual one. As we know, it is not only young adults in search of a mate who evaluate others for the pleasingness of their appearance and character. Rather the aesthetic is a frame (one among many) through which we all seek value in the world. An interest in and fascination with human beauty, of both appearance and character, is pursued by and directed to all, regardless of age and gender.

As regards natural environments, the suggestion is that our ancestors took delight in environments suited to their hunter-gatherer way of life. They were drawn to landscapes that offered prospects, shelter, and refuges, along with water and food. (Even in today's cities, the most sought-after properties overlook parkland and rivers, seas, or lakes.) They found beautiful those habitats in which they and their children could flourish (Heerwagen & Orians 1993).

Some evolutionary psychologists claim that the African savannah, where the first humans evolved, is aesthetically privileged by children wherever they are born. In any case, the human capacity to adjust to a variety of physical environments suggests that the general principles undergirding the aesthetic stance toward habitats can be applied to suit the local conditions.

ART AS AN ADAPTATION

The natural aesthetic preferences so far described would not help us discriminate swimsuit and landscape calendars from paintings by Rembrandt or Constable, so how does evolution apply to art more specifically? Some argue that the creation and appreciation of art are adaptive behaviors. Notice that this presupposes that art is probably pan-cultural and ancient, which invites the view that art is typically humble and functional, being tied to decoration, religion, and ritual. The eighteenth-century Western concept of fine art then must be viewed as only one species within a wider genus. Indeed, the abstruse appeal of such art and the cult of disinterested connoisseurship associated with it might be considered as a perversion of what was originally adaptive.

Some theories present the arts in general as adaptations. Ellen Dissanayake (1988) argues that art is an ancient, universal behavior that falls alongside play and ritual under the heading of "making special." Making special is adaptive because those who engage in it thereby create communities in which human families can more readily thrive. Geoffrey Miller (2000), by contrast, holds that sexual selection drives artistic creation, which is an honest because costly display of male fitness, somewhat like the peacock's tail. Though women are primarily styled as consumers of male art, Miller emphasizes that they must match men's subtle creativity with equally sophisticated and complex modes of aesthetic appreciation. Very general theories, like these, run the risk of reducing the arts to denominators so low and common that what they identify as evolutionarily relevant is not characteristic of art as such.

Other theories treat specific arts as distinctively adaptive. For instance, Ian Cross (2007) argues that, because it is significant yet lacking in definite meaning, music facilitates social interaction even in the face of disagreement. Moreover, its semantic openness and its capacity to be integrated with other activities underpin our ability to integrate information across different cognitive domains. Meanwhile, Joseph Carroll (2007) and J. Tooby & L. Cosmides (2001) argue that literature and its oral antecedents create emotionally and morally imbued models of human action which provide psychological maps that allow us to assess others and to explore hypothetical courses of action and engagement. Such accounts sometimes make claims for the adaptive value of the given art that seem unduly inflated or implausible; alternatively, the significance of the artistic contribution to the adaptive result is difficult to discern.

THE ARTS AS SPANDRELS

Theorists who argue that art is merely a by-product of evolutionary adaptations need show only that something of uncontroversial adaptive value has the incidental benefit of promoting artistic activity.

Several writers, including Mithen (1996) and Pinker (1997), suggest that the arts are a by-product of our large and developed brain or of the evolution of intelligence. This makes the connection between art and evolution trivial, however, since science, technology, and almost everything else can similarly trace their roots to the same source.

A more useful theory might first argue for the adaptive importance of our propensity to construct narratives in understanding ourselves, others, cosmology, and the world at large, and then describe narrative drama and literature as the artistic bonus. Or it could discuss how our concerns with the prosodic and expressive features of speech, the informational content of environmental sound, and the interplay of sonic forms and patterns lay the foundation for our delight in music. And so on for the other arts. (Denis Dutton (2009) suggests, however, that on such theories, the arts are best understood as deliberate enhancements or extensions of adaptations rather than as byproducts of adaptations.)

Others are interested in the way that universal features of our evolved perceptual, cognitive, and affective systems, and connections among these, are reflected in art and our engagement with it (Ramachandran & Hirnstein 1999; Zeki 2000; Solso 2003). The operation of such systems can give rise to aesthetic reactions, as when we take pleasure in pattern, symmetry, or closure, in tracking meanings or narratives, in tracing the ebb and flow of affect, and so on. Often, rather than telling us about the artwork as such, these accounts use art merely to illustrate the aesthetically appreciable workings of the relevant systems. They are more to the point when they address how art achieves its potency and appeal by the way it concentrates and amplifies features that not only trigger but also overstimulate these systems or bring them into unusual and provocative juxtapositions. And they are at their most interesting when doing this helps explain how the artist tackled some technical problem posed by the work's aesthetic goals, style, or content.

See also ART OF THE PALEOLITHIC; COGNITIVE SCIENCE AND ART; OBJECTIVITY AND REALISM IN AESTHETICS; UNIVERSALS IN ART.

BIBLIOGRAPHY
Carroll, Joseph. 2007. "Evolutionary Approaches to Literature and Drama." In *The Oxford Handbook of Evolutionary Psychology*. R. I. M. Dunbar & L. Barrett (eds.). Oxford: Oxford University Press, 637–48.

Cross, Ian. 2007. "Music and Cognitive Evolution." In *The Oxford Handbook of Evolutionary Psychology*. R. I. M. Dunbar & L. Barrett (eds.). Oxford: Oxford University Press, 649–67.

Dissanayake, Ellen. 1988. *What is Art For?* Seattle: University of Washington Press.

Dutton, Denis. 2009. *The Art Instinct: Beauty, Pleasure, and Human Evolution*. Oxford: Oxford University Press.

Gottschall, Jonathan & Wilson, David Sloan (eds.). 2005. *The Literary Animal: Evolution and the Nature of Narrative*. Evanston: Northwestern University Press.

Heerwagen, Judith H. & Orians, Gordon H. 1993. "Humans, Habitats, and Aesthetics." In *The Biophilia Hypothesis*. S. R. Kellert & E. O. Wilson (eds.). Washington, DC: Island Press, 138–72.

Miller, Geoffrey. 2000. *The Mating Mind: How Sexual Choice Shaped the Evolution of Human Nature*. New York: Doubleday.

Mithen. Steven. 1996. *The Prehistory of the Mind: A Search for the Origins of Art, Religion, and Science*. London: Thames & Hudson.

Pinker, Steven. 1997. *How the Mind Works*. New York: Norton.

Ramachandran, Vilayanur S. & Hirstein, William. 1999. "The Science of Art: A Neurological Theory of Aesthetic Experience," *Journal of Consciousness Studies*, 6, June–July, 15–51.

Solso, Robert L. 2003. *The Psychology of Art and the Evolution of the Conscious Brain*. Cambridge, MA: MIT Press.

Tooby, J. & Cosmides, L. 2001. "Does Beauty Build Adapted Minds? Toward an Evolutionary Theory of Aesthetics, Fiction and the Arts," *SubStance*, 94/95, 6–27.

Voland, Eckart and Grammer, Karl (eds.). 2003. *Evolutionary Aesthetics*. Berlin: Springer.

Zeki, Semir. 2000. *Inner Vision*. New York: Oxford University Press.

STEPHEN DAVIES

experience and art   *see* SENSES AND ART, THE.

expression   Something is expressed when it is laid out to public gaze. Hence, the minutes might express the view of the meeting, or *Lisa of Lambeth* the plight of the urban poor. There is a set of more particular problems in discussing the expressive qualities of art and it is this on which this entry will focus. A natural place to start is with expression in the central (i.e., nonartistic) case and to take that as the model for expression in art. Some make a distinction between "betraying" one's emotion and expressing it. The former is merely the venting of emotion with little or no intention behind it. The latter involves some attempt (conscious or otherwise) to mold one's appearance or behavior for communicative intent. This distinction is useful when it comes to thinking about the arts, however it is not well marked in ordinary language; betrayals of emotion are often counted as expressive: just think of bursting into tears. Hence, I shall assume a generous definition of expression, which has three parts. An inner state is expressed when it is made publicly available, by a person, by means of appearances or behavior characteristically associated with that state. Furthermore, the term describing that inner state can be transferred to states of affairs that give a reason for being in that state: for example, weddings are happy occasions and funerals are sad occasions.

There are various means by which a work could be expressive (none invariably successful). It might represent a person being expressive. It might represent a situation that gives a reason for being in an emotional state. However, the philosophical literature has tended to focus on ways by which a work can become expressive that do not involve the representation of states of affairs; paradigmatically, it has focused on instrumental music although there is also a small literature on expression in paintings. I shall deal with each in turn.

An account of expression in music is only philosophically (as opposed to psychologically) interesting if it fits in with an account of artistic understanding. Hence, philosophy needs to take account of only those properties that are part of our experience of music. Thus, the question of which properties of instrumental music *cause* us to experience it as expressive is not relevant to our inquiry unless those properties figure in our experience, in which case it is better to study the experience directly. Thus we can put the causal question to one side, and focus on the issue of what constitutes expression. I shall divide the accounts into three types, defined according to what they take to be

involved in the experience of expression: an imagined state, an experience of resemblance, or an aroused feeling.

Jerrold Levinson takes the experience to be an imagined state. Of all the theories, his follows most closely expression in the central case. Thinking of the tripartite account of expression offered above, Levinson claims that to hear music as expressive is to hear it as an inner state made publicly available, by a persona. The third part of the tripartite account he must reject. Obviously, we do not hear music as "the appearance or behavior characteristically associated with that state." That is, we do not hear it as, for example, the sound of weeping and wailing. In other words, our experience of the music is an imaginative one: we hear the music as the expression of an emotion by a persona – an emotion expressed in a *sui generis* musical manner (even if we might not articulate that final thought to ourselves as an element of the experience) (Levinson 2005). Kendall L. Walton also claims that expressive music is that which prompts us into an imagined state, albeit one of a very different sort. Walton allows expression of much the sort Levinson describes, but goes on to claim that there is an additional form of expression. Walton's suggestion is that some music will prompt us to imagine, of our actual introspective awareness of our auditory sensations, that it is an awareness of our own (emotional) states of mind (Walton 1988: 359). If it does so, it is expressive.

Whatever the individual merits of these suggestions, they suffer from the drawback that there is no generally accepted account of the imagination on which we can draw. We have no independent grasp of whether we are in fact exercising these imaginative capacities of ours in these ways; it is in the nature of the case that what it feels like to do so will simply be what it feels like to experience expressive music. We have no way of being sure that the reconstruction of our experience offered by Levinson and Walton corresponds to what is going on in our minds. This is not to say that we have nothing to go on; we can ask whether the elements of the accounts are or are not metaphysically dubious, and whether the accounts have intuitive appeal. However, I am not sure whether this is robust enough to allow us to decide between alternative proposals. It is not clear that either of our other types of view is in any stronger position on this point.

My second type of solution relied on the experience of resemblance. Stephen Davies claims that there is a type of appearance – "an emotion characteristic in appearance" – that gets its character from the appearance characteristically linked to the expression of emotion in the central case. It is not, however, necessarily caused by any feeling or emotion; such an appearance can be worn by someone whatever they are feeling. We experience some pieces of music as possessing such appearances, or at least some aspects of such appearances: "the expressiveness of music depends mainly on a resemblance we perceive between the dynamic character of music and human movement, gait, bearing, or carriage" (Davies 1994: 229). We do not notice such appearances and infer the music is expressive; rather, our experience of such resemblances is (or is in part) our experience of music as expressive.

The movement properties Davies specifies are possessed by many things apart from music and human beings, so one might wonder why it is this resemblance that is brought to our notice. However, it is not fair to demand such an account of Davies; there will be some causal account of why this is so, while Davies is giving us a constitutive account. This does, however, raise another worry. The experience of resemblance seems inadequate as a characterization of the experience of expression: they simply do not seem equivalent. It is open to Davies here to say that he need not provide a full characterization, it is enough that all and only music we experience as expressive, we experience as resembling a human being in the appropriate way – whatever more there is to be said about the experience. There is a danger in such an answer, however, for it raises the question as to whether we have a characterization of expression, and not merely of a property that is constantly conjoined with expression.

The third type of solution was accounts that rely on some aroused noncognitive state. The bare claim that sad music is music that makes us sad will not do for many reasons, not least because not all feelings that are aroused by music are related to expression (we can be

made sad by music that is badly played) nor does all sad music arouse our feelings (we can experience expression in music without being aroused to that feeling of which it is expressive). Furthermore, the experience of music as expressing sadness is different from the experience of the music conjoined to a feeling of sadness. However, it need not be the case that the aroused feeling has this simple form. We might hold that there are pieces of music that arouse the feeling that "sadness is being felt around here," without being any more specific (see Walton 1999). Nonetheless, more work would need to be done to show this was an adequate account of the experience of expression.

Although I have divided these accounts into distinct types, experience suggests that the connections between music and emotion might be various. Malcolm Budd has suggested "a basic and minimal" account of the musical expression of emotion, which is a cross-categorial likeness perception (a theory of our second type). However, Budd argues that it is likely that there are others, and countenances the possibility of accounts of our first and third types as well (1995: 138–59). This has the virtue of explaining the interminable nature of the debate: that one theory is correct does not mean that the alternatives are incorrect.

Finally, I shall say something about expression in painting, which also seems capable of embodying emotion. Here the literature is less developed. Richard Wollheim has given an account that relies on the mechanism of "complex projection." A scene is such that it is particularly apt for us to "project" our mental states upon it, in such a way that we come to see it as "of a piece" with our emotions. If a painting is made with the intention that this take place, and that intention is successful, the painting has the requisite expressive property (1986: ch. 7). There is much in the theory that requires further elaboration, not least the phenomenon of complex projection and, particularly, how the projection could take place in the absence of the felt emotion (as it is not plausible to hold that gallery-goers occurrently experience all the emotions they subsequently find in the works) (Budd 2001). Dominic Lopes has a less ambitious theory. He defines a notion of an "expression look": "a physical configuration that has the function, in the circumstances, of indicating an emotion" (2005: 73). He rightly points out that, for reasons gone into above in the case of music, philosophy does not owe an account of the mechanism or mechanisms that underlie such indication.

Progress on this issue has been made in some respects. The nature of the problem has been clarified, and there are interesting solutions to be compared. However, in one other crucial respect progress has been less marked: namely, the relation between expression in the art and the value of art.

See also EMOTION; EXPRESSION THEORY; MUSIC AND SONG.

BIBLIOGRAPHY
Budd, Malcolm. 1995. *Values of Art: Pictures, Poetry, Music*. Harmondsworth: Penguin.
Budd, Malcolm. 2001. "Wollheim on Correspondence, Projective Properties and Expressive Perception." In *Richard Wollheim on the Art of Painting*. R. van Gerwen (ed.). Cambridge: Cambridge University Press, 101–11.
Davies, Stephen. 1994. *Musical Meaning and Expression*. Ithaca: Cornell University Press.
Levinson, Jerrold. 2005. "Musical Expressiveness as Hearability as Expression." In *Contemporary Debates in Aesthetics and the Philosophy of Art*. M. Kieran (ed.). Oxford, Blackwell, 192–204.
Lopes, Dominic McIver. 2005. *Sight and Sensibility: Evaluating Pictures*. Oxford: Oxford University Press.
Walton, Kendall L. 1988. "What is Abstract about the Art of Music?" *Journal of Aesthetics and Art Criticism*, 46, 351–64.
Walton, Kendall L. 1999. "Projectivism, Empathy, and Musical Tension," *Philosophical Topics*, 26(1–2), 407–40.
Wollheim, Richard. 1986. *The Thread of Life*. Cambridge: Cambridge University Press.

DEREK MATRAVERS

expression theory The term "expression theory" has a broad and a narrow usage. Broadly, it is the thought that, in creating a work of art, artists somehow embody a state of mind in it, which the work then brings about in the spectator. Narrowly, it refers to a theory of art associated with Benedetto Croce and R. G. Collingwood, which draws on this idea.

The broad expression theory found its best exponent in Leo Tolstoy (1828–1910). The argument that drove him to this has its merits.

Tolstoy assumes that if art is to be taken seriously as a human activity, it must prove itself morally worthwhile; it must have a purpose connected to the meaning of life. Religion captures exactly such serious purposes, so art must embody the religious ideas of its time. In our time, Tolstoy held, that means that art needs to embody the Christian ideals of the union and brotherhood of man. There must be a transmission of these ideals from artist to audience, with the purpose of conveying such ideals. Work that fails to convey this sense of unity with the artist and others in the community fails as art. Tolstoy sums up his version of the expression theory as follows:

> To evoke in oneself a feeling one has once experienced and having evoked it in oneself then by means of movement, lines, colours, sounds or forms expressed in words, so to transmit that feeling that others experience the same feeling – this is the activity of art. Art is a human activity consisting in this, that one man consciously by means of external signs, hands on to others feelings he has lived through, and that others are infected by these feelings and also experience them. (1962: 123)

This theory suffers from a number of problems. However, the central problem, from which we can learn most, is that the work of art is being used as a vehicle for the transmission of ideas that can be specified independently of the work. The artist has these "feelings he has lived through," and by certain mechanical means embodies them in a work "so to transmit that feeling." However, if the vehicle and the content can be separated in such a way, then it is possible that another vehicle could transmit the same content. That is, one work of art could be replaced by another and the content not be disturbed. That this is not possible (at least in the case of great works) is one of our central intuitions about art.

An alternative account construes expression, not in terms of what the creator puts into the work, but in terms of what the audience gets out. That is, a work is expressive of an emotion if it arouses an emotion in some suitably qualified audience. This suffers from a number of problems. First, not all objects that arouse emotions in us are thereby expressive. A dentist might arouse apprehension without expressing apprehension. Perhaps such problems can be overcome by specifying some psychological role any aroused feeling needs to fulfill. It might be the case that the aroused feeling needs to track our experience of the object in a particularly intimate manner: our apprehension does not change as we experience the dentist in the way that our feelings change as we experience the music (Matravers 1998: ch. 8). However, the account would still have to overcome the problem that to claim that a work of art is expressive is to claim that there is some phenomenally objective quality to the form or character of the work, and it is unclear how the purported analysis proposes to capture this (Tormey 1971; Davies 1986).

For the narrow expression theory I shall focus on Collingwood's account in his *Principles of Art*. The account suffers from several drawbacks. First, there is Collingwood's idiosyncratic philosophical system, which serves as background. One can only understand certain of his claims (e.g., that "art must be language" (1945: 273)) by taking this system into account. Second, there is a tendency to overstate his case, or at least state it in a way that easily misleads. Notoriously, he holds that works of art do not exist in the world, but in their creators' minds: "the music, the work of art, is not the collection of noises, it is the tune in the composer's head" (1945: 139). Finally, the central theses of the work cannot be abstracted and stated clearly and independently. Collingwood makes a point, but then returns to it later to integrate it in yet another part of his philosophical system that has since arrived on the scene. All this makes it difficult to summarize the account while doing it justice (it also means that Collingwood, more than most, suffers from being anthologized). Hence, in what follows I shall tend more toward clarity than I will toward being respectful to the text.

Collingwood contrasts what he calls "art proper" with various other human activities. The primary contrast is with craft, and the points of contrast are as follows. (1) Craft exhibits a distinction between means and end. That is, there are objects and processes that we manipulate in producing (say) a tennis racket, but not in producing a poem (1945: 20). (2) Craft exhibits a distinction between planning and execution. We might plan our garden and then create it; we (generally) do not do the

same with a poem. (3) Craft exhibits a distinction between raw material and finished product. The wood, strings, and cat gut are worked on to produce a tennis racket; nothing analogous happens in the case of a poem. It is important to realize that Collingwood is not here making a distinction between art objects and craft objects; rather, he is making a distinction between types of activity. Individual objects might be the product of both craft and art: the sculptor uses certain means to carve the stone, he or she might well plan it before executing it (although not down to the finest detail), and there is a distinction between raw material and finished product (1945: 20–6). Collingwood also contrasts art proper with "art as magic" (art designed to elicit emotions "useful to the work of living" (1945: 66)) and "art as amusement" (art designed merely to gratify and amuse (1945: 78)).

In contrast, Collingwood's view is that art is a matter of expressing, and hence clarifying, our mental states.

> When a man is said to express emotion, what is being said about him comes to this. At first, he is conscious of having an emotion, but not conscious of what this emotion is. All he is conscious of is a perturbation or excitement, which he feels going on within him, but of what nature he is ignorant. While in this state, all he can say about his emotion is: "I feel . . . I don't know what I feel." From this helpless and oppressed condition he extricates himself by doing something which we call expressing himself . . . As unexpressed, he feels it in what we have called a helpless and oppressed way; as expressed, he feels it in a way from which this sense of oppression has vanished. His mind is somehow lightened and eased. (1945: 109–10)

It is important to distinguish this process from what Collingwood calls "betraying an emotion." This involves no process of clarification; it is simply externalizing an emotion – venting it. In expressing something, a person "becomes conscious of what it is that he is expressing, and enables others to become conscious of it in himself and in them" (1945: 122).

The account looks simple, but it captures that central intuition about art violated by the broad expression theory (Ridley 1998: 28). The artist clarifies their mental state by means of creating an object (broadly construed – this might be a poem or a piece of music that exists only in the artist's mind). That object – and I shall, for ease of exposition, talk of it as an object in the world – has the form it does as a result of that clarification. Colin Lyas provides an example that has some intuitive force. Some youth, filled with inchoate feelings of frustration, picks up a brick and throws it through a window. That act would betray the emotion felt. However, if he or she then starts to remove bits of glass and replace others, sculpting the glass until the jagged hole is "of a piece" with their now clarified mental state, then they have expressed their emotion (Lyas 1997: 70–1). As we saw, the problem with the broad expression theory is that the work is taken to be a mere vehicle for a previously existing state. For Collingwood, it is not a vehicle; rather, the work is the exploration and clarification of that particular mental state; one could not exchange the work without exchanging the content. For Collingwood the pay-off, the value of art, is in the clarification of our mental states. We thus avoid what he calls "the corruption of consciousness." This is something to which Collingwood returns, always with horror at its individual and social effects (1945: 284–5). However, this is not the only value of art available to the expression theorist: there is also the intrinsic benefit of communing with the refined expression of a self-aware mind.

What of the drawbacks? First, we need to say something about the claim that works have their primary existence in their creator's heads. This claim has been roundly (and rightly) criticized (Wollheim 1972). There have been various attempts to defend Collingwood on this, but he does seem to argue that the aesthetic work is "an imaginative experience" (1945: 305). This is odd, in that it would seem natural for Collingwood to regard externalizing the mental state as a necessary part of clarifying it. Whatever the true account of why he held the view (and there are various theories), it is something that can be excised from the theory without loss. Second, there is a more general problem for the expression theory, that all action is caused by our mental states and hence everything we do is art. This view is embraced by Collingwood (1945: 285), and at least one advocate of the expression theory

(Lyas 1997: 104). However, we can argue for differences here. Although all our actions are (by definition) caused by our mental states, not all of our actions seek to refine and clarify such states. The final problem with the theory rests with its self-imposed limitations. What account can the expression theory provide of a work of art such as Raymond Chandler's *The High Window*? Among the salient properties of this novel are its intricate plot, its evocation of mood, and vivid imagery. No light is thrown on these by thinking of them as the expression and clarification of an emotion. The expression theorist might reply in two ways. First, that while this is not the expression and clarification of an emotion, it might be of some other mental state; for example, some notion of what makes a good hard-bitten detective novel. However, the burden of the explanation here would be carried by the content of that state, rather than its being expressed and clarified. Second, the expression theorist might try to restrict the theory to the visual arts, or perhaps the visual arts and music. However, once the objection has been conceded in the case of the novel, one can see that many works of visual art and of music possess the kinds of properties that were salient for the novel, and the expression theory will throw no light on these either.

See also TWENTIETH-CENTURY ANGLO-AMERICAN AESTHETICS; COLLINGWOOD; CREATIVITY; CROCE; EMOTION; EXPRESSION; TOLSTOY.

BIBLIOGRAPHY
Collingwood, R. G. (1945). *The Principles of Art*. Oxford: Clarendon.
Davies, Stephen. (1986). "The Expression Theory Again," *Theoria*, 52, 146–67.
Lyas, Colin. (1997). *Aesthetics*. London: UCL Press.
Matravers, Derek. 1998. *Art and Emotion*. Oxford: Clarendon.
Ridley, Aaron. (1998). *R. G. Collingwood*. London: Phoenix.
Tolstoy, Leo. (1962) [1898]. *What is Art? And Essays on Art*. A. Maude (trans.). New York: Oxford University Press.
Tormey, Alan. 1971. *The Concept of Expression*. Princeton: Princeton University Press.
Wollheim, Richard. (1972). "On an Alleged Inconsistency in Collingwood's Aesthetic." In *On Art and the Mind*. London: Allen Lane, 250–60.

DEREK MATRAVERS

F

feaminist **aesthetics** is a somewhat contested notion. Some feminists are content with the phrase (Ecker 1985) while others prefer to call a gendered approach to the philosophy of art – one that is now inclusive of the various but interrelated perspectives of race, religion, sexuality, class, and ethnicity as well as gender – simply a feminist critique of aesthetics (Brand & Korsmeyer 1995). This approach links feminism with aesthetics but stops short of proposing anything like a cohesive and mutually agreed upon body of work that can be strictly called feminist aesthetics (Felski 1989). No one theory of what might constitute a codified and accepted core of feminist aesthetic principles has arisen because of the many perspectives on what counts as "feminist" – dependent as they are on social context and identity. In terms of basic politics, a feminist is a person – male or female – who believes that biological sex differences should play no role in a person's access to equal opportunity, equal representation under the law, and equality in the workplace. However, gender, unlike sex, is socially constructed, and its constructions take multiple forms that infuse culture and its products. A sophisticated body of literature already exists from feminists who have systematically – from a gendered point of view – criticized the existing inequalities and historical discourses of literature, art, music, theater, film, video, and other modes of performance and representation. Within aesthetics, feminists have substantively questioned basic philosophical concepts like art, genius, pleasure, disinterestedness, and taste (Battersby 1989). However, current thinking suggests that no one feminism can capture the diversity of perspectives comprising such a massive challenge to centuries-old thought, and that feminist systems of criticism and creativity have arisen all over the world that are too complex and idiosyncratic to be united under one umbrella concept, especially one as indeterminate as "feminist aesthetics."

"Global feminisms" – note the plural form – is a term that aptly captures the sentiment most prevalent today among feminists in the visual arts who, unified in their goals of equality, celebrate the achievements of today's women and those of the past – particularly artists of the original feminist art movement (from the late 1960s on) who worked primarily in the US, Great Britain, and France. With the dispersion of information through exhibition catalogues, monographs, and more recently the Internet, goals first manifest in Euro-American feminism have become known, adopted, and adapted in various ways across the globe, creating a multiplicity of "transnational feminisms": a network among women who continually rethink the shared tenets of feminism and the art it produces (Reilly 2007: 17). Thus "feminism" is an evolving concept; it has proven itself resistant to constraints on time (it has already survived its first, second, and third "waves"), place (it has spread beyond the homogeneous culture of the so-called "first world"), and identity (no longer a white middle class movement, there are black, lesbian, Chicana, postcolonial, as well as liberal, socialist, Marxist, radical, or cultural feminists). Moreover, feminism has survived its own demise, announced prematurely in the 1980s when the phrase "postfeminism" was introduced to refer to a new phase of self-referential and postmodern art, which in fact acknowledges and endorses its feminist roots. With the inclusion of more voices within feminist discourse, divergent views have naturally spawned lively debate. Like philosophy itself, feminism continually questions the ever growing complexities of its own enterprise and challenges its own assumptions. But how did it reach this point? What is the foundation for its current role of critique within the field of aesthetics?

First, the feminist critique of aesthetics is an outgrowth of the more general questioning of philosophy as a traditionally male-dominated, gender-biased enterprise focused on mind over matter/body, reason over emotions, and (covertly) male over female. Second, it parallels similar challenges to subdisciplines within philosophy such as feminist epistemology, feminist philosophy of science, feminist ethics, feminist social/political philosophy, and feminist bioethics, which question basic, longstanding principles. Third, as a cross-disciplinary field, aesthetics participates in the critiques and revisions of art history, music, literature, film studies, and the like. Within aesthetics and the philosophy of art, a feminist might ask not only traditional questions about the parameters of the definitions of art versus craft, an artwork's beauty or formal features, aesthetic and nonaesthetic value, but also how an artwork came to be, who created it, and how the power structure of the socioeconomic context operable at the time of its production either facilitated or complicated its creation: all factors operating below the surface of standard exploration, factors which Carolyn Korsmeyer appropriately terms "deep gender" (2004: 3).

Feminists argue that artistic creativity is doubly bound up within (1) the general fabric of one's society – which, for most cultures over the history of time, has been patriarchal, that is, dominated by men who have not allowed women full equality, and (2) the specific organization of the institutions of the artworld, which has been uniformly organized and operated by male artists, writers, musicians, actors, critics, philosophers, museum directors, and investors. The concept of art as a source of elevated aesthetic pleasure belies its role as a commodity created by persons whose social identity affects the production and success of artistic goals. Consider such familiar terms as "old master," "masterpiece," or "genius" and one immediately thinks of male icons such as Rembrandt, Shakespeare, or Mozart. Few women who are similarly accomplished, well known, and routinely valorized in histories of art, literature, or music easily come to mind.

When art historian Linda Nochlin asked the provocative question in 1971 "Why have there been no great women artists?" two specific agendas were born (Nochlin 2006). One was the task of rediscovery of numerous women artists, writers, and musicians of the past. In some cases, the work of these women had been erroneously attributed to male artists; in other cases, women who were notable in their day – publishing, securing commissions, earning a living at their craft – had subsequently been forgotten. When a pattern emerged that revealed the systematic devaluing of women's achievements throughout history, the second agenda of exploring the reasons *why* became necessary for understanding the social conditions by which history had been written to exclude women's voices. This theoretical exploration was closest to the work done by aestheticians, since to question attributions of greatness is to challenge the assumptions of aesthetic value, a concept long contemplated by (primarily male) philosophers as well as art historians. The impetus to challenge other established judgments – about who counted as a genius, why crafts like needlework were not considered fine art, whose beauty was on display and for whose pleasure, and how disinterestedness applied to a heterosexual man gazing at the nude body of a voluptuous woman – became overriding interests of feminist scholarship in the arts.

Philosophical aesthetics was somewhat slower to develop feminist critiques than were the critical disciplines, although a German volume, *Feminist Aesthetics* (Ecker 1985) contained an essay by Sylvia Bovenshen from 1977 that asked whether there was a particularly unique *feminine* aesthetic exhibited in the art women made. Similarly, certain French theorists posited "writing from the body" that might distinguish female from male linguistic production. Among other feminists, this attribution of female identity was critiqued as essentialist – whereby all women are reduced to an essence tied to their sex, their physical bodies, or their ideal nature as the givers of life and nurturers. Critics of essentialism emphasized the differences among women and women's art and stressed the diversity of voices such as artists like Adrian Piper, also a Kant scholar, who inject race into the feminist critique, along with many others who challenge power relations beyond those of gender by focusing on issues of identity, genealogy, and cultural diversity (Robinson 2001).

Feminist writing continues to be concerned with issues that preoccupy many women artists and writers: the body, beauty and disgust, the sublime, pleasure, the intersection of ethics and aesthetics, the role of emotions, political art, connections between art and the law, strategies of interpretation and evaluation, and metacritical analyses of feminism itself (Brand & Devereaux 2003). British scholars have stressed the interdisciplinary nature of art practice and theoretical observation while proposing a new approach through differential aesthetics (Florence & Foster 2000). The future of the feminist critique is open-ended amid a rich variety of possibilities: explorations of nature and the environment, gender differences in perception and the role of the emotions, feminist politics in cultural climates where rape is a weapon of war, infusions of video and film recordings that literally give voice to the oppressed, and transnational feminisms that bypass traditional gallery and museum representation, thereby subverting continuing power structures and artworld institutions (Musgrave 2009). The shifting terrain of feminist art and aesthetics attests to its ever expanding and limitless boundaries, a sure sign of its future good health.

See also CANON; FEMINIST CRITICISM; FEMINIST STANDPOINT AESTHETICS; ONTOLOGICAL CONTEXTUALISM; PORNOGRAPHY; RACE AND AESTHETICS.

BIBLIOGRAPHY
Battersby, Christine. 1989. *Gender and Genius: Towards a Feminist Aesthetics.* Bloomington: Indiana University Press.
Brand, Peg Zeglin & Devereaux, Mary (eds.). 2003. "Women, Art, and Aesthetics," *Hypatia: A Journal of Feminist Philosophy*, 18 (special issue).
Brand, Peg Zeglin & Korsmeyer, Carolyn (eds.). 1995. *Feminism and Tradition in Aesthetics.* University Park: Pennsylvania State University Press.
Ecker, Gisela (ed.). 1985. *Feminist Aesthetics.* H. Anderson (trans.). Boston: Beacon.
Felski, Rita. 1989. *Beyond Feminist Aesthetics: Feminist Literature and Social Change.* Cambridge, MA: Harvard University Press.
Florence, Penny & Foster, Nicola (eds.). 2000. *Differential Aesthetics: Art Practices, Philosophy and Feminist Understandings.* Aldershot: Ashgate.
Hein, Hilde & Korsmeyer, Carolyn (eds.). 1993. *Aesthetics in Feminist Perspective.* Bloomington: Indiana University Press.
Korsmeyer, Carolyn. 2004. *Gender and Aesthetics: An Introduction.* New York: Routledge.
Musgrave, L. Ryan (ed.). 2009. *Feminist Aesthetics and Philosophy of Art: Critical Visions, Creative Engagements.* Dordrecht: Kluwer/Springer.
Nochlin, Linda. 2006. "Why Have There Been No Great Women Artists? Thirty Years After." In *Women Artists at the Millenium.* C. Armstrong & C. De Zegher (eds.). Cambridge, MA: MIT Press, 21–32.
Reilly, Maura & Nochlin, Linda (eds.). 2007. *Global Feminisms: New Directions in Contemporary Art.* New York: Merrell/Brooklyn Museum of Art.
Robinson, Hilary (ed.). 2001. *Feminism – Art – Theory: An Anthology, 1968–2000.* Malden: Blackwell.

PEG ZEGLIN BRAND

feminist criticism In "A Criticism of Our Own: Autonomy and Assimilation in Afro-American and Feminist Literary Theory" Elaine Showalter (1989) discerned five ideologies that have been influential in feminist literary criticism and theory. The first, "androgynist poetics," denies that there is any specifically male or female way of writing or approaching texts, maintaining that the human imagination is essentially genderless. With the rise of the women's movement, feminists initiated a critique of male culture and advanced a "female aesthetic" celebrating women's culture. Believing that our sexual identities cannot be separated from our expressions and creations, advocates of the female aesthetic maintained that women's writing expresses a distinct female consciousness, is more discursive and conjunctive than classifying and linear.

By the mid 1970s the emphasis had shifted to "gynocriticism," or the study of literature by women. Arguing that the female aesthetic is problematic in its presupposition of an eternal, universal feminine "essence" shared by all women, gynocritics preferred to focus on locating and examining texts by women, and undertook a historical analysis of the problems of talented women attempting to create in a male tradition. In the early 1980s, proponents of "gynesis" charged that gynocritics were confining themselves to a women's literature ghetto, and advocated a confrontation with the patriarchal canon. Following the lead of French writers such as Hélène Cixous and Luce Irigaray, these feminists explored representations and expressions of the feminine in Western thought. The French feminists in particular also suggested that women should discover, explore and "write their bodies" and that this writing of the body will lead to a style of "openness, fragmentation, non-linearity, and disruption."

Although gynocriticism and gynesis continued to be strong, the late 1980s were characterized by the rise of "gender theory," concerned with integrating the study of gender differences into the various disciplines. Rather than concentrating on women and "reifying feminine marginalization," gender theorists sought to produce comparative studies of men and women and their works, and to focus on social constructs of gender rather than on biology (Showalter 1985).

More recently, feminist literary criticism has further expanded to include more diverse voices (black, lesbian, "third world") that respect differences among women, experimenting with various expressions of female experience, and undertaking more complex analyses that connect a revised literary canon with history, psychoanalysis, linguistics, philosophy, film, sociology, religion, law, economics, anthropology, cultural, and media studies (Plain & Sellers 2007). Feminist literary criticism continues to generate fresh approaches to the written text against the backdrop of myriad representations of women, including those of the nonliterary virtual world. Given that today's women more freely create and enjoy the limitless possibilities of a multiple gendered subjectivity, their critical perspective has come to include masculinity studies, postcolonialism, and queer theory. Rejecting monolithic feminism, theorists now speak of multiple feminisms that "produce constructive new readings of the world, its texts and its bodies" (Plain & Sellers 2007: 213).

A feminist approach has also been taken to art, architecture, theater, film, and dance. Joanna Frueh has offered a history of feminist art criticism in three stages that echo the categories of feminist literary criticism presented above (1988: 155–7). The first stage, comparable to gynocriticism, was a resurrection of lost or ignored women artists. In highlighting supposedly "minor" artists, this stage led to new perspectives on art history and to new bodies of knowledge. Traditionally, portraits, still-lifes, miniatures, and crafts have been prominent among women artists, and the presentation of craft or craft-like art in "high" art contexts by contemporary women artists has served to blur the distinction between "high" and "low" art. The second phase, comparable to the female aesthetic and equally controversial, posited a women's art distinct from the tradition of patriarchal culture, an art based on a "female imagination" or "female sensitivity." Active in the mid 1970s, advocates of a female artistic sensibility maintained that women's art is characterized by central core imagery of apertures, rifts, and cracks (thought to symbolize female genitalia); circular or repeated patterns; open, fluid forms; soft colors; repetitive patterning; the decorative; and subjective or personal subject matter. The third phase of feminist art criticism was more theoretical, and centered on gender analysis of the art of both women and men, and interconnections between an artwork and its historical and cultural context, giving rise to more philosophical work in feminist aesthetics.

Frueh's own performance pieces are examples of this new and profound body of knowledge about women's art and its production through her ongoing evolution of these feminist principles (Frueh 2007). Through photography and video of performed texts, she creates models of presentation that focus on the female-centered body in terms of physicality, playfulness, and female pleasure. Her lived body within its physical environment – the arid desert of the American southwest – functions as a continuing presence within and against a cultural context of patriarchy. She exhibits a female agency that replaces centuries of representations of female passivity previously depicted by male artists, thereby attracting and empowering female viewers (Broude & Garrard 2005).

These phases in literature and art can also be instructive for the development of a feminist criticism in music. Researchers in music identify, analyze, perform, and record musical works by women throughout history, considering the contexts in which women in music have been active, and assessing the status of women in various musical disciplines (Bowers & Tick 1987). The possibility of a music analogous to *l'écriture féminine*, the writing claimed to arise out of women's bodies and sexual experience, has been proposed (Cox 1992; Duran 2007). While "phallocentric" culture is based on the singularity, identity, and specificity of male genitalia and sexual experience, female genitalia are multiple and contiguous, and the sexual experience of women tends to be indefinite, cyclic, without set beginnings and endings. Correspondingly, *l'écriture féminine* is said to be heterogeneous, process-oriented, and fluid. Growth and development are continuous, and boundaries are unclear. There are frequent repetitions, and phrases are rephrased or conjoined. There is a resistance to the definitive, the highly structured; to closure, hierarchies, and the dialectical process. A music comparable to *l'écriture féminine* would have a flexible, cyclical form, and would involve continuous repetition with variation, the cumulative growth and development of an idea. It would serve to deconstruct musical hierarchies and the dialectical juxtaposition and resolution of opposites, disrupt linearity, and avoid definitive closures. Such music would not be reflective of the experience of all women, and could be and has been composed by both men and women. Yet discerning this style in the music of women would provide an opportunity for interested feminists to celebrate what has been identified or culturally conditioned as feminine or womanly.

There have been a few works written on musical expressions of the feminine and the masculine in canonical masterworks. Susan McClary (2002) has suggested that in Bizet's *Carmen* chromaticism is associated with a seductive, deadly feminine sexuality. The music of the slithery, slippery Carmen is predominantly chromatic, while Don José and the pure, chaste Micaëla sing diatonically. Because Carmen makes us so aware of her body and her sexuality when she sings, we come to associate her sexuality with the chromaticism; we likewise associate Don José's and Micaëla's diatonicism with the abstract ideals of society, Church, and state that they strive to uphold. These associations become significant when we look at how chromaticism is handled within the opera and

the tonal system in general. Although Carmen and her music are interesting and attractive, there is something in us that seeks resolution of the instability of the chromaticism, that seeks the clarity and closure of diatonicism and the tonic triad. In seeking this resolution, we may on some level – probably an unconscious one – be expecting or even wanting Carmen to be somehow overcome, to be appropriated into the system both musically and socially. In the opera and literature of the time, women who do not conform to the social order may eventually submit to marriage, enter a convent, or be committed to an asylum, but those who will not be tamed usually wind up dead. And when Carmen dies, her unstable music resolves into diatonicism. The stability and order of the tonic is "violently imposed."

Dramatic music, song, and programmatic music from all eras are ripe for gender analysis of this kind, which has come to be known as "New Musicology." Discerning the masculine and feminine in instrumental music (as with abstract visual art), however, proves to be more difficult. Romantic conceptions of the masculine and feminine in music are already fairly well known. The so-called "masculine" music or theme of the Romantic era is characterized by a dramatic quality, large intervals, volume, sforzandos, full orchestral scoring, and predominant wind and brass instruments, while "feminine" music is more likely to be lyrical and legato, with delicate instrumentation, small intervals, and regular rhythms (Rieger 1985: 139–40). The "masculine cadence" is definitive and achieves closure, while the "feminine cadence" is inconclusive or implicative. All of this helps to explain why the work of certain composers is easily read as "gendered" by feminist critics: the forceful and definitive music of Beethoven, for example, seems masculine relative to the lyrical, inconclusive, and disruptive music of Chopin or Debussy. But McClary's reading of tonality, rhythm, and musical form as an erotic metaphor for the physical – and in the case of Beethoven, particularly violent – sex act, strikes some as narrow and overly negative: one that ignores the positive pleasure association with a sexual aesthetic (Higgins 1993: 184). Moreover, gay and lesbian musicologists question the attribution of "masculine" to the music of a composer like Tchaikovsky

271

who, in light of his homosexuality, resists a simplistic interpretation along the lines of gender.

It seems clear that conceptions of women's writing, art, or music can be quite similar to expressions of the feminine in traditional works by men. Yet there is an important difference between the types of expression, in that the traditional works often present the feminine as trivial, weak, or dangerous, while women's art may reconstruct this subject matter and cast it in a positive light. However similar the aesthetic content of the works, radically different perspectives will be brought to this content. Feminist critics, whatever their opinions of traditional notions of the feminine or of women's art, can identify, consider, and critique these perspectives, thereby enriching the available range of interpretations and aesthetic judgments.

See also CANON; CRITICISM; FEMINIST AESTHETICS; FEMINIST STANDPOINT AESTHETICS; KRISTEVA; PORNOGRAPHY; PSYCHOANALYSIS AND ART; RACE AND AESTHETICS.

BIBLIOGRAPHY

Bowers, Jane & Tick, Judith (eds.). 1987. *Women Making Music: The Western Art Tradition 1150–1950*. Urbana: University of Illinois Press.
Broude, Norma & Garrard, Mary D. (eds.). 2005. *Reclaiming Female Agency: Feminist Art History After Postmodernism*. Berkeley: University of California Press.
Cox, Renée. 1992. "Recovering *Jouissance*: Feminist Aesthetics and Music." In *Women and Music: A History*. K. Pendle (ed.). Bloomington: Indiana University Press, 331–40.
Duran, Jane. 2007. *Women, Philosophy and Literature*. Aldershot: Ashgate.
Frueh, Joanna. 1988. "Towards a Feminist Theory of Art Criticism." In *Feminist Art Criticism: An Anthology*. A. Raven, C. Langer, & J. Frueh (eds.). Ann Arbor: UMI Research Press, 153–65.
Frueh, Joanna. 2007. *Clairvoyance (for Those in the Desert): Performance Pieces, 1979–2004*. Durham: Duke University Press.
Higgins, Paula. 1993. "Women in Music, Feminist Criticism, and Guerilla Musicology." *Nineteenth-Century Music*, 17, 174–92.
McClary, Susan. 2002 [1991]. "Sexual Politics in Music." In *Feminine Endings: Music, Gender and Sexuality*. Minneapolis: University of Minnesota Press, 53–79.
Plain, Gill & Sellars, Susan (eds.). 2007. *A History of Feminist Literary Criticism*. New York: Cambridge University Press.
Rieger, Eva. 1985. " 'Dolce semplice'? On the Changing Role of Women in Music." In *Feminist Aesthetics*. G. Ecker (ed.). H. Anderson (trans.). Boston: Beacon, 135–49.
Showalter, Elaine (ed.). 1985. *The New Feminist Criticism: Essays of Women, Literature and Theory*. New York: Pantheon.
Showalter, Elaine. 1989. "A Criticism of Our Own: Autonomy and Assimilation in Afro-American and Feminist Literary Theory." In *The Future of Literary Theory*. R. Cohen (ed.). New York: Routledge, 347–69.

RENÉE LORRAINE & PEG ZEGLIN BRAND

feminist standpoint aesthetics is a relatively new name for a view that has its roots in the social history of art and feminist epistemology. It takes as its point of departure the idea that taste – broadly speaking, our capacity to produce, appreciate, and judge aesthetic value – is deeply social. More specifically, the view is committed to three theses: (1) Social location systematically shapes how art – broadly construed – is made, and how both art and nature are understood, appreciated, and evaluated. *Social location* refers to a person's ascribed social identities – for example, gender, race, class, ethnicity, sexual orientation, etc. – and the social roles and relationships considered appropriate to them (Anderson 2007: 4). (2) Taste is normative: judgments of taste admit of degrees of success and competence, and correct judgments of taste have legitimate claims on others. (3) Standpoints – that is, social positions that yield uniquely perceptive awareness of particular features of the world – can be aesthetically privileged in certain crucial respects.

Despite their many differences, feminist philosophers of art agree that taste is gendered; more precisely, that gender – the different roles, norms, and meanings assigned to people based on real or imagined anatomical characteristics of the different sexes – is a constitutive element of aesthetic production, experience, and judgment (Korsmeyer 2004). This presents a difficulty, namely that taste's perceptival and partial nature appears to undermine its normativity, which, it has traditionally been thought, requires impartiality in judgment.

This result would be particularly unwelcome for feminists since our intervention into art history and the philosophy of art depends on taste's being normative. For instance, feminists criticize the artistic canon for its androcentric bias (Korsmeyer 2004; Eaton 2008). Reducing this bias to just one of the myriad ways that social location inflects taste strips feminism of a substantive critique of the canon. If we are to denounce these androcentric biases as genuine "errors," then we must endorse the normativity of taste. This apparent tension between normativity and the ineliminable effects of social location is what feminist epistemologists call "the paradox of bias" (Antony 2002).

The tension can be resolved by rejecting the presumption that bias is always bad (Antony 2002; Wylie 2003; Anderson 2007). Bias may in specifiable cases have constructive effects on taste, while in other cases it may lead taste astray. Distinguishing between generative and detrimental forms of bias is an ongoing project for standpoint aesthetics.

Bias yields errors in taste when any of the following circumstances obtains. (1) The bias stems from an irrational attitude of hostility directed against an individual or a group (or their supposed characteristics). (2) It results in aesthetic dogmatism: (a) blinding its proponents to counterevidence and other viewpoints, and (b) insulating its proponents from critical scrutiny by others. (3) It blocks the possibility of discovering new aesthetic values. (4) It serves primarily to reinforce social hierarchies (see Bourdieu's 1984 critique of Kant). (5) It closes off values that would be unwelcome to some because they empower disenfranchised groups. Such forms of bias are often referred to as *prejudices*: judgments formed without sufficient grounds and motivated, whether consciously or not, by a concern for one's own wellbeing or the wellbeing of one's group.

Generative bias, by contrast, is a perspective that is partial – that is, both *slanted* and *incomplete* – yet marked by an awareness of the effects, both positive and negative, of social location. Generative bias enables the discovery of aesthetic value, whether in the form of merits or defects, producing new aesthetic concepts and principles. Generative bias can bring neglected perspectives into view, thereby allowing us to see beauty, ugliness, and other aesthetic values where they had been missed, or new forms of these values, or old forms of these values in new and surprising places. This, in turn, can enable the identification of prejudices in matters of taste.

The distinction between prejudice and generative bias is well illustrated with the case of the female nude, that category of European art (especially painting, sculpture, and most recently photography) that focuses on the unclothed female body. For all of the differences in style throughout the ages, most works comprising the genre, especially the most prized works, embody a gendered *way of seeing*, to use a term from art historian John Berger (1972). From Titian to Matisse, female nudes are most often anonymous, passive, vulnerable, and objectified bodies positioned so as to provide the viewer with maximal visual access to erogenous zones (Saunders 1989; Nead 1992). The term "the male gaze," first coined by film theorist Laura Mulvey (1989), captures this dimension of the tradition: female nudes typically address a heterosexual male viewer and aim primarily at arousing his carnal appetites. This is not an empirical claim about actual viewers and their responses but, rather, a normative concept regarding ideal viewers and the objectifying responses called for by these works (Korsmeyer 2004: 51–6).

The fact that the genre of the female nude is biased toward heterosexual men is not in itself a problem. As noted earlier, standpoint theorists do not automatically condemn all bias. What makes this a case of *prejudice* can be seen only by situating the genre in the context of the history of Western art. First, the genre eroticizes women in ways that reinforce social gender hierarchies, and this coincides with the primary way that women in general are represented throughout the history of Western art. Second, there is no comparable genre that eroticizes inert, passive, anonymous, objectified male nudes. The male body, by comparison, is rarely subjected to an objectifying erotic gaze. Third, this one-sided abundance of objectified female flesh occurs within the context of women's general disenfranchisement from the artistic canon. Strolling through the great museums of the world, or even skimming an art history textbook, one observes that women are connected to great art *not* as its *creators* but simply as sexual bodies serving as the raw material from which men forge masterpieces (Nochlin 1988: esp. chs. 1, 6, 7; Nead 1992; Duncan 1993; Guerilla Girls 1998).

There are, however, exceptions, one of which provides an example of how the effects of social location can be a *resource* for taste. Artemisia Gentileschi was born in Rome and painted during the first half of the seventeenth century at a time when there were almost no female painters. Although the female nude was, as in the centuries to follow, one of the most popular subjects for art, life drawing classes relied almost entirely on male models (Garrard 1989: 200). In order to meet the demands of realism in depicting the female nude, artists had to rely on their extra-studio experience with female bodies, filtered through current conceptions of women as well as standards of female beauty. As a result, female nudes of the period are typically idealized, generic, and objectified.

Artemisia had distinct advantages in representing the female body. First, she had opportunities to observe many different kinds of female bodies, including her own, in different contexts and engaged in a variety of activities. Second, she had the perspective of being *embodied* in such a body: she knew what it feels like – from the *inside* – to have, say, breasts and hips and fleshy thighs. As a result, her exacting naturalism outshines her predecessors and contemporaries. Third, as a heterosexual woman, Artemisia's *way of seeing* women differed starkly form the dominant artistic paradigm: from her perspective women were not primarily passive objects of sexual desire but, rather, strong capable individuals. Artemisia's nudes come with the blemishes and personality of individuals, and they often adopt dynamic Michelangelesque postures that bespeak vitality and strength rather than passivity and vulnerability (Garrard 1989).

Consider, for instance, Artemisia's *Susanna and the Elders* (1610). The painting offers an original interpretation of the biblical story according to which lascivious male elders spy on Susanna bathing and attempt to blackmail her into sexual relations. Susanna resists the blackmail and the elders are punished. The standard way of representing this story in and before Artemisia's time gave it a kind of pornographic visual appeal, offering the viewer tantalizingly revealing views of a supple and sexually available body (Garrard 1989). Artemisia's picture differs starkly: Susanna is not eroticized and her nudity feels entirely motivated by the story instead of by the aim to kindle carnal desires. Furthermore, rather than depict the moment *before* the villains approach when Susanna luxuriously displays herself in a relaxed atmosphere, Artemisia depicts the moment of the attack with a strong emphasis on Susanna's physical and psychological resistance. This emphasis on Susanna's predicament rather than the viewer's erotic pleasure (Garrard 1989: 189) represents a significant shift away from appeal to the male gaze.

Artemisia's gender identity enabled this unique and powerful take on both the female nude and Susanna's story. Not only was Artemisia striving for recognition in an all-male field at a time when women had few rights and opportunities but she was herself the victim of persistent sexual harassment that eventuated in rape – an attack that she fought and doggedly pursued in court (Garrard 1989: ch. 3). This dimension of her social location afforded a clearer and more discerning view of the sort of plight Susanna faced, as well as of her resistance, than was available to Artemisia's male colleagues. This privileged perspective yielded one of the strongest pictures ever made on the subject.

Standpoint aesthetics is committed to the idea that taste is always biased, imbued with a partial perspective that has been shaped by the material conditions of the judging subject. The case of the female nude illustrates how social location can issue in prejudices that are damaging for taste, whereas Artemisia's case shows how social location can yield artistically privileged interpretations of time-worn subjects.

Feminist standpoint theory thus recommends the use of perspectives from particular socially located points of view for understanding, appreciating, and judging art. Artemisia's work, to return to our example, was woefully undervalued both at the time that she produced it and in modern times. It took a standpoint sensitive to the artistic effects of gender to see both the androcentric distortion of the canon and what so many had missed in Artemisia's work. This is not to claim that feminist consciousness will be more discerning in every, or even most, cases. Rather, a feminist standpoint allows certain features of certain kinds of works to come into focus, making us in these cases better and more exacting judges of taste.

See also CANON; FEMINIST AESTHETICS; FEMINIST CRITICISM; RELATIVISM.

BIBLIOGRAPHY

Anderson, Elizabeth. 2007. "Feminist Epistemology and Philosophy of Science." In *The Stanford Encyclopedia of Philosophy*. E. N. Zalta (ed.). Available at http://plato.stanford.edu/entries/feminism-epistemology/

Antony, Louise. 2002. "Quine as Feminist: The Radical Import of Naturalized Epistemology." In *A Mind of One's Own: Feminist Essays on Reason and Objectivity*. L. M. Antony & C. E. Witt (eds.). 2nd edn. Boulder: Westview, 110–35.

Berger, John. 1972. *Ways of Seeing*. London: Penguin.

Bourdieu, Pierre. 1984 [1979]. *Distinction: A Social Critique of the Judgment of Taste*. R. Nice (trans.). Cambridge, MA: Harvard University Press.

Brand, Peggy Zeglin. 1998. "Disinterestedness and Political Art." In *Aesthetics: The Big Questions*. C. Korsmeyer (ed.). Malden: Blackwell, 155–71.

Duncan, Carol. 1993. *The Aesthetics of Power: Essays in Critical Art History*. Cambridge: Cambridge University Press.

Eaton, A. W. 2008. "Feminist Philosophy of Art," *Philosophy Compass*, 3(5), 873–93.

Garrard, Mary. 1989. *Artemisia Gentileschi*. Princeton: Princeton University Press.

Guerilla Girls. 1998. *Bedside Companion to the History of Western Art*. Harmondsworth: Penguin.

Korsmeyer, Carolyn. 2004. *Gender and Aesthetics: An Introduction*. New York: Routledge.

Mulvey, Laura. 1989 [1975]. "Visual Pleasure and Narrative Cinema." In *Visual and Other Pleasures*. Bloomington: Indiana University Press, 14–26.

Nead, Lynda. 1992. *The Female Nude: Art, Obscenity and Sexuality*. London: Routledge.

Nochlin, Linda. 1988. *Women, Art, and Power and Other Essays*. Boulder: Westview.

Pollock, Griselda. 1999. *Differencing the Canon: Feminist Desire and the Writing of Art's Histories*. New York: Routledge.

Saunders, Gill. 1989. *The Nude: A New Perspective*. New York: Harper & Row.

Wylie, Alison. 2003. "Why Standpoint Matters." In *Sciences and Other Cultures*. R. Figueroa & S. Harding (eds.). New York: Routledge, 26–48.

A. W. EATON

fiction, nature of   There are at least two senses of the word "fiction" that are easy to run together, but need to be distinguished. In one sense, a fiction can simply be a type of falsehood. If I say, "Your PhD is a fiction," I am using "fiction" in this sense. I am simply saying that it is false that you have a PhD. On the other hand, if I say that *Middlemarch* is a fiction, I am *not* saying that it false that there is such a novel. I am saying that it is a certain type of book, story, or representation. The book, story, or representation clearly does exist.

There is probably *some* connection between the two senses of "fiction," which explains the ease with which they are run together. Works of fiction typically contain an element of "unreality." In reality, there is no such town as Middlemarch and no such people as the characters Dorothea or Casaubon who in the fiction inhabit the town. In fact, unlike the novel, the town Middlemarch and the people Dorothea and Casaubon are fictions in the *first* sense. On the other hand, it is important to realize that the logical relationship between the two senses of fiction is loose. Fictions in the first sense can be lies and always involve falsehood or "unreality." Works of fiction – a class of representations – are never lies, can refer to real things such as historical personages (Julius Caesar, Napoleon) and actual places (Rome, Moscow), and can contain truths about them. In fact, the purpose of a work of fiction, or one of its purposes, can be to convey certain truths.

The sense of "fiction" that primarily interests us is the second one, which refers to a class of works: works of fiction. Having identified it, our job is to figure out what characterizes it and makes it distinct from other representations. But before directly tackling that issue, there is one further preliminary one. This is to get some sense of the range of works of fiction.

Fiction is sometimes identified with a type of discourse. So understood, fiction is a linguistic phenomenon. Novels, stories, and dramas are preeminent example of fictions. However, it is obvious that there is lots of nonliterary fiction. Media like cinema and television constantly trade in stories that are fictional. Songs often tell fictional stories. Many paintings also present fictional representations. Consider Vermeer's *A Woman Weighing Gold*. A woman stands before a balance beneath a picture of the Last

Judgment. Light from a nearby window divides the picture into two diagonals, the upper one light, the lower one dark. The picture does not tell a story; it is not a narrative. But it is also not a portrait of an actual woman. Though Vermeer almost certainly used a model to paint it, the picture is not a portrait of her. The scene is an imaginary one, a fiction.

We are now ready for the main question: what is fiction? There is one large class of answers I will simply ignore: those that define fiction as a type of linguistic discourse (see Walton 1990: 75–89 for a survey and critique of these.) We know in advance that these will be inadequate because of the ample existence of nonlinguistic fiction. There are two broad classes of answers that remain. One defines it in terms of a special type of reference. A second kind defines fiction in terms of pretense or make-believe.

FICTIONAL REFERENCE

Most fictional works appear to refer to people and other things that do not exist. For some, this is strictly appearance. We are not really referring to anything. We may make believe such reference to fictional entities occurs, but it really does not.

However, there are others who hold that some sort of reference to fictional things really occurs. Among these, some claim we refer to fictional people and other fictional things even though they deny that fictional things exist (Zemach 1997; Dilworth 2004). If they are right about this, perhaps they have a way of answering the question "what is fiction?" In fiction, we refer to things that do not exist, while in nonfiction we refer to things that do. Alternatively, in fiction we intend to refer to things that do not exist and in nonfiction we intend to refer to things that do.

The view under discussion makes two interesting claims. One is that we can define fiction through reference to nonexistent things. The second is simply that such reference is possible and actually occurs. The first claim obviously depends on the second, which is very controversial. By contrast, the majority view (which obviously does not mean it is the true one) is that one can refer only to what exists. When we refer to something, we pick it out, and what does not exist cannot be picked out because there is

nothing to be picked out. If there were something, it would exist. The things we refer to are distinguished from others in virtue of their properties or characteristics, but nothing can have properties unless it exists in the first place. Existence is not just another property, but is the condition for having properties. What does not exist is nothing and so cannot have properties.

Those who believe we can refer to nonexistents deny that they lack properties. Compare Hamlet and Macbeth, that is, the characters from the two plays by Shakespeare. Hamlet is a prince of Denmark. Macbeth is a Scottish lord, a usurper, a king. They have different properties, it is claimed, so they must have properties. One property that Hamlet and Macbeth both lack is being real or existing. For those who believe that there is fictional reference to nonexistents, existence *is* just another property, and not a condition for having properties.

Can appealing to fictional reference provide a plausible answer to the question "what is fiction?" It does not. Even if there is reference to nonexistents, it can occur both inside and outside fiction. If I am a habitual liar, and lie about where I spent my vacation, claiming it was on the golden mountain, I referred to a nonexistent object and did so intentionally (according to those who believe such reference occurs), but I did not create a fiction in the relevant sense. I merely told a lie. If a write a historical novel, I may refer only to existents (past or present), but I still create a fiction. Hence, fictional reference does not provide a route to answering the question "what is fiction?"

PRETENSE AND MAKE-BELIEVE

One might think that the standard function of a mode of representation like language or pictures is to inform us about the actual world, to assert or show us things about it. Fiction could then be thought of as something derived from this standard use. Instead of actually asserting something, a fictional story or its author pretends to assert it. Instead of showing us something about the actual world, in a picture like *A Woman Weighing Gold* the painter Vermeer pretends to show us something about it (Searle 1975).

This proposal would need to be refined to even approach adequacy. Consider an epistolary novel – one whose story is told not through a narrative but through a series of letters written by one or more characters. Here the author does not pretend to assert something but, if the pretense view is correct, pretends to present letters that, among other things, make assertions. Such adjustments, while needed to make the pretense view work, are not hard to make and hence do not pose a serious problem for the view.

There is another problem with the pretense view that is not fixable. Pretense does not always seem to be the right description of what artists are doing in their works. Consider a clear case of pretense. I am pretending to sing by lip-syncing. There is no intent to deceive, just as there usually is not when an artist produces a fiction, but I am doing one thing in order to pretend to do another. Is Vermeer pretending to show us a real scene by painting an imaginary one? That is what does not seem right. To adequately describe what Vermeer is doing it is enough to say that he is painting an imaginary scene without adding anything about something he is thereby pretending to do. In fact, there would be a certain irony if we did say that because it is very likely that Vermeer painted an imaginary scene by using a real one as a model.

So what is it to write a fictional story if not to engage in a sort of pretense? What is it to paint an imaginary scene if not to pretend to do something? One might think that one has represented an imaginary scene if there is no real scene "corresponding" to the one that is painted or described. This will not work. Misdescriptions satisfy this condition without being imaginary scenes. Further, in the Vermeer case, there might have been a real scene corresponding to the one represented in the painting.

The make-believe view offers an alternative answer. In order to understand this view one has to recognize that "make-believe" is being used in a restricted, somewhat technical sense. There are some ordinary uses of "make-believe" in which it is a synonym for pretense. "Let's make-believe we are pirates" and "Let's pretend we are pirates" say the same thing.

Make-believe in the relevant sense involves two special features. First it involves props. Props are publicly accessible objects that guide imaginings. Suppose children are playing school with dolls. The dolls are props. Painting, novels, and poems are also props on the make-believe view. Second, make-believe, unlike some other imaginings, operates according to underlying rules about these props, which authorize or mandate certain imaginings. For example, the game of school might operate according to the rule that the number of students in the classroom is equal to the number of dolls arranged in a certain way. Similarly, a given art form or genre will have certain rules that guide the audience's imaginings (Walton 1990).

A fiction, on this view, is a work that is intended or has the function of being a prop in a game of make-believe. What makes *A Woman Weighing Gold* fictional is that it is first of all a work – a painting in this case – and second that it is intended or has the function of being a prop of the kind described above. It authorizes us to imagine certain things: that we are seeing a woman before a balance in the act of weighing gold, standing beneath a picture of the Last Judgment, etc.

The make-believe view has become one of the most widely held accounts of the nature of fiction. However, there are some differences among those who accept it. One of these is embodied in the very definition of fiction just given. It concerns whether a work must be intended by its maker to be a prop (Currie 1990) or whether it is enough that it functions as a prop (Walton 1990). The latter condition is too weak. We can treat almost anything, from a police report to a scientific paper to a shopping list, *as if* they were fictions, and for the nonce they acquire the function of being props. But treating something as if it were a fiction does not create a work of fiction. On the other hand, perhaps regular treatment or conventions can render a work a prop for make-believe without an original intention that it be so treated. We tend to treat the ancient "myths" of other cultures not only as if they were fiction, but as fiction. (Let us assume they were not originally so intended.) *Perhaps* this use creates a work of fiction. If so the original intention requirement is too strong. The most plausible view lies somewhere between the two thus far discussed. We can express it this way: *F* is a fiction only if it is a work with the *proper* function of being a prop in a game of make-believe. To speak of a proper function is to screen out items treated as if they are fictions or that acquire the function of being props on an ad hoc basis. This typically is the result of an original intention that it be so used, but the function can perhaps be acquired in other ways.

We have just claimed that a *necessary condition* for being a fiction is properly functioning as a prop for a game of make-believe. Another disagreement concerns whether this condition also is sufficient on its own to pick out works of fiction or whether a second condition is needed. Here is one type of situation that, according to some, gives rise to the need for a second condition. Suppose that I think my life contains the stuff of a great narrative. I could present this as my autobiography, but I think it would have greater significance to present it as a fictional story: a novel. The only thing is, every sentence states a fact. The question here is whether I am attempting to do something that is impossible – make a fiction out of nothing but fact. There are those who answer this question affirmatively (Currie 1990) and so claim that we need a second condition on the definition stipulating that a narrative that is "nonaccidentally" true throughout is not a work of fiction.

There is another problematic set of cases that this condition eliminates. These cases involve perfectly familiar items. Suppose that I do in fact present my story as autobiography, but in such a way that you can vividly imagine the events of my life. Then it appears that my work fulfills two functions. One is to inform you about my life. A second is to enable you to engage in the kind of guided imagining that is constitutive of make-believe in our technical sense. (Since this imagining is about real events, it is hardly make-believe in its ordinary sense.) Something similar happens with certain works of history, journalism, as well as the "nonfiction" novel like Truman Capote's *In Cold Blood*. All these works are props that authorize certain imaginings and hence meet our first condition. There are some who claim that because of this, these works are fictional even if the primary purpose lies elsewhere (Walton 1990). However, this does not seem right. Historical novels are fictional; history is not, even if it uses techniques that produce guided imaginings. It is cases like these that provide

the strongest argument for adopting the second condition.

See also LITERATURE; FICTION, TRUTH IN; FICTIONAL ENTITIES; GENRE; IMAGINATION; NARRATIVE.

BIBLIOGRAPHY

Currie, Gregory. 1990. *The Nature of Fiction.* Cambridge: Cambridge University Press.

Dilworth, John. 2004. "Internal versus External Representation," *Journal of Aesthetics and Art Criticism*, 62, 23–36.

Lopes, Dominic. 1996. *Understanding Pictures.* Oxford: Oxford University Press.

Searle, John. 1975. "The Logical Status of Fictional Discourse," *New Literary History*, 6, 319–32.

Walton, Kendall L. 1990. *Mimesis as Make-Believe.* Cambridge, MA: Harvard University Press.

Zemach, Eddy. 1997. *Real Beauty.* University Park: Pennsylvania State University Press.

ROBERT STECKER

fiction, the paradox of responding to   It is a fact about most of us that we can be emotionally affected by our engagement with stories and other works of narrative fiction; and we often characterize experience of this sort as involving emotions directed at fictional characters and events: I feel pity for Anna Karenina, I am terrified of Nosferatu the vampire, I loathe Iago, and so on. Indeed, it is arguable that the very point of certain genres of fiction – ghost stories, "tear-jerkers," and horror movies, for example – is to engage us emotionally in such ways. At the same time, however, it seems obvious that in engaging with narrative fiction – reading a story or a novel, watching a play or a movie – most of us, most of the time, are aware that what we are engaging with *is* fiction: we do not believe that Anna really did jump under a train, or that Nosferatu left his home in eastern Europe to threaten people farther afield, or that Iago betrayed Othello; and we do not believe any of these things just because – or inasmuch as – we know that neither Anna nor Nosferatu nor Iago ever existed. But if we know that Anna and Nosferatu and Iago do not and never did exist, why, and what, do we feel for them? For emotion would appear to depend on belief, or at any rate something like belief, in the existence of and the possession of certain attributes by their objects: it is because I take the rabid dog charging toward me to be actually a threat that I am terrified of it; and only if I take a person to be in some sense a victim of misfortune can I pity her.

We have three thoughts, then: (1) we may experience emotions such as fear of and pity for fictional characters; (2) we do not believe that these characters exist; and (3) the experience of emotions such as pity and fear requires belief in the existence of the objects of those emotions. The puzzle often referred to as "the paradox of fiction" consists in the fact that while each of these thoughts has at least prima facie plausibility, they cannot all be true.

One strategy for dissolving the paradox lies in questioning the second thought outlined above – the thought that in engaging with fictional narratives we are perfectly well aware that the characters and events depicted *are* fictional. Perhaps the fact that we are moved by such things itself demonstrates that we are *not* "perfectly well aware" of their fictionality. Thus Jonathan Barnes has suggested that it is the fact that poetry can affect us emotionally that led the Pre-Socratic philosopher Gorgias to hold that poetry can "persuade and deceive the soul" and that in responding to poetry "the deceived [is] wiser than he who is not deceived" (1979: 161ff.). This idea is echoed in different ways in Samuel Taylor Coleridge's notion of "that willing suspension of disbelief for the moment, which constitutes poetic faith" (1907: 6), and in what Noël Carroll (1990) has called "the illusion theory" of engagement with fiction. In none of its manifestations to date has the idea been convincingly worked out. Whatever support the audience's emotional response to a fiction may be thought to provide for the idea that it loses its awareness that what it is responding to *is* fiction, other aspects of its response seem to support the opposite conclusion: as Dr. Johnson suggests, for example: "The delight of tragedy proceeds from our consciousness of fiction; if we thought murders and treasons real, they would please no more" (1969: 27–8).

Another obstacle faced by any attempt to substantiate the idea that our emotional responses to fiction are based on illusion or suspension of (dis)belief is the charge – a variant of part of Plato's critique of poetry in the

Republic – that if this were the case, these responses would be fundamentally irrational. This is a conclusion reached via a different route by Colin Radford, in a series of articles that initiated contemporary philosophical interest in the paradox of fiction. Radford in effect amends the third of the thoughts outlined above – the thought that the experience of emotions such as pity and fear requires belief in the existence of the objects of those emotions. As Radford argues (1975), emotional experience *normally* requires such belief, and evaporates in cases in which a person becomes aware that the beliefs on which an emotional response is grounded are false; in responding emotionally to narrative fiction in the absence of the relevant sort of belief, then, we are behaving inconsistently, incoherently, and irrationally.

A different approach to the paradox that proceeds by rejecting the idea that emotional responses require belief, sometimes labeled "Thought Theory," begins by asserting that in all sorts of circumstances merely the thought of danger or suffering, for example, without any belief that one is actually in danger or that anyone is actually suffering, is sufficient to generate emotion. (See for example Lamarque 1981; Carroll 1990; Meskin & Weinberg 2003; Robinson 2005. Different versions of Thought Theory offer different, and varyingly sophisticated, accounts of the ways "unasserted thought" can generate emotional response.) So responding emotionally to fiction without believing in the actuality of its characters and events is not, contra Radford, inconsistent with our responses in other contexts, and so need not be irrational.

Thought Theory construes and rejects the claim that emotional response requires certain sorts of belief as a claim about the *causal* conditions of emotional response. However, the claim has also been understood as making a *conceptual* point: as asserting that whatever the facts about the generation of a particular response, for that response to count as one of fear, for example, the subject must believe or in some way take himself to be somehow threatened or in danger. Thus it may be granted that (as Thought Theory maintains) I need not take Nosferatu to pose a threat to me in order to feel as I do when he appears on the screen, but maintained that what I feel cannot coherently be characterized as fear unless I do take him to be a threat. While Thought Theory offers an answer as to *why* I feel anything when confronted with the depiction of Nosferatu, that is, it does not settle the question of *what* it is that I feel.

An alternative strategy for dissolving the paradox argues for a qualified rejection of the claim that emotional responses require – in a conceptual, rather than a causal, sense – belief in the existence of the objects of those responses. On this view, at least certain varieties of emotion can be grounded – conceptually, if not causally – in beliefs about what is fictionally the case, or what is true in the fiction (Neill 1993). Thus, for example, it may be argued that my belief that it is fictional that Anna Karenina suffers as she does in the story, together with certain other facts about me, including my desires and the character of my feeling, may make it true that what I experience amounts to pity for Anna; and if the beliefs in question are themselves appropriately grounded, and the feelings are within appropriate limits, that pity may be rational.

However, while I can coherently believe that it is fictional that Anna Karenina suffers, I cannot coherently believe, given that he does not inhabit the world that I inhabit, that I am threatened by Nosferatu. In which case – if the conceptual version of the claim that belief is necessary for emotion is correct – whatever I feel in the face of his depiction, those feelings cannot without distortion be described as amounting to fear of Nosferatu. While we may pity fictional characters, it may be argued, we cannot be afraid of them. But then how are our feelings – phenomenologically speaking, our fear-like feelings – in the face of the depiction of Nosferatu best characterized?

Answering this question in effect involves a qualified rejection of the first of the thoughts outlined at the beginning of this piece – that we may experience emotions such as pity for and fear of fictional characters. And at least three ways of rejecting this thought – whether in a qualified or wholesale fashion – have been suggested. One is given by Dr. Johnson: fictions move us not because they are mistaken for realities, but because they bring realities to mind (1969; see also Levinson 1990). On this view, our affective

responses to fiction are grounded (both causally and conceptually) in beliefs about the actual world, and those responses have actual rather than fictional objects: what I may at first be inclined to describe as fear of Nosferatu is in fact fear of something (or some possible something) in the actual world; what may misleadingly be described as pity for Anna Karenina is in fact directed at actual people in the kind of situation that she is depicted as being in. A second approach (Charlton 1984; Neill 1993) describes the responses in question in terms of nonintentional, non-belief-dependent states such as moods or sensations: what I may unreflectively be inclined to describe as fear of a horror movie monster, for example, may turn out (particularly when we consider the manner of the monster's depiction) to be less misleadingly described in terms of responses such as startle and shock.

The most theoretically sophisticated and interesting attempt to dissolve the paradox of fiction by denying the claim that we experience emotions the objects of which are characters and events that we know to be fictional has been developed by Kendall L. Walton (1990). Walton argues that the contexts in which we may be inclined to describe ourselves as fearing or pitying (for example) fictional creatures are contexts in which we engage in games of make-believe, using the works of fiction in question as "props." And just as a work of fiction generates fictional truths concerning its characters and events (such as that Nosferatu is a vampire, and deadly), the game that the reader or spectator plays in engaging with it generates fictional truths which refer to himself or herself, as well as to the inhabitants of the fictional world of the work: thus in the game of make-believe I play when watching a vampire movie it will be make-believe that I am threatened if, in a scene where the camera's point of view is that of the audience, the vampire begins to advance threateningly toward the camera. And if in response to the scene I experience the feelings that typically partially constitute fear (increased pulse rate, adrenalin surges, and so on), then it will be make-believedly the case that I am afraid. And so, *mutatis mutandis*, for my "pity" for Anna Karenina, my "loathing" of Iago, and so on. Walton thus dissolves the paradox of fiction by denying the first of the thoughts outlined at the beginning of this piece: it is not *literally* true that we experience emotions such as fear of and pity for fictional characters; it is, rather, sometimes *fictional* that we experience such emotions.

As philosophical debate in aesthetics on the paradox of fiction has developed in recent years, it has drawn on an increasingly wide range of cognate areas in philosophy and psychology, and connections between questions concerning the nature of our emotional responses to fiction and adjacent issues – for example, concerning the moral implications of and constraints upon our engagement with fiction, and concerning the nature of our emotional engagement with nonrepresentational forms of artistic representation – have emerged. Progress on the topic will be driven by increasing discrimination with regard to the different ways in which different kinds of narrative (and indeed other sorts of) fiction elicit different kinds of emotional response.

See also EMOTION; FICTIONAL ENTITIES; HORROR; IMAGINATIVE RESISTANCE; TRAGEDY; WALTON.

BIBLIOGRAPHY

Barnes, J. 1979. *The Presocratic Philosophers*, vol. ii: *Empedocles to Democritus*. London: Routledge & Kegan Paul.
Carroll, Noël. 1990. *The Philosophy of Horror*. London: Routledge.
Charlton, W. 1984. "Feeling for the Fictitious," *British Journal of Aesthetics* 24, 206–16.
Coleridge, Samuel Taylor. 1907. *Biographia Literaria*. 2 vols. J. Shawcross (ed.). Oxford: Oxford University Press.
Johnson, Samuel. 1969 [1765]. *Preface to Shakespeare's Plays*. Menston: Scholar Press.
Lamarque, Peter. 1981. "How Can We Fear and Pity Fictions?" *British Journal of Aesthetics*, 21, 291–304.
Levinson, Jerrold. 1990. "The Place of Real Emotion in Response to Fiction," *Journal of Aesthetics and Art Criticism*, 48, 79–80.
Meskin, Aaron & Weinberg, Jonathan M. 2003. "Emotions, Fiction, and Cognitive Architecture," *British Journal of Aesthetics*, 43, 18–34.
Neill, Alex. 1993. "Fiction and the Emotions," *American Philosophical Quarterly*, 30, 1–13.
Radford, Colin. 1975. "How Can We be Moved by the Fate of Anna Karenina?" *Proceedings of the Aristotelian Society*, supp. vol. 69, 67–80.
Robinson, Jenefer. 2005. *Deeper than Reason: Emotion and Its Role in Literature, Music and Art*. Oxford: Oxford University Press.
Walton, Kendall L. 1990. *Mimesis as Make-Believe*. Cambridge, MA: Harvard University Press.

ALEX NEILL

fiction, truth in   Consider Thomas Hardy's 1895 novel, *Jude the Obscure*. It is *true in the fiction* that in spite of his humble origins, Jude Fawley aspires to a life of scholarship. It is also true in the fiction that the stonecutter sends letters to five academics expressing his desire to study at Christminster University. The only answer he receives is from T. Tetuphenay, the master of Biblioll College, who curtly advises him to abandon his scholarly ambitions. It is true in the fiction that Fawley never recovers from this blow, even though Hardy's narrator does not state the point explicitly.

It is easy to give uncontroversial examples of fictional truths of this sort, but hard to answer philosophical questions concerning their status and justification. Truth requires a truth-bearer, such as a belief, proposition, or assertion; it also requires a truth-maker, such as objects, events, persons, and states of affairs. Even though Hardy obviously based his fictional Biblioll College on the actual Balliol College at Oxford, and Tetuphenay may have had a particular model in the Oxonian classical scholar Benjamin Jowett, such real-world sources are not the truth-makers for Hardy's fiction. Even if he wanted to insinuate that the master of the actual Balliol College of his day was inhospitable to aspiring working class intellectuals, Hardy did not make any direct, literal assertion to that effect in the novel. He certainly did not absurdly accuse the master of Balliol of rejecting Jude Fawley, and the latter is not Hardy himself. Why and in what sense is it true, then, that some nonexistent Fawley unsuccessfully tried to study at a nonexistent college?

In David K. Lewis's (1978) influential paper on the topic, the first step is to recognize that what is true in a given fiction is based on, but not reducible to, a string of declarative sentences (or accurate translations of them). Fictional truth is not just a matter of sentences but of propositions true in a world where the fiction is "told as known fact." And for Lewis that is a possible world, or more accurately, a collection of possible worlds, logically compatible with what the storyteller tells as known fact. Lewis's second step is to acknowledge that competent interpreters have to understand the storyteller's sentences correctly and use them as a basis for making any number of inferences to propositions or beliefs that are unstated in the text yet also "true in the fiction." The propositions expressed in the text alone, standardly interpreted in the language in which it was written, underdetermine fictional truth. For example, Hardy's narrator does not say so, but it is true in the fiction that Fawley never responds to Tetuphenay's letter. Any minimally competent understanding of the story requires the reader to reason to unstated story truths, and the problem is specifying the principled basis of such a competence.

Lewis tentatively advances a pair of proposals for the analysis of fictional truth. One, which Kendall L. Walton (1990) has usefully dubbed "the Reality Principle," is roughly the idea that what is true in a fiction is what is true in our actual world, with minimal changes required to accommodate what the storyteller in the fiction explicitly relates as known fact. This proposal may seem to work for realist fiction, but is hopeless as an analysis of fictional truth in general. As John Heinz observes (1979: 85), inferences about what is *implicitly* true and false in some fictions require premises incompatible with our beliefs about the actual world (as when the spaceship must be traveling faster than the speed of light, yet the narrator does not explicitly present us with an alternative physics). Knowing which actual world beliefs to revise or delete is another problem. Should Oxford be deleted to make room for Christminster, or does the latter figure in the worlds of the story as a third venerable British site of learning? It would seem inappropriate to import scads of irrelevant beliefs about the actual world into every fiction.

Lewis's other analysis hinges on a different way of amplifying the storyteller's explicit indications. Instead of importing beliefs about the actual world wholesale, the interpreter draws on what was mutually believed about the actual world in the community within which the fiction originated. According to some such belief systems, magic really works, and such

beliefs can carry over into a story even if the narrator does not say so explicitly. This would appear to get us the premises we need to draw the right inferences about fictions where acts of conjuring are followed by some desired result, the implicit proposition or story truth being that the relation between such events is a causal one. Yet the analysis does not really fit all such examples. In some cases, the storyteller invokes a familiar, but to his community nonveridical, system of supernatural beliefs. And in many cases, there is no single, coherent system of beliefs to be associated with the community within which a work was created.

Where else might one look for principles determinative of fictional truth? One place is generic or other artistic conventions. It is conventional in some types of comedy that violent blows and accidents do not have the same serious consequences they would have in the actual world or in other kinds of fiction. The pain is not so bad, and recovery is swift. This blocks inferences concerning the negative moral status of such actions as hitting one's friends on the head with a hammer and taking delight in the fool's misfortune. Yet not every fiction having determinate, comprehensible contents falls squarely within a single genre having well-established story-constitutive conventions. What is more, the very classification of fictions in genres could require independent recognition of what is true and false in the story. If I have to know whether the consequences are seriously harmful in order to say whether the fiction is genuinely comic, I cannot first help myself to comic conventions in order to identify the story's content. There is also the related question of saying how genres get started. If someone needs to know the generic conventions in order to devise or understand a fiction having determinate content, how could the first instance of the genre ever be created or understood?

Interpretative intentionalism is another family of approaches to the topic. "Constructivist" proposals in this vein are based on the idea that given a text created by some actual author, it is the intentions of an interpreter-constructed "author" that determine fictional content. To figure out what is true in a fiction, the reader is to take the text (interpreted standardly given relevant linguistic conventions) and augment its content by including propositions intended by an *interpreter-constructed* "author." The interpreter's construction of this authorial persona (variously named the "postulated," "fictional," "hypothetical," or "ideal" author) is guided by evidentiary strictures specified by the philosopher. For example, William Tolhurst (1979) proposes that it is the actual author whose intentions determine what kinds of evidence are relevant to the reader's construction of the "hypothetical author's" intended fictional content. In other words, it is the author who decides what should count as a suitably "informed" interpreter. In another constructivist proposal, the interpreter's evidentiary base in constructing an authorial persona is selected in function of the goal of making a work the contents of which enhance the work's value. Unlike the actual author, the constructed author has infallible intentions.

An objection to all constructivist proposals is that once it has been recognized that the text alone underdetermines fictional content, it is hard to see why any particular set of evidentiary restrictions on the construction of an authorial model should be accepted. Why not use diaries, letters, or websites indicative of the actual author's plans and intentions, whether or not the actual author intended for the audience to use such evidence? For example, why should interpreters consult Hardy's wishes in deciding whether to study his private correspondence for clues about how he conceived of Sue Bridehead's sexuality? Why should critics not pursue the goal of trying to understand the *actual* author, using all available evidence to that end?

Many philosophers (e.g., MacDonald 1954; Wolterstorff 1980; Currie 1990) reckon that it is the intentions of the actual author (or authors) that make the difference between fiction and nonfiction. Roughly, the idea is that to make fiction is to imagine that such and such is the case and to invite others to do the same, providing props (such as a text, performance, or audiovisual display) to that end. Some philosophers also reckon that if the text or other prop is successfully designed and created, the actual author's choices and intentions help constitute fictional truth. Fictions in which the narrator is unreliable make the importance of recourse to authorial intention

especially salient, since it is uptake of authorial irony that warrants recognition that a proposition asserted by the narrator may be false in the fiction.

One outstanding issue among "actual intentionalists" concerns the nature of the success conditions on the realization of intended fictional content, as it is implausible to think that artist's semantic intentions infallibly determine the content of the finished work. One idea (Livingston 2005) is that intended imaginings are part of what is true in the fiction only when they mesh or are integrated with the coherence-constitutive rhetorical structures of the text or display. Another proposal is Robert Stecker's (2005) view that there must in principle be evidence indicative of intended fictional content if that content is to be part of the work's actual meaning. More generally, intentionalism allows us to recognize that authors can flexibly draw on various sources as they select content-constitutive assumptions and patterns of reasoning in creating a fiction. Those sources include convictions about the actual world as well as devices specific to artistic genres and conventions, historically remote systems of belief, alternative psychological theories and value schemes, or creative recombinations of any of the above.

See also LITERATURE; COGNITIVE VALUE OF ART; FICTION, NATURE OF; FICTIONAL ENTITIES; IMPLIED AUTHOR; INTENTION AND INTERPRETATION; "INTENTIONAL FALLACY"; INTERPRETATION; MEANING CONSTRUCTIVISM; TRUTH IN ART.

BIBLIOGRAPHY
Currie, Gregory. 1990. *The Nature of Fiction.* Cambridge: Cambridge University Press.
Davies, David. 2007. *Aesthetics and Literature.* London: Continuum.
Heinz, John. 1979. "Reference and Inference in Fiction," *Poetics*, 8, 85–99.
Kirkham, Richard L. 1992. *Theories of Truth: A Critical Introduction.* Cambridge, MA: MIT Press.
Lamarque, Peter. *Fictional Points of View.* Ithaca: Cornell University Press.
Lewis, David K. 1978. "Truth in Fiction," *American Philosophical Quarterly*, 15, 37–46.
Livingston, Paisley. 2005. *Art and Intention.* Oxford: Clarendon.
MacDonald, Margaret. 1954. "The Language of Fiction," *Proceedings of the Aristotelian Society*, supp. vol. 27, 165–84.

Pavel, Thomas. 1986. *Fictional Worlds*. Cambridge, MA: Harvard University Press.

Rossholm, Göram. *To Be and Not to Be: On Interpretation, Iconicity, and Fiction*. Bern: Peter Lang.

Stecker, Robert. 2003. *Interpretation and Construction: Art, Speech, and the Law*. Oxford: Blackwell.

Stecker, Robert. 2005. *Aesthetics and the Philosophy of Art: An Introduction*. Lanham: Rowman & Littlefield.

Tolhurst, William. 1979. "On What a Text Is and How It Means," *British Journal of Aesthetics*, 19, 3–14.

Walton, Kendall L. 1990. *Mimesis as Make-Believe: On the Foundations of the Representational Arts*. Cambridge, MA: Harvard University Press.

Wolterstorff, Nicholas. 1980. *Worlds and Works of Art*. New York: Oxford University Press.

PAISLEY LIVINGSTON

fictional entities Among artworks there are stories told by storytellers in words or in pictures, or acted out on stage or film. We call some "fiction," some "history"; what distinguishes these? One answer is: the teller of a fictional story creates imaginary characters, events, and places – Madame Bovary, the War of the Worlds, and Lilliput – whereas the historian describes actual people, events, and places. But imaginary objects, it seems, do not exist, and so this answer raises difficult philosophical problems.

First, how can we think about entities that are not there to be thought of? This is one of the problems of intentionality (the "aboutness" of mental representation). That we can think about the imaginary Madame Bovary is a particular problem for contemporary "naturalistic" theories of intentionality, which aim to explain thought in terms of relations between physical objects.

Second, how can names that do not refer to anything be meaningful, or sentences containing such names be true? If what gives my name meaning is the fact it labels or points to me, how can the name "Hamlet," which does not label or point to anything, have meaning? This is the problem of empty reference. If "Hamlet" is meaningless, then the sentence "Hamlet killed his stepfather" fails to express a complete thought, and so cannot be true. (Also, this sentence fails to express a different thought from "Polonius killed his stepfather.") Yet intuitively "Hamlet killed his stepfather" is

true, just as "Hamlet killed Homer Simpson" is false.

Third, how are emotional responses to non-existent objects possible? What do I respond to? And how can I feel pity for Little Nell or fear of Hannibal Lecter, when I know that no one is actually dying or in danger? Emotions, like thoughts, have intentional objects, and also seem to be belief-dependent (e.g., the difference between my envying Fred and my being jealous of him – my behavior and raw feelings may be the same – is that I believe Fred possesses what is rightfully mine).

Fourth, talk about nonexistent objects appears to violate a rule of elementary logic. According to the existential generalization rule, if Gordon Brown is a Labour politician, then there is something that is a Labour politician. If I think, then there is something that thinks. And so on. Fictions, it seems, break this rule: Harry Potter is a boy wizard even though there is nothing that is a boy wizard.

Despite these difficulties, several philosophers have argued for nonexistent objects. Broadly speaking, there are two rival philosophical approaches to discourse about fictional characters, events, and places. The *realist* about fiction takes sentences such as "Hamlet killed his stepfather" more or less at face value: the name "Hamlet" (or the whole sentence) picks out some entity. The canonical realist is Alexius Meinong, who notoriously wrote in 1904, "There are objects of which it is true that there are no such objects" (1960: 83).

In contrast, the *reductionist* aims to "analyze away" such sentences: "Hamlet killed his stepfather" looks like (i.e., is grammatically similar to) the sentence "Henry VIII killed his second wife," but in fact is used to make a (logically) different claim. The canonical reductionist is Bertrand Russell, for whom Meinong's theory lacked a "robust sense of reality" (1919: 170). According to Russell, "There is only one world, the "real" world: Shakespeare's imagination is part of it, and the thoughts that he had in writing Hamlet are real . . . But it is of the very essence of fiction that only the thoughts, feelings, etc., in Shakespeare and his reader are real, and that there is not, in addition to them, an objective Hamlet" (1919: 169). Meinong said that this type of view exhibits a "prejudice in favor of the actual" (1960: 78) – for Russell, only the actual is real.

One problem for Meinong's thesis that there are nonexistent objects is that it appears to generate a contradiction, and (in classical logic) we can prove anything from a contradiction. (Russell said: "[H]owever hot the flames of Hell may become, I will never so degrade my logical being as to accept a contradiction" (1954: 34).) Consider a fiction about a round square. According to Meinong, it is plainly true that, in thinking of the round square, I am thinking about a nonexistent (because impossible) object that is nevertheless both round and square. Russell replied: if so, then it is plainly true that, in thinking about the existent round square, I am thinking about a nonexistent object that is round, square, and exists! Meinong (according to Russell) attempted to avoid this contradiction by saying: the existent round square is existent but does not exist. Russell said he could see no difference.

On Russell's own theory, the fictional name "Hamlet" is shorthand for a (definite) description – for example, "the Danish prince who said 'To be, or not to be, that is the question . . .'." When we say "Hamlet killed his stepfather," we are claiming: *there exists one (and only one) Danish prince who said "To be, or not to be . . ." and that prince killed his stepfather*. Without postulating nonexistent objects, "Hamlet killed his stepfather" is meaningful (because the italicized sentence is meaningful) and "Hamlet does not exist" is true (since nothing fitting the description exists). However, difficulties remain. Which features should we include in the description of "Hamlet"? On Russell's theory, if some actual person fitting Hamlet's description killed his stepfather, "Hamlet killed his stepfather" would be true, but independently of Shakespeare's play – and in this case "Hamlet does not exist" would be false. Moreover, unless some actual person does behave like Hamlet, "Hamlet killed his stepfather" is false. Intuitively, these outcomes are incorrect.

Modern Meinongians (e.g., Parsons 1995; Zalta 2003) make various technical moves, aiming to avoid Russell's objections. These include: a distinction between two senses of "are" in "There are objects of which it is true that there are no such objects"; nonstandard accounts of "negation" (so the round square can without contradiction be both round and nonround); a distinction between "existence-entailing" and "nonexistence-entailing" properties (so the round square can be round, and even existent, although it does not exist – and Sherlock Holmes both live in London and be a fictional character); or a distinction in "modes of predication" (Gordon Brown, but not Sherlock Holmes, really has the property of living in London). Other neo-Meinongians have argued for the possibility of true contradictions.

However, outside the formal machinery, what exactly are these nonexistent objects (and the proposed properties and modes of predication) – and how many are there? Some theorists come close to saying that nonexistents are sets of properties (e.g., Hamlet is the set of properties that in Shakespeare's play are attributed to the man named "Hamlet"), but it seems that sets exist. (Sets are also abstract entities, which is a problem for Meinongians who claim that Hamlet is a concrete object like you or me.) The formal machinery itself is puzzling: if the round square is both round and nonround, can "nonround" mean the same as "not round"? And even if we can make sense of nonexistents, if no fictional character exists, what is the difference between Hamlet and Lucianus (in Shakespeare's play one is a flesh-and-blood prince and the other a fictional character)? Moreover, how can a storyteller create objects that do not exist? On the other hand, if, as some contemporary realists claim, these objects do exist, what makes them fictional?

A *possible worlds* analysis of truth in fiction (e.g., Lewis 1983) can in principle be either realist or reductionist (depending on our view of "possible worlds" talk). On this theory, "In the Conan Doyle fictions, Holmes is a detective" is true if and only if the sentence "Holmes is a detective" is true in the world(s) of the fiction. The "In the . . . fiction" prefix respects our intuition that fictions are cut off from reality (even if the actual 221B Baker Street was a Chinese restaurant, Holmes did not live in a Chinese restaurant) and the notion of the "world(s)" of a fiction allows background truths in fiction that are not explicitly stated (although Conan Doyle did not say so, Holmes did not have two heads). However, problems remain. If the background of a fiction is determined by the actual world, is it true in the Sherlock Holmes stories that Blackwell published *A Companion to Aesthetics* in 2009? Since there is no possible world in which contradictions are true, how can it be true (in *Le Voyageur Imprudent*) that a man travels back in time and prevents his own birth? (Some theorists assume that impossible fictions are few or peripheral, but many important fictions are impossible (Proudfoot 2006). And, since in the fiction Sherlock Holmes exists, what makes "Sherlock Holmes does not exist" true?

Some modern reductionists (e.g., Evans 1982; Walton 1990; Brock, 2002) propose *fictionalist* theories: Shakespeare's audience merely pretends or makes believe that things are as they seem – for example, that "Hamlet" refers, "Hamlet killed his stepfather" is meaningful and true, and there is a "world" of the play. I make believe (when watching the film) that I see Hannibal Lecter kill his victim; when my heart races (this natural reaction is a "prop" in an open-ended "game of make-believe" based upon the film), I make believe that I am afraid. "I am afraid" is make-believedly true, although actually false.

Fictionalism, however, raises more questions. If the name "Hamlet" is meaningless, how can the sentence "Hamlet killed his stepfather" express even a "make-believe" thought? What is it for a sentence to be "make-believedly true"? Why, when my heart races, do I pretend I am afraid – rather than believe I am having a heart attack? To answer these questions, fictionalists introduce such technical notions as: "quasi-information" (the content of the empty name "Hamlet") and "make-belief" (my psychological attitude to fictional stories); an "In the . . . make-believe" prefix, with a formal notation and rules; and "quasi-fear" (my response to a horror movie). However, often these notions are merely programmatic; fictionalists assume that we already understand what it is to "suspend disbelief" or think "within the scope of a pretense."

Recently some fictionalists have added *simulation theory*, with the associated psychological research (e.g., Currie 1995). (Using simulation theory, to know what another person thinks or feels, I imagine being that person; I actually experience "off-line" versions of his or her psychological states. According to the fictionalist, if I imagine being an observer of a real Hamlet, and this observer is herself imagining being Hamlet, I actually experience off-line versions of a real Hamlet's beliefs and emotions.) Some realists postulate impossible worlds. Other theorists provide combination realist-reductionist accounts, or use "deflationist" approaches (e.g., Proudfoot & Copeland 2002). Analyzing talk about fiction remains an important challenge for contemporary philosophy.

See also LITERATURE; EMOTION; FICTION, THE PARADOX OF RESPONDING TO; FICTION, TRUTH IN; IMAGINATION; WALTON.

BIBLIOGRAPHY
Brock, Stuart. 2002. "Fictionalism about Fictional Characters," *Noûs*, 36, 1–21.
Currie, Gregory. 1995. "Imagination and Simulation: Aesthetics Meets Cognitive Science." In *Mental Simulation: Evaluations and Applications*. M. Davies & T. Stone (eds.). Oxford: Blackwell, 151–69.
Evans, Gareth. 1982. *The Varieties of Reference*. Oxford: Clarendon.
Everett, Anthony & Hofweber, Thomas (eds.). 2000. *Empty Names, Fiction, and the Puzzles of Nonexistence*. Stanford: CSLI.
Lewis, David K. 1983. "Truth in Fiction." In *Philosophical Papers*, vol. i. New York: Oxford University Press, 261–80.
Meinong, Alexius. 1960 [1904]. "The Theory of Objects." In *Realism and the Background of Phenomenology*. R. M. Chisholm (ed.). I. Levi, D. B. Terrell, & R. M. Chisholm (trans.). London: Allen & Unwin, 76–117.
Nichols, Shaun (ed.). 2006. *The Architecture of the Imagination: New Essays on Pretence, Possibility, and Fiction*. Oxford: Clarendon.
Parsons, Terence. 1995. "Meinongian Semantics Generalized," *Grazer Philosophische Studien*, 50, 145–61.
Proudfoot, Diane. 2006. "Possible Worlds Semantics and Fiction," *Journal of Philosophical Logic*, 35, 9–40.
Proudfoot, Diane & Copeland, B. Jack. 2002. "Wittgenstein's Deflationary Account of Reference," *Language and Communication*, 22(3), 331–51.
Russell, Bertrand. 1919. *Introduction to Mathematical Philosophy*. London: Allen & Unwin.
Russell, Bertrand. 1954. "The Metaphysician's Nightmare." In *Nightmares of Eminent Persons*. London: Bodley Head, 31–5.
Thomasson, Amie. 1999. *Fiction and Metaphysics*. Cambridge: Cambridge University Press.

Walton, Kendall L. 1990. *Mimesis as Make-Believe: On the Foundations of the Representational Arts.* Cambridge, MA: Harvard University Press.

Walton, Kendall L. 1997. "Spelunking, Simulation, and Slime: On Being Moved by Fiction." In *Emotion and the Arts.* M. Hjort & S. Laver (eds.). Oxford: Oxford University Press, 37–49.

Zalta, Edward N. 2003. "Referring to Fictional Characters," *Dialectica,* 57(2), 243–54.

DIANE PROUDFOOT

film   *see* MOTION PICTURES.

forgery   raises various questions concerning the nature and value of the arts. I divide them into three.

WHAT IS FORGERY, AND WHERE IS IT POSSIBLE?
The forgeries that come naturally to mind are fraudulent copies of individual paintings or sculptures. However, historically most forgery in the visual arts involves a modern original posing as an instance of an earlier type. Van Meegeren and Bastianini did not copy existing Vermeers and works by the school of Donatello, but passed off their own works as previously undiscovered pieces by those masters. Here the type is already recognized – however seriously the addition of these false examples threatens to weaken our understanding of it. In yet other cases, the type itself might be invented, as when forgery is of the entire oeuvre of a fictitious, or long lost, artist.

At least some types of forgery are also found in all the other arts. Perhaps literature and music do not allow for forging an individual work. Anyone reproducing the text or notes has, arguably, merely produced a fresh inscription of the original novel or another performance of the original piece. Musical and literary *manuscripts* might be forged, but works cannot be. But type forgeries are certainly possible in these arts. James MacPherson faked a set of poems by Ossian in his "translations" from the Gaelic bard, and we can at least imagine someone offering her own compositions as Sibelius's (unwritten) atonal symphonies. Nor is forgery by any means confined to the fine arts. Its targets have included furniture, coins, stamps, weapons, costumes, and carpets, to name but a few (Arnau 1961).

What, then, is forgery? At its core lies deception: producing something with the intention that it pass as other than it is – either as an individual, or as a member of a kind. Now, decoy ducks are intended to deceive in this second way, but they are not forgeries of ducks. A deceptive duck, however lifelike, and who- or whatever (other ducks, bird-watchers, duck-breeders) it is intended to fool, while it might be a *fake* duck, will not count as a forgery of one. Why? What condition on forgery is the phony duck doomed not to meet? The answer cannot be that only artifacts can be forged, for we can raise the same question for a "decoy" door: a *trompe-l'oeil* painting of a door is intended to deceive, yet it too will not be a forgery of a door, but at most a fake one. Nor can it be that a forged *F* cannot be a representation *of an F* – at least not until we are convinced that forged banknotes do not count as representations of them. Rather, I suggest, the concept of forgery requires a particular sort of practice to be in place, one in which we value items at least in part for their origin in a particular agent. The agent might be an individual, as in the case of a signature; a group, as with the paintings of a particular school; or an institution, as in the case of banknotes, passports, and other official documents. The item's origin might play a greater or smaller role in explaining *why* the thing is of value to us. In the case of official documents, their originating where they do more or less secures that they will perform the tasks we want them to (e.g., getting us into other countries); in the case of paintings and the like, we presumably care about their origin because we think that feature will bring others we care about (such as artistic merit) in its train.

So a forgery is a work produced or altered with the intention that it pass for some other individual or as belonging to some type, where there is a practice of valuing such things in part as the product of a certain agent. Successful forgeries are those where the intention to mislead is itself successful. This definition has two consequences. First, for any forgery it is always possible that there be a nonfraudulent copy – something as like (or unlike) the original as the forgery, but not intended to mislead anybody. Second, forgeries need not resemble their originals. Sometimes there will be no relevant individual for them to resemble (think of the atonal works by Sibelius). But even when there is, the forgery might bear little relation to it. Since we have scant idea how the statue of Zeus at Olympia looked, someone might produce a successful forgery of it however thin the resemblance between the two.

THE PERFECT COPY

Let us concentrate on forgeries in art. Although forgeries need not be like their originals, they might be. What then? What, in particular, if a forgery of an individual artwork were so good that no one could tell it and the original apart? Could the two nonetheless differ in their value *as art* (Goodman 1969)? Although this question could be asked about a nonfraudulent copy, the forgery dramatizes it nicely. For, on the one hand, how can the two not differ, given that one might be a sublime artistic achievement, such as Picasso's *Les Demoiselles D'Avignon*; the other merely a slavish reproduction? Yet, on the other hand, how can the two differ? For surely the value of art lies in the experiences to which it gives rise. And surely the two works, being indistinguishable, give rise to precisely the same experiences.

One influential response to this dilemma is to distinguish two kinds of value a work of art might possess (Lessing 1965). *Aesthetic* value is indeed bound up with experience. The two works can no more differ aesthetically than identical twins can differ in how handsome they are. But the value of works as art does not reduce to their aesthetic merit: they also have *artistic* value. That is a matter of their contributing to the tradition – of Japanese landscape painting, piano music, epic poetry, or whatever – to which they belong. Artistic value is about creativity and innovation, about reflecting on the achievements of other artists and adapting, incorporating, reacting to, or rejecting them. It essentially involves the history of the art form. As such, it often eludes our senses. We cannot *see* that in *Les Demoiselles* Picasso broke, decisively and for the first time, with the Western tradition of the group portrait. Its being innovative in that way is not therefore an aspect of its aesthetic value. But it is part of its value *as art*, nonetheless: a value the copy, as merely imitative, does not share.

However, it is not clear that we can neatly divide the value of art in this way. *Les Desmoiselles D'Avignon* is not *separately* startling looking and a radical challenge to the tradition of the group portrait. Its startling quality lies in part in what it does to that tradition. For sure, one will not see that unless one knows something of that tradition. Indeed, extensive exposure to other group portraits, by Van Dyck, Hals, and nineteenth-century academicians, might be needed. But for someone suitably acculturated, the revolution *Les Demoiselles* effects *is* there to be seen. Does this render its value aesthetic? It certainly seems to involve the very elements (innovation, reflection on tradition, etc.) taken to define artistic value. If artistic value too can be experienced, then perhaps the sharp distinction above is not needed for meeting the dilemma.

The alternative is to accept that all the value of art shows up in experience, while freeing experience from the limits of discrimination. How you experience a work (how it looks, sounds, or reads to you) is not simply a matter of what you can distinguish it from. It also turns on the "cognitive stock" (Wollheim 1987) you bring to bear: your knowledge of the work and the tradition from which it comes, your habits and aptitudes in (say) looking at paintings, the visual culture in which you have been raised. Being told that these are the Van Meegerens, these the Vermeers, will make certain features of each salient to you, as the key likenesses within a group and differences between them. Paintings that once looked strikingly alike can thus come to look radically different. Again, viewers looking at Van Meegerens now may be struck by features that, as visual "ticks" of the forgeries' time, largely escaped contemporary viewers – features that the real Vermeers lack. These examples concern type forgeries. They help explain how pictures that now look so unlike Vermeers might have been taken, even by leading experts, for them. But the points carry over to our present concern, the way we experience a perfect copy and its original. How something looks depends on the thoughts, knowledge, and experience of other works one can bring to bear. If we bring knowledge of their origins, and the right contrast and comparison classes, to bear on the two works, we may thus experience the original differently from the forgery. And this, even though we remain unable to tell the two apart.

This response to the dilemma has proved popular. However, as it stands it is only the beginning of a reply. First, the challenge was to say how the two works differ in value, given that they cannot be told apart. Being told that they can be experienced differently helps only if that reflects the differing value of the objects experienced. But, quite generally, thought can affect how we experience things without reflecting their nature. If some comedian prompts me to hear humorous English sentences in the lines of an Italian opera, that shows nothing about the artistic value of the aria. Why should my ability to see the forgery one way, the original another, be any more revealing (Radford 1978)? The question bites especially hard when we remember that either experience is possible before either work: we merely need to approach the forgery thinking it to be the original, or vice versa. What, then, makes one experience the *right* way to see the original, the other the *right* way to see the forgery?

Nelson Goodman is among the few to face this question. His answer is that what makes each experience appropriate to just one of the pair is that by experiencing them thus we open the way to being able to distinguish them one day (1969: ch. 3). The works differ in value now, even for those (and that, we are supposing, is everyone) who cannot currently distinguish them. The two experiences reflect that value. But their claim to do so turns on the fact that, seeing the one as a forgery, and so belonging with Van Meegerens, Bastianinis, and the like; the other as *Les Demoiselles*, and so belonging with the rest of Picasso's output, will lead to our eventually being able to tell the two apart. But what, we may wonder, if we never come to discriminate the fake from the original? What if the copy is so good that no one ever could tell the two apart? Goodman has various things to say in reply (1969: 106–8), but few have found them compelling.

We may do better simply to appeal to the facts here. We should see the forgery as a forgery, the Picasso as a Picasso, simply because that is how things really are (Hopkins 2005). But even if that reply is found adequate, a second difficulty looms. It remains the case that either experience could be had before either work. Is there any reason, then, to look at the original, rather than the copy; or any reason to preserve

the former that is not equally a reason to preserve the latter? The key experience may only be veridical before the Picasso, but the fake would seem just as useful as a prop for inducing that experience. Thus even if the two differ in value as art, we may wonder whether that thought, in the form in which we have preserved it, connects in the right way with what we have reason to do.

IS FORGERY BAD ART?

Forging is wrong – or so at least the sanctions against it suggest. But it does not follow that the wrongness is artistic, rather than ethical; let alone that the wrongness of the act infects its product, the forgery itself, with an artistic defect. So is forgery bad as art? Does a forgery necessarily lack artistic value? (Since we have set aside the distinction between artistic and aesthetic value, by "artistic value" I simply mean value as art, whatever that turns out to be.)

Any deficiency here might lie in forgery's lacking an artistic virtue, or its possessing an artistic vice. The obvious candidate for the missing virtue is originality, in the sense of creative novelty. *Les Demoiselles* might be groundbreakingly original, but a forgery of it can hardly be. (It could at most be groundbreaking as forgery, in terms of the techniques, etc. used, not as art.) Not that all forgery necessarily lacks originality. Our hypothetical atonal symphonies "by" Sibelius might break ground in many ways. But at least some kinds of forgery will necessarily lack this virtue, and other kinds will perhaps be unlikely to possess it, even if they are not excluded from doing so.

Perhaps mere lack of virtue will seem insufficient: intuitively, if forgery is bad at all as art, it is so seriously so that it must manifest some vice. If so, we might look for that vice in the strong parallel forgery bears to other forms of deception, and in particular lying. (The wrongness of lying is presumably ethical, but for all that the comparison might be useful.) There is controversy over what exactly *is* wrong with lying. Crudely put, views divide into those that consider it a crime against trust, and those that consider it a crime against truth (Macintyre 1967). On the latter account it involves a sort of corruption of the central function of language, that of conveying truth.

It may be that we can make sense of something analogous in the case of forgery.

Suppose we thought that one central function of art was to express the emotions, thoughts, and other states of mind of its maker. Forgery seems ill-suited to do this. Not that every form of forgery is absolutely incapable of it. Forgeries of new specimens of old types, or of new types, might manage it. Forgeries of individual artworks that are very little like their originals may also do so (think of the statue of Zeus). But when the individual work that has been forged is known, the forgery will certainly be blocked from expressing its maker's feelings: even if the forger happens to share the states of mind the original expressed, his work is not expressive of those states of mind as a result of his feeling them. And while other kinds of forgery might express their maker's attitudes, the chances of their doing so seem slim. Too many other pressures are at work, dictated by the intention to deceive. Thus, as a whole forgery seems destined to forsake what we are supposing to be a central function of art. To that extent, its products are fated to stand as corruptions of the project of art itself. They would be a crime against art, somewhat as lying is (on some views) a crime against truth. That, I take it, would be an artistic defect, and a serious one.

Of course, defending such a view requires us to defend a rather old-fashioned conception of art. Nonetheless, if the badness of forgery lies in any substantial artistic vice at all, this would seem to be the best place to look for it.

See also CONSERVATION AND RESTORATION; EXPRESSION THEORY; FUNCTION OF ART; ONTOLOGY OF ARTWORKS; ORIGINALITY; SENSES AND ART, THE.

BIBLIOGRAPHY

Arnau, Frank. 1961. The Art of the Faker: Three Thousand Years of Deception. J. Maxwell Brownjohn (trans.). Boston: Little, Brown.

Danto, Arthur C. 1981. The Transfiguration of the Commonplace. London: Harvard University Press.

Dutton, Denis (ed.). 1983. The Forger's Art: Forgery and the Philosophy of Art. Berkeley: University of California Press.

Goodman, Nelson. 1969. Languages of Art. 2nd edn. Oxford: Oxford University Press.

Hopkins, Robert. 2005. "Aesthetics, Experience and Discrimination," Journal of Aesthetics and Art Criticism, 63, 119–33.

Lessing, Alfred. 1965. "What is Wrong with a Forgery?" Journal of Aesthetics and Art Criticism, 23, 461–72.

Macintyre, Alasdair. 1967. Secularization and Moral Change: The Riddell Memorial Lectures 1964. Oxford: Oxford University Press.

Radford, Colin. 1978. "Fakes," Mind, 87, 66–76.

Wollheim, Richard. 1987. Painting as an Art. London: Thames & Hudson.

ROBERT HOPKINS

formalism is primarily a view about what it takes to determine the aesthetic characteristics or features or properties of things. Which characteristics are aesthetic? "Aesthetic" is an elastic term. One approach to giving it a sense is simply to give a list of examples of the kind of features that are aesthetic: beauty, ugliness, daintiness, dumpiness, elegance, and so on. A more ambitious approach is to say that the list of aesthetic characteristics is nonarbitrary in virtue of a crucial role that beauty and ugliness play: other characteristics, such as, elegance, are ways of being beautiful or ugly. Either way, it is clear that works of art have many nonaesthetic characteristics, and nature has many aesthetic characteristics. (Formalism is sometimes thought of as a view of the nature of art, but that is probably because a view about aesthetic characteristics is conjoined with an aesthetic view of the nature of art.)

FORMAL AND NONFORMAL PROPERTIES

Now, what of formal aesthetic characteristics? These are a subclass of the aesthetic ones. Rather than offering a definition, we can gain an indication of which aesthetic properties they are by considering debates over various art forms.

Clive Bell (1914) and Roger Fry (1920) thought that formal aesthetic features of paintings are those that are determined by the lines, shapes, and colors that are within the frame. By contrast, the meaning and representational characteristics of paintings are not entirely determined by what is in the frame but also by the work's history of production. What a painting means or represents is determined in part by the intentions of the person who made it (Wollheim 1980, 1987). Such intentions are not sufficient, but they are necessary for the meanings or representational properties of paintings. Thus meaning and representation are not formally relevant. The aesthetic formalist about paintings believes that all their aesthetic properties are formal; they are all determined solely by what is in the frame and not at all by their history of production. By contrast, the antiformalist about paintings believes that all their aesthetic properties are determined in part by their history of production. Sometimes antiformalists appeal to the context of interpretative practices in which works are embedded, instead of their history of production, or they invoke some combination of interpretative practices and history of production, or some other extrinsic factor. I shall assume, however, that antiformalists insist on the aesthetic importance of the history of production of works.

Eduard Hanslick claimed that musical beauty was determined by structures of sound (1986: ch. 3). On this view, even if music sometimes has meanings, they are of no relevance to its formal aesthetic properties. The emotions leading a musician or composer to make music, and the emotions generated in listeners are formally irrelevant. In a performance of a piece of classical music, for example, the "frame" around the sounds that determines formal aesthetic properties is the tapping of the conductor's baton and the applause (Cone 1968). That structure of sounds determines the formal properties of the music. Anything outside that, such as the history of production of the sounds or their emotional causes or effects, is aesthetically irrelevant.

FORM AS STRUCTURE
There is another sense of form and formal properties that has currency – especially in reflections on literature, but also in music, architecture, and painting – and that is of form as *structure*. This is a matter of the arrangement of the elements of a work with respect to each other. Consider three cards arranged in a line: the six of hearts, the six of spades, and the seven of hearts. There is a sense in which they have an *ABA* structure, and another in which they have and *AAB* structure. Perhaps they have both. Now consider a painting with three human figures in a line: a king in a red cloak, a bishop in a red cloak, and a king in a blue cloak. There is a sense in which it has an *ABA* structure and a sense in which it has an *AAB* structure. But note that the *AAB* structure is formal in the previous sense that it is determined by what is in the frame – by the lines, shapes, and colors on the surface – while the *ABA* "structural form" is determined by what they represent (king or bishop), and on most plausible views that structure is not determined just by the lines, shapes, and colors that are in the frame, but is determined in part by the artist's intention. So the sense of form as structure does not overlap with the sense of form as the determination of aesthetic features by what is in the frame. Let us put structural form to one side here, interesting though it is.

FORMALISM VERSUS ANTIFORMALISM
Antiformalists say that in order to appreciate a work of art aesthetically we must always see that work as historically situated. Aesthetic antiformalism, with its emphasis on historical determination, has its roots in Hegelian history and philosophy of culture (*Kulturgeschichte*) that was popular in prewar Germany and Austria. This was imported to English-speaking countries by refugees from Nazism becoming very influential in English-speaking art history, and beyond. Consider Ernst Gombrich's bestselling *The Story of Art* (1950). The antiformalism is right there in the title! The idea became commonplace that the aesthetic value and even the identity of a work of art depend on its place in the story of art. Contrast Bell, the formalist, who writes "what does it matter whether the forms that move [us] were created in Paris the day before yesterday or in Babylon fifty centuries ago?" (1914: 45–6).

Gottlob Frege famously said that a word has meaning only in the context of a sentence (1967), and similarly most aestheticians would assert that the elements of a work have significance only in the context of the whole work. W. V. O. Quine equally famously said that a sentence has meaning only in the context of other sentences of the language (1951), and similarly aesthetic antiformalists assert that a work has aesthetic significance only in the context of other works in the tradition in which the work is located. Aesthetic formalists deny this and insist that works sustain their aesthetic properties by themselves. (There was a similar debate, conducted in different terms, in the Renaissance: see Mitrovic 2004.)

Antiformalists believe that all aesthetic properties are historically determined and that aesthetic judgments should always be made, and experiences always had, in the light of appropriate historical categories (Walton 1970). Formalists deny this. Antiformalists charge formalists with a naive belief in the "innocent eye" according to which knowledge of history is irrelevant to the aesthetic appreciation. Formalists celebrate the innocent eye, preferring it to one cluttered with irrelevances. Innocence is sometimes a good thing, they say.

ARGUMENTS?

What can be said in favor of either view? In favor of antiformalism, Gombrich put forward an imaginary example of physically identical works by different artists and invited us to judge that they are aesthetically different (Gombrich 1959: 313). Philosophers like Danto (1964) and Walton (1970) followed suit. Such arguments are supposed to show that a work's physical nature does not suffice for its aesthetic properties and that history also plays a role. But the appeal to imaginary examples has limited dialectical efficacy. Fanciful thought experiments – sometimes involving Martians – are supposed to generate possible examples of physically identical artworks with different aesthetic properties; but whether such cases are really possible is far from uncontroversial. The dialectical pressure exerted by such examples is minimal since formalists and antiformalists will simply interpret the examples differently. Physically identical cases with different histories may have *other* interesting differences. For example, they might differ in originality; but that difference may not contribute to a difference in their beauty, elegance, or delicacy – that is, it may make no aesthetic difference. Or so the formalist will say, and merely imaginary examples will not sway them. Similarly, it is controversial whether being a fake makes an aesthetic difference.

Arguments for or against formalism should probably be less purely philosophical and involve more attention to actual cases. The apparently abstract metaphysical issue about what it takes to determine aesthetic properties is probably not answerable without practical critical engagement with works of art in various art forms. Here it is worth transgressing disciplinary boundaries. This need not mean the vacuous kind of "interdisciplinarity" that is mere deference to the apparent authority of another discipline (so as to avoid the authority of one's own!). It can be an active engagement with the subject matter of both disciplines with whatever genres of intellectual thought are available (so long as the disciplines really do engage with the subject matter, rather than being an excuse for undisciplined philosophy).

It is likely that the issue or issues over formalism needs to be discussed art form by art form; there may be no one correct view that applies universally. And even within art forms, it may be that no general theory is right.

MODERATE FORMALISM

Both formalism and antiformalism have something to be said for them, and yet both also seem too extreme. A possible middle course is what we might call "moderate formalism" (Zangwill 2001). On this view, many aesthetic properties are formal and many are not; and many works have only formal properties and many do not have only formal properties. Moderate formalism admits some, and indeed many nonformal properties of works. For example, marching music or religious music is music with a nonmusical function; it is music *for* marching or praying; but the way it realizes that extramusical function may be part of its aesthetic excellence. This is unlike music that is for shopping. There the question is simply "Does it make people buy more?" or perhaps "Does it make shopping more pleasant?" Shopping music is not the aesthetically appropriate expression of the activity of shopping in the way that music may be the appropriate aesthetic expression of marching or praying. Sometimes musical beauty arises when music serves some nonmusical function or purpose in a musically appropriate way. The music has a certain nonmusical function and the aesthetic qualities of the music are not separate from that function but are an expression, articulation, or realization of it. This is what Kant calls "dependent" beauty (1928: §16). Similarly, there can be a representation that is beautiful, elegant, or delicate *as* a representation, and a building may be beautiful *as* a mosque, station, or library.

So nonformal aesthetic properties are important. Bell, Fry, and Hanslick overshot in denying that. However, there are many aesthetic properties that are purely formal, and there are many purely formal works. Some paintings are entirely abstract and quite a lot of music is "absolute." Moreover, most representational paintings have formal aesthetic features among their other aesthetic features. Extreme antiformalism, which denies the existence of formal aesthetic properties and purely formal works, goes too far. Moderate formalism insists on the importance of both formal and nonformal properties.

See also EIGHTEENTH-CENTURY AESTHETICS; TWENTIETH-CENTURY ANGLO-AMERICAN AESTHETICS; AESTHETICISM; BELL; DANTO; FORGERY; GOMBRICH; HANSLICK; INTENTION AND INTERPRETATION; ONTOLOGICAL CONTEXTUALISM; REPRESENTATION; SENSES AND ART, THE; WALTON.

BIBLIOGRAPHY

Bell, Clive. 1914. *Art*. London: Chatto & Windus.

Cone, Edward. 1968. *Musical Form and Musical Performance*. New York: Norton.

Danto, Arthur C. 1964. "The Artword," *Journal of Philosophy*, 61, 571–84.

Frege, Gottlob. 1967. "The Thought: A Logical Inquiry." In *Philosophical Logic*. P. F. Strawson (ed.). Oxford: Oxford University Press, 17–38.

Fry, Roger. 1920. *Vision and Design*. London: Chatto & Windus.

Gombrich, Ernst. 1950. *The Story of Art*. London: Phaidon.

Gombrich, Ernst. 1959. *Art and Illusion*. London: Phaidon.

Hanslick, Eduard. 1986 [1854]. *On the Musically Beautiful*. G. Payzant (trans.). Indianapolis: Hackett.

Kant, Immanuel. 1928 [1790]. *Critique of Judgement*. J. C. Meredith (trans.). Oxford: Oxford University Press.

Mitrovic, Branko. 2004. *Learning from Palladio*. New York: Norton.

Quine, W. V. O. 1951. "Two Dogmas of Empiricism." In *From a Logical Point of View*. Cambridge, MA: Harvard University Press, 20–46.

Sibley, Frank. 1959. "Aesthetic Concepts," *Philosophical Review*, 68, 421–50.

Walton, Kendall L. 1970. "Categories of Art," *Philosophical Review*, 79, 334–67.

Wollheim, Richard. 1980. "Seeing-In, Seeing-As and Pictorial Representation." In *Art and Its Objects*. 2nd edn. Cambridge: Cambridge University Press, 205–26.

Wollheim, Richard. 1987. *Painting as an Art*. London: Thames & Hudson.

Zangwill, N. 2001. *The Metaphysics of Beauty*. Ithaca: Cornell University Press.

NICK ZANGWILL

Foucault, Michel (1926–1984) French intellectual, historian, and social critic, professor of history of systems of thought at the Collège de France (1970–84).

During the last three decades of his life, Michel Foucault produced thought-provoking volumes that contributed significantly to philosophy, psychology, sociology, historical studies, culture criticism, and art criticism. Their engaging literary style, searching detail, ingenious interpretations, and implicit social critique have secured his influence among intellectuals from all walks of life.

Foucault's initial writings (1954 to early 1960s) address, directly or tangentially, the nature and history of mental illness and of creative personalities who radically deviate from the norm. Included here is his literary-critical study of the eccentric French writer, Raymond Roussel (1877–1933), who captured Foucault's interest through his fascination with language and his imaginatively intense and yet mechanically methodical use of it.

As Foucault became a major European intellectual during the 1960s, his interests extended to include the history of medical clinics, the history of conceptions of knowledge, and more reflectively during the late 1960s and early 1970s, alternative methods of investigating history itself. Foucault's own method emphasizes "discourse formations," which are formal regularities between sets of objects, types of statement, concepts, or thematic choices. His parallel interests in literature, painting, and art criticism inform all of these studies.

Foucault's final decade highlights the themes of power and discipline insofar as they exert a controlling factor in the formation of individual personalities and social institutions. Central to this period is his history of the prison system and his multivolume history of sexuality, whose origins go back to his 1957 studies on the concept of love in French literature, from Sade to Genet. In 1984, an AIDS-related illness cut short Foucault's life as he approached the age of 58, but he was able to publish three volumes of his history of sexuality and begin the study of disciplines related to self-mastery, which he referred to as "technologies of the self." In relation to the latter he developed an "aesthetics of existence," described below.

Foucault's initial publications on the nature and history of mental illness issued from his diploma studies in psychopathology, his psychology teaching position at the University of Lille, and his experiences as a psychology assistant at both the Sainte-Anne psychiatric hospital in Paris and at the main medical facilities of the French prison system, housed at Fresnes. His homosexuality also shaped his outlook, for it placed him within an unpopular minority group associated with sexual practices that were more often than not legally prohibited. He was also motivated to break away from the Marxism, phenomenology, and existentialism that had grounded his education.

These assorted experiences motivate Foucault's larger project of understanding in terms of a variety of psychological and historical dimensions, how different societies treat their minority members. One of his key questions is how the prevailing social evaluations of the mentally ill, the unemployed, lepers, and eccentric members of a society in general, establish their legitimacy. In the course of answering this question throughout his oeuvre, he often refers to artists and their work, not simply because their productions represent the themes he is discussing but because artists themselves have a reputation for often being rebellious social critics and outcasts. Aesthetics-related concepts also inspire Foucault's writings, since the notions of "artifactuality," "creativity," and "technique" underpin his main theses about the nature of historical change.

With respect to this last point, a leading and recurring assertion is that what *seems* to be timelessly true, essential, and eternally patterned, is in fact the upshot of arbitrary strands of happenings that have coalesced – periodically with dramatic speed – into a particular social system, set of values, practices, attitudes, or common assumptions. Foucault observes, for example, that concepts such as the "author" or "man" (human being) were not always prominent within the socially prevailing discourse, but

came into currency at a particular place and time. His writings accordingly focus on the processes of historical emergence and mutation that give birth to such concepts, and address themes such as madness, mental hospitals, medical doctors as social authorities, styles of imprisonment, and techniques of self-discipline. Foucault's underlying assumption is that social systems, values, and practices are artifactual: as such, they are constructed, they change, and they remain open to evaluation. Impressed by the artificiality of social institutions, Foucault observed their numerous discontinuities with a penetrating eye.

Although Foucault did not compose a systematic philosophy of art, the assumption that concepts are historically constructed implies a way to interpret those that constitute such philosophies. We refer here to notions such as beauty, sublimity, art, works of art, aesthetic value, aesthetic judgment, creativity, representation, expression, modernity, and so on. Following Foucault's own examples, each of these can be analyzed historically to reveal how and when the concept emerged, and to intimate that the contemporary use of this or that concept holds only for the time being and will either transform or fade away "like a face drawn in sand at the edge of the sea," as he states concerning "man" at the conclusion of *The Order of Things* (1973a). Foucault's essay "What is an Author?" (1969) provides a further example by characterizing "the author" as an ideological product and as a function of a style of discourse that was once not present and that can and does change. Like people, Foucault regards concepts as having finite lifetimes that come into and go out of fashion.

In a more selective, piecemeal manner, Foucault also rhetorically utilizes references to works of art to introduce and illustrate the respective themes of his manuscripts. These are usually masterpieces of fine art, but he sometimes mentions those that, independent of their artistic quality, represent the spirit of the times. In the first chapter of *Madness and Civilization* (1965), for instance, he invokes the allegory of the Ship of Fools (e.g., as painted by Hieronymus Bosch (1490–1500), but which appears also in woodcuts and in literature) to encapsulate his claim – often challenged – that mentally deficient individuals were treated with a greater measure of humanity and freedom during the 1400s and 1500s, in contrast to the dehumanizing incarcerations they suffered in later centuries. In the first chapter of *The Order of Things* (1966), he similarly describes Diego Velázquez's *Las Meninas* (1656), in order to show how the painting's structure represents that of classical representation in general and, accordingly, the epistemological spirit of the times. According to Foucault, the classical style of representation duplicates the relationships between the objects it represents within the relationships between the signs that it uses (e.g., in the way the grooves on a phonograph record are isomorphic with the sounds the record produces). The style of representation remains naive insofar as the presence and influence of the person who is doing the representing is thought to remain outside the representation.

In *This is Not a Pipe* (1973b), Foucault highlights René Magritte's painting, *La trahison des images* (*The Treachery of Images*) (1928–9), in conjunction with works by Paul Klee and Vassily Kandinsky. These serve as contemporary examples that challenge the principles Foucault believes "ruled Western painting from the fifteenth to the twentieth century." Magritte's painting contains a realistic image of a pipe with the words "Ceci n'est pas une pipe" ("This is not a pipe") written below it, and Foucault calls on this arrangement to show how word and image are equally valued, how their meanings are ambiguous, and how we should not confuse a thing's image with the thing itself (as when we look at a photograph of the Eiffel Tower and feel that we are actually looking at the tower). His references to Magritte, Klee, and Kandinsky document a break with earlier tradition, where this tradition is understood to privilege images over words, to strive for literalistic exactness, and to confuse image with reality.

"Theatrum Philosophicum" (1977b) mentions Andy Warhol's Pop Art as exemplary of a liberating outlook where repetition, monotony, and evenness prevail, where traditional hierarchies and orderings are leveled, and where on such a homogeneous field, we are set free to perceive new types of differences and multiplicities. In literature, Foucault addresses the same theme in *Maurice Blanchot: The Thought from Outside* (1966), where he finds Blanchot's

works expressing the idea of an emptiness situated at the edge of language which, when met, undermines already ossified forms of speech to create new forms of discourse. Reiterating the point, *The Order of Things* begins with a passage from one of Jorge Luis Borges's short stories that refers fictionally to "a certain Chinese encyclopedia" that (dis)organizes the sphere of animals into a set of confusing, contradictory, and conceptually entertaining categories. Basic to these literary references is the theme of pushing one's present perspective to the limit, such as to undermine established orders and hierarchies.

In connection with architecture, an image at the other end of the spectrum is Jeremy Bentham's ideal prison design, the Panopticon (1785), which Foucault uses in *Discipline and Punish: The Birth of the Prison* (1977c) to embody the idea of an ossifying, all-seeing watchman. Representing an omniscient monitor, the Panopticon captures the image of an Orwellian society whose leaders, fixated on power and control, try to stifle creativity by holding everyone under their surveillance in a quasi-sadistic manner.

In each of these cases, Foucault employs works of art to present themes that the works themselves, as a rule, were not intended by their creators to represent. The series of examples also displays Foucault's own intellectual trajectory, telling us as much about his interest in liberation as they do about the themes they are used to supplement.

The bulk of Foucault's artistic examples coalesce, on the one hand, into a group whose genius expresses a touch of madness and/or whose works creatively challenge the status quo. Opposing this is a group that has close affinities to scientific objectivity and that regards the world with the detached, analytic eye of a medical doctor or all-seeing God that embodies ultimate veracity. The latter group represents the stable world of established truths, the former the disrupting world of new, unexpected, and unforeseen truths.

The artist has yet a further role in Foucault's works, if we conceive of an artist broadly to include society and language themselves as artists of a nonpersonal sort. In his studies of madness, medical clinics, and prisons, Foucault describes how various social institutions historically emerge and shape individuals into appropriately behaving kinds of people. In the production of "soldiers," for example, he notices how the process of social formation became increasingly manipulative: during the early 1600s, men who became soldiers were "found," owing to their natural display of an alert manner, broad shoulders, and the like. By the late 1700s, soldiers had "become something that can be made; out of a formless clay, an inapt body, the machine required can be constructed; posture is gradually corrected . . ." (1977c: 135). Here, society acts like an artist who works (unconsciously and sometimes cruelly) on the human materials that stand as formless clay. Education becomes a sinister form of manipulation within this perspective, and the prevailing society, when seen in retrospect, often becomes a Ship of Fools as it continues on contentedly and obliviously, failing to realize the distortions inherent in its conception of truth.

Most of Foucault's writings significantly, but not completely, adopt the detached perspective of an onlooker who considers how the particular society at large organizes its people into various privileged and marginalized groups, orders, and institutions. This detached perspective is tempered by Foucault's self-awareness that his historical constructions are his own interpretations that inevitably harbor a fictional or creative element. The result is a complicated mixture of descriptive science and imaginative art, where it is often difficult to discern the line between history as the depersonalized assemblage of hard facts, and history conceived of as personally or politically motivated fiction. This tension mirrors the dynamics of the traditional, self-conscious knower, who is a fundamentally active and creative consciousness, but who becomes a fixed object of knowledge in the act of reflection.

Aware of this dynamic, Foucault explores nontraditional notions of subjectivity that involve the liberating dissolution and dispersal of the subject within the field of language. He finds examples of this type of personal abandon in the literary tradition that includes Nietzsche, Mallarmé, Artaud, Bataille, Klossowski, and, most importantly, Blanchot, interpreting them as expressing the latter half of the transition between Descartes's "I think," which directs our gaze inward and coalesces our personality,

and the twentieth century's "I speak" and "I write," which direct our gaze outward and disperse it into linguistic activities and structures. In this transition from thought to language, Foucault perceives a change in our orientation toward truth, within the context of which writing fiction serves epistemologically better than writing science.

In his final period, Foucault focuses on the "technologies of the self." These describe practices where an individual becomes his or her own artist through a set of objective procedures or self-disciplines whose purpose is to produce an enhanced state of being such as happiness, wisdom, health, purity, or perfection. In this aesthetics of personal existence, one exercises a skill or technique upon oneself, as if one were an object to be manipulated, aiming to recreate oneself into a new person thereby. This activity of self-liberation and self-transformation has a paradoxical and complicating recoil, since the character who initially engages in this process of self-recreation becomes a different character by the end of it.

Since Foucault did not prescribe determinate goals toward which this self-recreation ought to be directed, he can be seen as advocating that only aesthetic criteria apply meaningfully to how one reconstitutes one's life. We can also interpret Foucault's position with less moral disengagement, as expressing merely the preliminary importance of being open to new possibilities. This reflects his 1982 remark that "the main interest in life and work is to become someone else that you were not in the beginning . . . The game is worthwhile insofar as we don't know what will be the end" (Martin 1988: 9). In 1969, he said the same: "I am no doubt not the only one who writes in order to have no face. Do not ask who I am and do not ask me to remain the same: leave it to our bureaucrats and our police to see that our papers are in order" (1972: 17).

Foucault intends here to explode limiting definitions and implicitly to advocate a notion of universal contingency where everything is a perishable good. As a breaker of the tablets and as an intellectual renegade, he embodies the spirit of Friedrich Nietzsche's iconoclasm; as a philosopher of ever open possibilities and universal contingency, he reiterates Jean-Paul Sartre's thought that we are absolutely free, and that existence precedes essence; as a philosopher of continual self-questioning and as cognizant that we are always already situated within a linguistic and social milieu, he reflects Descartes's skepticism in league with Martin Heidegger's historical and hermeneutical sensitivity. Along each dimension, Michel Foucault presents himself as a philosopher of social freedom, inspired by unconventional and innovative artistic personalities and by masterpieces of fine art, which he believes can guide us to a more liberated sense of self and world.

See also NINETEENTH- AND TWENTIETH-CENTURY CONTINENTAL AESTHETICS; INTERPRETATION; INTERPRETATION, AIMS OF; MODERNISM AND POSTMODERNISM.

BIBLIOGRAPHY

Primary sources
[1961] 1965. Madness and Civilization: A History of Insanity in the Age of Reason. R. Howard (trans.). London: Tavistock.
[1963] 1986. Death and the Labyrinth: The World of Raymond Roussel. C. Ruas (trans.). Garden City: Doubleday.
1966. Maurice Blanchot: The Thought from Outside. B. Massumi (trans.). New York: Zone.
[1966] 1973a. The Order of Things. A. Sheridan (trans.). New York: Vintage.
[1968] 1973b. This is Not a Pipe. J. Harkness (trans.). Berkeley: University of California Press.
[1969] 1972. The Archaeology of Knowledge and the Discourse on Language. A. M. Sheridan Smith (trans.). New York: Pantheon.
[1969] 1977a. "What is an Author?" In Language, Counter-Memory, Practice: Selected Essays and Interviews. D. F. Bouchard (ed. & trans.). Ithaca: Cornell University Press, 113–38.
[1970] 1977b. "Theatrum Philosophicum." In Language, Counter-Memory, Practice: Selected Essays and Interviews. D. F. Bouchard (ed. & trans.). Ithaca: Cornell University Press, 165–96.
[1975] 1977c. Discipline and Punish: The Birth of the Prison. A. Sheridan (trans.). London: Penguin.

Secondary sources
Carroll, David. 1987. Paraesthetics: Foucault, Lyotard, Derrida. London: Methuen.
During, Simon. 1992. Foucault and Literature: Towards a Genealogy of Writing. London: Routledge.
Martin, Rux. 1988. "Truth, Power, Self: An Interview with Michel Foucault." In Technologies of the Self: A Seminar with Michel Foucault. L. Martin, H. Gutman & P. H. Hutton (eds.). Amherst: University of Massachusetts Press, 9–15.
Nilson, Herman. 1998. Michel Foucault and the Games of Truth. New York: St. Martin's.

ROBERT WICKS

function of art The belief that works of art are functional and serve certain important ends has a very long and distinguished history – one that begins with Plato and has persisted in a variety of forms to the present day. The opposing idea that genuine art is nonfunctional, that it is always autonomous and is produced merely for its own sake, is a comparatively recent invention.

The distinction between the useful arts (or crafts) and arts that serve no purpose and are attended to solely as ends in themselves is not to be found in Plato or Aristotle; nor is it to be found in medieval theories of art. It was only at the time of the Renaissance that the notion of fine art began to take root as a way of distinguishing the functional from the nonfunctional arts. Up until then, all of what we now call fine art was considered to have a purpose – although in the case of some art forms like music and decoration the precise nature of its function was specified only with difficulty.

Functional views of art take at least two distinct forms. Some are normative, and insist that art *ought* always to serve a specified function. To the extent that a work of art performs its designated function, it is considered meritorious; reciprocally, when a work fails to serve its function it is considered inadequate or bad. In this article, this is referred to as normative functionalism. Descriptive functionalism, by contrast, contends that by their very nature works of art serve certain metaphysical, psychological, or cultural functions, and do so whether or not the artist knows or intends it. Descriptive functionalism treats a particular function as a *necessary* feature of all art, although it is true that both descriptive and normative functionalists are generally quite happy to allow that particular works of art may contingently serve a function on a certain occasion – where this function is entirely unrelated to its status as art.

Those functional views of art that are normative in character tend often to hold that art ought to act as a medium of instruction. Thus, for instance, Plato tells us that art ought not to deceive, and ought instead to imitate the "Forms" and thereby convey intellectual insights into reality. In book 10 of the *Republic* Socrates is said to have advocated the banishment of those poets who either could not or would not abide by his injunction. Their art imitated appearances rather than the eternal forms, and was, for that reason, irredeemably bad. Aristotle in the *Poetics* also believed that art should imitate the real nature of things, but his account of real essences differed from Plato's and he believed that the proper function of art was both the imitation of the functions of things and the achievement of certain pleasurable and cathartic effects. The medieval Church, long after, wanted an art that would illustrate the gospels and so convey the glory of God. One can continue in this way: Leonardo thought that art should imitate physical reality, while John Constable believed that painting should convey appearances scientifically, and would be especially good if it did so. Leo Tolstoy thought that good literature ought to convey truths about human nature and morality; while realist painters of the nineteenth century and twentieth-century socialist realists argued that serious art should convey the realities of social and political life.

Descriptive functionalism, by contrast, while clearly concerned with the functions served by works of art, is not concerned to isolate those functions that are thought to make art worthwhile or good. Indeed, descriptive functionalists seem often to be of the opinion that the functions served by a work of art need have very little, if anything at all, to do with artistic merit. They are more concerned with social and psychological theory and with the role that art plays in our lives than with the critical assessment of works of art. Sigmund Freud, for example, sees all art as the imaginative expression and fulfillment of certain deep-seated desires that cannot be fulfilled in the artist's everyday life. On his view, thwarted desires in the real world lead most people to daydream or fantasize. However, the artist learns to control these fantasies, and to mold them into works of art. Of course, good artists will do this more effectively than poor artists; but irrespective of whether they do it well or badly, on Freud's view all works of art perform this function, and they do so whether or not the artist knows it.

In much the same way, Karl Marx, as a descriptive functionalist, sees art as a phenomenon that arises out of the economic interests of groups of individuals within the economy and that helps reinforce or else advance these interests. Although he qualifies this in important respects by allowing that certain periods of art are not directly connected to the growth and development of society and its economy, he does nonetheless believe that art somehow expresses and, in this way, helps reinforce, various economic interests within the economic "base" of the society.

In an altogether different vein, Ortega y Gasset (1925) sees art as a social safety valve: an early-warning system that can, if properly attended to, inform us of social directions and so promote an understanding of our society. There is no shortage of such theories. Using gestalt theory, Rudolf Arnheim (1974) has argued that the function of art is to symbolize the entire pattern of feelings and meanings (what he calls "expressiveness") that is embodied in the perception of the artist. In a similar, but more philosophical, way Susanne Langer (1953) argues that art always captures and symbolizes nonverbal human feelings.

Freud, Marx, Ortega, Arnheim, and Langer are each in their own way descriptive functionalists. All hold that art serves certain psychological and social ends, and that it must do so whether or not an artist intends it to. It is however, no part of the descriptive functionalist's view that the performance of these functions is sufficient for something's being a work of art; the same functions can be, and often are, performed by nonart. Freud and Marx treat their chosen functions only as a necessary feature of art, although Freudians are not entirely consistent in this matter, and are inclined at times to treat the functions that they isolate as a contingent feature of art. It is arguable, for instance, that while Freudian critics believe that representational painting necessarily performs a specific psychological function, this need not be the case, say, with minimalist or conceptual art. They veer between being descriptive functionalists for specific genres, and contingent functionalists for others.

Of course, if the performance of a particular function is a necessary feature of an artwork, it cannot be a mark of its merit. This notwithstanding, it is entirely consistent for a descriptive functionalist to approve of the way in which a function is performed. Thus, for instance, a work that exposes the corrupt structure of bourgeois society may be praised on that account by Marxists and socialist realists, while one that lends strength to a free market ideology may be criticized. In much the same way, Freudian critics are often inclined to praise a work on the basis of how subtly and efficiently it fulfills its psychological function.

Quite often one and the same thinker turns out to embrace both normative and descriptive functionalism. We find, for instance, that Tolstoy believes that a work of art must always express the emotions of its artist and infect its audience with similar emotions. To this extent Tolstoy is clearly a descriptive functionalist. However, he also argues that in order for a work to be good, the emotions it expresses must be moral: it must encourage progress toward the wellbeing both of individuals and of humanity. To this extent, he is also a normative functionalist. This suggests that the distinction I have drawn between descriptive and normative functionalism marks ideal positions that often merge in subtle and quite complex ways. In part, this is why traditional aesthetics has tended to criticize functionalism as if it were a single, homogeneous position. Edward Bullough's (1912) arguments, for instance, against the normative functionalist account of evaluation, leads him to the undefended conclusion that art is always nonfunctional. In a similar way, Stuart Hampshire (1959) tries to show that aesthetic judgments are not informed by practical interests, but from this concludes that descriptive functionalism is false: that art is necessarily gratuitous and so always nonfunctional.

This tendency to ignore the distinction between normative and descriptive functionalism can further be explained by the fact that as High Renaissance art shaded into Mannerism, baroque and eventually neoclassicism, the emphasis came to be placed not just on the functions of the artwork, but also, and increasingly, on the formal properties of the work. As a result, the status of objects as art, as well as their critical assessment, gradually became detached from their function. In this climate of increasing hostility to functionalist views of art, subtle distinctions between types of functionalism were not of interest, and were never drawn.

The antagonism to functionalist views of art was brought to a head in the second half of the nineteenth century. The demise of feudalism and, with it, the disappearance of an aristocratic class that was willing to act as patron of the arts, threw all practicing artists on the mercy of the marketplace. Many artists refused absolutely to pander to what the market demanded: they refused to produce art that would serve some or other fashionable end, and instead insisted on producing art for its own sake. The aesthetic movement, and with it the cry of art for art's sake, had come of age.

The pursuit of purely artistic values and the production of art for the sake of art alone meant that many artists were no longer concerned with what ordinary people wanted from art. Their attention was wholly absorbed by the demands of the medium, and it was largely because of this that artists grew increasingly out of touch with what their audiences expected and could understand. The result was that the rank and file of society grew disillusioned with much fine art, and began to attend instead to what they found interesting and entertaining. In this way, painters, poets, musicians, and sculptors gradually began to lose their audience, and in the process they lost whatever impact they had once had on the broader society.

On one functionalist view, this series of historical accidents meant that the fine arts had effectively neutered themselves, had chosen the path of silence, and could no longer challenge the hegemony of the ruling classes (Novitz 1989). Partly because of this, those in positions of power found art for art's sake congenial and helped entrench its position in the broader society. Quite soon, the "proper" appreciation of art as an end in itself came to signal one's inclusion in the upper classes, and was taken as a sign of refinement and high culture. Those who looked for a message in art, and who, worse still, attempted to evaluate art in terms of that message, were considered vulgar and uninitiated: they failed in the round to understand what art and culture were all about.

If this is right, it helps explain the strong allegiance that some people have to the view of art as an end in itself. It is arguably a political allegiance, since commitment to it is thought to assure one of a place in an intellectual, cultural, and class elite. One result of all of this was that in the middle years of the twentieth century aesthetics became little more than an apologetic for a specific and very restricted view of the fine arts. Its concern, for the most part, was to defend the view that art was properly an end in itself, that it existed for its own sake, and that our understanding and evaluation of it should not concern itself with matters extraneous to the work such as its intended function.

One standard argument against functionalist views of art and in favor of autonomist views maintains that if a work of art serves a particular function – say, the function of informing you about the workings of American or British society – then anything which performs the same function – say, a sociology text – ought to be capable of serving as a substitute for a work of art. But this conclusion, it has been argued, is counterintuitive. For if I cannot locate a copy of *Bleak House*, I do not refer you instead to a report on the practice of law in nineteenth-century London, even if it turns out to be the case that both texts are equally instructive in this respect. Autonomists infer from this that what is important about a work is not its function but its formal properties. However, functionalists have generally contended that the function of a work of art, while artistically important, is not all-important. The *way* in which the function is performed is what is of singular importance about a work of art (Beardsmore 1971).

In arguing for the possibility of artistic values that are not tied to practical interests, traditional aestheticians have failed to acknowledge the extent to which the values that attach to art are dependent on the roles that works of art play in our lives: that is, on their functions. It is wrong, of course, to think that there is a single function that art invariably performs. Rather, there are many different functions, which vary from genre to genre and from period to period.

Traditionally an art was conceived of as a practice consisting of an organized package of more or less integrated, but invariably useful, skills (Sparshott 1982: 25–6). In this sense, medicine and shoemaking are arts, as are plumbing and sheep-shearing. All consist of sets of skills, often housed within institutional frameworks that perpetuate and regulate them. It is precisely because doctors, shearers, and cobblers have an interest in doing their job well that they think about and try to improve their skills. Consequently, the skills themselves, and not merely the ends that they serve, become objects of attention. It is, according to Sparshott, when an art (an organized body of skills) comes to be treated as an end rather than as a means that the fine arts begin to emerge.

This is why we should not allow the work of art to occlude our awareness of the useful skills that are exercised in its execution and of the value that we attach to these skills. It is all but impossible to look at a painting, a drama, a sculpture, or a dance without being aware, however remotely, of the practical skills exercised in these works of art. The skills of pictorial representation, for instance, have an obvious practical value, for they not only facilitate the communication of attitudes and information, but enable us to negotiate situations of which we have no first-hand experience. Again, we find that poets and novelists are normally skilled not just in the use of language (which is itself highly prized), but also in inventing a world of people and in telling a story about them. The capacity to invent, to be innovative and original, has obvious utility in a world that requires people to respond in new and useful ways to the problems that confront them. And, of course, skills of invention are praised everywhere in the fine arts.

One can continue in this way to outline the many practical interests and concerns that mediate our appreciation of all art forms. We can learn about our world from works of art; they may sharpen our moral sensitivities, and in so doing either unsettle or entrench certain of our commitments, enlist loyalties, and thereby foment or resolve social conflicts of one sort or another. Although these are not the only functions that works can serve, they greatly influence our assessment of, and hence the values that we attach to, particular works of art. It is simply a fact, then, that our religious, economic, moral, ecological, and intellectual values can, and often do, intrude on our response to a work of art. The remoteness and concern of Titian's madonna in his *Madonna with Saints*, for instance, is valued not just because of the formal correctness of the painting, but also because of the religious and gender-related values that we bring to it.

The assumption that art is wholly nonfunctional, and that our evaluation of it has nothing at all to do with our practical interests and concerns, is simply misleading. This, of course, is not to deny that works of art are sometimes appreciated for their textures, colors, timbre, and other formal properties. But such appreciation is not determined by the nature of art itself. On the contrary, people learn to appreciate art in this way, and they do so because they are the beneficiaries of a particular art education. The threat of being considered incompetent, insensitive, or ignorant about art gives them an interest in attending to textures and grains rather than messages or themes. In such a case, the viewer's artistic (or aesthetic) values are clearly mediated by social considerations. And at least part of their reason for subscribing to formal artistic values is that they want to be accepted and acknowledged within a certain social network. In this case, art and its appreciation can fairly be said to serve a specific social function: the function, that is, of assuring oneself of a place in a specific social group.

See also AESTHETICS IN ANTIQUITY; AESTHETICISM; ARISTOTLE; DEFINITION OF "ART"; EVOLUTION, ART, AND AESTHETICS; FORMALISM; LANGER; MARXISM AND ART; PLATO; PSYCHOANALYSIS AND ART; REALISM; THEORIES OF ART; TOLSTOY.

BIBLIOGRAPHY

Arnheim, Rudolf. 1974. *Art and Visual Perception.* Berkeley: University of California Press.

Beardsmore, R. W. 1971. *Art and Morality.* London: Macmillan.

Bullough, Edward. 1912. " 'Psychical Distance' as a Factor in Art and as an Aesthetic Principle." *British Journal of Psychology*, 5, 87–98.

Davies, Stephen (ed.). 1997. *Art and Its Messages: Meaning, Morality, and Society.* University Park: Pennsylvania State University Press.

Hampshire, Stuart. 1959. "The Logic of Appreciation." In *Aesthetics and Language.* W. Elton (ed.). Oxford: Blackwell, 161–9.

Langer, Susanne. 1953. *Feeling and Form.* New York: Scribner.

Novitz, David. 1989. "Ways of Artmaking: The High and the Popular in Art." *British Journal of Aesthetics*, 29, 213–29.

Ortega y Gasset, José. 1972 [1925]. *The Dehumanization of Art and Other Writings on Art and Culture.* H. Weyl (trans.). Princeton: Princeton University Press.

Shiner, Larry. 2001. *The Invention of Art.* Chicago: University of Chicago Press.

Sparshott, Francis. 1982. *The Theory of the Arts.* Princeton: Princeton University Press.

Wolff, Janet. 1981. *The Social Production of Art.* London: Macmillan.

DAVID NOVITZ

G

Gadamer, Hans-Georg (1900–2002) German philosopher; a pupil of Heidegger, and the leading "hermeneutical" theorist of the late twentieth century. Gadamer once described his approach to art as an attempt to transform the systematic problem of aesthetics into the question of the experience of art (1976: 97). Broadly speaking, his concerns might be described as phenomenological: the question of our access to the artwork and the need to guard against misdescribing our experience of it under the influence of unwarranted philosophical prejudices. However, as is clear from the first part of *Truth and Method* (1960), his major work, where Gadamer gives his most sustained account of art, art plays an exemplary role for him in illuminating the hermeneutical notion of truth.

Gadamer legitimates the hermeneutical idea of truth by showing how, once one has dropped the restriction of truth to its scientific conception, the artwork can also be understood as making a claim to truth. Although written primarily as a critique of aesthetic consciousness, his discussion exemplifies hermeneutics by showing that the historical tradition of reflection on art itself makes a claim to truth. Gadamer rehabilitates the tradition by recalling the legitimate experiences that underlie traditional terminology – for example, when he finds the much maligned concept of *mimesis* appropriate even to "pure poetry" and to nonobjective painting (1986: 36, 103, 117). One does not find in him a wholesale rejection of the conceptual language that has mediated the experience of art in the West. In this he differs from his teacher, Martin Heidegger. But it is striking that Gadamer at the same time had more success than Heidegger at taking account of our experiences of specifically modern works of art, such as nonobjective art (1986: 52–3), even though many of these works were designed to disrupt traditional aesthetic concepts. Gadamer's success in this can be understood as a result of his insistence on giving this priority to the experience of art over any determinate framework. It is noteworthy that already in the 1940s he challenged Beissner's approach to Hölderlin – and implicitly Heidegger's too – for basing their interpretation on Hölderlin's famous letters to Böhlendorf instead of acknowledging the content of the poem as first appeal (1994: 176). The same approach is still in evidence many years later in his brilliant readings of the challenging poetry of Paul Celan (1997).

Gadamer employs the term "aesthetics" in a technical sense to refer to a specific consciousness of art that, though prepared for earlier, became clearly apparent only toward the end of the eighteenth century. *Truth and Method* records in its first part the rise of aesthetic consciousness in the passage from Kant's *Critique of Judgment* to the writings of Schiller. In the course of that transition, the concept of genius is said to take the place of judgments of taste, and at the same time the artwork loses its connection with the world. Gadamer's challenge to aesthetic consciousness does not take the form of denying that its experience of art is genuine. The point is, rather, that aesthetic consciousness misunderstands its experience; it is more than it knows itself to be.

Gadamer, typically, does not ask his readers to open themselves up to new experiences so much as to awaken themselves to familiar experiences. So, even the term "consciousness" in the phrase "aesthetic consciousness" is ultimately found inadequate insofar as the artwork is the underlying subject of the experience of art, rather than the human subject. His frequent appeals to the model of play are in large measure introduced to render this idea more acceptable. What draws and holds the player is the game, which thus itself becomes the *subjectum* of the playing (1989: 106, 490).

It is striking to find that Gadamer's first scholarly essay, "Plato and the Poets," anticipates, and even illuminates, his subsequent writings on art. Plato's critique of mimetic art in book 10 of the *Republic* is read by Gadamer as a critique of the moral consequences of aesthetic consciousness. Plato banished the poets from the ideal state, on Gadamer's interpretation, because the joy taken in their imitations led to a kind of self-alienation in which one forgets oneself. Losing oneself in a poem or a piece of music in this way was precisely the frame of mind that aesthetics cultivated. In other words, Gadamer understands Plato to have attacked the attitude that would subsequently become known as "aesthetic" (1980: 65). What aesthetic consciousness tended to forget, but which was well known to Plato, was that there are forms of art that clearly escape these limitations and thus serve as a corrective to the interpretation. Hymns of praise sung to a god or some outstanding individual bind those who hear it to each other. They prepare their audience to meet its obligations.

In this early essay from 1934, Gadamer appears to accept Plato's distinction between different kinds of poetry, and simply follows Plato's displacement of the question of poetry into philosophical dialogue. Philosophical dialogue has its own poetry, which makes it the song of praise most appropriate for those politics that are "almost incurable" (1980: 66). Subsequently, Gadamer would likely have concluded that all works of art, and not just hymns of praise, make a claim on their audience. That is to say, self-alienation is only one moment of the experience of art which, properly described, also includes a return to self.

Nevertheless, the self to whom one returns following the experience of art is not the self with which one began. "The experience of art . . . does not leave him who has it unchanged" (1989: 100). Art does not represent a realm into which one can escape, only to return subsequently to the life one had temporarily bracketed. The artwork issues a challenge to everybody who experiences it. By its dissolution of the familiar, the artwork says not only, "You are this," but, with Rilke, "You must change your life [*Du musst dein Leben ändern*]" (*Archaïscher Torso Apollos*, cited in Gadamer

1976: 104). In German, one would say that the experience of art is an *Erfahrung*, in the Hegelian sense of a transformative experience that one undergoes, and not an *Erlebnis*, the lived experience described by Dilthey.

Aesthetics is not only a frame of mind, it has an institutional reality, for example, in the museum. Just as aesthetic consciousness attempts to take up the aesthetic quality of the work independently of its moral or religious content, thereby abstracting from the conditions of the work's accessibility, its purpose, and its function, so the isolation of works from their contexts by placing them in "collections" can seem to disregard everything in which a work is rooted. Gadamer calls this abstraction "aesthetic differentiation" (1989: 85). Whereas cultural historians respond to aesthetic differentiation by attempting to reconstruct the conditions of the original construction, as if one could thereby reproduce an understanding of the original purpose of the work, Gadamerian hermeneutics takes a somewhat different approach. The point at which aesthetics becomes reabsorbed in hermeneutics, beyond anything that simply historiological investigations can accomplish, is when one attains a living relationship with the work, such that it still has something to say to us as people in history (1989: 164–9).

See also NINETEENTH- AND TWENTIETH-CENTURY CONTINENTAL AESTHETICS; AESTHETIC ATTITUDE; AESTHETICISM; BAUMGARTEN; HEIDEGGER; HERMENEUTICS; MUSEUMS.

BIBLIOGRAPHY

Primary sources
[1934] 1980. "Plato and the Poets." In *Dialogue and Dialectic*. P. C. Smith (trans.). New Haven: Yale University Press, 39–72.
[1947] 1994. "Hölderlin and the Future." In *Literature and Philosophy in Dialogue*. R. Paslick (trans.). Albany: State University of New York Press, 87–108, 176.
[1960] 1989. *Truth and Method*. J. Weinsheimer & D. G. Marshall (trans.). 2nd edn. New York: Crossroad.
[1964] 1976. "Ästhetik und Hermeneutik." In *Philosophical Hermeneutics*. D. E. Linge (trans.). Berkeley: University of California Press, 95–104.
1967. *Kleine Schriften*, vol. ii: *Interpretation*. Tübingen. (Some of the essays in this volume

may be found in translation in *The Relevance of the Beautiful and Other Essays* (see below).)

[1977] 1986. *The Relevance of the Beautiful and Other Essays*. N. Walker (trans.). Cambridge: Cambridge University Press.

[1986] 1997. "Who Am I and Who Are You?" In *Gadamer on Celan*. R. Heinemann & B. Krajewski (trans.). Albany: State University of New York Press, 63–165.

ROBERT BERNASCONI

gardens Although some of the "founding fathers" of aesthetics, including Shaftesbury, Kant, and Hegel, made interesting, if only passing, remarks on garden appreciation, neither gardening nor gardens have attracted great attention in modern philosophical aesthetics. The many reasons for this comparative neglect include the perception of gardening as an activity too useful and practical to belong among the Fine Arts, and the relative immunity of garden design to the avant-garde gestures, familiar in several twentieth-century arts, that have shaped the preoccupations of modern aesthetics. The outdoor analogues to experimental artworks in the studio are more likely to be found in "earthworks" and other environmental interventions than in gardens, perhaps because of the constraints implied by gardens being, typically, places that people live in and with.

A more general reason for neglect has been the "ambiguous" status of the garden as a prime example of what Malcolm Budd (2002: 7) calls "nature as affected by humanity." For Hegel (1975: 627), gardening's reliance on nature makes it an "imperfect art," while its intervention in the natural world makes of the garden an equally imperfect specimen of nature. The garden, it has seemed to some, is a fit object of reflection neither for the philosophy of art nor for natural or environmental aesthetics. Ironically, however, this same "ambiguity" has become, in an intellectual climate hospitable to the "deconstruction" of dichotomies like that of art versus nature, a reason for renewed philosophical attention to the garden. The garden is important, writes Mara Miller, as "an attempt at the reconciliation of opposites which constrain our existence" (1993: 25). Certainly the image of the gar-

dener as a creative agent who is nevertheless thoroughly dependent on the cooperation of natural processes has a popular resonance at the beginning of the twenty-first century.

There are a number of themes closely related to the question of the garden's "ambiguity," on which contemporary aestheticians have focused. But before articulating these, mention should be made of the increasing attention being paid to the application to gardens of some familiar issues in aesthetics. Unsurprisingly, for example, there has been discussion of the adequacy or otherwise, in the case of gardens, of the "institutional" theory of art. Given the creation of such unusual gardens as Charles Jencks's "Garden of Cosmic Speculation" or Ian Hamilton Finlay's "Little Sparta," should we describe something as a garden just in case it is deemed to be one by the "gardenworld," the horticultural equivalent of the "artworld"? Again, proposals have been made, parallel to familiar ones in the ontology of artworks, about the kind of existence that gardens enjoy. It has been urged, for example, that rather as we distinguish a novel from the printed physical object on a bookshelf, so we should distinguish the garden as a "virtual" entity – a "world" imaginatively to explore and appreciate – from the physical garden, "a particular chunk of Surrey," say (Ross 1998: 179).

The three most prominent themes addressed in contemporary philosophy of gardens, however, are those relating to the perception of the garden as "nature as affected by humanity." These themes are, moreover, recognizable descendants of ones that were prominent in eighteenth- and nineteenth-century debates.

The debate that dominated eighteenth-century garden writing, and which has recurred ever since, is whether gardens should, like the formal, regular ones at Versailles and Hampton Court, wear their art on their sleeves or, instead, like the informal "English" garden, more closely resemble natural places. (Joseph Addison boasted that his garden would strike a foreigner as a "natural wilderness.") The debate was one to which both Kant and Hegel contributed, with the former preferring the "English" garden – in keeping with his calls for art to be "free from the constraint of arbitrary rules" and to "look like Nature" – and the latter denouncing as a deception what was, after all, a carefully designed "natural wilderness." The main issue that descends from this debate and has been addressed by later philosophers is no longer the normative one of what gardens should look like – artworks or natural places – but the relationship of garden appreciation to the appreciation of art and nature respectively. (It does not follow from a garden's looking natural that it is to be appreciated in the way natural places are. Maybe, as with many Chinese and Japanese gardens, the intention is that they be enjoyed as skillful representations of mountains, islands, or whatever.) Some writers (e.g., Miller 1993: ch. 4) stress how very different appreciation of a garden is from that of, say, a painting. A garden is not a discrete, "framed" object to stare at, but something we are surrounded by, move about in, and engage with using all our senses: and, unlike the case with a painting, our perception and hence enjoyment of the garden is crucially subject to changes in the weather, the season, the light, and other factors.

Other writers, though, emphasize the difference between garden and nature appreciation, arguing in particular that it is a necessary feature of people's authentic enjoyment of a natural place that they recognize that it is not, to any significant degree, a human product. (The discovery that the "natural" scene was, like Addison's garden, an artifice would cause the enjoyment to evaporate, or to modulate into a different type of enjoyment – in the designer's skill, say.) It is tempting to steer a middle course here and maintain that the appreciation of a garden should be a fusion of art and nature appreciation. But this suggestion is problematic. It is surely not the case that enjoyment of a garden factors out, as it were, into admiration of artistic contributions and pleasure at the sight of natural objects, like trees. Arguably, garden appreciation is *sui generis*, and not the joint product of two other modes of appreciation to which it is therefore reducible (see Cooper 2006: ch. 3).

A second normative debate in the eighteenth century concerned the desirability or otherwise of making gardens with symbolic purposes. Opinions differed, for example, on the attempt at Stourhead to represent scenes from Virgil's *Aeneid* or on the aim of "picturesque" gardens to recall famous paintings.

While some garden historians lament the decline of these symbolic ambitions, the focus of contemporary philosophers – in keeping with a wider tendency in modern aesthetics – has not been on the issue of whether or what gardens ought to signify, but on distinguishing the various and very different ways in which gardens can signify or have meaning (e.g., see Ross 1998). Distinctions are consequently drawn between, for example, the representational, the expressive, and the allegorical powers of gardens, or between the meaning a garden may have for a person and the cultural significance it may possess as a symptom or reflection of an age or society.

Particular attention has been paid to distinctive aspects of meaning that gardens, in virtue of their "ambiguous" place between art and nature, are especially apt to convey. It has been argued, for example, that some Japanese temple gardens paradigmatically exemplify the Zen Buddhist antipathy to drawing any sharp distinction between nature and artifice. Certainly the reliance of a garden, if it is to flourish, not only on the commitment of the gardener but on the cooperation of nature makes it an apt symbol or epiphany of an intimate relationship – a "codependence," one might say – between human creativity and the world in which it is exercised (see Cooper 2006: ch. 7).

Closely associated with the debates surrounding the relations between gardens, art, and nature in the eighteenth and nineteenth centuries was a further debate with a distinctly moral edge. We noted above Hegel's hostility to the informal "English" garden on the ground that it was a deceptive imitation of nature. For Schopenhauer (1969: 404–5), by contrast, it was formal "French" gardens that deserved censure, as blatant "tokens of [nature's] slavery" and mirrors of "the will of the possessor." These morally charged positions have their contemporary descendants. While few people now worry about being "deceived" into thinking that an informal garden is really "wild" and "natural," some writers are concerned that the garden presents an all too benign and anodyne image of nature, which thereby obstructs a proper, informed appreciation of nature itself. And Schopenhauer's strictures against the "French" garden are prescient of a contemporary animus, especially marked among "deep ecologists," against gardens in general. For them, all gardens signify a human enslavement of nature.

It is important to recognize that these moral concerns are not disjoined from aesthetic ones. For Schopenhauer, after all, aesthetic contemplation involves a suspension or quietening of the will – something hard to achieve if the objects being contemplated are, like the gardens at Versailles, themselves unmistakable "mirrors" of the will. A more moderate implication of Schopenhauer's strictures than those drawn by "deep ecologists" would be that gardens should be – and appear to be – places where care and effort is taken to cooperate with natural processes and to attend to the good of the plants and creatures that belong there. This would not, for example, exclude all topiary (a particular bugbear of ecological critics of gardens), but it would militate against shaping foliage into Mickey Mouse, a giant phallus, or anything else that singularly fails to honor the integrity of the tree or bush (see Brook & Brady 2003).

It is, more generally, a salient feature of contemporary philosophical discussions of gardens that they address issues at the interface of aesthetics and ethics. In doing so, the discussions belong to a long tradition of garden writing – from Virgil and Pliny the Younger to Karel Čapek, Hermann Hesse, and Michael Pollan in the twentieth century – that proposes a close relationship between the informed enjoyment of both gardens and gardening and the good life. For some time to come, one may surmise, philosophers will continue to explore the attractive vision expressed in this tradition that much of the significance and satisfaction people find in the garden owes to its being a theater for the creative exercise of such virtues as hope, humility, and respect for the integrity of living things.

See also AESTHETICS OF THE ENVIRONMENT; AESTHETICS OF THE EVERYDAY.

BIBLIOGRAPHY

Adams, William H. 1991. *Gardens through History: Nature Perfected*. New York: Abbeville.

Brook, Isis & Brady, Emily. 2003. "Topiary: Ethics and Aesthetics," *Ethics and the Environment*, 8, 128–41.

Budd, Malcolm. 2002. *The Aesthetic Appreciation of Nature: Essays on the Aesthetics of Nature*. Oxford: Clarendon.

Cooper, David E. 2006. *A Philosophy of Gardens*. Oxford: Clarendon.

Hegel, G. W. F. 1975 [1835–8]. *Aesthetics*. J. Knox (trans.). Oxford: Clarendon.

Miller, Mara. 1993. *The Garden as Art*. New York: State University of New York Press.

Pollan, Michael. 1996. *Second Nature: A Gardener's Education*. London: Bloomsbury.

Richardson, Tim & Kingsbury, Nöel (eds.). 2005. *Vista: The Culture and Politics of Gardens*. London: Frances Lincoln.

Ross, Stephanie. 1998. *What Gardens Mean*. Chicago: University of Chicago Press.

Schopenhauer, Arthur. 1969 [1819/44]. *The World as Will and Representation*. 2 vols. E. F. J. Payne (trans.). New York: Dover.

DAVID E. COOPER

genre A type or kind (of art); the term is frequently used as a substitute for a general concept of stylistic kind.

There is a slightly special sense of the word that applies to a certain sort of painting – namely, to paintings of low life or "real" or "ordinary" life. Elsewhere, the idea of genre has come to mean a kind of art in a rather specific sense, which has far more to do with subject matter than with style, so that style may indicate genre but not define it.

In the case of literature and the narrative arts generally, recognizing genre is a precondition for any sort of fair critical judgment. To read *Macbeth* as a detective story, as James Thurber suggested, or the first two books of *Paradise Lost* as if they were an early form of science fiction, would clearly be absurd. Similar mistakes may be more subtle, hence more misleading. Some people object to the sort of fairy-tale that ends with the princess and the woodcutter getting married and "living happily ever after," insisting that such tales are grossly unrealistic; or that the stories of P. G. Wodehouse lack deep sexual motivation. But, with stories of that sort, that genre, such objections are not to the point. "Living happily ever after" is how it is in fairy-tales, and indeed, that style of ending itself indicates the genre to which the story one has been told belongs, just as Wodehouse's style indicates the sort of story he is telling. It seems as inappropriate to object to the lack of psychological depth in a "standard" detective story or science fiction fantasy as to object of

Gilgamesh that it is hard to identify with the main character.

The tacit principles here are roughly these: we are invited by fictional narratives to assume certain events or situations, so that what we may be told happens next will be against a background of the nonfictional expectations that we, as readers, will have. Our capacity to be surprised, reassured, unconvinced, or astonished by the outcome we are in fact given constitutes our intelligently understanding the narrative. In the case of a purely factual narrative, we bring to bear on this all that we know or believe about the "real" world, whether in terms of general principles of inference, laws of nature, or, more loosely, how we suppose facts and situations to "hang together." Thus, if a factual report has it that someone called Pickwick or Holmes did such and such at such a place and time, any further information – birth certificates, meteorological records, the latest discoveries in medical science, and so on – will be relevant to assessing the truth or plausibility of the story we are told. But, if a story about Holmes or Pickwick is a fiction, clearly neither the failure to find the birth certificates, nor a check on the weather at the time of the events, will be relevant. Yet, for all that, plausibility must be in question at some point. Snow in London in August would, in a Sherlock Holmes story, clearly count against its plausibility and thus be relevant first to our understanding of the narrative, and then to our critical judgment. For a narrative, however fictional, to be intelligible at all there must be a minimal, normally very rich, reference to what both reader and author take to be the way the real world actually is. Narrative genre essentially has to do with how this may play a part in our understanding of the work.

It can be useful to distinguish between the fictional elements in a story (fictional characters, places, events) and the quite differently fictional assumptions that we, the readers, will have to make in order to follow the kind of story we are being told. These latter have to do with genre. L. C. Knights (1964) rightly objected to those who, reading the line of Lady Macbeth's, "I have given suck, and know / How tender 'tis to love the babe that milks me," deemed it appropriate to ask how many children we should suppose her to have had. (It is clearly not an appropriate question, even though it is a logical truth that if anyone has had some children she must have had some number of children.) A then fashionable stricture to limit the reader's interpretative attention to the "words on the page" is misleading: questions about tacit psychological motivation are, clearly and especially for Shakespeare, of central relevance, yet plainly involve questions that go well beyond the merely verbal text.

In a detective story, precisely the sort of question that Knights ruled out for *Macbeth* would be relevant, though other questions may not be. Again, when Rapunzel lets down her hair for her lover to climb up, questions about the subsequent state of her scalp are no more relevant than are questions about the likelihood of giants exceeding escape velocity when they put on seven-league boots: though such questions might well matter for some science fiction.

In the central genre of narrative fiction that F. R. Leavis identified as the canon of the "great tradition," concerns with the plausibility of motivation are all-important, since questions for the reader about what it would have been like to be a protagonist in such a story are central to that genre. Yet the assumption that such characters have a peculiar psychological transparency is no more part of the fictional narrative than it is part of the plot of a play staged "naturalistically" before an audience that one of the walls of the room is transparent, or part of the narrative that when Hamlet speaks in soliloquy the other fictional characters at Elsinore go strangely deaf. Such devices control those judgments of plausibility that we need to make in order to construe the narrative. They define this fictional genre.

Fictional genres such as fairy-tales, the heroic epic, fantasy, nonsense fantasy that makes fiction out of the logically absurd (such as the stories of Lewis Carroll), science fiction, detective fiction, the novel of psychological insight, and so on are loose yet familiar classifications. Often stylistic devices in the manner of telling the story or in the ways in which the reader is addressed can be relied on to indicate what sort of assumptions the reader should make when construing the story – what to expect, what to take for granted. But there have always been deliberately ambiguous fictional genres. Tragicomedy was for the seventeenth century something of this sort, as was so-called "magic realism" 200 years later: in such cases the point is to challenge the reader, via a self-conscious awareness that it is with fiction that he or she has to deal, into a direct confrontation with the very idea of plausibility or verisimilitude itself. For what might be termed "genre unease" can be one of the most effective ways of enforcing a reader's reflection, via those devices of art that exploit these very capacities, on the nature of imagination and belief.

In the case of nonliterary, nonnarrative art these issues press in on us in slightly different ways. Various forms of figurative and non-figurative painting and sorts of music that can be hard to classify, raise similar embarrassments: all have to do with the propriety of critical presuppositions. What, for instance, does one have the right to expect of, say, popular music, rock music with a political content, popular art as opposed to Pop Art, graffiti art, amateur art with pretensions toward something else, highly professional painting with the superficial appearance of amateur art, various forms of minimalist and conceptual art, and so on? To present the list, even at random, is to indicate a further twist to the puzzle – namely, that it is very much integral to the subject matter of modernist and postmodernist art to make such embarrassments a central theme of the process of art itself (compare Danto 1981). From Dada onwards, what might be called deliberate "genre shock" can seem to be what the arts are about. In effect, this is to incorporate within the content of art "philosophical" anxieties about the status of the works, and hence philosophical questions valid in their own right.

See also LITERATURE; FICTION, NATURE OF; FICTION, TURTH IN; NARRATIVE; STYLE; WALTON.

BIBLIOGRAPHY

Danto, Arthur C. 1981. *The Transfiguration of the Commonplace*. Cambridge, MA: Harvard University Press.

Dodsworth, Martin. 1973. "Genre and the Experience of Literature." In *Philosophy and the Arts*. Royal Institute of Philosophy Lectures, vol. 6. G. Vesey (ed.). London: Macmillan, 211–27.

Fowler, Alastair. 1982. *Kinds of Literature*. Oxford: Clarendon.

Knights, L. C. 1964 [1933]. "How Many Children Had Lady Macbeth? An Essay in the Theory and Practice of Shakespeare Criticism." In *Explorations*. New York: New York University Press, 15–54.

Walton, Kendall L. 1970. "Categories of Art," *Philosophical Review*, 79, 334–67.

Walton, Kendall L. 1990. *Mimesis as Make-Believe: On the Foundation of the Representational Arts*. Cambridge, MA: Harvard University Press.

ANDREW HARRISON

Gombrich, Sir Ernst (Hans Josef) (1909–2001) Austrian-born historian and theorist of the visual arts.

"There really is no such thing as Art. There are only artists," are the opening words of Gombrich's immensely popular *The Story of Art* (1950: 5). Still, until the twentieth century at least, and despite some deviations, painters and sculptors have, since the very earliest times, been inspired by a predominant endeavor – to provide "convincing representations" of the visible world (or "illusions" as Gombrich, perhaps misleadingly, calls them). That is why a story of art is possible. And not just a story, for Gombrich's starting point is the fact – one which he urges us to find surprising – that painting and sculpture have a *history*. Despite its subtitle, the "central problem" of his most influential work, *Art and Illusion: A Study in the Psychology of Pictorial Representation*, is "why representation should have a history; why it should have taken mankind so long to arrive at a plausible rendering of visual effects that create the illusion of life-likeness" (1980: 246).

That painting has a history, and not simply a chronology, is evident from the existence of styles and traditions that enable us, usually without much trouble, correctly to allocate anonymous paintings to their periods. More than that, we should recognize with Heinrich Wölfflin that "not everything is possible in every period" (quoted in Gombrich 1980: 4). A thirteenth-century work that looked very like a Monet would not be an Impressionist painting, since Impressionism is intelligible only as a response to the canons of the Academy. Gombrich (1984) has hailed Hegel as "the father of art history" precisely because of the latter's acute awareness that painting not only develops but that in crucial respects the stages of this development could not have occurred in a different order.

That certain fashionable views, old and new, about the nature of artistic activity make it impossible to understand how art could have a history is sufficient reason for rejecting them. If painting were simply a matter of an individual's "copying what he sees" or "only . . . an expression of personal vision, there could be no history of art" (1980: 3). But these views are anyway inadequate on psychological and philosophical grounds. According to Gombrich, no clear sense can be attached to the notion of "copying what one sees"; and even the "Abstract Expressionist" must rely on tradition not only to furnish an inherited vocabulary of "affects" but as something which gives a point – albeit a rebellious or nihilistic one – to his work.

Granted that art has a history, we require an adequate psychology if this history is to be properly characterized. It is implausible, for example – despite the favored rhetoric of many contemporary art teachers – to suppose that in any serious sense of "see," Egyptian artists, Giotto, Constable, and Monet "saw" the world differently from one another. Perception may have altered in marginal ways, but not in the massive ways we should have to suppose if we took all these artists as accurately recording what they perceived. This may encourage us to jump to an opposite extreme and argue that their paintings merely manifest a number of different "conventions" for representing the world, barely constrained by – and not to be judged by – any ideal of fidelity to how that world actually looks. But not only is this contradicted by the stated aim of many such artists to provide "convincing representations," it also denies the obvious. One should indeed "stress the conventional element in many modes of representation," but carried to an extreme this is "also nonsense." For while Constable's *Wivenhoe Park* "is not a mere transcript of nature . . . it still remains true that it is a closer rendering of the motif than is that of the child" (1980: 252). *Pace* Herbert Read, perspective is no mere convention, but enables a genuine and objective similarity between a painting and a scene viewed through a window to be achieved (Gombrich 1980: ch. 8; 1982).

But it is to the ideal of the "innocent eye" that Gombrich devotes most critical attention. On this view (e.g., Ruskin's), painting has progressed through artists' gradually setting aside the assumptions and knowledge that intrude between their recognition or interpretation of the scenes before them and what they actually and directly *see* – colored specks, shimmers, etc. Only with Turner and the Impressionists have painters achieved this disengagement and succeeded in recording the deliverances of "innocent" perception. Gombrich is not entirely unsympathetic to this view, for he too wants to stress the role that knowledge of the real world, or "expectations" based on experience of it, play in our recognition of what is there to see. Indeed, his objection is that these "expectations" play such a crucial role in perception that there can be no complete "disengagement" from them. "[W]e cannot disentangle seeing from knowing, or rather, from expecting" so as to "see" anything free from all interpretation and thereby proceed to paint what we "innocently" "see" (1980: 187). There is another obstacle to "innocence": our perception of the world has been indelibly shaped by the traditions of painting itself. Even if we could "bracket" the world of material objects so as to focus on shapes, colors, etc., how we focus on these and how we would record them in our own paintings will have been irredeemably influenced by the Claudes, Constables, or Monets that belong to our cultural inheritance.

Debates about the roles of convention and tradition, and about the possibility of "pure" observation, are familiar of course in the history and philosophy of science. Gombrich, inspired by Constable's rhetorical question "Why . . . may not landscape painting be considered as a branch of natural philosophy, of which pictures are but the experiments?" takes this parallel very seriously. Indeed, it is Sir Karl Popper's "logic of scientific discovery," Gombrich believes, that provides a key to the understanding of artistic discovery as well. According to Popper, scientific theories cannot result from unaided observation and induction since, except against the background provided by some hypothesis, one would have no idea what observations were relevant or what they could possibly show. Science proceeds, rather, through a process of "conjecture and refutation," with scientists *creating* hypotheses that indicate observable data which would, if obtained, serve to falsify the hypotheses. Science, therefore, is *essentially* historical, for without a context of earlier theories succumbing to refutation, there would be nothing to motivate the conjecturing of new hypotheses. While science progresses, through refutations of earlier theories, no theory can pretend to truth since, if it has real empirical content, it too must stand open to falsification.

Analogously, for Gombrich, painting proceeds, not through artists copying unguided observations of nature, but through "schemas and corrections." " 'Making comes before matching' . . . the matching process itself proceeds through the stages of 'schema and correction.' Every artist has to know and construct a schema before he can adjust it to the needs of portrayal" (1980: 99). At a more macro level, the "schemas" that characterize the style of an age are "corrected" when the paintings they generate fail to "match" aspects of experience that have become important to people to capture. So art, like science, is essentially historical. And just as no scientific theory can pretend to truth, nor can any genre of painting: for we can never exclude new dimensions of experience that only an artist of genius is able both to reveal and to record. It takes a Van Gogh, for example, to discover that "you can see the visible world as a vortex of lines" (1980: 203).

While Gombrich's account of the activity and history of art has been extremely influential, it has also been criticized on a number of counts (e.g., see Woodfield 1996). Some later art historians, for instance, have argued that *The Story of Art* in particular is excessively "traditional" in approach, too much focused on "great *men*" and "style" (Arnold 2004: 35). Of greater philosophical interest has been criticism of Gombrich's rejection of the "innocent eye" approach. It is unclear for a start, so it is argued, that we should compare too seriously the artist's "problem" of representing the scene before him with that of the scientist erecting a theory on the basis of the data he or she observes. Does the former really have to "interpret" in the same sense as the latter?

Second, critics have wondered whether, without the "innocent eye," it is possible, as Gombrich insists it is, to speak of paintings

having an "objective likeness" or "fidelity" to our experience of the world. He defines "objective likeness" in terms of the accurate information about the world that a painting may afford us. But this seems to elide the difference between a "convincing representation" and a correct verbal description. It is difficult not to suspect that the analysis is the wrong way round: a painting gives accurate information, typically, because it really is like its motif.

Finally, Gombrich's confidence in experimental psychology's having established that seeing is always a matter of interpreting may be misplaced. Doubtless, there is a sense of "see" in which a person can only be said to see *X* if that is what he takes it to be. But it is a philosophical issue whether there is not a different, and possibly more basic, sense in which one can be said to see *X* without conceptualizing it as such (Dretske 1983). At the very least, it sounds exaggerated to hold that "To 'see' *means* to guess at something 'out there' " (1980: 254; emphasis added), or that "it is *always* hard to distinguish what is given to us from what we supplement in the process of projection" (1980: 203; ; emphasis added). Is it really that hard to distinguish the bare lines of the famous duck/rabbit drawing from my "projection" onto them of a rabbit (or a duck, as may be)?

See also DRAWING, PAINTING, AND PRINTMAKING; SCULPTURE; ART HISTORY; DEPICTION; HEGEL; ILLUSION; PERSPECTIVE; PICTURE PERCEPTION; REPRESENTATION; STYLE; TRADITION.

BIBLIOGRAPHY

Primary sources
1950. *The Story of Art*. London: Phaidon.
1973. "Illusion in Art." In *Illusion in Nature and Art*. E. Gombrich & R. Gregory (eds.). London: Duckworth, 194–243.
1980. *Art and Illusion: A Study in the Psychology of Pictorial Representation*. Oxford: Phaidon.
1982. *The Image and the Eye*. Oxford: Phaidon.
1984. "The Father of Art History: A Reading of the *Lectures on Aesthetics* of G. W. F. Hegel." In *Tributes: Interpreters of Our Cultural Tradition*. Ithaca: Cornell University Press, 51–69.

Secondary sources
Arnold, Dana. 2004. *Art History: A Very Short Introduction*. Oxford: Oxford University Press.

Dretske, Fred. 1983. *Knowledge and the Flow of Information*. Boston: MIT Press, esp. ch. 6.
Woodfield, Richard (ed.). 1996. *Gombrich on Art*. Manchester: Manchester University Press.

DAVID E. COOPER

Goodman, Nelson (1906–1998) American philosopher who made major contributions to epistemology, metaphysics, and philosophy of science, as well as to aesthetics. In his youth he ran an art gallery, and throughout his life he was an avid collector of art. He was professor emeritus of philosophy at Harvard University.

The arts enhance understanding, Goodman (1976) contends, and aesthetics explains how they do so. Aesthetics, then, is a branch of epistemology. He maintains that understanding a work of art is not a matter of appreciating it, or finding beauty in it, or having an "aesthetic experience" of it. Like understanding an utterance or inscription, understanding a work of art consists in interpreting it correctly. This involves recognizing how and what it symbolizes, and how what it symbolizes bears on other visions and versions of our worlds. Works of art, then, belong to symbol systems with determinate syntactic and semantic structures. Much of *Languages of Art* (first published in 1968) is devoted to delineating the structures of the systems that the various arts employ, detailing their powers and limitations.

Goodman recognizes two basic modes of reference: denotation and exemplification. A symbol denotes whatever it applies to. A name denotes its bearer; a portrait its subject; a predicate the members of its extension; and so on. Fictive symbols fail to denote. Their significance, he believes, depends on what symbols denote them. Because the term "Ophelia description" denotes a range of names and descriptions in Shakespeare's play, those names and descriptions collectively fix Ophelia's fictive identity (1972: 221–38).

Some symbols – including abstract art, most instrumental music, much dance – do not even purport to denote. They deploy other modes of reference exclusively. Prominent among these is exemplification, whereby a symbol refers to some of its own properties. A Mondrian painting, for example, exemplifies squareness. It not only consists of squares, but points up this fact

about itself. That is, it refers to the squareness of the shapes it contains. No more than denotation is exemplification peculiar to the arts. It is critical in commerce and science as well. A commercial paint sample exemplifies its color and sheen; a blood sample, the presence of antibodies. In art and elsewhere, exemplifying symbols afford epistemic access to properties that they sample.

Exemplification and denotation are not mutually exclusive. Works of art that denote typically exemplify as well. *Wivenhoe Park* exemplifies Constable's style while denoting the park. Tolstoy's description of the Battle of Borodino describes the battle and exemplifies his attitude toward war. Critical to Goodman's aesthetics is the recognition that symbols can, and often do, simultaneously perform a variety of referential functions.

Denotation and exemplification need not be literal. A distinctive feature of Goodman's theory is that metaphorical symbols genuinely refer to their figurative subjects. "Bulldog" genuinely denotes Churchill; the *Pietà* genuinely exemplifies sorrow. Reference, then, is not restricted to literal reference, nor truth to literal truth.

Symbols typically belong to schemes – systems of signs that collectively classify the objects in a realm. "Bulldog" belongs to a scheme that, in its literal application, sorts the realm of dogs. In metaphor, Goodman maintains, the scheme transfers to a new realm. The organization of dogs into breeds is reapplied to classify people. Because under that transfer Churchill falls within the extension of "bulldog," Churchill is metaphorically a bulldog. New patterns and distinctions in the human population emerge; for the metaphor sorts people into classes that no literal predicate exactly captures. This is one reason why metaphors resist literal paraphrase.

In referring to a property that it metaphorically possesses, an object metaphorically exemplifies that property. Thus, Churchill metaphorically exemplifies bulldoggishness when serving as an example of that trait. Expression, Goodman contends, is a form of metaphorical exemplification. A work of art, functioning as such, expresses the properties that it metaphorically exemplifies. Being inanimate, the *Pietà* cannot literally exemplify sorrow. But it can and does exemplify that property metaphorically. It therefore expresses sorrow. Expression, as Goodman construes it, is not restricted to feelings. For aesthetic symbols metaphorically exemplify other features as well. Music may express color; sculpture, motion; painting, depth. There is evidently no a priori limit on the features that works of art can express (1976: 45–95).

Reference need not be exclusively denotational or exclusively exemplificational. Sometimes, Goodman maintains, reference is transmitted via chains consisting of denotational and exemplificational links. Allusion is a case in point. The simplest allusions involve three-link chains. A symbol alludes to its referent by exemplifying a feature that it shares with its referent, or by denoting an object that exemplifies its referent. Thus, passages in *Ulysses* allude to Roman Catholic prayers by exemplifying the cadences of those prayers. And the figure of a dog in a Dürer print alludes to loyalty by denoting dogs, which exemplify loyalty. Longer and more complex chains also occur. And multiple routes of reference may secure an allusion. Regardless of length or configuration, so long as reference is transmitted across such a chain, indirect reference occurs (1984: 55–71)

A variation must be like its theme in some respects and different from it in others. But merely having shared and contrasting features is not enough. Otherwise, every passage would be a variation on every other. A passage does not qualify as a variation, Goodman contends, unless it refers to the theme via the exemplification of both sorts of features. Variation, then, is a form of indirect reference (Goodman & Elgin 1988: 66–82).

Scientific symbols, Goodman urges, are relatively attenuated. They symbolize along comparatively few dimensions. Aesthetic symbols, by contrast, are relatively replete. Comparatively many of their aspects function symbolically. The same configuration of ink on paper might be an electrocardiogram or a drawing. If the former, only the shape is significant. If the latter, the precise color and thickness of the line at each point, the exact shade of the background, the exact size and shape of the paper and of the line on the paper, even the quality of the paper itself, may be significant. Moreover, the electrocardiogram is referentially austere. It

denotes a heartbeat and perhaps exemplifies certain symptomatology. The drawing is apt to perform myriad complex and interanimating referential functions. Via denotation, exemplification, expression, and allusion, it refers to a multiplicity of referents through a variety of routes (Goodman 1976: 229–30).

The status of a line as an electrocardiogram or a drawing depends on its function. It counts as a work of art so long as it functions as an aesthetic symbol. And it may function aesthetically at some times and not at others. The crucial question, then, is not "What is art?" but "When is art?" Although Goodman supplies no criterion of aesthetic functioning, he identifies its symptoms: exemplification, relative repleteness, complex and indirect reference, syntactic and semantic density. A symbol system is syntactically dense if the finest differences among signs make for different symbols. It is semantically dense if it has the resources to mark the finest differences among objects in its domain. As symptoms, these features are neither necessary nor sufficient, but they are indications that an object is functioning as a work of art (1978: 71–89).

Interpreting a work involves discovering what symbols constitute it, how they symbolize, what they refer to, and to what effect. Because of the richness and complexity of aesthetic symbols, the task may be endless. And multiple, divergent interpretations may be correct. But it is not the case, Goodman maintains, that every interpretation is correct. Only such interpretations as make maximally good sense of the work's symbolic functions are acceptable. His pluralism consists in his recognition that more than one interpretation may do so (Goodman & Elgin 1988: 222).

To construe works of art as symbols and the aesthetic attitude as a quest for understanding might seem to anaesthetize art. It does not. For the feelings that a work evokes are sources of understanding. Emotional sensitivity, like perceptual sensitivity, enables us to discern subtle but significant features. In the arts, Goodman maintains, emotions function cognitively (Goodman 1976: 245–52).

Merit, too, transforms from an end to a means. Rather than seeking to understand a work in order to evaluate it, we use evaluations as sources of understanding. An unexpected assessment kindles curiosity, prompting us to attend more carefully to the work – to search for features that previously eluded. The knowledge that a given work has (or lacks) aesthetic merit may then help us to understand it better (1972: 120–1).

See also TWENTIETH-CENTURY ANGLO-AMERICAN AESTHETICS; DEPICTION; EXPRESSION; METAPHOR; NOTATIONS; ONTOLOGICAL CONTEXTUALISM; ONTOLOGY OF ARTWORKS; PERSPECTIVE; REPRESENTATION.

BIBLIOGRAPHY

Primary sources
[1968] 1976. *Languages of Art*. Indianapolis: Hackett.
1972. *Problems and Projects*. Indianapolis: Hackett.
1978. *Ways of Worldmaking*. Indianapolis: Hackett.
1984. *Of Mind and Other Matters*. Cambridge, MA: Harvard University Press.
1988. (with Elgin, Catherine Z.) *Reconceptions*. Indianapolis: Hackett.

Secondary sources
1974. "Supplement: Symposium on Skills and Symbols in the Arts," *Monist*, 58.
1978. "The Philosophy of Nelson Goodman," *Erkenntnis*, 12 (special issue), 3–179.
2000. "Symposium: The Legacy of Nelson Goodman," *Journal of Aesthetics and Art Criticism*, 58, 213–53.
Elgin, Catherine Z. (ed.). 1997a. *Nelson Goodman's Philosophy of Art*. New York: Garland.
Elgin, Catherine Z. (ed.). 1997b. *Nelson Goodman's Theory of Symbols and Its Applications*. New York: Garland.
Elgin, Catherine Z. 2001. "The Legacy of Nelson Goodman," *Philosophy and Phenomenological Research*, 62, 679–90.

CATHERINE Z. ELGIN

H

Hanslick, Eduard (1825–1904) Austrian music critic, the most famous critic of his day, and an acerbic enemy of excessive romantic tendencies in nineteenth-century music. His verdicts on contemporary compositions greatly affected their reception, especially in Vienna, where he lived for most of his career. His first important publication, *The Beautiful in Music* (first edition 1854), is deservedly the most famous work of musical aesthetics.

Hanslick's aim in writing the book was to establish the thesis that, in his own terms, "the beauty of a composition is *specifically musical.*" In other words, he attempted to show that musical value is autonomous, in the sense that the value of music as an art, or the value of any piece of music *as music*, is independent of its relation to anything extramusical. Instrumental music has no subject matter extraneous to its combinations of musical sounds, and its artistic value is determined only by the intrinsic beauty of the audible forms that compose it, so that its aesthetic appeal resembles that of an ever changing kaleidoscope or a mobile arabesque that pleases in itself rather than subserving a further function. The illustrative power of music is minimal, consisting only in the imitation of sounds (e.g., bird calls); and the introduction of reproductions of sounds of the natural world into a musical work always serves a poetic, not a musical, purpose.

The principal target of the book is the doctrine that the aim of music as an art is the representation of feelings or emotions. This doctrine maintains that the proper subject matter of music is the emotional life and that the musical value of a work is determined by how successful it is in representing emotional feelings and, perhaps, by the nature of the feelings it represents. This doctrine, Hanslick believed, is buttressed by the thesis that the aesthetic function of music is to arouse feelings. This is his subsidiary target.

He brings three main considerations against the supporting thesis. First, there is no invariable causal nexus between a musical work and the feelings, if any, it arouses: the feelings excited by a particular work vary both from person to person and within a single life. But a composition's musical merit is unvarying. Second, the power to awaken feelings is not confined to music, and the feelings excited by any musical work could be aroused by another, nonmusical, stimulus. So music does not possess an aesthetic monopoly of the function of evoking feelings. Third, emotional feelings are states either of satisfaction or of discomfort. But a musical work that arouses a discomforting feeling is not valued for doing so, and its capacity to arouse such a feeling is not a musical merit.

To establish his principal negative thesis, Hanslick uses three main arguments. The first and most important of these is designed to restrict the scope of the musical representation of feeling. A definite feeling, such as a feeling of love, anger, sorrow, or fear, is not only a state of pleasure or dissatisfaction, but a state that possesses "intentionality": the felt pleasure or dissatisfaction is not free-floating but has an object – namely, the state of affairs represented by the thought that is partly constitutive of the feeling. For example, the feeling of hope involves the thought of a desired outcome and the feeling of grief the thought of someone's death. Hanslick argues that music cannot represent definite feelings, since it cannot represent the thoughts in which such feelings partly consist: music can represent only the "dynamic" properties of definite feelings, the ways in which feelings vary in intensity and the changing aspects of the movements in or of the body that are felt in an episode of emotion.

But the argument is not yet finished. For music cannot represent these dynamic properties *as* being properties of feelings, and feelings are not the only phenomena that can change in strength and kind of movement. So Hanslick reaches the conclusion not only that music cannot represent definite feelings, but also that it can neither represent indefinite feelings nor indefinitely represent feelings.

He brings two additional arguments against his prime target. The first asserts that it cannot be necessary for music, considered from the point of view of its being an art, to represent definite feelings, since at least some musical works are admitted by all listeners not to do so. The second claims that even if music could represent definite feelings, its doing so would not be a requirement of musical value. Hanslick offers two reasons why this requirement would not apply. The first is the existence of valuable music that does not have feelings as its subject matter. The second is that, if there were any music that represented feelings, it would not be valuable to the degree that it represented feelings accurately; for, so Hanslick argues, musical value would always be inversely proportional to representational accuracy.

Despite its clarity and boldness, Hanslick's philosophy of music is not entirely successful. It places a salutary emphasis on the fact that music as an art must be appreciated for its own sake, rather than merely for the feelings it may awaken. It certainly demolishes the unvarnished thesis that music has no other aesthetic function than the arousal of feelings. It follows that, if there is an aesthetically significant role for the musical excitation of feelings, music must possess other aesthetic functions in virtue of which it elicits definite feelings. It is also clear that, if representation is understood as a relation which involves a noticeable resemblance between the related items, instrumental music cannot represent the thought that forms the core of a definite feeling, so that the musical arousal of feelings cannot be an aesthetic response to music's representation of the emotional life. But this is not sufficient to show that the appreciation of musical value cannot require hearing music in a manner that relates it to a definite emotion. If there is such a mode of perception, an aesthetics of music that does not recognize and explicate it is incomplete.

See also MUSIC AND SONG; EMOTION; EXPRESSION; FORMALISM; FUNCTION OF ART.

BIBLIOGRAPHY

Primary sources
[1854] 1885. *Vom Musikalisch-Schönen*. 7th edn. Leipzig.
[1885] 1891. *The Beautiful in Music*. G. Cohen (trans.). London: Novello & Ewer. (Translation of 7th edn.)
[1891] 1986. *On the Musically Beautiful*. G. Payzant (trans.). Indianapolis: Hackett. (Translation of 8th edn.)
1894. *Aus meinem Leben* [From My Life]. Berlin: Allgemeiner Verein für Deutsche Literatur.
1988. *Hanslick's Music Criticisms*. H. Pleasants (ed. & trans.). New York: Dover.

Secondary sources
Budd, Malcolm. 1980. "The Repudiation of Emotion: Hanslick on Music," *British Journal of Aesthetics*, 20, 29–43.
Davies, Stephen. 1994. *Musical Meaning and Expression*. Ithaca: Cornell University Press, 202–20.

MALCOLM BUDD

Hegel, Georg Wilhelm Friedrich (1770–1831)

The most important German philosopher of the early nineteenth century; his all-embracing absolute idealism was an immense influence on later thinkers, including such critics as Kierkegaard and Marx. Hegel's writings provide what is arguably the most systematic and comprehensive aesthetic theory of the modern world (and a fortiori for all time, since aesthetics, in the strict sense, is a discourse that begins only in the eighteenth century).

It has become customary to describe as "Hegelian" all approaches to the arts that understand them in terms of a meaningful succession of styles, or as expressions of the worldviews of cultures or historical periods. While this is a rather loose designation, it is indeed the case that Hegel's aesthetics played a fundamental role in the formation of literary history and the history of art in the nineteenth century. It would be only a slight exaggeration to say that every philosophical aesthetician in the nineteenth and twentieth centuries has been either a Kantian or a Hegelian. Kantian aesthetics focuses on those characteristics of aesthetic experience that differentiate it from others (knowledge and action) and insists, in one way or another, on the contemplation of form as the defining characteristic of the aesthetic. Hegelian aesthetics emphasizes the meaning and the content of works of art and takes those works to be superior, everything else being equal, which have as their content the most concrete and fully articulated idea.

Despite this contrast, Hegel's aesthetics (like his entire philosophical project) would not have been possible except for Kant's thought and for post-Kantian romanticism, which regarded art and beauty as providing our most profound access to the real. Hegel's early writings show him to be first a participant in and then an early critic of this romantic aestheticism. In "The Earliest System-Programme of German Idealism" (which apparently emerged out of youthful exchanges between Hegel, Hölderlin, and Schelling), Hegel writes that "the highest act of reason, the one through which it encompasses all ideas, is an aesthetic act and . . . truth and goodness only become sisters in beauty" (1972: 511); and he speaks of the need for philosophy to become poetic and poetry to become philosophical, in order that a new aesthetically appealing religion of reason may arise.

By the time of his first major work, *The Phenomenology of Spirit* (1807), Hegel had become a critic of aestheticism and spoke now of the absolute priority to be accorded to *Wissenschaft* (science, wisdom, or knowledge) over the representational, intuitive, and figurative knowing that mark the limits of art and religion. Nevertheless, the *Phenomenology* contains some of the most significant philosophical writings on the arts, including a speculative analysis of tragedy, a theory of the development and dissolution of Greek art, and a commentary on Diderot's comic and satiric masterpiece *Rameau's Nephew*. The *Phenomenology* can be read as a contest between the claims of art and those of philosophical science, and while it is clear where Hegel's final allegiance lies, recent philosophers (notably Jacques Derrida in *Glas*) have pointed out that, despite his assurances, Hegel's text is less scientific and more artistic than he would have us believe.

Beginning after his arrival at his final teaching position in Berlin, Hegel began to lecture periodically on the philosophy of fine arts, or aesthetics. The text that is called Hegel's *Aesthetics* is a collation of various student transcripts and some of Hegel's own manuscript notes for these lectures, over a number of years (the publication and editing of such materials is still going on, and while the main outlines of Hegel's mature aesthetics are clear, we ought to expect some new emphases and analyses to emerge). Hegel – in a way that is documented of no earlier philosopher – took a comprehensive and many-sided interest in the arts, traveling to picture galleries and reading extensively in the literatures of the world; this artistic concern reached a peak in Berlin, where he took a passionate interest in opera and the theater and befriended a number of actors. Nevertheless, by the time of the lectures Hegel is announcing what is (somewhat misleadingly) called his "death of art" thesis, opening his lectures with the claim that art has exhausted its potential and that "it is now, on its highest side, a thing of the past" (1975: 11). Art, he argues, has not merely been displaced by science (a science of dialectical wisdom, we should recall), but is now a subject matter for science; in other words, this is the era of institutions such as the museum and the formation of such intellectual constructions as "world literature" (a notion apparently invented by Hegel's contemporary, Goethe), in which it is possible to know peoples and cultures by a comparative study of their literary expressions.

HEGEL'S DIALECTICAL THEORY OF ART
THE PHENOMENOLOGY OF SPIRIT

Most accounts of Hegel's aesthetics are based almost exclusively on the lecture course. This is unfortunate, because the lectures tend to focus on the meaning of art independently of the role of the artist and the audience. In the *Phenomenology*, in the sections entitled "Natural Religion" and "The Religion of Art," Hegel develops a complex account of the dialectic of the production and reception of artworks, or of intention and interpretation, in which the meaning of the work is a triadic relation between the artist, the artifact, and the audience. Although Hegel's concrete material for this analysis is taken only from the ancient world (Egypt, the Near East, and Greece), the lines of analysis are arguably applicable to all artistic production and reception; this is not surprising if we recall that he thinks of the Greeks as the supremely artistic culture. Hegel provides a narrative account of how art first emerges from a more mechanical, craft-like endeavor; he then proceeds to explain the development of Greek art as the increasingly conscious and articulate attempt to overcome the gaps of sympathy and understanding that arise when an artifact must mediate between producer and consumer; the story ends, like so many Hegelian narratives, with a moment of attained recognition or identity in difference among all the parties to the artistic transaction.

In the initial form of the religion of art, which Hegel calls "abstract," a created work such as a sculpture stands as something of an obstacle between artist and audience. Those who admire the finished piece do not really comprehend it if they focus only on its surface beauty and fail to grasp the thought, activity, and labor that the artist put into his work. The artist, too, will reflect on the discrepancy between the static form (of the god or hero) and the life or vitality it was meant to embody. By implication, Hegel is critical of a major tradition in German thought (represented by Winckelmann and Kant, among others) according to which Greek sculpture is an unsurpassable model; for Hegel it is a failure, despite its beauty. Faced with this failure or impasse artists turn, on Hegel's analysis, to forms that aim at collapsing the distinction between artist and audience; these are works of "living art" such as hymns, Dionysiac revels, or Olympic games (twentieth-century analogies would be participatory theater or "happenings," just as Hegel's "abstract art" would find its parallel in such movements as minimalist art).

The problem that Hegel finds with the living work of art is that it fails to achieve a fully conscious wholeness, or totality, because it must be either completely transient (in active forms like the revel) or static and detached (as in more disciplined, choreographed displays of human bodies). What is needed, he says, is a medium that is both internal and external, exhibiting characteristics of both motion and rest. This he finds in language, which offers the possibility of an identity of meaning for artist, work, and audience. Even within this "spiritual" art, however, Hegel sees a series of approximations to this identity in the forms of epic, tragedy, and comedy. The content of these genres has to do with the relations of men and gods, and for Hegel

that relation is a figurative way of talking about the relation between finite and infinite mind.

The epic presents an ultimately confused picture of all action in which the ostensible agents, the gods, sink to trivial and all too human behavior, while men can obtain a heroic stature apparently not accessible to immortals. The same situation is reflected in the communicative structure of the epic itself, in which the singer claims to be nothing but a mouthpiece for the muse and the audience is alienated from the poem's content by the realization that the latter tells of human beings of a long-lost heroic era beside which they appear insignificant. Hegel takes the presence of fate in the epic to be the sign that there is something seriously flawed in the way that this artwork understands itself and the task of art. The development of art requires a more daring and less qualified form of consciousness that will expel fate, depopulate the heavens, and leave all the participants with the deep sense that they have learned about their own humanity.

Tragedy takes a significant step in this direction because its characters are themselves poets who are artists insofar as their speeches "give utterance to the inner essence" (1979: 444). However, the chorus and the spectators are still relatively passive and removed from the life of the poet-actors. While the gods tend to be reduced to the single figure of Zeus or to an impersonal fate, either of these still leaves tragedy subject to an uncomprehended necessity.

Comedy, the ultimate form of the religion of art, demonstrates the identity of artist-actors and their audience. While Zeus is dethroned and the vortex reigns in his place, all recognize that the only ones here are us human beings. The mask which stood between artist and audience in tragedy now becomes dispensable, and a mutual recognition is achieved which coincides with an unparalleled "state of spiritual well-being" – that is, a celebration of human self-consciousness. Hegel marks this achieved identity with a profound pun: "The actual self of the actor [*Schauspieler*] coincides with his persona or mask [*Person*], just as the spectator [*Zuschauer*] is completely at home in the drama performed before him and sees himself playing in it" (1979: 452). Production and consumption or intention and interpretation

317

are not, on this dialectical view, always and necessarily distinct; it is in fact the task of art to bring them together.

HEGEL'S SYSTEM OF AESTHETICS

For Hegel, aesthetics is concerned essentially with the beauty of art rather than with natural beauty or some free-floating aesthetic experience. This is because art is one of the modes, along with religion and philosophy, or absolute spirit, in which mind comes to know itself and its activities. Hegel defines the beauty of art as the manifestation of the idea in sensuous form. The idea is not any random thought or concept, but the idea of the whole, or totality, the self-expression and self-understanding that is the aim of all human thought. Art is a way in which the mind comes home to itself, displaying and reflecting on its truth. Much of the content of art is religious, but it must be remembered that for Hegel religion is not intrinsically mysterious; it is, rather, a revelation of what mind is.

In the lectures, Hegel distinguishes three main forms of art that are differentiated in terms of the relation that holds in each between idea and sensuous form. In *symbolic art* there is a discrepancy between the idea grasped in a relatively crude and minimal way and a profusion of specific forms that attempt to embody the idea. The paradigm of such art for Hegel is the religious art of India and Egypt in which, as he sees it, there is a restless search for the appropriate form for the gods. Symbolic art is typically sublime insofar as it testifies to the insufficiency of artistic means. Hegel manages thus to demote the sublime from the position it occupied in eighteenth-century aesthetics (for instance, in Burke and Kant) as coordinate with or even more significant than the beautiful; for him, the sublime is a lower or preparatory stage of beauty itself, and its relative inadequacy is a function of that indeterminacy and formlessness which impressed earlier thinkers.

The most sophisticated form of symbolic art are works like the sphinxes of Egypt, which embody a sense of mystery and hint at its solution as the human form begins to emerge from animal and geometrical shapes. While Hegel's account of non-Western art may sound naively chauvinistic, it is based on an extraordinary range of knowledge for a thinker of his time; and the lectures on aesthetics themselves were a major impetus in the Western movement, gathering momentum in the nineteenth century, to accord a significant status to non-Western art.

The middle term of the three great art forms is *classical art*, and here Hegel's material is drawn mainly from ancient Greece. Here the form "is the free and adequate embodiment of the idea in the shape peculiarly appropriate to the idea itself in its essential nature" (1975: 77). Although Hegel is still regarded by some as an extreme idealist and rationalist, he argues that the anthropomorphism of this form of art is absolutely necessary, "since spirit appears sensuously in a satisfying way only in [a human] body" (1975: 78). The beautiful bodies of Greek sculpture are echoed in Greek poetry, where word and action are perfectly adequate to conception and all residues of mystery have been eliminated. The price that must be paid for the supreme beauty of classical art, however, is a certain limitation in the depth and intensity of its spiritual world.

In *romantic art*, spirit is known as "infinite subjectivity" and "absolute inwardness," such that its riches could never be presented in any sensuous form. This romantic art (which Hegel sometimes identifies as Christian art) often takes as its theme the very inadequacy and insufficiency of bodily beauty; representations of the crucifixion, for example, can be seen as negations of the perfect, unblemished bodies of Greek sculpture. If classical art is supremely beautiful, romantic art is more spiritual. Hegel traces the development of romantic art from its explicit concern with Christian themes, through their gradual secularization in the literature of chivalry, which deals with themes of honor, love, and fidelity, to the formation of modern characters (like those of Shakespearean drama) that have an independence and freedom not known in art's earlier phases. It is here that he begins to speculate about the dissolution (*Auflösung*) of art, sometimes referred to (a bit simplistically) as "the death of art." His claim is that the romantic concentration on inwardness and subjectivity has led to a condition in which art is no longer determined by any specific content; rather, the artists themselves have been liberated through criticism and reflection, and now they are radically free in their choice of styles and themes. Interest in art has shifted to the artist's persona, and the artist of the late romantic phase may exploit this interest in a humorous or ironic mode (we might think of Picasso's many styles, or the irony of Marcel Duchamp, as suggesting the plausibility of Hegel's projection of art's new vocation). Hegel never claimed that the production and appreciation of art would simply cease; in that sense he held no "death of art" thesis. He did argue that a certain essential history of art had come to an end, and that once this history had become an object of knowledge (for aesthetics, the history of art, the museum, and so on) artists themselves would become inspired and cheerful players in an inexhaustible game of the imagination.

Coordinate with Hegel's distinction between the general symbolic, classic, and romantic forms of art is his theory of the individual arts and their system. He thinks of the individual arts as forming a hierarchy, rising from those most tied to the constraints of the material world (e.g., architecture) to those that are first, or most ideal, in this respect (e.g., poetry). Art becomes actual only in particular works in specific media, and every concrete work must be understood in terms of the specific potentials and limits of the individual art of which it is an instance. Architecture is the attempt to master and subordinate an external inorganic medium to make it an appropriate vehicle for spirit. Because of the obstinacy of its medium, it is typically a symbolic art; however, it is not exclusively so, and Hegel comments penetratingly on architecture's development from such enclosed symbolic forms as the Egyptian pyramids to structures of a more human scale, such as Greek temples, and then to Gothic architecture which dematerializes matter in soaring cathedrals where light transforms the resistant stone. Similarly, sculpture is paradigmatically but not exclusively a classical form of art. In the first instance it presents the image of a god or a human being conceived on the model of the gods' tranquillity and self-sufficiency. Sculpture no longer processes its material externally as architecture does, simply in order to bear and distribute weight or provide shelter from the elements, but constructs its works under the aspect of the bodily form.

The individual arts are further dematerialized in painting, which is a relatively ideal medium because it is limited to two dimensions and is concerned with appearance as such, where appearance is understood as something that must be subjectively entertained. This play with appearance allows painting a far greater range of subjects, styles, and treatments than the preceding more material arts. Painting portrays not only the many forms of human consciousness by capturing expression and nuances of mood; it also conveys the subjective act of perception as such, when (as in Dutch painting of the seventeenth century, which seems to be, for Hegel, the highest variety of painting) it exhibits human vision as such in manifesting evanescent qualities of light, atmosphere, and texture. Music moves further into the inner world by abandoning spatial form altogether; sound has no obvious material embodiment and it must be heard sequentially – that is, perceived only in time – which is, of course, the form of the inner life. Even more specifically, the musician's ability to repeat a theme with variations and the listener's capacity to grasp and recall it are forms of what Hegel calls *Erinnerung*, *re*internalization or a making inward again, at a higher level. (For Hegel, *Erinnerung* is the very form of spirit's activity in realizing and becoming aware of itself; the English "recollection" is at best a pale translation of this fundamental concept.)

Poetry, by which Hegel designates what we would call imaginative literature, is the supremely inward art. He claims that its external embodiments are relatively accidental and that it exists completely in the imagination, so that it is fully translatable from one language to another. "Poetry is the universal art of the spirit which has become free in itself and which is not tied down for its realization to external sensuous material; instead, it launches out exclusively in the inner space and the inner time of ideas and feelings" (1975: 89). Poetry is the most philosophical art, exhibiting dialectical relations and structures in the imaginative worlds it creates; Hegel devotes about as much space to it as to all of the other arts together. Where much philosophical aesthetics claims that the meaning of poetry is ambiguous, implicit, metaphorical, or suggestive, Hegel holds that its meaning is explicit – although we must grasp this explicit meaning in a dialectical way, rather than in terms of the propositional logic of the understanding. He analyzes these dialectical structures in considering the three genres of epic, lyric, and drama with respect to their various transformations of the subject–object relation.

The *epic* poet might seem to be a subject passively recording a world external to him. Yet the content of the epic (he is thinking of Homer in particular) yields a different view. The hero of the epic is neither simply a product of his world nor its cause; epic society cannot be understood either as a collection of human atoms nor as a holistic unit whose properties determine all its members. The hero emerges from his world and is of it, yet he transcends it in his individuality, as Achilles does with his towering wrath and his demand for honor from Zeus. The epic world is a poetic one, prior to the fixed ordinances of law and based on more flexible forms of individual allegiance. Even the items or objects of this world are understood in terms of their makers and their histories, rather than as neutral objects. The *lyric* stance is that of the individual poet who has reflectively withdrawn from a regularized world in which he or she had been engaged. The lyric is not a merely solipsistic meditation or retreat, however, but the site of a conflict between the independent freedom of the poet and its infinitely variable subject matter.

The *drama* is the most dialectical of poetic forms because it exhibits both subjects becoming objective (the character's action constituting the dramatic world) and the objective becoming subjective (the world giving rise to individual expression). Drama is concerned specifically with conflict and its (possible) resolution. Hegel's analysis of ancient tragedy is that it is an art demonstrating the inevitable conflict of two forces, each having its own legitimacy. In *Antigone*, which he calls the supreme tragedy, it is the clash between the male, explicit law of the public world (or state) and the female, implicit law of the private world or family. Such clashes are necessary in the ancient world because human beings there are split between their public and private dimensions; poetry is the way in which that world becomes conscious of itself. In modern drama, dialectical developments are more complex and are not tied to the social structures of the ancient world; modern drama deals with individuals who are no longer types of the different social spheres into which the ancient world was divided. At the height of modern drama (e.g., Shakespeare), these individuals become poets themselves, showing by their beautiful speeches that they have risen beyond their terrible circumstances to a poetic vision of their own careers (see the last soliloquies of Macbeth and Cleopatra). It is this rise to self-consciousness that is typical of Hegel's understanding of art, and which forms the guiding theme of his metanarrative of art's history.

See also NINETEENTH- AND TWENTIETH-CENTURY CONTINENTAL AESTHETICS; ART HISTORY; BEAUTY; DANTO; FUNCTION OF ART; LUKÁCS; RELIGION AND ART; SUBLIME.

BIBLIOGRAPHY

Primary sources
[1796] 1972. "The Earliest System-Programme of German Idealism." In *Hegel's Development: Toward the Sunlight*. H. S. Harris (trans.). Oxford: Oxford University Press, 510–12.
[1807] 1979. *Hegel's Phenomenology of Spirit*. A. V. Miller (trans.). Oxford: Oxford University Press.
[1835–8] 1975. *Hegel's Aesthetics: Lectures on Fine Art*. 2 vols. T. M. Knox (trans.). Oxford: Oxford University Press.
1962. Hegel *on Tragedy*. A. Paolucci & H. Paolucci (eds.). New York: Harper & Row.

Secondary sources
Bungay, Stephen. 1984. *Beauty and Truth: A Study of Hegel's Aesthetics*. New York: Oxford University Press.
Derrida, Jacques. 1986 [1974]. *Glas*. J. P. Leavey Jr. & R. Rand (trans.). Lincoln: University of Nebraska Press.
Desmond, William. 1986. *Art and the Absolute: A Study of Hegel's Aesthetics*. Albany: State University of New York Press.
Houlgate, Stephen (ed.). 2007. *Hegel and the Arts*. Evanston: Northwestern University Press.
Maker, William (ed.). 2000. *Hegel and Aesthetics*. Albany: State University of New York Press.
Pöggeler, Otto (ed.). 1981. *Hegel in Berlin*. Berlin: Staatsbibliothek Preubischer Kulturbesitz.
Shapiro, Gary (ed.). 1982. "Hegel on Art and Literature," *Clio*, 11, 4.
Shapiro, Gary. 1986. "An Ancient Quarrel in Hegel's *Phenomenology*," *Owl of Minerva*, 17, 165–80.
Steinkraus, Warren & Schmitz, Kenneth (eds.). 1980. *Art and Logic in Hegel's Philosophy*. New York: Humanities Press.

GARY SHAPIRO

Heidegger, Martin (1889–1976) German philosopher; a pupil of Husserl, and a main inspiration for such philosophical movements as existentialism, hermeneutics, and postmodernism.

Heidegger's essays on art and poetry have mystified the uninitiated and frustrated traditionally minded philosophers. Most frustrating to aestheticians is that Heidegger does not offer a philosophy of art in the familiar sense, so that it is far from easy to assess where he stands in relation to the standard debates. But for his followers this is the measure of his greatness as he was engaged in the overcoming of aesthetics. He showed how certain characteristics of Western metaphysics have governed the philosophical approach to art: its conceptions of truth as correctness and of space as something to be occupied, as well as its reliance on the distinction between form and matter, and its appeal to the lived experience of the isolated individual. The challenge his writings pose is to determine how successfully he broke with those conceptions without succumbing to other pitfalls.

Poetry, and the arts more generally, became central to Heidegger's presentation of his thought during the period immediately after the disastrous rectoral address of May 1933 in which he aligned himself with National Socialism. During the 1934–5 semester he lectured on the poetry of Hölderlin (1770–1843), from which the essay "Hölderlin and the Essence of Poetry" was largely drawn; in 1935 he gave the lecture course "An Introduction to Metaphysics," which included a close reading of the chorus on man from Sophocles' *Antigone*; in 1935 and 1936 he gave in various places the lecture "The Origin of the Work of Art" which was first published in 1950; during the semester 1936–7, under the title "The Will to Power as Art," he delivered the first of four lecture courses on Nietzsche; and in 1941 and 1942 he again lectured on Hölderlin's poetry. However, although at one time there was a tendency to believe that Heidegger had retreated into art and poetry as a result of his disillusionment with the reality of National Socialism, the texts themselves tell a different story.

To see this one needs to understand what Heidegger meant when he described Hölderlin not simply as "the poet of poets" (2000b: 52), but also as "the poet of the Germans" (1980: 214). He did not mean that Hölderlin was already established as a great poet. That remained to be decided, and it will be decided only by the German people – or rather, on the basis of whether the German public becomes a people, a *Volk*, in listening to Hölderlin's poetry. In opening up a world, the poet also founds a people. Reading Hölderlin is thus engaging in politics "in its highest and most authentic sense" (1980: 214). The artwork functions in a way that reflects Heidegger's understanding of the Greek sense of *polis* as the place around which all beings appear to a people as what they are (1992: 89–90). Hence authentic politics is not so much concerned with an already established people as it is about a people finding itself, which happens in part through an engagement with art.

Heidegger locates the origin of the work of art not in the genius of the artist or the taste of the observer, but in art itself. The claim of the lecture "The Origin of the Work of Art," that art is an origin, translates into philosophical language Hölderlin's line, "But what remains the poets establish." It is in this sense that Heidegger talks about the truth of art: it opens up the new, the excess, over what has gone before. However, with Hölderlin as his guide to poetry and the arts in general, Heidegger seems more often to be concerned with translating philosophical language into poetic language than vice versa. According to Heidegger, poetic language has a unique capacity to introduce and preserve novelty, which is why he refers all the arts, and language itself, to poetry (2002: 45). He attaches an importance to poetry virtually unparalleled in the philosophical tradition. It might not be too much to say that he resolves the "old quarrel between philosophy and poetry" by placing philosophy at the service of poetry (1979: 190).

The brief history of aesthetics and art to be found in the 1936–7 course on Nietzsche establishes the philosophical context for reading Heidegger's writings on art (1979: 77–91). He claims that aesthetics, in the sense of reflection on feelings inspired by the beautiful, did not begin until Plato and Aristotle, who came after the great period of Greek art, and that it attained its highest point with Hegel and the claim that great art, "in its highest vocation," had become "a thing of the past" (Hegel 1975: 11). But Heidegger ends his history of aesthetics with Nietzsche and not Hegel. Whereas Hegel turned to religion and philosophy as the place where the absolute was to be established following the sublation of art, Nietzsche thought that religion and philosophy had lost their creative force and that art was to be pursued as the countermovement of nihilism. Heidegger shares Nietzsche's conviction that turning to art is the thinker's best recourse in this crisis, and he assigns to the thinker the task of overcoming aesthetics and so preparing for the possible return of great art.

In "The Origin of the Work of Art" Heidegger takes up that task by addressing aesthetics, and especially Hegel's *Aesthetics*, in at least two different ways. First, "The Origin of the Work of Art" confronts the Greek interpretation of art in terms of *technê*. According to Heidegger, *technê* does not mean "art" or "craft" so much as "know-how," the mode of knowing appropriate to *poiêsis*, which itself is to be understood not just as "production" but as "bringing forth" (2002: 35). The breadth of the Greek conception determines not only subsequent philosophical reflection on art, but also the basic categories in terms of which all things are understood, and not just things produced by human beings for their own use. So, according to Heidegger, the form/matter distinction derives from the experience of making things. That this distinction provides one of the most pervasive frameworks in terms of which art and poetry are analyzed within aesthetics underlies the originality of Heidegger's suggestion that the artwork would be better approached in terms of world and earth. It opens up a world and sets the world back on the earth of a historical people as the ground on which and in which they dwell. By highlighting the emergence of the earth as nevertheless self-secluding in the stones of the temple or the sounds of the words of a poem, Heidegger attempts to leave all talk of form and matter behind. The work of art does not use up its materials as the worker does when he produces something.

The culmination of Heidegger's reflections on *technê* can be found in "The Question concerning Technology." In this 1953 essay, he refers the dominance of technology within the West to the dominance within Greek thought of the experience of *poiêsis* and *technê*. Whereas he was earlier somewhat ambiguous on this point, in this context he regards it as something positive that the Greeks lacked a special word for art and employed the pair of terms *poiêsis* and *technê* to cover all man-made products. Heidegger reminds his readers that in a technological world one has the impression of living in an environment in which human beings seem to encounter only themselves and their products. This description recalls the basis that Hegel gave for establishing the place of art within his system: art is "born of the spirit and born again" (Hegel 1975: 2), and so constitutes a site where spirit recognizes itself in its own products.

However, according to Heidegger, this widespread impression and the Hegelian philosophy that appeals to it are misleading. Human beings do not everywhere encounter themselves in such a world, because they nowhere encounter human essence as such. More precisely, they do not see themselves as addressed by what Heidegger refers to as "the historical determinations of Being." And yet the very proximity of making, on the one hand, and poetry and the arts, on the other – as suggested by the fact that they were both understood by the Greeks in term of *poiêsis*, or revealing – comes to suggest to Heidegger that poetry may possibly rescue us from this impasse by reawakening our sense of being as that which grants to things their appearance (1977: 35). Although the language is obscure at this point, it would seem to correspond closely to what he understands by the "excess" or "overflowing" of the origin in the earlier essay on art (2002: 47). To put it another way, essences do not endure permanently so as to underwrite timelessly valid concepts. Essences, including the essence of poetry, are historical and belong to a specific time (2000b: 65).

A second way in which "The Origin of the Work of Art" can be said to contribute to the overcoming of aesthetics is in its approach to the question of the so-called death of art. Hegel is not mentioned explicitly by Heidegger in the published version of "The Origin of the Work of Art" until the epilogue, but the question of the end of art, reformulated as the question of whether great art is still possible, dominates the text and is left open at its conclusion. For Heidegger, the vocation of art is to be an origin, a distinctive way in which truth, in the Heideggerian sense of "unconcealment," becomes historical. Two of his examples have since become famous. Van Gogh's painting of peasant shoes reveals more about such shoes than any direct examination of them would show; Heidegger says that the painting reveals their truth and that of the world to which they belong. More telling still is the example of the Greek temple. That the temple gave "to things their look and to men their outlook on themselves" exemplifies what it means to write of the truth of the artwork, because it seems clearer in this case in what sense art might be an origin. The example also suggests that an artwork ceases to be a work when it no longer opens up a world – which happens, in this case, when the gods have fled from it (2002: 21).

Hegel's question of the death of art, therefore, becomes the question of whether art is to serve simply as a way of cultivating our feelings and of maintaining contact with the past, or whether it may still open up or found a world. This was an open question for Heidegger, and neither his reference to Vincent Van Gogh in "The Origin of the Work of Art" nor his subsequent discussions of Igor Stravinsky, Paul Klee, Gottfried Benn, Rainer Maria Rilke, Stefan George, or Georg Trakl provide an answer. He contemplated writing an essay on Klee that would serve as a continuation of the reflections begun in "The Origin of the Work of Art," but when this was abandoned in the late 1950s he returned to Hölderlin. In 1959 Heidegger wrote a major essay, "Holderlin's Earth and Heaven" that, with its reference to "other great beginnings," hints that he finally abandons his single-minded fixation on the relation of the Germans to the Greeks, and allows that other peoples have and can make similar contributions (2000b: 201). Nevertheless, this does not eradicate the impression that Heidegger's essays on art are more about how a people is formed than they are about art.

Even so, by referring art to the people Heidegger did at least expose the isolating tendency characteristic of so much of modern aesthetics, where the aesthetic experience has often been largely a matter of subjective feeling. After World War II Heidegger attempted to counter that tendency without taking the political route he had employed in the 1930s. In essays from the 1950s that addressed poems by Stefan George and Georg Trakl, Heidegger sought an experience with language that would be not just a matter of the feelings of a human subject, but transformative of historical existence. These essays represent one further step in his longstanding attempt to break the grip of the so-called rational or calculative thinking of modern philosophy, and return to the "poetic thinking" characteristic of early Greek thinkers. As the debate continues about how successfully Heidegger's writings on art twist free of aesthetics, so does the question of how readily one can separate these writings from his disastrous political engagement in National Socialism. However, there is no doubting the massive impact Heidegger has had on the theory and practice of literary criticism and on the philosophical reflections on the work of art of thinkers like Hans-Georg Gadamer, Gianni Vattimo, and John Sallis.

See also NINETEENTH- AND TWENTIETH-CENTURY CONTINENTAL AESTHETICS; GADAMER; HEGEL; HERMENEUTICS; TRUTH IN ART.

BIBLIOGRAPHY

Primary sources
[1950] 2002. "The Origin of the Work of Art." In *Off the Beaten Track*. J. Young & K. Haynes (trans.). Cambridge: Cambridge University Press, 1–56.
[1953] 2000a. *Introduction to Metaphysics*. G. Fried & R. Polt (trans.). New Haven: Yale University Press.
[1954] 1977. "The Question concerning Technology." In *The Question concerning Technology and Other Essays*. W. Lovitt (trans.). New York: Harper & Row, 3–35.
[1960] 1979. *The Will to Power as Art*. D. F. Krell (trans.). New York: Harper & Row.
[1971] 2000b. *Elucidations of Hölderlin's Poetry*. K. Hoeller (trans.). Amherst: Humanity Books.
1980. *Hölderlin's Hymnen "Germanien" und "Der Rhein."* In *Gesamtausgabe* [Collected Works], vol. 39. Frankfurt: Klostermann.
[1982] 1992. *Parmenides*. A. Schuwer & R. Rojcewicz (trans.). Bloomington: Indiana University Press.
[1984] 1996. *Hölderlin's Hymn "The Ister."* W. McNeill & J. Davis (trans.). Bloomington: Indiana University Press.

Secondary sources

Bernasconi, Robert. 1992. *Heidegger in Question*. Atlantic Highlands: Humanities Press.

De Beistegui, M. 2005. *The New Heidegger*. London: Continuum, ch. 5.

Gadamer, Hans-Georg. 1976 [1960]. "Heidegger's Later Philosophy." In *Philosophical Hermeneutics*. D. E. Linge (trans.). Berkeley: University of California Press, 213–28.

Hegel, G. W. F. 1975 [1835–8]. *Aesthetics*. T. M. Knox (trans.). 2 vols. Oxford: Oxford University Press.

Pöggeler, O. 1987 [1963]. *Martin Heidegger's Path of Thinking*. D. Magurshak & S. Barber (trans.). Atlantic Highlands: Humanities Press, 167–90.

Taminiaux, J. 1993 [1982]. "The Hegelian Legacy in Heidegger's Overcoming of Aesthetics." In *Poetics, Speculation, and Judgment*. M. Gendre (trans.). Albany: State University of New York Press, 127–52.

ROBERT BERNASCONI

hermeneutics Construed as *that* theory of interpretation that begins more or less with the work of Friedrich Ast (1778–1841) and Friedrich D. E. Schleiermacher (1768–1834), and includes among its principal lights Wilhelm Dilthey (1833–1911), Hans-Georg Gadamer (1900–2002), and Paul Ricoeur (1913–2005), hermeneutics appears to be the unique philosophical tradition spanning two continuous centuries. It centers on the analysis of human understanding as inseparable from a grasp of cultural context, intention, and historical change.

As a distinct movement, hermeneutics begins at the turn of the nineteenth century, in the interval just starting to reflect on the significance of the French Revolution for the metaphysics and methodology of history and human culture, for the understanding of history, and for the historical nature of understanding and interpretation. It has preserved through its disputatious career a distinct constellation of conceptual themes that, until very recently, has been effectively marginalized, at times even pronounced pernicious, in the Anglo-American literature focused on extensional logic, physicalism, and the philosophy of the physical sciences.

All that changed – quite radically – with late twentieth-century doubts about the supposed canons of genuine science, reductionism, the elimination of intentionally complex phenomena, and the adequacy of extensionalism, together with the dawning realization of the global importance of the Kantian theme of the symbiosis of the structure of the intelligible world and the structure of thinking, and the Hegelian theme of thinking's being inherently historicized. Since at least the early hermeneutic efforts of Heidegger in *Being and Time*, the latter theme has come to dominate the hermeneutic tradition.

The principal figure of post-Heideggerian hermeneutics, Gadamer, particularly in *Truth and Method*, has effectively installed the notions of the flux of history, the transience and contingency of cultural tradition, the social emergence and constructive nature of human selves, and the impossibility of giving logical and methodological analysis priority over the metaphysics of human existence. One finds cognate developments in any number of distinct philosophical programs that have no particularly close connection with hermeneutics – and which affect the theory of artworks and the theory of their interpretation – for instance, Deweyan pragmatism, Marxian and early Frankfurt critical philosophy, Kuhnian-like philosophies of science, and poststructuralism. Late phenomenology shows similar tendencies, but phenomenology and hermeneutics have been inextricably linked since the work of Dilthey and Heidegger.

Hermeneutics has developed along the following lines:

1 the replacement of a psychologistic interpretation of speakers' linguistic intentions by an interpretation that is more directly centered on the collective *Geist* (Spirit) of particular cultures;

2 the replacement of a model of universal human rationality by a more constructivist view of the self, partly adjusted to the divergent traditions of different historical cultures (the theme of so-called classical historicism, as in the work of Leopold von Ranke (1795–1886)), and partly adjusted (particularly toward the end of the twentieth century) to the radical historicity of human existence;

3 the subordination of logical, methodological, and epistemological questions to

questions concerning the metaphysics of the historicity of thinking (Heidegger's and Gadamer's essential theme);

4   the attempt to recover, under radical history, some more perspicuous sense of the discipline of interpretative judgment itself, particularly in the work of Ricoeur and Habermas – also, more reactively (against Gadamer), in the work of Emilio Betti (1890–1969) and E. D. Hirsch Jr. (b.1928).

Hermeneutics is becoming increasingly difficult to distinguish from theories of interpretation that have quite different pedigrees. This is largely because, first, the theme of historicity came to dominate late twentieth-century thought; and, second, hermeneutics has so far failed to recover in a compelling way a theory of interpretative judgment or, indeed, a theory of the clear connection between interpretation as (self-)understanding (*Verstehen*) and as the description and explanation (*Erklären*) of physical nature.

Dilthey has exerted an immense influence on the late development of hermeneutics by entrenching an overstrong disjunction between *Verstehen* and *Erklären* with regard to the human and natural sciences. But more recent efforts (notably by Ricoeur and Habermas) to integrate understanding and explanation have foundered in skirmishes that have postponed a recovery of the methodological side of hermeneutics. All such efforts have failed to claim the notion of radical history that is endorsed in views as disparate as those of Marx, Nietzsche, Heidegger, Gadamer, and Foucault. The problem is still very much with us, but it is difficult to suppose that late contributions to the matter can be expected to continue to single out hermeneutics as a distinct, privileged, relatively homogeneous stream of philosophical analysis.

Technically, what is now needed is a systematic reconceptualization of the central notions that were originally called into play in the methodologically minded early phases of hermeneutics, and remain central to the largely ahistorical orientation of Anglo-American philosophy: namely, reference, predication, numerical identity, reidentification, truth, and the assignment of truth values and the like. The seemingly restricted question of

the methodology of "hermeneutic" treatments of interpretative judgment is really a special case of the more general question of the possibility and structure of objective judgment *under conditions of radical history.*

By "radical history" is meant the following orientation:

1   Thinking has a history, is an artifact of history, hence is not reliably invariant in terms of rationality, norms, values, rules of coherence, and the like.

2   Human existence is distinguished by the nature of reflexive or self-interpreting thinking.

3   The real structures we impute to physical nature are inseparable from the conditions of reflexive (self-)understanding.

4   However embedded in physical nature, the human world is understood only in terms of the understanding, mutual and self-directed, of the members of a common cultural tradition or society.

5   Human beings and the things of their world are interpretatively altered and affected by their ongoing efforts at understanding themselves and their world.

6   The intelligible world, as historicized, has no necessary fixity.

Put this way, "the" hermeneutic question is the essential philosophical puzzle of the late nineteenth century, addressed as much to logic and the physical sciences as to the human sciences, history, and the interpretation of art.

Hermeneutics in the narrow sense may be divided, very roughly, into two phases: one spanning the tradition from Schleiermacher to Dilthey and, somewhat reactively, even retrogressively (following the appearance of Gadamer's *Truth and Method*), to Betti, Hirsch, Ricoeur, and Habermas; the other spanning the tradition from Heidegger and Gadamer, reaching back to Nietzsche and pressing forward also to nonhermeneuts interested in interpretation under the flux of history, such as Foucault. The first is methodologically and epistemologically centered, intent on identifying a clear sense of the objectivity with which the real meaning of a text, linguistic utterance, action, pattern of social life, artifact, or artwork is uniquely and reliably determined.

Originally, in Ast and other early figures, hermeneutics was compartmentalized in terms of specific procedures for determining original intent within a given historical *Geist*, with respect to the law or to religion or the like. In Schleiermacher, a common discipline is generalized for written texts, still strongly cast in terms of personal intention, though with some appreciation of the tacit influence of an encompassing culture. In Dilthey, it is enlarged still further to range over more than literary remains, and is more and more centered on the recovery of historical rather than biographical intention, though with the same emphasis on a rigorous recovery of meanings. These conceptions somewhat justify Gadamer's well-known charge against romantic hermeneutics: that the pertinent theorists failed to grasp satisfactorily that their interpretation of historical materials was itself historical – historicized, preformed by the historical "fore-structuring" of their consciousness (*wirkungsgeschichtliches Bewusstsein*: "effective-historical consciousness"); hence, that the past cannot be literally recovered though it can be reconstructed in relation to some present "horizon."

The second phase is distinctly *not* methodological but metaphysical, focused on the inherent conditions of human existence – on the fact that humanity is and becomes what, under preformative "prejudice," it understands its own "being" to be (see, especially, Taylor 1985). Human beings live, are formed by, and change as a result of living in the historical tradition to which they belong. They *are* histories in a sense, whose "present" is already preformed by the historical "past" that they claim to recover and understand. Hence, the interpretation of the "texts" ("text" now signifying, for Gadamer particularly, any suitably interpretable historicized referent: persons, artworks, literary texts, events of history) produced in the past already implicates a present "horizon" (a tacit, conceptual as well as affective and practical, orientation in life) – indeed, a "fusion of horizons" (*Horizontverschmelzung*), a fusion of recovered past and active present, operative in and only in the present ongoing life of actual societies. In this sense, Gadamer sets certain strenuous conditions on any would-be theory of interpretation. His own contribution to the theory of interpreting artworks holds that the interpretation of art (or texts) and self-interpretation are inseparable and affect one another (*subtilitas applicandi*).

No standard form, therefore, can be ascribed to hermeneutics. It ranges from a methodologically focused account of interpretation committed to the recovery of original authorial intent or original *geistig* meanings suited in principle to any historical period, to a metaphysically focused account of interpretation that holds that humanity and our world are constituted and continually reconstituted by our reflexive efforts at interpretative understanding. These efforts are tacitly skewed in a perspectival or horizonal way by the conditions of historical formation and ongoing life.

The decisive mark of these large changes in the hermeneutic tradition, particularly bearing on the interpretation of artworks, rests with the changes in the conception of the *hermeneutic circle* that the tradition has favored at one time or another. For Ast, for example, there is apparently one supreme ("infinite") *Geist*, of which all the diverse cultures of the world are alternative manifestations. Understanding, therefore, is simply the human capacity to find in particular texts "the spirit of the whole," proximately, through the various "spirits" of particular cultures, ultimately in terms of an all-encompassing *Geist*. Schleiermacher is more doubtful about the likelihood of recovering a truly "general hermeneutics" or of grasping the "infinite" that is language, which appears to be required in order to resolve the problem of the hermeneutic circle adequately. But within these troubling limits, Schleiermacher emphasizes an author's "thought" and the formation of his thought through the genres in which he expresses himself, which capture the "whole" of his historical language and culture.

An institution of this sort is fundamental to all versions of romantic hermeneutics, if we understand by that term the extension of the appropriate methodology, beyond narrowly biographically focused thought, to what is historically *geistig* at large, as in Dilthey, Betti, and Hirsch. But even in Schleiermacher, as with the interpretation of the New Testament, "a minimum of psychological interpretation is needed," he says, "with a predominantly objective subject." Interpretation begins, then, with a guess that probably fails at once to recover either pertinent genres of discourse (which effectively fix the whole of a text's meaning) or the thought that produces a particular text. Hermeneutic skills rework such commentaries in order to bring them into congruity with these criterial constraints.

One sees here the incipient structure of a relatively late romantic hermeneutic position such as Hirsch's, which is characteristically sanguine about the benign form of the hermeneutic circle. The tell-tale difficulty in Hirsch (1967) is a dual one that adversely affects all more or less essentialist conceptions of the circle: (1) there is no satisfactory way of demonstrating that there *are* relatively fixed constitutive genres of discourse, in accord with which every properly formed "thought" (author's or artist's original intent) is formed and then interpretatively recovered by suitably informed respondents; and (2) there is no satisfactory way of fixing constitutive genres so that new poetic or other artistic acts or utterings, presumably formed within them, are truly governed by them.

Such genres function only heuristically, then. Only on the assumption that human nature and understanding were essentially fixed through the whole of history could the contemporary solution of the hermeneutic circle possibly be sustained. Hirsch probabilizes the treatment of genres, but he fails to resolve the problem just indicated. The hermeneutic circle begins to mean only that human understanding proceeds by constructing part/whole constellations of meaning, without relying on methodological rules of any fixed sort.

Once the insolubility of the puzzle is acknowledged, it cannot but be difficult to resist Gadamer's twin doctrines of "effective-historical consciousness" and "fusion of horizons." The hermeneutic circle becomes a characterization of the metaphysics of human existence, rather than a criterial principle for canonical interpretation. One might almost say, trivially, that human understanding proceeds by way of generating open-ended part/whole relations of meaning, since meaning and rationality are inherently holistic notions. There would then be no sense in speaking of the right closure of interpretation: closure merely becomes practical or heuristic. There would

then also be no need for closure, since every change in experience would invite the construction of a new circle. The admission, in this new sense, of the hermeneutic circle confirms the irreducibility of what is interpretable to the nonintensional (or nonintentional) features of physical nature. But to put matters thus still leaves unresolved the methodologically insistent question of the rigor of interpretation under the conditions of radical history.

We may risk, here, one last finding that the hermeneutic tradition would be willing to support: that is, it would be impossible to recover *any* viable sense of the objectivity of an interpretation of a text or artwork without supposing that such objectivity lies within the competence of the consensual practices of an actual historical society. Would-be norms would then be constructed rather than discovered, would be provisional rather than fixed, pluralistic and relativistic rather than universalized.

This means that all presumptions of canonical objectivity, which assume that the interpreted "world" is independent of the "world" of the interpreter, utterly fail. The interesting fact remains that the devices of truth-claiming discourse – reference, predication, individuation, identity, the ascription of truth values – must *all* be inherently dependent on the processes of historical self-understanding. But then, too, there are no privileged cognitive universalities by which to recover any interpretative canon. The idea that interpretation may be disciplined in a public way remains entirely coherent – even ruggedly attractive.

See also NINETEENTH- AND TWENTIETH-CENTURY CONTINENTAL AESTHETICS; GADAMER; HEIDEGGER; INTERPRETATION; TEXT.

BIBLIOGRAPHY

Ast, Friedrich. 1808. *Grundlinien der Grammatik, Hermeneutik und Kritik*. Landshut: Thomann.

Dilthey, Wilhelm. 1976 [1900]. "The Development of Hermeneutics." In *Dilthey: Selected Writings*. H. P. Rickman (ed. & trans.). Cambridge: Cambridge University Press, 247–63.

Gadamer, Hans-Georg. 1975 [1960]. *Truth and Method*. G. Barden & J. Cumming (trans.). New York: Seabury.

Heidegger, Martin. 1962 [1927]. *Being and Time*. J. Macquarrie & E. Robinson (trans.). New York: Harper & Row.

Hirsch, E. D., Jr. 1967. *Validity in Interpretation.* New Haven: Yale University Press.

Ricoeur, Paul. 1981. *Hermeneutics and the Human Sciences.* J. B. Thompson (ed. & trans.). Cambridge: Cambridge University Press.

Schleiermacher, Friedrich D. E. 1977 [1838]. *Hermeneutics: The Handwritten Manuscripts.* H. Kimmerle (ed.). J. Duke & J. Fortman (trans.). Missoula: Scholars Press.

Taylor, Charles. 1985. *Philosophical Papers.* 2 vols. Cambridge: Cambridge University Press.

JOSEPH MARGOLIS

horror Although the horror genre, which dates back at least as far as the nineteenth century, covers several art forms, and has its roots in English and Gothic Romanticism, this discussion focuses almost exclusively on horror film. It summarizes key theoretical debates regarding the following topics: (1) definitions of horror, (2) attempts to explain the appeal of horror, and (3) representations of women in horror film.

For several decades, horror has been among the most popular and widely discussed film genres. Filmmakers have produced hundreds of horror films and created numerous subgenres. There are currently dozens of websites, blogs, and film festivals devoted exclusively to horror film. Some of Hollywood's most respected and commercially successful directors have made horror films, including Alfred Hitchcock (*Psycho*, 1960), Roman Polanski (*Repulsion*, 1965 and *Rosemary's Baby*, 1968), Steven Spielberg (*Jaws*, 1975), Ridley Scott (*Alien*, 1979), Stanley Kubrick (*The Shining*, 1980), and Quentin Tarantino (*Death Proof*, 2007). Horror film has also been widely discussed by cultural theorists, film scholars, and philosophers.

WHAT IS HORROR?

Most philosophers and film theorists approach the study of horror film from either a cognitivist or a psychoanalytic perspective. Cognitive film theorists often appeal to research in cognitive science and typically employ some version of the method of explanation and generalization developed by Aristotle in the *Poetics*. In contrast, psychoanalytic film theorists and critics draw on thinkers such as Freud, Lacan, and Kristeva and concentrate on hidden meanings in horror film. Not surprisingly, these two approaches tend to yield very different interpretations and analyses of horror films.

Psychoanalytic accounts of horror film tend to focus less on necessary and sufficient conditions of the genre than on determining its core meanings and underlying themes. Robin Wood (2003) argues that horror films are fundamentally about the struggle for recognition of the forces and desires our culture represses, such as surplus sexual energy, female sexuality, bisexuality, and children's sexuality. Since these desires threaten the cultural norms of heterosexual monogamy and the family, they must be repressed within the self. But according to Wood, "what is repressed must always strive to return" (2003: 72). Horror films symbolize the failure of repression through the return of unconscious and dangerous desire, which is embodied by a monstrous "other."

Otherness represents something that the dominant ideology can neither recognize nor accept, and so must deal with in one of two ways, either by destroying it or by rendering it harmless through assimilation. Otherness can refer to things that exist outside of the culture and the self or to one's own culturally unacceptable desires that one first represses and then projects outward onto someone or something else in order to safely disown and discredit it.

Wood interprets horror films as dramatizing the battle between social order and personal desire, or "normality" and otherness. As the embodiment of otherness, the figure of the monster stands in for whatever repressed desires or forces threaten to disrupt the social order of a given time. In other words, different monsters reflect different fears. For example, it has been argued that the monsters in *Cat People* (1982), *The Exorcist* (1973), *The Brood* (1979), and *Alien* (1979) all represent dangerous female sexuality, that the monsters in James Whale's *Frankenstein* (1931) and *The Texas Chainsaw Massacre* (1974), in which the monsters are a family of retired slaughterhouse workers who have been displaced by society, represent the rampant desire of the proletariat, and that the monsters in *Nosferatu* (1922) *Dressed to Kill* (1980), and *Silence of the Lambs* (1991) represent repressed bisexuality and homosexuality.

Wood's general theory of horror films does not develop a clear classificatory scheme yet it nevertheless offers a framework for categorizing horror films in social and political terms and a criterion for distinguishing progressive from reactionary films. We can interpret films that depict monsters as at least somewhat sympathetic as doing social critique and challenging the dominant norms. Films in which monsters are depicted as pure evil, however, are interpreted as reactionary since these films almost always end with the annihilation of the monster and the restoration of social order. Examining the monsters and their meanings provides insight into whatever has been repressed in a given culture and thus into whatever is perceived as most threatening at a given time.

At the opposite end of the theoretical spectrum from Wood is analytic philosopher and leading proponent of cognitive film theory Noël Carroll. Carroll's book-length study of the horror genre *The Philosophy of Horror; or, Paradoxes of the Heart* (1990) convinced analytic philosophers and other theorists suspicious of psychoanalysis that horror is not only a legitimate object of study, it is an especially philosophical genre.

In contrast to most scholars, Carroll takes a bold position on the nature of horror, identifying a set of conditions that must be met in order for a work to be categorized as horror. Utilizing an Aristotelian approach, Carroll defines the horror genre in terms of the emotional effect it is intended to elicit, which he labels "art horror." "Art horror" is a combination of fear, disgust, and physical agitation that occurs in response to particular types of monsters and that typically parallels the emotional experience of the film's main characters.

To qualify as horrific, a monster must be threatening, impure, and inconceivable. Impure in this case refers to something that is "categorically interstitial, categorically contradictory, or formless" (Carroll 1990: 32). In short, horrific monsters must be category violations of some kind. There are multiple types of category violation. For example, some horrific beings are structurally fused, that is, they combine qualities or attributes that are categorically distinct or transgress categorical distinctions such as inside/outside, living/dead, insect/human, or flesh/machine (1990: 43).

Ghosts, zombies, vampires, and mummies are all both living and dead, and demonically possessed characters combine two people in one body. It is in virtue of the fantastic nature of their biologies that horrific beings elicit art horror. Consider the monster in John Carpenter's *The Thing* (1982). A famously terrifying scene occurs when it takes the form of a disembodied head that grows spider-like legs and then walks away. Another famous example of a fused being is Regan (Linda Blair) in *The Exorcist* (1973). The film begins to get scary when unexplainable things happen in the house and Regan starts behaving abnormally (e.g., urinating on the carpet during her mother's dinner party) and saying spooky things (e.g., when she tells the astronaut that he is going to "die up there"), but it grows horrifying when clear signs indicate that Regan is fused with an evil entity, such as the first time she speaks with the demon's voice or when scratches spelling the word "HELP" are discovered on her torso, looking as if they have been scrawled from within. Carroll's theory of horrific beings fits these examples and explains why they are so effective at eliciting fear and disgust.

THE PARADOX OF HORROR

The "paradox of horror," which is closely related to the "paradox of tragedy," concerns the question of why we take pleasure in watching horror films. Why do we seek out experiences that in ordinary life we try to avoid? Why do we delight in being terrified and repulsed?

According to Carroll, we do not. The pleasure we derive from horror films does not come from our experience of fear and disgust. It comes from curiosity. Carroll contends that horror plots engage audiences in processes of discovery, proof, explanation, hypothesis, and confirmation, all of which are directed at horrific monsters. Since these monsters are impossible beings that cannot be explained in terms of our existing conceptual schemes, they are intrinsically fascinating. Human characters must search for clues to determine what the monsters are, how they can exist, and how they can be defeated. Like the human characters, we yearn to understand these horrific beings due to their anomalous nature, and yet this is precisely what frightens and disgusts us about them. In essence, we tolerate the fear and disgust of art horror because of our deep desire to comprehend the monsters.

Most solutions to the paradox of horror place far less emphasis than Carroll does on the cognitive. Some theorists argue that it is genuinely fun to be scared during a movie, just as it is genuinely fun to ride a roller coaster. In neither case are we in any real danger and so our fear is exhilarating. Wood (2003) sees horror as representing the struggle between oppressive social norms and our repressed desires. We are ambivalent toward the monster; it is loathsome and threatening but it is also a symbol of a disowned part of ourselves. Even as we recoil from the monster, we find its destructive power gratifying since it expresses desires we have been compelled to deny.

Daniel Shaw (2001) proposes that a major source of the pleasure we derive from horror films is the vicarious feelings of power and mastery they provide. Appealing to Nietzsche's notion of "will to power," Shaw asserts that we experience increases in power as pleasurable. We delight in the power struggles in horror, often finding monsters and psychotic killers like Hannibal Lecter compelling due to their awe-inspiring destructive force. At the same time, we recognize that the suffering the monster causes is undeserved and so identify with the human victims as well. This is why our experience of horror is ambivalent. Shaw thinks most of the major solutions to the paradox tell part of the story about our attraction to horror, but the full story requires us to recognize how much we enjoy feeling powerful and dominant, even if only vicariously.

GENDER AND HORROR

Horror is frequently viewed as an essentially misogynist genre, one that reveals fear and hostility toward women and female sexuality. Horror films sexualize violence, celebrate graphic and sadistic violence against women, and punish female sexuality. Many of them are also believed to privilege the male gaze, rendering men as active agents who control and dominate and women as passive victims subject to male power.

Feminists from a variety of traditions have analyzed the representation of women in horror in order to uncover what it reveals about cultural attitudes and fears. Linda Williams (2002) maintains that horror films associate women with the monster. Monsters and women are both "other" because they both threaten the heterosexual male norm. This is why they both must be controlled and dominated. Barbra Creed (1993) analyzes horror's depiction of women in terms of the psychoanalytic conception of abjection, as elaborated by Julia Kristeva. According to Creed, horror depicts women as monstrous by representing them and their bodies in particular as abject, and therefore as something to be expelled, disowned, or tamed. Although neither Williams nor Creed suggests that horror is completely bad, they both find it deeply problematic.

In her groundbreaking study of the horror subgenre the "slasher" film, Carol Clover (1992) complicates traditional accounts of gender in horror films by identifying multiple respects in which they challenge and transform representational codes of gender and standard modes of identification. Films like *The Texas Chain Saw Massacre* (1974), *Halloween* (1978), *Alien* (1979), *Friday the 13th* (1980), and *Nightmare on Elm Street* (1984) all feature a female protagonist who survives a killing spree, confronts a villain, and triumphs in the end. Clover coined the term "final girl" to label this character type. According to Clover it is not only the final girl who defies standard cinematic conventions in slasher films. The killers do as well. Unlike most powerful male characters, the killers in slasher films are effeminate and childlike, expressing infantile rage and disturbed sexuality (e.g., Jason Vorhees, Michael Myers, etc.).

Representations of a strong and triumphant female and a sexually disturbed and childlike male are now generic conventions, and according to Clover, they are what enable horror films to play with gender identity. She concludes that the female characters in slasher films are "masculine," and the male characters "feminine."

Clover's provocative theory of the slasher film has been extremely influential, inspiring debates and discussion not only within academic circles but also in popular culture at large, but there is a serious problem with Clover's account. Although she successfully identifies a generic formula featuring a triumphant female, she argues that this female is actually a stand-in for an adolescent male. The protagonist in slasher films has to be a girl, Clover explains, because viewers are uncomfortable with men represented as vulnerable and terrified.

According to Clover then, the atypical characteristics that set final girls apart from the other females in slasher films – that they are survivors, that they are not sexualized, that they are intelligent and resourceful, and that they employ an active investigating gaze – make them masculine. It is true that the final girl's characteristics are unusual given that so many cinematic representations of female characters depict them as highly sexualized objects, passive, dependent on men, or concerned solely with finding a male partner or taking care of others. In contrast, the final girl is an active and effective agent whose beauty and sexuality are not on display. But this does not make her less feminine, unless we accept the cultural stereotypes that equate femininity with being sexualized, passive, and dependent on men.

Cynthia Freeland (2002) insists that there is greater room for individuality in reactions to horror films and resists the assumption that all audiences respond the same way. Freeland acknowledges that there is much that is objectionable in horror's representation of women but points out that horror films often call into question traditional value and gender roles associated with patriarchal institutions. Freeland is less interested in how audiences respond to horror films than in what horror films say, that is, in how women are presented. If horror gives us healthy representations of women, why explain that away? Why accept outmoded notions of femininity and masculinity in order to label characters such as Ellen Ripley (Sigourney Weaver) and Clarice Starling (Jodi Foster) as masculine?

See also CATHARSIS; FEMINIST CRITICISM; FICTION, THE PARADOX OF RESPONDING TO; KRISTEVA; TRAGEDY.

BIBLIOGRAPHY

Carroll, Noël. (1990). *The Philosophy of Horror; or, Paradoxes of the Heart*. New York: Routledge.

Clover, Carol J. (1992). *Men, Women, and Chainsaws: Gender in the Modern Horror Film*. Princeton: Princeton University Press.

Creed, Barbara. (1993). *The Monstrous Feminine*. London: Routledge.

Freeland, Cynthia. (2002). *The Naked and the Undead: Evil and the Appeal of Horror*. Boulder: Westview.

Grant, Barry Keith (ed.). (1996). *The Dread of Difference: Gender and Horror Film*. Austin: University of Texas Press.

Jancovich, Mark (ed.). (2002). *The Horror Film Reader*. London: Routledge.

Pinedo, Isabel Cristina. (1997). *Recreational Terror: Women and the Pleasures of Horror Film Viewing*. Albany: State Univesity of New York Press.

Schneider, Steven J. (ed.). (2004). *Horror Film and Psychoanalysis: Freud's Worst Nightmare*. Cambridge: Cambridge University Press.

Schneider, Steven J. & Shaw, Dan (eds.). (2003). *Dark Thoughts: Philosophic Reflections on Cinematic Horror*. Lanham: Scarecrow.

Shaw, Dan. (2001). "Power, Horror, and Ambivalence," *Film and Philosophy*, special issue on "Horror," 1–12.

Williams, Linda. (2002). "When the Woman Looks." In *The Horror Film Reader*. Mark Jancovich (ed.). London: Routledge, 61–6.

Wood, Robin. (2003). *Hollywood from Vietnam to Reagan . . . And Beyond*. Rev. edn. New York: Columbia University Press.

AMY COPLAN

Hume, David (1711–1776)   One of the leading figures of the Scottish Enlightenment, David Hume applied the precepts of British empiricism to topics in philosophy, economics, history, and politics. Hume's essay "Of the Standard of Taste" (1757) is his longest sustained examination of art and it is generally regarded as his major contribution to aesthetics. However, it is merely one facet of his larger project and it can be misunderstood if approached without due consideration of his other writings and his intellectual context.

Hume's first publication, *A Treatise of Human Nature*, sold poorly. Dismayed, he confined most of his subsequent philosophical writing to the more accessible format of the short literary essay. Consequently, he never produced the planned segment of the *Treatise* that was to address "criticism." So we must reconstruct Hume's aesthetic theory from a handful of essays and from scattered comments in his *Treatise* and the two *Enquiries*. Readers seeking a clear statement of Hume's philosophy of art will therefore suffer disappointment. In the *Treatise*, for example, the short chapter on beauty and deformity ignores art and focuses on human physical beauty. The discussion is offered solely as a confirmation of Hume's general theory of the emotions. The *Enquiry concerning the Principles of Morals* contains a few short remarks that emphasize the parallels between aesthetic and moral judgment. In keeping with his moral theory, these sources suggest (but do not expand on) utilitarian dimensions of aesthetic judgment. Hume repeatedly endorses the standard idea that critical judgments rely essentially on pleasures of the human imagination. However, he does not provide an account of that doctrine. (He removed his only extended discussion of the topic when he edited his final version of *An Enquiry concerning Human Understanding*.)

Hume's essays on aesthetics are chiefly concerned with negotiating among a series of conflicting theses. He concentrates on how judgments of taste are formed and how they might be justified. He departs from his contemporaries by abandoning the thesis of a distinct faculty of taste. He consistently emphasizes the parallels between moral and aesthetic judgments and grounds both kinds of judgment in our felt experiences of pleasurable approval. Relying on a fundamental dichotomy between feeling and reason, he contends that judgments of taste do not involve "knowledge of truth and falsehood" about objects, but instead "gild" objects with "the sentiment of beauty and deformity" (1998: 163). Yet Hume denies that taste can be reduced to mere subjective preferences. Some works of art are superior to others. "Of the Standard of Taste" directly tackles the resulting paradox. If a poem's elegance or clumsiness is a "sentiment" or emotion felt by its various readers, how do we support the commonsense view that some poets merit praise but others do not? Although Hume rejects a priori aesthetic principles and entertains a sweeping academic skepticism about all universal principles, he says that causal regularities provide an objective basis for distinguishing between better and worse taste. In summary, Hume's aesthetic theory is primarily an account of how evaluative judgments can be justified in the absence of their possessing a truth value.

Writing at a time when other Enlightenment authors actively debated the definition of fine art, Hume ignores that issue. His examples are drawn almost exclusively from literature and theater. In passing, he recognizes that music, painting, and "eloquence" are to be grouped with poetry and essay writing as the "polite," "finer," and "nobler" arts. This group is notable within the arts and sciences for offering beauty, elegance, and wit that is agreeable to refined audiences. In "Of the Rise of the Arts and Sciences," Hume speculates that the polite arts encourage civility and therefore flourish in civilized monarchies. A republic of laws has less need of civility and is more likely to permit and encourage the sciences than the fine arts. These broad remarks are as close as Hume comes to offering an explicit theory of art.

Hume treats beauty and virtue as equivalent, or at the very least as two closely related species of value. In one of his early essays on the arts, "Of the Delicacy of Taste and Passion" (1742), Hume links them so closely that he proposes that developing and refining our taste concerning beauty and deformity in the arts will improve our general character. Working within the mimetic theory that still prevailed in his century, Hume assumes that the arts are primarily concerned with representing human affairs. Hence, one cannot be an apt judge of the arts without first becoming a sound judge of human nature. Developing a delicate taste for art can be a step toward forming "just" evaluations of human life, including one's own situation in the face of varying fortunes. This argument prefigures the closing paragraphs of Hume's 1757 essay "Of the Standard of Taste," where he endorses moral evaluation of art. Fifteen years before he links aesthetic and moral evaluation in that essay, Hume has already proposed that the fine arts demand delicate taste, good sense, and sound moral judgment of human character.

Written to fill out a planned book of essays when other, more controversial essays were deemed unpublishable, "Of Tragedy" and "Of the Standard of Taste" provide Hume's final thoughts on aesthetic issues. "Of Tragedy" addresses the established philosophical paradox of how depictions of displeasing events (e.g., in melodramas, tragic theater and literature, and historical writing) elicit approval. Hume wonders why our naturally disagreeable experience of fear, terror, or anxiety does not override our pleasurable feelings of "approbation" or approval. More to the point, why is the pleasure enhanced in proportion to the degree to which we feel the disagreeable emotions? The solution, Hume claims, is that any emotion can amplify a different or contrary one. Different features of the same work generate the agreeable and disagreeable responses. Imitation is naturally agreeable to the imagination. This pleasure can be supplemented by our sense of taste, which responds pleasurably to the work's aesthetic achievement. As long as the unpleasant responses to the depicted content remain subordinate to these pleasures, anxiety and fear strengthen the predominant sentiment, pleasure. Hence, fictional tragedy is aesthetically satisfying. Hume suggests that, by extension, we have a general theory of the pleasures of poetry, painting, and music.

Unfortunately, Hume complicates his theory in two ways. First, he sometimes proposes that the pleasure "weakens" and even eradicates the disagreeable sentiments. He also talks as if one emotion is "converted" into the other. However, these formulations are difficult to reconcile with the idea of a proportion between the two feelings, which implies that both are maintained. Second, Hume allows that the degree of pleasure depends on the degree of refinement of taste. Unrefined, "vulgar" tastes are pleased by excessive violence that spoils theatrical works. Lacking admiration for a play's more subtle beauties, why do unrefined audiences respond with approval? In their case, the pleasure of imitation enhances the disagreeable emotions aroused by the work's content. So it is unclear why pleasure, not pain, is the predominant emotion for those with unrefined tastes. For these and related reasons, "Of Tragedy" generates more puzzles than it solves.

"Of the Standard of Taste" concentrates on conflicts between refined and unrefined tastes. Hume begins by invoking the parallel between moral and aesthetic judgment. Not every opinion on morality deserves equal consideration, and the same holds for critical judgments of art. It is absurd to suppose that everyone's taste is equally valid and that everyone's evaluation of Milton's poetry has equal standing. Hume thus announces his central problem as that of distinguishing better from worse critical responses. However, there is considerable disagreement about the precise details of his proposed standard. First, Hume emphasizes the importance of rules or principles. Yet he is notoriously unclear about their nature and role (Mothersill 1984: 188–204). Second, Hume's argument appears to be circular. Hence, there is a disagreement about the explanatory adequacy of the proposed standard (Kivy 1967). Third, the essay's closing remarks on art's moral dimension introduce additional complications. Hume entangles moral and aesthetic sentiment in a way that makes it psychologically impossible to appreciate most art unless one is already capable of making unprejudiced moral judgments (Mason 2001).

In outline, the essay is clear. In conformity with Hume's revisions to his *Enquiry concerning Morals*, "Of the Standard of Taste" proposes that matters of fact are necessary but not sufficient to justify evaluative judgments. Hume is an inner sense theorist who treats aesthetic pleasure as an instinctive and natural human response. Natural objects and works of art are beautiful or ugly only because humans respond to them with subtle "sentiments" or feelings of pleasurable approval and disagreeable disapproval. If humans lacked emotions, they would neither formulate nor grasp evaluative judgments. Good art elicits our positive sentiments by employing appropriate composition and design.

Hume argues that levels of taste are supported by the analogy between taste and ordinary perception. Yet he recognizes differences between "mental" and "bodily" taste. As with sound moral judgment, the "proper sentiment" is cognitively complex. It requires that our first impressions be "corrected by argument and reflection" (1998: 76). Hence, a sound critic must possess sound understanding. This requirement leads some interpreters to think that Hume's "true" critic consults aesthetic principles. However, that reading conflicts with the essay's clear warning that such principles are of little value in ethical evaluation. At best, Hume recognizes "rules" of good and bad art in order to make the point that human responses are governed by causal regularities, ensuring that the complex object that is Milton's *Paradise Lost* will have the same effect on similarly constituted audiences. Aesthetic principles play an explanatory role, but they risk rendering Hume's account incoherent by relegating sentiment to a felt pleasure that lacks the normative element of genuine approval (Shiner 1996).

Building on the hypothesis of causal regularities, Hume proposes that taste improves with experience. Invoking a parallel with wine-tasting, he argues that practice and comparison allow some judges to develop a "delicate" taste that recognizes objective elements overlooked by most people. Hence, acquired delicacy furnishes greater complexity in the resulting sentiments. Because few people have the requisite exposure and practice, few people are accurate, capable judges of art.

Finally, Hume emphasizes impartiality. For Hume, the most serious form of corrupting "prejudice" is parochial judgment. Good sense enables a critic to consider a work in light of its originating purpose and context. A "prejudiced" response treats everything as if designed for the evaluator's own situation, or it "perverts" the assessment by judging "the persons introduced in tragedy and poetry" without due consideration of their own point of view.

Hence, good taste is a "delicate imagination" that is guided by sound reasoning, "improved" and "perfected" by extensive practice and comparison, and applied with appropriate and unprejudiced understanding of the object's originating circumstances. Hume explicitly identifies the "joint verdict" of judges possessing such taste as the only standard of taste. Because both the qualifications and the consensus of judges are subject to verification, the normative problem is replaced by two factual questions: Who satisfies this description? What do they jointly recommend?

Unfortunately, "good sense" is itself an evaluative category, so Hume actually replaces one normative category with another (Kivy 1967). Furthermore, the absence of fully articulated rules of art invites the charge that Hume argues in a circle. A taste that rightly ranks works of art is superior because it derives pleasure from the best art. The best art is whatever the superior critics admire. Superior critics are initially identified, in part, by their agreement about those same works. In the end, Hume leaves us with the puzzle of why we ought to develop a taste for those works (Levinson 2002).

See also EIGHTEENTH-CENTURY AESTHETICS; CRITICISM; FICTION, THE PARADOX OF RESPONDING TO; KANT; OBJECTIVITY AND REALISM IN AESTHETICS; RELATIVISM; TASTE.

BIBLIOGRAPHY

Primary sources
[1739] 2000. *A Treatise of Human Nature*. D. F. Norton & M. J. Norton (eds.). Oxford: Oxford University Press.
[1748] 1999. *An Enquiry concerning Human Understanding*. T. L. Beauchamp (ed.). Oxford: Oxford University Press.
[1751] 1998. *An Enquiry concerning the Principles of Morals*. T. L. Beauchamp (ed.). Oxford: Oxford University Press.
1987. *David Hume: Essays Moral, Political, and Literary*. E. F. Miller (ed.). Indianapolis: Liberty Classics.

Secondary sources
Costelloe, Timothy. 2007. *Aesthetics and Morals in the Philosophy of David Hume*. London: Routledge
Kivy, Peter. 1967. "Hume's Standard of Taste: Breaking the Circle," *British Journal of Aesthetics* 7, 57–66.
Levinson, Jerrold. 2002. "Hume's Standard of Taste: The Real Problem," *Journal of Aesthetics and Art Criticism*, 60, 227–38.
Mason, Michelle. 2001. "Moral Prejudice and Aesthetic Deformity: Rereading Hume's 'Of the Standard of Taste'," *Journal of Aesthetics and Art Criticism*, 59, 59–71.
Mothersill, Mary. 1984. *Beauty Restored*. Oxford: Clarendon, 177–209.
Neill, Alex. 1998. " 'An Unaccountable Pleasure': Hume on Tragedy and the Passions," *Hume Studies*, 24, 335–54.
Shiner, Roger A. 1996. "Hume and the Causal Theory of Taste," *Journal of Aesthetics and Art Criticism*. 54, 237–49.
Townsend, Dabney. 2001. *Hume's Aesthetic Theory: Taste and Sentiment*. London: Routledge.

THEODORE GRACYK

humor Despite the fact that most of the great philosophers from Plato onward have had something to say on the matter, the question of what humor is remains notoriously problematic. Standardly, most explanations are placed into one or other of three theoretical traditions, which attempt to explain the phenomenon in terms of incongruity, superiority, or the release of energy. But before discussing these traditions a warning about terminology should be sounded.

Many thinkers mentioned below write about laughter rather than humor. But laughter can arise as a result of experiences other than humor, such as joy, hysteria, or exposure to nitrous oxide. Though several theorists have attempted to explain *all* laughter in terms of a single theoretical formula, most at least *include* an attempt to explain humor (and laughter threat), so in what follows, such theories will be judged according to their success, or otherwise, in this enterprise. Also, humor should be understood in what follows as the general term of which wit, satire, jokes, etc., may be viewed as subcategories.

That said, we can go on to identify the three main humor theoretical traditions.

THE INCONGRUITY TRADITION

Probably the most popular of the three among contemporary humor researchers, the incongruity tradition is often viewed as originating in a comment by Kant. For Kant, "laughter is an affection arising from a strained expectation being suddenly reduced to nothing" (1952: 199). The idea seems to be as follows. Many jokes set up the mind to follow a particular path, but the outcome suddenly makes us realize that we have followed completely the *wrong* path: the one we have followed turns out to lead nowhere; or at least not to the same place as the punch line of the joke. If understood in this way, Kant can be seen as having given birth to the kind of incongruity theory more explicitly outlined by Schopenhauer. The core of Schopenhauer's formulation is that "In every case, laughter results from nothing but the suddenly perceived incongruity between a concept and the real object that had been thought through it in some relation; and laughter itself is just the expression of this incongruity" (1966: i.59).

Some recent writers in this tradition have argued that what is amusing is not the perception of an incongruity itself, but rather the *resolution* of that incongruity: amusement results from fitting what appears to be an anomaly into some conceptual schema. (For instance, John Sparkes's story about his grandmother's strange phobia: fear of the floor. When asked by a psychiatrist why she is not afraid of

"something sensible, like heights," she replies that it is not heights that kill you; it is the floor.) However, though some humor is well explained by incongruity resolution, in other cases – such as the opening lines of Lewis Carroll's *Jabberwocky* or nonsensical riddles ("What's the difference between a duck?" "One of its legs is both the same") – our amusement seems connected precisely to our inability to find a conceptual schema that allows us to make sense of the material.

Humor theorists have used the word "incongruity" to describe a very wide range of humorous phenomena:

1 logical impossibility ("Lincoln was a great Kentuckian. He was born in a log cabin, which he built with his own hands.").
2 ambiguity (including *double entendres* and the literal interpretations of figures of speech, such as Steven Wright's "I woke up one morning and my girlfriend asked me if I slept good. I said, 'No, I made a few mistakes.' ").
3 irrelevance (Woodly Allen: "How is it possible to find meaning in a finite world given my waist and shirt size?").
4 general "inappropriateness": "the linking of disparates . . . the collision of different mental spheres . . . the obtrusion into one context of what belongs in another" (Monro 1951: 235).

Many examples of humor can be subsumed under one or other of these headings, yet there remain doubts as to whether all of the above may be said to be genuinely interchangeable with the term "incongruity." Just as we cannot explain all humor in terms of incongruity resolution, neither can we do so in terms of incongruity without stretching the meaning of the term so far that it ceases to be very informative.

Perhaps the most important objection to incongruity theories is that, even if, in any given example of humor, it is possible to identify an element of incongruity, it is not necessarily this incongruity itself that causes amusement. Putting all the emphasis on incongruity leaves mysterious why one joke will be rated as much funnier than a structurally identical joke on a different topic. (*Ceteris paribus*, some subjects, e.g., sex, tend to "get a laugh" far more easily than others.)

335

Moreover, the incongruity theorist must explain why some incongruities are perceived as funny while others are not, and why a particular incongruity will amuse some but not others. To focus exclusively on incongruity is to stress form or structure at the expense of content or context: we need also to consider factors such as the subject matter, the context within which the humor is set, and the attitude of the hearer or reader, as well as the structure of jokes and the cognitive side of humor on which the incongruity tradition concentrates. This has led some to reject the incongruity tradition, and others to suggest that incongruity is a necessary but not sufficient condition.

THE SUPERIORITY TRADITION

Though Plato and Aristotle's brief comments on laughter arguably justify placing them in this tradition, the most commonly quoted superiority theorist is Thomas Hobbes. For Hobbes, "laughter is nothing else but sudden glory arising from some sudden conception of some eminency in ourselves, by comparison with the infirmity of others, or with our own formerly" (1840: 46). We laugh when we realize we are, or perceive ourselves as being, superior in some way to the object of our laughter.

Clearly, important areas of humor can be explained in this way: much humor has a "victim" and involves, in one way or another, laughing at the perceived "infirmities of others." (Consider racist and sexist jokes, or the flaws of many a stock comic character.) But a similar objection arises as was raised against the incongruity theorist: why do some feelings of superiority result in laughter, while others do not? Hobbes pays insufficient attention to the object of amusement. It is perfectly possible to be amused by a piece of humor for its own sake: in other words, it can often be the object of amusement itself, rather than the hearer's feelings, that causes laughter. If the incongruity tradition puts excessive emphasis on the structure of humor at the expense of the attitude or feelings of the laugher, Hobbes seems to make the opposite mistake.

Another philosopher who should be mentioned in this section is Henri Bergson. For Bergson, laughter's function is to act as a social corrective. The key elements in the comic are mechanism and inelasticity: what is

funny is "something mechanical encrusted on the living" (1956: 84). Each member of society must pay constant attention to his social surroundings, and those who fail to do so thereby demonstrate unsociability, a kind of inelasticity, which renders them comical. Since nobody likes being thought of as comical and laughed at, having this experience, or seeing a comic character treated thus, therefore coerces the individual, by humiliation, into acting as a social being, as society demands.

It is difficult to see why, on Bergson's view, an individual should value a sense of humor as strongly as we do: from the individual's point of view, all that can be said in favor of laughter, on Bergson's account, is that it allows society to pursue "a utilitarian aim of general improvement" (Bergson 1956: 73). Both Hobbes and Bergson tend to overlook the attitude of childlike playfulness that is so important to the enjoyment of much humor based on nonsense and absurdity, for instance. Also, superiority theorists have great difficulty in adequately explaining the phenomenon of laughing at oneself. Hobbes claims that the self at whom we laugh is a former self to whom we are now superior. But this explanation ignores the fact that it is perfectly possible to find one's current self genuinely amusing.

THE RELEASE TRADITION

The central idea in this third main tradition is that laughter provides a release of tension: nervous or psychical energy built up in the nervous system can be discharged through laughter. Though relatively simple versions of this view were propounded by Christian defenders of the Feast of Fools and by Herbert Spencer, the most important and elaborately worked out theory in the tradition is that of Sigmund Freud. Freud divides jokes into two main categories: "innocent" and "tendentious," the latter being subdivided into "hostile" and "obscene" jokes. The pleasure attainable from innocent jokes comes from their "technique" alone, whereas tendentious jokes have "purpose" (*Tendenz*) – such as aggressiveness or "exposure" – as well as technique. Civilization forces us to repress both our aggressive and our sexual desires. Tendentious jokes allow us to enjoy these pleasures, by circumventing the obstacle that stands in the way of the hostile or lustful instinct. Such obstacles are of two kinds: external (the difficulty of venting our aggression on someone more powerful than ourselves, for instance) and internal (our inner, civilization-induced aversions to smut and hostility). A tendentious joke either saves us from having to create the inhibition necessary for self-restraint, or allows an already existing inner obstacle to be overcome and the inhibition lifted. This works as follows: the technique of the joke provides a small amount of pleasure, the "fore-pleasure," which acts as an "incentive bonus" by means of which the suppressed purpose gains sufficient strength to overcome the inhibition and allows the enjoyment of the much greater amount of pleasure which can be released from the purpose (Freud 1976: 188). Since in creating or maintaining an inhibition we expend psychical energy, Freud claims, it is plausible to conclude that the yield of pleasure derived from a tendentious joke corresponds to the psychical expenditure that is saved, and the psychical energy saved can be discharged in laughter. (Freud gives a similar explanation of the pleasure derived from innocent jokes: in the enjoyment of nonsense and absurdity, for instance, the psychical energy saved is that which one would normally expend on obeying the rules of coherence, reason, and logic.)

The central idea of laughter's serving as a release of tension is a plausible one in much humor; the very phrase "comic relief" lends some support to such a view, and it does seem reasonable to say that we operate under a number of constraints, and that laughter can act as a "safety valve." While these constraints are not, *pace* Freud, limited to the pressure to restrain sexual and hostile urges – indeed, the pressures to live up to the ideals of sexual potency and "macho" aggressiveness might themselves be felt as constraints – it is true that we are under pressure to conform to various social and moral norms, and to act rationally. It makes sense to claim that humor which breaks these rules can afford us a release, albeit transitory, from these constraints.

However, Freud's claims are stronger than this, and his key error is to offer his theory as a scientific one: his view that all phenomena are determined by physical and chemical laws leads him to take the notion of "psychical

energy" literally, and thereby to attempt to quantify it. Aspects of the details of the theory remain highly dubious too. For example, Freud maintains that those who expend most psychical energy in repressing their sexual and hostile urges will laugh most at humor which affords relief from these inhibitions. Yet experimental research has suggested the opposite: that it is those who readily express sexual and aggressive feelings who laugh most at sexual and aggressive humor. It is also difficult to see why the fore-pleasure, which on Freud's own admission is a small amount of pleasure, is enough to overcome deep-rooted inhibitions. Finally, we could object that any explanation of humor in terms of energetics merely attempts to explain what happens *when* I find something funny; it does not explain *why* I find it so.

BEYOND ESSENTIALISM?

Perhaps unsurprisingly, the essentialist presupposition that there is some feature common to *all* instances of humor does not seem to have yielded a fully satisfactory account of humor. Furthermore, a synthesis of such theories would still not cut the mustard, since their inadequacies are not merely those of omission: some of the most important defects are *intrinsic* to the theories, such as the stretching of terminology observed in the incongruity tradition. In the light of this, it becomes very tempting to be as skeptical about the likely success of essentialism in humor theory as elsewhere in aesthetics. We also need to be careful about shoe-horning some thinkers into one or other of the three main traditions, as approaching the matter with the traditional trio of theories in mind can lead us to overlook the significance of some thinkers to the topic. To illustrate this, consider finally a figure typically included as just another incongruity theorist: Kierkegaard.

HUMOR AND HUMAN EXISTENCE

Kierkegaard gives humor an important role in an ethical and religious worldview, his richest and most extended discussion of this being in the *Concluding Unscientific Postscript*, published under a pseudonym, Johannes Climacus, who describes himself as a "humorist." Climacus develops important existential roles for irony and humor (subcategories of his more generic term "the comic"). Irony and humor serve as "boundary zones" between the "aesthetic," "ethical," and "religious" existence-spheres. The ironist stands at the boundary between the "aesthetic" and the "ethical" life, having seen the limitations of the former – a fragmented life which involves an endless evasive toying with existential possibilities – but without moving to the ethical, in which serious choices and commitments for one's own life are made. Whereas irony is proud, and tends to divide one person from another – Climacus describes it in terms of self-assertion and "teasing" (1992: 551) – humor is rather more gentle, and is concerned with those tragicomic elements of the human condition shared by all human beings. Humor thus has a *sympathy* that irony lacks (1992: 582), and the humorist understands more profoundly the role of *suffering* in human life. This insight into such aspects as suffering places humor, rather than irony, at the boundary of the ethical and the religious.

The overall idea seems to be that, as one ascends the existence-spheres from the aesthetic, to the ethical, to the religious, one develops an ever deeper and more profound sense of the comical in life. Hence Climacus' claim that a sense of and taste for the comic is intimately related to one's existential capabilities: "the more competently a person exists, the more he will discover the comic" (1992: 462).

More recently, this idea has been developed by others to suggest that prolonged exposure to humor of an appropriate sort can have an important role to play in the development of the virtues, as part of the process of moral education as "habituation" espoused by Aristotle. Thus Kierkegaard's work can be seen as one way of expanding the scope of philosophizing about humor beyond the three standard theoretical traditions, and into a discussion of the connections between humor, emotion, virtue, and the very nature of being human.

See also COMEDY; IRONY; KIERKEGAARD; PSYCHO-ANALYSIS AND ART; TRAGEDY.

BIBLIOGRAPHY
Bergson, Henri. 1956 [1900]. *Laughter*. C. Brereton & F. Rothwell (trans.). In *Comedy*. W. Sypher (ed.). Baltimore: Johns Hopkins University Press, 61–190.

Critchley, Simon. 2002. *On Humour*. London: Routledge.
Freud, Sigmund 1976 [1905]. *Jokes and Their Relation to the Unconscious*. J. Strachey (trans.). Harmondsworth: Penguin.
Hobbes, Thomas. 1840 [1640]. *Human Nature*. In *The English Works of Thomas Hobbes*, vol. iv. W. Molesworth (ed.). London: John Bohn, 1–76.
Kant, Immanuel. 1952 [1790]. *The Critique of Judgement*. J. C. Meredith (trans.). Oxford: Clarendon.
Kierkegaard, Søren. 1992. [1846]. *Concluding Unscientific Postscript*. H. V. Hong & E. H. Hong (trans.). Princeton: Princeton University Press.
Lippitt, John. 2000. *Humour and Irony in Kierkegaard's Thought*. London: Macmillan.
Monro, D. H. 1951. *Argument of Laughter*. Carlton: Melbourne University Press.
Morreall. John. 1983. *Taking Laughter Seriously*. Albany: State University of New York Press.
Morreall, John (ed.). 1987. *The Philosophy of Laughter and Humor*. Albany: State University of New York Press.
Schopenhauer, Arthur. 1966 [1819/1844]. *The World as Will and Representation*. 2 vols. E. F. J. Payne (trans.). New York: Dover.

JOHN LIPPITT

Hutcheson, Francis (1694–1746)

Hutcheson, Francis (1694–1746) Scottish moral and aesthetic philosopher; professor at Glasgow University, and a leading representative of the "moral sense" school.

Three important and substantial treatises, published in the first quarter of the eighteenth century, inaugurated the modern discipline of aesthetics and, at the same time, by no means coincidentally, established what Paul O. Kristeller has called the "modern system of the arts." They are J. P. de Crousaz's *Traité du beau* (1714), the Abbé Du Bos's *Réflexions critiques sur la poësie et sur la peinture* (1719), and Francis Hutcheson's *Inquiry concerning Beauty, Order, Harmony, Design* (1725), the first of two works published together under the title, *An Inquiry into the Original of Our Ideas of Beauty and Virtue*. These must be considered the first book-length studies in the field of aesthetics and the philosophy of art, at least in the way we now conceive of them – which is to say, as a fully autonomous intellectual enterprise within the general confines of philosophy. And although Hutcheson's work is neither the first of the three nor the most expansive, it is unique in the clear philosophical direction that he was able to give to the subject as he understood it, in his brief but concentrated monograph.

The model of aesthetic perception that Hutcheson chose derived from the Lockean account of how we perceive secondary qualities. Take, for example, my perception of a red barn. As Hutcheson would have understood Locke, here is what is happening. The microstructure of the material object – the "primary qualities" – causally interacts with my sense of sight, to produce in me the sensation of redness. Strictly speaking, the term "red" refers to the sensation or "idea" that is experienced, because if there were no such idea, there would be no occasion for me to call the object "red." It is customary, nevertheless, also to call the object itself "red" and the "power" it possesses of causing the idea of sensation in us "redness." Redness is a simple quality – which is to say, the sensation or idea is a simple idea, not a complex one. And the perception of it is nonepistemic in the sense that we need know nothing about the causal apparatus, or what it is in the red object that possesses the appropriate powers, to perceive redness. This basic outline is followed, point for point, by Hutcheson in his account of how we perceive what he calls "absolute beauty," although some of the points are in the nature of analogies rather than literal.

On his view, "the word *beauty* is taken for *the idea raised in us*, and a *sense* of beauty for *our power of receiving this idea*" (1973: 34). The "property" in "objects" that causes this idea of beauty to be raised in us is a relation among the parts of the object that Hutcheson called (the French had already used the phrase) *uniformity amidst variety*; and so "where the uniformity of bodies is equal, the beauty is as the variety; and where the variety is equal, the beauty is as the uniformity" (1973: 40). This we know, presumably, by inductive inference.

Analogous to the physical object, the red barn, that raises in us the idea of redness, is not a physical object that raises the idea of beauty, but rather a different kind of "object" – namely, a complex of ideas of primary and secondary qualities, perceived not by an outer but by an "inner" sense: what Hutcheson tended to call, in his later writings, "*reflex* or subsequent, by which certain new forms or perceptions are received, in consequence of others previously observed" (Hutcheson 1747: 12–13). Thus the property in "objects" that raises the idea of beauty, although it plays the same kind of causal role that the primary qualities of external objects do in arousing ideas of secondary qualities, is not a congeries of primary qualities, not a property of the external world at all, but the relational property of the internal world of ideas.

There are, then, three different "ideas," properly so called by the Lockean, that are involved in Hutcheson's account of aesthetic perception. There is the complex idea, consisting of ideas of primary and secondary qualities, that possesses the relational property of *uniformity amidst variety*. There is the simple idea of beauty, aroused by that property, that Hutcheson sometimes describes as something like a secondary quality but more often as a "pleasant idea" – by which, clearly, he means "pleasure." And there is, finally, the complex idea of uniformity amid variety that one forms when one comes to know that uniformity amidst variety is the cause of the idea of beauty.

Now each of these ideas can, on the Lockean scheme with which Hutcheson is working, be called with some propriety the "idea of beauty"; and this has led some to falsely assert that Hutcheson believed the idea of beauty to be complex. But, speaking with the learned, only the simple idea of beauty, the pleasure raised by the sense of beauty, is "beauty" properly so called. That is the genuine doctrine. And we know that the idea is simple by virtue merely of the fact that a special "sense" is required for its perception. (Locke required no such "sense" of beauty because for him beauty *was* a complex idea.)

Another mistake to guard against is that of concluding that Hutcheson is really maintaining an epistemic account of aesthetic perception because, on his account, we can consciously perceive that certain objects possess uniformity amidst variety, the cause of the idea of beauty, whereas we cannot consciously perceive the microstructure of matter that causes the ideas of secondary qualities. However, Hutcheson does *explicitly* say that uniformity amidst variety functions in a way exactly analogous to the way the microstructure of matter functions in causing the ideas of secondary qualities; and he does say *explicitly* that uniformity amidst variety causes us to have the idea of beauty without our necessarily being aware that the object possesses uniformity amidst variety, or that uniformity amidst variety has anything to do with beauty, just as people were seeing red long before they knew anything of Locke's account of perception. Indeed, in one place Hutcheson says both in the same breath.

> But in all these instances of beauty let it be observed that the pleasure is communicated to those who never reflected on this general foundation, and that all here alleged is this, that the pleasant sensation arises only from objects in which there is *uniformity amidst variety*. We have the sensation without knowing what is the cause of it, as a man's taste may suggest ideas of sweets, acids, bitters, though he be ignorant of the forms of the small bodies, or their motions, which excite these perceptions in him. (1973: 47)

I have explicated at length Hutcheson's account of what he calls "absolute beauty" because that is the part that was most influential in the eighteenth century. But, in fact, the larger portion of the *Inquiry concerning Beauty* is taken up with what he calls "relative beauty," which is to say, the beauty of "imitation." Naturally, what he has uppermost in his mind in this regard is representation in the fine arts.

One might have expected that tackling the beauty of imitation would force Hutcheson to abandon, for that very different-seeming kind of beauty, the causal, nonepistemic account that served for absolute beauty. For, after all, it would seem palpably obvious that seeing something as a representation or "imitation" of something else is a clear case of "perceiving that . . ." Such, however, is not how he saw things. The foundation, for him, is still the same: *uniformity amidst variety* – "this beauty [of imitation] is founded on a conformity, or a kind of unity between the original and the copy" (1973: 54), with the variety, it must be supposed, being supplied by the fact that the original and the copy are *different* sorts of things altogether, although unified by the similarity of their appearances.

On the assumption, then, that uniformity amidst variety must be functioning in the same way in the case of relative beauty as in the case of absolute – or it would not have been introduced in the former at all – Hutcheson must be maintaining, it is clear, that although the complex idea we have of X imitating Y is composed of various "knowings" as well as "perceivings that . . . ," the uniformity amidst variety that these conscious "knowings" and "perceivings that . . ." possess we are not aware of at all. And it is this hidden property of our conscious "knowings" and "perceivings that . . ." that causes to arise in us, through our internal sense, the simple, pleasurable idea of relative beauty. Whatever may be said of the plausibility of Hutcheson's position here, its consistency is undoubted.

See also EIGHTEENTH-CENTURY AESTHETICS; BEAUTY.

BIBLIOGRAPHY

Primary sources
[1725] 1738. *An Inquiry into the Original of our Ideas of Beauty and Virtue.* 4th edn. London.
[1738] 1973. *Inquiry concerning Beauty, Order, Harmony, Design.* P. Kivy (ed.). The Hague: Nijhoff.
1747. *A Short Introduction to Moral Philosophy.* Glasgow.

Secondary sources
Kail, Peter J. 2000. "Function and Normativity in Hutcheson's Aesthetic Epistemology," *British Journal of Aesthetics*, 40, 441–51.
Kivy, Peter. 1976. *The Seventh Sense: A Study of Francis Hutcheson's Aesthetics and Its Influence in Eighteenth-Century Britain.* New York: Burt Franklin.
Kivy, Peter. 2007. "The Perception of Beauty in Hutcheson's First *Inquiry*: Response to James Shelley," *British Journal of Aesthetics*, 47, 416–31.
Matthews, Patricia M. 1998. "Hutcheson on the Idea of Beauty," *Journal of the History of Philosophy*, 36, 233–59.
Michael, Emily. 1984. "Francis Hutcheson on Aesthetic Perception and Aesthetic Pleasure," *British Journal of Aesthetics*, 34, 241–55.
Shelley, James. 2007. "Aesthetics and the World at Large," *British Journal of Aesthetics*, 47, 169–83.
Townsend, Dabney. 1987. "From Shaftsbury to Kant: the Development of the Concept of Aesthetic Experience," *Journal of the History of Ideas*, 48, 287–305.

PETER KIVY

I

iconoclasm and idolatry Assaults against images – iconoclasm – occur in all cultures. In analyzing the various forms of aggression against images, one may want to distinguish between acts of vandalism (including acts of war), pathological or psychotic violence, and destruction or mutilation for reasons of principle (political or religious); but in practice the motives are much less clear and much more difficult to unravel. There is also more of a continuum than may first be apparent between spontaneous acts of individual violence and concerted and organized group hostility. In situations where public or theological motives are adduced for the iconoclastic deed or event, individual psychological motives may well appear to receive a kind of legitimation in the social, legal, theological, or philosophical domain.

The term "iconoclasm" is popularly used in a metaphorical sense; it will not be so discussed here. At issue are physical acts against physical images, whether two- or three-dimensional, and sometimes buildings.

The more clearly definable motivations for iconoclasm include the following:

1 the desire for publicity (as in the *locus classicus* of this motivation, the destruction of the temple of Diana at Ephesus by Herostratus, and in any number of psychopathic assaults on images in the twentieth century, where the targets have been exceptionally well-known works of art);
2 the fear of the life inherent in an image (whether because of the imagined conflation of sign and signified, or in the case, as often in the Reformation, of images operated by deceptive mechanical means);
3 the desire to demonstrate that an image is not a live thing, in the end, but merely dead material;

4 the belief that an image is pornographic or may be sexually arousing;
5 the view that too much wealth is invested in a material object, relative to perceived social need;
6 the sense that an image is too beautiful or too stylish to convey the message it is meant to convey (as in those cases where art and artistry are believed to be too distracting, such as the sixteenth-century polemics against Michelangelo's style);
7 the desire to draw attention to a felt social or personal injustice;
8 the need to avenge such an injustice by attacking or destroying a work that is known to be popularly venerated – or one which has become a particularly important local or national symbol (as with the attacks on Rembrandt's *Nightwatch* in Amsterdam, or those on paintings by Dürer in Munich).

Finally, there is the whole gamut of cases where the image or building is taken to be a symbol of an oppressive, hated, or overthrown order or individual. This includes the occasions when all images that might recall a deposed regime are removed (as in the persistent removal of images in Old Kingdom Egypt and in the great Soviet iconoclasm of 1989), or where images that stand in one way or another for a suppressed religion are destroyed. It is in such contexts that one can understand the many instances where the pictures and statues of a hated authority have one or another form of violence visited upon them, or on parts of them. In almost all such cases it is not hard to see the plausibility of the rationale. Only in those instances where the assailant believes that he or she has been instructed by God or some other supernatural being or force to attack a work is it difficult

341

to see the possible continuity with normal rational behavior.

The range of iconoclastic acts is great: they vary from surface defilement to total destruction. Among the commonest examples are partial mutilation, as in the removal of sexual organs (in attempts to reduce the putative sexual affectiveness of the image) or of the limbs of unjust judges; or in the removal of those parts of the body – generally the face (the eyes, but often the mouth or nose), or a limb or two – which most betoken the imagined life of the image. The passage from censorship to iconoclasm – and vice versa – is a common one.

Perhaps the commonest basis for iconoclasm is the belief that the image must be destroyed, or have its putative power reduced, because it is something other than it ought to be; or that it has powers that it ought not to have; or that it is testimony to skills which are regarded as supernatural. The aim in all such cases is to deny the power of the image.

Among the more characteristic of the iconoclastic injunctions is one to be found in Exodus 20: 3–5 (the first or the first and second of the commandments, depending on one's church), where the injunction, "thou shalt have no other gods before me . . . [nor] bow down thyself to them, nor serve them," is followed by the firm prohibition (sometimes regarded simply as part of the first commandment and sometimes – more rigorously – as the second), "thou shalt not make unto thee any graven image, or any likeness of anything that is in heaven above, or that is in the earth beneath, or that is in the water under the earth." Equally typical is the passage in the Islamic *hadith*, where the artist who has the temerity to create figurative images is summoned, in the next world, before God, and is instructed to breathe life into his creations. Failing to do so (since that ability is reserved only to God), he is cast into outer hell for his effrontery in attempting to enter, by imitation, what is God's province alone – namely, the creation of living beings. In both cases the crime is one that falls under the rubric of idolatry.

One of the more persistent allegations against images, especially in Christian cultures, is that pictures and statues, being essentially material, are by their very nature incapable of adequately circumscribing the divine, the spiritual, and the essentially immaterial. To attempt to do so is also to make false gods, which have to be cast down in order to preserve the purity of religion or the state.

The notion that images are idolatrous forms an important element in the motivation for many iconoclastic acts and attitudes. Images are taken to be idols when they do not represent the true god; when they are identified with the god or divinity itself (rather than simply as mediators); and when they are wrongly or abusively worshipped or venerated (the German *Abgott* and Dutch *Afgod*, for example, convey more closely the sense of a deceptive deviation from the genuine god). They are seductive because they give the illusion of the godly or divine (as in the original sense of *eidolon*, ghost, phantom). With idolatry there is always a sense of devotion to a substitute for what ought to be the real object of devotion: hence idolatry can occur in the case of real, physical images, and in the more metaphorical sense in which we speak of "false gods," usually something that is the subject of moral disapprobation. For the sixteenth-century Protestant reformers, avarice was regarded as an idol just as much as any image. Indeed, one consistent element in all allegations of idolatry is the moral dimension. There are no cases in which idolatry is taken to be something good or morally acceptable.

In iconoclastic movements, as well as in some individual cases, the iconoclasts may allege that the images of god (or the approved images of a particular society, whether god, ruler, or symbol of the regime) are not godly but, rather, idolatrous. As if to demonstrate that they do not in fact have the powers attributed to them, or which true gods are supposed to have, they are mutilated, overthrown, or destroyed. At the end of the sixth century, Gregory the Great threw the pagan idols – that is, the statues of classical antiquity – into the Tiber. They were idols not only because they were beautiful and therefore seductive but also because they were the replete symbols of a corrupt religion, only recently hostile to the true one.

One of the most consistent bases of all those reservations about images that terminate in their mutilation, removal, or total elimination is the association between material images and sensuality. Precisely because of their materiality they cannot mediate with the world of the spirit. Both their materiality and their form engage and provoke our senses, through the channel of sight. Excessive engagement with the aesthetic pleasures of art leads only to luxury and seduction (as is frequently alleged in the case of the history of the Roman republic); the purity and primitive virility of the people are better preserved if images are not allowed to corrupt such virtues. Exotic images, and excessive interest in art, make people soft. Images, especially artistic ones, are thus proscribed in the interests of the commonweal, of moral purity, and of a spirituality untrammeled by sensuality or materiality.

The same fears concerning images surface in modern societies, not simply in relation to the varieties of pornography, but also, in general, in relation to television. And just as in the old arguments, words and texts are assigned a truth value and a spiritual and cultural status that images, by their very nature, are not believed to have. They cannot attain this status, because they are material and sensual, and are perceived by the eyes, the most direct channel of all to the senses. Hearing now takes the place of seeing, not only as a more reliable form of perception, but also as a less potentially dangerous one. Words replace images in societies that are purified of idolatry: written texts in literate societies, the spoken word in illiterate ones. The way is prepared first by censorship, and then, increasingly, by one or more of the varieties of iconoclasm

See also CENSORSHIP; MORALITY AND ART; PORNOGRAPHY; RELIGION AND ART.

BIBLIOGRAPHY
Freedberg, David. 1985. *Iconoclasts and Their Motives.* Maarssen: Schwartz.
Freedberg, David. 1989. *The Power of Images: Studies in the History and Theory of Response.* Chicago: University of Chicago Press.
Latour, Bruno & Weibel, Peter (eds.). 2002. *Iconoclash: The Image Wars in Science, Religion, and Art.* Cambridge, MA: MIT Press.
Warnke, Martin (ed.). 1973. *Bildersturm: Die Zerstörung des Kunstwerks.* Munich: Hanser.

DAVID FREEDBERG

illusion Roughly, an illusion is an error rooted in perception. A little more precisely, it

is an error occurring when what one perceives reliably elicits a response that would be appropriate to something of a rather different nature. I will first attempt to be more precise still about the notion, or notions, of illusion; and then turn to illusion's significance for art.

WHAT IS ILLUSION?
Psychology revels in the study of illusions, and offers many examples. In the Müller-Lyer illusion, two lines of equal length, topped with arrowheads pointing in different directions, look to be different lengths. The "impossible triangle" is an open-jawed, three-dimensional object. Viewed from the right position, any one of its corners appears both nearer and farther away than each of the others. The Mach band effect leads a square of uniform color, set against a suitable background, to appear to vary in shade across its width. Shepard tones sound as if they are constantly rising in pitch, even though what one is listening to is stable in that respect. But everyday life also throws up examples. The stationary train you are on seems to move when the adjacent carriage pulls out of the platform. The moon looks far larger when near the horizon than when high in the sky. Given the right size of tile and width of grout, you see faint spots at the center of the grout crossings in your shower. As these examples suggest, illusions come in many forms. They may be in two dimensions or three. They may involve shape, color, movement, or pitch. They might be visual, auditory, or involve proprioception. What one seems to see may merely not exist, or it might be (as in the case of the impossible triangle) something that could not do so.

An illusion is always the illusion of something. There is a way things seem to be, a way other than they really are. Sometimes the seat of error is belief. On first encountering the Müller-Lyer illusion, subjects are likely to believe that one line is shorter than the other. Learning the facts is not, however, always enough to banish illusion – the two lines may continue to look different lengths, even when one no longer believes they are. Thus illusion might be a matter of error in belief, or it might involve error in experience. We can call the former *cognitive* and the latter *experiential* illusion. In either case, the error concerns something perceived. The illusory object is perceived, and either belief or experience ascribe to the thing properties it does not really possess. Unless the first part of this condition is met, the case is not one of illusion, but of hallucination.

It is natural to think that cognitive illusion will normally occur only when experiential illusion does. What, though, is involved in experiential illusion? The simplest thought would be that one's experience of whatever one perceives matches that one would have if perceiving something else, something with a different nature (Clark 1993). However, we might wonder whether this is in fact the best way to define experiential illusion. For one thing, differences in experience will not matter unless they somehow register with the subject. My experience before object 1 might count as the illusion of perceiving object 2 even though the two experiences differ, provided those differences are as nothing to me. Of course, the differences that do matter cannot be differences in what I *believe*. Matching belief is definitive of cognitive illusion, and we are currently trying to define its experiential form. But there are other responses to experience to which we might appeal – action and feeling, for example. For another thing, some illusions certainly do not involve an experience that matches that we would have before the object illusorily presented. The illusory spots on the grout, for instance, have an insubstantial, floating quality quite unlike any that a real spot could display. If we are right to describe this as the illusion of seeing spots, then it is not always true that the illusory experience is exactly like that we would have before the object we seem to see. To distinguish this from illusions in which that is the case, I will talk of *perfect* and *imperfect* experiential illusion.

ILLUSION AND ART

How do the various notions of illusion bear on art? Do works of art themselves sustain illusion? Some do, for sure. A *trompe-l'oeil* painting of ornately molded plasterwork on a ceiling might, seen from far below, look exactly like the molding it depicts. The result might be not merely perfect experiential illusion, but cognitive illusion too, at least in those ignorant of the trick. And it is at least not hopeless to argue, as some have done, that perfect experiential

illusion might be found more widely than in *trompe-l'oeil* painting alone – that there are aspects of it in other painting of a realist nature (Gombrich 1977), that cinema and theater might sometimes sustain it (Allen 1995), and that it is what modern technology aims for in reproducing recorded music.

However, even if the attempt to argue this point is not hopeless, it does not in the end succeed. The *trompe-l'oeil* ceiling painting is able to work its magic in part because the context severely constrains the position from which we can see the work. Other painting, even of a highly realistic nature, is all too easily seen for what it is, given the spectator's ability to move from side to side and back and forth relative to the canvas, her ability to compare the light falling in the gallery with that apparently falling in the space depicted, the visibility of cracks in the picture's surface and highlights reflecting the incident light, and so forth. Parallel points hold for cinema, in which, however hard it is to see many features of the screen, one is aware of its flatness, and one's experience is sensitive to the fact that the light reflected from it usually varies in intensity far less than would light coming from the scenes represented.

There are more general obstacles to illusion's having a major role in art. Cognitive illusion is surely very rare. Almost always, in engaging with artworks we know that that is what they are, and do not mistake them for what they represent. If this were not so, it would be hard to appreciate them *as art*, for that in part surely involves appreciating that a certain effect has been achieved, and wondering (and wondering at) how it has been. If we simply took artworks for other objects, we could not appreciate what is (in one sense) their art. We would be left appreciating only the qualities of whatever it is they seem to put before us. But this point also curtails the role of experiential illusion. The central vehicle of our appreciation of art is experience. It is in experiencing the work that we are alert to what there is to value in it. If we avoided cognitive illusion but remained in the grip of illusory experience, we would still be confronted merely with whatever the work illusorily presents. Our appreciation that an effect has been achieved would be limited to belief, to our knowledge that what is before us is in fact a work of art. And the prospects for investigating how the effect has been achieved would be very limited indeed. These points strongly suggest that the place of illusion, both experiential and cognitive, will be strictly limited, even in those arts, such as painting, where illusion most readily occurs.

In response, advocates of illusion will weaken their claims. Not much art sustains continuous illusion, they concede. But perhaps our experience of a good deal of art is illusory some of the time. We swing between succumbing to experiential illusion and falling out of it again. In doing so, we can appreciate art for what it is, and have some chance of discovering how it achieves its effects (Gombrich 1977). Thus we have one last distinction between forms of illusion: continuous and discontinuous.

There is no space here to explore whether the appeal to discontinuous illusion will restore the notion's claim to be central to at least some arts. Even if it does, when we turn to the arts more generally, the situation is bleaker. The prospects for illusion in any form look so poor, in music (as opposed to its reproduction), in sculpture, and especially in literature, that surely no one would try to persuade us that illusion is central to art per se.

ART, ILLUSION, AND IMAGINATION

Yet, strangely, that is just what some have claimed. In *Laocoön*, G. E. Lessing suggested that both painting and sculpture on the one hand, and the literary arts on the other, can engender illusion. He went on to explore the differences in what each can illusorily present, and the means by which they do so. More recently in *Feeling and Form* Susanne Langer constructed a comprehensive theory of the arts, allocating to each a distinctive form of illusion it is its peculiar mission to create. What did these thinkers have in mind? Did they mean by "illusion" something different from any of the phenomena described above? If not, were they simply blind to the objections to its role in the wider arts just canvassed?

I suggest that for Lessing and Langer, as for others who have attempted to apply the notion of illusion to the arts in general, the notion of illusion is inextricably bound to that of imagining. Art engenders illusion by stimulating particularly vivid imaginings in its audience.

Those imaginings often, in the visual and musical arts, affect the perceptual experience we have of the work. (In the literary arts, in contrast, the thought must be, our distinctive engagement with the work lies in imagining alone.) The claim that art sustains illusion is thus equivalent to the claim that it provokes certain vivid imaginings.

The insight at the heart of this view is that imaginative engagement is central to a great deal of art. The error lies in tying these imaginings to the notion of illusion. For there is no reason to think that illusion involves the imagination. Psychological study seeks to locate its origins in the workings of our perceptual systems. To understand why the lines in the Müller-Lyer illusion look to be different lengths, we need to discover what aspects of the figure are operative, and how they interact with those features of the visual system used in perceiving relative length, so as to produce on the system the effect that lines of equal length would have. Why think that at any point in this explanation we will need to appeal to the imagination?

True, there is a sense of "imagine" in which if someone did not perceive something (but only seemed to), then he must have imagined it. But in that use of the word, it is simply a gloss on the idea of misperception or false belief. The insight that art engages our imagination appeals to a quite different and more substantial notion, albeit one that is hard to define. Now, it would be natural to think of illusion as involving imagining if we took imagination, at least in its sensory forms, in something like the way that Hume and many other empiricists have done, as involving mental states that differ, in their phenomenology at least, from perceptions in only one dimension, a dimension Hume famously labeled "force, or vivacity" (1977: book 1, pt. 1, sec. 3). For a maximally "forceful" or "vivid" imaginative episode will then indeed be indistinguishable, to the subject, from perception. Within this framework, it is natural to think of illusory experience as constituted by imaginings that attain this unusual level of vivacity. But this view of sensory imagining, despite its perennial appeal to layman and expert alike, came under severe criticism in the last century. At the least, to appeal to it to explain illusion is to take on a significant theoretical commitment.

There is one last possible attraction in deploying illusion in giving an account of art. Above I have concentrated my criticisms on views that appeal to perfect experiential illusion, be it continuous or discontinuous. It may seem that the defender of illusion would do better to appeal to it in its imperfect form, such as that obtaining when we see the shifting, insubstantial spots on the grout. The way the spots are given to us – half-present, half not – may seem strikingly akin to the way some forms of art present us with their objects. After all, one might think, if we see Cromwell in a portrait, or Coriolanus brought to life before us on the stage, these objects too have a tenuous perceptual presence, neither fully there nor wholly absent. Perhaps so. But even if some forms of art are significantly like imperfect illusions, in certain respects, it does not follow that we should explain the former in terms of the latter. For each of these phenomena is as puzzling as the other. We should not assume that we already have the sort of theoretical insight into imperfect illusions that could help us in theorizing about art.

See also GOMBRICH; IMAGINATION; LANGER; LESSING; PICTURE PERCEPTION; REPRESENTATION.

BIBLIOGRAPHY
Allen, Richard. 1995. *Projecting Illusion: Film Spectatorship and the Illusion of Reality.* Cambridge: Cambridge University Press.
Clark, Austen. 1993. *Sensory Qualities.* Oxford: Clarendon.
Gombrich, Ernst. 1977. *Art and Illusion: A Study in the Psychology of Pictorial Representation.* 5th edn. Oxford: Phaidon.
Gregory, Richard. 1997. *Eye and Brain: The Psychology of Seeing.* 5th edn. Princeton: Princeton University Press.
Hume, David. 1977 [1739]. *A Treatise of Human Nature.* London: Dent.
Langer, Susanne. 1953. *Feeling and Form.* New York: Scribner.
Lessing, G. E. 1962 [1766]. *Laocoön: An Essay on the Limits of Painting and Poetry.* E. A. McCormick (trans.). Indianapolis: Bobbs-Merrill.

ROBERT HOPKINS

imagination The word "imagination" is used in a variety of ways, usually to denote a mental capacity. As a technical term of philosophy it has at least two senses: First, the capacity to experience "mental images," and, second, the capacity to engage in creative thought. The connection between these two senses is obscure, partly because each is obscure in itself, and very much dependent upon the theory with which it is associated.

THE CAPACITY TO EXPERIENCE MENTAL IMAGES
Mental images occur in thinking, in dreaming, in perceiving, and in remembering. They also occur when we are trying to imagine something (in the second sense of the term). Because they occur in so many different contexts, it would be quite misleading to suppose that a theory of mental images is the same as a theory of imagination, in the second sense, or even a necessary *part* of such a theory. For one thing, there seems nothing wrong in the suggestion that animals have mental images: certainly they perceive, dream, and remember (after a fashion). But it strains credibility to say that they have imagination in the second sense – if we mean by this that they can engage in the thought processes involved in storytelling, painting, or creative science.

A mental image is like a thought in the following ways:

1 It is "of" or "about" something. This feature – "intentionality" – implies that a creature's capacity for mental imagery strictly depends upon its cognitive powers. For example, if it cannot have *thoughts* about the past, then it cannot have "memory images" either.
2 It may be true or false: a true image of your friend's face is one that *shows him as he is*, that is, which corresponds to the reality.
3 It stands to thoughts in relations of implication and contradiction. My image of Venice may contradict your thoughts about the town; it may also imply them.

However, a mental image is *not merely* a thought. Images are like perceptions: they have a component that we are inclined to call "sensory," and which relates them to the experiences that we obtain through our senses.

IMAGES AND SENSORY EXPERIENCES
It is not easy to say, in precise terms, what the "sensory" character of imagery consists in.

The following features of images are, however, shared with various other "sensory" experiences, and could be assumed to provide a prephilosophical definition of the idea:

1 Images can be precisely dated in time: they begin at a certain moment, last for a while, and then cease.
2 They may be more or less intense (like a pain, or a visual experience). This is not a matter of being more or less *detailed*, but is something *sui generis*.
3 They can be fully described only by reference to a corresponding *perceptual* experience: my image of Venice can be conveyed only by describing what it would be like to *see* such and such a vista; my image of a piece of music must, likewise, be described in terms of how the music is *heard*, and so on.
4 There is a "subjective" aspect to every image, which we may express by saying that there is a phenomenology or a "what it's like" to have the image. It is doubtful that there is a phenomenology in the case of a *thought*.

CREATIVE IMAGINATION AND MENTAL IMAGERY

Mental images occur when we dream, when we remember, and also when we *imagine* things. Sometimes we describe a person as imagining what he thinks is there but is not. In this sense "imagining" means something like "suffering an illusion," and to "imagine things" is to acquire *false beliefs* about the real world. Creative imagination, however, is not a matter of illusion. The person with a strong imagination does not suffer more false *beliefs* than his less imaginative neighbor: rather, he thinks more widely, more creatively, less literally. His thought roams among possibilities and is more ready to "suspend" both belief and disbelief. Imaginative thoughts in this sense are not illusions about the real world, but depictions of a world that is not only unreal but also known to be so. (To be *taken in* by this world – for example, by the world of a play – is to exhibit a deficiency of imagination rather than a superabundance of it.)

Imagery has a part to play in creative imagination, although it is neither necessary nor sufficient for it. When I imagine, for example, a dialogue between Socrates and Xanthippe,

I may also imagine what it would be like to *see* and *hear* the encounter between them. In such a case, my imaginative thoughts are partly embodied in images. Such images differ from dream images and perceptual images, in that they lie within the province of the will. It makes no sense to command a person to dream something or to see something. But we can certainly command her to imagine something, and she may "summon" or "construct" the image without further ado, and using no method other than the direct application of her will.

One of Wittgenstein's most interesting observations in this area is that mental states can be classified according to whether they are or are not "subject to the will," and that the distinction cuts across the traditional divisions between the sensory and the intellectual, between the animal and the rational, between the affective and the cognitive, and even the "passive" and the "active" (as these were described, for example, by Spinoza). There are perceptions that are subject to the will (seeing an aspect) and also cognitive states (supposing, hypothesizing); but wherever belief or sensation is involved, the will, as it were, withdraws. I can command you to suppose that the moon is made of rock (rather than cheese), but not to believe it; I can command you to injure your finger, but not to have a pain in your finger; and so on.

One reason for thinking that memory and creative imagination are closely related is that both involve imagery, and in both cases the imaging process remains at least partly within the domain of the will. When I "summon up remembrance of things past" I am *doing* something that I might have refrained from doing. I deliberately call to mind the appearance and character of past events and objects, so as to undergo again, in some faint and helpless version, the experiences which were once imprinted on my senses. There is an art in this, which is not unlike the art employed in fiction, and while not everyone is able to achieve what Proust achieved in reworking the past as though it were entirely the *product* of creative imagination, there is no doubt that "powers of recall" and "powers of creation" have, in this area, much in common and speak to a single emotional need.

CREATIVE IMAGINATION

The voluntary nature of imaginative acts gives a clue to creative imagination. For, whether or not it involves imagery, imagination always involves the summoning or creating of mental contents which are *not otherwise given* (as they are given, e.g., in perception and judgment). When I stand before a horse it involves no act of creative imagination to entertain the image of a horse – this image is implanted in me by my experience, and is *no doing of mine.* Likewise, if I listen to a story of some battle, or read an account of it in the newspaper, my thoughts are not my own doing, and I play no creative role in the unfolding of them. In general, things perceived and things believed, in the normal course of our cognitive activity, are imprinted upon us, and are both passive and independent of our own creative powers.

When, however, I summon the image of a horse in the absence of a real horse, or invent the description of a battle which I have heard about from no other source, my image and my thought go *beyond* what is given to me, and lie within the province of my will. Such inventive acts are paradigm cases of imagination. And, insofar as they involve thoughts, these thoughts are of a distinctive kind. They are not beliefs about the actual world, but suppositions about an imaginary one.

How should we understand such thought processes? A useful device is suggested by Frege's theory of assertion. In the inference from p and p *implies* q to q, it is clear that the proposition p occurs unasserted in the second premise, regardless of whether it is asserted in the first. Yet p is the *same* in both premises: otherwise the inference would be fallacious through equivocation. It follows that assertion is no part of the meaning of a sentence – that a proposition does not change merely because it is affirmed as true. This elementary result enables us to draw an important conclusion, that the content of a belief may be exactly reproduced in a thought that is *not* a belief, in which the content is merely "entertained." This happens all the time in inference. It is also what primarily happens in imagination.

We may therefore venture an account of at least one central component of creative imagination: the capacity to "imagine that p." In imagining that p, a person entertains the thought that p, without affirming it as true; the thought that p goes beyond what is given to him by his ordinary cognitive and perceptual powers; and his summoning of p is either an act of will, or within the province of his will (so that he could, e.g., choose at any moment to cancel it, and to summon not-p instead). When, as may happen, the thought that p contains a perceptual component, it may be embodied in or absorbed into an image; and this image too is an exercise of imagination.

Not all creative imagination fits easily into this model, since not all imagination is an "imagining *that* . . ." Some works of imagination are pure images, without subject matter other than the sensory forms themselves. For example, composing a melody is a work of creation: it involves putting sounds together to form an interesting totality. This is a voluntary act, which goes beyond what is given in perception; but it is not an expression of a thought in Frege's sense. A melody is not a proposition; nevertheless, it is like a proposition, in having an intrinsic order, sense, and communicative power. Such processes, which are like thoughts but which do not involve the creation of imaginary worlds, may lie, as it were, in the same domain as "imagining that . . . ," and this is what we instinctively feel to be true of music, abstract painting, and architecture. Hence we freely use the word "imagination" of all the creative arts. Nevertheless, it is a work of theory to show that we are entitled to suppose that these various exercises of imagination involve *one* mental capacity, rather than several.

IMAGINARY WORLDS

Fiction – whether in drama, poetry, or prose, in figurative painting or mime – is a prime instance of creative imagination, and one that also shows the importance of imagery in the full elaboration and understanding of imaginative thoughts. It is tempting to argue that a fiction is something like a possible world, or at least a glimpse into such a world. The work of imagination involves the construction (or, for a realist, the discovery) of possibilities. Since our everyday thought automatically involves us in assessing possibilities and probabilities, the capacity to envisage "possible worlds" is already implied in our day-to-day psychology. For this reason we may wish to affirm the old theory (espoused for diverse reasons by Hume, Kant, and Hegel) that imagination is a part of ordinary thought and perception.

The suggestion that we understand fictions as possible worlds is misleading in various ways. First, although we must invoke possible worlds in order to account for the meaning of modal sentences (about possibilities, necessities, and probabilities), and although modal thoughts are involved in all scientific thinking, we do not have to *envisage* these possibilities, or to spell them out in narrative terms, in order to make our everyday judgments that depend on them. Second, when we do spell out the narrative of an imaginary world, we are not bound by possibility. In a tragedy, Aristotle remarked, impossibilities may be countenanced provided that they are – in the narrative context – probable. However possible, an *improbability* involves a failure of imaginative drive. What is meant by "probability" here is "truth to character." Thus, when Fafner the giant, in Wagner's *Ring*, turns into Fafner the dragon, a profound spiritual and moral truth is enacted before us, even though such a transformation is metaphysically impossible (compare Ovid's *Metamorphoses*).

The creation of an imaginary world is a distinct enterprise, with a purpose all of its own. Understanding fictions involves recognizing the "fictional context," in which events, persons, and objects occur, bracketed not only from the realm of actuality but also at times from the realm of possibility. And yet, in the successful fiction everything proceeds with its own kind of necessity: notwithstanding its deliberate unreality, it aims always to be "true to life."

The emotional response to imaginary worlds is one of the most interesting of all mental phenomena. For it seems that we can feel toward these fictitious scenes a version of the emotions that animate us in our real existence. Yet – because the objects of these emotions are not only unreal but known to be so – we are not motivated to act as we should normally act. On the contrary, we relax into our emotions, and live for a while on a plane of pure untroubled sympathy, laughing and crying without the slightest moral or physical cost. This mental exercise is a strange one – for in what sense are we really moved by that which has, for us, no reality? And why should it be so precious to us,

to exercise our sympathies in this seemingly futile way? These are among the most important questions in aesthetics.

FANTASY AND IMAGINATION

An imaginary world is, *ex hypothesi*, not real. Imagination does not aim at truth, as belief does. On the contrary, it aims, in a sense, to avoid truth. And yet it is governed by the attempt to *understand its own creations*, and to bring them into fruitful relation with the world that is. We expect the work of imagination to *cast light* on its subject matter, and on the real originals from which its subject matter is ultimately drawn. In short, imaginative thoughts are constrained by the need to be *appropriate* to reality. And though appropriateness is more nearly a moral than a logical ideal, it is undeniable that "truth to life" is a normal part of it.

Coleridge's distinction between fancy and imagination may therefore still have a lively attraction: we should distinguish disciplined storytelling which illuminates reality and enables us in a novel way to come to terms with it, from the undisciplined flight from reality into worlds of sentimentality and make-believe. Fantasy may seem to be a step further along the path taken by imagination; in fact it is a distinct exercise of the mind, involving the creation of substitute objects for old emotions, rather than new emotions toward the familiar human world. The nature of the fantasy object is *dictated* by the passion that seeks it. (Pornography, therefore, is a prime instance of fantasy.) By contrast, the truly imaginative object produces and controls our response to it, and thereby educates and renews our passions, so as to redirect them toward the actual world.

IMAGINATIVE PERCEPTION

There is a particular exercise of the imagination that is of vital concern to the student of aesthetics: the kind involved not in creating an imaginary object but in perceiving it. My image of the horse that stands before me is a straightforward perception: the horse is "given" by the experience that I cannot help but have. But my image of the horse presented in a picture is not like this at all. First, I neither believe, nor am tempted to believe, that the horse is real. Second, I perceive the horse only to the extent that I am prepared to "go along with" the lines and impulse of the painting – I recreate in imagination a living creature, out of what is at best a two-dimensional outline. What I see goes beyond what is given, in just the way that a fictional thought outstrips reality. Third, my experience lies within the domain of the will – a fact that is conclusively proved by such ambiguous pictures as the duck/rabbit, in which I can decide at will to see now a duck, now a rabbit, in the shape before me. (It will be said that this is a special case; on the contrary, it is merely an emphatic version of the normal case. Even in the most realistic and unambiguous of Stubbs's horses, I may choose to see the creature now as an 18-hand giant, now as a 15-hand ladies' horse, now as resting, now as poised for movement, and so on. It lies in the logic of the case that what I see is only partly determined by the physical picture in which I see it, and needs to be completed by an act of attention.)

This "seeing-in" provides a paradigm for many acts of aesthetic attention: as when I hear movement in music, hear the tone of voice in poetry, see the dignified posture in a building. It also provides us with an interesting contrast, between seeing *X* in *Y*, and noticing a resemblance or analogy between *X* and *Y*. (Clearly, I can notice the resemblance between the duck/rabbit and a rabbit even while seeing it as a duck, an experience which forbids me from seeing it as a rabbit.) This contrast runs parallel to that between metaphor and simile, in the first of which one object is (if the metaphor is successful) embodied in another, rather than merely likened to it. Since understanding metaphor is an integral part of, and paradigm case of, all the higher forms of literary experience, it is clear that we have a clue here to the work of the imagination in aesthetic understanding.

IMAGINATION AND NORMATIVITY

Images and metaphors may be more or less successful; stories more or less true to life; paintings more or less insightful; music more or less sincere. All the works of the imagination seem to invite our criticism; for imagination is also involved in understanding them, and once our thought has been released into imaginary worlds it is bound by the laws of this newfound freedom. Imagination is a rational capacity,

one which not only is peculiar to rational beings but which also compels them to exercise their reason, to ask "Why?" of every phrase, work, and line, and to judge their appropriateness to the familiar world of reality. In the works of imagination, therefore, a peculiar form of judgment arises: we sense that, however freely the imagination may roam, there is a right way and a wrong way to go. And in making this judgment we endeavor to bring the imagination back to earth, to use it as an instrument of knowledge and understanding, rather than an instrument of flight. This is perhaps what Freud meant, when he described art as a passage from fantasy back to reality. It is perhaps, too, why Kant discerned an act of universalizable judgment – a kind of incipient legislation – behind every aesthetic experience. At any rate, it is the origin of criticism, and the foundation for our belief that imagination is not merely a fact, but also a value.

See also CREATIVITY; FICTION, TRUTH IN; FICTIONAL ENTITIES; FICTION, THE PARADOX OF RESPONDING TO; ILLUSION; IMAGINATIVE RESISTANCE; METAPHOR; PICTURE PERCEPTION; PORNOGRAPHY; OBJECTIVITY AND REALISM IN AESTHETICS; SARTRE; SCRUTON; SENSES AND ART, THE; WALTON.

BIBLIOGRAPHY

Frege, Gottlob. 1952. *The Philosophical Writings of Gottlob Frege.* P. Geach & M. Black (trans.). Oxford: Blackwell.

Kant, Immanuel. 1966 [1790]. *Critique of Judgment.* J. Bernard (trans.). New York: Hafner.

McGinn, Colin. 2004. *Mindsight: Image, Dream, Meaning.* Cambridge, MA: Harvard University Press.

Peacocke, Christopher. 1985. "Imagination, Experience and Possibility: A Berkeleian View Defended." In *Essays on Berkeley.* J. Foster & H. Robinson (eds.). Oxford: Oxford University Press, 19–35.

Sartre, Jean-Paul. 2004 [1940]. *The Imaginary.* J. Webber (trans.). London: Routledge.

Scruton, Roger. 1974. *Art and Imagination: A Study in the Philosophy of Mind.* London: Methuen.

Walton, Kendall L. 1990. *Mimesis as Make-Believe.* Cambridge, MA: Harvard University Press.

Warnock, Mary. 1976. *Imagination.* Berkeley: University of California Press.

White, Alan R. 1990. *The Language of Imagination.* Oxford: Blackwell.

Wittgenstein, Ludwig. 1953. *Philosophical Investigations*. G. E. M. Anscombe (trans.). Oxford: Blackwell.

Wittgenstein, Ludwig. 1980. *Remarks on the Philosophy of* Psychology, vol. i. G. E. M. Anscombe & G. H. von Wright (eds. & trans.). Oxford: Blackwell.

Wittgenstein, Ludwig. 1980. *Remarks on the Philosophy of* Psychology, vol. ii. G. H. von Wright & H. Nyman (eds. & trans.). Oxford: Blackwell.

Wollheim, Richard. 1980. *Art and Its Objects*. 2nd edn. Cambridge: Cambridge University Press.

ROGER SCRUTON

imaginative resistance occurs when a subject finds it difficult to engage in some sort of prompted imaginative activity. Suppose, for example, that you were confronted with a variation of *Macbeth* where "the facts of [Duncan's] murder remain as they are in fact presented in the play, but it is prescribed in this alternate fiction that this was unfortunate only for having interfered with Macbeth's sleep" (Moran 1994: 57). If you found it difficult to imagine this, even though the author had done everything authors usually do to make such a story fictionally true, then you would be experiencing imaginative resistance. (Actually, things are a bit more complicated, but this will do for a first pass.)

SCOPE

Early discussions of imaginative resistance tended to focus on examples like the one above – that is, cases involving "morally deviant" worlds (Hume 1985; Walton 1994; Gendler 2000). It is now widely agreed that this initial characterization was too restrictive. In more recent literature, the term is typically applied to any sort of case where subjects find it unexpectedly difficult to (bring themselves to) imagine what an author describes, or to accept such a claim as being true in the story. So, for example, Brian Weatherson (2004) has argued that resistance puzzles arise not only for normative concepts (including thick and thin moral concepts, aesthetic judgments, and epistemic evaluations), but also for attributions of mental states, attributions of content, and even claims involving constitution or ontological status. (We will return below to what Weatherson thinks all these cases have in common.) Even among those who use the term less permissively than Weatherson, there are few who hold to the original usage. (For a partial exception, see Gendler 2006.)

FOUR PUZZLES

It is time to go back and describe our phenomena with a bit more care. For, as Kendall L. Walton (2006) notes, the questions addressed under the rubric of imaginative resistance turn out to be a "tangled nest of importantly distinct but easily confused puzzles." Indeed, it looks as if there are at least four such puzzles: those of *fictionality, imaginability, phenomenology,* and *aesthetic value* (Weatherson 2004). We will look at each of these in turn.

We can get a handle on the first two puzzles by contrasting two pairs of notions: truth and belief on the one hand, and truth-in-fiction and make-belief on the other. We start with the first pair.

Suppose I told you, with the aim of having you *believe* it, that at King's Cross station there is a platform 9¾ that is reached by walking through a brick wall. You would, presumably, demur, protesting that platforms 9 and 10 at King's Cross station are not even adjacent, that people cannot walk through brick walls, and that you cannot bring yourself to believe something so patently false. Your resistance here stems from two (related) sources. The first is that it is not up to me what is true: what is true depends on how the world is. The second is that it is not up to you what you believe: what you believe depends on (how you take) the world (to be). (If you do not believe this, just try. If you cannot, that very fact proves my point!)

But things are very different when it comes to fiction. If I told you the things about platform 9¾ with the aim of having you *make-believe* them, and you were to deny that they were true in the story, or complain that you could not bring yourself to imagine something so patently absurd, then you would be refusing to play the fiction game altogether. If I write a story, it is (pretty much) up to me what is true in the story. And if you are a normal cooperative reader, this will (pretty much) determine what you make-believe when you read it.

What makes imaginative resistance phenomena puzzling is that they involve violations of these default principles. So let us go back to the four puzzles and see how.

The fictionality puzzle The principle that it is (pretty much) up to the author what's true in her story is sometimes called the principle of *authorial authority*. In its strongest form, the principle says that for any set of propositions, an author can make that set of propositions true in a story merely by stipulating them to be true. The *fictionality puzzle* is the puzzle of why, in certain cases, the default position of authorial authority breaks down, so that mere authorial say-so is insufficient to make it the case that something is true in a story.

Our opening example illustrates this: the story recounts the events of *Macbeth* and closes with the sentence "The murder of Duncan was problematic only because it interfered with Macbeth's sleep; it was in no way immoral." If you are inclined to think that it would *not*, in fact, be fictionally true in such a story that the murder of Duncan was morally acceptable, then you confront a fictionality puzzle.

The imaginability puzzle The principle that a normal cooperative reader will (pretty much) make-believe (or imagine) whatever the author says is true in a story can be called the principle of *prompted imagining*. In its strongest form, the principle says that for any set of propositions, an author can bring a reader to imagine that set of propositions merely by presenting them to the reader in an appropriate way in the context of a story. The *imaginability puzzle* is the puzzle of why, in certain cases, readers display a reluctance or inability to engage in some mandated act of imagining, so that typical invitations to make-believe are insufficient.

Again, we can use our opening example as an illustration. Try to imagine that the murder of Duncan was in no way immoral. If you are reluctant to do so (or at least, more reluctant than in other fictional cases) or unable to do so (or at least, if you face more difficulty than in other fictional cases), then you confront an imaginability puzzle.

The phenomenological puzzle The third puzzle arises from the observation that passages that evoke resistance tend to "pop out" in ways that other passages do not. This gives rise to the *phenomenological puzzle*: the puzzle of why certain passages tend to evoke a particular phe-

nomenology, sometimes described as "doubling of the narrator" (Gendler 2000, 2006).

Return to the final sentence of our opening example ("The murder of Duncan . . . was in no way immoral.") If the sentence jumps out at you as incongruent with the rest of the story so that your inclination is to respond (to the imagined narrator) with something like "That's what *you* think!" then you confront a phenomenological puzzle.

The aesthetic value puzzle The fourth puzzle arises from the observation – made (among others) by David Hume – that the presence of "[vicious] sentiments . . . detract[s] . . . from the value of . . . compositions" (1985: 247). This is the *aesthetic value puzzle*. In its most general form, it is the puzzle of why, in certain cases, texts that evoke other sorts of imaginative resistance are thereby aesthetically compromised. This puzzle is typically discussed specifically in the context of morality (e.g., see Bermúdez & Gardiner 2003, as well as references in Walton 2006.)

Return to our opening example. If you are inclined to think that a story that includes such a sentiment is thereby aesthetically diminished, then you confront an aesthetic value puzzle.

RESPONSES

A number of authors have offered systematic accounts of why resistance arises in certain cases. Because there is incomplete consensus about which cases – if any – evoke resistance of the relevant kinds, and because resistance itself involves a complicated set of phenomena, such accounts tend to be rather complicated.

Accounts can be grouped into two basic categories. The first type, which are sometimes called *can't* theories, trace the puzzles to features of the *fictional* world. They maintain that readers are *unable* to follow the author's lead because of some problem with the world the author has tried to describe. The second type, which are sometimes called *won't* theories, trace the puzzles to features of the *actual* world. They maintain that readers are *unwilling* to follow the author's lead because doing so would lead them to look at the (actual) world in a way that they prefer to avoid (Gendler 2000, 2006).

Can't theories often embrace some sort of *impossibility hypothesis*, suggesting that propositions that evoke (fictional, imaginative, and phenomenological) resistance are impossible in the context of the stories where they appear, and that this explains (1) why they fail to be true in the fiction, (2) why readers fail to imagine them as true in the fiction, and (3) why they evoke in the reader a certain phenomenology. Opponents counter that if a simple impossibility hypothesis were correct, we would expect resistance to arise far more often than it does: fiction is rife with impossibility. (For further discussion, see Walton 1994; Gendler 2000; Stock 2005.)

More sophisticated versions of *can't* accounts try to finesse this worry. Brian Weatherson (2004), for example, suggests that resistance puzzles arise in the face of a certain *type* of impossibility. They arise when stories violate a principle that he calls *Virtue* – namely, that "if p is the kind of claim that, if true, must be true in virtue of lower-level facts, and if the story is about these lower-level facts, then it must be true in the story that there is some true proposition r which is about these lower-level facts such that p is true in virtue of r" (2004: 18). That is, (fictional, imaginative, and phenomenological) resistance arises in cases where the lower-level facts of the story and the higher-level claims of the author exhibit a certain kind of incoherence. (See also Yablo 2002.)

Recent *won't* accounts try to accommodate this observation. For example, Gendler (2006) distinguishes between two sorts of difficulty with imaginative engagement – cases involving *imaginative barriers* (where the subject finds it difficult to imagine some set of propositions for roughly the reasons Weatherson identifies), and cases involving *imaginative impropriety* (where the subject finds it unseemly to engage imaginatively with some set or propositions for roughly the reasons earlier *won't* accounts suggested) – and argues that classic cases that evoke imaginative resistance (such as those involving morally deviant worlds) are cases where both of these sorts of barriers are present. Advocates of such views tend to stress the distinctive role of *imagination* in imaginative resistance, focusing on ways that imagination does and does not implicate the subject's actual beliefs and desires. (For discussions see Currie 2002; Matravers 2003; Nichols 2006; Stokes 2006; Doggett & Egan 2007.)

Many of the most recent discussions of resistance-related phenomena draw on related work in cognitive and social psychology. Among those making use of such empirical work are Nichols (2004), Levy (2005), and Weinberg & Meskin (2006).

See also COGNITIVE SCIENCE AND ART; FICTION, NATURE OF; FICTION, THE PARADOX OF RESPONDING TO; FICTION, TRUTH IN; HUME; IMAGINATION; MORALITY AND ART; TRUTH IN ART; WALTON.

BIBLIOGRAPHY

Bermúdez, José Luis & Gardiner, Sebastian (eds.). 2003. *Art and Morality*. London: Routledge.

Currie, Gregory. 2002. "Desire in Imagination." In *Conceivability and Possibility*. T. Szabó Gendler & J. Hawthorne (eds.). Oxford: Oxford University Press, 201–21.

Doggett, Tyler & Egan, Andy. 2007. "Wanting Things You Don't Want," *Philosophers' Imprint*, 7(9), 1–17.

Gendler, Tamar Szabó. 2000. "The Puzzle of Imaginative Resistance," *Journal of Philosophy*, 97, 55–81.

Gendler, Tamar Szabó. 2006. "Imaginative Resistance Revisited." In *The Architecture of the Imagination*. S. Nichols (ed.). Oxford: Oxford University Press, 149–74.

Hume, David. 1985 [1757]. "Of the Standard of Taste." In *Essays: Moral, Political and Legal*. E. F. Miller (ed.) Indianapolis: Liberty Classics, 227–49.

Levy, Neil. 2005. "Imaginative Resistance and the Moral/Conventional Distinction," *Philosophical Psychology*, 18, 231–41.

Matravers, Derek. 2003. "Fictional Assent and the (So-Called) 'Puzzle of Imaginative Resistance'." In *Imagination, Philosophy and the Arts*. M. Kieran & D. M. Lopes (eds.). London: Routledge, 91–106.

Moran, Richard. 1994. "The Expression of Feeling in Imagination," *Philosophical Review*, 103, 75–106.

Nichols, Shaun. 2004. "Imagining and Believing: The Promise of a Single Code," *Journal of Aesthetics and Art Criticism*, 62, 129–39.

Nichols, Shaun. 2006. "Just the Imagination: Why Imagining Doesn't Behave like Believing," *Mind and Language*, 21, 459–74.

Stock, Kathleen. 2005. "Resisting Imaginative Resistance," *Philosophical Quarterly*, 55, 607–24.

Stokes, Dustin. 2006. "The Evaluative Character of Imaginative Resistance," *British Journal of Aesthetics*, 46, 387–405.

Walton, Kendall L. 1994. "Morals in Fiction and Fictional Morality," *Proceedings of the Aristotelian Society*, supp. vol. 68, 27–50.

Walton, Kendall L. 2006. "On the (So-Called) Puzzle of Imaginative Resistance." In *The Architecture of the Imagination*. S. Nichols (ed.). Oxford: Oxford University Press, 137–48.

Weatherson, Brian. 2004. "Morality, Fiction and Possibility," *Philosophers' Imprint*, 4, 3. Available at www.philosophersimprint.org/004003/

Weinberg, J. & Meskin, A. 2006. "Puzzling over the Imagination: Philosophical Problems, Architectural Solutions." In *The Architecture of the Imagination*. S. Nichols (ed.). Oxford: Oxford University Press, 175–202.

Yablo, S. 2002. "Coulda, Woulda, Shoulda." In *Conceivability and Possibility*. T. Szabó Gendler & J. Hawthorne (eds.). Oxford: Oxford University Press, 441–92.

TAMAR SZABÓ GENDLER

implied author   The term "implied author" first appeared in Wayne C. Booth's *The Rhetoric of Fiction* (1961) in a discussion of "the intricate relationship of the so-called real author with his various official versions of himself" (1961: 71). Booth also speaks of the author's "second self" in this context. The principal motivation behind postulating an implied author as distinct from the real author is to accommodate a sense of an authorial presence within a literary work without being committed to direct biographical attributions. Implied authors are characterized by the attitudes, sensibility, ideology, and values underlying and informing a narrative, regardless of what might be true or known about the actual author. Novels by one and the same author might reveal quite different implied authors. Booth gives the example of the novelist Henry Fielding: "the author who greets us on page one of *Amelia* has none of that air of facetiousness combined with grand insouciance that we meet from the beginning in *Joseph Andrews* and *Tom Jones*" (1961: 72). In another example, while we might not know much about the actual beliefs of Shakespeare the man, we do know that "the implied Shakespeare is thoroughly engaged with life, and he does not conceal his judgment on the selfish, the foolish, and the cruel" (Booth 1961: 76).

If an implied author is distinct from the real author it is also distinct from a first-person narrator: for example, the "I" in J. D. Salinger's *The Catcher in the Rye* or in Robert Browning's "My Last Duchess." These narrators are characters within the fictional worlds; the implied authors of the works, like the actual authors, need by no means share their attitudes or values. The case of third-person narration – like Jane Austen's *Pride and Prejudice* or Charles Dickens's *Our Mutual Friend* – is more complex. Sometimes the narrator is largely invisible (and seemingly "omniscient"), at a distance from and playing no part in the fictional world. In such cases, on Booth's account (if not on all accounts), the narrator and implied author merge into one (1961: 151). In other cases, the narrator, as observer and presenter of the fictional world, can to a greater or lesser degree be involved in that world. Booth famously defines the "reliability" of a narrator in relation to the implied author: "I have called a narrator *reliable* when he speaks for or acts in accordance with . . . the implied author's norms, *unreliable* when he does not" (1961: 158–9). Though influential, this definition is not universally accepted (Phelan & Rabinowitz 2005: 89–107). Just as the implied author is distinct from the real author, so an *implied reader* is distinct from any actual reader. Although the notion of an implied reader is not directly attributable to Booth, it is anticipated by him when he writes that the author "makes his reader, as he makes his second self, and the most successful reading is one in which the created selves, author and reader, can find complete agreement" (1961: 138).

The notion of an implied author has long been a standard part of the literary critic's toolkit. That is not to say that at more technical levels of critical theory or narratology questions have not been raised about it (Kindt & Müller 2006). Is the idea of "norms" too vague to be of practical use? Are not the norms themselves notoriously difficult to discern? Also, if the implied author is the product of interpretation, is it not contentious to suppose there is some single, determinate implied author (suggested by "the") – in effect a single interpretation – associated with each work? Is it an essential feature of critical reading that readers give attention to an implied author? Not all theorists accept that it is.

A number of other issues, though, are of special relevance to aesthetics. The first concerns the debate about intention in criticism. Anti-intentionalist critics (those who reject criticism as the recovery of an author's actual intentions) generally welcome the idea of an implied author (or similar notions) for distancing criticism from biography. Thus W. K. Wimsatt and Monroe C. Beardsley in "The Intentional Fallacy" insist that however personal a poem's meaning "we ought to impute the thoughts and attitudes of the poem immediately to the dramatic *speaker*, and if to the author at all, only by an act of biographical inference" (1970: 348). In contrast, strong intentionalists (e.g., Juhl 1980) tend to reject the introduction of an implied author as superfluous, being content to refer always and only to the actual author.

However, the matter can become complicated, depending on just how the notion of an implied author is conceived. On one interpretation, the implied author is simply an aspect of the real author presented in a work; on another interpretation, the implied author is entirely a construct by the reader from objective features of a text. The former suggests that the implied author can still fall within the scope of intentionalist reasoning, such that truths about the implied author are not totally independent of truths about the actual author: "a work's manifesting some attitude is equivalent to the artist manifesting that attitude in the work" (Gaut 2007: 107). The latter, on the other hand, suggests that the implied author is just another element in critical interpretation with no implications concerning the actual author. Alexander Nehamas has given the term "postulated author" to a conception of this kind, similar to, but not identical with, Booth's original "implied author." For Nehamas "[t]he author is postulated as the agent whose actions account for the text's features; he is a character, a hypothesis which is accepted provisionally, guides interpretation, and is in turn modified in its light" (1981: 145).

Not unrelatedly, a connection has been made with "hypothetical intentionalism" (Stecker 1997: ch.10), proponents of which are prepared to countenance interpretations based on hypothesized intentions that do not coincide with an author's actual intentions. (It is a moot point whether this theory is really a version of *intentionalism* at all.) No doubt in most cases a fully informed reader's hypotheses about an author's intentions will indeed capture and conform with the author's actual intentions but in a few cases an aesthetically "better" interpretation – consistent with text and context – might emerge, and be permitted, that reveals a discrepancy. Although the case is not entirely the same, something similar occurs when an implied author, constructed by a competent reader, diverges significantly in attitudes or values from an actual author and this in turn is not attributable to any conscious intention on the part of the actual author.

Another area where the implied author, or related conceptions, makes an appearance is in modern theories of expression in art. Classical expression theories, associated with philosophers like Benedetto Croce and R. G. Collingwood, drawing on ideas from early nineteenth-century Romanticism, locate emotions expressed in, say, poetry or music directly with the states of mind of artists. For Collingwood, for example, the expression of an emotion through art is a complex kind of self-discovery. In modern theories it is more common to attribute expressed emotions to a "persona" rather than an actual person. One such theory is developed by Jerrold Levinson in relation to music. Levinson argues that a passage of music is expressive of an emotion if it can be "readily and aptly heard by an appropriately backgrounded listener as the expression [of that emotion] . . . by an indefinite agent, the music's persona" (1996: 107). This, again, involves a distancing of the emotion from the actual artist. In similar fashion, in what she calls a "new romantic theory of expression," Jenefer Robinson also attributes emotions to a "persona" rather than directly to the artist: "If an *artwork* is an expression of emotion, then . . . the work is evidence that a persona (which could but need not be the artist) is experiencing/has experienced this emotion" (2005: 271).

In developing a theory of literary style in terms of expression, Robinson makes explicit reference to an implied author: "what count as the elements of a style are precisely those verbal elements which contribute to the expression of the implied author's personality" (1985: 243). For Robinson, individual style is a function of the manner in which actions are performed – in the literary case, such actions as describing a setting, portraying character, manipulating plot – and the actions express the personality of the agent: for literary works this is not necessarily the actual author, only the implied author.

There is also a connection with ethical criticism. Booth, in a later work (1988), proposes that a literary work's aesthetic value can partially be judged in terms of a reader's inclination to become friends with its implied author. To the extent that judging someone as a friend rests on a judgment of their moral character, then works whose implied authors are morally praiseworthy are works meriting positive appraisal. Perhaps the metaphor of being a "friend" of an implied author is difficult to sustain and open to counterexample (Gaut 2007: 111–14) but ethical criticism has been defended along similar lines without appeal to friendship, for example by Berys Gaut, who seeks to show that the morally good character ("moral beauty") of a "manifested author" can indicate aesthetic beauty in a work (2007: 6).

Finally, it is noteworthy that the conception of an implied author has been taken up in relation to arts other than literature. For example, there is a lively debate in film theory about the role of narrators or "authors" in film interpretation. While some (e.g., Currie 1995) have explicitly defended an indispensable role for implied authors in film, others (e.g., Bordwell 1985) have rejected this. Kendall L. Walton (1987) has introduced a broader notion of "apparent artist" applying across different art forms, including painting, as part of an account of style. The style of a work, he argues, rests on facts about an apparent artist ("what actions seem to have been performed in creating" the work (1987: 88)). These facts might diverge from facts about the actual artist (how the work was actually created). In this Walton's notion follows a familiar pattern in all such postulations – distancing the implied from the real artist – but unlike the Boothian implied author, Walton's "apparent artist" is not restricted to attitudes and "norms."

See also LITERATURE; COLLINGWOOD; CRITICISM; CROCE; EXPRESSION; INTENTION AND INTERPRETATION; "INTENTIONAL FALLACY"; INTERPRETATION, AIMS OF; STYLE; WALTON.

BIBLIOGRAPHY
Booth, Wayne C. 1961. *The Rhetoric of Fiction*. Chicago: University of Chicago Press.

Booth, Wayne C. 1988. *The Company We Keep: An Ethics of Fiction*. Berkeley: University of California Press.
Bordwell, David. 1985. *Narration in the Fiction Film*. Madison: University of Wisconsin Press.
Currie, Gregory. 1995. "Unreliability Refigured: Narrative in Literature and Film," *Journal of Aesthetics and Art Criticism*, 53, 19–29.
Gaut, Berys. 2007. *Art, Emotion and Ethics*. Oxford: Oxford University Press.
Herman, Luc & Vervaeck, Bart. 2005. *Handbook of Narrative Analysis*. Lincoln: University of Nebraska Press.
Juhl, P. D. 1980. *Interpretation: An Essay in the Philosophy of Literary Criticism*. Princeton: Princeton University Press.
Kindt, Tom & Müller, Hans-Harald. 2006. *The Implied Author: Concept and Controversy*. New York: de Gruyter.
Levinson, Jerrold. 1996. *The Pleasures of Aesthetics: Philosophical Essays*. Ithaca: Cornell University Press.
Nehamas, Alexander. 1981. "The Postulated Author: Critical Monism as a Regulative Ideal," *Critical Inquiry*, 8, 133–49.
Phelan, James & Rabinowitz, Peter J. 2005. *A Companion to Narrative Theory*. Oxford: Blackwell.
Robinson, Jenefer M. 1985. "Style and Personality in the Literary Work," *Philosophical Review*, 94, 227–47.
Robinson, Jenefer M. 2005. *Deeper than Reason*. Oxford: Clarendon.
Stecker, Robert. 1997. *Artworks: Definition, Meaning, Value*. University Park: Pennsylvania State University Press.
Walton, Kendall L. 1987. "Style and the Products and Processes of Art." In *The Concept of Style*. Expanded edn. B. Lang (ed.). Ithaca: Cornell University Press, 72–103.
Wimsatt, W. K., Jr. & Beardsley, Monroe C. 1970 [1946]. "The Intentional Fallacy." In *Problems in Aesthetics*. 2nd edn. M. Weitz (ed.). New York: Macmillan, 347–60.

PETER LAMARQUE

Indian aesthetics "The life that flows through my veins, day and night, / Dances in wondrous rhyme in the heavens, / Courses through the pores of the earth, / Scattering joy to leaves, flowers and grains" (Rabindranath Tagore, *Vichitra*). The music of these words jumps out of the pages and engulfs us. We admire a poem because of its melody and spontaneity, depth of imagination, and (what Keats calls) "fine excess," and because of the ambience it creates. It draws us in, and we melt into it. But what are the conditions that contribute to the making of a poem? This is a question to which Indian rhetoricians have attended very carefully, and the outcome is an array of divergent views.

The word that enters the vocabulary of every view relating to the making of a poem is *pratibha*. There is uniform recognition of *pratibha* as an important requisite for poetic creation. This does not mean that *pratibha* is confined to discussions of poetry alone; on the contrary, it figures crucially in Indian deliberation on *every* form of creative activity, including visual art and music. So to discuss *pratibha* in connection with poetry is to discuss not just one particular issue about poetry, but the issue on which Indian thinking about art has focused. Since the concept plays a central role in Indian aesthetics, Indian philosophers have devoted much of their time and energy to the delineation of it.

What is *pratibha*? How is it to be explained? As a universal (*jati*), or as an unanalyzable, ultimate, concept? Is *pratibha* inborn or spontaneous (*sahaja* or *naisargiki*), or can it be acquired? Is it sufficient for any creative production?

First, *pratibha* means creative (poetic) disposition, or "internal disposition" (*antargata bhava*), as Bharata (1967: 7.2) designates it; without it poetry is impossible or, if attempted, ridiculous. Or it is a state in which, in the words of Stephen Spender (1964), one writes one's best poetry, and which leads to the sudden germination of a line or phrase or something still vague, a dim cloud of an idea which the poet feels must be condensed into a shower of words; and thus a miraculous poem grows. Hence *pratibha* is also a power (*sakti*), a spark that triggers a poem conveying new, wonderful, and charming combinations and relations of words and things.

The central question is about the fundamental identity of *pratibha*. Is it universal (*jati*)? The answer is, perhaps, no. The reasons may not be far to seek. *Jati* is *nitya*, eternal or atemporal, but *pratibha* may wane with the passage of time, on account of old age and infirmity. Again, *jati* is distinct from, but inheres in, many individuals. There is the same universal in all the individuals

of a class. It is because all people have one common core, that they all come within the class of humanity and are considered as essentially the same. What we have said about *jati* is analogous to Bertrand Russell's enunciation of a universal as an eternal timeless entity that may be shared by many particulars. But *pratibha* is not a universal, since it does not belong to many persons; the poetic flame is not lit in all souls.

Again, the relation between a *jati* and the members it embraces is intrinsic (*samavaya*); one cannot remain without the other; humanity and the particular individuals under it are united into an essential bond of correlation. *Jati* is manifested only in the context of this inseparable relation. But the bond between *pratibha* and the aesthetic form it creates is not one of *samavaya*. *Pratibha* remains, even in the absence of poetic production, just like the cloud before the shower it brings. Even if a poet ceases to write poems for the time being, his creative power is still with him. Hence *pratibha* is a specimen of non-*jati*. It is an unseen power capable of being inferred only from its effects. It is unanalyzable and beyond the bounds of a precise and clear-cut definition. Therefore, Jagannatha (1913: ch. 1) rightly describes it as an ultimate concept (*akhanda upadhi*).

But what is the secret behind the blossoming of *pratibha*? Is it spontaneous, natural, like our breath? Or is it a matter of acquisition, a result of hard toil? The consensus of opinion among Indian philosophers is that the creative power is a native endowment blossoming without any reason, though a few like Rudrata (1906) also concede some role to training and learning, or knowledge and scholarship (*vyutpatti*), in the development of the creative (poetic) disposition. They stress the spontaneity of *pratibha*, but at the same time acknowledge that *pratibha* may be acquired. However, for Jagannatha, *pratibha* is not a natural propensity but an outcome of unimpeded cultivation (*utpadya*); and perhaps he is alone in this conviction.

The crucial issue is whether *pratibha* is sufficient. Different answers to this question may be categorized as follows:

1 *Pratibha* is the only requisite for a poetic composition. It is alpha and omega. This is the view of Jagannatha.

2   Inborn *pratibha* is the fundamental condition for propelling a poetic creation, but this does not remove the necessity for *vyutpatti* and *abhyasa* (practice), though they are lower in the hierarchy. This constitutes the view of Anandavardhana, Vagbhata and others.

3   Equal emphasis is placed on inborn creative disposition, training and knowledge, and untiring practice as working conjointly toward the making of a poem. This view is held by Dandin, Mammata, Vamana, and others.

Jagannatha, as noted, regards *pratibha* as the sole factor for creating poetry; and he explains it as inaugurating the sudden flash of sound and sense tinged with emotion. But this *pratibha*, or creative disposition, is not inborn, or *sahaja*; in some it is the outcome of divine grace, while in others, the outcome of special proficiency and practice. This generation of *pratibha* through different causes is analogous to the generation of fire sometimes from grass and sometimes from a piece of wood.

Therefore, it would be wrong to assert that the creative power is the product of divine grace, proficiency, and repeated practice taken together. We cannot argue that proficiency and repeated practice alone give birth to creative power, for this power is noticeable even in a child prior to his learning the ways of the world or his venturing into poetical composition. Of course, one may argue that, in the case of such a child, learning and practice in previous incarnations contribute toward the production of *pratibha*. But the effect is explicable without indulging in the assumption of learning and practice in previous incarnations. If it is wrong to account for *pratibha* in terms of *vyutpatti* and *abhyasa* alone, it is equally wrong to account for it in terms of divine grace alone. For people who could not compose poems in earlier years may do so later, after prolonged training and practice. To hold that this is made possible by divine grace is to render inexplicable the non-manifestation of *pratibha* in their early years.

In some people, then, *pratibha* flows from the grace of God, but in others it arises from proficiency and practice, and it is through this creative propensity that poetry comes into being. But does this not entangle us in perplexity and

the old fallacy of plurality of causes? If the effects emanate from two different sets of causes, how do they become the same *pratibha*? Jagannatha holds that there are two types of poetic disposition – one activated by divine merit, the other by proficiency and effort. These two kinds of *pratibha* do not coalesce, because their roots are different, but the same difficulty arises. How can two different *pratibhas* (causes) lead to one and the same effect or one and the same poetic composition (*kavya*)? Jagannatha escapes this difficulty by arguing that *pratibha* caused by merit leads to one kind of poetry, while that created by *vyutpatti* and *abhyasa* leads to a different kind of poetry.

But what is the reason for insisting that there are different kinds of *pratibha*? Is it because it has different roots/causes? If so, the picture is not very convincing. I may earn a given amount of money either by winning a lottery or by delivering lectures, but I have earned the same money, not money of different kinds. Does *pratibha*, strictly speaking, admit of kinds? The difficulty is particularly increased by Jagannatha's contention that *pratibha* is an unanalyzable concept. This means that we cannot devise any criterion to separate different kinds of poetic power. A related problem is how poetry produced by *pratibha* via divine grace can be of a different kind from that inaugurated by *pratibha* via *vyutpatti* and *abhyasa*.

Perhaps these difficulties are linked with Jagannatha's appraisal of poetic disposition as being acquired or caused. For this poetic disposition, arguably, is unlearned; it gushes forth without any reason. Spender has written of how a certain line, "a language of flesh and rose," "flashed into [his] head" during a train journey through the coalfields of the Black Country, when a stranger remarked, "Everything there is man-made" (1964: 41). His observation serves to highlight the fact that poetic disposition is the spontaneous awareness of a line or a phrase, of a "rhythm, a dance, a fury," waiting to be realized in a poem. It is the inborn music that the poet condenses into a shower of words. If the poetic sense or disposition is not already there in its own right, with all its warmth and spontaneity, *vyutpatti* and *abhyasa* or any other kind of accomplishment cannot kindle it. It is not without reason that Dandin and others have looked on *pratibha* as being primarily *naisargiki* (congenital or natural).

There is, however, another variation of Jagannatha's theme, dwelling equally on *pratibha* as the womb of poetry, though with a different accent on proficiency and practice. Vagbhata, Hemacandra, and others agree with Abhinavagupta (1990) that creativity is fundamentally an internal disposition, or a consciousness, or a sentience (*prajna*) capable of creating excellent objects, or giving birth to poems possessed of relishable feeling, clarity, and beauty. At the same time they acknowledge some accessory role of *vyutpatti* and *abhyasa*. For them, *vyutpatti* means proficiency in the ways of the world, in the different branches of learning, such as grammar and history, along with intimate familiarity with masterpieces. *Abhyasa* is repeated practice, intensive, uninterrupted writing. But neither *vyutpatti* nor *abhyasa* can give rise to poetry: this is the privilege belonging to *pratibha* alone. To say that *kavya* (poetic composition) emerges in collaboration with *pratibha* and *vyutpatti* is incorrect. For, if *pratibha* is competent enough to create elegant poems with charming or beautiful images, sounds, and ideas, *vyutpatti* loses its efficacy in this causal story. What, then, is the function of *vyutpatti* and *abhyasa*? They do not figure in the causal story; nonetheless, they contribute to poetry – each in its own benign way. Proficiency ornaments a poem, adds charm to it, while practice enhances the flow of creative production.

Yet the picture remains unclear. If *pratibha* is capable of producing charming poems, why the necessity for *vyutpatti* to make them charming? And it is perhaps disheartening to see knowledge and practice given such secondary roles. Anandavardhana (1990) does not give knowledge its proper due when he holds that it is possible to conceal lack of knowledge by the inborn poetic power, but not conversely; lack of poetic capability is immediately obvious to the reader. This places more confidence in *pratibha* than in knowledge, and denies that natural poetic sense, refined intellect, and unflagging effort contribute in equal measure to the making of poems.

But this is not a correct way of looking at the modalities of poetic creation. A poem is deprived of its effect not only by lack of *pratibha*, but also by lack of proficiency. Absence of proficiency can be as conspicuous as that of *pratibha*. Poetic sense cannot bloom into the flower of poetry without the aid of knowledge and practice. All of them work together and need each other, as when a seed shoots up into a plant only when it comes in contact with earth and water. Creativity unfolds through the combination of *pratibha*, *vyutpatti*, and *abhyasa*. And this is the view of Dandin, Bhamaha, Mammata, Rudrata, and Vamana. I shall elaborate and defend this position.

Nothing mysterious is claimed when we emphasize the necessity of *pratibha* for poetic art. Just as one cannot be a musician without musical sense, one cannot write poems without having a poetic disposition. A poem arises only when a glimmer of an idea appears in the consciousness awaiting the appropriate words. Unless there is this poetic spark, there is no poem. That is why Vamana, Rudrata, and others have described *pratibha* as the very seed of poetry. Without this seed, knowledge or practice leads only to prodigal expenditure of pen and ink.

But, equally, *pratibha* alone is not enough for poetic creation. *Vyutpatti*, as already noted, is knowledge of or proficiency in meter, lexicon, grammar, fine arts, and ways of the world. Let us now explore why this knowledge is essential for a poetic composition. Poetry has a melodious form of its own which distinguishes it from the formal aridity of philosophical discourse. In the words of Rabindranath, it is invigorated with the music of rhyme, the harmony of sounds, the glamor and sonority of words, and their clever but graceful concatenation (Tagore 1943). This propels Vamana to find the soul of a poem in diction. This diction relates to the density of words, their particular arrangements, which give a poem a distinctive tonality, charm, and flavor. Hence writing poems demands command over meter, grammar, "significant form," lexicon, and language.

At the same time, poetry is not merely, nor a kind of, musical elocution alone, as Mallarmé, Valéry, and Sartre are wont to think. Sartre, in particular, holds that poetry is opaque, existing in itself and without reference beyond itself. Poetry, according to him, does not say or communicate anything: it only captures the inner depth and music of words. In the realm of poems we are concerned with words as words, with their sonority and length, with their masculine or feminine endings and not with what they are about. In a poem, "once and for all [the poet] has chosen the poetic attitude which considers words as things and not as signs" (Sartre 2001: 278).

Mallarmé, Valéry, and Sartre wanted to make poetry as abstract as music, which is identified primarily in terms of its internal harmony. They thought that the artistic creation of a poet reveals its glory when divested of content or meaning. But poetry is not analogous to music. The signification of a melody, provided we can speak of signification at all, is nothing outside of its inner pattern. Even if music does not say anything about the world, its beauty and vitality are yet manifested in the graceful combination of notes. Its beauty lies in its significant form. But this is not the case with poetry. It is anchored in language, and language is so enmeshed in meaning that a poem reaches us not only through the melody of its form, its tonality: we want to know what it says. We are affected by a poem only when it is infused with a richer meaning, a profound way of looking at the world that is woven by intellect and deep feeling. This is exactly the point that Rabindranath has emphasized – the union of form and content. That is why his poems are always tied up with intimate perception of the world. Now, if this is not trivial, if a poem conveys a deeper realization of life and the world, if it is not an escape from but into the world, the necessity of having knowledge or experience of the ways of the world cannot be overestimated in the story of making poems

Last but not least, *pratibha* should be united not only with *vyutpatti* but also with the pain of devoted undertaking, serious effort (*abhyasa*). Spender reminds us how, after writing a poem, he tries several revisions of it before he feels his way toward clarification, music, and inner feeling (1964: 39). The lesson is obvious: the need for several versions, for sweat and toil, before a poem emerges in its complete grandeur.

Along with *pratibha*, *vyutpatti*, and *abhyasa*, brief mention should be made of another important factor contributing to the making of a poem. This is what Vamana calls concentration (*cittaikagryamavadhanam*). Concentration for the purposes of writing poetry is, to invoke

Spender again, "different from the kind of concentration required for working out a sum. It is a focusing of the attention in a special way, so that the poet is aware of all the implications and possible developments of his idea" (1964: 35). This expresses the kernel of what Vamana would like to say about concentration. But he also wants to drive home how concentration requires a right time and place: the place should be secluded, and the time is the fourth quarter of the night (1977: 92–3). The seclusion and silence constitute the conditions within which a poem comes to life.

See also POETRY; ART HISTORY; CONSERVATION AND RESTORATION; RASA; RELATIVISM.

BIBLIOGRAPHY
Abhinavagupta. 1990 [1928]. *The "Dhvanyāloka" of Ānandavardhana with the "Locana" of Abhinavagupta*. D. H. H. Ingalls, J. M. Masson, & M. V. Patwardhan (trans.). D. H. H. Ingalls (ed.). Cambridge, MA: Harvard University Press. Based on *Dhvanyalokalocana*. Bombay: Nirnaya Sagara, 1928.
Bharata. 1967 [1894]. *Natya Sastra*. M. Ghosh (ed. & trans.) 2 vols. 2nd rev. edn. Calcutta: Granthalaya.
Dandin. 1965. *Kavyadarsa*. H. Bhattacharya (ed.). Calcutta: Sanskrit Book Depot.
Jagannatha. 1913. *Rasagangadhara*. Bombay: Nirnaya Sagara.
Mammata. 1991. *Kavyaprakasa* [The Poetic Light]. Poona: Anandasrama.
Rudrata. 1906. *Kavyalamkara*. Bombay: Nirnaya Sagara.
Sartre, Jean-Paul. 2001 [1947]. "What is Literature?" In *Continental Aesthetics: Romanticism to Postmodernism*. R. Kearney & D. Rasmussen (eds.). Malden: Blackwell, 276–87.
Spender, Stephen. 1964. "The Making of a Poem." In *Creativity in the Arts*. V. Tomas (ed.). Englewood Cliffs: Prentice-Hall, 35–48.
Tagore, Rabindranath. 1943. *Sahityer Svarupa*. Calcutta: Visva Bharati.
Tagore, Rabindranath. 1978. *Angels of Surplus: Some Essays and Addresses on Aesthetics*. S. Ghose (ed.). Calcutta: Visva-Bharati.
Vamana. 1977. *Kavyalamkarasutravrtti*. A. C. Basu (ed.). Calcutta: Sanskrit Pustak Bhandar.

KALYAN SEN GUPTA

ineffability That which cannot be communicated, nor even expressed perhaps, by words (in their literal uses, at least). Reviewing a performance of Beethoven's Fifth Symphony in 1810, E. T. A. Hoffmann wrote that "music opens up an unknown realm to man . . . in which he leaves behind all the feelings which are determinable by concepts in order to devote himself to the unsayable" (quoted in Bowie 1990: 184). The date is of some significance in that one does not find, much before the beginning of the nineteenth century, many similar claims for the power of art, especially music, to "open up" the ineffable – meaning what cannot be represented or communicated through (literal) language, and deriving from a Latin verb meaning "to speak."

Ancient thinkers, indeed, tended to regard art as an obstacle to insight into the ineffable realm – whether because, as in Plato's *Republic*, it anchors us in the world of mere appearance or because, as for Chuang Tzu (Zhuangzi), its artificiality is inimical to the "natural" attitude that responds to the intimations of the Tao, which is "beyond words." It is important, here, not to confuse the rather modern claim that art can communicate what is ineffable with an older one to the effect that it can and should remind us that there exists such a realm. Zen artists, one reads, aimed at "the evocation . . . of an atmosphere of mystery (*yūgen*)," but insisted that this mystery "remained inexpressible" in *any* medium (Hrdlička & Hrdličková 1989: 56).

Over the last two centuries claims like Hoffmann's have multiplied to the point of becoming clichés in some circles. Developments in both art and philosophy help to explain this. Within the growth of art forms that were neither representational in aim nor, as with Beethoven's music, designed merely to amuse or entertain, the question of the function and justification of art assumed some urgency. A tempting answer has been that the artist's role is to communicate what cannot be communicated through ordinary, literal language – a view encapsulated in Dewey's dramatic remark that "if all meanings could be adequately expressed by words, the arts of painting and music would not exist" (quoted in Kennick 1961: 309). The doughtiest opponents of "realism" and "representationalism" seem to find it difficult totally to renounce a signifying role for art. "Even in the most extreme experiments in abstraction . . . *something* is being represented . . . even if

the something is not identifiable" (Dufrenne 1973: 119).

The urge to carve out an autonomous role for art was strengthened by various philosophical developments. These include the Romantics' elevation of the emotions to crucial cognitive functions and the German idealists' view of consciousness and reality as a seamless unity, with its corollary that "to attempt to objectify our relationship to nature" through the categorizing apparatus of language "must be a failure. The turn to art became the attempt to say the unsayable" (Bowie 1990: 80). Later there emerged theories of meaning, like the verificationism of the Vienna Circle, which so restricted the range of what is literally signifiable by words that, if meanings outside this range can be conveyed at all, it must be through the medium of poetic language or other arts.

As these remarks suggest, there is no single thesis of art and the ineffable, and the true complexity of the discussion becomes apparent from the plethora of answers to the following questions: What kinds of item are ineffable? Why are they ineffable? How does art nevertheless succeed in acquainting us with them? Answers to the "what?" question range from "subjective" items like feelings to "objective" ones like a thing's true essence; from "intentional" items, such as meanings, to minute perceptual features of an artwork. Reasons why items may be ineffable range from the uncanniness of certain feelings evoked by a painting or poem to the unarticulated "oneness" of the reality revealed in a work.

As to how a work might convey the ineffable, schematic suggestions include mimicry (as Schopenhauer seemed to think, in the case of music's depiction of the unconceptualizable will), showing or presenting, incorporating or embodying, and evoking or evincing. There is no unanimity, moreover, as to the meaning of the term "ineffable." For some, "that is ineffable for which there . . . can be no suitable words" (Kennick 1967: 181); for others, there may be suitable words, but ineffability remains if we possess no procedure for correctly applying them; and for yet others, more moderately, something is ineffable when no description, however correctly applied, serves to communicate its nature to people lacking direct acquaintance with it. (It is in this last sense, of course, that several philosophers, such as Rudolf Carnap, have regarded colors and other "simple" qualities as ineffable.)

To lend some order to the motley of claims on behalf of art's capacity to "eff" the ineffable, it is useful to distinguish two broad directions from which most such claims are reached. The first takes as a datum the experience that people may have when, trying to describe an encounter with an artwork, they find themselves unable, to their satisfaction, to tell other people just how it was (Cavell 1976: 191–3). The attempt is then made to diagnose this frustrating situation. Thus it might be concluded, in the manner of Schleiermacher, that what resists communication – words being general in their application – is the "complete determinacy of the singular," unique work (quoted in Bowie 1990: 169).

Proceeding from the second direction, one begins with a theory of language and its limits and then proposes how artworks sometimes manage to transcend those limits. For example, the young Wittgenstein held, roughly, that only contingent propositions stating empirical facts can strictly *say* anything, for they alone have informational content. Other kinds of utterance may nevertheless *show* what is unsayable (for instance, that the world is a totality). Wittgenstein is therefore able to write, apropos of a poem by Ludwig Uhland, that the unutterable is "unutterably *contained* in what has been uttered," and that the poet succeeds in conveying it precisely through not trying to state it (and thereby producing nonsense) (in McGuinness 1988: 251).

Some authors take both directions. Susanne Langer, for instance, explains the difficulty in communicating an experience of an artwork by the fact that the knowledge of feeling and sentience it affords is too exact to be captured by the "crude designations" – "joy," "sorrow" and so on – of our psychological vocabulary. She claims, in addition, that literal language communicates by means of structured propositions that are "incommensurable" with the unarticulated stream of our "inner life." Art manages to express the relevant knowledge of feeling and sentience because its devices – melodies, for example, or Joycean "stream of consciousness" monologues – are commensurable with these "inner" processes (1957: 91–5, 22–6).

Critics of aesthetic ineffabilism, then, must reject both the diagnoses of our difficulties in telling of aesthetic encounters and the theories of meaning that make ineffabilism seem tempting or even inevitable. Thus a critic may concede to Schleiermacher that, in one sense, no description can do full justice to the "complete determinacy" of an artwork, but argue that this is due not to its language-defying uniqueness, but to the unsurprising fact that there is always more that *can* be said about a work – or any individual object, for that matter – however long we go on describing it.

Again, if "communicating a feeling" means producing that feeling in another person, then a description of a painting is unlikely to communicate what the painting does. But, a critic will point out, this is an attenuated sense of "communicate," and one in which a painting is no more ineffable than a wasp sting, which also causes a feeling that a description of the sting fortunately does not. As for the theories of meaning that inspire aesthetic ineffabilism, these are typically guilty, it is charged, of a "mimetic fallacy" in assuming that for a sentence to express or state X, it must somehow be *like* X – in terms of shared elements or structure, say. Langer is surely mistaken to hold that the natural resemblance between a melody and an emotion – both may rise and fall, and have climaxes – automatically makes the melody a more adequate expression of the emotion than a description of it (unless, of course, she is stipulatively defining "expression" as resemblance, in which case her point is trivial).

More sympathetic critics try to discern in the claims of ineffabilism expressions, exaggerated or misleading though they may be, of what are nevertheless important insights into art and our responses to it. Thus it is at once true and of significance for sensibility and taste that artistic performances (in music, dance, or whatever) possess features that are perceptually discriminable, but which could only be linguistically differentiated in a language too complex and cumbersome to be manageable by speakers. This is why sensitive listeners can hear, yet not describe, the differences between two violinists' renditions of a certain trill; and why, more generally, a performance may have a "corona" that the audience, while sensitive to it, is unable to articulate (Raffman 1993).

Note, though, that such ineffable features are not peculiar to artistic performances, since car engines may have them as much as violins; and that it would be wrong to speak, in connection with such features, of works "expressing" or "communicating" anything ineffable.

Again, it is of the first importance that some paintings, like Van Gogh's of a pair of old shoes, inspire a vivid sense of the sheer materiality, the "mere thingness," of what they depict, so that in viewing them the usual categories in terms of which we categorize the things (e.g., as shoes) are put in abeyance, as it were. But it will not follow, as Heidegger perhaps thinks, that we are thereby acquainted with "a nameless, preconceptualizable . . . stuff." For, as one critic puts it, "to confront an entity simply as a material object in its own right rather than as a specific *kind* of thing, is not to strip away all conceptual structures" (Mulhall 1990: 154). All that may be "stripped away," rather in keeping with Kant's criterion for the "disinterested" aesthetic attitude, are the everyday functional and pragmatic categories in which we usually characterize things.

Is it possible to be still more sympathetic and discern truth, and not simply misleadingly voiced insights, in some versions of ineffabilism? Two very different, though not incompatible, claims deserve close consideration. The first begins with the frequent observation that in giving expression to, say, a feeling, the artist does not always, nor even often, start with a clear, determinate experience that he or she only later translates into paint, stone, or sounds. Rather, it is precisely *through* constructing the work that the feeling assumes a determinate shape and identity. If the artist is right to insist, as many artists do, that no other work would have been an expression of just that feeling, it will follow that the feeling cannot be identified in isolation from its manifestation in that work. In the terminology of the later Wittgenstein, the work will be an *Äusserung* ("utterance," "expression") of the feeling: something that is a *criterion* for the feeling and not a symptom or causal product of some "inner" state identifiable independently from the work (Mulhall 1990). The feeling will then be ineffable in the sense, at least, that it could not be communicated to someone unacquainted with the work, since it is defined by means of ostensive reference to the latter – "that *Grande Jatte* feeling," "that *Appassionata* mood," or whatever (see Collingwood 1938 for a somewhat similar view).

A second claim deserving serious attention extrapolates to works of art a point sometimes made concerning certain metaphors – some of which, after all, merit Paul Ricoeur's label "poems in miniature" (Cooper 1986). Literal descriptions of the world, it is argued, presuppose that things "open" or manifest themselves to us in some ways (e.g., as tools) and not others. The purpose or effect of some metaphors may be to open up new ways, so that they prime us to experience things under aspects less sedimented than the usual ones. In his sonnet, "The world is too much with us," Wordsworth deploys a range of metaphors to induce in us a pantheistic perception of the natural world as replete with purpose and significance. But why should this vision not be conveyable by literal statements of the poet's pantheistic beliefs? The reply will be that having such a vision is no more exhausted by assenting to such propositions than, say, the moral point of view is equivalent to subscribing to a set of ethical propositions. In both cases, the propositions are intelligible only to those who, as Heidegger puts it, "comport" themselves toward the world in certain ways, who display a readiness to behave, respond, feel, and speak in appropriate manners.

Propositions and the beliefs they state are then derivative, intellectualized registers of the "comportments." If some metaphors may be usefully regarded in the above light, there is no obvious reason why certain paintings and other artworks should not also be so regarded. Perhaps, indeed, it was a similar point, in connection with music, that Hoffmann was trying to make in the quote with which we began. Beethoven's music, like Wordsworth's metaphors, might "open" us to, and give voice to, a "comportment" toward things which, as the precondition for articulated statements of a view of the world, cannot be reduced to such statements.

See also EXPRESSION; FUNCTION OF ART; LANGER; METAPHOR; TESTIMONY IN AESTHETICS; WITTGENSTEIN.

BIBLIOGRAPHY

Bowie, Andrew. 1990. *Aesthetics and Subjectivity: From Kant to Nietzsche*. Manchester: Manchester University Press.

Cavell, Stanley. 1976. *Must We Mean What We Say?* Cambridge: Cambridge University Press.

Collingwood, R. G. 1938. *The Principles of Art*. Oxford: Clarendon.

Cooper, David E. 1986. *Metaphor*. Oxford: Blackwell, ch. 4.

Dufrenne, Mikel. 1973. *The Phenomenology of Aesthetic Experience*. A. Anderson (trans.). Evanston: Northwestern University Press.

Hrdlička, Z. & Hrdličková, V. 1989. *The Art of Japanese Gardening*. London: Hamlyn.

Kennick, W. E. 1961. "Art and the Ineffable." *Journal of Philosophy*, 58, 309–20.

Kennick, W. E. 1967. "The Ineffable." In *Encyclopedia of Philosophy*, vol. iv. P. Edwards (ed.). New York: Macmillan, 181–3.

Langer, Susanne K. 1957. *Problems of Art*. New York: Scribner.

McGuinness, B. F. 1988. *Wittgenstein, A Life: Young Ludwig, 1889–1921*. Berkeley: University of California Press.

Mulhall, Stephen. 1990. *On Being in the World: Wittgenstein and Heidegger on Seeing Aspects*. London: Routledge.

Raffman, Diana. 1993. *Language, Music and Mind*. Boston: MIT Press.

DAVID E. COOPER

Ingarden, Roman (1893–1970) Polish philosopher, best known for his application of phenomenology to the study of literature. He studied under Kazimierz Twardowski and Husserl and wrote voluminously in many areas of philosophy, most notably aesthetics. Here his work remains unrivaled in its scope and depth of analysis, especially in the philosophy of literature, mostly discussed in his *The Literary Work of Art* and *The Cognition of the Literary Work of Art*.

The main theses of the first book are as follows:

1 The literary work of art is a multilayered creation consisting of (a) the stratum of word sounds and higher sound formations, (b) the layer of meanings of words and sentences, (c) the layer of schematized aspects (*Ansichten*) through which the objects are presented, and (d) the layer of the presented objects themselves.

2 The artistically valuable work of art contains the aesthetically valuable qualities in potentiality.

3 Most of the sentences of the literary work of art are *quasi-judgments*: unlike the predicative statements of nonliterary text, they have no referents outside the presented world.

4 The literary work has also a *quasi-temporal* dimension in the succession of its sentences and larger units.

5 The work itself should be distinguished from each of its *concretizations* constituted during the reading or staging (filming) of it.

6 Unlike the concretizations, the work itself is schematic – it contains "places of indeterminacy," which in the course of reading are to a large extent eliminated.

7 The literary work is a *purely intentional object*, which originated in the creative acts of the author and which is embodied in some form of material substratum. Yet it has an enduring identity that transcends the multiplicity of acts of consciousness and mundane reproductions. In principle, it can be shared by anyone, and always as identically the same despite the differences in interpretations and evaluations. (1973b: preface)

Phenomenologically speaking, *The Literary Work of Art* presents the content of the idea of any literary work of art whatsoever, arrived at through Husserl's famed method of *eidetic intuition*, which Ingarden favored over any empirical studies. Similarly, in his subsequent books he presents the results of his phenomenological analyses of the various types of cognition of the literary work; of the ontological peculiarities of other types of art (1989); of the nature of artistic creation; of the ontology and phenomenology of artistic and aesthetic values; of the nature of the aesthetic experience and the constitution of the aesthetic object; of problems of the cognition of the constituted aesthetic object; of the study of aesthetic and metaphysical qualities; and of the seven different notions of truth in art. All these analyses are supported not only by rigorous argumentation, but also, and most importantly, by intuitive evidence – that is, the description of the phenomena as they are directly experienced.

Ingarden's thesis of works of art as *purely intentional* bears close affinities with Husserl's treatment of "objectivities of understanding" as *irreal* in his *Formal and Transcendental Logic* (see preface to *The Literary Work of Art* for Ingarden's discussion of similarities and differences between Husserl and himself). Ingarden's thesis entails the following claims. First, against physicalism: works of art are logically and essentially distinct from their material embodiment – musical works from the concrete physical sounds or material notation, pictures from the pigment on canvas, film from the ribbons of celluloid. Second, against psychologism: works of art cannot be identified with the mental processes of the artists and perceivers. Third, against Platonic idealism: works of art derive their existence from the acts of the artist's consciousness, and can be appreciated only through aesthetic concretizations – their "life" comes to an end when they are forgotten. Fourth, against traditional realism: a work of art is schematic and two-sided. One side is the work itself, the history of its composition, its reception, and its intentional stratification. The other side is its content, which is the proper object of our aesthetic appreciation.

It is the content that contains "places of indeterminacy." For example, some of the qualities of characters in a novel, of tones in music, or of action in a film are simply not specified by the author. Since they cannot be appreciated as such, the performers of a musical work, for example, have to decide "which tones in the totality of tonal material should be emphasized . . . and whether the tones should sound 'soft' or 'hard,' and so on" (1989: 106). Similarly, the reader is free to envision his favorite characters in the way he likes, within the limits delineated by the text. Each successful aesthetic concretization carries with it various aesthetic qualities synthesized into a coherent, valuable whole, which is its aesthetic value. Since perceivers differ in individual preferences, education, expectations, imagination, temperament, and so forth, they complete the indeterminacies and constitute the aesthetic qualities in ways that also exhibit significant differences. Add to this the changes in the whole cultural atmosphere, in language, in musical instruments – and the puzzle of differences obtaining between various interpretations and evaluations of the same work of art is solved in a way precluding both essentialist and relativist conclusions. The aesthetic values differ, but so do the objects of which they are values. The artistic value of the work of art itself remains the same, and it is the function of the work's ability to inspire a multiplicity of valuable aesthetic experiences and concretizations.

Aesthetic qualities and values were the subject of Ingarden's many analyses, published in 1969 and in many collections of articles and lectures. He made lists of hundreds of words denoting such qualities in both German and Polish, and was aware of the necessity of creating new words capable of expressing further differentiations between them.

Over 70 years after the publication of *The Literary Work of Art*, Ingarden's contribution to the philosophy of art remains unmatched – and virtually unknown, especially among Anglo-American philosophers. His two main works on literature were translated only in 1973, and in such a way that his dazzling constructions and captivating style were lost in the complexity of the argument. In Europe, his influence has already been considerable: Nicolai Hartmann, Emil Steiger, and Mikel Dufrenne have appropriated some of his findings, and others have used his methodology in their analyses of concrete texts, especially art critics in Poland and Germany. Many philosophers have taken an interest in the problems that Ingarden thematized – among others, Heidegger, Sartre, Langer, Wollheim, and Margolis.

New translations should attract more interest in Ingarden's aesthetics, but appreciation of the complete system is hardly possible without knowledge of the ontological and phenomenological foundations for the grand ontologico-metaphysical edifice begun in the three-volume *Der Streit um die Existenz der Welt* ("The Controversy over the Existence of the World"). The metaphysical part was not completed, but these volumes contain many significant distinctions important for a comprehensive view of Ingarden's philosophy of art: for instance, the distinction between existential, formal, and material ontology; the problem of the identity of real, ideal, and purely intentional objects, and of states of

365

affairs, processes, and relations; nine conceptions of matter–form relations; and no fewer than 64 possible solutions of the realism/idealism controversy.

Like every great philosophical system, Ingarden's is both comprehensive and incomplete, which makes it all the more fascinating for students of aesthetics, not least because it invites us to continue where Ingarden left off.

See also NINETEENTH- AND TWENTIETH-CENTURY CONTINENTAL AESTHETICS; DUFRENNE; ONTOLOGY OF ARTWORKS; PERFORMANCE.

BIBLIOGRAPHY

Primary sources
[1931] 1973a. *The Literary Work of Art.* G. G. Grabowicz (trans.). Evanston: Northwestern University Press.
[1937] 1973b. *The Cognition of the Literary Work of Art.* R. A. Crowley & K. R. Olsen (trans.). Evanston: Northwestern University Press. (From 1968 German-language edn.)
[1962] 1989. *Ontology of the Work of Art: The Musical Work, the Picture, the Architectural Work, the Film.* R. Meyer & J. T. Goldthwait (trans.). Athens: Ohio University Press. (From 1962 German-language edn.)
1964, 1965, 1974. *Der Streit um die Existenz der Welt.* 3 vols. Tübingen: Niemeyer.
1985. *Selected Papers in Aesthetics.* P. J. McCormick (ed.). Washington DC: Catholic University of America Press.

Secondary sources
Mitscherling, Jeffrey Anthony. 1997. *Roman Ingarden's Ontology and Aesthetics.* Ottawa: University of Ottawa Press.

WOJCIECH CHOJNA

intention and interpretation It is commonplace for us to judge the things people do by reference to their purposes and intentions. It is equally commonplace to assume that what we understand when we understand an utterance is what its speaker intended to convey. Given these propensities, it is tempting to assume that since a work of art is something that someone has made, it is to be judged, at least in part, by reference to the purposes of its creator. And since, additionally, many works of art, notably literary works, have a meaning, it is equally tempting to assume that the meaning of a work is what its creator intended to say.

These two assumptions have, however, been under continuous attack in twentieth-century literary theory. Thus Eliot wrote in 1919 that "honest criticism . . . is directed not upon the poet but the poetry." At the same time the Russian Formalists lay emphasis on the effect of the public words of the poem and excluded any interest in the private psychology of the poet, a view echoed by the New Critics and canonized in Beardsley and Wimsatt's "The Intentional Fallacy" (1946). Again structuralists such as Barthes and Sartre and poststructuralists such as Derrida have directed attention to the words of the text, which may in their view yield infinitely more than the creator of the work could intentionally have conceived.

A battery of arguments has been offered against the relevance of reference to artists and their intentions. The most important of these consist of three major lines of attack. First, there is what may be called the "two-objects argument." The first premise (Beardsley 1981: 25) is that the work itself is one thing, and the creator of the work, including his or her intentions, quite another. To that is added the premise that the critic's task is solely to concentrate on the work itself. And from that it follows that any references to artists, including reference to such states of mind as intentions, is irrelevant.

Those, such as Beardsley, who deploy this argument do not deny that inferences can be made from facts about the work to facts about its creator, and from facts about its creator to facts about the work. But inferences *from* facts about the work to facts about its creator are relevant only to biographical inquiries, not to criticism of the work. When the inference is from facts about the artist to facts about the work, the inference is dispensable. To test the inference, we must eventually go to the work to check that it actually has the inferred properties. But, then, we could have gone directly to the work without taking a detour through the artist. Thus, inferences from artist to work are dispensable and inferences from work to artist are irrelevant.

One objection to the two-objects argument (Lyas 1973) is that it is not always possible to distinguish talking about works from talking about their creators. The distinction does work when terms such as "graceful" are being used. Again, we can distinguish calling a requiem sad from saying of its creator that he or she was sad when composing it. But when a critic calls *Lady Chatterley's Lover*, say, "pretentious," or Swift's *A Modest Proposal* "ironic," then a reference seems to be made to qualities that the creator displays *in* his or her work.

A second major argument against the relevance of references to intention attempts to establish the irrelevance of intention to the interpretation of *meaning*. The claim is that the meanings of words, singly or in combinations, depend on the public rules of syntax and semantics and not on the private intentions of speakers. Hence, to interpret a poem we need only dictionaries and grammars. Here a powerful argument can be derived using the practices of Lewis Carroll's Humpty-Dumpty, who claimed to be able to make a word mean whatever he wanted by his mere act of will. This meant, of course, that he had to explain each of his words as he used them. Suppose, now, that Humpty-Dumpty decides that by "glory" he will mean "fine knock-down argument." He explains this by saying. "By 'glory' I mean 'fine knock-down argument'." But, on his own account, he now has to explain what he means by "fine knockdown argument." Suppose he says, "By that phrase I meant 'stickleback'." But now the question repeats itself: "And what did you mean by 'stickleback'?" Now, either there is an infinite regress of such explanations, in which case the speaker can never succeed in making his meaning clear, or eventually he will have to use words that have an agreed public meaning independently of his will. And then his claim that meaning can be given only by private acts of will refutes itself.

There is a kind of linguistic meaning, then, that is ultimately grounded in public *structures* of rules and agreements and not private intentional acts. Call this semantic meaning. Since a literary work is nothing other than a set of words, it would seem that we can set aside artists and their intentions and let the words speak for themselves.

Powerful though this argument is, it does not eliminate authors and their intentions. First – a point made by Derrida in breaking with structuralism – the set of structural rules

of a language is not closed. I can extend the system, as when – and this is commonplace in poetry – I project a word into new contexts: for example, when I take the word "vivid" from its original use to talk of colors and use it to characterize turns of phrase. This projection is not something done by the language itself, but something that speakers of the language must do. This is related to a point made by Merleau-Ponty (1964: 30): the language is inert until put into force by individual speakers. And to that I add that, although the words used by speakers must have, antecedently, a public meaning, literary interpretation is not typically concerned with the semantic meaning of words or sentences. That is usually not in question. Rather it is the point of using those words and sentences that is the interpretative problem. For example, in Kafka's story "Report to an Academy," an individual who claims formerly to have been an ape reports the story of his transformation to a scientific society. The words of this fictional speaker are easy to understand. Nor is *his* point in question. What cries out for interpretation is the point (Kafka's) of this strange story told by its strange speaker.

It is sometimes said that, all the same, the reader is allowed a complete liberty to play with the infinite possibilities of interpretation allowed by the words of a language. That suggestion invites two responses. First, it becomes unclear, if there is such a complete liberty, what the study of literature as a discipline is to become. How, if at all, will interpretations be assessed? Second, although a work may contain more than its writer ever intended, it may still be the case that the greater part of what the work contains will be due to the controlling intelligence of its creator. To ignore this will be to ignore part of what is actually there in the work: and since critics are supposed to report what is there, to ignore this aspect is to fail one's critical duty.

The third major argument derives from the fact that we sometimes do not realize the intentions with which we set out to act. This implies that even if an artist intended to say or do something in a work, there is no guarantee that this intention will always be realized. When one does fail in trying to carry out an intention, one will end up doing something else. I may intend to shoot the hostage-taker but shoot the hostage instead. Notice that in this situation I fail to do what I intend, but I also do something, something I did not intend. What can happen with shooters can happen with authors – they may intend to represent one thing, but fail in carrying this out and end up representing something else.

This is a successful argument against the identity thesis: the view that the meaning of a literary work is identical to what the author intended to do in the work. Since some of these intentions might go unrealized, they won't contribute to work meaning.

If intentions cannot be the whole story about meaning in works, it does not follow that they cannot be part of the story. That leaves the challenge of making explicit what the exact role might be. In the last 20 years, there have been two major projects that attempt to do this: hypothetical intentionalism and moderate actual intentionalism.

The guiding thought behind both views is that we should distinguish between intended or utterer's meaning and utterance meaning. Work meaning is a species of the latter kind of meaning. Each view interprets this idea in a different way.

Hypothetical intentionalists still use the concept of intention to characterize work meaning, but eliminate reference to the actual intentions of actual artists as a constituent of work meaning. The meaning of a work is a hypothetical intention that may differ from the author's actual intention. There are different versions of hypothetical intentionalism that result from different conceptions of the target audience, the basis of their hypothesis, and the intention hypothesized. There are indefinitely many possible versions of hypothetical intentionalism, but here are some conceptions of the meaning-constituting hypothesis that have actually been advanced: the hypothesis of the intended audience about what the actual author's intentions might be using the evidence that would be available to them in the public realm (Tolhurst 1979), the hypothesis of an ideal audience – one that knows the artist's whole oeuvre and other publicly available facts concerning the context of creation – about what the actual artist's intention might be (Levinson 1996), the hypothesis about the intention of an ideal utterer of the text who is

fully aware of context and convention and uses them flawlessly to say or do what she intends (Nathan 1993). One can add a more relativistic version of this view that would claim the meaning of the work is variable depending on the artist hypothesized to be behind it, and it is reasonable to posit any number of such hypothetical artists for the sake of enhanced appreciation of the work (Currie 1993).

Unlike hypothetical intentionalism, moderate actual intentionalism makes a subclass of actual intentions – the successfully realized ones – constitutive of work meaning. However, they could not be the only constituents, since we already know that when an intention fails to be realized, something meaningful can result, though it diverges from intended meaning. The challenge for a proponent of moderate actual intentionalism is threefold: to give a coherent account of a realized intention, to identify other constituents of meaning, and finally to explain how these various constituents hang together to result in a work's meaning. At present there are several versions of moderate actual intentionalism which vary in their conceptions of realized intentions and the degree to which they tackle the other two challenges (Iseminger 1993; Carroll 2001; Stecker 2003; Livingston 2005). A rough but not inaccurate idea of the position advocated by moderate actual intentionalism is that the meaning of a work is a function of the realized intentions of its creator in combination with the relevant conventions in place when the work was created and the context of creation.

See also LITERATURE; POETRY; BEARDSLEY; IMPLIED AUTHOR; "INTENTIONAL FALLACY"; INTERPRETATION; INTERPRETATION, AIMS OF; STRUCTURALISM AND POSTSTRUCTURALISM.

BIBLIOGRAPHY
Beardsley, Monroe C. 1981. *Aesthetics: Problems in the Philosophy of Criticism*. 2nd edn. Indianapolis: Hackett.
Beardsley, Monroe C. & Wimsatt, W. K., Jr. 1946. "The Intentional Fallacy," *Sewanee Review*, 54, 468–88.
Carroll, Noël. 2001. *Beyond Aesthetics*. Cambridge: Cambridge University Press, 157–213.
Currie, Gregory. 1993. "Interpretation and Objectivity," *Mind*, 102, 413–28.

Davies, Stephen. 2006. "Authors' Intentions, Literary Interpretation, and Literary Value," *British Journal of Aesthetics*, 46, 223–47.

Eliot, T. S. 1953. *Selected Prose*. Harmondsworth: Penguin.

Iseminger, Gary. 1993. "An Intentional Demonstration." In *Intention and Interpretation*. G. Iseminger (ed.). Philadelphia: Temple University Press, 76–96.

Levinson, Jerrold. 1996. *The Pleasures of Aesthetics*. Ithaca: Cornell University Press, 175–213.

Livingston, Paisley. 2005. *Art and Intention*. Oxford: Oxford University Press, 135–74.

Lyas, Colin. 1973. "Personal Qualities and the Intentional Fallacy." In *Philosophy and the Arts*. G. Vesey (ed.). London: Macmillan, 194–210.

Merleau-Ponty, M. 1964. *Signs*. R. McCleary (trans.). Evanston: Northwestern University Press.

Nathan, Daniel O. 1993. "Irony, Metaphor and the Problem of Intention." In *Intention and Interpretation*. G. Iseminger (ed.). Philadelphia: Temple University Press, 183–202.

Stecker, Robert. 2003. *Interpretation and Construction: Art, Speech and the Law*. Oxford: Blackwell.

Tolhurst, William. 1979. "On What a Text Is and How It Means," *British Journal of Aesthetics*, 19, 3–14.

COLIN LYAS & ROBERT STECKER

"**intentional fallacy**" takes its name from a seminal article with that title published by Monroe C. Beardsley and William K. Wimsatt in 1946. The initial emphasis of the article is on a denial of the relevance of a reference to intention in literary evaluation: the denial that "in order to judge a poet's performance we must know what he intended" (Beardsley & Wimsatt 1976: 4), where "intention" is understood as "the design or plan in the author's mind."

However, and somewhat confusingly, the article has a wider scope than this. In addition there is, first, the denial that reference to intention has any relevance to the *interpretation* of a literary work. Second, there is the claim that the true speaker of a poem is a "dramatic speaker" *in* the poem who is not to be identified with its creator (who may be pretending to speak in that voice). Third, there is the much more general claim that "personal studies" – that is, investigations into the biography and psychology of writers can be distinguished from "poetic studies." The belief is that a work of art

and its creator are two discrete entities, the critic's sole proper concern being the former.

Influential though "The Intentional Fallacy" was, it is more a set of assertions than a clearly articulated body of argument, and the target of its attack is not always clear. Beardsley (1970, 1981) and Wimsatt (1976) later attempted to redress this unclarity. It is possible, however, to detect at least two suppositions on which "The Intentional Fallacy" is based. First, there is the supposition that a work of literature is a public object available for "objective" scrutiny and an intention is a "private" object in the writer's mind unavailable to the audience of a work. Granted that the work is one thing and the author's intention another, and granted that the job of a critic of a work of literature is to talk about that work and nothing else, it follows that reference to the author is irrelevant. For the author just is a different object from the work itself. Hence the intentional fallacy is a fallacy of irrelevance: required to talk about the work itself, the critic who commits this fallacy digresses into talk about a different thing altogether – the author and her or his intentions.

This first supposition, that an intention is a private event in a mind and a work a public event in the world, seems committed to a view of mind that would occasion severe problems for an account of knowledge of other minds. Here there is a dilemma for Beardsley and Wimsatt. On the one hand, if intention is a private event in a mind, knowledge of it seems in jeopardy. At times this conclusion seems almost welcome (Wimsatt 1976): intention really is unavailable and private, so we are left only with the public work of art. But that buys the irrelevance of intention only at the cost of making *any* knowledge of *any* mind impossible. The alternative is to adopt an account of intention according to which states of mind, such as intentions, can be seen *in* and known through their manifestations in action and behavior. But then intention, though undoubtedly a psychological state, ceases to be unavailable to others because it can display itself in action: and since a literary work may be the product of a complex set of actions, it is unclear why we should not see its creator's intentions made manifest in it (as they clearly are in, say, Milton's *Paradise Lost*).

It should be noted, as Beardsley and Wimsatt stress, that an author may not be the most reliable source of information about his or her intentions. But that does not mean we should ignore authorial assertions about intentions but only that we should not ignore other evidence of their intentions that their works themselves provide, which can sometimes override what the writer says about his or her work. As Wimsatt (1976: 131) somewhat inconsistently says, a poet's denial of ironic intent may be belied by his or her performance.

The second supposition made in "The Intentional Fallacy" is about meaning. The claim is that the meaning of a word is a public matter, to be determined by dictionaries and not by references to the intentions of its users. A poet cannot make the word "cup" mean "saucer" just by declaring an intention so to use the term. He or she may mean that by it, but that is not what the word means. And what words used in sentences mean is decided by equally public rules of syntax and semantics. From this it seems to follow that if we wish to know the meaning of a poem, we can determine this by reference to dictionaries and grammars. We do not need to make reference to the intentions of authors. Beardsley and Wimsatt say, "The poem belongs to the public. It is embodied in the language, the peculiar possession of the public" (1946; Beardsley 1981: 25). Hence the distinction in "The Intentional Fallacy" between "internal" evidence of the meaning of the poem, discovered through "syntax and semantics, grammar and dictionaries," and "external" evidence, such as letters and diaries of the author, which are "not part of the work as a linguistic fact."

Critics (Cioffi 1963–4) have queried this distinction between internal and external evidence, which is anyway muddied by Beardsley and Wimsatt, who introduce an intermediate category of "semi-private" meaning (1946). Further, although at one level the meaning of a poem can be settled by dictionaries and grammars, this still leaves scope for references to authorial intentions. For there remains the question about what the author was doing in using those words: Was he being ironic? Did he wish to make allusions? Those questions seem prima facie to involve reference to intention, since the semantically encoded meaning of a sentence used on one occasion to make an ironic utterance and on another occasion to make a nonironic one is the same in both cases. The difference between an ironic and nonironic utterance must lie elsewhere, and a plausible place to look is in the communicative intention of the utterer. Attempts in "The Intentional Fallacy" to show that allusion in poetry can be handled without reference to intention are not happily framed (see Wheeler 1977).

Recent defenders of anti-intentionalism (Levinson 1996; Nathan 2006) have attempted to reply to this objection. One proposal is that, although we cannot account for irony merely by appeal to dictionaries and grammars, the ironic nature of a passage is not grounded in the intention of its actual author. Rather it is grounded in contextual clues to be found either in the work itself or the situation in which it is "uttered." Thus, it is claimed that what makes ironic the suggestion found in *A Modest Proposal* that fricasseeing Irish babies would have the double advantage of controlling and feeding the local population is "a confluence of linguistic clues found in the text of the essay as a whole and the connotation of words like 'fricassee' . . ." (Nathan 2006: 285). However, this very example reveals a problem with the idea. For *A Modest Proposal* to work ("as intended," one is very tempted to say) we have to imagine that a fictional author is seriously proposing cooking Irish infants. So at one level – call it the level of representation – it make sense to read the proposal as serious. How do we come to understand that the level of representation is not the ultimate level at which to understand the work? Linguistic clues might be of some use here but only once we understand what they are clues to. Clearly they are not clues to what is represented in the text or even the attitude of the fictional author of it. They are clues to the point of creating the representation and its fictional author. They are clues to Swift's communicative or literary intention in creating this work. It is that which is satirical rather than serious. Of course, it is not enough for Swift to have this intention for the work to be a satire and for the proposal to be ironic. He must provide clues in the text so the intention can be grasped and in that way be successfully realized. But that is just what Swift does.

Ultimately, even the anti-intentionalists have to admit that we cannot avoid appealing to intentions in interpreting works for without such an appeal we lack a reason to move beyond the level of representation. Their fallback position is that when we ask about the point of a representation we are not asking about an actual intention but a purely hypothetical one. It is simply a convention of interpretation to ask what intention would best explain the significant features of the work and the best interpretations provide the best explanations, whether the actual artist had them or not.

But that seems just incorrect. If we could establish that Swift really intended to argue in *A Modest Proposal* that cannibalism was the best solution to Ireland's food problems, then it would turn out not to be a satire, and it would have meant just what it says at the level of representation. If some of the choice of words might be taken as clues to the contrary, that would signal a degree of ineptitude, or perhaps mental instability, rather than irony. After all, Swift's contemporary Bishop Berkeley wrote works in which he advocated incredible powers to tar water and others where he expressed equally strange views about the nature of tables. The works could easily be read as satires of contemporary medicine and philosophy respectively, if we did not know they were meant in all seriousness.

See also LITERATURE; POETRY; BEARDSLEY; IMPLIED AUTHOR; INTENTION AND INTERPETATION; INTERPRETATION; INTERPRETATION, AIMS OF; IRONY.

BIBLIOGRAPHY

Beardsley, M. C. 1970. *The Possibility of Criticism.* Detroit: Wayne State University Press.

Beardsley, M. C. 1981. *Aesthetics: Problems in the Philosophy of Criticism.* 2nd edn. Indianapolis: Hackett.

Beardsley, M. C. & Wimsatt, W. K., Jr. 1946. "The Intentional Fallacy," *Sewanee Review*, 54, 468–88; extensively reprinted.

Cioffi, Frank. 1963–4. "Intention and Interpretation in Criticism," *Proceedings of the Aristotelian Society*, 64, 85–106.

Levinson, Jerrold. 1996. *The Pleasures of Aesthetics.* Ithaca: Cornell University Press, 175–213.

Nathan, Daniel O. 2006. "Art, Meaning and Artist's Meaning." In *Contemporary Debates in Aesthetics and the Philosophy of Art.* M. Kieran (ed.). Oxford: Blackwell, 282–95.

Wheeler, M. 1977. "Biography, Literary Influence and Allusion as Aspects of Source Studies," *British Journal of Aesthetics*, 2, 149–60.

Wimsatt, W. K. 1976. "Genesis: A Fallacy Revisited." In *On Literary Intention.* D. Newton-de Molina (ed.). Edinburgh: Edinburgh University Press, 116–38.

COLIN LYAS & ROBERT STECKER

interpretation   The theory of interpretation has changed so rapidly that one could not have anticipated the radical themes favored in the 2000s from their sources in the 1950s. The salient disputes about the nature of interpretation have indeed taken the most extreme forms in our time, and exhibit a certain dialectical boldness that justifies confining our attention to a handful of conceptual options. The suggestion here is that nearly everything of importance about interpretation can be recovered through the economies of a small number of alternative strategies.

A first pass at managing the unwieldy spread of contemporary theories follows the lead of organizing answers to cognate questions regarding the nature of the human sciences. Two opposing intuitions dominate our thinking there. On one, every would-be science preserves objectivity more or less in accord with the model that treats physics as the paradigm of all science. The Vienna Circle, logical positivism, and the unity of science movement all accept this model.

The other intuition, drawn from an entirely different post-Kantian tradition that counts Wilhelm Dilthey as its most distinctive champion, emphasizes that:

1   the human sciences are, methodologically, *sui generis*;

2   objectivity cannot be construed in the same way as in the physical sciences;

3   the human sciences are primarily centered on the meanings and the semiotic and interpretable features of the things of the human world; and

4   the actual properties of the "objects" of that world – those that are interpretable – may (the matter is disputed) be altered in a distinctive way as a direct result of their interpretation under the conditions of changing history.

On the first intuition, knowledge is essentially ahistorical, even in admitting historical progress among the sciences; on the second, particularly as we approach the viewpoint of the 2000s, the historicity of knowledge becomes deeper and more problematic.

The methodological treatment of interpretation in the arts within the Anglo-American literature (critical as well as philosophical) that dominated the 1950s through the mid 1970s noticeably favored the New Criticism and romantic hermeneutics. In the philosophical literature, there can be little doubt that the influential views of Monroe C. Beardsley characteristically defined the task of interpretation in a strongly empirical manner that deliberately approached the supposed rigor favored by the unity of science program without ever formally urging a specific connection.

Beardsley conveys the conviction that artworks – literature preeminently but not exclusively – may be treated, for the purpose of objectively testing interpretative claims, as "objects" not significantly different for methodological purposes from the objects of any other bona fide science. Even their "meanings," certainly a mark that differentiates poems from stones, are objectively "there, in" the poem, according to Beardsley.

On the view he professed, the historical and biographical circumstances of an artist's life could only be causally – that is, extrinsically – connected with the production of particular artworks, and could not bear directly in any pertinent way at all on the empirical analysis of their actual properties or meanings. For similar reasons, the artist's or author's intention in producing particular poems or paintings proved quite irrelevant in determining the specific meaning that an interpretative critic might correctly explicate. These are the essential themes of "The Intentional Fallacy" – probably one of the most celebrated (and condemned) of contemporary philosophical essays on the arts.

These claims also deliberately rule out as illicit the master thesis of the alternative interpretative methodology of romantic hermeneutics. Beardsley explicitly excoriates the views of E. D. Hirsch Jr., a well-known American literary critic and theorist who has sought to redeem a conservative sense of interpretative objectivity and rigor from the extravagances of so-called post-Heideggerian hermeneutics, as practiced, for instance, by the doyen of contemporary Western hermeneutics, Hans-Georg Gadamer. For the moment, we may simply take note of the fact that Hirsch's methodology is utterly opposed to Beardsley's as well as to Gadamer's; Hirsch simply favors an entirely different model of the human sciences from that of the unity program; and, within the German tradition of the *Geisteswissenschaften*, he opposes Gadamer's relatively radical historicizing of hermeneutics.

Beardsley advances three principles regarding art and its interpretation: first, the "principle of independence" – that literary works exist as individuals and can be distinguished from other things; second, the "principle of autonomy" – that literary works are self-sufficient entities, whose properties are decisive in checking interpretations and judgments; and third, the "principle of the intolerability of incompatibles" – that if two interpretations are logically incompatible, they cannot both be true.

Beardsley's model, then, brings critical discourse into a congenial alliance with empiricism. In this sense, it marks one extreme pole of interpretative theory. Romantic hermeneutics may be straightforwardly characterized as opposing Beardsley's first two principles, but not in the interest of opposing the third; and post-Heideggerian hermeneutics, particularly Gadamer's, opposes (at least implicitly) all three principles. The hermeneuts, of course, adhere one way or another to the post-Kantian bifurcation of the sciences. Also, one finds no discussion within any of these three models of the necessity of adhering to a bivalent logic.

Hirsch's model is probably the most ramified version of the romantic theory that may be found in English. Opposing Beardsley, Hirsch is extremely cautious about speaking of a poem or story as of an actual "object" that is "given" or encountered in experience. He speaks instead of "manuscripts," "holographs," written remains, and the like – which, properly examined, permit us to construct or reconstruct a reasonable conception of a text or artwork open to interpretation. Both phases of this effort – the imaginative reconstruction of a text and the proper reading of the text thus constructed – involve interpretation, in the sense that they involve the recovery of original authorial intent. Evidence may be adduced, then, including biographical, historical, and stylistic remains, that enables us to form a correct conception of the "text" that some inscription imaginatively subtends.

The text is a representation of an author's creative intention; the author, as an apt member of a particular culture, intends, in uttering some inscription or other, to conform to the essential organizing literary genres of his own cultural world; and apt readers, guided by an understanding of those genres, are able to recover an author's meaning from his inscription. The poem is reconstructed in the shared space of common culture, through imagination.

Hirsch is committed to texts having uniquely determinate meanings. Still, he admits that it may be impossible to recover those meanings with certainty. But this fact signifies our limited access to the *Geist* of a culture, rather than the arguable truth that the supposed constitutive genres are themselves no more than heuristic artifacts: (1) contingently posited within the changing course of history, (2) not necessary for the intelligibility of any creative or interpretative act, and (3) themselves freely altered and affected by ongoing artistic and critical efforts. Hirsch opposes (1)–(3).

This bears directly on Gadamer's seemingly unanswerable challenge to the romantic hermeneutic view. Gadamer claims that the romantic fails to acknowledge that his own interpretation of a text is itself historicized – structured, oriented, limited, biased by the process of enculturation. Gadamer explicitly holds that the events to be interpreted must be constructed and reconstructed from a changing present vantage point in history, and that the interpretation of that construction cannot fail to reflect the historically contingent "prejudice" from which any critic or historian makes his effort. So the historical past – a fortiori, "original historical intent" – is itself an interpretative construction from the present; and the interpretation of what is thus constructed is organized by a consciousness itself shaped by ongoing history.

Gadamer radicalizes the famous "hermeneutic circle." The circle – that is, the thesis that the meaning of an entire text depends on its parts and the meaning of its parts depends on the meaning of the whole text – now cannot be assigned more than a provisional or heuristic

closure; whereas, for the romantic, closure is objectively and uniquely imposed on interpretation by reference jointly to original intent and constitutive genres. The upshot is that Gadamer construes hermeneutics only in terms of the metaphysics of culture and human existence, not in terms of the logic and methodology of interpretation, about which he has next to nothing to say.

Gadamer's theory precludes the fixity and determinacy of texts or other interpretable referents. There are no such "objects." Similarly, it precludes the adequacy of a bivalent logic applied to interpretation. Interpretation is at best "authentic," rather than true or accurate.

It will pay us to collect, here, certain general philosophical doctrines regarding interpretation that may help to offset the impression (otherwise nearly ineluctable) that recent currents in theorizing are simply irresponsible, inadequately developed, even incoherent. Recent theories of interpretation are conceptually inseparable from equally radical larger reconstructions of the very nature of science, philosophy, intellectual inquiry in general.

The master themes of the larger reconstruction may be roughly tallied as follows:

1 There is no privileged access to what is true about the world.
2 There is no principled disjunction between the structures of human thinking and the structures of the encountered world.
3 Human thinking, reason, science, inquiry, logic have a history, hence are not reliably invariant over the whole of history.
4 There are no *de re* or *de dicto* necessities.
5 The reflexive critique of thinking and inquiry is subject to the same constraints of history that infect the thinking and judgment that it seeks to organize in a rationally systematic way.

It would not be unreasonable to affirm that these five doctrines dominated Western thinking by the end of the twentieth century. They are certainly not incontestable, but it would be extremely difficult to specify any thesis that either had a stronger backing among the pertinent professions. So (1)–(5) constitute a very distinct revolution of sorts; each doctrine has made its way against formidable opposition over the centuries. The result is that the remarkable flurry of recent radical theories of interpretation that converge with the general thrust of (1)–(5) also entrenches the expectation that the assessment of their advantage will accord with those same developments.

Once this much is in place, we may go on to add some further doctrines that cohere with (1)–(5) but are more narrowly pertinent to the radical claims of recent interpretative theories. These are bound to be more controversial. But the argument may be made that if (1)–(5) were conceded, it would be very difficult indeed to deny these further claims. Here, then, is a compendium of the most important of them:

6 The referents of the human world – artworks, in particular – lack fixed natures, have only histories (predicatively) or are (referentially) only histories.

7 Interpretation is primarily addressed to those features of given referents that are linguistic, semiotic, significative, symbolic, rhetorical, stylistic, historical, traditional, or the like, but they are real features of the (human) world, irreducible to the physical, and subject to change through the processes of history and reinterpretation.

8 Objectivity with respect to the description and interpretation of the human world is methodologically distinct from that accorded physical nature. It makes no sense to suppose that the human world is in any regard independent of the actual process of human (reflexive) understanding, in contrast to what is often conjectured regarding physical nature.

9 Whatever is interpretable is, in principle, open to infinitely many interpretations, both synchronically and diachronically.

The important point is that each member of the set of (1)–(9) is internally coherent, and the entire set is consistent and coherent. More than that, the entire thrust of the late twentieth century very strongly favors large subsets of (1)–(9).

This may be shown, for instance, in the critical practice and/or theories of Barthes, Foucault, and Bloom, at least. For instance, Foucault (1973), in the interpretation of Velázquez's painting *Las Meninas*, pursues a rigorous application of his (our) own conceptual orientation to that of the earlier period (reconstructed, of course, in a way not altogether different from the hermeneut's). The meaning of Velázquez's painting may be assigned in terms that would have been inaccessible to Velázquez himself and would have been incompatible with any canon rightly drawn from his period; and yet Foucault's interpretation is strongly congruent with the details of the painting viewed in terms of the history of its reception as well as Foucault's own theory of the historicity of interpretation.

Foucault is nearly unique in pursuing his thesis in the radically historicized way in which he does. Both Bloom (1975) and Barthes offer what may be called formal analogues of Foucault's fully historicized notion of *epistemes*, in a sense not altogether unlike that in which Wittgenstein's notion of *Lebensformen* is a formal (i.e., nonhistoricized) analogue of Foucault's *epistemes*. Bloom easily confirms the energy, promise, and distinctive rigor of an interpretative practice that deliberately works through the "misprision" of a "strong" poet or ancestral text. (Here, one might think of Euripides' *Iphigenia* as a misprision of Homer.) For Bloom, poetry is interpretative criticism ("verse-criticism"), and criticism is an attenuated poetry ("prose-poetry"). That is, both may be said to depend on the same logic, although interpretation makes explicit truth claims.

Barthes's *S/Z* (1974) may well be the most sustained, explicitly poststructuralist attempt at an interpretative practice that tests the limits of arbitrariness within the familiar boundaries of the whole of Western culture. In the process, Barthes explores the difference between what he (elsewhere) calls "readerly" reading (interpretation) and "writerly" reading, which in effect demonstrates, by example, the compatibility of an interpretative practice more or less in accord with a large subset of (1)–(9) and a more conventional practice – one that converges, say, with something like the limiting models championed by Beardsley or Hirsch. That is, one can actually construe "canonical" theories – those that insist on a determinate object of interpretation, or on a strong bivalence for determinate authorial intentions or the like – as special cases falling within the terms of reference of a larger practice. Reading Barthes thus, a comprehensive overview of interpretative theories may be formed, admittedly prejudicial to the exclusionary pretensions of the "canon," but coherent and hospitable enough in terms of the rising themes of the end of the twentieth century. There is every reason to believe that the larger vision has introduced relatively permanent changes in the theory of interpretation. In any case, its innovations cannot be discounted without recovering the older canons of general philosophy.

See also BARTHES; BEARDSLEY; CANON; CRITICISM; FOUCAULT; GADAMER; HERMENEUTICS; "INTENTIONAL FALLACY"; INTERPRETATION, AIMS OF; MEANING CONSTRUCTIVISM; STRUCTURALISM AND POSTSTRUCTURALISM; TEXT; TRUTH IN ART.

BIBLIOGRAPHY

Barthes, Roland. 1974. *S/Z*. R. Miller (trans.). New York: Hill & Wang.

Beardsley, Monroe C. 1970. *The Possibility of Criticism*. Detroit: Wayne State University Press.

Bloom, Harold. 1975. *A Map of Misreading*. Oxford: Oxford University Press.

Foucault, Michel. 1973. *The Order of Things*. A. Sheridan (trans.). New York: Vintage.

Gadamer, Hans-Georg. 1975. *Truth and Method*. G. Barden & J. Cumming (trans.). New York: Seabury.

Hirsch, E. D., Jr. 1967. *Validity in Interpretation*. New Haven: Yale University Press.

Ingarden, Roman. 1973. *The Cognition of the Literary Work of Art*. R. A. Crowley & K. R. Olsen (trans.). Evanston: Northwestern University Press.

Iser, Wolfgang. 1978. *The Act of Reading: A Theory of Aesthetic Response*. Baltimore: Johns Hopkins University Press.

Margolis, Joseph. 1989. "Reinterpreting Interpretation," *Journal of Aesthetics and Art Criticism*, 47, 237–51.

Wimsatt, William K., Jr. 1954. *The Verbal Icon*. Lexington: University of Kentucky Press. (Contains both "The Intentional Fallacy" and "The Affective Fallacy," coauthored with Monroe C. Beardsley.)

JOSEPH MARGOLIS

interpretation, aims of Interpretation is an essential element in our appreciative engagement with works of art of all kinds. In the case of narrative or representational artworks this is uncontroversial, since the appreciation of such works requires that we ascribe "thematic" content that goes beyond what can be given in a description of the artistic manifold. But the appreciation of abstract paintings and "pure" music also involves interpretation, since we must ascribe some overarching structure to the artistic manifold in terms of which we can see the elements of that manifold standing in certain relations to one another. interpretation also plays an ineliminable role in the performance arts, where the interpretative burden falls upon performers or presenters of works.

It is also undeniable that artworks admit of differing interpretations in both the critical and the performative sense. While aficionados of Mozart debate the merits of different interpretations of a given string quartet, literary criticism is rife with differences, such as that between Cleanth Brooks and F. W. Bateson over whether the final stanza of Wordsworth's poem "A Slumber Did My Spirit Seal" expresses, as Brooks maintained, the poet's horror at the inertness of his beloved, or, as Bateson argued, the pantheistic sentiment that she is now part of the greater life of Nature. Indeed, Robert Matthews (1977) claims that it is the essence of interpretation, as opposed to description or mere execution, that the interpreter is not in a position to know whether the claims made are *true*, and thus that interpretations are underdetermined by the available evidence. Thus, any situation that involves interpretation is one in which alternative and even incompatible interpretations may be equally acceptable.

While openness to different performative interpretations is generally celebrated in the performing arts, there is disagreement as to the significance of differences in critical interpretation. Much of this disagreement is grounded in a deeper disagreement about the aims of critical interpretation. For those who adhere to the idea that the goal of criticism is what Richard Wollheim (1980) termed "retrieval," the indeterminacy identified by Matthews is merely *epistemic*, and the work, taken to be the product of its creator's working in a particular art-historical context, admits in principle of a single "true" interpretation that captures those meanings the artist succeeded in realizing in her work. The aim of interpretation, as retrieval, is to furnish the reader with such an interpretation. Apparently conflicting interpretations of a work either admit of reconciliation as elements in a single correct interpretation, or cannot both be correct. Interpretation, if aimed at retrieval, can admit of incompatible right interpretations only if there are conflicting right accounts of the meanings that the artist succeed in realizing in her work – if, for example, the correct interpretation of the work depends on the intentions of the artist, which are themselves taken to be genuinely (and not merely epistemically) indeterminate.

Matthews himself subscribes not only to an epistemic thesis about the indeterminacy of interpretation but also to the substantive thesis that, in artistic interpretation, there is typically no "fact" independent of the evidence available to interpreters that could make one of a pair of conflicting interpretations true. While some interpretations are more acceptable than others, this is to be explained in terms of relative plausibility, as measured against some disciplinary norm of acceptability, rather than in terms of truth. Opponents of such a view, however, challenge these claims, arguing that a plausible interpretation is one that is plausibly *true*, and that the underdetermination thesis rests on too thin a conception of available evidence (Stecker 1994: 198–9).

But, once the retrievalist goal of truth is called into question, a more pluralistic conception of the aims of interpretation becomes attractive. Susan Feagin (1982), for example, suggests that we see the tolerance, in critical practice, of a plurality of apparently incompatible readings of a literary work as a reason to reevaluate our understanding of the legitimate goals of interpretation and the sorts of standards to which it is accountable. She argues that we should not think of radically differing interpretations of a literary work as "incompatible." Such a characterization rests on the mistaken assumption that literary interpretation aims at discovering some independently existing meaning of a work. Rather, we should view interpretation as a creative activity whose goal is to provide the reader with "a theoretical framework of understanding" for a work, a framework that renders it coherent and permits the reader to ascribe a sense to it. We then evaluate different such frameworks not according to whether they correspond to the "true meaning" of the work but in terms of how the readings they engender enrich our

experience of both the work and the world. Even historically anachronistic interpretations, she claims, "contribute to the enrichment of experience . . . of the work" (1982: 141). Alan H. Goldman (1990) argues for a similar conclusion, holding that the aim of interpretation is "to maximize the artistic value of the interpreted work," where to accomplish this goal may require that we depart from what would be regarded as historically accurate interpretation.

A similar conception of *literary* interpretation as essentially creative has been proposed separately by Roland Barthes (1977) and Michel Foucault (1986). Advocating what he terms the "proliferation of meaning," Foucault rejects, as repressive and ideologically based, the practice of constraining the interpretation of literary texts by referring them to an author. According to what Barthes terms the *écriture* thesis, the texts generated by literary authors are to be viewed as pieces of writing that are, by the very process of their creation, divorced from their origins. "Texts," as Barthes terms them, are to be distinguished from "works," the kinds of semantically constrained entities with which literary critics have traditionally taken themselves to deal. A text, for Barthes, "answers not to an interpretation, even a liberal one, but to an explosion, a dissemination" (1977: 159).

It is clearly possible to treat the products of literary activity as "texts," in Barthes's sense, and to seek various values in the "proliferation of meaning," and the fruits of such a practice may on occasion prove significant. But this is quite compatible, as it stands, with the retrievalist's claims about what is involved in the interpretation of *works*. Writers like Feagin and Goldman, on the other hand, take themselves to be offering an alternative to the retrievalist conception, and it is less clear how such views might be reconciled. Robert Stecker, however, has argued for such a reconciliation between what he terms "critical monism" and "critical pluralism" (1994: 193): critical pluralism is the view that "there are many acceptable interpretations of many artworks that cannot be conjoined into a single correct interpretation." *Critical monism*, on the other hand, is the view that "there is a single, comprehensive, true (correct) interpretation for each work of art."

The claim that critical pluralism and critical monism are compatible turns on the distinction between (1) truth or correctness, and (2) acceptability. The quest for "true" or "correct" interpretations of artworks is the retrievalist project of understanding a work as the product, for the most part, of design by its historical creator. But critical monism can be reconciled with critical pluralism once we recognize that there are other legitimate aims of art interpretation, and that the acceptability of an interpretation is relative to interpretative aim. Such aims might include "making a work relevant or significant to a certain sort of audience, identifying what is cognitively valuable in a work, or . . . enhancing the reader's aesthetic experience of a work" (Stecker 2003: 54). Interpretations of works that satisfy such alternative aims can be acceptable, insofar as they try to achieve *an* understanding of a work, where the acceptability of the latter is a matter of rendering the work coherent in a way that promotes appreciation. Acceptable interpretations that aim in this way at maximizing the value of the work to the receiver are constrained to a certain extent in that they must be "consistent with *some* facts about the work" (1994: 194), but this also allows them to conflict with other such facts.

In what respects, however, can an interpretation conflict with certain facts about a work while still being an interpretation *of the work*, rather than a reading of a Barthian text? This question is addressed by Stephen Davies. He claims that interpretation is pursued for the pleasure that goes with understanding a work, where such understanding is achieved by considering the readings that can be "put upon" that work. In response to the charge that this licenses anachronistic interpretations, he states that all right interpretations must respect the identity of the work: "If a particular work becomes the work that it is in virtue of being embedded in a particular culture, time, and social practice, a concern with interpreting *that* work must consider only the readings consistent with the conventions of language and literature at the time of the work's creation . . . An interpretation is true if it is true-to-the-work, that is, if it deals with at least one of the meanings the work (as opposed to a context-less text) can support" (1995: 9–10).

If Davies's point holds for "acceptable" interpretations of a work just as much as for true

interpretations, this suggests a difficulty with Stecker's proposal for reconciling critical monism and critical pluralism (David Davies 1996). For, while critical monism seems to presuppose a broadly contextualist conception of the literary work, it is not obvious how such a conception can support an interesting form of critical pluralism. Certainly, if Stephen Davies is right about the implications of contextualism, the anachronistic interpretations canvassed by Feagin and Goldman cannot be interpretations of works but only interpretations of their decontextualized artistic vehicles. In what sense can an anachronistic interpretation of *Hamlet*, for example, be an acceptable interpretation of the *work*, if, as the defense of critical monism requires, we take the work to incorporate aspects of the context of creation of the text which rule out the possession of anachronistic properties?

Stecker, however, counters this objection by insisting on the legitimacy of interpretations that identify what a work *could* mean in what he terms the "pragmatic" sense: "We assert that a work could mean something relative to a point of view or set of constraints. We ignore or bracket off something we do know about the work for the purpose of pursuing a particular interpretive aim" (2003: 66). It might be asked, however, whether works, construed contextually, have "pragmatically possible" interpretations in this sense? Once we "bracket off" what are, for the contextualist, constitutive features of the work, why think that it is *the work* that can be taken to have the ascribed meanings, rather than an entity, or a class of entities, that would resemble the work in certain respects? However we resolve these questions, it should be clear that the legitimacy of claims about the aims of artistic interpretation depends on the position we adopt on the nature of artworks themselves. Thus we cannot unproblematically appeal to interpretative pluralism to settle questions about the ontology of art, as some have sought to do (Goodman & Elgin 1988).

See also LITERATURE; BARTHES; CRITICAL MONISM AND PLURALISM; FOUCAULT; IMPLIED AUTHOR; INTENTION AND INTERPRETATION; INTERPRETATION; MEANING CONSTRUCTIVISM; ONTOLOGICAL CONTEXTUALISM; PERFORMANCE; TEXT; WOLLHEIM.

BIBLIOGRAPHY

Barthes, Roland. 1977. "From Work to Text." In *Image–Music–Text*. S. Heath (ed.). Glasgow: Fontana, 155–64.

Davies, David. 1996. "Interpretive Pluralism and the Ontology of Art," *Revue Internationale de Philosophie*, 198, 577–92.

Davies, Stephen. 1995. "Relativism in Interpretation," *Journal of Aesthetics and Art Criticism*, 53, 8–13.

Feagin, Susan L. 1982. "Incompatible Interpretations of Art," *Philosophy and Literature*, 6, 133–46.

Goldman, Alan H. 1990. "Interpreting Art and Literature," *Journal of Aesthetics and Art Criticism*, 48, 205–14.

Goodman, Nelson & Elgin, Catherine Z. 1988. *Reconceptions in Philosophy and Other Arts and Sciences*. London: Routledge.

Foucault, Michel. 1986. "What is an Author?" In *The Foucault Reader*. P. Rabinow (ed.). New York: Pantheon, 101–20.

Matthews, Robert. 1977. "Describing and Interpreting Works of Art," *Journal of Aesthetics and Art Criticism*, 36, 5–14.

Stecker, Robert. 1994. "Art Interpretation," *Journal of Aesthetics and Art Criticism*, 52, 193–206.

Stecker, Robert. 2003. *Interpretation and Construction*. Oxford: Blackwell.

Wollheim, Richard. 1980. "Criticism as Retrieval." In *Art and Its Objects*. 2nd edn. Cambridge: Cambridge University Press, 185–204.

DAVID DAVIES

irony is a topic of interest to philosophy, not least the philosophy of literature, for several reasons. To begin, it is a many-sided concept within which distinctions need to be made and connections sought. Second, since irony involves a kind of simulation – the Greek *eironeia* means "simulated ignorance" – we need to explain both why we indulge in it and how we manage to communicate through it. There is, third, a recurrent claim to the effect that the *world* or *existence* is inherently ironic which requires investigation. Finally, we need to understand and assess the surprisingly frequent claims that irony is central to serious literature, that – in Roland Barthes's words – it is "the essence of writing" (quoted in Culler 1983: 86).

TYPES OF IRONY

Whether or not it is actually ambiguous, "irony" is certainly applied to several categorically

different kinds of objects – single utterances, discursive styles, and events, for example. There is irony as a particular trope or figure of speech, classically illustrated by a remark like "What a fine friend!" said of someone who turned out to be treacherous. But it is wrong to generalize from this example and define irony, as many dictionaries do, as "meaning the opposite of what is actually said." Not only does that definition fit lying as much as irony, but the ironist by no means always intends to convey the *opposite* of what the words literally say. "Ah, some Raphaels!" said at an exhibition of a new third-rate artist, is not meant to convey, pointlessly, that the paintings are not by Raphael. So the usual definition needs double amending. While an ironic trope must convey something that vividly contrasts with what is literally meant by the words, this need not be the "opposite" of the latter. And the utterance is not intended to deceive generally, since some people, at least, are meant to "catch on."

Ironic speech and writing do not, typically, consist in the production of ironic tropes, and it is not for the production of these that writers such as Swift, Voltaire, Heine, and Anthony Powell are celebrated as masters of irony. That there are other modes of ironic discourse is established by the existence of so-called "Socratic irony." In Plato's dialogues, Socrates characteristically feigns modest ignorance of a topic and sympathy with his opponent's position, thereby leading him on until the absurdity of that position becomes clear. Another ironic device – employed, for example, by Voltaire, in *Candide* – is an *ingénu* character, the exaggerated naivety of whose questions and observations throws into relief the pomposity and pretentiousness of the views expressed by other characters in the work.

Such devices of irony have at least two broad features in common with the trope of irony. The words used by a speaker or a character in a book are not intended to convey, to an alert audience at least, the attitude they superficially convey. And the purpose of the devices, as with the "Raphael" example, is a critical one – typically ridicule, mockery, and the like.

It is less easy to perceive connections between these forms of verbal irony and that which we attribute to events or circumstances

– such as those in the O. Henry story where a husband sells his watch to buy a comb for his wife who, in the mean time, has sold her hair to buy a chain for the husband's watch. But here too, ridicule is effected through vivid contrast, for the wonderful incongruence between the actions of husband and wife serves to mock the sentimental optimism that pervades a certain romantic and literary tradition. So viewed, the irony belongs not to the events in themselves, but to the mute comment they pass on certain beliefs and sentiments. In so-called "tragic irony," too – though ridicule is no longer quite the point – the irony owes to the incongruence between the actual dispensation of Fate and the protagonist's own understanding of events.

EXPLAINING IRONY

The typical purposes of ironic devices are ridicule, mockery, and the like. But why should we achieve this by using words to convey something different from what they standardly convey? A plausible suggestion is that irony has the same kind of attraction as criticism through *mimicry*. The ironist "echoes" the words that someone holding the opinions mocked actually or might well have used (Sperber & Wilson 1981, and, for some reservations, Cooper 1986.) Thus, Socrates ridicules his opponents through mimicking the speech of their obsequious disciples. But why should we so often prefer this roundabout tactic instead of coming "straight out" with our criticisms? One explanation appeals to our fondness for belonging to in-groups. It is a feature of much of the best irony that it is recognized only by people with the appropriate knowledge, acumen, and intimacy with the speaker or writer. *A Modest Proposal*, in which Swift "advocated" eating Irish babies to solve the population problem, was taken by many readers as a serious recommendation. Why we should take an in-group pleasure in having the right credentials for catching on to "coded" communications is a question that belongs, presumably, in the recesses of philosophical anthropology.

The problem of *how* an audience catches on to the ironist's intentions is a vexed one. One proposal appeals to the recognition that *if* the writer intended his or her words literally there would then be a violation of some "maxim" of proper discourse, such as truth-telling. The reader then searches, by way of interpretation, for an intention behind the utterance that would save the writer from the charge of culpably having violated any "maxims" (Grice 1975). But while this may fit some cases, it suffers from the false assumption that the ironist must always intend to convey some particular propositional message. While Swift must certainly be understood as ridiculing the solutions to "the Irish problem" offered by contemporary politicians, there is no reason to assume he was also trying to communicate some specific proposition(s) about Ireland. Generally speaking, irony aims more to express fairly unspecific attitudes than to communicate particular beliefs.

"WORLD-IRONY"

It is not only words, but events too, which get described as ironic, and some philosophers have even wanted to describe the world – or history, or existence – as ironic. Thus Hegel's reference to "the universal irony of the world" was picked up by the young Kierkegaard, who took it to mean that "each particular historical actuality . . . bears within itself the seeds of its own destruction" (Kierkegaard 1965: 278). But it is hard to see why something's containing the seeds of its own destruction should, by itself, make us regard its existence as ironic. Time-bombs are not ironic. As with "the irony of events," however, perhaps the point should be not that the world (history, etc.) is per se ironic but that there is an ironic contrast between how it really is and certain conceptions of it – as the arena of undisturbed progress, for example. To the naive observer, the stages of world history have a meaning that the real processes of history, as discerned by Hegel or Kierkegaard, serve to mock.

IRONY AND THE ESSENCE OF WRITING

While many writers are esteemed precisely because of their mastery of irony, there are many others who would not usually be thought of as ironists, but who are also admired – Tennyson, Dostoevsky, Zola, and Hemingway, for example. So it comes as a surprise to be told that irony is of the essence of good literature. Yet, since the time of Friedrich Schlegel at least, this is the claim of several literary critics.

The nineteenth-century Romantic Karl Solger called irony "the most complete fruit of the artistic understanding" (quoted in Schmitt 1980: 115); for Thomas Mann "irony . . . is the sense of art itself" (1974: 353); while for Barthes, as we saw, it is "the true test of writing as writing . . . the essence of writing." (For further claims of this kind, especially ones made by French poststructuralists, such as Jacques Derrida, see Wilde 1981; Colebrook 2003.)

One version of these large claims is inspired by the idea of world-, or historical, irony mentioned above. Kierkegaard, for example, argues that since "actuality" is itself ironic, it is the writer's duty to take a "negative," distanced stance toward it. And Lukács holds that since existence, in modernity at least, is one of intrinsic "dissonance, breakdown or failure," the novel which is true to existence must be "essentially ironigenic" (quoted in Muecke 1982: 96). Such views will not, of course, be appealing unless one shares these writers' visions of existence. And even if one does share them, one might think that there are other aspects of existence with which literature might respectably deal. Moreover, an unrelenting diet of novels about failed aspirations or the burgeoning of the seeds of self-destruction might soon become indigestible. One can read *Tender is the Night* or *The Heart of Darkness* only so many times.

More common, however, is an appeal not to the irony of the world that literature is about, but to something inherent in literature itself. The general thought is that paradox and irony necessarily infect authorship and literary texts, and can be mitigated only by writing in a self-consciously ironic manner that reveals to the reader the contradictions inherent in the craft.

The emphasis, in one development of this thought, is on the ironic contrast or "contradiction" between a text's status as an *artifice* and its effect on readers of immersing them in a world of events and characters that can seem as real and natural as the actual world. Related to this is the contrast between the apparent passion and commitment that may pervade a text and the comparatively cool detachment the author requires in order to craft it. Schlegel, who makes much of such "contradictions," urges that the honest author who is

properly aware of them should visibly "hover" above the text, reminding readers of its artificial nature through such devices as "authorial interference" (Schlegel 1958). (A classic example of this device is Thomas Mann's use, in *Doktor Faustus*, of a narrator who continually intrudes himself between the story and the reader.)

In a different development, favored among structuralists and deconstructionists, the focus is on the alleged ironic gap between the author's effort to convey a certain message and his inability to "control" how the text will in fact be understood. This gap is due to a "play of codes" that intervenes between the author's intentions and the readers and may severely refract the text's intended meaning. The honest author, once again, will admit to this "contradiction" and, like Flaubert according to Roland Barthes, will write in a manner "fraught with uncertainty" by way of confirming that "the meaning of the work" is not governed by the author (quoted in Culler 1983: 86).

It is not possible here properly to assess these claims about the nature of literature, but we can question the appropriateness of expressing them in the form of a thesis about literature's essential irony. At least four observations are pertinent.

(1) It is misleading to speak of the ironic nature of writing when what is apparently meant is that there is something ironic in the act of writing or the condition of being a writer. There is irony, no doubt, in a virgin writing a novel of torrid sexual passion, but it need not therefore be an ironic novel.

(2) We should note how much of our familiar concept of irony is being left out in the claim that all writing is ironic and in the recommendation that authors should therefore write in a self-consciously ironic manner. In particular, the typical purpose of irony – ridicule, and the like – is being ignored. The alleged contrast between the artificiality of the text and its realistic effect on readers, for example, hardly serves to mock or pass critical comment on anything. Nor is it clear that a device like "authorial interference" has a purpose that deserves to be called ironic in the way that, say, Socrates' "simulated ignorance" does.

(3) Where connections between the ironies discussed by the theorists mentioned and our familiar concept can be discerned, they are tenuous and superficial. It may be that the author is "detached" from the story he tells, and that the ironic speaker is also detached from the words she utters. But the two kinds of detachment are quite different. The author is detached from, say, the passions and commitments of his characters, whereas the speaker is detached from her words in that she does not believe what they literally express. Again, there may be a gap between what the author intends and the meaning of his or her text, and a gap between the ironic speaker's intention and the meaning of her words. But, once more, the gaps are quite different. In the one case, it is between what the author wants to convey and how his or her readers – because of a "play of codes" or whatever – interpret the text. In the other case, the gap is between what the speaker wants to convey and what is literally conveyed by the words uttered. It is certainly not part of our ordinary understanding that an ironist must fail to communicate what he or she intends to.

(4) Even if the author's position is inherently ironic, it will not follow that the text should be written in a manner that makes this painfully visible to readers – through "authorial interference," say, or a style "fraught with uncertainty." Only someone who would welcome "the death of the novel" and other genres could want all authors to emulate Thomas Mann, Samuel Beckett, and others who parade their predicament as writers. There are, after all, many important features of the writer's situation – from the need to make a living to the influence of certain literary traditions. But it is not desirable, obligatory, or even possible for the author to keep reminding readers of all these aspects of the literary enterprise. An author who tries to do this may soon be without readers.

See also LITERATURE; BARTHES; DECONSTRUCTION; HUMOR; "INTENTIONAL FALLACY"; METAPHOR; SCHLEGEL, F.; STRUCTURALISM AND POSTSTRUCTURALISM.

BIBLIOGRAPHY

Booth, Wayne C. 1975. *A Rhetoric of Irony*. Chicago: University of Chicago Press.

Colebrook, Claire. 2003. *Irony*. London: Routledge.
Cooper, David E. 1986. *Metaphor*. Oxford: Blackwell.
Cooper, David E. 1989. "Irony and 'the Essence of Writing'," *Philosophical Papers*, 18, 53–73.
Culler, Jonathan. 1983. *Barthes*. London: Fontana.
Grice, H. P. 1985. "Logic and Conversation." In *Syntax and Semantics*, vol. iii. P. Cole & J. Morgan (eds.). London: Academic Press, 41–58.
Kierkegaard, Søren. 1965 [1841]. *The Concept of Irony*. New York: Harper & Row.
Mann, Thomas. 1974. *Gesammelte Werke*, vol. x: *Die Kunst des Romans* [The Art of the Novel]. Frankfurt: Fischer.
Muecke, D. C. 1982. *Irony and the Ironic*. London: Methuen.
Schlegel, Friedrich von. 1958 [1797]. "Lyceum-Fragmente." In *Kritische Friedrich-Schlegel-Ausgabe*, vol. ii. 35 vols. E. Behler (ed.). Munich: F. Schöningh, 147–63.
Schmitt, H.-J. (ed.). 1980. *Romantik*, vol. i. Stuttgart: Reclam.
Sperber, Dan & Wilson, Deirdre. 1981. "Irony and the Use–Mention Distinction." In *Radical Pragmatics*. P. Cole (ed.). London: Academic Press, 295–318.
Wilde, Alan. 1981. *Horizons of Assent: Modernism, Post-Modernism, and the Ironic Imagination*. Baltimore: Johns Hopkins University Press.

DAVID E. COOPER

Islamic aesthetics A number of aesthetic issues arise in Islamic culture. Many countries in the Islamic world produced, and continue to produce, exquisite forms of art, and their composition has often been linked with Islam as a religion. There has been an extensive debate on whether Islam allows art, what sorts of art it allows, and how the religion has played a role in the sorts of art that have evolved in the Islamic world. There is also a protracted discussion of the beauty of the Qur'an and its aesthetic nature, since the inimitable beauty of the Book is taken by many commentators to be a proof of its veracity. There has also been among the classical Islamic philosophers a protracted discussion on how to use Aristotelian logic to understand the structure of literary art.

THE AESTHETICS OF THE QUR'AN

The Qur'an is not taken to be poetry (*shir*) on the lines of ordinary Arabic poetry, but it is certainly regarded as eloquent, designed as it was to impress a community, the Arabs, who valued language and the evocative uses to which it could be put. The Qur'an challenges (*tahaddi*) those who do not accept it to produce something like it, or better than it, and here is meant usually a combination of the excellent doctrines that it includes, plus the wonderful style of the Book. A tradition of exposition has arisen that defends and promotes the beauty of the text, and that explores alternative formulations of the verses of the Book, but these alternatives have been judged inferior to the original. The Qur'an is said to be the direct word of God, unmediated by human beings, and to have been expressed in such a perfect way that everyone can understand it, and also be impressed with its aesthetic qualities. It is not the only revelation sent to humanity, but it is the final, most complete, and most perfect revelation, which is reflected in its aesthetic quality.

Despite this emphasis on beauty, the Qur'an makes clear that it does not regard itself as poetry, although parts of it clearly are poetic. The disinclination to refer to itself as poetry is probably due to a desire not to link itself too closely with the sort of poetry common in the *jahaliyyah*, the pre-Islamic period, which while often excellent tended to focus on secular or even romantic themes that might be thought inappropriate to associate with a religious text such as the Qur'an. The trouble with poetry is perhaps that it seeks to manipulate and impress its audience entirely through its form and not necessarily through its matter, and this is far too superficial for the sort of message that the Qur'an produces. On the other hand, there are problems with the emphasis on the beauty of the Book, since it is not clear how the challenge to produce something similar would cope with those who honestly endeavor to do just that, and who prefer their results to the Qur'an. Also, there are those who speak Arabic and who remain unimpressed with the style of the Book, and even criticize it for what they take to be its tendentious form and repetitive nature.

It is very difficult to judge the Qur'an aesthetically since it has played such a large role in the construction of what has come to be known as classical Arabic. The rules of the language itself are highly informed by the Qur'an, and even for non-Muslims in the Arab world, the Qur'an is an important document for understanding the Arabic language, so it is problematic to use the standards of that language to assess the style of the Qur'an. Yet even having accepted that, it has been possible to criticize the style of the Book from the point of view of the Arabic language, and this suggests that the beauty of the text is not as evident as has been suggested. It is worth pointing out, though, what a high standard that Qur'an sets itself here, since other religions do not on the whole base their acceptance on the beauty of their main text. Not only is the Qur'an taken to be beautiful, it is taken to be miraculously beautiful, so no human being could have been capable of producing such a text. This is a very powerful claim, and throughout Islamic history there have been many attempts to establish it on a sound theoretical basis. It is worth adding that Islam classically regards beauty to be an objective feature of the world (it is one of God's names, for instance), and so the definition of the Qur'an as miraculously beautiful is often accepted as a matter of fact, not opinion.

BEAUTY AND PERFECTION

This stress on the objectivity of aesthetics has been very much a theme in Islamic thought. In the earliest philosophical approaches Pythagoreanism was popular, with its theory that the structure of the universe leads to beauty, which is a reflection of celestial motion. Beauty is a function of perfection, and since God is the most perfect being, he is also the most beautiful. The harmony of the spheres represents divine beauty to a degree. Al-Kindi (c.805–c.873) defended a theory of this kind. This view came to be replaced by a version of Neoplatonism. This approach interprets art as expressive of greater levels of truth and perfection mediated through the use of imagination, and considers literary work in particular as comprehensible through its use of the syllogistic form to work toward a conclusion. This conclusion is usually taken to be experienced as an emotion. Poetry is certainly not the most secure form of reasoning that one could employ, since it starts not with demonstrative principles nor even with legal or theological ideas, but with the sorts of ideas that move people and that they generally accept. However, once these ideas are accepted, the skillful poet moves his audience to the conclusion that he has in mind through his careful and considered use of language. A reasoning process is involved here, since the conclusion is not something that arbitrarily follows from what precedes it. The main Islamic philosophers in the Peripatetic tradition, including al-Farabi (c.872–950), Ibn Sina (d.1037), and Ibn Rushd (1126–98) all developed forms of this theory, and adapted Aristotle's thought on poetry to the sort of verse that had arisen in the Islamic world. Imagination is significant in assessing art, since imagination represents a combination of rationality and emotion, both of which are essential in aesthetics. Rationality operates by making our ideas more abstract and logical, while our physical nature demands that our emotions are also engaged. Aesthetic statements are then both logical and emotional.

ISLAMIC ART AS SPECIFICALLY ISLAMIC

A popular way of analyzing Islamic art is very much in line with its foundations in Islam. Why would we call it "Islamic," after all, unless it shared some features with the religion of Islam, and was influenced by Islam? This type of analysis is often combined with an approach to Islam on Sufi or mystical lines, where Islam is seen as having an essence and that essence is best represented by Sufism. The fact that Sufis believe that God is everywhere can be represented by the geometrical designs so common in much Islamic art, which seem to be unending and constantly self-generating. The fact that some interpretations of Islam are critical of the representation of living things is seen as an explanation for the enthusiasm for abstract shapes and calligraphy, rather than pictures of human beings and animals. Calligraphy itself, with its very beautiful multiplicity of styles and shapes, is seen as a reflection of the Islamic concentration on the word, especially the word of God, and on the idea that with that word one possesses everything worth having, with the result that figurative art becomes unnecessary and superfluous.

There have been iconoclastic schools of thought in Islam, as in other religions, but how influential they were in structuring art is a matter of opinion. It is certainly the case that there has been much figurative art in Islam, especially in civilizations such as Persia that have a long tradition of such work, and even today there seems to be little theological difficulty in most Islamic societies with representation of animals and people, given the ubiquity of photographs, paintings, and other representations of the human form. The idea that there is just one essence of Islam that is embodied in its art is neat, but it is difficult to accept when one is confronted with the variety of artistic styles found throughout the Islamic world, which continues to produce art today in very different ways in different places. Islam is not the only culture to have produced a sophisticated calligraphic tradition, for example, and some of the others like those of China or western Europe have very different ideological bases for wishing to express themselves through lettering. There are huge problems, then, in seeking a simple explanation for the nature of Islamic art in a particular definition of Islam itself, a problem that exists in relation to other "religious" art also.

MUSIC

There has been a protracted controversy in Islamic law about the acceptability of music. Some think that all music is forbidden. Others refer to an apparently approving comment made by the Prophet to a particular event which would have involved music, and take it to be allowed, albeit perhaps with restrictions. These could involve limiting instruments to those contemporary with the Prophet, and not listening to women singing. Music, like art in general, can be classified as distracting Muslims from the important things in life, like worship, but some Muslims argue that music can be used as an aid to religion by encouraging participation and devotion. Indeed, the *adhan*, the call to prayer, is often very beautiful, and the recitation of the Qur'an can also be a potent aesthetic event.

See also ART HISTORY; CONSERVATION AND RESTORATION; RELIGION AND ART.

BIBLIOGRAPHY
Black, Deborah. 1990. *Logic and Aristotle's "Rhetoric" and "Poetics" in Medieval Arabic Philosophy*. Leiden: Brill.
Kemal, Salim. 1991. *The Poetics of Alfarabi and Avicenna*. Leiden: Brill.
Kemal, Salim. 1996. "Aesthetics." In *History of Islamic Philosophy*. S. Nasr & O. Leaman (eds.). London: Routledge, 969–78.
Leaman, Oliver. 2004. *Islamic Aesthetics: An Introduction*. Edinburgh: Edinburgh University Press.

OLIVER LEAMAN

J

Japanese aesthetics Historically, the Japanese aesthetic tradition has emphasized discipline-specific teachings for practitioners of artistic activities. Manuals provide instruction not only in techniques and rules for such disciplines as literature, painting, calligraphy, flower arrangement, garden-making, Noh theater, and tea ceremony, but also in the appropriate attitude and worldview required to master them. Only after wide-ranging Western influences entered Japan in the late nineteenth century did intellectuals begin to produce general and comprehensive overviews of Japanese aesthetics. These efforts were partly inspired by the sudden exposure to systematic Western philosophy and aesthetics. They were also motivated by Japan's struggle at the time to come up with something "truly" or "purely" Japanese in order to secure its national identity (and superiority in some cases) against a rising tide of Westernization.

Despite this historically contextual attempt at a general aesthetic theory and its origin as discipline-specific instructions, certain principles emerge that characterize the Japanese aesthetic tradition.

First, from the earliest written artistic instructions, Ki no Tsurayuki's preface to *Kokinshū* ("Collection of Ancient and Modern Poems," 905) and Tachibana-no-Toshitsuna's *Sakuteiki* ("Records of Garden Making," 11th century), one principle that predominates in the Japanese tradition of art-making is that artistic inspiration comes directly from a subject matter or material object. As explained more fully by eighteenth-century nativist philologist Motoori Norinaga in his theory of *mono no aware* (sensitivity to things), the art of poetry-making is to express one's empathy with the emotive quality of an object, which is often taken from nature. Similarly, in *Sakuteiki*, Toshitsuna describes the art of garden-making as arranging rocks to clarify and enhance their native characteristics, a process referred to as *kowan ni shitagau* (obeying the request of the object).

The same exhortation to observe, respect, and give expression to the object's distinctive qualities extends to other aesthetic disciplines. The aim of flower arrangement is to let flowers articulate themselves (*ikasu*: "let live"). Mimesis in painting is intended to capture "the spirit of the object." Noh actors are urged to "enter into" the characters and express their "essence" rather than simply to mimic their outward appearances and actions. In his instructions on haiku-making, the seventeenth-century master poet Matsuo Bashō wrote, "of the pine-tree learn from the pine-tree" and "of the bamboo learn from the bamboo." When successful, a resulting work is said to exude the air of "naturalness" or "spontaneity," identified as the most important artistic virtue in a Japanese aesthetic tradition that emphasizes the art of artlessness.

This object-centered creative process also underlies the making of everyday artifacts, as in the production of lacquerware, pottery, textiles, woodwork, and metalwork. In addition, Japanese packaging that makes use of such materials as bamboo, paper, straw, and wood is designed to maximize the materials' own characteristics. This same principle is applied to food preparation, both in cooking and presentation.

The respectful attitude toward objects that informs the artistic and design process can be found in Shintoism, Japan's indigenous religion, and in Zen Buddhism, which was transmitted to Japan from China between the late twelfth and early thirteenth centuries. Both emphasize the sacredness of this world rather than of the other world. Zen Buddhism also urges "forgetting" or "overcoming" one's ego as a necessary condition for enlightenment.

Artistic discipline similarly consists not only of sharpening skills and cultivating creativity but more importantly of practicing a way of life thoroughly dedicated to art-making without any ulterior motive, such as fame or fortune. Thus, the traditional terminology for each artistic medium ends with the suffix *dō*, meaning "the way." *Sadō*, *kadō*, *shodō*, and *kadō* refer, respectively, to "the way" of tea, flower arrangement, calligraphy, and poetry. All are subsumed under the term *geidō*, meaning "the way of the arts." The attitude of disinterestedness that is often considered necessary for one to have an aesthetic experience in Western aesthetics is thus rather required of the artist, craftsperson, or designer in the Japanese tradition.

This thoroughgoing transcendence of self as a "way" of mastering an artistic discipline also applies to the Japanese martial arts, such as *kyūdō* (the way of archery) and *kendō* (the way of swordsmanship). Martial arts training manuals emphasize cultivation of a correct attitude and composure rather than of specific skills. Success is said to result from overcoming one's self-consciousness and desire for winning.

While not imbued with the same spiritual significance, Japanese appreciation of nature also depends on how an object or phenomenon is defined by its distinctive characteristics. This is best illustrated by the appreciation of seasonableness. With four distinct seasons, Japan has always celebrated the aesthetic appeal of each. For example, the *Kokinshū* and subsequent court-sponsored anthologies of poems are organized according to season; and one of the most influential works of Japanese literature, the eleventh-century *Makura no Sōshi* (*Pillow Book*) by court lady Sei Shōnagon, begins its collection of essays and vignettes by extolling the beauty of each season. Sensitivity toward, and appreciation of, each season applies even to elements which in themselves might not ordinarily be "appreciated," such as heat and humidity or freezing wind. This aesthetic appreciation is clearly evident in the rules of composition for haiku poetry, established in the seventeenth century, which require that one season word (*kigo*) be included in each 17-syllable poem. This same appreciation gave rise to festivals celebrating the beauty of each season, the best-known of which is cherry-blossom

viewing in spring, still practiced today. Furthermore, seasons are considered important in food preparation and interior decoration, not only for such formal occasions as the tea ceremony, but also in people's everyday lives.

Another important principle in the Japanese aesthetic tradition is also other-regarding: the respectful attitude toward the experiences of other people. While not involving formal art objects or activities, the court sensibility in the Heian period (794–1185) sets the stage for this ethos and its subsequent development. This sensibility is perhaps best illustrated in the courtship ritual carried out by exchanging letters. All aesthetic details, such as paper, poetry, calligraphy, folding, infused fragrance, and attached flower or leaf, are selected by considering what would most please the recipient of the letter. This other-directed concern, sometimes referred to as elegance, characterizes "a good person," according to Heian sensibility.

Considered a moral virtue, concern for the other person's experience is similarly expressed aesthetically in the art of tea ceremony. The host's utmost effort to welcome and please the guests is reflected in the meticulous attention to details. These include the choice and placement of the utensils, tea bowls, and interior decorations; the preparation of food, tea, and the tea hut; the care of the garden and its various implements such as a water basin and stepping-stones; and even the preparation of the toilet.

This consideration for others' experience also enriches the content of aesthetic experience through multisensory appeal. Just as the aesthetics of courtship letters engages not only the visual and literary but also the tactile and olfactory sensations, Japanese garden design, architecture, packaging, food, pottery, and tea ceremony all highlight various sensations. The tactile sensation is emphasized when holding a pottery piece, or when walking on stepping-stones, an aged wooden corridor, or a straw mat. Straw mats also impart a distinctive smell, as do such packaging materials as bamboo leaves or cedar. Visual attraction is important for food arrangement, while bodily engagement is required not only in eating but also in performing the tea ceremony or opening a package. Furthermore, sensitivity to the temporal sequence in which the experience unfolds is reflected in various techniques of garden design. It is also expressed in the several steps required for opening a carefully wrapped package, and in the arrangement and simultaneous serving of different food items that allow one to compose one's own order of eating.

Japanese aesthetics thus emphasizes multisensory bodily engagement as a way of gaining aesthetic experience. This lack of distinction between higher and lower senses, as well as that between mind and body, results in what might be characterized as a kind of egalitarianism, another important principle in Japanese aesthetics. During the Westernization period, Japanese aestheticians were concerned with developing a comprehensive aesthetic theory focused on what would be equivalent to the modern Western notion of "fine arts." However, Japanese aesthetic tradition is more diverse, embracing not only those art media familiar to the West, but also the tea ceremony, flower arrangement, and martial arts, as well as what in the West are considered "crafts," such as the design of everyday objects.

This tendency toward egalitarianism also extends to the qualities for aesthetic appreciation. Opulent, gorgeous, and luxurious beauty, typically considered worthy of aesthetic appreciation, certainly exists in Japanese arts and other objects. However, more challenging qualities that are not normally appreciated in the West, such as imperfection, defect, desolateness, and impoverished or aged appearance, are appreciated equally, or sometimes more than their opposites. These qualities are referred to as *wabi* and *sabi*, originally designating desolateness in tea ceremony and rusticity or forlornness in haiku. They are highly valued in Japan for their aestheticization of contingency and the transience of life, and for their power to stimulate the imagination. This aesthetic taste results in minimalism, which is expressed in literature and painting through implication and suggestion, rather than clarity and explicitness. It is also reflected in the extreme brevity of haiku, the sparse interior of Japanese built structures, such as the tea hut, and the minimum movement of the actors in Noh theater. It also extends to a preference for phenomena that are less than optimal, such as the moon obscured by clouds and cherry blossoms falling from their branches. Finally, there exists a special attraction for signs of aging, such as cracked pottery or lacquerware worn from repeated usage.

Even within the Japanese tradition, such qualities are considered challenging to the experiencing agents, because flowers in full bloom, gold-gilded objects, and clear and straightforward artistic expressions are assumed to be easier to appreciate. Thus, just as the Japanese aesthetic tradition challenges the makers of objects to be open-minded, that is, to let the object and materials speak for themselves in the creative process, it also encourages the experiencing agents to be open-minded enough to accept and appreciate those qualities not normally appreciated. Furthermore, if a certain moral stance, such as care and respect for the experiencing agents, is expected of the makers of art and other objects, the sensitivity to recognize and appreciate its aesthetic expression is required on the part of the experiencing agent. In short, moral and spiritual discipline is inseparable from engaging in aesthetic experience, whether as a provider or as a recipient.

Thus, the Japanese aesthetic tradition opens possible areas for inquiry not often explored in modern Western aesthetics. They include the relationship between the aesthetic and its moral and spiritual considerations in the sense explained above, creative activity that is object/material-centered, and the appreciation of multisensory experiences and those qualities that are typically depreciated.

See also AESTHETICS OF FOOD AND DRINK; AESTHETICS OF THE EVERYDAY; CHINESE AESTHETICS; FORGERY; GARDENS.

BIBLIOGRAPHY

Hume, Nancy (ed.). 1995. *Japanese Aesthetics and Culture: A Reader*. Albany: State University of New York Press.

Izutsu, Toshihiko & Izutsu, Toyo. 1981. *The Theory of Beauty in the Classical Aesthetics of Japan*. The Hague: Nijhoff.

Keene, Donald (ed.). 1955. *Anthology of Japanese Literature*. New York: Grove.

Marra, Michael (ed. & trans.). 2001. *A History of Modern Japanese Aesthetics*. Honolulu: University of Hawai'i Press.

Marra, Michael (ed.). 2002. *Japanese Hermeneutics: Current Debates on Aesthetics and Interpretation*. Honolulu: University of Hawai'i Press.

Marra, Michael (ed. & trans.). 1999. *Modern Japanese Aesthetics: A Reader*. Honolulu: University of Hawai'i Press.

Saito, Yuriko. 1998. "Japanese Aesthetic Appreciation of Nature." In *Encyclopedia of Aesthetics*, vol. iii. M. Kelly (ed.). New York: Oxford University Press, 343–6.

Saito, Yuriko. 1998. "Japanese Aesthetics." In *Encyclopedia of Aesthetics*, vol. ii. M. Kelly (ed.). New York: Oxford University Press, 553–5.

Tsunoda, Ryūsaku, de Bary, Wm. Theodore, & Keene, Donald (eds.). 1964. *Sources of Japanese Tradition*. 2 vols. New York: Columbia University Press.

Ueda, Makoto. 1967. *Literary and Art Theories in Japan*. Cleveland: Press of Case Western Reserve University.

Yanagi, Sōetsu. 1972. *The Unknown Craftsman: A Japanese Insight into Beauty*. B. Leach (adapted). Tokyo: Kodansha International.

YURIKO SAITO

judgment, aesthetic *see* AESTHETIC JUDGMENT.

K

Kant, Immanuel (1724–1804) The greatest eighteenth-century German philosopher, and one of the subject's most influential figures, in epistemology, ethics, and metaphysics as well as aesthetics; a leading champion of European Enlightenment.

Kant's analysis of the nature of aesthetic judgment forms the first part of his third *Critique*, the *Critique of Judgment* (1790), the second part of which is an investigation into the role of teleological judgments in our descriptions of the natural world. This division corresponds to the ways in which the apparent purposiveness of natural forms may be viewed: either subjectively (the aesthetic standpoint), or objectively (the teleological standpoint). The most influential part of Kant's theory of aesthetic value concerns the notion of beauty, which he treats as applying primarily to natural objects and only secondarily to works of art. However, he considers the value of a work of fine art to depend not only on its beauty, but also on its being the vehicle for aesthetic ideas.

An aesthetic idea is an intuition of the creative imagination for which an adequate concept can never be found. It is the counterpart of an idea of reason for which no intuition is adequate. The latter include such nonempirical notions as God, eternity, virtue. Aesthetic ideas may go some way toward giving sensory embodiment to such ideas, but without imparting knowledge of any kind. Their other role is to "body forth to sense" empirical notions such as love, death, and fame, but "with a completeness of which nature affords no parallel" (1952: 177). They provide the imagination with a powerful incentive "to spread its flight over a whole host of kindred representations that provoke more thought than admits of expression in a concept determined by words." Their expression is typically symbolic, but as no truth is being asserted, there would be no point in trying to paraphrase them. This free flight of the imagination is an activity that is worthwhile for its own sake, giving to works of art an intellectual as well as a purely aesthetic appeal, without which, says Kant, they would lack "soul." The invention of aesthetic ideas is ascribed to genius, while their expression in beautiful forms, on which their communicability depends, is ascribed to the faculty of taste.

The "Critique of Aesthetic Judgment" (part 1 of the third *Critique*) is chiefly concerned with the question of how aesthetic judgments can be subjective and yet universally valid. Kant distinguishes two main types of aesthetic judgment: judgments about the beautiful, or pure judgments of taste, and judgments about the sublime. The most obvious difference between them is that, whereas the beautiful is grounded in the spatial and temporal form of objects (figure and play), and thus on that which is limited in space and time, the sublime depends on that sense of limitlessness which is evoked by the unimaginably vast (the mathematically sublime) and the overwhelmingly powerful (the dynamically sublime).

Strictly speaking, our experience of the sublime is only partly aesthetic because, unlike the beautiful, it needs to be mediated by ideas of reason and morality. In the case of the mathematically sublime, such as the starry heavens, reason is exalted by enabling us to think of what lies outside the reach of the imagination as a totality; and in the case of the dynamically sublime, such as a storm at sea, we are reminded of our worth as moral beings in contrast to the weakness of our empirical selves. In both cases, an otherwise unpleasing experience is tempered by feelings of admiration and respect. It would be fair to say, however, that although Kant's account of the sublime contains many points of interest, it lacks both the plausibility and the overall importance of his account of the beautiful.

To find a thing beautiful, whether it be natural or humanly made, is to take pleasure in it simply on account of how it looks or sounds. This means, says Kant, that judgments of beauty – or judgments of taste, as he calls them – are based on the feelings of pleasure or displeasure that denote nothing in the object and so cannot be other than subjective. Such judgments can be neither true nor false, since to discriminate on the basis of feeling alone is to contribute nothing to knowledge. The most they can aspire to is a kind of intersubjective validity.

In the four sections, or "moments," of his "Analytic of the Beautiful," Kant attempts to define beauty in terms of the type of pleasure it affords. From this it emerges that beauty is a perceptual form whose subjective finality is *felt* as a disinterested, universally communicable, and necessary pleasure. Its finality assures us that it is worth contemplating for its own sake, although it is only through feeling that this feature can be apprehended. Thus, to understand the nature of beauty, we need to understand the nature of aesthetic pleasure.

Kant distinguishes three types of pleasure: pleasure in the agreeable, or gratification; pleasure in the good, or approval; and pleasure in the beautiful, or free liking. Only the last is disinterested. To reflect on a thing in a disinterested way is to adopt a nonmoral, nonpractical, nonegoistic attitude toward it. Hence any value that we attach to it belongs to it alone and is not dependent on considerations of morality, utility, personal advantage, or sensory gratification. If aesthetic merit is conferred on things as a result of such a contemplative attitude, then it follows that aesthetic values are nonderivative and so autonomous – as Kant claimed moral values also to be. Few ideas in the history of aesthetics have been more pervasive than that of the disinterestedness of the aesthetic attitude. It has figured prominently, in various guises, in the writings of eighteenth-century English empiricists and of nineteenth-century German idealists, and in much twentieth-century writing. The idea can be traced back to Lord Shaftesbury, but Kant was the first to incorporate it into a theory about the logical character of aesthetic judgment.

Kant's own criterion of disinterestedness is stricter than the one given above, for he defines "interest" as "the delight which we connect with the representation of the real existence of the object. Such a delight, therefore, always involves a reference to the faculty of desire, either as its determining ground, or else as necessarily implicated with its determining ground" (1952: 42). Further, "one must not be in the least prepossessed in favour of the real existence of the thing, but must preserve complete indifference in this respect in order to play the part of judge in matters of taste" (1952: 43).

Part of what is being claimed here is that aesthetic delight is delight in what *appears* to the subject regardless of its ontological status. Compare, for example, the indifference of the traveler in a desert who admires the beauty of what he takes to be a lake, on learning that it is only a mirage, with the disappointment of the traveler who is dying of thirst. Since aesthetic value resides in the pleasure taken in the intentional object, the real nature of the object is irrelevant. On the other hand, the same might be said of the reflective pleasure we sometimes take in smells, tastes and colors, which Kant regards as being merely sensory and so "interested."

This shows that disinterestedness on its own is not a sufficient condition for pleasure to count as aesthetic, despite some suggestions to the contrary (e.g., at 1952: 49), although it might still be a necessary condition. However, if Kant's other three conditions – universal communicability, necessity, and the subjective finality of the intentional object – are taken into account, then a more adequate criterion emerges.

Clearly, Kant is mistaken in supposing that disinterested pleasure can be taken only in the perceptual form of the object and never in what he terms "the matter of sensation." If smells and tastes are to be excluded from the realm of the aesthetic, it should be on grounds other than interest; for example, their incapacity for formal organization or the more personal and idiosyncratic nature of our response to them, which would breach the universality condition. Again, Kant's insistence on treating our delight in color as merely sensory seems to be a mistake, since it is no more dependent on our antecedent needs or desires than is our delight in perceptual form. Moreover, colors are capable of formal arrangement, although it must be admitted that one's response to color is likely to be more personal than one's response to shape, say; people have their favorite colors but not their favorite shapes.

A more general objection might be raised against Kant's insistence that we "must preserve complete indifference" as to the real existence of the thing in order to judge it aesthetically on the grounds that most aesthetically sensitive people would in fact regard an object's beauty as a very good reason for wanting to preserve it. This objection is perhaps unfair to Kant, since nothing he says rules out the possibility of treating one's disinterested pleasure in beautiful things as a first-order attitude, and one's approval of their existence as a logically independent second-order attitude. Thus one might, for example, feel, as Aristotle did, that one had a duty to develop one's perceptual and cognitive powers to their fullest extent, and to see this as a practical benefit of, albeit not the purpose of, aesthetic reflection. One would then have a moral reason for preserving beauty. Kant, too, might have a further motive for doing so in that he sees the beautiful as a *symbol* of the moral. Nevertheless, the first-order attitude in no way determines the second-order attitude, and may even be in conflict with it. For example, it is quite possible to disapprove of beautiful things and want to destroy them, as some Puritans have done, while being fully sensible of their beauty. This might be a way, albeit an extreme one, of asserting the supremacy of moral or religious values over aesthetic ones.

According to Kant, the disinterestedness of pure judgments of taste helps to explain the possibility of their universal validity, which is what chiefly distinguishes them from judgments upon the merely agreeable. Both are *singular* judgments in which the subject makes his judgment on the basis of an immediate, and therefore subjective, response to a particular object; for instance, "This is delicious," "This is beautiful." In each case, the proof of the pudding is in the eating, as it were. The crucial difference is that, whereas in the case of the agreeable the subject only judges for himself – for instance, "This Canary wine is agreeable to me" – in the case of the beautiful the subject

judges "not merely for himself, but for all men, and then speaks of beauty as if it were a property of all things" (1952: 52); for example, "This rose is beautiful."

To call something beautiful is to put it "on a pedestal" and *demand* the same delight from others. The disinterestedness helps to explain why we feel entitled to do this. "For where any one is conscious that his delight in an object is with him independent of interest, it is inevitable that he should look on the object as one containing a ground of delight for all men" (1952: 50). In other words, if one is aware that one's delight in the beautiful is not dependent on any fact about oneself that might be peculiar to oneself, as with needs, desires and appetites, then one is entitled to assume – or at least one has no reason for not assuming – that it is grounded on something which one shares with all human beings, that is, with beings who are both animal and rational and who share one's perceptual and cognitive faculties.

This does not, of course, prove that our aesthetic feelings must in principle be universally communicable, but it does help to explain why we should feel them to be so. It helps to explain, for instance, in a very general way, why we would be extremely puzzled by someone who genuinely considered a typical multi-storey car park to be more beautiful than the Taj Mahal, but not surprised by an Inuit who genuinely preferred the taste of raw whale blubber to lobster soufflé. It is true that one can often predict with a fair degree of accuracy what others will find agreeable or disagreeable, and thus make judgments with which most, if not all, people would concur, for example, that the smell of freshly roasted coffee is delicious. However, to demand universal assent to a pure judgment or taste is not to predict a similar reaction in others, but to require it. In other words, others *ought* to agree, even if they do not. Judgments upon the agreeable, on the other hand, can at best aspire only to a general validity and contain no hidden "ought."

The aesthetic "ought" differs from the "ought" of practical judgment in not resting on the concept of an end. This is because when an object pleases aesthetically in the Kantian sense, it does so apart from any concept. To judge a thing purely beautiful is to judge it on the basis of perceptual form alone without reference to how it might be described or what purpose, if any, it might serve. The case is otherwise with the good, whether morally good or only usefully good, for a thing can be good or bad, right or wrong, only under a description which must include reference to an end: in the case of an object, its purpose; in the case of an action, the intention behind it. All such judgments are "interested" in Kant's sense, for "the good is the object of will" and "to will something, and to take a delight in its existence, that is to take an interest in it, are identical" (1952: 48).

For this reason, an object cannot be judged beautiful or ugly on the basis of a general description of it, as can the rightness or wrongness of an action. Thus aesthetic disagreements cannot be settled by rational argument in the way that moral and practical disagreements can; that is to say, "there can be no rule according to which any one is to be compelled to recognize anything as beautiful." For where there are no concepts there can be no rules, or at least no rules capable of formulation. Thus holds good the dictum that there can be no disputing about tastes.

The only procedure for settling aesthetic disagreements is for the parties concerned to attend to the object with greater care, in case the perceptual form has not been properly apprehended. But even when those features of the object that contribute to its beauty can be named, no rule can be formulated which says that any object possessing such features must be beautiful. One can, of course, improve one's taste by exercising one's perpetual and imaginative faculties in the right way on objects which are considered exemplary in respect of their beauty, but one cannot be forced to abandon a judgment simply because others disagree with it (1952: 137–9).

A pure judgment of taste is, then, one that expresses a disinterested and universally communicable pleasure in the perceptual form of an object, considered apart from any concept. The subjective principle that determines what it is about the perceptual form that pleases or displeases by feeling alone, Kant calls the "Form of Finality." Since the form of finality can only be felt and not known, there is very little that can be said about it apart from its effect on the subject, which is to induce a harmonious interaction between the faculties of imagination

and understanding. We know a priori, Kant says, that such harmonious interaction is possible because it is a necessary condition of the possibility of all empirical knowledge. In other words, the mere possibility of the universal communicability of empirical truth, which is objective, assures us of the possibility of the universal communicability of aesthetic feeling, which is subjective.

There are two types of form: figure, which is the product of design; and play, which is the product of composition. Painting is an example of the first and music of the second. Dance combines the two. Subjective finality can be ascribed to the form when it is so well adapted to our powers of cognition that it is found pleasing for its own sake. When this happens, the imagination, whose normal role is to supply data for the understanding to synthesize, enters into a free, self-sustaining, and harmonious interaction with understanding, whose normal role is to bring the data under concepts with a view either to knowledge or to action. The interaction is free, because unconstrained by determinate concepts. Thus, the form of finality has the appearance of purposiveness or design, but without purpose. It is that for the sake of which we exercise our perceptual powers, when we have no practical or theoretical interest in the object.

See also EIGHTEENTH-CENTURY AESTHETICS; AESTHETIC ATTITUDE; AESTHETIC JUDGMENT; AESTHETIC PLEASURE; BEAUTY; CREATIVITY; LUKÁCS; RELIGION AND ART; SUBLIME; SHAFTESBURY; TASTE.

BIBLIOGRAPHY

Primary sources
[1790] 1952. *The Critique of Judgement.* J. C. Meredith (trans.). Oxford: Clarendon. (Translation 1st pub. 1928.)
[1790] 1987. *Critique of Judgment.* W. S. Pluhar (trans.). Indianapolis: Hackett.
[1790] 2000. *Critique of the Power of Judgment.* P. Guyer & E. Matthews (trans.). Cambridge: Cambridge University Press.

Secondary sources
Cohen, Ted & Guyer, Paul (eds.). 1982. *Essays in Kant's Aesthetics.* Chicago: University of Chicago Press.
Coleman, Francis X. J. 1974. *The Harmony of Reason: A Study in Kant's Aesthetics.* Pittsburgh: University of Pittsburgh Press.

Crawford, Donald W. 1974. *Kant's Aesthetic Theory*. Madison: University of Wisconsin Press.

Gasché, Rodolphe. 2003. *The Idea of Form: Rethinking Kant's Aesthetics*. Stanford: Stanford University Press.

Guyer, Paul. 1997. *Kant and the Claims of Taste*. 2nd edn. Cambridge, MA: Harvard University Press.

Kemal, Salim. 1986. *Kant and Fine Art*. Oxford: Clarendon.

McCloskey, Mary A. 1987. *Kant's Aesthetic*. London: Macmillan.

Osborne, Harold. 1968. *Aesthetics and Art Criticism*. London: Longman.

Schaper, Eva (ed.). 1979. *Studies in Kant's Aesthetics*. Edinburgh: Edinburgh University Press.

Scruton, Roger. 1982. *Kant*. Oxford: Oxford University Press.

Warnock, Mary. 1976. *Imagination*. Berkeley: University of California Press.

Wicks, Robert. 2007. *Routledge Philosophy Guidebook to Kant on Judgement*. London: Routledge.

DAVID WHEWELL

Kierkegaard, Søren (1813–1855) Danish philosopher and theologian; an inspiration, in the twentieth century, for both existentialism and Protestant thought.

In *Either/Or* (1843) Kierkegaard writes pseudonymously to his *symparanekromenoi* ("fellow-moribunds") of his own sense of the nihilism of his age (1987: i.168). Describing the "music of the storm," he comments: "People do say that the voice of the divine is not in the driving wind but in the soft breeze, but our ears, after all, are constructed not to pick up the soft breeze but to swallow the uproar of the elements." The vortex is the world's core principle, and he wishes that "it might erupt with deep-seated resentment and shake off the mountains and the nations and the cultural works and man's clever inventions."

Whether or not he was right to find the sources of nihilism in the work of Fichte, in the Romantics, or in Hegelianism, he searched for an understanding of "the aesthetic" (an existential category) in relation to this vortex, loving poetry and art and all the works of the imagination (aesthetics as artistic practice) while setting limits to them (1987: ii.273). For, as he says (under one of his pseudonyms), "they provide only an imperfect reconciliation with life . . . when you fix your eye upon poetry and art you are not looking at actuality."

Kierkegaard's manner of presenting his views on aesthetics was possible only for a writer capable of the range of experiments in style and thought exhibited in his private papers as well as in his published work, and it is this which gives his writing special distinction (the modern editions of 1983 and 1987 collate material from the private papers with the published work). His pseudonymous writing has to do, he says, with deliberately created "author-personalities" (1987: ii.451) by means of which he enables his readers to explore aesthetics, and themselves, and to discover what finally matters to them.

There are three main aesthetic "ideas," which represent the lyric (Don Juan – sensuous immediacy), the epic (the wandering Jew – despair), and the dramatic (Faust – doubt). Don Juan belongs to the Middle Ages, while Faust is a parody of the Reformation, abandoned to himself and needing completion in the wandering Jew. The latter is the unhappiest of men because he cannot die; he stands for the aesthetic, without meaning or purpose, and powerless against the boredom of the modern age. In "The Seducer's Diary" (a story within *Either/Or*), he entertains himself by creating in a young girl, "the motions of infinity" (1987: i.392), in which she learns "to swing herself, to rock herself in moods, to confuse poetry and actuality, truth and fiction, to frolic in infinity."

There are, then, those like the Seducer for whom life becomes a stage and those who perform, for example, "The Immediate Erotic Stages; or, The Musical Erotic," of which the supreme example is Mozart's *Don Giovanni*. In this work is to be found the "thoroughgoing mutual permeation" of form and subject matter, like for like (1987: i.52–3). The Don's sensuous immediacy has its absolute medium in music, in its power, life, movement, continual unrest, continual succession (1987: i.71). We lose ourselves in the music in which the Don unfurls himself. But a different form, and therefore a different response, is appropriate for different subject matter. So in a comedy like *The First Love*, a play Kierkegaard saw, what is important is that:

> In it there must not be a single character, not a single situation, that could claim to survive the downfall that irony from the outset prepared for

each and all in it. When the curtain falls, everything is forgotten, nothing but nothing remains, and that is the only thing one sees; and the only thing one hears is a laughter, like a sound of nature, that does not issue from any one person but is the language of a world force, and this force is irony. (1987: i.273).

It is a reflection on Emmeline (a character in *The First Love*) and her illusions, disclosed by the comedy, remaining afterwards for contemplation, and fostered by repeatedly seeing the comedy, which distinguishes watching it from losing ourselves in the Don's music.

Kierkegaard also explores the relation between the ancient and the modern in tragedy. The crucial difference is that modern tragedy has no "epic foreground," for the hero or heroine stands or falls entirely on his or her own deeds. "The wrath of the gods is terrible, but still the pain is not as great as in modern tragedy, where the hero suffers his total guilt, is transparent to himself in the suffering of his guilt" (1987: i.148). And in a remarkable piece of necromantic fantasy, he sketches how he would recharacterize *Antigone* (in marked contrast to Hegel, in his *Aesthetics*). It is precisely that capacity for reflection associated with comedy, but now, as it were, attributable to a character in tragedy itself, which robs tragedy of something essential to it; for "the power which is the source of the suffering has lost its meaning" and the spectator has lost the compassion which is tragedy's authentic expression.

Reflection can still leave one with illusion, or drive one from aesthetics to ethics, from the masks of the self's shadow-play as in *Repetition* (1983: ii.156), which have their place in a life, to feel oneself present as a character in a drama that the deity is writing, in which poet, prompter and actor are at one (1987: ii.137). And some things, such as daily dying, or the patience that contends against time (1987: ii.135–6), cannot be portrayed in poetry or art – there is no form for them.

Finally, it is an image taken from the theater that provides Kierkegaard with the form for the content of his own authorship. "In a theater, it happened that a fire started offstage. The clown came out to tell the audience. They thought it was a joke and applauded. He told them again, and they became still more hilarious. This is the way, I suppose, that the world will be destroyed – amid the universal hilarity of wits and wags who think it is all a joke" (1987: i.30). He is to be ridiculed if there is only the endless shadow-play to see, rather than the need to give birth to the self (1987: ii.206). "Therefore it is quite all right that in modern drama the bad is always represented by the most brilliantly gifted characters, whereas the good, the upright, is represented by the grocer's apprentice. The spectators find this entirely appropriate and learn from the play what they already knew, that it is far beneath their dignity to be classed with a grocer's apprentice" (1987: ii.228).

See also NINETEENTH- AND TWENTIETH-CENTURY CONTINENTAL AESTHETICS; HUMOR; IRONY; MORALITY AND ART.

BIBLIOGRAPHY

Primary sources
[1843] 1983. *Fear and Trembling, Repetition*. H. V. Hong & E. H. Hong (eds. & trans.). Princeton: Princeton University Press.
[1843] 1987. *Either/Or*. 2 vols. H. V. Hong & E. H. Hong (eds. & trans.). Princeton: Princeton University Press.

Secondary sources
Pattison, George. 1991. *Kierkegaard: The Aesthetic and the Religious*. London: Macmillan.
Walsh, Sylvia. 1994. *Living Poetically: Kierkegaard's Existential Aesthetics*. University Park: Pennsylvania State University of Press.

ANN LOADES

kitsch is a category term referring to a type of aesthetically impoverished art, artifact, performance, or practice that commonly relies on banal subject matter and stock emotional responses. The term, however, is used more or less loosely, sometimes in reference to a wide variety of somewhat incongruous items made in a slapdash manner, sometimes making no reference to absurdity or poor technique but instead to a particular type of emotional appeal.

Given the cluster of associations that has grown around the term, a precise definition of "kitsch" is difficult to formulate. The term was originally used in connection with sketchy tourist art that became popular in Germany in the latter half of the nineteenth century. Such sketches were cheap and produced in large quantity. (Indeed, the German verb *verkitschen* means "to make cheaply.") Kitsch has accordingly become associated with consumer society and mass production, although being produced on a mass scale is not a necessary criterion. Early kitsch products appealed to middle class sensibilities, and the term has acquired the association of pandering to those who seek easy gratification and are not very selective about the style or quality of what they buy. In light of the fact that souvenir art was the initial paradigm of kitsch, moreover, the association of emotional appeal is a basic connotation of the term.

Kitsch always involves some kind of deficiency, but a variety of particular inadequacies are associated with it, and this adds to the difficulty of defining it. Among its alleged faults are insincerity, bad taste, tackiness, a formulaic and facile character, incongruous juxtaposition, vagueness, incompatibility between form and function, overly simplistic presentation, and false representation of reality. The label has been applied to objects and performances on the basis of some but not all of these characterizations.

A further complication for a definition of kitsch is that while the term is commonly used to identify certain objects, the nature of the appeals that kitsch makes is typically a basis for considering them to be kitsch. This being the case, it is possible that objects that are not themselves kitsch might be employed in a manner that yields kitschy results. An example might be the use of the image of the American flag on neckties or suspenders. The American flag itself is not kitsch, nor is an image of the flag. Serious historical paintings and works by Jasper Johns can utilize the flag in a way that is not kitsch. But by virtue of the incompatibility of form (the image of a banner celebrating a nation state) and function (to accessorize an outfit of clothing or to hold up a pair of pants) the flag on these items of clothing may well be kitsch.

What, then, makes kitsch kitsch? Analysts of kitsch commonly associate at least three criteria with it:

1 Kitsch involves the formulaic and makes use of stock elements.

2 Kitsch evokes emotion that is enjoyed in an effortless way.
3 Kitsch presents reality in an unrealistic way.

The formulaic character and the effortless enjoyment associated with kitsch were among the features that led Clement Greenberg to denounce it in his famous 1939 essay "Avant-Garde and Kitsch." Greenberg claimed that kitsch debases aesthetic sensibilities by encouraging mindlessness in its audience. He objected that its formulaic character effectively pre-digested kitsch for its audience. By contrast with the avant-garde, which aimed to confront the viewer and demand reflection, kitsch was an artistic type of pabulum, offering only familiar elements to elicit trained responses from spectators. Perhaps ironically, the primary example of kitsch that Greenberg employs, a painting by Repin that allegedly appealed to peasants, appears to have been an amalgam of various paintings that he had seen rather than a particular actual work.

Thomas Kulka emphasizes the formulaic character and the effortless enjoyment of kitsch when he defines kitsch as being charged with stock emotions, involving themes or objects that are effortlessly identifiable, and failing to substantially enrich our associations relating to the depicted themes or objects. Like Greenberg, Kulka faults the derivative nature of kitsch and the unchallenging entertainment that it offers. These two features work together, so that one responds effortlessly to what is presented precisely because it is so familiar. Typically, the themes or objects depicted resonate with important concerns in human life, such as family, friendship, patriotism, etc. Kulka points out that the spectator responds to the gestalt of what is depicted, not to the representation as such.

Strictly speaking, then, the viewer is not responding aesthetically to the object at all, but using the object's representational gesture as a basis for emotional response. The effect, as Kulka puts it, is entirely parasitic on the referent. Kitsch tends to be representational, and its representations refer to some element in a network of cultural associations. Kitsch treats subject matter that we associate with some basic human concern, and we respond to this general concern more than to the object itself. The object itself is relevant only to the extent that it conjures up an important human theme and prompts an emotional reaction to it.

Kitsch, generally speaking, trades in atmospheres. It evokes feelings, and the enjoyment of kitsch is largely a matter of taking satisfaction in the fact of having these feelings. Milan Kundera, in his novel *The Unbearable Lightness of Being*, proposes that the emotions kitsch elicits are inherently reflective and involve our indulging the impression that the rest of the population shares our emotions with us.

> Kitsch causes two tears to flow in quick succession. The first tear says: How nice to see children running on the grass!
>
> The second tear says: How nice to be moved, together with all mankind, by children running on the grass! It is the second tear that makes kitsch kitsch. (Kundera 1984: 251)

Kitsch, on this view, appeals to our sense of human solidarity and promotes the belief that the rest of the world values just what we do.

Despite its universal pretensions, the images (broadly construed) that kitsch presents make reference to cultural beliefs about the world and important human goals. These beliefs are semiconscious but reinforced through many cultural practices. They are also connected to other beliefs in a network of associations. Thus, an image of the American flag is related for many Americans, at least, to ideas of the United States, power, prestige, home, the American population, the American landscape, a comforting sense of membership, patriotism, etc. The image of the flag serves as an icon that brings to partial awareness the whole background structure of associations. And the satisfaction one takes in the kitsch is generalized to implicate this entire structure.

A consequence is that the kitsch object reinforces culturally embedded beliefs about the way the world is organized and where one fits within it. Kitsch allows one to enjoy one's feelings about these beliefs, and the kitsch object seems to affirm these feelings. Milan Kundera, in *The Unbearable Lightness of Being*, takes the May Day parade in eastern bloc Czechoslovakia as an instance of kitsch. The aim of the parade is to arouse patriotic feelings by presenting organized formations of beautiful young people, who metonymically remind viewers of all that is great about their country.

Many critics of kitsch have argued that it presents reality in an unrealistic way, and for this reason they see it as morally objectionable. Kitsch excludes whatever is objectionable in our world, thereby encouraging a distorted view of reality. Kitsch is "the absolute denial of shit," in Kundera's striking phrase (1984: 248). This deceptive portrayal of reality can be pernicious because it encourages a sense that some aspects of the world (children or one's country, for example) are absolutely good, with the implication that some others are absolutely bad. Kitsch thus imposes an absolutistic schema of good and evil on whatever we encounter. This in turn can motivate a sense that the absolutely good features of the world must be protected against anything that would threaten them, that is, the completely evil.

By virtue of the binary values that kitsch imposes, kitsch is particularly serviceable for propagandistic purposes. It facilitates absolute distinctions that propagandists can seize on. Merely presenting one's party as the sponsor of some kitsch entertainment, such as the May Day parade, facilitates associations between one's cause and the pleasure one takes in the kitsch. The propagandist can suggest, moreover, that one is really sharing one's feeling, not with all people in the world, but with the *good* people, that is, those on the side of their cause by contrast to their opponents. The fact that kitsch was a favored propagandistic tool of the Nazis indicates that the ends supported by kitsch have sometimes been sinister.

Despite these objections to kitsch and the general complaint that it is aesthetically shallow, some commentators see kitsch as relatively harmless. Some accept the verdict that kitsch is aesthetically worthless, but nevertheless think it is morally innocent. These critics tend to doubt that kitsch plays a very significant role in how people understand reality. Others consider kitsch to be innocently enjoyable if one approaches it from an ironical point of view. Such critics sometimes relabel the kitsch that is appropriated in this tongue-in-cheek manner "camp." They tend to consider the bad taste or incongruity of kitsch to be part of its charm.

Even some of those who take kitsch to be morally damaging believe that its harms can be defused by seeing its appeals for what they are. Kundera, for example, contends, "As soon as kitsch is recognized for the lie it is, it moves into the context of non-kitsch, thus losing its authoritarian power and becoming as touching as any other human weakness." An ironical stance is essential, as he sees it, for we cannot do without kitsch with its pretensions of human brotherhood and its oversimplifications. As he concludes, "No matter how we scorn it, kitsch is an integral part of the human condition" (1984: 256).

See also MASS ART; SENTIMENTALITY.

BIBLIOGRAPHY
Boyers, Robert & Boyers, Peg (eds.). 1990. "On Kitsch: A Symposium," *Salmagundi*, 85–6, 198–312.
Calinescu, Matei. 1987. *Five Faces of Modernity: Modernism, Avant-Garde, Decadence, Kitsch, Postmodernism*. Durham: Duke University Press.
Crick, Philip. 1983. "Kitsch," *British Journal of Aesthetics*, 23, 48–52.
Dorfles, Gillo. 1968. *Kitsch: The World of Bad Taste*. New York: Universe.
Greenberg, Clement. 1961 [1939]. "Avant-Garde and Kitsch." In *Art and Culture*. Boston: Beacon, 3–21.
Harries, Karsten. 1968. *The Meaning of Modern Art*. Evanston: Northwestern University Press.
Higgins, Kathleen. 1992. "Sweet Kitsch." In *The Philosophy of the Visual Arts*. P. Alperson (ed.). New York: Oxford University Press, 568–81.
Kulka, Tomas. 1996. *Kitsch and Art*. University Park: Pennsylvania State University Press.
Kundera, Milan. 1984. *The Unbearable Lightness of Being*. New York: Harper & Row.
Solomon, Robert C. 1991. "In Defense of Kitsch," *Journal of Aesthetics and Art Criticism*, 49, 1–14.

KATHLEEN MARIE HIGGINS

Kristeva, Julia (b.1941)   Naturalized French theorist of language, literature, and psychoanalysis: an important influence on several late twentieth-century intellectual developments, including feminist criticism.

Born in Bulgaria, Kristeva studied linguistics and literature at the University of Sofia, while working as a journalist on a newspaper for communist youth. She went to Paris in 1966 on a French government doctoral research fellowship, and worked as research assistant at Claude Lévi-Strauss's Laboratory of Social Anthropology. Lucien Goldmann directed her doctoral thesis, a study of the emergence of the novel in the late medieval period as exemplified by the writings of Antoine de la Sale. Published in 1970 as *Le texte du roman* ("The Text of the Novel"), this study draws upon the "postformalism" of Mikhail Bakhtin, in particular his account of the heterogeneity of the textual and cultural materials making up the novel form, and analyzes the shift in the concept of the "sign," from meaning as closure to open-ended processes of signification.

In *Séméiotiké: recherches pour une sémanalyse* (1969), the neologism "semanalysis," stemming from the conjunction of semiotics and psychoanalysis, is defined as a "critique of meaning, of its elements and laws," "conceiving of meaning not as a sign-system but as a *signifying process*." Rejecting the static model of language upheld in much semiotic and linguistic theory, Kristeva focuses attention on the conditions of meaning-production. Psychoanalytic theories of language and signification, particularly Jacques Lacan's reformulations of Freudian thought, become increasingly central to this project. Kristeva's intention is to bring issues of subjectivity and the role of the "speaking subject" into play: questions largely excluded from semiotic and linguistic theory – social and psychic processes, the pre- or extralinguistic, and the dynamic and "wild" language of literary texts – thus become central.

These concerns are developed in one of her most important works, originally her doctoral thesis, published as *La révolution du langage poétique* (first published in 1974; *Revolution in Poetic Language*, 1984). This ambitious study is both an account of avant-garde literary and linguistic practices at the end of the nineteenth century, making particular reference to works by Lautréamont and Mallarmé, and an attempt to produce a comprehensive theory of poetic language, drawing on a variety of theoretical traditions and modes of analysis – philosophical, linguistic, and psychoanalytic. Of its many theoretical strands, two of the most important are Kristeva's use of psychoanalysis and of Hegelian dialectics, particularly her reformulation of Hegelian negativity as motion and process, expulsion or "rejection" (*rejet*). In articulating an account of the "semiotic" and the "symbolic" as the two modalities of all processes of signification, she draws on Freud's distinction between pre-oedipal and oedipal sexual drives and Lacan's concepts of "imaginary" and "symbolic." Following Plato's *Timaeus*, she defines the place of the presymbolic or "semiotic" (where the symbolic is understood as the condition of ordered, "rational" signification) as the space of the maternal *chora* (enclosed space, womb, receptacle), which in turn corresponds to the "poetic" function of language. "The *chora*," Kristeva writes, "as rupture and articulations (rhythm), precedes evidence, verisimilitude, spatiality and temporality." It is also seen as the space of instinctual drives and of a "bodily" relationship to the rhythmic-intonational aspects of language.

The "semiotic," then, is represented as the transgressive, "feminine" materiality of signification, which becomes evident in "madness, holiness and poetry" and surfaces in literary texts, particularly those of the avant-garde, as musicality and linguistic play. It should be noted, however, that Kristeva's concept of the relationship between "semiotic" and "symbolic" is a dialectical one: the order of the "symbolic" and the "thetic" allows the "semiotic" entrance into social and psychic relations, allowing negativity a mode of articulation. The "semiotic" has to work through the very order of logical and syntactic functioning that it subverts, in order to enter into representation at all; the "symbolic," which is the realm of the speaking subject, makes positionality (psychic, social, and political) possible.

Kristeva's relationship to the contemporary avant-garde should be understood in the context of her involvement with the journal *Tel Quel*, her primary intellectual forum from the late 1960s until 1983, when it was reformulated under the title *L'Infini*. Philippe Sellers, avant-garde novelist and essayist, has edited it in both its manifestations, and Kristeva has been closely involved with his work. In her collection of essays, *Polylogue*, the title essay is a review of Sellers' novel *H*, which she describes as "external polylogue" rather than "internal monologue"; the collection also contains essays on Antonin Artaud and Georges Bataille. The dominant theme of these essays is, in accord with the *Tel Quel* project, the articulation of the links between language, subjectivity, and transgression in the avant-garde text. The influence of Roland Barthes's work was of paramount importance to this project, not least in the correspondences he claimed between the challenge to literary conventions and subversion at a social and political level.

The more overtly "political" involvements of the *Tel Quel* group were at their height at the beginning of the 1970s, when it broke off relations with the French Communist Party and declared its support for the Chinese Cultural Revolution. Kristeva's account of her visit to China was published as *About Chinese Women* (1977). The *Tel Quel* group's Maoist affiliations did not survive long after this visit, and Kristeva has ascribed her own more pronounced withdrawal from direct political involvement to her disillusionment with aspects of Chinese society. Similarly, despite the centrality of her work to feminist theory, she has expressed ambivalence toward feminism as a social and political movement, though repeatedly emphasizing the importance of addressing women's psychic and social condition.

The consolidation of Kristeva's theoretical concerns with "the individual life" may be linked to her increased professional and intellectual engagement with psychoanalysis. During the mid 1970s she trained as an analyst, starting her own psychoanalytic practice in 1979. Since 1980, her theoretical work has demonstrated a very close engagement with psychoanalytic theory, and art and literature are used extensively to explore psychoanalytic concepts and psychic processes. In *Powers of Horror* (1982), she analyzes the concept of "abjection" and "horror," incorporating in these terms her earlier focus on "negativity" and *rejet*. "Abjection" is described as "what disturbs identity, system, order"; the "abject" can be exemplified by those "unclean" and "improper" aspects of corporeality and instinctual life which are disavowed in order for the subject to enter into the "symbolic order." Drawing on Freud's cultural criticism, particularly *Totem and Taboo* and *Civilization and Its Discontents*, and Mary Douglas's *Purity and Danger*, Kristeva's "anthropological" focus is also on the ways in which societies and religions have erected taboos against the "abjects" (food, waste, and the bodily signs of sexual difference). What is expelled, however, is never wholly destroyed, but remains as an ambiguous, liminal area of instability threatening the individual's assumption of unity and cohesion.

In the last part of *Powers of Horror*, Kristeva turns to the work of Céline, whose writing "speaks" horror and whose political vision, including a violent antisemitism, is to be understood as a symptom, which both enacts and exposes the horror and fascination of psychic violence. More generally, in her later work she emphasizes that "the problem of art in the twentieth century is a continual confrontation with psychosis . . . a crisis of subjectivity which is the basis for all creation." In *Black Sun: Depression and Melancholy* (1989), she discusses the work of Holbein, Dostoevsky, Nerval, and Duras, writers and artists for whom "the experience of art was lived as a salvation" or, as in Nerval's case, where art failed to save.

Other works include a volume on Proust and the experience of literature, *Time and Sense* (1996), and *Tales of Love* (1987), in which images of Western love are analyzed in myth and religion and through figures such as Don Juan and Romeo and Juliet, which "have woven our amorous imaginary." The concept of maternal love also plays a crucial role in this text, as elsewhere in Kristeva's work. She has also addressed the themes of foreignness, exile, and nationalism in her *Étrangers à nous-mêmes* (*Strangers to Ourselves*) (1991) and *Lettre ouverte à Harlem Désir* ("An Open Letter to Harlem Désir") (1990). Kristeva has confronted the common tendency to associate genius exclusively with males through her *Le genie féminin* (1999–2002), a trilogy of intellectual biographies focusing, respectively, on Hannah Arendt, Melanie Klein, and Colette. Kristeva's engagement with the aesthetic took a different turn when she served as the invited curator of an exhibition of artworks on the theme of decapitation at the Louvre, entitled *Visions capitales*. More theoretically, in *The Sense and Nonsense of Revolt* (2000), she considers the role art (in particular, installation art) can play in helping to restore a sense of connectedness to bodily sensation, which she considers a common malaise in the contemporary world.

Published in 1990, Kristeva's first novel, *The Samurai* (1990), which is a *roman-à-clef* about Parisian intellectuals, marks a turn in her career toward fiction writing. She has since written several additional novels, including *The Old Man and the Wolves* (1994), *Possessions* (1998), and *Murder in Byzantium* (2006).

See also BARTHES; FEMINIST CRITICISM; HORROR; PSYCHOANALYSIS AND ART.

BIBLIOGRAPHY
1969. *Séméiotiké: recherches pour une sémanalyse*. Paris: Seuil.
1970. *Le texte du roman: approche sémiologique d'une structure discursive transformationnelle*. The Hague: Mouton.
[1974] 1977. *About Chinese Women*. A. Barrows (trans.). London: Boyars.
[1974] 1984. *Revolution in Poetic Language*. M. Waller (trans.). New York: Columbia University Press.
[1977] 1984. *Polylogue*. Paris: Seuil. (Part trans. as *Desire in Language* by T. Gora, A. Jardine, & L. Roudiez. Oxford: Blackwell.)
[1980] 1982. *Powers of Horror*. L. Roudiez (trans.). New York: Columbia University Press.
[1983] 1987. *Tales of Love*. L. Roudiez (trans.). New York: Columbia University Press.
[1987] 1989. *Black Sun: Depression and Melancholy*. L. Roudiez (trans.). New York: Columbia University Press.
[1988] 1991. *Strangers to Ourselves*. L. Roudiez (trans.). Brighton: Harvester.
1990. *Lettre ouverte à Harlem Désir*. Paris: Rivages.
[1990] 1992. *The Samurai*. B. Bray (trans.). New York: Columbia University Press.
[1991] 1994. *The Old Man and the Wolves*. B. Bray (trans.). New York: Columbia University Press.
[1994] 1996. *Time and Sense: Proust and the Interpretation of Literature*. R. Guberman (trans.). New York: Columbia University Press.
[1996] 1998. *Possessions*. B. Bray (trans.). New York: Columbia University Press.
[1996] 2000. *The Sense and Nonsense of Revolt*. J. Herman (trans.). New York: Columbia University Press.
[1997] 2002. *Intimate Revolt: The Powers and Limits of Psychoanalysis*. 2 vols. J. Herman (trans.). New York: Columbia University Press.
1998. *Visions capitales*. Paris: Réunion des musées nationaux.
1999–2002. *Le génie féminin: la vie, la folie, les mots: Hannah Arendt, Melanie Klein, Colette*. Paris: Fayard.
2002. *The Portable Kristeva*. K. Oliver (ed.). New York: Columbia University Press.

2004. *Colette*. J. M. Todd (trans.). New York: Columbia University Press.

[2004] 2006. *Murder in Byzantium*. C. J. Delogu (trans.). New York: Columbia University Press.

2005. *La haine et le pardon*. Fayard: Paris.

Secondary sources

Beardsworth, Sara. 2004. *Julia Kristeva: Psychoanalysis and Modernity*. Albany: State University of New York Press.

Fletcher, J. & Benjamin, A. (eds.). 1990. *Abjection, Melancholia and Love*. London: Routledge.

Keltner, Stacy & Oliver, Kelly. 2008. *Julia Kristeva: Between Politics and Aesthetics*. Albany: State University of New York Press.

Kolocotroni, Vassiliki. 1991. "Interview with Julia Kristeva," *Textual Practice*, 5(2), 157–70.

Lechte, John. 1990. *Julia Kristeva*. London: Routledge.

Moi, T. (ed.). 1986. *The Kristeva Reader*. Oxford: Blackwell.

LAURA MARCUS

L

Langer, Susanne (1895–1985) American philosopher, best known for her contributions to philosophical anthropology and aesthetics; one of the most important aestheticians of the twentieth century. Her views on art are integrated with a general philosophical position of some intricacy. Her aesthetic theory had its genesis in her book on the nature of symbolism and meaning, *Philosophy in a New Key* (first published in 1942), became the focus in its sequel, *Feeling and Form* (1953), and was expanded in the three volumes of *Mind: An Essay on Human Feeling* (1967, 1972, 1982) In all these works, Langer wove together an astounding variety of influences with a sensitive understanding of art. The writings of A. N. Whitehead, Ernst Cassirer, Wittgenstein, C. S. Peirce, and Rudolf Carnap feature strongly in her work, not to mention those of biologists, psychologists, anthropologists, and numerous writers on art. Only the portion of her work directly concerned with the aesthetic is considered here.

Langer began by accepting the great division made by positivism between cognitive and emotive expression, but it was her intention to rescue the emotive from being dismissed as meaningless by describing how it exhibits an alternative *form* of meaning best illustrated by art. Human beings are essentially *symbolic* animals; this capacity cannot be regarded as a mere extension of animal psychology. Her last work undertook to describe the "great shift" from the rhythmic patterns of organisms, to symbolic meaning, to mind. By then, in her view, feeling mediated between the biological and the symbolic, lying as it does at the very basis of rationality (1967: 23).

Symbolism is the capacity to think *about* something without implying that object's existence, differing in this way from the denotative function of a sign (or "signal"). Experience exhibits certain *forms* that provide the basis of abstractive rationality. With the early Wittgenstein, Langer holds that our discursive thought, expressed in language, offers logical pictures of states of affairs in the world. Because of its complex syntactic nature and immense vocabulary, language must build up its picture from discrete units governed by logical laws. It cannot even begin to present the world *simul totum*. Langer believes that here a crucial error has been made: since discursive language has been the medium of philosophical reflection, philosophy has been willing to identify meaning with discursivity. Hence the question "What is the meaning of art?" became an undesirable either/or: either a work had *no* meaning or its meaning could be *translated* into literal, propositional language. Her challenge is to offer a *nondiscursive* mode of symbolism, a "presentational" mode, which begins with the "grammar of the eye and ear" in sensation and then becomes highly articulated in art (1957a: 89).

Through symbolism we gradually organize our world of meaning. Even in perceiving ordinary objects, we are transforming a complex manifold of sensation into a "virtual world" of general symbols (1957a: 144). Beginning with dreams, our awareness of meaning grows through the use of metaphoric thinking. In tribal culture, the awareness of presentational meaning lies at the root of totemism. Myth constitutes a further development toward a symbolic understanding of the great forces governing human existence. But here, with Cassirer, Langer believes that a fork in the road is taken: discursive understanding must drop the metaphoric for the literal mode, aiming at metaphysical rigor and scientific description; the myth, further developed, becomes the epic – that is, art. Science and art are the two ultimate refinements of meaning, the one consuming our practical concern with nature, the other our power of "envisagement."

In *Philosophy in a New Key*, Langer discusses music as the paradigm instance of presentational meaning because it best exhibits the distinctive concern with "pure form" (1957a: 208). All works of art aspire toward "significant form," she claims, adopting Clive Bell's term while rejecting his psychologistic view that it expresses a distinct "aesthetic" emotion. Music is not a psychological expression of emotions, but a logical, symbolic expression *about* feelings. Thus it reflects the composer's knowledge of human feeling, not his emotional constitution at the time. Music seems to resemble language; we speak of its syntax and vocabulary. But it has no literal meaning: it is an "unconsummated symbol" expressing "vital import." It cannot achieve the denotational conditions of conventional linguistic reference. Music expresses the "forms of human feeling" and is "our myth of the inner life" (1957a: 235, 245; see also 1953: 27).

While the plastic arts, like painting, easily become "model-bound" and so become confused with the goal of literal representation, music demonstrates that art is truly about significant form. The plastic arts can express significant form *through* depicting objects; music does not. It is the work as a *whole* which bears artistic or "vital import," conveying "knowledge by acquaintance" rather than indirect "knowledge about." The arts in the past have drawn on myth and religion, but no longer need to do so. Art, thus liberated, can freely serve human expressivity.

Feeling and Form continues these general themes, applying them to the entire range of the arts. One of the strengths of this work lies in Langer's concrete applications. Her grander claim is to organize the whole of aesthetics by focusing on the question of creation. "Once you answer the question 'What does art create?', all the further questions of why and how, of personality, of talent and genius, etc., seem to emerge in a new light from this central thesis" (1953: 10). The perennial paradoxes that have stymied aesthetics, most notably that between "feeling and form" (feeling leading to subjectivist theories, form to objectivist ones), will disappear. Feeling and form are not opposed. Feelings may be objectively symbolized in certain forms, which then are capable of being abstracted in experience. Hence "art works

contain feelings, but do not feel them" (1953: 22). Since "significant form" is the essence of art, art is defined as "the creation of forms symbolic of human feeling" (1953: 40). "Creation" must refer, then, to the creation of such symbols, not to the ordinary production of artifacts. One can produce painted canvases, but one may or may not create significant forms in the process.

Langer's discussion of "semblance" contains the cardinal points of her theory. Artworks are distinguished from ordinary objects above all by their sheer "otherness," their "unreality," giving a sense of illusion. The art image is not copied, but created, making a "virtual object." Unlike ordinary objects, the virtual object does not exist for all the senses, but focuses instead on one or two. Adopting Jung's term, Langer calls this character "semblance," though it also has strong affinities to what Schiller called *Schein*. The semblance or *Schein* of a work disengages us entirely from the practical demands of belief, making it a "strange guest" among "the highly substantial realities of the natural world." Like discursive meaning, the presentational symbol reveals "a new dimension apart from the familiar world," the dimension of articulate but nondiscursive feeling (1953: 50). Works of art are not representations of objects in the natural world so much as explorations in this dimension of meaning. And yet Langer insists that what art expresses are the forms *of life*, of vital feeling, "forms of growth and of attenuation, flowing and stowing, conflict and resolution," and so on – "the elusive yet familiar patterns of sentience," as she calls it elsewhere (1953: 27, 52). Art is "essentially organic," creating the *appearance* of life (1953: 373). Her *Essay* itself addresses the question, "Why must artistic form, to be expressive of feeling, always be so-called 'living form'?" (1967: xv).

The artist abstracts the significant form from experience and uses it to create an object that directly expresses it. Thus there can be no real distinction between the form and its "content." The "content" of a work is its import, and this accounts for its "transparency," its alien presence that reveals immediately a dimension of meaning, the *idea* of feeling. Insofar as a work of art confuses this significant form with other aims, such as utilitarian or representational ones, or simply fails to create a truly expressive form, it ceases to be art. There are no high or low arts, simply good and bad artworks. A great work, presumably, is one that powerfully expresses a highly significant feeling. This symbol of feeling is intuitively grasped. Even though a work may take time to unfold, from the beginning there is an "intuition of the whole presented feeling" (1953: 379).

All of these themes are developed in her last work, a work at once in the tradition of a philosophy of symbolic form, like Cassirer's, and a process metaphysics which, like that of her "great mentor" Whitehead, makes feeling and creativity the basis of nature. It would be easy to question some of the sharp distinctions she sets forth (especially the fundamental one of presentational versus discursive meaning); her eclecticism; the repetition of such central terms as "significant form" which remain nonetheless vague; the fact that, for all her stress on the "logical" nature of presentational symbols, they are objects of intuition pure and simple; and her claim that language has an origin in an expressive rather than a communicative need. But this would be to miss the fact that, in a century dominated by factual description and logical justification, Langer saw the problem of mind also in terms of symbol, ritual, myth, expression, and feeling. She argued for a view of nature in which form and creativity are at work in the very heart of things.

See also TWENTIETH-CENTURY ANGLO-AMERICAN AESTHETICS; AESTHETIC EDUCATION; BELL; EMOTION; EXPRESSION; ILLUSION; INEFFABILITY; SYMBOL.

BIBLIOGRAPHY

Primary sources
[1942] 1957a. *Philosophy in a New Key*. 3rd edn. Cambridge, MA: Harvard University Press.
1953. *Feeling and Form*. New York: Scribner.
1957b. *Problems of Art*. New York: Scribner.
1967, 1972, 1982. *Mind: An Essay on Human Feeling*. 3 vols. Baltimore: Johns Hopkins University Press.

Secondary sources
Bertocci, Peter. 1970. "Susanne K. Langer's Theory of Feeling and Mind," *Review of Metaphysics*, 23, 527–51.
Budd, Malcolm. 1985. *Music and the Emotions: The Philosophical Theories*. London: Routledge & Kegan Paul, ch. 6.
Danto, Arthur C. 1984. "Mind as Feeling; Form as Presence," *Journal of Philosophy*, 81, 641–6.
Davies, Stephen. 1994. *Musical Meaning and Expression*. Ithaca: Cornell University Press, ch. 3.
Hagberg, Garry. 1984. "Art and the Unsayable: Langer's Tractarian Aesthetics," *British Journal of Aesthetics*, 24, 325–40.
Laird, Addis. 1999. *Of Mind and Music*. Ithaca: Cornell University Press.
Welsh, Paul. 1955. "Discursive and Presentational Symbols," *Mind*, 64, 181–99.

THOMAS M. ALEXANDER

Lessing, Gotthold Ephraim (1729–1781) German dramatist and literary critic, and eminent figure in the German Enlightenment.

Lessing's contribution to philosophical aesthetics is both prescriptive and systematic. In *Laocoön: An Essay on the Limits of Painting and Poetry* (1766) and the *Hamburg Dramaturgy* (1767–9) he reflects normatively on the constraints that guide artists working within different forms of art, constraints which he presents as systematically derivable from the nature of their chosen media and genres. What these constraints are and why they arise are the central topics of these two works. The former structures discussion around the provenance and aesthetic character of the famous statue in the Vatican Museum that depicts the death of the Trojan priest Laocoön; the latter discloses aesthetic principles that guided two years of theater reviewing in Hamburg.

The arts discussed are painting, sculpture, poetry, and drama. All are mimetic in their content, and what they all represent are bodies in space or events in time. In either case they present those things to the senses; to the eye, as in painting and sculpture and drama, or to the ear, which takes in the recital of poetry as a prelude to the formation of vivid images in the mind's eye.

Normatively, medium determines content in these arts, Lessing holds, because the prime measure of artistic success lies in the power a work has to affect its beholder or audience. Within any particular art, that power will be greater as the artist exploits to the limit the potentialities that are offered by the medium that bounds it. Reflection on fundamental differences between the various mimesis-permitting media shows how wrong it must be to think in the traditional way of painting as a sort of visual poetry or of poetry as a kind of painting for the ear. Horace's dictum *Ut pictura poesis* could not be farther from the truth.

The medium of statuary and painting is a two- or three-dimensional material object, a canvas or a block of stone; in poetry and drama it is the temporally extended reading of a text or the performance of a play. These truths will encourage successful practitioners of the figurative arts to concern themselves with the representation of bodies, and those of the narrative ones with representation of actions, bodies being things that, like the canvas or the block of stone that depict them, exist all at once, while drama and poetry best represent what takes place over time, like the reading of the poem or the performance of the play (1984: ch. 16).

The large normative claim here is reached in two steps. Step one: medium bears on content because what carries the representation, the canvas or stone in the one case, the performance or the reading in the other, either exists entirely at any one moment or else only comes to be complete as it is produced through time from beginning to end. So the beholder takes in all the represented content in the former cases more or less at once as he contemplates the canvas or moves around the statue, whereas audiences only take in a play or a poem bit by bit in the temporally extended process of viewing the performance or reading the work.

Step two: in the figurative arts, the content best fitted to evoke powerful affect is the human body in space; in the narrative arts, it is action that takes place over time. In either case what effect can be achieved depends on the way the spectator or hearer apprehends the content that the works represent. Perception of a statue or a picture of beautiful Helen, say, taken in at one go may make an indelibly vivid impression on us that no poetic description of her could match. Compare that with the image a poem conjures up by means of its temporally extended presentation of the whole. That will inevitably suffer from our reliance on memory of parts that are no longer present by the time the whole is complete. The vivacity of what is then summoned up to the mind's eye is compromised just because in constructing it we draw on something other than what is most immediately present as we read.

By way of contrast, we must presume that any sequence of actions presented in the theater or in an epic may be made increasingly vivid to our imagination as the elements presented at any given moment of apprehension are understood in terms of the remembered past that leads up to them. That is, the represented action has its own vivacity of the moment as we are taken through it scene by scene, which vivacity is itself amplified in consciousness as our memory of the previously presented elements fills out what we encounter at this or that moment of the poem's or the play's development. In terms of the effects they produce, figurative and narrative arts are systematically quite different here. The artist ignores this difference at his peril.

Of course, the nature of the medium does not set the limits of poetry and art utterly inflexibly. A painting or a statue can indeed present an action in progress or a moment of an action, as does the Laocoön group itself; equally, a poem can well enough represent a body, as does Homer in his depiction of Achilles' shield. However, for Lessing these divergences from the norm are achieved indirectly, so that in the former case we see a body as it is at the "pregnant moment" of the action (1984: ch. 19), allowing us to envisage in imagination the stages that led up to that moment and the effects to which it gave rise. Analogously, in the case of Achilles' shield, the poet can describe it piece by piece, but hardly in a way that allows the hearer to build up a picture of the shield that is almost as vivid as that which the artist can present to the eye. What the poet does to avoid the flatness that must threaten is to describe the object in terms of either its effect on others (1984: ch. 18), or else, as in the case of Achilles' shield, the process of making its various panels.

The way in which medium constrains content is thus highly normative. The poem is *most successful* as it takes us through action in time; the painted or sculpted work of art so as it presents a human body to view, and any artist striving for greatness and renown needs to be guided by the differential potentialities of his medium. "What each genre does best, and what no other genre can do as well determines its own essential province" (1962: §77). To convince ourselves of this Lessing holds we need only consider the paradigms of art, the finest works inherited from classical antiquity.

The normative character of the story presumes it settled what the fundamental goal of the various mimetic arts should be, and while Lessing never discusses that issue at length, remarks he makes *en passant* and his own dramas reveal the leading assumptions that guide him. The most important thing he says comes in the course of a seemingly banal reflection about painting. This is that while the painter can represent just about anything, if his work is truly to belong to fine art, it must aim at the production of "agreeable feelings" (*angenehme Empfindungen*) (1984: ch. 24). Such feelings are the natural and proper response to beauty. If this is the model the figurative artist follows, success will be achieved by those beautiful representations of objects that are apt forcefully to produce that response in the beholder's mind.

The questions that then open up are just what forms are beautiful ones, and how they are related to the spectator's all-important agreeable response. Once more Lessing is not very forthcoming. In chapter 20 of *Laocoön* he speaks of beauty as the harmonious balance of the manifold parts of an object that can be taken in by the eye all at once, but that familiar trope is uninformative about the beautiful object itself, and in its allusion to harmony inevitably throws the weight of the idea onto the nature of the response, onto those "agreeable feelings."

Yet, any hasty accusation of banality would be misplaced. To arrive at Lessing's considered view, we must first set aside the too easy assumption that the agreeable feelings on which everything turns are just sentiments or sensations that it is agreeable or pleasant for the subject to entertain. Rather, the requisite feelings or responses are agreeable at large, and agreeable just through being fully suited to their objects, to the mimetic content that the artist offers. The agreeableness in question is thus more answerable to the rightness of the induced emotion in its place than to the way the subject feels himself affected by the represented content.

That this is a thought Lessing would acknowledge and endorse is clear from the *Dramaturgy*'s discussion of tragedy (see §§75–7), which, following Aristotle, Lessing holds to be essentially concerned with the purification (*Reinigung*) or clarification of the spectator's feelings through the arousal of fear and pity. To achieve that at all effectively our imaginative engagement needs to be with the suffering of people not too dissimilar from ourselves. There our emotions are agreeably "purified" by being directed at their truly appropriate and proper objects. And because tragic theater provides its greatest satisfactions through such effects, it is liable to provide a schooling of the emotions and an outlook on the world that Lessing holds to be firmly tied to the formation of dispositions to properly virtuous action in our wider lives (1962: §§75–6).

The fear that is so central to tragedy is the fear that the sort of stress that the dramas' central figures undergo could well befall ourselves, and it is that thought that remains alive when the final curtain comes down in the form of the pity that we carry away with us even as the fear the performance has induced fades. Furthermore, being sympathetic to Aristotle's doctrine of the mean, Lessing likes to think that the agreeable feelings schooled in the theater are liable to be engendered in any spectator who is initially devoid of feeling, as well as tempered in one whose reactions are initially unruly and excessive.

The systematic nature of Lessing's thought is at its sharpest in the way in which he holds the norms that apply to one form of art to be constant across the others, differing only insofar as is demanded by the specific genre and medium in which it represents its objects. Speaking of tragedy, he says: "A tragedy is a poem which arouses pity. By genus, it is the representation of an action; according to its species, one that represents an action worthy of pity. From these two notions all its rules may be completely deduced: they even fix its dramatic form" (1962: §77). In critical mood, one might suspect that there is little here that carries over systematically to figurative art or poetry. However, Lessing is not talking here about drama in general, but about just one of its specific genres. Taking a step back, we have a higher generic classification of dramas as representations of action through acted performance. It takes the species, namely tragedy, to introduce the particular responses of pity, which Lessing insists extends "to all philanthropic feeling," and fear, which covers not just distress before imminent misfortune, but also distressing attitudes to present or past ill, affliction, and grief. Other passions can be refined and clarified elsewhere, since "not all genres can improve everything, at least not as completely as any other."

This suggests that we should expect "agreeable feelings" to be generated not just by other species of drama than tragedy, such as comedy, but also by other sorts of art as well. In respect of sculpture this is just what we do find Lessing saying about the Laocoön group. For the pregnant moment of that episode is represented by the priest fighting off the snakes constricting him and his sons, not shrieking out in agony, but wearing an expression which mingles pain and beauty. That, says Lessing (1984: ch. 6), gives rise to the idea of manly dignity and courageous endurance, clearly attitudes which are based in feeling and which he thinks it proper for us to adopt in the face of extreme adversity. On that score those attitudes will count as relevantly "agreeable," making the group beautiful in its way and an outstanding artistic success.

When Lessing hazards his definition of beauty as pertaining to something that can be surveyed all at once, he says that that is the proper business of painting, so that "it and it alone can represent bodily beauty" (1984: ch. 20). Understandably enough, that has inclined critics to suppose that since Lessing thinks of beauty as what gives rise to mere pleasing sentiment, there is little system in his thought and also that he must hold the artist in far lower esteem than the poet or dramatist. Yet once we understand the "agreeableness of feeling" more generously, the apparent trivialization and denigration of the figurative arts that depends on such a narrow conception of beauty dissolves. Nor does the criticism revive in the face of Lessing saying that the depiction of bodily beauty belongs to painting alone and lies without the poet's range, since we must not overlook the fact that he simply gives a different name to the poet's "transitory beauty," one to which "we wish to return time and again," to wit, "charm" (*Reiz*) (1984: ch. 21). So beauty does have its place in poetry as well as in painting; it is just not the bodily beauty peculiar to the painter that we find there. That being so,

beauty's crucially defining feature will be common to the arts that possess it, namely their liability to arouse agreeable, properly clarified, feeling in their respective audiences. Interestingly, Lessing even allows that in poetry ugliness can agreeably refine our sense of the risible and ludicrous (as does Homer's *Thersites*) or, when it is combined with evil, horror, as does Shakespeare's *Richard III*. Both sorts of case involve attitudinal reactions that the narrative arts are adapted to "purify," clarify, and refine. Beauty then has extensive place at the core of fine narrative as well as fine figurative art. Lessing's claim to be a systematic thinker stands.

See also EIGHTEENTH-CENTURY AESTHETICS; DRAMA; POETRY; SCULPTURE; ARISTOTLE; BEAUTY; CATHARSIS; DEPICTION; GENRE; TRAGEDY.

BIBLIOGRAPHY

Primary sources
[1766] 1984. *Laocoön: An Essay on the Limits of Poetry and Painting*. E. McCormick (trans.). Baltimore: Johns Hopkins University Press.
[1767–9] 1962. *Hamburg Dramaturgy*. H. Zimmern (trans.). New York: Dover

Secondary sources
Allison, H. E. 1966. *Lessing and the Enlightenment*. Ann Arbor: University of Michigan Press.
Lamport, F. J. 1981. *Lessing and the Drama*. Oxford: Clarendon.
Savile, Anthony. 1987. *Aesthetic Reconstructions: The Seminal Writings of Lessing, Kant and Schiller*. Oxford: Blackwell.
Fischer, Barbara & Fox, Thomas C. (eds.). 2005. *A Companion to the Works of Gotthold Ephraim Lessing*. Rochester: Camden House.

ANTHONY SAVILE

Lewis, C(larence) I(rving) (1883–1964)
Although this distinguished Harvard professor is primarily known for his groundbreaking work in modal logic, his rarely cited contributions to aesthetics include an account of aesthetic experience as well as an early articulation of a contextualist position in the ontology of artistic and aesthetic objects. Lewis's discussion of these topics occupies two chapters of his 1946 treatise, *An Analysis of Knowledge and Valuation*.

To understand Lewis's views in aesthetics, one must first grasp some of his positions in the theory of value. Lewis followed W. D. Ross (1930: 130) in espousing an axiological "experientialism": were there no sentience or subjective experience in the universe, value would not exist. Experiences can be instrumentally useful in promoting other ends, but every experience has some positive or negative intrinsic valence: there is no "zero" to be plotted on a linear dimension of value (1946: 402). This valence or "felt quality" of experience is not a matter of a second-order belief to the effect that a given stretch of experience has a particular sort of intrinsic merit or demerit; instead it is a "mode of presentation." "Value–disvalue is that mode or aspect of the given or the contemplated to which desire and aversion are addressed; and it is that by apprehension of which the inclination to action is normally elicited" (1946: 403). Lewis is careful not to equate this claim about the positive or negative immediate valence of all experience with any form of reductive hedonism, according to which pleasure and pain are the only bases of noninstrumental value. An experience can be distressing, challenging, or tense, yet nonetheless carry an overall positive valence, and not only in terms of perceived longer-term payoffs. An experience's immediate, positive valence can, for example, derive from "the sense of integrity in firmly fronting 'the unpleasant' as well as 'pleasure' " (1946: 405). When an experience carries a strong, positive intrinsic valence, the experience is valued for its own sake and the person would not rationally choose to forego it, other things being equal.

Lewis uses the term "inherent value" to refer to an object's capacity to give rise to immediately valenced experiences. The term "inherent" may have led some philosophers to believe that Lewis blurred two different axiological distinctions, namely, the distinction between instrumental and final value, on the one hand, and the distinction between a value based entirely on some item's intrinsic or inherent properties, and a value that emerges or supervenes on a broader, relational basis. For Lewis, to say that something has inherent value is to say that it is prone, when contemplated under the right circumstances, to give rise to experiences that are positively or negatively valenced in a *primarily* (but not exclusively) noninstrumental way. The inherent value is "in" the object, but only

as a capacity to give rise to a certain type of experience when contemplated in the right circumstances and by the right kind of contemplators. Lewis comments that "to say that a value is inherent in an object, is not necessarily to locate this value in the physical properties of it" (1946: 477).

Lewis's remarks on the ontology of the aesthetic object (which he labeled "aesthetic essences") are consonant with this more general point about value. He examines the idea that all objects of aesthetic experience are either physical individuals, abstract entities, or an "ideal" intended by some artist. Deeming these options unsatisfactory, he asserts that although aesthetic experience often involves contemplation of particular artistic artifacts or natural objects or scenes, the aesthetic object is *never* only the physical object. Nor can it be a purely abstract type and still be the object of a genuinely aesthetic experience. Instead, the aesthetic object "is to be located in an associated context of the physically presented thing" (1946: 475).

Lewis traces a spectrum, at one end of which he locates those cases, such as poetry, where "the aesthetic essence" is presented by a physical entity (the spoken or written string of words) yet is clearly not reducible to that particular item because its appreciation requires attention to the context associated with the physical entity that presents the poem – part of that context being the linguistic and other conventions that govern both the creation and interpretation of the work of art. Whatever the subject must bring to the presentation in order to understand the poem correctly belongs to the poem, and anyone who fails to take this "associated context" into account fails to apprehend the object's actual aesthetic character. At the other end of Lewis's spectrum are natural objects the aesthetic appreciation of which is more a matter of the contemplation of the object's purely physical properties, and less a matter of their contextualization by the observer. Yet Lewis asserts that "there is no physical object the esthetic evaluation of which is altogether independent of its relations to some context," if only because the qualitative essence which is incorporated in the object is "theoretically repeatable in some other physical object" (1946: 477). Lewis considers that the theoretical possibility of *indistinguishable objects* cannot be squared with the idea that the object of aesthetic value could be a particular physical object. The object is instead a physical thing that serves to present the aesthetic essence, as contextualized in a manner which is neither arbitrary nor subjective.

Lewis suggests that as a result of the intrinsic valence of experience there is a broad sense in which all experiences or "direct apprehensions" are aesthetic. Yet he goes on to delineate a more limited concept of aesthetic experience corresponding to the appreciation of art, nature, and aspects of everyday life. He prefaces his attempt to elucidate this narrower concept of aesthetic experience with some reflections concerning the status and purpose of such an elucidation. He begins by underscoring his recognition of the multifarious nature of usage of "aesthetic" and related terms. The task of the elucidation cannot plausibly be described as that of providing a philosophically precise identification of "the" concept of aesthetic experience that lies latent in current usage. As several different coherent elucidations are possible, the key question is what grounds could motivate the selection of any one of them. Lewis was enough of a student of John Dewey to believe that classifications and reasoning are motivated by practical interests as well as purely epistemic grounds. In the case of "the aesthetic," Lewis adverts to the idea that universal or near-universal human interests are the final court of appeal. His point is that all people tend to have an interest in knowing what kinds of experiences are and are not intrinsically worth having, and the concept of aesthetic experience that he seeks to identify responds to and serves that interest.

Lewis's distinction between aesthetic experience in the broad and narrow senses is based on several logically distinct conditions. He states that in the narrow sense, aesthetic experience must carry an intrinsic, *positive* valence. Lewis does not require that to be aesthetic, an experience must involve *only* this kind of positive valuation, as in the angelic idea that the aesthetic attitude requires the adoption of a "purely disinterested" relation to some object. For Lewis, an experience's intrinsic quality is also commonly accompanied by various instrumental valuations and means–end calculations,

which are in turn connected to beliefs about the final ends to be served by various actions. He does, however, require that the intrinsic value be "predominant" in relation to instrumental assessments. He also requires that the positive valence must be possessed to a "high degree": there are no negative, or even mildly positive, aesthetic experiences.

Another condition involves the necessity of what Lewis somewhat misleadingly labels "the esthetic attitude." Lewis does not mean by this that the subject must *voluntarily* adopt a special attitude or stance, and he explicitly criticizes the thought that "deliberateness of attention" is characteristic of "the more truly esthetic attitude" (1946: 384). What Lewis does require is that the subject be absorbed in the content of the experience. The subject must be attentive to the object and must not be distracted from its contemplation by thoughts about what it can later be used for (1946: 456). Lewis does not expand on what he means by "contemplation," but it may be surmised that in using the word to evoke a fully attentive and active condition, he drew upon the one source he explicitly cites in his two chapters on aesthetics, namely, D. W. Prall's *Aesthetic Analysis* of 1936.

Lewis goes on to sketch additional constraints on the kinds of contemplative, positively valenced experience that should bear the name "aesthetic" given his reconstruction of the concept. More specifically, Lewis believes that any possessive or contemplative attitudes vitiate the experience and prevent it from being aesthetic. The consumer who relishes acquisition or ownership may be contemplating the acquired object and thereby having a positively valenced experience, but this is not, according to Lewis, an aesthetic experience (in his narrow sense). Lewis does not give much of a justification for this claim, and one may be led to wonder whether it does not lead him in the direction of a content-based conception, the thought being that the reason why possessive attitudes are inappropriate is that they lead the contemplator's attention away from those properties of the object that deserve to be identified as its specifically aesthetic qualities. Yet Lewis does not develop an independent, nonaxiological account of the distinction between aesthetic and nonaesthetic qualities. A possible justification for what

Lewis calls the "moralistic" conditions on aesthetic experience might be found in his emphasis on the universality of the interests to be served by the concept, the thought being that the contemplation of possessive or competitive relations does not correspond to such an interest.

Gathering these points, we can say that for Lewis, an experience is aesthetic just in case it has a strongly positive intrinsic value that is preponderant in relation to whatever instrumental value the experience may also have; the experience must correspond to the distinctive character of some external object and be indicative of that object's reliable and distinctive power to occasion strong, positive intrinsic valuation; furthermore, it must involve an absorbed and active contemplation of the object and cannot be a matter of a competitive or possessive attitude.

Critical discussion of Lewis's work on aesthetics has largely focused on the problem of justifying aesthetic judgments (e.g., Garvin 1949; Stolnitz 1960), a principal worry being that Lewis does not tell us under what conditions valenced experiences of an object are or are not indicative of its inherent value. It is far from obvious, however, that this epistemological problem has disastrous implications for all of Lewis's arguments, or for a neo-Lewisian account of aesthetic experience (Livingston 2004, 2006). Although Lewis's discussions of aesthetic experience and the ontology of art have been mentioned briefly in passing by such figures as Monroe C. Beardsley, Richard Wollheim, and Francis Sparshott, his contributions to the field, and in particular his precocious contextualism, merit broader recognition and renewed consideration.

See also AESTHETIC ATTITUDE; AESTHETIC PLEASURE; AESTHETIC PROPERTIES; ONTOLOGICAL CONTEXTUALISM.

BIBLIOGRAPHY

Primary sources
1946. An Analysis of Knowledge and Valuation. La Salle: Open Court.
1969. Values and Imperatives: Studies in Ethics. J. Lange (ed.). Stanford: Stanford University Press.
1970. Collected Papers of Clarence Irving Lewis. J. Goheen & J. Mothershead Jr. (eds.). Stanford: Stanford University Press.

Secondary sources
Garvin, Lucius. 1949. "Relativism in Professor Lewis's Theory of Esthetic Value," Journal of Philosophy, 46, 169–76.
Livingston, Paisley. 2004. "C. I. Lewis and the Outlines of Aesthetic Experience," British Journal of Aesthetics, 44, 378–92.
Livingston, Paisley. 2006. "Utile et dulce: A Response to Noël Carroll," British Journal of Aesthetics, 46, 274–81.
Prall, D. W. 1936. Aesthetic Analysis. New York: Thomas Y. Cromwell.
Ross, W. D. 1930. The Right and the Good. Oxford: Clarendon.
Schilpp, Paul Arthur. (ed.). 1968. The Philosophy of C. I. Lewis. La Salle: Open Court.
Stolnitz, Jerome. 1960. "On Objective Relativism in Aesthetics," Journal of Philosophy, 57, 261–76.

PAISLEY LIVINGSTON

Lukács, Georg [György Szegedy von Lukács] (1885–1971) Hungarian Marxist philosopher and literary critic; a member of Nagy's shortlived government in 1956. His work on aesthetics includes theory and its application in a wide range of literary studies. His career and his study of aesthetics falls into two main parts: his pre-Marxist period extending until the end of World War I, and that following his conversion to Marxism. His interest in aesthetics is a main factor connecting his pre-Marxist and his Marxist writings. When he converted to Marxism, he had already written two books on aesthetics. Marx and Engels provided hints, but did not develop a systematic theory of the subject. Lukács's claim that his own contribution is the first attempt to work out a Marxist aesthetic theory in systematic form has gained acceptance.

His brilliant early Marxist work, History and Class Consciousness (1923), has profoundly influenced the Marxist discussion but has had little impact on non-Marxist philosophy. His contribution to aesthetic theory may ultimately turn out to be his most important contribution to philosophy in general. Although his views on aesthetics have attracted more attention than other aspects of his position, they have not been discussed as often as their intrinsic importance seems to merit. With some exceptions, studies of his aesthetic ideas seem mainly to be confined to his later Marxist position, with little attention to his pre-Marxist writings.

His views on aesthetics cannot be understood without reference to his cultural background. Lukács, who spoke German at home – his mother was Austrian – grew up bilingual. Although widely read, with the exception of the Marxist classics he rarely refers to writers outside the German cultural sphere, and then usually in a disparaging manner. Before he began to work out his theory of aesthetics, he had already acquired extensive experience in literary criticism and a solid literary background. Lukács regarded his work in aesthetics as his main theme. But it is clear that his early views on the subject underwent a transformation in the course of his long career. During his period in Heidelberg before World War I, he was already interested in Hegel's position. This interest only deepened in later years. But his early work on aesthetics was strongly Kantian and Neo-Kantian, with particular attention to the views of Emil Lask. In his later, Marxist, writing, Lukács was reacting, as he was aware, against his own earlier views. His later understanding of aesthetics, like his Marxist position in general, is marked by flashes of insight, but also by great intellectual rigidity. Lukács is never an indifferent writer, even in his most dogmatic moments. Yet it is often the case that his insights need to be sought out and separated from the rigid Marxist framework in which they are housed.

It would be a mistake to see Lukács's profession of Marxist faith as marking a radical break in his thought, for it exhibits rather greater continuity than is often realized. He stresses that in his initial work as a literary critic and essay writer he sought to base himself on Kant's and then later on Hegel's aesthetics. The failure of his early work in aesthetics, begun in the winter of 1911–12, was followed by his book, *The Theory of the Novel*, which already showed a turning toward problems of the nature and interpretation of history, with respect to which the specifically aesthetic questions are merely symptomatic. Further attention to ethics, history, and economics was followed by his conversion to Marxism and a period of political activity. His renewed attention to aesthetic questions around 1930, after he withdrew from overt political activity, led to the systematic aesthetics that arose as the natural consequence of a lengthy concern and, in this way, from a somewhat different perspective, completed the realization of his youthful dream.

The manuscripts of Lukács's pre-Marxist writings on aesthetics were lost for more than 50 years. They started to reemerge in the 1960s, and have been published as two separate works, representing successive versions of his pre-Marxist aesthetic theory: *The Heidelberg Philosophy of Art* and *The Heidelberg Aesthetics*. Both texts are strongly Kantian in flavor, and both begin with the Kantian question: "Works of art exist – how are they possible?"

Although in some ways similar, these two aesthetics are also very different. One observer has described the difference as that between a synthesis of life philosophy (*Lebensphilosophie*) and Kantianism on the one hand, and an extremely dualistic form of Kantianism on the other. The former work seems almost unrelated to Hegelian influence, and Hegel is never named in it. In the latter, Hegel is an important presence, although the influence of the Heidelberg Neo-Kantian Emil Lask, whom Lukács knew and thought well of, is even more significant. Yet there is a Hegelian aspect even in the first text, since he states here the importance of the conception of the aesthetic object as a concrete totality (alluding to the central Hegelian category), and in the second text he insists on the Hegelian view of spirit as a concretely developing totality.

The first book is based on an insight of Lukács's friend Leo Popper concerning the transcendent character of the work of art that cannot be reduced to any experience of it, and the spectator's or receiver's view of it. The work of art is, then, located in a sphere beyond the world of everyday experience within which it is manifested. In this study Lukács develops the twofold relation between the creator and the receiver to the work of art. In his phenomenological sketch of the creative and receptive aspects, he draws a quasi-Kantian distinction between phenomenological experience and imaginative reconstruction. In his analysis of the historicity and timelessness of the work of art, he follows Lask's view of the timeless validity (*Geltung*) of value, which he here applies to the problem of aesthetics. Aesthetic perception, according to Lukács, is the timeless relation to value.

The second study is a wholly new attempt to work out his own theory. It begins with the injunction to analyze the transcendental philosophical significance, objective structure, and value of the sensory form of the aesthetic object – what Last describes as the logically naked givenness of its aesthetic character. The art object is here understood as a complex form whose autonomous value requires elucidation. In the discussion of the subject–object relation in aesthetics, Lukács considers the irreducible distance between subject and object, whose absolute value is essentially grasped as a transcendental ought and endless task for the subject. Turning finally to the idea of beauty, he provides an ideal-typical analysis of beauty posited as absolute. Then follows a discussion of the speculative conception of the development of the idea of beauty, with special attention to Hegel, as well as to Kant and to Goethe. There is no discussion of the so-called substantial-ethical idea.

The third, specifically Marxist, aesthetics, the massive work known as *The Specific Nature of the Aesthetic*, is often regarded as Lukács's most nearly finished work – in effect, his masterpiece. Its Marxist perspective differentiates it from his pre-Marxist aesthetic writings. Influenced by Neo-Kantianism, life philosophy, Kierkegaard, Dostoevsky, and many others including Hegel, Lukács became resolutely Marxist. He made important contributions to Marxist theory and defended the idea of an independent Marxist aesthetics, which he began to work out in a systematic form. Yet there is an obvious continuity between his pre-Marxist and Marxist aesthetic positions. In his earlier writings, Lukács took a determinedly dualist line in his emphasis on the independence of form. In his Marxist works, he held that form was determined by content. His Marxist approach to aesthetics resolves the dualism of his Heidelberg period, which had opposed the work of art as transcendent and artistic experience as immanent.

In general terms, Lukács's Marxist aesthetics is strongly Hegelian. Like Hegel, he is concerned with aesthetics as a form of knowledge, and regards it as concerned with a specific type of activity arising out of ordinary life (*Alltagssein*). Again following Hegel, he understands the specifically aesthetic as constituting an ever more concrete objective totality through a process of gradual development.

Lukács departs from Hegel in his adoption of a version of the reflection theory of knowledge (*Widerspiegelungstheorie*) developed by Engels and Lenin. It is fair to regard his Marxist aesthetics as a persistent effort to apply the official Marxist materialist theory of reflection to aesthetic objects. His aesthetic theory is realistic, since the problem is less that of beauty than of objective knowledge. He regards mimesis, or imitation, as a mere species of reflection. The work of art forms a structured unity spanning concrete contradictions. The greater its span, the better the work. A successful work of art is said to be a microcosm that reflects or evokes the social context out of which it arises, including intentions, ethical life, good and evil. Art has a specifically human meaning, since it functions as the human memory, so to speak.

The key category of Lukács's Marxist aesthetics, particularity (*Besonderheit*) (1987: ii.180), is borrowed from Goethe and interpreted from a Hegelian perspective. Hegel discusses particularity as the mediating factor between universality and individuality, as the reality of the individual. For Lukács, drawing on his earlier concern with this category, particularity is best adapted to the essential structure of aesthetics. In his view, the world of art is the world of human being, and through particularity one can grasp the objective unity of the subjective and the objective elements in the artwork.

See also HEGEL; KANT; MARXISM AND ART.

BIBLIOGRAPHY

Primary sources
[1912–14] 1974. *Heidelberger Philosophie der Kunst.* G. Markus & F. Benseler (eds.). Darmstadt: Luchterhand.
[1916–18] 1974. *Heidelberger Ästhetik.* G. Markus & F. Benseler (eds.). Darmstadt: Luchterhand.
[1920] 1971. *Theory of the Novel.* A. Bostock (trans.). Cambridge, MA: MIT Press.
[1923] 1971. *History and Class Consciousness.* R. Livingstone (trans.). London: Merlin.
1987. *Die Eigenart des Ästhetischen.* 2 vols. Berlin: Aufbau.

Secondary sources
Jung, Werner. 1989. *Georg Lukács.* Stuttgart: Metzler.
Királyfalvi, Béla. 1975. *The Aesthetics of Gyorgy Lukács.* Princeton: Princeton University Press.

TOM ROCKMORE

M

Margolis, Joseph (b.1924)   American philosopher who has written extensively on the philosophy of mind, metaphysics, epistemology, and philosophy of language, as well as making significant contributions in aesthetics. His extra-aesthetics writings are closely integrated with his major themes in the philosophy of art, and help ground them. Though there is hardly an important topic in aesthetics that Margolis has not touched on (from the definition of art to the question of metaphor, to the "autographic" identity of dance, to the nature of pictorial representation), and though his thought has continuously evolved not only in terms of particular issues but also in terms of general philosophical approach (from mainstream analytic philosophy to a new pragmatism which attempts to blend the analytic and post-Hegelian Continental traditions), his philosophy of art is perhaps best represented by three main themes.

The first is works of art as physically embodied and culturally emergent entities. This ontological position aims to find a middle ground between idealist theories of the artwork (Crocean, phenomenological, and so on) and the opposite extreme of a reductive materialist nominalism, where artworks are simply identified with the physical objects (the material tokens) through which they are manifested. Margolis's position, which is an analogue of his (Strawsonian) account of persons as irreducibly complex individuals bearing two different (though structurally related) categories of predicates rather than as compound entities of body and mind, is that artworks are similarly irreducibly complex. They are and must be embodied in the spatiotemporal world in order for them to serve their aesthetic functions and to allow for stable reidentification for art criticism, but their identity or constitutive properties transcend their physical make-up. These properties, largely those of meaning, emerge through the work's situation and role in a matrix of cultural practice, in the world of human culture and history. This, in turn, leads Margolis back to general ontological concerns about the metaphysics of culture and history, and their relation to the natural world (which he treats in his trilogy, *The Persistence of Reality*).

Recognition of the cultural constitution of art also supports the second dominant theme of Margolis's aesthetics: relativism. This theme has always been central to his philosophy, even before his theory of culture emergence. But it is deeply reinforced by it. For, given the variety and change of cultures – or of change historically within a culture – if the work's meaning is culturally constituted and if the culture allows for various ways of constituting or appropriating artworks – authorially or nonauthorially directed, Christian, Marxist, Freudian, and so on – relativism of some sort seems hard to avoid. Margolis (1980) has labored to articulate a "robust relativism" that avoids the charges of logical inconsistency and "anything goes" subjectivism that are usually advanced against relativism. Though he eschews foundationalist ideas of transparency and cognitive privilege, he recognizes that our account of an artwork is always somehow constrained by relevant realities, and that some accounts are therefore better, more plausible, and more justifiable than others. For a time he located some of these constraints in a fixed, determinate core of descriptive properties of the work on which interpretations and evaluations had to be based, but during the 1980s he abandoned this idea through increasing emphasis on the role of interpretation (Margolis 1989b), for the distinction between what is a descriptive fact about an artwork and an interpretation of it is often itself a matter of interpretation.

Margolis's third theme of interpretation, long central to his aesthetics of relativism, latterly has been developed in wider ways which dovetail with his metaphysics of culture (including the ontology of artworks) and which reflect his shift away from traditional analytic philosophy and aesthetics. This shift involves "hermeneuticizing" naturalism, recognizing that interpretation not only functions to explain or elucidate the entities or texts that we encounter but that it is already actively involved in constituting those entities as entities for interpretation. In other words, the cultural world – that is, not merely the artworld but the human *Lebenswelt* – is one whose objects are constructed through interpretative efforts, which means through language, and thus its objects are better understood as texts rather than as "objects" in the traditional naturalistic sense. Margolis's most recent work focuses on the relations between constitutive and explanatory interpretation.

See also HERMENEUTICS; INTERPRETATION; MEANING CONSTRUCTIVISM; ONTOLOGICAL CONTEXTUALISM; RELATIVISM; TEXT.

BIBLIOGRAPHY

Primary sources
1965. *The Language of Art and Art Criticism*. Detroit: Wayne State University Press.
1978. *Persons and Minds*. Dordrecht: Reidel.
1980. *Art and Philosophy*. Atlantic Highlands: Humanities Press.
1983. *Culture and Cultural Entities*. Dordrecht: Reidel.
1986, 1987, 1989a. *The Persistence of Reality*. 3 vols. Oxford: Blackwell.
1989b. "Reinterpreting Interpretation," *Journal of Aesthetics and Art Criticism*, 47, 237–51.
1995. *Interpretation Radical but Not Unruly*. Berkeley: University of California Press.
1999. *What, After All, Is a Work of Art?* University Park: Pennsylvania State University Press.

RICHARD SHUSTERMAN

Marxism and art   Marxism has proved very fertile in the areas of aesthetic and literary criticism, though less so in the actual production of works of art in virtue of certain limitations associated with the rigid application of the Marxist point of view. The Marxist view of art follows from the Marxist theory of the relation of superstructure and base. In general terms, the basic principle is that art, like all higher activities, belongs to the cultural superstructure and is determined by sociohistorical conditions, in particular economic ones. It is argued that a connection can always and must be traced between a work of art and its sociohistorical matrix, since art is in some sense a reflection of social reality.

Marxist writers on aesthetics, particularly Georg Lukács, have gone to some lengths to construct a Marxist aesthetics on the basis of hints contained in the writings of Marx (1818–83) and Engels (1820–95). The list of Marxist and non-Marxist writers influenced by the Marxist approach to art in general is long and distinguished, including, apart from Lukács, Edmund Wilson, Peter Demetz, Theodor Adorno, Frederic Jameson, Ernst Bloch, Lucien Goldmann, Hans Mayer, Bertolt Brecht, Maurice Merleau-Ponty, and Christopher Caudwell. There are a number of different, even incompatible, views of Marxist aesthetics, all of which claim to find support in the classical Marxist texts, above all in the writings of Marx and Engels.

The official Marxist insistence on social realism, prominent in Lukács's writings, has no clear anticipation in Marx's position but is based squarely on certain indications in the later Engels. The positions of Marx and Engels are demonstrably different (although this difference is not often observed by commentators). For political reasons, it was routinely denied by official Marxism for decades. The usual tendency to conflate the views of Marx and Engels is present as well in the Marxist approach to art. Although their writings have been seen as providing the basic principles of a Marxist theory of art and aesthetics, the precise relation of the resultant theory to the views of the founders is controversial.

Both Marx and Engels had early literary ambitions that largely evaporated when, still young and unknown left-wing radicals, they became acquainted in the early 1840s. Both retained a lifelong interest in literature, although their backgrounds and literary tastes differed widely. In the field of literature as elsewhere, Engels was largely self-taught. As a young man, he wrote poetry and literary criticism. He also translated Thomas Carlyle. Engels's literary taste was formed by nineteenth-century Romanticism, and included an appreciation of nationalist German poetry.

Marx had an excellent education in classical languages in the German high school (*Gymnasium*), which influenced his later appreciation of art and literature. His literary tastes remained within the framework of eighteenth-century classicism. He shared the widespread German intellectual grecophilia, illustrated by Winckelmann, Goethe, and Hegel. His favorite authors were Aeschylus, Shakespeare, and Goethe. When he began his university studies in Bonn, Marx spent most of his time studying Greek art and mythology as well as writing poetry. He also attempted a novel (uncompleted) and wrote the draft of a tragedy. After 1837 he did not return to the study of aesthetics, although there is an aesthetic cast to some of his writings, and on occasion he concerned himself with specific aesthetic questions.

An important example of the aesthetic bent to Marx's thought is his conception of human being. In the *Paris Manuscripts* (1844), he argues that alienation is the result of the institution of private property, characteristic of capitalism. As a result of the transition to communism, in which private property is abolished, Marx foresees the opportunity for what might be called the full development or fulfillment of human being. In the third of the *Paris Manuscripts*, full human development is described as the full development of the various senses. It is characterized from a slightly different perspective in *The German Ideology* (1845–6) – in a famous passage often criticized for its romantic idealism – as the real possibility, following on from the abolition of the division of labor that prevails in capitalism, for each person to perform a full variety of tasks. The aesthetic view of human being as self-realizing in its free activity is indebted to Schiller's idea of the aesthetic as the basic harmonizing element of human life.

The fragmentary nature of Marx's comments on aesthetic themes does not represent a mature aesthetic theory. In his writings, the most considered passage on aesthetic themes occurs in the introduction to the *Grundrisse* ("Rough Draft") (1857–8). Here he advances the idea of the uneven development of material production in relation to artistic development.

He refers to the well-known fact that artistic flowering is on occasion unrelated to the general development of society, to its material foundation. He maintains that Greek art specifically presupposes Greek mythology. The problem, as he remarks, is not that Greek artistic production is bound up with a certain social stage, but, rather, that Greek art has a universal value unrelated to its material conditions.

Here, Marx is more faithful to his aesthetic judgment than to his theoretical commitment. The result is a clear contradiction between his artistic sensitivity, honed by his classical education, and the theory he recommends. His evident appreciation of the permanent value of Greek art clearly contradicts his effort, in this and other texts, to comprehend all forms of culture as a function of the underlying economic organization of society.

The difference in literary background and taste is evident in the different reactions of Marx and Engels to specific literary works, particularly the Greek classics. Whereas Marx was deeply interested in the artistic merits of Greek literature, Engels more than once treated the world classics merely as illustrations of basic economic principles – for instance, he once remarked that Homer's *Iliad* represents the highest point of Greek barbarism.

Nonetheless, Marx and Engels share a broad perspective. The common element that subtends their rather different approaches is their basic commitment to a contextualist approach to aesthetics. In aesthetics, contextualism of all kinds differs from isolationism in insisting on the importance of context to comprehend the work of art. Hegel is a contextualist in virtue of his insistence on the inseparability of the result from the process leading up to it. Typically, he is concerned with art less as a form of beauty than as offering a particular access to truth. In Marxism, art is typically held to offer insight into the nature of the society in which it emerges.

The central shared insight, that takes many different forms even in the works of Marx and Engels, is the approach to art and other forms of culture as a function of an underlying economic dimension of society. This is the famous relation of superstructure to base, or the effort to comprehend all spiritual or mental phenomena – everything that for Hegel would fall under the heading of spirit (*Geist*) – as directly or indirectly a function of material relations. In this approach, the meaning of the term "material" is left undefined. Although Marxism is widely identified with historical materialism and even dialectical materialism, Marx's own position, unlike Marxism, is independent of any particular view of matter. Yet it is clear that Marx and Marxism share the idea that all cultural phenomena can be regarded against the background of the form of society in which they arise.

The central view that matter determines spirit, including art, underlies the specifically Marxist approach to aesthetics. It is possible to distinguish stages in the development of the superstructure–base relation. In *The German Ideology*, in opposition to the usual view of German philosophy, Marx and Engels assert:

> The production of ideas, of conceptions, of consciousness, is at first directly interwoven with the material activity and the material mental intercourse of men, the language of real life. Conceiving, thinking, the mental intercourse of men, appear at this stage as the direct efflux of their material behaviour. The same applies to mental production as expressed in the language of politics, laws, morality, religion, metaphysics, etc. of a people. (1970: 47)

A different form of this view is provided in the famous preface to *A Contribution to the Critique of Political Economy* (1859). In an influential passage, Marx writes:

> In the social production of their life, men enter into definite relations that are indispensable and independent of their will, relations of production which correspond to a definite stage of development of their material productive forces. The sum total of these relations of production constitutes the economic structure of society, the real foundation, on which rises a legal and political superstructure and to which correspond definite forms of social consciousness. The mode of production of material life conditions the social, political and intellectual life process in general. It is not the consciousness of men that determines their being, but, on the contrary, their social being that determines their consciousness. (Tucker 1978: 4)

Instead of the more indeterminate relation, Marx here substitutes a causal determinism of the form of society on the cultural phenomena, including aesthetic phenomena, that occur within it.

With respect to the precise understanding of the relation of superstructure and base, the inconsistency of Marx's texts no doubt reflects his inability to resolve the problem in his own mind. It is notable that in a number of letters written after Marx's death, toward the end of his own life, Engels took a somewhat softer, interactionist line. Examples include the letter to J. Bloch (September 21, 1890) in which Engels asserted that "according to the materialist conception of history the determining element in history is *ultimately* the production and reproduction in real life," as well as the letter to H. Starkenburg (January 25, 1894) in which, in a passage that weakens the concept of economic determination beyond all intelligibility, Engels writes: "The further the particular sphere which we are investigating is removed from the economic sphere and approaches that of pure ideology, the more shall we find it exhibiting accidents in its development, the more will its curve run in a zig-zag" (Marx & Engels 1942: 475–518).

The view of aesthetics, as well as all other cultural phenomena, as deriving from – in effect, as produced by – the economic structure of society is independent of the realist cast of most Marxist aesthetics. Marx's position is often regarded as realist, but there is absolutely nothing in his writings to indicate a view of aesthetic realism. On the other hand, this doctrine finds support in the later Engels, in the period following Marx's death. In letters to two aspiring novelists, Minna Kautsky and Margret Harkness, Engels made clear his rejection of so-called tendency literature, which directly espoused the "correct" political message, in favor of a realist approach from which the "correct" perspective could emerge. In his objection to Harkness, who regarded her novel as realist, Engels maintained that it was not realist enough. Realism, he argued, requires the faithful reproduction of detail as well as truthful representation of typical characters under typical circumstances.

Several examples will serve to illustrate the range of Marxist aesthetic theory. Before the Russian Revolution, Plekhanov, Lenin's teacher, attacked doctrines of art for art's sake and the separation of the artist, in either theory or practice, from society in *Art and Social Life* (1912). After the revolution, there was a debate between Marxists and formalists. Trotsky argued in *Literature and Revolution* (1924) that art has its own peculiar laws and cannot be reduced to economic motifs. In line with his doctrine of "partyness" (*partiinost*), Lenin maintained that the writer should put art at the service of the party. At the First All-Union Congress of Soviet Writers in 1934, the party established control over the topic in adopting the view expressed by Engels in his letter to Margret Harkness. According to this view, in order to forward the revolutionary developments himself, the artist is to reveal the moving social forces and portray his or her characters as expressions of these forces.

In the twentieth century, Marxist aesthetics has developed in a series of different directions. One theme is the contemporary viability of the concept of realism that led to an important debate between Lukács, who represents the classical nineteenth-century literary perspective, and Brecht, who argues that this perspective is no longer appropriate for twentieth-century audiences. A second view is the theory of art as ideology, now prominently represented by Terry Eagleton (1990). A third topic is the link of aesthetics and politics that is developed, for instance, in Marcuse's (1978) view of aesthetics as pointing toward a better world. Fourth, there is the effort to relate forms of art to forms of society, as in Caudwell's (1937) discussion of poetry. A fifth theme is the notion of aesthetic value. Lukács (1964), for example, insists on realism, as exemplified by Balzac, since great literature is said to penetrate beneath the surface to reveal social reality, with all its contradictions. Conversely, the same author dismisses the importance of such writers as Beckett and Kafka as mere reflections of a decadent capitalist society. Although Marxist aesthetics has traditionally been one of the most viable branches of Marxist theory, it remains to be seen if it will maintain its vigor after the political collapse of official Marxism in eastern Europe.

See also ADORNO; AESTHETICISM; LUKÁCS; REALISM.

BIBLIOGRAPHY

Caudwell, Christopher. 1937. *Illusion and Reality: A Study of the Sources of Poetry*. London: Macmillan.
Eagleton, Terry. 1990. *The Ideology of the Aesthetic*. Oxford: Blackwell.
Lukács, Georg. 1964. *Studies in European Realism*. E. Bone (trans.). New York: Grosset & Dunlap.
Marcuse, Herbert. 1978. *The Aesthetic Dimension: Towards a Critique of Marxist Aesthetics*. Boston: Beacon.
Marx, Karl. 1973 [1857–8]. *Grundrisse*. M. Nicolaus (trans.). Harmondsworth: Penguin.
Marx, Karl & Engels, Friedrich. 1942. *Selected Correspondence*. D. Torr (trans.). New York: International Publishers.
Marx, Karl & Engels, Friedrich. 1970 [1845–6]. *The German Ideology*, pt. 1. C. J. Arthur (ed.). New York: International Publishers.
Tucker, R. C. (ed.). 1978. *The Marx–Engels Reader*. New York: Norton.

TOM ROCKMORE

mass art is art that is mass produced, typically by an automated technology, for mass consumption. The category of mass art includes motion pictures, television, radio dramas, photography, music (recorded and broadcast), bestselling novels, comics, fiction magazines, and so forth. Mass artworks are such that they can be tokened in multiple instances. The last installment of the Harry Potter series, for example, sold literally millions of copies.

Although there are examples of certain ancient, mass-produced artifacts with some claim to the status of art – such as coins, tiles, and engravings – prototypical mass art really only comes to the fore and emerges with mass industrial society. Indeed, one might think of it, first and foremost, as art for the teeming populations of urban, industrial centers. Pulp fiction is an early example of mass art. Printed on cheap pulp paper – from which the category derives its name – items like Harry Enton's *Frank Reade and His Steam Man of the Plains* (1878) were affordable by city workers who consumed this and other pulp fictions in great quantities. Likewise, in time, photographs, motion pictures, radio, vinyl recordings, and so on were added to the list of affordable, mass-produced art, or, as some might prefer to call it, entertainment.

Since it is mass produced, mass art needs a mass audience. Initially it was aimed at a working class audience, although by now it is consumed by virtually everyone across class lines in modern, industrialized societies. Perhaps in large measure because of this association with the lower classes, for much of its history, mass art has been disparaged by the proponents of elite art, including philosophers of art who have, for the most part, either ignored mass art altogether, or even argued that it is not art, properly so called, at all. So one task for a philosophy of mass art is to address the reasons previous philosophers have invoked to cashier mass art from the order of art. However, before that can be done, we need an account of what it is to be a mass artwork.

DEFINING MASS ART

Mass art is designed and produced for large audiences, usually by automated, industrial procedures, such as printing, which gave rise to one of the first mass art forms, the novel. Mass artworks are such that they can be consumed at two or more – often many more – reception sites simultaneously. The movie *Jumper* opened in 3,428 theaters in the United States alone. For our purposes, each copy of a mass-market novel can be considered a reception site, as is your television set, your radio, your iPod, and so forth. Mass artworks, like TV programs such as *Lost*, can be seen by millions of people in different cities, countries, and continents at the same time, in contrast to live theatrical performances, which can be played only before one audience, at one place, at one time. A similar contrast can be drawn between a live concert and a mass-produced CD and a handmade painting versus a photograph.

Mass art can be consumed at multiple reception sites because mass art is art that can be instantiated in multiple tokens or instances. These instances are produced and/or distributed to often far-flung audiences by means of mass production technologies. In capitalist countries, this is done for profit, but noncapitalist regimes may also take an interest in the production and distribution of mass art, frequently as a means for disseminating ideology.

So far, then, we see that something is a mass artwork only if (1) it is an artwork, (2) of the multiple-instance variety, that is, (3) produced and/or distributed by a mass production technology. However, although these represent necessary conditions for membership in the category of mass artwork, they are not conjointly sufficient. They are not sufficient because there can be avant-garde artworks, such as experimental films, that meet these three criteria, but which no one would count as examples of mass art. Andy Warhol's *Empire* and Stan Brakhage's *Scenes from under Childhood* are artworks of which there can be multiple copies and they were produced and distributed by the same network of mass production technologies as were *Casablanca* and *The Bandwagon*, but no one imagines them to be mass art.

Why not? Because mass art is intended for mass consumption. That is not to say that all mass art is massively consumed. Most mass-market music, for example, flops. Nevertheless, mass art aspires to command a mass audience. Mass art is a subcategory of popular art, its differentiating mark being that it is mass produced whereas popular art, as such, need not be multiple-instance art. On the other hand, neither *Empire* nor *Scenes from under Childhood* was designed to attract mass audiences.

Undoubtedly, Warhol and Brakhage would have been very happy had their films broken box office records. But they did not do what one needs to do in order to assure that outcome. They did not make films that were accessible to broad audiences with diverse backgrounds. Warhol and Brakhage made work that was accessible primarily for the narrow band of people who had knowledge of the issues and strategies of the avant-garde cinema, as well as a feeling, an appetite, and an appreciation for it.

Avant-garde art is esoteric; mass art is exoteric. Mass art is designed to engage mass audiences. In order to secure a mass audience, the mass artwork has to be comprehensible to the average man or woman on the street. To this end, it trades in widely shared stereotypes and narrative and pictorial structures that are easily mastered by nearly anyone. Mass art, in contrast to avant-garde art, is prototypically designed with the intention that it be very user-friendly. Ideally, the mass artwork is structured in such a way that large numbers of people will be able to understand it effortlessly, virtually on first contact. Avant-garde art – including that which is multiply tokenable due to its provenance in mass production technologies – is typically made to be difficult, to defy, to rebuff, and even to outrage the plain viewer, reader, and/or listener.

With this contrast with technologically based, avant-garde art in mind, we are now in a position to say that something is a mass artwork if and only if it is (1) an artwork of (2) the multiple-instance variety, that (3) is produced and/or distributed by a mass production technology, and (4) which artwork is intentionally designed to gravitate in its creative choices (e.g., its narrative forms, symbolism, sonic structures, intended affect, and/or even its content) toward those choices that promise accessibility with minimum effort, virtually on first contact, for the largest numbers of relatively untutored or plain viewers, listeners, and/or readers.

However, if it is the accessibility condition that enables us to zero in on the concept of mass art, it is also this very condition that has prompted some philosophers to deny categorically that mass art can be genuine art, properly so called.

CAN MASS ART REALLY BE ART?

Putatively what makes a recording of the musical *South Pacific* a token of a mass artwork in contrast to a recording of Schoenberg's *Moses and Aaron* is that the former but not the latter is accessible to the plain listener, untutored in modernist music. In order to be extensively accessible, the mass artwork exploits stereotypes, formulas, simple contrasts (e.g., stark oppositions of good and evil), highly legible harmonic patterns, and so forth. Features like these make the mass artwork easy for the untutored viewer, listener, or reader to negotiate. But philosophers and theorists of art who are suspicious of the credentials of mass art think that mass art is too easy to be the real thing. Instead it is something else – kitsch or perhaps pseudo-art.

Among the arguments that mass art is not genuine art, there are two interconnected arguments that can be labeled the formulaic argument and the passivity argument. The formulaic argument correctly points out that mass art is formulaic. For example, it is comprised of many genres that employ routine plot structures and stock characters and situations. No one could deny this. However, the next step in the argument lays down the premise that authentic artworks, as opposed to pseudo-artworks or kitsch, do not employ formulas. Genuine art abides the modernist imperative to "make it new." Thus, if certain alleged artworks traffic in the formulaic, they are not truly artworks. Mass artworks are formulaic.

Therefore, mass artworks are not truly artworks. They are kitsch.

The passivity argument builds upon notions with which we are already familiar from the formulaic argument. Mass artworks are formulaic. The use of formulas makes mass artworks easy to absorb. In fact, the audience can process the mass artwork with so little effort that following a mass artwork does not call on the viewer, listener, or reader to do anything. The art is spoon-fed to the consumer. The audience is passive.

But genuine art requires activity on the part of the audience. Real art encourages the audience to participate – to interpret the work, to struggle with ambivalent feelings, to be open to new experiences, to concentrate, to adopt new perspectives, and so on. Authentic art is difficult in a way that demands effort and activity from the audience. This too fits nicely with the modernist preference for difficult art that compels the audience to actively co-construct the artwork. So, if something is a real artwork, it engenders active or participatory engagement on the part of its audience. Mass artworks are passively absorbed. Mass artworks do not engender active engagement. Therefore, mass artworks are not real artworks. Thus, mass artworks are kitsch.

These arguments rest respectively on the ideas that genuine art is not formulaic and that it engenders activity, whereas mass art is formulaic and induces passive absorption. With respect to the charge that mass art is formulaic, the defender of the potential art status of mass art will agree that this is true. However, the friend of mass art can then go on to challenge the idea that genuine art is not formulaic. Shakespeare's sonnets adhere to certain formulas as do Beethoven's sonata allegros. Many Greek tragedies follow the patent distilled by Aristotle; they possess beginnings, middles, and ends, with reversals, recognitions, and calamities, etc.

It is stupendously false that all genuine art is nonformulaic. Thus, the fact that mass art is formulaic should not weigh against the possibility that mass art can be art, properly so called. Indeed, that Charlie Chaplin may share certain formulas with *commedia dell'arte* should encourage us to count his work as art and not to discount its art status.

Furthermore, the passivity argument overstates the degree to which, in the pursuit of accessibility, a mass artwork reduces its audiences to inaction. Mass artworks can call for a great deal of co-construction from spectators. Consider *The Sopranos*, with its multiple storylines and large cast of central characters. Simply following it requires a great deal of mental activity from the audience. The audience is hardly passive. As we watch the story unfold, we are constantly on the lookout for clues as to what might happen next. Moreover, we are constantly struggling with our feelings toward Tony Soprano – sympathizing with him one moment, horrified by him in the next. He is certainly not the sort of stock character that the formulaic argument claims populates mass art throughout.

Nor does the suggestion that genuine art must be difficult ring true. *Pride and Prejudice* is not difficult, but no one has suggested that it is not properly identified as art. Not even all modernist art is difficult. Who does not get Picassos' visual joke involving the bull's head made out of a bicycle seat and handlebars? But does that require more audience activity or participation than following an episode of *The Sopranos*?

Two of the most frequent arguments against the proposal that mass artworks can be art are the formulaic argument and the passivity argument. Neither carries the day. Thus, although there may be some putative examples of mass artworks that are not genuine artworks, there are others that are not only artworks but great artworks.

See also MOTION PICTURES; PHOTOGRAPHY; KITSCH; POPULAR ART; TECHNOLOGY AND ART.

BIBLIOGRAPHY

Adorno, Theodor W. 1991. *The Culture Industry: Selected Essays on Mass Culture*. J. M. Bernstein (ed.). London: Routledge.

Carroll, Noël. 1998. *Philosophy of Mass Art*. Oxford: Oxford University Press.

Collingwood, R. G. 1969 [1938]. *The Principles of Art*. Oxford: Clarendon.

Greenberg, Clement. 1986. "The Avant-Garde and Kitsch." In *Clement Greenberg: Collected Essays and Criticism*, vol. i. J. O'Brien (ed.). Chicago: University of Chicago Press, 5–22.

Nehamas, Alexander. 1988. "Plato and the Mass Media," *Monist*, 71, 214–35.

Novitz, David. 1989. "Ways of Artmaking: The High and The Popular in Art," *British Journal of Aesthetics*, 29, 213–39.

Novitz, David. 1992. "Noël Carroll's Theory of Mass Art," *Philosophic Exchange*, 23, 51–62.

NOËL CARROLL

meaning constructivism is a convenient label for a collection of views about the objects and nature of interpretation, including the interpretation of artworks. *Radical constructivism* is the view that interpretations create new objects. *Moderate constructivism* is the view that interpretations alter their objects. *Historical constructivism* is the view that changes that occur in an artwork's historical or cultural context change its meaning. One kind of change that can do this is the way the work is interpreted, but for the historical constructivist, this is not the only way such change can occur.

All of these views oppose a certain picture of what goes on when we interpret artworks and other "intentional" objects. According to this picture, interpretations attempt to discover relevant truths about their objects, truths that are not obvious before we interpret them. For example, interpretations of artworks attempt to discover what artistically important properties works possess, when it is not obvious which properties these are. On this picture interpretation is discovery. It neither brings any object into existence nor changes any of its artistically important properties. We have to now inquire how each version of constructivism diverges from this picture and what might motivate this divergence.

Radical constructivism differs from this picture in asserting that the object of interpretation is in some sense created by the interpretation. That sounds paradoxical because (among other reasons) it raises the question: why was an interpretative act undertaken in the first place? Did there not have to be something that we wanted to understand or appreciate that we were thinking about when we undertook this act, and while we were engaged in it? Since this object exists prior to interpretation, it cannot be an object created by an interpretation. The radical constructivist does not deny the existence of this prior object of interpretation. He or she asserts that when we interpret, beside this object and the interpretation it elicits, there is a third object the interpretation brings into existence.

One motivation for this is the thought that objects of interpretation are intentional objects construed as objects of thought. But this by itself does not get us very far. "Intentional object" is ambiguous in many ways and anything can be an object of thought from artworks to aardvarks. Those who appeal to intentional objects sometimes think of them as objects that exist in thought, or depend on thought for their existence. A straightforward proposal is this: the initial object of interpretation is either an object that exists independently of the interpreter's thoughts, or an object as conceived by the interpreter prior to interpretation. The subsequent object is one conceived by the interpreter after interpretation. These objects have different properties, so they are two.

This proposal can be criticized on several grounds. Even if we agree that objects of interpretation are objects that exist in thought, why suppose we have two objects rather than one that has undergone change? The initial object exists at the start of an interpretative act. The subsequent object exists at the end of an interpretative act. The same object can have different properties at different times. So, unless we have a clear way to count objects that exist in thought, it is not clear how to choose between radical and moderate constructivist construals of what has happened.

But it is not clear that either construal is desirable. Both seem to make the object of interpretation dependent on the mind of the interpreter. It is more plausible to think of the object as a public one. The conceptions we have of it may change over time, but why think it changes, with every change in our conception? Unless constructivists can propose a way of construing objects of interpretation as public objects, their proposals lack plausibility.

Artworks are objects that exist in the public domain, but they also depend for their existence on human practices and institutions. There are other objects like this that behave in ways a constructivist might predict. Consider words, in particular, the word "Madagascar." Originally it referred to a part of the African mainland. Through misunderstanding some

people started using it to refer to a large island off the east coast of Africa. Eventually this usage stuck. There are two ways of looking at what happened. (1) Because some "interpreted" (misinterpreted) "Madagascar" in a certain way, a new word came into existence spelled just like the old one for which the "interpretation" was correct. (2) Because some interpreted "Madagascar" in a certain way, the original word came to take on a new meaning.

Both construals are plausible accounts of what happened. On each construal both the word referring to the African mainland and the word referring to the island are public objects. So the question is: can either construal be plausibly carried over to the interpretation of artworks?

In favor of the radical constructivist approach to these matters, consider the following supposedly analogical case. Suppose Attawamp makes a sign that, in his language (Wampian) means "no trespassing." A thousand years later Sue discovers this sign in her garden in remarkably good shape and sees a string of symbols on it that looks like "be back in five minutes." Being an English speaker, Sue realizes she can use these symbols in a sign for her shop to indicate that she will be back soon when she has to close it to run a short errand. Notice what has happened. Because different meanings are assigned to the string of symbols, we end up with two signs, though they are "embodied" in a single physical object. In a sense, Attawamp and Sue "interpret" the string differently in terms of the different meanings assigned to the string by their respective languages. So perhaps different interpretations of the same public artwork (prior object) end up creating new works (subsequent objects).

However, this proposal is much less plausible when applied to artworks than in the case of the signs. There, it is the different uses of the string of symbols (shapes) within two different languages to say two different things that plausibly creates two signs. When we give an interpretation of an artwork, we are not using the artwork to say or do something, as the artist might plausibly be said to do, but we are making an assertion about it. Just as I cannot use your utterance to say something that I intend to convey, the interpreter cannot use an artwork to say something he intends to convey. He can assert that the work conveys what he has in mind, but then his assertion would be false. He can assert that the work could be construed as conveying what he has in mind. That might be true and a worthwhile interpretation of the work, but it would create no new object. It would simply say something about the original object – that it could be construed in a certain way. Notice that if Sue gave an interpretation in this sense of the original sign and asserted that in Wampian it says "be back in five minutes" she would be mistaken and create no new sign.

Let us now turn to the moderate constructivist idea that interpretations alter their objects by what they say about them. Do artworks undergo changes in their meaning as the word "Madagascar" perhaps did? An argument in favor of this position turns on the idea that artworks are indeterminate in certain respects, and when an interpretation "imputes" a property to a work, it removes an indeterminacy, thereby altering the work. To illustrate this idea, assume that the play *Hamlet* does not provide a definite answer to the question: what motivates the character Hamlet to delay revenging the death of is father? The play is in a sense indeterminate with respect to that property of Hamlet's motivational structure. Different interpretations of *Hamlet* nevertheless impute different motives to the character in delaying action.

However the sort of indeterminacy we have been considering is to be understood, it has so far provided no reason to think that the imputation of properties to works changes the works in any way. The works themselves would appear to remain indeterminate regarding the interpretative issues, and what the interpretation does is provide a way the work can be taken – an optional way at that since the work, by hypothesis, does not require or prescribe the assignment of the property in question. Further, since a work that is indeterminate about an interpretative issue may permit imputations of incompatible properties by different interpretations of it, a moderate constructivist could not claim that the *work* has been altered in all the ways it has been interpreted, since no one work could actually come to have all those properties. It might be true that the work can plausibly be taken in all those ways,

but there is no reason so far to think that was not always true.

Historical constructivism provides such a reason. The historical constructivist claims that changes in the work's historical or cultural context change its meaning. It may have one meaning when it first appears and a different meaning 100 years later in virtue of the new context it is in at the later time. So it may be plausible to claim, after the appearance of Freudian psychoanalytic theory, that Hamlet hesitates because of Oedipal feelings of guilt but not plausible to impute this at an earlier time. If this claim is coupled with the idea that a work's meaning at any time is constituted by the properties plausibly imputed to it, then its meaning would change over time.

This proposal is among the more reasonable constructivist claims. Nevertheless, there are grounds to doubt that it is correct. The proposal assumes that a property applies (or plausibly applies) to a work only when people become equipped with the concept of that property. Arguably, people did not become equipped with the concept of an Oedipus complex until the early twentieth century. But it is a mistake to make this assumption. If that were true, nothing would have any properties at all prior to the existence of concept users, and that is absurd. The same evidence that Hamlet is motivated by an Oedipus complex – such as the scene in Gertrude's bedroom – existed at the work's creation. What awaited the twentieth century was the ability to use the evidence to apply the concept. Here is an analogy. The concept of the baroque came into existence well after baroque works were composed. For this reason, composers of the baroque period did not apply the concept of the baroque to their work. Nevertheless, their works always belonged to the baroque style and period because they always had the properties that make them baroque.

A complication in this argument is introduced by the use of the word "plausible" in the formulation of the constructivist thesis. Perhaps the evidence for the Oedipal interpretation of *Hamlet* always existed, but the interpretation would not have been found plausible until the twentieth century. Since the constructivist thesis is put in terms of the properties plausibly imputed to it at a time, it might still be argued that these properties change over time. To evaluate this claim, we have to distinguish between what is found plausible and what is plausible. Presumably, plausibility per se is a function of the evidence or reasons that exist for a hypothesis. If evidence was always there, the plausibility of the Oedipal interpretation does not change over time. What changes is people's ability to appreciate the evidence.

Constructivists still may not be convinced. They could perhaps argue that the meaning of a work at a time is a function of the plausible interpretations that its audience can appreciate at that time. This surely does vary over different times. But why should we suppose that a work's meaning must always be accessible to a given actual audience and capable of being "appreciated" by it? The debate between proponents and opponents of constructivism will not be definitively settled until we have a clearer idea of what artworks are and what properties, including meaning properties, they possess.

See also CRITICAL MONISM AND PLURALISM; INTERPRETATION; INTERPRETATION, AIMS OF; MARGOLIS; RELATIVISM.

BIBLIOGRAPHY

Krausz, Michael. 1993. *Rightness and Reasons: Interpretation in Cultural Practices*. Ithaca: Cornell University Press.

Krausz, Michael. (ed.). 2002. *Is There a Single Right Interpretation?* University Park: Pennsylvania State University Press.

Lamarque, Peter. 2000. "Objects of Interpretation," *Metaphilosophy*, 31(1/2), 96–124.

McFee, Graham. 1992. "The Historical Character of Art: A Reappraisal," *British Journal of Aesthetics*, 32, 307–19.

Margolis, Joseph. 1995. *Interpretation Radical but Not Unruly: The New Puzzle of the Arts and History*. Berkeley: University of California Press.

Margolis, Joseph. 2000. "Relativism and Interpretive Objectivity," *Metaphilosophy*, 31(1/2), 200–26.

Percival, Philip. 2002. "Can Novel Critical Interpretations Create Artworks Distinct from Themselves?" In *Is There a Single Right Interpretation?* M. Krausz (ed.). University Park: Pennsylvania State University Press, 181–208.

Stecker, Robert. 1997. "The Constructivist's Dilemma," *Journal of Aesthetics and Art Criticism*, 55, 43–51.

Stecker, Robert. 2003. *Interpretation and Construction: Art, Speech and the Law*. Oxford: Blackwell.

Thom, Paul. 2000. *Making Sense*. Lanham: Rowman & Littlefield.

ROBERT STECKER

Merleau-Ponty, Maurice (1908–1961) French philosopher of the period following World War II, best known for his analyses of human existence, perception, and action in *Phenomenology of Perception* (1945); cofounder with Jean-Paul Sartre of the literary magazine *Les Temps modernes*, and professor at the Universities of Lyons and Paris; later (1952–61) held the chair of philosophy at the Collège de France. His writings cover a wide range, from philosophical psychology and philosophy of language to political philosophy, philosophy of history, and the philosophy of art.

Like his friend (and sometimes friendly opponent) Sartre, with whom his thought had much in common, Merleau-Ponty had no fully developed aesthetics. Yet, again as with Sartre, he often wrote critical essays on the arts – chiefly on painting, but also on the novel and film (some are included in *Sense and Non-Sense*). Moreover, his entire approach to the human situation was aesthetic and has implications for aesthetics.

At the core of Merleau-Ponty's philosophy is an attempt to recapture in experience (and to analyze) what it is like to encounter the world in a "primordial" way – that is, prior to describing and explaining it in objective, scientific terms. Drawing on the gestaltists, he proposes that one's primordial experience is to exist toward things through a living (perceiving, feeling, and acting) body. It is to struggle to achieve equilibrium with things against the background posed by the global environment, on the one hand, and one's "body schema," one's developed repertoire of perceptual-motor skills and habits, on the other. Through this reciprocal interplay, as he sees it, one's way of being in the world and the primary perceptual world itself become formed and instituted. Since the environment includes others, one becomes an embodied social being and one's perceived world becomes a social world as well. Each bodily movement, each object one sees and responds to, each performance one carries out, is thus, in a sense, an aesthetic achievement – an expression of the meaning of one's individual style within a concrete situation. The involved, living body is to be understood as an expressive medium, and every perception, feeling, and action as a work of art.

From this starting point, it is quite natural for Merleau-Ponty to go on to say that a work of art is itself a kind of expressive body: like the body, "a novel, a poem, a picture, a piece of music are individuals, that is to say beings in which it is impossible to distinguish the expressive vehicle from its meaning, whose meanings are accessible only in direct contact, and which radiate their significance without leaving their temporal and spatial position" (1962: 151).

Works of art thus have a kind of gestural meaning. Of course, they exhibit a complex vocabulary and syntax. But we comprehend them, Merleau-Ponty suggests, in much the way that we grasp the meanings of bodily gestures – not, in the first instance, by thinking about them, by trying to decipher them, but rather by lending our bodies to them, by living through their words, lines, colors, or sounds, and following out their tacit perceptual implications. The process of creating artworks is also best understood as a prereflective, bodily one. In this way it is like creative speech: "Like the functioning of the body, that of words and paintings remains mysterious to me: words, lines, colors which express my thoughts come from me like gestures; they are forced upon me by what I want to say as my gestures are by what I want to do" (1964b: 75). Descartes was therefore wrong: neither in speaking nor in painting are there two actions, one of thinking and another of mobilizing the body – on the contrary, one thinks with one's words and with one's hand, brush, and paints. Nor is there an idea *behind* the word or the work, or somewhere *beyond* them, but only *in* them and inseparable from them. Merleau-Ponty's thesis throughout is that the possibility of both language and painting rests upon the primordial, expressive possibilities of the human body.

Merleau-Ponty was enamored of Cézanne. He saw in Cézanne a philosopher – indeed, he saw himself – working with paint. In "Cézanne's Doubt" (1945), he shows how Cézanne struggled to define his own style in the face of academic painting, with its linear, "objective" realism, on the one hand, and his friends the Impressionists on the other, who, like him, wished to reject that sort of realism, but who seemed to leave natural things behind entirely and focus solely on light, air, and patches of color. What Cézanne finally managed to do, Merleau-Ponty thinks, was to cut through the conceptual biases of these other styles and, like a faithful phenomenologist, let the solid, weighty, voluminous presence of perceived things appear. By attending to surfaces and the structures perceptible beneath them, by painting the modulations of color at the edges of things and including perspectival distortions, he made canvases in which these elements "are no longer visible in their own right, but rather contribute, as they do in natural vision, to the impression of an emerging order, of an object in the act of appearing, organizing itself before our eyes" (1964a: 14).

In the last work that he saw published ("Eye and Mind" (1960), in 1964c: 159–90), written for the first issue of *Art de France*, he returns to Cézanne, as well as Klee, Matisse, and others, to suggest that painting can have a distinctive ontological function. Precisely because painting does not "copy" things, and because it does not offer things to thought as does science but presents them immediately and bodily, in their depth and movement, so that we seem to be "present at the fission of Being from the inside" – for these reasons painting gives us a true sense of "the internal animation" of the world and what it means "to see" it (1964c: 186).

See also NINETEENTH- AND TWENTIETH-CENTURY CONTINENTAL AESTHETICS; DUFRENNE; EXPRESSION; SARTRE.

BIBLIOGRAPHY

Primary sources
[1945] 1962. *Phenomenology of Perception*. C. Smith (trans.). New York: Humanities Press.
[1948] 1964a. *Sense and Non-Sense*. H. L. Dreyfus & P. A. Dreyfus (trans.). Evanston: Northwestern University Press.
[1960] 1964b. *Signs*. R. McCleary (trans.). Evanston: Northwestern University Press.
1964c. *The Primacy of Perception*. J. M. Edie (ed. & trans.) Evanston: Northwestern University Press.

Secondary sources
Kaelin, Eugene F. 1966. *An Existentialist Aesthetic.* Madison: University of Wisconsin Press.

JOHN J. COMPTON

metaphor A verbal composition which, on the basis of novel semantic relations among its components, evokes a complex and productive set of mental responses. Ever since Aristotle's *Poetics*, there has been widespread agreement on the important role played by metaphor in literature, especially poetry. Metaphor has been seen – by, among others, Shelley, Valéry, and I. A. Richards – as a main source of both the pleasure and the interest to be gained from poems. More recently, philosophers have become aware of the considerable difficulties surrounding this concept, and it is on these theoretical problems that this essay concentrates.

Theories of metaphor may be divided into those that see metaphor as a secondary use of language, a departure from its basic function of describing our responses to the outside world, and those that see it as an essential characteristic, inherent in the nature of language itself.

Implicit in this is the assumption that language is a means for transacting relations between the thoughts that a speaker has and conditions as they obtain in the world. One of the inferences from this assumption is, then, that a speaker, in carrying out such a transaction, can use the language in a manner which is factually objective and epistemically neutral – a use, thus, in which the function of language is purely descriptive and its use strictly literal. Metaphor on this view is some modification or extension of literal language and is to be explicated by the use of linguistic analysis or the theory of speech acts.

Alternatively, one may regard the role played by one or another of the components in the linguistic transaction as functioning not neutrally but with a characteristic predilection. Thus, one may regard the thought component as so indoctrinated by human experience that all such transactions are epistemically tendentious and the language consequently biased. It is a corollary of this position that language is congenitally and pervasively metaphoric, and that explication is to be achieved by examining the conceptual prepossessions of the speaker.

Another approach centers on language; it holds that, in routinely accommodating itself to broader and broader segments of human experience, a language acquires a metaphoric character as an autonomous function of its historical development. Explication here involves the study of linguistic change – in particular, an examination of how the words of a language widen their extensions in consequence of their use to comprehend new objects and ideas. A variant of this position makes an even stronger claim – that language is metaphoric *ab origine*, its metaphoric character deriving from the very fact that, as we might put it, words are not the things they refer to.

It might appear that the remaining component in our analysis is not capable of prejudicially asserting itself – that is, that the constitution of the world is simply what it is and cannot be made to function other than passively in the linguistic transaction – and thus that the role played by the world in that transaction cannot be exploited for metaphoric purposes. This is no doubt true; at the same time, however, nothing prevents someone from employing in the interpretation of metaphor a *conception* of the world that is at variance with empirical conditions. Thus, flowers may not laugh or feel happy in our world, but one can *conceive of* a world in which such states of affairs are possible. Conceptions of this sort, it should be noted, are not (conceptual) prepossessions; they come into being in the act of interpreting metaphors literally.

When regarded as the modified use of literal language, metaphor may take one of two basic forms: in one, the modification reflects itself in an incongruity between the literal sense of the expression and the (nonlinguistic) environment in which it occurs; in the other, the incongruity is reflected in the expression itself. Thus, in responding to an opponent's argument, a speaker might say, "That's a pile of garbage"; a poet, to describe the formation of dew at nightfall, might say, "When the weak day weeps." The latter expression – Shelley's – is syntactically well formed, but it is semantically deviant, in that the grammar of English does not "sanction" predicating *weak* and *weep* of *day*. In the first type of metaphor, on the other hand, nothing in the expression is linguistically unorthodox; there is, however, a form of deviance in the *use* to which the expression is put; we might refer to metaphors of this type as pragmatically deviant.

As the example in the preceding paragraph indicates, the deviant character of metaphor is a consequence of collocations that comprise incompatible semantic valences. Beardsley (1962) remarks on this semantic opposition or "tension" in metaphor, and argues that from this opposition a "twist of meaning" is forced; in "the spiteful sun," for instance, the predicate "spiteful" acquires a new intension, "perhaps one that it has in no other context."

Black (1954–5) characterizes his approach to the analysis of metaphor as "interactional." Taking as his example "Man is a wolf," he defines two subjects: principal ("man") and subsidiary ("wolf"). To each of these subjects there pertains a "system of associated commonplaces," these being beliefs that the average person holds about the referents of the names. In the construal process these commonplaces interact, some being, as it were, transferred from one to the other subject and its import assimilated into the "meaning" of that subject, others being filtered out as incompatible. Black does not explicitly invoke semantic deviance in his discussion, but it figures implicitly in that his interactional process is a nontrivial function only if some sort of deviance is assumed.

In the face of semantic deviance, Searle (1979) refers, in his analysis of metaphor, to the difference between sentence meaning and speaker's meaning. This prizing apart of the speech act into two separate components is a tactic used by Searle also in his analysis of irony and indirect speech acts. In all these cases, the speaker says one thing but intends another. Thus, in "Sally is a block of ice," the rationalization of its metaphoric function does not take the form of operations performed on the utterance itself; the metaphoric meaning devolves, rather, on what the speaker had in mind when uttering the sentence – namely, that Sally is a cold, unresponsive person. It is a significant aspect of Searle's approach that the words in a metaphoric expression comprise or have conferred on them no additional, special, ad hoc, or "metaphoric" meaning – in this respect differing from Beardsley and Black.

Davidson (1979) is in agreement with Searle that the words in a metaphoric utterance have only their literal meaning. However, the consequence for Davidson is not semantic deviance but patent or obvious falsity. Moreover, rationalization of the expression's metaphoric quality is not accomplished by adverting to the speaker's meaning; instead, the interpretative activity is localized in the reader of the metaphor, who will be set to calibrating a series of novel and provocative juxtapositions of objects and ideas. It is in the prompting of these novel relationships, which the "patently" false expression causes the reader to notice, that the metaphoric function consists.

That metaphor is a question primarily of thought and only secondarily of language is the argument of Lakoff and Johnson (1980). According to them, our experience of the world – its physical features and human activities – implicitly conditions our mental development in such a way that certain concepts become so impressed on our thought processes that we are predisposed to respond "metaphorically" to the affairs of everyday life. Thus, such notions as "Argument is war," "Time is money," and "Happy is up" are for Lakoff and Johnson conceptual metaphors, mental figures in which elements from one domain are mapped onto correlative elements of another. In a conceptual metaphor like "Time is money," elements like concreteness, short supply, and value are mapped from the source domain, money, on to the target domain, time – the mapping manifesting itself in such locutions as "I spent a solid week on that problem," "I can't spare the time," "That cost me a night's sleep."

As these examples make evident, conceptual metaphors (which need not be articulated as such) leave their traces in (and may be inferred from) the expressions that we use in everyday speech. Of the linguistic expressions themselves, Lakoff and Johnson claim that they too are metaphoric; in fact, vitally metaphoric, and this despite the fact that the senses of the words occurring in these expressions are "conventionally fixed within the lexicon of English."

In the treatment provided by Levin (1988) it is again the thought component that figures as the essential focus. Instead, however, of that focus bearing on preconceived experiential notions (the conceptual metaphors of Lakoff and Johnson), it bears, rather, on the responses that one might make to metaphors that one encounters in poetry. Consider again Shelley's "When the weak day weeps." However one approaches their analysis, it is clear that, if taken literally, the truth claims made by most metaphors (Shelley's example being paradigmatic in this regard) describe conditions that are ontologically and empirically bizarre. Levin proposes that instead of trying to rationalize the meaning of such metaphors – make their interpretation conform to conditions in the actual world – one takes them at face value and attempts, rather, to conceive of a "world" in which what the metaphor purports to describe represents a possible state of affairs. This approach to metaphor might be called conceptional in nature.

It is a natural proclivity of language to widen the scope and applicability of its semantic units. Thus, in its normal use and development the meaning of a word will automatically gain new senses as the range and nature of its reference is extended. A large part of this process is routine, raising no theoretical problems and requiring no particular comment. When a word like "leaf," say, is applied successively to different individual leaves, to various species of leaves, and further extends its range to designate the sections of a shutter or the pages of a book, the semantic consequences of the extension are comparatively unproblematic. This is because the referents, throughout the extension, are uniformly concrete. Something significant emerges, however, when the extension in question represents a move from the domain of physical to that of mental activities. For inasmuch as a good deal of the scientific and philosophical literature is conducted via words which have made just this semantic transfer, the question is raised as to whether language can still be used to describe reality straightforwardly; or whether language is not in fact fundamentally and ineluctably metaphoric.

Derrida (1974) adopts the latter of these alternatives, and educes from it the following argument: if it is the case that philosophical language is intrinsically metaphoric, then it follows that no noncircular account can be given of metaphor, since the language of that account would itself be metaphoric. As a temper to the drastic nature of this conclusion, one might raise the issue of dead metaphor, in the case of

which the emergent sense gets registered in the lexicon of the language. Additionally, one might invoke the role played in these developments by catachresis, in which the range of a word is extended not to replace an already existing word but, rather, to fill a lexical gap.

See also POETRY; INEFFABILITY; IRONY.

BIBLIOGRAPHY
Beardsley, Monroe C. 1962. "The Metaphorical Twist," *Philosophy and Phenomenological Research*, 22, 293–307.
Black, Max. 1954–5. "Metaphor," *Proceedings of the Aristotelian Society*, 55, 273–94.
Carroll, Noël. 2001. "Visual Metaphor." In *Beyond Aesthetics*. Cambridge: Cambridge University Press, 347–68.
Cohen, Ted. 1999. "Identifying with Metaphor: Metaphors of Personal Identification," *Journal of Aesthetics and Art Criticism*, 57, 399–409.
Cooper, David E. 1986. *Metaphor*. Oxford: Blackwell.
Davidson, Donald. 1979. "What Metaphors Mean." In *On Metaphor*. S. Sacks (ed.). Chicago: University of Chicago Press, 29–45.
Derrida, Jacques. 1974. "White Mythology: Metaphor in the Text of Philosophy," F. C. T. Moore (trans.), *New Literary History*, 6, 5–74.
Gaut, Berys. 1997. "Metaphor and the Understanding of Art," *Proceedings of the Aristotelian Society*, 97, 223–41.
Kittay, Eva F. 1987. *Metaphor: Its Cognitive Force and Linguistic Structure*. Oxford: Clarendon.
Lakoff, George & Johnson, Mark. 1980. *Metaphors We Live By*. Chicago: University of Chicago Press.
Levin, S. R. 1988. *Metaphoric Worlds: Conceptions of a Romantic Nature*. New Haven: Yale University Press.
Ortony, Andrew (ed.). 1979. *Metaphor and Thought*. Cambridge: Cambridge University Press.
Ricoeur, Paul. 1977. *The Rule of Metaphor: Multi-Disciplinary Studies in the Creation of Meaning in Language*. R. Czerny (trans.). Toronto: University of Toronto Press.
Sacks, Sheldon (ed.). 1979. *On Metaphor*. Chicago: University of Chicago Press.
Searle, John R. 1979. "Metaphor." In *Metaphor and Thought*. A. Ortony (ed.). Cambridge: Cambridge University Press, 92–123.

SAMUEL R. LEVIN

modernism and postmodernism Modernism held sway over creative activity in most of the arts for the greater part of the twentieth century, and it is only since the 1970s with the rise of postmodernism that its dominance has been significantly challenged. The critical element of the modernist aesthetic was its commitment to originality; the objective being, in the poet Ezra Pound's ringing declaration, to "make it new" each time around (1934). Creative artists were to be prized above all for their "imaginative individuality" (Gay 2007: 1). In practice this commitment led to systematic experimentation with form, with artists rejecting most of the norms that had governed artistic practice hitherto. Tradition was no longer to be taken as a guide, with what Peter Gay has dubbed "the lure of heresy" proving a much stronger force (2007: 3).

The notion of progress so embedded in modernity came to be just as critical a requirement in the creative domain. Painting and sculpture became abstract, music atonal, fiction fragmented in terms of its plot and narrative and often deliberately opaque in style, architecture geometrically regular in shape and unornamented (the "International Style," or the "new brutalism" as it came to be called by detractors). Vassily Kandinsky and Pablo Picasso emerged as the new models in art, Arnold Schoenberg in music, and James Joyce in literature; although it is worth noting that modernism is varied enough in styles and practices for some commentators to prefer to speak of "modernisms" instead.

One of the most influential theorists of modernism was the art critic Clement Greenberg, for whom the defining quality of modernist painting was its "painterly" quality. What this entailed was that painting was supposed to be about the art of painting itself: "The essence of modernism lies, as I see it, in the use of characteristic methods of a discipline to criticize the discipline itself, not in order to subvert it but in order to entrench it more firmly in its area of competence" (1961: 101). Painters were in consequence expected to distance themselves from the realist tradition and its use of the technique of perspective. Greenberg advocated "flatness" and abstraction instead, with formal features coming to dominate the artist's concerns; Cubism and Abstract Expressionism being pertinent examples of this ethos in practice.

Roland Barthes was to come up with a similar criterion for judging literature when he championed the cause of "writerly" fiction in his famous essay "The Death of the Author." Writerly fiction challenged the reader by leaving gaps that were open to multiple interpretation, thus involving the reader in the act of creation; whereas its opposite, "readerly" fiction, left no such loose ends and constrained the reader into the interpretation of the narrative that the author wanted. For Barthes, writerly fiction marked the "death of the author" and the "birth of the reader" (1977: 148). Although writerly fiction could be found throughout literary history (Laurence Sterne's *Tristram Shandy* (1759–67) manifestly fits the description), it was most obviously to be found in the modern era in the work of such authors as Virginia Woolf and James Joyce, and their often highly complex experiments in form (e.g., the use of stream of consciousness). Readerly fiction could be found in abundance in the realist tradition of novel writing, as in the nineteenth century.

The self-referential quality that Greenberg so admired in modernist painting carried over into literature too, and writing about the act of writing became a recurrent motif among modernist authors. This was a tendency that eventually came to be attacked by critics like John Barth, one of the leading figures in the development of the postmodernist style in fiction, for whom ultimately it led to the "literature of exhaustion" (1967), and with that a worrying loss of interest on the part of the general public.

Postmodernism, on the other hand, has largely rejected the obsession with originality and formal experiment, reviving older styles and modes in a deliberate attempt to open up more of a dialogue with the past than modernist aesthetics permitted. Cultural commentators speak of a condition of postmodernity developing in the latter decades of the twentieth century, when political and institutional authority in the West came to lose much of their aura among the general public. For Jean-François Lyotard "incredulity toward metanarratives" (1984: xxiv) was the dominant feature of this trend, and postmodernism is to be regarded as an attempt to theorize this across the many areas of our culture. An attitude of incredulity toward the dominant metanarratives in the aesthetic realm is certainly to be noted among both critics and creative artists from about the

1960s onward. John Barth called for a return to plot and linear narrative in literature, for example, arguing that this would constitute a "literature of replenishment" to counteract modernism's "literature of exhaustion" (1980). Many artists have returned to figurative painting, and composers have reembraced tonality (although minimalism tends to have a very restricted range in this latter respect, with rhythm coming to be the dominant feature in many cases).

The architectural theorist Charles Jencks has been one of the most significant influences in postmodern aesthetics, particularly through his concept of "double coding." Jencks devised the concept as a way of encouraging architects to take more account of public opinion by moving away from the "new brutalism," which was far more popular with architects than it ever was with the general public, who tended to find the tower blocks so closely associated with this style, and still so prominent a part of cityscapes across the globe, soulless and alienating in the main. The ideal for Jencks was buildings that could appeal to both professionals and lay persons alike, buildings that were "double coded," having elements that could be appreciated by both constituencies. Architects were asked to bring back ornamentation and to experiment with mixing styles from the past and present, on the assumption that the public would be more willing to accept the new when it came accompanied by the familiar. There was a clear sense of a dialogue with the past when this was adopted as architectural practice, with such buildings being conspicuously more user-friendly.

The architectural style which has developed from ideas like Jencks's is unashamedly eclectic, combining past and present styles with abandon, and largely jettisoning the obsession with straight lines and geometrical regularity that had characterized the new brutalism. (Jencks himself had notoriously claimed that modern architecture had died at the precise moment in July 1972 when the typically new brutalist Pruitt-Igoe housing scheme in St. Louis was demolished by the city authorities (1991: 23).) There was also a move to introduce more popular elements into architectural practice as well, with bright colors coming back into play, as well as playful and often eccentric shapes (e.g., twists and spirals). Some architectural theorists insisted that the divide between serious and popular needed to be abolished as well, and that the playful qualities of the latter were being undervalued by the profession; ideas that are most memorably argued for in *Learning from Las Vegas* (Venturi et al. 1977), where commercial architecture is taken as a source of aesthetic inspiration.

Overall, the postmodern aesthetic in architecture has been heavily biased toward pastiche – what the theorist Kenneth Frampton has rather frostily called "the cannibalization of architectural form" (1992: 306) – and indeed that has proved to be a critical aspect of the postmodern aesthetic in general, one of its major methods of constructing a dialogue with the past.

Arguably the quintessential example of the double coding ethic is to be found in Umberto Eco's novel *The Name of the Rose* (1983), simultaneously a murder mystery much in the classic style of Sherlock Holmes – the lead character is called William of Baskerville, for example, echoing the Holmes adventure *The Hound of the Baskervilles* (1902) – and a reflection on semiotic theory, as well as on the conflicting claims of Aristotelian and Platonic aesthetics. The book was a bestseller, largely on the grounds of its cleverly constructed murder mystery set in what for the twentieth-century reader was the exotic world of a medieval monastery; but it was also an intellectual triumph, offering many important insights into the nature and workings of semiotic theory and classical aesthetics. It remains a model of how to double code creative work, as well as an excellent example of the art of pastiche. An even more self-conscious use of pastiche can be found in the work of the British author Peter Ackroyd, who in his novel *Hawksmoor* (1985) set half the action in present-day London and half back in the early eighteenth century, cleverly imitating the writing style of eighteenth-century fiction throughout the latter sections.

Postmodernism's dialogue with the past also comes with a dose of irony, however, and that is another key aspect of the postmodernist aesthetic. There can be a very "knowing" quality to postmodern creative practice, an acknowledgment that although older forms and themes are being reappropriated, they can never mean the same thing to us now as when they were fresh to their original creators. Whether future generations will be as amused by this ironic attitude remains to be seen, and there are already signs that it is losing its effectiveness and coming to be regarded as rather trite. Gilbert Adair's critical observation, that "the past (mostly the recent past) has been transformed into a mammoth lucky dip . . . All you have to do, if you are a maker of TV commercials, or pop promos, a designer of shop windows or record sleeves, . . . an architect, a painter, even a marketing entrepreneur, is plunge in and scoop out whatever happens to address your particular need" (1992: 17), is evidence of a growing concern that postmodern artistic practice can be lazy and often lacking in real creativity. Perhaps the wheel has come full circle and a new form of modernism is due to come on stream.

See also NINETEENTH- AND TWENTIETH-CENTURY CONTINENTAL AESTHETICS; ABSTRACTION; ARISTOTLE; BARTHES; DECONSTRUCTION; IRONY; PLATO; STRUCTURALISM AND POSTSTRUCTURALISM.

BIBLIOGRAPHY
Adair, Gilbert. 1992. *The Postmodernist Always Rings Twice: Reflections on Culture in the 90s.* London: Fourth Estate.
Barth, John. 1967. "The Literature of Exhaustion," *Atlantic Monthly*, 220, 29–34.
Barth, John. 1980. "The Literature of Replenishment: Postmodernist Fiction," *Atlantic Monthly*, 245, 65–71.
Barthes, Roland. 1977. "The Death of the Author." In *Image Music Text*. S. Heath (ed. & trans.). London: Fontana, 142–8.
Eco, Umberto. 1983. *The Name of the Rose.* W. Weaver (trans.). London: Secker & Warburg.
Frampton, Kenneth. 1992. *Modern Architecture: A Critical History.* 3rd edn. London: Thames & Hudson.
Gay, Peter. 2007. *Modernism: The Lure of Heresy from Baudelaire to Beckett and Beyond.* London: Heinemann.
Greenberg, Clement. 1961. "Modernist Painting," *Arts Yearbook*, 4, 101–8.
Jencks, Charles. 1991. *The Language of Post-Modern Architecture.* 6th edn. London: Academy Editions.
Lyotard, Jean-François. 1984 [1979]. *The Postmodern Condition: A Report on Knowledge.* G. Bennington & B. Massumi (trans.). Manchester: Manchester University Press.
Pound, Ezra. 1934. *Make It New.* London: Faber.
Venturi, Robert, Brown, Denise Scott, & Izenour, Steven. 1977. *Learning from Las Vegas: The Forgotten Symbolism of Architectural Form.* 2nd edn. Cambridge, MA: MIT Press.

STUART SIM

morality and art The relation between art and morality has been of recurrent interest to Western philosophy and literary criticism since at least the time of Plato. Some concerns have been about the causal effects of art on people's morals. Popular films, music, and videogames have been condemned on grounds of their alleged tendencies to produce moral depravity. This causal claim is essentially empirical and is best determined by psychological and sociological studies. Some questions concerning the relation of art to morality are more properly philosophical. One might wonder how artistic evaluations stand in relation to moral evaluations: do they differ, for instance, in their realism, objectivity, or relativity? A distinct question is whether the moral features of artworks are relevant to their artistic value, and if so, whether the moral merits of artworks always count toward their artistic value. This question has dominated much of the recent debate about the relation of art to morality, and it is the issue that we will address here.

An initial puzzle concerns what it means to call an artwork morally good or bad. Moral properties apply to people and their actions but not, it seems, to mere objects. A willow might metaphorically weep, but no willow has ever done anything morally wrong. In this spirit Oscar Wilde denies that artworks can properly be called moral or immoral: "There is no such thing as a moral or an immoral book. Books are well written, or badly written. That is all" (1992: 3). One reply is that when we morally judge works it is really their effects that we are morally assessing. However, this returns us to the causal question and its properly empirical resolution. And even morally bad books may have morally good effects (and vice versa), due to adventitious circumstances of their reception: the publication of a racist work might alert readers to racism and enhance their efforts to combat it. A better response to the Wildean worry is to note that works are the products of actions and we can talk about what the author (whether the actual, implied, or postulated) is doing in the work; so we can morally assess the author's actions manifested in the work (Devereaux 2004).

If it makes sense to assess works morally, the question arises of whether this has anything to do with their artistic or aesthetic value. (I will use "artistic" and "aesthetic" interchangeably here.) *Autonomists* or *aestheticists* deny that moral values are ever relevant to the artistic value of works. Autonomism, which owes a debt to formalism (Beardsley 1981), appeals to various considerations, but two stand out. One is an adherence to the idea that there is an aesthetic attitude, characterized in terms of disinterest, that is, by a lack of concern with practical engagement with the object of aesthetic attention. Since the moral attitude grounds a practical concern, the aesthetic and the moral are, it is held, independent of each other. Some have responded by denying the existence of an aesthetic attitude (Dickie 1964). But it can also be queried whether, even if it exists, the attitude is characterized by disinterest in the sense of lack of practical concern for its object: the artist, the student studying for an exam, and the art valuer can all have practical concerns, but nevertheless be adopting an aesthetic attitude toward the art object.

A second autonomist point is that a great deal of good and indeed great art has been morally suspect or just downright evil: "Rape, pillage, murder, human and animal sacrifice, concubinage, and slavery in the *Iliad*; misogyny in the *Oresteia* and countless other works; bloodcurdling vengeance; anti-Semitism in more works of literature than one can count, including works by Shakespeare and Dickens; racism and sexism likewise" (Posner 1997: 5; see also Gass 1993). The examples might be disputed, but the general point has force: great works may have considerable ethical flaws. The opponent of autonomism would be thus well advised to concede that lack of moral blemish cannot be a necessary condition for an artwork to be good, still less for it to be great. But if the anti-autonomist is a pluralist about artistic values, she can hold merely that *one* ground for holding a work to be artistically flawed is that it is morally flawed. And she may note that a great deal of artistic and critical practice has been informed by moral ambitions.

If autonomism is rejected, moral flaws are sometimes aesthetically relevant. Two rival positions are compatible with this claim. The first is *moralism* or *ethicism*, which in one formulation holds that a work of art is *always* aesthetically flawed insofar as it possesses an aesthetically relevant ethical flaw (Gaut 2007: ch. 3). This position does not hold that all moral flaws of artworks are aesthetically relevant; but when they are, moral flaws always count as aesthetic flaws. The position is pluralist, holding that there is a plurality of artistic values, so that an ethical flaw is only one ground for aesthetic condemnation of a work. In contrast, a position that has been variously called *immoralism* (Kieran 2003) or the *antitheoretical* view (Jacobson 2006) agrees that moral flaws are sometimes aesthetically relevant, but holds that when they are so, *sometimes* a work is aesthetically flawed insofar as it is morally flawed, and *sometimes* it is aesthetically meritorious insofar as it is morally flawed. Whether a moral flaw counts as an aesthetic flaw depends on its context in the work; so I will term this view *contextualism*. The participants in this debate can be marshaled in terms of this distinction. But it should be noted that, while Carroll (1996) describes his position as moderate moralism, at some points he seems to allow that moral defects may contribute positively to the aesthetic value of a work, in which case he is a contextualist. But I will classify him here as a moralist.

Moralists have given a variety of arguments in favor of their view. An argument from friendship holds that artistically evaluating a literary work is akin to evaluating its implied author as a friend; since a person's moral goodness counts toward him being a good friend, the moral goodness of works contributes to their artistic worth (Booth 1988). The moral beauty argument holds that if a person has a morally good character, then she possesses a kind of inner beauty; so the moral worth of the author, as manifested in a work, counts under certain circumstances as an aesthetic excellence in the work (Gaut 2007: ch. 6). And the two most widely employed arguments are the cognitive and merited response arguments.

The cognitive argument appeals to a claim about the cognitive value of art (Nussbaum 1990; Carroll 1998). Most broadly, it holds that the fact that a work teaches us something is, under certain circumstances, an artistic merit in the work; so if a work teaches us something morally important, this is, under the relevant circumstances, an artistic merit in the work. This argument has to specify the relevant circumstances, since clearly not everything a work teaches us is germane to its artistic value. Ian Rankin's wonderful John Rebus novels are so geographically accurate that one can navigate around parts of Edinburgh using them, but that fact does not constitute an artistic merit in them. The argument also requires a defense of cognitivism about artistic values and that claim has been attacked by autonomists (Lamarque 2006). Some moralists have developed a specification of the relevance condition and a defense of cognitivism, by arguing that one can learn through the imagining deployed in artworks (Gaut 2007: chs. 7–8).

The merited response argument holds, roughly, that when a work manifests attitudes, it standardly does so by prescribing (inviting) its audience to have certain responses. The responses a work prescribes are of aesthetic relevance. Prescribed responses are not always merited, which is an aesthetic failure in the work; and one ground for holding these responses to be unmerited is that they are unethical. So if a work manifests unethical attitudes in its prescribed responses, then the work has an aesthetic flaw. For instance, de Sade manifests approval of sexual torture by inviting his readers to enjoy torture scenarios; these prescribed responses are aesthetically relevant to assessing his works; enjoying spectacles of sexual torture is unmerited because unethical; so his works are aesthetically flawed insofar as they possess this ethical flaw (Gaut 1998; 2007: ch. 10; see also Carroll 1996).

Contextualists have argued for their position mainly by attacking the arguments for moralism. Jacobson (2006) maintains that the merited response argument is invalid, since it moves from the claim that it is wrong to adopt a response to the claim that the response is unwarranted: for instance, it may be wrong to be amused by a joke but the joke might nevertheless be funny. The moralist can reply that there is no invalid transition: the claim is that the joke is not funny, or is at least flawed in its humor, by virtue of its immorality; and that is something that has intuitive support, including in what we

think about racist and sexist humor (Gaut 2007: 237–51). Jacobson's antitheoretical version of contextualism, which apparently holds that nothing in general can be said about when and why ethical flaws count as aesthetic merits and when as aesthetic flaws, also exposes him to an autonomist attack. For the autonomist can claim that the reason that no general account can be given is because there is no relation between the aesthetic and the ethical realms.

Matthew Kieran has developed a contextualist position that has the salient advantage that it provides an account of when and why ethical flaws are sometimes aesthetic flaws and sometimes aesthetic merits. Kieran is a cognitivist, but denies that cognitivism entails moralism. On the contrary, we can sometimes learn from a work precisely because it advocates immoral views; so an ethical flaw will be an aesthetic merit when it promotes learning (Kieran 2003). Autonomists will question the cognitivist assumption that the argument shares with most versions of moralism. A moralist response is that the argument elides the distinction between whether the work merely asks its audience to *imagine* the morally bad views without advocating them (say, inviting the audience to imagine the attitudes of a serial killer) or whether it actually *endorses* those views (advocates serial murder). We can be taught something by the former act of imagining, which in itself is not morally problematic (a detective might imagine the killer's attitudes in the course of trying to catch him). But if the work advocates something that is morally bad and false (that murder is good), it is cognitively as well as morally flawed. Endorsing immoral views introduces a cognitive flaw into a work, so a cognitivist ought to be a moralist, not a contextualist (Gaut 2007: 184–6).

The question of the relation between moral and artistic values has, then, been the subject of an intriguing three-cornered fight between autonomists, moralists, and contextualists. Since this dispute has in one form or another been with us since Plato, the only prediction that one can make with confidence is that the debate will continue.

See also AESTHETICISM; CENSORSHIP; COGNITIVE VALUE OF ART; EROTIC ART AND OBSCENITY; IMAGINATIVE RESISTANCE; PORNOGRAPHY.

BIBLIOGRAPHY

Beardsley, Monroe. 1981. *Aesthetics: Problems in the Philosophy of Criticism.* 2nd edn. Indianapolis: Hackett.

Booth, Wayne. 1988. *The Company We Keep: An Ethics of Fiction.* Berkeley: University of California Press.

Carroll, Noël. 1996. "Moderate Moralism," *British Journal of Aesthetics,* 36, 223–38.

Carroll, Noël. 1998. "Art, Narrative, and Moral Understanding." In *Aesthetics and Ethics: Essays at the Intersection.* J. Levinson (ed.). Cambridge: Cambridge University Press, 126–60.

Devereaux, Mary. 2004. "Moral Judgments and Works of Art: The Case of Narrative Literature," *Journal of Aesthetics and Art Criticism,* 62, 3–11.

Dickie, George. 1964. "The Myth of the Aesthetic Attitude," *American Philosophical Quarterly,* 1, 56–65.

Gass, William. 1993. "Goodness Knows Nothing of Beauty: On the Distance between Morality and Art." In *Reflecting on Art.* J. Fisher (ed.). Mountain View: Mayfield, 108–15.

Gaut, Berys. 1998. "The Ethical Criticism of Art." In *Aesthetics and Ethics: Essays at the Intersection.* J. Levinson (ed.). Cambridge: Cambridge University Press, 182–203.

Gaut, Berys. 2007. *Art, Emotion and Ethics.* Oxford: Oxford University Press.

Jacobson, Daniel. 2006. "Ethical Criticism and the Vice of Moderation." In *Contemporary Debates in Aesthetics and the Philosophy of Art.* M. Kieran (ed.). Oxford: Blackwell, 342–55.

Kieran, Matthew. 2003. "Forbidden Knowledge: The Challenge of Immoralism." In *Art and Morality.* J. Bermúdez & S. Gardner (eds.). London: Routledge, 56–73.

Lamarque, Peter. 2006. "Cognitive Values in the Arts: Marking the Boundaries." In *Contemporary Debates in Aesthetics and the Philosophy of Art.* M. Kieran (ed.). Oxford: Blackwell, 127–39.

Nussbaum, Martha. 1990. *Love's Knowledge: Essays on Philosophy and Literature.* Oxford: Oxford University Press.

Posner, Richard. 1997. "Against Ethical Criticism," *Philosophy and Literature,* 21, 1–27.

Wilde, Oscar. 1992. *The Picture of Dorian Gray.* Ware: Wordsworth.

BERYS GAUT

museums Despite its evident centrality to the modern experience of art, the museum has been largely absent, as idea or institution, from the contemporary literature of aesthetics. The word scarcely appears in texts of the most different philosophical persuasions, and it is only within the last decade that journals like the *Journal of Aesthetics and Art Criticism* have carried articles devoted to the subject. This leakage from Cultural Studies and the new discipline of Museum Studies has, however, hardly affected the reigning orthodoxy in aesthetics, which identifies the autonomy of art with a transcendence of social and historical context. And yet it is in large part the museum that, by providing an institutional (and physical) form for art's autonomy, has created the possibility of aesthetic experience as conceptualized by aesthetic theory.

The transformative effect of the museum on the nature of art objects was noted in 1815 by Quatremère de Quincy, for whom the display of works removed from their original political, religious, and moral uses could mean nothing "but to say that society has no use for them" (1989: 37). Yet, even while protesting against Napoleon's removal of classical statues from Rome in 1796, Quatremère saw that city as itself a museum: a prototype of history museums, theme parks, and allied forms of display that aim at presenting an experience to which the viewer, distanced by history and cultural difference, can have only a spectator's, an aesthetic, relation.

Quatremère's complaint was echoed by John Dewey, who contrasted his own understanding of art as enhanced experience with "the museum conception of art." The museum, by separating artworks from their indigenous status, had given them a new one, "that of being specimens of fine art and nothing else." By the same token, Dewey was careful to note, it also set these objects "apart from common experience" and enabled them to "serve as insignia of taste and certificates of special culture" (1980: 6–9). Although he identified the museum and the notion of art associated with it as peculiar to modern, originally Western, society, Dewey followed the chief convention of aesthetic theory in constructing a theory of art in abstraction from historical specificity and so without further mention of museums.

However, it can well be said that without the museum the idea of art as a cross-cultural, transhistorical phenomenon, which underpins even Dewey's account, would not have achieved social visibility. It is no coincidence that

431

the onset of what has been named "the Museum Age" coincided, in the later eighteenth century, with the development of the modern system of the arts, as a domain of objects and practices sharing what were now called "aesthetic properties." The museum's role in this development was to represent, in the display of the objects collected in it, their shared character as "works of art." Its organization came to embody the classification of artworks, by nationality and period, and as between "high" and "decorative" arts: over time its inclusion of ever more types of object – ancient Middle Eastern, Asian, "primitive," "folk," and so on – actualized the extension of the label "art" over an expanding domain. It was the new uses that these items, stripped of any original functions, acquired in the museum – as elements of history and as materials for the construction of a mode of sensibility characterized by distance from material necessity and so free to cultivate responsiveness to experience – that appeared as the autonomy of art.

The establishment of the museum both responded to and fostered the modern idea of art as the product of individual creative acts, rather than as the performance of a contracted service. "Set at a distance from their original uses, past works can be joined by new ones produced specifically for display as works of art" (Mattick 2003: 112). The museum thus provides the ideal context, at once physical and ideological, for new as well as old art, a model for the other main locations of display, the gallery and the collector's home. In particular, by deciding what to collect and what part of their collections to display, museums play a central role in shaping and reshaping the artistic canon operative at any moment.

The princely art gallery, from which the museum evolved, typically aimed at impressing visitors with the power and wisdom of the prince. Accordingly, the collection was used decoratively; in the hanging of pictures, "size, colour and subject matter determined the arrangement, and paintings were often cut down or enlarged to fit into the ensemble" (Duncan & Wallach 1980: 455; see also Bazin 1967: ch. 7). In contrast, museums early on made the works displayed the center of attention. For example, the transformation of the Royal Collection in Vienna into a public museum in 1776 involved the rehanging of paintings in simple, uniform frames, with clear labels, grouped by national schools and art-historical periods.

The official in charge of this installation, Chrétien de Mechel, described his aim in the institution's catalogue as the construction of "a Repository where the history of art is made visible." This aim was criticized at the time (in von Rittershausen's commentary on the Vienna collection, 1785) as an elevation of science over aesthetic sensibility (Bazin 1967: 159). An ideal of the museum as an institution dedicated to purely aesthetic experience is visible also in such texts as Goethe's description of the Dresden Gallery in 1768 as a "temple," a "place consecrated to the holy ends of art" (Bazin 1967: 160). The conflict between historical knowledge and aesthetic contemplation – a conflict inherent in the modern idea of art, which seeks transcendent meaning in a historically diverse range of objects – has structured debate in the museum field ever since. The former seems the clear victor in the practical terms defined by the average visitor, who rarely pauses in contemplation of an individual work but tends to be drawn by the architecture of the institution toward a survey of the entire collection. Nonetheless, the museum remains at once the repository of art history and a testimony to the supposedly nonhistorical character of art's meaning.

R. G. Saisselin has noted resemblances between the museum and that other institution of the modern era, the department store, "an anti-museum of modern, productive, dynamic capitalist production in which *objets d'art* [are] but one possible line of goods." While the store displays the world of (mass-produced) commodities, the museum presents an array of (unique) items not for sale, but nonetheless bearing the high prices earned by being objects "beyond price." Taking the place occupied in earlier European society by the church, palace, and villa, these two spaces define the nature of art in modern society, as they "correspond to the internal contradictions of bourgeois aesthetics which are founded on idealism in a world that in its daily business is anything but ideal" (Saisselin 1984: 42, 47).

Beginning most notably with the dislocation of art in Europe during the French Revolution and the Napoleonic wars, the great museum collections were shaped by way of conquest and purchase, and today bear testimony to such political-economic processes as imperialistic expansion and the rise of economic powers in North America and Japan. While its omnivorous collecting exemplifies the unique openness of bourgeois culture to the practices and products of other societies, the museum also embodies the redefinition of all cultures in terms of its own. In particular, by exhibiting works of many types and from many disparate cultures in the same space, the museum activates the modern concept of art and so implicitly proclaims the essential, timeless character of modern social constructs generally. Thus the museum has celebrated both the innovative individual – artist and collector – central to bourgeois ideology and proclaimed the freedom of art from the constraints of social history.

Whether instituted under royal, papal, parliamentary, or revolutionary auspices, the museum was from the start "one of the fundamental institutions of the modern state" (Bazin 1967: 159). Indeed, as Duncan and Wallach observe, "in common with ancient ceremonial monuments, museums embody and make visible the idea of the state," traditionally "by the use of a Roman-derived architectural rhetoric" (1980: 449). Analogously to the way in which the state is supposed to incarnate the social interest in contrast to the competitive conflict of wills that structures civil society, the realm of art signifies the claim of capitalism's higher orders to rise above the confines of commerce as worthy inheritors of the aristocratic culture of the past. Involvement with the autonomous artwork represents detachment from the claims of practical life, even while its ownership and enjoyment require both money and the time made possible by money, and so signify financial success along with cultural superiority

As modern society has changed, forms of museum have changed with it. The converted European palaces and the neoclassical structures that in the USA expressed the imperial ambitions of turn-of-the-century robber barons have been joined – sometimes literally – by the modernist building styles favored by the corporations which after World War II became the primary funders of museum construction and exhibition programs. The change in architecture is

only one sign of the adaptation of the museum to corporate culture, along with organizational restructuring and such gambits as their self-promotion as locales for business social affairs. During the last decade, as contemporary art "has more and more clearly come to symbolize, and even generate, a city's identity as modern, up-to-date, part of the fast-paced international world of the moneyed and cutting-edge elite . . . museums have increasingly emphasized collecting and exhibiting contemporary art" and there has been a flurry of construction of new museums dedicated to it (Siegel 2006). A particularly noteworthy form of this is the phenomenon of museums devoted to the collections of wealthy individuals, celebrating their personal prowess as business people and collectors.

An exhibition space open to all, the museum not only created new modes of object display but also called for a new collective subject to experience them. "This new collective in the face of which all future art will exist and agonize is 'the public.' It is for the public that society in the new democratic age retraces in social space – through the creation of zoos, libraries, parks, museums, and concert halls – the amenities of leisure and privilege once held by a few within the private space of moneyed or aristocratic property" (Fisher 1975: 598–9). As a public institution, the museum suggests the idea that aesthetic experience is in principle universal; variations in the understanding and appreciation of art seem, then, to be a matter of individual ability, of the "eye." But this ability – "artistic competence," as Bourdieu and Darbel (1990) call it – depends on possession of a store of knowledge derived from the formal and informal education in general reserved for the upper classes. Given the class character of culture, the love of art – or the capacity for aesthetic experience – serves to legitimate privilege, in a differentiation of haves from have-nots that renders its social and economic basis invisible.

During the last half-century, what might be described as capitalism's overcoming of its former sense of inferiority with respect to the social order it replaced in Europe, and its forthright celebration of market-certified success, have led to a striking decline in the felt antipathy between art and bourgeois life central to the nineteenth-century ideal of culture. One

433

element of this is the transformation of the museum from a hallowed haunt of an aesthete minority into a thronged station of touristic pilgrimage. As art has become a central element of upper-income people's leisure activity, museums have become more visitor-friendly (with more explanatory labels, brochures, acoustiguides, etc.) while expanding auxiliary services like shops and restaurants (see Merriman 1989). It nevertheless remains true that a chief function of museums "is to reinforce for some the feeling of belonging and for others the feeling of exclusion" (Bourdieu & Darbel 1990: 112). The possibility that the powers of subjective response called for by the museum's appropriation of aristocratic pleasures could truly become the property of all remains to be realized by a future social transformation.

See also ART HISTORY; CULTURAL APPROPRIATION; DEWEY.

BIBLIOGRAPHY
Bazin, G. 1967. *The Museum Age*. New York: Universe.

Bourdieu, P. & Darbel, A. 1990 [1969]. *The Love of Art*. C. Beattie & N. Merriman (trans.). Stanford: Stanford University Press.

Dewey, John. 1980 [1934]. *Art as Experience*. New York: Perigree.

Duncan, C. & Wallach, A. 1980. "The Universal Survey Museum," *Art History*, 3, 448–74.

Fisher, P. 1975. "The Future's Past," *New Literary History*, 6, 587–606.

Mattick, Paul. 2003. "Context." In *Critical Terms for Art History*. R. S. Nelson & R. Shiff (eds.). Chicago: University of Chicago Press, 110–27.

Merriman, N. 1989. "Museum Visiting as a Cultural Institution." In *The New Museology*. P. Vergo (ed.). London: Reaktion, 149–71.

Quatremère de Quincy, A.-C. 1989 [1815]. *Considérations morales sur la destination des ouvrages de l'art* [Moral Considerations on the Purpose of Works of Art]. Paris: Fayard.

Saisselin, R. G. 1984. *The Bourgeois and the Bibelot*. New Brunswick: Rutgers University Press.

Siegel, E. K. 2006. "On Wisconson." In *Between the Lakes: Artists Respond to Madison*. Madison: Madison Art Center.

PAUL MATTICK

N

narrative   "Narrative" appears in the English language in the sixteenth century first as designating a legal document (1537) "which contains a statement of alleged or relevant facts closely connected with the matter or purpose of the document; *spec.* a statement of the parties to a deed and the cause of its granting" (*Oxford English Dictionary*), and then, a few years later (1571), in the more general and nontechnical sense of "An account of a series of events, facts, etc., given in order and with the establishing of connections between them." It is only in the mid nineteenth century (1843) that it enters the vocabulary of literary criticism as designating "The part of a text, esp. a work of fiction, which represents the sequence of events, as distinguished from that dealing with dialogue, description, etc." (*Oxford English Dictionary*). The conditions for what counts as a narrative as it appears in these usages are simple and define a phenomenon that is of little intrinsic interest.

Certain negative conclusions can be drawn about narrative on the basis of this very simple definition. The notion of narrative is distinct from notions such as fiction, story, tale, and plot, though all of these may have narrative as an element. There is nothing in the notion of narrative itself that licenses the conclusion that narratives have a special cognitive function, that is, that they have or do not have a referential function; that they necessarily constitute or construct fact rather than describe them; that they do or do not make claim to truth; that they have the function generally of imposing meaning and structure on "the world," on one's "life."

Narrative in this traditional sense can be of different kinds. There are literary narratives (and within this kind there is narrative poetry, epics, novels, etc.); there are fictional narratives, historical narratives, scientific narratives (the Big Bang Theory of the origin of the universe), etc. And while narrative itself is theoretically innocuous and of minimal theoretical interest, various *types* of narrative can and do have great cultural and, indeed, epistemological interest. But the interest is not due to the fact that something is a narrative but that it is literary, fictional, historical, etc.

This point is worth making since there has been a tendency in recent literary and cultural theory to assign to narrative a "deep" significance. Until the early 1960s, the notion of narrative was employed essentially as a nontheoretical, nontechnical concept in literary criticism. Then, with the effort to establish the disciplinary respectability of literary criticism by "theorizing" it, narrative became a technical concept. The theorizing of criticism was based in Saussurean structuralist linguistics, and rested on the assumption that there was a strong analogy between linguistic entities like the sentence and the literary work. The literary work could be segmented in the same way as a sentence, and the structure into which these segments entered could be described in a "grammar." Just as Saussure had developed a structural description of the sentence and rules for how to combine its constituent entities, one could develop a structural description of the literary text, breaking it down into constituent minimal units, and look for general rules for how these units could combine to yield (literary) meaning. Structuralist theory did not, however, stop at applying the analogy to literary works, but suggested that it would also hold for all kinds of cultural expressions.

For structuralist theory the concept of narrative was particularly suitable as a technical concept. It enabled theorists to emphasize what they saw as the commonalities between different kinds of stories: folktales, myths, novels, epics tales, historical accounts, scientific accounts, etc., and thus enabled them to develop a theory that would ostensibly apply to a wide range of cultural phenomena rather than just to literature. This gave the theory explanatory power. It enabled theorists to explore the elements common to all "narrative forms," oral and written, verse and prose, factual and fictional (Scholes & Kellogg 1966). However, this exploration was based in a theory of the novel, and was essentially an attempt to extend the theory of the novel to other kinds of story types. Literary narrative became the paradigmatic type of narrative and it was this kind of narrative that became the object of study in "narratology," a name modeled on "biology" and "sociology" (Todorov 1969), the "science of narrative" created by structuralism.

The assimilation of narrative per se to literary narrative might have some initial plausibility because there are certain features that all types of narrative share. They are narrated by a narrator, and insofar as they are narrations, narratives are human creations. The narrator employs a specific language, which is not neutral (transparent) but has a range of rhetorical features chosen by the narrator for a specific purpose. The narrator always presents a certain kind of perspective and exercises choice in picking out the events that make up the narrative. All types of narrative have a structure, even though it may be minimal: the events of a narrative must be linked in some way even though the link may simply be a chronological one ("The king died and then the queen died"). And all narratives have a temporal dimension.

The consequence of adopting literary narrative as paradigmatic was that those features that are characteristic of this type of narrative were assumed to be features of narrative per se and assumed to play the same role and to receive the same emphasis in other types of narrative as they do in literary narrative. Literary narratives are made up in a strong sense: they create characters, objects, and events and structure these in accordance with certain conventions (literary narratives have a beginning, a middle, and an end); they present a perspective on the events they describe, a perspective which is defined through a variety of rhetorical devices; and through these various means the literary narrative creates coherence and meaning but it does so without employing reference to a world external to the narrative.

The assimilation of narrative per se to literary narrative had two particularly important consequences. The view of narrative as imposing order and creating meaning gave narrative a new importance. It could be seen as a way of imposing order and meaning on "reality," whether that reality was the historical past, the identity of the individual, the physical world, the social world, or the world of ideas. This new importance assigned to narrative also led to its being sought and found everywhere. Or to put it in slightly different terms, a number of different kinds of human discursive practices came to be conceptualized as narratives in the literary sense, thus giving the new science of narrative an object worthy of attention and inquiry. This science of narrative also identified for itself precursors which had established the deep significance of certain kinds of narrative: Vladimir Propp's *Morfologiya skazki* (1928; *Morphology of the Folk Tale*), which created a model for folktales based on seven "spheres of action" and 31 "functions" of narrative, and Claude Lévi-Strauss's *Anthropologie structurale* (1958; *Structural Anthropology*), which outlined a "grammar" of mythology.

The view of narrative as imposing order and meaning was attacked in poststructuralist theory. As in so many areas of poststructuralism, the criticism of the structuralist theory of narrative was conservative rather than radical. It did not reject the concepts and framework of analysis, but only the thesis that the meaning and order produced by narrative was substantive and true. In fact, the attack on the meaning-producing function of narrative took its point of departure in the second important consequence of assimilating narrative per se to literary narrative: the adoption of the view that narrative did not have referential function and consequently could not be true or false. In this perspective, the order and meaning created by narrative were seen as social constructs without any basis in the world outside the narrative. Indeed, narrative created not only the order and meaning it presented but also the objects and events that constituted that order. There was no final narrative (*grand récit*) about the world, which could reveal an objective order, nor a final narrative about the historical past, the self, the social world, or the world of ideas, which was the *true* narrative. There were just different narratives.

When the concept of narrative was introduced first in literary theory and then into a broader cultural theory, it was employed as a critical primitive. It was assumed that the concept as such was unproblematic and that it referred to a phenomenon, which could be the object of study and be described in a theory. The question that was raised neither in literary theory nor when the concept of literary narrative was extended to other forms of cultural discourse was whether the concept of narrative was a useful critical instrument. Narrative in the sense in which it appears in cultural theory is a theoretical construct: narrative is not a given that awaits discovery and description. The question of usefulness is therefore centrally important.

The question can be briefly answered insofar as the application of the concept to discourses other than literature is concerned, and written history provides a touchstone. First, historical accounts are not necessarily constituted through a narrative. An article presenting the results of an inquiry into the income of hand-loom weavers in Flanders from 1650 to 1660 will not in any sense constitute a narrative. When a historical account does make use of narrative it is subject to constraints that are absent in the case of literary narratives: in a historical narrative the referential function is central, and it is subject to the requirement that it be a true and accurate account of events. On the other hand, a historical narrative does not have a formulaic structure that can be captured in a theory. It can be fairly clearly structured or it can have only a very loose structure. It needs only to be "An account of a series of events, facts, etc., given in order and with the establishing of connections between them." And it does not present a story with a meaning. Indeed, the establishment of the academic discipline of historiography came about through a series of steps where the moralizing of history was rejected as were those historians who wrote grand narratives employing an attractive literary style. So in relation to history, the concept of literary narrative is not helpful. Indeed, in the philosophy of history the notion of narrative has been developed in another direction in an attempt to develop a notion of "narrative explanation."

In literary criticism and theory, where narrative as a technical concept was first introduced, the answer about usefulness can be somewhat more positive. The "science of narrative" has been unable to answer the question about the "nature of narrative," that is, unable to reach any sort of agreement concerning the elements and structural principles of narrative. Also in this area, the concept of narrative and, consequently, the nature of narrative itself remains Protean. However, narrative theory, inspired in particular by Gérard Genette's work, has produced a vocabulary for discussing narrative which can be used eclectically and which has provided critics of the novel, the epic, and, indeed, of film with a useful toolbox. To that extent the attempt to move from a nontechnical concept of narrative as designating "The part of a text, esp. a work of fiction, which represents the sequence of events, as distinguished from that dealing with dialogue, description, etc." to a well-defined technical concept of narrative has brought the disciplines of literary studies and film studies a step forward.

See also LITERATURE; FICTION, TRUTH IN; STRUCTURALISM AND POSTSTRUCTURALISM.

BIBLIOGRAPHY

Chatman, Seymour. 1978. *Story and Discourse: Narrative Structure in Fiction and Film*. Ithaca: Cornell University Press.

Danto, Arthur C. 2007. *Narration and Knowledge*. 3rd rev. edn. New York: Columbia University Press.

Genette, Gérard. 1980. *Narrative Discourse*. J. E. Lewin (trans.). Oxford: Blackwell.

Hutto, Daniel D. (ed.). 2007. *Narrative and Understanding Persons: Royal Institute of Philosophy Supplements*. Cambridge: Cambridge University Press.

Lamarque, Peter. 2004. "On Not Expecting Too Much from Narrative," *Mind and Language*, 19, 393–408.

Lévi-Strauss, Claude. 1993 [1958]. *Structural Anthropology*, vol. i. C. Jacobson & G. Grundfest Schoepf (trans.). Harmondsworth: Penguin.

Mitchell, W. J. T. (ed.). 1981. *On Narrative*. Chicago: University of Chicago Press.

Phelan, James & Rabinowitz, Peter J. (eds.). 2005. *A Companion to Narrative Theory*. Oxford: Blackwell.

Propp, Vladimir. 1968 [1928]. *Morphology of the Folk Tale*. 2nd rev. edn. L. Scott (trans.). Austin: University of Texas Press.

Scholes, Robert & Kellogg, Robert L. 1966. *The Nature of Narrative*. Oxford: Oxford University Press.
Todorov, Tzvetan. 1969. *Grammaire du Décaméron*. The Hague: Mouton.

STEIN HAUGOM OLSEN

nature, aesthetics of *see* AESTHETICS OF THE ENVIRONMENT; GARDENS.

Nietzsche, Friedrich (Wilhelm) (1844–1900) German philosopher and poet; at first a champion of Wagner, but later his bitterest critic. Unrecognized during the sane years of his life, he has exerted a huge influence in the twentieth century, for example, on existentialism and postmodernism. Nietzsche's thought about art (indeed, his philosophy in general) may be divided into four sharply contrasting periods: an early period centered on *The Birth of Tragedy* (1872); a "positivistic" period centered on *Human, All Too Human* (1878); the period of *The Gay Science* (1882–7) and *Thus Spoke Zarathustra* (1883–6); and his last year before the onset of madness, 1888, the central work of which is *Twilight of the Idols*. (It must be added, however, that this opinion, as with almost everything to do with Nietzsche, is highly controversial.)

THE BIRTH OF TRAGEDY

Nietzsche's interest in art is marked by an intense seriousness, an attribute he shares with his mentor, Schopenhauer. Fundamentally, he asks but one question: what can art do for life? How can it help us flourish, or at least survive? And he possesses but one evaluative criterion: good art is art that "promotes" life, bad art that which "hinders" it. At some stages in his career he sees art as, literally, a life-saving activity, our only salvation from "nausea and suicide." At others, he sees it as useless, hostile even, to the promotion of life. At these moments, with the radicalism of a Plato, he does not hesitate to demand its elimination from our culture.

The sense of life as deeply problematic is something Nietzsche took over from the self-confessed pessimist, Schopenhauer. In *The Birth of Tragedy* (alternatively titled *Hellenism and Pessimism*) he emphasizes that the radical insecurity of the individual in the face of the "terror and horror" of (Darwinian) nature belongs inalienably to its metaphysical essence: "Socratism," the conviction that science is capable of knowing and even "correcting" being, is a destructive illusion. History is a mere flux of generation and destruction to which we are powerless to impart direction or significance.

Faced with such nausea-inspiring "absurdity," we cannot do better than learn from the Greeks. They, though deeply sensitive to the "wisdom of Silenus" – "best of all is not to be born, not to be, to be nothing. But the second best for you is to die soon" – not only survived but also constructed a culture the like of which has never since been seen. The Greeks, Nietzsche holds, survived through their art: more specifically, through their two types of art – "Apollonian," the art of, for example, Homer; and "Dionysian," the later art of the great tragedians Sophocles and Aeschylus. (The claim that the music dramas of Richard Wagner represent a rebirth of Dionysian art constitutes the main propaganda point of *The Birth of Tragedy*.)

Nietzsche describes Apollonian art as a "radiant glorification" of the phenomena of human existence by means of which the Greeks "overcame . . . or at any rate veiled" (1966a: §3) from themselves the horrors of life. In the "dream-birth" of their gods and heroes they produced a beautiful, "transfigured" portrait of *themselves* that "seduced" them into a favorable evaluation of life as such. Typically, Nietzsche elucidates transfiguration in terms of "illusion" and even "lies." But we cannot understand Apollonian seduction as sentimentality, a simple censoring of the horrible, for he also says that in Apollonian art "*all* things, whether good *or evil* [*böse*] are deified" (1966a: §3; emphasis added). The way to understand this idea of a beautiful illusion that is yet in some way truthful is to think of Uccello's *Battle of San Romano* or of that modern epic, the Western. In art (or, more generally, consciousness) of this kind, war, pain, and death exist yet are "overcome," swamped, by our sense of the power and magnificence, the *style* of its heroes. Dazzled by their beauty, we are desensitized to the horrors they confront.

What now of the Dionysian solution to the problem of living? To understand this, we have to take account of the fact that *The Birth of Tragedy* takes over, assumes as given, Schopenhauer's version of Kantian idealism. According to this, the everyday world of plurality and individuality is mere appearance or phenomenon. Beyond or behind the *principium individuationis* lies reality itself, the monistic thing in itself called by both Schopenhauer and Nietzsche "the will," and by the latter also "the primal unity." According to the metaphysics in question, this is what constitutes our true identity.

Nietzsche's account of Dionysian art comes as an answer to Aristotle's question as to the nature of the "tragic effect." Why is it that we voluntarily subject ourselves to depictions of the terrible in life, the downfall and destruction of human beings of more than usual power and quality? Presumably, we must derive some kind of satisfaction. But what is its nature?

Schopenhauer had classified the tragic effect as the highest species of the "feeling of the sublime," the feeling of fearless exultation that we sometimes experience when confronting the normally fearful – for example, a storm or waterfall. He, following Kant, explains this as a becoming alive to the "supersensible," supra-individual aspect of one's being. And Nietzsche does the same: the "artistic taming of the horrible" is, he says, "the sublime" (1966a: §7). In tragedy, though forced to witness the destruction of its hero, "we are not to become rigid with fear: a metaphysical comfort tears us momentarily from the bustle of changing figures. We really are, for a brief moment, the primordial being itself" (1966a: §17). In Greek tragedy this effect is achieved through the singing of the chorus. Though we partially empathize with the tragic hero, our primary identification is with the chorus. This leads us to view the action from a Dionysian, metaphysical perspective, and through this we experience an exultant affirmation of our supra-individual identity. Tragedy has the quasi-religious function of "redeem[ing] us from the greedy thirst for this existence." With an "admonishing gesture" it "reminds us of another existence and a higher pleasure" (1966a: §21).

HUMAN, ALL TOO HUMAN

In 1876, unable to sustain his friendship with Wagner any longer, Nietzsche abruptly departed from Bayreuth in the middle of its first festival. This dramatic change in his personal life was the outward manifestation of a profound change in philosophical outlook, a change that found expression in *Human, All Too Human*. *The Birth of Tragedy*, dominated by Schopenhauer's pessimistic transcendentalism and its musico-dramatic expression in Wagner's *Tristan and Isolde*, had been the product and expression of romantic alienation from worldly reality in general, and from the materialism and scientific optimism of the nineteenth century in particular. But in *Human, All Too Human* all such "untimeliness" disappears. The idea of a "metaphysical world" relative to which nature is mere appearance is held up to ridicule. All that exists is material reality. Moreover, it is a reality in principle capable of being understood, even controlled, by human beings. In short, the hitherto despised position of Socratism comes now to be *occupied* by Nietzsche.

In line with this newfound optimism, art comes to be seen as useless – an object, even, of contempt. Its function, as conceived in *The Birth of Tragedy*, was to *protect* us from the horrors of human reality. But now we need no such protection or "narcoticizing." On the contrary, we need to look at reality as unflinchingly as possible. The more we look, particularly, to the metaphysical comforts of art, the less we are inclined to change that in the world which disturbs us. Art, like religion, is the opiate of the neurotic. (Indeed art *is* religion: the *feelings* served and promoted by religion are able to survive because, submerged in the vagueness of art, they have been severed from those cognitive claims that have become ludicrous to the post-Enlightenment thinker.) Thankfully, however, concludes Nietzsche, we are moving into a postartistic culture. We live in the "evening twilight of art": "the scientific man is the further evolution of the artistic" (1986: §§222–3).

THE GAY SCIENCE

Here we confront yet another abrupt shift in Nietzsche's stance toward life and toward art. As "aesthetic phenomenon," we are told, "existence is still *bearable* for us." But without the aestheticization of life, the realization that "delusion and error are conditions of human knowledge" would lead us to "nausea and suicide"

(1968a: §107). We are back, in short, with the failure of Socratism: the brief reconciliation is over. We face, once again, our powerlessness ultimately to know and hence to impose significant form on the world. Its character is "in all eternity chaos" (1968a: §109).

Faced with this terrible knowledge brought by that intellectual "honesty" which defines the scientist in general and the philosopher in particular, we must turn from science to art, that "cult of the untrue" (1968a: §107) – not, or not primarily, the art of artworks, but art, rather, which has our own life as its product. We must learn from artists, learn in particular to utilize "artistic distance" (1968a: §§78, 107) so that by standing back from an object "there is a good deal that one no longer sees and much the eye has to add if we are still to see [anything] . . . at all." Yet we must be "wiser" than they. For their subtle powers of transfiguration usually stop with the artwork, whereas "we want to be poets of our lives" (1968a: §299). We want and need to write for ourselves, in particular, not the suicide-threatening life of honesty, but, rather, a "mocking, light, fleeting, divinely untroubled, divinely artificial" kind of life that "like a pure flame licks into unclouded skies." Above all, we must learn from the Greeks, who knew that to live requires one to "stop courageously at the surface," to be "superficial – *out of profundity*" (1968a: §4).

It is not difficult to recognize here a return both to the pessimism of *The Birth of Tragedy* and to the Apollonian solution of redemption through illusion. As in *The Birth of Tragedy*, however, Nietzsche contemplates a *second* art solution to the predicament of living. This crucially involves the idea of willing the "eternal recurrence" of *everything* in one's life (1968a: §341), an idea which may be seen as equivalent to the injunction to *amor fati, to love* everything that has happened in one's life – indeed in the world.

How is such "redemption" of the totality of the past possible? By discovering a "personal providence" even in the most problematic events in one's past; through seeing "how palpably always everything that happens to us turns out for the best" (1968a: §277). But to do this one must be an artist: one must script for oneself such a personality that the vicissitudes of one's past acquire a cumulative value

rather like a well-constructed *Bildungsroman*. Construing one's life so that one can will its eternal recurrence, unlike "profound superficiality," is entirely "honest": one wills, loves *all* of one's life, and there is none of the "looking away," evasion, falsification, self-deception, and repression that is involved in the life of artifice. But it is an honesty achievable only by that ideal fiction, the *Übermensch* (overman). Only such a being would have the "overflowing" psychic health necessary to incorporate the horrors of the world into a lovable, beautiful whole. We, like Nietzsche's alter ego Zarathustra, remain "convalescents," unable to will the eternal recurrence. Lacking *übermenschlich* health, *we* cannot but retreat into profound superficiality.

TWILIGHT OF THE IDOLS

The idea of the beautifying illusion as a solution to the predicament of living continued to have a powerful hold over Nietzsche in the last year of his productive life: "Truth is ugly. We possess *art* lest we perish of the truth" (1968b: §822), runs an unpublished note from 1888. But what distinguishes *Twilight of the Idols* from *The Gay Science* is a renewed interest in the tragic effect. What the tragedian communicates, Nietzsche says, is a state of "[being] *without* fear in the face of the fearful . . . courage and freedom of feeling before a powerful enemy, before a sublime calamity" (1966b: §9, 24). What is this freedom of feeling? It is "the will to life rejoicing over its own inexhaustibility . . . be[ing] oneself the eternal joy of becoming." And, he points out, "herewith I again touch the point from which I once went forth: *The Birth of Tragedy*" (1966b: §10, 5). There is, that is, a cyclical quality to Nietzsche's thought about art: at the end of his career, as at the beginning, he offers us not merely the beautiful but also the sublime as solutions to the problem of living: not merely the transfiguration of the world of individuals, but also its transcendence.

Different though they are, Nietzsche's Apollonian and Dionysian solutions share with each other (and with Schopenhauer) the desire to escape the actuality of human life. Though he would not wish to admit this, they are both species of – to use his own language – "romanticism." For all his tough talk about honesty, courage, and facing up to life as the "will to power," Nietzsche's thought about art is, at the end as at the beginning, the product of a wounded consciousness.

See also NINETEENTH- AND TWENTIETH-CENTURY CONTINENTAL AESTHETICS; FUNCTION OF ART; SCHOPENHAUER; TRAGEDY; WAGNER.

BIBLIOGRAPHY

Primary sources
[1872] 1966a. *The Birth of Tragedy.* W. Kaufmann (trans.). New York: Vintage (Includes *The Case of Wagner.*)
[1878] 1986. *Human, All Too Human.* R. Hollingdale (trans.). Cambridge: Cambridge University Press.
[1882] 1968a. *The Gay Science.* W. Kaufmann (trans.). New York: Vintage.
[1901] 1968b. *The Will to Power.* W. Kaufmann & R. Hollingdale (trans.). New York: Vintage.
1966b. *The Portable Nietzsche.* W. Kaufmann (ed. & trans.). New York: Vintage. (Contains *Thus Spoke Zarathustra* (1883–5), *Twilight of the Idols* (1888), and *Nietzsche contra Wagner.*)
1983. *Untimely Meditations,* vol. iv. R. Hollingdale (trans.). Cambridge: Cambridge University Press. (Contains *Richard Wagner at Bayreuth* (1876).)

Secondary sources
Heller, Erich. 1988. *The Importance of Nietzsche.* Chicago: University of Chicago Press.
Higgins, Kathleen Marie. 1987. *Nietzsche's Zarathustra.* Philadelphia: Temple University Press.
Nehamas, Alexander. 1985. *Nietzsche: Life as Literature.* Cambridge, MA: Harvard University Press.
Ridley, Aaron. 2007. *Nietzsche on Art.* New York: Routledge.
Schacht, Richard. 1983. *Nietzsche.* London: Routledge & Kegan Paul.
Silk, M. S. & Stern, J. P. 1981. *Nietzsche on Tragedy.* Cambridge: Cambridge University Press.
Young, Julian. 1992. *Nietzsche's Philosophy of Art.* Cambridge: Cambridge University Press.

JULIAN YOUNG

non-Western art   *see* AFRICAN AESTHETICS; AMERINDIAN AESTHETICS; CHINESE AESTHETICS; INDIAN AESTHETICS; ISLAMIC AESTHETICS; JAPANESE AESTHETICS; RASA.

notations   Musical scores are paradigmatic of artistic notations, as is their function of specifying works for performance. The work's creator writes them and through them addresses the per-former, indicates what is to be achieved, and effectively mandates "make it so!" Playscripts are equivalent. These are *work-specifying notations.*

To be correctly interpreted, scores must be read according to the appropriate notational and performance conventions. Sometimes the notation is not to be read literally; for instance, sometimes a note is to be sharpened or flattened without this being shown in the notation. Sometimes what is notated has the force merely of a recommendation, such as fingering indications. Sometimes what is required is not shown in the notation, for example, that melodies are to be decorated when repeated. The relevant conventions and practices have changed over time. Phrasing indications had the status of recommendations in 1700 but were mandatory by 1850; the same is true of the specified instrumentation. In general, the historical trend was for scores both to indicate and to mandate more detail. This is likely to be connected to the standardization of instruments and of orchestras, a more consistent and higher quality of professionalism among performers, and the composer's decreasing involvement in performances of his works.

What is indicated may be precise (middle C) or vague (the tempo indication "fast"). Instructions of the latter kind indicate not that the notation is inadequate to specifying its work, but rather that the given work is vague (within conventionally established limits) in some aspects of its constitution.

However detailed the notation is, it underdetermines much of the concrete detail of its accurate performances and so they differ. Performances always are richer in properties than the works they are of. Typically, a playscript indicates what is to be said, but not its accent, phrasing, pace, or tone; as well, it is rare that accompanying gestures, facial expressions, physical interactions between the actors, and so forth are specified. These matters are left to the performers' (or director's) discretion. The decisions taken on such matters contribute to the performers' interpretation of the work.

A difficult case to classify is that of the architect's plan. It is addressed to those who will instance the work, but their doing so is not usually regarded as a performance or as allowing much interpretative freedom. Yet, if we allow that the architectural work is created when the plan is done, whether or not the building is built, just as we allow for finished but unperformed musical works and plays, the plan might best be regarded as work-specifying. A similarly difficult case is that of the movie script. Again, if we think of a remake based on the same script as a further instance of the same work, the script looks to be work-specifying. The alternative to these conclusions holds that the remake is a different but related movie, even when based on the same script, in which case the script is best thought of as a sketch or design for the work, but not as work-specifying. The corresponding view for architecture would hold that an architectural work is not created until the building is built. How we should settle such problem cases depends on the ontology appropriate to works of the kinds in question.

It can be clear that sketches, drafts, and designs prefigure the work, as aspects of the process of its creation, rather than functioning as work specifications. This is especially apparent where the artwork is singular and not for performance, such as a hewn statue or an oil painting. In formulating or experimenting with the work, the artist might make preparatory drawings and models. These are not work notations. Though the distinction can be more difficult to draw in practice, the same applies to notes and drafts of dramatic works, musical works, novels, and poems, and also to unused movie takes.

Not all works for performance are transmitted via work-specifying notations. Instead, a model performance might be given, and the work then be passed on by performers who recall the work-relevant details of that performance. This is commonly the case with dance, as well as in folk and oral traditions of music, saga, and drama. Several notations for dance exist, though none is as entrenched as is the standard musical notation. These could be and have been used to specify dance works. More often, though, they are written down after the fact, and often not by the choreographer, as a way of recording the work. In the musical case, such notations are called "transcriptions," though I will use the general term "work-recording notations." A notation that is work-recording *describes* the work and lacks the normative, directive force of notations with a work-specifying function.

Notational recordings may be made of performances that do not instance works; for instance, the transcriber might notate a freely improvised jazz solo from a recording of it. Where they are of work performances, notational recordings might target the performance, the interpretation, or the work. That is, there may be *performance-recording* and *interpretation-recording notations*, as well as work-recording ones. Typically, a notational record of a performance would record all its individual idiosyncrasies, nuances, and micro-details, perhaps even its errors. A notational record of an interpretation would capture not only the work but also the way it is shaped for performance in the given interpretation. A notational record of a work would indicate only what is work-constitutive. Notational records of interpretations or performances are likely to include nonstandard notational characters, drawings, or written descriptions, because they aim to capture the kinds of details not usually covered in notations designed for work specification. The transcriptions by Béla Bartók of Serbo-Croatian folksongs employ so many supplementary signs that they are almost unreadable.

A special instance of a notational recording is that of *mnemonic notations*. These have the function of reminding performers (or their teachers) of a piece with which they have a prior familiarity. These frequently underspecify the work, leaving memory to fill in what is missing. For instance, one might record a melody simply by its direction of movement (*First note, Up, Down*, and *Same*), which may be sufficient to bring the melody to mind. For instance, the last movement theme of Beethoven's Ninth Symphony then would be *FUUSDDDDUUSD-SUUUSDDDDUUDDS, UUDUUUDDUUUDD-DUD*, etc. The earliest musical notations were mnemonics, often of a rather simple kind.

Another anomalous work-recording notation is that of the pictographs that accompany some purely electronic musical works. Such notations are not addressed to performers – such pieces are for playback, not performance – and they would be difficult to interpret sonically in any case. One reason for their production was that, at one time, composers could copyright only scores, not musical works as such.

On a liberal view of what counts as a notation, we could regard photographs of singular paintings and statues as notational records of those works. The same might apply to copies in the same or similar media, as well as to verbal descriptions of their appearance. And to return to the sketches made in advance of the work, we might regard these, if not as records, then as notational predictions or precursors of their works.

So far the focus has fallen here on the relation between notations and works for performance. Other kinds of works, especially multiply instanced ones, can be or are notated. A novel, for instance, is characterized by a certain word sequence, and we might reasonably characterize an inscription of that sequence as a *work-constituting notation*. Instead of being addressed to performers, that notation realizes the work, with the first instance that comes complete from the author's hand setting the standard by which the faithfulness of later copies or clones is judged.

Here poetry is problematic. If one thinks of poetry as to be read out, in effect to be performed, the text of the poem is work specifying, but if it is not to be read out the text is work constituting. Again, ontological analysis would be needed to settle the issue, or to demonstrate that poems come in a variety of ontological types, some of which are for performance and some not.

I call the written text of the novel work constitutive because its analogic nature gives the audience direct access to the work. On this basis, we might distinguish work-constitutive notations from *work-encoding notations*. Examples of the latter might include printouts of text, music, or movies as a sequence of 1s and 0s, or electromagnetic tapes and computer files, or grooves in vinyl records. To provide access to the work, these must be decoded in some appropriate fashion, where decoding is a mechanical rather than an interpretative process. In this schema, prints of movies are work-encoding notations because, though the frames are analogic, it is only when a print is screened that the movie moves as it should. Other borderline cases include silkscreens, etched plates, woodcuts, statue molds, and photo negatives.

Earlier I suggested that, on a liberal account, we might count one picture as a notational record of another. The philosopher who wrote most on notations, Nelson Goodman (1976), would object. Paintings are *autographic*; every

feature is relevant to the work's identity. By contrast, it is a hallmark of *allographic* arts that they are notational; such works are defined by their "spelling" and any accurate rendition of this spelling instances the work, whatever other differences there are between renditions.

Goodman goes on to consider the features that must be met by a notation if it is to unequivocally specify a work and concludes it must be unambiguous and both syntactically and semantically disjoint and differentiated. In other words, the notational elements cannot overlap and every mark can be assigned to only one of any two notational elements. Where elements in actual musical notations fall short of these standards, Goodman denies that they specify work-identifying features. In consequence, he regards tempo, improvised cadenzas, trills, figured basses, and the like as not part of the work, but rather as aspects of the performer's interpretation.

Goodman's attempt to exclude social conventions and practices, so that the work can be specified purely in terms of its notation, means that he must either strip the work of features that seem essential to its identity or treat every work as created under a symbol system that is unique to it (or, perhaps, to its composer) (Davies 2001). This *reductio* should lead us to conclude both that there are no purely allographic works and that acknowledgment of the sociohistorical context as relevant to the artwork's identity undermines Goodman's distinction between autographic and allographic works (Levinson 1990).

See also DRAMA; MUSIC AND SONG; AUTHENTICITY AND ART; GOODMAN; ONTOLOGICAL CONTEXTUALISM; ONTOLOGY OF ARTWORKS; PERFORMANCE.

BIBLIOGRAPHY
Benesh, Rudolf & Benesh, Joan. 1956. *An Introduction to Dance Notation*. London: Adam & Charles Black.
Davies, Stephen. 2001. *Musical Works and Performances: A Philosophical Exploration*. Oxford: Clarendon, ch. 3.
Goodman, Nelson. 1976. *Languages of Art*. 2nd edn. Indianapolis: Hackett.
Laban, Rudolf. 1956. *Principles of Dance and Movement Notation*. London: Macdonald & Evans.
Levinson, Jerrold. 1990. *Music, Art, and Metaphysics*. Ithaca: Cornell University Press, ch. 5.

STEPHEN DAVIES

O

---

objectivity and realism in aesthetics   There is objectivity in an area if it makes sense to think of judgments on those matters as in some way correct or incorrect, as right or wrong. Realism about a given area, in contrast, is the claim that judgments on that topic are right or wrong *because* they describe distinctive aspects of reality, the nature of which determines which of our judgments are correct. Thus, while questions of objectivity focus on our judgments, questions of realism focus on the world those judgments concern. (That, at least, is how I will use the terms. Some writers treat the two as more or less synonymous.)

We can distinguish three aspects to any area of discourse: the judgments we make on the topic (either the mental act of judging that an object has some feature, or the act of expressing that judgment verbally); the reactions to the world on which we base those judgments, be they perceptions, feelings, or other mental states; and the features of the world that provoke those reactions. Where not only realism but realism in the strongest form is appropriate, we get something like the following picture. (1) The judgments in the discourse represent certain facts as obtaining. (2) Those facts are represented as holding independently of the particular judgments we make about them. (3) We can make sense of what those facts are without referring to our practice of making such judgments, or the reactions on which those judgments are based. (4) Those reactions are cognitive: they, like the judgments they ground, represent those facts as obtaining. (5) In favorable conditions, the pattern in our judgments (finding these things to be *F*, and these things not to be) reflects some pattern in the world. (6) That correlation takes the most straightforward form: judgments ascribing a single feature will be made in response to the presence of a single feature in the world. We may think that something like this picture holds in the case of shape. Our judgments of shape represent facts about the shape of things as obtaining, facts that we take to be independent of those judgments, and indeed which we can make sense of independently of our judging shape at all. The judgments are based on responses, perceptions of shape, that themselves represent certain things as the case (that what is before me is such and such a shape). Moreover, when things go right, our judgments align with reality in the simplest way: for example, we judge to be cubes all and only things that have a certain feature – they are cubic.

Aesthetic matters might be thought to fit this strong realist picture too (Moore 1993: 248–51). Below we will see some reasons for doubting that they do. I begin, however, with views that take aesthetic discourse to lack certain features required for strong realism. Indeed, I start with views that lie at the other end of the spectrum, views that reject, not only realism, but objectivity too.

The *expressivist* about aesthetics (Ayer 1952) denies that our aesthetic judgments represent at all. Claim (1) is thus false of aesthetic discourse, and so therefore are (2) and (3). But the reason aesthetic judgments fail to represent is that the mental states that ground them are not representational either. The reactions on which I base my judgments in aesthetic matters are feelings, in key part of pleasure and displeasure. These do not purport to capture how things are. They may be caused by certain aspects of the world around me, but they no more represent those aspects than a stinging sensation represents the nettle that was its cause. Thus the expressivist about aesthetics takes (4) to be false too, and to provide the fundamental point of contrast with matters such as shape. In consequence, when we say, for instance, that something is beautiful, we are not describing the world but giving voice to ("expressing") the pleasure the object has stirred. The classic analogy here is with expressions of pain or of approval such as "ouch" or "hooray." Note the suggestion is not that these various expressions *mean* "I take pleasure in/feel pain at/approve of this." For they would then be representations of facts after all – facts about my responses. Rather, the claim is that language here does not perform a representational function at all, but an expressive one.

There is something to be said in favor of expressivism's claim that neither (1) nor (4) holds in aesthetics. The idea that aesthetic judgment is rooted in noncognitive responses, of pleasure, displeasure, and perhaps other feelings, is one with a distinguished history (Kant 2000: §1; Hume 2004: 495). And it is very plausible that when we utter aesthetic judgments at least part of what we do is to express responses provoked by the object judged. As many have noted, in some sense the right to offer an aesthetic judgment requires one to have experienced the object for oneself, and to have responded to it in the appropriate way (Kant 2000: §33; Wollheim 1980: 234; Mothersill 1986). The expressivist can explain what goes wrong in such cases, and why. Since the judgment's role in our language is to express a certain response, to utter the judgment when one lacks the response is to misuse the words. (Compare "ouch" as uttered by someone in pain, and by someone who is not.)

However, expressivism is too crude. It implies that the *only* way in which our aesthetic judgments can be appropriate (or otherwise) is as sincere (or not) expressions of feeling. There seems more room for right and wrong here than this allows. For one thing, each individual's aesthetic judgments should reflect the supervenience of aesthetic on nonaesthetic matters. If you take two items to be perfectly alike in nonaesthetic respects, you cannot reasonably take them to differ aesthetically. For instance, two paintings that present the same appearance and that share a history (perhaps they were painted simultaneously by an ambidextrous artist) cannot differ in beauty or artistic merit: if one is a masterpiece, the other is. At least to this limited extent, your judgments of aesthetic quality are answerable to

other facts about the object. For the expressivist, however, my feelings alone govern what I appropriately say, and nothing renders the feelings themselves appropriate or otherwise. If only one of a pair of identical nettles stings me, the situation is odd; but there is nothing wrong in my saying "ouch" to one and not to the other. Thus, if we model the aesthetic case as closely on that of pain as the expressivist suggests, some of the normativity of aesthetic judgment is left out. Nor is this the only omission. Given that the feelings that supposedly ground aesthetic judgment can be neither appropriate nor otherwise, the expressivist can make no sense of the idea that my judgment conflicts with yours. Yet we do take disagreement to be possible in aesthetics. There must, it seems, be more to aesthetic judgment than the expression of a noncognitive response.

The *error theorist* (Mackie 1977) takes this moral to heart. On this view, aesthetic judgments are just as much claims about the world as are judgments of shape. There is a gulf between them, but it lies at the level of the world described, rather than the semantics of our claims. For while our aesthetic talk describes a realm of distinct aesthetic properties, there are in fact no such properties for it to describe accurately or otherwise. There are shapes, colors perhaps, various properties studied by the sciences and captured in everyday perception. But there is not, in addition to these, beauty and elegance, ugliness or lack of grace. When we examine the world reflectively, we find that the subject matter of aesthetic discourse goes missing. Thus, while the expressivist denies that aesthetic judgments are even candidates for truth, the error theorist accepts that they are candidates, but denies that any are in fact true. (They are either false or lack a truth value altogether.) In aesthetics, strong realism's (5) and (6) fail to hold.

Error theory is first and foremost a rejection of realism. However, in effect it rejects objectivity too. It does so on the basis of three assumptions. First, the content of our aesthetic claims is very committing: a realm of metaphysically distinctive mind-independent properties, the distribution of which would provide the standard of correctness for our aesthetic judgments. Second, the only correctness that could apply to those judgments would be truth and falsity. Third, truth should itself be understood as correspondence between the content of one's judgments and the nature of mind-independent reality. Given these assumptions, objectivity in aesthetics requires realism. (See Zangwill 2001: ch. 9 for someone who accepts this entailment, but uses it to reason *to* realism from objectivity.) Arguments against a realm of distinct mind-independent aesthetic properties, some of which we will consider below, then persuade the error theorist that, since realism is false, objectivity also fails.

Each assumption has been questioned. One way to undermine the second is to consider *quasi-realism*. In effect, this is expressivism back in more sophisticated form. The quasi-realist project (Blackburn 1984, 1993) is to retain the idea that aesthetic judgments are at root grounded in noncognitive responses such as pleasure, while explaining how aesthetic discourse nonetheless comes to have many of the features a realist would expect. The project has been worked through furthest in ethics. There, one can perhaps see how we might not merely express our moral attitudes, of approval or disapproval toward certain actions, social structures, character traits, and the like, but seek to find a way to bring others to share those attitudes. A form of language that at first merely expresses feelings might thus come to mimic some of the features of descriptive discourse – allowing, for instance, that if my feelings and yours do not align, there is something undesirable in the situation (an expressivist analogue of disagreement over matters of fact). One upshot of working this program through might be that the quasi-realist can make sense of some analogue of truth, as that at which utterances in this ultimately expressive discourse should aim. That would provide us with right and wrong in aesthetics, without truth proper – contra the error theorist's second assumption. It is far from clear whether this project can succeed in any area (Geach 1965; Hale 1993), and its prospects in aesthetics in particular have been explored to only a limited degree (Scruton 1974; Hopkins 2001). However, its ambitions alone raise the possibility of making sense of correctness without truth.

Some consider that possibility unstable. If our judgments in a given area are directed toward a certain goal, and they sometimes attain it, why

is that not already enough for *truth*? (See Wright 1992: ch. 2.) The idea that there is at least *a* notion of truth that is minimal in this way challenges the error theorist's third assumption. Even if he is right that truth provides the only option for correctness in aesthetics (assumption two), truth may not require reality to be as, according to assumption one, aesthetic judgments claim. Instead, there can be truth provided aesthetic talk exhibits enough "discipline": in effect, that it is governed by norms that ensure that not anything goes. Undermining the error theorist's third assumption in this way prevents him from building his position around the claim that no aesthetic claim is true, at least until he says more about the notion of truth he has in mind.

However, it is the error theorist's first assumption that is his Achilles heel. What compels us to interpret talk about beauty, elegance, or clumsiness in such a way as to ensure that it all comes out false? It is a familiar idea that interpretation, either of others' utterances or our own, should in part be guided by charity: it should ascribe error to speakers only where their mistake is comprehensible (Davidson 1984). The error theorist's first assumption flies in the face of this principle. What, then, justifies his understanding of our aesthetic talk? Of course, we do talk of aesthetic properties. But why think that the properties we are describing are to be understood as the error theorist construes them – as wholly independent of our engagement with them?

The alternative is to take aesthetic talk to concern properties that are in some sense anthropocentric. They are to be understood in part by reference to our responses to them – thus rejecting the strong realist's (3). (The natural analogy here is with secondary qualities, such as color.) This idea appears repeatedly in one form or another throughout the history of aesthetics. In its latest guise, it takes the form of the idea that aesthetic properties are *response-dependent*. What it is for something to be, say, beautiful, is for it to elicit a certain response (pleasure, perhaps) in us. Such a view will see aesthetic properties as fitting the following template: X is F (e.g., beautiful) if and only if X would elicit response R (e.g., pleasure) from subjects S under conditions C. With the gaps filled in, this might be offered as a claim about what, for example, "X is beautiful" *means*; but need not be so. The thought might be only that the right-hand side of the biconditional states the conditions under which the left-hand side is true. (Compare: X is water if and only if X is H₂0.) Either way, the response-dependence account of aesthetic properties promises to state conditions for the truth of our aesthetic claims (thus offering more than the expressivist would accept) without (as error theory does) beefing up those conditions to the point at which they prove impossible to meet.

There are certainly grounds for thinking that, if there are aesthetic properties, they take the anthropocentric form response-dependence describes. For, whatever aesthetic properties are, they are surely either themselves values (e.g., beauty or artistic merit), or intimately connected to such values (e.g., elegance or clumsiness). How can we make sense of values, without invoking the fact that they are *valued* by someone (Railton 1998)? Again, aesthetic properties seem to play no role in the order of things except via their effects on conscious subjects. Perhaps it was the ugliness of Quasimodo that led to his life being so hard, and beauty is as often made as found. But such properties play a causal part only via affecting, or being affected by, us. Like colors, they have no "cosmological role" (Wright 1992: ch. 5) independently of their causes and effects in conscious states. Why, then, suppose that there *is* any property here independently of those states? Finally, it is surely plausible in aesthetics, as in ethics (Nagel 1986: ch. 8), that the truth cannot in principle lie beyond our reach. Could the majority of our collective aesthetic judgments be seriously wrong? The possibility is not clearly coherent. But why not, if we can make sense of the aesthetic facts independently of our reactions to them?

Some might counter that it is just as hard to make sense of properties, and facts involving them, that *do* need characterizing by reference to our responses: real properties cannot implicate observation of them in this way. Those drawn to that thought may find in response-dependence a source of objectivity for aesthetic judgment, but not a form of realism. Others, however, are less fastidious. They wonder whether the contrast between "real" properties understandable independently of our

responses to them, and "mere" complexes of world-plus-response, can in the end be sustained (McDowell 1988). For these thinkers, response-dependence offers a way to make sense of aesthetic properties without metaphysical excess: it promises a moderate form of realism (e.g., Pettit 1983). All should agree, however, that there can be no realism without objectivity, and that response-dependence has yet to earn even that. To do so, it needs to fill the gaps in the template above. In particular, it has to find a way to specify the observers whose responses fix what is (say) beautiful, and the conditions under which those responses occur. If it can do that, objectivity will have been secured. Judgments will be right or wrong, as for that matter will be the responses on which they are based, depending on whether they accord or not with the responses and judgments of those observers under those conditions. (Strong realism's (2) will have been preserved.) The question, however, is whether those specifications can be made. Can we, without falling into triviality or simply assuming objectivity, make sense of some judgers and conditions as those whose judgments determine the aesthetic facts?

There are certainly the materials with which to begin. We might borrow ideas from Hume (2004), who made the first, and still one of the most thorough, attempts to solve this problem. For instance, one of his thoughts was that the key observers are those who are most discriminating, that is, those who are best at telling one possible object of aesthetic appraisal (in the relevant category, be it mountain views, or baroque cello concertos) from others. Or we might appeal to ideas that Hume did not consider, such as that of a trajectory within an individual's taste. If everyone who enjoys P. G. Wodehouse, on reading the comic novels of Evelyn Waugh comes to prefer those, then the "ideal critic," at least of comic literature, should be one who has made that transition, rather than one who has not.

A more serious challenge to the response-dependence project, and indeed to the prospects for aesthetic objectivity or realism more generally, lies in the seemingly ineradicable presence of disagreement. The threat takes two forms. First, the extent of actual disagreement threatens to show that aesthetic discourse is not objective (so we should stop attempting to make sense of how it can be so). Given how far folk disagree on what is beautiful or artistically worthwhile, why think there is any room here for right or wrong? The question is all the more pressing once we compare judgments across cultures and historical periods, and once we note that there may be more disagreement than is at first apparent. For, as Hume noted, people may agree that, say, the works of Shakespeare are excellent, and yet still disagree about *why* they are so. And we may think (although Hume did not) that there is no corresponding chance of finding real agreement beneath apparent dispute. For in aesthetics, unlike morals, there do not seem to be principles underlying our particular judgments, principles on which we might agree; the disagreement lying merely in whether, or how, they apply to the case in hand.

Serious as this challenge is, we should not give in too readily. The mere fact of disagreement proves nothing: the most objective matter can provoke conflict in views, sometimes of an entrenched and widespread nature. (Consider past debates over whether the earth is flat.) What matters is what *explains* disagreement. Realist and objectivist views can do this. If the conditions for discovery are unfavorable enough, anyone can make the wrong judgment. However, disagreement does tend to exert dialectical pressure in the other direction. There must be *some* explanation for every judgment reached on a given question. The more disagreement there is, the more judgments must be explained without appeal to the idea that they are correct, or that they reflect how reality is. But the richer our explanatory resources for explaining judgments without appeal to their rightness/reality, the better able we are to use those resources to explain *every* judgment on the matter. If no such judgment needs explaining by leaning on these ideas, we have one reason fewer for supposing that judgments on that matter *can* be right, or that there are facts of the matter for them to reflect.

The second problem posed by disagreement confronts the response-dependence view more directly. The worry is that, however "ideal" conditions and observers are specified, it will always be possible for those observers to disagree. Our aesthetic responses are not driven simply

by the nature of the object we are judging, but also by irreducibly idiosyncratic aspects of our personalities and sensibilities. Ideal observers could avoid dependence on such features only by ceasing to be recognizable as responding aesthetically at all. Disagreement deriving from these differences between observers is blameless: it impugns neither judgment. Since it is the responses of ideal observers in those conditions that fix which judgments are right and wrong, and hence fix the aesthetic facts (as the response-dependence view conceives them), if ideal observers can issue conflicting judgments, it seems there cannot after all be one right judgment, or any fact of the matter for judgments to reflect (Goldman 1995; Bender 1996). The question facing such views, and the moderate realism they offer, is whether they can specify conditions and observers so as to exclude this possibility.

Less moderate forms of realism might avoid this difficulty. By locating the reality that underpins the correctness of judgment in facts independent of the responses of observers (ideal or otherwise), they need not let the presence of correctness turn on how certain observers would respond. Above I have sketched other objections that such views might instead face. Let me close by indicating what sorts of position the theoretical space offers, at the more determinedly realist end.

Stronger forms of realism might be naturalist or not. *Nonnaturalist realisms* are closest to the strong form with which we began. *Naturalist realism* is in some ways more subtle. The naturalist will try to identify aesthetic properties with properties of the kind science studies. To uncover what those naturalistic properties are, she may appeal to the evolutionary benefits of engaging with them. It is highly unlikely that, say, beauty corresponds in a straightforward way to some simple property studied by science. What, after all, do the many and various things we call beautiful have in common? But it might be that some complex or disjunctive property can be found to play this role. Suppose, for instance, it turns out that health in one's mate offers reproductive advantage, and that symmetry in features is an indicator of long-term health. Such symmetry might then be one natural property correlating with beauty. It would not be alone

– sometimes we find asymmetrical things beautiful, perhaps precisely *for* that reason. But symmetry might form one element in a complex disjunction, one disjunct from that disjunction always being present when beauty is. (Thus, while the response-dependence view takes beauty to be a disposition to elicit a certain response; the naturalist identifies beauty with the complex property that is that disposition's categorical ground.) So the naturalist will accept every claim the strong realist makes bar (6): there is no simple correspondence between patterns in judgment and patterns in the world. As a corollary, she is likely to take the judgments we make as representing the complex disjunctive natural property in a way that conceals, to some extent, its true nature.

See also AESTHETIC JUDGMENT; AESTHETIC PROPERTIES; COGNITIVE SCIENCE AND ART; EVOLUTION, ART, AND AESTHETICS; HUME; KANT; RELATIVISM; TASTE.

BIBLIOGRAPHY

Ayer, A. J. 1952 [1936]. *Language, Truth and Logic*. New York: Dover.
Bender, John. 1996. "Realism, Supervenience and Irresolvable Aesthetic Disputes," *Journal of Aesthetics and Art Criticism*, 56, 283–97.
Blackburn, Simon. 1984. *Spreading the Word*. Oxford: Clarendon.
Blackburn, Simon. 1993. *Essays in Quasi-Realism*. Oxford: Oxford University Press.
Budd, Malcolm. 1995. *Values of Art*. London: Penguin.
Davidson, Donald. 1984. *Inquiries into Truth and Interpretation*. Oxford: Clarendon.
Geach, P. T. 1965. "Assertion," *Philosophical Review*, 74, 449–65.
Goldman, Alan H. 1995. *Aesthetic Value*. Boulder: Westview.
Hale, R. 1993. "Can There be a Logic of Attitudes?" In *Reality, Representation and Projection*. J. Haldane & C. Wright (eds.). Oxford: Oxford University Press, 337–63.
Hopkins, Robert. 2001. "Kant, Quasi-Realism and the Autonomy of Aesthetic Judgement," *European Journal of Philosophy*, 9, 166–89.
Hume, David. 2004 [1757]. "Of the Standard of Taste." In *Philosophy: Basic Readings*. N. Warburton (ed.). London: Routledge, 493–507.
Kant, Immanuel. 2000 [1790]. *Critique of the Power of Judgment*. P. Guyer & E. Matthews (trans.). Cambridge: Cambridge University Press.
McDowell, John. 1988. "Values and Secondary Qualities." In *Essays on Moral Realism*. G. Sayre-McCord (ed.). Ithaca: Cornell University Press, 166–80.
Mackie, John. 1977. *Ethics: Inventing Right and Wrong*. New York: Penguin.
Moore, G. E. 1993 [1903]. *Principia Ethica*. T. Baldwin (ed.). Rev. edn. Cambridge: Cambridge University Press.
Mothersill, Mary. 1986. *Beauty Restored*. Oxford: Clarendon.
Nagel, Thomas. 1986. *The View from Nowhere*. Oxford: Oxford University Press.
Pettit, Philip. 1983. "The Possibility of Aesthetic Realism." In *Pleasure, Preference and Value*. E. Schaper (ed.). Cambridge: Cambridge University Press, 17–38.
Railton, Peter. 1998. "Aesthetic Value, Moral Value and the Ambitions of Naturalism." In *Aesthetics and Ethics*. J. Levinson (ed.). Cambridge: Cambridge University Press, 59–105.
Scruton, Roger. 1974. *Art and Imagination: A Study in the Philosophy of Mind*. London: Methuen.
Wollheim, Richard. 1980. *Art and Its Objects*. 2nd edn. Cambridge: Cambridge University Press.
Wright, Crispin. 1992. *Truth and Objectivity*. Cambridge, MA: Harvard University Press.
Zangwill, Nick. 2001. *The Metaphysics of Beauty*. Ithaca: Cornell University Press.

ROBERT HOPKINS

ontological contextualism proposes that sociohistorical contingencies play an essential role in fixing the identity and content of artworks. For example, a work's level of originality depends on what else has been done in its genre, and a poetic or musical allusion cannot exist without the prior existence of the work to which it alludes. According to Arthur C. Danto's version of the theory, "the aesthetic qualities of the work are a function of their own historical identity" (1981: 111). Hence, contextualists deny that any work of art would be the very same work if it were instead created in a significantly different time and place, or by means of different art practices.

For example, contextualists propose that a twenty-first-century painting that looks exactly like a nineteenth-century Dutch still-life will have artistic and aesthetic properties that cannot belong to the seventeenth-century painting, and vice versa. These differences are crucial to the interpretation and appreciation of each painting. This point is independent of whether the recent painting has been put forward as a faked seventeenth-century still-life. Even if it is clearly labeled as a new work, perhaps with the title *Homage to a Dutch Still-Life*, the newer painting has at least one important property, that of paying homage to the seventeenth century, that cannot be possessed by any seventeenth-century still-life.

As this example suggests, contextualists often discuss cases of perceptually indiscernible objects with distinct identities. As such, contextualism extends Danto's influential explorations of two sorts of indiscernibles. First, artists such as Duchamp and Warhol created works of art with content not possessed by indiscernible nonart counterparts. Second, two works of art can be perceptually indiscernible and possess very different content. Either way, audience indifference to a work's art-historical context will lead to superficial and inappropriate responses.

Where Danto concentrates on visual and literary works, many contextualists concentrate on puzzles generated by the performing arts. Joseph Haydn's String Quartet in F minor (Op. 20, no. 5) was composed for four instruments. But suppose four cellists follow the score on four cellos, transposing three of the parts in order to accommodate the cello's lower range. There is overwhelming consensus among contextualists that, questions of musicality aside, the result is simply not a performance of that musical work. Haydn created a musical work for violins, viola, and cello. In the string quartet tradition, three cellos cannot be substituted for the violins and viola. Furthermore, it is not merely a question of whether the performance sounds as Haydn intended it to sound. Contextualists also hold that playing the string quartet on four electronic keyboards that are programmed to sound like the appropriate string instrument does not yield a performance of that string quartet. An instance must be derived by the correct process in order to be an instance of that work. At best, a sonic replica is a derivative work whose identity is, in turn, dependent on the historical fact of its derivation from the earlier work. Such examples confirm that the essential properties of works of art cannot be restricted to their perceptually accessible features. Many of a work's essential

features depend on art practices that exist at the time and place of its creation.

Beyond this core idea about identity, contextualists disagree on the scope of the relevant context. Three important areas of disagreement are the relevance of events and interpretations that occur after a work has been created, the relevance of historical authorship to artwork identity, and the extent to which different identity conditions hold for artworks of the same general type. Contextualists contend that these disagreements can be resolved only by acknowledging and understanding art's fundamental historicity. However, if we must consult historical practices in the art of painting in order to determine whether a planned restoration of an early Renaissance fresco would actually have the effect of destroying it, then we have already granted that distinct criteria might apply in different eras and for the various arts. It might turn out that some works gain or lose essential properties due to their ongoing histories, that authorship is more relevant for some kinds of works, and that two works in what seems to be a unified art form might be very different kinds of things. The remainder of this entry will take up these three issues in turn.

Contextualism is frequently defended with the insight that some features of artworks become accessible only to respondents who grasp the art-historical context in which they were actually created. Because the piano is a percussive instrument, the "singing" quality of a piano melody emerges only through its contrast with other piano compositions and performing styles (Walton 1970). Consequently, ontological contextualism highlights connections between ontological and epistemological issues.

However, many works of art have features that cannot be identified or appreciated until they are evaluated in light of later art history. As a result, some contextualists contend that properties gained after a work's creation can be relevant to its identity. A work's history of influence and critical reception can transform its identity (McFee 1980; Danto 1981; Bacharach 2005). Most contextualists respond that, with rare exception, the relevant history is restricted to events and actions preceding a work's creation. So we must take care not to conflate the conditions that allow audiences to recognize a property with the art-historical facts that make it possible in the first place. Relationships that create a relational property are not always sufficient to reveal its presence; hence many works of art remain misunderstood or wrongly valued until subsequent art history reveals them in a new light. This is not to deny that some properties, such as being an influence on later generations, arise due to subsequent history. However, there is no good reason to treat these properties as essential to the works in question (Levinson 1990; Stecker 2003).

Contextualists also debate whether the artist's identity is always part of an artwork's identity. Some contend that Claude Monet could not have painted *Sunset and Fog at Eragny* simply because that painting was the work of Camille Pissarro. Here, being painted by Pissarro is regarded as essential to that painting. Had Monet painted an indiscernible painting, at least one of its essential properties would be different and so it would be a different work of art. Jerrold Levinson (1990) argues that the artist's identity is crucial in just this way. His primary argument is that a work's position within an artist's oeuvre determines a number of its properties, and so the work's identity depends on the artist's identity. For example, suppose Igor Stravinsky never composed *The Rite of Spring* and Serge Prokofiev composed a work late in his own career that sounds just like it; Prokofiev's work would have very different expressive properties than Stravinsky's *Rite of Spring*. Similarly, Monet's frequent practice of repeatedly painting the same scene was not adopted by Pissarro, so the existence of only one painting of a particular scene at Eragny would be significant for Monet in a way that is not true of Pissarro's actual painting. Generalizing, it appears that another artist could not have created any work of art that another artist did create (Rohrbaugh 2005). Levinson's argument explicitly identifies an underlying principle that any two artists invariably inhabit different art-historical contexts. Each artist's own personal history is a relevant historical context that cannot be duplicated by any other individual.

Other contextualists respond that consideration of oeuvre is relevant for only a limited number of recent art movements. Excessive focus on a relatively narrow range of Western art diverts attention from the many art traditions that are indifferent to the place of a work within an individual's oeuvre. Furthermore, even in those cases where oeuvre is relevant, we need more information about the art-historical tradition in order to decide whether the resulting difference involves an essential rather than an accidental property. Not every difference is equally relevant to work identity. For example, art history provides examples of works wrongly assigned to one artist and then subsequently reassigned. On Levinson's hypothesis, any such reassignment involves recovery of a different and previously unknown work. Many philosophers find it more plausible to say that the same work was previously misunderstood in some way. Epistemic access has changed rather than the identity of the work. Finally, Stephen Davies (2001: 73–86) denies that two artists invariably carve out distinct creative contexts. After all, collaborations between artists are sometimes followed by significant independent careers (e.g., Salvador Dali and Luis Buñuel, and John Lennon and Paul McCartney). For a time, the two artists shared a common creative context. If later achievements in an oeuvre are relevant to the identity of earlier works, then the later, independent works of *both* collaborators are equally relevant to the identity of their earlier, shared work. Since collaboration demonstrates that two artists can share an art-historical context, we cannot generalize to the desired conclusion that any two artists invariably inhabit different art-historical contexts.

Turning to our final issue, contextualists need not assume that all paintings or musical works are of a single ontological kind. Although ontological theorizing is greatly simplified by the thesis that each art form has a uniform ontology, contextualists question this hypothesis. Different artworks are of distinct ontological types and these types are themselves the product of sociohistorical contingencies. Hence, any art form can develop ontological variety.

For example, a pair of indiscernible paintings might be distinct works of art because they belong to distinct ontological categories. Although a seventeenth-century Dutch still-life ceases to exist if the canvas is destroyed, an indiscernible twenty-first-century painting might be created by a process that permits its multiple instantiation. Suppose the newer painting was generated by a computer-controlled process that mass produces oil paintings. Like an etching or a cast sculpture, the computer program could allow for the painting's subsequent reinstantiation and thus permit its survival despite the destruction of its first instance. In contrast, painting a new canvas to replace a seventeenth-century painting yields a second painting rather than a second instance of the first, so the replacement painting does nothing to preserve the first's existence. (This point should not be confused with the fact that copies often provide epistemic access to important features of lost works. In a context that distinguishes between originals and copies, epistemic access does not ensure ontological equivalence.) Although some contextualists contend that the history of painting is such that paintings, unlike prints, are incapable of multiple instantiation (Levinson 1990), others contend that the historical record includes numerous paintings for which no original/copy distinction can be made among multiple versions (Gracyk 2001).

Music offers rich evidence of art's ontological variety. Knowing that something is a musical work does not itself inform us of its ontological kind, nor of its proper mode of appreciation. For example, although performances of Haydn's String Quartet in F minor have a stipulated instrumentation, some of J. S. Bach's works are for unspecified *Klavier* or keyboard. Although these works by Bach and Haydn belong to a single art-kind in being notated works for performance, Bach's *Klavier* compositions permit far more variability of timbre than do Haydn's string quartets. Furthermore, Haydn did not expect performers to engage in extensive improvisation when playing his string quartets, whereas many of Bach's notated works rely on figured bass, a practice in which the composer supplies a bass line and basic chords and then expects performers to supply improvised middle lines. Although Bach and Haydn share a common tradition in the same century, their shared reliance on notation specifies neither the kinds nor degree of heard properties that are essential to work identity. To complicate matters, many musical works are not notated and still others cannot be realized through performance. A great deal of music arises in oral traditions where it does not make sense to consult composers' intentions about instrumentation. At the other extreme, Pierre Schaeffer's *musique concrète* was composed on recorded tape, so its public presentation involves playbacks of recorded sound rather than performance on instruments. These and countless other examples show that, depending on which musical tradition generates a particular work, fewer or more audible properties are essential to work identity and thus to the identity of whatever is heard by an audience. Furthermore, these differences demonstrate that different kinds of entities can be musical works, leading Stephen Davies to defend the position that music is created in at least six different ontological categories.

Some ontologists challenge contextualism on the grounds that we can construct a simpler, unified ontology (D. Davies 2004). Others distinguish between artistic and aesthetic properties and argue that contextualism holds for artistic but not aesthetic properties (Zangwill 2001). In reply, contextualists deny that works of art always fit comfortably into ontological categories developed to handle philosophical problems unrelated to philosophy of art. It is not obvious that art-kinds can be collapsed into familiar ontological categories. Theories that rely on only one (Currie 1989; D. Davies 2004) or two (Wollheim 1980) ontological categories are revisionist recommendations that downplay art's fundamental historicity. In contrast, contextualism is a descriptive enterprise that requires mapping out the ontological categories generated by historical and contemporary practices. Repositioned to the meta-ontological level, contextualism supports methodological openness to ontological variety.

Amie Thomasson (2004) defends ontological variety by appeal to theories of reference. The correct reference of any unit of language is determined by the beliefs and practices of language users. Hence, the name of a particular work of art refers to one object rather than to another as a result of sociohistorical contingencies. The same holds true for general art-kind terms, such as "painting" and "symphony." There is no alternative, a priori method for connecting terms with their referents. As a result, there is some remote possibility that additional historical inquiry will reveal that Vermeer did not paint *Girl with a Pearl Earring*, in which case the phrase "Vermeer's *Girl with a Pearl Earring*" incorrectly describes the object it is commonly thought to describe. However, there is no plausible account of language and meaning that would allow us to be similarly mistaken about the meaning of an art-kind term like "painting." Thus, the only method for determining what paintings are, and thus for determining their ontological status, is to examine the beliefs and practices that link these terms to their referents. Consistency among the relevant beliefs and practices must take priority over theoretical elegance or uniformity. The final step is to admit that the beliefs and practices governing the identity conditions of Vermeer's paintings diverge significantly from those governing "string quartet" in the phrase "Haydn's last string quartet." Again, we might prove wrong about which work is Haydn's last string quartet, but we certainly have a handle on which practices are relevant to distinguishing string quartets from symphonies, much less from paintings. These divergences are so substantial that we must regard paintings and string quartets as distinct kinds of things. Hence, contextualism endorses ontological variety.

See also TWENTIETH-CENTURY ANGLO-AMERICAN AESTHETICS; "ARTWORLD"; AUTHENTICITY AND ART; DANTO; FEMINIST AESTHETICS; FORMALISM; MEANING CONSTRUCTIVISM; ONTOLOGY OF ARTWORKS; PERFORMANCE.

BIBLIOGRAPHY

Bacharach, Sondra. 2005. "Toward a Metaphysical Historicism," *Journal of Aesthetics and Art Criticism*, 63, 165–74.

Currie, Gregory. 1989. *An Ontology of Art*. New York: St. Martin's.

Danto, Arthur C. 1981. *The Transfiguration of the Commonplace*. Cambridge, MA: Harvard University Press.

Davies, David. 2004. *Art as Performance*. Malden: Blackwell.

Davies, Stephen. 2001. *Musical Works and Performances*. Oxford: Clarendon.

Gracyk, Theodore. 2001. "Who is the Artist if Works of Art are Action Types?" *Journal of Aesthetic Education*, 35(2), 11–24.

Levinson, Jerrold. 1990. *Music, Art, and Metaphysics: Essays in Philosophical Aesthetics*. Ithaca: Cornell University Press.

McFee, Graham. 1980. "The Historicity of Art," *Journal of Aesthetics and Art Criticism*, 38, 307–24.

Rohrbaugh, Guy. 2005. "I Could Have Done That," *British Journal of Aesthetics*, 45, 209–28.

Stecker, Robert. 2003. *Interpretation and Construction: Art, Speech, and the Law*. Malden: Blackwell.

Thomasson, Amie. 2004. "The Ontology of Art." In *The Blackwell Guide to Aesthetics*. Peter Kivy (ed.). Oxford: Blackwell, 78–92.

Walton, Kendall L. 1970. "Categories of Art," *Philosophical Review*, 79, 334–67.

Wollheim, Richard. 1980. *Art and its Objects*. 2nd edn. Cambridge: Cambridge University Press.

Zangwill, Nick. 2001. *The Metaphysics of Beauty*. Ithaca: Cornell University Press.

THEODORE GRACYK

ontology of artworks   Branch of aesthetics which examines the kind(s) of existence possessed by works of art (including literary and musical works). Not until the twentieth century did the ontology of artworks become a regular and sustained topic of discussion among philosophers. Of course, one finds remarks on the topic in the writings of earlier philosophers; but those remarks were either undeveloped or, as in the case of Hegel, not picked up by other philosophers. In this century, Roman Ingarden has been far and away the most prominent figure on the Continent and, after him, Benedetto Croce. By contrast, in the Anglo-American tradition contributions have come from many different quarters, and no one thinker has stood out from the others in the way that Ingarden has stood out among Continental philosophers.

The phenomena which a satisfactory ontology of art must organize and account for are extraordinarily rich and diverse. Let us begin with a quick survey, couched in ordinary language, of those phenomena; and then move on to look at some of the theories.

In several of the arts (e.g., music, dance, and drama) we regularly work with the distinction between a performance of something and that which is (or can be) performed. Let us call the latter a *performable*. In music, at least, one may have either of two quite different entities in mind when speaking of a *performance*. One may have in mind an *act of performing* the work. Or one may have in mind an *occurrence* of the work performed. Let us regiment our use of the language a bit, and call only the latter a *performance*.

That we do in fact operate with the distinction between performables and performances is

453

clear from the following three considerations (of which the second and third are, strictly speaking, applications of the first). First, a performance will always diverge in certain of its properties from the work of which it is a performance; and often, where it need not diverge, it will in fact diverge. Thus it comes about that critics make such remarks as "All the energy of the first movement of the concerto was missing in last night's performance." To speak thus is to work with a performable/performance distinction, and to claim that, though the first movement of the performable has the property of being energetic, the first movement of last night's performance lacked that property.

Second, our way of using the language of identity and diversity indicates that we are working with the performable/performance distinction. For we speak of the *same* work as having *distinct* performances (occurrences). But in general, two distinct things cannot both be identical with some one thing. That leaves open the abstract possibility that one of the performances is identical with the performable and the other is not; but that just seems incoherent. The conclusion must be that our way of using the concepts of identity and diversity in speaking of the performance arts indicates that we do indeed operate with a distinction between performables and performances.

Third, our way of using the concept of *existence* indicates the same thing. We often speak of works as existing *before* any performance of them has taken place. Then, after the work has existed for some time, a performance of it takes place; after a while, the performance is over, while the work endures. Here too, then, we assume the distinction. It is worth adding that in dance and drama we regularly find reason to introduce an entity that comes in between the work and its performances. We speak of a *production*. And a certain production of a work is neither the work itself nor is it a particular performance. (It is, in fact, another sort of performable.)

In certain of the nonperforming arts we work with distinctions closely similar to the performable/performance distinction. When dealing with graphic art prints, for example, we regularly distinguish between a particular *impression* and the *work* of which it is one of the impressions. When dealing with cast sculpture, we distinguish between a particular casting and that work of which it is one of the castings. And now and then in architecture we find need for a counterpart distinction – between, say, an example of one of Frank Lloyd Wright's usonian houses, and that Usonian House itself of which the house is one of the examples.

The considerations which compel these distinctions are, in their structure, exactly the same as those which compelled the distinction between performables and their performances. A given impression of a print may well have come into existence after the print itself had been created, and may well go out of existence before the print does. We speak of two *different* castings of the *same* sculpture. And a particular usonian house may, to cope with the high rainfall of its climate, have a drain spout where the Usonian House itself, of which it is an example, has none. In literature and film we also work with such distinctions. For most works of literature, there are many *copies* of the same literary work – and when there are not in fact many copies, there could always be. And in film there are many copies of the same work of cinematic art – or, once again, if there are not, that is purely accidental; there could be.

It will be convenient to have one set of terms to mark all these different, but parallel, distinctions. Let us follow an increasingly common practice, and borrow from C. S. Peirce the terms "type" and "token." Peirce introduced these terms to mark the distinction between a word understood as something that can be repeatedly inscribed or pronounced, and a word understood as an inscription or sounding out. The former he called a *type* and the latter he called a *token*. We will call an impression of an art print a *token*, and the work of which it is an impression a *type*; a performance of musical work a *token*, the work of which it is a performance a *type*; and so on.

One notices a tendency, in those who first begin reflecting on the ontology of artworks, to think that the performed work in music is the same as its score, when there is a score, as there is a tendency to think of the performed work in drama as identical with its script. But, quite clearly, this is mistaken; and our ordinary distinction between a work of music and its score, a work of drama and its script, and so on, is to be honored. For not only may a work of music exist without ever having been scored; all the score impressions may be destroyed and the work still endure – by virtue, for example, of being lodged in people's memories. It may be added that the type/token distinction also has applications to scores, scripts, and drawings.

We speak of paintings and noncast sculptures differently. Here we do not operate with anything like the type/token distinction. Of course, there are reproductions of paintings and copies of noncast sculptures. But these are not originals in the way in which impressions of prints and castings of sculptures are originals. In the field of graphic art prints, we distinguish between an impression and a reproduction of the impression; this is exactly like the distinction between a painting and a reproduction of the painting. What is missing in our talk of paintings is that other distinction that we work with in the field of graphic arts – the distinction between an original impression of a print and the print of which it is an impression.

The type/token distinction has even more pervasive application in the arts than so far indicated. And where it does have application, it is often worth reflecting on the subtle differences in how the distinction finds application. So the above must be taken as an *indication* of the phenomena that an ontology of artworks must take into account, not as an ample and suitably qualified *description* of the phenomena.

In my statement of the phenomena I have highlighted the distinction between those arts in which we make use of one or another version of the type/token distinction, and those arts such as painting in which we do not make use of any such distinction. Some of those who have written on the ontology of art have regarded this distinction as not ontologically significant, and have gone on to develop ontologies of artworks that are uniform across the distinct arts. We may call them *uniform* theories – in distinction from nonuniform theories. Of course, there may be uniformity across the arts with respect to the type/token distinction and nonuniformity in respect to other ontologically significant distinctions; for example, some of the arts are obviously temporal in ways that others are not. Unfortunately, it will be necessary here to exclude those other distinctions from consideration. In turn, a good many of the uniform theories that have been developed in the twentieth century have also been *unitive*, in the sense that they deny any fundamental ontological distinction as that between types and tokens. Let us begin by considering some of these uniform and unitive theories.

In the first half of the twentieth century, *mentalistic* theories of the ontological nature of artworks enjoyed a good deal of popularity. We can take the theory of R. G. Collingwood as representative. In *The Principles of Art*, Collingwood (1970) observed that one can compose tunes and poems in one's head; he went on from there, and from a few other considerations, to conclude that the work of art *is* a mental object. He conceded, of course, that musicians make sounds with instruments, that painters cause viscous pigment to adhere to canvas, that sculptors chisel away at marble and wood, and so forth. But no such physical entities are works of art, insisted Collingwood; they are devices that serve, when perceived with appropriate imagination, to communicate a work of art from one mind to another – from the creator's mind to the minds of members of the public. On this view, performances, impressions, castings, copies, and the like are not works of art – as paintings are not. They are, all of them, "mere" devices for transmitting the work of art from the mind of the artist to the minds of his or her public.

Collingwood's theory has a rather large number of consequences that, in combination or singly, have by most thinkers been regarded as a *reductio ad absurdum*. Among such are these: on this view one can, in principle, create a "painting" entirely in one's head, without ever making pigment adhere to surface; and the object that one hangs on a wall and puts in a crate for shipping to an art show is not a work of art. What is called "Van Gogh's *Starry Night*" does not hang on any wall. Furthermore, on this view, a work is not in existence when no one has it in mind. Works typically go in and out of existence; they exist intermittently.

Nominalistic theories of the ontology of artworks deny that there are any such entities as those we have singled out as *types*; there are only tokens. Thus, they too are unitive uniform theories. Of course, as indicated above, it certainly *appears* that in our discourse about the arts we commit ourselves to the existence of types.

Thus, to make his theory plausible, the nominalist has to make it seem plausible that we do not thus commit ourselves – for example, by making it seem plausible that reductive analyses can be given of all true sentences that appear to commit their users to the existence of types, a "reductive analysis" of such a sentence being another sentence which asserts the same proposition but clearly does not commit its users to the existence of types. It is probably fair to say that no nominalist theorists have in fact made it seem plausible that reductive analyses can be given of all such sentences. Nelson Goodman is the most aggressively nominalistic of all those who have written about the arts. But nominalism functions for Goodman more as ideal than as project; and, certainly, it is not in his hands a *completed* project. In his *Languages of Art*, Goodman (1968) makes clear his commitment to a nominalistic ontology. But he says that in the book he will speak with the "vulgar" rather than with the "learned"; and he offers very few suggestions as to how vulgar talk might be replaced with learned.

A complex variant on the more or less standard nominalism to which Goodman is attracted has been developed by Joseph Margolis (1980). On Margolis's view, works of art are all tokens of a special sort; namely, they are "culturally emergent entities" which, though embodied in physical objects, are not to be identified with those objects. Margolis concedes that in our discourse about the arts we also refer to types; but in his ontology he insists that there exist no such entities. As he realizes, this commits him to the position that it is possible to refer to entities that do not exist – indeed, to entities that in no sense whatsoever "are."

The observation that the nominalist tries to achieve a unitive uniform theory by denying the existence of types leads one to wonder whether anyone has tried to achieve a unitive uniform theory by moving in the opposite direction – denying tokens rather than types. Exactly such a theory has been proposed by Gregory Currie in *An Ontology of Art* (1989). Currie thinks that an artist, in composing or creating, discovers a certain structure – of words, of sounds, of colors, or whatever. He adds that the artist always does this in a certain way; and he insists that not only is *what* the artist discovers

relevant to aesthetic appreciation, but also some features of *how* he discovers it are relevant. He calls those features that are thus relevant the artist's *heuristic path*. And his ontological proposal is that works of art are action types of the following sort: someone's discovering a certain structure via a certain heuristic path. Discoveries of the same structure via different heuristic paths are instances of different works, as are discoveries of different structures via the same heuristic path. The structures as such are not works at all.

Currie is led to this unusual view from his conviction that "distinct works may possess the same structure." For example, though it is theoretically possible that Beethoven and Brahms should independently have discovered and composed the same musical structure, their works would nonetheless have different properties – for instance, Brahms's might be Liszt-influenced, Beethoven's would not be. But one and the same entity cannot both have and lack a certain property. "In cases like that," says Currie (1989: 65), "what differentiates the works is the circumstances in which the composer or author arrived at the structure."

But is it decisively clear that the property we wish to attribute to what Brahms composed is *being Liszt-influenced*? May it not rather be the relational property of *being such that this composing of it was Liszt-influenced*? Obviously, one and the same entity may have both that property and this other one: *being such that that composing of it was not Liszt-influenced*. Thus it is questionable that the argument even gets off the ground. To this we may add that the theory has a good many counterintuitive consequences; for example, since on this view a work of music is a *composing*, and composings are not the sorts of things that can be heard, it follows that works of music cannot be heard.

The views that we have considered are all *unitive* uniform theories. A *dualist* uniform theory, by contrast, would contend that, though our ordinary ways of speaking do not reveal it, the type/token distinction does in fact have application in the arts of painting and noncast sculpture. It is rather often said, for example, that we might well have a technology for making *copies* of paintings – not reproductions, but copies – looking as much like the "original" as you please. All those copies would then be "originals," in the same way that all the impressions of a print are "originals"; and it is purely accidental, of no ontological significance, that we have no such technology – or that we do have it but do not use it.

But the argument is fallacious, in an interesting way. What brings it about that a set of print impressions are all impressions of the same print is not that they are indiscernibly alike; they may be very far from that. So, too, what brings it about that a series of musical performances are all performances of the same work is not that they sound indiscernibly alike; they may sound very different indeed. Two performances are performances of the same work if they are brought about under the guidance of the same set of rules for correctness in performance. And they may satisfy that condition, while yet sounding very different. Our practice of painting might have been such that painters ordained rules for correctness of instances; but in fact it is not like that.

A *nonuniform* theory of the ontology of artworks will regard the type/token distinction as present in some of the arts and not in others. It turns out that the main work of accounting for this difference will have to be done by an appropriate theory of the nature of artistic types. Ingarden on the Continent, and I myself in the Anglo-American tradition, have developed the most elaborate theories of artistic types. Taking as my cue the phenomenon just mentioned of *rules for correctness*, I argue that artistic types are a special sort of *kinds*; I call them *norm kinds*. It is typical of natural kinds that there can be both well-formed and malformed examples; there are, for instance, malformed examples of the horse. In a similar way, there are incorrect performances of musical and dramatic works, defective castings of sculptures, and so on. Thus, artistic types are not *sets*; for a set cannot have different members from those it does have, whereas artistic types can have more or fewer tokens than they do have. Artistic types are instead *kinds*; for kinds can have more or fewer examples than they do have. But, more specifically, they are *norm kinds*. One composes a work of music by selecting a set of rules for correctness of (musical) performance; thereby one selects a certain norm kind. That, then, is the work that one has composed, which is then available for performance.

Many significant positions staked out during the twentieth century in the extraordinarily rich discussion concerning the ontology of artworks have not been presented here; many significant contributors to the discussion have not been cited. In particular, nothing has been said about any of the so-called ontological contextualist theories that have emerged in recent years.

See also TWENTIETH-CENTURY ANGLO-AMERICAN AESTHETICS; COLLINGWOOD; DEFINITION OF "ART"; GOODMAN; INGARDEN; MARGOLIS; NOTATIONS; ONTOLOGICAL CONTEXTUALISM; PERFORMANCE.

BIBLIOGRAPHY
Collingwood, R. G. 1970 [1938]. *The Principles of Art*. Oxford: Clarendon.
Currie, Gregory. 1989. *An Ontology of Art*. New York: St. Martin's.
Goodman, Nelson. 1968. *Languages of Art*. New York: Bobbs-Merrill.
Ingarden, Roman. 1973 [1931]. *The Literary Work of Art*. G. G. Grabowicz (trans.). Evanston: Northwestern University Press.
Levinson, Jerrold. 1990. *Music, Art, and Metaphysics*. Ithaca: Cornell University Press.
Margolis, Joseph. 1980. *Art and Philosophy*. Atlantic Highlands: Humanities Press.
Wollheim, Richard. 1971. *Art and Its Objects*. New York: Harper & Row.
Wolterstorff, Nicholas. 1980. *Works and Worlds of Art*. Oxford: Clarendon.

NICHOLAS WOLTERSTORFF

originality   A work of art can be an original, in the sense that it can be an authentic work by so-and-so, without having any degree of originality. What is originality and what, if anything, does it have to do with artistic or aesthetic value? A common response to the first question holds that to have originality is to be a historical first in some important respect – the historically first instance of a kind that might have other instances, produced by other artists. (An example would be the first expressionist painting.) We can begin by working with this definition of "originality," refining it as necessary. However, if this is what originality is, it at least needs explaining why originality is relevant to artistic or aesthetic value. Presumably the first work to attain a certain level of artistic or aesthetic awfulness is original in the sense in question. If being original (in that sense) is sufficient for having value, a work can be of positive historical significance because it has negative artistic value. It is at least unclear how having this significance could at the same time guarantee the work some positive artistic value.

On one view, originality (in the sense of being a historical first) is not an aesthetic value by itself, though it is a component of a work of art's total value (Meiland 2004). Critiquing this position requires fixing what falls under the notion of total value. Does total value include any value the work of art might have, such as economic value or even its value as a potential source of heat? If so, originality could add to a work's total value by giving it historical value. But as yet we have no reason to think that an increase in total value is an increase in artistic value. After all, a work's total value can be increased without increasing its artistic value – by, say, increasing its economic value. Perhaps total value is supposed to be restricted to only those values that arguably are forms of artistic value. Even if so, the question remains how being original contributes to total value in that sense.

Some philosophers hold that the contribution a work's originality makes to its aesthetic value cannot be understood by considering originality in isolation from other forms of artistic value. For example, Alan H. Goldman (1995) claims that a work must have other positive artistic values if originality is to add to its value as art. Being a historical first adds value only to art that would otherwise have artistic value. Generalized to historical matters of any sort, this explains why not everything that is a historical first has historical value. What it does not explain is why the value added when the historical first involves an artistically valuable work of art is artistic rather than historical.

Is there some special way of being a historical first that ensures that a work of art displaying originality has positive artistic or aesthetic value? If there is, perhaps this special way can be used to refine the notion of artistic originality, so as to secure its link to artistic value. Consider Dabney Townsend's view.

Townsend (1997) argues that for originality to be an aesthetic value, it has to be understood in the context of some theory of art. Townsend is clear that merely giving originality some important role in a theory of art does not suffice to show how originality adds aesthetic value. The expression theory, Townsend observes, can appeal to originality as part of its account of what distinguishes aesthetic from nonaesthetic expression of emotion. However, all this shows is how originality might be a condition on being a work of art. It does not show how being original adds to a work's aesthetic value. What is wanted, according to Townsend, is a theory in which the role originality plays in art supports the claim that originality confers artistic value. Townsend offers his own theory of art as an example. This theory links originality and creativity to what happens when artists think of themselves as part of their work. For Townsend, originality is an aesthetic value when what is novel in the work is its giving creative expression to a new power of the artist's mind.

Is expressing a new power of the artist's mind artistically valuable? It might be, if the new mental power can find creative expression only in a work art. But, even if a certain mental power can find creative expression only in a work, it is not clear why that power must be new for its expression to be of artistic value. Whether the historical novelty here lies in the newness of the power or in its expression (or both), it remains unclear why novelty adds value over and above the value the work derives from being the creative expression (novel or not) of some power (new or not) of the artist's mind.

A view made popular by Arthur C. Danto (1984, 1997), if not one he would necessarily claim as his own, has it that originality in art is a matter of the work's occupying a special place in the development of art. This fits Townsend's bill, in that it accounts for the artistic value of originality in the context of a theory of art. It does so in a way that explains what is special about a work's being a historical first. For it limits originality in art to those works that found new art movements. This kind of originality is directly relevant to a work's artistic value, since the value of a work is determined by the extent to which it advances art's evolution, an evolution that ultimately, for Danto, sees art transformed into philosophy.

One problem with this view is that it seems too narrow, implying as it does that very few works have the relevant sort of originality. The view also implies that a work's originality cannot be cited to explain its impact on art history, since its originality just consists in its having the impact it does. The cost of connecting originality to artistic value in this way is having to adopt a very narrow understanding of the latter.

Francis Sparshott's understanding of originality and its relation to artistic value, like Townsend's, is part of his theory of art. Sparshott holds that a work of art has artistic value merely in virtue of having originality, which he equates with a specific sort of uniqueness. Arguably, the uniqueness that Sparshott has in mind is not that something has through being a historical first in some special way. Sparshott stresses that the uniqueness of a work of art does not require (or ordinarily involve) breaking from past traditions or initiating new movements. What matters for a work's originality is not its doing something for the first time, but the way in which it does what other works do. To explain what he has in mind, Sparshott draws an analogy with the special sort of uniqueness a loved one has for his lover. Someone is loved for the special way he does the things we all do, a way that makes him irreplaceable. Similarly, it is the special way in which a work does what other works also do, not its independence from existing traditions or movements, or its possession of other artistic or aesthetic values, that makes it unique.

What is compelling about Sparshott's analogy is its applying to art the notion of someone who is unique in that he is irreplaceable in our affections, not because of positive qualities that can be found in no one else, but because of just how positive qualities are present in him. Those qualities are part of the way the loved one is who he is, and so are in part constitutive of what about him is loved. The positive value of the loved one's being just who he is can be found in no one else, however like him they may be. Technically, Sparshott's notion of originality entails that every original work is a historical first, since it is the only work that presents its qualities just as it does. But for Sparshott, the value of originality does not derive from historical novelty. What matters is the way in which positive artistic qualities are present in a work when they constitute part of what it is for it to be the work it is, and thus, in one sense of the words, unique, irreplaceable. Unlike Goldman, Sparshott is not saying that originality adds value if a work of art has other artistic values. It is the way in which the work has the values it does that makes it unique. It is unique in virtue of having the positive artistic qualities it does in just the way it does, whether or not it is the first to have them.

See also AUTHENTICITY AND ART; CREATIVITY; DANTO; EXPRESSION THEORY; FORGERY; THEORIES OF ART.

BIBLIOGRAPHY
Crowther, Paul. 1991. "Creativity and Originality in Art," *British Journal of Aesthetics*, 31, 301–9.
Danto, Arthur C. 1984. "The End of Art." In *The Death of Art*. B. Lang (ed.). New York: Haven, 5–35.
Danto, Arthur C. 1997. *After the End of Art: Contemporary Art and the Pale of History*. Princeton: Princeton University Press.
Goldman, Alan H. 1995. *Aesthetic Value*. Boulder: Westview.
Guyer, Paul. 2003. "Exemplary Originality: Genius, Universality and Individuality." In *The Creation of Art: New Essays in Philosophical Aesthetics*. B. Gaut & P. Livingston (eds.). Cambridge: Cambridge University Press, 116–37.
Levinson, Jerrold. 1980. "Aesthetic Uniqueness," *Journal of Aesthetics and Art Criticism*, 38, 435–50.
Meiland, Jack. 2004. "Originals, Copies, and Aesthetic Value." In *Aesthetics and the Philosophy of Art*. P. Lamarque & S. H. Olsen (ed.). Oxford: Blackwell, 375–82.
Sibley, Frank. 1985. "Originality and Value," *British Journal of Aesthetics*, 25, 169–84.
Sparshott, Francis. 1982. *The Theory of the Arts*. Princeton: Princeton University Press.
Sparshott, Francis. 1983. "The Disappointed Art Lover." In *The Forger's Art*. D. Dutton (ed.). Berkeley: University of California Press, 246–63.
Townsend, Dabney. 1997. *An Introduction to Aesthetics*. Oxford: Blackwell.
Vermazen, Bruce. 1991. "The Aesthetic Value of Originality," *Midwest Studies in Philosophy*, 16, 266–79.

GEORGE BAILEY

P

painting *see* DRAWING, PAINTING, AND PRINT-MAKING; DEPICTION; PICTURE PERCEPTION; REPRE-SENTATION.

performance Within the major performing arts of the Western tradition – drama, ballet, opera, both instrumental and vocal music, and, possibly, narrative forms of poetry – performance need not involve the presentation of an independently identifiable work; that is, performances may be improvised, as is often the case with mime, for example. Moreover, within these arts, some works do not require performance; a musical work may consist of taped natural sounds. Usually, though, the performing arts involve the presentation of works that derive their independence from their instances either from the existence of notated specifications for performances (such as scripts or musical scores) or from the creation of model instances, faithfulness to which is preserved within the performance tradition. Ballet typifies this latter case.

Works in the performing arts have sometimes been identified with their notations (or with classes of performances compliant with their notations). But notations need not be involved in the creation of such works. More to the point, notations sometimes leave work-constitutive elements unspecified and sometimes include specifications that are not work-constitutive. For instance, in an early eighteenth-century musical work it may be understood that the performer is required to embellish the notated melody or to fill in the figured bass, whereas written phrasing or dynamics in the score of the same piece might make interpretative recommendations that the performer is free to ignore. Whether all constitutive aspects of the work are notated and whether everything that is notated is constitutive depends on the background of conventions against which the piece's creator works.

Works in the performing arts typically admit of multiple instances and frequently involve notations, but these features do not distinguish them from many works in the other arts. For example, novels may have multiple instances; statues may be produced on the basis of sketches and models. In the performing arts, the work is conceived for performance and is completed when a specification for performance or a model instance is produced. The work is not identical with the script or score, but comes into existence through, and usually at the same time as, the production of the specification. As a result, a play is completed when it is scripted, even if it is destined never to be performed. A novel must exist in at least one instance, but a performing work need have no instances. And, while a statue may be produced from plans, the existence of the work relies on the execution of the plan. That is, the plan in these cases is a plan for the *creation* of the work itself; whereas, where the performing arts use notations, those notations specify not how the work is to be created, but, instead, how the created work is to be instanced. In terms of the distinction drawn here, cinema is not a performing art as such, though dramatic (and musical) performance usually is involved in the *creation* of the cinematic work.

Specifications of works intended for performance are frequently minimal, leaving considerable freedom to the performer in the realization of the work. Typically this is the case with jazz, for example. Even where the specification is detailed, it underdetermines vital aspects of any performance. For instance, playwrights do not usually notate the timing and nuances of phrasing to be employed by the actors. To the extent that performers, in presenting the work, must go beyond what is provided by the work's creator, performance is essentially creative. At this minimal level, creativity in performance is consistent with dull, mechanical rendition, however. Primarily we value the performer's creativity when this involves skills that bring the work vividly to life.

Where performance takes as its point the presentation of an artist's work, achieving a fair degree of accuracy must be its first goal. One can perform a Balanchine ballet only if one attempts to preserve what constitutes the work as the particular piece that Balanchine created. Audiences are interested in works, generally, as the works of artists. Given this, it is reasonable to regard performers as having a duty to the audience to do what is in their power to render the work accurately. Performances also serve other goals, though. They should be stimulating, revelatory, and so on. Perhaps a first performance should aim for as much clarity of form and content as is consistent with the artist's instructions, but if a work is already well known to the audience it can be appropriate to aim for adventurous and idiosyncratic approaches to its interpretation. This may be why Shakespeare's best-known plays or Mozart's operas are often radically transformed in modern-day productions.

How should inaccuracies in performance be regarded? One might deny that a performance differing in the smallest detail from what is constitutive of the work is a performance of it, as Goodman (1976) notoriously does. This approach is counterintuitive, however, given that works often remain identifiable in performances with many inaccuracies. A normative approach to the issue is more reasonable. An inaccurate rendition is a performance of a given work if it is the performer's intention to perform that work and if the work remains recognizable within the performance. A performance may be the worse for inaccuracies, but it can be good overall, because accuracy is not the sole criterion of value for performances. We would not usually condemn a live performance that achieves spontaneous vibrancy at the cost of minor errors.

Within classical music, since the 1960s there has been a marked move toward "authentic" or "historically informed" performance. The goals and achievements of this movement are hotly debated. Two lines of argument should be distinguished.

(1) There is disagreement about the ontological character of musical works, with some authors seeing them as "pure" sound structures and others viewing them as including among their constitutive elements the instruments and performance practices known to and specified by the composer or mandated by the conventions of the time. What one takes to be required of an accurate performance depends on one's view of the ontological character of the work. Authors in the first camp, who see musical works as thin in properties, regard the authenticity movement as going beyond what is required in the name of accuracy. "Authentic" performances have no more claim to legitimacy than do many "inauthentic" performances. By contrast, those who take the view that musical works are thick with properties regard the pursuit of accuracy as requiring the approach adopted by the authenticity movement. But it should be noted that what composers can determine as constitutive of their works varies considerably from place to place and time to time, which suggests that musical works display considerable ontological variety. If authenticity is mainly a matter of accuracy, then the authentic performance of jazz or fifteenth-century masses is far less restrictive of performers than is the authentic performance of Berlioz.

(2) There is also dispute over the desirability of authenticity in musical performances of works of the past. If the aim of authenticity is to provide access to the experience of the music that the composer's contemporaries should have had, and if historical and cultural differences between us and them prevent our sharing that experience, then the pursuit of authenticity is pointless. In this view, works are reconstituted through time so that, strictly speaking, it is not Beethoven's symphonies (as he would have recognized them) that we appreciate. An alternative position holds that we can narrow the gap that separates us from the past and from other cultures, and thereby experience works of these times and places as the works of their creators, though doing so requires sensitivity to the art-historical conventions and practices presupposed by the works' creators and original performers, along with suspension of expectations and habits acquired in appreciating different, more familiar kinds of works.

A final, different issue: sometimes it is said that the critic is like the performer in generating the work's properties through his or her interpretation of it. There are parallels between the two activities – both the performer and the critic must understand the work if they are to perform their jobs convincingly, even if the performer's understanding is more practical and may be difficult to articulate. But if the suggestion is that critics and performers do essentially the same thing, the distinction between the performing and nonperforming arts drawn above collapses. Yet that distinction does seem to be widely acknowledged, and on the following grounds.

The playwright and the composer create works for performance. The contribution of the performer is anticipated and desired by the work's creator. The performer mediates between the artist and his or her public, most of whom would otherwise lack access to the artist's work. By contrast, the critic's efforts, useful and interesting though they may be, are not necessary for the work to reach its audience and, in that sense, are uninvited. Moreover, criticism concerns itself with performances of works, as well as with the works themselves, but we would not normally consider the presentation of the critic's views as a performance of the performance. Performance interpretations present a way of playing the piece, whereas critics' interpretations are concerned with explaining its meaning or import (Levinson 1993).

See also DANCE; DRAMA; MUSIC AND SONG; AUTHENTICITY AND ART; GOODMAN; NOTATIONS; ONTOLOGICAL CONTEXTUALISM; ONTOLOGY OF ARTWORKS; PERFORMANCE ART; STYLE.

BIBLIOGRAPHY

Brown, Lee B. 2000. " 'Feeling My Way': Jazz Improvisation and Its Vicissitudes – A Plea for Imperfection," *Journal of Aesthetics and Art Criticism*, 58, 112–23.
Davies, Stephen. 1987. "Authenticity in Musical Performance," *British Journal of Aesthetics*, 27, 39–50.
Davies, Stephen. 2001. *Musical Works and Performances*. Oxford: Clarendon.
Dipert, Randall R. 1988. "Toward a Genuine Philosophy of the Performing Arts," *Reason Papers*, 13, 182–200.
Godlovitch, Stan. 1998. *Musical Performance*. London: Routledge.
Goodman, Nelson. 1976. *Languages of Art*. 2nd edn. Indianapolis: Hackett.
Hamilton, James R. 2001. "Theatrical Performance and Interpretation," *Journal of Aesthetics and Art Criticism*, 59, 307–12.
Hamilton, James R. 2007. *The Art of Theater*. Malden: Blackwell.
Kivy, Peter. 1995. *Authenticities: Philosophical Reflections on Musical Performance*. Ithaca: Cornell University Press.
Levinson, Jerrold. 1993. "Performative vs. Critical Interpretation in Music." In *The Interpretation of Music*. M. Krausz (ed.). Oxford: Clarendon, 33–60.
Osipovich, David. 2006. "What is a Theatrical Performance?" *Journal of Aesthetics and Art Criticism*, 64, 461–70.
Saltz, David Z. 2001. "What Theatrical Performance Is (Not): The Interpretation Fallacy," *Journal of Aesthetics and Art Criticism*, 59, 299–306.
Thom, Paul. 1993. *For an Audience: A Philosophy of the Performing Arts*. Philadelphia: Temple University Press.
Thom, Paul. 2007. *The Musician as Interpreter*. University Park: Pennsylvania State University Press.

STEPHEN DAVIES

performance art The performing arts are those artistic practices whose primary purpose is to prepare and present "artistic performances" – performances that make perceptually manifest to receivers qualities that bear on the appreciation of works of art. A performance may be artistic in this sense if either (1) it is itself an object of artistic appreciation, or (2) it plays an essential part in the appreciation of one or more other things that are objects of artistic appreciation. We are most familiar with performances that, whether or not they are artistic in the first of these senses (see Kivy 1995; Davies 2003), are artistic in the second sense. Examples would be performances of independently identifiable works such as Shakespeare's *Hamlet* or Beethoven's *Hammerklavier* sonata. We may term the latter "performed works" and the former "work-performances."

In attempting to locate works of "performance art" in this more general context of artistic performance, the most obvious strategy would be to identify them with particular performance events that – in contrast with work-performances – are artistic in the first but not in the second of the above senses. But this would conflict in at least two ways with our antecedent classification of artworks. First, it would make free jazz improvisations works of performance art. Second, it would exclude accepted works of performance art that are themselves performed works admitting of multiple performances (e.g., works by Robert Wilson and Laurie Anderson). While some have sought to restrict performance artworks to nonrepeatable events – Alan Kaprow, for example, so restricted the use of the term "happening" – artistic practice does not conform to these suggestions, and neither shall we.

Given these difficulties, it is perhaps better to identify works of performance art through their relation to certain historically situated traditions of artistic making, traditions from which they emerge or by reference to which they define themselves. This is the approach taken by two prominent writers on this issue, RoseLee Goldberg (2001), who has authored an authoritative history of performance art, and Noël Carroll (1986), who situates performance artworks in relation to theoretical and practical innovation in the visual and theatrical arts in the latter half of the twentieth century. Both authors resist the invitation to define "performance art," on the grounds that the phenomena we seek to capture under that label are too diverse. Goldberg (2001: 9) stresses that much twentieth-century performance art stems from artists' dissatisfaction with more established artistic practices, and with working within the limitations of particular artistic media. Performance art often draws in a single work upon different such media – literature, poetry, theater, music, dance, architecture, and painting, as well as video, film, slides, and narrative – deploying them in ways that by their very novelty defeat any attempt at definition: all that can be said is that performance art is "live art by artists," but, as we have seen, this is at best a necessary condition for being performance art in the accepted sense.

Goldberg traces the roots of performance art in the second half of the twentieth century to such earlier movements as Italian Futurism, Russian Constructivism, Dada, Surrealism, and Bauhaus. In each case, she maintains, the "object" works customarily associated with these movements come out of an artistically revolutionary impulse whose initial, but now

widely ignored, expressions were in performance. Often, this involved theatrical performances that stressed provocation, interaction with the audience, and the rejection of the traditional theatrical idea that performance is work-performance. Such performances drew upon such nonartistic practices as the circus, vaudeville, cabaret, and puppet shows, and sought to relocate art in public space rather than in galleries. The focus was not, as in theater traditionally conceived, on the representation of action and the rendering of a text, but on the performers themselves and the visual aspects – the spectacle – of the performance. The conjoining of different traditional artistic media in such performances is well illustrated in the Bauhaus conception of the "total artwork," something echoed in the "happenings" of the 1950s and 1960s and also in later works by artists such as Robert Wilson.

Carroll takes avant-garde theater, as represented in particular by Artaud, to be one of two sources of the interest in performance in the art of the 1970s and the 1980s. He distinguishes between what he terms "art performance" and "performance art." The former originated in the 1960s as a reaction to certain perceived problems with the ways in which visual artworks were presented in galleries. The doctrine of "medium-purity," promoted most forcefully by Clement Greenberg, was seen as denying the relevance of the artist's performance, as exemplified in the action painting of Jackson Pollock. "Art performance" manifested itself initially in "happenings" that rejected both the idea of the purity and autonomy of different artistic media, and the focusing of artistic interest on formal properties of objects divorced from the activities of artists. One of the most famous such performances took place at Black Mountain College in North Carolina in 1952, and involved collaborations, under the aegis of John Cage, between musicians, choreographers, poets, painters, and film-makers. Later exponents of "art performance" included individual artists such as Vito Acconci, who used his body as a medium for exploring and expressing themes relating to human interaction, and Gilbert and George, who produced works of "live sculpture." While their artistic vehicles are performances, these works, like traditional visual artworks, are made accessible to audiences in art galleries, but through the visual or verbal "records" or "documentations" of the performances. Carroll, like Goldberg, stresses the awareness, on the part of those involved in the development of "art performance," of the earlier traditions of Futurism and Dada.

"Performance art," in Carroll's sense, developed out of traditional theater, as a reaction against the idea that dramatic performance should be a vehicle for a literary text. It stressed, rather, the performative aspects of group or individual activity on a stage, and the values, such as spectacle, realizable through such activity. The orientation of traditional theater toward representation, spectatorship, and fidelity to the text was replaced by a concern with the presentational, the participatory, and the visual and gestural. In dance, this manifested itself in the interest in the body in motion in the work of choreographers like Yvonne Rainer – something that echoes the interests of the Futurists in the body as mechanism and in "Taylorism," the study of efficient movement in the work environment. Rather than the performer mediating between the audience and a character that she represents, there is a focus on performativity, the unmediated interaction between the performer and her audience. Recent work in "performance art" in Carroll's sense has generated and in turn been influenced by philosophically inflected studies of performativity by those working in "performance studies" (e.g., see Parker & Sedgwick 1995).

Performance art of both kinds raises a number of distinctive philosophical questions. First, as already noted, it is difficult to delimit the extent of the art form other than by reference to various historical traditions, which themselves comprise much that is not obviously itself performance art. The latter, as noted, overlaps with and incorporates other art forms in significant respects. Attempts at clarifying the nature of performance art are also likely to be frustrated by the generally transgressive agenda that has driven much work in the field. In the case of total artworks, this is perhaps not a serious problem, because, while such works incorporate different artistic media, the multiplicity of media itself provides a distinguishing criterion. In the case of the overlap between performance artworks and works of theater, the most useful distinguishing marks may be the reliance, in the articulation of content in performance art, on the visual and the spectacular rather than the textual and the narrative, and on the performer *as* performer rather than as representation. (For the contrary view that theatrical performances are themselves works of performance art, see Hamilton 2007). In the case of what Carroll terms "art performance," on the other hand, difficulties arise from the intimate relations between much recent art performance and conceptual art. Goldberg, for example, notes that performance art fits very naturally with the conceptualist's hostility toward the "art object" as commodity. Performance art, as event, is by its very nature transient and, insofar as it involves the artist's body as material, cannot be bought and sold in the standard way.

In cases where the performance seems designed to function as a materialization, in and through the artist's activity, of the conceptual content of the work, the line between performance art and conceptual art becomes difficult to draw. For example, as with some works by Yoko Ono (Goldberg 2001: 154), the work may offer a set of instructions for a performance, with no apparent requirement that those instructions be put into practice in order for the work to be fully appreciated. It is the *very idea* of carrying out a particular performance that serves to articulate an artistic content, it seems. More problematic still are early works by Vito Acconci – normally classified as paradigm examples of performance art – such as *Following Piece*, a particular extended activity undertaken by Acconci in 1969 in New York City. The piece required that, on 23 consecutive days, he followed people at random until it became impossible to do so. While many of Acconci's other performances of that time are documented by a cinematic record, *Following Piece* is represented in galleries by just a few still photographs staged by Acconci after the event – indeed, he failed to perform the required actions on some of the 23 specified days. It is tempting to say, again, that the artistic content is articulated by the *idea* of carrying out such a performance, given that we are offered only sparse visual assistance if we try to appreciate the work. Other late modern works prescribing particular performances raise similar issues (see Davies 2003, 2007).

These examples are troubling because, as we have noted, the stress on "performativity" in works of performance art suggests that appreciating such works requires an immediate, or at least a cinematically mediated, engagement by the receiver with the performance itself. Where the performance is a singular event presented to an audience on a given occasion, we are prepared to say, as with unrecorded work-performances of musical works, that "you had to be there" to appreciate the performance. But, where no opportunity for such an engagement is ever offered, the status of a piece as performance art becomes unclear.

Finally, there is a further issue about the accessibility of much performance art. Even if we are present during the performance event(s), a proper grasp of the work will often require that we bring considerable contextualizing knowledge to bear upon what is manifest to us. Many performance works are motivated by social and political concerns of the artist. For example, the use of the artist's body in a performance lends itself to the expression of themes about gender and embodiment that have been central to feminist thinking. Performance art therefore provides an interesting challenge to those "empiricist" theories of artistic appreciation that try to exclude such contextualizing knowledge from the proper appreciation of artworks.

See also CONCEPTUAL ART; PERFORMANCE.

BIBLIOGRAPHY

Carroll, Nöel. 1986. "Performance Art," *Formations*, 3(1), 63–79.

Davies, David. 2003. *Art as Performance*. Oxford: Blackwell, ch. 9.

Davies, David. 2007. "Telling Pictures: The Place of Narrative in Late-Modern Visual Art." In *Philosophy and Conceptual Art*. P. Goldie & E. Schellekens (eds.). Oxford: Oxford University Press, 138–56.

Goldberg, RoseLee. 2001. *Performance Art: From Futurism to the Present*. Rev. & expanded edn. London: Thames & Hudson.

Hamilton, James. 2007. *The Art of Theater*. Oxford: Blackwell.

Kivy, Peter. 1995. *Authenticities: Philosophical Reflections on Musical Performance*. Ithaca: Cornell University Press, ch. 5.

Parker, Andrew & Sedgwick, Eve (eds.). 1995. *Performativity and Performance*. New York: Routledge.

DAVID DAVIES

perspective In the pictorial arts, the term "perspective" generally refers to the system of artificial perspective, whereas "aerial perspective" refers to the depiction of the loss of clarity in form and color in the far distance. Artificial perspective, the subject of this article, is the method for depicting space which was invented by Filippo Brunelleschi in Florence in the 1420s and perfected by writers and artists in the course of the fifteenth century, notably Leon Battista Alberti, Lorenzo Ghiberti, and Piero della Francesca. The invention of artificial perspective marks a watershed in the history of changing attitudes toward images, their use, and their manufacture in western Europe, dividing the mystery of the icon from the secular magic of illusionism. For this reason, it has always fascinated historians of art. However, it has become the subject of philosophical controversy only in the twentieth century, as a result of an article published by Erwin Panofsky in 1927.

Panofsky's ideas were partly influenced by the German mathematician Guido Hauck, who had elaborated a curvilinear alternative to the system of artificial perspective some 50 years earlier. But the influence of the Neo-Kantian philosopher Ernst Cassirer was more important. Following Kant, Cassirer (1953–7) believed that the mind imposes a form on the ultimate material of experience, that this is an absolute and invariable prerequisite for cognition, and that the form itself is determined not by the objects we apprehend, but by the structure of human sensibility and understanding. However, Cassirer argued that human knowledge and experience are conditioned in this way not only by the fixed and unalterable canons of space, time, and causality but also by the variable "symbolic forms" of language, mythology, art, and science.

Panofsky's article, entitled "Die Perspektive als 'symbolische Form'," presents the case for regarding artificial perspective as a symbolic form. It cannot, Panofsky argues, claim to be a uniquely valid method for representing space as we see it because it is based on two important assumptions: "first, that we see with a single motionless eye; and second, that the plane section through the cone of sight is an adequate reproduction of our visual image. The fact is, however, that these assumptions involve an extremely bold abstraction from reality (if, in this context, we may call the subjective visual impression 'reality')" (1927: 260).

The first assumption is evidently false; the second, Panofsky argues, is no closer to the truth than the first. His argument is obscure and somewhat confused. However, he claims that perspective pictures represent the visual field as if it were flat, whereas in fact it is shaped like a sphere; that the system of perspective records the influence of distance on apparent size in a way which accords more closely with the images on our retinas than with our visual impressions, where the influence of distance is compensated for by psychological mechanisms; and that the system of perspective is designed to produce pictures on flat surfaces and represents straight lines as straight, whereas the retina is concave, and so straight lines are represented on its surface by curves. It follows, Panofsky argues, that artificial perspective is – to borrow a phrase that Cassirer used to describe language – "a magic mirror which falsifies and distorts the forms of reality in its own characteristic way" (1946: 137) and which influences our perception and our imagination accordingly.

Since the publication of Panofsky's paper, many distinguished theorists of art, psychologists, and philosophers have addressed the question of whether the system of artificial perspective is best regarded as an elaborate code or as a discovery about the form of visible space. Following Panofsky, Read claims that "the theory of perspective . . . is a scientific convention; it is merely one way of describing space and has no absolute validity" (1956: 67). Goodman argues that "the bundle of light rays delivered to the eye by the picture [of a building] drawn in standard perspective is very different from the bundle delivered" by the building itself, and he therefore maintains, as do Read and Panofsky, that "the behavior of light sanctions neither our usual nor any other way of rendering space" (1968: 19).

On the other hand, Gombrich describes artificial perspective as "the most important

trick in the armoury of illusionistic art" (1977: 205). The trick is turned by applying a set of rules, but the impression it causes in a spectator proves that artificial perspective is far from being an arbitrary code. "What may make a painting like a distant view through a window . . . is the similarity between the mental activities that both can arouse" (1973: 240), and therefore "the goal which the artist seeks . . . [is] a psychological effect" (1982: 228). Artificial perspective, he argues, tends to produce this effect. Pirenne argues in a similar vein that a picture painted in perspective will "produce visual percepts in the observers . . . which resemble those which would be given by the (actual or imaginary) scene represented" (1970: 10).

As these quotations reveal, not only is the status of artificial perspective disputed, it is also uncertain what would settle the matter. In order to prove that artificial perspective has or does not have a singular authority, independent of custom and convention, should we attempt to measure the geometrical differences between a picture painted in perspective and a retinal image? Should we compare the pattern of light reflected by such a picture with the pattern reflected by the scene depicted? Or should we investigate the psychological episode that the picture is apt to cause?

I suspect that none of these strategies is the right one. In order to decide whether Brunelleschi and his followers devised an ingenious code or discovered a method for reproducing the visible form of space, we must first appreciate that the system of artificial perspective is a synthesis of the various techniques for depicting nonplanar spatial relations that already existed – overlapping, foreshortening, and perspective diminution. (No special techniques for depicting planar spatial relations – above, below, to the left of, to the right of – are needed, for they can be reproduced on the painted surface.) If we can explain what these relatively primitive techniques accomplish, and how they accomplish it, we shall find it easier to understand their harmonious integration into a unified system, and the awkward puzzle that Panofsky created may be solved more easily.

Overlapping, which is the simplest technique for depicting nonplanar spatial relations, was already used by Egyptian artists in the Old Kingdom to depict the partial occlusion of one object by another. The object that is partly hidden from sight is only partly depicted, and the part of the painted or carved surface that would otherwise depict this hidden part depicts instead the part of the object in front that hides it.

Foreshortening and perspective diminution are more sophisticated techniques, but they serve essentially similar purposes. Foreshortening allows a painter to depict what philosophers have misleadingly called "apparent shape" – that is, an object's outline or silhouette. "Occlusion shape" is a less tendentious term. A circular plate viewed obliquely has an elliptical occlusion shape: it will occlude an elliptical patch on a plane perpendicular to the line of sight. An object's occlusion shape is a function of its actual shape and its orientation relative to the line of sight of a spectator, and so foreshortening allows a painter to depict not only the shape of an object, but also its orientation. Thus, a panel by Uccello in the National Gallery, London, which depicts the battle of San Romano, includes a fallen knight lying along a line orthogonal to the picture plane. Needless to say, this is a feat of artistry that was beyond the powers of the artists who depicted the many fallen warriors on the Bayeux Tapestry or the Narmer Palette.

Perspective diminution allows a painter to depict relative occlusion size. If I hold out my hands in front of me, and extend one arm further than the other, my hands will not appear to differ in size, but the greater occlusion size of the nearer hand will be evident: the nearer hand will occlude a larger patch on a plane perpendicular to my line of sight. The relative occlusion size of two objects is a function of their relative size and their relative distance from the spectator, and so perspective diminution allows a painter to make a picture in which one object is further from the spectator than another without depicting partial occlusion. (It seems likely that painted scenery employing perspective diminution was introduced by Sophocles, and that the technique was perfected by Agatharcus of Samos, when he painted a backcloth for a revival of a play by Aeschylus in the 430s BCE.)

Many philosophers have mistakenly supposed that occlusion shape and relative occlusion size are not visible properties of the physical world, but features of our subjective visual impressions. To take a recent example, Christopher Peacocke writes as follows:

> Suppose you are standing on a road which stretches from you in a straight line to the horizon. There are two trees at the roadside, one a hundred yards from you, the other two hundred. Your experience represents these objects as being of the same physical height and other dimensions; that is, taking your experience at face value you would judge that the trees are roughly the same physical size . . . Yet there is also some sense in which the nearer tree occupies more of your visual field than the more distant tree. This is as much a feature of your experience itself as is its representing the trees as being the same height. (1983: 12)

In Peacocke's view, this shows that visual experience has certain features that do not "represent the environment of the experiencer as being in a certain way," because "no veridical experience can represent one tree as larger than another and also as the same size as the other" (1983: 5, 12). I do not intend to say anything about Peacocke's view that visual experience involves mental representations. What is relevant for present purposes is the idea, plainly present in this passage, that the relative occlusion size of the two trees is not actually a feature of the visible environment but of the visual impressions of the person who sees the trees.

This idea is mistaken. Their relative occlusion size is a visible property of two trees, no less than their relative size. (And the occlusion shape of a plate is a visible property of the plate, no less than its shape.) This is clear from the fact that I can mistake the relative occlusion size of two trees, and my mistake can be corrected by measurement and geometrical calculation. For example, I might guess that the nearer tree has double the occlusion size of the further tree, and be surprised to discover that the correct ratio is three or four to one. By and large, painters with a traditional academic training will be good at giving accurate reports of occlusion shape and relative occlusion size, and the rest of us not so good.

Perhaps the temptation to deny that occlusion shape and relative occlusion size are visible features of our physical environment is due to the fact that the shape of an object's outline will change as we move around it, although the object itself does not undergo any change; and the relative occlusion size of the two trees in Peacocke's example will change as we move from one end of the avenue to the other, although the trees do not change or move. However, it does not follow that occlusion shape and relative occlusion size are not visible features of our physical environment, or that when we describe them we are talking about our visual impressions (let alone about features of these impressions which do not in themselves "represent the environment of the experiencer as being in a certain way"). After all, the distance between me and the door changes as I walk toward it, without the door moving; but this does not show that the changing distance between me and the door is not really a feature of my physical environment, but is in some peculiar way merely a feature of my subjective experience.

Relative occlusion size, like partial occlusion, is relative to a point of view, and occlusion shape is relative to a line of sight, but this does not impugn their objectivity in the least, or imply that they are nebulous, merely apparent, or unreal. Nor does it imply a contradiction to suppose that two trees appear to be (and actually are) the same height while their occlusion size, relative to my point of view, appears to be (and actually is) different. Despite what Peacocke says, this is no more contradictory than the fact that a single object may be big relative to one thing and small relative to another.

The notion that occlusion properties are merely apparent, subjective, or unreal is one of the commonest errors in the philosophical canon, and its influence on the theory of painting is unmistakable. For if we imagine that the elliptical occlusion shape of a circular plate viewed obliquely belongs in the metaphysically subordinate category of mere appearance, or that it is a feature of the subjective visual experience of a person looking at the plate, then we are bound to conclude that a painting which depicts a plate foreshortened shows the plate *as it appears to us* rather than *as it is*, or that the technique of foreshortening aims to reproduce a feature of our subjective visual experience. Indeed, this conclusion was already drawn by Plato, in the *Sophist* (235d–236c). Twenty-three centuries later the same notion, but given a Kantian inflection, led Panofsky to

suppose that artificial perspective aims at "an adequate reproduction of our visual image." (There is an important ambiguity here, since in this context "reproduce" can mean either "make a copy of" or "produce artificially." This ambiguity, which recapitulates an ancient ambiguity in the meaning of "mimesis," has had its own repercussions, but they are beyond the scope of this entry.)

Once the mistake has been corrected, we can see overlapping, foreshortening, and perspective diminution for what they are: techniques for depicting nonplanar spatial relations. Overlapping allows the painter to make a picture in which one object is further from the spectator than another, in the manner described above. (However, their relative distance from the spectator will be indeterminate.) Foreshortening allows the painter to depict orientation relative to the line of sight of the spectator, by making the shape of the part of a picture that depicts an object the same as the object's occlusion shape. Perspective diminution allows the painter to depict relative distance from the spectator, by making the relative size of the parts of a picture that depicts various objects the same as the objects' relative occlusion size. (Shading is a close cousin of foreshortening: it allows an artist to depict orientation relative to the source of illumination.)

Before the invention of artificial perspective, these techniques for depicting nonplanar spatial relations were used independently. They were also used inconsistently. For example, in the panel from Duccio's *Maestà* that depicts the flagellation, Pontius Pilate appears to be standing both behind and in front of a column. The invention of artificial perspective was a systematizing achievement: it integrated the existing techniques for the depiction of nonplanar spatial relations into a harmonious unity, and thereby guaranteed a consistent pattern of spatial relations between the parts of a depicted scene.

What conclusions should we draw about the debate initiated by the publication of Panofsky's paper? Panofsky himself was right to deny that "we see with a single motionless eye," but wrong when he maintained that artificial perspective is based on the assumption that we do; and wrong when he stated, in the concluding paragraph of his paper, that artificial perspective is "an ordering of visual appearance . . . transforming *reality* into *appearance*." Goodman was right to insist that "the bundle of light rays delivered to the eye by the picture [of a building] drawn in standard perspective is very different from the bundle delivered" by the building itself, but wrong to conclude that artificial perspective is merely a conventional method of projection which has been sanctioned by habit. Gombrich was right to deny this, but wrong to base his view on the claim that "what may make a painting like a distant view through a window . . . is the similarity between the mental activities that both can arouse." Alberti was closest to the truth when he stated that "the function of the eye in vision need not be considered in this place" (1966: 47), and confined his discussion of perspective to geometry.

See also DEPICTION; GOMBRICH; GOODMAN; ILLUSION; PICTURE PERCEPTION; REPRESENTATION.

BIBLIOGRAPHY

Alberti, Leon Battista. 1966 [1435]. *On Painting.* J. R. Spencer (trans.). New Haven: Yale University Press.

Cassirer, Ernst. 1946 [1925]. *Language and Myth.* S. Langer (trans.). New York: Harper.

Cassirer, Ernst. 1953–7 [1923–9]. *The Philosophy of Symbolic Forms.* 3 vols. R. Manheim (trans.). New Haven: Yale University Press.

Gombrich, E. H. 1973. "Illusion in Art." In *Illusion in Nature and Art.* E. H. Gombrich & R. L. Gregory (eds.). London: Duckworth, 193–243.

Gombrich, E. H. 1977. *Art and Illusion.* 5th edn. Oxford: Phaidon.

Gombrich, E. H. 1982. "Experiment and Experience in the Arts." In *The Image and the Eye.* Oxford: Phaidon, 215–43.

Goodman, Nelson. 1968. *Languages of Art.* Indianapolis: Bobbs-Merrill.

Kemp, M. 1990. *The Science of Art.* New Haven: Yale University Press.

Panofsky, E. 1927. "Die Perspektive als 'symbolische Form'." In *Vorträge der Bibliothek Warburg.* Leipzig: Teubner, 258–330.

Peacocke, Christopher. 1983. *Sense and Content.* Oxford: Oxford University Press.

Pirenne, M. H. 1970. *Optics, Painting and Photography.* Cambridge: Cambridge University Press.

Read, Herbert. 1956. *The Art of Sculpture.* London: Faber.

White, J. 1967. *The Birth and Rebirth of Pictorial Space.* 2nd edn. London: Faber.

JOHN HYMAN

picture perception Pictures present us with aspects of our worlds. We can see in pictures landscapes, familiar or unknown faces, or any of the numerous objects that inhabit our environment, but what is the nature of this perceptual experience? Specifically, how does it relate, in terms of its character and content, to ordinary perception? This is a question that philosophical studies of pictorial perception aim to answer, in an effort to understand the nature of pictorial representation and the source of the distinctive pleasure that it can afford the viewer.

One way to think of pictorial perception is as continuous with ordinary perception. One might think, for instance, that in seeing a picture of a tree one has an experience that exactly matches in phenomenology the experience of seeing the depicted tree face to face. In pictorial theory this idea has been associated with Ernst Gombrich who, in that context, describes pictorial perception as a case of illusion. This description seems apposite since such a perceptual experience would misrepresent the physical properties of the object of perception. Is this, however, a correct description of pictorial perception? It seems not. If in seeing a picture we had an experience as of really seeing the objects depicted therein then (1) pictorial space would be experienced as actual three-dimensional space, while (2) recognition of the subject matter would "absorb" properties of the medium so that, for instance, an etching and a color photograph of the same scene would look the same to the viewer, as they would both look indistinguishable from the actual scene depicted. Obviously this is not so. With the exception of *trompe-l'oeil* pictures, we appreciate the two-dimensionality of a pictorial configuration, while we know from our experience with pictures that a color photograph of a given scene looks different from an etching or a drawing of the same scene. How these pictures look different has to do *not* with their subject – which is shared – but with the medium, that is, with what materials have been used and how these have been handled by the artist to represent the relevant subject.

Against the illusion theory it thus seems that, ordinarily, seeing an object in a picture is not continuous with seeing that object face to face, to the extent that in pictorial seeing the perceiver is aware of the medium (i.e., of the pictorial surface and the marks on that surface) as well as the object of representation. This insight has been central to Richard Wollheim's account of pictorial representation. According to Wollheim, the capacity to generate a twofold perceptual experience is distinctive of pictorial forms of representation. Specifically, the perceptual experience that pictures foster has a distinctive phenomenology; it is a single experience that consists of two aspects of awareness: the *configurational* aspect of awareness, which relates to the marked surface; and the *recognitional* aspect of awareness, which relates to the object of representation. Wollheim names this twofold perceptual experience "seeing-in" and explains that it is not unique to pictorial representation: although commonly triggered by pictures, seeing-in may further occur in our encounter with adequately differentiated surfaces that are not, and are not believed to be, representational (for instance, rock formations). In contrast to such surfaces, however, pictures, according to Wollheim, do not just permit but *require* seeing-in; while, further, there is a standard of correctness set by the intentions of the artist, for what is to be seen in a picture.

The success of Wollheim's theory rests, in part, on the intelligibility of seeing-in: we need to understand how two disparate (and, in certain respects, incompatible) objects of awareness – one of which, furthermore, is actually absent from the viewer's visual field – merge, in the viewer's experience, into an integrated whole. Wollheim only provides a negative specification. We are not to model our understanding of each aspect of seeing-in on the face-to-face experience after which it can be described, and to which it is partly analogous, as the phenomenology of the relevant experiences is incommensurable. If so, however, we seem to have no resources to understand the phenomenological character and the content of seeing-in. Unless more can be said by way of explanation – an explanation that Wollheim does not provide – the notion of seeing-in is incomprehensible.

An attempt to meet this challenge can be found in the work of Robert Hopkins. Hopkins agrees with Wollheim that in seeing a pictorial representation the viewer is aware of the pictorial marks as *marks,* as well as of the object that the picture represents. He argues however that this twofold experience, seeing-in, has to be understood as an experience of resemblance: the marks on the pictorial surface are seen as resembling something else, that is, the object that the picture thereby represents, in terms of outline shape. Outline shape, Hopkins explains, is a visible property of things, albeit a property that they have only in relation to some point: it is a matter of the combined directions of the parts of an object from a point in its surroundings. To the extent that outline shape ignores the third dimension it is a property that pictures and their objects can share.

When the viewer experiences a resemblance in outline shape between the marks on a pictorial surface and the object represented therein, both the marks and the object figure in her awareness. The experience thus exhibits twofoldness, so it can be properly characterized as an experience of seeing-in. However, Hopkins's account of seeing-in deviates from Wollheim's characterization of the experience in one important respect: whereas Wollheim takes seeing-in to involve perceptual awareness of the represented object (which is actually absent from the viewer's visual field), for Hopkins it is only the thought of the object – specifically of the object's outline shape – that is part of the experience. Hopkins thus escapes the illusionistic insights that lurk in Wollheim's description of seeing-in. Although the viewer is not perceptually aware of the represented object, still (1) the thought of the object transforms the look of the marks in a way that we could characterize, in part, by reference to the object and its properties; (2) the object is thereby part of the experience, in accordance with the requirements of seeing-in. The experienced resemblance theory thus seems to provide a coherent characterization of seeing-in. Doubts have been expressed (e.g., in Lopes 2005), however, about Hopkins's claim that outline shape is a visible property, moreover a property of pictorial designs that we can perceive before we identify what a picture depicts.

An alternative characterization of seeing-in has been suggested by Kendall L. Walton. Pictures are, for Walton, props in visual games of make-believe, that is, they prescribe visual imaginings with a particular content. In looking at a picture of *X* one is to imagine that one's looking at the canvas is looking at X. For instance, it is appropriate (but also required), according to Walton, that on observing Meindert Hobbema's *The Water Mill with the Great Red Roof*, one imagines one's observation of the canvas to be of a mill (1990: 293). Walton argues that the imaginings thus prescribed could plausibly amount to seeing-in, since (1) both the marked surface and the object depicted therein are in some way part of the experience, and (2) the experience is visual since it is a case of visual imagining exercised on an actual act of seeing. There has been some concern, however, over this claim. It is a requirement of seeing-in that the viewer is aware of the pictorial marks *as marks*. This condition does not seem to hold in Walton's account, where the viewer is expected to imagine that the marks are, or her looking at them is, something else, that is, her looking at the represented object. Besides, it is doubtful whether the imaginary experience that Walton describes is indeed one we customarily have, and are *expected* to have, in front of pictures.

Philosophical debate regarding seeing-in does not focus solely on the characterization of the experience. Wollheim's claim that seeing-in is definitive of pictorial representation, that is, that pictures do not just permit but require seeing-in, is another source of disagreement among pictorial theorists. Lopes (1996), for instance, acknowledges that pictures often trigger a twofold perceptual experience, but he doubts that pictorial perception is, by default, a case of seeing-in. Seeing-in, he argues, is relevant to art pictures, especially art pictures of a certain "painterly" style, but it is arguable whether documentary or illustrative pictures require awareness of their medium. Moreover, an account of pictorial representation in terms of seeing-in would exclude *trompe-l'oeil* pictures (i.e., pictures designed to produce an illusion, prohibiting awareness of their media properties) from the domain of pictorial representation by fiat. But *trompe-l'oeil* pictures, Lopes notes, *are* pictures and a comprehensive account of pictorial representation ought to recognize them as such.

It should be acknowledged, however, that *trompe-l'oeil* pictures are quite extraordinary pictures – perhaps they even lie at the boundaries of pictorial representation, as Wollheim

claims – and the seeing-in theory at least explains why this is so. Moreover, as John Hyman notes, the belief that *trompe-l'oeil* pictures are designed to produce an illusion and sustain it for as long as the viewer sees the painting, is an exaggeration "which distorts the aim and the effect of *trompe-l'oeil* painting. The play element would be lost and the enjoyment of skill and virtuosity, which *trompe-l'oeil* cultivates and caters to, would be frustrated if it were true. That is why, as Ruskin remarks, *trompe-l'oeil* invariably 'has some means of proving at the same time that it is an illusion' " (Hyman 2006: 132). If this is the case, the *trompe-l'oeil* objection to the seeing-in theory is met – once the representational character of what is seen is acknowledged, the technique comes to the fore and the medium is thereby evident. At this point the *trompe-l'oeil* picture not just is but also can be *seen* as a pictorial representation.

As the case of *trompe-l'oeil* pictures illustrates, the representational character of an object should be manifest in our visual experience (along with what the object represents) if this object is to be seen as a picture. Although the precise character and scope of seeing-in is still an object of debate among pictorial theorists, it seems that it is only within a theory that appeals to seeing-in that we can accommodate this fact. The analysis of seeing-in is, for this reason, among the most vital projects in pictorial theory.

See also DRAWING, PAINTING, AND PRINTMAKING; PHOTOGRAPHY; DEPICTION; GOMBRICH; ILLUSION; PERSPECTIVE; REPRESENTATION; STYLE; WALTON; WOLLHEIM.

BIBLIOGRAPHY

Budd, Malcolm. 1992. "On Looking at a Picture." In *Psychoanalysis, Mind and Art: Perspectives on Richard Wollheim*. J. Hopkins & A. Savile (eds.). Oxford: Blackwell, 259–80.

Gombrich, Ernst. 1977. *Art and Illusion: A Study in the Psychology of Pictorial Representation*. 5th edn. London: Phaidon.

Hopkins, Robert. 1998. *Picture, Image and Experience*. Cambridge: Cambridge University Press.

Hopkins, Robert. 2003. "What Makes Representational Painting Truly Visual?" *Proceedings of the Aristotelian Society*, supp. vol. 77, 149–67.

Hopkins, Robert. 2005. "The Speaking Image: Visual Communication and the Nature of Depiction." In *Contemporary Debates in Aesthetics and the*

Philosophy of Art. M. Kieran (ed.). Oxford: Blackwell, 145–59.

Hyman, John. 2006. *The Objective Eye: Color, Form, and Reality in the Theory of Art*. Chicago: University of Chicago Press.

Levinson, Jerold. 2001. "Wollheim on Pictorial Representation." In *Richard Wollheim on the Art of Painting*. R. van Gerwen (ed.). Cambridge: Cambridge University Press, 28–38.

Lopes, Dominic McIver. 1996. *Understanding Pictures*. Oxford: Oxford University Press.

Lopes, Dominic McIver. 2005. "The Domain of Depiction." In *Contemporary Debates in Aesthetics and the Philosophy of Art*. M. Kieran (ed.). Oxford: Blackwell, 160–74.

Nanay, Bence. 2005. "Is Twofoldness Necessary for Representational Seeing?" *British Journal of Aesthetics*, 4, 248–57.

Walton, Kendall L. 1990. *Mimesis as Make-Believe*. Cambridge, MA: Harvard University Press.

Walton, Kendall L. 1992a. "Seeing-In and Seeing-Fictionally." In *Psychoanalysis, Mind and Art*. J. Hopkins & A. Savile (eds.). Oxford: Blackwell, 280–91.

Walton, Kendall L. 1992b. "Looking at Pictures and Looking at Things." In *The Philosophy of the Visual Arts*. P. Alperson (ed.). New York: Oxford University Press, 103–13.

Wollheim, Richard. 1980. *Art and Its Objects*. 2nd edn. Cambridge: Cambridge University Press.

Wollheim, Richard. 1987. *Painting as an Art*. London: Thames & Hudson.

Wollheim, Richard. 2003. "What Makes Representational Painting Truly Visual?" *Proceedings of the Aristotelian Society*, supp. vol. 77, 131–47.

KATERINA BANTINAKI

Plato (c.427–347 BCE) Greek philosopher: disciple of Socrates and teacher of Aristotle. His dialogues are arguably the most influential philosophical works ever written. They contain the first extended investigations of many of the central issues of ethics, metaphysics, politics, and representational art.

Plato can be regarded, with equal reason, as both the founder of philosophical aesthetics and the fiercest critic of aesthetics' right to an autonomous existence. Questions about poetry, music, painting, and dance, as well as broader reflections on the nature of beauty, are approached from diverse angles throughout his works. The unifying thread is a requirement that the possibilities of artistic form, meaning, and beauty should be appraised within a larger framework – ultimately a metaphysics – of truth and goodness. Behind Platonic concerns with the musico-poetic and figurative arts, therefore, lies a conviction of the unity of all value. This appears, for example, in dissatisfaction with functional and relativist definitions of "beauty," and the assumption of the latter's inseparability from goodness, in *Hippias Major*. A related impetus emerges in the *Republic*'s claim (5.475–6) that "lovers of sights and sounds," including devotees of poetry, music, and painting, perceive only sensory reflections of beauty and cannot grasp the principle of "beauty (in) itself." In the *Symposium*, Diotima's speech (201–12), a mixture of logic and visionary mysticism, makes beauty the object of a desire (whose roots are erotic) for what is intrinsically and permanently valuable: among much else, Diotima locates poetic creativity within this expanded model of the soul's erotic aspirations.

Because of its importance in education and its general cultural prestige, poetry was of particular importance to Plato. Following earlier Greek philosophers like Xenophanes who had pursued the "ancient quarrel between philosophy and poetry" (*Republic* 10.607b), he challenges poetry's ethical, psychological, and religious credentials; but he also evinces an unceasing fascination for poetry's emotional and dramatic power, which he tries to rival in his own writing. One recurrent issue is whether poets create from knowledge and conscious skill (*technê*) or are reliant on non-rational inspiration. The *Ion* approaches this question obliquely, via an examination of the basis for critical interpretation of poetry. But its famous image of the poet composing when ecstatically possessed by a divine force (533–4) is an arguably ironic hypothesis that the dialogue's quest for an understanding of "the art of poetry as a whole" (532c) leaves unresolved. In the *Phaedrus*, Socrates at one point ranks *technê* below inspiration in poetic creativity (245a), but at another (268–9) he suggests that expert poets have systematic knowledge of how to produce unified works. As always with Plato, individual passages have dramatic contexts that do not reveal a fixed authorial viewpoint.

The two most important Platonic critiques of poetry, with subordinate consideration of other mimetic art forms, occur in the *Republic*. The first, in Books 2–3 (376–98, with related discussion of music at 398–403), starts by repudiating the ideas of vengeful gods and volatile heroes found in the greatest Greek poets, especially Homer and the tragedians. It then proceeds to an analysis of narrative form, focusing in particular on the special psychological power of dramatic impersonation (for which the term "mimesis" is here reserved): this is said to mold the mind and "self" of anyone who identifies with the viewpoint of a character. The critique as a whole evaluates poetic works by three interlocking criteria: "truth" (construed here as partly normative); the ethical paradigms conveyed (explicitly or implicitly) by poetic narratives; and the psychological benefit or harm to an audience of internalizing those paradigms. Socrates' proposed exclusion of the most imaginative poets from the ideal city (3.398a) should not be reduced to crude censorship: it is a symbolic challenge to the values of Plato's culture rather than a blueprint for action. Despite a passing allusion to the possibility of aesthetic "play" (3.396e), the argument refuses to allow artistic representation an autotelic status: its power to "enter the interior of the soul" (401d) and influence the lives of both individuals and groups is too great for that. Far from propounding a narrow puritanism, the eventual goal of the discussion is claimed as "the erotics of the beautiful" (3.403c), a principle that applies to music, painting, architecture, and other forces that shape the city's cultural environment (400–2). Characteristically, Plato leaves sensitive readers with the impression that artistic image-making has been both questioned and potentially reclaimed for a better world.

After the *Republic*'s elaborate exploration of psychology and metaphysics in its middle books, the dialogue returns to poetry in book 10 (595–608). Here mimesis assumes a broader sense of depictive representation; the argument accordingly starts from an analogy with painting. In a gesture which can be read as a provocation to "lovers of sights and sounds" (above), Socrates asks what mimesis can offer that a mere mirror cannot; and he uses a tripartite metaphysical hierarchy (of unchanging "forms," individual objects, and mere

simulations) to demote mimetic art to a level "twice removed from the truth." In addition, after he has trenchantly questioned the common Greek view of poets as knowledgeable, wise "guides to life," Socrates suggests that mimesis appeals only to "low" parts of the soul: painting to a sensory susceptibility to illusions, poetry to the irrational grip of emotion. The latter charge is given special weight: "even the best of us," Socrates says (605c–d), cannot resist the emotional power of the greatest poetry, especially tragedy. But as in book 3, something more than a puritanical impulse is at work in the text. Socrates concludes the discussion by actually hoping that poetry's "banishment" can be reversed: admitting his own quasi-erotic attachment to poetry, he invites the defenders of the art to produce a new justification of it that will harmonize ethical benefit and psychological pleasure (10.607–8).

The combination of arguments in *Republic*, books 2–3 and 10, as elsewhere in Platonic treatments of mimetic art, is more ambivalent than might appear at first glance. Socrates shows a troubled awareness of the capacity of poetry and music to touch deep psychic roots in ways that can bypass rationality; but he remains open to the possibility that such power might be harnessed to the good of the soul and the community. Plato's own writing, indeed, with its wealth of imagery and dramatic finesse, can be considered as an attempt to pursue that possibility: Plato was recognized as a "poetic" philosopher by some ancient readers, as well as by his Renaissance and Romantic admirers. The *Republic* itself ends with an eschatological myth that uses intense narrative and visionary imagination to emulate poetic myths of the afterlife, especially Homer's *Odyssey*.

But engagement with existing art forms is also sustained, right up to the final dialogues, through critical analysis. The *Laws* contains several passages that sketch issues and problems for aesthetics, some of them complex, obscure, yet probing (and still relatively neglected). The richest are in books 2 (653–71) and 7 (796–817): they encompass ideas about mimetic art and cultural recreation; the psychological roots of aesthetic form and order; the importance of moral feelings in art; the value of certain types of artistic tradition; the nature of representation in poetry, music, dance, and painting. Nowhere do Plato's arguments relinquish the underlying demand that the expressiveness of artistic images be grounded in a unified conception of value; the beauty of art depends on ethical beauty (*Laws* 2.654b–c). This principle betokens something more than a moralistic denial of aesthetics. Just as in other dialogues (e.g., see *Republic* 4.420c–d, *Phaedrus* 268–9 on the importance of formal unity), the *Laws* intimates an awareness of the need for "internal" principles of artistic excellence and recognizes unsolved problems: the relationship between pleasure and other criteria of artistic value remains vexed (*Laws* 2.667). The dialogues do not claim to have the final answers.

Plato is the only great questioner of art and aesthetic experience who can also count as a profound lover of art; even Tolstoy was not both these things simultaneously and throughout his life. In the *Laws*, Plato calls philosophy itself "the most beautiful and truest tragedy" (7.817), an alternative vision of life's fundamental meaning. There is a vital sense in which Plato's aesthetics is embodied in the entirety of his own philosophical creativity.

See also AESTHETICS IN ANTIQUITY; MEDIEVAL AND RENAISSANCE AESTHETICS; ARISTOTLE; CREATIVITY.

BIBLIOGRAPHY

Primary sources
1997. *Plato: Complete Works*. J. M. Cooper (ed.). Indianapolis: Hackett.

Secondary sources
Asmis, Elizabeth. 1992. "Plato on Poetic Creativity." In *Cambridge Companion to Plato*. R. Kraut (ed.). Cambridge: Cambridge University Press, 338–64.
Burnyeat, Myles. 1999. "Culture and Society in Plato's *Republic*," *Tanner Lectures on Human Values*, 20, 217–324.
Halliwell, Stephen. 2002. *The Aesthetics of Mimesis: Ancient Texts and Modern Problems*. Princeton: Princeton University Press.
Janaway, C. 1995. *Images of Excellence: Plato's Critique of the Arts*. Oxford: Clarendon.

STEPHEN HALLIWELL

pleasure, aesthetic   *see* AESTHETIC PLEASURE.

Plotinus (204–c.270)   Greek philosopher of the Christian era; the best-known Neoplatonist thinker, and a major influence on Western mysticism.

Born in Egypt and educated at Alexandria, Plotinus joined the emperor Gordian III on an expedition to Persia in 242, hoping to learn about Persian mystical philosophy. In the event, Gordian was killed and Plotinus traveled to Rome, where he established an academy and came to be favored by the emperor Gallienus. He was regarded as a spiritual master, known for gentility and kindness and reputed to be a mystic.

Porphyry, one of his students, was his biographer and edited his works. These are known collectively as the *Enneads*, and consist of six books each of nine chapters (*ennea*: "nine"). Chapter 6 of book 1, entitled "On Beauty," contains Plotinus' most systematic treatment of this issue. Aesthetics is prominent within Plotinus' entire system, and from this single chapter one may learn much of his general philosophical outlook. For many centuries, the essay "On Beauty" was the only known part of the *Enneads*.

Plotinian philosophy is essentially Platonistic, and this provides a key to understanding his emphasis on the importance of aesthetic experience in advancing from miserable ignorance to mystical transcendence. From the earliest speculative philosophers (the Pre-Socratics) Plato had inherited a belief in the possibility of comprehending reality by relating apparently disparate phenomena to some deeper ordering and unifying principles. Plotinus follows Plato in taking the ordering principles to be *forms* that organize quantities of matter into intelligible unities. Variants on this basic theme are common within ancient and medieval philosophy, and are important to the aesthetic theories of these periods, which generally treat the experience of beauty as a mode of knowledge of (or identification with) reality.

Plotinus' version of the "philosophy of form" is esoteric but recognizably related to aspects of Christian theology, which it deeply influenced. At the heart of things is a transcendent divine reality that escapes all categories of description. Nonetheless, it has three modes, or aspects (*hypostases*). First and foremost it is ultimate unity (*the one*); second, it is both intellect and what intellect knows (*mind or thought*); and, third, it is the source of life (*the soul*). Emanating out of this "primal core" is the remainder of things, ordered according to their degree of existence or participation in the nature of innermost reality. All entities seek union with the divinity, and strive to move inwards toward it, seeking to realize their potential for perfection and aspiring to the condition of pure, self-originating, matterless *form*.

Aesthetic experience plays an important role in this process of self-perfection. In "On Beauty," Plotinus wonders what precise conditions are necessary and sufficient for beauty, and first considers the suggestion that the essence of beauty is *symmetry* (*Enneads* 1.6.1). This is dismissed, however, because some beautiful things, such as single colors and musical notes, are simple (without parts) and hence lack symmetry; while some symmetrical things, such as some faces, lack beauty. Also, Plotinus assumes a principle of composition according to which a complex entity can have a given property only if its parts have it independently of their membership of the whole. Instead, beauty is taken to be *unity* or oneness, by which he means formal unity: "In what is naturally unified, its parts being all alike, beauty is present to the whole" (*Enneads* 1.6.2). This is a comprehensive notion covering both simples and complexes. Different answers to the question "What is it?" – for instance, "red," "middle C," "a square," "a horse," and so on – all introduce unifying forms which impose an integrated nature on the matter in which they inhere. When we experience such forms we derive pleasure from this perceived unity, and the soul is also awakened to its co-natural affinity with the source of empirical and other forms – namely, divinity in its aspects of oneness, mind and soul.

Beauty is generally a *supervenient* quality – that is to say, one which results from the organization of matter by formal principles. The beauty of a (near-)perfect pattern, say, consists in the ordering of stuff (wood, paint, and so on) according to a geometrical ideal, and this is true also of the constituent parts of the pattern, such as lines and curves, considered in their own right. Since it does not identify empirical beauty with any particular form, this view allows for indefinitely many kinds of beautiful

things – beauty is "variably realizable." Equally, however, it raises the question of nonempirical beauty, such as that of a proof, or a virtuous character. Plotinus not only recognizes the aesthetic quality of these, but regards nonsensible beauty as being of a higher order, and claims that the ascent through the hierarchy of beauty-inducing forms is the pathway to mystical union with *the one*, an aspect of which (in its hypostasis as *mind*) is the dazzling self-existent form of beauty:

> Like anyone just awakened the soul cannot look at bright objects. It must be persuaded to look first at beautiful habits, then the works of beauty produced not by craftsmen's skill but by the virtue of men known for their goodness, then the souls of those known for beautiful deeds . . . Only the mind's eye can contemplate this mighty beauty . . . So ascending, the soul will come first to Mind . . . and to the intelligible realm where Beauty dwells. (*Enneads* 1.6.9)

These ideas may strike us as extravagant and even unintelligible. But Plotinus is worth reading, both in order to make sense of work in medieval and Renaissance thought, and to see how aesthetics could have a central place within a well-built philosophical and religious system.

See also AESTHETICS IN ANTIQUITY; MEDIEVAL AND RENAISSANCE AESTHETICS; BEAUTY; INEFFABILITY; PLATO.

BIBLIOGRAPHY

Primary sources
1988. *Plotinus*, vol. vi: *Ennead 6.1–5*. Loeb Classical Library. A. H. Armstrong (trans.). Cambridge, MA: Harvard University Press.
1989. *The Essential Plotinus*. E. O'Brien (ed. & trans.). Indianapolis: Hackett.

Secondary sources
Anton, J. P. 1964. "Plotinus' Refutation of Beauty as Symmetry," *Journal of Aesthetics and Art Criticism*, 23, 233–7.
Beardsley, Monroe C. 1975. *Aesthetics from Classical Greece to the Present Day*. Montgomery: University of Alabama Press.
Geerson, L. (ed.). 1996. *The Cambridge Companion to Plotinus*. Cambridge: Cambridge University Press.
Gurtler, G. M. 1989. "Plotinus and Byzantine Aesthetics," *Modern Schoolman*, 67, 275–84.

Miller, C. L. 1977. "Union with the One, *Ennead* 6, 9, 8–11," *New Scholasticism*, 51, 182–95.

O'Meara, Dominic J. 1993. *Plotinus*. Oxford: Oxford University Press.

JOHN HALDANE

popular art is a contested topic. Even its name evokes controversy. While those sympathetic to popular art call it such, those who traditionally opposed it prefer to label it "mass art" – the term "mass" suggesting an undifferentiated (and possibly even subhuman) conglomerate rather than merely the idea of mass-media technology. The idea of entertainment for the masses as a ploy of capitalist domination is associated with the notion of the "culture industry" (an influential term coined by Horkheimer & Adorno 1986) but some theorists use the term "mass art" more neutrally to define it in terms of appeal to the largest audience (Carroll 1998). Popular art can be usefully distinguished from this notion of mass art in that popular art does not require a mass audience but only a sufficiently multitudinous one to establish adequate popularity (Shusterman 1992). In this way, genres or styles that are clearly oppositional to mainstream culture (e.g., rap or heavy metal music) can be recognized as popular art though they never try to reach the largest possible audience.

The main aesthetic issue is not the definition of popular art but whether it really deserves artistic status and can exhibit genuine aesthetic merit. Cultural critics through the latter part of the twentieth century tended to consider it intrinsically and necessarily an aesthetic failure and a corruptive danger to high art. Though it was never a central concern of traditional philosophical aesthetics, the value of popular art has recently become an important aesthetic topic, because of the increasing dominance of mass-media culture and the growing alienation of much of the public from contemporary avant-garde forms of high art.

The most reasonable position on this issue lies between the condemnatory pessimism shared by reactionary high-culture elitists and left-wing Marxists of the Frankfurt school, and the celebratory optimism of popular culture enthusiasts. It is a position of *meliorism*, which recognizes popular art's flaws and abuses, but also its merits and potential. It holds that popular art should be improved because it leaves much to be desired, but that it can be improved because it can achieve real aesthetic merit and serve worthy social goals (Shusterman 1992).

Though we should focus on the aesthetic arguments against popular art, it is important to note that perhaps the most damaging indictments are not directed at popular art's aesthetic status but at its pernicious sociocultural influence. Yet these more general indictments seem to rest on aesthetic considerations. For example, the charges that popular art corrupts high culture by borrowing from it and by luring away potential artists and audiences presume that popular art's borrowings are to no good aesthetic purpose (since works of high art borrow from each other with no consequent complaint). Similarly, the charges that popular culture is emotionally destructive because it produces spurious gratification, and is intellectually destructive because of its superficiality and escapism, rest on the presumed aesthetic inability of popular art to produce genuine aesthetic pleasure through meaningful form and content. Further, the charges that popular art "not only reduces the level of cultural quality . . . but also encourages totalitarianism by creating a passive audience peculiarly responsive to the techniques of mass persuasion" (Gans 1974: 19) rest on the assumptions that popular art's products are invariably of negative aesthetic value and so necessarily lower taste, and that they necessarily require a mindless, passive response because they can neither inspire nor reward any aesthetic attention beyond uncritical passivity.

In considering the arguments against the aesthetic legitimacy of popular art, it would be futile to attempt a total whitewash, for much of popular art is lamentably unaesthetic and socially noxious. What philosophers need to consider, however, is the validity of arguments claiming to show that popular art is necessarily an aesthetic failure – that, in the words of Dwight Macdonald, "there are theoretical reasons why Mass Culture is not and can never be any good" (1957: 69). We shall consider six such charges.

(1) Popular art fails to provide real aesthetic satisfactions but provides only spurious ones,

which are "washed-out," vicarious, escapist, and ephemeral. There are several problems with this charge, apart from the problem of knowing what "spurious" satisfaction is. For most of the public, the pleasures of popular art (such as movies and rock music) are surely as intense, real, and direct as those derived from high art, which also has an escapist dimension. Nor do high and low art always differ with respect to the ephemerality of their pleasures. But even if our pleasure from a pop song is briefer than that from a sonnet, this does not entail this pleasure's illegitimacy or unreality. Moreover, the argument that popular art can produce only ephemeral pleasures is flawed in forgetting that many of the great classics of high art (for instance, Greek and Shakespearean drama) were originally produced and consumed as popular art.

(2) It is argued that popular art can provide no real aesthetic pleasure because it requires no effort but only passivity. As Horkheimer and Adorno remark, its "pleasure hardens into boredom because it must not demand any effort . . . No independent thinking must be expected from the audience"; anything "calling for mental effort is painstakingly avoided" (1986: 137). One of the problems with this argument is that it equates all effort with "mental effort" or "independent thinking." Critics of popular art tend to forget that there are forms of aesthetically rewarding activity other than intellectual exertion (e.g., dancing). Moreover, these critics too often make the mistake of assuming that because some popular art can be enjoyed without intellectual effort it can never sustain or reward intellectual interest. But from the fact that something can be enjoyed on a shallow level, it does not follow that it must be so enjoyed and has nothing else to offer.

(3) The charge of popular art's intellectual shallowness typically breaks down into two subcharges. The first is that it cannot deal with the real problems of life in a serious way because its aim is to distract the masses and keep them in a false contentment by showing them only what they can easily understand and accept. But this argument falsely assumes that consumers of popular art are just too stupid to understand more than the obvious, and that they are incapable of appreciating views with

which they disagree. Empirical studies of television watching (see Fiske 1987) show this is false. Second, there is the charge that popular art's products necessarily lack sufficient complexity, subtlety, and levels of meaning so that they may be comprehensible to the large audiences that popular art seeks to please. But again, the argument presumes the inability of popular art's audience to appreciate any intellectual complexity, and, again, empirical evidence shows that they do. Intellectualist critics typically fail to recognize the multilayered and nuanced meanings of popular art.

(4) The common claim that popular art is necessarily uncreative relies on three lines of argument: its standardization and technological production preclude creativity because they limit individuality; its group production and division of labor frustrate original expression because they involve more than one artists' decisions; the desire to entertain a large audience is incompatible with individual self-expression, hence with creativity. All these arguments rest on the premise that aesthetic creation is necessarily individualistic – a questionable romantic myth nourished by liberalism's ideology of individualism, and one which belies art's essential communal dimension.

The sonnet's length is just as rigidly standard as the TV situation comedy's, and the use of technology is present in high as well as popular art, where it serves less as a barrier than as a spur to creativity. As for the second argument, we can grant no contradiction between collective production and artistic creativity without thereby challenging the aesthetic legitimacy of Greek temples, Gothic churches, and the works of oral literary traditions. The third argument, that popular art cannot be creative because it must offer homogenized fare to meet an average of tastes, involves a number of errors. It confuses a "multitudinous audience" with a "mass audience." Popularity requires only the former. A particular taste group sharing a distinct social or ethnic background or specific subculture may be clearly distinguishable from what is considered the homogeneous mass audience.

Moreover, popular artists are also consumers of popular art and form part of its audience, often sharing the tastes of those toward whom their work is directed. Here there can be no real conflict between wanting to express oneself creatively and wanting to please one's large audience. Finally, the argument that popular art requires conformity to accepted stereotypes rests on the empirically falsified premise that its consumers are too simple-minded to appreciate views that are unfamiliar or unacceptable to them.

(5) A fifth charge often leveled at popular art is that it lacks the autonomy necessary for true artistic status (see Adorno 1984; Bourdieu 1984). Popular art forfeits this status by its desire to entertain and serve human needs rather than purely artistic ends. Such inferences rest on defining art as essentially opposed to life. But why should this view be accepted? Originating in Plato's attack on art as doubly removed from reality, and reinforced by Kant's aesthetic of disinterestedness (defined as indifference to real existence and praxis), this view allows philosophy, even in defending art, to assert art's difference from the real so as to ensure philosophy's sovereignty in determining reality and the conduct of life.

But surely art forms part of our reality and practical life? Music is used to lull babies to sleep. Poetry is used for prayer and courtship, fiction to inculcate moral lessons, architecture to create living and working spaces. Moreover, today's developments in postmodern culture suggest the increasing implosion of the aesthetic into all areas of life.

(6) Finally, popular art is condemned for not achieving adequate form. Usually it is not unity but formal complexity that is denied to popular artworks, and used to distinguish them from genuine art. For Bourdieu, popular art involves "the subordination of form to function" and "content," and thus cannot achieve the complex formal effects of high art, "which are only appreciated relationally, through a comparison with other works which is incompatible with immersion in the . . . [content] given" (1984: 4, 34). But this formal complexity of intertextuality is also often present in works of popular art, many of which self-consciously allude to each other. Nor are these allusions and their formal aesthetic effects unappreciated by the popular art audience, who are generally more literate in their artistic traditions than are the audiences of high art in theirs. The formal quality of popular art can be

properly assessed only by examining concrete examples, and the reader is referred to Cavell (1981), Shusterman (1992), Carroll (1998), and Irwin & Gracia (2006).

See also MUSIC AND SONG; ADORNO; MASS ART.

BIBLIOGRAPHY
Adorno, Theodor W. 1984 [1970]. *Aesthetic Theory*. G. Adorno & R. Tiedemann (eds.). C. Lenhardt (trans.). London: Routledge & Kegan Paul.
Bourdieu, Pierre. 1984. *Distinction*. Cambridge, MA: Harvard University Press.
Carroll, Noël. 1998. *Mass Art*. New York: Oxford University Press.
Cavell, Stanley. 1981. *Pursuits of Happiness*. Cambridge, MA: Harvard University Press.
Fiske, John. 1987. *Television Culture*. London: Routledge & Kegan Paul.
Gans, Herbert. 1974. *Popular Culture and High Culture*. New York: Basic Books.
Horkheimer, M. & Adorno, T. W. 1986. *The Dialectic of Enlightenment*. New York: Continuum.
Irwin, William & Gracia, Jorge (eds.). 2006. *The Philosophical Interpretation of Popular Culture*. Lanham: Rowman & Littlefield.
Macdonald, Dwight. 1957 [1946]. "A Theory of Mass Culture." In *Mass Culture: The Popular Arts in America*. B. Rosenberg & D. White (eds.). Glencoe: Free Press, 59–73.
Shusterman, Richard. 1992. *Pragmatist Aesthetics: Living Beauty, Rethinking Art*. Oxford: Blackwell.

RICHARD SHUSTERMAN

pornography Etymologically, the word means writing associated with the brothel, and it applies most specifically to a genre of fiction which draws its materials from sexual fantasy and consists almost exclusively of detailed descriptions of sexual activity, tireless and sometimes elaborately perverse. It typically lacks any interest of character or plot. In its "ideal type," developed by the Marquis de Sade (1740–1814) in such works as *Justine* and *The 120 Days of Sodom*, the apparatus also includes, for instance, an isolated, luxurious chateau, and silent servants. Such features are now less common, though they can still sometimes be found in examples with more literary pretension, such as *The Story of O*, published under the pseudonym Pauline Réage, a well-known book which also preserves the Sadean emphasis on cruelty. In recent times the strictly sadistic aspect has generally been more cultivated in other media.

Written pornography seems to have first appeared, at any rate in Europe, in the middle of the seventeenth century. The first original English prose pornography (as opposed to translations), and also the first to take the form of a narrative rather than a dialogue, was John Cleland's *Memoirs of a Woman of Pleasure* (1748) – better known as *Fanny Hill*. However, visual representations with an explicit sexual content go back to ancient times and appear in almost all cultures, and some of them (such as murals at Pompeii and some Attic vase painting) seem designed to elicit the same kind of interest as written pornography. The word "pornographic" is now applied to works in any medium, and by far the largest proportion of pornography now current consists of material in mechanically reproduced visual forms, such as photographic magazines, cinema films, and images available through the Internet.

Particularly in relation to this visual material, a distinction is often drawn between "hard-core" and "soft-core" pornography. The distinction has a complex structure, but roughly speaking the subject matter of soft-core pornography excludes violence, and if males are represented at all, they are not visibly aroused. It is interesting for the psychology of pornography that magazines of the kind standardly for sale in respectable newsagents in Europe and North America, which have soft-core illustrations, often contain writing which, if the distinction is applied to text, must count as hard-core. In the case of films, soft-core pornography may possess more ambitious production values than hard-core, sometimes aiming for distribution in ordinary cinemas as opposed to specialist porno houses.

Although the term "pornography" is applied to works in any medium, it may still be taken to refer to what is, in a very broad sense, a genre. A pornographic work is one that combines a certain content, explicitly sexual representation, with a certain intention, sexual arousal. (Pornographic material is, of course, often sold in sex shops and used in connection with sexual activity, particularly masturbation.) A feature of this definition, as opposed to more wide-ranging or, again, evaluative proposals for the use of the word, is that it leaves open questions about the relation of pornography to other notions – in particular, those of the *obscene* and the *erotic*. Even leaving aside its technical use in English law, "obscene" in its ordinary use is a strongly negative term, suggesting the hideous, repulsive, or unacceptable; "erotic," on the other hand, has more positive connotations in contemporary society. Pornography is sometimes taken to be necessarily associated with obscenity; sometimes it is contrasted with the erotic. If pornography is defined merely in terms of a certain content and a certain intention, it will remain for discussion whether all pornography is obscene, or to what extent it can be erotic.

Such discussions naturally bear on a further question – whether there can be a pornographic work of art. There is strong pressure to use "pornographic" in an unequivocally negative way, to imply condemnation on moral and social grounds, or aesthetic grounds, or both. In this sense, the pornographic is often contrasted with art. It may also be contrasted with the erotic, pornography being specially associated with cruelty and violence, particularly against women, while the erotic is taken to imply sexual relations that are both gentler and more equal. If the term is used in this way, there is a danger that different issues may be run together, and some important questions begged: it may be harder, for instance, to separate, intellectually and politically, the question of whether some objectionable work has merit from the question of whether it should be rejected (for instance, banned) whatever its merit.

It would be naive to suppose that in this area definitional issues could be uncontentiously settled without ideological implications. For one thing "pornography" is a candidate for legal use in regulating, and perhaps trying to suppress, objectionable material. More generally, and more deeply, the nature and definition of pornography are necessarily at issue when it is asked what exactly is objectionable about such material. Pornography is found in varying degrees offensive by many people, and some of it is deeply offensive to almost everybody. Is this best explained by general psychological theory, or in cultural (and therefore perhaps more local) terms? To what extent can any such questions be discussed without bringing in considerations that are in a broad sense political?

The most radical cultural analysis of pornography since around 1980 has come from feminist critics. Most pornography is intended for and used by men, and consists of representations of women and of heterosexual activity serving male fantasies. Most pornography involving same-sex activity between women is also intended for men (there is usually at least one sequence of this kind in the standard pornographic film). However, pornography is not exclusively related to men's fantasies about women. There is a great deal of male homosexual pornography intended for male homosexuals, and also pornography which is used by women and on an equal basis by heterosexual couples. Moreover, it is not necessarily true that the more extreme or the "harder" a piece of pornography is, the more sexist it is. Much of the most extreme pornography indeed expresses violence against women; but, with more widely available material, it is significant that the distinction between hard core and soft core, mentioned above, is itself drawn on sexist lines: it is soft-core pornography that exclusively offers women to the view of a male figure who is either outside the representation or unaffected within it.

The radical feminist thesis is that not just the fantasy but also the reality of male domination is central to pornography, and that sadistic pornography involving women is only the most overt and unmediated expression of male social power. Moreover, the objectifying male gaze to which pornography offers itself is thought to be implicit not only throughout the commercial media, but in much high art. This outlook reinterprets the relation of pornography to other phenomena. Traditional views, whether liberal or conservative, are disposed to regard pornography as a particular and restricted phenomenon, and extreme sadistic pornography as even more so; but a radical feminist approach is likely to see the overtly sadistic varieties of pornography, and the phenomenon in general, as merely less reticent versions of what is more acceptably expressed elsewhere.

This approach leads to new emphases in the definition of pornography, but they involve a conflict. On the one hand, it should be less significant in this perspective to pick out a class of works distinguished by the extremity of their sexual content – or indeed, at the limit, by their having explicit sexual content at all. On the other hand, a radical feminist critique is likely to want to distance itself from conventional puritanism, and to encourage the expression of some rather than other kinds of sexuality and eroticism. It is thus involved, just as much as are traditional approaches, in making discriminations between kinds of sexual content – discriminations which inevitably run into familiar ethical, psychological, and (if enforcement is proposed) legal complexities of separating some kinds of sexual representation from others.

See also CENSORSHIP; EROTIC ART AND OBSCENITY; FEMINIST AESTHETICS; FEMINIST STANDPOINT AESTHETICS; IMAGINATION; MORALITY AND ART.

BIBLIOGRAPHY
Dworkin, Ronald. 1985 [1981]. "Do We Have a Right to Pornography?" In *A Matter of Principle*. Cambridge, MA: Harvard University Press.
Dwyer, Susan (ed.). 1995. *The Problem of Pornography*. Belmont: Wadsworth.
Eaton, A. W. 2007. "A Sensible Antiporn Feminism." *Ethics*, 117, 674–715.
MacKinnon, Catherine A. 1987. *Feminism Unmodified*. Cambridge, MA: Harvard University Press, 335–72.
Peckham, Morse. 1969. *Art and Pornography*. New York: Basic Books.
Shrage, Laurie. 2007. "Feminist Perspectives on Sex Markets." In *The Stanford Encyclopedia of Philosophy*. E. N. Zalta (ed.). Available at http://plato.stanford.edu/archives/fall2007/entries/feminist-sex-markets/
West, Caroline. 2005. "Pornography and Censorship." In *The Stanford Encyclopedia of Philosophy*. E. N. Zalta (ed.). Available at http://plato.stanford.edu/archives/fall2005/entries/pornography-censorship/
Williams Committee Report. 1979. *Obscenity and Film Censorship*. Cmnd 7772. London: HMSO.

BERNARD WILLIAMS

pragmatist aesthetics Like pragmatism itself, pragmatist aesthetics is a tradition with different voices that, nevertheless, tend to converge on certain key themes. Perhaps the most crucial points of convergence are the centrality of experience in aesthetics and the way that aesthetic experience extends well beyond the circumscribed field of fine art to pervade manifold dimensions of life, action, and culture. Hence for pragmatism, aesthetics cannot be narrowly equated with the philosophy of art, at least when art is understood in the modern institutional sense of the established fine arts of high culture.

Pragmatist aesthetics received its first systematic formulation in John Dewey's classic *Art as Experience*, first published in 1934. Charles S. Peirce and William James had an appreciation of the aesthetic but did not substantively theorize about it (though Peirce had a very substantive semiotics). Ralph Waldo Emerson and the African American philosopher and cultural critic Alain Locke (both sometimes associated with pragmatism) anticipated several of the key ideas that Dewey developed into the first systematic pragmatist aesthetic. We can introduce it in terms of eight themes.

(1) Naturalism. Though art can be correctly described as cultural and even spiritual, pragmatism insists on art's deep roots in the natural world, in the elemental desires, needs, and rhythms of the human organism interacting with that world. Emerson defines art as "nature passed through the alembic of man" (1990: 133), just as Dewey held that "underneath the rhythm of every art and every work of art, there lies . . . the basic pattern of relations of the live creature to his environment" (1987: 155–6). For Emerson and Dewey, art is not pursued purely for its own sake but for the sake of better living and the highest art is "the art of life."

(2) Art's service to life implies a rejection of the traditional aesthetic/practical opposition that defines art by its contemplative noninstrumentality. Dewey's pragmatist aesthetics contrastingly insists on art's wide-ranging functionality, while affirming the pleasures of its immanent experience (including its pleasures of dynamic form). "The work of esthetic art satisfies many ends . . . It serves life rather than prescribing a defined and limited mode of living" (1987: 140). Emerson likewise demands that art, in serving life, be both practical and moral.

(3) Recognition of art's deep functionality and immediate experience of vital delight leads Emerson to celebrate art over science as representing the peak of human experience. Dewey was, of course, extremely appreciative of science, but he still claims that "art, the mode of activity that is charged with meanings capable of immediately enjoyed possession, is the culmination of nature," and that " 'science' is properly a handmaiden that conduces natural events to this happy issue" (1987: 33).

(4) Pragmatism is a philosophy of continuities rather than dichotomies. Hence Dewey affirmed the continuity of art and science, since both disciplines are creative, symbolic, well-formed expressions that emerge from and restructure life's experience and that demand intelligence, skill, and trained knowledge in order to improve experience. Pragmatism is critical of the dualisms that dominate aesthetic theory (e.g., art/life, art/nature, fine/practical art, high/popular art, spatial/temporal art, aesthetic/practical, artists/ordinary people). Emerson famously critiques the institutional compartmentalization of human life that produces fragmentary monsters instead of complete humans, while Alain Locke's aesthetics suggests that the richness and value of an artwork (or a culture as a whole) tend to be enhanced through the tasteful mixing and interaction of different elements.

(5) One of contemporary theory's most popular dualisms is that between nature and culture. Defying these dichotomies, Emerson and Dewey explain art as much through cultural history as through nature, showing that not only the content but the very concept of art has altered through historical change. As Dewey outlines the historic reasons for "the compartmental conception of fine art" in terms of the growth of museums through modern nationalism, imperialism, and capitalism, so Emerson traced our culture's evolution from the aesthetic unity of beauty and use in ancient Greece to modern art's romantic, antifunctional aestheticism.

(6) Among pragmatism's most distinctive features is its attitude of meliorism, its desire not simply to understand reality but to improve it. Aesthetics' prime goal should not be formal definitions of art and beauty but rather improved aesthetic experience. Locke appreciatively studied the negro spirituals not for mere theory but to develop its potential for new creativity and transformation. Moreover,

pragmatism includes Emerson's view that art itself has higher ends than its objects: "nothing less than the creation of man and nature is its end" (Emerson 1990: 192).

(7) One vital area for melioristic transformation is the democratization of art, the goal of broadening the notion of art to embrace the experience and expression of more people from more classes, races, and walks of life. Opposing the elitism of high culture that divides society and dries up the fountains of invention, Emerson recommends "the literature of the poor, the feelings of the child, the philosophy of the street, the meaning of household life" as "the topics of the time" that art should treat (1990: 50). Dewey similarly blasted the stultifying elitism of "the museum-conception of fine art" that denies legitimacy to popular art. Unfortunately, Dewey fails to provide popular art with any of the sort of careful, appreciative, legitimizing critical study that by his own account seems necessary. In contrast, Locke provides very detailed practical criticism and legitimizing study of the African American popular arts, not only the musical arts (especially of spirituals and jazz) for which African Americans were most respected, but also the arts of literature, drama, painting, and sculpture.

(8) Central to Dewey's pragmatist aesthetics is the primacy of experience in art. Dewey famously distinguishes the physical object as mere "art product" from the heightened experiential activity that is the real artwork: "the actual work of art is what the product does with and in experience" – first, the creating artist's experience, then that of the work's audience (1987: 9, 87, 121, 167). For Dewey, the aesthetic experience that defines art is an intensified, well structured, directly fulfilling experience that involves heightened vitality and feeling and that stands out from the ordinary flow of experience as something special, as *an* experience that is strongly felt, unified, distinctive, and memorable. Emerson also stressed the concept of deeply felt experience in art and in life more generally. Since life means movement, a life-serving art cannot be a matter of lifeless artifacts but implies dynamic, changing, lived experience. Hence "true art is never fixed, but also flowing." "The true poem is in the poet's mind," for "the poet has . . . a new experience to unfold," and through the

sharing of this experience with his audience makes them into new artists (1990: 119, 189, 192, 200).

DEWEY'S INFLUENCE

Dewey's ideas had impact on the artworld, influencing such important painters as Robert Motherwell, Thomas Hart Benton, Jackson Pollock, Alan Kaprow (who helped create the genre of performance art known as the "happening"). In academic philosophy, however, his influence in aesthetics fell into decline between the 1950s and 1990s through the rise of analytic philosophy. Though Monroe C. Beardsley was clearly influenced by Dewey's theory of aesthetic experience and made it the key to his own definitions of art and aesthetic value, Beardsley's analytic definitions and aims were remote from Dewey. Other philosophers grounded in analytic philosophy, however, have built on Deweyan insights to develop pragmatist approaches to such traditional topics as the interpretation and definition of art and to more distinctively contemporary issues ranging from mass-media arts and multi-culturalism to postmodernism and the stylizations of the art of living.

Nelson Goodman develops Dewey's theme of the continuity of art and science. Rejecting the idea of "autonomous aesthetic objects," valued merely for the pleasure of their form, Goodman urges the fundamental unity of art and science through their common cognitive function. Hence, aesthetics should be placed with philosophy of science and should be conceived as an integral part of metaphysics and epistemology. Aesthetic value is subsumed under cognitive excellence. Despite his attempt to supply extremely strict definitions of works of art in terms of the conditions of identity and authenticity of the material objects that exemplify them, Goodman insists with Dewey (and Beardsley) that what matters aesthetically is not precisely what the material art object is but how it functions in dynamic experience. He therefore advocates that we replace the question "what is art?" with the question "when is art?" (1969: 259; 1978: 70, 102; 1984: 6, 148). Moreover, Goodman offers a critique of contemporary museum practices and ideology that greatly resembles the spirit of Dewey's critique of the museum conception of fine art, though Goodman (1984), of course, has a very different style of argumentation. Both thinkers warn against the fetishization and compartmentalization of art objects, arguing instead that our purpose should be the maximization of the active use of such objects in the production of aesthetic experience.

Other philosophers trained in the analytic tradition (e.g., Joseph Margolis, Richard Rorty, and Richard Shusterman) have used pragmatist ideas to show how the interpretation of artworks can be meaningful and valid without the need to posit fixed entities as the unchanging objects of these valid interpretations. Their arguments explain how traditionally entrenched but dialogically open practices can be enough to secure identity of reference for discussion of the work (and thus ensure that we can meaningfully talk about the same work) without positing that there is therefore a fixed, substantive nature of the artwork that permanently defines its identity and grounds all valid interpretation. This basic strategy of distinguishing between substantive and referential identity is formulated in different ways by these contemporary pragmatists. These theorists stress the historicity and culturally embedded nature of artworks. Opposing the idea (shared by Rorty, Margolis, and the literary pragmatist Stanley Fish) that all our aesthetic experience is interpretative, Shusterman (1992) deploys Dewey (but also Wittgenstein) in arguing for some level of experience "beneath interpretation" and even beneath language.

As Goodman revived Dewey's continuum of art and science, so Rorty (1989) extends Dewey's pragmatist blending of aesthetics and ethics by advocating "the aesthetic life" as an ethics of "self-enrichment," "self-enlargement," and "self-creation." Rorty's vision of the aesthetic life has been criticized for its reductive isolation in the private sphere, its narrowing focus on language, and its failure to engage with popular art forms. In contrast, Shusterman urges greater appreciation of the aesthetic experience of popular arts by providing detailed aesthetic analyses of contemporary popular art genres (e.g., rap and country music) and of somatic-centered disciplines that can augment our aesthetic experience and creative power in the art of living. Rorty counters not only by questioning the idea of a somatic aesthetics but even by expressing "scepticism about 'aesthetics' as a field of inquiry" formulating general principles about the arts and judgments of aesthetic value, calling it "another of Kant's bad ideas" (2001: 156).

See also BEARDSLEY; GOODMAN; MUSEUMS; ONTOLOGICAL CONTEXTUALISM.

BIBLIOGRAPHY

Beardsley, Monroe C. 1958. *Aesthetics: Problems in the Philosophy of Criticism*. New York: Harcourt, Brace & World.
Dewey, John. 1987 [1934]. *Art as Experience*. Carbondale: Southern Illinois University Press.
Emerson, Ralph Waldo. 1990. *Ralph Waldo Emerson: A Critical Edition of the Major Works*. Richard Poirier (ed.). Oxford: Oxford University Press.
Goodman, Nelson. 1969. *Languages of Art*. Oxford: Oxford University Press.
Goodman, Nelson. 1978. *Ways of Worldmaking*. Indianapolis: Hackett.
Goodman, Nelson. 1984. *Of Mind and Other Matters*. Cambridge, MA: Harvard University Press.
Locke, Alain. 1925. *The New Negro*. New York: Albert & Charles Boni.
Margolis, Joseph. 1999. *What, After All, is a Work of Art?* University Park: Pennsylvania State University Press.
Rorty, Richard. 1984. *Consequences of Pragmatism*. Minneapolis: University of Minnesota Press.
Rorty, Richard. 1989. *Contingency, Irony, and Solidarity*. Cambridge: Cambridge University Press.
Rorty, Richard. 1991. *Objectivism, Relativism, and Truth*. Cambridge: Cambridge University Press.
Rorty, Richard. 2001. "Response to Richard Shusterman." In *Richard Rorty: Critical Dialogues*. M. Festenstein & S. Thompson (eds.). Cambridge: Polity, 153–7.
Shusterman, Richard. 1992. *Pragmatist Aesthetics: Living Beauty, Rethinking Art*. Oxford: Blackwell.
Shusterman, Richard. 1999. "Emerson's Pragmatist Aesthetics." *Revue Internationale de Philosophie*, 207, 87–99.
Shusterman, Richard. 2000. *Performing Live*. Ithaca: Cornell University Press.
Shusterman, Richard. 2002. *Surface and Depth: Dialectics of Criticism and Culture*. Ithaca: Cornell University Press.

RICHARD SHUSTERMAN

properties, aesthetic   *see* AESTHETIC PROPERTIES.

483

psychoanalysis and art Psychoanalysis is a field of inquiry into the human mind and mental development, aimed at therapy for mental disorders. Psychoanalysis is committed to the premise that unconscious motives are the fundamental impetus and determinants of form for human productions and behavior. It seeks to translate the obvious import of everyday human activities into their hidden, unconscious messages. Art figures in psychoanalytic discussion primarily as a product of human creation, to be decoded into the unconscious motives that it represents.

A number of psychoanalytic theorists, however, provide suggestions regarding the pleasure the audience takes in artworks. In addition, psychoanalytic theory has served as the starting point for certain twentieth-century schools of art and art criticism. Thus, while psychoanalysts' accounts of art rarely amount to aesthetic theory as such, their writings touch on many matters of relevance to aesthetics.

Sigmund Freud (1856–1939), the founder of psychoanalysis, elaborates a theory of mind that treats the human psyche as comprising multiple dynamic components. An entirely unconscious segment, which Freud calls the "id," is comprised of basic instinctual drives. Another, largely conscious, component, called the "ego," attempts to reconcile the demands of the instincts with the demands of the larger world. In the course of the ego's efforts, a part of it branches off into a third component of relative independence. This component is called the "superego." It internalizes parental and social demands, and it serves as an internal control and censor over the ego's activities.

Freud analyzes mental disorders in terms of disharmony among these components. Disorders arise, for example, as the result of a conflict between the id's demands – frequently sexual – and the ego's and the superego's efforts to steer the mind into conformity with socially imposed criteria for respectability. They may also result from the ego's inability to maintain some autonomy from the superego or external reality. Normal childhood development involves a series of stages in which the id's demands are gradually brought under the control of the ego. The route involves numerous conflicts among the elements of the psyche and external reality, conflicts which may be only partially resolved and may continue to plague an individual throughout adulthood.

The conflicts between instinctual desires and the demands of society and the superego lead to many desires becoming repressed – that is, exiled into unconsciousness. Similarly, memories of experiences that conflict with the psyche's internalized notions of acceptability tend to be repressed. Psychoanalysis attempts to recover and treat the motives for neurotic behavior by unburying repressed ideas, memories, and desires. Among the techniques that psychoanalysis employs in this effort are the analysis of dreams (which are believed to express repressed ideas in a disguised way) and free association (in which a patient freely says to the analyst whatever comes to mind, in the hope that these may trigger forgotten but significant memories).

Although he describes his own artistic sensitivity to form and artistic methods as deficient, Freud contends that psychoanalysis can legitimately approach artworks in the same manner as it approaches dreams or neurotic symptoms. "The product itself after all must admit of such an analysis, if it really is an effective expression of the intentions and emotional activities of the artist" (1966–74: xiii. 212). Freud's writings on the artist and artworks are, consequently, focused on the artist's psychobiography and its relation to his or her artworks.

Freud approaches the creative work and products of artists with the full arsenal of his psychoanalytic methodology. In artworks as in dreams, he takes the surface or "manifest content" to be a deceptive camouflage for underlying, "latent" meanings. He also seeks the formal determinants of an artwork, as of all products of human making, in the artist's personal biography. The form of Michelangelo's *Moses*, for example, is motivated, according to Freud, by his longstanding irritation over many inconsiderate outbursts made by the pope whose grave the sculpture adorns. Michelangelo depicted Moses as one who overcomes rage as posthumous critique of the dead pope, who lacked the dignified restraint of the sculpture.

Freud's account of the psychology motivating art is unlikely to charm many artists. He compares artists to children, their activity to neurosis, and their achievements to symptoms of narcissism. Artists, according to Freud, are "people who have no occasion to submit their inner life to the strict control of reason" (quoted in Spector 1972: 33). Through art, they indulge desires that most adults have put aside. The original motivation of psychic life, in the Freudian account, is the desire to pursue pleasure, a driving force that Freud terms "the pleasure principle." Maturation involves the individual's recognition that pleasure is more certain if one submits to the constraints of reality – and a constraining "reality principle" emerges. The artist, however, unlike the average adult, continues through creative activity to gratify the pleasure principle without accepting limitation by the reality principle.

Freud's "Creative Writers and Daydreaming" compares artistic activity directly to immature behavior. He considers both daydreaming and literary art to be psychologically akin to children's play. All three are motivated by unconscious desires. Children's play is motivated by the wish to be grown up. But the overriding wishes of adults are more embarrassing desires of an erotic and ambitious nature. The average adult, therefore, does not freely display his or her motives in public, as the playing child does, but satisfies them only in imagination, in the form of fantasies. The artist, by contrast, is a kind of exhibitionist who publicly displays his or her fantasies.

That literature serves the same function as fantasy is suggested, Freud claims, by the number of works that have a hero who is the center of the reader's interest and sympathy. The hero of all novels is "His Majesty the Ego" – the very hero of daydreams (1966–74: ix.150). The ego is the hero even in novels that treat several characters with similar sympathy. In such cases, the ego is simply divided into several component egos.

The artist's creativity is, in Freud's view, primarily motivated by repressed sexual desires. He sees the artist as an introvert whose erotic desires are more powerful than those of the ordinary human being, but whose impulses are diverted into the nonsexual activity of art. Artistic activity might be taken as the paradigm for what Freud labels "sublimation," a process in which sexual urges are given an indirect outlet for their expression. He contends that all forms of cultural achievement are products of sublimation. He writes in *Three Essays on Sexuality*: "There is to my mind no doubt that the concept of 'beautiful' has its roots in sexual excitation and that its original meaning was 'sexually stimulating' " (1966–74: vii.156 n.).

Artists, then, are sufficiently in control of themselves to be able to sublimate their raging desires. Despite their relative developmental immaturity, a good artist is, in Freud's view, sufficiently connected to intersubjective reality to communicate with his or her audience. Nonetheless, the artist's motivations are personal and fundamentally narcissistic. The audience might be repelled were it not for what Freud describes as "the essential *ars poetica*." This technique involves the artist's use of disguises to conceal the work's egoistic character in aesthetic form. The latter is akin to sexual forepleasure, for it is an incentive, providing an increment of pleasure in order to provoke the release of greater pleasure. In the literary case, the reader's ultimate enjoyment is a release of mental tensions that is available through the work's providing a context in which his or her own daydreams can be enjoyed without shame.

Although Freud does not analyze the techniques utilized by artists in giving form to their work, his analysis of the formative principles at work in dreams (and jokes) is suggestive in this connection. Among the formative principles active in what Freud calls "the dreamwork" are "condensation" (which conjoins elements of two or more constituent images into a composite image); "displacement" (in which the psychological significance of one object is assumed by a substitute); "representation" (in which thoughts are translated into images); and "secondary revision" (a vaguely described process that renders the disparate elements comprising the dream into a coherent, intelligible whole).

Otto Rank (1884–1939) explicitly set out to extend Freudian psychoanalytic theory to illuminate art, myth, and creativity. He initially attracted Freud's attention with his study *The Arts*, which elaborates a psychology of the artist's personality on the basis of Freudian theory. Rank analyzes the artist as intermediate between the dreamer, as described in Freud's *Interpretation of Dreams* of 1900, and the neurotic, similar to both in being motivated by repressed sexual wishes.

Rank's later work, *Art and Artist: Creative Urge and Personality Development* (1932), departs from Freudian theory in emphasizing will as the guiding force in the development of the creative personality, and in analyzing artistic creation as a function of the interaction of both individual and collective factors. The latter stem from social environment and societal ideology, and ensure the intelligibility of the artwork's form. Analyzing all human creative impulses as aimed at the "constructive harmonization" of the independent individual and the collective, Rank contends that the creative person succeeds where the neurotic fails. The artist triumphs over biology, mastering the ego to a greater degree than most individuals. Rank postulates that the collective factor involved in artistic creation is a spiritual principle – "genius" – working in the artist, and he contends that the artist has a rather spiritual aim – the achievement of a kind of immortality through art.

Rank does, however, follow the lead of Freud's biologism (the belief that psychological processes can be reductively explained in terms of physiological ones) in his analysis of artistic form. Speculating on the significance of the birth trauma for the individual's psychological life, Rank believes that artistic form refers back to the primal form of the mother's body. The mother's body is also the content of much art, according to Rank, albeit presented in an idealized form.

Carl G. Jung (1875–1961) argues that Freud's analysis does not do justice to the real significance of art, as either a psychological or an aesthetic phenomenon. In general, he contends that Freud is too reductivist in his theorizing, attempting to explain all psychic phenomena in terms of the vicissitudes of the individual's repressed sexual desires. Jung denies that sexual desire can account for all varieties of psychic phenomena (unless one broadens the definition of "sexual" to the point of vacuity). Moreover, he denies that personal psychobiography is the ground on which all psychological structures develop.

While eager to distance himself from Freud, Jung follows him in distinguishing the psychoanalytic approach to art from an aesthetic approach. The former can give an account of art as a phenomenon derived from psychic motives; but aesthetics alone considers art in its essential nature. The two approaches ought to complement one another, but the influence of Freud's psychoanalytic theory has led many to the erroneous expectation that Freudian analysis can explain art. Given that Freud treats art on a par with a psychopathological symptom, Jung considers this view pernicious, for it misses the deeper significance of art.

Jung distinguishes two different types of artistic creation, the psychological and the visionary. The psychological type involves a calculated project on the part of the artist. Such creation draws from conscious life, and deals with matters assimilated by the poet's psyche. The material is the stuff of human experience generally, and the artist offers the audience a greater depth of insight into ordinary matters than they typically have. Nevertheless, the resulting artwork remains within the sphere of what is psychologically intelligible to the artist and (presumably) to his or her audience.

Visionary artistic creation, by contrast, involves an imagistic richness that outstrips the artist's capacity for expression. The material is unfamiliar and surpasses understanding. The work disturbs its audience; nonetheless it is pregnant with meaning. Jung describes this kind of art as "sublime," and compares the act of its creation to Nietzsche's Dionysian experience. The experience from which the artist draws in such work is not personal, but collective. The images provided by the work represent archaic psychic structures that are commonly active in the unconscious of every individual.

Such structures populate what Jung describes as the "collective unconscious," a psychic layer that exists along with, but deeper than, the personal unconscious. The basic structures inhabiting the collective unconscious are what he calls "archetypes." Archetypes are deeply rooted, nearly automatic patterns of instinctive behavior that are aroused when an individual's circumstances correspond to a typical, universal human experience (for instance, losing a loved one, becoming a parent). The archetypes themselves are unconscious, but they appear to consciousness in the form of images that represent instincts. The characters of the world's mythologies, for example, are archetypal images for archetypes, as are provocative images of visionary art.

Art, according to Jung, is indispensable for culture. Just as he contends that dreams provide compensatory images to correct the errors of consciousness, he argues that art provides compensation for the errors of nations and eras. Art serves this role only insofar as it is a symbol – that is, only insofar as primordial images are active behind artistic ones. By definition, visionary art serves this role. Jung grants, however, that psychological art, too, may be symbolic. In such cases, both artist and the contemporary audience typically have similar difficulty recognizing this content. Sometimes, though, such art becomes the focus of a revival in a later epoch, when the consciousness of the age has grown to such a point that it can recognize what an earlier era missed.

Whichever mode of creation is involved in the making of the work, the creative impulse is an autonomous complex, a split-off part of the psyche that leads its own life outside the control of consciousness. The difference between the two modes of creation depends on the artist's conscious relation to the complex. The psychological artist, who feels at one with the creative process, has acquiesced to the unconscious orders of the complex from the beginning; the visionary artist, who has not acquiesced in this way, has been caught unawares.

Jung emphatically denies that artistic activity is comparable to psychopathology, but he does contend that artistic activity makes artists, as a group, more susceptible to certain kinds of psychopathological conditions. Any autonomous complex draws energy away from consciousness. Thus, the energy that fuels the unconscious direction of creative work is drawn away from conscious control of the personality. For some artists, this diversion of energy results in "the instinctual side of the personality" prevailing over the ethical, "the infantile over the mature, and the unadapted over the adapted" (Jung 1966: 79).

According to *Julia Kristeva* (b.1941), linguistic signification has two aspects, the semiotic and the symbolic. The symbolic aspect is meaning in a narrow sense, which for Kristeva is a function of words' syntactic roles within a grammatical system. A sign refers to other elements within the language by virtue of their relative roles within the structure of grammar. Semiotic meaning involves tones and rhythms; it includes the affective dimension of language. According to Kristeva, these tones and rhythms are means for the discharge of bodily drives, which is how language comes to have its significance for us. Communication is a matter of interaction with others, and this depends on our language having emotional force. The semiotic side of language reflects and conveys the nuances of feeling and interconnection. Our engagement with the social world is a matter of emotion, and signs need to be related to our interactions with others, not just to other signs. Language has vitality because it is more than the manipulation of signs; it also expresses our drives and emotions. Poetic language, in particular, is heavily infused with semiotic meaning. In general, Kristeva contends that poetic and artistic expression aims to express the semiotic in the symbolic.

Many other psychoanalytic theorists have deviated from Freud's views, while nonetheless building on elements of his model. *Ernst Kris* (1952) describes the process of artistic creation as "regression in the service of the ego." He is convinced, contra Freud, that art is considerably more controlled than is fantasy, and that the ego plays the role of critic and director for the material that emerges from the unconscious. *Ernest Schachtel* grants the ego's role in directing unconscious material, but claims that the artist has greater than average access to unconscious material because he or she is unusually open to the world and trusts his or her own perception. *Jack J. Spector* (1972) suggests taking further Freud's concept of "ideational mimetics," which draws on the tendency to form mimetic representations of concepts that one is entertaining, often as a consequence of observing others' behavior or receiving communications from others. Spector believes that an elaboration of this concept might have led to an aesthetics based on empathy, which would be particularly illuminating with respect to performance.

THE IMPACT OF PSYCHOANALYSIS ON ART AND ART CRITICISM

Much twentieth-century art is informed by Freudian themes (for instance, the Oedipal complex, the psychological significance of dreaming, the importance of the unconscious). Indeed, the impact of Freudian theory on the populace at large is so pervasive that the burden of proof would rest on anyone who claimed that a given artwork or school was completely uninfluenced by psychoanalytic thought.

Certain schools of art have explicitly drawn inspiration from Freud. Most notorious among these are the Surrealists. Growing out of the Dada movement, which was not unified in its responses to Freud, Surrealism employed Freudian concepts to its own purposes. Surrealist poets employed free association (a method they valorized as a form of "automatism") as a means of tapping the unconscious. They enlisted the resultant dreamlike imagery in their poetry, aiming to jar and provoke their audience into an altered state of responsiveness. Surrealist theorists, notably André Breton, also attempted to expand Freud's theories regarding the importance of sexuality into a new collective mythology, focused on achieving the heights of sexual satisfaction with a mythic female principle. Breton developed images of a number of female love deities, who were to supplement the collection of psychologically significant figures (such as family members) so important to Freud's theory.

The Surrealists took issue with Freud on many points, particularly on matters concerned with therapy. Unlike Freud, they aimed to liberate the id, giving it dominant control over the psyche. They also valued mental disorder as a means of breaking down the barriers between art and life. The Surrealists' interest in spiritualism also clashed with Freud's clinical, biologistic approach to aberrant mental phenomena. Freud himself took issue with his Surrealist followers; and in general, he disliked modern art. He rejected the products of another school motivated by his theories, the expressionist movement, which attempted to represent the primitive processes of inner life. A more recent artistic trend that Freud's theories partially inspired is the post-World War II tendency in some American painting to work with mythic elements. Perhaps this phenomenon draws greater inspiration from Jung, whose concept of the archetypes provides a means of theoretically bridging personal images and collective themes.

Many twentieth-century art and literary critics have seen in the theories of Freud and other psychoanalytic theorists (among them Jacques Lacan and Julia Kristeva) tools for unpacking the significance of art. Critics have employed psychoanalytic theory in diverse projects, such as seeking repressed content in the manifest form of artworks; interpreting the behavior of literary characters in psychoanalytic terms; analyzing artworks in terms of the artist's psychobiography; and utilizing psychoanalytic concepts (such as "displacement" and "condensation") as fundamental terms in criticism.

While formalists and others have opposed the Freudian emphasis on the artist's biography as a key to the artwork, the range of employments of psychoanalytic theory in criticism suggests that it will continue to be a major catalyst for art and literary criticism, as well as a stimulus for art.

See also AESTHETIC PLEASURE; CREATIVITY; CRITICISM; HUMOR; KRISTEVA; NIETZSCHE; SYMBOL.

BIBLIOGRAPHY

Bersani, Leo. 1986. *The Freudian Body: Psychoanalysis and Art*. New York: Columbia University Press.

Freud, Sigmund. 1966–74. *The Standard Edition of the Complete Psychological Works of Sigmund Freud*. 24 vols. Vols. iv & v: *The Interpretation of Dreams*. Vol. vii: *A Case of Hysteria, Three Essays on Sexuality, and Other Works*. Vol. ix: *Jensen's "Gradiva" and Other Works*. Vol. xiii: *Totem and Taboo and Other Works*. J. Strachey (ed. & trans.). London: Hogarth.

Jung, C. G. 1966. *The Collected Works of C. G. Jung*. 24 vols. Vol. xv: *The Spirit in Man, Art, and Literature*. R. F. C. Hull (trans.). Princeton: Princeton University Press.

Kofman, Sara. 1988. *The Childhood of Art: An Interpretation of Freud's Aesthetics*. W. Woodhill (trans.). New York: Columbia University Press.

Kris, Ernst. 1952. *Psychonalytic Explorations in Art*. New York: International Universities Press.

Kristeva, Julia. 1980. *Desire in Language*. T. Gora, A. Jardine, & L. Roudiez (trans.). L. Roudiez (ed.). New York: Columbia University Press.

Kristeva, Julia. 1980. *Revolution in Poetic Language*. T. Gora, A. Jardine, & L. Roudiez (trans.). L. Roudiez (ed.). New York: Columbia University Press.

Rank, Otto. 1932. *Art and Artist: Creative Urge and Personality Development*. New York: Tudor.

Spector, Jack J. 1972. *The Aesthetics of Freud: A Study in Psychoanalysis and Art*. New York: Praeger.

Wollheim, Richard. 1974. *On Art and the Mind*. Cambridge, MA: Harvard University Press.

KATHLEEN MARIE HIGGINS

R

race and aesthetics Theoretical reflection on the connections between aesthetics and race may appear to be a relatively recent phenomenon, associated with the emergence of postcolonial theory and critical race studies. Yet, philosophers have long developed their accounts of the nature and social effects of taste by reference to presumed differences between the aesthetic propensities and practices of the white subject of cultivation and his racial others (West 1982; Roelofs 2005). Shaftesbury, Hume, Burke, and Kant are among the thinkers who have delineated taste's ethical and political functioning with the help of racial designations. They implicitly consider aesthetic creation and judgment instrumental in the realization of cultural constellations that observe moral, epistemic, social, and political hierarchies among white European men and women of the middle classes on the one hand, and blacks, Arabs, Indians, and peasants on the other hand. This intellectual history, conjoined with traditions of (neo)colonialism and other cultural institutions that render racism a systemic phenomenon, leave the field of aesthetics mired in racial constellations that contemporary critics are working to undo (Anzaldúa 1987; Bhabha 1994; Davis 1998; Chow 2002). Given the depth of racialization as a structural register of sociality, community, and individual agency, such theorists do not aspire to color blindness but hope to supplant problematic forms of racialized experience, creation, and evaluation by more just and less oppressive modes of meaning production.

RACE AND THE BODY

One prominent resource for understanding aesthetics in light of its imbrications with race is theories of racial embodiment. Referring to the body image, that is to say, the implicit sense of the body that organizes and directs bodily comportment, Frantz Fanon formulates the notion of the historico-racial schema of the body, which is made up by "the white man, who had woven me out of a thousand details, anecdotes, stories" (1967: 111). This influential idea points to the role of aesthetic fantasies, images, and narratives in the production of racialized modes of corporeal consciousness and orientation. In addition, Fanon identifies ruptures in the body schema wrought by racism. Addressing the violence summarily comprised under the repetitive, fearful, stereotyped phrase "Look, a Negro!" he writes: "My body was given back to me sprawled out, distorted, recolored, clad in mourning in that white winter day" (1967: 110–13). Racialization fundamentally structures embodiment, instituting social asymmetries, norms, and hierarchies at the level of corporeal life. As such it pervades the embodied reality inhabited by those who are categorized as white people of Anglo-European descent, whose bodies are implicitly normalized, no less than that of those who are marked as people of color, who are alternately rendered invisible and hypervisible under regimes of seeing that privilege whiteness while implementing detailed rankings among multiple racial identifications. Extrapolating from the visual register of racialization, we can bring into view the racial workings of feeling, touching, smelling, tasting, sounding, listening, mobility, proximity, distance, togetherness, and isolation, which contribute to the distinctive patterns of racialization characterizing embodied existence. Given that these bodily modes participate in aesthetic production and reception, aesthetic agency can be seen to lend support to and, in turn, acquire support from structures of racialization. Critical approaches to matters of race thus both demand and enable critical perspectives on aesthetic questions.

RACE AND THE EVERYDAY

The bodily dimensions of racialization testify to the functioning of race as a regulatory force controlling quotidian aesthetic life. Race operates not merely as a naturalist postulate – a presumption about the biological characteristics of populations – but is to be comprehended as a set of cultural regimens, casting ethnicities as identities to be managed and policed, and to be produced as a form of labor (Chow 2002). An aesthetic technology guiding daily occupations and interactions, race can be found at work in the systemic organization of social space through surveillance procedures, commodified transactions, and official as well as incidental encounters between embodied subjects (Ahmed 2000). To reflect on the racialization of everyday existence is to think about the ways racial norms and histories delineate the constraints and possibilities of social exchanges and individual itineraries of becoming. Aesthetic values are implicated in such racialization, both as products and carriers of racial meanings. Transnational capitalism and the racialized global division of labor that sustain the contemporary world order thrive on the flows of ever renewing aesthetic desire for consumption goods that underwrite a sense of the ordinary and the unusual. Yet, while aesthetic conduct constitutes a powerful motor of modes of racialization under late capitalism, cultural critics also attribute oppositional capacities to tactics of aesthetic dislocation. Nelly Richard (2004) describes how aesthetic performances disturb the transparent vocabularies of market rationality that render commercial pleasure compelling and efface state-sanctioned violence from the public domain. Such performances unsettle linguistic practices that lock the affective implications of historical violence in an unspeakable past and sustain the collective illusion of having broken with this past. Likewise, pointing to the role of racial representations as a form of sociopolitical imagination, Robert Gooding-Williams (2006) considers aesthetic protest capable of unhinging racial ideologies, for example, by demythifying powerful political allegories, such as the fantasy, repeated in movies as well as courtrooms, that considers blackness antithetical to social order.

RACE AND CULTURE

For many philosophers, including Scottish Enlightenment thinkers, Kant, Schiller, and Hegel, the aesthetic participates in the realization of a progressive trajectory of cultivation, leading from less developed stages of culture to more advanced ones. The ensuing picture of culture institutes a divide between modernity and the premodern that, postcolonial critics have argued, keeps reiterating a racialized and colonial framing of subjectivity, and yet at the same time creates a space for critical reconfigurations of cultural agency and identification. Homi Bhabha witnesses a split between developmental trajectories that are imagined as realizing a static ethical model of the nation, and ongoing significatory processes that keep the nation's image in motion, incessantly renewing the alterity of the nation and of its representations, and resisting stabilization. He contends that modern cultures are marked by disparate, incommensurable, temporal frameworks. Far from homogeneous, fixed grounds or origins for identity, national cultures constitute liminal formations that are continually being reproduced. Eluding any singular, unambivalent cultural order, liminal positions, according to Bhabha, hold out resources for resistance and transformation. They enable us to shift and tweak given conditions for cultural production. Artistic and cultural critiques, specifically, can allow for what Bhabha calls "a postcolonial translation of modernity" (1994: 241), making room for the articulation and negotiation of hybrid identities and differences. Such hybridity is not to be hailed as a utopian condition – far from that – but must be interrogated with respect to the structures of profitability, entrapment, and abjection it entails (Chow 2002). More generally, in view of slavery, colonialism, labor markets, cultural capital, and other forms of racialized power, postcolonial perspectives challenge aesthetics to rethink the web of interconnected assumptions about culture, the public, and the nation underlying philosophical theories of the meaning and ontology of artworks and other cultural artifacts.

Racial hierarchies are crisscrossed by other hierarchies in which they find support and that help to buttress them (see below). Divisions between high or avant-garde art and popular or mass culture are among the binaries that shore up and find sustenance in normatively marked racial differentiations (as inflected by and inflecting differences of class, gender, and so on). Oppositions between theoretical abstraction and the realm of cultural praxis (including art) are also among the hierarchies that carry socially normative codings. Challenging racialization by other names, such as "culture," "value," "the sublime," or "taste," critics place such dualities under suspension, initiating methods of cultural analysis designed to work around the proliferating logics of difference just outlined.

RACE AND THE INTERPRETATION, CRITICISM, AND PRODUCTION OF ART

While some explicitly reject the notion of the aesthetic on account of its entanglements with ethnocentric and racist formations of difference, it is unlikely that we can simply cast off this pervasive, globally circulating web of norms and idioms in which we are mired. Faced with the limitations of liberal conceptions of artistic interpretation, criticism, and creation in capturing the operations of race in the cultural field, thinkers have adopted Marxist, feminist, psychoanalytical, phenomenological, and deconstructive approaches that recognize the embeddedness of artworks and interpreters in encompassing frameworks of symbol production. Numerous contemporary theorists and artists draw on aesthetic concepts and strategies as resources for cultural invention and critique. Philosophers and cultural critics have devised strategies of reading that trace the racial production of aesthetic meanings, experiences, and judgments (Anzaldúa 1987; Bhabha 1994; Davis 1998; Chow 2002; Roelofs 2005; Gooding-Williams 2006). Accordingly, cultural participants and analysts have begun critically to factor race into the delineation of the artworld and the concept of art. They have brought race to bear on the nature of aesthetic evaluation and the idea of aesthetic value. Artistic value still tends to be differentiated from market status (see Richard 2004) notwithstanding its historical imbrications with racial economies. While matters of race throw a wrench into theoretical frameworks that separate the aesthetic from the political and the economic, more complex perspectives are being developed that can acknowledge ethically desirable as well as undesirable dimensions of racial subjectivity and community.

RACE AND INTERSECTIONALITY

Since the 1970s, numerous theorists have argued that racial formations both rely on and influence constructions of gender, economic disparity, and other dimensions of difference. There is no generic racial identity shared by all members of a given race. A person's racial identity is shaped, in part, by this person's economic background, nationality, ethnicity, gender, age, and degree of able-bodiedness. The list goes on. The concept of intersectionality refers to the ways in which racial identities are inflected by notions such as gender and class, and, more generally, analytically entwined with an extensive range of social categories. Given the mutual imbrications of racial formations with structures of class and gender, the aesthetic workings of race cannot be comprehended apart from their entanglements with the operations of other categories. To sidestep the collaborations among multiple axes of difference in the production of racial constellations is to project an overly homogeneous notion of racialized subjectivity. Likewise, to ignore the functioning of race in inquiries addressed at aesthetic constructions of, say, masculinity or national identity is to efface the heterogeneity of these formations. Intersectionality demonstrates that approaches to race in aesthetics share fundamental interests with other disciplinary subfields such as feminist, cross-cultural, and queer aesthetics, as well as studies of the connections between the aesthetic and what is construed as the political, the economic, the public, the domestic, the local, the national, and the transnational.

A great deal of philosophical work on the intersection of aesthetics and race has taken place in interdisciplinary contexts, and this field of inquiry represents a theoretically rich and growing area of reflection that goes to the heart of the epistemological, metaphysical, historical, ethical, and political concerns that are often considered to constitute philosophy's core preoccupations in various philosophical traditions.

See also CANON; FEMINIST AESTHETICS; FEMINIST STANDPOINT AESTHETICS.

BIBLIOGRAPHY

Ahmed, Sara. 2000. *Strange Encounters: Embodied Others in Post-Coloniality*. London: Routledge.

Anzaldúa, Gloria. 1987. *Borderlands/La Frontera: The New Mestiza*. San Francisco: Spinsters/Aunt Lute.

Bhabha, Homi K. 1994. *The Location of Culture*. New York: Routledge.

Chow, Rey. 2002. *The Protestant Ethnic and the Spirit of Capitalism*. New York: Columbia University Press.

Davis, Angela Y. 1998. *Blues Legacies and Black Feminism: Gertrude "Ma" Rainey, Bessie Smith, and Billie Holiday*. New York: Random House.

Fanon, Frantz. 1967. *Black Skin, White Masks*. C. L. Markmann (trans.). New York: Grove.

Gooding-Williams, Robert. 2006. *Look, a Negro! Philosophical Essays on Race, Culture and Politics*. New York: Routledge.

Richard, Nelly. 2004. *Cultural Residues: Chile in Transition*. A. West-Durán & T. Quester (trans.). Minneapolis: University of Minnesota Press.

Roelofs, Monique. 2005. "Racialization as an Aesthetic Production: What does the Aesthetic do for Whiteness and Blackness and Vice Versa?" In *White on White / Black on Black*. G. Yancy (ed.). Lanham: Rowman & Littlefield, 83–124.

West, Cornel. 1982. "A Genealogy of Modern Racism." In *Prophesy Deliverance! Towards an Afro-American Revolutionary Christianity*. Philadelphia: Westminster Press, 47–65.

MONIQUE ROELOFS

rasa is a Sanskrit term meaning "taste," "juice," or "flavor." In the context of aesthetics, it refers to the experience of the full savor of an emotion provoked in an audience member through an artistic performance. By extension, the term is also sometimes used in reference to visual artworks that analogously convey emotional savor to the spectator.

The canonical text in which the term *rasa* is used aesthetically is the *Nāṭyaśāstra*, attributed to Bharata but composed over three centuries (200–500). This text is a compendium of practical knowledge about producing dramatic performances, which were assumed to include music and dance as well as performed scripts. The *Nāṭyaśāstra* presents the production of *rasa* in audience members as the aim of a dramatic production. The technical features of drama that it prescribes are presented as means for fulfilling this ultimate goal.

The *Nāṭyaśāstra* analyzes various affective elements of drama, each of which plays a role in the production of *rasa*. Although the text does not clearly distinguish the terms, a *rasa* is generally taken to be an emotional state achieved by the spectator, while a *bhāva* is an emotion represented in a drama. Ideally a drama presents a *sthāyibhāva* (durable emotion), a stable emotion that is the overarching affective tone of the work as a whole. This tone, however, may be accomplished by means of various emotions presented over the course of a work. Only certain emotions are both so essential within human experience and sufficiently presentable to serve as the overall emotional quality of an entire dramatic presentation. The *Nāṭyaśāstra* lists eight: erotic love (*rati*), mirth (*hāsya*), sorrow (*śoka*), anger (*krodha*), energy (*utsāha*), fear (bhaya), disgust (*jugupsā*), and astonishment (*vismaya*).

Several components are involved in the production of a *sthāyibhāva* within the play. First, there are the persons, objects, and circumstances that incite the emotion. These are called the *vibhāvas*, or "determinants" in the translation of Manomohan Ghosh (Bharata-muni 1967). Second, there are those expressive gestures and behaviors that reveal that a character is in a particular emotional state. These are called the *anubhāvas*, or "consequents," in that they are the result of an emotional condition. Third, there are the various transitory mental states that figure in the extended experience of an overall emotional tone. These are the 33 *vyabhichāribhāvas*, or "complementary psychological states." These include a mixed assortment of conditions, specifically,

> discouragement, weakness, apprehension, envy, intoxication, weariness, indolence, depression, anxiety, distraction, recollection, contentment, shame, inconstancy, joy, agitation, stupor, arrogance, despair, impatience, sleep, epilepsy, dreaming, awakening, indignation, dissimulation, cruelty, assurance, sickness, insanity, death, fright and deliberation. (Bharata-muni 1967: 102)

The list of *rasas*, or emotional savors, that may be produced in the audience, correlates with the list of *sthāyibhāvas*. While the *sthāyibhāvas* are emotions that a particular character undergoes in specific situations, the *rasas* are understood to be the essences or universal forms of basic emotions. The *Nāṭyaśāstra* lists eight *rasas*: the erotic (*śṛṅgāra*), the comic (*hāsya*), the pathetic (i.e., sorrowful) (*karuṇa*), the furious (*raudra*), the heroic (*vīra*), the terrible (*bhayānaka*), the odious (*bībhatsa*), and the marvelous (*adbhuta*). A ninth *rasa*, tranquillity or quiescence (*śānta*), was later added to this list by some commentators.

Whether the presentation of a *sthāyibhāva* leads to the experience of a *rasa* depends not only on the skill of those involved in the production. The cultivation of the spectator is also crucial. Bharata suggests that one should not expect individuals of inferior character to experience *rasa*, no matter how good the performance. The ideal candidate for an experience of *rasa* would be an audience member who is

> possessed of [good] character, high birth, quiet behaviour and learning, are desirous of fame, virtue, are impartial, advanced in age, proficient in drama in all its six limbs, alert, honest, unaffected by passion, expert in playing the four kinds of musical instrument, very virtuous, acquainted with the Costumes and Make-up, the rules of dialects, the four kinds of Histrionic Representation, grammar, prosody, and various [other] *Śastras*, are experts in different arts and crafts, and have fine sense of the Sentiments and the Psychological States. (Bharata-muni 1967: 523)

In addition, such a person should be of "unruffled sense" as well as "honest, expert in the discussion of pros and cons, detector of faults and appreciator [of merits]" and also experience "gladness on seeing a person glad, and sorrow on seeing him sorry," and be one who "feels miserable on seeing him miserable" (Bharata-muni 1967: 523–4). Bharata grants that this combination of social status, education, artistic skill, and moral character is unlikely to coincide fully in the same person. Nevertheless, his list provides insight into the degree to which the experience of *rasa* is an achievement on the part of the audience member.

The *Nāṭyaśāstra* was lost and rediscovered in the nineteenth century in the context of a commentary by Abhinavagupta (11th century). Abhinava associates *rasa* with spiritual development in a way that the *Nāṭyaśāstra* does not. According to Abhinava the experience of *rasa* involves breaking through egotistic obsession with one's personal emotions to an appreciation of emotional types that are transpersonal. This requires empathy, and the achievement of *rasa* is an accomplishment.

Abhinava claims that unconscious memory traces (*saṃskāra*), built up through previous lives as well as the present one, enable the spectator to empathize with an emotion presented in a dramatic production. Latent impressions of the same kind of emotion are stimulated by the performance (or some other kind of affect-producing stimulus, such as a scene that might move a poet to write). The *rasika*, or cultivated spectator, recognizes the congruence between the remembered emotion and that experienced by the character. This is possible because the *rasika* has broken through the sense that one's emotion is one's own possession and come to see it as a type that all human beings share, and which one can savor reflectively.

Abhinava identifies seven obstacles that can interfere in the production of *rasa* by a drama, several of which occur through faults in the play, but some through faults in the viewer. First, one might find the play unconvincing, and thus be unable to take the emotions portrayed seriously. Second, one might relate to the drama in a manner that is too self-interested, and find oneself reminded of one's personal problems. Third, one might be too absorbed in one's own feelings to move beyond an egotistical outlook. Fourth, one may be obstructed by an incapacity in a sense organ that is needed in order to experience the drama. Fifth, the play might not be clear enough to convey emotion effectively. Sixth, the play may be too diffused to convey a dominant mental state. Seventh, one might be confused by certain particular expressions and be in doubt as to what emotional content they are intended to convey.

Abhinava accepts *śānta*, or tranquillity, as a *rasa* in itself, and he claims that it is the aim toward which all other *rasas* lead. This is because *śānta* is the most serene mental state. In this respect it resembles the supreme human goal of *mokṣa*, or spiritual liberation. A monist, Abhinava understands *mokṣa* as complete identification with the universal consciousness, the one reality, which he identifies as *Śiva*. Each of us is a manifestation of this single consciousness, and our ultimate spiritual goal is to realize that we are not distinct beings but one with *Śiva*, our true Self. While *Śānta* falls short of complete liberation, it gives us a taste of *mokṣa* by lifting us above our ordinary sense of identification with our egos and offering us a glimpse of the transpersonal outlook of the liberated being.

Abhinava is not the only theorist who associates *rasa* with spiritual aims. According to Rūpagisvāmin and other Bengali Vaiṣṇavites (i.e., devotees of Vishnu) of the sixteenth century, *śṛṅgāra* (the erotic) is the supreme *rasa*. The ultimate form of this *rasa* occurs in the context of *bhakti*, devotion to god (understood here as Vishnu, often in the form of his avatar Krishna), expressed in a variety of sometimes ecstatic devotional practices.

Aesthetic issues relating to *rasa* include the status of the specific eight types identified by Bharata. Is this to be taken as a complete list? Is the addition of *śāntarasa* by later commentators acceptable? One might question this not only on the basis of Bharata's authority, but also on the ground that tranquillity might be understood as the absence of certain distressing emotions rather than an emotion itself. Or one might raise pragmatic concerns: if *rasa* is experienced when a performer conveys a related *sthāyibhāva* to the spectator, how would a performer theatrically express the appropriately peaceful *sthāyibhāva* of *śāntarasa*? If the addition of *śāntarasa* is justified, moreover, one might conclude that the list could in principle be further expanded.

Another issue concerns the universality of *rasas*. Certain Indian commentators have accepted *rasa* theory as applicable to poetry and other art forms. But does it apply in all cultures as well? Granted that the production is an explicit aim of both performers and spectators in the Indian dramatic tradition, and in the Indonesian and Malaysian traditions that were influenced by Indian drama, is a spectator likely to experience *rasa* through dramas in other traditions? And more generally, is *rasa* theory universally relevant to art?

Rasa theory also raises questions about whether there are certain universal emotions to which art may appeal. Bharata's specific list does not converge with contemporary proposals for a list of basic emotions, which are frequently individuated in terms of patterns of brain activation and/or hard-wired facial expression. Even if some subset of Bharata's list coincides with lists of basic emotions, there would still be cultural differences in the way these emotions are understood and the appropriate occasions and means for expressing them. Nevertheless, *rasa* theory offers an account of the power that art sometimes has to speak beyond its time and place and to widen the capacity of its audience for empathic emotional concern.

See also INDIAN AESTHETICS; RELATIVISM.

BIBLIOGRAPHY
Ānandavardhana & Abhinavagupta. 1990. *The "Dhvanyāloka" of Ānandavardhana with the "Locana" of Abhinavagupta*. D. H. H. Ingalls, J. M. Masson, & M. V. Patwardhan (trans.). D. H. H. Ingalls (ed.). Cambridge, MA: Harvard University Press.
Bharata-muni (ascribed). 1967. *The Nāṭyaśāstra*. 2 vols. Rev. 2nd edn. M. Ghosh (ed. & trans.). Calcutta: Granthalaya.
Bharata-Muni (ascribed). 1970. *Aesthetic Rapture: The Rasādhyāya of the Nāṭyaśāstra*, J. M. Masson & M. V. Patwardhan (ed. & trans.). Poona: Deccan College.
Chakrabarti, Arindam. 2002. "Disgust and the Ugly in Indian Aesthetics." In *La Pluralità Estetica: Lasciti e irradiazioni oltre il Novecento, Associazione Italiana Studi di Estetica, Annali 2000–2001*. Torino: Trauben.
Chari, V. K. 1990. *Sanskrit Criticism*. Honolulu: University of Hawai'i Press.
Gerow, Edwin. 1994. "Abhinavagupta's Aesthetics as a Speculative Paradigm," *Journal of the American Oriental Society*, 114, 186–204.
Gerow, Edwin. 1997. "Indian Aesthetics: A Philosophical Survey." In *A Companion to World Philosophies*. E. Deutsch & R. Bontekoe (eds.). Malden: Blackwell, 304–23.
Goswamy, B. N. 1986. "Rasa: Delight of the Rason." In *Essence of Indian Art*. San Francisco: Asian Art Museum of San Francisco, 17–30.
Keith, Arthur Berriedale. 1924. *The Sanskrit Drama: Its Origin, Development, Theory and Practice*. Oxford: Oxford University Press.
Masson, J. Moussaieff & Patwardhan, M. V. 1969. *Śāntarasa and Abhinavagupta's Philosophy of Aesthetics*. Poona: Bhandarkar Oriental Research Institute.
Shweder, Richard A. & Haidt, Jonathan. 2000. "The Cultural Psychology of the Emotions: Ancient and New." In *Handbook of the Emotions*. M. Lewis & J. M. Haviland-Jones (eds.). 2nd edn. New York: Guilford, 397–414.

KATHLEEN MARIE HIGGINS

realism The English term "realism" was introduced into literary criticism by Samuel Taylor Coleridge in 1817, and into art criticism by John Ruskin in 1856, by which time the French and German equivalents were already well established. Almost as soon as *réalisme* appeared in print, both the term and the style were regarded with suspicion and distaste. Baudelaire described it as "a vague and elastic word"; and Flaubert – who was considered one of the "high priests" of realism, as he himself put it – vehemently denied that it applied to him.

During the twentieth century, the feeling of unease increased, and today art history, philosophy, and literary studies are all gripped by skepticism about the idea that art or literature can reveal the world to us *as it is in reality*, independently of the conventions and local perspectives, the prejudices and values, that limit and control art, as they limit and control the whole of human life. Presumably, realistic art must be closer to reality than other kinds of art. But does art of this kind exist, or is the name propaganda and a sham, like "The Ministry of Truth" in Orwell's *1984?*

I believe that the concept of realism can serve a useful purpose, as long as we abandon the idea that realistic art has a unique sanction, or a unique ability to express the truth, and instead consider what the art that historians and critics describe as "realist" or "realistic" is really like. Philosophers who write about realism generally focus on the visual arts, and for the most part I shall do the same.

Among philosophers, Nelson Goodman was the most influential twentieth-century skeptic about realism in painting and sculpture. "The literal or realistic or naturalistic system of representation," Goodman writes, "is simply the customary one." Realism, he argues, is not a matter of fidelity to nature, and cannot be measured by resemblance. For our judgments of resemblance are influenced by our visual habits, and our visual habits are influenced in turn by the kinds of representations we are used to seeing. Hence, resemblance cannot be a "constant and independent" standard against which works of art can be measured, because "the criteria of resemblance vary with changes in representational practice" (Goodman 1968: 39 n. 31; see also Jakobson 1921).

It is easy to exaggerate the extent to which our visual experience is modified by art. Oscar Wilde famously remarked that nobody had noticed the fog in London until it appeared in Impressionist paintings, but in fact writers have generally described optical effects long before painters learned to represent them. For example, the spinning highlights on a chariot wheel were described by the Latin poet Prudentius many centuries before Velazquez captured this effect in paint.

Be that as it may, if the art we see modifies our visual habits and influences the resemblances we perceive, it does not follow that fidelity to nature is a vacuous idea. For this may also be something that we must learn to see and judge correctly, and art may be a source from which we learn. In a similar way, progress in the physical sciences has enabled us to refine our observations of natural effects, and these observations have in turn enabled us to test scientific theories. There is nothing suspicious about this interaction between theory and observation, and nothing that should make us wonder whether we possess a "constant and independent" standard, with which scientific theories can be assessed. Science sometimes progresses in this way, step by step, placing its weight on one foot while it moves the other one; and there is no reason why art should not sometimes do the same.

Nevertheless, Goodman is right to think that the concepts of resemblance and fidelity to nature are too vague and too metaphorical to explain what realism is. In fact, it is unwise to assume that realism is a single phenomenon or style. We need to look at art-historical and theoretical texts, and try to discern what their authors were referring to when they used the terms "realism" and "realistic," without assuming that they are unambiguous, or that realistic works of art in one period or tradition must resemble realistic works in another.

We can begin to map the ground the term covers by distinguishing between subject matter and technique. Let us take subject matter first. Realism, in this sense, is about the choice of subject matter and the manner in which it is treated.

For example, compare Ingres's painting of 1808, *The Valpincon Bather* and Degas's (mistitled) pastel of 1885, *Girl Drying Herself,* in the National Gallery of Art, Washington DC. (Readers are invited to search for images online.) One salient difference between these works is that the surface of Ingres's painting is almost transparent – the brush strokes are barely visible – whereas Degas draws attention to the individual strokes that were deposited on the surface of the paper as the pastel crayon was rubbed back and forth. But let us set this difference in the use of materials aside, and consider the ways in which the two artists treated the theme of the female nude. In Ingres's painting, sensuality is perfectly translated into line and surface: the refined outline of the bather's body, and the surface of her shoulders and broad back, beautifully modeled by the diagonally falling light. Compare the ungainly pose of the woman in Degas's drawing, her feet planted steadily on the ground, her bottom sticking out just enough to balance the weight of her head, and the rapid gesture with which she pulls her shift over her head. There is clearly a sense in which Degas's drawing is the more realistic treatment of the theme.

Realism, in this sense, is opposed to idealism, classicism, or romanticism. It represents the lower social classes, comic as opposed to tragic material, daily life as opposed to myth. In the paintings of Courbet, Manet, and Degas, and in the novels of Balzac and Flaubert, the so-called hierarchy of genres, which promoted the representation of history, myth, or allegory, is definitively set aside, and the everyday lives of people belonging to the lower classes are taken seriously, and placed in a definite period of contemporary history. "Realism" becomes the name of a self-conscious movement only in the nineteenth century, but its themes appear in art in every age. In his famous study of realism in literature, from Homer to Virginia Woolf, Erich Auerbach (1969) argues that it is in the gospels, where God lives among the humblest members of society, that the roots of modern realism first appear.

Realism in technique is an entirely different phenomenon, which can be traced back to the revolutionary developments in Greek art between the sixth and fourth centuries BCE. For example, compare two paintings of runners on Panathenaic amphorae, which were made about 50 years apart (New York, Metropolitan Museum of Art: items 301692 and 303085 at

www.beazley.ox.ac.uk/xdb/ASP/databaseGeneral.asp). On the earlier vase, which was decorated by the Euphiletos painter in about 530 BCE, the exertion of the burly runners is conveyed in a marvelously vivid way, but their anatomy is sketchy and their posture is wrong. By contrast, the Berlin Painter, who painted the later vase, evidently preferred grace to exertion, and these men look as if they are setting out on a gentle jog. But their anatomy is depicted with a plausible economy of means, and the forward arm is placed, as it is in nature, opposite the forward leg. The differences we would have in mind if we described the later painting as more realistic than the earlier one are not differences in subject matter. They are differences in the technical resources the artist was able to control.

Realism in technique can be defined in terms of three main properties, which I shall call *accuracy, animation,* and *modality.*

By *accuracy,* I mean the accurate depiction of a kind of material or object or activity, such as water or satin, a palm tree or a dove, sleeping, galloping, or making love. (The accurate depiction of people, places, and events is related, but distinct.) Accuracy combines a degree of individuation or precision with the avoidance of idealization, fantasy, error, and deceit, and it is a salient characteristic of realistic art. For example, neither of the two vase paintings of runners is artificial or unskilled. But the depiction of posture in the later painting is more accurate, because when a man runs, his forward arm really is opposite his forward leg. It was not necessary to use a camera with a rapid shutter speed to discover this, as it was necessary to discover how a horse gallops. But both discoveries made it possible for artists to represent motion with greater accuracy than before.

The second element of realism in technique is *animation,* which combines mobility with the expression of emotion, character, or thought. For example, the first painful grimace in a surviving Greek vase painting is in the tondo of a cup decorated by the Sosias Painter in about 500 BCE, which represents Achilles binding the wound on Patroclus' arm (Berlin, Antikensammlung; item 200108 at www.beazley.ox.ac.uk/xdb/ASP/databaseGeneral.asp). The tense expression on Patroclus' face is marked by three curved lines between his mouth and cheek and the artist has added a little white pigment to show him baring his teeth with pain. He has also depicted him turning away from Achilles, and bracing his foot against the tondo's frame.

Animation points toward the third and most general measure of realism in technique, namely, *modality*, by which I mean the extent of the range of questions it is possible to ask about a depicted scene. The principal measure of realism in Greek art in particular, and of realism in technique generally, is the range of questions we can ask about what a work of art represents: Is this man angry or impassive? Is he despondent or alert? Is he Semitic or Egyptian? Is he young or old? Is he fat or thin? Is his cloak made of linen or of wool? Is he standing in the shade or in the sun? Is he running, walking, jumping, or standing still?

The most popular way of arguing that realism is a myth is to compare art and language. Philosophers and art historians like to describe art as if it were a kind of language, both to emphasize the extent to which artists rely on systems of conventions, and also to discourage the idea that some styles are more truthful, or closer to reality, than others. The things we say are not truer or closer to reality if we say them in French; and it turns out that they are not truer or closer to reality if we paint them in French either. We call art "realistic," it has been said, when we find the artist's style easy to absorb or understand, because the conventions are familiar – like our native tongue.

The comparison between artistic styles and languages makes sense, as long as languages are not confused with scripts or codes. For example, the hieroglyphic and hieratic Egyptian scripts do not differ in the information they can be used to record, and neither do Morse code and semaphore. But languages obviously differ widely in their expressive powers. The Psalms are not inferior as poetry to Shakespeare's sonnets, but the language at Shakespeare's disposal was much richer than the language available to the Psalmist. "All you need is love" can probably be translated into every human language that is known, but the same is not true of "Energy is equivalent to mass."

The analogy between artistic styles and languages is useful, if we get it right. But we should not compare the difference between, for example, Giotto and Caravaggio to the difference between Morse code and semaphore or to the difference between English and French. We should compare it to the difference between the English of Chaucer's *Canterbury Tales* and the English of Milton's *Paradise Lost*. The technical resources of pictorial art are always limited in their expressive range, as languages are also bound to be; and these technical resources, like languages, can expand in different directions to express new ideas and new observations. The development of realistic technique is the expansion of the modality of art, in other words, the expansion of what it is possible for art to represent.

The critics (e.g., Roman Jakobson), philosophers (e.g., Nelson Goodman), and art historians (e.g., Leo Steinberg) in the twentieth century who were skeptical about realism wanted to deny that art can be judged by a single standard that is valid at all times and in all places, and they wanted to insist that the art that is described as "realist" or "realistic" proceeds from the artist's values, methods, and viewpoints, no less than other kinds of art. They were right on both counts. But it does not follow that the idea of realism is a myth, invented to pretend that one kind of art is the most universal and genuine, sanctioned by reason and the destiny of all mankind. Nor does it follow that "realism" is merely an honorific term, which we apply to art in a familiar style. We can be pluralists about art without denying the reality and the importance of realism.

See also GOODMAN; ILLUSION; REPRESENTATION; TRUTH IN ART.

BIBLIOGRAPHY
Auerbach, Erich. 1969. *Mimesis*. Princeton: Princeton University Press.
Gombrich, E. H. 1977. *Art and Illusion*. 5th edn. Oxford: Phaidon.
Goodman, Nelson. 1968. *Languages of Art*. Indianapolis: Hackett.
Goodman, Nelson. 1983. "Realism, Relativism, and Reality," *New Literary History*, 14, 269–72.
Hyman, John. 2006. *The Objective Eye*. Chicago: University of Chicago Press.
Jakobson, Roman. *Language in Literature*. K. Pomorska & S. Rudy (eds.). Cambridge, MA: Harvard University Press. (Includes "On Realism in Art" (1921), 19–27.)

Nochlin, Linda. 1971. *Realism*. Harmondsworth: Penguin.

Rosen, Charles & Zerner, Henri. 1984. *Romanticism and Realism: Mythology of Nineteenth-Century Art*. London: Faber.

JOHN HYMAN

relativism assumes variant forms, the most common being (1) dogmatic relativism, which denies either the existence or the knowability of ahistorical, universal, or eternal truths about art's alleged intrinsic nature or the qualities of aesthetic appreciation, concluding that all truth claims about art and our modes of understanding it are unverifiable and, consequently, equivalent to each other; and (2) a pragmatic or commonsense relativism, which simply recognizes an evident plurality of criteria between cultures concerning what counts as an artwork, as the beautiful, or as meaning in the interpretation of art, without claiming, as dogmatic relativism does, that "anything goes." Pragmatic relativism recognizes the possibility of talking about "truths" within distinct cultural horizons, without laying claim to a universality other than that which constitutes a specific cultural community.

Dogmatic relativism is commonly associated with a belief in the absence of, or loss of faith in, immutable critical standards in aesthetics and art criticism. It is allied with similar pessimistic convictions in epistemology and moral theory. Nietzsche is often taken to be one of the most modern sources of contemporary dogmatic relativism, insofar as from the pronouncement that "everything is false" he drew the conclusion that "everything is permitted" (Nietzsche 1968: §602). Such extreme relativism is associated with a form of nihilism that denies the possibility of any lasting foundation to either epistemological or interpretative principles, and that historical pessimists such as Paul Johnson have seen as the dominant *Weltanschauung* of the twentieth century: "a world adrift, having left its moorings in traditional law and morality" (Johnson 1983: 48). Similar sentiments have been repeatedly echoed across twentieth-century Europe, as avant-gardism, Dadaism, modernism and Abstract Expressionism, and, more recently, deconstruction have challenged every supposed critical verity and boundary

between different modes of artistic and cultural practice. Yet dogmatic relativism in both its aesthetic and epistemological forms is far from a contemporary phenomenon, having its roots both in the pluralist outlook of Michel de Montaigne (1533–92) and the skepticism of Pyrrho of Elis (c. 360–270 BCE).

Dogmatic relativism is, arguably, doubly inconsistent. First, the conviction that the absence or unknowability of universal truths about art and artistic interpretation implies that *all* views about the nature of art or aesthetics are as good as one another, self-defeatingly proclaims precisely the universalism that it denies. Second, all views about art's character or the qualities of aesthetic response are equivalent only insofar as they fail to match up to the supposed universal criteria of artistic and aesthetic truth. Yet to claim this is inadvertently to lay down what such criteria are or ought to be, which, in turn, is to contravene the premise of the argument – namely, that there are no such criteria or that, even if there are, they are unknowable. Dogmatic relativism can consequently be accused of an inverted absolutism and an attitude of *ressentiment* – that is, it implicitly lays down the conditions whereby all truth claims would not be equivalent and, insofar as it is forced to realize that such universal conditions are unattainable, it closes its eyes to the rich plurality of truth claims in variant artistic traditions by consigning all to an indifferent equivalence.

Whereas dogmatic relativism defines itself in relation to a yearning for a universal standard of truth and appraisal in the arts that is unattainable, pragmatic aesthetic relativism does not. It simply recognizes the de facto existence of a plurality of modes of appreciation and idioms of truth claim, not only in a culture but also between cultures. The possibility of rival, if not contradictory, practices and conceptual employments is accepted, and an attempt to formulate a general theory of art that might sublate such difference is eschewed. Most important, pragmatic or cultural relativism is not wedded to the pernicious indifference of the "anything goes" doctrine, but, on the contrary, defends the possibility of localized truth claims integral to different artistic and cultural horizons. Whereas dogmatic relativism inadvertently endorses the foundational in truth claims (that is to say, because no universal foundation can be established, no universal truth can be endorsed), pragmatic relativism does not. It perceives truth claims to rest on and to be relative to distinct cultural practices. In other words, pragmatic relativism is plainly not a variant of subjectivism, but it is consistent with appeals to intersubjective criteria for aesthetic appraisals within particular aesthetic communities.

David Hume recognized that the denial of universal truth claims about art's essential nature does not lead to the conclusion "everything is permitted." Although the proposition that beauty "exists merely in the mind that contemplates" things and not in things themselves "seems to have attained the sanction of common sense, there is . . . [also] a species of common sense which opposes it" (Hume 1995: 257). That "species of common sense" recognizes that established critical consensus, shared practices of critical discernment, comparative knowledge of different artistic traditions, and the suppression of overt personal or cultural prejudice, all serve the attainment of a standard of taste by which the various sentiments of men may be reconciled. Though the judgments legitimated by such standards will not have the binding force of a priori reasoning, Hume recognizes the solid consensus and experimental reasoning which sustain them; and he understands, furthermore, how aesthetic education is dependent on the recognition and acceptance of such argumentation.

Though belonging to a very different philosophical tradition, Gadamer presents a similar line of reasoning. He shares Hume's skepticism regarding a priori claims to fixed epistemological foundations, and yet is vehemently opposed to any form of subjectivism. In *Truth and Method*, he argues that all truth claims by and about art are inevitably preconditioned by the norms and values of the cultural horizon that shape them and are, in a foundational sense, relative. Nevertheless, the localized cultural claims to truth that Gadamer defends gain their authority from what can be argumentatively validated by a community of interpreters whose experience is such as to substantiate and reendorse their warrant. Gadamer does not suggest an ahistorical or transcultural platform from which conflicting truth claims in

aesthetics can be appraised. On the contrary, we can attempt only to reconcile any "conflict of interpretation" by appeal to those standards forged in the course of a culture's development. Pragmatic relativism in effect attempts to bypass or neutralize the issue of the absence of objective foundations, by showing that truth claims in and about the arts gain their warrant from the competence of those practices which forward them. Thinkers such as Habermas and Apel have consequently examined the parameters of such competence in order to establish intersubjective criteria for such truth claims, while recognizing that such criteria are historically malleable and to an extent renegotiable within a given community. Nevertheless, though the truth claims of different cultural practices never have the force of universal claims, they are not made on subjectivist grounds. The weight of the traditions and practices that support them is such as to make them relatively objective – that is, in Gadamer's phrase "beyond our willing and doing" (1989: foreword).

Pragmatic relativism is therefore wedded to the view that no work of art possesses a universal property that makes it universally a work of art, and recognizes that works of art are only what they are within specific cultures. Furthermore, it holds that how works of art are perceived, evaluated, interpreted, described, and judged depends on the norms and practices of different cultures. The plurality of such practices does not, on a critical level, imply a crude subjectivism, as each culture can establish its own intersubjective criteria for truth claims and aesthetic evaluation.

Of the problems associated with pragmatic relativism, three stand out:

1 The position cannot be formally substantiated without self-contradiction. Pragmatic relativism cannot simultaneously declare itself to be *the* most appropriate way of looking at the arts *and* advocate a plurality of interpretative values.
2 Consequently, the pragmatic relativist can only "show" rather than demonstrate his commitment. Nietzsche and Derrida recognize in different ways that perspectivism and stylistic pluralism (both variants of pragmatic relativism) can be merely insinuated rather than proved. It is for this reason that

pragmatic relativism has been treated with such ridicule in some academic communities.

3   Though pragmatic relativism can successfully challenge subjectivism on the grounds that the truth claims relative to a given tradition are not arbitrary but gain their warrant from a historically established consensus, it can do little when a consensus and the norms which sustain it are challenged by competing values. Reasoned arbitration is possible only when the disputants within a tradition agree as to the identity of their tradition. When what constitutes a tradition is in question, appeal to shared norms or practices to warrant a given claim is obviously impossible.

Despite its difficulties, pragmatic relativism is both plausible and persuasive. First, it is essentially a modest position, seeking not to impose the truth claims of, say, the Western tradition of aesthetics over the *rasa* (taste) doctrine of India, but to recognize and learn from the nature and conceptual parameters of both. Second, pragmatic relativism is primarily an open-spirited stance that, by being receptive to the truth claims of other traditions and cultures, places great emphasis on understanding through difference rather than similarity. Third, pragmatic relativism entails presuppositions that, in effect, allow it to add to an understanding of an artwork. If there are fixed truths about art and the norms of its appreciation, the task of criticism would merely be to identify their concrete exemplifications. Interpretation would be replaced by descriptive typology. However, the lack of universal foundations implies that what is accepted as an artwork is differently determined by different interpretative traditions. Changes and alterations to those traditions will, historically speaking, cumulatively expand our understanding of art. Pragmatic relativism not only recognizes but extends the knowledge-constitutive role of interpretation, whereas, commitment to any form of foundationalism limits interpretation to the mere rendition of the art's alleged timeless essence.

See also FEMINIST STANDPOINT AESTHETICS; GADAMER; HUME; INDIAN AESTHETICS; NIETZSCHE; RASA; TASTE; TRADITION.

BIBLIOGRAPHY

Bernstein, Richard J. 1983. *Beyond Objectivism and Relativism*. Oxford: Blackwell.

Craige, B. J. 1983. *Relativism in the Arts*. Athens: University of Georgia Press.

Gadamer, H. G. 1989 [1960]. *Truth and Method*. J. Weinsheimer & D. G. Marshall (trans.). 2nd edn. New York: Crossroad.

Hermerén, Göran. 1988. *The Nature of Aesthetic Qualities*. Lund: Lund University Press.

Hollis, Martin & Lukes, Stephen. 1982. *Rationality and Relativism*. Oxford: Blackwell.

Hume, David. 1995 [1757]. "Of the Standard of Taste." In *The Philosophy of Art: Readings Ancient and Modern*. A. Neill & A. Ridley (eds.). New York: McGraw-Hill, 254–68.

Johnson, Paul. 1983. *A History of the Modern World: From 1917 to the 1980s*. London: Weidenfeld & Nicolson.

Margolis, Joseph. 1982. "The Reasonableness of Relativism," *Philosophy and Phenomenological Research*, 42, 91–7.

Margolis, Joseph. 1986. *Pragmatism without Foundations: Reconciling Realism and Relativism*. Oxford: Blackwell.

Nietzsche, Friedrich. 1968 [1901]. *The Will to Power*. W. Kaufmann & R. Hollingdale (trans.). New York: Vintage.

NICHOLAS DAVEY

religion and art   In the Middle Ages, art, science, philosophy, history, and practical life were all offshoots of religion. Nowadays, however, they are usually treated as separate discourses. The most sustained attempts to chart their boundaries have been made within the idealist tradition. Here each is assumed to be a particular mode, or phase, of *Geist* (the German word for both "mind" and "spirit"). Typical idealist thinkers in this respect are Kant, Schiller, Hegel, Croce, Collingwood, Oakeshott, and (up to a point, since he also has naturalistic leanings) Santayana.

The key tenet of idealism is that reality is first and foremost mental. (Nature and the physical world are, quite literally, abstractions from reality so defined.) That is, reality is virtually indistinguishable from consciousness or its contents. Anything wholly transcendental – that is, permanently inaccessible to consciousness – might as well, at least for a strict Hegelian, not exist. A thing exists, ultimately, only so far as it can exist *for us*.

Nevertheless, for many idealists, the phenomenal world (the world as it appears to consciousness) is shot through with intimations of transcendence. For Kant, since the transcendental is *ex hypothesi* inscrutable, traditional theology is impossible. The divine (which is normally thought of as transcendental) cannot be known, "proved," or reasoned about. At best it can be intuited from the manifest facts of ethical and aesthetic life.

Judgments in both spheres ("this is good," "that is beautiful," etc.) possess a peculiar subjective immediacy that seems to confirm their implicit claim to objective, universal validity. The self is necessarily their focus, but their intrinsic structure is such as to point away from it, toward the transcendental. The reality of the transcendental is underwritten by the fact that the experiencing self must logically belong to it, since it cannot simultaneously be an object of its own observation.

In ethical life, according to Kant, we are governed by an imperative that no naturalistic or utilitarian considerations can fully explain. No doubt the cohesion of society, like our aggregate self-interest, is furthered by observance of the moral law, but that is not, subjectively speaking, why we observe it. We observe it simply because we know we must; and that inscrutable, but undeniable, "must" points to a transcendent source. A command cannot issue from nowhere.

Aesthetic judgment similarly legislates for all observers. A thing can be pleasing, but not beautiful, for me alone. If it really is beautiful, you too are in a sense "obliged" to see it as such. The beautiful, like the good, is not independent of the observer's subjectivity, since a thing's beauty, though objective, must be subjectively experienced. It cannot simply be taken on authority or accepted as a piece of information.

The beautiful is, however, independent of the observer's self-interest. This makes it apprehensible only by those, the good, who can suspend their self-interest. On the other hand, unlike goodness, it is also independent of the observer's moral interests and enthusiasms. It is not its goodness that makes a thing beautiful, but its appearance of "free" or self-governed purposiveness. (Not, be it noted, its appearance of serving some extraneous purpose,

that being the principle behind the so-called "functionalist" aesthetic.)

Though Kant has illuminating things to say about art, he invariably regards its beauty as inferior to that of nature. (According to his biographers, Kant was notoriously indifferent to art, especially music, which not only "plays merely with sensations," but also disturbs the neighbors.) But what he says about the relation of the aesthetic and the moral to the transcendental is clearly suggestive in respect of any joint consideration of art and religion, particularly as regards the sublime. Our response to the sublime in nature (or, one might add, in art, though Kant doubts whether art can ever be truly sublime) prefigures the religious attitude. It consists in the awareness of an awesome limitlessness and unbounded power, but one in which our natural fear of such a power is qualified by the sense of our own righteousness and innocence when confronted by it.

This ambivalent response differs from the superstitious, self-abasing terror of the savage. The civilized person's fortitude and self-respect – that is, his own sublimity of character – at once enable him to triumph over a threatening nature and reconcile him with it (quite how is unclear), so that he not only participates in its power but also discerns in it an underlying, and ultimately benevolent, divinity.

Schiller's account of the sublime, as of aesthetic experience generally, has much in common with Kant's. Hegel's aesthetics, however, are different. They are art- rather than nature-centered. Art is superior to nature as a vehicle of the divine, because, like the Absolute Mind (or Idea) of which the universe as a whole consists, and unlike nature, it too is self-conscious, or a product of self-consciousness. The divine, however, is not transcendent, since there is no transcendence. Hegel's "God," therefore, is more or less a figure of speech, being simply the immanent Absolute risen to self-consciousness in the world which it has itself created or "posited." A prime medium through which it rises to self-consciousness is art, defined as "the sensuous embodiment of the Idea."

In primitive or "symbolic" art the Absolute fails to achieve full articulation, being overwhelmed by the "crassness" (as Hegel calls it) of the natural world. This is because humankind, or incarnate Mind, is yet undeveloped, and is hence still too deeply enmeshed in that world. At the other extreme, in modern or "romantic" art, form has been outstripped by content. Mind is now so self-aware that representations of nature (which is not self-aware) are inadequate fully to embody it. Art has finally been superseded by philosophy (most notably Hegel's own), in which alone the Absolute is completely realized, and of which even religion is a mere shadow. (This is inevitable, and no cause for regret.) Only in "classical" art, epitomized by Greco-Roman sculpture, are form and content wholly in balance, since only then was the evolving Idea precisely matched to the natural forms available for its representation – that is, the human body, used to depict the gods.

Hegel's aesthetics, like his ethics, are a branch of his metaphysics. The Beautiful is essentially an "appearance" of the True, of ultimate reality. If it be asked why the Real should manifest itself in beauty, the reason lies in its essential organic harmony, or unity in diversity, which is also the principle of the Beautiful.

The earlier Collingwood, like Hegel, sees religion as a more "advanced" phase of *Geist* than art. For religion, though defective, deliberately aims at truth, while art (like primitive man) is indifferent to truth, making no distinction between fact and imagination. Religion is the prototype of science, history, and philosophy. Other thinkers (including Santayana and the later Collingwood) have seen art as superior to religion, precisely because, in its purest or most mature form, it actively asserts nothing. "The poet nothing affirms," said Sir Philip Sidney, "and therefore never lieth."

The idea that art (or the highest art) is essentially nondeclarative points in two directions. On the one hand it leads to aestheticism, the view central to the so-called aesthetic movement (e.g., Pater, Whistler, Wilde), to Bloomsbury aesthetics (e.g., Fry, Bell), and to Oakeshott, that aesthetic experience, and thus art, is *sui generis*. A wholly distinct and autonomous province of experience, it is reducible to no other and is valuable precisely on that account, as satisfying a similarly unique human need.

On the other hand, art's nondeclarative character is taken by some (mostly critics, such as Matthew Arnold and F. R. Leavis, rather than philosophers) merely to indicate that, unlike religion (or at least, dogmatic religion), it recognizes the limits of the sayable. Nevertheless, what cannot be said can still be suggested; and art's suggestiveness, for all that its medium is fiction, is actually truer to the complexities of experience than the cut-and-dried factual claims of religion or philosophy.

A tacit presupposition of this view is that all art, even nonrealist art, is in some sense representational. (So-called "expressive" art may be thought to represent inner, "subjective" experience, which eludes one-to-one pictorial or linguistic articulation.) Art points beyond itself to a reality apprehensible by no other means. It elicits meaning and coherence from experience. It reconciles us to life by exposing some of its mysteries as superficial, and persuading us humbly to accept the rest. In short, it does what religion offers to do, only more honestly. It achieves symbolic "truth" precisely by forswearing any claim to literal veracity.

All this raises the question as to whether religious art can be called art at all, unless religion itself is somehow to be regarded as imperfect art. Clearly, on the idealist view, both art and religion offer to reveal structure and meaning in the cosmos. The difference is that art knows itself to be fiction, whereas religion claims to be true. It demands active belief, where art demands at most Coleridge's "willing suspension of disbelief."

Excluding jokes such as *trompe-l'oeil*, where the delight lies precisely in the illusion's being detected, art that invites literal or near-literal belief is fantasy art. Its aim is to excite pleasurable emotions by presenting an illusory world more submissive to the subject's self-indulgent desires than the real one can be. Accordingly it will usually employ more surface verisimilitude, and less obvious stylization, than art which has no such extraneous purpose, or whose purpose is simply to focus attention on the object for its own sake.

Hence there arises the paradox that fantasy art often seems more "real" than what Collingwood called "art proper," or even than nature. An obvious example is pornography, which has come overwhelmingly to rely on photographic images. For a photograph seems to present the object directly, rather than to depict it; to be not art, but fact. It thus exacts a minimum of imaginative effort from the spectator.

Collingwood (1938) stigmatized pornography as typical of "amusement art," while regarding religious art as "magical art". Amusement art excites emotions simply in order that we may enjoy the sensation of having them without the responsibilities involved in acting on them. It is, in Collingwood's view, a substitute for action.

These reservations, of course, could apply equally to sentimental or any other amusement art. Following Mill's somewhat erratic train of thought in his *On Liberty* and *Utilitarianism*, I. A. Richards suggested that any "impulse" might legitimately be satisfied so long as its being so did not thwart the satisfaction of "superior" impulses. Ignoring the question as to what "superior" might mean, however, it may be felt in general that amusement art is tolerable or even valuable so long as the consumer himself understands it to be such, and is therefore in no danger of being mastered by his fantasy, that is, of mistaking it for reality.

But clearly we have to do here not with fantasy in a pejorative sense, rather with something like play (a category central to Schiller's aesthetics). Play may be considered either as a necessary liberation from the practical (or, some would say, "serious") business of life, or as a rehearsal for it. (Indeed, both functions seem on reflection to be intrinsic to the idea.) In the first capacity it recalls the aestheticist view of art, in the second the Arnold–Leavis view, that is, of art as a means of grasping and mastering a complex reality. But either option must render dubious the distinction between amusement art and "art proper." The real distinction is between "art proper" and fantasy art as previously defined.

Magical art stimulates emotions (martial, patriotic, revolutionary, religious, acquisitive, moral, etc.) with a view to their being discharged in the appropriate actions. Its value therefore will depend entirely on that of the ends it serves. The sole criterion will be technical or pragmatic, concerning the efficiency with which the required emotion is stimulated. Beauty might conceivably do this (though not on Kant's view), but will otherwise be incidental. For crudity, either of execution or of the emotion demanded, will not matter so long as the emotion is, in fact, evoked and acted upon.

A vulgar advertisement may sell a product better than a sophisticated one. A sentimental religious print may conduce to piety as effectively as an artistic masterpiece, and more. From a religious standpoint, as from any other of a primarily purposive character, "good" art, or "art proper," is superfluous, except as a lexicon of proven techniques of emotional stimulation.

Indeed, in and for itself, "art proper" might even be harmful. The object of religion is to open the mind to transcendent things, and thereafter to close it. In the religious view the complexities of experience to which "art proper" exposes us are at best irrelevant, and at worst a return to the chaos and doubt from which religion rescues us.

It might be said, nevertheless, that "art proper" is itself insufficiently distinguishable from magical art. The outlook that Arnoldians believe it to promote is effectively moral, even quasi-religious, and can scarcely fail to find expression in behavior. Certainly, nineteenth-century realists such as George Eliot, Trollope, and Tolstoy claimed to be writing with a moral purpose, revealing the hidden order of things and extending human sympathies. How much difference is there, logically speaking, between an art that professes (and achieves) such aims, and explicitly magical art (i.e., emotionally manipulative art governed by an extrinsic, nonartistic purpose)?

The answer might be that whatever such authors intended, and whatever effects their work actually had, what made it "art proper" was the fact that in practice it did not subordinate the immediate aesthetic aim (either truth to the object represented, or fidelity to the integrity of the artistic creation as such, or both) to any prior goal, moral or otherwise. This patient refusal to jump to conclusions, or to bend the artistic process into premature conformity with them, would itself constitute a moral phenomenon and a moral example.

Science and history present parallel cases. How far religion also does so – and here obvious political analogies suggest themselves – will depend on whether we see religion primarily as a "world-open" receptivity to the transcendent, or as a "world-closed" claim finally to have captured it in doctrine. If the first, how is religion to be distinguished from art or from its supposed effects?

503

Those are questions that can be answered neither simply, nor here. However, many post-Enlightenment thinkers have been struck by the likeness of artistic experience, not to religious belief or doctrine, but to religious practice, of the kind based on myth, custom, and ritual. Here the underlying beliefs demand no intellectual assent, because they are already tacitly embodied in the practice itself, as it is communally experienced and renewed.

The most notable champion of this view was Richard Wagner, who thought of his own art precisely as renewing the human community despite being self-consciously mythic. (He was greatly influenced by Greek tragedy.) His last work *Parsifal* (1882) is actually *about* religion, and certainly excites religious emotions. But so far from requiring religious belief in the spectator, it could even be seen as an effectual, humanistic substitute for it. Wagner was not a literal believer, but said he had written *Parsifal* to give a nonreligious age some idea of what religion might mean, and to activate that meaning in his audience. The whole work is about community, how it lapses through sin and consequently decays, and how the offender is reintegrated and is restored, through compassion, forgiveness, and sacrifice. *Parsifal*, in fact, functions as a myth, but one that, being explicitly fictional, is merely entertained, not asserted (if it were, it could not be *perceived* as myth).

Wagner thought the essential functions of religion could be fulfilled by art, at least of this kind. But it could be objected that an emotional substitute for religion is easily found, since what is depicted in *Parsifal* is religious experience, and one needs only to empathize with it. And indeed there have been many, starting with Nietzsche, who regard *Parsifal* as mere decadent religiosity. However, this view might equally betray a deep-seated fear of that primal trust – T. S. Eliot's "awful daring of a moment's surrender" – without which there is no true intimacy, or real relationship with others and the world. Significantly, *Parsifal* is the ultimate subtext of Eliot's modernist landmark *The Waste Land* (1922).

See also PHOTOGRAPHY; AESTHETICISM; CATHARSIS; COLLINGWOOD; HEGEL; INEFFABILITY; ISLAMIC AESTHETICS; KANT; PORNOGRAPHY; SCHILLER; SUBLIME; TESTIMONY IN AESTHETICS; TRUTH IN ART; WAGNER.

BIBLIOGRAPHY
Collingwood, R. G. 1924. *Speculum Mentis; or, The Map of Knowledge*. Oxford: Clarendon.
Collingwood, R. G. 1938. *The Principles of Art*. Oxford: Clarendon.
Croce, Benedetto. 1909 [1902]. *Aesthetic: As Science of Expression and General Linguistic*. D. Ainslie (trans.). London: Macmillan.
Hegel, G. W. F. 1979 [1835–8]. *Introduction to Aesthetics*. T. M. Knox (trans.). C. Karelis (ed.). Oxford: Clarendon.
Kant, Immanuel. 1969 [1790]. *The Critique of Judgement*. J. C. Meredith (trans.). Oxford: Clarendon.
Leavis, F. R. & Wellek, René. 1964. "Literary Criticism and Philosophy," *Scrutiny*, 5. 4; 6, 1–2; repr. in *The Importance of Scrutiny*. E. Bentley (ed.). New York: New York University Press.
Santayana, George. 1922 [1905]. *Reason in Art: The Life of Reason*, vol. iv. New York: Scribner.
Schiller, Friedrich von. 1966. *Naïve and Sentimental Poetry* (1795) and *On the Sublime* (1801). J. A. Elias (trans.). New York: Ungar.
Scruton, Roger. 2003. *Death-Devoted Heart: An Account of Wagner's "Tristan und Isolde."* London: Continuum, esp. ch. 1.
Wagner, Richard. 1897 [1880]. "Religion and Art." In *Prose Works of Richard Wagner*, vol. vi. W. A. Ellis (trans.). London: Reeves, 211–52; also available at http://users. belgacom. net/wagnerlibrary/prose/wlpr0126.htm

ROBERT GRANT

representation One of the most general and important notions in philosophy as a whole and the philosophy of art in particular. Despite, or perhaps because of this, it is very hard to say anything illuminating about the nature of representation per se, a difficulty that also hampers adequate discussion of the nature and significance of representation in art. I concentrate on the notion of representation considered independently of art, clarifying it as best I can, and introducing some useful distinctions within the phenomenon as a whole. When I turn to representation in art, I do little more than identify the key questions it raises, questions that will find proper discussion in other entries. (Sometimes "representation" is used to mean something only pictures and perhaps sculptures do. I intend by it something very much more general. The representation unique to pictures (depiction) is just one of many forms representation, in my sense, might take.)

REPRESENTATION IN GENERAL

It is often said that one thing represents another when it stands for, symbolizes, or is in some sense "about" it. Thus my name represents me; a photograph in a newspaper represents a scene in some troubled African city; a performance of *Julius Caesar* represents the long-dead dictator and the excesses of power; and a bit of old wood, in the hands of a child, represents a rifle. Where there is representation, there is meaning or content, that is what is represented, along (where appropriate) with how it is represented as being. So the meaning of my name is me, and the content of the photograph above is (in part) a dirty street of ramshackle houses, with a road block at the end, manned by soldiers lolling in the midday heat. It is easy for most of us to know that this is what is represented; we only have to look at the picture. In the case of my name, in contrast, looking will not suffice. In addition to recognizing the marks as that symbol, we need to know whom the name is used to refer to. But, easy or not, the possibility of working out or otherwise coming to know content, that is of *interpretation*, is always present where representation is.

It would be a mistake, however, to take our usage of any of the terms now before us as reliable guides to the phenomenon. It is natural enough to say that the dark skies in the north represent the coming storm; that the difficulties in our recent relations are not about you, but about me and my insecurities; or that America stands for the freedom to be selfish, or represents the last best hope for mankind. With a bit of ingenuity, we could redescribe these phenomena in terms of "symbolizing," "meaning," "content," and allowing for "interpretation." Yet, while various phenomena are here described, none is the one that interests us. The moral is that ordinary language does not mark that phenomenon at all neatly.

One of the most significant turns in Anglophone philosophy in the last half-century has been the extension of the scope of representation to cover, not merely external symbols, but our own mental states. The claim is that it is not only words, pictures, gestures, and the like that bear content: our beliefs, desires, emotions, imaginings, and perceptual states do so too. The idea is not uncontroversial, though it is more controversial as applied to particular mental states – sensations and perceptions are, in different ways, particularly contentious cases – than in the claim that at least some mental states represent. If representation is found in both "inner" and "outer" meaning-bearing entities and states, this places further pressures on any claims we make about it.

One thing we can do without running into trouble is to draw some distinctions. First, while some representations take propositional content, others are object-directed. The belief or fear that the world is warming fall into the former camp, as, moving to nonmental representations, does the sentence I utter when I tell you what I believe. A picture of the consequences of climate change, in contrast, has a content that is not propositional. Perhaps it shows a dried-up lake, the surrounding trees withered, the bottom cluttered with the rotting bodies of grounded fish. Although we can capture some of this content in propositions, the whole resists summary in a series, however long, of "that" clauses. This is something the picture has in common with some mental states, such as (arguably) perceptions and visual imaginings. That is one reason why the natural way to convey such a state to someone else is to draw a picture of what one has seen or imagined, rather than describing it in words. Second, object-directed representations might ascribe properties to the objects, or they might not. My name does not convey a proposition, but nor does it tell you anything about me: you might guess my sex from it, but if you guess wrong you will not blame the name for misdescribing me. A portrait of me, in contrast, will represent me as having certain features. If I do not have that long nose or thick head of hair, the representation is inaccurate. Accuracy and inaccuracy are the analogues in object-directed representations of truth and falsity in those with propositional contents. Third, both accuracy and truth, and their opposites, are in play only if the representation seeks to show how things are. There are other options, including showing how things *are to be*, ordering them to be that way, exploring the merely possible (how things might be), and so on. The easiest purchase on these differences comes from considering language. The distinctions between asserting, supposing, ordering, expressing a wish, and so on find analogues in other representations, both external and mental. Finally, reflection on language naturally suggests a fourth distinction, between literal and metaphorical uses or meanings. With an eye on the role of representation in art, we might think this last distinction will be of particular importance. However, it is at least unclear how far the notion of metaphor can apply beyond linguistic representations in their assertoric mode. (For an attempt to describe pictorial metaphor, see Wollheim 1987: ch. 4.)

By now we have uncovered a framework of ideas rich enough to find no easy parallel beyond the realm of genuine representation. But none of this amounts to a definition of the notion. That is not something we will attempt to do. But we can at least consider two more substantive claims that promise to hold at something like the right level of generality. Although each starts from an everyday idea, each has found a sophisticated working out within the philosophy of language – that part of philosophy that, despite its natural focus, has most thoroughly investigated the notion of representation per se.

The first idea is simply that there must, as it were, be some gap between a representation and the object or state of affairs it represents. Perhaps the most useful form of this idea lies in the dictum that where there is representation there must be the possibility of misrepresentation – falsity or inaccuracy, depending on whether the representation is propositional or object-directed. And the most sophisticated development of that dictum that might direct us to a claim about representation per se is the thought that the meaning of language ultimately lies in the conditions under which utterances in it would be true. That is, the meaning of a sentence is given by its truth conditions. What it is for a bit of language to have meaning is thus for it to have truth conditions. And since nothing counts as language unless it counts as meaningful, having truth conditions is what defines those of our noises and scribblings that count as linguistic representations from those that do not. (For a highly influential advocacy of this approach see Davidson 1984.)

Although the claim thus far is limited to language, it is not hard to see in broad outline how to generalize it. We merely add accuracy to truth, and claim that there is representation

where there are conditions under which the individual, state, or event in question might usefully be described as accurate or true. What is harder to see is how to fill out this sketch so as to accommodate the various options noted above. Applied to language alone, the approach needs extending (somehow) to cover (1) meaningful parts of truth-bearing sentences, such as names and property terms; (2) utterances that are not apt for truth at all (such as orders and expressions of wishes); and (3) metaphorical uses. Applied to representations in general, we can add to these challenges their analogues for object-directed external symbols and mental states.

The other idea is that nothing is a representation intrinsically; representing requires the right context. If we restrict our attention to external representations, that context seems to be one of certain human purposes. External representations are all artifacts – that is one reason for thinking that the dark sky does not (in our sense) represent the oncoming storm. More precisely, they are artifacts designed for communication. A sophisticated working through of this idea can be found in the writings of Paul Grice (1989). For Grice, external representations are items, states of affairs, or events we produce with a complex intention. At its core lies the intention to bring about a certain effect in another's mind – to get her to entertain a certain thought. But the overall intention includes the intention that the other recognize that this is our intention. She is to grasp the thought, and to grasp that we produced whatever noises, marks, or gestures we produced precisely in order to get her to have that thought. Indeed, this higher-level intention (that our intention be recognized) is itself one we intend her to recognize.

Grice's idea applies from the first to external representations that are nonlinguistic; some of his own examples include gestures. Although initially confined to the communication of propositional contents, the strategy might generalize to cover object-directed property-ascribing representations, such as pictures (see Abell 2005). Although it is not clear how to extend the ideas to cover all representational moods (asserting, ordering, wishing, supposing, . . .), there are no compelling grounds for pessimism on that count. What the Gricean approach certainly cannot do, however, is to give an account of mental representation. It takes that notion for granted, in helping itself to speakers' intentions and the thoughts they aim to engender in the listener. The gain that accompanies this cost is that Grice can hope to say more about how external representation comes to be than the appeal to truth conditions can.

Our discussion so far has stuck stubbornly at a stratospheric level of generality. If we were to drop a little toward the specific, we would discuss the various forms external representation can take. Pictures and words, gestures and theatrical performances, three-dimensional models and numerical symbols all represent, but they do so in very different ways. Whatever representation per se is taken to be, there are different ways of fitting the template thus laid down. Moreover, these different forms of representation have different features and powers – not just in the terms above, such as whether they are propositional or object-directed, whether they are capable of, or perhaps stuck with, assertion as opposed to the other "moods"; but also in terms of the sorts of thing they can represent. For instance, while pictures, one might think, can represent only what can be seen, language suffers no similar limitation. Conversely, pictures might be taken to capture appearances as words cannot. The differences between the various forms of representation would repay far more intense study than philosophy has so far granted them. One, but only one, reason for correcting this neglect lies in the philosophy of art.

REPRESENTATION IN ART

Although representation is central to a good deal of art, and although a considerable part of the philosophy of art is concerned with representing in one way or another, the philosophical questions concerning art's relation to representing per se can be framed very simply. Can art be defined in terms of representation? And does representation somehow hold the key to some or all of the value of art? Let us very briefly consider each in turn.

Representation cannot alone provide a definition of art. Our discussion has been structured around the thought that a good deal of representation is found outside art. Even setting aside mental representation as at best the precursor, rather than an instance, of art proper; there are many external symbols that do not begin to qualify as artistic. Thus if art is representation, it is representation under certain conditions, with a certain purpose, in a certain context, or with certain further features. But even so modified, the proposal still faces a serious challenge. Much art is representational, it is true; but some, apparently, is not. The challenge is usually framed by appeal both to certain traditional fine arts (music and abstract painting) and to the decorative arts (pottery, intaglio work, and the like). The discussion above allows us to note one factor that complicates the dialectic here. It is usually suggested that nonrepresentational art is art nonetheless at least in part because it is expressive. Whether this bolsters or undermines the challenge these examples pose turns on whether expression can itself be treated as just another form of representation. For all the intuitive appeal of the distinction between the two, it is far from clear that our efforts to clarify the notion of representation leave expression distinct from it. Once we have extended the appeal to truth/accuracy conditions, or to Gricean communicative intentions, to the point at which they cover all uncontroversial cases of representation, how can we be sure that they will not equally apply to expression? Thus, until further progress is made in understanding the notion of representation, the force of the prime objection to the representational theory of art remains uncertain.

Let us turn to the idea that representation holds the key, if not to art's nature, then to its value, to why it matters to us. Again, the extent of nonartistic representation suggests that a full account will have to say more. (At least assuming that art does matter to us in ways that mere representations do not.) The bare idea will need supplementing, for instance by appeal to the idea that art, unlike humdrum representations, somehow bears many meanings all at once, that its meanings resonate at the margins with rich connotations, or that it captures the ineffable. All these ideas – perhaps they are only facets of a single idea – have found repeated advocates in the history of aesthetics. (For a recent example, see Danto 1981.) Again, the threat from nonrepresentational artworks will require a different treatment.

Whether or not that approach is ultimately fruitful, there is a related line of inquiry to explore. Representation per se may not hold the key to the value of art per se, but it could still be that the differing value of the different representational arts turns in key part on the different forms of representation they involve. To take just one prominent example, representing in the way it does, that is depicting, is surely a deep feature of painting, one that aligns it with sculpture and opposes it to literature. Understanding what these different art forms offer might in part involve appreciating the differing ways they represent.

See also DRAWING, PAINTING, AND PRINTMAKING; ABSTRACTION; DEPICTION; EXPRESSION; ILLUSION; METAPHOR; PERSPECTIVE; PICTURE PERCEPTION; REALISM; SYMBOL; THEORIES OF ART.

BIBLIOGRAPHY

Abell, Catharine. 2005. "Pictorial Implicature," *Journal of Aesthetics and Art Criticism*, 63, 55–66.

Danto, Arthur C. 1981. *The Transfiguration of the Commonplace*. Cambridge, MA: Harvard University Press.

Davidson, Donald. 1984. *Inquiries into Truth and Interpretation*. Oxford: Clarendon.

Goodman, Nelson. 1969. *Languages of Art*. 2nd edn. Oxford: Oxford University Press.

Grice, Paul. 1989. *Studies in the Way of Words*. Cambridge, MA: Harvard University Press.

Walton, Kendall L. 1990. *Mimesis as Make-Believe: On the Foundations of the Representational Arts*. Cambridge, MA: Harvard University Press.

Wollheim, Richard. 1987. *Painting as an Art*. London: Thames & Hudson.

ROBERT HOPKINS

Ruskin, John (1819–1900)   English art critic, educator, economist, and social reformer. Ruskin is Britain's greatest critic of art and society. His aesthetics is grounded in his thinking on the morality of art (his refusal to separate aesthetics from ethics is always in evidence), and focuses on three relationships:

1   between art (man's creation) and nature (God's creation);
2   between art (including architecture, "the distinctively political art") and the values of the society in which it was created;
3   between the viewer and the object.

To teach people how to "see clearly" was the project that shaped Ruskin's life-work, as reflected in his writing on a vast range of topics, from Turner and the Pre-Raphaelites to Tintoretto and Carpaccio, from Venetian Gothic architecture and the Alps to minerals and birds. (The Library Edition of the Works extends to 39 volumes.)

Three problems associated with defining Ruskin's aesthetics actually help to explain its nature. First, he is contradictory, not only from work to work, but sometimes within a single work. Ruskin himself claimed that he was never satisfied that he had "handled a subject properly" until he had contradicted himself "at least three times." (R. G. Collingwood compares Ruskin with Hegel, both "historicists," in this regard; see Hewison 1976: 206.) Second, although there are many continuities in Ruskin's aesthetics (and these might be called "Ruskinian"), his individual observations must always be read in relation to the immediate context in which they were first made. Much of his writing – particularly in the middle and late periods – was for a specific purpose, and was addressed to a specific audience or readership. Ruskin enjoyed working against the grain, and was a master of irony that is easily missed when read out of context. Third, although he stated that no true disciple of his would ever be a "Ruskinian," we find that not only his admirers, but also many Victorian public buildings that he himself hated, were frequently described as "Ruskinian," both during and after his lifetime.

Ruskin's mind can in certain respects be compared to that of Coleridge: both are multifaceted, encyclopedic, dynamic, religious. Unlike Coleridge's concept of the imagination, however, Ruskin's concept is based on what he understood to be the truth of "fact" (including such Old Testament "facts" as the Fall). As Hewison summarizes Ruskin, the "penetrative imagination" deals with external fact and the inner truth it reveals, seeing the object or idea in its entirety: the "associative imagination" expresses the artist's thought, conveying the vision of the penetrative imagination: the "contemplative imagination" deals with remembered or abstract ideas, and acts as a metaphor-making faculty. This last became increasingly important in practice from the 1860s, when Ruskin's interest in myth deepened, but contemplation (Greek: *theôria*) had been central to his thought since *Modern Painters*, vol. ii (of 1846): "Now the mere animal consciousness of the pleasantness [the pleasures of sight] I call Aesthesis; but the exulting, reverent, and grateful perception of it I call Theoria. For this, and this only, is the full comprehension and contemplation of the Beautiful as a gift of God" (1903–12: iv.42).

The "theoretic faculty" perceives two kinds of beauty. "Typical Beauty" is that external quality of bodies which "may be shown to be in some sort typical of the Divine attributes," while "Vital Beauty" is "the appearance of felicitous fulfillment of function in living things, more especially of the joyful and right exertion of perfect life in man." Landow (1971: 178–9) argues that, unlike vital beauty, the idea of typical beauty lost its force when Ruskin's religious beliefs changed.

Unlike Coleridge, the evangelical Ruskin makes no claim for the creative power of the imagination, guarding against the danger that the self might usurp God's role as creator. He invented the term "pathetic fallacy" (in *Modern Painters*, vol. iii) to describe the "error" of projecting onto external things attributes of the perceiving mind under the influence of emotion. Charles Kingsley's "They rowed her in across the rolling foam – / The cruel, crawling foam" evokes from Ruskin the dry comment, "The foam is not cruel, neither does it crawl."

The work that first made a great impact on the artworld when Ruskin was only 24 – the anonymous first volume of *Modern Painters* – proclaimed the undervalued Turner to be the greatest English artist because he painted the facts of nature truthfully. Its subtitle reflects the youthful ambition of its author, who was ignorant of the German founders of modern aesthetics: "Their Superiority in the Art of Landscape Painting to all the Ancient Masters, proved by examples of The True, The Beautiful and The Intellectual, from the Works of Modern Artists, especially from those of J. M. W. Turner, Esq., R.A." Having developed his aesthetic theories in vol. ii, Ruskin interrupted his work on *Modern Painters* in order to study architecture, defining its "Seven Lamps" as those of sacrifice, truth, power, beauty, life, memory, and obedience, and writing his history of *The Stones of Venice*, from an apocalyptic perspective in which the city is seen as being under judgment after the "fall" that was the Renaissance. The famous chapter in vol. ii on "The Nature of Gothic" had a separate and influential afterlife as a key text for the Working Men's College Movement, and for William Morris, who reprinted it in the beautifully designed Kelmscott edition.

Having completed *Modern Painters* in the years immediately before and after his "unconversion" from evangelical dogma (1858), Ruskin developed the social ramifications of his thought (already present in *The Seven Lamps of Architecture* and *The Stones of Venice*) in a series of books and lectures in the 1860s. (A statement from *Unto This Last* is characteristic: "There is no wealth but life.") In the subsequent decade two new platforms became available to him: the newly founded Slade Professorship of Fine Art at Oxford, and his monthly *Fors Clavigera: Letters to the Workmen and Labourers of Great Britain*. Much autobiographical writing is woven into the latter, and then reworked in *Praeterita*, written in the 1880s in increasingly difficult circumstances associated with his mental decline in retirement at Brantwood, in the Lake District. *Praeterita* is the autobiography of a brilliant draughtsman, art critic, and social critic, for whom theory and practice, art and society, are interrelated rather than separate entities.

See also IMAGINATION.

BIBLIOGRAPHY

Primary sources

1903–12. *The Works of John Ruskin*. 39 vols. E. T. Cook & A. Wedderburn (eds.). Library Edition. London: Allen.

1843–60. *Modern Painters*. Vols. iii–vii in Library Edition.

1849. *The Seven Lamps of Architecture*. Vol. viii in Library Edition.

1851–3. *The Stones of Venice*. Vols. ix–xi in Library Edition.

1859. *The Two Paths*. Vol. xvi in Library Edition.

1871–84. *Fors Clavigera: Letters to the Workmen and Labourers of Great Britain*. Vols. xxvii–xxix in Library Edition.

Secondary sources

Fraser, Hilary. 1986. *Beauty and Belief: Aesthetics and Religion in Victorian Literature*. Cambridge: Cambridge University Press.

Hewison, Robert. 1976. *John Ruskin: The Argument of the Eye*. Princeton: Princeton University Press.

Hilton, Timothy. 1985. *John Ruskin: The Early Years, 1819–1859*. New Haven: Yale University Press.

Hilton, Timothy. 2000. *John Ruskin: The Later Years*. New Haven: Yale University Press.

Landow, George P. 1971. *The Aesthetic and Critical Theories of John Ruskin*. Princeton: Princeton University Press.

Wheeler, Michael. 1999. *Ruskin's God*. Cambridge: Cambridge University Press.

MICHAEL WHEELER

S

Santayana, George (1863–1952) Spanish philosopher and novelist; for many years at Harvard University. Santayana somewhere notes that philosophers come to aesthetics through opposite routes – as metaphysicians who need to complete their systems, and as artists who need to generalize about their experiences. He belonged in both camps, with emphasis on the latter. He was an obvious literary artist in his poetry and fiction, but he was a poet-philosopher all the time, even when he was a metaphysician. While he wrote *about* art intermittently, particularly in *The Sense of Beauty* and *Reason in Art*, he sought to be artful in all of his writings, including his "theoretical" ones.

His central work in aesthetics is that early and most remarkable book, *The Sense of Beauty*: its subtitle is *Being the Outline(s) of Aesthetic Theory*. Santayana reveals his hand, and his approach, when he says at the very outset: "The sense of beauty has a more important place in life than aesthetic theory has ever taken in philosophy." And, indeed, the stylistic beauty of this treatise is as telling as its philosophical or theoretical side, and must properly be seen as part of its "statement." Santayana also says: "To feel beauty is a better thing than to understand how we came to feel it." He certainly feels it, and might even be said to explain how he comes to feel it. But, as always, he explains it more as a literary critic than as a metaphysician. He addresses himself to the task of creating literary art as surely as he works at discovering any principles of art in a theoretical fashion.

Santayana is cavalier about distinctions, even the distinction between theory and art, between comprehension and inspiration: "But the recognition of the superiority of aesthetics in experience to aesthetics in theory ought not to make us accept as an explanation of aesthetic feeling what is in truth only an expression of it." This might be seen as a form of self-scolding, or a way of guarding against the neglectful obliteration of an important distinction. But the distinction that he makes does not actually mark out different phases or moments of experience, or different sections of his own texts.

As further indication of his way with distinctions, Santayana objects, on theoretical grounds, to calling beauty a "manifestation of God to the senses." Such an observation is obscure and beyond truth or falsehood, albeit high-minded. But then an analysis of what is meant by God, an unpacking of the metaphor, reveals how and why the attributes of God are indeed an appropriate way to reach an understanding of beauty. In a word, a good metaphor can give a scrawny theory some divine afflatus and some cognitive force. Art and philosophy always were one enterprise! The presumed structure of Santayana's "theoretical" work is the barest skeleton upon which various comments, or "little essays," are hung. The parts of the treatise, which *The Sense of Beauty* might be said to be, are quite incidental to a process that is fundamentally critical, literary, and ironic. The dynamic of making and unmaking distinctions, the play of perspectives – not the semblance of structure which these distinctions might have been thought to have created – constitute the essential quality of Santayana's presentation.

The organization of the book, such as it is, consists of part 1 on the nature of beauty; parts 2, 3, and 4 on matter, form, and expression. In part 1, Santayana distinguishes the moral and the aesthetic, or work and play. He teases the distinction and accords it some initial and conventional deference. But then he undermines it and shows in effect how any adequate value theory must ambiguously embrace both the moral and the aesthetic.

Beauty is defined in part 1 as "objectified pleasure," or "pleasure regarded as the quality of an object." It suggests a psychological tendency or process in us, whereby we attribute or affix our feelings to things. It is a provocative definition, but leaves the locus of pleasure somewhat problematic. The lower senses, taste and touch, are mostly bodily and not objectifiable. Smell seems mildly but vaguely objectifiable. Hearing and seeing take us entirely from the organs whereby we perceive, to the objects out there that we esteem and enjoy. Santayana was never entirely satisfied with this approach, and at a later date wrote self-critically of his tendency to "skirt psychologism."

Part 4, on the concept of expression, is most startling and unusual. Expression is an evocation of memory, the bringing of some association to mind, in the presence of sensed matter and form. The memory may be vague; some emotion may persist, with the details of its occasion forgotten. Indeed, vagueness sometimes helps make possible the fusion of present and past. Santayana's theory of expression, if it can be called a theory, undermines any clear and traditional notions about the fixity of the art object. In principle, any sensation or idea or concept can conjoin or fuse with any other, and this is what his "theory" asserts. But in practice, as we know from the associations we attempt in the making of metaphors, not everything tossed into the air can be said to fly. Theory cannot quite account for art, or substitute for it.

Santayana's concept of expression, one might say, is the general case of which certain late twentieth-century and radical views about art are so many special instances. Theories can attach to sensuous objects as surely as sentimental memories can. That an object is offered for appreciation by the artworld demonstrates an "expressive value" in it. Expression allows any association – a previous sensuous memory, a mood, a thought, a theory – to attach itself to the presently perceived object. More exactly, Santayana's notion of expression allows this, and our experience of art confirms that such things happen. But it is a question of sensibility, and criticism, as to whether an association "works," and whether or not it succeeds effectively in affiliating with a sensuous object.

Santayana's *The Sense of Beauty* fits into no clear tradition of aesthetic writing, yet is rich in historical antecedents. It has no clear influences and effects, yet shows remarkable anticipation of what is happening in aesthetic theory and criticism one hundred years after its appearance. It is at once *sui generis* yet full of perennial wisdom.

See also EXPRESSION; RELIGION AND ART.

BIBLIOGRAPHY

Primary sources
[1896] 1988. *The Sense of Beauty*. W. G. Holzberger & H. J. Saatkamp Jr. (eds.). Cambridge, MA: MIT Press.
[1905] 1955. *The Life of Reason*, vol. iv: *Reason in Art*. New York: Scribner.

Secondary sources
Schilpp, P. A. (ed.). 1951. *The Philosophy of George Santayana*. New York: Tudor.

MORRIS GROSSMAN

Sartre, Jean-Paul (1905–1980) French novelist, playwright, journalist, literary critic, political activist, and philosopher, and one of the most influential intellectuals of the twentieth century. Sartre's voluminous writings never included a philosophy of art in the traditional sense, although a case can be made (and he himself insisted) that aesthetics is implicit in everything he wrote (Schilpp 1981: 15).

Sartre is best known for his philosophy of "existentialism" – the view that in human beings "existence precedes essence," that humans first come on the scene and only then define who they are or who they ought to be. In early writings, such as the novel *Nausea* (1938), the wartime plays *The Flies* (1943) and *No Exit* (1945), and up through the massive philosophical work *Being and Nothingness* (1943) and the lecture "Existentialism is a Humanism" (1946), he develops a view of freedom according to which each human being, facing whatever "coefficient of adversity" in his situating conditions, is completely responsible for the fundamental values he or she chooses to follow.

Sartre described this "human condition" as similar to the challenge confronting an artist – to invent without being given any standards in advance. However, he thought, that as people invent they should strive to avoid forms of "bad faith" in which they cover up their freedom; they should assume full responsibility for their actions and act so as to recognize and promote freedom for everyone. In the case of the French writer after World War II, Sartre argued that this meant a new kind of literature, an "engaged" literature. So in 1945, with a group of friends, he founded a literary magazine, *Les Temps modernes*, to encourage writers who would recognize their social role and work "to change simultaneously the social condition of man and the concept he has of himself" (Sartre 1988: 255). On this basis, he criticized "art for art's sake" and the cult of "genius," and he indicted a number of earlier writers, including Baudelaire, for elaborate efforts to hide their freedom and social responsibility from themselves.

In later years, Sartre seemed to judge less and interpret more. In plays such as *The Devil and the Good Lord* (1951) and *The Condemned of Altona* (1960), in critical studies like that of the criminal literary figure Jean Genet, and the never completed study of the novelist Flaubert, *The Idiot of the Family* (1971–2), Sartre recognized far greater complexity and force of circumstance in human life, and in the creative artist's life in particular. He came to believe that human values are largely interiorized from one's family history and one's situating institutions and practices. Still, he thought that we never simply return what we have been given. There is always an element of freedom. Indeed, in a figure such as Genet, Sartre thinks, one can come to see this freedom "at grips with destiny, crushed at first by its mischances, then turning upon them and digesting them little by little . . . [one can learn] the choice that a writer makes of himself, of his life and of the meaning of the universe, including even the formal characteristics of his style and composition, even the structure of his images and of the particularity of his tastes" (1963a: 584).

As Sartre saw it, a work of literature, and any work of art, is a free, imaginative creation addressed to other freedoms. It has a kind of autonomy and offers aesthetic enjoyment simply in arousing the reader's (viewer's, listener's) free response. At the same time, it discloses the world in some of its aspects and, often, for a determinate audience. The function of literary

(or art) criticism is to exhibit, in the work, the interplay between freedom and situation which constitutes the creator's distinctive view of things; and also, since the work is "an act of confidence in the freedom of men" (1988: 67), the critic must assess its import for the human situation of freedom and unfreedom in which it speaks. In his essay "Black Orpheus" (1948), Sartre admires African poetry for its dynamism and because it makes blackness a symbol of openness, of freedom. He praises the sculptor Giacometti's embodiment of the forces of repulsion and attraction which keep people at a distance while together; and he prefers Tintoretto to Titian because he sees in the former's expressiveness and violence a rejection of the Venetian establishment which Titian, with his smooth and idealized figures, served so slavishly (Sartre 1963b).

The theoretical basis for Sartre's view of the work of art lies not only in his ontology of freedom but in his early phenomenological analysis of the imagination in *Psychology of the Imagination* (1940). Here he describes imagining not as "having images" somehow internal to consciousness, but as a distinctive way of having a world – a way of intending an object, of making it present, but in a mode of absence, or as *"irréel."* In imagining the Parthenon, he says, one takes a certain sensuous content or physical object (perhaps a sketch) *as* something that is not, *as* the Parthenon that is elsewhere. One conjures the world not present.

One may also conjure a world that is not real at all. This is what happens on seeing a performance of *Hamlet*, on hearing a performance of Beethoven's Seventh Symphony, or when viewing a Matisse. One picks up the solicitations of the perceived thing (the actor's voice and movements, the scraping of strings and hooting of horns, the colored shapes on canvas) and transforms them into an imaginative consciousness of the Prince of Denmark, the symphony, or a dancing woman – with all the feelings appropriate to those things.

All works of art are, in this sense, beyond the real, not anywhere. "Aesthetic contemplation is an induced dream," Sartre says, and "Beauty is a value which applies only to the imaginary and which entails a negation of the world" (1948: 282). This is its seductive power. The artist is, in a way, an escapist (Sartre thinks

Flaubert was almost neurotically so). None-theless, the sort of imaginative negation at stake, not only in creating but in responding to a work of art, may also *disclose* the world as it is – through *Hamlet*, the symphony, and the flying figure, we are afforded a fresh perspective on ordinary things. This is particularly true for literary texts. And, Sartre points out, our own freedom is inevitably engaged with the freedom of others, and with the freedom of the artist, in the aesthetic response we make to such works and in the moral and social response we make to them as well.

See also NINETEENTH- AND TWENTIETH-CENTURY CONTINENTAL AESTHETICS; IMAGINATION; INDIAN AESTHETICS; MERLEAU-PONTY; TRUTH IN ART.

BIBLIOGRAPHY

Primary sources
[1940] 1948. *Psychology of the Imagination*. B. Frechtman (trans.). New York: Philosophical Library.
[1946] 1947. *Existentialism*. B. Frechtman (trans.). New York: Philosophical Library. (Includes "Existentialism is a Humanism.")
[1952] 1963a. *Saint-Genet, Actor and Martyr*. B. Frechtman (trans.). New York: Braziller.
1963b. *Essays in Aesthetics*. W. Baskin (ed. & trans.). New York: Philosophical Library.
1988. *"What is Literature?" and Other Essays*. S. Ungar (intro.) Cambridge, MA: Harvard University Press. (Includes "Black Orpheus," 289–330.)

Secondary sources
Kaelin, Eugene F. 1966. *An Existentialist Aesthetic*. Madison: University of Wisconsin Press.
McBride, William L. (ed.). 1996. *Existentialist Literature and Aesthetics*. New York: Routledge.
Schilpp, Paul Arthur. 1981. *The Philosophy of Jean-Paul Sartre*. La Salle: Open Court.

JOHN J. COMPTON

Schelling, Friedrich Wilhelm Joseph von

(1775–1854) German idealist philosopher. The first philosopher to write a philosophy of art. Schelling was educated together with Hegel and Hölderlin in a Tübingen seminary. He occupied various chairs of philosophy, in, for example, Jena, Würzburg, and Munich, finishing his career in what had been Hegel's chair of philosophy in Berlin, which he took on in 1841 and occupied until his death. His *Philosophy of Art* (1802–3) attempts a systematic philosophical articulation of the arts, in which art has a status equal to philosophy.

In his earlier *System of Transcendental Idealism* (1800) he saw art as the "organ of philosophy," because it can show what philosophical concepts cannot: the absolute. By the middle of the nineteenth century such ideas, which had been the foundation of romantic art and philosophy, often came to be regarded, particularly in the English-speaking world, as mere mystical hyperbole. They did live on in artistic movements such as Symbolism, but they played less and less of a role in the dominant strands of philosophy. Behind the ideas of the early Schelling lies the notion that art has truth status, a notion that lost currency in the light both of the advances of the natural sciences and of the clarification of the truth status of propositions in analytical philosophy.

The notion of the truth of art was revived in a philosophically viable way by the work of T. W. Adorno, as well as by Hans-Georg Gadamer, on the basis of the work of his teacher, Heidegger, and plays a subterranean role in poststructuralism (Bowie 1990). If we take account of these approaches we are now in a better position to understand why Schelling's early work gave such importance to art than if we rely on philosophical approaches oriented toward the natural sciences as the sole arbiters of truth. This essay concentrates on the *System of Transcendental Idealism* as it is Schelling's most important and influential contribution to the understanding of art's importance to philosophy; despite some remarkable insights into art's relationship to mythology and into some of the specific arts, especially music, the *Philosophy of Art* does not have the same degree of importance.

The work of the early Schelling is part of the flowering of philosophy in Germany initiated by Kant's critical philosophy. In common with many of his contemporaries, and J. G. Fichte in particular, Schelling regarded Kant's division of the world into "representations" and "things in themselves," and the concomitant division between theoretical and practical reason, as a failure to achieve Kant's own stated aim. As Kant had made clear, philosophy had to arrive at an explanation of the world and our place in it with its own means, without using theology as a basis. This could not, though, be done at the expense of separating thought and being. The desire to avoid this separation led to an orientation toward monism, and its key exponent, Spinoza. At the same time, the fear was that Spinoza's philosophy led, as F. H. Jacobi saw it, to "nihilism," to the world of reductionist conceptions of modern science.

This reductionist view was precisely what Kant's insistence on practical reason was meant to overcome, in the name of reason, the capacity to have purposes that are not determined by natural causality. Fichte made Kant's practical philosophy primary: even the subject's cognitive relationship to the world was grounded in its "activity." This activity, which Kant himself saw as a "spontaneity," in that it could not be explained in terms of the law of causality, Fichte made into the very principle of reality. Without the cognitive activity of the subject there would not be a world to know (though there might still be a world). The reason the world is intelligible has to lie, as Kant had shown, in the subject. Fichte dealt with the problem of the resistance of the "external" world by making it the reflection back into the subject of its own activity. If this were not the case it would, he claimed, be impossible to understand how it is that we can feel the resistance of the world; without an identity between what can feel and what is felt, one is stuck with the Cartesian problems which Kant had not fully escaped. The prior factor has to be that which allows one to be *aware* of even the most mechanical phenomena, which, for Fichte, was self-consciousness.

How is it that Schelling's version of these ideas leads him to privilege art over philosophy? The linking factor between Spinoza and Fichte is, for Schelling, the notion of that which is the cause of itself. In Spinoza, this is "God," in Fichte the "I" (as a spontaneity). Schelling's early key idea was that, instead of being the inaccessible thing in itself that Kant made it in the *Critique of Pure Reason*, nature in itself was "productive." Kantian synthetic judgments deal with the world as "product," as that which appears at a particular moment; *Naturphilosophie*, in Schelling's sense, deals with the "productivity," which gives rise to transient "products" by opposing itself to itself, like the

flowing molecules of a stream when they form an eddy. The very need for synthetic judgments derives from the fact that what is being synthesized is split within itself: objects are determined by their not being other objects; they cannot be fully themselves without the other objects from which they are separated. Nature must, then, unite itself because it is divided within itself.

If the objects of scientific knowledge are to be subsumed under general laws that interrelate, they must, as Kant had realized in the *Critique of Judgment*, ultimately share the same status. The model of this is the organism, whose parts cannot be themselves without each other. This notion of the relation of parts to whole made Kant link the natural organism to the artwork. Schelling went beyond Kant by suggesting that, as we ourselves are part of nature, what knows in us must have an organic relationship to what is known; there can be no ultimate division between the two. This is what he means by the absolute. The question is how philosophy can explicate this link between knowing and being known.

Schelling suggests, with prophetic consequences, that the forces of Fichte's conscious philosophical "I" have an "unconscious" history, which it is the task of transcendental philosophy to retrace. The structure of this argument prefigures both Hegel's genetic account of self-consciousness in the *Phenomenology of Spirit*, and psychoanalysis. How can it be, though, that philosophy should have access to what is unconscious? Schelling argues that we will never understand the forces that give rise to self-consciousness if we try to do so in terms of conceptual knowledge. How can *unconscious* forces appear as themselves to the *conscious* mind? Freud will later make it clear that we do not have cognitive access to drives, only to their "representations," though he still thinks we can make psychoanalysis into a positive science; Schelling is led to the idea of the object that cannot be conceived of merely as a causally determined natural object, in order to suggest how we can understand "unconscious activity" via "conscious activity." This object is a product of spontaneity, the work of art.

The artwork begins with the conscious intention of the artist, but it must be the result of more than conscious reflection and technique if it is to achieve aesthetic status. A work of art is not art because it shares the same determinable attributes as some other objects but rather because it reveals the world in a way which only it can: a chemical or physical analysis of a Rembrandt painting tells us nothing about it as a work of art. There is no cognitive criterion that allows us to judge whether something is art or not. The work of art is what unifies "unconscious" production – the productivity which gives rise to natural products – with "conscious" production, which allows us to know nature as an object of science. As such, the work of art is the only means of direct access to the absolute, because it overcomes the division between the conscious subject and the object world by revealing the ground they both share. Philosophy cannot represent this ground because this would entail making it into an object of reflexive knowledge by saying what it is (matter, mind, energy, or whatever). As soon as one attempts to do this one is forced to *relate* the absolute to what it is not, and it thereby loses any possibility of being absolute.

Talk of the absolute makes everyone uneasy. However, what Schelling means becomes clear in the way he claims that both science and art are means of revealing the absolute. Science, though, is faced with an endless task, in that each new revelation is arrived at via the exclusion of other possibilities: successive networks of interdepending theories, as modern science shows (and as Kant realized in the *Critique of Judgment*), do not allow one to arrive at something noncontingent. In art this failure is constitutive: the very fact that artworks are "capable of an infinite interpretation," and our *awareness* of this fact, demonstrate the real nature of being, as that which cannot ever be known in its entirety. Each interpretation may disclose an aspect of the work, but at the same time it hides other aspects.

Science and art depend on the same activity, which we can regard, in the light of Heidegger (who relies on Schelling to a far greater extent than he ever admitted), as ways of disclosing the world that share the same source. Many of these ideas were the common property of the Jena Circle of Romantic thinkers, which included Friedrich Schlegel and Novalis, and to which Schelling belonged for a time, before moving away, after the beginning of the century, from the Romantic position. In the *Philosophy of Art* he moves toward the position of his identity philosophy, which, like Hegel's after it, claims to be able to show the absolute in philosophy by articulated insight into the finitude of particular knowledge. This leads him to a systematic philosophical presentation of the various forms of art, of the kind more familiar from Hegel's *Aesthetics*.

The hopes invested in art as the means of communicating a "mythology of reason" that will reconcile the contradictions in modern societies between sensuousness and reason, which are present in the *System of Transcendental Idealism* (and, in a different way, in the work of Schiller), give way in the work of the later Schelling to a conviction that great art depends on the right social conditions to flourish and thus cannot really help create these conditions. At the same time, the key philosophical thought of the *System of Transcendental Idealism*, that philosophy has to come to terms with a ground of reflexive thinking which transcends it, remains central to the later Schelling, particularly in his critique of Hegel, and has a significant influence on thinkers like Schopenhauer, Kierkegaard, Nietzsche, and Heidegger, all of whom see art as vital to philosophy.

See also NINETEENTH- AND TWENTIETH-CENTURY CONTINENTAL AESTHETICS; HEGEL; HEIDEGGER; KANT; SCIENCE AND ART.

BIBLIOGRAPHY

Primary sources
[1797] 1988. *Ideas for a Philosophy of Nature*. E. E. Harris & P. Heath (trans.). R. Stern (intro.). Cambridge: Cambridge University Press.
[1800] 1978. *System of Transcendental Idealism*. P. Heath (trans.). M. Vater (intro.). Charlottesville: Virginia University Press.
[1802–3] 1988. *Philosophy of Art*. D. W. Stott (ed. & trans.). Minneapolis: University of Minnesota Press.
1856–61. *Sämmtliche Werke*. K. F. A. Schelling (ed.). Stuttgart: Cotta.

Secondary sources
Bowie, Andrew. 1990. *Aesthetics and Subjectivity: From Kant to Nietzsche*. Manchester: Manchester University Press.

Frank, Manfred. 1989. *Einführung in die frühroman-tische Ästhetik* [Introduction to Early Romantic Aesthetics]. Frankfurt am Main: Suhrkamp.

Jähnig, Dieter. 1966, 1969. *Schelling: Die Kunst in der Philosophie* [Art in Philosophy]. 2 vols. Pfullingen: Neske.

ANDREW BOWIE

Schiller, (Johann Christoph) Friedrich von

(1759–1805) German dramatist, poet, and philosopher; a major figure in the *Sturm und Drang* movement and in the Weimar culture of the late eighteenth century. All Schiller's philosophical writings, with the exception of an early dissertation on the mind–body problem, were devoted to aesthetic topics and are in the form either of letters or of essays. His reputation as a philosopher rests largely on his major work, *On the Aesthetic Education of Man* (1794–5), a series of 27 letters written to his patron, the Duke of Augustenburg and sometimes called his *Aesthetic Letters*.

His aesthetics has often seemed enigmatic. Its character is apparent from the dictum: "It is only through beauty that man makes his way to freedom" (1967: letter 2, para. 5), which sets the practical concept of freedom alongside the theoretical concept of beauty, crossing boundaries between ethics, politics, and aesthetics. Why Schiller elected to treat aesthetics in this dynamic manner requires explanation. His dictum, which has the ring of a political slogan, presupposes that humans are in a condition of un-freedom, which, Schiller believed, resulted both from social and economic divisions, devised by the human intellect, and from crude sensuality encouraged by materialism. The way he envisaged that this condition could be corrected depended on his theory of human nature, that "the will is the genetic characteristic of man as a species, and even reason is only its eternal rule" (1966: 193). Thus a powerful means for changing the will was needed. Schiller identified this as beauty.

He describes his inquiry as "concerning art and beauty" (1967: letter 1, para. 1), but does not discuss these concepts, being primarily concerned with their effects on moral character and action. What effects works of art have, if any, is a contingent matter and the concern of psychologists and sociologists; but Schiller was

claiming an a priori connection between beauty and freedom. He defines beauty as "freedom in appearances," and also speaks of it as the necessary means for attaining freedom. The claim "freedom only through beauty" can be taken in different senses – practical, as saying that a liberal society requires the development of aesthetic sensibility; and also theoretical, as attempting to bridge the Kantian gulf between the worlds of nature and freedom. The dual nature of his thesis is the expression of the duality of his own make-up as poet and philosopher. This complexity does not make for easy understanding, but his relentless defense of his thesis presents a refreshing challenge.

Although he is generally regarded as a Kantian, he endeavored to correct Kant's formalism and criticized his treatment of beauty in a correspondence with C. G. Körner, between January and March 1793, which was intended as the basis of a dialogue that never materialized (the book was to be titled "Kallias"). He attacked the subjectivity of Kant's theory, which treated the aesthetic as yet another compartment in an already overcompartmentalized theory of mind; and rejected his distinction between free and dependent beauty, because the formality of the former notion was unacceptable and the linking of beauty with perfection of a kind in the latter was too rational. Instead, he advanced his own view of beauty as objective, as pertaining to objects in the world of appearances, which linked beauty to the senses, as opposed to the intellect or subjective pleasure. He saw his theory as resolving the controversy between rationalist, empiricist, and idealist theories of beauty. But his tactics ignore the fact of aesthetic disagreement, and endow beauty with a mystical power to create harmony.

His ambiguous concept of aesthetic education refers not to an education in the fine arts but to his interest in an ideal humanity that can be achieved only through beauty and art. For Schiller, the ideal was not beyond the world of sensible appearances, as it was for Kant. It referred to wholeness in which reason and the senses are in tandem. It had already been exemplified in the rounded humanity of the ancient Greeks, and he believed that in order to correct "barbarian" and "savage" tendencies in human nature it must reemerge. But this leaves open the question of whether his main interest was the concept of beauty or the perfectibility of human nature. His definition of beauty as "living form" (1967: letter 15, para. 3) not only characterizes beautiful objects, but, he also claimed, creates beautiful human beings, showing how closely the public world of appearances was associated by him with the realms of consciousness and moral character – which prompted Hegel to comment (favorably) that Schiller's aesthetics was one of "totality and reconciliation."

His strategy for proving this large claim is cumbersome, for he employs two methods: one relating to evolution, which pertains to the world of nature; and the other to transcendental deduction, which is the tool of reason. By the latter method, two fundamental and necessary drives in human nature – the formal (*Formtrieb*), representing the rational, abstract aspect, and the sensuous (*sinnliche Trieb*), representing the concrete aspect of experience – are shown to be capable of being brought into an ideal equilibrium. From this state of psychological harmony the play drive (*Spieltrieb*) emerges.

Although this concept is derived from Kant's view of aesthetic judgment as the free play of the cognitive faculties, the idea that human beings reach their fullest potential when "playing" with beauty is Schiller's unique contribution. It introduces the notion of an aesthetic attitude as detachment from practical or intellectual concerns. The play drive is also treated as evolving from animal play (1967: letter 26), which is the result of a superfluity of energy; but the essence of aesthetic play is that it employs both sense and reason in a recreative harmony. Schiller's argument becomes convoluted because he not only argues that beauty is necessary for human wellbeing, but also shows how our psychological make-up can be conditioned by the effects of two kinds of beauty, energizing and melting, so that ideal beauty will be attained. But causal accounts do not establish anything of importance for aesthetics. Furthermore, psychological conditioning is inimical to education.

A more plausible account, showing that the development of aesthetic sensibility is essential for a liberal society, is given in terms of semblance (*Schein*). Aesthetic semblance, which is distinguished from illusion (1967: letter 26, para. 5), has to do with our ability to distance ourselves from matter through the special aesthetic senses of sight and hearing, and to create appearances by giving form to what is formless. Although it can be argued that touch and smell are also aesthetic senses, Schiller rightly implies that in an aesthetic context we are not concerned with physical properties of objects such as weight, volume, and so on, but with appearance of color, shape, texture, and sound. For Schiller, an interest in semblance is the hallmark of a liberal society, in which the conditions for egocentricity to flourish have been eradicated. Within the "joyous Kingdom of play" the Kantian virtue of dignity has been replaced by grace, which is a kind of beauty, applying to character as well as appearance and implying spontaneity and lack of constraint. Only the sketchiest outline of the ideal society is given (1967: letter 27).

Whether Schiller succeeds in showing that beauty can bridge the gap between the worlds of nature and freedom depends on the sense in which these terms are taken. The thrust of his argument is to establish the priority of the aesthetic dimension in human development. But he is inconsistent, sometimes speaking of the aesthetic as a transitional stage between nature and morality or freedom, and at others as the ultimate achievement for humanity. With regard to his aim of showing that beauty creates beautiful human beings, the difficulty of proof is considerable and too much is uncritically assumed. For example, aesthetic education takes it for granted that emotions can be trained. There are times in his argument when an ideal human nature takes priority. For instance, his concern to show that the ability to instill a mood of serene disengagement from any proclivity to action or intellectual activity is the mark of aesthetic excellence, leads him to overlook differences between art forms (1967: letter 22).

Schiller occupies a rightful place in the development of post-Kantian idealist aesthetics, although he was an eclectic thinker who drew on the theories of Goethe, Herder, Fichte, and Wilhelm von Humboldt, as well as those of Kant. His theory of beauty has been seminal. Croce's expression theory defends the priority of the aesthetic over other areas of human activity; and the concepts of living form, semblance, and aesthetic education have had an extensive influence on twentieth-century aesthetics.

Schiller's aesthetics also provides an introduction to standard problems – the definition of beauty; the question of an aesthetic attitude; what constitutes aesthetic excellence; the relation between art and morality. He has become a focus of interest for late twentieth-century British and Continental philosophers, especially the hermeneutic philosopher, Gadamer, whose defense of a liaison between philosophy and poetry is after Schiller's own heart.

See also NINETEENTH- AND TWENTIETH-CENTURY CONTINENTAL AESTHETICS; AESTHETIC ATTITUDE; AESTHETIC EDUCATION; GADAMER; KANT.

BIBLIOGRAPHY

Primary sources
[1793] 1966. "On the Sublime." In *Two Essays by Friedrich von Schiller: Naive and Sentimental Poetry and On the Sublime*. J. A. Elias (trans.). New York: Ungar.
[1794–5] 1967. *On the Aesthetic Education of Man.* E. M. Wilkinson & L. A. Willoughby (eds. & trans.). Oxford: Clarendon.

Secondary sources
Gardiner, Patrick. 1979. "Freedom as an Aesthetic Idea." In *The Idea of Freedom*. A. Ryan (ed.). Oxford: Oxford University Press, 27–39.
Kooy, Michael J. 2002. *Coleridge, Schiller, and Aesthetic Education*. New York: Palgrave.
Miller, R. D. 1970. *Schiller and the Ideal of Freedom*. Oxford: Clarendon.
Savile, Anthony. 1987. *Aesthetic Reconstructions: The Seminal Writings of Lessing, Kant and Schiller*. Oxford: Blackwell.
Schaper, Eva. 1985. "Towards the Aesthetic: A Journey with Friedrich Schiller," *British Journal of Aesthetics*, 25, 153–68.

MARGARET PATON

Schlegel, August Wilhelm von (1767–1845)   German poet, critic, and scholar. By the time of his death, with his younger brother Friedrich, August Schlegel was recognized as a founder of the modern Romantic school of German literature. In the classical–modern debate he generally favored the modern over the classical. He is important for his success in clarifying the meaning of romanticism via his distinction between classical (or ancient) and Romantic (or modern) forms of literature.

He was born into a literary family. His father, Johann Adolf, a high official in the Lutheran church, was a religious poet and a friend and associate of Gottlieb Rabener, Christian Gellert, and Friedrich Klopstock. His uncle, Johann Elias, was a dramatist. His brother, Friedrich, was a well-known poet and thinker, regarded as the most penetrating mind among the founders of German Romanticism. August studied theology and then philology at the University of Göttingen. After three years as a tutor in a private family, he lectured on aesthetics in Jena beginning in 1798, where, with his brother, the philosopher and poet Novalis, and Ludwig Tieck he laid the critical foundations of Romanticism. While in Jena, his wife left him for the well-known idealist philosopher, F. W. J. Schelling. From 1804 to 1817 he traveled in the entourage of Mme de Staël, whose *De l'Allemagne* ("On Germany") expands many of his views. He also studied oriental languages and became, in 1818, the first professor of Indology in Germany. He became professor in Berlin in 1819.

August Schlegel wrote dramas in the classical style and much verse, though without great success. He was a critic, producing his *Lectures on Dramatic Art and Literature* – widely recognized as a crucial statement of Romanticism – in 1809, and a translator: he translated *Bhagavadgita* (1823), the dramas of Calderón, and the poetry of Petrarch and Dante. With Tieck, he is most important for his translations of Shakespeare's plays.

The term "romantic" emerged in the second half of the seventeenth century in both England and France. It then meant "as in the romances," with special reference to medieval romances and Ariosto and Tasso. When the term arrived in Germany in the late eighteenth century, it was used as a synonym for "Gothic." It appears that Novalis invented the words *Romantik* and *Romantiker* at the end of the eighteenth century. For Novalis, the former meant someone who composed romances and fairy-tales, and the latter was synonymous with *Romankünstler*. Friedrich Schlegel defined romantic poetry as "progressive *Universalpoesie*." Slightly later he connected the term "romantic" with Shakespeare, Cervantes, and Italian poetry.

He considered that in his unromantic age only the novels of Jean-Paul (Richter) were romantic. He also claimed that all poetry must be romantic.

Statements of August's in several series of lectures, especially those delivered in Vienna in 1808–9, were more influential in fixing the image of Romanticism. (The contrast of the classical and the romantic is implicit, but not yet explicit, in the lectures on aesthetics given in Jena in 1798.) In the lectures that he gave in Berlin from 1801 to 1804, he compared the difference between the classical and the romantic with that between ancient and modern poetry. In this formulation, the romantic is progressive and Christian. In his account of romantic literature, he distinguished between form and content. He described the great Italian writers Dante, Petrarch, and Boccaccio as the founders of modern romanticism; despite their admiration for classical literature they struck out on their own, and their own form and expression were unclassical. Thus Dante, who admired Virgil, produced something different from and better than the *Aeneid*. This is also the case with Michelangelo and Raphael in the field of art. In Schlegel's typology, examples of romantic literature include the *Nibelungenlied* and other German heroic poems, the King Arthur and Charlemagne romances, and Spanish literature from *El Cid* to *Don Quixote*. Schlegel took up the theme again in his Vienna lectures, published in 1809–11, which were quickly translated into the major European languages.

The object of the Vienna lectures is both a general survey of drama in different periods and nations, and the exposition of a series of general ideas in order to evaluate their true artistic merit. Schlegel insisted that it is for the philosophical theory of poetry and of the fine arts to establish the fundamental laws of the beautiful. He associated the romantic/classical antithesis with those of the organic/mechanical and the plastic/picturesque. He opposed ancient literature and its neoclassical successor, a form of poetry allegedly representing perfection, to the romantic drama of Shakespeare and Calderón, that is supposedly representative of so-called infinite desire.

The influence of Schlegel's identification of romanticism with modern literature, as opposed to classical or ancient literature, was spread by other writers, especially through the efforts of Mme de Staël. Her *De l'Allemagne* appeared in 1813 in London, and was then republished in Paris in 1814, several months after a French translation of Schlegel's *Lectures on Dramatic Art and Literature*. Her restatement of his parallels of classical and sculpturesque, romantic and picturesque, helped to popularize his view. In this way, Schlegel's ideas exerted a decisive influence, first in France, where Stendhal was the first to declare himself a Romantic, and then throughout Europe – particularly Italy, Spain, Portugal, and Poland. In Russia, Pushkin labeled his *Prisoner of the Caucasus* a Romantic poem; and Coleridge, in England, made use of Schlegel's ideas in his lectures delivered between 1808 and 1818 and published later as *Shakespearean Criticism*.

See also CRITICISM; SCHLEGEL, F.

BIBLIOGRAPHY

Primary sources
[1809] 1884. *Lectures on Dramatic Art and Literature*. J. Black (trans.). London: Bell.
[1809] 1884. *Vorlesungen über schöne Kunst und Literatur*. Heilbronn: Henniger.

Secondary sources
Beiser, Frederick C. 2006. *The Romantic Imperative: The Concept of Early German Romanticism*. Cambridge, MA: Harvard University Press.
Haym, R. 1972. *Die Romantische Schule*. Darmstadt: Wissenschaftliche Buchgesellschaft.
Pinkard, Terry. 2002. *German Philosophy 1760–1860: The Legacy of Idealism*. Cambridge: Cambridge University Press.
Wellek, René. 1955. *A History of Modern Criticism*, vol. ii. New Haven: Yale University Press.

TOM ROCKMORE

Schlegel, Friedrich von (1772–1829) A many-sided cultural figure, Schlegel is best known with his brother, August, as one of the leaders of the German Romantic movement. He made contributions to the theory and practice of painting and to the evaluation of Gothic architecture, and he established Sanskrit studies in Germany. He lectured on philosophy and history, and on literature, of which he published an important history. He was also active as a diplomat. The son of a Lutheran minister, he was the youngest of five brothers. For more than a century he was less well known than his elder brother, August, but he is now generally regarded as a more significant figure. Many of the views that August later popularized were either restatements or modifications of Friedrich's ideas.

Friedrich initially studied law in Göttingen and Leipzig, but quickly abandoned it for literary pursuits. In 1804 he married Dorothea Viet, the daughter of Moses Mendelssohn. His novel *Lucinde* (1799), advocating free love and written while he was courting his future wife, who was married to someone else at the time, caused an enduring scandal. Both he and Dorothea converted to Roman Catholicism in 1808 – a change that was to be important for the later evolution of Schlegel's thought. Although his conversion was sometimes seen as the indirect result of the failure of August's marriage and his own subsequent break with his brother, Schlegel understood it as part of a continuous process. The conversion later led him away from certain of his early concerns, including his interest in the East arising out of his study of Sanskrit, and his pantheism. His religious views subsequently colored all his later writings.

As a lecturer at the University of Jena, Schlegel studied the ideas of Kant (which he rejected); those of Fichte, which remained a basic influence on his thought; and those of Schelling. In Berlin, he studied Schleiermacher, Spinoza, Leibniz, and Schiller. Like Schelling, Schlegel knew Fichte, whom he regarded as the greatest living metaphysical thinker even though he objected to the abstract character of Fichte's thought; the parallels between the views of Schlegel and of Schelling, insofar as both were influenced by Fichte's, led each to accuse the other of plagiarism.

With August, Friedrich founded and edited the journal *Athenaeum* (1798–1800), which laid the conceptual foundations of German Romanticism and was regarded by his contemporaries as the organ of the Romantic school. In 1802 he went to Paris, where he studied Sanskrit and Persian, lectured on philosophy, and edited the journal *Europa*. In 1808 he published *Über die Sprache und Weisheit der Inder* ("On the Language and Wisdom of the Indians"). He was appointed court secretary to Archduke Charles in 1809 and, after the peace of 1814, Metternich's representative from the Viennese court in Frankfurt. In Vienna, he lectured on modern history in 1810 and on ancient and modern literature in 1812. From 1820 to 1823, with Adam Müller he edited the review *Concordia*. His *Philosophie des Lebens* ("Philosophy of Life") appeared in 1828.

After Novalis, Schlegel was the outstanding literary theoretician of the first phase of Romanticism (the *Frühromantik*, c.1795–1801), and as philosopher and historian he was one of the main representatives of later Romanticism. His Romanticism evolved from what was initially an entirely classical approach to literature. The term "romantic" was employed beginning in about 1810 by the opponents of this tendency; the term "Romantic school" was popularized by Heine in 1836. Schlegel's theory, never stated in systematic form, can be deduced from his writings. Here we can look to a series of important articles published in *Athenaeum*, in which the term "romantic" was understood in an imprecise sense as "not classical." As well as the Schlegels, the contributors to this journal included Novalis, Schleiermacher, Ludwig Tieck, and the *Naturphilosoph* ("philosopher of nature") Hülsen.

The typical Romantic mixture of idealistic philosophy and romantic poetry reflects an alienation from contemporary society that is exemplified by Friedrich Schlegel's writings. He was concerned to find a way to take up the difference between the ancient and the modern, or the classical and the romantic, into a wider unity. He wrote essays entitled "Athenaeum Fragments," "On Goethe's Wilhelm Meister," "Ideas" and "Conversation on Poetry." In the *Athenaeum Fragments* Schlegel commented on philosophy and politics and formulated his literary theory. His main ideas are illustrated in the following, frequently cited, passage:

> Romantic poetry is a progressive universal poetry. Its destiny is not merely to unite all the separate genres of poetry and to put poetry into contact with philosophy and rhetoric. Its aim and mission is, now to mingle, now to fuse poetry and prose, genius and criticism, the poetry of the educated and the

poetry of the people, to make life and society poetic, to poeticize wit, to fill and saturate the forms of art with matters of genuine cultural value and to quicken them with the vibrations of humor. It embraces everything that is poetic, from the most comprehensive system of art . . . to the sigh or kiss which the poetic child expresses in artless song. It can lose itself so completely in its subject matter that one may consider its supreme purpose to be the characterization of poetic individuals of every kind, and yet there is no form better suited to the complete self-expression of the spirit of the author, so that many an artist who merely wanted to write a *Roman* willy-nilly portrayed himself. It alone can, like the epic, become a mirror of the whole surrounding world, a portrait of the age. And yet it can, more than any other art form, hover on the wings of poetic reflection between the portrayed object and the portraying artist, free from all real and ideal interests . . . [The] essential nature [of the romantic genre is] that it is eternally becoming and can never be perfected. No theory can exhaust it, and only a divinatory criticism could dare to attempt to characterize its ideal. It alone is infinite, as it alone is free; its supreme law is that the caprice of the author shall be subject to no law. The romantic genre is the only one that is more than a genre, but is, as it were, poetry itself, for in a certain sense, all poetry is or ought to be romantic. (Quoted in Eichner 1970: 57–8)

Writing in the wake of the French Revolution, Schlegel here regards romantic poetry, like Fichte's *Wissenschaftslehre* ("Theory of Knowledge") and Goethe's *Wilhelm Meister*, as corresponding to the spirit of the times and as surpassing all limits. What he calls progressive universal poetry is intended to unite all the different forms of poetry that it will bring into contact with philosophy and rhetoric. The aim in view is to be reached through irony and wit. Irony surpasses every limit and wit is understood as a fragmentary expression of genius that knows no bounds. Unlike other types of literature that have already attained fixed form and, hence, can be described, romanticism is and will remain in a state of becoming. It follows that a romantic work of art, be it philosophical or poetical, must retain a fragmentary character. Schlegel finds in romantic poetry the literary equivalent of the idealist conception of the subject as unlimited and, hence, as free.

See also IRONY; SCHLEGEL, A.

BIBLIOGRAPHY

Primary sources
1966. *Kritische Friedrich Schlegel Ausgabe.* E. Behler (ed.). Paderborn: Schöningh.
1978. *Kritische und Theoretische Schriften.* A. Huyssen (ed.). Stuttgart: Reclam.

Secondary sources
Beiser, Frederick C. 2006. *The Romantic Imperative: The Concept of Early German Romanticism.* Cambridge, MA: Harvard University Press.
Eichner, Hans. 1970. *Friedrich Schlegel.* New York: Twayne.
Pinkard, Terry. 2002. *German Philosophy 1760–1860: The Legacy of Idealism.* Cambridge: Cambridge University Press.
Wellek, René. 1955. *A History of Modern Criticism*, vol. ii. New Haven: Yale University Press, 5–35.

TOM ROCKMORE

Schopenhauer, Arthur (1788–1860) German philosopher; one of Kant's greatest critics, and a major influence, especially in ethics and aesthetics, on later writers, including Nietzsche and Wittgenstein.

Schopenhauer is unusual among the great philosophers in according to the arts a central place in his philosophical system. Schopenhauer saw himself as a disciple of Kant in his general philosophy, with the crucial difference that he thought it possible to know the nature of the reality that lies beyond sensuous experience, without resorting to the elaborate jiggery-pokery in which Kant indulged in his metaphysics of morality. Schopenhauer believed that the ultimate reality is will – more precisely, the will-to-live – ubiquitous and undifferentiated.

In our own everyday activity of willing we come into contact with this ultimate reality, though in a deceptive form, since each of us believes that he is a separate will: this is the fundamental error of the *principium individuationis*, but if we accept his arguments on the subject, Schopenhauer believes, we shall grasp that in fact we are all parts of the single will. This leads him directly to his most celebrated view, his pessimism. Since in willing, which we do all the time, we are trying to change the state we are in, it follows that that state is felt to be unsatisfactory. But as soon as we achieve what we were willing (something that occurs less often than we would wish), we are propelled into willing something else, that being our essential nature. But it is also the essential nature of everything else, so the world is a scene of perpetual frustration, with brief respites of boredom.

This drastic account of things would seem to leave no room for any consolation or mitigation, and our general unwillingness to acknowledge our plight adds a strong element of delusion to the already gloomy picture. But there is help at hand, and in a form sufficiently impressive to compromise Schopenhauer's pessimism considerably. For under certain circumstances we are able to suspend, if only temporarily, the activity of willing; and those circumstances are, in the first (and, for most of us, the only) place, when we are having an aesthetic experience. Accepting Kant's aesthetic theory as enthusiastically as he rejects his moral theory, Schopenhauer argues that in the presence of beauty we can practice "disinterested contemplation," seeing objects for their own sakes and not having, as we always otherwise do, any palpable designs on them.

But to this he adds an element that makes his theory of the visual arts and literature (music is altogether different, as we shall see) radically different from Kant's. It is one of the surprises of his philosophy that he announces a belief in Platonic ideas, though they have only the ontological, and not the normative, status that they possess for Plato. What this amounts to is that, in the contemplation of a work of art, its content ceases to be particular and assumes universality. So Schopenhauer combines a Kantian account of aesthetic experience with an Aristotelian account of its objects. His account of art is thus essentially cognitive, not perceptual, since perception is of particulars, while art is concerned with universals. Why this should make us eager to have aesthetic experiences remains unclear, however, since the Schopenhauerian universe is quintessentially undesirable. If it is painful to experience any emotion, for instance, it is not clear why it should be pleasurable to contemplate any emotion in its universal form. The fact that we are briefly released from wanting to act seems insufficient to account for the delight we take in art, granted what its subject matter is bound to be.

It could be claimed that Schopenhauer is in no worse a position than other theorists of art when they deal with "negative states," such as jealousy and betrayal: it is just that he does not admit that there are any positive states, such as fulfilled love – or, indeed, any kind of fulfillment. So it could be said that for him the whole of art presents the kind of problem that tragedy has traditionally presented for everyone.

It is no surprise that Schopenhauer puts a very high value on tragedy, but not for any of the traditional reasons. He finds in it the portrayal of the nothingness of life, so that it can serve to prepare us for our own cessation – indeed, make that cessation seem something devoutly to be wished for. In other words it preaches, in Nietzsche's contemptuous term (for this very theory), "resignationism." It helps to detach us from life, which we otherwise so absurdly cling to, despite its pervasive wretchedness. Whatever may be said against this theory, at least it avoids the usual glibness about "tragic affirmation." On the other hand, given Schopenhauer's general metaphysical views, it is not clear that the enticing prospect of ceasing to exist is one that we can actually accomplish. Since our usual view of ourselves as separately existing beings is radically mistaken, my ceasing to exist can come to no more than my no longer having the illusion that I exist in the sense that I normally think I do. It is as if we are all – to use an image that is Schopenhauerian in spirit though not in letter – pimples on the ocean of cosmic pus that constitutes the will, and resignation to my non-existence is acquiescence in rejoining the rest of the undifferentiated ocean. What that would come to is, of course, unimaginable, but it would hardly be the same as simple nonexistence.

The paradoxes that lie just beneath the surface of Schopenhauer's account of the visual and literary arts become much more striking when we consider his account of music, to which he accords a uniquely exalted status. Whereas the other arts involve representations and concepts, music dispenses with both of these, with the minor exception of onomatopoeic music (for instance, the birdcalls at the end of the second movement of Beethoven's "Pastoral" Symphony). Not being mimetic or expressive in any ordinary sense, music is, according to Schopenhauer, a direct *presentation* of the will, and is therefore to be prized uniquely. He even writes of "music or the world," and means what he says. This certainly puts music in a remarkable ontological position, while at the same time it renders Schopenhauer's eulogies of it all the more puzzling. In the first place, he regards his claim as true of all music (with the exception mentioned above), so that comparative qualitative assessments of different works are out of place – which seems strange. But that is a minor point compared with the further point that music is esteemed for presenting a reality which, in the rest of his work, Schopenhauer so comprehensively condemns.

The mixture, in his philosophy, of traditional and innovative elements here emerges as something very close to contradiction. Since, with remarkably few exceptions, Western philosophers have taken a view of reality that has led them to place a positive value upon it, something that represents it accurately would automatically inherit the favorable estimate of what it depicts. An alternative way in which mimetic art may be prized is in that it somehow transforms what it imitates, giving value to something that lacks it – or even, in the case of tragedy, to something that is acutely painful or has an otherwise negative value. But since Schopenhauer makes it the special glory of music that imitation or transformation is sidestepped – and so music is, as Nietzsche was later to put it, "the truly metaphysical activity of mankind" because it gives us the actual movements of the will – how does it come about that he is so ecstatic about it? Music certainly cannot be accused of misleading us if Schopenhauer is right, but why should we not want to be misled over such a sordid matter? To this question, it seems, he has no answer except the traditional one – which he should certainly have queried – that it is better to know the truth.

It appears that what Schopenhauer did was to make an attempt, in itself praiseworthy, to account for the extraordinary power that music has over us, or at any rate over many people – though in general, it would seem, not over philosophers. But in accounting for this power he overplays his hand badly, and produces nonsense on at least two levels: in the first place, it is wholly unclear how music can be identified with will, whatever interpretation we put on that term or concept, which is both central to Schopenhauer's metaphysics and extremely vague in the context of it. In the

second place, granted that the claim is meaningful, he has not succeeded in his task of explaining the value of music: on the contrary.

If he did have a plausible answer, it would no doubt be related to his Kantian insistence that in aesthetic experience our own wills are in abeyance, even if we are contemplating the single will itself. But this seems to be putting far too great an emphasis on the concept of disinterested contemplation – or, rather, getting it to do work for which it was not designed. It may be that in aesthetic experience "we keep the sabbath of the penal servitude of willing," as Schopenhauer put it with characteristic color. But it does not follow that not willing is in itself pleasurable or worthwhile, irrespective of what we contemplate when we are in this condition. A fortiori, it does not follow that willlessly contemplating the will is pleasurable, but that must be Schopenhauer's view. Perhaps it would be most plausible if he claimed that, from that vantage point, life became a farce, but he does not; though, were he to, his fervent admiration for Rossini would thereby be explained. For in the works by which Rossini is best remembered, especially his *Barber of Seville*, we have a kind of parody of the will-to-live. His characters are puppets, animated by nothing more than a vague demonic energy; but the fact that in these works Rossini taps a vein of malicious humor which is peculiar to him gives the lie to the general claim about music.

It has been argued, above all by Erich Heller in his book on Thomas Mann, *The Ironic German*, that it is because, and not in spite, of the profound confusions and ambiguities in his metaphysics, and especially in his aesthetics, that Schopenhauer has had so powerful an influence: not indeed on philosophers, who have for the most part ignored him since he died, as they did while he was alive – to his immense chagrin. But the list of artists who have been influenced by him, to whom reading him has come with the force of a revelation, is uniquely long and impressive. At their head is Richard Wagner, who read him first in 1854, and incessantly thereafter.

But Tolstoy, an utterly different artist, also praised him in the most abandoned terms, and began to translate his *magnum opus*, *The World as Will and Representation*. Turgenev, Zola, Maupassant, and especially Proust were other

European novelists on whom he made a lasting impression. And for Thomas Mann he was part of the constellation whose other members were Wagner and Nietzsche, under whose light he wrote his entire output. Among writers in English, Hardy and Conrad are the most notable figures who admired him. Less often mentioned is his impact on the remarkable Brazilian novelist Machado de Assis, whose masterpiece *Epitaph of a Small Winner* is clearly written under his aegis. In all these cases it can be argued that it was Schopenhauer's elevation of art at the expense of existence that had the greatest impact. The incongruity of this elevation was something that they overlooked: what may well have excited them was his pessimism, refreshing among philosophers, combined with the idea that they were equipped, as artists, with the means of offering consolation, or even escape. The more appalling the world, the more heroic the achievement of art in effecting its transfiguration.

There are two philosophers on whom Schopenhauer made an impression, though in neither case did it last. The first was Nietzsche, for whom, as for Wagner, encountering him was a revelation. His first book, *The Birth of Tragedy*, was written under their joint spell; he soon rejected both of them, though not before writing to them panegyrics of a strange kind. But Schopenhauer's "Romantic pessimism" was something that Nietzsche soon felt he had to transcend, though his replacement of the will-to-live by the will to power shows a residual influence. In the case of Ludwig Wittgenstein, the effect of Schopenhauer is most striking in the *Notebooks 1914–1916* and in the concluding passages of the *Tractatus*. But by the 1930s he had come to feel that "where true depth begins, Schopenhauer's runs out," and that may be taken as a harsh but finally just estimate of his work.

See also NINETEENTH- AND TWENTIETH-CENTURY CONTINENTAL AESTHETICS; FUNCTION OF ART; KANT; NIETZSCHE; TOLSTOY; WAGNER, WITTGENSTEIN.

BIBLIOGRAPHY

Primary sources
[1819/1844] 1969. *The World as Will and Representation*. 2 vols. E. F. J. Payne (trans.). New York: Dover.

2000. *Pareraga and Paralipomena*. Rev. edn. 2 vols. E. F. J. Payne (trans.). Oxford: Clarendon.

Secondary sources
Gardiner, Patrick. 1967. *Schopenhauer*. Harmondsworth: Penguin.
Hamlyn, D. W. 1980. *Schopenhauer*. London: Routledge & Kegan Paul.
Heller, Erich. 1981. *The Ironic German*. Cambridge: Cambridge University Press, ch. 2.
Jacquette, Dale (ed.). 1996. *Schopenhauer, Philosophy, and the Arts*. Cambridge: Cambridge University Press.

MICHAEL TANNER

science and art This entry focuses on differences between the enterprises and purposes that distinguish science and art.

Although science and art are both human activities, and respond in various ways to human interests, our interests in scientific activity will be directly and successfully served only by theories that (approximately) correspond to the way the world is, at least in their observational consequences. Our interests in pursuing scientific activity are not, of course, confined to representing the world. We may pursue science in order to manipulate the world, build bridges, fly planes, produce energy, and so on. We may be interested in scientific theories in order economically to summarize a mass of data, or for religious, metaphysical, or ideological reasons. Nevertheless, each of these interests is best served by theories that, at the observational level at least, fit the facts, or are judged in terms of their successes and failures in this respect. Even the investigator who wishes to use science to subserve some grander ideological scheme will come to grief if others can show that the empirical facts fail to confirm his scientific theories.

In most scientific theories there are elements that go beyond our powers to verify or check. There will always be an element of construction in the postulation of scientific theories, of imaginative leaping beyond the data. But checkable data must always support a theory if it is to be deemed successful scientifically. The reason for the need for an embedding of science in fact is clear; science is concerned with the description, explanation, and manipulation of a world that has an objective existence

525

apart from anything we might believe or feel about it.

In dealing with the world as it is, science has tended since the seventeenth century to abstract from the way things appear to us as human perceivers. The search for causal regularities in the world, central to the scientific aims of explanation and manipulation of physical phenomena, may well go hand in hand with a downplaying of aspects of phenomena that are important to us as perceivers and agents in the world. In its search for an observer-independent view of the world, science has demoted the qualities of color, sound, feel, taste, and touch, with which our phenomenal world is filled, to the status of "secondary" or response-dependent qualities.

Together with the displacement of the perceptual, the scientific drive for an observer-independent account of the world characteristically tends to reductionism; it will tend to see what appear to be many different things in terms of smaller numbers of fundamental entities and processes. Where what we are interested in is causal explanation and manipulation of the world, successful reductions of this sort will represent considerable intellectual advances, in that we will thereby be enabled to ignore those aspects of reality which are important only at a human or perceptual levels.

Science, then, attempts to investigate the world as it is in itself. It rescinds from observer-relative properties, it seeks theories of far-reaching application that abstract from differences at the phenomenal level, and the success of its theories is judged in terms of the way they are empirically borne out. In all these respects there are significant differences between art and science.

Artistic activity and expression are characteristically directed to stimulating experiences and reactions of various sorts in perceivers. They work, in the first instance, insofar as they succeed in doing this in the manner intended by the artist. Contemplating a Turner canvas, let us say, evokes the swell and pull of the sea. A Bach fugue may combine a sense of beauty of the theme with one of an imposing quasi-architectural structure. The exterior of a Georgian house conveys a sense of calm simplicity and order together with an unostentatious grandeur. With art, success is bound up with the responses, thoughts, and attitudes it evokes or might evoke in those who perceive it.

A work of art is an attempt to express some vision or attitude to the world from a consciously human perspective, and it will communicate this vision through the way it works on the perceptions or sensibility of its audience. From this fundamental difference between the theories of science and works of art, it obviously follows that artists cannot overlook the effects of secondary or response-dependent qualities.

As the world of art is first and foremost the world of human experience, it is arguable that artists should not seek the type of beneath-the-surface simplification and generalization rightly pursued in scientific inquiry. Human experience and activity, once clothed in cultural forms, develop new complexities and meanings. Thus, a rude hut is transformed into a Doric building, with columns and capitals, porticoes and plinths. New possibilities of balance, proportion, light and shade, surface and depth are thus opened up (and in this context it is notable that in the Parthenon, the most famous of all Doric buildings, the effect of balance and harmony is achieved by deviating from the mathematical identities and lines that a scientific theory might favor in order to give the observer the impression of harmony and balance). To the reductionist mind, any building is a shelter from the elements. but to emphasize the deep way in which all buildings are the same is to overlook the ways in which they are all different and the way these differences appear, affect, delight, matter, or give pain to us.

As artists operate in the world of human meaning and experience, they cannot avoid the superficial richness, complexity, and diversity of that experience, or the way cultural practices endow our experience with values and meanings. There can naturally be forms and styles of art that ape reductionism and simplification, which purport to show the skull beneath the skin and the universal animal lurking behind the performances and rituals of civilization. But the decision to take this direction will be an aesthetic one, not something forced on us by the nature of the discipline. And, as with other aesthetic simplifications, it is a decision that leaves the artist open to criticism for failing to do justice to the complexity of human experience.

A similar point can be made against theorists of art and of human psychology who claim that a certain building or painting gives us satisfaction because it is based on some mathematical formula, such as the golden section, to which our perceptual systems naturally respond. Even if it true that this figure is disposed to induce in the perceiver a sense of order, the mathematical figure itself provides at most the framework for the full aesthetic experience offered by a particular building or painting. A Mexican palace, a Greek temple, the Cancelleria, a sketch by Le Corbusier, and a figure in a Euclidean textbook may all be examples of the golden section, but, from the point of view of the experience of the perceiver, just as important as what they have in common are the differences between them, and the different feel that each thing will have for a perceiver, which patient attention to surface detail can articulate and explain.

Much the same can be said about attempts to analyze paintings in geometric terms, as when someone speaking about Piero della Francesca's *Baptism of Christ* starts to trace out geometric lines and shapes over the canvas. Even if it were true that Piero was influenced by mathematical considerations, to treat and conceive works of art simply in terms of some hidden mathematical essence is to obliterate their human and aesthetic meaning. In the case of the *Baptism of Christ*, emphasizing formal relationships at the expense of the rest of what is on the canvas will be to downplay or overlook altogether its tenderness, its peace, its religiousness, its poignancy, and its human and religious meaning generally. Similarly, analyzing the Cancelleria as just an example of the golden section will be to leave out of account how the beauty of architecture requires the addition of ornament to the harmony of proportion. And, as already remarked in dealing with the Parthenon, what counts even in the harmony of proportion is perceived harmony, which may actually require deviation from strict mathematical or scientific harmony.

There is, finally, one further important respect in which science differs from art, which again arises directly from science's aim of representing a world that exists independently of human response. In the light of this central aim of science, it is possible to speak of scientific progress, which will be measured by the increasing adequacy of succeeding theories in representing, revealing, and predicting parts of the physical world. We all know now, simply because science has progressed, that the earth is not the center of the universe and that there is no such stuff as phlogiston. But it would not be possible to say that we are better poets than Homer or Shakespeare – or, indeed, that poetry has made progress since Homer or Shakespeare. Part of the reason for this is that in poetry, as in the other arts, there is no external goal that remains constant over time, in terms of which success can be judged.

It is true, as T. S. Eliot remarked, that there is a sense in which we know more than the dead writers knew; part of what we know is the dead writers and their works, and, insofar as we see ourselves as operating within a particular tradition, knowledge of authorities within the tradition will be very important to later artists and audiences in order to learn the expressive potential of the tradition. Of course, this too is a difference between art and science. Contemporary scientists are interested in the truth or the empirical adequacy of theories, and to discover this they do not have to know about the work of their predecessors. By contrast, in the human world, of which art is a significant part, judgment of works inevitably refers to the response they evoke among those schooled in the tradition to which artists and audience alike belong.

See also AESTHETIC ATTITUDE; AESTHETIC PROPERTIES; COGNITIVE SCIENCE AND ART; COGNITIVE VALUE OF ART; EVOLUTION, ART, AND AESTHETICS; FUNCTION OF ART; OBJECTIVITY AND REALISM IN AESTHETICS; ONTOLOGICAL CONTEXTUALISM.

BIBLIOGRAPHY

Goodman, Nelson & Elgin, Catherine Z. 1988. *Reconceptions in Philosophy and Other Arts and Sciences*. London: Routledge & Kegan Paul.

Leavis, F. R. 1972. *Nor Shall My Sword*. London: Chatto & Windus.

O'Hear, Anthony. 1988. *The Element of Fire: Science, Art and the Human World*. London: Routledge & Kegan Paul.

ANTHONY O'HEAR

527

Scruton, Roger (b.1944)   As well as being noted as a political theorist and commentator on political and cultural affairs both in Britain and the USA, Scruton has written widely on aesthetics and on matters of taste in architecture, music, and the other arts.

In his inaugural lecture as professor of aesthetics at the University of London, Scruton attempted to restore the subject of aesthetics to the place of philosophical eminence once accorded it by Kant and Schiller, and from which it has been deposed by generations of analytic philosophers. Scruton's view stems from a bifurcation between the world revealed by scientific inquiry and that in which we live our daily lives, the *Lebenswelt* of the phenomenologists. In the scientific paradigm, the human subject is, as far as possible, eliminated: Scruton agrees with many contemporary analytic philosophers and philosophers of science in seeing science as aiming at an impersonal and absolute view of the world as it is in itself, and not necessarily as it is revealed to us in everyday experience. But unlike, say, Quine, Scruton is concerned to stress what is absent from the scientific paradigm and its construal of objective knowledge.

What is absent is precisely that "intentional understanding" by which we describe, criticize, and justify the world as it appears. Intentional understanding fills the world with the meanings implicit in our aims, actions, and emotions. The concepts and explanations generated in this understanding have evolved in answer to the needs of generations, and cannot be replaced by the deeper-level scientific accounts of the world, which, in their abstraction from appearance, can lead to an estrangement of the human subject from the world of appearance in which, perforce, he lives his life. As we will see, in his later aesthetic writings, Scruton has been concerned to discover in the aesthetic a remedy for the resulting desacralization and dehumanization.

In his books *Art and Imagination*, *The Aesthetics of Architecture*, and *The Aesthetics of Music* Scruton has developed an analysis of aesthetic judgment, grounding that judgment in the imaginative experience of the perceiver. In an analogy he uses more than once, he contrasts the pigments and blobs of paint a painting such as the *Mona Lisa* consists in as a physical object, no doubt analyzable ultimately in terms of physics, with how we actually see it as a painting and what the painting means. Similarly, a work of music consists of separate and discrete sounds, ultimately wave patterns in the atmosphere, to be sure, but that is not how we hear it. We hear it in an "acousmatic realm" where the sounds have an inner logic of perceived or imagined feeling and movement, a movement in which the music, without being a self, nevertheless has many of the attributes of a living spirit, endowed with gesture, rational agency, and freedom of consciousness. Precisely because music is nonrepresentational, this human charge is stronger than in the other arts. In listening to a piece of music, we enter its spirit and that of the community of other listeners, actual and potential, all of whom will be attentive to how the music engages them.

In stressing the ways in which works of art have to be experienced in order to communicate, Scruton wishes to distance himself from accounts of works of art which locate their significance in some message hidden beneath or outside the surface of their appearance, or which postulate the need for some quasi-linguistic decoding of the aesthetic. Aesthetic experience is, for Scruton, on the level of our shared everyday recognition of the fitting, the beautiful, the funny, the tragic, the bizarre, and so on. In works of art we have some kind of disinterested manifestation of the sensibility of the everyday; they and the criticism of works of art can be seen as the refinement of our understanding of the everyday. Aesthetic experience, indeed, is for Scruton as for Kant that which reveals the sense of the world for us as human beings, that sense of which science cannot speak and from which scientific accounts, while in their own terms presenting a complete account of what is, deliberately prescind. Some readers of Scruton may find at this point a trace of the very scientism from which he would rescue us. For at times he speaks of the aesthetic realm as if it were in some sense metaphorical, constructed by the imagination (visual, musical, or whatever), a realm of "as if," supervening on the physical. But why "as if"? Why metaphorical, *unless* we accord ontological priority to the perspective of science? Is the Mona Lisa's smile not as real as the underlying paint, the tragedy of Brahms's Fourth Symphony as real as the sound waves of which it is constituted?

In *The Aesthetics of Architecture*, Scruton is concerned to demonstrate by means of examples what the sense of particular given buildings is to the perceiver; how, by means of detail (or lack of it), a given building may come to appear serene or balanced or lively or theatrical or pompous, and so on. In his writings on music (and on popular culture), following in the honorable tradition of Plato and Nietzsche, he is anxious to show why some music (nearly all pop music) is banal and worse, and other music (much classical music) often by contrast deep and profoundly moving; he does so by pointing in detail to elements of the works he is describing which would be apparent to any attentive listener (which, in Leavis-like spirit, roots criticism in an implied community in which these judgments will be forged and tested). On one level, then, aesthetics is the systematic study of our experience of works of art, discussing them and judging them among a community of perceivers, which is itself developed in having those experiences and testing those judgments. In turning its attention to specific works and scenes in this way, it might be said to reveal the sense of the world, and for the reasons adduced first by Plato doing it well will be a work of the utmost importance both to individual sensibility and to public culture.

But in his subsequent writings, Scruton makes grander claims for aesthetics, linking it to religion and the decline of religion. Placing himself in the tradition of Kant, Arnold, Ruskin, and Wagner, Scruton wants aesthetics to reveal the sense of the world in the way natural theology tried to do and failed. It is through aesthetic contemplation that we feel the purposiveness and intelligibility, and even the personality, of everything that surrounds us; in it we get those imitations of the transcendental, of the world as somehow grounded, and of human life as sacred, which people once found in religion. It is precisely because they cannot accommodate this sense that Scruton rejects both the imperialistic claims of science to explain everything and the tenets of moral systems such as utilitarianism, which would treat human beings in accordance with some norm of scientific detachment and objectivity, analyzing their actions in abstraction from the contexts and contents which make them meaningful for their agents.

It is in a study of Wagner's *Tristan und Isolde* that Scruton has done most to develop his account of the religious dimension of art, and indeed to develop Wagner's famous claim that it is given to art to salvage the kernel of religion by revealing the deep truth concealed in the symbols of religion. The assumption of both Wagner and Scruton appears to be that as beliefs, the symbols are not true, not on their literal surface. What is true in religion, and what we are also given in *Tristan* and many great works of art, including in Wagner's case his other late operas, is a ritual in which redemption is enacted before us, and in which we participate. These works of art, in being experienced, give the lie to the modern temptation to see ourselves as animals, products of the natural order merely. They clear a way for us to regain the psychic space necessary to reinforce our sense of ourselves as sacred, free, individual, and responsible to an order other than the Darwinian. In experiencing them, like Parsifal, we redeem and are redeemed.

In the case of *Tristan* the redemption occurs because the lovers value their love to the point of renouncing all else for it, thus showing the nobility, worthwhileness, and transformative power of carnal love. In the experience of the opera we learn in a unique and practical way the inadequacy of treating sex as a purely animal function, as an entertainment in the service of the causality of our genes. For Wagner and for Scruton, in contrast to the orthodox Christian, it is not that the ritual symbolizes the doctrine but that the doctrine is an allegory of the ritual. Redemption occurs in the sacrifice itself, not (as in Christian orthodoxy) after or as a result of the sacrifice. Wagner (and some other artists) resacralize the key elements of our lives in a world desecrated by the effects of science and the loss of religion, by recovering a sacred order and meaning within.

While many readers would accept Scruton's analysis of aesthetic experience at what might be called the lower level, the quasi-religious role he claims for aesthetics and for works of art is likely to cause problems. For one thing, it is not clear how works of art can restore meaning of a sacred sort to the world in the absence of any religion or natural theology to frame them. Just what are the intimations of the transcendental intimating if, as Scruton says, the idea of God is something we can grasp only negatively? (The fact that similar problems are wrestled with in the poetry of Rilke is, though, testament to Scruton's depth, and to his distinctiveness in the world of analytic philosophy.) Moreover, the relationship between the world of science and the *Lebenswelt* of freedom, responsibility, and beauty is more difficult to understand than Scruton's simple Kantianism suggests. Nonetheless, many will admire his successive attempts to link the analysis of aesthetic experience and judgment with the experiences that perceivers of works of art actually have, and to place aesthetics firmly within the *Lebenswelt*. They will also admire his attempt to bring thinkers such as Arnold, Ruskin, Wagner, and Leavis within the scope of contemporary philosophy – which normally neglects such figures, and even the problems they wrestled with; philosophy's neglect notwithstanding, the problems that they and Scruton address are and remain central to the future of our culture.

See also TWENTIETH-CENTURY ANGLO-AMERICAN AESTHETICS; IMAGINATION; RELIGION AND ART; SCIENCE AND ART; WAGNER.

BIBLIOGRAPHY

Primary sources
1974. *Art and Imagination.* London: Methuen.
1979. *The Aesthetics of Architecture.* London: Methuen.
1984. *The Aesthetic Understanding.* London: Methuen.
1990. *The Philosopher on Dover Beach.* Manchester: Carcanet.
1997. *The Aesthetics of Music.* Oxford: Oxford University Press.
2004. *Death-Devoted Heart: Sex and the Sacred in Wagner's "Tristan and Isolde."* Oxford: Oxford University Press.

ANTHONY O'HEAR

seeing-in   *see* PICTURE PERCEPTION

senses and art, the   Art would seem to be linked to sense perception as other forms of human endeavor, such as mathematics or natural science, are not. These involve the senses as sources of evidence or channels for communication. In the case of art, in contrast, it is tempting to give the senses a more fundamental role. That role might be in defining the very idea of art – for instance, if it is essential to art of any form that it be the object of possible sense experience. Alternatively, it might be that particular senses play key roles in individual art forms – painting, for instance, being in some important way a visual art, music an art of hearing. Let us consider these in turn.

THE SENSES AND ART IN GENERAL
Could there be art among the angels? Beings with (let us suppose) intellect but no body, and hence no sense experience could, we might think, pursue mathematics or even – given access to observations made by others – science. But what could they know of art? Art, we might think, *exists in* the sensory. Certainly that idea runs through the writings of some of the most important philosophers of art – Plato, Kant, and Hegel are all committed to it in one way or another. It also plays a role in our everyday thinking. Consider, for instance, two central kinds of failure we take to be possible. An artist can fail by producing a work that does not embody in sensory form the ideas to which she aspired; and criticism of art can fail by presenting us with information that, while no doubt true, does not help us to perceive the work in novel ways.

Precisely what link between art and the senses do these thoughts motivate? Call *artistic properties* those features of a work the possession of which make it art, and give it whatever value it has as art. Then the following possibilities open up:

Knowledge: sense experience plays an essential role in our coming to know the artistic properties of the work.
Appreciation: sense experience plays an essential role in our appreciating (i.e., not merely knowing but enjoying or otherwise engaging with) the artistic properties of the work.
Constitution: sense experience plays an essential role in the work's having its artistic properties – and so in its being art, and possessing artistic value, at all.

Constitution looks better placed than *Knowledge* to capture the idea that art is importantly connected to the senses. For it promises to explain *Knowledge*. If the senses play a key role in objects' even possessing whatever properties make them works of art, it is easy to see why sense experience is the primary route to knowing those properties. In contrast, *Knowledge* does not seem well placed to explain *Constitution*. If *Constitution* is not to be brute, its explanation will lie not in *Knowledge* but in *Appreciation*. There is something very odd about the idea of artistic properties that could not be appreciated (by anyone, at any time). Artistic properties are essentially appreciable. But then, if appreciation involves sense experience, as *Appreciation* claims, artistic properties will be essentially experienceable, as *Constitution* asserts. Now, we could as easily run the explanation in the other direction. It is because artistic properties are effects on sense experience that appreciation of them is a matter of experiencing the work in the right way. *Appreciation* and *Constitution* are thus best seen as two aspects of a single important fact about art, with *Knowledge* as a consequence.

If this is the way to articulate the idea that art is bound to the senses, it faces two serious challenges. The first is that some arts seem much less intimately related to sense experience than others. Perhaps, if there is to be music it must be heard; and if there is to be painting it must be seen. But what of literature? Of course, if literature is to be shared, it must be taken in somehow, and the senses provide that service. But why think that their role here is greater than in mathematics? A poet could presumably write and appreciate his own verse using only thought and memory. Only contingent limitations on the power of those two faculties prevent a novelist from doing the same. Thus individuals can in principle create and appreciate literary art without using the senses. If the senses play a major role in our actual engagement with art, that reflects only the fact that we generally choose to share art, and have limited means for doing so.

We might offer two responses. The first is that literature is an art of sound. This was true of its origins – the first literary works were the spoken paeans, odes, and epic poems of the ancient world. But even once it became customary to write works down, and to appreciate them by reading in silence, this heritage lived on. Even when reading silently to oneself, one appreciates literature in key part by engaging with the sound of the words out of which it is composed. The same will be true of our soliloquizing poet: he is appreciating ideas expressed in sound, for all that he is not literally hearing anything. He does so by using hearing's nearest neighbor: the auditory imagination. To allow such a role for the imagination is to refine, rather than abandon, the idea that art is bound to the senses. The various sensory modes (sight, hearing, touch, and so forth) have their analogues in imagining (visualizing, imagining sounds, imagining the touch of things, etc.). If *Appreciation* and *Constitution* have to be interpreted as describing roles played by either sensory experience or sensory imagining, they still make substantive claims.

The thought that we might legitimately supplement sense experience with sensory imagining also leads naturally to the other response. This gives a role to the sensory in defining, not the vehicle of literary art, but its content or subject matter. On this proposal, literature, like all art, is *about* the sensory. Poetry in any form, drama, short stories, and novels all concern the world as we experience it through our various senses. They are able to do so because the sensory imagination brings that world before us even when our current sensory experience is confined to the sight of words on a page, or – if we silently recite a poem from memory – less.

Is it, however, true that art is always about the sensory? Of course a great deal of literature concerns the world we experience through the senses. But that might simply be because that is how so much of the world is known to us at all. As soon as we move beyond our own feelings and the most abstract ideas, we are concerned with things our senses make available to us. If the response is not to exploit unfairly the sheer reach of the senses, it should be more precise. The claim should be that literature necessarily concerns, not merely those things that can be experienced by the senses, but the sensory aspect of things. So refined, however, the claim is not obviously true.

That leaves untouched the first response, that sound is the vehicle of literary art. But even if this is true of literature, there are other art forms at least as tenuously connected to the senses, for which no parallel maneuver is possible. Conceptual art in particular seems not to involve the senses in any but banal ways. Of course, if conceptual art is to be shared, others must somehow grasp its nature, and that inevitably involves sense experience. But, sharing aside, it is not clear that a conceptual artist need produce anything that might be sensed As with our lone poet, she might simply do it all "in her head." Nor is it at all obvious that whatever she does must involve the sensory imagination, as providing either the content of the work or its vehicle. Nothing stands to conceptual art as, arguably, sound stands to literature. And conceptual art's topic, we might think, is also without sensory character. As the name perhaps suggests, ideas form both its subject matter and its medium.

The other serious challenge to *Appreciation* and *Constitution* applies even in the context of those arts for which the senses do play a central role. In every art some of what we appreciate apparently lies beyond the reach of sense experience, and so hardly depends on that experience for its existence. We value, for instance, the various ways in which works of art develop, challenge, or overturn the artistic traditions from which they spring. Their doing this is a matter of the history of that tradition, of how the work relates to those that came before and after it. Is this the kind of property we can take in through the senses? Not obviously – but if not, not every artistic property fits the bill *Appreciation* and *Constitution* describe.

Faced with this second challenge, those seeking to establish a close tie between art and the senses have generally resorted to one of two strategies. Some (Beardsley 1958; Lessing 1965) seek to limit their claims to a subset of artistic properties. Properties such as beauty, grace, clumsiness, and harmoniousness are indeed essentially sensory. Properties such as breaking with tradition are not. Given the word's etymology, it is natural to label the first group of properties *aesthetic*.

Others hope to stick with the idea that *all* artistic properties are bound to the senses. They see the second challenge above as turning on an impoverished conception of what the senses provide. If sense experience must stand alone, then it is true that a good deal of what we value in art eludes its grasp. It need not, however, stand alone. We see and hear more when we draw on knowledge of what we are perceiving than when we do not. Knowledge of what is before us can inform how we experience it, thereby drawing within the reach of experience even such properties as breaking with tradition. Perhaps some artistic properties elude the experience of the ignorant. That of the well-informed, however, reaches out to all that is of consequence in art (Wollheim 1987, 1993; see also Davies 2006).

Whether either strategy succeeds is open to question. The first threatens to divide the realm of artistic properties implausibly. As just noted, even historical properties, such as breaking with tradition, *can* be experienced, given the right background knowledge. Why, then, privilege the experience of the ignorant in drawing the line between those artistic properties that are aesthetic and those that are not? The second strategy avoids this issue, since it does not divide artistic properties at all. But it does make claims about the way knowledge extends the reach of the senses that might be challenged on empirical grounds (Danto 2001). Even if those claims are correct, questions remain. Molding experience, in the light of knowledge, to reflect every aspect of a work's artistic nature will be of little use if the relation between the two remains too tenuous to count as appreciation. That would certainly be so if the experience reflected the thing's nature only *by accident*. Appreciation should involve more than mere coincidence between how the work is and how it seems to the spectator – it requires the latter to count as *perception* of the former. Now, provided experience has been aligned with the work's nature by deploying knowledge of that nature, the alignment between the two will not be accidental. It does not follow, however, that their relation is perceptual. That, we might think, precisely requires experience to reflect the work under its own steam, and not only with the assistance of independently acquired knowledge. If appreciation does require perception, expanding the reach of sensory experience in this way is not enough to save *Appreciation* (and so *Constitution*) from the original counterexamples (Hopkins 2006).

PARTICULAR SENSES AND PARTICULAR ART FORMS
Whether or not art in general is bound to sense experience in its various forms, particular arts may be bound to particular senses in important ways. Certainly this thought has a long history (Herder 2002 [1778]). It is easy to see why. How could we begin to understand painting without the idea that it is an especially visual art, or music without the acknowledgment that it is an art of sound? Other arts may be harder to place. There has been vigorous debate over whether sculpture, for instance, is an art of touch (Read 1956), of sight (Carpenter 1960), or both. However these debates should be settled, it is not hard to feel that the answer promises to reveal something important about that art form.

Those attracted to such ideas again face the question of precisely how art and sense experience are related. We might frame art- and sense-specific versions of our key options earlier:

Appreciation: sense experience in modality M (e.g., vision) plays an essential role in our appreciating the artistic properties of works in art form A (e.g., painting).
Constitution: sense experience in M plays an essential role in works in A having their artistic properties, and so in their being art, and possessing artistic value, at all.

Note that the earlier distinction between the vehicle and content of a work in effect divides *Appreciation* in two. In the case of painting, for instance, the proposal might be that vision plays a role in our appreciating key properties of the vehicle – the color and distribution of the paint on the surface; or that it plays such a role in our appreciating key aspects of what is represented – the shapes, colors, and other properties of the depicted scene. (Of course, it might be that painting is visual in both these ways.) However, these are not the only ways in which we might seek to link art forms to senses. Painting might be visual in the sense that the *way* in which it represents the space it depicts has important structural similarities with the way in which vision represents the world (Hopkins 2004). And, while the options just described naturally apply only to representational art forms (for where there is no representation, there is no content, or way of representing things), analogues of some form might be available even in some abstract arts. We might, for instance, explore the idea that even absolute music can be appreciated as expressing emotion only by those with sense experience of emotional behaviors.

It may even be that some of these ways of connecting arts to senses reveal something important about the senses themselves. For instance, if what links painting (and the other pictorial arts) to vision is the way in which each represents space, that might be because that way of representing space is what defines the category of the visual – a category that has a perceptual manifestation (vision), an imaginative one (visualizing – assuming that it too represents its objects in this way), and a manifestation in the realm of external representations (picturing) (Hopkins 1998: ch.7).

However that may be, we should beware overconfidence about these connections. There is a strand of thinking in contemporary cognitive science and philosophy of mind that is skeptical about the very idea that perceptual experience neatly divides into different sensory modalities. And even those art forms that seem most securely tied to particular forms of sense experience (supposing there are such), turn out to be related to the senses in ways that are more fluid than we might have thought. Painting, we might think, is deeply visual only because that is true of the pictorial arts in general – drawing, etching, and photography included. Yet it is possible for people who lack vision, and indeed have done so since birth, to understand and even to create raised-line drawings that, prima facie, have good claim to count as pictures (Lopes 1997). This suggests that picturing, and so in principle the pictorial arts, are at least as tactual as visual – if, indeed, it is at all useful to categorize by their relations to the traditional five senses. Pictures may be visual in the sense that they are accessible to/appreciable in vision, but they are not so, it is tempting to conclude, in the sense that that is the *only* sense through which we may engage with them.

See also LITERATURE; MUSIC AND SONG; POETRY; SCULPTURE; ABSTRACTION; AESTHETIC PROPERTIES; CONCEPTUAL ART; DEPICTION; FORGERY; REPRESENTATION; TRADITION; TRAGEDY.

BIBLIOGRAPHY

Beardsley, Monroe C. 1958. *Aesthetics: Problems in the Philosophy of Criticism*. New York: Harcourt, Brace & World.

Carpenter, Rhys. 1960. *Greek Sculpture*. Chicago: University of Chicago Press.

Danto, Arthur C. 2001. "Seeing and Showing," *Journal of Aesthetics and Art Criticism*, 59, 1–9.

Davies, David. 2006. "Against Enlightened Empiricism." In *Contemporary Debates in Aesthetics and the Philosophy of Art*. M. Kieran (ed.). Malden: Blackwell, 22–34.

Herder, Johan Gottfried. 2002 [1778]. *Sculpture*. J. Gaiger (trans.). Chicago: University of Chicago Press.

Hopkins, Robert. 1998. *Picture, Image and Experience*. Cambridge: Cambridge University Press.

Hopkins, Robert. 2004. "Painting, Sculpture, Sight and Touch," *British Journal of Aesthetics*, 44, 149–66.

Hopkins, Robert. 2006. "Painting, History and Experience," *Philosophical Studies*, 127, 19–35.

Lessing, Alfred. 1965. "What is Wrong with a Forgery?" *Journal of Aesthetics and Art Criticism*, 23, 461–72.

Lopes, Dominic M. M. 1997. "Art Media and the Sense Modalities: Tactile Pictures," *Philosophical Quarterly*, 47, 425–40.

Read, Herbert. 1956. *The Art of Sculpture*. London: Faber.

Wollheim, Richard. 1987. *Painting as an Art*. London: Thames & Hudson.

Wollheim, Richard. 1993. "Danto's Gallery of Indiscernibles." In *Danto and His Critics*. M. Rollins (ed.). Oxford: Blackwell, 28–38.

ROBERT HOPKINS

sentimentality Michael Tanner, no doubt with an eye to Oscar Wilde's remark that "One would have to have a heart of stone to read the death of Little Nell without laughing," tells of his reaction to Dickens's *Martin Chuzzlewit*. Whatever the book's other merits, Tanner complains about certain characters who, he claims, "hijack" its final chapters. These characters are "examples of impossibly virtuous, endlessly put-upon, shockingly exploited figures who remain trusting, gentle, only happy in the happiness of others, resilient to the point of imbecility, and of course unafflicted by the desires of the flesh, by jealousy of those they love but are not loved by – the kind of thing that any cultivated reader of this very great novelist

comes to expect and to dread" (2006: 312). Tanner suggests that the best way to express his reaction to these characters is to acknowledge that they are "intolerably sentimental." Tanner stands in good company with many other philosophers and aestheticians who see sentimentality as an aesthetic, and possibly also an ethical, flaw or fault.

Things were not always so. A perusal of the literature shows at least three broad reactions to sentiment and sentimentality that emerge in something like a historical sequence. First, philosophers such as Adam Smith and authors of fictions such a Henry Mackenzie's *The Man of Feeling* felt that the sentiments were an important feature of human psychology and that works of art that focused on issues concerning them were good and desirable. Indeed, the education of the sentiments was considered a positive thing to which the arts generally, and the narrative arts in particular, can contribute. In due course, however, sentiment and sentimentality came under attack as weak and possibly deplorable ways to engage audiences' interest in works of art, including works of narrative arts. Robert C. Solomon lays the blame for the move from an ethical theory interested in cultivating the emotions to an ethical theory interested in reason at the expense of the emotions squarely at the feet of Immanuel Kant. Recently, the view that sentimentality is an aesthetic and ethical scourge has been challenged. Solomon, who is very much interested in rehabilitating a pre-Kantian view of the sentiments, has been paramount in coming to the defense of sentimentality.

There is no particular class of objects that characteristically elicits a sentimental response. Nor, obviously, is there agreement that sentimental responses are inevitably objectionable on either aesthetic or ethical grounds. Sentimental responses keyed to the so-called tender emotions (i.e., compassion, fondness, caring, and so forth) can take a variety of objects, ranging from fictional heroes struggling to succeed in a quest to particularly adorable children. Sentimental responses can be triggered by narrative fictions, musical works, sporting events, public events, and ceremonies ranging from the Rose Bowl Parade to weddings, infant mammals of nearly all sorts including babies, and so on. Sentimental responses are often keyed to objects deemed to be poignant, stirring, cute, sweet, darling, charming, cuddly, or pretty. It is a question just when the sentimental turns into kitsch. Anne Geddes' charming photographs of children might teeter on the borderline, but arguably Thomas Kinkade's paintings of impossibly romantic cottages and idyllic townscapes have crossed over. However, not everyone agrees that sentimentality is primarily a matter of appealing to the tender emotions. Anthony Savile has argued that sentimentality is not itself an emotion or even a group of emotions but rather a mode of thought and feeling. Sentimentality, Savile would say, distorts particular thoughts and emotions. Thus emotional responses such as anger or pride, jealousy or patriotism, could be distorted and thus sentimentalized.

When philosophers of art and aestheticians complain about sentimentality – and of course not all do complain – the negative view is usually presented in terms of an excessive appeal to easy or cheap emotions. The objection is that sentimental emotions are easily tapped and are thus somehow of lesser value than emotions that require more challenging or compelling circumstances in order to be elicited. To clarify, opponents of sentimentality do not necessarily reject the importance of emotional responses to works of art. Savile's nice phrase captures what he finds objectionable in sentimentality: he says it causes us to "false-color the world." Some argue that sentimental responses typically inhibit us from taking necessary real-world action because we remain basking in the luxury of our own mostly self-regarding sentimental responses. Critics agree that sentimentality is not just an aesthetic fault but an ethical fault as well. Works of art that prescribe sentimental responses are thought to pander, and people who are disposed to excessively emotional responses are thought to be self-regarding, self-deceived, or worse.

To say that sentimentality in the post-Wilde period is typically condemned is no overstatement. Consider Mark Jefferson: "It is generally agreed that there is something unwholesome about sentimentality: it would certainly be a mistake to think it a virtue" (1983: 519). Joseph Kupfer (1996) goes the extra step and calls

sentimentality "a deceptive, dangerous vice." Where Savile suggested that sentimentality "false-colors" the world, Kupfer argues that the sentimentalist – to adapt Savile's language – comes to "false-color" herself. To respond sentimentally to life or to art, Kupfer claims, is to respond in a morally impoverished, apathetic, yet oddly self-aggrandizing way. The sentimentalist fails ethically as well as aesthetically by making herself the focus of a sentimental, or perhaps more accurately, a sentimentalized experience, and thus is incapable of treating the stimulus situation or object with the proper degree of distance and analysis.

I use the feminine pronoun intentionally in this example since sentimentality is typically associated with overly emotional reactions by women, a point noted by Solomon (2004: 6). Historically, this prejudice goes back to the emergence in the eighteenth century of so-called sentimental literature written by women (pot-boilers, melodramas, and such). It is noteworthy that sentimental literature, in its prime, was also written by men and that some examples, for instance Flaubert's *L'Education sentimentale*, are still considered canonical. Not only is sentimentality condemned by its critics for reasons that perpetuate tiresome gender stereotypes (the sentimentalist is passive, emotional, self-indulgent, in short, womanish). The complaint is that, judged in either aesthetic or ethical terms, the sentimentalist gravitates toward the easy, the shallow, the fantastic, or the irrational. Solomon sees here the workings of a Kantian-inspired rejection of the emotions at the expense of reason in ethical judgments.

It is hard to see how to mount an effective defense of sentimentality even if one finds the sorts of criticisms typically lobbed at the sentimentalist and at sentimental art reductive and predictable. The agenda concerning sentimentality appears to be very much in the control of sentimentality's critics. Apparently, as Jefferson has remarked, sentimentality just cannot be a virtue. Hume once told us that the word "virtue" implies praise. It does not seem logically possible, Hume might have continued, to treat "virtue" as a term of criticism or condemnation, although Nietzsche goes some way to proving Hume wrong. Still, it is hard to envisage "sentimentality" being treated positively, as for instance something aesthetically meritorious or ethically virtuous. The terms of the debate seem to be set against the recuperation of sentimentality. Excessive emotional responses undertaken by the sentimentalist for her own self-indulgence just do seem an ethical weakness, and if the object of those responses is a work of art, it is at least possible that the weakness is in part aesthetic as well.

Notwithstanding the consensus against the sentimental, Robert Solomon defends sentimentality against its critics. His view is that there is "*nothing wrong*" with sentimentality as such. Solomon admits that excessively emotional responses can be a problem, but the problem lies in the excess, not in the sentiment. Sentimentality, as Solomon understands it, is nothing more nor less than the "appeal to tender feelings." Sentimentality has at least four distinct senses, which Solomon distinguishes as follows. The so-called "minimal definition" says that sentimentality should be understood in terms of the tender emotions. The "loaded definition" invokes emotional weakness or excessive emotional response. The "diagnostic definition" points to the self-indulgence of sentimental responses. Finally, the "epistemological definition" looks to false or fake emotions (2004: 8). It is the minimal definition that Solomon is interested in, since plainly the other three are committed to a negative view of sentimentality.

The idea that sentimentality should be construed as "a matter of moral bad taste" strikes Solomon as wrong-headed. Indeed, it is Solomon's view that narratives that count as sentimental because they draw attention to emotions such as pity, sympathy, fondness, adoration, compassion, and so forth (2004: 9) contribute to the general education of the emotions. Rather than condemning sentimental narratives for overstepping their emotional warrant, Solomon insists that engagement with narratives that foreground emotional response helps readers and viewers to rethink and therefore develop their own emotional capacities. Key to Solomon's position is that from roughly Wilde onward, mere sensitivity – which is to say, openness to the tender emotions – has been conflated with, and dismissed as, sentimentality. Yet it is hard to see just what exactly is wrong with the viewer who cries or

is otherwise emotionally distressed at the end of Vidor's *Stella Dallas* or Curtiz's *Casablanca*. To fail to appreciate the poignancy of these films – the thwarted hopes of the protagonists, their decisions to put the welfare of others before their own, in short their self-sacrifice – is in an important way to miss their point. Only those with a real antipathy to emotional responses would imagine that there is something pathological or irrational about responding emotionally to such narratives. Whether our examples are genre films such as *Stella Dallas* and *Casablanca*, or literary works such as *Pride and Prejudice* and *Atonement*, we must acknowledge that as competent viewers and readers, we are required to respond in emotionally appropriate ways. If it is acceptable to respond in an emotionally appropriate way to *Oedipus Rex* or *Hamlet*, why should it not be equally appropriate to respond emotionally to other works that involve emotions such as compassion?

But of course, sentimentality is thought to involve an excessive, possibly irrational emotional response that causes the sentimentalist to misrepresent her world to herself. The question in part becomes, who decides, and on what basis, what counts as excessive? As Solomon notes, the usual complaints about sentimentality involve the idea that "sentimentality is distorting, self-indulgent, self-deceptive." Where this is true, it is arguably blameworthy. If Solomon is right, these extreme sorts of emotional responses are atypical and signs that the responses in question are unwarranted. While sentimentality, understood in terms of excess and distortion, will arguably continue to be a term of condemnation, there is clearly both room and reason to consider positively our emotional responses to works of art.

See also KITSCH.

BIBLIOGRAPHY

Jefferson, Mark. 1983. "What is Wrong with Sentimentality?" *Mind*, 92, 519–29.

Knight, Deborah. 1999. "Why We Enjoy Condemning Sentimentality: A Meta-Aesthetic Perspective," *Journal of Aesthetics and Art Criticism*, 57, 411–20.

Kupfer, Joseph. 1996. "The Sentimental Self," *Canadian Journal of Philosophy*, 20, 543–60.

Newman, Ira C. 2008. "The Alleged Unwholesomeness of Sentimentality." In *Arguing About*

Art. 3rd edn. A. Neill & A. Ridley (eds.). London: Routledge, 342–53.

Savile, Anthony. 1982. *The Test of Time: An Essay in Philosophical Aesthetics.* New York: Oxford University Press.

Solomon, Robert C. 2004. *In Defense of Sentimentality.* New York: Oxford University Press.

Tanner, Michael. 1976. "Sentimentality," *Proceedings of the Aristotelian Society,* 77, 127–47.

Tanner, Michael. 2006. "Review of Solomon's In Defense of Sentimentality," *British Journal of Aesthetics,* 46, 312–13.

DEBORAH KNIGHT

Shaftesbury, Lord [Anthony Ashley Cooper, third Earl of Shaftesbury] (1671–1713) English moral philosopher and man of letters; prevented by ill-health from the political life usual in his family. Shaftesbury has some claim to the title of founder of modern aesthetics. He was brought up in the household of his grandfather, the first earl, who was actively involved in the politics of the Restoration. His education was placed in the hands of the first earl's friend and supporter, John Locke, though it took a more classical pattern than Locke's own model. Shaftesbury acknowledges this debt, though he later qualifies its extent:

> From the earliest infancy Mr. Locke governed according to his principles . . . I was his more peculiar charge, being as eldest son taken by my grandfather and bred under his care, Mr. Locke having the absolute direction of my education, and to whom next my immediate parents, as I must own the highest obligation, so I have ever preserved the highest gratitude and duty. (1900: 332)

One of the interesting questions about Shaftesbury concerns the way in which his classicism is modified by Lockean empiricism, even though Shaftesbury himself specifically rejects Locke's ideas.

Shaftesbury was fundamentally a moralist. Three factors shaped his moral theory. He was a country Whig who defended both the rights and the obligations of his class. He was an opponent of Hobbes, and attempted to establish a public interest in place of the self-interested egoism that he attributed to Hobbesians. And he was a sentimentalist who found the basis for moral judgment in a moral sense.

In practice, Shaftesbury advocated a Neoplatonic form of classicism. His first published work was an introduction to a collection of sermons by Benjamin Whichcote, and he was familiar with the Cambridge Platonists. The internal sense that Shaftesbury introduces into his Neoplatonism is not bare sense perception, and it undoubtedly retains something of earlier, Augustinian, connotations. Augustine, also, spoke of an interior sense which "is in some kind of way a ruler and judge among the other senses . . . The interior sense judges the bodily senses, approving their integrity and demanding that they do their duty, just as the bodily senses judge corporeal objects approving of gentleness and reproving the opposite" (1983: 37; see also Augustine 1993). Augustine subordinates the interior sense to reason, however, and Shaftesbury likewise distrusts mere sense. The difference between them lies in Shaftesbury's conversion of interior sense into a moral source, so that virtue is known by the feelings that it is capable of producing under the influence of a moral sense. Thus Hobbes's total reliance on egoistic self-interest is countered by a natural impulse for the good that is nonegoistic, according to Shaftesbury. One has direct empirical verification of that good through the moral sense.

The connection between virtue and beauty is close. It begins with a typical Neoplatonic equation: "I am ready enough to yield there is no real good beside the enjoyment of beauty. And I am as ready, replied Theocles, to yield there is no real enjoyment of beauty beside what is good" (1964: 141). That identity is explicated in terms of an immediate sense response, which can be taken as an aesthetic sense paralleling the moral sense:

> [The mind] feels the soft and harsh, the agreeable and disagreeable in the affections; and finds a foul and fair, a harmonious and a dissonant, as really and truly here as in any musical numbers or in the outward forms or representations of sensible things. Nor can it withhold its admiration and ecstasy, its aversion and scorn, any more in what relates to one than to the other of these subjects. So that to deny the common and natural sense of a sublime and beautiful in things will appear an affectation merely, to any only who considers duly of this affair. (1964: 251–2)

Thus Shaftesbury moves from a harmony between the intelligible and sensible worlds to a harmony within the senses themselves. In so doing, he shifts aesthetic judgment in the direction of Locke, no matter how much his own classicism leads him to distrust Locke's bourgeois reliance on mere sense. Francis Hutcheson sees the possibilities implicit in this shift, and develops them into a full theory of aesthetic sensibility.

Shaftesbury is also given credit for introducing "disinterestedness" into modern aesthetics (Stolnitz 1961). For example, Shaftesbury claims: "In all disinterested cases, [the heart] must approve in some measure of what is natural and honest, and disapprove what is dishonest and corrupt" (1964: 252). But the case is complex. Shaftesbury is not concerned to eliminate interest, but to guide and correct it so that one's true interests are discovered. In an essay entitled "Plastics," that is plastic form, he explains that "the great business in this (as in our lives, or in the whole of life) is 'to correct our taste'. For whither will not *taste* lead us?" (1914: 114). Neither the aesthetic sense nor taste can be relied on, in the absence of reflection. Disinterestedness is a possibility in contrast to pure self-interest, but both must be corrected by a number of practical tests, including the approval over time of an educated public and correction by discourse and even raillery. Shaftesbury's use of "disinterestedness" does not denote a special aesthetic attitude, therefore, and it is not opposed to moral and critical examination.

Shaftesbury's place as a founding father of modern aesthetics rests on his practical concern with art and the education of taste more than on any single theoretical innovation. His influence on Hutcheson and Hume is clear. He writes unsystematically, but there is a coherent view of aesthetics as a harmony of the person with the values of beauty and taste, which is often far more persuasive in Shaftesbury's way of approaching problems than it is in his largely traditional Neoplatonic language.

Before Shaftesbury, harmony is the music of the spheres; after Shaftesbury, it is the soul's sensory response to art and style. Taste in its aesthetic mode is naturalized and added to the five external senses. Shaftesbury's overt debt to Locke is not large, but in subtle ways he relies as heavily on his own experience and his ability to use that experience as a basis for judgment as does Locke. That spirit is absorbed into eighteenth-century aesthetics, even as Shaftesbury's own writings come to seem mannered and his patrician classicism is replaced by a more egalitarian aesthetic sense.

See also EIGHTEENTH-CENTURY AESTHETICS; AESTHETIC ATTITUDE; HUTCHESON; TASTE.

BIBLIOGRAPHY

Primary sources
[1705] 1900. *The Life, Unpublished Letters and Philosophical Regime of Anthony, Earl of Shaftesbury*, B. Rand (ed.). London: Swan & Sonnenschein.
[1711] 1914. *Second Characters*. B. Rand (ed.). Cambridge: Cambridge University Press.
[1711] 1964. *Characteristics*. J. M. Robertson (ed.). Indianapolis: Bobbs-Merrill.

Secondary sources
Augustine. 1983. "On Free Will." In *Philosophy in the Middle Ages*. 2nd edn. A. Hyman & J. J. Walsh (eds.). Indianapolis: Hackett, 33–64.
Augustine. 1993. *On Free Choice of the Will*. T. Williams (trans.). Indianapolis: Hackett.
Kivy, Peter. 1976. *The Seventh Sense*. New York: Burt Franklin.
Stolnitz, Jerome. 1961. "On the Significance of Lord Shaftesbury in Modern Aesthetic Theory," *Philosophical Quarterly*, 43, 97–113.
Townsend, Dabney. 1982. "Shaftesbury's Aesthetic Theory," *Journal of Aesthetics and Art Criticism*, 42, 205–13.
Voitle, Robert. 1984. *Anthony, Earl of Shaftesbury*. Baton Rouge: Louisiana State University Press.

DABNEY TOWNSEND

Sibley, Frank Noel (1923–1996) British philosopher of art. Although perhaps cited most often as the author of the seminal paper, "Aesthetic Concepts" (1959), that work is only one of a lengthy set of essays, some published only after Sibley's death, which fit together to give a systematic view of a central set of aesthetic problems.

The first part of "Aesthetic Concepts" begins with instances of aesthetic concepts used in judgments of taste. These are contrasted with what are called "non-aesthetic concepts" – examples of which would be *red, curved, square*, and *in iambic pentameters*. Examples of aesthetic concepts are *graceful, balanced*, and *tightly knit*. The distinction is offered in the expectation that the reader will recognize that the ability to apply aesthetic concepts requires a power to discriminate ("taste") that goes beyond an ability merely to say that something is square, curved, or possessed of a certain pattern of rhymes and stresses.

The features designated by aesthetic concepts depend on and emerge from the nonaesthetic features that a work possesses. Thus the aesthetic balance in a painting may depend on and emerge from such nonaesthetic features as a patch of red in a certain position. Although anyone possessed of normal eyesight could see the position of this color patch, it takes something more to see that it contributes to the balance in the work. "Aesthetic Concepts" and the related "Aesthetic and Non-Aesthetic" (1965) explore the relationships between aesthetic and nonaesthetic concepts. The central, and much debated, claim is that the presence of aesthetic features is not positively condition-governed by that of the nonaesthetic features on which they depend and from which they emerge. No description of the work in nonaesthetic terms (e.g., a description of a painting in terms of the position of color patches) will entail the conclusion that it has an aesthetic feature, such as balance, even though it is the position of those color patches that is responsible for the possession of an aesthetic feature, such as balance. By contrast, the description "is a closed figure with four sides and four equal angles" will entail that the figure in question is a square. Another way of putting this is that one could see that a painting had color masses in a certain configuration without thereby seeing that it had balance.

This account has profound implications. First, a certain kind of proof will not be possible in cases of aesthetic dispute. If someone doubts a figure to be a square, a *conclusive demonstration* is possible, for squareness is positively condition-governed. But no nonaesthetic description of a picture (to which the contending parties are likely to agree) will entail the conclusion that it is aesthetically balanced. This has to be seen. Aesthetic judgment is *perceptual*.

The second part of "Aesthetic Concepts," which has important implications for aesthetic education, describes how we might bring someone to see what we see by way of aesthetic qualities in a work of art. In "Aesthetic

and Non-Aesthetic," too, important conclusions are drawn about criticism. Criticism will not be a matter of demonstration but of perceptual proof, bringing someone to see something. This goes hand in hand with critical explanation, in which, having seen the aesthetic qualities of a work, one points to the nonaesthetic features that are responsible for the aesthetic features. Thus, knowing that a poem, say, has a certain rhyme pattern will not guarantee that we will see its aesthetic unity: but once we have perceived the unity, we may point to the rhyme scheme as the factor on which that unity depends.

It might be asked whether criticism, in the sense of the activity of pointing to the perceptual aesthetic features of a work, can be objective. This question is addressed in the two papers "Colours" (1967–8) and "Objectivity and Aesthetics" (1968). The former investigates the conditions that underpin our propensity to say that certain things are, say, red or green. The latter argues that a case can analogously be made for saying that things are, say, graceful or delicate. For our language, which imputes colors to objects, depends in the last resort on an agreement in judgments, and it is argued that that sort of agreement holds, with variations, in the aesthetic case as well.

Criticism is dealt with further in "General Criteria and Reasons in Aesthetics" (1983). (And see, here, Dickie 1988.) In this paper Sibley addresses whether reasoning is possible in aesthetics. The traditional problem here is that a reason, to be a reason, must be *general*: if courage is to be a reason for praising one person, it must be a reason for praising anyone who shows it. The difficulty in aesthetics is that what seems to be a reason for saying that this picture is, say, balanced (as when we say that the reason it is balanced is this patch of red in this position) might be the very thing that makes another picture unbalanced. Here Sibley distinguishes between "merit" features, such as grace and balance, and neutral features, such as the possession of a red patch in a certain position. Those who focus on the latter are right that the presence of such features cannot constitute general reasons for saying that the work has merit. But the former are general in the sense that they prima facie count only for a judgment of merit (although in some cases, carefully described by Sibley, their pro-judgment force may be neutralized).

The claims of "Aesthetic Concepts" are central to Sibley's work. And they have been vigorously contested. Thus, Meager (1970) has maintained that concepts other than aesthetic concepts display the property of being nonpositively condition-governed. Provided, however, that some indubitably aesthetic concepts do display this property, Meager's claim does not undermine the claims that Sibley makes about the nature of aesthetic judgment and its non-demonstrative perceptual nature. What her claim does do is raise the question of what makes a nonpositively condition-governed concept an aesthetic one. Others (e.g., Cohen 1973) have attempted to show that there are positively conditioned-governed aesthetic concepts, thus striking at the roots of Sibley's account. Cohen has further asked whether the initial distinction between aesthetic and nonaesthetic concepts, on which everything in Sibley's "Aesthetic Concepts" rests, can be drawn without circularity.

These controversies continue, their existence testifying to the important bearing that Sibley's work is seen to have on questions about the nature of aesthetic appreciation and criticism.

See also TWENTIETH-CENTURY ANGLO-AMERICAN AESTHETICS; AESTHETIC EDUCATION; AESTHETIC JUDGMENT; AESTHETIC PROPERTIES; CRITICISM; SENSES AND ART, THE; TASTE; TESTIMONY IN AESTHETICS.

BIBLIOGRAPHY

Primary sources
1959. "Aesthetic Concepts." *Philosophical Review*, 68, 421–50; repr. in Sibley 2001: 1–23.
1965. "Aesthetic and Non-Aesthetic." *Philosophical Review*, 74, 135–59; repr. in Sibley 2001: 33–51.
1967–8. "Colours." *Proceedings of the Aristotelian Society*, 68, 145–66; repr. in Sibley 2001: 54–70.
1968. "Objectivity and Aesthetics," *Proceedings of the Aristotelian Society*, supp. vol. 42, 31–54; repr. in Sibley 2001: 71–87.
1983. "General Criteria and Reasons in Aesthetics." In *Essays on Aesthetics*. J. Fisher (ed.). Philadelphia: Temple University Press, 3–20. Repr. in Sibley 2001: 104–18.
2001. *Approaches to Aesthetics* J. Benson, B. Redfern, & J. Roxbee Cox (eds.). Oxford: Clarendon.

Secondary sources
Brady, E. & Levinson, J. (eds.). 2001. *Aesthetic Concepts: Essays After Sibley*. Oxford: Clarendon.
Cohen, Ted. 1973. "Aesthetic and Non-Aesthetic," *Theoria*, 39, 113–52.
Dickie, George. 1988. *Evaluating Art*. Philadelphia: Temple University Press.
Meager, Ruby. 1970. "Aesthetic Concepts," *British Journal of Aesthetics*, 10, 303–32.

COLIN LYAS

structuralism and poststructuralism
Structuralism is an aesthetic theory based on the following assumptions: all artistic artifacts (or "texts") are exemplifications of an underlying "deep structure"; texts are organized like a language, with their own specific grammar; the grammar of a language is a series of signs and conventions which draw a predictable response from human beings. The objective of structuralist analysis is to reveal the deep structures of texts. The roots of structuralism lie mainly in structural linguistics, in particular the theories of the Swiss linguist Ferdinand de Saussure (1857–1913), whose *Course in General Linguistics* provides structuralism with its basic methodological model. Other major sources of structuralist aesthetic theory have been Russian Formalism (a school of literary theorists who flourished in postrevolutionary Russia) and structural anthropology (Claude Lévi-Strauss being a key figure in this area).

Poststructuralism is a broad-based cultural movement embracing several disciplines, which has self-consciously rejected the techniques and premises of structuralism, particularly the notion that there is an underlying pattern to events. Nevertheless, it owes a great deal to the earlier theory, and has been variously described as "neo-structuralism" and "superstructuralism."

For Saussure language is a self-regulating system, in the sense that a game like chess can be considered as self-regulating:

> In chess, what is external can be separated relatively easily from what is internal. The fact that the game passed from Persia to Europe is external; against that, everything having to do with its system and rules is internal. If I use ivory chessmen instead of wooden ones, the change has no effect on the system; but if I decrease or increase the

number of chessmen, this change has a profound effect on the "grammar" of the game . . . everything that changes the system in any way is internal. (1960: 22–3)

Chess is a whole system, with its own specific rules and procedures ("grammar") that prescribe what can happen during the game. Language is similarly held to be a self-contained, self-regulating system with an underlying structure of rules that allow a certain degree of freedom to the individual language-user; the rules specify general principles and practices that can be varied (or "transformed") at the local level by the individual. It is in the *structure* of the language, rather than in the utterances made within it, that Saussure's interest lies, and he distinguishes sharply between the former (*langue*) and the latter (*parole*). Jean Piaget has noted that "the notion of structure is comprised of three key ideas: the idea of wholeness, the idea of transformation, and the idea of self-regulation" (1971: 5), and these will remain primary considerations for structuralist theorists and critics in their analyses of phenomena.

Saussurean linguistics is based on a series of critical distinctions that have been taken over by structuralists: in particular, *langue/parole*, signifier/signified, synchronic/diachronic, and syntagmatic/paradigmatic. Signifier/signified refers to the distinction between a word, spoken or written, and the mental concept lying behind it. The union of signifier and signified, word and concept, in an act of understanding, creates what Saussure calls the "sign."

The study of language is for Saussure the study of signs and how they work. He subsumes this study within the wider discipline of "semiology," which takes all sign systems as its field of inquiry. The connection between signifier and signified is described as being arbitrary, which means that it is subject to change over time as long as there is general agreement as to that change within a given linguistic community. "The principle of change is based on the principle of continuity," as Saussure (1960: 74) puts it, thus introducing the distinction between synchronic and diachronic. Synchrony deals with the totality of a phenomenon over time, whereas diachrony deals with some aspect of that totality at a given point in time. In chess terms, the game

plus its grammar constitutes an example of synchrony; an actual move of any of the pieces within the game itself is a diachronic event. Diachronic events must always be examined in terms of their relationship to the whole system.

Saussure's theory of relations involves the distinction between syntagmatic and paradigmatic. A syntagm is a combination of words consisting of two or more consecutive units, constructed according to the rules of syntax of the relevant language, for example, "God is good," "If the weather is nice we'll go out" (1960: 123). Each word is linked to the next word in the sequence, as it unfolds, in linear relationship. Paradigmatic – or, as Saussure originally termed them, "associative" – relations are more akin to John Locke's notion of "association of ideas," and fall into no predictable pattern since they depend on the particular mental processes and experience of the individual; in Locke's words of 1690, "there is another connexion of ideas wholly owing to *chance or custom*. Ideas that in themselves are not at all of kin come to be so united in some men's minds that it is very hard to separate them; they always keep in company" (1964: 250–1). Deconstruction relies heavily on the notion of paradigmatic relation, which it interprets in a radical fashion in its critical theory and practice.

Saussure's theory of value has had important implications for the development of structuralism. He equates value with function: units have value only in that they can be compared, or exchanged, with other units in their own sign system. There is no such thing as intrinsic value in Saussure, and he takes a purely formal, function-oriented approach to the question of value. Structuralism is similarly form- and function-oriented.

Structuralists have adopted the bulk of the terminology and methodology of Saussure's *Course in General Linguistics*. The basic concerns of a structuralist critic are to identify the boundaries of the system under analysis, to establish the nature of its syntax and the relations obtaining between its syntactical elements, and then to view her findings in both synchronic and diachronic perspective where transformations of the syntactical elements can be traced in detail. Russian Formalists like Vladimir Propp have shown how a range of folktales could vary subtly from one example of the genre to another by the transformation of basic narrative units. The supernatural, for example, might appear in every case, but in a different form each time around, to different effect, and at a variety of points in the plot.

The study of transformation can lead to some very sophisticated comparative analysis of narratives within and across genres, and that is one of structuralism's great strengths. Lévi-Strauss's work on primitive myth is a model of how to catalogue transformations within a genre for the purposes of comparative cultural analysis. In *The Raw and the Cooked*, his investigations into a range of South American Indian myths are directed toward proving that, "in all these instances we are dealing with the same myth," and that "the apparent divergences between the versions are to be treated as the result of transformations occurring within a set" (1969: 147). Unity remains an overriding concern of structuralists. The major virtue of structuralist analysis for Lévi-Strauss is that its "unique and most economical coding system" enables the critic to "reduce messages of a most disheartening complexity" to a determinate order in terms of their deep structures. Roland Barthes is similarly concerned with coding in narrative but, as his reading of Balzac's novella *Sarrasine* in *S/Z* suggests, he is committed to demonstrating how *complex* rather than how economical such coding can be: "the codes it mobilizes," he remarks of the literary text, "extend *as far as the eye can reach*, they are indeterminable" (1974: 5–6).

As an aesthetic theory, structuralism has been criticized on a variety of counts, most notably as being mechanical in operation, ultra-formalist, committed to determinism and idealism, and lacking in evaluative power. It can easily decline into a highly predictable form of analysis in which codes are checked off, signs cataloged, and comparisons made on a formal level that says little about content or psychological effect. Since it stays at a formal level, structuralism tends to avoid evaluation, the critic's interest lying in the way a text and its units are organized rather than with what it might be saying. The notion of a deep structure seems to deny human agency (deep structures work *through* individuals), and has deterministic

connotations: structuralists are notorious for claiming the "death of the [individual] subject."

Structure remains a highly problematical concept, and in practice most structuralists have tended to analyze individual artworks in terms of an assumed ideal structure, which suggests an underlying Platonism to the enterprise. Jacques Derrida, among others, has been very critical of this aspect of structuralist methodology (see "Force and Signification" (1978: 3–30)). Structuralism is a superbly efficient theory when it comes to describing and comparing phenomena in formal terms, but arguably seriously deficient when it comes to evaluating them.

Evaluation has traditionally been a central concern of criticism, and structuralism's weakness in this respect has been heavily criticized by, for example, Marxists, who consider the refusal to evaluate to be almost a dereliction of a critic's duty toward readers. So-called "structuralist Marxists" have tried to have the best of both worlds by adapting structuralist methodology to Marxist political purposes; but although Pierre Macherey's "reading against the grain" techniques, in which the text is ransacked for evidence of ideological contradictions and "false" authorial resolutions of "real" sociopolitical debates, had a considerable vogue in the 1970s and 1980s (see particularly Macherey 1978; Eagleton 1976), the respective theories are generally felt to be largely incompatible, given their differences over value.

Structuralism's implicit determinism has exercised poststructuralist thinkers considerably. Many poststructuralists, drawing on developments in recent science, stress the importance of chance and indeterminacy in human affairs. Whereas structuralists invariably seek to find an underlying unity in texts or events, poststructuralists search out instability. Derrida has described structuralism as being authoritarian and totalitarian in operation, as forcing artworks to conform to preestablished schemes. The emphasis in poststructuralist analyses is on the contingent, the different, the unsystematic and unsystematizable. Poststructuralism is a wide-ranging movement that encompasses not just Derrida and deconstruction, but also Michel Foucault-inspired "discourse theory" and the postmodernism of theorists like Jean-François Lyotard and

Jean Baudrillard. In general it can be said that poststructuralists reject the certainties of structuralism and the ideas that structure can be pinned down and all textual "messages" ultimately reduced to preexisting codes.

Discourse theory studies the way that discourses (e.g., of aesthetics) arise in a society, and how they construct notions of value and make claims to power. Foucault rejects the idea of history as a teleological process, and emphasizes difference and discontinuity instead. In *Madness and Civilization* (1967) he explores how the discourse of "madness," as a recognizable phenomenon with its own set of social practices and institutions, arose in seventeenth-century Europe as a method of social control, and how it represented a break with past practices. Foucault can find no pattern or reason to history, and resists totalizing theories and analyses (both structuralism and Marxism would be so describable). His "archaeological" investigations into history often concentrate on bringing to the surface hidden or subjugated discourses – as in the case of his studies of sexuality – in order to illustrate just how lacking in rational pattern or teleological progress history actually is.

Lyotard's postmodernism involves a wholesale rejection of large-scale, all-embracing theories of explanation ("grand narratives" or "metanarratives" in Lyotard's terminology), such as Marxism or Hegelianism. Once again, as in Derrida and Foucault, the reaction is against "authoritarian" theories – that is, theories that assume an underlying pattern to events. Lyotard regards all theoretical discourses, including philosophy, as forms of narrative and as having no ultimate purchase on truth or knowledge. Ordinary narrative is taken to be just a fact of human existence requiring no further justification or license from any grand narrative: "it certifies itself in the pragmatics of its own transmission" (1984: 27). He supports the cause of "little" narrative, which he identifies with the individual, over that of "grand," which he identifies with systems and institutions. The world is seen to consist of a multiplicity of little narratives, all of which have their own particular integrity and sense of importance, but none of which can be considered to take precedence over any of the others. Grand narrative dominates and suppresses little narrative, and is therefore to be resisted.

In aesthetic terms this skepticism about authority has led to a rejection of programmatic theories like modernism. Postmodernist artists are quite happy to rework older styles and forms, feeling no need for a break with tradition in the manner of their modernist counterparts. Although this has led to postmodernism being criticized as innately conservative, it should be noted that postmodern artists generally use older forms in an irreverent and even cynical way. Irony and pastiche, it has frequently been pointed out, are the staples of the postmodernist repertoire.

Jean Baudrillard espouses an even more radical attitude to signs and systems than Lyotard, completely rejecting the idea that signs communicate the deep structure of artifacts or phenomena, or exemplify the workings of preestablished codes. Indeed, signs do not seem to communicate anything much at all in Baudrillard's world, where image has taken over from reality – "the cinema and TV are America's reality," he remarks at one point (1988: 104). His work registers as an updated version of Marshall McLuhan: "the medium is the message" stated in apocalyptic terms. We live in a "hyperreality" surrounded by simulacra and simulations in Baudrillard's view, and there is no longer any point in trying to engage in interpretation of texts or events. He might more correctly be dubbed the purveyor of an anti-aesthetics than an aesthetics, but he has nevertheless inspired an art movement in America ("simulationist" or "neo-geo" art) which has claimed to provide visual equivalents of his theories. Ironically enough, Baudrillard did not like the art that his theories generated, and dissociated himself from the group's efforts.

What all of these poststructuralist thinkers share is a distrust of totalizing theory and of notions of unity. They bequeath to criticism a commitment to contingency and discontinuity, and it is a commitment that has provoked considerable debate. Given that they have rejected the notion of authority in general, it is hard to see on what grounds poststructuralists can claim authority for their own theories – a problem that traditionally plagues relativists and antifoundationalists. Neither is it clear how we are even to understand their theories if signs really are as unstable as they are arguing. Perhaps poststructuralism is more successful in drawing attention to the excesses of structuralism than in offering a truly viable alternative to traditional ways of going about criticism and aesthetic theory.

See also NINETEENTH- AND TWENTIETH-CENTURY CONTINENTAL AESTHETICS; BARTHES; CRITICISM; DECONSTRUCTION; DERRIDA; FOUCAULT; IRONY; MARXISM AND ART; MODERNISM AND POSTMODERNISM; NARRATIVE; RELATIVISM.

BIBLIOGRAPHY

Barthes, Roland. 1974 [1970]. *S/Z*. R. Miller (trans.). New York: Hill & Wang.

Baudrillard, Jean. 1988 [1986]. *America*. C. Turner (trans.). London: Verso.

Derrida, Jacques. 1978 [1967]. *Writing and Difference*. A. Bass (trans.). London: Routledge & Kegan Paul.

Eagleton, Terry. 1976. *Criticism and Ideology*. London: NLB.

Foucault, Michel. 1967 [1961]. *Madness and Civilization: A History of Insanity in the Age of Reason*. R. Howard (trans.). London: Tavistock.

Lévi-Strauss, Claude. 1969 [1964]. *The Raw and the Cooked: Introduction to a Science of Mythology I*. J. & D. Weightman (trans.). London: Jonathan Cape.

Locke, John. 1964 [1690]. *Essay concerning Human Understanding*. A. D. Woozley (ed.). London: Fontana/Collins.

Lyotard, Jean-François. 1984 [1979]. *The Postmodern Condition: A Report on Knowledge*. G. Bennington & B. Massumi (trans.). Manchester: Manchester University Press.

Macherey, Pierre. 1978 [1966]. *A Theory of Literary Production*. G. Wall (trans.). London: Routledge & Kegan Paul.

Piaget, Jean. 1971 [1968]. *Structuralism*. C. Maschler (trans.). London: Routledge & Kegan Paul.

Saussure, Ferdinand de. 1960 [1915]. *Course in General Linguistics*. C. Bally, A. Sechehaye, & A. Reidlinger (eds.). W. Baskin (trans.). London: Peter Owen.

STUART SIM

style   The concept of style can seem simple enough. We can think of style merely as a way of doing things, or a way in which something is made. But this captures little of the complexity of the relevant issues. It is by no means a straightforward matter to identify precisely what qualities should properly be considered stylistic, nor indeed to what sorts of things such qualities should properly be applied. Generally, style applies to those sorts of artifacts and performances that communicate partly by inviting our conscious recognition that they are to be regarded as artifacts or performances.

Stylistic qualities invite our attention, legitimately or otherwise, to the maker's or performer's activity in producing the object or performance – what in art we think of as a "work." To ascribe stylistic qualities to a natural object is at best metaphorical: neither a volcano nor a potato can have a style (though a picture of either might). Much the same applies to activities and actions that are not performances. To refer to the style of someone's sweeping a room or running to catch a bus is to imply that somehow they are making a performance out of the business, but one might refer with propriety to the style in which someone greets another or serves a meal. Similarly, one might properly talk of the style of a highly domesticated, artifact-saturated landscape. Hence to refer to the style (or stylishness) of what we normally suppose should not be a self-conscious performance, nor a self-consciously produced artifact, is normally pejorative. It is, for example, not normally a compliment to refer to the style in which someone makes love, or to the style with which a student explains the lateness of an essay; to the style of a mechanic's cleaning rags, or an academic's rough notepaper. Style in the wrong place can be meretricious.

Yet even this is not straightforward. There is a central tradition of aesthetic judgment that places the highest value on the forms of useful artifacts following their "unselfconscious" fitness for their function, as if their very absence of "style" in this pejorative sense were itself a style. Similarly, an ability to apologize, or to show affection to another naturally, without any sense of "making a performance" out of the business, may be regarded as a style, a natural manner of the highest order – a sign of integrity. Evaluative disputes about style tend inevitably to look toward concepts of integrity and honesty (in design, performance, or in unperformed behavior), and to their polar opposites. Our concepts of stylishness, of the mannered or the naturally simple (whether in or outside art), inevitably take us to the brink of some of our subtlest moral concepts. For they have to do with our sense of how we may, or may fail to, see through the ways in which something is made or performed to deeper matters of the agent's thought and intention.

To suppose that style can be thought of as a manner, or a characteristic manner, of doing or making something that might have been done differently, is to treat matters as if one might "peel off" the external manner of production from an inner kernel that could be given a different casing. In this sense it can be an intelligible exercise to rewrite a poem or a musical piece in the style of another or of another period. This is how we might construe the concept of style as "signature." Individual artists, authors, composers, types of people, and identifiable periods and movements have their characteristic styles. The recognition of such stylistic signatures, therefore, may be the central skill of a certain kind of connoisseurship, a highly saleable skill for antique dealers, a taught skill in many English literature courses, an examined skill in "dating" documents; and a rich source not only for the forger's art but, more importantly, for a high variety of fictional devices, elegantly discussed by Walton (1987). Such identifications of style and of stylistic change are, moreover, central to the fact that art inevitably has a history, the dynamic traces of which are those of stylistic development. For style as signature announces, and may thus misannounce, whose mind, thought, intention one is to be properly receptive to in responding to the work.

However, a sharp distinction between a stylistic skin and an inner kernel is unconvincing, for much of the content of a work inevitably resides in a celebration of how it is made or performed, a content that is essentially stylistic. Goodman (1978) objects that the distinction rests on an unintelligible concept of synonymy to make sense of different works having the same "content" and different styles. In part his point rests on a general skepticism over the concept of synonymy, but it might equally rest firmly enough on any reasonably applicable idea of aesthetic content.

Such an idea of aesthetic content requires a concept of style other than that of style as signature alone. The development of an artist's style is essentially linked with the development of the work's communicative authority. In this sense style is a "direction of salience," similar to what Wollheim (1987b) calls "thematisation": stylistic devices invite us to attend to certain features of the work as central, thereby responding to the work as the artist demands. When an artist's use of style achieves this sort of authority our responses flow, as it were, in the direction the work demands, not merely as our whim as beholder, audience, or reader dictates.

This is best illustrated by examples from particular arts. Let us start with painting. A representational painting presents to us a set of objects depicted for our imagination such that they, and the masses of color and form they invoke, are arranged in a certain way within the depicted space defined by the frame of the picture. It thus presents a pictorial space. Also, given familiar forms of perspective, we may think of the depicted space as if it had a limit, like the view beyond the plane of a framed window. It may then invoke this as a picture plane. And all of this will be achieved by an elaborately and carefully marked, that is handled, pigmented surface. Thus a painting may present us with a pictorial space, a pictorial plane, and a depicting surface (these last two are notoriously easy to confuse if we are inclined to think of a picture as like a glass window through which we can look, but at an imaginary landscape rather than at a real one some distance beyond the glass).

Gombrich (1960) has argued that the "illusion" of the pictorial requires that we cannot attend simultaneously to the depicting surface of a painting or drawing and to what is depicted by it. But as Wollheim (1973, 1987b), Podro (1987), and others have insisted, it is essential to any proper response to pictures that we should attend to each in terms of our attention to the other: any understanding of pictorial style that goes beyond the mere concept of "signature" requires this. For the capacity of style in painting and drawing to communicate to us derives from how we may be led, by various means, to attend simultaneously to a wide variety of quite different types of topics of aesthetic and imaginative interest: to the objects as depicted, to the balance and structure of their pictorial space, to the picture plane with its magical sense of the celebration of optical phenomena; and, in the case of pictures that celebrate their painterly qualities of touch and graphic vigor, to the depicting surface itself. The control of pictorial style – what gives an integrated, dominant authority to the picture as a coherent expression of an artist's visual intelligence – requires that the direction of our attentive interest traverse this terrain in ways that cohere with the absorbed attention of the artist's own thought in making the work.

It is central to any idea of stylistic development that, as an artist's style matures, the demands that the works make on our attention and judgment – their imaginative authority – will be more firmly insistent. But a meretricious development of style may also occur. For it is all too easy for a certain sort of facility on the part of an artist to be engaged in the mere production and reproduction of style as signature. Then it is only too obvious who, or what type or "school" of artists, produced the work or the performance; only too easy for an individual artist or performer to engage in facile self-imitation, or for a teacher to encourage a facile academicism. The difference seems to be that mere signature need pay little attention – and thus demand none – to the integrity of a work's levels of significance and interest. Under those conditions it may be depressingly easy to "disintegrate" the work, to "peel off" a skin or manner of "performance" from a kernel of "content."

Much the same can be said about each of the arts. In the design of useful objects (see Dormer 1990) stylistic excellence can also best be thought of as being about salience – with how our attention may be controlled by the interrelation of forms, qualities of finish (or the lack of it), patterns of decoration or of noticeable plainness, and thus directed to what is more or less important. This might be function alone, or the celebration of grandeur, of modesty or simplicity or, perhaps, pride in possession. Here, therefore, while the concept of style itself is not a moral concept, discussion of style – whether it be the style of a Shaker chair, a grandiose sideboard, a slot machine, or a Coca-Cola bottle – leads us inevitably toward such concerns in terms either of stylistic integrity itself or of the integrity of what the style may be taken to imply. Mere style as signature is again inadequate to deal with these facts.

An actor or musician may perform with a style that is manifestly, and all too dismally, recognizable as the style of that performer, but the stylistic integrity of a performance must achieve more than that. What is required is a kind of seriousness that controls the direction of our attention to the salient elements in the work, so that each aspect of what we are shown (often at quite different levels of attention) can be understood by us in terms of how it is understood by the performer. Integrity of style makes the concentrated thought of the performer *to* the work manifest *in* the performance. Inevitably, as with style in painting, this form of understanding must involve a grasp of the complexity of different "levels" in a work (the "formal" structure of the work, its patterns of narrative, of themes, of dramatic developments and interactions, together with the "texture" of a performer's "patterns" of expressive stress and emphasis) and at the same time integrate them into a whole for our attention.

Similarly, in literature, it is notoriously easy to imitate (as pastiche) the style of another writer. Mock Shakespeare, Milton, T. S. Eliot, or Henry James is disturbingly easy to achieve. It is a dull skill to learn the trick of writing merely in the manner of such authors. Occasionally they may even do it themselves; few great writers are ever quite free from the faults of self-imitation. But, as the study of rhetoric and literary criticism have always insisted, this is not stylistic integrity. Integrity of style both celebrates the differences between, say, meter, stress, emphasis, and the literal and metaphorical meanings of the words and phrases, and, at the same time, "orchestrates" these distinct elements into an authoritative unity, so that an apparently simple distinction between literary form and content ceases to be in place.

Concepts of style enter in when we embrace what can seem to be two paradoxical features of art. The first is that art both communicates and celebrates the fact of its ways of communication, yet must, with stylistic honesty (as with other forms of honesty), eschew self-conscious posturing. The second is that the responses that stylistic integrity demands of us involve our distinguishing radically different aspects of a work and of our attention to a work, while still responding to the work as an ordered unity. Style resolves the first apparent paradox in terms of the second.

See also GENRE; GOMBRICH; ILLUSION; PERFORMANCE; PICTURE PERCEPTION; WOLLHEIM.

BIBLIOGRAPHY

Dormer, Peter. 1990. *The Meanings of Modern Design*. London: Thames & Hudson.

Gombrich, E. H. 1960. *Art and Illusion*. London: Phaidon.

Gombrich, E. H. 1968. "Style." In *International Encyclopedia of the Social Sciences*. D. L. Sills (ed.). New York: Macmillan, 352–61.

Gombrich, E. H. 1975. "Mirror and Map: Theories of Pictorial Representation." In *Philosophical Transactions of the Royal Society*, 270, 119–49; repr. in *The Image and the Eye*. London: Phaidon, 1989.

Goodman, Nelson. 1978. "The Status of Style." In *Ways of Worldmaking*. Hassocks: Harvester, 23–40.

Podro, Michael. 1987. "Depiction and the Golden Calf." In *Philosophy and the Visual Arts: Seeing and Abstracting*. A. Harrison (ed.). Dordrecht: Reidel, 3–22.

Walton, Kendall L. 1987. "Style and the Products and Processes of Art." In *The Concept of Style*. 2nd edn. B. Lang (ed.). Ithaca: Cornell University Press, 72–103.

Wollheim, Richard. 1973. *On Art and the Mind*. London: Allen Lane.

Wollheim, Richard. 1987a. "Pictorial Style: Two Views." In *The Concept of Style*. 2nd edn. B. Lang (ed.). Ithaca: Cornell University Press, 183–202.

Wollheim, Richard. 1987b. *Painting as an Art*. London: Thames & Hudson.

ANDREW HARRISON

sublime Defined by the *Concise Oxford Dictionary* as "so distinguished by . . . impressive quality as to inspire awe or wonder, aloof from . . . the ordinary"; but used by Kant and others in the special, though closely related, senses discussed below.

The world of letters has its own dialect, one that reflects and at the same time serves to fix the stylistic preferences of a particular place and time. The vocabulary of criticism mirrors the history of taste. Fifty years ago someone who wanted to join a discussion of poetry or fiction would have to have mastered such terms as "objective correlative," "ambiguity," "existential," "paradox," "symbol." Nowadays you can get along quite well without them. The lexicon is born in the classroom. Students and grown-up beginners need guidance: What do you look for? What should you appreciate? What needs to be analyzed? The key terms offer answers, and when the answers begin to seem inadequate, the terms become obsolete. Such terms are characteristically ill-defined; they have to be to serve their purpose. Philosophers and grammarians can say pretty clearly what makes a word ambiguous, but what they say will not replace William Empson's *Seven Types of Ambiguity*, where definition is all by way of example. And then, since it is easier to ape your elders and master the lexicon than it is to come to grips with the examples, the key terms come to carry less and less information: they become clichés, and outsiders make fun of the critics' jargon. It is in this company that we find "the sublime."

By the second third of the eighteenth century, the term was firmly entrenched, both as an adjective and as noun. Every man of taste (another stock phrase) had at his fingertips a catalogue of examples – volcanoes, raging seas, towering cliffs, the pyramids, ruined castles, blasted heaths, and so forth. That there is an interesting and subtle distinction to be drawn between the true and the false sublime was taken for granted. Curious intellects pondered the question of how to make psychological sense of that "agreeable horror" (Addison's phrase) that marks an encounter with the sublime. By the middle of the nineteenth century, the term "sublime" had largely disappeared from the critical vocabulary, and had begun to sound archaic.

The story of the sublime begins with Longinus, a second-century Greek rhetorician, if it was indeed he who was the author of *Peri Hupsos* (meaning "on impressiveness of style"; it went into Latin as *De Sublimitate*; from Latin to French, and thence to English; Dr. Johnson's *Dictionary* (1755) says of "the sublime" that it is "a Gallicism now naturalized"). Longinus provides a handbook for orators who want to develop their speaking skills, but later audiences were not much interested in his helpful hints: on such technical matters, they had Cicero and Quintilian, not to mention Aristotle, as mentors. What captured their attention was what Longinus has to say in passing about content rather than about style, and the poetic examples he gives. Here are some Longinian dicta that were endorsed and elaborated by every subsequent exponent of the sublime.

1   The grand style is suited only to subjects that are in themselves lofty, magnificent, and astonishing. For ordinary topics, everyday language is good enough.
2   The grand style may, but need not be, ornate: the sublime often calls for extreme simplicity, as in the Mosaic account of creation. Sometimes stupendous effects are achieved just by mention and display, without any oratory at all. The silence of Ajax in the eleventh book of the *Odyssey* is an example.
3   The grand style has great emotional force: it not only persuades, but "ravishes and transports" the hearer. It is irresistible.
4   The speaker who succeeds in presenting an exalted subject in a suitably elevated style thereby reveals an inward greatness of soul.
5   The products of a lofty mind (what would later be called works of genius) are often rough-hewn and imperfect in detail. That is to be excused and not blamed: it is part of their intrinsic grandeur.
6   Nature as well as art affords instances of the sublime: mighty rivers, in contrast to little streams; Mount Etna in eruption, the sun, the stars – all are astonishing.
7   Since the sublime, wherever it occurs, is like a force of nature rather than a product of skill, it is destined to please all people, everywhere, and at all times.

Translations of *Peri Hupsos* appeared in the sixteenth century without attracting much notice. The real inauguration came in 1674, when Boileau produced both *L'Art poétique* ("Poetic Art") and *Traité du sublime ou du merveilleux dans le discours traduit du grec de Longin* ("Treatise on the Sublime or the Marvelous in the Discourse translated from the Greek of Longinus"). Neither Boileau nor his audience was much taken by the sublimity of natural wonders – that came later with the English and then with the Germans. His French readers were more interested in the arts and with the idea that great art, especially tragedy, has power to stir the deepest passions. In the protracted and tiresome debate about

the comparative merits of the ancients and the moderns, Boileau, a champion of the ancients, frequently draws on Longinus. But the other side could use him too: it depends on who you think is more sublime.

Longinus' views were also put into play by both parties to the dispute about French and English drama. Corneille was sublime in his laconic understatement, Shakespeare was sublime in his roughness and grandeur. (*King Lear* was a favorite example of an awe-inspiring though "irregular" work.) On an even broader scale, Longinus was pressed into service both by neoclassical critics who deferred to Aristotle and believed in the "rules," and by the avant-garde who thought that Milton, especially in *Samson Agonistes* and the descriptions of Satan in *Paradise Lost*, teaches, by precept and by example, iconoclasm and the need to transcend the rules. The competition was bitter, although in retrospect it is hard to see what was at issue. The neoclassicists always allowed space for genius to take liberties, and their opponents, the forerunners of Romanticism, were willing to grant that where stupendous effects were achieved, following the rules was all right. (Pope's *Essay on Criticism* (1711) presents an elegant set of balanced oppositions in compromise.)

Once the sublime had taken root, nobody paid attention to Longinus. Not everyone was an enthusiast, though. Dr. Johnson, who disliked the wilder aspects of nature and thought enthusiasm for the Scottish highlands was absurd – almost as bad as approving of the landscape of Norway or Lapland – had a low opinion of poetic evocations of the natural sublime. Satirists such as Swift and Pope, in the meantime, had a field day at the expense of the enthusiasts. Belief in a kind of experience that ravishes and transports and at the same time ennobles and elevates is certainly appealing, and many people said silly things and at great length. Numerous comedies caricatured pretentious persons (mostly women) who expatiate on the sublime.

In an influential series of articles in *The Spectator* (1711–12), Joseph Addison studies Milton more carefully than anyone before him, pointing out the "beauties" and the "blemishes" and arguing the Longinian point that, since the poetry is sublime, readers should be indulgent toward the blemishes. Addison was the first to suggest a distinction, that rapidly caught on, between the beautiful and the sublime. He is not consistent: "beauty" is still the genus, and "sublime" is the word for the greatest preeminent beauties. But he does hold that there is a difference, not just of degree but in kind. "Beauty," which properly applies to what is regular, pleasing, well constructed, is ceded, as it were, to Boileau and his party. The sublime – Addison's actual term is "elevated" – is a different genre. Beauty and sublimity are two varietal species of artistic excellence. Addison was also one who encouraged his readers to appreciate the sublime in nature – he favored "a vast Desert, a huge Heap of Mountains." The Alps he found a source of "agreeable Horror," and his oxymoron was echoed and paralleled in many contemporary writings. (Kant, who knew, at least at second-hand, the whole literature, says that our response to the sublime is a "negative pleasure.")

For those given to reflection on their encounters with the sublime, there were questions. How are we to explain the fact that we enjoy what we find frightening and hence painful? Why, in confrontation with large and menacing things, should we feel elevated and somehow above it all? These are old questions, raised before sublimity was invented. The phenomena had been noted by Plato, who observes that we are repelled and yet somehow drawn to look at decaying corpses, that we *enjoy* the enactment of horrible and disgusting deeds on the stage.

In 1757 Edmund Burke published *A Philosophical Enquiry into the Origin of Our Ideas of the Sublime and the Beautiful*. Burke really liked popular graveyard poetry and Gothic fiction with all their stock props – the screeching owls, the ravenous beasts, the ghosts, the ruined battlements, and the like. He stipulates a distinction between "positive" or "independent" pleasure on the one hand, and on the other, "delight," which signifies relief from pain and danger and is therefore "relative." Delight is connected in some way that is not explained with the instinct for self-preservation. It is with delight, not pleasure, that we respond to the sublime. This sounds more like a rephrasing of the question than an answer. One's general impression is that Burke thinks that violent

and unfocused emotions, negative as well as positive, have intrinsic value (which means that no explanation is either necessary or possible).

Kant's treatment of the sublime is of great interest, but difficult to summarize without assuming knowledge of his overall philosophical project – knowledge not easy to come by. Kant's initial foray, *Observations on the Feeling of the Beautiful and Sublime*, appeared in 1763, 18 years before his first *Critique*, and his developed position is presented in the first part of the *Critique of Judgement* in 1790. The *Observations* are informal and discursive, rather in the manner of Hume's essays. They offer little that is new, and no arguments, but seem rather to be a compendium of currently received opinion. Kant writes:

> Finer feeling . . . is . . . of two kinds: the feeling of the *sublime* and that of the *beautiful*. The stirring of each is pleasant, but in different ways . . . The description of a raging storm, or Milton's portrayal of the infernal kingdom, arouse enjoyment but with horror; on the other hand, the sight of flower-strewn meadows . . . or Homer's portrayal of the girdle of Venus, also occasion a pleasant sensation but one that is joyous and smiling . . . Night is sublime, day is beautiful . . . The sublime *moves*, the beautiful *charms* . . . The sublime must always be great; the beautiful can also be small. The sublime must be simple; the beautiful can be adorned and ornamented. (1960: 46–9)

Two of the four sections of the *Observations* are devoted to sexual differences – men are sublime, women beautiful; and to national characters – English, Spanish, and Germans have an affinity with the sublime, French and Italians with the beautiful. The Dutch, who care for neither, go in for being neat and making money. The effect of this parade of popular prejudice and illiberal bias is somewhat mitigated by a point that is original with Kant and anticipates the developed views of the third *Critique*. It is that virtue based on benevolence, though variable and not to be depended on, is beautiful and inspires love, while virtue based on adherence to principle is sublime and commands respect. Previous authors had assumed that only exceptional persons can aspire to sublimity – great works of art argue a lofty mind; works of genius transcend the rules. But Kant claims that the sublimity that supervenes on acting from principle is open to every human being – even women and savages. (The Indians of Canada get particularly high marks.)

Kant's final word on sublimity comes 27 years later. In the *Critique of Pure Reason* he had argued that, while we cannot know the future in detail, there are nonetheless certain things we *can* know with complete certainty, such as that whatever comes our way will be spatiotemporal and describable under causal laws. The price to be paid for such certainty is that we have to acknowledge that the world of science, the world we live in, is a world of appearance, not the really *real* world. What Kant calls "the noumenal world" has somehow got to *be* there, but we can know nothing about it. Attempts to find out, for instance, whether God exists, or whether the will is free, are futile: just raising such questions leads to a series of contradictions, symptoms of the breakdown of our intellectual apparatus. In the *Critique of Practical Reason* Kant argues that, while we cannot know anything about the real, noumenal world, we have a foothold in it; and so, even though everything we do can be explained scientifically, we are subject to the moral law and, as such, endowed with a capacity for acting on principle no matter how great the temptations to be selfish or greedy may be. The categorical imperative, which says that human beings have dignity and must be treated with respect, overrides every ignoble impulse that would lead us to use and exploit other people for our own ends.

In the third *Critique* Kant again distinguishes the beautiful from the sublime, but now he is much more systematic and has dropped all the chatty bits about national character and sexual difference. The beautiful is what is found to be a source of pleasure by someone who is not concerned with satisfying his appetites, or with classification, or with utility, or with the moral good – in short, someone who is disinterested, who responds to the item in question, whether natural phenomenon or work of art, not for what it stands for but for what it is. Beauty is not, on Kant's view, a *property* of objects, but we talk – and not incorrectly – as if it were. The sublime is different. When we confront something so vast, so powerful and potentially dangerous as to defeat our attempts to grasp it, we incline to say that the object – a storm at sea, for instance

– is sublime: but that is a plain, though understandable, mistake. A storm is only a storm: what moves us is the reminder of something in ourselves – our unique status as centers of moral authority in the noumenal world. We try, and necessarily fail, to imagine infinity:

> Still the mere *ability even to think* the given infinite without contradiction is something that requires the presence in the human mind of a faculty that is itself supersensible . . . Therefore the feeling of the sublime in nature is respect for our own vocation which we attribute to an Object of nature by a certain subreption (substitution of a respect for the Object in place of one for the idea of humanity in our own self – the Subject); and this feeling renders, as it were, intuitable, the supremacy of our cognitive faculties on the rational side over the greatest faculty of sensibility. (1964: §27)

An interesting idea, even if not very persuasive. To see why Kant was so taken with it, we need to consider the project of the third *Critique* as a whole. He thought he had finished, but two considerations led him to think there was something more to be done. First, he discovered an anomaly in aesthetic judgment – what he calls the "judgment of taste." To say seriously of some individual that it is beautiful is not just to confess that one likes it but to claim that it merits admiration, that everyone *ought* to like it. Kant also saw that such a claim cannot be backed by a generalization, since there are not and cannot be laws or principles of taste.

The second consideration that moved him is more difficult to describe: having made a point of distinguishing the world of nature, what science studies, from the moral realm where freedom reigns, he complained (perhaps unreasonably) that there is too little connection between the two and that a "bridge" is needed. He thought that an explication of the beautiful and the sublime could provide such a bridge. What he meant to do and the extent to which his efforts are successful are questions in dispute, but here is a tentative suggestion: Kant was committed to rejecting all arguments for the existence of God, since they pretend to say something about ultimate reality, but he seems to have been haunted by the so-called "argument from design," according to which God is not only all-powerful but intelligent and just. If that argument were valid, then life would have

9

coherent meaning, morality would comport with science, virtue would be rewarded. A telling observation of Kant's is that when we find some natural object, such as a wild flower, beautiful, we see it as having a purpose although we know that it does not: and that when we find a work of art beautiful, we imagine it as having just grown, like a wild flower, rather than having been made, as we know it to have been, with a purpose. Therefore, if we find beauty in the universe as a whole, we see it *as if* it were the creation of an artist. There is no reason to think that the world *has* been planned, but it is cheering and invigorating to think that it *might* have been.

What gap is the sublime supposed to bridge? Perhaps it is the division, again one established by Kant himself, between the moral realm where action accords with principle and the aesthetic realm where there is perception and feeling but no principle. On Kant's view, an action has moral worth only if the agent is moved by respect for the moral law rather than by any hope of reward, here or in the afterlife. The sublime is marked by feelings of awe and respect, but remember that it is also a source of *pleasure*. Kant's idea may be that a correct interpretation of my response to mountains and storms will provide me with an incentive to do my duty. Vast and powerful forces give me a sense of elation: I think, "They can crush me and yet I am still (like Pascal's 'thinking reed') superior to them." Then I realize that the storms and mountains represent or symbolize my strong inclinations to act as I wish without reference to the moral law, and that I have the power to triumph over such temptation. ("My strength is as the strength of ten because my heart is pure.")

If the foregoing speculations are correct, then Kant's motive in the third *Critique* is not to bridge gaps and achieve unity: the distinctions insisted on in the first two *Critiques* are a priori and necessary, not to be overridden. His wish is, rather, to make the whole system less austere and more congenial. That, one might argue, is a retrograde step: it is not the philosopher's job, any more than it is the scientist's, to come up with results that are attractive and inspiring. In Longinus the sublime is a matter of style and feeling and so, despite Kant's efforts, it remains. You can master the grand style and pick sublime topics, and yet write something that is no good at all. You can be thrilled in a storm by fantasies about your own omnipotence, and yet remain a selfish and inconsiderate person. The sense of spiritual elevation is not an indication of actual spiritual elevation.

See also AESTHETICS IN ANTIQUITY; EIGHTEENTH-CENTURY AESTHETICS; AESTHETIC PLEASURE; BEAUTY; BURKE; KANT.

BIBLIOGRAPHY
Addison, Joseph. 1966 [1711–14]. *The Spectator*. 4 vols. G. Smith (ed.). Dutton: Everyman.
Burke, Edmund. 1958 [1757]. *A Philosophical Enquiry into the Origin of Our Ideas of the Sublime and the Beautiful*. J. T. Boulton (ed.). London: Routledge & Kegan Paul.
Kant, Immanuel. 1960 [1764]. *Observations on the Feeling of the Beautiful and Sublime*. J. T. Goldthwait (trans.). Berkeley: University of California Press.
Kant, Immanuel. 1964 [1790]. *The Critique of Judgement*. J. C. Meredith (trans.). Oxford: Clarendon.
Monk, Samuel H. 1960. *The Sublime*. Ann Arbor: University of Michigan Press.

MARY MOTHERSILL

symbol   A semantic construct which substitutes one term or entity for another. At this level of generality the notion of a symbol can easily be equated with that of a sign, usually a broader category, or that of metaphor, which is a narrower one.

Indeed, one of the difficulties in using the term "symbol" results from lack of agreement as to whether all signs are symbols or all symbols are signs. If one regards all signs as symbols, one usually turns "symbolizing" into a variety of semantic or rhetorical operations, most of which involve substitution or "standing in for." An example would be using a picture of parched earth to symbolize a drought. So understood, symbolizing has little specific aesthetic meaning. But if symbols are understood as a subcategory of signs, matters may stand otherwise. True, it is not enough for symbolizing to be aesthetically significant that it merely be an instance of semiosis. But in aesthetics, symbols are often treated as a special or privileged case of the semiotic. Indeed, there are those who claim that the symbol is central to works of art, and is therefore more than merely a matter of the substitution of one semantic term for another or the generation of sign-making possibility. In this context, the symbol is understood as an inherently aesthetic entity or act.

For those who make this larger claim, the symbol partakes not only of the semiotic realm but also of the psychological and even of the ontological. Symbols are, then, not what make up art but rather what make art possible. This larger claim rests on a tradition most importantly developed in the Romantic era, a tradition that culminated in the Symbolist art of the later nineteenth century. But even before this tradition developed its complex genealogy, the understanding of the concept of sign was influencing the possible meanings of "symbol." In Augustine's hermeneutics, for example, the ancient distinction between natural and conventional signs is extended into an at least incipient understanding that the entire created world can be a symbol – or a repository of usable symbols – since it is the incarnate word of God. Though Augustine more often uses the term "sign" instead of "symbol," his larger claims about the symbolic (as opposed to the literal) meaning of sacred scripture make most sense if read as the foundation of much medieval aesthetics.

But it was at the end of the eighteenth century and the beginning of the nineteenth that the symbol began to play a crucial role in aesthetics. In 1801, August Schlegel argued that "making poetry (in the broadest sense of the poetic that is at the root of all the arts) is nothing other than an eternal symbolizing" (quoted in Todorov 1984: 198). For Schlegel the symbol was the way (the semantic structure, if you will) by which the infinite was able to appear in finite expression. Todorov (1984: 198) argues convincingly that this is the cornerstone of Romantic aesthetics and that all modern meanings of symbol flow from it.

But part of the Romantic understanding of the symbol is knowing what it is not, what it is being defined against: allegory. Allegory, for Romantic writers such as Goethe, was a lesser aesthetic form because it represented the spiritual world in a way that was too literal (paradoxically reversing the medieval sense of allegory, which meant all that went beyond the literal). For Goethe, the "allegorical differs from the symbolic in that what the latter designates indirectly, the former designates directly." For him, works of allegory "destroy our interest in representation itself" (Todorov 1984: 199); in other words, allegory betrays or fails adequately to convey spiritual meaning. In part, the distinction here is between natural and conventional signs; allegory is too reliant on convention, whereas symbol is more expressive of natural forms and truths.

Also reminiscent, at least in part, of Augustine's notion of the world as constituted as a symbolic rendering of divine will is the Romantic emphasis on the flux involved in the Romantic symbol, as opposed to allegory's static structure. One property of the symbol for Wilhelm von Humboldt is that "the representation and what is represented [are] in constant mutual exchange," an exchange which can "incite and constrain the mind to linger longer and to penetrate more deeply" (Todorov 1984: 215). This sense of "symbol" is connected with a notion of delay, which suggests that the symbolic meaning occurs only through temporal unfolding. Furthermore, it begins to suggest that symbols have a mystical dimension that surpasses their natural semiosis but builds upon it. These two features of the symbol, its diachronic and its supra-rational dimensions, are what usually mark it off from signs in the broad or common sense. Allegory, like conventional signs, usually involves an intentional and one-to-one correspondence that is regulated and codified. Symbolism, like natural signs, takes its force from laws and an understanding that cannot be so easily limited or contained within definable concepts.

The mystical aspects of Romantic aesthetics were encouraged by writers such as Swedenborg, who said that nature is a system of correspondences between the heavenly and the human, and that these correspondences are manifest through symbols. However, it was more from Swedenborg's many expositors that the symbol came to be thoroughly aestheticized. Emerson, reading Swedenborg in the middle of the nineteenth century, lamented his lack of a developed poetics and went on to supply one for him, in *Nature* (1836). The Symbolists in France were also heavily indebted to Swedenborgian mysticism. Mallarmé's claim that to name a thing is to destroy it, while to suggest it is to give it life, is an extension of the idea that symbolic expression is necessary to establish and uncover connections that are otherwise lost to merely rational cognition.

Another major development in the aesthetic use of the symbolic came about through Freud, whose model of the psyche, with its language of condensation and displacement, can be seen as a semiosis which makes considerable use of symbolic substitution. Indeed, it is possible to see Freud as offering a thoroughly secularized view of the correspondence theory of meaning, as the semiotic processes of projection and introjection establish connections between the realms of objective existence and subjective experience. The landscape of the psyche is filled with symbols, usually in the form of images that are invested with emotion and contain the residue of traumatic events. One of Freud's main expositors, Jacques Lacan, goes so far as to use the term "symbolic" to refer to the whole realm of language and semantic meaning, a realm in which the real and imaginary are mediated. Since in the Freudian scheme the unconscious can be imagined as a place of immeasurable depth, and as a place where the "normal" sense of logical identity does not apply, it can be regarded not only as a locale but as a source of symbolic forms or symbolizing energies.

Such psychological adaptations of the complex uses of symbols and symbol-making are themselves part of a larger development in what is called "the problematic of language." This very complex set of ideas, interrelated and also contradictory, questions the assumption that language is "merely" a transparent medium through which meaning passes unobstructed. Language, especially its symbolizing properties, is more accurately seen as constituting meaning rather than reflecting it. The problematic developed in the nineteenth century, partly in tandem with Romantic aesthetics, in a sense culminated with Nietzsche, who saw most concepts or ideas as tropes or metaphors that have become calcified by long use; thus all ideas are symbolic transformations whose changes are now hidden from view. But this problematic also involves a cross-fertilization with many writers on myth. For example, Herder's notions of the relations between language and national or ethnic identity add to the sense of languages as containing certain crucial prelogical truths that are best expressed in symbolic form. For such writers, mythological thinking is a special case of symbolizing activity, where an otherwise ineffable meaning, such as national identity, can be embodied in, or at least expressed through, a collective activity such as the development of a vernacular literature. Here, the symbolic is at once natural and conventional.

The conception of the symbol as a special instance of condensation also shows up in a poet such as Pound, whose theory of imagism, according to which an image is a complex of emotional and intellectual truth in an instant of time, is related to late Romantic, anti-allegorical notions. Pound also said that "the natural object is always the adequate symbol," thus bringing to a peak the bias in favor of natural over conventional signs. In very broad terms, the symbol is used frequently in post-Romantic thought to convey either a realm or a construct of meaning in which more is compressed than can be spelled out. Wherever an aesthetician needs to discuss an experience or a meaning in which both the substitution of terms and the compression of meaning occur, there is likely to be some reference to the concept of the symbol.

See also HERMENEUTICS; INEFFABILITY; LANGER; METAPHOR; PSYCHOANALYSIS AND ART; REPRESENTATION; SCHLEGEL, A.

BIBLIOGRAPHY

Adams, Hazard. 1983. *The Philosophy of the Literary Symbolic*. Gainesville: University Presses of Florida.

Balaikian, Anna. 1973. *The Symbolist Movement*. New York: New York University Press.

Emerson, Ralph Waldo. 1982. *Selected Essays*. Harmondsworth: Penguin.

Todorov, Tzvetan. 1984 [1977]. *The Theory of the Symbol*. C. Porter (trans.). Ithaca: Cornell University Press.

CHARLES MOLESWORTH

T

taste   The ability to judge the aesthetic and artistic aspects of works of art and nature, or (sometimes) whatever capacity or sensibility underlies that ability. Since it is obvious that we do make aesthetic and artistic judgments, it is uncontroversial that there is such a thing as taste in the former sense. The idea that that ability is underpinned by some further capacity, especially one with the features described below, is more contentious. As a philosophical idea, taste's heyday was the Enlightenment, in the work of Shaftesbury, Hutcheson, Hume, Reid, Kant, and others. However, outside philosophy the term still has some prominence, and provides many people with their strongest intuitive purchase on some key issues in philosophical aesthetics.

The most obvious feature of the word "taste" is the analogy it invites us to draw with the activities of eating and drinking, and our preferences therein. Three aspects to that analogy particularly merit attention. The first is the idea that our ability to make aesthetic and artistic judgments is, like that for gustatory discriminations, rooted in something affective – in pleasure or displeasure. Perhaps that casts the net too narrowly. Sometimes we base our judgments of art on other responses: for instance, shock or boredom, sorrow or nostalgia. But the idea that those judgments are rooted, not in purely cognitive states, such as thinking or perceiving, but at least in part in feelings, has proved persistent in its appeal.

The second aspect of the analogy is related. While cognitive states are rule-governed, feelings are not. My judgment that what is before me is a chair commits me to thinking that the object meets certain conditions – that it is an artifact designed for sitting. I cannot comprehensibly make that judgment unless I take those conditions to be met. The cognitive state is thus subject to a rule – I can make that judgment only if I am prepared to make certain others. Pleasure and displeasure (whether gustatory or aesthetic) and other feelings, in contrast, are not similarly rule-bound. Perhaps they must be stable across different encounters with a given thing. If I liked the pie, or the painting, last time, and if neither it nor I have changed, there is something wrong if this time I feel otherwise. But there is certainly no requirement for stability across different objects. I may like one kind of pie while quite legitimately disliking another; or find beautiful one painting in a certain style while feeling entirely indifferent to another from that school. Kant, who first expressed this idea clearly, captured it in the claim that there are no "principles of taste," general claims from which one could deduce that the object before one is beautiful (2000: §34). More recently, Frank Sibley (1959) offered an alternative expression of the idea in claiming that there are no logically sufficient conditions in non-aesthetic terms for the application of aesthetic concepts. For both these philosophers, since grasping the mundane features of what is before one is insufficient for judging its aesthetic or artistic aspect, that ability requires one to exercise some further capacity – "taste" in the more controversial of the two senses with which we began.

We should distinguish three forms of freedom from rules. Kant is surely right that we often make aesthetic judgments without being *guided* by such principles. To discover whether a piece of music is beautiful I will merely listen to it carefully; I will not usually also ponder general claims about what beauty in music consists in. It is another thing to say that our various judgments cannot be *systematized* into principles, principles I might then use to justify a judgment already made, or to guide me in those cases in which exposure to the work leaves me uncertain of its quality. Whether such systematization is possible is moot. I can usually say what I like in one piece of music or another, but I am far from confident that I could produce general principles capturing precisely my likes and dislikes, however much time I had to formulate them. The liveliness of a Bach partita is pleasing, but a similar quality grates in some of Telemann's work; and parallel counterexamples confront every principle for which I reach. Does this merely reflect lack of ingenuity on my part, or are such principles unobtainable? That question has been much debated (Hume 2004; Kant 2000; Mothersill 1986; Dickie 2006; Goldman 2006). Finally, there is the issue whether aesthetic judgment is subject to *explanatory* rules. What, we might ask, explains why I respond to some objects by finding them, for example, beautiful, and others by finding them not so? If the explanation lies in some feature or features common to the former and lacking in the latter, even if those are features I could never discover by merely reflecting on my assessments of them, then there is a kind of rule-governedness to aesthetic judgment after all. We might think this could hardly fail to be the case. *Something* must explain my responses, and what else is available? However, there is an alternative: that the response (here, finding something beautiful) emerges only from the way objects and my psychophysiological system interact, so that objects quite varied in themselves nonetheless all have that effect on me. Certainly that may be the way to explain other responses of ours – some have argued that our experience of color fits this model (Hardin 1993).

Together, the role of feeling in aesthetic judgment and its failure to be (in at least some senses) governed by rules raise the question whether aesthetic judgment can be objective. Unlike cognitive states such as perceptions and thoughts, feelings do not even purport to represent how things are in the world to which they are a response. While a visual experience, for instance, presents the objects that cause it as being a certain way, a feeling such as pleasure does not. What sense, then, can we make of some of these responses being right, others wrong (Hume 2004: 495; Kant 2000: 89)? If the responses were themselves systematically related to conditions obtaining in the world to which we respond, we might be able to

answer. But they are not so related, for, it is claimed, neither the responses nor the judgments they ground are rule-governed. Hence aesthetic judgment threatens to be as much a matter of personal preference as one's likings in food or wine. Both are, it would seem, "only a matter of taste."

However, while the threat may be there, it is too hasty to assume that it cannot be met. For a start, there is the question of the sense in which aesthetic judgment is free from rules. At first glance, its being bound by explanatory rules would be enough to give it some kind of objectivity – there would be some pattern in the world which my aesthetic judgments reflect, even if the way those judgments present the relevant objects (as, for instance, beautiful) is rather different from the way we think of them in identifying the relevant pattern (as having whatever features are responsible for our finding them beautiful). Of course, aesthetic judgment may not be bound by explanatory rules. But even if it is not we can hope to make sense of its objectivity. The attempt to do this lies at the heart of Kant's thinking in aesthetics. He tries to locate the explanation for our aesthetic responses in features sufficiently entrenched and universal to guarantee that we would, given ideal conditions, all respond the same way to the same things. It is unclear whether Kant succeeds. This is not the place to examine that question, or those hanging over the various other attempts to reconcile the objectivity of aesthetic judgment with the features described above. Suffice to say that what they are trying to do is not clearly impossible. Indeed, optimism about their prospects is encouraged by certain platitudes about taste. For, much as we are inclined to dismiss matters of taste as beyond reasoned dispute, we also acknowledge that not all tastes are equal. A person "of taste" has a personal quality that is not merely different from ours, but something to which we might intelligibly aspire. And try looking back on your earlier preferences in art without considering them *inferior* to those that have taken their place. Taste, it would seem, can be educated – that is, made *better*.

Nonetheless, even if some tastes are better than others, I am not obliged to bring my own tastes into line with superior ones in any comprehensive way. Here we encounter the last aspect to the analogy between taste in aesthetics and taste in food and drink – the thought of taste as something personal, and legitimately so. This may seem simply to return us to the idea that in matters of taste there is no objectivity; but that is quite wrong. Consider the notion of personal taste as contrasted with the canon. The latter is a list of the works the greatness of which all ought to acknowledge – something that would seem to make sense only on the assumption of some form of objectivity. The former, in contrast, is a list of works that particularly appeal to the individual. Perhaps one must *admire* all that is great, but one need not like it, or want to spend time with it. Conversely, there is leeway (at least up to a point) to like, and to want to live with, works which are not masterpieces. This aspect to the notion of taste *requires* the canon, and hence objectivity, as the background against which it is defined. As Hume noted, what pleases the young man may not suit him so well in his middle or later years (2004: 504). As his character and situation in life shift, so do those works that he finds most amenable. Although Hume does not himself draw this moral, it is tempting to think that, while our likings and dislikings, along with other affects, (arguably) ground all aesthetic judgments, there is nonetheless room to distinguish between those likings that reflect the merits of the work, and those more tailored to the idiosyncrasies of our own nature.

Although philosophers of art talk about taste rather less than they once did, there is some justification for claiming that the notion has lost none of its importance to philosophy in general. The idea that a form of judgment might be both objective and, in certain key senses, free from rules has in recent years attracted attention beyond aesthetics. *Particularists* in ethics argue that ethical judgment shares these features. There too, we base our judgments not on general principles, but on how, guided by sensibility, we respond to the specifics of the case before us (Dancy 2004). Others (McDowell 1979; Bell 1987), reacting to Wittgenstein's profound inquiry into what following a rule could amount to, have thought that *every* form of judgment must, in the end, turn on something itself not rule-governed. If so, far from being distinctive in combining these features, judgments based on the exercise of taste provide the true model for the act of judging itself.

See also AESTHETIC EDUCATION; AESTHETIC JUDGMENT; AESTHETICS OF FOOD AND DRINK; BEAUTY; CANON; HUME; HUTCHESON; KANT; OBJECTIVITY AND REALISM IN AESTHETICS; SHAFTESBURY; SIBLEY.

BIBLIOGRAPHY
Bell, David. 1987. "The Art of Judgement." *Mind*, 96, 221–44.
Dancy, Jonathan. 2004. *Ethics without Principles*. Oxford: Clarendon.
Dickie, George. 2006. "Iron, Leather and Critical Principles." In *Contemporary Debates in Aesthetics and the Philosophy of Art*. M. Kieran (ed.). Oxford: Blackwell, 313–26.
Goldman, Alan. 2006. "There are No Aesthetic Principles." In *Contemporary Debates in Aesthetics and the Philosophy of Art*. M. Kieran (ed.). Oxford: Blackwell, 299–312.
Hardin, C. L. 1993. *Color for Philosophers*. Expanded edn. Indianapolis: Hackett.
Hume, David. 2004 [1757]. "Of the Standard of Taste." In *Philosophy: Basic Readings*. N. Warburton (ed.). London: Routledge, 493–507.
Kant, Immanuel. 2000 [1790]. *Critique of the Power of Judgment*. P. Guyer & E. Matthews (trans.). Cambridge: Cambridge University Press.
McDowell, John. 1979. "Virtue and Reason," *Monist*, 62, 331–50.
Mothersill, Mary. 1986. *Beauty Restored*. Oxford: Clarendon.
Sibley, Frank. 1959. "Aesthetic Concepts," *Philosophical Review*, 68, 421–50.

ROBERT HOPKINS

technology and art Technology has always played a central role in the fine arts and has had a decisive impact on their development historically. Changes in the arts have frequently reflected changes in the technologies available to artists. Examples abound: the development of oil paint led to easel painting in the sixteenth century; the invention and development of the piano (1700–1860) enabled the development of new genres of classical music such as the piano sonata; and, in more precipitate fashion, the invention of the electric pickup, solid body electric guitar, and multitrack recording made rock music possible. On top of this, there are art forms that were from the beginning based on a new technology, those that Noël Carroll calls the "self-consciously invented arts of film, video, and photography" (1996: 3).

Technologies have affected both the construction of artworks and the way that they are communicated and experienced. Accordingly, there is a distinction between those technologies that create new ways to make or arrange the elements of works (e.g., photography, music synthesizers) and those that create new means of communication (e.g., TV, the Internet). Then there are technologies that have greatly affected the presentation of art without changing the nature of the art presented, for example, the use of electric lighting in museums and European cathedrals – this latter enabling viewers to see frescos more accurately and arguably differently than in earlier times. However, presentational technology can also so change the art presented as to lead to a new art form. Amplification and recording of music is a case in point. Early in its development it merely made live musical performances accessible to a wider audience. But the development of rock music and advancements in recording technology since the 1960s, according to Theodore Gracyk (1996), have led to and been constitutive of a new type of autographic musical work: the rock recording. Thus, a technology for recording an art form precipitated an evolution from a sonic record of live performance to a separate studio-based art form.

Although technology has always been intertwined with the arts, when writers worry about the impact of technology on the arts and on the very notion of fine art they usually have in mind technologies developed after the industrial revolution, technologies of mass production and distribution, as well as the contemporary explosion of digital media. (For an extensive review of these worries see Carroll 1998.) Noël Carroll proposes that we call these new technologies "mass technologies" (1998: 3). These are technological developments beginning with the invention of photography in the nineteenth century and film in the twentieth, recording technologies leading to sound and visual media, broadcast media (TV and radio), and including new digital technologies, for example, interactive web-based art, video games, etc. These technologies have made both traditional and new sorts of artworks or their reproductions available to almost everyone in a high-tech society.

This explosion of technology brings with it categorizing questions. First, if technology makes possible a novel cultural form with significant resemblance to previous art, is it art? Video games are a case in point. Their enormous popularity and increase in sophistication have made them prime candidates for the status of art. Smuts (2005) argues that if we evaluate them from the perspective of the various definitions of art currently debated, such as institutional or aesthetic definitions, or even from traditional points of view involving expression and representation, we should conclude that *some* video games merit the status of art and some probably do not (see also Tavinor 2005). The same question is debated concerning other mass-technology products that have roots in commerce (software projects) or in entertainment (YouTube mashups) rather than in regular artworld contexts such as galleries. Proponents of the usefulness of definitions of art could argue that this situation confirms their position: the constant growth of technology arguably makes it more imperative than in the past to have some principal way to justify applying or denying the status of fine art to new media products.

If a technology is applied to traditional arts, such as poems and novels, the question is not likely to be "Is it art?" but rather, "Is it the *same* art form?" For example, so-called hypertext poetry, often found online, uses visuals and links so that the text (and visuals) have no set order in which to be read, and the text may alter and be interactive. This invites the question: are "hypertext poems" *poems*, merely a hybrid of other forms, or a new art form?

Hypertext poetry is an application of new media to an established art form embedded in old media (words printed on a page). Art forms that were originally based on mass technology, such as film, are hostage to technological development from their beginning. As the technology underlying a technologically embedded art form evolves, does it eventually bring about a new art form worthy of its own aesthetic account? For example, is the march from silent black and white movies, through sound and color, to computer-generated imagery and on to digital movies with CGI merely an expansion of the art of film or is it the evolution of new art forms? Questions about the nature of technologically created art forms have been explored extensively in film theory. The notion that film is a specific medium with essential features received much favorable attention by early film theorists; more recently, such notions have come in for substantial criticism in the work of Carroll (1996, 2008).

What is the relation of technology to media and of media to art forms? Is a medium defined by the technologies it uses, and does a medium dictate the nature of the art form that is embedded in it? One set of answers to such question is given by the view called medium essentialism. Medium essentialism is "the doctrine that each art form has its own specific medium – as painting has paint, and film has film" (Carroll 2008: 36). Medium essentialists hold that this doctrine has normative implications both for how to evaluate works and also what artists can and should strive for. Roughly the view is that the medium dictates distinctive effects and possibilities that artists working within the medium should exploit; hence the medium can be viewed as determining what the art form is about, what makes it a film or a painting. (For a historical overview of medium specificity positions from Lessing's *Laocoön* to photographic and film theorists, and for criticisms, see Carroll 1996, 2008.)

But can we pair up art forms and media, as this view requires? One problem is that there may be some art forms that do not have distinctive media, such as poems and novels; poems need *a* medium to encode words, but that could be ink on a page, chiseled grooves in stone, sound waves, or digital files. If it is said that the medium is words, this does not dictate which uses of words constitute a poem. If media are thought of as defined by technological possibilities, then some media underlie multiple art forms (e.g., digital media or image printing on paper underlie lithographs and comics). Moreover, it is not obvious how to individuate technologies (e.g., image-editing programs or types of photography), nor how to individuate material media, much less to figure out how to correlate the two.

There is, in addition, a serious ambiguity in writing about media. On the one hand, media are treated as providing a way to make the artist's idea "physically manifest for reception" (Carroll 2008: 35). This notion of medium is of the materials (paints) and tools (brushes) needed to create the work and make it available. In contrast, it is also common to refer to the artistic medium, as in the "film medium" or "the medium of comics." In this sense, a medium may be described in terms that are in reality standard or defining features of the art form, such as describing the medium of comics as sequential pictures and texts (or speech balloons) intended to convey a narrative. It is in this sense that Meskin says, "Comics are among those media – like film and photography – that can be used to make art, but can also be used non-artistically" (2007: 370). But if the "medium" of an art form turns out to be its formal features – line, space, shape, motion, temporal and narrative structures for film (Carroll 1996: 52) – then no particular technology appears necessary or to imply the art form's features.

That said, it seems clear that new digital technology, with its shift from physically mechanical to computational technologies, has provided potentially radical new possibilities for art forms. Binkley claims that there is a deep inherent difference between analogue and digital media; he claims that digital media are "vital" because they involve both virtual reality and interactivity. "If images make their subjects present to us, digital representations make us present to them" (1997: 108).

Although rock records are not essentially embedded in digital media, one effect of so embedding them may be to bring about a change in cultural notions of their identity, and this may turn out to be true of all art forms now embedded in digital media, such as digital movies. The general willingness to illegally download, to sample and produce mashups, the multiple mixes and remixes of songs, all suggest that digital works may already be treated as having different or very loose identity conditions compared to traditional rock recordings, movies, or traditionally notated pieces of music.

A different impact that technology may have on work identity occurs because of how museums and other cultural venues have digitalized and multiplied images of traditional artworks. This challenge concerns the way these practices encourage a severing of artworks from their original cultural context, whether by appropriating paintings for use on T-shirts or projection on video screens, or the use of music in commercials and movies. The question is whether such practices are bringing about a change in our concept of what an artwork is, namely, that artworks are historically indexed individuals to be most properly appreciated as the products of their time and place.

New technologies have not only expanded established art forms, generated new art forms, and affected the way traditional art forms are experienced, but perhaps also diluted the very status of the fine arts in general. Walter Benjamin was one of the first to argue that the new mass technologies would in fact undermine the traditional status of art. In his much cited essay, "The Work of Art in the Age of Mechanical Reproduction" (1935), he proposed an account of how the development of mass technologies of various sorts – photography, film, music recordings, and radio – by enabling the multiplication and distribution of artworks and their reproductions, would destroy the traditional "aura" that Benjamin thought attached to artworks before the twentieth century. This quasi-religious aura attached to past artworks, such as paintings, plays, and classical music, because of their scarcity; such art was handmade, unique, and available only in museums and concert halls. By contrast, the production and distribution of multiple copies of artworks made possible by the new mass technology allows the masses to experience and even possess artworks, which undermines, so Benjamin argued, the auratic character of traditional art: "that which withers in the age of mechanical reproduction is the aura of the work of art . . . By making many reproductions it substitutes plurality of copies for unique existence" (1969: 221).

Recently, Carroll has developed an account of the effects of mass technology on the arts that draws a different conclusion. He proposes that such technologies have generated a new subcategory of art that he calls "mass art." He characterizes a mass artwork as any sort of artwork – whether involving music, moving images, TV, or whatever – that inherently has multiple copies and is "produced and distributed by a mass technology" (1998: 196). Because such art, by definition, aims at a mass audience, it must also be designed and structured in such a way as to aim for "accessibility with minimum effort, virtually at first contact, for the largest number of untutored (or relatively untutored) audiences" (1998: 196). He suggests that all mass artworks merit being categorized as art, although not necessarily as good art (see Carroll 2004; Fisher 2004). Categorizing mass arts as art argues that, contrary to the views of many cultural critics, the use of mass technologies in making and distributing art forms does not prevent some of them, such as great movies, from being great works of art.

See also MUSIC AND SONG; MOTION PICTURES; DEFINITION OF "ART"; MASS ART; POPULAR ART.

BIBLIOGRAPHY
Benjamin, Walter. 1969 [1935]. "The Work of Art in the Age of Mechanical Reproduction." In *Illuminations*. H. Zorn (trans.). H. Arendt (ed.). New York: Schocken, 217–51.
Binkley, Timothy. 1997. "The Vitality of Digital Creation." *Journal of Aesthetics and Art Criticism*, 55, 107–16.
Carroll, Noël. 1996. *Theorizing the Moving Image*. Cambridge: Cambridge University Press.
Carroll, Noël. 1998. *A Philosophy of Mass Art*. Oxford: Clarendon.
Carroll, Noël. 2004. "Mass Art as Art: A Response to John Fisher," *Journal of Aesthetics and Art Criticism*, 62, 61–5.
Carroll, Noël. 2008. *The Philosophy of Motion Pictures*. Malden: Blackwell.
Fisher, John Andrew. 1998. "Rock 'n' Recording: The Ontological Complexity of Rock Music." In *Musical Worlds: New Directions in the Philosophy of Music*. P. Alperson (ed.). University Park: Pennsylvania State University Press, 109–23.
Fisher, John Andrew. 2004. "On Carroll's Enfranchisement of Mass Art as Art," *Journal of Aesthetics and Art Criticism*, 62, 57–62.
Fisher, John Andrew & Potter, Jason. 1997. "Technology, Appreciation, and the Historical View of Art," *Journal of Aesthetics and Art Criticism*, 55, 169–85.
Gracyk, Theodore. 1996. *Rhythm and Noise: An Aesthetics of Rock*. Durham: Duke University Press.
Meskin, Aaron. 2007. "Defining Comics?" *Journal of Aesthetics and Art Criticism*, 65, 369–79.
Saltz, David. 1997. "The Art of Interaction: Interactivity, Performativity, and Computers," *Journal of Aesthetics and Art Criticism*, 55, 117–27.

Smuts, Aaron. 2005. "Are Video Games Art?" *Contemporary Aesthetics*, 3. Available at www.contempaesthetics.org/newvolume/pages/article.php?articleID=299

Swanson, Will. 2006. "Beautiful Noise." *Contemporary Aesthetics*, 4. Available at www.contempaesthetics.org/newvolume/pages/article.php?articleID=464

Tavinor, Grant. 2005. "Videogames and Interactive Fiction," *Philosophy and Literature*, 29, 24–40.

Youngblood, Gene. 1989. "Cinema and the Code," *Leonardo*, supp. issue 2, "Computer Art in Context," 27–30.

JOHN ANDREW FISHER

testimony in aesthetics   In general, there are various means by which we might legitimately form belief on a given topic. Perception, reasoning, and memory are all – at least when the subject matter is of a suitable kind – central examples. For most subject matters, the testimony of others also plays this role. Most of my scientific beliefs, and almost all that I know of history, geography, and what my acquaintances get up to when I am not there is directly dependent on what I have been told about these things. But is testimony a legitimate source of belief on every topic? Some think that aesthetic matters are an exception.

Normally, when we learn from another on a topic, testimony mingles with other sources of belief. Our informants often offer us reasons to believe what they say, as well as baldly asserting things we are intended to take on trust. If we are to identify the contribution of testimony to knowledge in general, and thus to examine the claim that it cannot play this role in aesthetic matters, we should concentrate on pure cases – those in which our informant merely asserts the claim in question, and does not offer us any reasons for believing it. Such cases are rather artificial, and perhaps especially so in the aesthetic realm, but they help focus the issue before us.

Suppose you read a neglected novel and tell me that it is excellent. Is it legitimate for me to adopt this view, simply on your say-so? No doubt if there is to be any chance of an affirmative answer, certain conditions must be met. If I know nothing of you and your tastes, or if I know that in general your judgment is terrible, I should not take your word on the matter. But suppose the situation is more favorable. In the past, I have found your opinions to tally closely with my own. You have no interest that might tempt you into an unduly favorable judgment (it is not, say, that you are a relative of the author, or have shares in the publisher). Perhaps you are even a well-respected critic. Even so, many feel, I cannot simply base my judgment on yours. Maybe your view should carry some weight. But can it justify my forming the matching belief? That seems more suspect. Certainly, your claim does not leave me in a position to make the same assertion to someone else. If I now say the book is excellent, without citing you as the source of that opinion, my audience is liable to feel misled. Yet in other matters, I can readily assert what I have come to believe through testimony without having always to flag the fact that the opinion I offer comes from someone else.

Considerations such as these motivate some to deny that testimony is a legitimate source of belief on aesthetic matters (Hopkins 2000). Let us call them *pessimists* about aesthetic testimony, and those who take the opposite view *optimists*. It might seem that the issue between these two camps is rather elusive. In no area is it plausible that one can *always* take another's word: some informants are too obviously incompetent, or have too strong an interest in one's adopting a certain view, for blanket trust to be rational. It is equally implausible that in aesthetic matters one can *never* rely on another's testimony. Surely aesthetic judgment needs educating, and surely that process will involve taking some aesthetic beliefs on trust. So one might expect the pessimist and the optimist to differ only in quite *how often* they consider it acceptable to take aesthetic testimony – an issue that looks rather intractable. However, we can find a more focused disagreement between the two, by appeal to the idea of a difference in kind. Can I legitimately take another's word on an aesthetic issue? Pessimists say "no" – aesthetic matters differ in kind, in this respect, from most others. Optimists disagree – one can take aesthetic testimony, and any difference here is merely one of degree.

The issue of testimony should be distinguished from others in aesthetics. One is whether we can legitimately form aesthetic belief by appeal to principles of taste. Such principles are generalizations to the effect that anything with a certain nonaesthetic feature has (or will tend to have) some aesthetic feature. Knowledge of these principles would allow us to construct arguments from nonaesthetic premises to aesthetic conclusions. The debate over principles is thus in effect over whether we can form aesthetic belief on the basis of a certain kind of reasoning. The question concerning testimony is different. One need not think that learning from testimony involves any form of reasoning, but, even if it does, it will not be reasoning from principles of taste. Moreover, while testimony might play a role in arguments that appeal to such principles, it would be as a source of knowledge of their premises, not of the aesthetic judgment that forms the conclusion. Similarly, the issue of testimony should not be confused with whether forming aesthetic belief requires us to exercise "taste." Since taste is meant to be a sensitivity that goes beyond our ability to perceive the nonaesthetic properties of the object judged, the question here is whether ordinary perception suffices for aesthetic judgment. Again, the question of testimony is distinct. For even if in general an exercise of taste lies at the root of our knowledge of the aesthetic properties of particular things, that leaves open the question whether such knowledge, once acquired, can be passed on via testimony.

Why does the debate over aesthetic testimony matter? It does so because, if pessimism is true, the failure of testimony may point to deeper features of aesthetic judgment. After all, if aesthetic judgments cannot be passed on via testimony, when judgments of most other kinds can, it is natural to ask why this should be.

A simple answer, perhaps to be found in Kant (2000), lies in the claim that the canonical ground of aesthetic belief lies in experience. Experience is our ultimate guide to the aesthetic character of things. Forming one's belief on any other basis is thus to put oneself in a position that is epistemically second-rate. Unfortunately, although the key claim here is certainly true, it fails to yield the desired explanation. Experience is the canonical ground of other judgments, too – color provides one obvious example. Yet we can quite unproblematically learn the color of things on the say-so of others. Why is the same not true in aesthetic matters?

A more sweeping explanation appeals to anticognitivism in aesthetics. Testimony is a way of passing on knowledge. It will thus fail if there is no knowledge to pass on. A variety of positions on the metaphysics and semantics of aesthetic judgment claim precisely that. We need not enter into the details here, for in any form the proposed explanation faces a serious objection. Those who think testimony is not a legitimate source of aesthetic belief do not, in general, think that there is no such source. On the contrary, they urge us to exercise perception and careful thought to make up our own minds – to study the novel, or film, or natural landscape for ourselves. What is the point of this strenuous activity, if there is no aesthetic knowledge for it to yield? Perhaps the anticognitivist will hope to find something other than knowledge to make sense of thinking for ourselves here. But that just raises the question why *that* is something testimony cannot pass on.

A final prominent explanation appeals to the extent of disagreement in aesthetic matters. Where informants disagree, some must be unreliable. The more disagreement there is in an area, the more unreliable we must in general take informants on those matters to be. Aesthetic testimony fails to deliver knowledge because, given the widespread disagreement in aesthetic matters, it is too difficult to identify reliable informants (Meskin 2004). The problem for this account is to explain the failure of aesthetic testimony without mandating agnosticism. The more widespread disagreement, the less reason there is to think that *anyone* is a good judge in the matter in hand – oneself included. Thus it is unclear how this account justifies resisting testimony without requiring one to eschew aesthetic belief altogether.

The failure of these explanations might lead us to wonder whether pessimism could be true. Why would testimony fail in aesthetics, if none of the obvious accounts of how it does so are successful? Such defeatism is premature. The three explanations above share a common form. They all assume that the problem with aesthetic testimony will be epistemic. Aesthetic testimony is not a legitimate source of aesthetic belief because it cannot, for one reason or another, meet the epistemic norms governing testimony in general. (For current purposes, we can just treat "knowledge" as the name for belief that meets those norms.) However, another form of explanation is possible. It might be that aesthetic testimony is epistemically kosher, but problematic in some other way. In other words, perhaps aesthetic testimony meets all the epistemic norms governing testimony in general, but fails to meet some further norm specific to the aesthetic case. Aesthetic testimony makes knowledge available, but that further norm renders it illegitimate to make use of that resource.

What could that further norm be? Although various candidates suggest themselves, I will describe just one. Richard Wollheim (1980: 234) suggested that our aesthetic thinking is governed by what he called the "Acquaintance Principle." Roughly, this states that having the right to an aesthetic belief requires one to have experienced for oneself the object it concerns. Discussion of Wollheim's principle has tacitly assumed that it is intended as an epistemic norm, that it governs the conditions under which one's aesthetic belief might count as knowledge. However, it is clearly possible to treat it instead as a norm governing the use that can be made of whatever aesthetic knowledge testimony makes available.

Wollheim probably intended the Acquaintance Principle to prohibit more than aesthetic testimony. It certainly also excludes forming aesthetic belief by reasoning from principles of taste. Moreover, Wollheim restricted the scope of the principle to pure verdicts, judgments to the effect that a given object has or lacks aesthetic merit, rather than those ascribing to it more substantive aesthetic properties, such as gracefulness or garishness. He may have been wise to formulate a position that limits the ban on aesthetic testimony in this way. The more an aesthetic belief ascribes a substantive property to the object it concerns, the weaker the intuition tends to be that such belief cannot legitimately be taken from another. Even in this cautious form, the Acquaintance Principle has come in for a good deal of critical discussion. But a pessimist about aesthetic testimony, including one who advocates the sort of view I have sketched, need not defend Wollheim's principle. What she must do, apart from defending pessimism by tackling apparent counterexamples to her claims, is to articulate her position fully, by offering some account of the norm specific to the aesthetic case. That done, she must also turn to the still deeper question why aesthetic discourse is governed by such a norm, when our interactions on many other matters are not.

See also COGNITIVE VALUE OF ART; OBJECTIVITY AND REALISM IN AESTHETICS; SIBLEY; TASTE.

BIBLIOGRAPHY
Budd, Malcolm. 2003. "The Acquaintance Principle," *British Journal of Aesthetics*, 43, 386–92.
Hopkins, Robert. 2000. "Beauty and Testimony." In *Philosophy: The Good, the True and the Beautiful*. A. O'Hear (ed.). Cambridge: Cambridge University Press, 209–36.
Hopkins, Robert. 2001. "Kant, Quasi-Realism and the Autonomy of Aesthetic Judgement," *European Journal of Philosophy*, 9, 166–89.
Kant, Immanuel. 2000 [1790]. *Critique of the Power of Judgement*. P. Guyer & E. Matthews (trans.). Cambridge: Cambridge University Press.
Meskin, Aaron. 2004. "Aesthetic Testimony: What Can We Learn from Others about Beauty and Art?" *Philosophy and Phenomenological Research*, 69, 65–91.
Pettit, Philip. 1983. "The Possibility of Aesthetic Realism." In *Pleasure, Preference and Value*. E. Schaper (ed.). Cambridge: Cambridge University Press, 17–38.
Scruton, Roger. 1974. *Art and Imagination*. London: Methuen.
Wollheim, Richard. 1980. *Art and Its Objects*. 2nd edn. Cambridge: Cambridge University Press.

ROBERT HOPKINS

text   The term "text" is very widely and differently used in contemporary aesthetics. Its denotation ranges from a specific concrete verbal inscription or utterance (existing as a particular spatiotemporal object or event) to an abstract verbal entity manifested in different concrete texts, and beyond that, to any object, event, or action that is construed or interpreted as meaningful. Deconstruction's textualism, with its denial of a *hors-texte* or referent outside of language, can be linked to the latter usage (Derrida 1976: 158).

The meaning of "text" is best understood in its particular theoretical context through its relationship and contrast to the notion of "work" (i.e., literary work, artwork, etc.). Roughly speaking, Anglo-American aesthetics has concentrated on the move from text to work, where textual identity was regarded as something clearer, more determinate, and more precise through which we could determine the more problematic and vague identity and meaning of the work. In contrast, poststructuralist Continental aesthetics has concentrated on the move from work to text, where the work instead is regarded as the clear, determinate, and fixed entity from which we must be liberated into text, conceived now much more broadly and dynamically as the activity of creatively constituting meaning through reading and interpreting. This is a move away from reified meanings and fixed and closed objects of criticism to the flux of textual creation and the play of language, a move sometimes linked (e.g., in Barthes) with a shift of criticism's goal from the truth about the work to the pleasure of the text. Understanding the notion of "text" requires looking more closely at these two contrasting moves.

FROM TEXT TO WORK

Criticism attempts to determine the correct meaning and value of works of art, but this, it is argued, requires determining their identity. We cannot judge the meaning or value of a novel by a bad translation or a drastically abridged version, which does not represent the work's crucial features and aesthetic qualities. But how do we determine the work's identity without already engaging in interpretation and evaluation? One way traditional theory could avoid this problem was to posit the identity of the work in the artist's intention, which even if it was practically unavailable provided a fixed intentional object with which the work could be identified. This option lost its appeal once the authority of authorial intention was challenged by New Criticism's doctrine of the intentional fallacy (see Beardsley 1973: 16) and poststructuralism's doctrine of the death of the author (Barthes 1977). In certain circles of analytic aesthetics, there have been vigorous attempts, since the 1990s, to revive varieties of intentionalism and confront the Beardsleyan, poststructuralist, and other arguments (e.g., see Iseminger 1992; Livingston 2005).

It thus became increasingly convincing to identify the literary work with its text and to view the meaning of the work as the meaning of the text. As Beardsley insisted (1973: 32–4), that textual meaning is more available than authorial intention, being determined by public rules of linguistic meaning. Finally, identifying the work with the text rather than with an authorial intention allows the meaning of the work to change over time while still maintaining its identity. This, it is argued, is because the very same text can change its meaning if its words acquire new meanings over time through linguistic change.

What then is the identity of a text? First, following a terminology introduces by C. S. Peirce, a distinction must be made between different "token" texts and the same "type" text they manifest. The former are concrete spatitemporal particulars, the latter an abstract entity they exemplify. While two copies of *The Wasteland* and an oral declamation of it constitute three different token texts they manifest the same type text, if they present the very same words in the same order. Nelson Goodman, one of the most rigorous in defining literary work identity as textual identity, defines textual identity more precisely in terms of two features: syntactic identity (identity of all the characters of the text including punctuation marks) and identity of language (1969: 209). Most aestheticians find Goodman's criterion of textual identity far too strict, since it rejects as different all sorts of texts that critical practice normally accepts as the same. Not only translations and variant versions are excluded but even texts that have a single unimportant misprint or omit an inconsequential punctuation mark. Moreover, the criterion is obviously inadequate to deal with the important critical question of the comparative authenticity of rival texts of a given work (e.g., whether the folio or second quarto text of *Hamlet* best conveys that work's identity), since for Goodman different type texts mean different works. To avoid this difficulty, some aestheticians (e.g., Stevenson 1957; Margolis 1965) have proposed viewing the work not as a "type" text but as a "megatype," which can embrace different type texts having the same general design or meaning, and thus can include translations and even adaptations to different media.

But with this greater flexibility of textual identity, there is greater vagueness. How do we determine similarity of design or meaning, and what is the semantic standard from which similarity must not depart? At this point, we encounter an intentionalist backlash, which argues that work identity and even textual identity require an appeal to authorial intention. For, as Hirsch (1976) argues, if the same syntactic text can embody different meanings or designs (hence different semantic texts), we obviously need more than textual identity to give us the identity of the work, or indeed to establish the identity of the text itself as a meaningful piece of language. Other intentionalists (Knapp & Michaels 1985) further insist that, since all meaning is intentional, textual meaning is identical with authorial meaning. But this has been shown to involve a false identification of all meaning-giving intentions with those of the historical author (Shusterman 1992: 96–7).

In contrast to attempts to fix the identity of the text through authorial intention or through the syntactic standard, some literary theorists have preferred more radically to question the need for defining or securing a fixed textual identity. We see one form of this strategy in Stanley Fish, who insists that since texts are only constituted through interpretations, different interpretations entail different texts and since the goal of interpretation or explanation is to say something new, there can be "no distinction between explaining a text and changing it" (1989: 98). This view conflates the identity of the text with its interpretative meaning and thus does not adequately account for the possibility that different interpreters or interpretative communities can differ in interpreting the same text. But if interpretative debate is to be meaningful, the same text must be able to sustain different interpretations. To resolve this problem and avoid the conflation of textual identity and interpretation, one can distinguish between a text's logical or referential identity, which allows us to refer to it, and, its substantive identity, the essential nature or full meaning of what we have identified in the first sense (see Shusterman 1992: 94). And as Rorty points out, to secure the first sort of identification there is no need to posit a fixed textual identity or

essence of the text, all we need is agreement on a reasonable number of propositions; and as the particular group of propositions can change over time, so can a text's identity. But the importance of a permanently fixed identity wanes once we are confident that in any situation we can agree on (or assume) enough identifying propositions to agree about which text we are talking about. Rather than trying to insure permanent sameness, "we should dissolve . . . texts . . . into nodes within transitory webs of relationships" (1985: 12). This vision converges with the poststructuralist move from work to text heralded by Barthes.

FROM WORK TO TEXT

The postructuralist theory of the text, developed in France in the late 1960s and early 1970s by Barthes, Kristeva, and Derrida, aims to replace the fixed work with the changing text as the object of literary study and source of aesthetic pleasure. While the work is viewed as closed and permanent, a finished product having certain limits of meaning and bearing the authority of its author, the text is instead conceived as an open, transgressive process and an endless field of meaning production. It is a practice rather than an object, "a methodological field . . . experienced only in the activity of production"; and it "cannot stop" its productive activity (Barthes 1977: 157). Text is thus limited neither to literature nor to verbal artifacts but involves the entire realm of meaning. "All signifying practices can engender text: the practice of painting pictures, musical practice, filmic practice, etc." (Barthes 1981: 41).

Rather than a fixed signification, text involves a perpetual play of "signifiance" (a term introduced by Julia Kristeva), which involves associative movements, overlappings, and connections of meaning, an idea that can be associated with Derrida's theme of the irreducible play and generativity of "différance" (Derrida 1976: 93). Thus, the text is not constrained by affiliation to the author (as the work presumably is). "It is not that the Author may not come back in the Text, in his text, but then he does so as guest" (Barthes 1977: 160). If the work is produced by an author for consumption by the reader, the text instead is not consumed as an object but creatively produced as an activity of play and practice. While the work directs the reader to uncovering the truth of its meaning or to consuming the pleasure its author has provided, the text aims neither at such truth nor pleasure but rather at a more powerful "jouissance," "a pleasure without separation" (Barthes 1977: 164).

Apart from "signifiance," Barthes's theory of the text employs three other concepts derived from Kristeva: phenotext, genotext, and intertextuality. The phenotext is "the verbal phenomenon as it presents itself in the structure of the concrete statement" (Kristeva 1972: 335), and thus represents the sense of text that is closest to the meaning of "text" in Anglo-American thought. The genotext is the structuring background for the phenotext and includes both verbal dimensions and psychological drives. More important is the idea of intertextuality: "that any text is an intertext; other texts are present in it, at varying levels, in more or less recognizable forms: the texts of the previous and surrounding culture" (Barthes 1981: 39). This notion captures the etymological root of "text" as a tissue or woven texture. Finally, the idea of intertextuality is used to assimilate all dimensions and kinds of language into the idea of text. Together with the philosophical premise that our reality (or at least its human experience) is always linguistically given, the notion of intertexuality often leads theorists to a general ontological textualism (in some way a linguistic analogue of classical idealism) which views all the world as text.

See also DECONSTRUCTION; DERRIDA; INTENTION AND INTERPRETATION; "INTENTIONAL FALLACY"; INTERPRETATION, AIMS OF; MEANING CONSTRUCTIVISM; ONTOLOGY OF ARTWORKS.

BIBLIOGRAPHY
Barthes, Roland. 1977. "The Death of the Author" and "From Work to Text." In Image–Music–Text. London: Fontana, 142–8, 155–64.
Barthes, Roland. 1981. "Theory of the Text." In Untying the Text: A Poststructuralist Reader. R. Young (ed.). London: Routledge & Kegan Paul, 32–47.
Beardsley, Monroe C. 1973. The Possibility of Criticism. Detroit: Wayne State University Press.
Derrida, Jacques. 1976. Of Grammatology. G. C. Spivak (trans.). Baltimore: Johns Hopkins University Press.
Fish, Stanley. 1989. Doing What Comes Naturally. Durham: Duke University Press.
Goodman, Nelson. 1969. Languages of Art. Oxford: Oxford University Press.
Hirsch, E. D. 1976. The Aims of Interpretation. Chicago: University of Chicago Press.
Iseminger, Gary (ed.). 1992. Intention and Interpretation. Philadelphia: Temple University Press.
Knapp, S. & Michaels, W. B. 1985. "Against Theory." In Against Theory. W. J. T. Mitchell (ed.). Chicago: University of Chicago Press, 11–30.
Kristeva, Julia. 1972. "Sémanalyse: Conditions d'une sémiotique scientifique," Semiotica, 5, 324–49.
Livingston, Paisley. 2005. Art and Intention: A Philosophical Study. Oxford: Oxford University Press.
Margolis, Joseph. 1965. The Language of Art and Art Criticism. Detroit: Wayne State University Press.
Rorty, Richard. 1985. "Texts and Lumps," New Literary History, 17, 1–16.
Shusterman, Richard. 1992. Pragmatist Aesthetics: Living Beauty, Rethinking Art. Oxford: Blackwell.
Stevenson, Charles. 1957. "On 'What is a Poem?' " Philosophical Review, 66, 329–62.

RICHARD SHUSTERMAN

theater   see DRAMA; TRAGEDY.

theories of art   Attempts to understand the "essence" of art in terms of a single key concept, such as "expression" or "representation."

ART AS REPRESENTATION

By "the representational theory" is meant here a historically persistent complex of views that see the chief, or essential, role of the arts as imitating, or displaying, or setting forth aspects of reality in the widest sense.

A typical representational account sees art as portraying the visible forms of nature, from a schematic cave drawing of an animal to the evocation of an entire landscape in sun or storm. The particularity of individual objects, scenes, or persons may be emphasized, or the generic, the common, the essential. The scope of representation can involve perspectives, slants on the world, ways of seeing the world. A representational artist may seek faithfulness to how things *are*. He or she may dwell selectively on the ugly and defective, the unfulfilled; or on the ideal, the fully realized potential. The artist opens our eyes to the world's perceptual qualities and configurations, to its beauty, ugliness, and horrors.

At the level of detailed philosophical analysis, what exactly it is to represent is a problem of some complexity (Wollheim 1987: 76–100). However we analyze it, it is very doubtful that representation possesses the explanatory power it would need in order to yield a one-concept theory of art. Clearly, there is art that is not at all representational: music is seldom directly representational; painting and sculpture can be abstract as well as figurative. Although in prose a subject may often be important, in poetry its importance can be much reduced and the poem be appreciated as an artifact in its own right rather than as a window on the nonart world. The work of representing may seem insufficiently ambitious. As the *repre*senting or imitating of what nature or God has already created, it can at its best be technically notable, but must always be derivative and repetitious. The beauties of art are very seldom transcriptions, into a medium, of preexisting natural beauties.

The representational theory, say its critics, must deflect attention from the work of art and its distinctive values, to what is always other than itself. Artworks, however, call attention upon their own unique forms, lines, colors, images, meanings, patterns of sound. What we encounter in them we have not encountered and cannot encounter elsewhere in the world. An artwork does not become "disposable" once we have extracted from it a message, a way of looking, a perspective.

Could we not attempt to save the representational theory by a shift to the speculative: art is always a mimesis of nature, if not of nature's visible appearances, then of its fundamental energies and laws and their endless transformations. We could say this, but at a price. We may be overextending the concept of representation in a way that unhelpfully conceals what would be better seen as distinct and different aims of art. Even with a clearly representational painting we may say, "The objects are represented – in such a way as heightens their crucial *expressive* qualities." Or again, "The forms of nature have no more than stimulated the artist to create a *new* world." Often, too, we shall say, "The formal ordering of the artwork

does not reproduce nature's order; it has its own distinctive order – invented, not discovered."

ART AS EXPRESSION

So let us start again, this time putting *expression* at the center. Music expresses feelings, emotions, moods, their conflicts, triumphs, defeats. A painted landscape may engage us as expressive of peace, melancholy, or menace; so too a lyrical poem, a semi-abstract sculpture, a scene or situation in drama. They may express highly particularized modes of feeling, even new emotions. In R. G. Collingwood's account, the artist struggles to clarify and articulate his initially unfocused feeling. Coming to grasp it and to express it by way of the fashioning of an artwork constitutes a single task.

It is not only sensations, feelings, moods, and emotions that may be expressed, but also attitudes, evaluations, atmospheric qualities, expectation, disappointment, frustration, relief, tensings, and relaxings; not only brief bursts of lyrical feeling evoked by specific, intensely felt events, but also the inner quality of a whole lifeworld. Even when art argues a case, its real interest is always to express the felt experience of arguing; and when it depicts or describes, its concern is with the human affective analogues of the objects and events of the outside world that make up its ostensible subject matter. Its real subject is always the human subject.

But what exactly am I reporting when I say, "I find this phrase for clarinet poignantly expressive" or, "The harmonic twist in the final cadence expresses foreboding"? Not necessarily that I am emotionally excited – I do not need to be, in order to "read" the emotional quality – nor that I am necessarily directly sharing the artist's emotions, though I certainly hope that my experience will be related to the artist's intentions, if these are well realized in his work. It is the work of art itself that is the primary locus of relevant emotional qualities. The *music* is tender; the *painting* is tranquil. We seem driven to say that, although we are well aware that there must be metaphor in the claim.

A critic of the expression theory, however, will argue that there are other factors no less essential to the creating and appreciating of art. Clive Bell, for instance, wrote, "If art expresses anything, it expresses an emotion felt for pure form" (1914: 132): and form must be our primary concern. The expressive qualities we most value are those which steer clear of clichéd, stereotyped, or trite forms of feeling – innovative qualities, perhaps exclusive to a single work of art. But if we say that, we are showing our allegiance to a criterion of creativity or originality, and not to expression alone.

FORMALIST THEORIES: "ORGANIC UNITY"

Art, it can be argued, is not a window on the world: it is on the artwork itself that appreciative attention must primarily be focused, on its distinctive structure, its design, unity, form. "Does the work *hang together?*" is always a relevant and surely a vital question, a question that shows the primacy of formal unity. Concepts of form and of unity applicable to works of art have been developed from suggestions first made by Plato and Aristotle.

We distinguish different kinds of wholes: some, like a pile of stones, are no more than loose aggregates; others, like a plant or animal, are tightly integrated ("organic") complexes, where each part exists only to serve the whole. A work of art is, characteristically, a complex unity whose elements do not impinge on us as isolated units, but are determined in their perceived qualities by the context of all the *other* elements and their relationships. The character of the whole in turn modifies, controls these components as we perceive them. The spectator's "synoptic" grasp of the unity will be quite vital (Osborne 1968).

In the unities that, on this theory, the arts seek to provide, our efforts toward synoptic perceptual grasp are neither defeated nor gratified on the instant. The very intricacy of an artwork's structure can challenge and stimulate our perceptive powers, making its appreciation both a strenuous and a rewarding activity. Within the various arts, the generic forms themselves are constantly open to creative revision. The unifying principles must be *perceivable* in the work – audible, visible, or, in literature, discernible in the meaning and sustainable interpretations of the actual text.

Why should we attach high value to formal unities of this kind? Basically, because of the quality of consciousness they make possible. Where the items of a complex lend themselves to perception because of their thematic inter-connections, as do those of a successful work of art, we are enabled to synthesize a far greater totality than in any other context. Consciousness can often be attenuated, meager, sluggish: here it is at its most active and zestful. Again, as finite beings, we are necessarily always vulnerable to the threat of diminished personal integration, of being fragmented – as we are, finally and literally, in death. We are seldom farther from that state than when we are rapt in enjoyment of a well-integrated work of fine art.

The temporal arts, although presenting motifs, brief melodies, rhythms, phrases of poetry which constantly pass into silence, effect a partial transcendence of that evanescence in time, precisely on account of their formal structuring whereby early notes (or images) are retained, remain active, ingredient in the total experience, recalled even as a movement (or poem) comes to its close. Something parallel happens in spatial art also, where the mutual connectedness and formal contribution of every represented object overcome the normal mutual "indifference" of objects in space.

Can formalism, then, constitute a single all-sufficient theory of art? Are there not many cases where one may justifiably question whether a work's formal structure is so decisively the essential thing that its other features must be given subordinate place? The formal structure of a work of art may be valued for its controlling, its focusing, of the work's unique (and treasured) *expressive* qualities. In other cases we may say that the expressive and the formal properties are coequally important. There are putative works of art the structure of which is so remote from traditional instances of "configurational unity," that the claim that their form is their essential feature, qua artwork, becomes drastically attenuated. It has also been argued that the theory has most plausibility with regard to *complex* works of art, but has little power to illuminate in the case of *simple* ones. Or is simplicity always deceptive, illusory, in significant works of art?

Even more elusive is precision in defining the "formal unity" that is thought exclusive to works of art. Too loose definitions may extend over the unity of a living organism, the features of a face or a mathematical formal system;

overnarrow definitions will demand, too strin-
gently, that in a fine work of art, *nothing* could
be altered but for the worse (Alberti 1988).

ART AS CREATION

Representation theorists and expression theorists
do, of course, allow that art can be innovative
– reworking nature's materials in a "new"
nature, or drastically modifying life experiences in the fashioning of expressive art. The
formalist or organic unity theory makes the
artist's innovative role more central: the unities
of art are nowhere paralleled in nature. But
why not, then, acknowledge *creation* as the
leading concept in a theory of art? And it has
indeed been made central by a variety of theorists and artists. To some, "creative imagination"
is that power by which, in a display of freedom
that echoes the divine prerogative of creation *ex
nihilo*, we summon up to actuality possible
worlds – worlds that have, as it were, been left
for us to create.

Obvious implications follow for artistic practice and for criticism. The development toward
abstraction in the visual arts can be proclaimed as a "purifying away" of objective reference. Originality and individuality become
criteria of high merit.

So, could "creation" yield a complete theory
of art? To play this role, it would surely have to
mean "new *and* aesthetically valuable, worthwhile, rewarding." Even for the God of Genesis,
after the work of creation there remained a
question of evaluating what had been done: a
question favorably answered – "Behold, it was
very good." For the human artist, the possibility surely exists that he make something from
(nearly) nothing, but . . . behold, it is very *bad*.
Novelty is not enough; an object can be original, in the sense of a perceptually distinct,
unique addition to the beings already in the
world, and yet be *un*rewarding to contemplate.

Among products of high creativity we must
include some scientific theories, mathematical
calculi and theorems, philosophical systems.
But they are not art. However creative my daydreams, they are not art either: they are not
worked in a medium, intersubjective, shared.
Moreover, not every movement, style, or
period in art sets a high evaluation on originality.
We should also be cautious in accepting that
ideal of "purifying" visual art from all depen-

dence on natural appearances. To purify can be
to attenuate, if it means to cut oneself off from
any allusion to the world beyond the canvas, for
such allusion can add immensely to the wealth
of meanings in a work of art.

Nevertheless, even if we reject a theology of
man as co-creator with God – perhaps particularly if we reject it – the creation theme rightly
spotlights the artist's distinctive dignity. His
imagination intensifies, transforms, perfects
nature's own doings. It is not merely a fanciful
metaphor to speak of the artist as bringing
into being what nature has not created, and
"awaits" creation.

DEVELOPING TRADITIONS

Emphasizing the freestanding character of
works of art as created objects encourages
us to see them as autonomous, independent,
and self-explanatory. For countless individual
works of art, however, that statement needs
correction. We shall not understand or appreciate them without at least an outline knowledge of the tradition in which they stand, the
genre to which they belong – and thus some
understanding of whether they simply continue or modify or rebel against these. Indeed,
it is tempting for an aesthetician, who despairs
of any of the unified theories of art to fulfill
their promise, to abandon all such theorizing and
urge instead that we take those ongoing developing traditions, genres, and media (and the
complex actual vocabulary of criticism) as the
basic data for reflection on the arts in all their
diversity.

THE INSTITUTIONAL THEORY

One strategy for coping with these last-
mentioned issues is that of the "institutional
theory of art." In a strong form it takes the
unifying factor to be not the possession of common perceptual features by artworks, but the
conferral on certain objects, by representatives
of the "artworld," of the status of "candidate for
appreciation" as works of art (Dickie 1974:
34). The artworld is thought of, roughly, as
the set of art critics, organizers of exhibitions,
owners of galleries, and the public of art appreciators. The theory may, however, provide me
with little illumination, when bewildered
before an object like Duchamp's *Fountain* (a
ready-made urinal) or Carl Andre's *Equivalent*

VIII (a rectangle of bricks), when it tells me that the artworld representatives have indeed conferred art status upon it. I cannot prevent myself asking on account of what features this status has been conferred. Either we must look for an answer – an answer that will render needless the artworld's conferral, since, once we have "reasons" for their decisions, these may be made public and applied by all. Or, if no reasons are disclosed, the artworld's decisions cannot be defended from arbitrariness (Wollheim 1987: ch. 1). Being deemed a work of art, given space in a gallery, publication, or performance imply judgments that the work will reward the attention solicited for it. But, again, we have a legitimate interest in knowing the features of the work that have led to its promotion.

A later version of the institutional theory drops the notion of conferral, and claims that a work of art is to be understood as an artifact made for presentation to an "artworld public" (Dickie 1984). The artworld becomes the totality of "frameworks for the presentation of a work of art by an artist to an art-world public," a public prepared to understand such objects. But what this leaves altogether unclarified is the point and value of these activities.

INEXHAUSTIBILITY AND DENSITY OF MEANING

"The heresy of paraphrase" is a familiar phrase expressing the fact that a significant work of literary art cannot be reduced to a summary of its plot. No more can a painting be reduced to an inventory of the objects it represents. Inexhaustibility of interpretation is a mark of authentic art. The coexistence of multiple levels of meaning gives a sense of richness and "depth." There is also a kind of "aesthetic transcendence" where the expressive quality, say, of a passage of operatic music, far surpasses in gravity or poignancy the unconvincing human situation to which it ostensibly refers, or where a deceptively commonplace still-life has a resonance beyond the reach of analysis.

In each of the arts there occurs the fullest possible assimilation of its materials. In poetry the sound and the rhythm matter as well as the sense; in a painting the picture plane and the traces of brush strokes, as well as the represented depth. Simultaneously sounding notes of music are each heard as continuing a "horizontal" line, parts, and melodies, as well as a "vertical"

succession of chords with distinctive harmonic qualities. The timbre of each instrument contributes uniquely to the overall resultant sound.

KEY CONCEPTS AND THEIR INTERRELATIONS

Supposing that none of those germinal concepts can generate a complete theory of art, we are not left with an unrelated plurality of notions. We can remain sensitive to aesthetically important creative and appreciative tensions between them.

A theory must do justice to the fact that certain media and materials lend themselves to our doing several significantly different things simultaneously in and through them. We can at once represent and express and construct new configurational unities in and through the skilled handling of paints, inks, or crayons, carved wood or chiseled stone. Some of our appraisals of artworks draw explicitly on these multiple possibilities, tensions, and challenges. For instance, we marvel at a composer's success in managing a demanding and potentially cramping form, while yet attaining a high degree of expressiveness and inventiveness within it, or at a novelist who represents a wide range of human activity and experience and whose work thoroughly assimilates it with unimpaired unity.

Some writers have seen the history of theorizing about the arts as a gradual realization that works of art are to be properly appreciated as "objects in their own right"; while other concerns – with truth to human nature and experience outside art, with moral or political or religious impact – are to be relegated to the inessential. If, however, representational art fashions an image of human life, it cannot be of indifference whether in particular cases it is an adequate, defensible image or a grotesquely reduced parody. This question can obviously be raised only where a work, or an oeuvre, does set out to characterize human experience as such, the human life-world rather than a selected fragment. Major works of art do typically attempt something close to this. We cannot properly rule out a moral scrutiny and appraisal as irrelevant to such works, even though we should be equally misguided to judge any works of art solely by their moral quality.

Furthermore, in its exploration of the widest range of human experience, art cannot fail to be concerned with the boundaries of experience, where the expressible begins to yield to the inexpressible. This is not to demand of art that it labor in defense of particular metaphysical or religious beliefs, but only that, where some approach to a comprehensive image of the life-world is attempted, neither the seeming bounds of that world, nor the peculiar ability of the arts to bring them to vivid awareness in a transcending movement of the mind, be ignored.

THE STATUS OF THEORIES OF ART

The multifariousness of the arts, their traditions, developing genres, idioms, and media, their self-transcending *nisus*, make a one-concept theory an unrealistic, even undesirable, goal. To seek it obstinately results in oversimplification and distortion. But to lurch too far in the opposite direction is to overstress complexity and difference, and prematurely give up any attempt to see an intelligible structure of relationships among the phenomena of the arts.

The aspiration to produce a unitary theory, even if it fails to result in one, remains legitimate and often fruitful. We may enhance our understanding of art by seeing how much work a given key concept can do for us, and finding where it ceases to be as illuminating as some alternative concept. The interrelations and tensions within and among the key concepts may illuminate the inner dynamics of creation.

See also "ARTWORLD"; BELL; COLLINGWOOD; CREATIVITY; DEFINITION OF "ART"; DEPICTION; DICKIE; EMOTION; EXPRESSION; FORMALISM; IMAGINATION; INTERPRETATION; ONTOLOGICAL CONTEXTUALISM; ORIGINALITY; REALISM; REPRESENTATION; TRADITION; TRUTH IN ART.

BIBLIOGRAPHY

Alberti, L. B. 1988 [1486]. *De re aedificatoria*. J. Rykwert, N. Leach, & R. Taverner (trans.). Cambridge, MA: MIT Press.
Beardsley, Monroe C. 1958. *Aesthetics: Problems in the Philosophy of Criticism*. New York: Harcourt, Brace & World.
Bell, Clive. 1914. *Art*. London: Chatto & Windus.
Bell, Clive. 1934. *Enjoying Pictures*. London: Chatto & Windus.
Charlton, William. 1970. *Aesthetics*. London: Hutchinson.
Collingwood, R. G. 1938. *The Principles of Art*. Oxford: Clarendon.
Dickie, George. 1974. *Art and the Aesthetic*. Ithaca: Cornell University Press.
Dickie, George. 1984. *The Art Circle: A Theory of Art*. New York: Haven.
Dufrenne, Mikel. 1973 [1953]. *The Phenomenology of Aesthetic Experience*. E. S. Casey, A. A. Anderson, W. Domingo, & L. Jacobson (trans.). Evanston: Northwestern University Press.
Gaut, Berys & Lopes, Dom McIver (eds.). 2005. *The Routledge Companion to Aesthetics*. 2nd edn. New York: Routledge.
Goldman, Alan H. 1995. *Aesthetic Value*. Boulder: Westview.
Levinson, Jerrold (ed.). 2003. *The Oxford Handbook of Aesthetics*. Oxford: Oxford University Press.
Osborne, Harold. 1968. *Aesthetics and Art Theory*. London: Longman.
Schiller, F. 1982 [1794–5]. *On the Aesthetic Education of Man*. E. M. Wilkinson & L. A. Willoughby (eds. & trans.). Oxford: Clarendon.
Sharpe, R. A. 1983. *Contemporary Aesthetics*. Brighton: Harvester.
Tilghman, B. R. 1984. *But Is It Art?* Oxford: Blackwell.
Wollheim, Richard. 1980. *Art and Its Objects*. 2nd edn. Cambridge: Cambridge University Press.
Wollheim, Richard. 1987. *Painting as an Art*. London: Thames & Hudson.

RONALD W. HEPBURN

Tolstoy, Leo [Lev Nikolayevich] (1828–1910) Russian novelist, educator, and social reformer; one of the great moral influences in his own time and subsequently. Nearly all Tolstoy's writings on art appeared during the last, "messianic," phase of his life. These include a number of short articles on individual artists, his philosophical essay *On Art* (c.1895–7), his notorious attack on Shakespeare in *Shakespeare and the Drama* (1906), and his only major work on aesthetics, *What is Art?* (1898).

Shortly after completing *Anna Karenina* in 1877, Tolstoy underwent a spiritual crisis, and became preoccupied with moral and religious questions. This is evident not only in his overtly didactic writings, including those on art, but in all his later fiction. It has been more common in Russia than elsewhere for the writing of fiction to be seen as a high moral calling. The novelist as moralist, religious or political teacher, and even prophet has been a recurring phenomenon in Russian literature, from Gogol through Dostoyevsky and Tolstoy to Solzhenitsyn. Whatever the historical or cultural reasons for this attitude, its justification requires some sort of theoretical underpinning, and this is what Tolstoy's theory of art provides.

He assumes, without argument, that if art is to be an activity worthy of the very highest respect then it must be possible to justify it on moral grounds, since moral values have supremacy over all others. He is therefore opposed, on principle, to the idea that art is self-justifying or that its value is in any way self-evident. His approach to all human activities and institutions is similarly moralistic and practical. He is just as opposed to the doctrine of science for science's sake, for example, as he is to that of art for art's sake. This was the principal reason for his hostility to the eighteenth-century view of art as the creation of beauty. Beauty, he insists, has no objective worth and should never be placed above the demands of morality. There is, in any case, no common standard of beauty as there is of morality.

In Tolstoy's view, to justify art in terms of beauty is to treat mere enjoyment as the ultimate criterion of aesthetic merit. The enormous sacrifices in men, money, and materials made in the name of art over the centuries could be justified only if art were more than just entertainment and served some high moral or religious purpose, as it was intended to do in the Middle Ages. That purpose, he insists, must be looked for in the meaning and purpose of life itself. This, for Tolstoy, was what religion, stripped of its supernatural and superstitious accretions, is ultimately about. "Religions," he says "are the exponents of the highest comprehension of life accessible to the best and foremost men at a given time in a given society; a comprehension towards which all the rest of that society must inevitably and irresistibly advance" (1930: 127). On this view, the value of individual works of art will depend, as far as their content is concerned, on the extent to which they are in conformity with the highest religious perceptions of the age. For Tolstoy, this is the Christian ideal of the union and brotherhood of man. Conversely, art that is socially divisive or elitist is failing in its true function and so is bad or counterfeit art.

Relatively few works since the Renaissance, when artists reverted to the hedonistic values of Greece and Rome for their inspiration, manage, in Tolstoy's estimation, to survive this test, although he sees some improvement in his own day. His list of failures includes Shakespeare's *King Lear*, Michelangelo's *Last Judgment*, Wagner's *Ring of the Nibelungs* – and even his own two masterpieces, *War and Peace* and *Anna Karenina*. Many commentators have seen the apparent absurdity of this conclusion as sufficient grounds for rejecting the theory. However, any theory that proceeds rationalistically from first principles, as Tolstoy's does, cannot be overturned simply on account of the unwelcome nature of its conclusions.

Unlike most writers on aesthetics, Tolstoy does not assume that somehow we already know what is good or bad in art, but sets out to discover the principles by which we should judge. Moreover, disagreements about first principles are notoriously difficult to resolve without resorting to ad hominem arguments. There can be no common ground between Tolstoy and his opponents unless the latter are at least prepared to concede overall supremacy to moral values, but to do that is to give the moralist approach to art a firm foothold.

Terry Diffey has argued that while Tolstoy's attempt to justify art as a human activity or institution in terms of religious perceptions is perhaps defensible, he is clearly mistaken in using this as a criterion for evaluating individual works of art, since "the reasons why something in general is valuable may not be the reasons why an individual thing of that kind is good" (1985: 134). One might, for instance, value cricket as an activity on the grounds that it promotes physical fitness and is character-building, but it would be absurd to claim that one particular game of cricket was better than another because it produced more fitness or nobler characters.

This is clearly an important distinction, and one that Tolstoy patently ignores, but it is not entirely clear-cut. For there has to be some connection between the overall justification of an activity and particular evaluations made within it. For instance, one could not consistently place a high value on the character-building potential of cricket and rate highly a particular game that was dogged by bad sportsmanship.

Similarly, if the most exalted function of art is to unite mankind in common bonds of feeling, then socially divisive works cannot be rated as masterpieces. It has to be admitted, however, that Tolstoy's moralistic approach fails to yield the sort of criteria that an art critic might find useful. This is partly due to the fact that Tolstoy, the theorist, has very little interest in what are normally regarded as the formal or aesthetic properties of a work of art – or, indeed, in the work of art itself apart from its effect on the audience. Critics, by contrast, tend to interest themselves chiefly in the internal properties of a work.

Tolstoy is of course untroubled by this because for him the aesthetic properties have value only as a means to an end, the immediate artistic end being the transmission of feelings from artist to audience, and the ultimate moral end being the transmission of feelings that unite us. Thus, if a work fails in its proper effect then it is worthless, and nothing the critics can say in its defense will alter the fact.

As Tolstoy's moralistic approach rides on the back of an expression theory of art, it is indirectly vulnerable to attacks on his version of that theory, which he summarizes as follows:

> To evoke in oneself a feeling one has once experienced and having evoked it in oneself then by means of movements, lines, colours, sounds or forms expressed in words, so to transmit that feeling that others experience the same feeling – this is the activity of art.
>
> Art is a human activity consisting in this, that one man consciously by means of external signs, hands on to others feelings he has lived through, and that others are infected by these feelings and also experience them. (1930: 123)

Aesthetic experience for Tolstoy is the experience of being united with the artist, and others affected by the work, in a common bond of feeling. When in this state, the recipient feels as if the work is her own and that what it expresses is what she has longed to express. This quality of infectiousness is what distinguishes true art from its counterfeit, and "the stronger the infection the better is the art, as art" (1930: 228).

Works that fail in expressiveness, as do "brain-spun or invented works" (1930: 196), are necessarily counterfeit. Other works will be limited in their capacity to infect others, especially where the feelings involved are accessible only to people of a certain class, creed, or culture; for instance, art which appeals to patriotic, aristocratic, or sectarian feelings. Such art is "exclusive," and is morally bad rather than counterfeit. The best art must be accessible to all and must therefore appeal to feelings that are common to all.

This criterion of universal accessibility devalues all art that makes any real demand on the audience's intelligence, learning, or powers of concentration. Any work that needs to be explained is a failure, for "to say that a work of art is good but incomprehensible to most men, is the same as saying of some kind of food that it is very good but most people can't eat it" (1930: 176). Thus arises Tolstoy's preference for simple folk art over sophisticated metropolitan art.

According to Tolstoy (1930: 228), the infectiousness of a work depends on three conditions: first, the degree of sincerity of the artist – that is, the artist should be impelled by an inner need to express his feelings; second, the degree of individuality of the feelings transmitted; and third, the beauty (that is, lucidity) of their expression. The first condition, to which Tolstoy attaches particular importance, contradicts the view that the genesis of a work is irrelevant to its evaluation. The second makes it improbable that exactly the same effects could be produced in some other way – something that instrumentalist theories are often accused of making possible. The third condition draws our attention to the work's internal organization, but it is a characteristic weakness of Tolstoy's theory of art that he has nothing of interest to say about that.

See also NINETEENTH- AND TWENTIETH-CENTURY CONTINENTAL AESTHETICS; TWENTIETH-CENTURY ANGLO-AMERICAN AESTHETICS; EXPRESSION; FUNCTION OF ART; MORALITY AND ART; RELIGION AND ART.

BIBLIOGRAPHY

Primary sources
[1898] 1930. "What is Art?" and Essays on Art. A. Maude (trans.). Oxford: Oxford University Press.

Secondary sources

Diffey, Terry. 1985. *Tolstoy's "What is Art?"* London: Croom Helm.

Fenner, David. 2005. "Production Theories and Artistic Value," *Contemporary Aesthetics*, 3, 1–15.

Garrod, H. W. 1935. *Tolstoy's Theory of Art*. Taylorian Lecture. Oxford: Clarendon.

Gifford, H. 1982. *Tolstoy*. Oxford: Oxford University Press.

Redpath, T. T. 1960. *Tolstoy*. London: Bowes & Bowes.

DAVID WHEWELL

tradition In considering the relevance to aesthetics of tradition, we can begin by looking at aesthetic reactions in terms of practical knowledge. Practical knowledge is knowledge of how to act and, by extension, of how to feel. It is the sort of knowledge that underlies moral activity and aesthetic appreciation.

Someone who responds to circumstances or to objects on impulse or at random manifests lack of such knowledge. There would be no room here for the application of any notion of appropriateness between stimulus and response, but only a causal connection between the two, with no room for any normativity. As human beings we have impulses and animal needs, to be sure, but we are also endowed with self-consciousness. We cannot avoid reflecting on the rightness or wrongness, the appropriateness or inappropriateness, of what we do, what we feel, and what we perceive. Separating ourselves in this way from the immediacy of our impulses, we live in a realm of *intelligibilia*, where things, feelings, and actions have meaning, and can be judged as appropriate or inappropriate, reasonable or unreasonable.

Practical knowledge, then, is knowledge of what action or feeling would be appropriate to a given situation. It is not merely theoretical, since it is knowledge of how to respond. But this raises the question of how one acquires this knowledge. In the aesthetic case, this is the question how perceivers form aesthetic responses; and how artists are able, as the precondition for intelligent activity on their part, to judge in advance, as they work, the likely reactions of perceivers to what is produced. Shared practical knowledge on the part of artist and perceiver alike, then, forms the basis of communication in the aesthetic realm.

Our aesthetic responses, like our moral practices, are certainly rooted in our existence as biological beings, and constrained by our physical nature. Sounds we cannot hear can never form part of a musical tradition, nor could such a tradition be based on intervals too close for us to distinguish. Our taste for certain types of harmony, say, or color contrasts may also have roots in biology. Nevertheless, it is also clear that a great deal of our aesthetic knowledge and perception is learned, and learned in traditions of practice and experience.

Westerners find the rhythms of Tchaikovsky's ballet scores so obvious as to appear entirely natural, but students in the Chinese school of ballet have to be taught what the rhythms are before they can pick them up. No doubt the response of Westerners to the "natural" elements of Chinese music would stand in analogous need of instruction. Studies of the psychology of perception and their application to art by Gombrich and others have shown the extent to which the perception of what appear to us to be realistic images also depends on upbringing in the relevant traditions and cultures. Judgments of the worth and success of particular works of art thus presuppose in the critic or perceiver some understanding of the tradition from which they stem, for only then are we in a position to understand just what is communicated, and what aimed at, by the works in question.

It is important to appreciate the extent to which the knowledge embodied in an artistic or moral tradition is tacit, the unarticulated context for action and judgment. But it is this untheoretical readiness of an audience to respond in specific ways to what they are presented with that forms the basis on which artists can plan their work.

There have nevertheless been periods in the history of art in which artists have been bent on dispensing with tradition and starting afresh. The most notable example of this trend is artistic modernism in the twentieth century, and along with the composer Schoenberg the most notable theorist and proponent of modernism is Le Corbusier. Le Corbusier explicitly advocated an architecture based on engineering and mathematics. In *Towards a New Architecture*, he advocates the elimination of all "dead" concepts with regard to the house. In their place we are to build from a "critical and objective" point of view, so as to arrive at the geometric and mathematical purity of the "house machine." Despite the pretension and the rhetoric, Le Corbusier was not dispensing with traditional knowledge altogether. His architecture, though devoid of ornament, is still based on geometric forms which humans have, through the centuries, found pleasing to the eye – as Le Corbusier implicitly admitted in his efforts to show that his buildings were based on the forms underlying classical architecture.

But Le Corbusier was dispensing with much of the architectural knowledge embodied in more recent traditions of architecture, which he and his followers regarded as moribund. It was because of this that his architecture aroused, and continues to arouse, such strong passions, as did the work of Schoenberg in the case of music and Herbert Read and others in the case of the visual arts. Even here, though, the modernists initially achieved much of their effect precisely by the contrast with what had gone before, and through producing works that were parasitic on it. In the twenty-first century, some 80 or more years after the first stirrings of artistic modernism, and when in some fields the initially revolutionary view has become the established policy, we are in a good position to evaluate what was being proposed by the antitraditionalists.

In the case of architecture, for example, and in the face of the continuing widespread unpopularity of modernist architecture, the traditionalist will emphasize the cost of wiping away too much of a tradition at any one time. Echoing Burke and Hayek in politics, the traditionalist will point to the way a traditional style encompasses a vast pool of implicit knowledge, of styles, designs, and solutions, which have survived because they have turned out to respond to human needs and desires. In doing this, and in becoming established, they have then in turn become constitutive of the needs and desires of succeeding generations. Until one disturbs a traditional order, one may not know just what the role of any particular element in it may be. This is because much of what is in any tradition will not have been explicitly planned, or even retained, with any precise knowledge of its significance. It will have endured through a process resembling biological natural selection, shaped invisibly by its actual, but often unseen, responsiveness to some need or taste.

The concept of a tradition as a spontaneously developing order, much of the value of which is implicit rather than explicit, can certainly be applied with profit in many fields, including the aesthetic. And it is not hard to find examples of the unforeseen costs, even in the aesthetic field, of going against traditional practices. An obvious example is the way many supposedly functional modern buildings have proved less well adapted to the functions they serve than their Victorian or Edwardian counterparts, particularly if function is taken in a wide sense to include the contentment or otherwise of the buildings' users. A less obvious, but no less pertinent, example would be the way a strongly developed tradition in the arts may allow for nuances of expression, and even for shock and inventiveness, in a way which the abrogation of that tradition will destroy. As the Canadian pianist Glenn Gould has pointed out, the straitlaced Mendelssohn can surprise the listener by the gentlest movement, whereas the technically crude Mussorgsky has to hit the listener over the head with a forte–piano contrast or a quasi-modal moment to make an effect felt.

However, even accepting that in various ways individual expression in the arts depends on the prior existence of traditions of expression, it does not follow that the only viable or possible response of an artist is blindly to follow what has gone before.

Again, to take an obvious example, Palladio, Hawksmoor, and Schinkel were all great architects, and great classical architects. But none of them simply copied classical models, and none built in the same way. Simply to repeat what has gone before can seem insipid, or worse. But once one allows that individual creativity and originality are important artistic values, it becomes impossible to say in advance just which departures from tradition should be sanctioned at any given moment. On the other hand, recognizing the importance of traditional styles and orders, and the way in which true originality depends on their existence, argues strongly in favor of teaching newcomers to a field of art the tradition relevant to them and their field.

See also ARCHITECTURE; ART HISTORY; CANON; GOMBRICH; MODERNISM AND POSTMODERNISM; ONTOLOGICAL CONTEXTUALISM; ORIGINALITY.

BIBLIOGRAPHY
Bantock, Geoffrey.1967. *Education, Culture and the Emotions*. London: Faber.
Hayek, Friedrich von. 1988. *The Fatal Conceit*. London: Routledge.
Oakeshott, Michael. 1962. *Rationalism in Politics*. London: Methuen.
O'Hear, Anthony. 1988. *The Element of Fire*. London: Routledge.

ANTHONY O'HEAR

tragedy held a special status as an important genre of dramatic art in the fifth and sixth centuries BCE, and the names of Sophocles, Euripides, and Aeschylus still resonate as among the most important authors of tragedy in the West. Plato criticized performances of tragedies as being morally and cognitively harmful, and it remained for Aristotle, in his *Poetics*, to develop the most systematic theory of tragedy that has come down to us from the ancient world. In describing its nature and justifying its special status, Aristotle takes the story of Oedipus as its paradigm case. In the nineteenth century, Nietzsche developed an account of the genre that drew on his own training as a classicist, and Hegel also proposed a strikingly different analysis of the genre that takes Sophocles' *Antigone* as its paradigm.

Even though the social context and the way tragedies were presented to audiences in the ancient world were strikingly different from those of the twentieth and twenty-first centuries, Aristotle's account contains a great deal that transcends the specific cultural environment in which it was developed. He attempted to explain how tragedy addresses what are, then and now, some of the most profound and important issues in human life. In particular, on his view, tragedy dramatizes how a good though far from perfect person who tries to do the right thing may nevertheless perform actions that, unknowingly, produce irreversible harm. Indeed, one's effort to do "the right thing" may be precisely what produces a catastrophe. Tragedies demonstrate how we

are all subject to forces larger and more powerful than ourselves, many of which we do not even contemplate as possibilities. Ultimately, we are all subject to luck, good and bad, and Aristotle takes the problem of how to act in the face of such uncertainty as a fundamental question that defines "the human condition" (Nussbaum 2001).

In order for a tragedy to speak to the ordinary person, the tragic figures that appear in ancient tragedies are, perhaps paradoxically, not ordinary people in their everyday lives but people who figure in well-known myths, in particular, men in important political positions. Such persons make decisions with implications that affect not merely their own personal lives but those of the people they govern – at a minimum, we are all subject to the effects of the actions of our leaders; in addition, we pay the price of the actions committed by members of our own family. Because ancient tragedies use well-known myths, audiences knew a great deal of the "backstory" for the events that take place during the play. We know that Oedipus is intelligent, industrious, and generally gifted, even if a bit headstrong and plagued by, as we might say, some anger-control problems. Such qualities are likely to be shared by leaders independently of where and when they rule, even though the particulars of Oedipus' own backstory may not seem plausible to an audience two and a half millennia later: his father, King Laius, angered the gods for ignoring their prophesy that if he had a son he would kill his father and marry his mother, so they took their revenge on Oedipus, his son, who left home in an effort to avoid making the prophesy come true, and as a consequence, albeit unknowingly, killed his father and married his mother. Nevertheless, there are alternatives to "prophecy from the gods" that have the status of modern myths, such as the possibility of brainwashing, which is employed in the film *The Manchurian Candidate* (John Frankenheimer, 1962). Tragedy is courted but ultimately averted in Woody Allen's *Mighty Aphrodite* (1995), which semi-seriously explores the forbidden search to discover the parentage of an adopted child along with a clever rendering of how the chorus may have functioned in Greek tragedy as dispensers of conventional wisdom. (In Allen's work as well as in many theories, comedy and tragedy have often been seen as bearing a special relation to each other.)

Aristotle's *Poetics* contains a great deal about what makes for the most compelling and effective tragedies, given their aim or function. Let us suppose, then, that tragedies dramatize how basically good people are subject to forces beyond their control so that actions they think will bring about something good may nevertheless produce irreparable harm. Such persons, according to Aristotle, are suitable for producing *pity* in the audience precisely to the extent that their suffering is undeserved, and *fear* when audience members perceive themselves to be vulnerable in the same way as the characters. In ancient times, various aspects of a performance drew attention to the ideas of the play and their perennial (and possibly universal) importance, rather than to the realism of the acting or the psychological peculiarities of the characters (which was one of the hallmarks of Shakespearean tragedy). For example, actors wore masks and elevated shoes, making them literally "larger than life." Tragedies were also written in verse and were hence a form of poetry, not prose, and Aristotle advises that the tone of the language should be suitably "elevated." (*Mighty Aphrodite* deliciously exploits the comic potential of formal verse that lapses into the colloquial.) Yet all of this is ancillary to the plot, according to Aristotle, which is the most important part of the play, and which should take place over a relatively circumscribed period of time or else it becomes unwieldy and loses its emotional impact. (The seventeenth-century French neoclassic theatrical tradition, epitomized most notably in the work of Corneille and Racine, rigidified Aristotle's guidelines for how to write tragedies that effectively evoke pity and fear by turning his astute psychological observations into "rationally" required rules.)

The part of Aristotle's theory that has probably garnered the most attention, perhaps because his extant work says so little about it, is the idea that tragedy is supposed to produce some type of catharsis. It is a domain ripe for speculation, and various interpreters have explicated it as a cleansing of one's psyche, a purification of the emotions of pity and fear, a source of pleasure as one learns to experience the right types of emotions to the right types of objects, and as features of the plot in the form of pitiable and fearful events.

As the social and political structures of Western civilization changed, so did the dramatic arts. The tragedies of Shakespeare, for example, played to a different audience. They were written as popular entertainments and contain scenes of comic relief (written in prose, not verse) that humanize the characters and provide a break in the intensity of the tragic action, a strategy for holding the interest of the audience that Aristotle explicitly condemned as inappropriate to the genre. Shakespeare's tragedies also concerned themselves not so much with figures of noble birth whose tragic destiny descends through the family line, but with how catastrophe is precipitated through the weaknesses and extremes of individual personalities, including some who are deeply evil. The tragedy is thus not prompted by the forces of fate or a lack of knowledge per se, though the tragic figure's character may well blind him to the significance of what a more rational or stable person would notice and take into account. Thus, Othello is ultimately destroyed by his jealousy, Hamlet by his chronic indecisiveness, Timon of Athens by his profligacy, Macbeth by his lust for power, and so on. One can apply this perspective to ancient tragedy as well, for example, by seeing Oedipus as destroyed by his arrogance and irascibility and Creon by his stubbornness and fear of being perceived as weak (because of being forced to back down by a *woman*), an interpretation that is unhappily abetted by a misunderstanding of Aristotle's use of the term *hamartia* as referring to a character flaw when it actually refers to an error or mistake.

Friedrich Nietzsche's analysis of tragedy was developed in his groundbreaking work *The Birth of Tragedy from the Spirit of Music*. Nietzsche sees the essence of tragedy as lying in the enduring struggle between the love of reason and the beauty of dreams or illusions, symbolized by the god Apollo and associated with the plastic arts, and the giving up of oneself to the joys of rapture and intoxication, symbolized by the god Dionysus and associated with music. Aristotle takes the dramatic *action* or *plot* of tragedy to be central and hence situates its origins in the way successive playwrights made members of the chorus into characters, that is, *agents* in the unfolding of the drama. Nietzsche instead emphasizes tragedy's origins in music, specifically, in a particular type of song, the dithyramb, which was sung during ecstatic, orgiastic Dionysian revels. During these rituals it was thought that one sees through the illusion that there can be either knowledge or beauty or goodness in the world to the *absurdity* of human existence. According to Nietzsche, no individual person can set the world right; rather, through song and dance, one expresses oneself as a member of a higher community, establishing a kind of Apollonian rapprochement between competing spirits. Through tragedy we subjugate our fear of the absurd and through comedy we are relieved of its tedium.

In the early nineteenth century, G. W. F. Hegel identified the origins of tragedy in conflict of a radically different sort: when a person must choose between two ethical goods, *knowing* that the choice of one entails the destruction of the other. *Antigone* thus became his paradigm case of tragedy. In this play, Creon, king of Thebes, must choose between enforcing his edict that anyone who buries the body of Polyneices (who led an attack against the city of Thebes) would be put to death, and having mercy on Antigone, who is engaged to be married to his own son, and who courageously defied Creon's edict out of loyalty to her fallen brother. It may be argued that Creon's behavior has significant *unforeseen* consequences, however, since he did not consider that Antigone's death would inaugurate a chain of suicides including those of his own son and his own wife. (The plot of *The Manchurian Candidate* also centrally involves a significant unforeseen consequence, though of malicious behavior that reveals the character's essential hypocrisy rather than an effort to do good.) An additional complicating circumstance, often neglected by commentators, is that Polyneices launched his attack against Thebes because his brother, Eteocles, refused to give up power after a year, as per their agreement. (How much catastrophe in our own time is generated by the refusal to give up power, even when the law demands it?) The most controversial aspect of Hegel's theory is its claim that conflicting ethical goods may

ultimately be reconciled (Bradley 1909). Even in *Antigone*, Creon's recognition that he should have mercy on Antigone comes too late to avoid catastrophe.

Gotthold Ephraim Lessing, in his notion of the domestic tragedy, and later Henrick Ibsen, opened up greater scope for the genre in eschewing the presumption that the tragic figure must be a person of great power and status. The intersection of various demands on the individual from politics, family, and religion have historically provided a nexus for tragic action for literally millennia in the history of the Western world. At its foundation, tragedy seems to depend at some level on recognizing that what *individuals* do matters, even if making a difference in the world for good or for ill also involves a bit of luck. If we are *only* pawns of forces beyond our control – whether the whims of mythical gods, inevitable forces of history, unknowable political conspiracies, hidden psychological forces within ourselves, or predestination – the human condition would seem to be more pathetic or absurd than tragic. In admitting the role of such forces, however, the genre links with general metaphysical views about the nature of the world and presses on the very human feeling of responsibility for our actions and their consequences.

See also AESTHETICS IN ANTIQUITY; ARISTOTLE; CATHARSIS; COMEDY; EMOTION; HEGEL; HORROR; HUMOR; LESSING; NIETZSCHE; SCHOPENHAUER.

BIBLIOGRAPHY
Belfiore, Elizabeth. 1992. *Tragic Pleasures: Aristotle on Plot and Emotion*. Princeton: Princeton University Press.
Bradley, Andrew C. 1909. *Oxford Lectures on Poetry*. London: Macmillan, 69–98.
Bushnell, Rebecca (ed.). 2005. *Blackwell Companion to Tragedy*. Oxford: Blackwell.
Else, Gerald. 1986. *Plato and Aristotle on Poetry*. Chapel Hill: University of North Carolina Press.
Feagin, Susan L. 1983. "The Pleasures of Tragedy," *American Philosophical Quarterly*, 20, 95–104.
Halliwell, Stephen. 1986. *Aristotle's Poetics*. London: Duckworth.
Hegel, G. W. F. 1975 [1835–8]. *Aesthetics: Lectures on Fine Art*. 2 vols. T. M. Knox (trans.). Oxford: Clarendon.
Hume, David. 1970 [1757]. "Of Tragedy." In *Four Dissertations*. New York: Garland, 3–24.

Lessing, Gotthold Ephraim. 1962. *Hamburg Dramaturgy*. V. Lange (trans.). New York: Dover.

Nietzsche, Friedrich. 2000. *Basic Writings of Nietzsche*. W. Kaufmann (trans.). New York: Modern Library.

Nussbaum, Martha C. 2001. *The Fragility of Goodness: Luck and Ethics in Greek Tragedy and Philosophy*. Rev. edn. Cambridge: Cambridge University Press.

Poole, Adrian. 2005. *Tragedy: A Very Short Introduction*. Oxford: Oxford University Press.

Ridley, Aaron. 2003. "Tragedy." In *The Oxford Handbook of Aesthetics*. J. Levinson (ed.). Oxford: Oxford University Press, 408–20.

Rorty, Amélie Oksenberg (ed.). 1992. *Essays on Aristotle's Poetics*. Princeton: Princeton University Press.

Schopenhauer, Arthur. 1966 [1819/44]. *The World as Will and Representation*. E. J. F. Payne (trans.). 2 vols. New York: Dover.

Wallace, Jennifer. 2007. *The Cambridge Introduction to Tragedy*. Cambridge: Cambridge University Press.

SUSAN L. FEAGIN

truth in art   Question 1: Are there true statements in works of art? Question 2: Does truth matter to the aesthetic value of a work of art? To answer these questions let us focus on literature, where true statements are more likely to be found, then briefly note how other arts may express truths. A true statement is expressed by a sentence whose terms (a) refer to something and (b) describe it rightly. So do artworks include terms that refer to something?

The target world of "Cigarette smoking causes cancer" is the real world; therefore that statement is true, for in reality cigarette-smoking does cause cancer. Were its target world one in which tobacco does not cause cancer, the statement would be false. Now, statements about Hamlet have a *set* of target worlds. A statement about Hamlet is true when satisfied in *all* the worlds of that set, false if satisfied in none, and truth-valueless if satisfied in some of them only. All of *Hamlet*'s target worlds satisfy "Hamlet is a Dane"; none satisfies "Hamlet married Ophelia"; and some (but not all) satisfy "Hamlet is tall." There is a world where Hamlet is a husband (for Hamlet might have married Ophelia), but that world does not belong to the set of target worlds defined by *Hamlet* as Shakespeare wrote it.

The description of the object referred to may be explicit, implicit, or metaphorical. What *Hamlet* tells us is mostly not stated by any protagonist; it is implied by the total drama – that is, by the nature of *Hamlet*'s target worlds. Hamlet does not say that fatalists tend to be cruel; we learn that by observing him in those target worlds. In much of literature descriptions are metaphorical. Literally construed, such works can have no target worlds, for they entail logical impossibilities; yet we can understand what worlds comply with the metaphorical description. Of course, metaphors cannot be reduced to literal descriptions, but this is not extraordinary. Many other features of an artwork cannot be reflected in its target worlds: its style, the order of narration, and so on. No artwork is exhausted by the target worlds it specifies, just as not *all* its merit comes from its truth. In abstract art, metaphorical description is the main way for a work to express true statements: architecture and music, while literally nonrepresentational, can portray a world metaphorically: its atmosphere, dynamic structure, and general "feel." A painting can be both literally and metaphorically true of its target worlds.

We now have a positive answer of sorts to question 1: we have seen that artworks do express true statements; but that is not a very interesting kind of truth. We wish to know whether artworks express statements that are true, not of some possible world *WI*, but of the real world (*WR*). Does *Hamlet* say something true about reality? The above discussion has answered that question too. If there is something, *a*, that occurs in world *WI* as well as in reality, then if we know that it is *F* in *WI*, we know that in reality it could be *F*, for possible worlds are the various possibilities of the real world. To let art instruct us about the real world we should therefore seek those entities that occur both in the world depicted in an artwork and in reality.

Are there such entities? So far we have discussed only things that do not occur in reality, such as Hamlet. What about names like "Rome" that occur in works of art? Do they denote the real things known by these names, or not? Ingarden (1973) has denied that in Sienkiewicz's novel *Quo Vadis* the word "Rome" refers to the real city, Rome. Reference, some say, is an intentional act, and in writing a novel one does not intend to refer to anything real, or say anything about it. But that cannot be right. If the terms "Rome," "Caesar," "the Christians," and so on in the said novel do not refer to what we refer to by these names, then the novel is incomprehensible. The novel does not explicitly say that Caesar was a man and not a machine, that the laws of nature in Rome are those that prevail in the real Rome. We can assume all these facts, without which nothing in the novel makes sense, only on the basis of our acquaintance with the real Rome and the real Caesar. Indeed, Rome as depicted in the novel is different from the real Rome; for instance, it is the home of some people that did not exist. I conclude that in the novel the term "Rome" refers to Rome, the city we know, but not as it is in reality; the Rome that the novel describes is an occurrence of Rome in another possible world. It retains all the properties of the real Rome except those that the novel explicitly modifies, and those that these imply. Things occur in the real as well as in other possible worlds, fiction describes them as they are in those worlds, and thus we learn how they could be in reality.

These truths about reality may still sound trivial, but that depends on what things a work can be about. Works can be about properties as well as individuals such as Rome and Caesar. If that is so, then *Hamlet* is about Hamlet, and about Denmark, but also about love, melancholy, and the quest for truth. The latter are things that occur not only in *Hamlet*'s target worlds but, as we know, in reality too. We know that the quest for truth of Hamlet caused (in *Hamlet*'s target worlds) the death of all those who loved him, and delivered his country into the hands of a bloodthirsty tyrant (Fortinbras); therefore, we also know what that quest *can* cause in *reality*.

A truth about a possible world is a possible truth about the real world, and as such it is highly interesting to us: *Hamlet* teaches us not only what happens in *WI*, but also what can happen here. Furthermore, we can discover the essence of a thing by examining an occurrence of it in one world; for example, by examining the occurrence of water in the real world we find that its essence, a property it has in all possible worlds, is H_2O.

Now the world at which a thing is examined may be a possible one: that is the procedure known as *thought experiment*, whereby we gain insight into the nature of some thing by imaginatively envisaging how certain actions and initial conditions will influence that thing. That method is used by historians, generals, and social planners, but its best example is in works of fiction that deal with human nature. So by examining the quest for truth that occurs in *WI*, we may reach the conclusion that the catastrophe that this quest leads to in *WI* is not an accidental but an essential feature of it. If so, if it is necessary to that quest that it leads to calamity, then that quest will end in a bloodbath in every possible world (including the real one) that has the relevant features. Such a truth that we learn by reading *Hamlet* is extremely important to us, for it tells us what the quest for truth, so typical to our culture, *will* lead us to. Thus, important truths can be gleaned from works of art.

Question 2 asked whether there is a connection between the truthfulness of an artwork and its aesthetic value. Classicists considered that connection self-evident, while formalists held it to be impossible, for the excellence criteria in art are alien to those pertaining to information-gathering and science. Romantic thinkers were divided: under the influence of Kant's distinction between phenomena (objects known to science) and *noumena* (things in themselves), some thought that art can gain us access to the latter (Schopenhauer 1961; Heidegger 2002) or to pure uncategorized-by-reason intuitions (Croce 1970). Others rejected all claims of art to knowledge, stressing the freedom of art from didactic strictures of morality and fact (Beardsley 1958; Valéry 1958). The latter view seems well supported, for the work of some great artists is permeated by heinous moral views (Gogol, Dostoyevsky, Griffith, Pound) or radical factual errors (Homer, Dante).

Moreover, factual and moral excellence do not guarantee aesthetic merit – Robert Nozik has versified Newton's laws, to show that great science can be atrocious poetry! Yet some philosophers (including Hospers 1960) rightly protest that the said divorce of excellence criteria flies in the face of common practice: we praise great art for providing insight into reality, mainly into human nature, and we censure a work for lack of deeper knowledge of social and personal phenomena. How can that be explained?

We said that much of a work's target world overlaps the real world. No writer, fantasy writers included, can forgo borrowing from reality. An artist's target world may differ from reality in detail, but not in basic features: the kind of beings in it, their beliefs and desires, what motivates them, the emotions they have, and most laws of nature, cannot but be those that occur in the actual world. Now if a work has considerable aesthetic value, its world (say, *WI*) is well organized; it is unified yet variegated, revealing a new, exciting kind of unity in a multifarious world. Since *WI* is mostly our world, the significance and unity that emerge in *WI* are relevant to us. An author is a world-sculptor, who mostly works on borrowed material. We, who are that material, are keenly interested in what is done with it, for the features salient in the target world may fashion our own life. Of course, the aesthetic achievement may be due to those elements in *WI* that are not taken from the actual world. In that case our aesthetic admiration is not due to the work's truth. Such works, however, must be rare.

Here is why. Suppose that a novel is based on a shallow view of some people and presents them falsely. In principle, this is no problem; we just assume that in *WI* these people are not as they are in *WR*. But, then, what else is different in *WI*? If the trait is deep and pervasive, we cannot isolate it from its conceptual environment in *WR*: that is inconsistent. Reading a racist novel, we cannot simply assume that the Jews in *WI* are malevolent, and go on aesthetically to appreciate the work. If we cannot import our beliefs about Jews into *WI*, some other changes must be made in it to keep it consistent. Those concepts that take on a novel significance are connected to other beliefs we have, which now we realize are all false in *WI*.

Withholding our real beliefs from *WI* may spread like cancer, so in the end *WI* collapses: it is not cohesive enough. Thus, just as a discovered truth about *WR* often makes *WI* beautifully structured, violating a basic truth about *WR* may make *WI* either so inchoate, or else so meager (since many beliefs must be excised to keep it consistent), that its aesthetic value becomes nugatory.

See also LITERATURE; AESTHETIC JUDGMENT; COGNITIVE VALUE OF ART; FICTION, NATURE OF; FICTION, TRUTH IN; FICTIONAL ENTITIES; IMAGINATIVE RESISTANCE; METAPHOR; REPRESENTATION.

BIBLIOGRAPHY

Beardsley, Monroe C. 1958. *Aesthetics: Problems in the Theory of Criticism*. New York: Harcourt, Brace & World.

Croce, Benedetto. 1970 [1902]. *Aesthetics*. D. Ainslee (trans.). London: Macmillan.

Graham, Gordon. 1995. "Learning from Art," *British Journal of Aesthetics*, 35, 26–37.

Heidegger, Martin. 2002 [1950]. "The Origin of the Work of Art." In *Off the Beaten Track*. J. Young & K. Haynes (trans.). Cambridge: Cambridge University Press, 1–56.

Hospers, John. 1960. "Implied Truths in Literature," *Journal of Aesthetics and Art Criticism*, 29, 36–46.

Ingarden, Roman. 1973 [1931]. *The Literary Work of Art*. G. G. Grabowicz (trans.). Evanston: Northwestern University Press.

John, Eileen. 1998. "Reading Fiction and Conceptual Knowledge," *Journal of Aesthetics and Art Criticism*, 56, 331–48.

Kripke, Saul. 1980. *Naming and Necessity*. Oxford: Blackwell.

Lamarque, Peter & Olsen, Stein Haugom. 1994. *Truth, Fiction and Literature*. Oxford: Oxford University Press.

Nussbaum, Martha. 1990. *Love's Knowledge*. Oxford: Oxford University Press.

Schopenhauer, Arthur. 1961 [1819/1844]. *The World as Will and Idea*. R. B. Haldane (trans.). Garden City: Doubleday.

Valéry, Paul. 1958. *The Art of Poetry*. New York: Random House.

Young, James O. 2001. *Art and Knowledge*. London: Routledge.

Zemach, Eddy. 1982. "A Plea for a New Nominalism," *Canadian Journal of Philosophy*, 12, 527–37.

EDDY M. ZEMACH

U

_____

universals in art   Traditionally, universals are held to be those properties or relations that hold for multiple particulars. An instance of a universal would be the property of having three angles; this property holds for all triangles. The problem of universals is the question of whether or not properties, relations, or principles hold universally, across time and place for particulars of the same kind, and how we could know this. Central themes in philosophy of art that raise questions about universals include the apparent ubiquity of art, the standard of taste, and aesthetic values.

THE UNIVERSALITY OF ART

Art is commonly said to be a human universal. Although the manifestations of the artistic impulse differ, societies across the world commonly produce artifacts and performances that are appreciated aesthetically. Some have argued that art-making is essential to human nature, suggesting that every human individual has a tendency toward artistic expression, despite divergences in talent.

According to many anthropologists and a growing number of philosophers, however, the universality of art should not be taken for granted. They argue that such terms as "art," "aesthetics," and "beauty" are laden with ethnocentric connotations derived from the West, such as the notions that art is in contrast with utility and that art's form should be appreciated for its own sake. One response is that cross-cultural employment of these terms merely needs to be tempered with the recognition that different societies may have different attitudes and beliefs about their cultural productions. Another is that art should be discussed in terms of its culture of origin. Still another is to propose an alternative terminology, such as Robert Plant Armstrong's notion of "affecting presence." Armstrong takes seriously the complaint

about ethnocentrism, but he thinks that all societies create objects and events that are powerful, have personalities of their own, and are evocative of affect, often beyond their cultures of origin.

The universality of art or art-like practices is sometimes explained by reference to our biological nature. Charles Darwin proposed that in many species males with aesthetically appealing traits, whether visual or auditory, are more attractive to females and thus have a greater chance at successful mating than others who are not so endowed. If the principle of sexual selection on the basis of aesthetic preference extends to humans, it might suggest that those who enhance the appearance of themselves or their environments might be at an evolutionary advantage over the less gifted.

Ellen Dissanayake defends the evolutionary value of art by arguing that it confers survival advantage to individuals as members of a social group. She contends that art (which she generically characterizes in terms of behaviors that make things "special" or "elaborate") promotes cooperation and social solidarity and emphasizes values important to the group. Art benefits the individual's chances of survival by improving the cohesiveness of the society to which the individual belongs.

Others who see grounds for art's universality in evolutionary psychology do not share Dissanayake's conviction that art is directly adaptive. Some take art to be a spandrel, that is, an agreeable by-product of traits selected for their centrality to species preservation. The convincingness of this ploy, however, depends on showing that the allegedly selected trait is more fundamental than artistic behavior. This may be difficult to demonstrate. The common allegation that music-making, for instance, is a spandrel while language was selected ignores the fact that the two capacities are built on many common components, some of which seem to have been selected, others of which may have been spandrels. However this dispute is resolved, those who focus on evolutionary psychology do tend to accept the universality of artistic activity.

THE UNIVERSALITY OF TASTE

The eighteenth-century debate about the foundation for taste also resulted in concern with artistic universals. The issue concerned the common but paradoxical acceptance of the idea that taste is radically subjective but that some people's tastes are better than others. David Hume attempted to explain this perplexity, contending that despite the subjectivity of taste, taste could be subjected to a standard. The standard by which a judgment of taste could be evaluated was the consensus of ideal judges, those who are optimally characterized by a sound state of mind and body, delicacy of imagination, freedom from prejudice, and considerable experience with the type of art in question. Lacking access to a clear consensus of ideal judges in most instances, the most reliable guidance we can typically get is provided by the standard of durable admiration, a standard which Hume articulates in universal terms. "The same Homer, who pleased at Athens and Rome two thousand years ago, is still admired at Paris and at London" (1995: 259). Hume also accepts the idea of general principles of approval or disapproval that influence all of our mental operations, and he contends that "some particular forms or qualities, from the original structure of the internal fabric, are calculated to please, and others to displease" (1963: 259).

Kant takes the capacity to please universally without conceptual mediation to be among the criteria of beauty, and thus of beautiful art. According to Kant, the beautiful pleases all individuals because it involves a heightened engagement of the basic faculties of cognition, imagination, and understanding in a state of "free play." Aesthetic experience is universally available because the faculties it involves are the very faculties employed in everyday cognition and the use of language. The accordance of these cognitive powers in relation to an object admit of universal communicability, according to Kant. So basic are these faculties and the condition of harmony between them in human experience that Kant terms our capacity for aesthetic pleasure to be based on a "common sense."

While Kant's analysis of beauty depends on universally available operations of standard human faculties, his paradigm for beauty is the beautiful object within nature. Where art (which he takes to be representational) is involved, he contends that we necessarily judge with concepts in mind, for we are concerned with whether or not the artwork presents an object in a manner that accords with our notion of it. Societies may have different relevant concepts, as they do, for example, in the case of human beauty. Nevertheless, Kant is a formalist, and he considers the focus of attention in genuine aesthetic experience to be the formal structure of an artwork. Presumably formal structure is recognizable through standard perceptual abilities, and we should expect a fair amount of convergence in what art members of various societies will find beautiful, particularly in the case of art that emphasizes geometric form as opposed to culturally specific content.

We should be cautious, however, when drawing conclusions about universality on the basis of our perceptual capacities. While typical human beings share the same perceptual apparatus, some of our perceptual abilities mature through the acquisition of mental templates for categorizing stimuli. We develop templates for musical pitch, for example, which we use to determine whether a particular tone is in tune or a plausible musical tone within its context. Once one has absorbed one's native musical style and learned the template for pitch relations that it allows, one will listen with the expectation of tones fitting the internalized pattern. Fortunately, we tend to assimilate closely proximate tones to pitches allowed by familiar scales. As a result, we are not disturbed, for instance, by small flaws in intonation. But if the distance is sufficiently large, which is often the case in foreign music that is tuned in an unfamiliar manner, we have the impression of the music being out of tune. What this suggests is that the learning involved in gaining mastery of a universal perceptual apparatus results not only in different preferences but a sense of wrongness in the foreign style.

UNIVERSAL VALUES IN ART

Evolutionary psychology proposes grounds for believing that at least some aesthetic preferences are universal. One study, for example, found that young children in a variety of societies preferred pictures of landscapes showing characteristics of savannahs, even when the children had never seen such a landscape. The explanation from evolutionary psychology is that aesthetic preferences developed during the late Pleistocene era, when the ancestors of contemporary humanity prospered in the savannahs of Africa. Another alternative, however, is to contend that our common biological nature and the experiences that come with it, along with the commonalities within environments that can sustain human beings, are sufficient to result in universal preference for certain artistic contents, regardless of how human beings initially acquired them.

Even if some preferences are common, artistic styles vary considerably across the world. Wilfried Van Damme points out, however, that even when societies' artworks exhibit contrasting superficial characteristics, they may nevertheless be organized in accordance with common principles. He distinguishes two types of universals, "transcultural universals," or the "*stimulus properties* which as such would seem to appeal to all human beings, regardless of cultural background," "*pancultural* universals," or "*principles* that are found to be operative in evaluating stimuli in all (pan) cultures," whether or not these are evident on the surface (2000: 258). Most people who refer to universals in art, he suggests, have in mind such transcultural universals as brightness, smoothness, clarity, balance, symmetry, and novelty.

However, differences in the stimulus properties that cultures favor in their art may themselves reflect an underlying universal. Van Damme cites the example of what is perceived to be ideal body weight. Cultures might disagree in their ideals but nonetheless agree in holding that the ideal should reflect health and physical wellbeing. Despite a transcultural disagreement, Van Damme contends that a pancultural universal is at work, the fact that "people in a particular culture find attractive those visual stimuli which in terms of that culture aptly signify its sociocultural ideals"

(2000: 274), that is, the qualities the culture considers worth pursuing. The same sociocultural ideals can be artistically expressed in many different ways. On the other hand, superficially similar presentations in artworks from different cultures might nevertheless reflect contrasting societal reasons for valuing them. While societies may share some ideas about qualities worth pursuing, forms that consolidate a variety of sociocultural ideals are likely to be particularly meaningful for the members of the society that holds them in a way that will not be fully accessible to nonmembers.

What this suggests is that what we superficially observe in the art of different cultures may not do justice to what is similar and what is different. Perhaps the most important consequence of considering universals in art is the new motive they produce for attending more closely to artworks, their contexts of production, and the range of reasons people have for finding them meaningful.

See also ART OF THE PALEOLITHIC; COGNITIVE SCIENCE AND ART; EVOLUTION, ART, AND AESTHETICS; HUME; KANT; OBJECTIVITY AND REALISM IN AESTHETICS; RELATIVISM.

BIBLIOGRAPHY

Armstrong, Robert Plant. 1971. *The Affecting Presence: An Essay in Humanistic Anthropology*. Urbana: University of Illinois Press.

Dissanayake, Ellen. 2000. *Art and Intimacy: How the Arts Began*. Seattle: University of Washington Press.

Dutton, Denis. 2001. "Aesthetic Universals." In *The Routledge Companion to Aesthetics*. B. Gaut & D. McIver Lopes (eds.). New York: Routledge, 203–14.

Higgins, Kathleen Marie. 2006. "The Cognitive and Appreciative Import of Musical Universals." *Revue Internationale de Philosophie*, 60/238, 487–503.

Hume, David. 1995 [1757]. "Of the Standard of Taste." In *The Philosophy of Art: Readings Ancient and Modern*. A. Neill & A. Ridley (eds.). New York: McGraw-Hill, 254–68.

Kant, Immanuel. 1987 [1790]. *Critique of Judgment*. W. Pluhar (trans.). Indianapolis: Hackett.

Orians, Gordon H. & Heerwagen, Judith H. 1992. "Evolved Responses to Landscapes." In *The Adapted Mind: Evolutionary Psychology and the Generation of Culture*. J. H. Barkow, L. Cosmides, & J. Tooby (eds.). New York: Oxford University Press, 555–79.

Shiner, Larry. 2001. *The Invention of Art: A Cultural History*. Chicago: University of Chicago Press.

Van Damme, Wilfried. 1996. *Beauty in Context: Towards an Anthropological Approach to Aesthetics*. Leiden: Brill.

Van Damme, Wilfried. 2000. "Universality and Cultural Particularity in Visual Aesthetics." In *Being Humans: Anthropological Universality and Particularity in Transdisciplinary Perspectives*. N. Roughly (ed.). Berlin: de Gruyter, 258–83.

KATHLEEN MARIE HIGGINS

V

value of art *see* AESTHETIC PLEASURE; CREATIVITY; COGNITIVE VALUE OF ART; INTERPRETATION, AIMS OF; OBJECTIVITY AND REALISM IN AESTHETICS; ORIGINALITY; RELATIVISM; THEORIES OF ART; TRUTH IN ART; UNIVERSALS IN ART.

W

Wagner, Richard (1813–1883) German composer (most famously of the four operas in the *Ring* cycle), poet, revolutionary, and author of books on art, religion, and politics. Wagner is unique among the greatest artists for having theorized a great deal, his topics ranging from vivisection and vegetarianism to the nature of art and its relations to religion and to revolution. This speculative work took the form of substantial books and essays, short fiction, and a copious correspondence (12,000 letters survive, some as long as 50 pages). Although not much of what Wagner wrote comes under the heading of aesthetics as such, he was not averse to philosophizing about it. He composed his prose mainly under the stress of needing to work out his position on the fundamental issues involved in composing operas, or, as he increasingly preferred to call them, "music dramas."

After composing his first three operas – *Die Feen* ("The Fairies"), *Das Liebesverbot* ("Forbidden Love") and *Rienzi* – which are highly competent and in some ways original works broadly in the German, Italian, and French traditions respectively, he began to realize that contemporary operatic forms and fashions, as well as operatic life and standards of performance, were unacceptable to him. For an artist destined to be more revolutionary than any other in his century, his awareness of his mission came to him slowly; he was not a precocious composer and the main thing in common between these three early works and his subsequent ones is that he wrote his own libretti from the outset – something that had rarely been done by his predecessors.

Like Verdi, his exact contemporary, Wagner never felt inclined to write substantial nonoperatic works, but, unlike Verdi, he was heir to an immensely impressive tradition of symphonic and instrumental composition, and

Beethoven was always his greatest idol. By the time he was in his late twenties, and living in Paris, he was beginning to have ambitions to bring closer together the achievement of the Austrian symphonists and the possibilities of operatic composition, contemporary examples of which he viewed with increasing distaste. Because he was living in acute poverty, he turned to journalism, and it was at this time that he produced his first substantial body of prose, consisting of short stories strongly influenced by E. T. A. Hoffmann, and reports on the Parisian musical scene. Most of these pieces make lively and enjoyable reading, unlike his later prose works, and in them there are the first signs of what became his lifelong obsession with the development of opera as a leading art form. In the story "A Pilgrimage to Beethoven," he presents the great composer on his deathbed giving expression to proto-Wagnerian ideas on the relationship between music and words, and on the kind of opera he would like to write: It "would contain no arias, duets, trios, and all the other things with which an opera is patched together these days."

Beethoven's Ninth Symphony was always a talismanic work for Wagner, and his returns, throughout his life, to writing about it might be said to reflect his developing thoughts on his deepest aesthetic concerns. In the explanatory program he wrote when he gave the work what was probably its first exemplary performance in Dresden in 1846, he claimed that the celebrated introduction to the last movement – in which the themes of the previous three movements are tried out and found wanting by the lower strings in passages of powerful and expressive recitative – was Beethoven's embodiment of the idea that purely instrumental music was not enough. So Beethoven introduced voices singing Schiller's "Ode to Joy" in order to complete a work that had, up to that point, been the greatest of all examples of a purely instrumental art form. Meanwhile, Wagner was himself producing operas in which the music and the drama were on ever more intimate terms, though he did not yet feel the necessity for working out the relationship between them at any great length. The three works of this decade, *Der fliegende Holländer* ("The Flying Dutchman"), *Tannhäuser*, and *Lohengrin*, are characterized by growing mastery in musical-dramatic presentation, but there was nothing here to alarm the operatic world of the time.

In 1848–9, Europe was shaken by a series of revolutions and Wagner participated, to an undetermined extent, in that of May 1849 in Dresden. The result was that he narrowly escaped arrest and imprisonment and was exiled from Germany for the next 12 years. He had already begun to think about various mythological subjects for a new work, but came to realize that he would not be able to accomplish anything without drastic speculations on the whole nature of his work as an artist, and as a member of a society which he had come to regard as fundamentally corrupt. The first fruits of this were his major theoretical works, *Art and Revolution* (1849), *The Art-Work of the Future* (1850), and *Opera and Drama* (1851). This last is the most important treatise in the history of operatic aesthetics. His basic premise in these works is that art has to reclaim the social function that it fulfilled in the classical Greek *polis*, and decisively reject its function as entertainment, which it has lapsed into in the decadent modern world. To achieve its proper aim, it must deal with the "purely human," that which is common to people of all times and places. Its subjects must therefore be mythological, not historical. And it must represent a new synthesis of the arts, which Wagner characterized as the *Gesamtkunstwerk*, perhaps best translated as "the total work of art." The focus of this kind of art was to be drama, to which the other arts, which had developed autonomously to their disadvantage, must all contribute.

In particular, the role of music in this new collective art must be reversed from that which Wagner alleged it had played in traditional opera, where it had been the end, the so-called drama having been the means. Music had to be subordinate, he declared, to make more powerfully expressive what was being enacted in the drama – which consisted, of course, not only of the text but also of the action. A great deal of what Wagner wrote in his historical reconstruction of the history of the various art forms is to be taken with a pinch of salt. What matters is that, without indulging in extensive special pleading – in which he borrowed heavily from Feuerbach, among many other, mostly German, thinkers – he would not have been able to return finally to his creative work, the composition of the *Ring*. He came to see that as he had originally conceived it, as a single music drama called *Siegfried's Tod* ("Siegfried's Death"), it was not sufficiently a drama because of the amount of narrative and explanation of former events that it contained. He therefore set about filling out the action, and the result was four dramas – or poems, as he called them – which he would not finish composing until 1874. The first, whose function was largely to clear the ground, is *Das Rheingold*, and in it he stuck very closely to the prescriptions he had set out in *Opera and Drama*. Because it is primarily an expository work, the theory translates remarkably smoothly into practice. But it is in the second of the dramas, *Die Walküre* ("The Valkyrie"), that his prodigious musical gifts begin to reassert themselves.

It so happened that at this time (1854) he was introduced by a friend to the works of Schopenhauer, and the effect of reading him, especially his magnum opus, *The World as Will and Representation*, was immediate and lasting. It also involved what amounted to a *volte-face* on the relationship of music to the other arts, but this was something that Wagner never explicitly acknowledged. It was left to Nietzsche, in *Towards a Genealogy of Morals* (1887), to point it out with typical firmness. For Schopenhauer, music was by far the most important of the arts, because unlike the others, which have an oblique relationship to the will – which is the sole reality, all else being appearance – music is the direct presentation of the will.

Wagner's conversion to this view was a smooth affair, as was his general acceptance of Schopenhauer's pessimistic evaluation of existence. Wagner's disillusionment with political events during the mid-century and his paradoxical combination of exuberant vitality with a yearning for death found what he took to be their ideal working out in Schopenhauer's philosophy. After writing two acts of the upbeat *Siegfried*, he broke off work on the *Ring* for 12 years, during which he wrote *Tristan und Isolde*, which he conceived in the spirit of Schopenhauer, whose influence is manifest in its text. But the philosopher would have been horrified by the lovers' achievement of "nothingness" by taking erotic love to a previously unimagined extreme. Wagner's next work, the ostensibly cheerful *Die Meistersinger von Nürnberg* ("The Mastersingers of Nuremberg"), is in fact far more imbued with pessimism. And by the time Wagner returned to the *Ring*, Schopenhauer's influence is pervasive, if elusive – it is more a matter of the overall tone of the work than of its conclusion, which is notoriously ambiguous.

During his later years Wagner continued to write prose works, though short ones. To celebrate the centenary of Beethoven's birth, in 1870 he produced a monograph on the composer in which his view of music is most explicitly Schopenhauerian. After the first performance of the *Ring* in 1876, he devoted himself to *Parsifal*, his "stage consecration festival drama," in which he put into practice the formulation at the opening of his essay "Religion and Art" (1880):

> It could be said that at the point where religion becomes artificial, it is reserved to art to salvage the kernel of religion, inasmuch as the mythical images which religion would wish to be believed as true are apprehended in art for their symbolic value, and through ideal representation of those symbols art reveals the concealed truth within them.

The clumsy expression, combined with depth of insight, in this piece of Wagnerian prose is typical of his mature thought on aesthetic matters.

See also NIETZSCHE; OPERA; SCHOPENHAUER.

BIBLIOGRAPHY

Primary sources
[1851]. *Opera and Drama*. E. Evans (trans.). London: Wm. Reeves.

Secondary sources
Borchmeyer, Dieter. 1991. *Richard Wagner: Theory and Theatre*. Oxford: Oxford University Press.

Skelton, Geoffrey. 1991. *Wagner in Thought and Practice*. London: Lime Tree.
Tanner, Michael. 1996. *Wagner*. London: Harper Collins.

MICHAEL TANNER

Walton, Kendall L(ewis) (b.1939)   Charles L. Stevenson Collegiate Professor of Philosophy at the University of Michigan, where he has taught since 1965. Past President of the American Society for Aesthetics (2003–5) and Fellow of the American Academy of Arts and Sciences, he received his doctorate in philosophy from Cornell University in 1967. He has made major contributions to a wide array of issues relevant to aesthetics and the philosophy of art, including: art interpretation, representation in the arts, fictional discourse, emotional responses to fiction, metaphor, the aesthetics of music, and aesthetic value. He is best known for his theory of make-believe, which he presented systematically in the seminal *Mimesis as Make-Believe*.

Walton's first publication in aesthetics (1970) has become a classic of analytic philosophy of art. Walton claims that knowing facts about the history of a work of art is relevant to the correct understanding and appreciation of it; in particular, it is relevant to the identification and experience of the work's aesthetic properties broadly conceived. The mere perception of an artwork will not disclose its aesthetic properties – whether, say, the work is serene, balanced, coherent, etc. – for the perception of such properties depends on which artistic *categories* the work is perceived in; that is, it depends on the work being perceived as a work of a certain kind, produced in a given medium, belonging to a certain genre, and so on. In agreement with Frank Sibley, Walton thinks that an artwork's aesthetic properties "emerge" from its nonaesthetic properties: a painting, for instance, is balanced in virtue of the color and shape configuration of its surface. Yet, an artwork never has its aesthetic properties just in virtue of its nonaesthetic properties, for the same nonaesthetic property may be or fail to be aesthetically relevant, or may be relevant in different ways, according to the category under which the work is perceived. Hence, the same physical object, such as a canvas with a marked surface, may lack realism when perceived as an Impressionist painting, but have realism when perceived as a Cubist painting (or may have neither property, when considered under an altogether different category, say, as an installation piece rather than a painting). That aesthetic judgments are category-relative does not mean that all judgments are admissible. Quite the contrary. For Walton, a number of factors contribute to determine which categories a work belongs to and, relatedly, the sort of investigations that an art critic ought to engage in. Such factors include facts about the work's origin, such as the intentions of its maker and the historical context of production of the work.

Mimesis as Make-Believe (1990) presents a theory of what representations (such things as paintings, sculptures, novels, plays, films, etc.) are and how they affect their perceivers. Walton considers all representations to be *fictions*, in the sense that they function, within the appropriate set of rules and for the appropriate perceivers, as prompters of imaginings (hence, for example, a documentary on real events is a fiction in this sense). Extending to art what is true of the games of make-believe that children play – say, when they pretend that globs of mud are pies – Walton claims that all representations are "props" in "games of make-believe." A prop in a game of make-believe makes certain propositions fictional (e.g., that there is a pie, that it is round, or that it was overbaked); it *prescribes* imaginings – prescribes, that is, that the relevant propositions be imagined. Likewise, representational works of art make propositions fictional: that a man named Robinson Crusoe was shipwrecked or that, as in Seurat's *A Sunday Afternoon on the Island of La Grande Jatte*, people are strolling in a park. Hence, Walton can speak of fictions without adding any fictional entities to our ontology. Rather, discourse about Robinson Crusoe, Willy Loman, or the strollers in *La Grande Jatte* is translated into talk regarding props (a novel, a play, a piece of canvas with colored marks on it). Which imaginings are prescribed in a given game depends on features of the prop: the *Grand Jatte* represents what it does in virtue of the color and line configuration of its surface, as a glob of mud represents a round pie in virtue of its size and shape. The

prescribed imaginings also depend on the rules of the game (the "principles of generation"), some explicit but many implicit. Children may agree, for instance, that globs of mud placed under a box are, fictionally, pies in the oven. Other rules apply even if not asserted, for instance, that larger, thicker globs correspond to larger, thicker pies. The interpretation of a representational artwork, then, largely has to do with identifying the principles of generation that apply to it. What is true in a game is independent of what individual players actually imagine; hence there may be disputes: children may argue, say, on whether there is a pie in the oven, art critics on whether *La Grande Jatte* represents tension between social classes. Which principles of generation apply to a representation, in fact even whether something is a representation or not, *may* but *need not* depend on the maker's intention. Representationality is a *function* and whether something has such a function depends only on the existence of "a social (or at least human) context or setting," not necessarily on someone's intentions (1990: 88–9). Hence, there may be naturally occurring representations: star constellations and faces in the clouds can be considered pictures and, in principle, the trace left by an ant in the sand could be a story.

The various kinds of representations are distinguished from each other by the sorts of games of make-believe that they authorize. When we read a narrative, for instance, we are invited to imagine that some narrator speaks or writes the words of, say, the novel. Pictorial representations are, instead, such that they authorize games of make-believe that are distinctively visual. When looking at *La Grande Jatte*, it is not just fictionally true that there are people strolling in a park, but also that our *act* of looking at the painting is an act of looking at such people (compare to what may be fictionally true in a child's game of hobbyhorse riding: not just that his broom is a horse, but also that the child's act of touching the broom, in the game, amounts to touching a horse). The distinctively visual nature of the make-believe games that we play with pictures also explains the sense in which resemblance plays a role in depiction. Rather than a resemblance between the picture and what it depicts, what is distinctive of pictures is the similarity between the two perceptual acts – that of looking at the picture and that of looking at whatever it depicts.

Among representations, photographs are a special case (1984). Since they essentially depend on the mechanism that produces them, photographs are in a special causal relation with what they portray. Accordingly, they are "transparent": not so different from such things as mirrors, microscopes, telescopes, etc., they are "aids to vision": they put us in contact with – literally, they allow us to *see*, if indirectly – what they portray.

That the propositions that are made fictional by representations include propositions about the perceiver himself or herself goes together with an important distinction Walton introduces – that between the *work world* and the *game world*. In the case of *La Grande Jatte*, the world of the work includes people strolling in a park. The world of the game, while it typically refers to much of what constitutes the world of the work, also refers to the perceiver. The distinction between work and game world makes it possible to explain, for instance, how when I look at *La Grande Jatte*, it is fictional (in my game world) that I am looking at people strolling in a park, although it is not fictional (in the work world) that they are being looked at by me.

That we are participants in games of make-believe is crucial to the investigation of our responses to fiction. Most notably, Walton (1990) explains in terms of make-believe what has become to be known as the puzzle, or paradox, of fictional emotions. The puzzle arises from the fact that, though we are often emotionally engaged, sometimes quite vividly, with fictional characters and events – we fear the monster in a horror film for example – our responses seem to lack the belief component necessary to an emotion (at least necessary to fear): normally, we know that there is no monster, hence that we are under no real danger. Walton solves the puzzle by maintaining that our emotional responses to fictional characters and events have themselves fictional status, that is, are fictional emotions. Specifically, when imagining the monster, it is fictional (i.e., fictionally true) of the physiological-psychological state we find ourselves in that such a state is fear of the monster. Whether we are aware of that or not, as consumers of fictions

we play a game of make-believe with the very sensations that naturally arise within us – sensations that Walton dubs "quasi-emotions" (in the case of fear, "quasi-fear"). Sometimes, this view is misleadingly characterized by Walton's commentators as the claim that people do not experience real emotions in appreciating works of fiction, or as the claim that responses to fictional characters *are* quasi-emotions. In fact, the view is about the status of our responses to fictional *characters* and *events*, which – by being fictional – produce the interesting puzzle; it is not about responses to *works*, which certainly can be the objects of emotions. Further, quasi-emotions are neither distinctive of responses to fictions nor unreal. By definition, bona fide emotions have quasi-emotions as an essential component and, of course, quasi-emotions are as genuine as sensations are. Quite simply, however, much as the real broomstick in a child's game of hobbyhorse-riding is, fictionally, a horse in the game, so is the really felt quasi-fear of the moviegoer, fictionally, an instance of fear of the monster.

The theory of make-believe, especially when applied to our affective responses to representations, rather naturally combines with simulation theories of the mind, and Walton has been investigating this link (forthcoming). Imagining in the way we do when we play games of make-believe involves running mental simulations and our responses to fictions can be seen as outputs of such simulations. It remains to note Walton's conviction that appeal to games of make-believe can illuminate as well both the nature of metaphor and the nature of response to music, and not simply that of representation.

Fictional worlds may deviate from the real world, either because of ignorance on the part of the author (e.g., making it fictional that the earth ends at the horizon, in a fiction produced at a time when the earth was believed to be flat) or intentionally so (making it fictional, say, that time travel is possible). Yet, when the deviation from reality surrounds ethical matters, authors' powers to prescribe whichever imaginings they like seems to break down. Partly by reference to David Hume's essay "Of the Standard of Taste," Walton has made a series of suggestions that have contributed to the arising of an ongoing debate on the so-called "puzzle of imaginative resistance" (1990: 154–5; 1994a; 2008). Walton's emphasis is mostly on the existence of a tangle of different issues here, ones that do not necessarily regard only moral deviance. Regarding one such issue, which he dubs "the fictionality puzzle," he brings to light our resistance to accept as true certain propositions, ones involving values, even just fictionally, for example, that "female infanticide is right and proper, or that nutmeg is the *summum bonum*, or that a dumb *knock-knock* joke is actually hilarious" (2008: 51). The impossibility of making it fictional that, say, genocide is good may have to do with the impossibility of imagining that certain dependence, or supervenience, relations between such things as genocide, slavery, and evil, are different from what they actually are. The issue can also be linked to the admittedly different question of the aesthetic value of immoral works. A work that celebrates genocide might lack in aesthetic value, the aesthetic value it has may be inaccessible because of the work's immorality, if the aesthetic value of an artwork does not just have to do with its capacity to produce a certain kind of pleasure but also with whether taking pleasure in such an object is *proper*, "reasonable," or "apt" to do (1994a: 30; 2008: 14, 50).

See also TWENTIETH-CENTURY ANGLO-AMERICAN AESTHETICS; DEPICTION; FICTION, NATURE OF; FICTION, THE PARADOX OF RESPONDING TO; HUME; IMAGINATION; IMAGINATIVE RESISTANCE; MORALITY AND ART; ONTOLOGICAL CONTEXTUALISM; PICTURE PERCEPTION; REPRESENTATION; SIBLEY.

BIBLIOGRAPHY

Primary sources

1970. "Categories of Art," *Philosophical Review*, 79, 334–67.
1984. "Transparent Pictures: On the Nature of Photographic Realism," *Critical Inquiry*, 11, 246–77.
1990. *Mimesis as Make-Believe: On the Foundations of the Representational Arts*. Cambridge, MA: Harvard University Press.
1993. "Metaphor and Prop Oriented Make-Believe," *European Journal of Philosophy*, 1, 39–57.
1994a. "Morals in Fiction and Fictional Morality," *Proceedings of the Aristotelian Society*, supp. vol. 68, 27–50.
1994b. "Listening with Imagination: Is Music Representational?" *Journal of Aesthetics and Art Criticism*, 52, 47–62.
2008. *Marvelous Images: Values and the Arts*. New York: Oxford University Press.
Forthcoming. *In Other Shoes: Music, Metaphor, Empathy, Existence*. New York: Oxford University Press.

Secondary sources

1991. *Philosophy and Phenomenological Research*, 51, 383–431. A symposium on *Mimesis as Make-Believe*, with articles by Kendall L. Walton, Noël Carroll, Patrick Maynard, George Wilson, Richard Wollheim, and Nicholas Wolterstorff.
Lamarque, Peter. 1991. "Critical Notice of Walton's *Mimesis as Make-Believe*," *Journal of Aesthetics and Art Criticism*, 49, 161–6.
Levinson, Jerrold. 1993. "Making Believe," *Canadian Philosophical Review*, 32, 359–74.

ALESSANDRO GIOVANNELLI

Wilde, Oscar

Wilde, Oscar [Fingall O'Flahertie Wills] (1854–1900) Irish playwright, poet, and man of letters; a luminary of late nineteenth-century cultural life, his career was cut short by imprisonment during the 1890s and consequent ill-health.

Various factors have stood in the way of appreciating Wilde's significance as a theorist of art – personal notoriety, a primary reputation for sparkling comedies of manners, and a penchant for paradox and irony. (*The Cambridge Companion to Oscar Wilde* (1997) has only one chapter devoted to Wilde as a theorist.) It is possible, however, to discern a coherent and challenging aesthetic informing the themes treated by his three main essays, "The Decay of Lying," "The Critic as Artist," and "The Soul of Man under Socialism" (all published during 1889–90): the themes of art's imitation by life and nature, of the role of criticism, and of the relation between art, politics, and morality.

Sounding a note that was to become dogma in the following century, Wilde proclaims that "art never expresses anything but itself," and so is "not to be judged by any external standard of resemblance" (1983: 987, 982). This is not intended to criticize representational art and plead for abstraction, but to point out that even the most "realistic" art acts only as a "veil, rather than a mirror." And insofar as imitation takes place at all, it is life and nature that imitate art, not vice versa. Part of Wilde's meaning here is, of course, that people's behavior is influenced by painting and literature. "The nineteenth century . . . is largely an invention of Balzac" (1983: 983). He is indicating, as well, the idea later developed by Ernst Gombrich that an artist's perception of nature is partly a function of the artistic tradition to which he or she belongs. It is Turner and the Impressionists, he suggests, who are responsible for London looking so foggy.

But Wilde is also making a more philosophical point. Nature, he writes, "is our creation. It is in our brain that she quickens to life. Things are because we see them" (1983: 986). Life and nature are in themselves a chaos, lacking in form and structure until humans impose these. And they impose them, not least, through the self-consciously form-giving activity of the arts. Art cannot, therefore, be answerable to an "external standard of resemblance"; for, prior to the constructive contribution of art, there exists nothing determinate for works of art to resemble. For Wilde, as later for Nelson Goodman, art is "a way of worldmaking" and not a mirror of something already in place.

This theme is continued through Wilde's contention, in "The Critic as Artist," that not only do critics have a vital role to play but that their calling is actually a higher one than that of the artists whose works they criticize. (Needless to say, the "true" critics Wilde has in mind are not the writers of hack columns in newspapers.) This would be an absurd contention, of course, if the critic's job were simply to describe works of art or to fathom the artist's intentions. But, for Wilde, the job is not at all to be a "fair, sincere and rational" commentator. On what has now become a familiar view, he holds that "criticism is itself an art," no more to be judged by fidelity to the works discussed than these works are by any "external standard of resemblance" (1983: 1026). Criticism should "treat the work of art simply as a starting-point for a new creation" (1983: 1029), as a peg on which the critic hangs some reflections. Such criticism, indeed, is "more creative than the [artist's] creation," primarily because the critic goes to work on superior materials. Artists are confronted by life, which is "deficient in form" and "incoherent

in its utterance." The advantage critics enjoy is that they "gain their impressions almost entirely from what art has [already] touched" and given form to (1983: 1034).

Wilde was a great admirer of Plato, but in these claims we can discern his divergence from, as well as his debt to, Plato. Wilde's contemplative critic, like Plato's philosopher, is superior to the artist, and for a similar reason – an acquaintance with forms. But whereas for Plato artists are simply poor imitators of reality – the forms – for Wilde they create forms, which then provide the cool, contemplative critic with the materials for a more self-conscious and refined intellectual creation.

This elevation of the critical thinker above the artist should give one pause before classifying Wilde, in the usual manner, as a fully fledged member of the "art for art's sake" school. After all, if art is to provide material for the thinker, it would seem to have a "sake" beyond itself. Many of Wilde's aphorisms, to be sure, ape the pronouncements of Théophile Gautier, Walter Pater, and other disciples of aestheticism – "All art is quite useless," "Art is the only serious thing in the world," "All art is immoral," and so on. But these need to be taken in context, and allowance has to be made for Wildean irony and a desire to épater les bourgeois. Moreover, it is easy to find "one-liners" that suggest a different attitude – for example, "The arts are made for life and not life for the arts," and "All beautiful things are made by those who strive to make something useful" (quoted in Ellmann 1987: 256, 246).

"Art for art's sake" is, anyway, a slogan that can be taken in various ways. Minimally, it proclaims that the only criteria that should govern the production of, or judgment upon, a particular work are aesthetic ones. Wilde seems generally to have subscribed to this. He would also accept the dictum read as a way of berating those artists whose works are motivated by commitment to social reforms. Not only does this tend to result in bad art or literature, as with Zola, but most social remedies for humanity's ills "do not cure the disease; they merely prolong it" (1983: 1079). However, he explicitly rejects "art for art's sake" if interpreted as a pronouncement on "the final cause of art" – or, rather, its lack of such a "cause" (see Ellmann 1987: 249). And despite the "immoralist" ring to some of his remarks, it is clear that the mature Wilde had a deep concern for the moral condition of humanity and believed that art had a vital role to play in improving it. As already implied, care must be taken with these remarks. Thus, having written that "the virtues of the poor . . . are much to be regretted" (1983: 1081), he then explains that these alleged virtues – obedience, say, and gratitude for charity – are nothing of the sort, but the symptoms, rather, of a degraded and crushed personality. More generally, his jibes at "the ethical" are attacks on what passes for morality in a society he despises.

"The Soul of Man under Socialism" is, in fact, a thoroughly moral manifesto for Wilde's ideals of freedom, individualism, and self-realization. Like Kierkegaard and Marx, he perceives the lives of people in his century as becoming increasingly mechanistic and anonymous. In part, the cure will be through radical economic and political change: the abolition of private property, for example, and guarantees against the tyranny of both government and public opinion. (This is a long way from Gautier's readiness to welcome the return of a tyrant, provided "he brings me back a hamper of Tokay" (1981: 39).) But the main vehicle of these ideals is art. "Art is the most intense mode of individualism," since it embodies a person's "unique temperament," thereby offering an escape from "tyranny of habit, and the reduction of man to the level of a machine" (Wilde 1983: 1090–1). Not only is artistic endeavor a particularly valuable route toward self-realization but it provides a model for every person's proper relationship to self. For, like Nietzsche, Wilde urges us to view our own lives as works of art to be constructed. Society is tending to "make men themselves machines . . . whereas we want them to be artists, that is to say men." Indeed, "to become a work of art is the object of living" (quoted in Ellmann 1987: 184–5, 292).

Fully to appreciate Wilde's position here, we must recall once again his persistent contrasting of the incoherent chaos of life and nature with the structured order of the artist's and critic's "worlds." Humans are distinguished from other beings by their capacity, which largely owes to language, for imposing form on chaos; and individuals are distinguished from one another by the particular styles with which this capacity is exercised. And it is in this capacity that the possibilities for true freedom and self-realization reside. "We are never less free than when we try to act": the free man or woman, rather, is one who "creates the age" by forging an individual perspective, by the artistic and contemplative construction of "a world more real than reality itself" (1983: 1040, 1021, 1049).

It would be quite wrong, argues Wilde, to regard this aesthetic individualism as a philosophy of selfishness. It is, in fact, the only effective antidote to egotism, for the person whose "primary aim is self-development" is content "letting other people's lives alone," in contrast with the egotist who manipulates their lives for self-advantage (1983: 1101). There is something here of the optimism of Socrates that the person whose soul is just will simply have no inclination to wrong others. As Wilde puts it, truly free and realized individuals will not sin, "not because they make the renunciations of the ascetic, but because they can do everything they wish without hurt to the soul" (1983: 1058).

See also AESTHETIC ATTITUDE; AESTHETICISM; CRITICISM; FUNCTION OF ART; MORALITY AND ART.

BIBLIOGRAPHY

Primary sources
1983. *Complete Works of Oscar Wilde.* Vyvyan Holland (ed.). London: Collins.
1991. *Aristotle at Afternoon Tea: The Rare Oscar Wilde.* Wyse Jackson (ed.). London: Fourth Estate.

Secondary sources
Ellmann, Richard. 1987. *Oscar Wilde.* Harmondsworth: Penguin.
Gautier, Théophile. 1981. *Mademoiselle de Maupin.* J. Richardson (trans.). Harmondsworth: Penguin.
Gide, André. 1938. *Oscar Wilde.* Paris: Gallimard.
Raby, Peter (ed.). 1997. *The Cambridge Companion to Oscar Wilde.* Cambridge: Cambridge University Press.

DAVID E. COOPER

Wittgenstein, Ludwig (1889–1951)
Youngest child of Karl Wittgenstein, the iron and steel magnate and patron of the arts, Ludwig

Wittgenstein wrote two philosophical master-pieces, *Tractatus Logico-Philosophicus* (1921) and the posthumously published *Philosophical Investigations* (1953). Neither has much to say about art, which did not lie at the center of his philosophical concerns.

But Wittgenstein had a deep and abiding interest in certain of the arts, and, though only briefly, practiced two of them, architecture and sculpture. In 1925 he assumed control of the project assigned to his friend Paul Engelmann, a pupil of Adolf Loos (whom Wittgenstein at one time admired), to design a house in Vienna for Wittgenstein's sister Gretl, applying himself to the task with characteristic fanatical zeal. The house still stands, at 19 Kundmanngasse, although its interior, to which Wittgenstein gave special attention, has been greatly altered. The house is a stark monument to his functional, antidecorative architectural ideal, which is perhaps most appealingly realized in the doors, radiators, and windows that enliven the other-wise drab appearance, and which he insisted were constructed to the precise millimeter. He also modeled a bust, which Gretl, who sat for it, displayed in the Kundmanngasse house. But Wittgenstein believed that he possessed only artistic taste, understanding, and good manners, rather than creative ability, and thought of his architectural work as merely the rendering of an old style into a language appropriate to the modern world. These were, therefore, isolated forays into artistic practice.

Perhaps his two favorite art forms were music and literature. He had a fairly extensive, although unsystematic and idiosyncratic, know-ledge of literature, made more accessible by his mastery of German, English, Norwegian, and Russian, and he immersed himself so intensely in his favorite works that he knew them almost by heart. He had a very good musical memory and an acute ear, and frequently played music in his head; he played the clarinet and was unusually adept at whistling music, sometimes performing complete works. He thought of music as having come to a full stop with Brahms. He confessed that it was impossible for him to say in *Philosophical Investigations* one word about all that music had meant in his life, so that it would be difficult for him to be understood. He seems to have had little interest in painting, his one

recorded remark on Michelangelo being banal. When, after World War I, he gave away the for-tune inherited from his father, part of it was dis-tributed to impecunious Austrian artists.

In his early philosophy are to be found a few gnomic utterances about art: "Ethics and aesthetics are one," "The work of art is the object seen *sub specie aeternitatis*." These show the influence of Schopenhauer, for whom the aesthetic attitude was one of pure will-less contemplation in which the subject's entire consciousness is filled by a single perceptual image, so that the object he contemplates becomes for the duration of his contempla-tion his whole world. But they do not invite prolonged thought, especially in the light of Wittgenstein's view at the time that what is of value in art must elude the net of language and therefore can never be spoken about.

The situation is not so bleak, however, if we turn to his later thoughts about art. Even here, though, the lack of an extended treatment of aesthetics in his writings means that an inter-pretation of the way in which he would have applied his new method of thinking to the philosophy of art must be largely speculative. But the lecture notes taken by students who attended his classes at Cambridge confirm that he had strong opinions about aesthetics; and these notes, and remarks in various writings, make it possible to identify a number of themes in his treatment of art, although the diversity of his thoughts precludes a comprehensive account, and many of these were not considered and carefully articulated opinions but sponta-neous remarks.

The least surprising feature is the application of one of the leading ideas of his later thought to the concepts of art and beauty. What do the arts have in common, in virtue of which they are all forms of art? What do all beautiful things have in common, in virtue of which they are beautiful? In both cases Wittgenstein rejects the supposition that the reason the items concerned fall within the concept is because they share a property common to and distinctive of them; but the alternative account that he offers appears to be different in the two cases. The reason the various art forms are all forms of art is not because they possess a distinctive common property, but because of the crisscrossing and overlapping of many resemblances: the arts form a "family." But the reason why the beauty of one kind of thing (a face, say) is very different from the beauty of another kind (e.g., a chair) is because "beautiful," like "good," is an attributive, rather than a predicative, adjective, so that it needs to be taken together with the substantive it qualifies, the nature of the judgment of beauty being determined by the kind of thing being judged.

Two of the most prominent themes concern the effects that the arts have on us. The first emphasizes the autonomy of artistic value against theories that deny works of art any distinctive value. There is a temptation, in reflection on the nature of art – one to which Tolstoy succumbed – to conceive of the appreciation of any work that we value as consisting in the work's inducing in us a rewarding experience, and, then, to conceive of this experience in abstraction from the work that gives rise to it. The result is that the value of a work of art is thought of as residing in its effects, and these effects are thought of as possessing a nature independent of the work that causes them. So the value of a work of art stands to the work in much the same relation that the value of a medicine stands to the medicine: just as the valuable results of the medicine can be fully characterized without mentioning the nature of the medicine that causes them, so the value of a work of art is located in an independently specifiable effect.

But, as Wittgenstein insisted, this is certainly a misrepresentation of artistic value. For if this conception were correct, the appreciation of a work of art would consist of two experiences – the experience of the work and another experience to which this gives rise; and the value of the work would be determined by the nature of the second, not the first, experience. But the experience of a work of art does not play a merely instrumental role in artistic appreciation. On the contrary, the value of the work is determined by the nature of the experience of the work itself, rather than any other experience it happens to generate. The only way of appreciating a work of art is to experience it with understanding – to read, listen to, imagine, look at, perform the work itself. When we admire a work, it is not replaceable for us by another that creates the same effect, for we admire the work itself; its value does not consist in its performing a function that another work could perform just as well. (As Wittgenstein pointed out, there is a similarity between, on the one hand, the doctrine that the value of a work of art is a function of an experience produced by the experience of the work and, on the other hand, the idea – one of the principal targets *of Philosophical Investigations* – that the sense of a sentence is a process that accompanies the utterance or perception of it.)

The second salient theme concerning the effects of works of art is opposition to the alleged relevance of psychological experiments to the solution of certain kinds of aesthetic puzzlement. When we are puzzled by our reaction to a work of art, our puzzlement, Wittgenstein insists, cannot be removed by a psychological investigation aimed at determining the cause of our reaction. For our reaction is "directed" or intentional, taking some aspect of the work as its object; the puzzlement will be removed only by identifying the reason why we react in this way to the work, rather than by identifying the cause of our reaction; and the criterion for a successful resolution of the puzzle is that we should *accept* or *agree with* the offered explanation – a clear mark that what is sought is a reason, not a cause.

This position is more difficult to evaluate, since there are different kinds of aesthetic puzzlement and Wittgenstein's examples are something of a medley. Moreover, it appears to rest on the contentious doctrine that the intentionality of an aesthetic impression is not susceptible of a causal analysis. The principal forms of aesthetic puzzlement that Wittgenstein seems to have had in mind concern what it is about a work of art that makes it so impressive, or impressive in a particular way; or what is wrong with a certain work or a performance of it; or why a work has just the distribution of features that it does. In such cases, what is needed to remove the puzzlement is, Wittgenstein claims, a certain kind of description of the art object. Such a description draws attention to the features that give the work the character in question, but does so in such a manner that we can now perceive these features in the work, with the result that our perception of it is modified.

One way in which this can be achieved is by placing side by side with the work other items that possess or lack these characteristics, or by indicating an analogy between the work and something else. So – to take one of Wittgenstein's favorite examples – one way of removing puzzlement about the particular pattern of variation in loudness and tempo in a musical theme would be to draw a comparison by pointing out that, at this point in the theme, it is as if a conclusion were being drawn; or that this part is, as it were, in parenthesis; or that it is as if this part were a reply to what came before. The explanation is persuasive, rather than diagnostic, effecting a clarification or change in the perception of the work; it differs from the causal diagnosis of a headache, where the sufferer's acceptance of the diagnosis is unnecessary and leaves his headache unchanged.

This example makes it clear that the principal focus of Wittgenstein's interest in aesthetic puzzlement is the enhancement of artistic appreciation: the kind of explanation that dissolves the puzzlement must further the understanding and appreciation of the work of art. This explains his emphasis on comparisons; the requirement that, if the proposed solution is to remove the puzzlement, the puzzled subject should agree with a proposed solution to his problem; and the resultant transformation of the subject's experience. But unless Wittgenstein's opposition to the relevance of psychological experiments to the solution of aesthetic puzzlement is narrowly restricted in this way, it is open to obvious counterexamples (Cioffi 1976).

This second theme is linked with another observation that Wittgenstein makes. Psychological experiments designed to determine which musical or pictorial arrangement produces the more pleasing effect on a particular person or set of people are irrelevant to aesthetics. For aesthetic appreciation is concerned, not with liking or disliking a work of art, but with understanding it and experiencing its features as right or wrong, better or worse, close to or distant from an ideal. This normative element in the appreciation of a work of art is misrepresented if artistic appreciation is thought of as merely a matter of what gives pleasure to the listener or spectator. In fact, artistic appreciation can be made sense of only by locating it in the cultural context to which it belongs and from which it derives its distinctive shape; different cultures determine different forms of artistic

and aesthetic appreciation; and any description of a culture that illuminates the nature of aesthetic judgments within that culture will be a description of a complicated set of activities from which the words used to express those judgments draw their life.

See also TWENTIETH-CENTURY ANGLO-AMERICAN AESTHETICS; EXPRESSION; INEFFABILITY; SCHOPENHAUER.

BIBLIOGRAPHY

Primary sources
[1921] 1922. *Tractatus Logico-Philosophicus.* C. K. Ogden (trans.). London: Routledge & Kegan Paul.
[1921] 1961. *Tractatus Logico-Philosophicus.* D. F. Pears & B. F. McGuinness (trans.). London: Routledge & Kegan Paul.
1953. *Philosophische Untersuchungen / Philosophical Investigations.* G. E. M. Anscombe (trans.). Oxford: Blackwell.
1966. *Wittgenstein: Lectures and Conversations on Aesthetics, Psychology and Religious Belief.* C. Barrett (ed.). Oxford: Blackwell.
1979. *Notebooks 1914–1916.* E. Anscombe (trans.). 2nd edn. Oxford: Blackwell.
1979. *Wittgenstein's Lectures, Cambridge 1932–1935.* A. Ambrose (ed.). Oxford: Blackwell.
[1994] 1998. *Culture and Value.* G. H. von Wright (ed.), with H. Nyman & P. Winch (trans.). 2nd edn. Oxford: Blackwell.

Secondary sources
Budd, Malcolm. forthcoming. "Wittgenstein on Aesthetics." In *Oxford Handbook of Wittgenstein.* M. McGinn (ed.). Oxford: Oxford University Press.
Cioffi, Frank. 1976. "Aesthetic Explanation and Aesthetic Perplexity," *Acta Philosophica Fennica,* 28, 417–49.
Elliott, R. K. 1993. "Wittgenstein's Speculative Aesthetics in its Ethical Context." In *Beyond Liberal Education: Essays in Honour of Paul H. Hirst.* R. Barrow & P. White (eds.). London: Routledge, 150–68.
Moore, George E. 1959. "Wittgenstein's Lectures in 1930–33." In *Philosophical Papers.* London: Allen & Unwin, 312–15.
Tanner, Michael. 1966. "Wittgenstein and Aesthetics," *Oxford Review,* 3, 14–24.

MALCOLM BUDD

Wollheim, Richard (1923–2003) British philosopher. Although his interests were exceptionally wide, Richard Wollheim's writings focused on two principal subjects: art and human psychology. His profound concern with human nature – to which he brought his unrivaled knowledge of psychoanalytic theory and his commitment to that development of it effected by Melanie Klein – combined with his passion for and knowledge of art, especially painting, architecture, and literature, endowed his philosophy of art with a rich, distinctive character. His originality, learning, sure feeling for what really matters and a highly personal style markedly free from technical jargon make his writings always fascinating, even where they do not command assent. He was the finest aesthetician of his generation, making outstanding contributions both to general aesthetics, beginning with his justly admired *Art and Its Objects*, and to substantive aesthetics, above all to the philosophy of painting, which culminated in his masterly *Painting as an Art*.

A defining feature of Wollheim's thought is his assigning conceptual priority to the philosophy of art over the aesthetics of nature, representing the aesthetic attitude to nature as that of regarding nature as if it were art. So for him the central problem of general aesthetics is the elucidation of the concept of art. The philosophy of art expounded in *Art and Its Objects* – one of the rare accounts that does justice both to the points of view of the artist and the spectator – is based on and shaped by the thought that both in the making and the appreciation of the objects of art the concept of art is operative. Although primarily concerned with exploring the nature of art and the ontological status of its objects, Wollheim's unique approach to the subject insured that he touched on nearly everything of interest and enabled him to deal en route with a number of the most important topics. Some of these he dealt with in detail – pictorial representation and artistic expression, for example, topics he returned to repeatedly in later work, developing, modifying, and defending his views; others – pictorial style, artistic meaning, and understanding – in a more sketchy fashion, the outlines of which he later refined, elaborated, and filled in. The outcome of his investigation of the concept of art is not an analytic definition of a traditional kind. Instead, there are two principal issues. One is the claim that art is a

form of life (in Wittgenstein's sense), artistic creativity and aesthetic understanding being possible only within a complex ramified structure of aesthetic practices, enterprises, and institutions, none of these being identifiable independently of the other elements in the structure – a claim that is elucidated by pursuing the analogy between art and language. He never deviated from this conception of art. The other is the suggestion of a recursive procedure for identifying which objects are works of art, art being an essentially historical phenomenon, the changes to which it is inevitably subject affecting the conceptual structure that surrounds it.

His account of the ontology of art consists of two main claims. The first is that the fundamental distinction within works of art is between individuals and types, some works of art being individuals, the rest types, every work of art belonging to the same art belonging to the same category, type, or individual as the case may be. The second is that, for all works of art, the identity of a work of art is determined by the history of its production. This last claim was of crucial importance for Wollheim, for it plays a vital role in his account of artistic meaning (and so of artistic understanding), an account that he worked out exclusively for painting but which he believed could be generalized over the other arts. The psychological orientation of his aesthetics is writ large in this account, as it is in his accounts of the nature of pictorial representation, artistic expression, individual artistic style, and artistic value: each concept is elucidated in psychological terms.

Wollheim conceived of artistic meaning in the following way. It is the aim of artists to endow the work they create with a meaning determined by the intentions that guide their activity, such an intention being understood as more or less any psychological factor that motivates the artist to paint as he does. If they succeed in fulfilling their intentions, the work has a meaning – its own, one and only, meaning. They succeed only if an adequately sensitive and informed spectator who engages with the work grasps that meaning, retrieves those intentions, through undergoing the experiences the artist intended it to provide. It is the distinctive function of the spectator to do this.

And, as indicated, the work that possesses this meaning is identified in part by its history of production.

Wollheim thought to capture the nature of pictorial representation and artistic expression by exploiting two species of perception that he attempted to articulate. His conception of pictorial representation has attracted a great deal of attention. The most important part of it can be put like this: when you look at a picture and see it as depicting something, a row of trees, say, you undergo a visual experience of a specific kind, one to which Wollheim gave the name "seeing-in." An experience of this kind possesses two aspects, each a visual awareness of something, the so-called "configurational" aspect being a visual awareness of the surface of the picture, the "recognitional" aspect being a visual awareness that involves the third dimension, an awareness of something being in front of or behind something else, a visual awareness of a row of trees, for example. This conception of pictorial perception presented a seemingly insoluble problem for Wollheim. For without a specification of the nature of the recognitional visual awareness – something he did not provide and was unhappy to concede the necessity or even the possibility of – the account is incomplete, and yet he rejected what appear to exhaust the possibilities: the (illusory) experience as of seeing a row of trees, the experience of in some way visually imagining a row of trees, the experience of seeing some kind of resemblance to a row of trees.

His account of artistic expression – which, although focused on the art of painting, he again thought could be adapted to apply across the arts – assumed many forms, which cannot easily be reconciled with one another, before eventually crystallizing around a hitherto unrecognized, or at least unnamed, form of the psychoanalytic notion of projection. In its final version "expressive perception," the perception of expression, is a perceptual experience that consists of three aspects: a representation of the world as "corresponding" to an affective psychological condition, an affect of the same kind as that of the corresponding condition, and a revelation or intimation of the origin in so-called "complex" projection, either of the experience itself or of the kind to which it belongs. Leaving aside the question whether there is such a

phenomenon as complex projection and the character of the unconscious fantasy it consists of, it is fair to say that Wollheim's account suffers from at least two defects. The first is that it introduces but fails to make clear the idea of a "correspondence" between inner and outer. The second is the obscurity of the idea of intimation in the third condition: what is this supposed to consist in?

Wollheim distinguishes between two different conceptions of style: general and individual, the first merely taxonomic, the second generative. Whereas a general style is a set of characteristics that are distinctive of paintings in that style, the constitution of this set varying as what is considered distinctive of these paintings changes, an individual style is not the set of characteristics associated with it but what in the artist's mind causes the set to be constituted as it is, this constitution being, not fluctuating, but fixed. Wollheim's claim is that each painter who is an artist has one and only one individual style, a style which will have been formed and which gives to his (stylistic) works their distinctive character. Not all a painter's works will derive from his individual style: there will be prestylistic works created before the formation of his style, and there may be poststylistic, when the artist's style has collapsed, or extrastylistic, when the artist attempts something his style cannot encompass. Wollheim allows that an artist's style can undergo change while remaining the same style, but only in exceptional cases of massive psychological disturbance can an artist change from having one individual style to having a different one, and he appears to disallow the possibility of a painter possessing more than one style at a given time. This is a plausible position and certainly there are few artists to whom one would want to attribute more than one style. But the last mentioned possibility is not ruled out by any considerations Wollheim advances and it fits easily with the analogy he exploits between two competences: having a style and knowing a language. Just as a speaker can have a competence in a number of languages, why shouldn't an artist possess a number of individual styles, as it might seem Picasso did, not, or not just, in the diachronic sense that Wollheim animadverts against, but at the same time, being able to work in one or another as he chooses? If works in an individual style are individuated, as Wollheim takes them to be, by reference to the common psychological or psychomotor processes that underlie them, the singularity of Picasso's style, its supposed constancy through the extraordinarily different manners of painting he practiced so close together in time, turns on the identification of the underlying processes – at present a distant goal.

As far as the evaluation of art is concerned, although Wollheim does not offer an analysis of a judgment of aesthetic value, he does, without explicitly embracing any of them, outline the only views – there are four of them – of the status of aesthetic value which he considers to have any plausibility. It is, I believe, clear that he favors one of them: the view he calls "subjectivism," understanding this term in an idiosyncratic sense to indicate a position that is resistant to easy summary. What can be said briefly is that subjectivism, like so-called "objectivism," represents aesthetic value as depending on the character of the experience of a work of art, by one who understands the work, a character that would justify the attribution of aesthetic value to it, such an experience being one that gives rise to certain directed thoughts. But subjectivism departs from objectivism in two ways by, first, requiring that the thoughts to which the experience gives rise should be complex enough to resist their being correctly characterized as being all or just about the character of the work, and, second, insisting that the causal pathway from the work to the experience is not a purely perceptual one but at some point essentially involves a projective mechanism. And it is because subjectivism incorporates the idea of projection that Wollheim likens the status of aesthetic value accorded by subjectivism to that of an expressive quality. Given Wollheim's conception of an expressive quality, the degree of likeness will depend on which idea of projection subjectivism incorporates and the manner in which it does so.

See also TWENTIETH-CENTURY ANGLO-AMERICAN AESTHETICS; DRAWING, PAINTING, AND PRINTMAKING; CRITICISM; DEPICTION; EXPRESSION; ONTOLOGY OF ARTWORKS; PSYCHOANALYSIS AND ART; PICTURE PERCEPTION; REPRESENTATION; STYLE.

BIBLIOGRAPHY

Primary sources
1980. *Art and Its Objects: An Introduction to Aesthetics.* 2nd edn (with 6 supplementary essays). Cambridge: Cambridge University Press.
1973. *On Art and the Mind: Essays and Lectures.* London: Allen Lane.
1987. *Painting as an Art: The Andrew W. Mellon Lectures in the Fine Arts.* London: Thames & Hudson.
1993. *The Mind and Its Depths.* Cambridge, MA: Harvard University Press.
2001. "On Formalism and Pictorial Organization," *Journal of Aesthetics and Art Criticism,* 59, 127–37.
2003. "What Makes Representational Painting Truly Visual?" *Proceedings of the Aristotelian Society,* supp. vol. 77, 131–47.

Secondary sources
Gerwen R. van (ed.). 2001. *Richard Wollheim on the Art of Painting: Art as Representation and Expression.* Cambridge: Cambridge University Press.
Hopkins, J. & Savile, A. (eds.). 1992. *Psychoanalysis, Mind and Art: Perspectives on Richard Wollheim.* Oxford: Blackwell.
Hopkins, Robert. 2003. "What makes Representational Painting Truly Visual?" *Proceedings of the Aristotelian Society,* supp. vol. 77, 149–67.

MALCOLM BUDD

work of art   *see* ARTIFACT, ART AS; DEFNITION OF "ART"; ONTOLOGICAL CONTEXTUALISM; ONTOLOGY OF ARTWORKS.

Index

Artists, writers, and philosophers form a separate sub-entry at the beginning of each relevant main entry, preceded by creative works if relevant, and followed by subject sub-entries.
Bold text *indicates the main article on a subject.*

Abbate, Carolyn 96–7
Abell, Catharine 506
Abhinavagupta 359, 493
abjection 330, 397–8, 490
Abstract Expressionism 108, 150–1, 426, 498
abstraction **107–9**, 148, 361
　see also drawing; music; painting; picture
　　perception; printmaking; representation
accessibility of art 417–18, 465, 559
　Gadamer 303; Tolstoy 572
Acconci, Vito 463
　Following Piece 202, 204, 464
Ackroyd, Peter, *Hawksmoor* 427
acquaintance principle *see* testimony in
　　aesthetics
Addison, Joseph 35–7, 216, 304, 547–8
　Burke 177
Adorno, Theodor W. 58, 91, **109–11**, 156, 236,
　412
　Benjamin 59, 174, 176; Schelling 514
　popular art 476–8
Aertsen, Jan 25
Aeschylus 14, 413, 438, 467, 575
aesthetic attitude 64, 67–8, **111–14**, 121, 129,
　137, 196, 363, 385, 429
　Bell 173; Dickie 114, 173, 247, 429; Gadamer
　　303; Goodman 312; Kant 33, 37, 111–13,
　　137, 363, 389–90, 478; Lewis 407; Schiller
　　518–19; Schopenhauer 64, 111; Shaftesbury
　　538; Wittgenstein 594; Wollheim 597
　see also aesthetic pleasure; aesthetic properties
aesthetic education 34, **114–17**, 118, 189, 194,
　218, 253, 301, 534–6
　Aristotle 114–15, 338; Dewey 115–16, 245;
　　Hume 46, 115, 499; Hutcheson 44; Kant 49,
　　115–16; Plato 47, 114, 194; Schiller 36,
　　47–9, 52–4, 517–19; Sibley 539
　see also function of art; morality and art; value
　　of art
aesthetic judgment 11, 14, 47, 65–6, 115,
　117–21, 127, 272, 292, 299, 351, 413,
　501, 544, 550, 554–6, 560–1

Beardsley 164; Foucault 294; Hume 117,
　332–3; Kant 51–2, 65, 118–22, 124, 164,
　388–9, 445, 483; Lewis 408; Schiller 518;
　Scruton 528; Shaftesbury 538; Sibley 65–6,
　539–40; Walton 589; Wittgenstein 120,
　596
　objectivity and realism 117–22, 444–7, 495–8
　see also aesthetic pleasure; beauty; relativism
aesthetic pleasure 8–9, 34, 38, 40–2, 44, 81, 115,
　121–4, 132, 139, 166, 203, 268, 343,
　476–7, 564, 582
　Aristotle 148; Beardsley 121–2, 164; Goodman
　　123; Hume 333; Kant 51–2, 65, 118–22,
　　124, 164, 388–9, 483; Schopenhauer 121;
　　Sibley 123
　see also aesthetic attitude; aesthetic judgment;
　　aesthetic properties; beauty; function of art;
　　value of art
aesthetic properties 44, 65, 67–8, 94, 111, 115,
　124–8, 128–9, 136, 138, 157, 204, 290–3,
　432, 445–9, 452, 561–2
　Beardsley 125, 164; Danto 226; Deleuze 234;
　　Sibley 65–6, 125–7; Tolstoy 572; Walton
　　588; Wittgenstein 67
　see also aesthetic judgment; aesthetic pleasure;
　　beauty; senses and art, the; taste
aestheticism 16, 92, **128–30**, 158, 196, 481,
　502
　Aristotle 148; Hegel 316; Kant 128–9;
　　Kierkegaard 130; Wilde 128–30, 428, 502,
　　592
　see also aesthetic attitude; formalism; function of
　　art; morality and art; value of art
aesthetics in Antiquity *see* Antiquity, aesthetics in
aesthetics of the environment 71, 76, 115, 117,
　134–6, 137, 269, 304
　see also aesthetic properties; aesthetics of the
　　everyday; aesthetics of nature; artifact, art as;
　　evolution, art, and aesthetics; gardens
aesthetics of the everyday 77, 92, 116–17,
　136–9, 407
　Dewey 136–8, 245–6; Shusterman 136–8

see also aesthetic attitude; aesthetic properties; aesthetics of food and drink; aesthetics of the environment; aesthetics of nature; evolution, art, and aesthetics

aesthetics of food and drink **131–4**, 384–6, 552
  Hegel 131; Hume 131; Sibley 132–3
  see also aesthetic properties; aesthetics of the everyday

aesthetics of nature 112–13, 123–4, 304–6, 384, 548–50
  Aurelius 17; Dewey 65, 137, 245–6, Hutcheson 35; Kant 48, 169, 501; Shaftesbury 34; Wilde 591–2; Wollheim 597
  see aesthetics of the environment; sublime, the

African aesthetics 78, 150–1, **139–42**, 150–1, 206–7, 222, 513

Agatharcus of Samos 467

Al-Fârâbî 27, 383

Al-Haytham, Ibn 24

Alain, Emile Chartier 249

Albert the Great 23–4, 146

Alberti, Leon Battista 29, 465, 469, 568

Aldrich, Virgil C. 66

d'Alembert, Jean le Rond 34, 47

Alexander of Hales 22

Alexander, Thomas M. 247

Alison, Archibald 37, 48

allegory 21, 169, 175, 294, 496, 529, 552

Allen, Richard 344

Allen, Woody, *Mighty Aphrodite* 575

Allhoff, Fritz 132

Allison, Henry E. 47, 50

allusion 76, 85, 162, 188–9, 230, 312, 370, 404, 449, 473, 478, 568

Alperson, Philip 92

Althusser, Louis 251

Amerindian aesthetics **142–5**, 159

Anandavardhana 358–9

Anderson, Elizabeth 272–3

Anderson, James C. 232

Anderson, Laurie 463

Andre, Carl, *Equivalent VIII* 568–9

anthropology 85, 238, 250, 270, 379, 396, 400, 436, 540

Antiquity, aesthetics in **10–22**

Antony, Louise 272–3

Apel, K.-O. 499

Aquinas, Thomas 23–5, 27, **145–7**, 167
  Aristotle 146

architecture 11, 22, 25, 28–9, 71, **74–6**, 83, 105, 170, 208, 270, 291, 348, 426–7, 432–3, 442, 454, 463, 478, 527, 573–4, 578
  Foucault 295; Goethe 46; Goodman 75; Hegel 319; Kant 75; Plato 473; Ruskin 508–9; Schlegel, F. 520; Scruton 528–9; Wittgenstein 76, 594; Wolff 40, 42; Wollheim 597
  African aesthetics 140

Japanese aesthetics 385
  see also aesthetics of the environment; function of art; gardens; modernism and postmodernism; technology and art

Arendt, Hannah 174, 398

Aristophanes, *Frogs* 12, 14

Aristotle 10–17, 19, 23, 29–30, 77, 91, **147–9**, 155, 182, 207, 217, 235, 254, 297–8, 321, 328, 336, 383, 390, 423, 547–8, 567
  Aquinas 146; Corneille 30–1; Plato 10–16, 472
  aesthetic education 114–15, 338
  beauty 15, 148, 169, 321
  catharsis 29, 182–3, 252
  tragedy 15, 30–1, 147–8, 252, 328, 349, 404, 417, 439, 575–6

Armstrong, Robert Plant 581

Arnheim, Rudolf 85, 298

Arnold, Dana 310

Arnold, Matthew 502–3, 529

art as artifact *see* artifact, art as

"art for art's sake" *see* aestheticism

art and experience *see* senses and art, the

art history 2, **149–52**, 205, 268, 270, 273, 291, 432, 459, 495
  Benjamin 174; Danto 227; Gombrich 149, 308; Hegel 150–1
  ontological contextualism 450–1

art of the Paleolithic *see* Paleolithic, art of the

Artaud, Antonin 296, 397, 463

artifact, art as 5, 7, 22, 25–8, 58–9, 70, 84, 89, 99–100, 125, 151, **152–4**, 159, 170, 203–4, 213, 287, 325, 373, 384, 393, 415, 482, 490, 506, 540, 544, 554, 566, 581
  Aristotle 147; Baumgarten 40; Bell 249; Benjamin 59, 176, 559; Collingwood 198, 203; Croce 221; Dickie 69, 248, 569; Foucault 60, 294; Hegel 316–17; Heidegger 56; Kant 206; Langer 401; Levinson 154; Lewis 406; Weitz 152–3; Wittgenstein 152–3; Wolff 40
  conservation and restoration 205–7
  definition of "art" *see* definition of "art"
  see also conceptual art; expression theory; mass art; technology and art

"artworld" 2, 83, 153, **155–6**, 203, 211–14, 226, 268–9, 304, 491, 509, 512, 557
  Danto 68, 155–6, 214, 226–8, 232; Dewey 245, 482; Dickie 68–9, 155–6, 226, 232, 248, 568–9; Dufrenne 250; Margolis 412

Ashfield, Andrew 36, 48

Ashworth, E. Jennifer 27

Asmis, E. 16

Assunto, Rosario 22

Ast, Friedrich 324, 326

attitude, aesthetic *see* aesthetic attitude

Auden, W. H., *Funeral Blues* 101

audience 2, 11, 14, 16, 31, 38, 46, 53, 58–9,
  61–3, 68, 71, 77, 81, 84, 88, 95–6, 113,
  116, 129, 153, 157–8, 264, 277, 283, 286,
  299, 345, 362, 377, 394, 415, 421, 430,
  443, 450, 452, 482, 492–4, 504, 526–7,
  534, 545, 547–8, 557, 559–60, 573
    Aristotle 148; Collingwood 198–9; Dickie 248;
      Gadamer 303; Hegel 316–17; Hume 332–3;
      Kierkegaard 393; Lessing 402–3, 405; Plato
      473; Ruskin 508; Sartre 513; Tolstoy 572
    African aesthetics 140
    Chinese aesthetics 188, 190
    expression theory 264
    fiction, the paradox of responding to 279–80
    horror 329–31
    intention and interpretation 230, 368–9, 378–9
    Islamic aesthetics 382
    mass art 415–18
    performance 461–2
    performance art 463–5
    popular art 476–8
    psychoanalysis 484–8
    tragedy 575–6
Augustine of Hippo, St. 21–6, 27, 537, 552
Austen, Jane 205, 210
    Pride and Prejudice 194–5, 354, 418, 536
authenticity and art 92, 97, 132, **156–9**,
  179–80, 461, 482, 563
    Benjamin 174; Deleuze 236; Herder 46
    see also conservation and restoration; cultural
      appropriation; forgery; ontology of artworks;
      originality
author, implied *see* implied author
Averroes 27, 29
Avicenna 27
Ayer, A. J. 444–5

Bach, J. S. 158, 171, 245, 452, 526, 555
Bach, Kent 132
Bacharach, Sondra 450
Bachelard, Gaston 251
Baeumker, Clemens 24
Bahn, Paul 4
Bakhtin, Mikhail 56, 396
Balanchine 77, 461
Balzac 160, 415, 496, 542, 592
Banes, Sally 78
Barry, Robert, *All the things I know but of which
  I am not at the moment thinking – 1:36 pm,
  June 15, 1969* 154, 203
Barth, John 426–7
Barthes, Roland 59–60, **160–2**, 249, 376, 378,
  380, 426, 563–5
    Dufrenne 249; Kristeva 397
    structuralism 366, 374, 542
Bataille, Georges 296, 397
Battersby, Christine 267

Batteux, Charles 13
Baudelaire, Charles 128, 175–6, 495, 513
Baudrillard, Jean 543
Baumgarten, Alexander G. 10, 32, 36–7, 40–1,
  115, **162–3**, 171
    Kant 162–3; Nietzsche 163
Bazin, G. 432–3
Beardsley, Aubrey 128, 257
Beardsley, Monroe C. 62, 66, 72, 77–8, **163–5**,
  209, 353, 355, 373, 374, 408, 424, 429,
  482, 532, 579
    Dewey 163
    aesthetic pleasure 121–2, 164
    aesthetic properties 125, 164
    definition of "art" 69, 164–5, 232
    "intentional fallacy" 66, 164, 355, 366,
      369–70, 563
Beardsmore, R. W. 300
Beatles, the 451
    "Revolution Nine" 93; "Something" 94
Beattie, James 45, 48
beauty 2–3, 9, 11, 13–17, 19–29, 31, 40, 60, 71,
  74, 100–1, 122, 128–9, 131, 156, **166–71**,
  204, 209, 216, 232, 331, 339–42, 356, 395,
  429, 481, 485, 496, 501–3, 526–7, 532,
  566, 580–2
    Adorno 110; Aquinas 24, 146–7, 167; Aristotle
      148, 169, 321; Baumgarten 10, 41, 163;
      Burke 36–8, 42, 177–8; Dewey 167, 171;
      Dickie 247; Diderot 34; Foucault 294;
      Goodman 311; Hanslick 314; Hegel 53,
      170–1, 316–18, 320; Heidegger 163,
      321; Hume 42–3, 45, 47, 167–9, 331–3;
      Hutcheson 34–5, 38, 42–4, 47, 126,
      338–40; Kant 24, 36–7, 43–4, 47–8, 51–2,
      54, 147, 166–9, 171, 292, 388–91, 503,
      582; Lessing 403–5; Lukács 410; Meier 41;
      Nietzsche 438, 440; Plato 16, 21, 28, 52,
      167–9, 171, 472–4; Plotinus 21, 474–5;
      Ruskin 509; Santayana 167, 511–12; Sartre
      513; Schiller 36, 48–9, 52, 54, 517–19;
      Schlegel, A. 520; Schopenhauer 523; Scruton
      528, 530; Shaftesbury 34–5, 537–8; Tolstoy
      571–2; Wilde 592; Wittgenstein 594–5;
      Wolff 42
    aesthetic attitude 111–12
    aesthetic judgment 117–19
    aesthetic properties 125–7
    African aesthetics 139–40
    Amerindian aesthetics 142–5
    evolution, art, and aesthetics 6, 259–60
    feminist aesthetics 268–9, 273–4
    formalism 290–2
    Indian aesthetics 359–60
    Islamic aesthetics 381–3
    Japanese aesthetics 385
    objectivity 445–9

relativism 498–9
sublime, the 548–51
taste 554–5
tragedy 576–7
Beckett, Samuel 184, 381, 415
Beethoven, Ludwig van 53, 61, 157–8, 250, 271,
    361, 417, 442, 456, 461, 513, 523, 586,
    588
    Hammerklavier sonata 452
Beiser, Frederick C. 520, 522
Bell, Clive 111, **172–4**, 245, 247, 293, 401, 502,
    566
    Kant 63; Dickie 249
    formalism 62–3, 121, 164, 237, 290–1
Bell, David 556
Belsey, C. 217–18
Bender, John 132, 448
Benjamin, Walter **174–7**
    Adorno 59, 174, 176; Goethe 174, 176
    art's technological reproduction 59, 176, 559
Bergson, Henri 202, 336
Berkeley, George 42, 167, 371
Berleant, Arnold 113, 116, 136–7
Bernasconi, Robert 324
Bernays, Jacob 183
Betti, Emilio 325–6
Bhabha, Homi K. 489–91
Bharata 357, 492–4
Bicknell, Jeanette 94, 159
Binkley, Timothy 204, 558
Bizet, Georges, *Carmen* 271
Black, Deborah L. 27, 383
Black, Max 424
Blackburn, Simon 446
Bloch, Ernst 412
Bloom, Harold 181, 229, 374
Boden, Margaret 193, 208, 210
Boethius 24–5
Boileau, Nicolas 36, 216, 548–9
de Bolla, Peter 36, 48
Bonaventure of Bagnoregio, St. 27
Booth, Wayne C. 354–6, 381, 429
Bordwell, David 356
Borges, Jorge Luis 86, 295
Bouguereau, William-Adolphe 57
Boulnois, Olivier 25–7
Bourdieu, Pierre 273, 433–4, 478
Bowie, Andrew 361–2, 514
Bradbury, Malcolm 215
Bradley, Andrew C. 130, 577
Brady, Emily 132, 136–7, 306
Brahms, Johannes 456, 529, 594
Brakhage, Stan, *Scenes from under Childhood* 416
Brand, Peg Zeglin 171, 267, 269, 275
Braque, Georges 62
Brecht, Bertolt 97, 175–6, 412, 415
Bredin, Hugh 147

Breton, André 55, 175, 488
Breuil, Abbé Henri 4
Brock, Stuart 286
Brook, Isis 306
Brooks, Cleanth 103, 215–17, 219, 375
Brown, Lee B. 92, 462
Browning, Robert, *My Last Duchess* 354
Brunelleschi, Filippo 465–6
Bruyne, Edgar de 22
Budd, Malcolm 103, 124, 128, 136, 241, 256,
    263, 304, 315, 402, 449, 562, 596
Buddhism, and Japanese aesthetics 305, 384
Bullough, Edward 64, 67, 111, 121, 299
Bungay, Stephen 320
Burke, Edmund **177–8**, 318, 489, 574
    Addison 177; Hume 177; Kant 177; Lessing 177
    beauty 36–8, 42, 177–8
    sublime, the 19–20, 36–7, 177–8, 549

Cage, John 463
canon 71, 79, **179–82**, 215, 284, 307, 324, 327,
    432, 468
    Burke 178; Deleuze 236; Gombrich 308; Hume
    45
    feminist criticism 270–1, 273–4
    interpretation 374–5
    taste 47, 556
    see also feminist aesthetics and criticism; race
        and aesthetics; tradition
capitalism 110, 413, 433, 481, 490
Capote, Truman 86
    In Cold Blood 278
Carlson, Allen 136
Carnap, Rudolf 362, 400
Carney, James D. 69, 232
Carpenter, John, *The Thing* 329
Carrier, David 151, 205, 207
Carroll, Joseph 260
Carroll, Lewis 307, 367
    Jabberwocky 335
Carroll, Noël 45, 69, 77, 91, 194, 201, 229, 233,
    279, 329–30, 368, 418, 425, 429–30,
    463–4, 476, 478, 556–9
Cassirer, Ernst 163, 465–6
Castelvetro, Lodovico 29
catharsis **182–3**, 252, 576
    Aristotle 29, 182–3; Corneille 30–1; Lessing
        183; Nietzsche 183
    see also fiction, the paradox of responding to;
        tragedy
Caudwell, Christopher 412, 415
Cavell, Stanley 68, 97, **183–5**, 247, 362, 478
censorship 71, **185–8**, 342–3, 484
    Plato 47, 473
    see also erotic art and obscenity; morality and
        art; pornography
Cézanne, Paul 57, 62, 108, 150, 172, 422

Charlton, William 280, 570

Chaucer, Geoffrey, *Canterbury Tales* 497

Chinese aesthetics 96, 100, 150–1, **188–91**, 207, 305, 397, 573

Chow, Rey 489–91

Chrysippus 17

Chuang-Tzu 361

Cicero 17, 22, 547

cinema *see* motion pictures

Cioffi, Frank 370, 596

Cixous, Hélène 270

classicism 109, 151, 413, 496, 537–8

Cleanthes 17–18

Cleiton 12

Cleland, John, *Fanny Hill* 479

Clover, Carol 330–1

cognitive science and art 71, 102, **191–4**, 210, 328, 533
    see also evolution, art, and aesthetics; science and art

cognitive value of art 115, **194–7**, 429–30
    see also function of art; literature; morality and art; Plato; truth in art; value of art

Cohen, Marshall 68

Cohen, Selma Jeanne 78

Cohen, Ted 202, 425, 540

Coleman, Elizabeth Burns 159, 225

Coleridge, Samuel Taylor 21, 216, 279, 349, 495, 502, 508–9, 520

Collingwood, R. G. 26, 61–2, **197–9**, 207, 209, 363, 455, 500, 502–3, 508
    Croce 199, 222; Dewey 246
    artifact, art as 198, 203
    audience 198–9
    creativity 198–9, 207, 209
    emotion 62, 197
    expression 197–8
    expression theory 198–9, 203, 264–6, 355, 566–7
    ontology of artworks 265–6, 455
    work of art 62, 198–9, 266

comedy 7, **199–202**, 216, 282, 308, 334–8, 477
    Cavell 184; Hegel 317, 319; Kierkegaard 337–8, 392–3; Lessing 405
    tragedy 576–7

comics 558

communication 53, 61, 76–7, 82, 98, 102, 183, 245–6, 300, 362, 379, 487, 506, 530, 546, 557, 573

composition, musical 134, 137, 217, 222
    see also ontology of artworks; work of art

composition, rules of 117–18, 385

conceptual art 2, 53, 154, **202–5**, 298, 308, 464, 532
    see also artifact, art as; definition of "art"; modernism and postmodernism; ontology of artworks; performance art

conservation and restoration 156, **205–7**, 450
    see also art history; museums; ontology of artworks

Constable, John 260, 298
    Wivenhoe Park 309, 311

contextualism *see* ontological contextualism

convention 59–60, 67–70, 86, 102, 109–10, 226–7, 238–9, 282–3, 309, 441, 443, 552–3

Cooper, David E. 305, 363, 379, 425

Cooper, James Fenimore, *The Last of the Mohicans* 127

Corneille, Pierre 30–1, 221, 548, 576

Cosmides, L. 260

Costelloe, Timothy 45

Courbet, Gustave 56, 496

Cousin, Victor 129

Cox, Renée 271

Craig-Martin, Michael, *An Oak Tree* 202

Crawford, Donald W. 47, 392

creativity 13, 20, 66, 71, 90, 153, 159, 193, **207–10**, 224, 259–60, 267–8, 288, 305, 346–8, 428, 458, 461, 477, 567–8, 574
    Beardsley 209; Collingwood 198–9, 207, 209; Deleuze 236; Dickie 248; Dufrenne 150–1; Foucault 294–5; Freud 208, 484–5; Herder 46; Kant 207–9; Kierkegaard 58; Langer 402; Levinson 210; Lyotard 61; Nietzsche 207; Plato 207–9, 472, 474; Sibley 209; Wittgenstein 597
    African aesthetics 139, 141
    Indian aesthetics 359
    Japanese aesthetics 385
    see also imagination; originality; value of art

critical monism and pluralism 26, **211–14**, 376–7
    see also canon; criticism; deconstruction; feminist aesthetics and criticism; implied author; intention; "intentional fallacy"; interpretation; literature; poetry; meaning constructivism; text

criticism 16–17, 33, 77–8, 80–1, 83, 101–2, 118, 171, **215–19**, 229–31, 350, 355–6, 366, 372–5, 379, 412, 428, 435–7, 462, 491, 495, 498, 500, 530, 542–4, 546–8, 563, 568
    Adorno 109; Baumgarten 163; Beardsley 62, 66, 163, 165; Bell 173; Benjamin 174–5; Cavell 183–4; Croce 221; Deleuze 234; Derrida 60; Dufrenne 251; Foucault 293; Hegel 318; Heidegger 323; Hume 331; Kames 37–9, 46; Kristeva 396–7; Lukács 409; Margolis 411; Santayana 512; Sartre 513; Schlegel, F. 521; Scruton 528–9; Sibley 539–40; Wilde 591–2
    canon 179–81
    feminism 71–2, 267, 269–70

see also critical monism and pluralism;
  deconstruction; feminist aesthetics and
  criticism; implied author; intention;
  "intentional fallacy"; interpretation; literature;
  meaning constructivism; New Criticism;
  poetry; text
Croce, Arlene 78
Croce, Benedetto 26, 197, **219–22**, 355, 411,
  453, 500, 579
  Collingwood 199, 222; Dewey 244; Hegel 219;
    Margolis 411
  expression theory 61–2, 264, 355, 518
Cross, Ian 260
Crowther, Paul 181, 459
Cubism 150–1, 426
Culler, Jonathan 162, 381
cultural appropriation **222–5**
  see also Amerindian aesthetics; authenticity and
    art; forgery; museums
Curran, Angela 91
Currie, Gregory 9, 91, 192, 277–8, 283, 286,
  353, 356, 368, 452, 456
Curtiz, Michael, *Casablanca* 356, 416

Dadaism 55, 308, 463–4, 488, 498
dance 11, 71, **76–8**, 87, 92, 192–3, 203, 270,
  300, 362, 442, 453–4, 492, 577
  Aristotle 147; Goodman 311; Kant 391;
    Margolis 411; Plato 472, 474
  African aesthetics 77, 141
  Amerindian aesthetics 142–3
  Chinese aesthetics 188
  Islamic aesthetics 77
  see also definition of "art"; expression; feminist
    aesthetics and criticism; music; performance
Dandin 358–9
Dante, Alighieri 25, 27, 29, 217, 245, 519–20,
  579
Danto, Arthur C. 68–70, 123, 203, **226–9**, 232,
  249, 292, 308, 449–50, 458, 507, 532
  Hegel 70, 227–8; Kant 227
  art history 227
  "artworld" 68, 155–6, 214, 226–8, 232
  interpretation 70
  ontological contextualism 449–50
Darbel, A. 433
Darwin, Charles 51, 210, 581
Davey, Nicholas 163
Davidson, Donald 213, 424, 446, 506
Davies, David 204, 283, 377, 452, 462, 465, 532
Davies, Stephen 69, 92–4, 96, 154, 157–8, 165,
  203, 231–3, 263, 265, 301, 315, 369, 377,
  402, 443, 451–2, 462
Davis, Angela Y. 489, 491
Davis, Whitney 8
De Clercq, Rafael 128
De Mechel, Chrétien 432

De Sanctis, Francesco 219
De Staël, Mme 519–20
Dean, Jeffrey 173
death of art *see* "end of art"
DeBellis, Mark 92
deconstruction 217–18, **229–31**, 304, 380, 498,
  541–2, 562
  Barthes 160; Derrida 229–31, 242–3, 562
  see also critical monism and pluralism; criticism;
    deconstruction; implied author; intention;
    interpretation; meaning constructivism;
    structuralism and poststructuralism; text
definition of "art" 2, 203, **231–4**, 482, 507,
  565–8
  Beardsley 69, 164–5, 232; Bell 63; Carroll 69,
    233; Davies 203, 231–3; Dickie 69, 164,
    232–3, 568; Hume 332; Kennick 66, 152;
    Levinson 69, 203, 232; Margolis 411; Weitz
    66, 152–3, 203, 233, 248; Wittgenstein 66,
    249; Wollheim 233, 597
  see also artifact, art as; "artworld"; conceptual
    art; Dickie, George; formalism; function of art
Degas, Edgar 257
  Girl Drying Herself 495
Deleuze, Gilles 60, **234–8**
Demetz, Peter 412
Democritus 13
Dennis, John 216
depiction 4–5, 7–8, 12, 21, 83, 92, 107, 216,
  224, **238–41**, 280, 330, 347, 361, 465,
  468, 496, 504
  Aristotle 148, Beardsley 66; Du Bos 39;
    Gombrich 84, 240, 310, 344, 469, 573;
    Goodman 67, 238–9, 312, 466, 469; Hume
    332; Kames 39–40; Langer 64; Lessing 405;
    Nietzsche 439; Walton 589; Wollheim 67,
    598
  photography 98–9
  see also abstraction; drawing; painting;
    perspective; picture perception; printmaking;
    realism; representation
Derrida, Jacques 60, **241–4**, 251, 380, 425, 499
  Hegel 241–2, 316; Heidegger 242–3; Kant
    242–3; Nietzsche 242; Plato 241–2
  deconstruction 229–31, 242–3, 562
  poststructuralism 366–7, 541–3, 564
Descartes, René 28, 162, 167, 184, 235, 241,
  296–7, 422
Devereaux, Mary 429
Dewey, John 64–6, 77, 133, 163, 167, 171,
  221–2, **244–7**, 324, 361, 407, 431, 482
  Croce 244; Collingwood 246; Kant 64;
    Shusterman 65, 116
  aesthetic education 115–16, 245
  aesthetics of the everyday 136–8
  aesthetics of nature 65, 137, 245–6
  pragmatist aesthetics 481–2

Dickens, Charles
  Martin Chuzzlewit 534; *Our Mutual Friend* 354
Dickie, George 37, 72, 77, 203, **247–9**, 539,
    555
  Bell 249; Weitz 248
  aesthetic attitude 114, 173, 247, 429
  "artworld" 68–9, 155–6, 226, 232, 248,
    568–9
  institutional definition of "art" 69, 164, 232–3,
    568
Diderot, Denis 34, 40, 316
Diffey, Terry 69, 571
Dilthey, Wilhelm 303, 324–6, 371
Dilworth, John 276
Diogenes Laertius, *Lives* 16
Dipert, Randall R. 154, 462
Dissanayake, Ellen 260, 581
Dodd, Julian 96, 154
Dostoevsky, Fyodor Mikhailovich 379, 398, 410,
    579
Douglas, Mary 397
drama 13–16, 29, 31, 47, 71, **78–82**, 84, 89,
    95–7, 102, 134, 169, 217, 261, 267, 270–1,
    275, 300, 348, 393, 415, 442, 460–4, 477,
    482, 531, 535, 546, 548, 566, 578
  Benjamin 174–5; Cavell 183–4; Du Bos 39;
    Hegel 317–18, 320; Hume 332; Kierkegaard
    392–3; Lessing 402–5; Nietzsche 438–41,
    576; Plato 47, 473; Schlegel, A. 520;
    Tolstoy 570
  Indian 115, 492–4
  Japanese 384
  ontology of artworks 453–4, 457
  rasa 492–4
  tragedy 216, 329, 575–8
  see also literature; Shakespeare, William;
    Wagner, Richard
drawing 7–8, **82–5**, 108, 191, 258, 274, 442,
    455, 469, 496, 533, 545, 565
  Gombrich 84, 240, 310, 344, 469, 573;
    Goodman 67, 238–9, 312, 466, 469;
    Kant 37, 84
  Chinese 100, 189
  Islamic 383
  Japanese 385
Dryden, John 217
Du Bos, Jean-Baptiste, Abbé 38–9, 45, 49, 338
Duchamp, Marcel 204, 319, 450
  Fountain 69, 153, 165, 202–3, 568
  ready-mades 2, 59, 227
Dufrenne, Mikel 56, 113, **249–51**, 361, 365
  Barthes 249; Heidegger 250–1; Ingarden
    249–50; Kant 250; Merleau-Ponty 250;
    Sartre 250
Dunbar, Robin 6, 8
Duncan, Carol 274, 432–3
Dutton, Denis 159, 261, 290, 583

Eagleton, Terry 33, 61, 85, 174, 415, 542
Eaton, A. W. 273, 480
Eaton, Marcia 115
Ecker, Gisella 267–8
Eco, Umberto 22, 24
  The Name of the Rose 427
education, aesthetic *see* aesthetic education
eighteenth-century aesthetics **32–51**
Eldridge, Richard 185
Eliot, George 503
  Middlemarch 275
Eliot, T. S. 210–11, 366, 504, 527, 546
  The Wasteland 563
Elliott, R. K. 173, 596
Ellmann, Richard 592
Elster, Jon 209–10
Emerson, Ralph Waldo 21, 184, 481–2,
    552
emotion 91, 182, 191–3, **252–6**, 349, 355,
    566
  Aristotle 252–4; Bell 63, 172–3; Burke 37;
    Collingwood 62, 197; Du Bos 39; Hanslick
    314–15; Hume 252, 333; Plato 148;
    Walton 590
  expression 262–4
  expression theory 264–6
  fiction, the paradox of responding to 252,
    278–81
  rasa 492–4
  sentimentality 534–6
  see also aesthetic education; aesthetic pleasure;
    catharsis; kitsch; tragedy
Empedocles 29
"end of art" 53, 70, 227–8, 318–19, 322
Engels, Friedrich 408, 410, 412–15
Enton, Harry, *Frank Reade his Steam Man of the
    Plains* 415
environmental aesthetics *see* aesthetics of the
    environment
Epicurus 16
Eriugena, John Scottus 27
erotic art and obscenity 11, 14, 187, **256–8**, 336,
    485
  Burke 178; Kierkegaard 392; Levinson 257–8;
    Plato 472–3; Wagner 588
  feminist aesthetics and criticism 271–4
  pornography 479–80
  rasa 492–4
  see also censorship; feminist aesthetics and
    criticism; morality and art; pornography;
    value of art
d'Errico, F. 3, 5
Euripides 14, 575
  Iphigenia 374
evaluation of art *see* value of art
evolution, art, and aesthetics 1–3, 7, 71, 92,
    259–61, 448

universals in art 581–3
see also cognitive science and art; objectivity;
Paleolithic, art of the
existentialism 58, 294, 321, 392, 438, 512
expression 11–12, 17, 19, 26, 48, 75, 77–8,
82–3, 88, 90, 93–4, 100, 102–3, 122, 129,
133, 150, 156–7, 191–3, 215, 252, **261–4**,
355, 362–3, 424, 445, 458, 507, 546, 566,
574
Adorno 109; Beardsley 66; Cavell 183–4;
Collingwood 197–8; Croce 220–1; Deleuze
235; Dewey 246; Freud 55, 484–5; Goodman
67, 311–12; Hanslick 91; Hegel 53, 318;
Kant 168, 388; Kristeva 487; Langer 64,
400–2; Nietzsche 55; Santayana 511–12;
Walton 71, 262–3; Wollheim 67, 263, 597–8
in African aesthetics 139–40
in Amerindian aesthetics 142–4
censorship 185–6
in Chinese aesthetics 189–90
feminist aesthetics and criticism 270–2
in Japanese aesthetics 386
see also emotion; expression theory
expression theory 61–2, **264–6**, 458, 566
Collingwood 198–9, 203, 264–6, 355, 566–7;
Croce 61–2, 264, 355, 518; Tolstoy 62, 264,
299, 572
see also artifact, art as; expression; ontology of
artworks; work of art
Expressionism, Abstract *see* Abstract
Expressionism

fake *see* forgery
Fanon, Frantz 489
fantasy 257, 307, 349–50, 478, 480, 485, 487,
490, 496, 502–3, 598
Feagin, Susan 376–7, 577
feeling *see* emotion
Felski, Rita 267
feminist aesthetics and criticism 71–2, **267–75**,
396
see also canon; criticism; pornography;
psychoanalysis and art; race and aesthetics
Ferry, Luc 33
Fichte, J. G. 392, 514–15, 518, 521–2
Ficino, Marsilio 28–30
fiction, nature of 86, **275–8**, 307, 348, 352,
435
Currie 277–8; Walton 277
see also cognitive value of art; fiction, truth in;
fictional entities; imagination; literature;
narrative; poetry
fiction, the paradox of responding to 71, 192–3,
252, **278–81**, 352
Radford 279; Walton 280, 590
see also emotion; fictional entities; horror;
imaginative resistance; tragedy

fiction, truth in **281–4**
Currie 281; Lewis, D. K. 281–2; Walton 282
see also cognitive value of art; fiction, nature of;
fictional entities; implied author; intention;
"intentional fallacy"; interpretation; meaning
constructivism; literature; text; truth in art
fictional entities 71, **284–7**, 354
Meinong, 284–5; Russell 284–5; Walton
589–90
see also emotion; fiction, the paradox of
responding to; fiction, truth in; imagination;
implied author
Fielding, Henry
Amelia 354; *Joseph Andrews* 354; *Tom Jones* 354
film *see* motion pictures
Fish, Stanley 483, 564
Fisher, John Andrew 91, 559
Fisher, P. 433
Flaubert, Gustave 128, 380, 495–6, 513–14, 535
folk art 53, 157, 572
forgery 156, **287–90**
Goodman 288–9; Wollheim 288
see also conservation and restoration;
expression theory; function of art; ontology
of artworks; originality; senses and art, the;
value of art
form and content 148, 360, 461, 476, 502, 520,
546
form, significant 63, 121, 172–3, 237, 243,
359–60, 401–2, 440
see also Bell, Clive; formalism; Fry, Roger
formalism 62–3, 77, 83–4, 111–12, 115, 150,
207, **290–3**, 429, 540, 567
Baumgarten 41; Bell 62–3, 121, 164, 237,
290–3; Danto 292; Fry 290, 293; Gombrich
291–2; Hanslick 291–3; Hegel 291; Schiller
517; Walton 292; Wollheim 290
Forster, E. M. 129
Foucault, Michel 59–60, 86, **293–7**, 325
Heidegger 297; Nietzsche 296; Sartre 296
interpretation 374, 376
poststructuralism 160, 542–3
Fraleigh, Sandra 77
Francesca, Piero della 465
Baptism of Christ 527
Frankenheimer, John, *The Manchurian Candidate*
575, 577
Freedberg, David 343
Freeland, Cynthia 91, 331
Frege, Friedrich Ludwig Gottlob 166, 291, 348
Frere, John 1, 3, 6
Freud, Sigmund 51, 55, 60, 183–4, 208, 242,
298–9, 328, 350, 397
humor 336–7
psychoanalysis 420, 484–8, 515, 553
Frith, William Powell, *Paddington Station* 172
Frueh, Joanna 270

Fry, Roger 62–3, 164, 172, 290, 293, 502
function of art 150–1, 158, 206, 232, 290, **297–301**
  Aristotle 297–8; Croce 220; Danto 227–8; Freud 298–9; Hegel 318–20; Langer 298; Marx 298; Plato 297–8; Tolstoy 53, 56, 61–2, 298–9, 572; Wittgenstein 67
  African aesthetics 140–1
  Amerindian aesthetics 144
  Chinese aesthetics 188–90
  Indian aesthetics 492–4
  Japanese aesthetics 384–6
  see also aestheticism; aesthetic pleasure; definition of "art"; evolution, art, and aesthetics; Marxism and art; psychoanalysis and art; realism

Gabo, Naum 104
Gadamer, Hans-Georg 58, 162–3, 236, **302–4**, 499, 514, 519
  Dilthey 303; Heidegger 302, 323; Hegel 303; Kant 58, 302; Plato 303; Schiller 302
  hermeneutics 302–3, 324–7, 372–3
Gans, Herbert 476
gardens 46, **304–6**, 384
  Hegel 304–5; Schopenhauer 305–6
  see also aesthetics of the environment; aesthetics of the everyday; aesthetics of nature
Gardiner, Patrick 519, 525
Gass, William 429
Gaut, Berys 69, 91, 194, 196, 207–9, 231, 233, 355–6, 425, 429–30
Gautier, Théophile 592–3
  Mademoiselle de Maupin 128
Gay, Peter 426
Gendler, Tamar Szabó 351–3
Genet, Jean 293, 513
Genette, Gérard 437
genre 68, 79–80, 166, 213, 282–3, **306–8**, 327
  Beardsley 165; Cavell 184; Lessing 403–5; Walton 588–9
  see also fictional entities; narrative; ontological contextualism; style
Gentile, Giovanni 220
Gentileschi, Artemisia, *Susanna and the Elders* 274
Geoffrey of Vinsauf 25
George, Stefan 323
Gerard, Alexander 38, 45, 49
Ghiberti, Lorenzo 465
Giacometti, Alberto 105, 513
Gilbert, W. S., *Patience* 128
Giotto 149, 172, 309, 497
Godlovitch, Stan 92, 158, 462
Goehr, Lydia 96

Goethe, Johann Wolfgang von 21, 46, 57, 316, 413, 432, 552
  Wilhelm Meister 522
  Benjamin 174, 176; Lukács 410; Schiller 518; Schlegel, F. 521
Gogol, Nikolai 571, 579
  Inspector General 202
Goldberg, RoseLee 463–4
Goldie, Peter 205
Goldman, Alan H. 124, 128, 376–7, 448, 458–9, 555, 570
Goldmann, Lucien 396, 412
Gombrich, Ernst 149, 197, 291–2, **308–11**, 592
  illusion 84, 240, 308, 345, 466, 469, 545
  pictorial representation 84, 240, 308–10, 344, 469, 573
Gooding-Williams, Robert 490–1
Goodman, Nelson 65, 67, 70, 75, 77, 123, 247, **311–13**, 443, 461, 592
  depiction 67, 238–9, 312, 466, 469
  forgery 288–9
  ontology of artworks 67, 377, 456
  pragmatist aesthetics 482–3
Gorgias 13–14
Gould, Carroll 173
Gould, Glenn 574
Gould, Timothy 185
Goya y Lucientes, Francisco de 112
  Disasters of War 192
Gracyk, Theodore 92–4, 225, 452, 557
Greenberg, Clement 62, 108, 150–1, 394, 426, 463
Grice, H. Paul 379, 506–7
Grosseteste, Robert 22–3
Guerilla Girls 274
Guyer, Paul 38, 44–5, 47–8, 112, 392, 459
gynesis 269–70
gynocriticism 269–70

Habermas, Jürgen 214, 325, 499
Hagberg, Garry 402
Halliwell, Stephen 12, 18, 149, 182, 474, 577
Hals, Frans 209, 288
Halverson, J. 9
Hamilton, Andy 92
Hamilton, James R. 82, 462, 464
Hampshire, Stuart 65, 299
Hanslick, Eduard 17, 91, 291–3, **314–15**
Hardin, C. L. 555
Hardy, Thomas 525
  Jude the Obscure 281–3
Hartman, Geoffrey 229–30
Hartmann, Nicolai 365
Hauck, Guido 465
Haydn, Franz Joseph 158, 205, 450, 452–3
Hayek, Friedrich von 574

Hegel, Georg Wilhelm Friedrich 52–3, 72, 77, 131,
    150–1, 219, 235, 241–2, 291, 303–5, 308,
    315–20, 324, 349, 379, 396, 411, 413, 453,
    490, 500–2, 508, 530, 543
  Danto 70, 227–8; Heidegger 321–3; Kant 53,
    315–18; Kierkegaard 315, 392–3; Lukács
    409–10; Marx 315; Schelling 316, 514–16;
    Schiller 518
  the absolute 316, 322, 501–2
  beauty 53, 170–1, 316–18, 320
  tragedy 316–17, 575, 577
Heidegger, Martin 56, 60, 156, 184, 234–6,
    242–3, 246, 250–1, 297, **321–4**, 363, 365,
    372, 579
  Aristotle 321; Baumgarten 163, 321; Gadamer
    302, 323; Hegel 321–3; Husserland 321;
    Nietzsche 321–2; Plato 321; Schelling 514,
    516
  hermeneutics 58, 321, 324–5
Heinz, John 282
Heller, Erich 441, 524
Hemacandra 359
Hepburn, Ronald W. 256
Heraclitus 12
Herbart, J. F. 219
Herder, Johann Gottfried 46–7, 49, 163, 518,
    533, 553
hermeneutics 56–8, **324–8**, 372–3, 552
  Gadamer 302–3, 324–7, 372–3; Hegel 324;
    Heidegger 58, 321, 324–5; Kant 324, Marx
    325; Nietzsche 325
  see also interpretation; semiotics; symbol; text
Hesiod 11–13
  Theogony 11
Hewison, Robert 508
Higgins, Kathleen Marie 396, 441, 583
Higgins, Paula 271
Hirsch, E. D., Jr. 325–7, 372–4, 564
Hirstein, William 261
history of art see art history
Hitchcock, Alfred, Psycho 328
Hobbema, Meindert, The Water Mill with the Great
    Red Roof 471
Hobbes, Thomas 85, 336, 537
Hoffmann, E. T. A. 361, 363, 586
Holbein, Hans 398
  Ambassadors 196
Hölderlin, Johann Christian Friedrich 302, 316,
    321, 323, 514
Holmes, Oliver Wendell Jr. 186
Home, Henry see Kames, Lord
Homer 11–13, 15, 18, 21, 30, 181, 320, 374,
    403, 438, 496, 527, 549, 579, 582
  Iliad 413; Odyssey 11, 473, 548; Thersites 405
Hopkins, Robert 104, 239–40, 289, 446, 470,
    532–3, 560, 599
Horace 11, 13, 170, 403

Horkheimer, Max 109, 476–7
horror 193, 252, 278, 280, 286, **328–31**
  Burke 177; Carroll, N. 329; Kristeva 397–8;
    Lessing 405; Walton 590
  and the sublime 547, 549
  see also catharsis; feminist aesthetics and
    criticism; Kristeva, Julia; tragedy
Hospers, John 209, 579
Hugh of St. Victor 26
Hülsen, August Ludwig 521
Humboldt, Wilhelm von 518, 552
Hume, David 31, 38, 99, 117, 131, 183, 234,
    252, **331–4**, 345, 349, 351–2, 489, 499,
    535, 549, 582, 590
  Burke 177; Kant 43–4, 47; Shaftesbury 538
  aesthetic education 46, 115, 499
  aesthetic judgment 117, 332–3
  beauty 42–3, 45, 47, 167–9, 331–3
  objectivity and realism 445, 447–8
  taste 44–7, 332–4, 554–6
  tragedy 44, 49, 332–4
humor 199–202, 259, **334–8**
  Bergson 336; Freud 336–7; Kant 335; Hegel
    317, 319; Hobbes 336; Kierkegaard 337–8,
    379–80, 392–3; Plato 334, 336; Schlegel, F.
    522; Wilde 130
  see also comedy; irony; tragedy
Humphrey, Nicholas 8–9
Husserl, Edmund 56, 60, 241–2, 244, 250, 321,
    364–5
Hutcheson, Francis 33–6, 38, **338–40**, 554
  beauty 34–5, 38, 42–4, 47, 126, 338–40
Hyman, John 241, 471, 497
Hyppolite, Jean 241–2

Ibsen, Henrik 577
iconoclasm **341–3**, 548
  see also censorship; pornography; religion and
    art; symbol
idolatry see iconoclasm
illusion **343–6**
  Carroll 279; Du Bos 39; Gombrich 84, 240, 308,
    345, 466, 469, 545; Hume 345; Langer 345,
    401; Lessing 345; Nietzsche 438, 440;
    Wollheim 471
  see also imagination; picture perception;
    representation; trompe l'oeil effects
images, mental see imagination
imagination 113, 193–4, 208–9, 345, **346–51**, 531
  Addison 36; Freud 350; Hegel 349; Hume 349;
    Kant 37–8, 349–50, 388; Plato 18–19; Sartre
    513–14; Scruton 528–9; Walton 67, 70–1,
    286, 470–1, 589–90; Wittgenstein 347
  see also creativity; fiction, truth in; fictional
    entities; fiction, the paradox of responding to;
    illusion; imaginative resistance; metaphor;
    picture perception

imaginative resistance **351–4**
  Currie 353; Hume 351–2; Walton 351–3, 591
  see also cognitive science and art; fiction, the
    paradox of responding to; fiction, truth in;
    imagination; morality and art
implied author **354–6**, 368, 429
  Beardsley 353; Collingwood 355; Croce 355;
    Currie 356; Gaut 355–6; Levinson 355;
    Nehamas 354; Robinson 355; Walton 356
  see also intention; "intentional fallacy";
    interpretation; meaning constructivism; style;
    text
Indian aesthetics 115, 150–1, 318, **356–60**,
    489
  rasa 492–4, 500
ineffability **360–4**, 507, 553
  Heidegger 363; Langer 362; Plato 361;
    Wittgenstein 362–3, 483; Schopenhauer 361
  see also expression; metaphor; testimony in
    aesthetics
Ingarden, Roman 56, 70, 249–50, **364–6**, 578
  Heidegger 365; Langer 365; Plato 365; Sartre
    365
  ontology of artworks 91, 365, 453, 457
Ingres, Jean-Auguste-Dominique 57
  Napoleon the Emperor 194; *The Valpincon Bather*
    495–6
institutional theory of art 69, 164, 232–3, 568
intention 67–8, 101, 199–200, 205, 230, 263,
    282–3, 287, 209–11, 355, **371–5**, 563–4
  Beardsley 164, 355, 366, 369–70, 563; Walton
    589–90; Wollheim 597
  authenticity and art 156, 158–9
  fiction, nature of 276–8
  interpretation 366–74, 376, 378–9, 462
  irony 379–8
  photography 99–100
  representation 506–7
  see also criticism; deconstruction; implied author;
    "intentional fallacy"; literature; poetry
"intentional fallacy" 66, 355, 366, **369–71**, 372,
    563
  Beardsley 66, 164, 355, 366, 369–70, 563;
    Wimsatt 66, 164, 355, 366, 369–70
  see also critical monism and pluralism; criticism;
    deconstruction; intention; interpretation;
    literature; meaning constructivism; New
    Criticism; poetry; text
interpretation 94, 97, 215, 217–18, 229, 324–7,
    354–5, **371–5**, 441–3, 482–3, 491, 563–4
  Augustine 27; Beardsley 372–4; Cavell 184;
    Danto 226–7; Davies 371; Foucault 374,
    376; Freud 60, 184, 484–5; Gadamer 302–3;
    Gombrich 309; Goodman 312; Kant 371–2;
    Levinson 368, 370, 462; Margolis 411–12;
    Sartre 366; Wittgenstein 374; Wollheim 375
  aims of 375–8

intention 366–74, 376, 378–9, 462
  "intentional fallacy" 369–71
  meaning constructivism 418–21
  performance 80–1, 461–2
  relativism 498–500
  see also criticism; deconstruction; intention;
    metaphor; New Criticism; poetry; text
Irigaray, Luce 270
irony **378–81**, 338
  Barthes 378, 380; Beardsley 164; Derrida 380;
    Hegel 379; Kierkegaard 337–8, 379–80,
    392–3; Plato 378; Searle 424; Schlegel, F.
    379–81, 522
  see also deconstruction; humor; "intentional
    fallacy"; metaphor; modernism and
    postmodernism; structuralism and
    poststructuralism; tragedy
Irvin, Sherri 137–8
Iseminger, Gary 368, 563
Islamic aesthetics 78, 151, 207, 224, **381–3**
  see also religion and art

Jacobi, F. H. 515
Jacobson, Daniel 429–30
Jacquette, Dale 132, 525
Jagannatha 357–9
Jakobson, Roman 86, 495, 497
James, Henry 546
James, William 115, 244, 481
Jameson, Frederic 412
Janaway, Chris 474
Japanese aesthetics 111, 150–1, 223, **384–7**
Jefferson, Mark 535
John, Eileen 580
Johnson, Barbara 218
Johnson, Mark 424
Johnson, Paul 498
Johnson, Samuel 216, 279–80, 547, 548
Jones Le Roi (Amiri Baraka) 224
Joyce, James 362, 426
  Ulysses 156, 187, 312
judgment, aesthetic *see* aesthetic judgment
Jung, Carl G. 401, 486–8

Kafka, Franz 176, 367, 415
Kames, Lord (Henry Home) 37–40, 46, 49
Kandinsky, Vassily 56, 107, 295, 426
Kania, Andrew 92–4
Kant, Immanuel 19, 58, 63–4, 75, 84, 184–5,
    242–3, 273, 304, 324, 335, **388–92**,
    409–10, 465, 528–30, 534–5, 561, 579
  Aquinas 147; Baumgarten 162–3; Burke 177;
    Hegel 53, 315–18; Hume 43–4, 47; Schelling
    514–16; Schiller 517–18; Schlegel, F. 521;
    Schopenhauer 439, 522–4
  aesthetic judgment 51–2, 65, 115, 118–22,
    124, 164, 388–91, 445, 483, 554–5

aesthetic attitude 33, 37, 111–13, 137, 363, 389–90, 478
aesthetic pleasure 51–2, 65, 115, 120–4, 164, 388–9, 445, 483
beauty 36–7, 43–4, 47–8, 51–2, 54, 147, 167–9, 171, 292, 388–91, 501, 503, 582
and Chinese aesthetics 190
on creativity 37–8, 207–9
formalism 63, 115, 129, 292, 391
imagination 37–8, 47, 349–50, 388
Kaprow, Alan 463, 482
morality and art 38–9, 47–9, 52, 54, 388–9, 391, 501
and race 489–90
the sublime 37, 54–5, 137, 388, 547, 549–51
taste 44, 47, 131, 388–91, 554–5
Kemal, Salim 27, 383, 392
Kennick, William E. 66, 152–3, 361
Kermode, Frank 215
Kieran, Matthew 194–6, 257–8, 429–30
Kierkegaard, Søren 56–8, 130, 315, **392–3**
Hegel 315, 392–3; Lukács 410; Schelling 516; Wilde 593
ironic humor 337–8, 379–80, 392–3
Kindt, Tom 354
Kingsley, Charles 509
kitsch **393–6**, 417, 535
Kivy, Peter 92–3, 97, 154, 157–8, 462
Hume 45, 333–4; Hutcheson 35
Kiyonobu I, Torii, *Erotic Contest of Flowers: Scenes of Lovemaking* 258
Klein, Melanie 398, 597
Klein, R. G. 1
Knapp, S. 564
Knight, Deborah 536
Knights, L. C. 307
Koed, Erik 105
Kohn, Marak 6
Koons, Jeff, *Made in Heaven* 257
Korsmeyer, Carolyn 45, 131, 133, 137, 267–8, 272–3
Kosuth, Joseph, *One and Three Chairs* 202–3
Kraus, Karl, *The Last Days of Mankind* 80
Krausz, Michael 421
Kraut, Robert 214
Krell, David Farrell 243
Kris, Ernst 149, 487
Kristeller, Paul Oskar 25, 28, 49, 338
Kristeva, Julia 328, 330, **396–9**, 487–8, 564–5
Kubrick, Stanley
Dr. Strangelove 201; *The Shining* 328
Kuehn, Glenn 133
Kulka, Thomas 394
Kulvicki, John 241
Kundera, Milan, *The Unbearable Lightness of Being* 395–6
Kupfer, Joseph H. 137–8, 535

Kurosawa, Akira
Ran 223; *Throne of Blood* 223

Labriola, Antonio 219
Lacan, Jacques 251, 328, 396–7, 488, 553
Lakis, Asja 175
Lakoff, George 424
Lamarque, Peter 82, 87, 102, 196, 279, 283, 421, 430, 437, 580, 591
Landow, G. P. 509
Langer, Susanne 63–4, 77, 91, 104, 247, 298, 345, 362, **400–2**
Ingarden 365; Schiller 401; Wittgenstein 400
Lask, Emil 409
Lawrence, D. H., *Lady Chatterley's Lover* 187, 367
Layton, Robert 142
Le Corbusier (Charles Edouard Jeaneret) 527, 573–4
Leaman, Oliver 383
Leavis, F. R. 307, 502–3, 529–30
Leddy, Thomas 138
Leibniz, Gottfried Wilhelm von 28, 40, 162, 167, 234, 521
Lenin, V. I. 410, 414–15
Leonardo da Vinci 28–9, 298
Mona Lisa 191–2, 528
Lessing, Alfred 288, 532
Lessing, Gotthold Ephraim 11, 19, 49, 183, 345, **402–5**, 558, 577
Lévi–Strauss, Claude 251, 396, 436, 540, 542
Levin, David Michael 77
Levin, Samuel R. 424–5
Levinson, Jerrold 91–3, 96, 124, 128, 154, 210, 256–8, 262, 280, 334, 355, 443, 457, 459, 472, 591
definition of "art" 69–70, 202–3, 232
intention and interpretation 368, 370, 462
ontological contextualism 451–2
Lewis, C. I. **405–8**
Lewis, David K. 281–2, 285
Lewis-Williams, David 3, 8
Lintott, Sheila 133, 136
Lippard, Lucy 202–3
Lippitt, John 338
literature 20, 22, 27–30, 37–41, 76, 78–81, **85–8**, 101, 103, 109, 151, 184, 194–5, 242, 260–1, 267–71, 306, 345, 354, 414–15, 425–9, 454, 482, 495–6, 531–2, 535, 542–3, 546, 563–5, 578
Barthes 160–1, 426; Croce 220–1; Foucault 293–5; Hegel 316–19; Hume 332; Ingarden 364–5; Kristeva 396–8; Sartre 513–14; Schlegel, A. 519–20; Schlegel, F. 521–2; Schopenhauer 523; Tolstoy 298, 571; Wilde 592, 594
canon 179–81

literature (*cont.*):
  criticism and interpretation 215–19, 366–81,
    435–7, 485
  irony 378–80
  Islamic aesthetics 381–2
  Japanese aesthetics 385
  see also deconstruction; feminist aesthetics and
    criticism; poetry
Livingston, Paisley 207–9, 283, 368, 408, 563
Livingstone, Margaret 191–2
Locke, Alain 481–2
Locke, John 28, 34, 339–40, 537–8, 541
Lomazzo, Gian Paolo 29
Longinus, Cassius 19–20, 36, 41, 547–8, 551
Lopes, Dominic McIver 82, 195, 239–40, 263,
  278, 470–1, 533
Lorusso, A. M. 27
Lucretius, *De rerum natura* 16, 29
Lukács, Georg 175, 380, **408–10**, 412, 415
  Goethe 410; Hegel 409–10; Kant 409–10;
    Kierkegaard 410; Marx 408
Lyas, Colin 266, 366
Lyotard, Jean-François 60, 251, 426, 542–3

Macdonald, Dwight 476
MacDonald, Margaret 283
Macherey, Pierre 542
Mackenzie, Henry, *The Man of Feeling* 534
Mackie, John L. 121, 445
MacKinnon, Catherine A. 256, 480
McClary, Susan 271
McCloskey, Mary 392
McDowell, John 121, 447, 556
McFee, Graham 77, 421, 450
McLuhan, Marshall 543
make-believe *see* imagination
Malevich, Kasimir 213
Mallarmé, Stéphane 296, 359–60, 396, 552
Malraux, André 129
Mammata 358–9
Man, Paul de 229, 243
Manet, Édouard 496
Mann, Thomas 122, 380–1, 524–5
  Death in Venice 122; *Doktor Faustus* 380
Mansfield, William Murray, earl of 186
Marcus Aurelius 17–18
Marcuse, Herbert 415
Margolis, Joseph 68, 77, **411–12**, 456, 483, 563
  Croce 411; Hegel 411; Ingarden 365
Maritain, Jacques 146
Marra, Michael 386–7
Marx, Karl 51, 53–4, 219, 235, 298, 325, 408,
  593
  Hegel 315, 413; Kant 53; Lukács 408–9, 412,
    415; Schiller 413
  and art 175, **412–15**, 543
  Marxism 412–14

Mason, Michelle 333
mass art 94, **415–18**, 476, 559
  see also kitsch; motion pictures; photography;
    popular art; technology and art
materialism 174, 176, 190, 414, 439, 517
Matisse, Henri 273, 422, 513
  The Red Studio 122
Matravers, Derek 265, 353
Matthews, Patricia M. 340
Matthews, Robert 375–6
Mattick, Paul 110, 432
Maurer, Armand 146
Mayer, Hans 412
Maynard, Patrick 85, 101
Meager, Ruby 173, 540
meaning constructivism **418–21**
  see also critical monism and pluralism; criticism;
    deconstruction; implied author; intention;
    interpretation; relativism; structuralism
    and poststructuralism; text
medieval and renaissance aesthetics **22–32**
Meier, Georg Friedrich 40–1, 163
Meiland, Jack 458
Meinong, Alexius 284–5
Mendelssohn, Moses 37, 39–42, 49, 163, 177,
  521, 574
Merleau-Ponty, Maurice 57, 77, 235, 367, 412,
  421–3
  Dufrenne 250; Sartre 421
Meskin, Aaron 82, 279, 353, 558, 561
metanarrative 320, 426, 543
metaphor 27, 102, 350, 363, **423–5**, 506, 578
  Aristotle 423; Beardsley 424; Danto 70;
    Derrida 425; Goodman 311–12; Nietzsche
    553
  see also irony
Michaels, W. B. 564
Michelangelo Buonarroti 83, 149, 151, 341, 520,
  594
  Last Judgment 571; *Moses* 484; *Pietà* 196
Mill, John Stuart 186, 503
Miller, Geoffrey 259–60
Miller, J. Hillis 229
Miller, Mara 304–5
Milton, John 44, 85, 168, 546
  Paradise Lost 246, 306, 333, 369, 497, 548–9
mimesis 11–12, 15, 17–21, 61, 70, 174, 302,
  384, 468, 566
  Aristotle 12, 15, 19, 147–8; Lessing 402;
    Lukács 410; Plato 12, 15, 20–1, 473;
    Plotinus 20–1; Walton 588–9
  see also depiction; representation
Mithen, Steven 6, 8–9, 260
modernism and postmodernism 59–62, 83, 110,
  161, 251, 321, **425–8**, 438, 482, 498,
  540–4, 573–4
  Barthes 426; Eco 427; Lyotard 426

Mondrian, Piet 107, 311

Monet, Claude 150, 308–9

   Sunset and Fog at Eragny 451

Monk, Samuel H. 36, 178, 551

Monro, D. H. 202, 335

Monroe, Dave 132

Montaigne, Michel de 241, 498

Montero, Barbara 192–3

Moore, George E. 172, 444

morality and art 130, 216, 298, **428–31**, 579

   Carroll 429–30; Gaut 429–30; Kant 48, 52, 54,
      388–9; Nietzsche 55; Plato 428, 430; Ruskin
      508; Schiller 49, 52, 518–19; Sidney 29–30;
      Wilde 591–3

   African aesthetics 141

   Chinese aesthetics 188–90

   see also censorship; erotic art and obscenity;
      imaginative resistance; pornography; value
      of art

Moran, Richard 351

Morreall, John 200, 338

Morris, William 509

Mothersill, Mary 171, 333, 445, 555

motion pictures **88–91**, 183–4, 328–31, 415–16,
   479

   see also photography; ontology of artworks;
      technology and art

Mozart, W. A. 157, 235, 268, 375, 461

   Don Giovanni 392

Mulhall, Stephen 363

Müller, Hans-Harald 354

Mulvey, Laura 273

museums 84, 205–7, 222–4, **431–4**

   Dewey 245, 431, 482; Goethe 432

   see also art history

music 5, 11–17, 24–8, 34, 37, 63–4, 75–8,
   91–5, 126–7, 184, 192–4, 198, 203, 222–3,
   234, 252, 260–6, 275, 292, 312, 345, 350,
   355, 360–3, 391, 426, 554–9, 566, 569,
   573, 582

   Adorno 109–10; Aristotle 148–9, 182;
      Hanslick 291, 314–15; Hegel 319; Hume
      332–3; Kant 501; Kierkegaard 392–3; Langer
      401–2; Nietzsche 576–7; Plato 169, 472–5;
      Schopenhauer 361, 523–4; Wagner 438–9,
      504, 529, 586–7; Wittgenstein 594, 596

   absolute or "pure" 92, 107–8, 293, 311, 360,
      375, 533

   African aesthetics 140

   Amerindian aesthetics 142–5

   Chinese aesthetics 96, 188–9

   feminism 268, 270–2

   Indian aesthetics 492–3

   Islamic aesthetics 383

   notation 287, 441–3

   ontology of musical works 153–4, 157–8, 365,
      450–7, 461–3, 528

opera 95–6, 157–8, 271, 392–3, 439, 460–1,
   504, 529, 586–7

   performance 157–8, 222–3, 460–2, 546

   popular 137, 157, 223, 308, 415–16, 428,
      476–8, 482–3, 529, 556–7

narrative 6, 79, 151, 191–3, 199, 201–2, 276–7,
   307–8, 426–7, **435–8**, 534, 536, 542–3

   Lessing 403, 405; Plato 473

Nathan, Daniel O. 368, 370

naturalism 9, 149, 274, 412, 481

nature, aesthetics of *see* aesthetics of nature

Nehamas, Alexander 211, 355, 418, 441

Neill, Alex 101, 280, 334

New Criticism 17, 62, 163, 215, 217, 230, 372,
   563

Newman, Barnett 107, 211

Newman, Ira 536

Nichols, Shaun 286, 353

Nietzsche, Friedrich (Wilhelm) 55, 57, 72, 183,
   207, 234–7, 242, 296, 325, 330, **438–41**,
   486, 498–9, 504, 529, 535, 553, 593

   Baumgarten 163; Heidegger 321–2; Kant 53,
      55, 439; Plato 438; Schelling 516;
      Schopenhauer 55, 438–9, 522–5; Wagner
      438–9, 587

   tragedy 14, 55, 438–40, 575–7

Nifo, Agostino 28

nihilism 322, 392, 498, 515

nineteenth- and twentieth-century Continental
   aesthetics **51–61**

Nochlin, Linda 61, 268, 274, 498

non-Western art

   African *see* African aesthetics

   Amerindian *see* Amerindian aesthetics

   Chinese *see* Chinese aesthetics

   Indian *see* Indian aesthetics

   Islamic *see* Islamic aesthetics

   Japanese *see* Japanese aesthetics

Norris, Christopher 230

notations 77–8, 287, **441–3**, 452, 460

   Goodman 67, 443; Ingarden 365

   see also dance; drama; music; authenticity and
      art; ontology of artworks; performance

Novalis (Friedrich von Hardenberg) 516, 519, 521

Novitz, David 137, 208–9, 299, 418

Nowell, A. 2, 5

Nozik, Robert 579

Nussbaum, Martha C. 21, 149, 184, 194, 429,
   575, 580

Oakeshott, Michael 500, 502

objectivity 65, 71, 117–19, 327, 371–2, 374,
   382, **444–9**, 495–8, 539, 555–6, 560–1

   Hume 445, 447–8; Kant 51–2, 65, 118–22,
      124, 164, 388–91, 445, 483; Scruton 446;
      Sibley 65–6; Wollheim 445

INDEX

objectivity (*cont.*):
  see also aesthetic judgment; aesthetic properties;
    cognitive science and art; evolution, art,
    and aesthetics; realism; relativism; taste;
    universals in art
Odin, Steve 111
Ofili, Chris, *Holy Virgin Mary* 224
Ogilby, John 44, 168
O'Hear, Anthony 527, 575
Olsen, Stein Haugom 82, 87, 102, 181, 210, 580
ontological contextualism 67, 71, 127, 377, 408,
    413, 429–30, **449–53**, 462
  Currie 452; Danto 449–50; Davies 451–2;
    Levinson 451–2; Walton 450
ontology of artworks 70–1, 77, 83, 89, 91, 94–7,
    103, 134, 137, 153–4, 157, 203–7, 217,
    222, 232–3, 442–3, 453–7, 461, 568–9
  Collingwood 265–6, 455; Croce 453; Goodman
    67, 377, 456; Hegel 453; Ingarden 91, 365,
    453, 457; Margolis 411–12, 456; Tolstoy
    571; Wollheim 70, 597
  ontological contextualism *see* ontological
    contextualism
  see also authenticity and art; artifact, art as;
    definition of "art"; formalism; type-token
    distinction; work of art
opera 93, **95–8**, 157–8, 271, 392, 439, 460–1
  Wagner 529, 586–7
  Chinese aesthetics 96
  see also music; ontology of artworks;
    performance
oriental aesthetics
  Chinese *see* Chinese aesthetics
  Indian *see* Indian aesthetics
  Japanese *see* Japanese aesthetics
originality 60, 122, 125, 156, 207–10, 289, 426,
    457–9, 568, 574
  Danto 458; Sparshott 459
  see also creativity; tradition
Orsini, Gian N. G. 220
Ortega y Gasset, José 298
Orwell, George
  1984 495; *Homage to Catalonia* 194
Osborne, Harold 128, 130, 171, 392, 567
Oshima, Nagisa, *Band of Ninja* 89
Osipovich, David 462

Paddison, Max 111
painting 12–15, 25, 28–9, 56–7, 66–7, 75, **82–5**,
    92, 104–5, 227, 361–3, 527, 533, 558
  Aristotle 13, 19, 148–9; Bell 62–3, 111, 172–3,
    290; Collingwood 198–9, 455; Deleuze
    236–7; Du Bos 38–9; Foucault 294–5, 374;
    Gombrich 84, 240, 308–10, 344, 469, 573;
    Greenberg 108, 151, 394, 426; Hegel 319;
    Heidegger 323; Kant 84, 391; Langer 401;
    Lessing 402–5; Merleau-Ponty 421–2;

Plato 14–15, 19, 472–4; Ruskin 309, 471,
    508–10; Sibley 539; Vasari 29, 149–51;
    Walton 588–9; Wollheim 263, 290, 597–9
  Abstract Expressionism *see* Abstract
    Expressionism
  African aesthetics 141
  Amerindian aesthetics 144, 159
  Chinese aesthetics 189–90
  and cognitive science 191–2
  Cubism *see* Cubism
  expression in 263–4, 566
  and feminism 273–4
  ontology 449–53, 455–7
  Paleolithic cave paintings 1–9
  Pop Art *see* Pop Art
  portrait *see* portrait
  style 545–6, 598
  Surrealism 55
  see also abstraction; conservation and
    restoration; depiction; drawing; forgery;
    illusion; mimesis; perspective; picture
    perception; realism; representation; seeing-in
Paleolithic, art of the **1–10**, 260, 583
Panaetius 17
Panofsky, Erwin 22, 24–5, 151, 465–6, 468
Papineau, D. 2
Parrhasius 12
Passmore, John 66
pastiche 427, 543, 546
Pater, Walter 128, 130, 502, 592
Peacocke, Christopher 241, 350, 467–8
Peirce, Charles S. 244, 400, 454, 481, 563
performance 77, 80–1, 91–7, 157–8, 403–4,
    441, 450–5, 457, **460–2**, 544, 546
  see also drama; music; opera; performance art
performance art 77, 156, 375, 454, **462–5**
  see also conceptual art; performance
perspective 24, 83, 436, **465–9**
  Danto 227; Goodman 239, 466, 469; Panofsky
    465–9; Peacocke 457–8
  Chinese aesthetics 189
  see also drawing; depiction; painting; perspective;
    picture perception; printmaking; realism;
    representation
Pettit, Philip 447, 562
phenomenology 56, 60, 77, 241–2, 249, 294,
    324, 364–5, 421–3
Philodemus 16–17
Philostratus 12
photography 57, 176, **98–101**, 469, 557, 590
  motion pictures 88–91
  see also representation
Piaget, Jean 541
Picasso, Pablo 2, 62, 108, 171, 222, 226, 319,
    418, 426, 598–9
  Les Demoiselles D'Avignon 288–9; *Guernica* 165
Pickering, John, *Horestes* 218

picture perception **469–72**
  Gombrich 309–10, 469; Hopkins 470; Walton
    470–1, 589–90; Wollheim 470–1, 506, 598
  see also drawing; depiction; illusion; painting;
    perspective; realism; representation; senses
    and art, the; style
Pindar 13, 15
Pinkard, Terry 520, 522
Pinker, Steven 259–60
Pirenne, M. H. 466
Pissarro, Camille 451
Plato 10–21, 47, 66, 70, 77, 111, 131, 147–8,
    155, 226, 230, 235, 238, 241–2, 257,
    297–8, 303, 334, 321, 336, 361, 378,
    397, 427–30, 438, 468, **472–4**, 478,
    523, 529–30, 542, 549, 567, 575, 592
  Aristotle 10–16; Plotinus 474; Socrates 12–15,
    168–9, 298, 347, 378–80, 472–3, 593
  aesthetic education 47, 114, 194
  beauty 16, 21, 28, 52, 167–9, 171, 472–4
  creativity 207–9, 472, 474
  poetry 21, 29–30, 217, 279, 472–3
pleasure, aesthetic *see* aesthetic pleasure
Plekhanov, Georgi Valentinovich 414
Pliny 149–50, 306
Plotinus 20–1, 30, **474–6**
pluralism 94, 186, 211–13, 312, 377, 499
Plutarch 11, 13, 16
Podro, Michael 85, 151, 545
poetry 11–18, 21, 25–31, 79, 86–7, **101–4**, 148,
    182, 215–17, 279, 557
  Aristotle 147–9; Baumgarten 36–7, 40; Burke
    37; Croce 220–1; Gadamer 302–3; Hegel 316,
    318–20; Heidegger 321–2; Hume 332–4;
    Kierkegaard 392–3; Lessing 402–5; Plato 21,
    29–30, 217, 279, 472–3; Sartre 359–60;
    Schlegel, A. 519–20; Schlegel, F. 521–2
  Amerindian aesthetics 144
  Chinese aesthetics 188–90
  Indian aesthetics 357–60
  Islamic aesthetics 381–3
  Japanese aesthetics 384–5
  see also canon; criticism; drama; intention;
    "intentional fallacy"; interpretation; literature;
    text
Pöggeler, Otto 320, 324
Polanski, Roman
  Repulsion 328; *Rosemary's Baby* 328
Pollock, Jackson 463, 482
Pop Art 70, 228, 295, 308
Pope, Alexander 216, 548
Popper, Sir Karl 197, 309
Popper, Leo 409
popular art 94, 137, 308, 416, **476–8**, 482–3
  Adorno 476–8; Carroll 476–8; Shusterman
    476–8
  see also mass art

pornography 187, 256–8, **478–80**
  Collingwood 502–3
  see also censorship; erotic art and obscenity;
    feminist aesthetics and criticism; morality
    and art
Porphyry 474
portrait 108, 189–90, 194, 238, 270, 276,
    288
Posner, Richard 429
postmodernism *see* modernism and postmodernism
poststructuralism *see* structuralism and
    poststructuralism
Pouillon, Henri 22
Pound, Ezra 426, 553, 579
pragmatist aesthetics 77, 407, **480–3**
  Dewey 481–2; Beardsley 482; Goodman 482–3
  see also aesthetics of the environment; aesthetics
    of the everyday; museums
printmaking **82–5**
  see also drawing; painting
Proclus 20–1
properties, aesthetic *see* aesthetic properties
Propp, Vladimir 436, 541
Proudfoot, Diane 286
Proust, Marcel 176, 347, 398, 524
Pseudo-Dionysius 22–3
psychoanalysis and art 183–4, 208, 298–9, 420,
    484–8, 515, 553
  Cavell 184; Freud 55, 60, 242, 328, 336–7,
    350, 397, 484–8; Jung 486–7; Kristeva
    396–7, 487–8; Nietzsche 486; Rank 485–6
Pullman, Philip, *His Dark Materials* 196
purpose of art *see* function of art
Pyrrho of Elis 498
Pythagoreanism 382

Quatremère de Quincy, A.-C. 431
Quine, W. V. O. 213, 291, 528

race and aesthetics 24, 482, **489–92**
  Hegel 490; Hume 490; Kant 489–90; Schiller
    490; Shaftesbury 489
  feminist aesthetics and criticism 267–8, 272
Radford, Colin 279, 289
Raffman, Diana 192, 362
Railton, Peter 447
Ramachandran, Vilayanur 261
Rank, Otto 485–6
Ranke, Leopold von 324
Rankin, Ian 430
Ransome, John Crowe 215
Raphael (Raffaello Sanzio) 151, 378, 520
Rapin, René 216
rasa **492–4**, 500
Rawls, John 184
Read, Herbert 104–5, 309, 466, 533, 574
Réage, Pauline, *The Story of O* 478

realism 2, 4, 98, 117–22, 444–9, **495–8**
  Ingarden 365–6; Merleau–Ponty 422;
    Ruskin 495; Walton 589; Wilde 495
  Marxism and art 414–15
  see also drawing; depiction; illusion; painting;
    perspective; picture perception; representation;
    trompe l'oeil effects; truth in art
Reid, L. A. 554
relativism 119–20, 211–14, 218–19, 376–6,
  498–500
  Gadamer 373–4, 499; Herder 46; Hume 44–5,
    333–4, 499; Margolis 411–12; Nietzsche
    498–9; Witelo 24
  see also canon; feminist aesthetics and criticism;
    objectivity; taste; truth in art; universals in art
religion and art 9, 260, 300–1, **500–4**
  Bell 172; Collingwood 197, 502–3; Hegel 53,
    316–18, 501–2; Kant 500–1; Nietzsche 439,
    504; Schiller 500–3; Scruton 529–30;
    Tolstoy 264, 503, 571; Wagner 504, 586–8
  Islamic aesthetics 381–3
  see also aestheticism; catharsis; iconoclasm;
    medieval and renaissance aesthetics;
    Paleolithic, art in the; sublime, the
Rembrandt van Ryn 150, 260, 268, 341, 516
renaissance aesthetics *see* medieval and
  renaissance aesthetics
representation 7, 11–12, 26, 38–42, 62–3, 70–1,
  83–4, 88–90, 96, 98–101, 238–41, 270,
  394, 444–5, 469–72, **504–8**, 533, 565–6
  Aristotle 147–8; Bell 172–3; Danto 226–7;
    Deleuze 235–7; Foucault 294–5; Gombrich
    84, 240, 308–10, 344, 469, 573; Goodman
    67, 238–9, 312, 466, 469; Hanslick 314–15;
    Langer 401; Lessing 403–4; Plato 472–3;
    Schelling 514–15; Walton 588–90; Wollheim
    597–8
  abstraction 107–9
  accuracy in 172, 227, 315, 496, 505–7
  aesthetic properties 125–7
  Chinese aesthetics 189–90
  cognitive science and art 191–3
  emotion 252–5
  erotic art and obscenity 256–7
  fiction, nature of 275–6
  formalism 111–12, 290–3
  horror 330–1
  Islamic aesthetics 383
  "intentional fallacy" 370–1
  motion pictures 88–90
  realism 495–6
  see also drawing; illusion; metaphor; painting;
    symbol
response, affective 129, 280, 590
restoration *see* conservation and restoration
Ribeiro, Anna Christina 101
Richards, I. A. 423, 503

Ricoeur, Paul 324–5, 363
Ridley, Aaron 92, 265, 441, 578
Riegl, Aloïs 151, 206
Rilke, Rainer Maria von 303, 323, 530
Rittershausen, Josef Sebastian von 432
Robinson, Hilary 269
Robinson, Jenefer M. 115, 193, 256, 279, 355
Robortelli, Francesco 29
Rodin, Auguste 105, 258
Roelofs, Monique 489, 491
Rogers, L. R. 105
Rogerson, Kenneth F. 47
Rohrbaugh, Guy 451
Rollins, Mark 193, 229
Romanticism 128, 174, 178, 184, 208, 215–16,
  271, 318–19, 328, 355, 361, 380, 392, 413,
  516, 519–22, 548, 552–3, 579
Rorty, Richard 483, 564
Ross, Stephanie 304–5
Rossini, Gioacchino Antonio, *The Barber of Seville*
  524
Rousseau, Jean-Jacques 47–9, 242
Rowe, Mark R. 231
Rubens, Peter Paul 150–1
Rudinow, Joel 92, 157
rules, aesthetic 118–20, 236
  see also aesthetic judgment; convention
Ruskin, John 309, 471, 495, **508–10**, 529–30
Russell, Bertrand 166, 284–5, 257

Sade, Donatien Alphonse François, Comte de 293,
  430
  The 120 Days of Sodom 478; *Justine* 478
Saenredam, Pieter 205
Said, Edward W. 224
Saisselin, R. G. 432
Saito, Yuriko 116, 132, 137–8, 387
Salinger, J. D., *The Catcher in the Rye* 354
Saltz, David Z. 81, 462, 559
Santayana, George 167, 500, 502, **511–12**
Santoro-Brienza, Liberato 147
Sappho 11
Sartre, Jean-Paul 58, 241, 250, 296, 359–60,
  366, **512–14**
  The Condemned of Altona 513; *The Devil and the
    Good Lord* 513; *The Flies* 512; *Nausea* 58, 512;
    No Exit 512
  Ingarden 365; Merleau-Ponty 421
  imagination 513–14
Sartwell, Crispin 137–8
Saussure, Ferdinand de 59, 160, 242, 435, 540–1
Savile, Anthony 48, 123, 405, 519, 535, 599
Scaliger, Julius 30
Schachtel, Ernest 487
Schaper, Eva 22, 392, 519
Scheler, Max 250
Schellekens, Elisabeth 205

Schelling, Friedrich Wilhelm Joseph von 54–5, 57, **514–17**
  Hegel 316, 514–16; Heidegger 514, 516; Kant 514–16; Kierkegaard 516; Nietzsche 516; Schiller 516; Schopenhauer 516; Schlegel, A. 519; Schlegel, F. 521
Schier, Flint 241
Schiller, Friedrich von 36, 55, 57, 302, 401, 413, 490, 500–3, **517–19**, 528
  Beethoven 586; Goethe 518; Hegel 518; Kant 517–18; Schelling 516; Schlegel, F. 521
  aesthetic education 36, 47–9, 52–4, 517–19; beauty 36, 48–9, 52, 54, 517–19
Schlegel, August Wilhelm von **519–20**, 552
  brother of Friedrich 519
  as critic 519
Schlegel, Friedrich von **520–2**
  Lucinde 521
  Goethe 521; Kant 521; Schelling 516
  brother of Auguste 520–1
  criticism 521
  irony 379–81, 522
  Romanticism 519–20, 521–2
Schleiermacher, Friedrich D. E. 324–6, 362, 521
Schoenberg, Arnold 109, 234, 426, 573–4
  Moses and Aaron 417
Scholem, Gershom 174
Schopenhauer, Arthur 54–6, 61, 64, 72, 91, 111, 121, 207, 305–6, 335, 361, 439, **522–5**, 579, 594
  Kant 439, 522–4, Nietzsche 55, 438–9, 522–5; Plato 523; Schelling 516; Tolstoy 524; Wagner 524–5, 587–8
science and art 1–3, 102, 115, 191–3, 328, 371–3, 481–3, **525–7**
  Baumgarten 162–3; Foucault 296; Gombrich 310; Goodman 65; Hegel 53, 316; Hume 332; Langer 400; Nietzsche 438, 440; Schelling 514–16
  see also evolution, art, and aesthetics; objectivity
Scott, Ridley, *Alien* 328
Scruton, Roger 66–7, 91–2, 113, 122, 129, 256, 446, **528–30**
  Kant 528–30; Nietzsche 529; Ruskin 529–30
sculpture 5, 28, 90, **104–6**, 150–1, 345, 495, 566
  Hegel 317–19; Gombrich 308; Herder 49; Langer 104; Lessing 402, 405
  ontology of artworks 454–7
  see also architecture; drawing, depiction; painting; printmaking; tradition
Searle, John R. 276, 424
seeing-in *see* picture perception
Sei Shônagon, *Makura no Sôshi* (*Pillow Book*) 385
semiotics 162, 396, 481
  see also hermeneutics; symbol
Seneca the Younger (Lucius Annaeus) 17–18

senses and art, the 38, 305, 343, **530–4**
  Hutcheson 43; Schiller 517–18; Shaftesbury 34–5, 537–8
  aesthetics of food and drink 131–2
  aesthetics of the environment 133, 134–6
  see also aesthetic properties; cognitive science and art; conceptual art; illusion; representation
sentimentality 41–4, 47–8, **534–7**
  Burke 177; Hume 333–4, 535; Kant 534–5; Lessing 404–5; Tanner 534–5; Wilde 534–5
  see also emotion; kitsch
Serrano, Andres, *Piss Christ* 224
Seurat, Georges Pierre 57
  A Sunday Afternoon on the Island of La Grande Jatte 589–90
Shaftesbury, Anthony Ashley Cooper, 3rd earl 33–5, 42, 304, 389, 489, **537–8**, 554
Shakespeare, William 61, 85, 102, 179, 216, 223, 268, 276, 284–6, 307, 354, 413, 417, 429, 448, 461, 477, 497, 527, 546, 548, 576
  Hamlet 55, 89, 201, 218, 246, 284–5, 420, 462, 536, 563, 578; *Julius Caesar* 505; *King Lear* 166, 548, 571; *Macbeth* 306; *A Midsummer Night's Dream* 201; *Richard III* 405
  Cavell 184; Croce 221; Freud 55, 420, 535; Goodman 311; Hegel 318, 320; Herder 46; Schlegel, A. 519–20; Tolstoy 570–1
Shapiro, Gary 320
Sharpe, R. A. 570
Shelley, James 340
Shelley, Percy Bysshe 208, 423, 425
  The Cenci 80
Shepard, Roger 343
Shiner, Larry 157, 159, 301, 584
Shiner, Roger A. 334
Showalter, Elaine 269–70
Shusterman, Richard 65, 77, 116, 137–8, 476–8, 483, 564
Sibley, Frank Noel 123, 132–3, 204, 209, **538–40**, 554, 588
  and aesthetic judgment 65–6, 539–40
  and aesthetic properties 65–7, 125–7
Sidney, Sir Philip 29–30, 502
Signac, Paul 57
significant form *see* form, significant
Silvers, Anita 156
Simonides 11
Smith, Adam 534
Smith, Barry C. 132
Smith, Ralph 114
Smith, William 36
Smuts, Aaron 557
Socrates 12–15, 168–9, 298, 347, 378–80, 472–3, 593
Solger, Karl 380
Solomon, Robert C. 396, 534–6

song *see* music
Sophocles 46, 250, 321, 438, 467
  Antigone 320–1, 393, 575, 577; *Oedipus Rex* 536
Souriau, Etienne 249
Sparkes, John 335
Sparshott, Francis 77, 125, 300, 408, 459
Spector, Jack J. 485, 487
Speer, Andreas 25
Spencer, Herbert 336
Spender, Stephen 357–8, 360
Spielberg, Steven
  Jaws 328; *Back to the Future* 201
Spinoza, Baruch 28, 162, 167, 234, 347, 515, 521
Spivak, Gayatri 229–30
Stecker, Robert 69, 86, 104, 123, 128, 203, 214, 233, 249, 283, 355, 368, 376–7, 421, 451
Steele, Richard 35–6
Steiger, Emil 365
Sterne, Laurence, *Tristram Shandy* 426
Stewart, Dugald 33, 46
Stevenson, Charles 563, 588
Stock, Kathleen 232–3, 353
Stokes, Dustin 353
Stolnitz, Jerome 111, 113, 121, 194, 247, 408, 538
Strabo 18
Stravinsky, Igor 110, 222, 323
  Firebird Suite 211; *Rite of Spring* 127, 451
Strawson, Peter 65
structuralism and poststructuralism 59–60, 160, 217, 242, 291, 324, 367, 425–8, 436, 514, **540–4**, 563–4
  Barthes 366, 374, 542; Derrida 366–7, 541–3, 564; Foucault 160, 542–3
  see also deconstruction; irony; formalism
style 86, 100, 222–4, 229–30, 232, 306, 355–6, 425–7, 495, 497, **544–7**, 574
  Danto 228; Foucault 294–5; Gombrich 310; Goodman 545; Walton 545; Wollheim 545, 597–9
  in Amerindian aesthetics 142
  in Chinese aesthetics 189
  in Islamic aesthetics 383
  in Japanese aesthetics 385–6
sublime, the 38, 60, 137, 501, **547–51**
  Addison 36, 549; Burke 19–20, 36–7, 177–8, 549; Hegel 318; Kant 54, 388, 547, 549–51; Longinus 19–20; Nietzsche 55, 439–40; Plato 549; Schiller 501; Schopenhauer 439
  see also aesthetic pleasure; aesthetics of nature; beauty; horror
Suger, Abbot of St-Denis 24–6
Sullivan, Sir Arthur, *Patience* 128

Sulzer, Johann Georg 40
Surrealism 174–5, 463, 488
Swedenborg, Emanuel 552
Sweeney, Kevin 132
Swift, Jonathan 370–1, 378, 548
  A Modest Proposal 367, 370–1, 379
symbol 3, 5–7, 9, 82–5, 91, 419, 487, **551–3**
  Augustine 552; Freud 484–8, 553; Goodman 67, 238–9, 311–12; Hegel 318–19; Kristeva 397; Lacan 553; Langer 63–4, 400–2; Schlegel, A. 552; Scruton 529
  iconoclasm and idolatry 341–2
  representation 505–7
  see also hermeneutics; ineffability; metaphor; psychoanalysis
symmetry 6, 23, 36, 259, 261, 448–9, 475, 583
Symons, A. J., *The Quest for Corvo* 128

Tagore, Rabindranath 356, 359
Tarantino, Quentin, *Death Proof* 328
taste 44–7, 118, 125, 168, **554–6**, 582
  Hume 44–7, 332–4, 554–6; Hutcheson 554; Kant 44, 47, 131, 388–91, 554–5; Shaftesbury 538, 554; Sibley 538–9, 554, 560–1
  aesthetics of food and drink 131–3, 552
  feminist standpoint aesthetics 272–5
  see also aesthetic education; canon; objectivity
Tatarkiewicz, Wladyslaw 22, 147
Tate, Allen 215
Tavinor, Grant 557
Tchaikovsky, Peter I. 271–2, 573
technology and art 92–3, 344, **556–60**
  Benjamin 59, 176, 559; Carroll 556–9; Heidegger 322; Lessing 558
  mass art 415–17
  ontology of artworks 456–7
  popular art 476–7
  see also motion pictures; definition of "art"
Telfer, Elizabeth 133
testimony in aesthetics 167, 347, 533, **560–2**
  Kant 561; Wollheim 562
  see also cognitive value of art; objectivity; taste
text 80–1, 86–8, 103, 462, 464, **562–5**
  Barthes 59, 564–5; Beardsley 563; Goodman 563; Kristeva 564–5
  canon 179–80
  deconstruction 218, 229–31
  fiction, truth in 282–3
  hermeneutics 325–7
  interpretation 372–4, 376–7
  irony 380–1
  music and song 92–4
  see also critical monism and pluralism; hermeneutics; interpretation; meaning constructivism; ontology of artworks; work of art

theater 78–82
see also drama
Theophilus 24
theories of art **565–70**
see also creativity; definition of "art"; depiction;
expression; formalism; interpretation;
ontological contextualism; originality;
realism; representation; tradition; truth
in art
Thom, Paul 96, 421, 462
Thomasson, Amie 154, 453
Thoreau, Henry David 184
Thucydides 13
Tieck, Ludwig 519, 521
Tilghman, B. R. 570
Tintoretto, Jacopo 508, 513
Titian (Tiziano Vecelli) 273, 513
Madonna with Saints 300
Todorov, Tzvetan 436, 552
Tolhurst, William 283, 368
Tolstoy, Leo 53, 264, 299–300, 311, 474, 503,
570–3, 595
Anna Karenina 571; *War and Peace* 195, 571
Schopenhauer 524
expression theory 62, 264, 299, 572
function of art 53, 56, 61–2, 298–9, 572
religion and art 264, 503, 571
Tomasello, Michael 1
Tooby, J. 260
Tormey, Alan 265
Townsend, Dabney 45, 334, 340, 458–9, 538
tradition 58, 101–3, 105, 125, 426, 451, 459,
463, 532, 568, **573–5**
Deleuze 236; Gombrich 309–10
Amerindian aesthetics 144–5
Chinese aesthetics 190, 573
Indian aesthetics 115, 494
Japanese aesthetics 384–6
see also art history; canon; creativity; originality
tragedy 216, 329, **575–8**
Aristotle 15, 30, 147–8, 252, 349, 404, 417,
439, 575–6; Corneille 30–1; Gorgias 14;
Hegel 316–17, 320, 575, 577; Hume 44, 49,
332–4; Kames 39; Kierkegaard 393; Lessing
404–5, 577; Nietzsche 14, 55, 438–40,
575–7; Plato 575; Schopenhauer 523–4
catharsis 182–3, 252, 576
dramatic *see under* drama
see also comedy; emotion; horror; irony; humor
Trakl, Georg 323
Trollope, Anthony 503
trompe l'oeil effects 105, 239–40, 287, 344, 469,
471, 502
see also illusion
Trotsky, Leon 415
truth in art 11–15, 102–3, 117, 195–6, 212,
215–17, 418, 578–80

Adorno 110; Benjamin 175; Croce 579;
Dufrenne 250; Gadamer 302; Hegel 318;
Heidegger 56, 321, 323, 579; Ingarden 364,
578; Plato 21, 472–3; Schelling 514;
Schopenhauer 55, 579; Tolstoy 298
beauty 166–9
objectivity 445–7
relativism 498–500
representation 505–7
see also literature; cognitive value of art; fiction,
nature of; fiction, truth in; fictional entities;
imaginative resistance; metaphor; realism
Turner, J. M. W. 236, 309, 508–9, 526, 592
Twardowski, Kazimierz 364
twentieth-century Anglo-American aesthetics
61–73
type-token distinction 89–90, 96, 415–17, 454–7,
563
see also ontology of art

Uccello, Paolo 438, 467
Ulrich of Strasbourg 23–5
universals in art 206, 486, 501, 555, **581–4**
Aristotle 15, 148; Burke 177; Croce 221;
Dissanayake 581–2; Hume 332, 582; Kant
37, 47, 52, 131, 389–91, 582; Schopenhauer
523
aesthetic judgment 118–20
relativism 498–500
see also cognitive science and art; evolution,
art, and aesthetics; objectivity; Paleolithic,
art of the
Urmson, J. O. 121
Ussher, James 48

Valéry, Paul Ambroise 359–60, 423, 579
Valla, Giorgio 29
value of art 9, 66, 121–5, 127, 194–7, 204, 209,
264, 266, 288, 352, 429–30, 507–8, 581
aesthetic education 114–17, 534–6
see also aestheticism; cognitive value of art;
criticism; evolution and art; formalism;
objectivity; taste; theories of art; truth in art
value, moral 17, 47–8, 52, 57, 130, 389, 429,
571
Vamana 358–60
Van Damme, Wilfried 583
Van Gogh, Theo, *Submission* 224
Van Gogh, Vincent 84, 113, 250, 310, 323, 363,
455
Van Meegeren, Hans 287–9
Vance, Robert D. 104–5
Vasari, G. 29, 149–51
Velázquez, Diego 495
Las Meninas 295, 374
Verdi, Giuseppe 586
Vermazen, Bruce 209, 459

Vermeer, Jan 150, 277, 287–8
  Girl with a Pearl Earring 452–3; *A Woman Weighing Gold* 275–6
Vico, Giovanni Battista (Giambattista) 197, 219
Vidor, King, *Stella Dallas* 536
Vienna Circle 361, 371
Virgil 306, 520
  Aeneid 305
Vivas, Eliseo 121
von Hardenberg, Friedrich *see* Novalis

Wagner, Richard 61, 97, 109, 234, 504, **586–8**
  Die Feen 586; *Der fliegende Holländer* 587; *Das Liebesverbot* 586; *Die Meistersinger von Nürnberg* 588; *Lohengrin* 587; *Parsifal* 504, 588, *Rienzi* 586; *Ring of the Nibelung* 349, 571; *Tannhäuser* 587; *Tristan und Isolde* 529, 588
  Nietzsche 438–9, 587; Schopenhauer 524–5, 587–8; Scruton 529–30
Wallach, A. 432–3
Walton, Kendall L. 67–8, 105, 107–8, 241, 280, 282, 292, 308, 356, 450, 508, 545, **588–91**
  expression 262–3
  fiction, nature of 276–8
  imagination 67, 70–1, 286, 350, 470–1, 589–90
  imaginative resistance 351–3, 591
Wang Huaiqing, *Bole, a Wise Old Man who Knows How to Choose Horses* 190
Ward, Andrew 121
Warhol, Andy 295, 450
  Brillo Boxes 68, 203; *Empire* 416
Warnock, Mary 350, 392
Warren, Robert Penn 215
Wartenberg, Thomas E. 91
Watson, George 217
Weatherson, Brian 351
Weber, Max 109
Webster, Anthony K. 144
Weinberg, Bernard 29
Weinberg, Jonathan 279, 353
Weitz, Morris 66, 152–3, 203, 233, 248
Wellek, René 504, 520, 522
Wenban–Smith, F. 6
Wheeler, Michael 510
Whistler, James Abbott McNeill 128, 502
White, Hayden 213
White, M. 6
Whitehead, A. N. 400, 402
Wicks, Robert 3 92
Wiggins, D. 206–7
Wilde, Oscar 495, 534–5, **591–3**
  aestheticism 128–30, 428, 502, 592
William of Auvergne 22
William of Conches 27

Williams, Bernard 480
Wilson, Deirdre 102, 379
Wilson, Edmund 412
Wilson, Robert 463
Wimsatt, William K. 66, 164, 355, 366, 369–70
Winckelmann, Johann Joachim 49, 57, 150, 317, 413
Wind, Edgar 206
Winters, Edward 75
Wiseman, Mary Bittner 162
Witelo 24
Wittgenstein, Ludwig 63, 66–7, 76, 120, 152–3, 235, 248–9, 347, 362–3, 374, 483, 556, **593–6**, 597
  Cavell 183–4; Danto 226; Langer 400; Schopenhauer 522, 525, 594
Wolff, Christian 40–2, 162
Wölfflin, Heinrich 68, 150–1, 308
Wollheim, Richard 7, 70, 107–8, 123, 233, 240, 288, 290, 365, 375, 408, 445, 452, 532, 545, 562, 566, 569, **596–9**
  expression 67, 263, 597–8
  picture perception 67, 263, 470–1, 506, 597–9
  style 545, 597–9
Wolterstorff, Nicholas 70, 91, 283, 457
Woodfield, Richard 310
Woolf, Virginia 426, 496
Wordsworth, William 164, 216, 363, 375
work of art 74, 77, 86–7, 90–2, 96, 99, 103, 125, 130, 134, 137, 203, 217, 222, 526, 567–9
  Bell 63, 172; Benjamin 59, 176; Collingwood 62, 198–9, 266; Danto 226–7; Dewey 116, 246, 482; Dickie 248; Duchamp 59; Dufrenne 56, 249–50; Foucault 60; Goodman 312; Heidegger 56, 321–3; Ingarden 56, 364–5; Kant 37–8; Lukács 409–10; Merleau-Ponty 422; Sartre 513; Schelling 54, 516; Tolstoy 299–300; Wollheim 597–9
  artifact, art as 152–3
  ontology of artworks 449–57
  see also conceptual art; definition of "art"; expression theory; ontological contextualism
Wreen, Michael 165
Wright, Crispin 446–7
Wright, Frank Lloyd 208, 454

Xenophanes 12, 16, 472
Xenophon 12

Yanal, Robert 249
Young, James O. 92, 159, 225, 580
Young, Julian 441

Zalta, Edward 285
Zammito, John 47
Zangwill, Nick 69, 115, 171, 292, 446, 452

Zeki, Semir 115, 192, 261
Zelle, Carsten 36
Zemach, Eddy 276, 580
Zen Buddhism 384

Zeno of Citium 17
Ziff, Paul 66, 152
Zilhão, João 5
Zola, Émile 379, 524, 592